ON COOKING

A TEXTBOOK OF CULINARY FUNDAMENTALS

SARAH R. LABENSKY

ALAN M. HAUSE

FRED L. MALLEY
Southern Alberta Institute of Technology and Canadian Culinary Institute

ANTHONY BEVAN
HRT Alliance, Humber College of Applied Arts and Technology

SETTIMIO SICOLI
Vancouver Community College

With STEVEN LABENSKY
Photographs by RICHARD EMBERY
Drawings by STACEY WINTERS QUATTRONE

Prentice Hall Canada Career & Technology
Scarborough, Ontario

President: Yolanda de Rooy
Vice President and Editorial Director:
    Laura Pearson
Senior Acquisitions Editor: David Stover
Senior Developmental Editor:
    Dawn du Quesnay
Field Editor: Nicole Lukach
Associate Editor: Susan Ratkaj
Production Editor: Avivah Wargon
Copy Editors: Wendy Thomas,
    Madeline Koch
Executive Marketing Manager:
    Jo-Ann DeLuca
Marketing Manager: Sophia Fortier
Production Coordinator: Kathrine Pummell
Art Director: Mary Opper
Interior and Cover Design: Monica Kompter
Cover Photograph: StockFood/Eising
Page Layout: Monica Kompter

Photo Credits:

Photograph of the CFCC/FCCC medallion—
used with the permission of the Canadian
Federation of Chefs and Cooks/Fédération
Canadienne des Chefs et Cuisiniers

Appearance of the CFCC medallion in this
publication does not constitute an official
endorsement. The Canadian Federation of
Chefs and Cooks is a professional trade
association providing educational, fraternal
and networking opportunities within
Canada's hospitality industry.

Portrait of Fannie Farmer—courtesty of The
Schlesinger Library, Radcliffe College

Portrait of Auguste Escoffier—courtesy of
Musée de l'Art Culinaire, Villeneuve-Loubet
(Village), France

Portraits of Alexis Soyer and Antonin
Carême—courtesy of Barbara Wheaton

Drawing of the Reform Club's kitchen—
courtesy of the Reform Club, London,
England

Canadian Cataloguing in Publication Data

Main entry under title:

On cooking : a textbook of culinary fundamentals

Canadian ed.
Includes bibliographical references and index.
ISBN 0-13-973892-4

1. Cookery. I. Labensky, Sarah R.

TX651.O5 1999   641.5   C99-931174-0

Prentice-Hall, Inc., Upper Saddle River, New Jersey
Prentice-Hall International (UK) Limited, London
Prentice-Hall of Australia, Pty. Limited, Sydney
Prentice-Hall Hispanoamericana, S.A., Mexico City
Prentice-Hall of India Private Limited, New Delhi
Prentice-Hall of Japan, Inc., Tokyo
Simon & Schuster Southeast Asia Private Limited, Singapore
Editora Prentice-Hall do Brasil, Ltda., Rio de Janeiro

ISBN 0-13-973892-4

Original English-language edition published by Prentice-Hall, Inc.,
Upper Saddle River, NJ. Copyright ©1999, 1995.

  2 3 4 5   RRD   03 02 01 00 99

Printed and bound in the United States of America

Visit the Prentice Hall Canada Web site! Send us your comments, browse our
catalogues, and more at **www.phcanada.com**. Or reach us through e-mail at
phabinfo_pubcanada@prenhall.com.

Contents

PART 3
COOKING

PART 5
MEAL SERVICE AND PRESENTATION

CANADIAN CHEFS' RECIPES

"My" Beurre Blanc Sauce (Recipe 10.17), *Marcel Kretz*, p. 218
Pine Nut and Pistachio Relish (Recipe 10.28), *Simon Smotkowicz*, pp. 229–30

Butternut Squash and Maple Soup (Recipe 11.11), *Anthony Bevan*, p. 251
Vichyssoise of Oysters with Caviar Chantilly (Recipe 11.13), *Anthony Borgo*, pp. 252–53

FOREWORD

Cornelia Patterson

Cornelia Patterson is a recognized professional chef, educator and culinary consultant. She has worked in a variety of capacities in the hospitality industry, including restaurant management, product distribution and promotion, and research and development. She has competed in and judged local and international culinary competitions, and for many years taught culinary arts and coordinated apprenticeship training. For seven years, Cornelia served on the Board of Directors of the Escoffier Society of Toronto and is currently the National President of the Canadian Federation of Chefs and Cooks.

Canadian culinary educators have long awaited a comprehensive instructional textbook to assist students entering a career in the culinary arts in this country. *On Cooking: A Textbook of Culinary Fundamentals,* Canadian Edition, provides a detailed approach to basic cook training in Canada, and introduces the requirements for becoming a great Canadian chef.

In years past, culinary educators in Canada have had to rely on foreign materials that lacked the focus on Canadian techniques, styles, regulations and food products provided in this text. By generating a text that exemplifies Canadian lifestyles and skill sets, we are helping to define a culinary culture unique to Canada. With the introduction of the Canadian Edition of *On Cooking,* we may now showcase our uniqueness while continuing to ensure the high standard of our learning outcomes.

Culinary students entering the hospitality industry must be equipped to meet the extensive requirements and challenges of their trade. Professional Canadian chefs and their recipes are featured in this text, providing students with the opportunity to explore career paths, food trends and cuisine styles from coast to coast. In addition, the articles and sidebars throughout the book depict a tradition rich in ethnic and cultural influences, and provide a grounding in culinary history. This exposure will create an awareness of the expectations and expertise required of an aspiring chef.

In short, *On Cooking* provides a framework within which to strengthen the skills of our cooks and chefs of tomorrow and launch them into careers of culinary excellence. We and generations to come will savour the rewards.

Cornelia Patterson
Toronto

PREFACE

Welcome to the Canadian Edition of *On Cooking: A Textbook of Culinary Fundamentals.* Learning to cook is much more than simply learning to follow a recipe. Consequently, this is neither a cookbook nor a collection of recipes. It is a carefully designed text intended to teach you the fundamentals of the culinary arts and to prepare you for a rewarding career in the food service industry.

Many chapters have extensive illustrated sections identifying foods and equipment. Throughout the book we emphasize culinary principles, not recipes (although we include more than 500 of them). Whenever possible, we focus on the general procedure, highlighting fundamental principles and skills, whether it be for preparing a yeast bread or grilling a piece of fish. We discuss both the *how* and *why* of cooking. Only then are specific applications and sample recipes given.

Numerous hotel and restaurant chefs throughout North America have contributed recipes to this book, including over 50 from Canadian chefs—usually accompanied by photographs of the dishes as prepared in their kitchens, or of the chefs themselves. These recipes and illustrations allow you to explore the different techniques and presentation styles used by a range of professionals.

In order to provide you with a sense of the rich tradition of cookery, informative sidebars on food history, chefs' biographies and other topics are scattered throughout the book. Also included are several short essays by prominent culinarians on topics ranging from tempering chocolate to tasting spicy foods.

We wish you much success in your culinary career and hope this text will continue to inform and inspire you long after graduation.

A Note on the Recipes

Recipes are important and useful as a means of standardizing food preparation and recording information. We include recipes that are primarily designed to reinforce and explain techniques and procedures presented in the text. Many recipe yields are intentionally low in order to be less intimidating to beginning cooks and more useful in small schools and kitchens.

All ingredients are listed in both metric and U.S. measurements (but not British imperial). The metric equivalents are rounded off to even, easily measured quantities. So, you should consider these ingredient lists as separate recipes or formulas; do not measure some ingredients according to the metric amounts and other ingredients according to the U.S. amounts or the proportions will not be accurate and the intended result will not be achieved.

Throughout this book, unless otherwise noted, *mirepoix* refers to a preparation of 2 parts onion, 1 part celery and 1 part carrot by weight; *pepper* refers to ground black pepper, preferably freshly ground; *butter* refers to whole, unsalted butter; and *TT* means "to taste."

A nutritional analysis is provided with each recipe. This information is provided as a reference only. There is a 20% margin of error, due primarily to choices for specific ingredients and variations in the size of fruits and vegetables. When a recipe offers a choice of ingredients, the first-mentioned ingredient was the one used in the calculations. Ingredients listed as "to taste" (TT) and "as needed" were generally omitted from the analysis. In addition, olive oil and 3% whole milk were used throughout for "vegetable oil" and "milk," respectively. When the recipe gave a choice of serving or weight, the first mentioned was used.

Recipes marked with the rainbow symbol are particularly low in calories, fat, saturated fat and/or sodium; some may also be a good source of vitamins, protein, fibre or calcium. These dishes are not necessarily dietetic; rather, they should be consumed as part of a well-balanced diet.

Detailed procedures for standard techniques (for example, "deglaze the pan" or "monter au beurre") are presented in the text and generally are not repeated in each recipe. No matter how detailed the written recipe, we must assume that you have certain knowledge, skills and judgment.

Variations appear at the end of selected recipes. These give you the opportunity to see how one set of techniques or procedures can be used to prepare different dishes with only minor modifications.

You should also rely upon the knowledge and skill of your instructor for guidance. While some skills and an understanding of theory can be acquired through reading and study, no book can substitute for repeated, hands-on preparation and observation.

Special Features of the Canadian Edition

- *Integrated Canadian Content:* The Canadian Edition of *On Cooking* contains information about Canadian regulations on, for example, cuts of meat, grading systems for meat and produce, and national standards for professional cooks.
- *Recipes by Canadian Chefs:* Spotlighting some of the tremendous culinary talent in our country, this variety of contemporary recipes adds a truly Canadian flavour. Accompanied by a photo of the chef and a brief caption describing some of the highlights of his or her career, these recipes will give students a glimpse of the many career paths they can choose from.
- *Learning Outcomes and Basic Procedures:* The Learning Outcomes at the beginning of each chapter correspond to the Basic Procedures taught in that chapter. Basic Procedures are now more prominent than before.
- *New Section on Sandwiches:* Chapter 33 now includes an extensive section on this important and often overlooked subject. The chapter has been renamed "Appetizers and Sandwiches."
- *Nutritional Analyses:* In keeping with our increasingly health-conscious society, every recipe in the text now has its own nutritional analysis to help readers make informed choices about the foods they prepare.
- *Weblinks:* A list of relevant Web sites is provided at the end of each chapter to take advantage of the constantly growing resources of the Internet and the World Wide Web.

Supplements

The following ancillary package is available to supplement the text.
- *Instructor's Resource Manual with Test Item File and Transparency Masters.* In addition to handy chapter outlines, lists of key terms, and pertinent discussion questions with answers, this Instructor's Manual contains multiple choice, matching and true-false test questions with an answer key. Test questions are also available in computerized format for easy manipulation.

- *Companion Website.* An online site devoted to *On Cooking* includes an interactive study guide with immediate feedback, over 280 additional recipes, links to other culinary sites, a syllabus builder, tips from the authors, informative supplementary articles on such topics as buffet presentation, and more.
- *Recipe Software on CD-ROM.* This indispensable disk includes all the recipes in the book plus over 280 additional recipes. It automatically generates shopping lists, allowing instructors to customize ingredients, class size, and yield. It also allows students and instructors to print out recipes. It includes a link to the text Website.
- *Knife Skills Video.* Featuring Noel C. Cullen, CMC, this excellent video demonstrates all the knife skills aspiring cooks need to know.
- *Study Guide.* Written by Christine Stamm, Linda Cullen and Daniel Esposito, this Study Guide provides a complete overview of the *On Cooking* text. It includes hundreds of multiple choice, terminology, fill-in-the-blank, short answer, matching, labelling and product identification questions.

ACKNOWLEDGMENTS

The authors of the Canadian edition would like to thank a number of people for their invaluable contributions to this edition. Tony Bevan's authorial team at H.R.T. Alliance, Humber College, included Michéal McFadden, Frank Formella, Klaus Theyer, David Jones, Robert McCann and Michael Elliott.

We are deeply indebted to chef-nutritionist Charles Bruce-Thompson of the Ontario Pork Producers Marketing Board for his meticulous work on the nutritional analyses for the Canadian recipes. Master pâtissier Hermann Greineder of SAIT proved an invaluable resource on the baking chapters.

We would also like to thank all those who graciously agreed to review the manuscript or who provided feedback throughout the development of the text:

Kim Coates (Cambrian College); Gerry Crewe (College of the North Atlantic); Glen Dahl (Sault College); Michael Durrer (Algonquin College); Daniel Esposito (Canadore College); Gabriel Ferron (Vancouver Community College); David Fleck (College of New Caledonia); Alan Fleming (Algonquin College); Nick Garcia (North West Community College); Hans Hamacher (East Kootenay Community College); Robert S. Haynes (Lambton College); Geoffrey Lough (George Brown Community College); Merle Maerz (Selkirk College); Bob Marchand (Matsqui Institution); Robert Mitchell (Nova Scotia Community College); Peter Neilsen (University College of the Caribou); Gilbert Noussitou (Camosun College); Charles Parker (Lethbridge Community College); Cornelia Patterson (CFCC); Robert Payette (Alberta Advanced Education and Career Development); Mario Ramsey (Algonquin College); Tony Rechstiner (Northern Lights College); Hubert Scheck (Malaspina University College); Olivier Schittecatte (Ministry of Education, Skills and Training, British Columbia); Tony Stoeckly (Mountain Institution); Ralph Walker (Northern Alberta Institute of Technology); Michael Wallace (North Island College); Wes Wilkinson (Lambton College); Michael Wilson (College of New Caledonia); Tony Wong (Northern Alberta Institute of Technology); and Tony Wood (Hospitality Industry Education Advisory Committee).

This book would not have been possible without the assistance and support of many people who contributed to the first American edition of *On Cooking*. The authors are particularly indebted to Steve Labenksy for his countless hours with a sharp pencil, his comments and criticism and his constant support, as well as to photographer Richard Embery for his talent, professionalism and commitment to quality. The nutritional analyses for the American recipes were prepared by William Miller. Special thanks go to Kristy Riding, Tim Moore and the entire kitchen staff of Continental Catering for their support. Thanks also to Leland Atkinson, Nancy Calomiris, Gaye Ingram, Lisa Kelly, Richard Martinez, Charlotte Morrissey, Ernst Reck, Chantal van de Brug and Stacey Winters Quattrone for their help. We are also grateful to the many chefs, restauranteurs, writers and culinary professionals who provided recipes and essays for this book.

The authors wish to thank the following companies for their generous donations of equipment and supplies: J.A. Henckels Zwillingswerk, Inc., All-Clad Metalcrafters, Inc. and Parrish's Cake Decorating Supplies, Inc. We also wish to thank Shamrock Foods Company, East Coast Seafood of Phoenix Inc., KitchenAid Home Appliances, Taylor Environmental Instruments, Hobart Corporation, Williams-Sonoma, architect Michael Apostolos, and Randy Dougherty of ISF International.

The authors would also like to acknowledge the following reviewers for their comments and assistance: Richard W. Alford, University of Akron; Earl Arrowood, Bucks County Community College; Mike Artlip, Culinary School of Kendall College; Leland Atkinson; James Belch, Pennsylvania Institute of Culinary Arts; Lane Berrent, Pennsylvania Institute of Culinary Arts; Thom Boehm, Pennsylvania Institute of Culinary Arts; James Bressi, New England Culinary Institute; John D. Britto, San Joaquin Delta College; Walter Bronowitz CEE, Edmonds Community College; Mark Clink, Pennsylvania Institute of Culinary Arts; George Conte, New York Restaurant School; Noel Cullen, CMC, Boston University; Jeanne Curtis, Newbury College; William Day, Johnson & Wales University; Jim Douglas CEC: CCE, Everett Community College; Rolf Epprecht, Swiss Hospitality Institute; John Fitzpatrick; Maureen Garfolo, Pennsylvania Institute of Culinary Arts; George Geary; Jeff Graves, University of Houston/Conrad N. Hilton Hotel School; Bill Greathouse, Ivy Technical College; Kimberly Harris; Brenda Harsh, Pennsylvania Institute of Culinary Arts; Elizabeth S. Leite, Scottsdale Culinary Institute; Robert Lombardi, Spokane Community College; Deborah Lynch, Middlesex County College; Sylvia Marple M.S., R.D., University of New Hampshire; Don McNicol, Madison Area Technical College; James Muth, Grand Rapids Community College; John Noe, Joliet Junior College; Philip H. Nudle CEC, Middlesex County College; Michael Piccinino, Shasta College; Marcia Rango; Ernst Reck; Christine Stamm, Johnson & Wales University; Clifford Steiner, New York Restaurant School; Cicely Stetson; Peter G. Tobin, Spokane Community College; and Susan Ward, Academy of Culinary Arts/Atlantic Community College.

PART ONE

PROFESSIONALISM

Chefs and cooks must be able to do
more than properly prepare and present foods. They must understand traditions and factors influencing
change. They are responsible for making sure that
the food served is wholesome and safe to eat and
that they and those around them work in a safe
and efficient manner. Further, chefs and cooks
must make sure that
the foods they serve
are nutritious or at
least should offer cus-
tomers sufficient
selection so they can construct a nutritious
meal. And, finally, chefs and cooks are
responsible for producing food in a cost-
effective manner as well as accurately calculating, tracking and controlling the cost of
food and labour in the kitchen.

Part I opens with a chapter on professionalism. It traces
the history of chefs, cooks and restaurants, discusses the modern
food service operation and factors influencing its
development and explains what attributes an apprentice cook must have to become a professional chef. The
following chapters address food safety and sanitation,
nutrition, menu planning and food costing.

CHAPTER 1
PROFESSIONALISM

> *"Cookery is become an art, a noble science; cooks are gentlemen."*
> —Robert Burton, British author, 1621

*S*ubstitute "professionals" for "gentlemen" and Burton's words are as true today as they were almost four hundred years ago. Like the fine arts, great cookery requires taste and creativity, an appreciation of beauty and a mastery of technique. Like the sciences, successful cookery demands a certain level of knowledge and an understanding of basic principles. And, like the "gentlemen" of Burton's days, today's professional chefs must exercise sound judgment and be committed to achieving excellence in their endeavours.

This books helps implement Burton's philosophy. It describes foods and cooking equipment, explains culinary principles and cooking techniques and provides recipes utilizing these principles and techniques. This book cannot, however, provide taste, creativity, commitment and judgment. For these we rely upon you.

LEARNING OUTCOMES

After studying this chapter you will be able to:

+ name key historical figures responsible for developing food service professionalism
+ discuss the development of the modern food service industry
+ explain the organization of classical and modern kitchen brigades
+ explain the role of the professional chef in modern food service operations
+ identify the attributes an apprentice or student cook needs to become a professional chef

Cooking—*(1) the transfer of energy from a heat source to a food; this energy alters the food's molecular structure, changing its texture, flavour, aroma and appearance; (2) the preparation of food for consumption.*

Cookery—*the art, practice or work of cooking.*

Professional cooking—*a system of cooking based upon the application of procedures to maintain the integrity of ingredients while providing wholesome and safe food.*

CHEFS AND RESTAURANTS

Cooks have produced food in quantity for as long as people have eaten together. For millennia, chefs have catered to the often elaborate dining needs of the wealthy and powerful, whether they be Asian, Native Canadian, European or African. And for centuries, vendors in China, Europe and elsewhere have sold to the public foods they prepared themselves or bought from others.

But the history of the professional chef is of relatively recent origin. Its cast is mostly French and it is intertwined with the history of restaurants. For only with the development of restaurants during the late 18th and early 19th centuries were chefs expected to produce, efficiently and economically, different dishes at different or the same times for different diners.

The 18th Century—Boulanger's Restaurant

The word "restaurant" is derived from the French word *restaurer* (to restore). Since the 16th century, the word "restorative" had been used to describe rich and highly flavoured soups or stews capable of restoring lost strength. Restoratives, like all other cooked foods offered and purchased outside the home, were made by guild members. Each guild had a monopoly on preparing certain food items. For example, during the reign of Henri IV of France (1553–1610), there were separate guilds for *rotisseurs* (who cooked *la grosse viande*, the main cuts of meat), *patissiers* (who cooked poultry, pies and tarts), *tamisiers* (who baked breads), *vinaigriers* (who made sauces and some stews, including some restoratives), *traiteurs* (who made ragouts), and *porte-chapes* (caterers who organized feasts and celebrations).

The French claim that the first modern restaurant opened one day in 1765 when a Parisian tavernkeeper, a Monsieur Boulanger, hung a sign advertising the sale of his special restorative, a dish of sheep feet in white sauce. His establishment closed shortly thereafter as the result of a lawsuit brought by a guild whose members claimed that Boulanger was infringing on their exclusive right to sell prepared dishes. Boulanger triumphed in court and later reopened.

Boulanger's establishment differed from the inns and taverns that had existed throughout Europe for centuries. These inns and taverns served foods prepared (usually off-premises) by the appropriate guild. The food—of which there was little choice—was offered by the keeper as incidental to the establishment's primary function: providing sleeping accommodations or drink. Customers were served family-style and ate at communal tables. Boulanger's contribution to the food service industry was to serve a variety of foods prepared on premises to customers whose primary interest was dining.

Several other restaurants opened in Paris during the succeeding decades, including the Grande Taverne de Londres in 1782. Its owner, Antoine Beauvilliers (1754–1817), was the former steward to the Comte de Provence, later King Louis XVIII of France. He advanced the development of the modern restaurant by offering his wealthy patrons a menu listing available dishes during fixed hours. Beauvilliers' impeccably trained wait staff served patrons at small, individual tables in an elegant setting.

The French Revolution (1789–1799) had a significant effect on the budding restaurant industry. Along with the aristocracy, guilds and their monopolies were generally abolished. The revolution also allowed the public access to the skills and creativity of the well-trained, sophisticated chefs who had worked in the aristocracy's private kitchens. Although many of the aristocracy's chefs either left the country or lost their jobs (and, some, their heads), a few opened restaurants catering to the growing urbanized middle class.

The Early 19th Century—
Carême and Grande Cuisine

As the 19th century progressed, more restaurants opened, serving a greater selection of items and catering to a wider clientele. By mid-century, there were several large, grand restaurants in Paris serving elaborate meals, decidedly reminiscent of the *grande cuisine* (also known as *haute cuisine*) of the aristocracy. **Grande cuisine**, which arguably reached its peak of perfection in the hands of Antonin Carême, was characterized by meals consisting of dozens of courses of elaborately and intricately prepared, presented, garnished and sauced foods. Other restaurateurs blended the techniques and styles of *grande cuisine* with the simpler foods and tastes of the middle class (*cuisine bourgeoise*) to create a new cuisine simpler than *grande cuisine* but more than mere home cooking.

Grande cuisine—*the rich, intricate and elaborate cuisine of the 18th- and 19th-century French aristocracy and upper classes. It is based upon the rational identification, development and adoption of strict culinary principles. By emphasizing the how and why of cooking,* grande cuisine *was the first to distinguish itself from regional cuisines, which tend to emphasize the tradition of cooking.*

The Late 19th Century—
Escoffier and Cuisine Classique

Following the lead set by the French in both culinary style and the restaurant business, restaurants opened in the Americas and throughout Europe during the 19th century. Charles Ranhofer (1836–1899) was the first internationally renowned chef of an American restaurant, Delmonico's in New York City. In 1893 Ranhofer published his "franco-american" encyclopedia of cooking, *The Epicurean*, containing more than 3500 recipes.

✦✦✦
MARIE-ANTOINE (ANTONIN) CARÊME
(1783–1833)

Carême, known as the "cook of kings and the king of cooks," was an acknowledged master of French *grande cuisine*. Abandoned on the streets of Paris as a child, he worked his way from cook's helper in a working-class restaurant to become one of the most prestigious chefs of his (or, arguably, any other) time. During his career he was chef to the famous French diplomat and gourmand Prince de Talleyrand, the Prince Regent of England (who became King George IV), Tsar Alexander I of Russia and Baron de Rothschild, among others.

His stated goal was to achieve "lightness," "grace," "order" and "perspicuity" in the preparation and presentation of food. As a *pâtissier*, he designed and prepared elaborate and elegant pastry and confectionery creations, many of which were based on architectural designs. (He wrote that "the fine arts are five in number, namely: painting, sculpture, poetry, music, architecture—the main branch of which is confectionery.") As a showman, he garnished his dishes with ornamental hatelets (skewers) threaded with colourful ingredients such as crayfish and intricately carved vegetables, and presented his creations on elaborate socles (bases). As a *saucier*, he standardized the use of roux as a thickening agent, perfected recipes and devised a system for classifying sauces. As a *garde-manger*, Carême popularized cold cuisine, emphasizing molds and aspic dishes. As a culinary professional, he designed kitchen tools, equipment and uniforms.

As an author, he wrote and illustrated important texts on the culinary arts, including *Le Maître d'hotel français* (1822), describing the hundreds of dishes

Photo courtesy of Barbara Wheaton.

he personally created and cooked in the capitals of Europe; *Le Pâtissier royal parisian* (1825), containing fanciful designs for *les pieces montées*, the great decorative centre-pieces that were the crowning glory of grand dinners; and his five-volume masterpiece on the state of his profession, *L'Art de la cuisine au XIXe siecle* (1833), the last two volumes of which were completed after his death by his associate Plumerey. Carême's writings almost

single-handedly refined and summarized five hundred years of culinary evolution. But his treatises were not mere cookbooks. Rather, he analyzed cooking, old and new, emphasizing procedure and order and covering every aspect of the art known as *grande cuisine*.

Carême died before the age of 50, burnt out, according to Laurent Tailhade, "by the flame of his genius and the coal of the spits." But this may have been the glory he sought, for he once wrote:

Imagine yourself in a large kitchen at the moment of a great dinner. . . . [S]ee twenty chefs coming, going, moving with speed in this cauldron of heat, look at the great mass of charcoal, a cubic metre for the cooking of entrees, and another mass on the ovens for the cooking of soups, sauces, ragouts, for frying and the water baths. Add to that a heap of burning wood in front of which four spits are turning, one which bears a sirloin weighing 45–50 pounds, the other fowl or game. In this furnace everyone moves with speed; not a sound is heard, only the chef has a right to speak, and at the sound of his voice, everyone obeys. Finally, the last straw; for about half an hour, all windows are closed so that the air does not cool the dishes as they are being served. This is the way we spend the best years of our lives. We must obey even when physical strength fails, but it is the burning charcoal that kills us. . . . [C]harcoal kills us but what does it matter? The shorter the life, the greater the glory.

One of the finest restaurants outside of France was the dining room at London's Savoy Hotel, opened in 1898 under the directions of Cesar Ritz (1850–1918) and Auguste Escoffier. Escoffier is generally credited with refining the *grande cuisine* of Carême to create *cuisine classique* or **classic cuisine**. By doing so, he brought French cuisine into the 20th century.

AUGUSTE ESCOFFIER
(1846–1935)

Escoffier's brilliant culinary career began at the age of 13 in his uncle's restaurant and continued until his death at the age of 89. Called the "Emperor of the world's kitchens," he is perhaps best known for defining French cuisine and dining during *La Belle Epoque* (the "Gay Nineties").

Unlike Carême, Escoffier never worked in an aristocratic household. Rather, he exhibited his culinary skills in the dining rooms of the finest hotels in Europe, including the Place Vendôme in Paris and the Savoy and Carlton Hotels in London.

Escoffier did much to enhance the *grande cuisine* that arguably reached its perfection under Carême. Crediting Carême with providing the foundation for great—that is, French—cooking, Escoffier simplified the profusion of flavours, dishes and garnishes typifying Carême's work. He also streamlined some of Carême's overly elaborate and fussy procedures and classifications. For example, he reduced Carême's elaborate system of classify-

ing sauces into the five families of sauces still recognized today. Escoffier sought simplicity and aimed for the perfect balance of a few superb ingredients. Some consider his refinement of *grande cuisine* to have been so radical as to credit him with the development of a new

cuisine referred to as *cuisine classique* (classic or classical cuisine).

His many writings include *Le Livre des menus* (1912), in which, discussing the principles of a well-planned meal, he analogizes a great dinner to a symphony with contrasting movements that should be appropriate to the occasion, the guests, and the season, and *Ma cuisine* (1934), surveying *cuisine bourgeoisie*. But his most important contribution is a culinary treatise intended for the professional chef entitled *Le Guide culinaire* (1903). Still in use today, it is an astounding collection of more than five thousand classic cuisine recipes and garnishes. In it, Escoffier emphasizes the mastery of techniques, the thorough understanding of cooking principles and the appreciation of ingredients: attributes he considered the building blocks professional chefs should use to create great dishes.

Escoffier was honoured as a Chevalier of the French Legion of Honour in 1920 for his work in enhancing the reputation of French cuisine.

The 20th Century—Point and Nouvelle Cuisine

This century has witnessed a trend towards lighter, more naturally flavoured and more simply prepared foods. Fernand Point was a master practitioner of this movement. But this master's goal of simplicity and refinement was carried to even greater heights by a generation of chefs Point trained: principally, Paul Bocuse, Jean and Pierre Troisgros, Alain Chapel, François Bise and Louis

FERNAND POINT
(1897–1955)

A massive man with a monumental personality, Point refined and modernized the classic cuisine of Escoffier. By doing so, he laid the foundations for *nouvelle cuisine*.

Point received his early training in some of the finest hotel-restaurant kitchens in Paris. In 1922 he and his family moved to Vienne, a city in southeast France near Lyon, and opened a restaurant. Two years later his father left the restaurant to Fernand, who renamed it

La Pyramide. During the succeeding years it became one of the culinary wonders of the world.

Point disdained dominating sauces and distracting accompaniments and garnishes. He believed that each dish should have a single dominant ingredient, flavour or theme; garnishes must be simple and match "like a tie to a suit." Procedure was of great importance. He devoted equal efforts to frying an egg and creat-

ing the marjolaine (a light almond and hazelnut spongecake filled with chocolate and praline buttercreams). His goal was to use the finest of raw ingredients to produce perfect food that looked elegant and simple. But simplicity was not easy to achieve. As he once said, " A bearnaise sauce is simply an egg yolk, a shallot, a little tarragon vinegar, and butter, but it takes years of practice for the result to be perfect."

Outhier. They, along with Michel Guérard and Roger Vergé, were the pioneers of **nouvelle cuisine** in the early 1970s.

Their culinary philosophy was principled on the rejection of overly rich, needlessly complicated dishes. These chefs emphasized healthful eating. The ingredients must be absolutely fresh and of the highest possible quality; the cooking methods should be simple and direct whenever possible. The accompaniments and garnishes must be light and must contribute to an overall harmony; the completed plates must be elegantly designed and decorated. Following these guidelines, some traditional cooking methods have been applied to untraditional ingredients, and ingredients have been combined in new and previously unorthodox fashions. For chefs with taste, skill, knowledge and judgment, this works.

INFLUENCES ON MODERN FOOD SERVICE OPERATIONS

From Monsieur Boulanger's humble establishment, a great industry has grown. Today there are more than 60 000 restaurants in Canada, as well as institutional and catering facilities. The dramatic growth and diversification of the food service industry is due in part to the Industrial Revolution and the social and economic changes it wrought, including the introduction of new technologies, foods, concerns and consumers.

New Technologies

Technology has always had a profound effect on cooking. For example, the development of clay and, later, metal vessels that could contain liquids and withstand as well as conduct heat offered prehistoric cooks the opportunity to stew, make soups and porridge, pickle and brine foods and control fermentation. But it was not until the rapid technological advances fostered by the Industrial Revolution that anything approaching the modern kitchen was possible.

One of the most important advancements was the introduction of the cast-iron stove. Prior to the 19th century, most cooking was done on spits or grills or in cauldrons or pots set on or in a wood- or coal-burning hearth. Hearthside cooking did not lend itself well to the simultaneous preparation of many items nor to items requiring constant and delicate attention. With the introduction of cast-iron stoves during the 1800s (first wood- and coal-burning, then, by mid-century, gas and, by the early 20th century, electric), cooks could more comfortably and safely approach the heat source and control its temperatures. They were also able to efficiently prepare and hold for later use or service a multitude of smaller amounts of items requiring different cooking methods or ingredients. This is a necessity at a restaurant simultaneously catering to different diners' demands.

Also of great importance were developments in food preservation and storage techniques. For thousands of years, food had been preserved by sun-drying, salting, smoking, pickling, sugar-curing or fermenting. Although useful, these procedures destroy or distort the appearance and flavour of most foods. By the early 19th century, preserving techniques that had minimal effect on appearance and flavour began to emerge. For example, by 1800 the Frenchman François Appert successfully "canned" foods by subjecting foods stored in sterilized glass jars to very high heat. An early mechanical refrigerator was developed by the mid-1800s; soon reliable iceboxes, refrigerators and, later, freezers were available. During the 20th century, freeze-drying, vacuum-packing and irradiation have become common preservation techniques.

While advancements were being made in preservation and storage techniques, developments in transportation technology were also underway. During the 19th century, steam-powered ships and railroads were able to bring foods quickly to market from distant suppliers. Indeed, by the early 1900s, live Atlantic oysters were available on the western plains. During the 20th century, temperature-controlled cargo ships, trains, trucks and airplanes all have been used as part of an integrated worldwide food transportation network.

Combined with dependable food preservation and storage techniques, improved transportation networks have freed chefs from seasonal and geographic limitations in their choice of foods and have expanded consumers' culinary horizons.

Engineering advancements also have facilitated or even eliminated much routine kitchen work. Since the start of the Industrial Revolution, chefs have come to rely increasingly on mechanical and motorized food processors, mixers and cutters as well as a wealth of sophisticated kitchen equipment such as high carbon stainless steel knife blades, convection steamers and combitherm ovens.

New Foods

Modern food preservation, storage and transportation techniques have made both fresh and exotic foods regularly available to chefs and consumers. Many of these foods are themselves more wholesome as the result of progress in agriculture and animal husbandry.

Advancements in agriculture such as the switch from organic to chemical fertilizers and the introduction of pesticides and drought- or pest-resistant strains have resulted in increased yields of crops. Traditional hybridization techniques and, more recently, genetic engineering have produced new or improved grains and, for better or for worse, fruits and vegetables that have a longer shelf life and are more amenable to mass-production handling, storage and transportation methods. Organic production is re-emerging in the marketplace in response to consumer demands for more natural foods.

Likewise, advancements in animal husbandry and aquaculture have led to a more reliable supply of leaner, healthier meat, poultry and fish. Moreover, foods found traditionally only in the wild (for example game, wild rice and many mushrooms) are now being raised commercially and are routinely available.

Food preservation and processing techniques have also led to the development of packaged, prepared convenience foods. After careful thought and testing, today's chef can rely on some of these products. Doing so allows greater flexibility and more time to devote to other preparations.

New Concerns

Consumer concerns about nutrition and diet, particularly during the last decade or so, have fuelled changes in the food service industry. Obviously, what we eat affects our health. Adequate amounts of certain nutrients promote good health by preventing deficiencies; good nutrition also helps prevent chronic diseases and increases longevity. Chefs should provide their customers with nutritious foods.

The public has long been concerned about food safety. Federal, provincial and local governments have helped promote food safety by inspecting and grading meats and poultry, regulating label contents for packaged foods and setting sanitation standards. All these standards, especially sanitation standards, affect the way foods are prepared, stored and served.

Concerns about nutrition and food safety have resulted in renewed interest in organically grown fruits and vegetables and free-range-raised animals. Consumers are more aware of additives and preservatives used in commercial food production.

◆◆◆

CULINARY FRENCH

Perhaps one of the most enduring legacies of French chefs and culinarians is the common usage of many French words in today's professional kitchens. Some, like *canapé* and *bain marie*, are simply the name of a food item or piece of equipment of French origin. Others, such as *sauté*, are French verbs with no equally terse and descriptive English counterpart. Still others, for example *julienne*, are not only used as nouns (julienne of carrot), but also as verbs (to julienne a carrot) and adjectives (julienned carrot). Often we forget the origins of these words and spell them without the original accent marks.

Here we list just a few of the more commonly encountered culinary French terms. As you study this book, note how many other words are of French origin.

Bain marie (bane mah-ree)—a hot-water bath for gently cooking foods or keeping cooked foods hot; the container holding the food in the hot-water bath is also referred to as a bain marie.

Brunoise (broo-nwahz)—cube-shaped cuts (1/16 inch × 1/16 inch × 1/16 inch/1–2 mm × 1–2 mm × 1–2 mm) of vegetables or other foods.

Canapé (kahn-ah-pay)—an hors d'oeuvre (another French term, meaning appetizer) usually composed of a small piece of bread or toast topped with a savoury spread and garnish.

Chef (chehf)—literally, "leader" or "chief," the person in charge of a kitchen or department.

Demi-glace (de-me glass)—literally, "half-glaze," a mixture of brown stock and brown sauce reduced by half.

Ganache (gah-nasch)—a rich pastry or candy filling made with chocolate, heavy cream and other flavourings.

Julienne (ju-lee-en)—noun: stick-shaped cuts (1/16 inch × 1/16 inch × 1–2 inches/1–2 mm × 1–2 mm × 2.5–5 cm) of vegetables or other foods; verb: to cut food into the stick-shaped pieces; adjective: stick-shaped.

Mayonnaise (may-o-nayz)—a basic cold emulsion sauce made of egg yolks and oil and seasoned with vinegar, mustard and seasonings.

Mirepoix (meer-pwa)—a mixture of onions, carrots and celery, used to flavour stocks, stews and other dishes.

Mise en place (meez on plahs)—literally, "everything in place," the preparation and assembly of all ingredients and equipment needed before a dish can be cooked.

Purée (pur-ray)—noun: food that is processed by mashing, straining or fine chopping to achieve a smooth pulp; verb: to process food to achieve a smooth pulp.

Rondeau (ron-doe)—a shallow, wide, straight-sided pot with two loop handles.

Roux (roo)—a thickener for sauces made by cooking together equal weights of fat and flour.

Sachet (sa-shay)—or Sachet d'épices (sa-shay day pees), literally "bag of spices," aromatic ingredients such as bay leaf, thyme, cloves, peppercorns and parsley stems, tied in a cheesecloth bag and used to flavour stocks and other dishes.

Sauté (saw-tay)—to cook in an open pan in a small amount of fat at high temperature.

Sous-chef (sue chehf)—literally "under chef," the chef who is second in command of a kitchen.

Vinaigrette (vih-nay-greht)—a temporary emulsion of oil and vinegar seasoned with herbs, spices and other flavourings.

New Consumers

Demographic and social changes have contributed to the diversification of the food service industry by creating or identifying new consumer groups with their own desires or needs. By tailoring their menu, prices and décor accordingly, food service operations cater to consumers defined by age (baby boomers and seniors, in particular), type of household (singles, couples and families), income, education and geography.

During this century, especially in the decades following World War II, there has also been a rapid increase in the number and type of institutions providing food services. These include hospitals, schools, retirement centres, hotels and resorts (which may, in turn, have fine dining, coffee shop, banquet and room service facilities), factories and office complexes. Each of these institutions presents the professional chef with unique challenges, whether they be culinary, dietary or budgetary.

Through travel or exposure to the many books and magazines about food, consumers are becoming better educated and more sophisticated. Educated consumers provide a market for new foods and cuisines as well as an appreciation for a job well done.

Although some consumers may frequent a particular restaurant because its chef or owner is a celebrity or the restaurant is riding high on a crest of fad or fashion, most consumers choose a restaurant—whether it be a fast-food burger place or an elegant fine dining restaurant—because it provides quality food at a cost they are willing to pay. To remain successful, then, the restaurant must carefully balance its commitment to quality with marketplace realities.

THE FOOD SERVICE OPERATION

To function efficiently, a food service operation must be well organized and staffed with appropriate personnel. This staff is sometimes called a **brigade**. Although a chef will be most familiar with the back of the house or kitchen brigade, he or she should also understand how the dining room or front of the house operates. Staffing any food service facility ultimately depends on the type and complexity of the menu. (Types and styles of menus are discussed in Chapter 4, Menu Planning and Food Costing.)

Brigade—*a system of staffing a kitchen so that each worker is assigned a set of specific tasks; these tasks are often related by cooking method, equipment or the type of foods being produced.*

The Classic Kitchen Brigade

Escoffier is credited with developing the kitchen brigade system used in large restaurant kitchens. From the chaos and redundancy found in the private kitchens of the aristocracy, he created a distinct hierarchy of responsibilities and functions for commercial food service operations.

At the top is the *chef de cuisine* or *chef*, who is responsible for all kitchen operations, developing menu items and setting the kitchen's tone and tempo.

His or her principal assistant is the *sous-chef* (the under chef or second chef), who is responsible for scheduling personnel and replacing the chef and station chefs as necessary. The *sous-chef* may function as the *aboyeur* (expediter or announcer), who accepts the orders from the dining room, relays them to the various station chefs and then reviews the dishes before service. Point of sales systems have modified this practice.

The *chefs de partie* (station chefs) produce the menu items and are under the direct supervision of the chef or *sous-chef*. Previously, whenever a cook needed an item, he or his assistants produced it; thus several cooks could be making the same sauce or basic preparation. Under Escoffier's system, each station chef is assigned a specific task based upon either cooking method and equipment or the category of items to be produced. They include:

✦ The *saucier* (sauté station chef), who holds one of the most demanding jobs in the kitchen, is responsible for all sautéed items and most sauces.

✦ The *poissonier* (fish station chef) is responsible for fish and shellfish items and their sauces. This position is occasionally combined with the sauté station.

✦ The *grillardin* (grill station chef) is responsible for all grilled items.

✦ The *friturier* (fry station chef) is responsible for all fried items.

✦ The *rotisseur* (roast station chef) is responsible for all roasted items and jus or other related sauces. The grill and fry stations are sometimes subsumed into the roast station.

✦ The *potager* (soup station chef) is responsible for soups and stocks.

✦ The *legumier* (vegetable station chef) is responsible for all vegetable and starch items.

✦ The *potager* and *legumier* stations are often combined into a single vegetable station whose chef is known as the *entremetier*. *Entremets* were the courses served after the roast and were usually composed of vegetables, fruits, fritters or sweet items (the sorbet served before the main course in some contemporary restaurants is a vestigial *entremet*).

✦ The *garde-manger* (pantry chef) is responsible for buffets and cold food preparations, including salads and salad dressings, cold appetizers, charcuterie items, pâtés, terrines and similar dishes. The *garde-manger* supervises:

> The *boucher* (butcher), who is responsible for butchering meats and poultry (fish and shellfish are usually fabricated by the fish station chef).

> Also under the *garde-manger*'s supervision are the chefs responsible for hors d'oeuvre and breakfast items.

✦ The *tournant*, also known as the roundsman or swing cook, works where needed, often covering for the chefs des parties' days off.

✦ The *patissier* (pastry chef) is responsible for all baked items, including breads, pastries and desserts. Unlike the several station chefs, the *patissier* is not necessarily under the *sous-chef*'s direct supervision. The *patissier* supervises the following:

> The *boulanger* (bread baker), who makes the breads, rolls and baked dough containers used for other menu items (for example, *bouchées* and *feuilletés*).

> The *confiseur*, who makes candies and petits fours.

> The *glacier*, who makes all chilled and frozen desserts.

> The *decorateur*, who makes showpieces and special cakes.

✦ Depending upon the size and needs of any station or area, there are one or more *demi-chefs* (assistants) and *commis* (apprentices) who work with the station chef or pastry chef to learn the area.

The Modern Kitchen Brigade

Today most food service operations utilize a simplified version of Escoffier's kitchen brigade.

The **executive chef,** working chef or kitchen leader is a team player who coordinates kitchen activities and directs the kitchen staff's training and work efforts. Taking into consideration factors such as food costs, food availability and popularity as well as labour costs, kitchen skills and equipment, the executive chef plans menus and creates recipes. He or she sets and enforces nutrition, safety and sanitation standards and participates in (or at least observes) the preparation and presentation of menu items to ensure that quality standards are rigorously and consistently maintained. The chef or kitchen leader may also be responsible for purchasing food items and, often, equipment. In some food service operations, the executive chef may assist in designing the menu, dining room and kitchen. He or she also educates the dining room staff so that they can correctly answer questions about the menu. The chef may also work with food purveyors to learn about new food items and products, as well as with equipment vendors, food stylists, restaurant consultants, public relations specialists, sanitation engineers, nutritionists and dietitians.

The executive chef is assisted by a **sous-chef** or **executive sous-chef**, who participates in, supervises and coordinates the preparation of menu

---

◆◆◆

THE DINING ROOM

Like the back-of-the-house (i.e., kitchen) staff, the front-of-the-house (i.e., dining room) staff is also organized into a brigade. The dining room brigade is led by the **dining room manager** (French *maître d'hotel* or *maître d'*), who generally trains all service personnel, oversees wine selections and works with the chef to develop the menu. He or she organizes the seating chart and may also seat the guests. Working with this manager are:

The **wine steward** (French *chef de vin* or *sommelier*), who is responsible for the wine service, including purchasing wines, assisting guests in selecting wines and then serving the wines.

The **headwaiter** (French *chef de salle*), who is responsible for service throughout the dining room or a section of it. In smaller operations, his or her role may be assumed by the *maître d'* or a captain.

The **captains** (French *chefs d'étage*), who are responsible for explaining the menu to guests and taking their orders. They are also responsible for any tableside preparations.

The **front waiters** (French *chefs de rang*), who are responsible for ensuring that the tables are set correctly for each course, foods are delivered properly to the right tables and the needs of the guests are met.

The **backwaiters** (French *demi-chefs de rang* or *commis de rang*, also known as dining room attendants or buspersons), who are responsible for clearing plates, refilling water glasses and other general tasks appropriate for new dining room workers.

Whether a restaurant uses this entire array of staff depends upon the nature and size of the restaurant and the type of service provided. With **American service** there is one waiter (also called a server) who takes the order and brings the food to the table. The table is then cleaned by a dining room attendant. With **French service** there are two waiters: a captain and a waiter. The captain takes the order, does the tableside cooking and brings the drinks, appetizers, entrees and desserts to the table. The waiter serves bread and water, clears each course, crumbs the table and serves the coffee. With **Russian service**, the entree, vegetables and potatoes are served from a platter onto a plate by the waiter. With **buffet service**, usually found in specialty restaurants and some institutional settings such as schools and correctional facilities, diners generally serve themselves or are served by workers assigned to specific areas of the buffet. Restaurants offering buffet service generally charge by the meal; if they charge by the dish they are known as cafeterias.

items. His or her primary responsibility is to make sure that the food is prepared, portioned, garnished and presented according to the standards established by the executive chef. The sous-chef may be the cook principally responsible for producing menu items and supervising the kitchen.

Large hotels and conference centres with multiple dining facilities may have several **sous-chefs**, each responsible for a specific facility or function. There could be, for instance, a restaurant chef and a banquet chef. Sous-chefs report to the executive chef, and each in turn has a brigade/team functioning with him or her.

Like Escoffier's station chefs, **line cooks** (or section cooks) are responsible for preparing menu items according to recipe specifications. Making the most of time, talent, space and equipment, the chef assigns responsibilities to each of the line cooks. Depending upon the size and type of operation, the sauté, broiler, fry, soup and vegetable stations may be combined into one position, as may the pantry, cold foods and salad stations.

The **pastry chef** is responsible for developing recipes for and preparing desserts, pastries, frozen desserts and breads. He or she is usually responsible for purchasing the food items used in the bake shop.

And, as in Escoffier's days, **apprentices** and **kitchen helpers** are assigned where needed in today's kitchens.

New styles of dining have created new positions since Escoffier's days. The most notable is the **short-order/line cook**, who is responsible for quickly preparing foods to order in smaller operations. He or she will work the broiler, deep-fat fryer and griddle as well as make sandwiches and even some sautéed items.

Another is the **institutional cook**, who generally works with large quantities of prepackaged or prepared foods for a captive market such as a school, hospital or prison.

Camp cooks often prepare food in remote locations with limited facilities. They usually work for an industrial catering firm contracting multiple sites.

The Professional Chef

Although there is no one career ladder for producing a good professional chef, we believe that with training, skill, taste, judgment, dedication and pride a student cook or apprentice will develop into a professional chef.

Training

Chefs must be able to identify, purchase, utilize and prepare a wide variety of foods. They should be able to train and supervise a safe, skilled and efficient staff. To do all this successfully, chefs must possess a body of knowledge and understand and apply certain scientific and business principles. Schooling helps. A culinary program—whether at the secondary or post-secondary level—should, at a minimum, provide the student cook with a basic knowledge of foods, food styles and the methods used to prepare foods. Student cooks must be able to apply sanitation, nutrition and business procedures such as food costing. They start their apprenticeship at this time. After approximately three years of work experience and technical training, they take the Journeyperson's exam and Interprovincial Red Seal. This can be followed by achieving Certified Chef de Cuisine (CCC) status.

This book is designed to help you learn these basics. Many chapters have extensive sections identifying foods and equipment. Throughout this book we emphasize culinary principles, not recipes. Whenever possible, whether it be preparing puff pastry or grilling a steak, we focus on the general procedure, highlighting fundamental principles and skills; we discuss both the how and why of cooking. Only then are specific applications and sample recipes given. We also want you to have a sense of the rich tradition of cookery, so informative sidebars on food history, chef biographies and other topics are scattered throughout the book.

In this way, we follow the trail blazed by Escoffier, who wrote in the introduction to *Le Guide culinaire* that his book is not intended to be a compendium of recipes slavishly followed, but rather his treatise should be a tool that leaves his colleagues "free to develop their own methods and follow their own inspiration; ... the art of cooking ... will evolve as a society evolves, ... only basic rules remain unalterable."

As with any profession, an education does not stop at graduation. The acquisition of knowledge continues after the student cook joins the ranks of the employed. He or she should take additional classes on unique or ethnic cuisines, nutrition, business management or specialized skills. Apprentices and professionals should regularly review some of the many periodicals and books devoted to cooking and should travel and try new dishes to broaden their culinary horizons. The professional cook should also become involved in professional organizations in order to meet peers and exchange ideas.

Skill

Culinary schooling alone does not make a student a cook. Nothing but practical, hands-on experience will provide even the most academically gifted student with the skills needed to produce, consistently and efficiently, quality foods or to organize, train, motivate and supervise a staff.

Many food service operations recognize that new workers, even those who have graduated from culinary programs, need time and experience to develop and hone their skills. Therefore, many graduates start at entry-level positions. They should not be discouraged; advancement will come and the training pays off in the long run. Today culinary styles and fashions change frequently. What do not go out of fashion are well-trained, skilled and knowledgeable cooks. They can adapt.

Taste

No matter how knowledgeable or skilled the cook, he or she must be able to produce food that tastes great or the consumer will not return. A cook can only do so if confident about his or her own sense of taste.

Our total perception of taste is a complex combination of smell, taste, sight, sound and texture. All senses are involved in the enjoyment of eating; all must be considered in creating or preparing a dish. The cook should develop a taste memory by sampling foods, both familiar and unfamiliar. He or she should think about what is being tasted, make notes and experiment with flavour combinations and cooking methods. But a cook should not be inventive simply for the sake of invention. Rather, cooks must consider how the flavours, appearances, textures and aromas of various foods will interact to create a total taste experience.

Gastronomy—*the art and science of eating well.*

Gourmet—*a connoisseur of fine food and drink.*

Gourmand—*a connoisseur of fine food and drink, often to excess.*

Gourmet foods—*foods of the highest quality, perfectly prepared and beautifully presented.*

Judgment

Selecting menu items, determining how much of what item to order, deciding whether and how to combine ingredients and approving finished items for service are all matters of judgment. Although knowledge and skill play a role in developing judgment, sound judgment comes only with experience.

Dedication

Becoming a cook is hard work; so is being one. The work is often physically taxing, the hours are usually long and the pace is frequently hectic. Despite these pressures, the cook is expected to efficiently produce consistently fine foods that are properly prepared, seasoned, garnished and presented. To do so, the cook must be dedicated to the job.

The dedicated cook should never falter. The food service industry is competitive and dependent upon the continuing good will of an often fickle public. One bad dish or one off night can result in a disgruntled diner and lost business. The chef should always be mindful of the food prepared and the customer served.

The cook must also be dedicated to co-workers. Virtually all food service operations rely on teamwork to get the job done well. Good teamwork requires dedication to a shared goal as well as a positive attitude. The chef is the individual who provides leadership and mentoring to the team.

Pride

Not only is it important that the job be well done, but the professional cook should have a sense of pride in doing it well. Pride should also extend to personal appearance and behaviour in and around the kitchen. The professional cook should be well-groomed and in uniform when working.

The professional cook's uniform consists of comfortable shoes, trousers (either solid white, solid black, black-and-white checked or black-and-white striped), a white double-breasted jacket, an apron and a neckerchief usually knotted or tied cravat style. The uniform has certain utilitarian aspects: Checked trousers disguise stains; the double-breasted white jacket can be rebuttoned to hide dirt, and the double layer of fabric protects from scalds and burns; the neckerchief absorbs facial perspiration; and the apron protects the uniform and insulates the body. Side towels are useful. This uniform should be worn with pride. Shoes should be polished; trousers and jacket should be pressed.

The crowning element of the uniform is the toque. The toque is the tall white hat worn by cooks and chefs almost everywhere. Although the toque traces its origin to the monasteries of the 6th century, the style worn today was introduced at the end of the 19th century. Most cooks now wear a standard 6- or 9-inch-high (15 or 24 cm) toque, but historically a cook's rank in the kitchen dictated the type of hat worn. Beginners wore flat-topped calottes; cooks with more advanced skills wore low toques and the master chefs wore high toques called *dodin-bouffants*. Culinary lore holds that the toque's pleats—101 in all—represented the 101 ways its wearer could successfully prepare eggs.

Some establishments are switching to other styles of hats. The change is usually part of a marketing plan. In addition, colours and designs have been introduced into uniforms. But functionality must always be kept in mind.

CONCLUSION

The art and science of cookery form a noble profession with a rich history and long traditions. With training, knowledge, skill, taste, judgment, dedication and pride, the student cook or apprentice can become part of this profession. In this book we provide you with the basic knowledge and describe the techniques at which you must become skilled. Dedicate yourself to learning this information and mastering your skills. Once you have done so, take pride in your accomplishments. Good luck.

QUESTIONS FOR DISCUSSION

1. Describe the kitchen brigade system. How does the classical brigade compare with modern teams?
2. What are the roles of a chef, sous-chef and line cook in a modern kitchen?
3. Describe the differences in a meal prepared by Carême and one prepared by Point.
4. List and explain three technological advances affecting food preparation.
5. Discuss the societal changes that have contributed to diversification in the modern food service industry.

WEBLINKS

Food and Culinary Links for the Culinary Historian
   www.foodbooks.com/foodlink.htm
New York Public Library Culinary History Research Guide
   www.nypl.org/research/chss/grd/resguides/culhista.html
All Things Culinary: Culinary Links on StarChefs
   www.starchefs.com/Links/menu.html
National Film Board of Canada: Documentary Films about Food and Food
   Industries
   www.onf.ca/FMT/E/cate/F/Food_and_Food_Industries.html
Canadian Federation of Chefs and Cooks
   www.cfcc.ca/
Cuisine Canada
   www.FoodserviceWorld.com/cuisine/home.html

CHAPTER 2 FOOD SAFETY AND SANITATION

LEARNING OUTCOMES

After studying this chapter, you will be able to:

◆ identify the causes of food-borne illnesses
◆ handle foods in a safe manner
◆ take appropriate actions to create and maintain a safe and sanitary working environment

*T**he Canadian Food Inspection Agency has overall responsibility for setting and monitoring food safety standards. The industry is assuming more responsibility and accountability for food safety, and the role of health inspectors is evolving. Providing consumers with safe food is the food handler's most important responsibility. Unfortunately food handlers include anyone coming into contact with food or food preparation equipment. Food handlers are also the primary cause of food-related illnesses.*

By understanding how food-borne illnesses are caused and what can be done to prevent them, you will be better able to protect your customers. This chapter is not meant to be a complete discussion of sanitation in food service operations. It should, however, alert you to practices that can result in food-borne illnesses.

Federal, provincial and municipal health, building and other codes are designed in part to ensure that food is handled in a safe and proper manner. Always consult your local health department for information and guidance. Take an approved safe food handling course or upgrade your present certificate. And always be conscious of what you can do to create and maintain a safe product and safe environment for your customers, your fellow employees and yourself.

Biological hazard—*a danger to the safety of food from disease-causing microorganisms such as bacteria, molds, yeasts, viruses or fungi.*

Chemical hazard—*a danger to the safety of food from chemical substances, especially cleaning agents, pesticides and toxic metals.*

Physical hazard—*a danger to the safety of food from particles such as glass chips, metal shavings, bits of wood or other foreign matter.*

Sanitation refers to the creation and maintenance of conditions that will control food contamination or food-borne illness. **Contamination** refers to the presence, generally unintended, of harmful organisms or substances. Contaminants can be (1) biological, (2) chemical or (3) physical. When consumed in sufficient quantities, food-borne contaminants can cause illness or injury, long-lasting disease or even death.

Contamination occurs in two ways: direct contamination and cross-contamination. **Direct contamination** is the contamination of raw foods, or the plants or animals from which they come, in their natural settings or habitats. Chemical and biological contaminants such as bacteria and fungi are present in the air, soil and water. So foods can be easily contaminated by their general exposures to the environment: Grains can become contaminated by soil fumigants in the field and shellfish can become contaminated by ingesting toxic marine algae.

Chemicals and microorganisms generally cannot move on their own, however. They need to be transported, an event known as **cross-contamination**. The major cause of cross-contamination is people. Food handlers can transfer biological, chemical and physical contaminants to food while processing, preparing, cooking or serving it. It is therefore necessary to view sanitation as the correction of problems caused by direct contamination and the prevention of cross-contamination during processing and service.

DIRECT CONTAMINATION

Biological Contaminants

Biologically based food-borne illnesses can be caused by several **microorganisms**, primarily bacteria, parasites, viruses and fungi. By understanding how these organisms live and reproduce, you can better understand how to protect food from them.

Bacteria

Bacteria, which are single-celled microorganisms, are the leading cause of food-borne illnesses. See Figure 2.1. Most bacteria reproduce by binary fission: their genetic material is first duplicated and the nucleus then splits, each new nucleus taking some of the cellular material with it. See Figure 2.2. Under favourable conditions each bacterium can divide every 15–30 minutes. Within 12 hours, 1 bacterium can become a colony of 72 billion bacteria, more than enough to cause serious illness.

Some rod-shaped bacteria are capable of forming spores. Spores are thick-walled structures used as protection against a hostile environment. The bacteria essentially hibernate within their spores where they can survive extreme conditions that would otherwise destroy them. When conditions become favourable, the bacteria return to a viable state. This is important in food sanitation because bacterial spores may not be destroyed by heating or sanitizing techniques.

Some bacteria are beneficial, such as those that aid in digesting food or decomposing garbage. Other bacteria spoil food, but without rendering it unfit for human consumption. These bacteria, called **putrefactives**, are not a sanitation concern. (Indeed, in some cultures, they are not even a culinary concern. Cultures differ on what constitutes "bad" meat, for example, and red meat is sometimes hung for a time or "aged" to allow bacteria to tenderize the meat.)

Microorganisms—*single-celled organisms as well as tiny plants and animals that can be seen only through a microscope.*

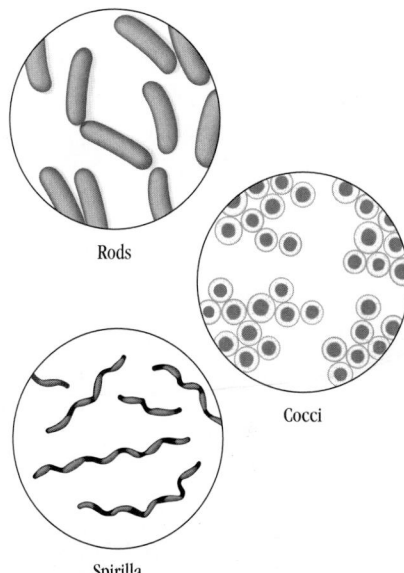

Rods

Cocci

Spirilla

FIGURE 2.1 *Bacteria can be classified by shape: Rods are short, tubular structures; cocci are disks, some of which form clusters; and spirilla are corkscrews.*

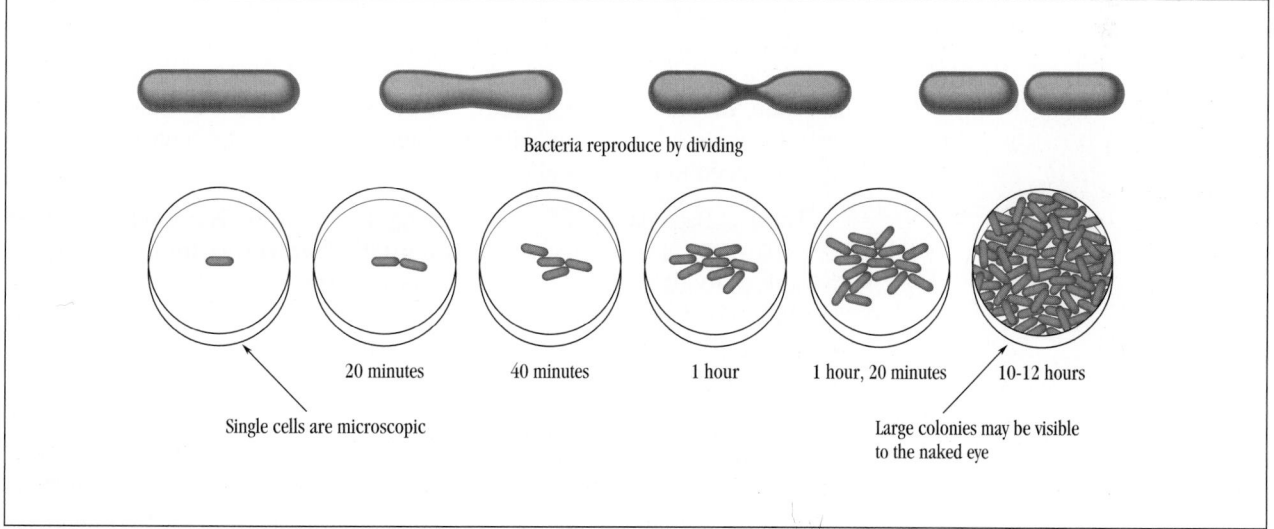

Bacteria reproduce by dividing

20 minutes   40 minutes   1 hour   1 hour, 20 minutes   10-12 hours

Single cells are microscopic

Large colonies may be visible to the naked eye

FIGURE 2.2 *One bacterium divides into 2; the 2 bacteria each divide, creating 4; the 4 become 16 and so on. It takes only a very short time for one bacterium to produce millions more.*

The bacteria that are dangerous when consumed by humans are called **pathogenic**. These are the bacteria that must be destroyed or controlled in a food service operation.

Intoxications and Infections

Depending upon the particular microorganism, pathogenic bacteria can cause illnesses in humans in one of three ways: by intoxication, infection or toxin-mediated infection.

Botulism is a well-known example of an **intoxication**. Certain bacteria produce **toxins**, a byproduct of their life processes. You cannot smell, see or taste toxins. Ingesting these toxin-producing bacteria by themselves does not cause illness. But when their toxins are ingested, the toxins can poison the consumer. Proper food-handling techniques are critical in preventing an intoxication, because even if food is cooked to a sufficiently high temperature to kill all bacteria present, the toxins they leave behind are usually not destroyed.

The second type of bacterial illness is an **infection**. Salmonella is the most well-known example. An infection occurs when live pathogenic bacteria (infectants) are ingested. The bacteria then live in the consumer's intestinal tract. It is the living bacteria, not their waste products, that cause an illness. An infectant must be alive when eaten for it to do any harm. Fortunately, these bacteria can be destroyed by cooking foods to sufficiently high temperatures, usually 165°F (74°C) or higher, and maintaining the temperature for sufficient time.

The third type of bacterial illness has characteristics of both an intoxication and an infection, and is referred to as a **toxin-mediated infection**. Examples are *Clostridium perfringens* and *Escherichia coli 0157:H7*. When these living organisms are ingested they establish colonies in human or animal intestinal tracts where they then produce toxins. These bacteria are particularly dangerous for young children, the elderly, the infirm or immunosuppressed individuals.

Preventing Bacterial Intoxications and Infections

All bacteria, like other living things, need certain conditions in order to complete their life cycles. Like humans, they need food, a comfortable temperature, moisture, the proper pH, the proper atmosphere and time. The best way to prevent bacterial intoxications and infections is to control the factors bacteria need to survive and multiply.

Food   Bacteria need food for energy and growth. The foods on which bacteria thrive are referred to as **potentially hazardous foods**. Potentially hazardous foods include those high in protein such as meat, poultry, fish and shellfish. Dairy products, eggs, grains and some vegetables are also sufficiently high in protein to support bacterial growth. These foods and items containing these foods (for example, custard, hollandaise sauce and quiche) must be handled with great care.

Temperature   Temperature is the most important factor in the pathogenic bacteria's environment because it is the factor most easily controlled by food service workers. Most microorganisms are destroyed at high temperatures. Freezing slows, but does not stop, growth nor does it destroy bacteria.

Most of the bacteria that cause food-borne illnesses multiply rapidly at temperatures between 60°F and 120°F (16°C–49°C). Therefore, the broad range of temperatures between 40°F and 140°F (4°C–60°C) is referred to as the **temperature danger zone**. See Figure 2.3. By keeping foods out of the temperature danger zone you decrease the bacteria's ability to thrive and reproduce.

This is known as the **time-and-temperature principle**. Potentially hazardous foods should be heated or cooled quickly so that they are within the temperature danger zone as briefly as possible.

To control the growth of any bacteria that may be present, it is important to maintain the internal temperature of food at or above 140°F (60°C), or 40°F (4°C) or below. Simply stated: *Keep hot foods hot, cold foods cold.*

Keep hot foods hot. The high internal temperatures reached during cooking (165°F–212°F/74°C–100°C) kill most of the bacteria that can cause food-borne illnesses. When foods are reheated the internal temperature should reach or exceed 170°F (77°C) for two minutes in order to kill any bacteria that may have grown during storage. Once properly heated, hot foods must be held at temperatures of 140°F (60°C) or above. Foods that are to be displayed or served hot must be heated rapidly to reduce the time within the temperature danger zone. When heating or reheating foods:

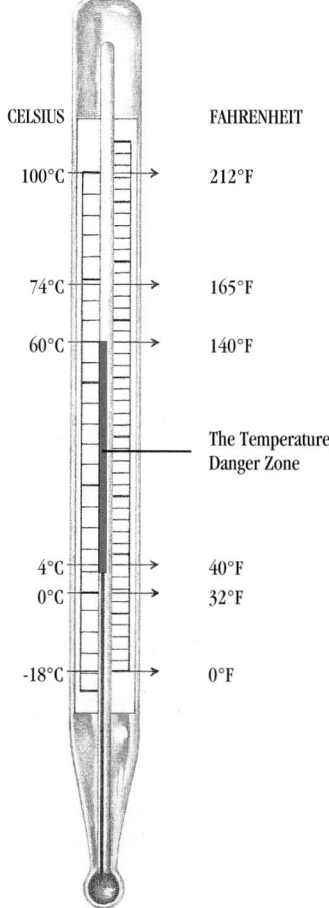

FIGURE 2.3

+ Heat small quantities at a time.
+ Stir frequently.
+ Heat foods as close to service time as possible.
+ Use preheated ingredients whenever possible to prepare hot foods.
+ Never use a steam table for heating or reheating foods. Bring the food to an appropriate internal temperature (at least 170°F/77°C) for two minutes before placing it in the steam table for holding.

Keep cold foods cold. Foods that are to be displayed, stored or served cold must be cooled rapidly. When cooling foods:

+ Refrigerate semisolid foods at 40°F (4°C) or below in containers that are less than 2 inches (5 cm) deep. (Increased surface area decreases cooling time.)
+ Avoid crowding the refrigerator; allow air to circulate around foods.
+ Vent hot foods in an ice water bath as illustrated in Chapter 10, Stocks and Sauces. Stir frequently.
+ Use prechilled ingredients, for example mayonnaise, to prepare cold foods.
+ Store cooked foods above raw foods to prevent cross-contamination.

Keep frozen foods frozen. Freezing at 0°F (–18°C) or below essentially stops bacterial growth but will not kill the bacteria. Do not place hot foods in a standard freezer. They will not cool more rapidly and the release of heat can raise the temperature of other foods in the freezer. Only a special blast freezer can be used for chilling hot items. If one is not available, cool hot foods as mentioned above before freezing them. When frozen foods are thawed, bacteria that are present will begin to grow. Therefore,

+ Never thaw foods at room temperature.
+ Thaw foods gradually under refrigeration. Place them in a container to prevent cross-contamination from dripping or leaking liquids.
+ Thaw foods under cold running water if items are wrapped in plastic.
+ Thaw foods in a microwave *only* if the food will be prepared and served immediately.

Time When bacteria are moved from one place to another they require time to adjust to new conditions. This resting period, during which very little growth occurs, is known as the **lag phase**. This phase may last from one to

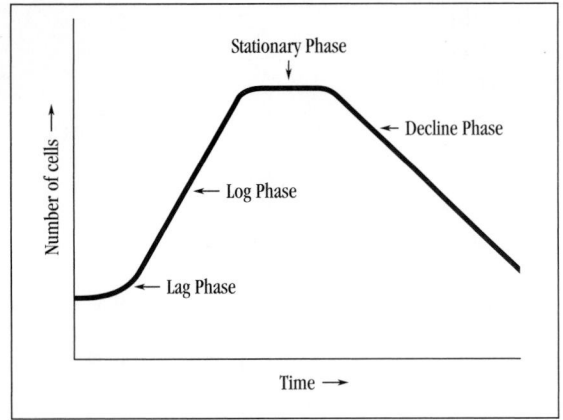

FIGURE 2.4 *Bacterial Growth Curve*

four hours. It is followed by the **log phase**, a period of accelerated growth, which lasts until the bacteria begin to crowd others within their colony, creating competition for food, space and moisture. This begins the **decline** or **negative growth phase**, during which bacteria die at an accelerated rate. See Figure 2.4.

Because of the lag phase, foods can be in the temperature danger zone for *very short periods* during preparation without an unacceptable increase in bacterial growth. Exposure to the temperature danger zone is cumulative, however, and should not exceed two hours total. The less time food is in the temperature danger zone, the less opportunity bacteria have to multiply.

Moisture   Bacteria need a certain amount of moisture, which is expressed as water activity or A_W. Water itself has an A_W of 1.0. Any food with an A_W of .85 or greater is considered potentially hazardous. See Table 2.1. Bacteria cannot flourish where the A_W is too low, usually below .85. This explains why dry foods such as flour, sugar or crackers are rarely subject to bacterial infestations. A low A_W only halts bacterial growth, however; it does not kill the microorganisms. When a dried food such as beans or rice is rehydrated, any bacteria present can flourish and the food may become potentially hazardous.

pH—*a measurement of the acid or alkaline content of a solution. Expressed on a scale of 0 to 14.0, 7.0 is considered neutral or balanced; the lower the pH value, the more acidic the substance. The higher the pH value, the more alkaline the substance.*

Acid/Alkaline Balance   Bacteria are affected by the **pH** of their environment. See Table 2.2. Although they can survive in a wider range, they prefer a neutral environment with a pH of 6.6 to 7.5. Growth is usually halted if the pH is 4.6 or less. Acidic foods such as lemon juice, tomatoes and vinegar create an unfavourable environment for bacteria. Simply adding an acidic ingredient to foods should not, however, be relied upon to destroy bacteria or preserve foods. The amount of acidity appropriate for flavouring is not sufficient to ensure the destruction of bacteria.

Atmosphere   Bacteria need an appropriate atmosphere. Some bacteria, known as **aerobes**, thrive on oxygen, while others, known as **anaerobes**, do not require the presence of oxygen. Others, known as **facultative**, can adapt and will survive with or without oxygen. Unfortunately, most pathogenic bacteria are facultative. See Table 2.3.

Canning, which creates an anaerobic atmosphere, destroys bacteria that need oxygen. But it also creates a favourable atmosphere for anaerobic and facultative bacteria. A complete vacuum need not be formed for anaerobic bacteria to thrive, however. A tight foil covering, a complete layer of fat, even a well-fitting lid can create an atmosphere sufficiently devoid of oxygen to permit growth of anaerobic bacteria. *Clostridium botulinum* is anaerobic and is one of the most deadly forms of food poisoning.

Parasites

Parasites are tiny organisms that depend on nutrients from a living host to complete their life cycle. Meat animals, fish, shellfish and humans can all play host to

TABLE 2.1	WATER ACTIVITY OF COMMON FOODS
0.0	
.1	
.2	
.3	
.4	
.5	dried pasta
.6	
.7	flour, dry milk
.75	jam, jelly, crisp cooked bacon
.8	
.85	MINIMUM FOR BACTERIAL GROWTH
.9	raw bacon
.95	soft cheese
.98	poultry and meat
1.0	distilled water

TABLE 2.2   pH OF COMMON FOODS

	0	
	1.0	
A	2.0	limes, lemons
C	3.0	commercial mayonnaise
I	4.0	orange juice
D	4.6	bananas
	5.0	most vegetables (5.0 to 7.0)
	6.4	chicken and fresh meats
NEUTRAL	7.0	distilled water, fish
	8.0	crackers.
A	8.5	baking soda in water
L	9.0	
K	10.0	
A	11.0	
L	12.0	household ammonia
I	13.0	
	14.0	

TABLE 2.3   CHARACTERISTICS OF BACTERIAL ILLNESSES

Common Name	Organism Name	Form	Sources	Prevention
Staph	Staphylococcus aureus	Toxin	Starchy foods, cold meats, bakery items, custards, milk products, humans with infected wounds or sores	Wash hands and utensils before use; exclude unhealthy food handlers; avoid having foods at room temperature
Perfringens or CP	Clostridium perfringens	Cells and toxin	Reheated meats, sauces, stews, casseroles	Keep cooked foods at an internal temperature of 140°F (60°C) or higher; reheat leftovers to internal temperature of 170°F (75°C) or higher
Botulism	Clostridium botulinum	Toxin, cells, spores	Cooked foods held for an extended time at warm temperatures with limited oxygen; rice, potatoes, smoked fish, canned vegetables	Keep internal temperature of cooked foods above 140°F (60°C) or below 40°F (4°C); reheat leftovers thoroughly; discard swollen cans
Salmonella	Salmonella	Cells	Poultry, eggs, milk, meats, fecal contamination	Thoroughly cook all meat, poultry, fish and eggs; avoid cross-contamination with raw foods; maintain good personal hygiene
Strep	Streptococcus	Cells	Infected food handlers	Do not allow employees to work if ill; protect foods from customers' coughs and sneezes
E. coli or 0157	Escherichia coli 0157:H7 (enteropathogenic strains)	Cells and toxins	Any food, especially raw milk, raw vegetables, raw or rare beef (especially ground), humans (fecal)	Thoroughly cook or reheat items
Listeria	Listeria monocytogenes	Cells	Milk products, deli meats, humans	Avoid raw milk and cheese made from unpasteurized milk; keep storage areas clean

parasites. Several types of very small parasitic worms can enter an animal through contaminated feed, then settle in the host's intestinal tract or muscles, where they grow and reproduce. The ones most commonly found in foods are *trichinella spiralis* and *anisakis*.

Trichinosis is caused by eating undercooked game or pork infected with trichina larvae. Trichinosis has been virtually eradicated by grain-feeding hogs and testing them before slaughter. Traditionally it was thought that pork must be cooked to internal temperatures of 170°F (77°C) or higher to eradicate the larvae. This generally resulted in a dry, tough product. Scientists have now determined that trichina larvae are killed if held at 137°F (58°C) for 10 seconds. The Canadian Food Inspection Agency currently recommends cooking pork products to an internal temperature of 150°F (66°C). (All commercially packaged cured or smoked pork products must be heated to an internal temperature of 155°F [68°C] during processing.)

Anisakiasis is another illness caused by parasitic roundworms. Anisakis worms reside in the organs of fish, especially bottom feeders or those taken from contaminated waters. Raw or undercooked fish are most often implicated in anisakiasis. Fish should be thoroughly cleaned immediately after being caught so that the parasites do not have an opportunity to spread. Cooking to a minimum internal temperature of 140°F (60°C) or freezing at –4°F (–20°C) for 24 hours is recommended, as they can survive even highly acidic marinades.

Cyclospora infections are caused by a single-celled parasite found in water or food contaminated by infected feces. Produce from undeveloped countries is a common source of cyclospora parasites, as is untreated water. Avoiding such products is the best prevention method.

Viruses

Other biologically based food-borne illnesses such as hepatitis A and Norwalk virus are caused by viruses. Viruses are the smallest known form of life. They invade the living cells of a host, take over those cells' genetic material, and cause the cells to produce more viruses.

Viruses do not require a host to survive, however. They can survive—but not multiply—while lying on any food or food contact surface. Unlike bacteria, viruses can be present on any food, not just a potentially hazardous food. The food or food contact surface simply becomes a means of transportation between hosts.

Unlike bacteria, viruses are not affected by the water activity, pH or oxygen content of their environment. Some, however, can be destroyed by temperatures higher than 176°F (80°C). Basically, the only way to prevent food-borne viral illnesses is to prevent contamination in the first place.

Hepatitis A often enters the food supply through shellfish harvested from polluted waters. The virus is carried by humans, some of whom may never know they are infected, and is transmitted by poor personal hygiene and cross-contamination. The actual source of contamination may be hard to establish, though, because it sometimes takes months for symptoms to appear.

The **Norwalk virus** is spread almost entirely by poor personal hygiene among infected food handlers. The virus is found in human feces, contaminated water or vegetables fertilized by manure. The virus can be destroyed by high cooking temperatures but not by sanitizing solutions or freezing. In fact, Norwalk virus has even been found in ice cubes.

Foods most likely to transmit viral diseases are those that are not heated after handling. These include salads, sandwiches, milk, baked products, uncooked fish and shellfish and sliced meats. The best techniques for avoiding viral food-borne illnesses are to observe good personal hygiene habits, avoid cross-contamination, and use only foods obtained from reputable sources.

Fungi

Fungi are a large group of plants ranging from single-celled organisms to giant mushrooms. Fungi are everywhere: in the soil, air and water. Poisonous mushrooms, a type of fungus, can cause illness or death if consumed. The most common fungi, however, are molds and yeasts.

Molds

Molds are algae-like fungi that form long filaments or strands. These filaments often extend into the air, appearing as cottony or velvety masses on food. Large colonies of mold are easily visible to the naked eye. Although many food molds are not dangerous, and some are even very beneficial, rare types known as mycotoxicoses do form toxins that have been linked to food-borne illnesses. For the most part, however, molds only affect the appearance and flavour of foods. They cause discolouration, odours and off-flavours.

Unlike bacteria, molds can grow on almost any food at almost any temperature, moist or dry, acidic or alkaline. Mold cells can be destroyed by heating to 140°F (60°C) for 10 minutes. Their toxins are heat resistant, however, and are not destroyed by normal cooking methods. Therefore, foods that develop mold should be discarded and any container or storage area cleaned and sanitized. The roots can grow one inch (2.5 cm) into the host product.

Yeasts

Yeasts require water and carbohydrates (sugar or starch) for survival. As the organisms consume carbohydrates they expel alcohol and carbon dioxide gas through a process known as **fermentation**. Fermentation is of great benefit in making bread and alcoholic beverages.

Although naturally occurring yeasts have not been proven to be harmful to humans, they can cause foods to spoil, developing off-flavours, odours and discolouration. Yeasts are killed at temperatures of 136°F (58°C) or above.

Chemical Contaminants

The contamination of foods by a wide variety of chemicals is a very real and serious danger, one about which the public has shown a strong interest. Chemical contamination is usually inadvertent and invisible, making it extremely difficult to detect. The only way to avoid such hazards is for everyone working in a food service operation to follow proper procedures when handling foods or chemicals.

Chemical hazards include contamination with (1) the residual chemicals used in growing the food supply, (2) food service chemicals, and (3) toxic metals.

Residual Chemicals

Chemicals such as antibiotics, fertilizers, insecticides and herbicides have brought about great progress in controlling plant, animal and human diseases, permitting greater food yields and stimulating animal growth. The benefits derived from these chemicals, however, must be contrasted with the adverse effects on humans when chemicals are used indiscriminately or improperly.

The danger of these chemicals lies in the possible contamination of human foods, which occurs when chemical residues remain after the intended goal is achieved. Fruits and vegetables must be washed and peeled properly to reduce the risk of consuming residual chemicals.

Food Service Chemicals

A more common contamination problem involves the common chemicals found in most every food service operation. Cleaners, polishes, pesticides and abrasives are often poisonous to humans. Illness and even death can result from foods contaminated by such common items as bug spray, drain cleaner, oven cleaner or silver polish. These chemicals pose a hazard if used or stored near food supplies. Even improperly washing or rinsing dishes and utensils leaves a soap residue, which is then transmitted via food to anyone using the item.

To avoid food service chemical contamination, make sure all cleaning chemicals are clearly labelled and stored well away from food preparation and storage areas. Always use these products as directed by the manufacturer; never reuse a chemical container or package. Follow WHMIS guidelines.

Toxic Metals

Another type of chemical contamination occurs when metals such as lead, mercury, copper, zinc and antimony are dispersed in food or water. For example:

+ Metals can accumulate in fish and shellfish living in polluted waters or in plants grown in soil contaminated by the metals.
+ Using an acidic food such as tomatoes or wine in a zinc (galvanized) or unlined copper container causes metal ions to be released into the food.
+ Antimony is used in bonding enamelware; it can be released into food when the enamel is chipped or cracked, so great care must be taken when using enamelware (terrines).
+ Lead enters the water supply from lead pipes and solder and is found in the glaze on some imported ceramic items.

Consuming any of these metals can cause poisoning.

To prevent metal contamination, use only approved food service equipment and utensils and re-tin copper cookware as needed. Never serve fish or shellfish that was illegally harvested or obtained from uninspected sources.

Physical Contaminants

Physical contaminants include foreign objects that find their way into foods by mistake. Examples include metal shavings created by a worn can opener, pieces of glass from a broken container, hair and dirt. Physical contaminants may be created by intentional tampering, but they are most likely the result of poor safety and sanitation practices or a lack of training.

CROSS-CONTAMINATION

Generally, microorganisms and other contaminants cannot move by themselves. Rather, they are carried to foods and food contact surfaces by humans, rodents or insects. This transfer is referred to as cross-contamination.

Cross-contamination is the process by which one item, such as your fingers or a cutting board, becomes contaminated and then contaminates another food or tool. For example, a chef's knife and cutting board are used in fabricating a potentially hazardous food such as a chicken. In this case, the chicken had been directly contaminated with salmonella at the hatchery. If the knife and board are not cleaned *and sanitized* properly, anything that touches them can also become contaminated. So, even though cooking the chicken to an appropriate internal temperature may destroy the salmonella in the chicken, the uncooked salad greens cut on the same cutting board or with the same knife can contain live bacteria. Health regulations require separate cutting boards for raw and cooked products.

Cross-contamination can occur with bacteria or other microorganisms, chemicals, dirt and debris. Side towels are an especially common source of cross-contamination. If a cook uses a side towel to wipe a spill off the floor, then uses that same towel to dry his hands after visiting the restroom, he has recontaminated his hands with whatever bacteria or dirt was on the floor. Cross-contamination also occurs when raw foods come in contact with cooked foods. Never store cooked food below raw food in a refrigerator, and never return cooked food to the container that held the raw food. Cross-contamination can also occur easily from smoking, drinking or eating, unless hands are properly washed after each of these activities.

Reducing Cross-Contamination

Cross-contamination can be reduced or even prevented by (1) personal cleanliness, (2) dish and equipment cleanliness and (3) pest management.

Personal Cleanliness

To produce clean, sanitary food, all food handlers must maintain high standards of personal cleanliness and hygiene. This begins with good grooming.

Humans provide the ideal environment for the growth of microorganisms. Everyone harbours bacteria in the nose and mouth. These bacteria are easily spread by sneezing or coughing, by not disposing of tissues properly and by not washing hands frequently and properly. Touching your body, then touching food or utensils, transfers bacteria. Human waste carries many dangerous microorganisms, so it is especially important to wash your hands thoroughly after visiting the restroom. An employee who is ill should not be allowed in the operation.

Current research shows that the human immunodeficiency virus (HIV), the causative agent of AIDS, is not spread by food. According to the United States Centers for Disease Control and Prevention, food service workers infected with HIV should not be restricted from work unless there is another infection or illness.

There are several things you can do to decrease the risk of an illness being spread by poor personal hygiene:

◆ Wash your hands frequently and thoroughly. Gloves are not a substitute for proper hand washing and may create a false sense of security.
◆ Keep your fingernails short, clean and neat. Do not bite your nails or wear nail polish.
◆ Keep any cut or wound antiseptically bandaged. An injured hand should also be covered with a disposable glove.
◆ Bathe daily, or more often if required.

+ Keep your hair clean and restrained.
+ Wear work clothes that are clean and neat. Avoid wearing jewellery or watches.
+ Do not eat, drink, smoke or chew gum in food preparation areas.

Dish and Equipment Cleanliness

Clean—*to remove visible dirt and soil.*

Sanitize—*to reduce pathogenic organisms to safe levels.*

Sterilize—*to destroy all living microorganisms.*

One of the primary requirements for any food service facility is cleanability. But there is an important difference between clean and sanitary. **Clean** means that the item has no visible soil on it. **Sanitary** means that harmful substances are reduced to safe levels. Thus, something may be clean without being sanitary; the visible dirt can be removed, but disease-causing microorganisms can remain.

The cleaning of dishes, pots, pans and utensils in a food service operation involves both removing soil and sanitizing. Soil can be removed manually or by machine. Sanitizing can be accomplished with heat or chemical disinfectants.

Procedures for manually washing, rinsing and sanitizing dishes and equipment generally follow the three-compartment sink set-up shown in Figure 2.5. The dish/pot washer must:

1. Scrape and spray the item to remove soil.
2. Wash the item in the first sink compartment at a temperature not lower than 113°F (45°C) using an approved detergent. A brush or cloth may be used to remove any remaining soil.
3. Rinse the item in the second sink compartment using clear, hot water of at least 113°F (45°C).
4. Sanitize the item in the third sink compartment by either:
   a. immersing it in 170°F (77°C) water for at least 2 minutes, or
   b. immersing it in an approved chemical sanitizing solution according to the manufacturer's directions. Use test strips to verify adequate concentrations.
5. Empty, clean and refill each sink compartment as necessary and check the water temperature regularly.

Food service items, dishes, silverware and utensils should always be allowed to air-dry, as towel-drying may recontaminate them.

Machine-washing dishes or utensils follows a similar procedure. The dishwasher should first scrape and rinse items as needed, then load the items into

FIGURE 2.5 *The Three-Compartment Sink* *Procedure – scrape, spray, wash, rinse, sanitize and air-dry each item.*

dishwasher racks so that the spray of water will reach all surfaces. The machine cleans the items with a detergent in wash water of at least 140°F (60°C) for hot-temperature machines, then sanitizes them with either a hot-water rinse (at least 180°F/82°C) for 10 seconds or chemical disinfectant. When the machine cycle is complete, items should be inspected for residual soil, allowed to air-dry, and stored in a clean area.

Work tables and stationary equipment must also be cleaned and sanitized properly. Equipment and surfaces, including floors, walls and work tables, should be easily exposed for inspection and cleaning and should be constructed so that soil can be removed effectively and efficiently with normal cleaning procedures. A thorough cleaning schedule should be implemented and closely monitored to prevent problems from developing.

The following points are important to the safety and cleanliness of any food service facility:

✦ Equipment should be disassembled for cleaning; any immersible pieces should be cleaned and sanitized like other items.

✦ All work tables or other food contact surfaces should be cleaned with detergent, then sanitized with a clean cloth dipped in a sanitizing solution.
An acceptable sanitizing solution is made by combining 1 gallon (4.5 L) of lukewarm water with 1 tablespoon (15 mL) of chlorine bleach. This solution must be replaced every 2 hours. Other chemical sanitizers should be prepared and used according to health department and manufacturer's directions.

✦ Surfaces, especially work surfaces with which food may come in contact, should be smooth and free of cracks, crevices or seams in which soil and microorganisms can hide.

✦ Floors should be nonabsorbent and should not become slippery when wet.

✦ Walls and ceilings should be smooth and light-coloured so that soil is easier to see.

✦ Light should be ample and well located throughout food preparation and storage areas. All light bulbs should be covered with a sleeve or globe to protect surroundings from shattered glass.

The design of a kitchen can also affect food safety and sanitation. Food preparation equipment should be arranged in such a way as to decrease the chances of cross-contamination. The work flow should eliminate crisscrossing and backtracking. Employees should be able to reach storage, refrigeration and cleanup areas easily. Dish- and pot-washing areas and garbage facilities should be kept as far from food preparation and storage areas as possible. Cleaning supplies and other chemicals should be stored away from foods.

In most communities, the design of a food service facility is controlled in part by public health regulations. The local health and building codes should be consulted when planning any construction or remodelling, or when purchasing and installing new equipment.

Pest Control

Food can be contaminated by insects (e.g., roaches and flies) and rodents (e.g., mice and rats). These pests carry many harmful bacteria on their bodies and defecate frequently, thus contaminating any surface with which they come in contact. An insect or rodent infestation is usually considered a serious health risk and should be dealt with immediately and thoroughly. Pests must be controlled by (1) building them out of the facility; (2) creating an environment in which they cannot find food, water or shelter; and (3) relying on professional extermination.

The best defence against pests is to prevent infestations in the first place by building them out. Any crack—no matter how small—in door frames, walls or window sills should be repaired immediately and all drains, pipes and vents should be well sealed. Inspect all deliveries thoroughly and reject any packages or containers found to contain evidence of pests.

Flies are a perfect method of transportation for bacteria because they feed and breed on human waste and garbage. Use screens or "fly fans" (also known as air curtains) to keep them out in the first place. Control of garbage is also essential because moist, warm, decaying organic material attracts flies and provides favourable conditions for eggs to hatch and larvae to grow.

Pest control also requires creating an inhospitable environment for pests. Store all food and supplies at least 6 inches (15 cm) off the floor and 6 inches (15 cm) away from walls. Rotate stock often to disrupt nesting places and breeding habits. Provide good ventilation in storerooms to remove humidity, airborne contaminants, grease and fumes. Do not allow water to stand in drains, sinks or buckets, as cockroaches are attracted to moisture. Clean up spills and crumbs immediately and completely to reduce their food supply.

Despite your best efforts to build pests out and maintain proper housekeeping standards, it is still important to watch for the presence of pests. For example, cockroaches leave a strong, oily odour and feces that look like large grains of pepper. Cockroaches prefer to search for food and water in the dark, so seeing any cockroach on the move in the daylight is an indication of a large infestation.

Rodents (mice and rats) tend to hide during the day, so an infestation may be rather serious before any creature is actually seen. Rodent droppings, which are shiny black to brownish grey, may be evident, however. Rodent nests made from scraps of paper, hair or other soft materials may be spotted.

Should an infestation occur, consult a licensed pest control operator immediately. With early detection and proper treatment, infestations can be eliminated. Be very careful in attempting to use pesticides or insecticides yourself. These chemicals are toxic to humans as well as to pests. Great care must be used to prevent contaminating food or exposing workers or customers to the chemicals.

HACCP SYSTEMS

Now that you understand what contaminants are and how they can be destroyed or controlled, it is necessary to put this information into practice during day-to-day operations. Although local health departments inspect all food service facilities on a regular basis, continual self-inspection and control are essential for maintaining sanitary conditions.

Hazard Analysis Critical Control Points (HACCP) is proving to be an effective and efficient method for managing and maintaining sanitary conditions in all types of food service operations. Developed by Pillsbury in 1971 for NASA to ensure food safety for astronauts, HACCP—and a similar system adopted by the National Restaurant Association known as Sanitary Assessment of the Food Environment/S.A.F.E.—is a rigorous system of self-inspection. It focuses on the

TABLE 2.4   HACCP ANALYSIS—THE FLOW OF FOOD

Control Point	Hazard	Critical Action
Menu and recipes	Potentially hazardous foods; human hands involved in food preparation	Plan physical work flow; train employees
Receiving	Contaminated or spoiled goods	Inspect and reject delivery if necessary
Storage	Cross-contamination to and from other foods; bacterial growth; spoilage	Maintain proper temperatures; rotate stock; discard if necessary
Preparation	Cross-contamination; bacterial growth	Wash hands and utensils; avoid temperature danger zone
Cooking	Bacterial survival; physical or chemical contamination	Cook to proper temperatures
Holding and service	Contamination; bacterial growth	Use clean equipment; maintain proper temperatures
Cooling leftovers	Bacterial survival and growth	Cool rapidly, cover and refrigerate
Reheating	Bacterial survival and growth	Heat rapidly to 170°F (75°C); maintain temperatures; do not mix old and new products

flow of food through the food service facility, from the decision to include an item on the menu through service to the consumer.

An HACCP critical control point is any step during the processing of a food when a mistake can result in the transmission, growth or survival of pathogenic bacteria. At each of these steps there is some hazard of contamination. The HACCP process begins by identifying the steps and evaluating the type and severity of hazard that can occur. It then identifies what actions can be taken to reduce or prevent each risk of hazard. See Table 2.4. The activities that present the highest risk of hazard should be monitored most closely. For example, a cook's failure to wash his hands before handling cooked food presents a greater risk of hazard than does a dirty floor. In other words, hazards must be prioritized and correction of critical concerns should take priority. See Figure 2.6.

Whatever system is followed, however, all personnel must be constantly aware of and responsive to problems and potential problems associated with the safety of the food they are serving. Accurate record keeping is a requirement of an effective HACCP program.

THE SAFE WORKER

Kitchens are filled with objects that can cut, burn, break, crush or sprain the human body. The best way to prevent work-related injuries is through proper training, adherence to good work habits and careful supervision.

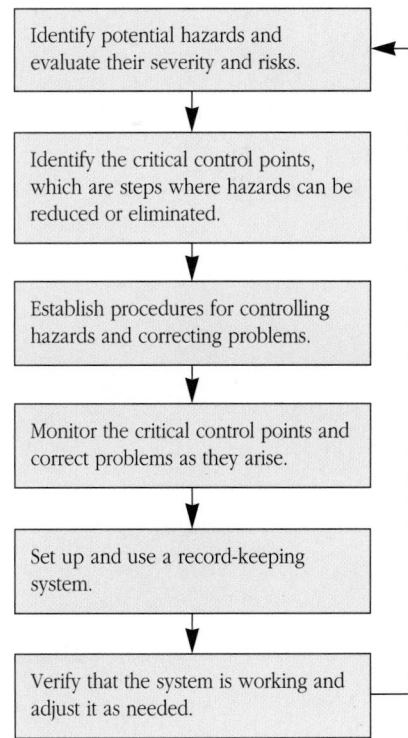

FIGURE 2.6 *An HACCP System Flowchart*

The federal government enacted legislation designed to reduce hazards in the work area, thereby reducing accidents. The Occupational Health and Safety Act (OHSA) covers a broad range of safety matters. Employers who fail to follow its rules can incur financial penalties. Unfortunately, human error is the leading cause of accidents, and no amount of legislation can protect someone who doesn't work in a safe manner.

Safe behaviour on the job reflects pride, professionalism and consideration for fellow workers. The following list should alert you to conditions and activities aimed at preventing accidents and injuries:

- Clean up spills as soon as they occur.
- Learn to operate equipment properly; always use guards and safety devices.
- Wear clothing that fits properly; avoid wearing jewellery, which may get caught in equipment.
- Use knives and other equipment for their intended purpose only.
- Walk, do not run.
- Keep exits, aisles and stairs clear and unobstructed.
- Always assume a pot or pan is hot; handle with dry towels.
- Position pot and pan handles out of the aisles so they do not get bumped.
- Get help or use a cart when lifting or moving heavy objects.
- Avoid back injury by lifting with your leg muscles; stoop, do not bend, when lifting.
- Use a well-placed ladder or stool for climbing; do not use a chair, box, drawer or shelf.
- Keep breakable items away from food storage or production areas.
- Warn people when you must walk behind them, especially when carrying a hot pan.

Some accidents will inevitably occur, and it is important to act appropriately in the event of an injury or emergency. This may mean calling for help or providing first aid. Every food service operation should be equipped with a complete first-aid kit. Municipal regulations may specify the exact contents of the kit. Be sure that the kit is conveniently located and well stocked at all times.

The Canadian Red Cross and St. John Ambulance offer training in first aid, cardiopulmonary resuscitation (CPR), and the Heimlich manoeuvre used for victims of choking. All employees should be trained in basic emergency procedures. A list of emergency telephone numbers should be posted by each telephone.

ONCLUSION

All food service workers are responsible for supplying food that is safe to eat. Microorganisms that cause food-borne illnesses are found in all types of food; they can be destroyed or their growth can be severely limited by proper food handling procedures. By learning about food contaminants, how they are spread and how they can be prevented or controlled, you can help ensure customer safety. You are also responsible for your own physical safety as well as that of your customers and fellow workers. Maintaining sanitary and safe facilities and high standards of personal hygiene is a necessary part of this responsibility.

QUESTIONS FOR DISCUSSION

1. Foods can be contaminated in several ways. Explain the differences between biological, chemical and physical contamination. Give an example of each.

2. Under what conditions will bacteria thrive? Explain what you can do to alter these conditions.

3. What is the temperature danger zone? What is its significance in food preparation?

4. Explain how improper or inadequate pest control can lead to food-borne illnesses.

5. Define the letters HACCP. How is this system used in a typical food service facility?

WEBLINKS

Foodnet: Food Safety
    foodnet.fic.ca/foodsafety.html

Agriculture and Agri-Food Canada: HACCP Implementation Manual
    foodnet.fic.ca/safety/haccp.html

North Carolina State University: Food Safety Main Page
    www.ces.ncsu.edu/depts/foodsci/agentinfo/

Centers for Disease Control and Prevention: Division of Bacterial and Mycotic
    Diseases: Foodborn Diseases
    www.cdc.gov/ncidod/dbmd/foodborn.htm

Health Canada: Food Quality and Safety Programs
    www.hc-sc.gc.ca/datahpsb/npu/agr1.htm

Canadian Food Inspection Agency/Agence canadienne d'inspection
    des aliments
    www.cfia-acia.agr.ca/

CHAPTER 3
NUTRITION

$\mathcal{S}$

◆◆◆

LEARNING OUTCOMES

After studying this chapter you will be able to:

◆ identify categories of nutrients and explain their importance in a balanced diet

◆ explain the evolution of Canada's Food Guide and its significance in planning nutritious menus

◆ describe the effects storage and preparation techniques have on various foods' nutritional values

◆ identify the use of ingredient substitutes and alternatives

◆ understand product nutrition labels

◆ provide diners with nutritious foods

ince the days of prehistoric hunters and gatherers, people have understood that some animals and plants are good to eat and others are not. For thousands of years, cultures worldwide have attributed medicinal or beneficial effects to certain foods, particularly plants, and have recognized that foods that would otherwise be fine to eat may be unhealthy if improperly prepared or stored.

But it was not until the past few decades that people have become increasingly concerned about understanding how all foods affect their health and what foods can and should be consumed in order to promote good health. These concerns comprise the study of nutrition.

This chapter cannot provide an in-depth study of the nutritional sciences. Rather, it sets forth basic information about nutrients, food additives, and ingredient substitutes and alternatives. It also provides guidelines for reading package labels and preparing nutritious meals.

Detailed nutritional information about many specific foods is found throughout the book. All recipes are accompanied by a nutritional analysis; recipes for dishes particularly low in calories, fat or sodium are marked with a 🍃.

Nutrition is the science that studies nutrients, (chemical) substances found in food, that nourish the body by promoting growth, maintenance and repair and by facilitating body functions. Some nutrients also provide energy.

The six categories of nutrients are carbohydrates, fats, proteins, vitamins, minerals and water. **Essential nutrients** are those that must be provided by food because the body does not produce them in sufficient quantities or cannot make them at all. (See Table 3.1.) Some nutritional components are considered nonessential because healthy, well-nourished bodies can make them in sufficient quantities to satisfy their needs.

Our bodies depend upon the various nutrients for different purposes and require different amounts of each depending on age, sex and health. In addition, some nutrients depend on one another for proper functioning. For example, calcium and vitamin D work together in the body: Vitamin D promotes the absorption of the calcium that the body utilizes for proper bone growth. Because foods differ with regard to their nutritional content, it is important to eat a variety of foods in order to achieve a proper nutritional balance.

TABLE 3.1	ESSENTIAL NUTRIENTS	

Essential nutrients are those that must be provided because the human body does not produce them in sufficient quantities. They are:

Energy Nutrients	Carbohydrates
	Fats (linoleic and linolenic acids)
	Proteins (the amino acids: histidine, isoleucine, leucine, lysine, methionine, phenylalanine, threonine, tryptophan and valine)
Water	
Vitamins	Thiamin, riboflavin, niacin, pantothenic acid, biotin, vitamin B_6, vitamin B_{12}, folate, vitamin C, vitamin A, vitamin D, vitamin E and vitamin K
Minerals	Calcium, chloride, magnesium, phosphorus, potassium, sodium, sulfur, selenium, zinc, chromium, copper, fluoride, iodide, iron, manganese and molybdenum

ESSENTIAL NUTRIENTS

Three of the essential nutrients provide calories or energy. Sometimes referred to as macronutrients, they are carbohydrates, fats and proteins.

A **calorie** (abbreviated *kcal*) is the way we describe the amount of energy in food. The number of calories in a food is measured by a device called a calorimeter, which burns the food and measures the heat the food gives off. From that measurement, an estimate for how the food would be burned in the body is calculated. The results of the calculation are the calorie designations assigned to the energy nutrients.

One gram of pure fat supplies 9 kcal; one gram of pure carbohydrate supplies 4 kcal, as does one gram of pure protein. Most foods are a combination of carbohydrates, proteins and fats; their kcal content may not be easily determined unless we know how much of each nutrient the food contains.

Vitamins and minerals are essential nutrients and must be provided through the diet because the body cannot manufacture them in quantities adequate to ensure good health. They have no calories. Because they are needed in smaller amounts that the other nutrients, they are sometimes referred to as micronutrients.

Calorie—*the unit of energy measured by the amount of heat required to raise 1000 grams of water 1°C; it is also written as* kilocalorie *or* kcal.

Carbohydrates

Carbohydrates are composed of carbon, hydrogen and oxygen and are found exclusively in plant foods and milk sugars. **Simple carbohydrates** include monosaccharides (single sugars) and disaccharides (double sugars). See Table 3.2. Simple carbohydrates are found in the naturally occurring sugars in fruit, vegetables and milk, as well as in sweeteners such as honey, corn syrup and table sugar. **Complex carbohydrates** are composed of long chains of the monosaccharide glucose. Starch is a complex carbohydrate. Complex carbohydrates are found in vegetables, fruits and cereal grains such as wheat, barley and oats. The body digests (or breaks down) these sugars and starches into glucose. Glucose, also known as blood sugar, is a very important source of energy for the body.

Another complex carbohydrate is fibre. Fibre is a unique carbohydrate because humans cannot digest it, so they do not derive calories from it. **Dietary fibre**, which generally comes from the seeds and cell walls of fruits, vegetables and cereal grains, plays an important role in health. Because the body cannot digest dietary fibre, it passes through the digestive system almost completely unchanged. This helps keep the digestive tract running smoothly. Fibre increases fecal bulk, which encourages proper elimination of waste products from the large intestines and helps avoid some forms of gastrointestinal distress. Some forms of fibre also reduce serum cholesterol.

TABLE 3.2	SUGARS
Monosaccharides	Disaccharides
Glucose (blood sugar)	Lactose (milk sugar)
Fructose (fruit sugar)	Maltose (malt sugar)
Galactose (part of milk sugar)	Sucrose (table sugar)

Fats

Fats, like carbohydrates, are composed of carbon, hydrogen and oxygen. The differences between carbohydrates and fats are the number and arrangement of the carbon, hydrogen and oxygen atoms. Fats are found in both animal and plant foods, although fruits contain very little fat. Fats provide calories, help carry fat-soluble vitamins and give food a creamy, pleasant mouthfeel.

Depending upon their structure, the fats in foods can be classified as saturated, monounsaturated or polyunsaturated. Most foods contain a combination of the three, although one kind may predominate. If saturated fat is the most abundant kind (as in the fat surrounding muscle meats), we describe the food as being saturated even though it contains a mixture of all three fats.

Saturated fats are found mainly in animal products such as milk, eggs and meats, as well as in tropical oils such as coconut and palm. Monounsaturated fats come primarily from plants and plant foods such as avocados and olives and the oils made from them. Polyunsaturated fats come from plants (soy and corn, for example) and fish.

Vegetable oils like canola and olive are high in monounsaturated fat. Cottonseed, sunflower, corn and safflower oils are high in polyunsaturated fat. All oils, however, are a combination of the three kinds of fat.

Saturated fats such as butter, lard and other animal fats are usually solid at room temperature. Monounsaturated and polyunsaturated fats are usually liquid at room temperature. Hydrogenation is a process by which a liquid fat is made more solid (or saturated) by the addition of hydrogen atoms. Hydrogenation increases the percentage of saturated fatty acids, resulting in a more solid product (such as margarine made from a polyunsaturated oil like corn oil). It also reduces the tendency to rancidity so shelf life is increased.

The body has more difficulty breaking down saturated fats than it does monounsaturated and polyunsaturated fats. Research suggests that high-fat diets, especially diets high in saturated fat, may be linked to heart disease, obesity and certain forms of cancer. Saturated fats are also linked to high levels of blood cholesterol, which are associated with arteriosclerosis (hardening of the arteries). Although the liver can produce all the cholesterol the body needs, additional cholesterol is often provided in the diet. Dietary cholesterol is found only in foods of animal origin. Meats, poultry, fish, shellfish, eggs and dairy products are all sources of dietary cholesterol. Fruits, vegetables and grains are cholesterol free.

Proteins

Proteins are found in both animal and plant foods. They differ from carbohydrates and fats in that they contain nitrogen as well as carbon, hydrogen and oxygen. Protein chains are composed of amino acids, the building blocks of protein. There are 20 amino acids, 9 of which are essential. People who eat a varied diet with adequate calories and protein can easily get all of the essential amino acids. The specific combination of amino acids gives each protein its unique characteristics and properties.

Proteins are necessary for manufacturing, maintaining and repairing body tissues. They are essential for the periodic replacement of the outer layer of skin as well as for blood clotting and scar tissue formation. Hair and nails, which provide a protective cover for the body, are composed of proteins.

Another important function of protein is the regulation of body processes. Proteins regulate the balance of water, acids and bases and move nutrients in and out of cells. Proteins contribute to the immune system by producing antibodies, which are necessary for combatting diseases. Proteins also form the enzymes that act as catalysts for body functions and the hormones that help direct body processes.

Water

The human body is approximately 60% water. Water is necessary for transporting nutrients and wastes throughout the body. It cushions the cells, lubricates the joints, maintains stable body temperatures and assists waste elimination. It also promotes functioning of the nervous system and muscles.

Although the principal sources of water are beverages, water is also the predominant nutrient by weight in most foods. Some foods such as tomatoes, oranges, watermelon and iceberg lettuce are particularly high in water. Others

---

Acidulated water—*a mildly acidic solution of water and lemon juice or vinegar used to prevent cut fruits and vegetables from darkening.*

Artesian-well water—*water obtained from an underground source; the water rises to the surface under pressure.*

Bottled water—*any water, either still or sparkling, that is bottled and sold.*

Deionized water—*water that has had the cations and anions removed by passing it over a bed of ion-exchange resins.*

Demineralized water—*water that has had all of the minerals and impurities removed by passing it over a bed of ion-exchange resins.*

Distilled water—*water that has had all of the minerals and impurities removed through distillation; it is generally used for pharmaceutical purposes.*

Drinking water—*water that comes from a government-approved source and has undergone some treatment and filtration; it can be bottled or available on tap and is used for drinking and general culinary purposes.*

such as dried fruits, nuts and seeds are lower. Water is also formed by the body when other nutrients are metabolized.

The average adult should consume at least 8 to 10 glasses (64 fluid ounces or 2 litres) of water a day to ensure adequate intake. People who perspire a lot should drink more water to replace body water lost through sweat.

Vitamins

Vitamins are vital dietary substances needed to regulate **metabolism** and for normal growth and body functions. They are essential and noncaloric, needed in the body in small amounts.

There are 13 vitamins. Table 3.3 lists them, their principal functions in the human body, the foods that contain high concentrations of these nutrients and some of the preparation and storage techniques that help retain the maximum amount of the various vitamins in their food sources.

Vitamins are divided into two categories: fat soluble and water soluble. The fat-soluble vitamins are A, D, E and K and are found in foods containing fat. Excess supplies of these vitamins may be stored in fatty tissues and the liver. Water-soluble vitamins are vitamin C and the B-complex vitamins, including thiamin (B_1), riboflavin (B_2), niacin (B_3), cyano-cobalamin (B_{12}), pyridoxine (B_6), pantothenic acid, biotin and folate. Vitamins B_1 and B_2 are commonly referred to by their names, thiamin and riboflavin, respectively; whereas, cobalamin and pyridoxine are commonly referred to by their letter designations, B_{12} and B_6, respectively. Water-soluble vitamins are not stored to the extent that fat-soluble vitamins are, and excesses may be excreted in the urine. Because of these differences, deficiencies in water-soluble vitamins usually develop more rapidly.

Virtually all foods contain some vitamins. Many factors contribute to a particular food's vitamin concentration: an animal's feed; the manner by which the produce is harvested, stored or processed; even the type of soil, sunlight, rainfall and temperature have significant effects on a food's vitamin content. For example, tomatoes have a higher concentration of vitamin C when picked ripe from the vine rather than when picked green. Also, different varieties of fruits and vegetables have different vitamin contents. A Wegener apple, for example, has 19 mg of vitamin C while a Red Delicious has only 6 mg.

You can control vitamin concentration and retention through careful food preparation:

1. Prepare vegetables as close to service time as possible; vegetables cut long before service lose more vitamins than those cut immediately before cooking.

2. Whether a vegetable is boiled, steamed or microwaved also determines the amount of vitamins it retains. Because the B-complex vitamins and vitamin C are water soluble, they are easily leached (washed out) or destroyed by food processing and preparation techniques involving high temperatures and water. Steaming and microwaving help retain nutrients (when steaming, keep the water level below the vegetables). But microwave cooking is best because it cooks vegetables with minimal water in less time.

3. In general, roasting and grilling meats, poultry, fish and shellfish preserve more vitamins than stewing and braising. The temperatures to which foods are cooked and length of time they are cooked may affect vitamin retention as well.

4. Storage affects vitamin concentrations. For example, long exposure to air may destroy vitamin C. Using airtight containers prevents some of this loss. Riboflavin is sensitive to light, so milk products (which are good sources of riboflavin) should be stored in opaque containers.

Fluoridated water—*water, either naturally fluoridated or treated with a fluorine-containing compound; intended to promote healthy teeth by preventing tooth decay.*

Hard water—*water with relatively high calcium and magnesium concentrations.*

Mineral water—*drinking water that comes from a protected underground water source and contains at least 250 parts per mineral of total dissolved solids such as calcium.*

Natural water—*bottled drinking water not derived from a municipal water supply; it can be mineral, spring, well or artesian-well water.*

Purified water—*bottled water produced by distillation, reverse osmosis, deionization or suitable processes that meet governmental standards.*

Seltzer water—*a flavourless natural mineral water with carbonation, originally from the German town of Nieder Selters.*

Soda water—*a flavourless water with induced carbonation consumed plain or used as a mixer for alcoholic drinks or soda fountain confections; also known as club soda and seltzer.*

Soft water—*water with a relatively high sodium concentration.*

Spring water—*water obtained from an underground source that flows naturally to the earth's surface.*

Well water—*water obtained from a hole bored into the ground to tap an aquifer.*

Metabolism—*all of the chemical reactions and physical processes that continually occur in living cells and organisms.*

TABLE 3.3   VITAMINS: THEIR FUNCTIONS, SOURCES AND TECHNIQUES FOR RETAINING MAXIMUM NUTRIENT CONTENT

Vitamin	Functions in the Human Body	Sources	Techniques for Nutrient Retention
Vitamin A	Keeps the skin healthy; protects eyes; protects mouth and nose linings; supports immune functioning	Deep yellow and orange vegetables, leafy green vegetables, deep orange fruits, egg yolks, liver, fortified milk	Serve fruits and vegetables raw or lightly cooked; store vegetables covered and refrigerated; steam vegetables; roast or broil meats
Vitamin D	Helps body absorb calcium; regulates calcium and phosphorus in the bones; assists bone mineralization	Fortified milk, butter, some fish oils, eggs yolks (exposure to sunlight produces vitamin D in the body)	It is stable under heat and insoluble in water, therefore it is unaffected by cooking
Vitamin E	Antioxidant; protects membranes and cell walls	Vegetable oils, whole grains, dark leafy vegetables, wheat germ, nuts, seeds, whole grains	Use whole grain flours; store foods in airtight containers; avoid exposing the food to light and air
Vitamin K	Assists blood-clotting proteins	Liver, dark green leafy vegetables (bacteria in the intestinal tract also produce some vitamin K)	Steam or microwave vegetables; do not overcook meats
Vitamin C (Ascorbic acid)	Supports immune system functioning; repairs connective tissues; promotes healing; assists amino acid metabolism	Citrus fruits, green vegetables, strawberries, cantaloupes, tomatoes, broccoli, potatoes	Serve fruits and vegetables raw; steam or microwave vegetables
Thiamin (Vitamin B_1)	Assists energy metabolism; supports nervous system functioning	Meats (especially pork), legumes, whole grains	Use enriched or whole grain pasta or rice; do not wash whole grains before cooking or rinse afterwards; steam or microwave vegetables; roast meats at moderate temperatures; cook meats only until done
Riboflavin (Vitamin B_2)	Assists energy metabolism	Milk, cheese, yogurt, fish, enriched grain breads and cereals, dark green leafy vegetables	Store foods in opaque containers; roast or broil meats or poultry
Niacin (Vitamin B_3)	Promotes normal digestion; supports nervous system functioning; assists energy metabolism	Meats, poultry, fish, dark green leafy vegetables, whole grain or enriched breads and cereals, nuts	Steam or microwave vegetables; roast or broil beef, veal, lamb and poultry (pork retains about the same amount of niacin regardless of cooking method)
Vitamin B_6	Necessary for protein metabolism and red blood cell formation	Meats, fish, poultry, shellfish, whole grains, dark green vegetables, potatoes, liver	Serve vegetables raw; cook foods in a minimum amount of water and for the shortest possible time; roast or broil meats and fish
Vitamin B_{12}	Helps produce red blood cells; assists metabolism	Animal foods only, particularly milk, eggs, poultry and fish	Roast or broil meats, poultry and fish
Folate	Necessary for protein metabolism and red blood cell formation	Orange juice, dark green leafy vegetables, organ meats, legumes, seeds	Serve vegetables raw; steam or microwave vegetables; store vegetables covered and refrigerated
Biotin	Coenzyme in energy metabolism, glycogen synthesis and fat metabolism	Widespread in foods	
Pantothenic acid	Coenzyme in energy metabolism	Widespread in foods	

Minerals

Minerals cannot be manufactured by the body. They are obtained by eating plants that have drawn minerals from the ground or the flesh of animals that have eaten such plants.

Minerals are a critical component in hard and soft tissues (e.g., the calcium, magnesium and phosphorus present in bones and teeth). Minerals also regulate certain necessary body functions. For example, nerve impulses are transmitted through an exchange of sodium and potassium ions in the nerve cells.

Minerals are divided into two categories: trace minerals and major minerals. Trace minerals such as iron are needed in only very small amounts. Major minerals such as calcium are needed in relatively larger quantities. Table 3.4

TABLE 3.4   MINERALS: THEIR FUNCTIONS AND SOURCES

Mineral	Functions in the Human Body	Sources
Major Minerals:		
Calcium	Helps build bones and teeth; helps blood clot; promotes muscle and nerve functions	Dairy products, canned salmon and sardines, broccoli, kale, tofu, turnips
Magnesium	Muscle entraction; assists energy metabolism; bone formation	Green leafy vegetables, whole grains, legumes, fish, shellfish, cocoa
Phosphorus	Helps build bones and teeth; assists energy metabolism; formation of DNA	All animal tissues, milk, legumes, nuts
Potassium	Maintains electrolyte and fluid balance; promotes normal body functions; assists protein metabolism	Meats, poultry, fish, fruits (especially bananas, oranges and cantaloupes), legumes, vegetables
Sodium	Maintains normal fluid balance; necessary for nerve impulse transmission	Salt, soy sauce, processed foods, MSG
Chloride	With sodium, involved in fluid balance; component of stomach acid	Salt, soy sauce, meats, milk, processed foods
Sulphur	A component of some proteins, insulin and the vitamins biotin and thiamin	All protein-containing foods
Trace minerals:		
Iron	Part of hemoglobin (the red substance in blood that carries oxygen); prevents anemia	Liver, meats, shellfish, enriched breads and cereals, legumes
Zinc	A component of insulin; enhances healing; a component of many enzymes; involved in taste perception; bone formation	Protein foods, whole grain breads and cereals, fish, shellfish, poultry, vegetables
Selenium	Antioxidant	Fish, shellfish, meats, eggs, grains (depends on soil conditions)
Iodine	Component of thyroid hormone	Iodized salt, fish, shellfish, bread, plants grown in iodine-rich soil
Copper	Facilitates iron absorption; part of enzymes	Meats, fish, shellfish, nuts, seeds
Fluoride	Necessary for bone and teeth formation; helps teeth resist tooth decay	Fluoridated drinking water, fish, shellfish
Chromium	Insulin cofactor	Liver, whole grains, brewer's yeast, nuts, oils
Molybdenum	Cofactor in metabolism	Legumes, cereals
Manganese	Cofactor in metabolism	Whole grains, nuts, organ meats
Cobalt	Component of vitamin B_{12} (cobalamin)	

✦✦✦
LIGHTEN UP!

On the night before their trials on the Colosseum floor, gladiators ate meat to make themselves strong. Until a few years ago, modern-day gladiators and coaches insisted that athletes needed meat the night before the game. Of course, being more scientific, they referred to their training-table steak as protein.

Times change, the pendulum swings, and who ever thought a brawny athlete would admit to being a vegetarian? The new message … is that we needn't stop eating meat entirely. Instead, we should reduce our consumption of beef, turning to alternative sources of protein such as fish, poultry, low-fat dairy products, nuts, beans and seeds, and increase our consumption of fresh fruits, vegetables, grains and other complex carbohydrates. The results: fewer fats, more fiber and lower cholesterol, helping to create a slimmer, energetic, longer-lasting body.

This new "fresh," "nutrient-dense," "light," "natural," "heart-healthy" approach to dining has gone from fad to fashion to fact of life. From formal French to Mexican fast food, facilities offering portions of innovative, tasty, eye-catching healthy cuisine will surely win allegiance and accolades from patrons. So lighten up. Replace the deep-fat fryer with a griddle. Garnish with fresh fruit. Serve whole grain bread, but take heed: Balance is paramount. An occasional indulgence is a joy. There will always be room for chocolate.

HARRIS GOLDEN, formerly Executive Chef of Elizabeth Arden's MAINE CHANCE HEALTH RESORT, currently owns and operates TRIANGLES RESTAURANT in La Jolla, CA. Golden is also the author of two cookbooks.

lists some minerals, their principal functions in the human body and the foods that contain high concentrations of these nutrients.

As with vitamins, food processing and preparation can reduce a food's mineral content. Soaking or cooking in large amounts of water can leach out small quantities of water-soluble minerals. Processing or refining grains, such as the wheat used to make white flour, also removes minerals.

EATING FOR HEALTH

It is generally recognized that a balanced diet is an important component of a healthy lifestyle. Eating well and exercising can contribute to a longer, healthier life.

Health Organization Recommendations

Planning a diet to enhance health is made simpler by diet and exercise recommendations from organizations such as the Canadian Heart Association and the Canadian Cancer Society. Both stress the importance of controlling the amount of fat in the diet and consuming in greater quantities plant foods such as vegetables, fruits and whole grains.

Another useful planning tool is *Canada's Food Guide to Healthy Eating*, published by Health Canada. The Food Guide recommends moderating the consumption of fats, cholesterol, sugar, salt and alcohol while increasing the consumption of grains, fruits and vegetables. Variety, energy, balance and moderation are the three central principles. Although some details of this guide are unique to Canada, the basic healthy eating principles that it promotes are much the same as the Food Pyramid used in the U.S. and the food guides of other international societies. By illustrating what foods are important and recommending a range of servings, they eliminate the guesswork of eating nutritiously.

The goal of healthy eating is to promote the shift from the traditional Canadian diet that is based heavily on protein-rich, higher-fat foods to one that includes more complex carbohydrates, fibre, key vitamins and minerals. This shift is presented visually in the Food Guide by the rainbow design illustrated in Figure 3.1. The larger outside arcs encourage eating proportionally more grain products, vegetables and fruits; the smaller inside arcs represent the smaller amounts required of milk and meat products. (See Figure 3.2.)

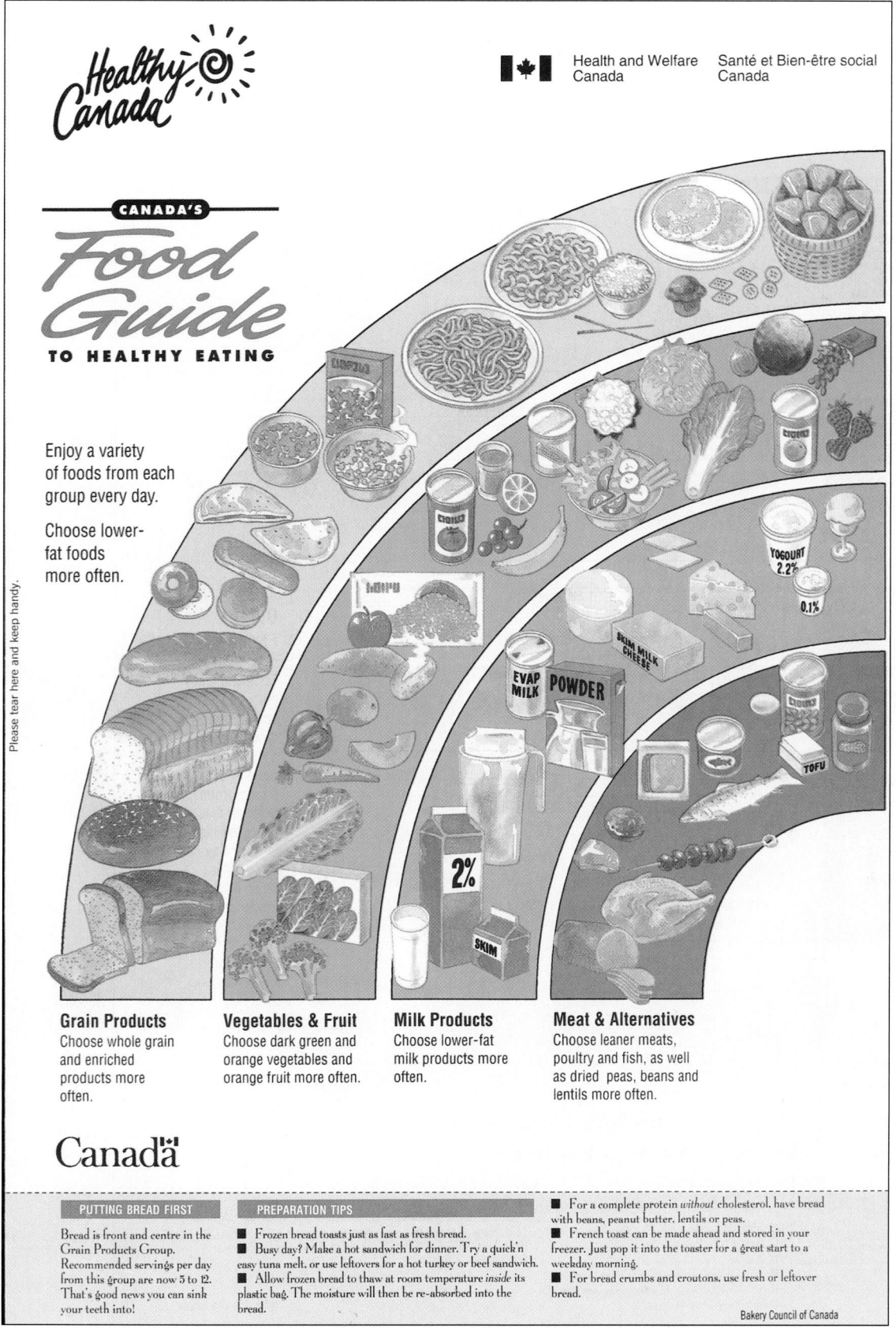

FIGURE 3.1   *Canada's Food Guide to Healthy Eating*
Source: Minister of Supply and Services Canada 1992, Cat. No. H39-252/1992E.

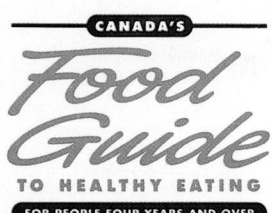

Different People Need Different Amounts of Food

The amount of food you need every day from the 4 food groups and other foods depends on your age, body size, activity level, whether you are male or female and if you are pregnant or breast-feeding. That's why the Food Guide gives a lower and higher number of servings for each food group. For example, young children can choose the lower number of servings, while male teenagers can go to the higher number. Most other people can choose servings somewhere in between.

Grain Products
5-12
SERVINGS PER DAY

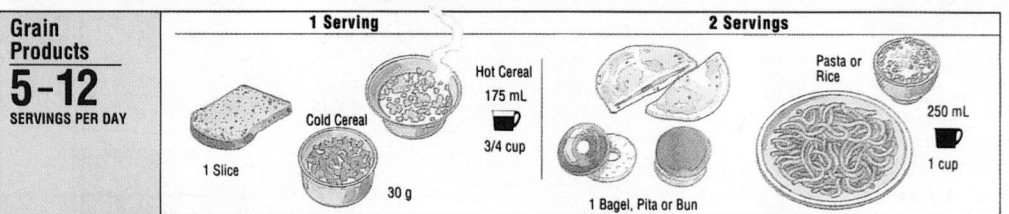

Vegetables & Fruit
5-10
SERVINGS PER DAY

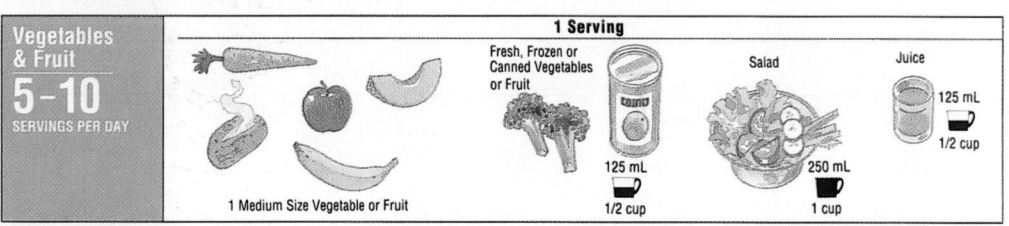

Milk Products
SERVINGS PER DAY
Children 4–9 years: 2–3
Youth 10–16 years: 3–4
Adults: 2–4
Pregnant & Breast-feeding Women: 3–4

Other Foods

Taste and enjoyment can also come from other foods and beverages that are not part of the 4 food groups. Some of these foods are higher in fat or Calories, so use these foods in moderation.

Meat & Alternatives
2-3
SERVINGS PER DAY

Enjoy eating well, being active and feeling good about yourself. That's VITALIT

GOOD NEWS

Now more than ever, you can enjoy a lot more bread in all its different shapes and textures each and every day.

NUTRITION TIPS

■ All bread is low in fat. One slice (one serving from the Grain Products group) averages just 75 calories.
■ Fibre is great for people who want to eat less. Bread's fibre helps satisfy your hunger without adding many extra calories.

■ When you have a sandwich, the bread provides you with 9 essential nutrients: thiamin, riboflavin, niacin, folacin, pantothenic acid, phosphorus, magnesium, iron and zinc.
■ All white flour in Canada is enriched. So *all* bread contains B vitamins and iron.

Bakery Council of Canada

FIGURE 3.2 *Servings and Selections from Canada's Food Guide to Healthy Eating*
Source: *Canada's Food Guide to Healthy Eating*, Minister of Supply and Services Canada 1992, Cat. No. H39-252/1992E.

INGREDIENT SUBSTITUTES AND ALTERNATIVES

More and more people are becoming health-conscious consumers. Many are trying to cut down on foods high in salt, fat, added sugar and cholesterol. To a degree, people can accomplish their goals—and cooks can assist them—by turning to ingredient substitutes and alternatives where possible.

Here we use the term **ingredient substitute** to mean the replacement of one ingredient with another of presumably similar—although not necessarily identical—flavour, texture, appearance and other characteristics. The substitute may be more nutritious, however. So, someone who is avoiding fats can use reduced fat or nonfat sour cream in place of regular sour cream when baking quick breads. The differences in flavour, texture, appearance and baking quality should be minimal.

We use the term **ingredient alternative** to mean the replacement of one ingredient with another of different flavour, texture, appearance or other characteristic, but one that will not compromise—although it may change—the flavour of the dish. As with the ingredient substitute, the ingredient alternative may be more nutritious. Lemon juice and herbs, for instance, can be used as flavouring alternatives to salt; a salsa of fresh vegetables can replace a cream-based sauce. The dishes will not taste the same, but they will still taste good.

In attempting to modify a recipe, the cook should first identify the ingredient(s) and/or cooking method(s) that may need to be changed. He or she can then use the following principles—reduce, replace or eliminate—to make a dish healthier:

1. Reduce the amounts of the ingredient(s); or
2. Replace the ingredient(s) with a substitute that will do the least to change the flavour and appearance of the dish; or
3. Eliminate the ingredient(s).

Salt Substitutes and Alternatives

A concern in the Canadian diet is excessive sodium (salt). Research has linked excessive amounts of sodium to hypertension (high blood pressure), heart and kidney diseases and strokes.

Cooks can contribute to a more healthful diet by decreasing the amount of salt and other high-sodium products such as soy sauce. Salt substitutes, which contain potassium chloride instead of sodium chloride, are available. "Lite" salt has a portion of the sodium content replaced by potassium but still contains some real salt for a truer flavour.

In addition, pepper, lemon, herbs, spices, fruits and flavoured vinegars can be used as salt alternatives to heighten flavour.

Sugar Substitutes

Saccharin, the oldest artificial sugar substitute, has been used for nearly a century. A petroleum derivative, it has no calories and tastes 300 times sweeter than table sugar. Saccharin has a bitter aftertaste, however, and many people find it unpalatable. Along with its sweetness come health concerns: some studies have linked saccharin with tumours in rats.

Aspartame (also known as Nutrasweet®), approved in Canada in 1982, is composed of the amino acids aspartic acid and phenylalanine. Unlike saccharin, aspartame does not have an aftertaste. It is 180 times sweeter than table sugar. It is now widely used in soft drinks, frozen yogurts, fruit spreads, candies and similar products. Aspartame breaks down when heated, so it cannot be used in cooked foods. According to the Health Protection Branch of Health Canada, aspartame is a safe substitute for sugar, although it is a risk for those people with the rare disorder phenylketonuria (PKU), who cannot metabolize the phenylalanine in aspartame. Appropriate warnings are printed on all aspartame-sweetened foods. It is not recommended for pregnant women.

Another sugar substitute is acesulfame K or acesulfame potassium (also known as Sunnette®), which is the most recent artificial sweetener to come on the market. The body cannot metabolize acesulfame K, so it passes through the digestive system unchanged. Like aspartame, it has no aftertaste. Acesulfame K is used in chewing gum, dry beverage mixes, instant coffees and teas, gelatins and nondairy creamers. It is more stable than aspartame, so it can be used in baking.

Sucralose (also known as Splenda®) is a noncaloric sugar substitute approved by the Health Protection Branch in 1991. Made from processed sugar, its tightly bound chlorine atoms pass through the body quickly without being broken down. Sucralose has a clean, sugar-like taste and no aftertaste. Because it remains stable in any temperature and storage conditions, it can be used in beverages, canning, baking and cooking.

Fat Substitutes and Alternatives

Several types of fat substitutes are available; they are either synthetic or derived from naturally occurring food substances. Two of the more recent products are Olestra® and Simplesse®.

Olestra is made of sucrose and vegetable oil. The two are bonded together and the final product consists of molecules too large to be digested. Because it cannot be digested, Olestra does not add any calories. Currently, Olestra is used in snack foods such as potato chips. It may become a useful substitute for fats in baking or cooking, but health concerns have kept it from being widely available. Approval is pending in Canada.

Simplesse is a fat substitute used in frozen desserts such as ice creams and yogurt. Simplesse, made from egg whites or milk proteins, has a rich, creamy texture similar to fat but is fat free. Products made with Simplesse are not usually fat free, however, because other fat-containing ingredients are added.

Caprenin and salarim are fat substitutes used in the candy industry and are not available for home or restaurant use.

Other Ingredient Substitutes and Alternatives

There are many other ingredient substitutes, some of which are identified in Table 3.5. Often ingredient substitutes and alternatives have a dramatic impact on the nutritional values of a completed dish. For example, in Figures 3.3A and B we list the ingredients for a sheet pan of traditional fudge brownies and one made with ingredient substitutes. Note the differences, especially in the values for fat and cholesterol.

Ingredient substitutes and, especially, ingredient alternatives change the nutritional values of a dish; they may also change its flavour, texture or appearance. Sometimes these changes will be acceptable; sometimes they will not. Because some ingredient substitutes and alternatives result in unsatisfactory flavours, textures or appearance, many recipes may not be suitable for substitution or alteration. Prepare a test batch first if you are unsure.

TABLE 3.5 INGREDIENT SUBSTITUTES

For	Use
Bacon	Well-cooked, drained bacon or soy-based bacon
Butter	Powdered butter granules plus liquid (either skim milk or water) or butter-flavoured oil sprays
Chocolate	Cocoa (vegetable oil may be added as needed)
Cream cheese	Reduced-fat cream cheese or fat-free cream cheese
Emulsified salad dressing	Start with a base of reduced-fat or nonfat yogurt, sour cream or mayonnaise, then thin with skim milk; or use a slurry-thickened broth or juice as the oil and add vinegar and other seasonings; or blend silken tofu with other ingredients for a creamy dressing
Light cream	Equal portions of 1% milk and skim evaporated milk
Mayonnaise	Reduced-fat mayonnaise (it can be mixed with reduced-fat or nonfat sour cream)
Sour cream	Reduced-fat or nonfat sour cream; drained reduced-fat or nonfat plain yogurt without gelatin
Whipped cream	Whipped chilled evaporated skim milk; the milk and beaters need to be very cold (needs to be stabilized)

TRADITIONAL FUDGE BROWNIES

Yield: 88 2-inch (5-cm) squares

Unsweetened chocolate	2 lb.	1 kg
Butter	2 lb.	1 kg
Eggs	20	20
Sugar	5 lb. 12 oz.	2.9 kg
Vanilla extract	2 oz.	60 mL
All-purpose flour	1 lb. 10 oz.	750 g
Pecan pieces	1 lb.	500 g

Nutritional values per 2-inch (5-cm) square:

Calories	343
Total carbohydrates	41 g
Total fat	17 g
Protein	4 g
Saturated fat	9 g
Sodium	16 mg
Cholesterol	70 mg
Vitamin C	0

FIGURE 3.3A

CALORIE-REDUCED BROWNIES

Yield: 88 2-inch (5-cm) squares

Unsweetened chocolate	4 oz.	120 g
Cake flour	1 lb.	450 g
Cocoa powder	9 oz.	270 g
Salt substitute	2 tsp.	10 mL
Egg whites	12	12
Whole eggs	8	8
Granulated sugar	2 lb. 2 oz.	1 kg
Corn syrup	2 lb.	900 g
Unsweetened applesauce	1-1/2 pt.	670 mL
Canola oil	7 oz.	210 g
Vanilla extract	2 Tbsp.	30 mL

Nutritional values per 2-inch (5-cm) square:

Calories	150
Total carbohydrates	26 g
Total fat	5 g
Protein	2 g
Saturated fat	0.8 g
Sodium	82 mg
Cholesterol	19 mg
Vitamin C	4 mg

FIGURE 3.3B

Great strides in agriculture have been made during the past two centuries. Pesticides, fungicides and herbicides now eliminate or control pests that once would have devoured, ruined or choked crops. Chemical fertilizers increase yields of many of the world's staples. But not everyone has greeted these developments with open arms.

During the past few decades, scientific and medical investigators have documented, or at least suggested, health risks associated with certain synthetic pesticides, fertilizers and other products. These findings have led to a renewed interest in a back-to-the-basics approach to farming: organic farming. Specialty farms, orchards and even wineries now offer organically grown products (or, in the case of wineries, wines made from organically grown grapes). These products come with few, if any, intentional additives and should be free of any incidental additives. Proponents argue that these products are better for consumers and better for the health of the farm workers.

There are no federal guidelines identifying what can be called "organic." There are provincial guidelines that address the production of organically grown foods. These laws vary widely, but generally, most provinces require that products marketed as "organically grown" must have been grown in soil certified free of synthetic pesticides, fungicides, herbicides or fertilizers. Depending on the province, the land can be certified free of these products one to three years after their use has ceased.

Additives—*substances added to many foods to prevent spoilage or improve appearance, texture, flavour or nutritional value; they may be synthetic materials copied from nature (e.g., sugar substitutes) or naturally occurring substances (e.g. lecithin).*

Incidental food additives—*those inadvertently or unintentionally added to foods during processing, such as pesticide residues on fruits.*

Intentional food additives—*those added to foods on purpose, such as the chemicals used to ensure longer shelf life or food colourings.*

PACKAGE LABELLING

To ensure that consumers have accurate information about packaged foods, the Consumer Packaging and Labelling Act and the Food and Drug Regulations require that most food products be clearly labelled. The language that may be used on these labels is closely regulated; even the minimum type size of the information is specified. The *Guide to Food Labelling and Advertising*, published by the Canadian Food Inspection Agency (1996), spells out requirements and is the source of most of the information that follows.

Mandatory Information

With few exceptions (such as one-bite confections sold individually), prepackaged products must be labelled. The label must include the common name of the product (e.g., "orange juice from concentrate," "mixed vegetables"), the net quantity, the name and address of the manufacturer or dealer, and a list of ingredients, in descending order of proportion by weight in the food. Certain ingredients used in small amounts, such as seasonings, vitamins, minerals and additives, may be given in any order at the end of the list. Most products with a durable life of less than 90 days must have a "best before" date. The net quantity must be given in metric measures—grams or millilitres—and may also be given in imperial or U.S. measures such as ounces or fluid ounces. If the package suggests a natural flavour (e.g., a picture of an apple) but an artificial flavour is used, this information must be given next to the image. In most cases, mandatory information must be shown in both French and English.

Nutritional Information

A breakdown of nutritional content is not required. However, if it is given, it must follow specific formats set out in the *Guidelines on Nutrition Labelling* (Health Canada, 1996) and the Food and Drug Regulations and must not be misleading or deceptive. Nutrition labelling must be given in both official languages. A serving size must be given in grams or millilitres, and a household measure (e.g., 1 cup) should be used as well.

Nutrient information must include a "core list": energy (in both calories and kilojoules), and protein, fat and carbohydrates (in grams). Other information is optional. If one fat component (e.g., monounsaturates) is given, the other three components (polyunsaturates, saturates, cholesterol) must be given as well. If vitamins and minerals are listed, they must be given as a percentage of recommended daily intake. The United States' "Nutrition Facts" information is not permitted on foods sold in Canada, since the two countries use different methods of calculating nutrient values.

Nutritional Claims

Many products carry nutrient claims, such as "a good source of...," "low in..." "sugar-free" or "low calorie." Such terms have specific definitions that must be used accurately. A food may not be listed as a source of a nutrient, for example, unless it contains at least 5% of the recommended daily intake for that nutrient. Standards for foods described as "a good source of" or "high in" a nutrient are specific to each nutrient. Figure 3.4 shows a label giving nutrient information and making appropriate nutrient claims.

This food may be labelled "fat-free" although it does contain a small amount of fat, because that amount is nutritionally insignificant: less than 0.5 grams of fat per serving and per reference amount.

Similar food products now list similar portion sizes, making nutritional comparison easier. The serving-size declaration must include the word "serving," must be given in grams or millilitres, and should also include a common or household measure.

If either sodium or potassium is listed, both must be stated.

Canadian Diabetes Association food choice values may be given, and are helpful for diabetics planning meals; the Canadian Celiac Association's gluten-free symbol is also allowed when applicable. Other endorsements may not be allowed, especially if they suggest a food may prevent disease.

No individual food may be called "essential" but nutrients assigned recommended daily intakes (RDI or RNI, recommended nutrient intake) may be. A food may not be called a "source" of a nutrient unless it contains at least 5% of the RDI.

Macronutrients are listed in grams; micronutrients are given as a percentage of RNI. RNI are usually for adult males and may be misleading for children or pregnant or lactating women.

The ingredient list, and most other mandatory information, must be shown in both English and French. In general, ingredients must be listed in descending order of proportion by weight in the food. Exceptions include spices, natural and artificial flavours, additives, vitamins and minerals, which may be shown at the end of the ingredient list in any order.

- Fat Free
- No Artifical Flavours or Colours
- No Preservatives

- Sans Matières grasses
- Sans Arôme ou Colorant Artificiels
- Sans Agent de Conservation

Nutrition Information

Information Nutritionnelle

Per 30 g serving cereal (250 mL, 1 cup)

Par portion de 30 g de céréale (250 mL, 1 tasse)

Per 30 g serving cereal with 125 mL partly skimmed milk (2%)

Par portion de 30 g de céréale avec 125 mL de lait partiellement écrémé (2%)

Energy	115 Cal	180 Cal	Énergie
	470 kJ	740 kJ	
Protein	2.2 g	6.5 g	Protéines
Fat	0.1 g	2.6 g	Matières Grasses
Carbohydrate	26 g	32 g	Glucides
Sugars	3.2 g	9.4 g	Sucres
Starch	22 g	22 g	Amidon
Dietary Fibre	0.5 g	0.5 g	Fibres Alimentaires
Sodium	245 mg	310 mg	Sodium
Potassium	30 mg	230 mg	Potassium

% of Recommended Daily Intake		% de l'apport quotidien recommandé	
Vitamin A	0%	7%	Vitamine A
Vitamin D	0%	23%	Vitamine D
Vitamin B1	46%	50%	Vitamine B1
Vitamin B2	1%	14%	Vitamine B2
Niacin	8%	13%	Niacine
Vitamin B6	10%	13%	Vitamine B6
Folacin	8%	11%	Folacine
Vitamin B12	0%	25%	Vitamine B12
Pantothenate	7%	13%	Pantothénate
Calcium	0%	15%	Calcium
Phosphorus	3%	14%	Phosphore
Magnesium	4%	11%	Magnésium
Iron	28%	29%	Fer
Zinc	12%	18%	Zinc

Canadian Diabetes Association Food Choice Value: 30 g (250 mL, 1 cup) cereal.
Le système des choix d'aliments de l'Association canadienne du diabète: 30 g (250 mL, 1 tasse) céréale = 1½ • choice/choix

Ingredients/Ingrédients

Corn, Rice, Sugar, Salt, Fancy Molasses, Barley Malt Syrup, Baking Soda, Colour, Vitamins (Thiamin Hydrochloride, Niacinamide, Pyridoxine Hydorchloride, Folic Acid, d-Calcium Pantothenate), Minerals (Iron, Zinc Oxide).
May Contain Traces of Soybeans.
Maïs, Riz, Sucre, Sel, Mélasse Qualité Fantaisie, Sirop d'orge Malté, Bicarbonate de Sodium, Colorant, Vitamines (Chlorhydrate de Thiamine, Niacinamide, Chlorhydrate de Pyridoxine, Acide Folique, d-Pantothénate de Calcium), Minéraux (Fer, Oxyde de Zinc). **Peut Contenir des Traces de Graines de Soja.**

FIGURE 3.4 *A Product Label Showing Nutritional Information in Approved Format*

As consumers express increasing concern about fat consumption, the term "fat free" has become particularly important. In 1997, Health Canada relaxed the definition of "fat free" to include foods that contain nutritionally insignificant amounts of fat: less than 0.5 grams of fat in a serving, and in a "reference amount" defined by regulation as the amount a person would typically consume at one time. The new definition matches U.S. and international standards.

Health Claims

Beyond simply making a claim about content, manufacturers sometimes want to claim certain benefits for a food. The language of health claims, too, is tightly regulated. For example, a food may be described as "wholesome" but should not be described as "healthy" where the word may suggest that simply eating the food will bring health. Manufacturers must not claim that a specific food may prevent a disease. Claims must be based on *Nutrition Recommendations for Canadians* or *Canada's Food Guide to Healthy Eating*, and must be substantiated by nutrient information. For example, it would be acceptable to claim: "Consuming a variety of fibre-containing foods is part of a healthy diet; this product is high in fibre." The package would then have to give the fibre content, which would have to meet criteria for "high." Table 3.6 shows the health claims that may be made for specific nutrients.

TABLE 3.6 ACCEPTABLE BIOLOGICAL ROLE CLAIMS FOR NUTRIENTS

Protein	Helps build and repair body tissues Helps build antibodies
Fat	Supplies energy Aids in the absorption of fat-soluble vitamins
Carbohydrate	Supplies energy Assists in the utilization of fats
Vitamin A	Aids normal bone and tooth development Aids in the development and maintenance of night vision Aids in maintaining the health of the skin and membranes
Vitamin D	Factor in the formation and maintenance of bones and teeth Enhances calcium and phosphorus absorption and utilization
Vitamin E	Protects the fat in body tissues from oxidation
Vitamin C	Factor in the development and maintenance of bones, cartilage, teeth and gums
Thiamine (vitamin B_1)	Releases energy from carbohydrate Aids normal growth
Riboflavin (vitamin B_2)	Factor in energy metabolism and tissue formation
Niacin	Aids in normal growth and development Factor in energy metabolism and tissue formation
Vitamin B_6	Factor in energy metabolism and tissue formation
Folacin	Aids in red blood cell formation
Vitamin B_{12}	Aids in red blood cell formation
Pantothenic acid	Factor in energy metabolism and tissue formation
Calcium	Aids in the formation and maintenance of bones and teeth
Phosphorus	Aids in the formation and maintenance of bones and teeth
Magnesium	Factor in energy metabolism, tissue formation and bone development
Iron	Factor in red blood cell formation
Zinc	Factor in energy metabolism and tissue formation
Iodine	Factor in the normal function of the thyroid gland

Source: *Guide to Food Labelling and Advertising*. Section 7.5.2, Specific Claims, Canadian Food Inspection Agency, 3/01/92, www.cfia-acia.agr.ca.

Nutritional Labelling for Restaurant Menus

Restaurants are not required to give nutritional information on menu items. If they do, the information must be accurate and meet the same standards as packaging material. Some restaurateurs like to use a heart symbol or claim that particular menu items are "heart smart choices." Such claims may be prohibited because they suggest that the food will prevent disease. However, a check mark may be used to identify menu items as healthy choices if it is part of a clearly identified nutrition information program.

CONSUMER CONCERNS ABOUT FOOD AND NUTRITION

Many food ingredients have been linked to medical conditions. Some of the links are tenuous at best; others may be well supported by research. Nutrition is a science and new information about the relationship of food to health and disease is always emerging.

Canadians have voiced concerns about the possible links of certain fats and dietary cholesterol to heart disease; they want to know if sugar intake is related to obesity, diabetes and heart disease. Some people are concerned that pesticide residues in produce may be dangerous and they will seek out restaurants that serve organically grown produce. Some people are curious about the alleged medicinal or health benefits of foods. Others have metabolic or digestive conditions that make it difficult or even dangerous for them to eat specific ingredients. Because of these concerns, patrons may request that their meals be prepared in special ways or that ingredients be deleted from or added to a dish.

The tremendous public interest in nutrition presents a special challenge to chefs. They should be able to prepare and serve food that meets the high standards for health demanded by some patrons, while maintaining the flavour and appearance important to everyone.

NUTRITION AND THE CHEF

Canada's Food Guide to Healthy Eating was designed to guide food consumption for a more healthful life. It presents a plan for a balanced diet. Chefs can use it to plan balanced menus as well. As the Food Guide suggests, chefs do not need to use only meat as the centre of the plate presentation. It demands that a variety of breads, pasta and grains be included on the menu along with an interesting selection of vegetable dishes. And it cautions against the use of too much fat and sugar.

Although not every food service operation can (or should) be devoted to "health food," to the extent appropriate you should offer healthful dining alternatives. Your ability to do so depends, or course, upon your facility. Chefs at hospitals, prisons and schools have much greater control over the foods they offer. Therefore, they have a far greater opportunity and responsibility to provide selections for a well-balanced diet. Chefs at most restaurants, however, do not have such captive audiences. But that does not mean that you can shirk your responsibilities.

You assist customers when you:

1. Use proper purchasing and storage techniques in order to preserve nutrients.
2. Offer a variety of foods from each arc of the food guide rainbow so that customers have a choice.
3. Offer entrees that emphasize plant instead of animal foods.
4. Offer dishes that are considerate of special dietary needs such as low fat or low salt.
5. Use cooking procedures that preserve rather than destroy nutrients.
6. Use cooking procedures that minimize the use of added fat (e.g., stocks, sauces and soups can be cooled and the congealed fats removed; foods can be browned in the oven instead of being sautéed in hot fat).
7. Use equipment that minimizes the use of added fat (e.g., nonstick pans).
8. Train the wait staff to respond properly to nutritional questions diners may have about menu items.
9. Use ingredient alternatives or substitutes where appropriate. If a dish does not lend itself to ingredient alternatives or substitutes, consider creating a new dish that replaces less nutritious traditional foods or preparations with more nutritious ones. For example, instead of serving a sauce made with butter, flour and cream, you can reduce an appropriately seasoned wine, stock or juice and then thicken it with fruit or vegetable purées or starches.

♦♦♦

THE CUSTOMERS WHO COUNT

I have spent 19 years of my professional life in the "fine dining" or "gourmet" field. As of the date of this publication, I will have completed more than 20 years in transition to what I now call a "Minimax" lifestyle.

Minimax is not the opposite of fine "gourmet dining." As a culinary philosophy it has its place about midway. Minimax is a constructed word that can be understood internationally. Mini refers to minimum, in this case to risks encountered by unwise or excessive consumption of food. Max, on the other hand, refers to maximum possible enhancement of food, using natural aromas, colors and textures rather than the classic western dependence on salts, fats and sugars.

Your future customers will be involved in a struggle when they read your menu. With their subjective right brains, they will be remembering former meals with enormous relish. With their objective left brains, they will apply what they know about fat, calories and sodium. Without some help they will either be confused, perplexed, rebellious or guilty.

Somehow then, you, who will make up the educated center of the restaurant business of the future, will have to address the needs of those who want to make changes and still celebrate a night out at a comforting restaurant.

My suggestion is that you devise recipes that avoid fat as a primary source of calories for at least two appetizers, two entrées and one dessert. I would simply describe these on the menu for what they contain and not call them "low-fat" or "diet" or, for that matter, by any special name (even Minimax!). I would then present a small, very attractive, folded menu card with a phrase such as "For Our Customers Who Count" on the outside, and then simply list the nutritional benefits from the low-fat specials in an attractive, easy-to-read manner.

If your management chooses to establish such a menu, it will be extremely important that you weigh each dish correctly and have it analyzed by an approved nutrition system.

The reason for accuracy is that some, if not most, of the "customers who count" do so for very critical reasons. To give someone an oversized portion of meat with a great sauce that far exceeds, say, 30% calories from fat is actually highly irresponsible and may even attract possible litigation in the future.

When you reduce fat in a classical dish, there will be a reduction in flavor, since "fat carries flavor." By drawing attention away from the taste change and enhancing the sense of smell (aroma), sight (color and presentation) and touch (texture), you can actually improve the finished dish.

I have found that the fusion idea has helped make this a reality. Fusion is simply merging seasonings from one culture with those from another. In this way it helps to see Northern European specialties that use abundant dairy products as "velvet memories," and North African and Asian seasonings as "future bright notes."

It is then possible to consider a modification to, say, sauce hollandaise by lowering the fat and adding a good Asian fish sauce to which shreds of mint and flecks of red pepper are added to spike interest with aroma, color and texture.

Whatever you choose to do, let me give you this last word of encouragement. Study hard, read the classics and see the future through them. If you've ever skipped smooth stones on flat water you'll know that the first bounce really matters. If your attitude to very rich classics is negative and condemning, then what you try to achieve will certainly fail to go the distance.

Therefore, don't condemn anyone's work. Aim to please today's customer with all the skills that our exciting profession has developed for thousands of years.

You have my very best wishes for a most successful career. Now go skip your stone...for your customers' sakes!

Graham Kerr, author, chef and host of
The Galloping Gourmet
and Graham Kerr's Kitchen,
seen on PBS-TV and The Discovery Channel

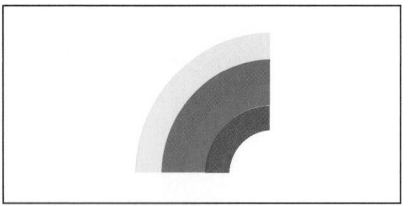

FIGURE 3.5   ***The Symbol for a Healthful Recipe***

The nutrient information provided here is for reference only. There is a 20% margin of error, due primarily to choices for specific ingredients and variations in the size of fruits and vegetables. Preparation techniques and serving sizes may also significantly alter the values of many nutrients. When a recipe offers a choice of ingredients, the first-mentioned ingredient was the one used in the calculations. Ingredients listed as "to taste" (TT) and "as needed" were omitted from the analysis. In addition, olive oil and 3% whole milk were used throughout for "vegetable oil" and "milk," respectively. When given a choice of serving size or weight, the first mentioned was used.

CONCLUSION

A basic understanding and appreciation of nutrition are important for both the consumer and those who prepare the foods consumed.

What you serve is important. Carbohydrates, proteins, fats, water, vitamins and minerals, in varying amounts, are all necessary for good health. *Canada's Food Guide to Healthy Eating* can guide selections to create and maintain a healthful diet.

How foods are prepared is also important. Remember that some cooking and storage techniques preserve nutrients; others do not. In addition, by substituting or modifying ingredients and preparation methods, many dishes can be made more nutritious.

QUESTIONS FOR DISCUSSION

1. Identify the six categories of nutrients and list two sources for each.
2. What are the differences between saturated fats and unsaturated fats? Identify two sources for each.
3. List four things you can do to reduce the loss of minerals and vitamins when storing or preparing foods.
4. Describe *Canada's Food Guide to Healthy Eating.* Explain how a chef can use it to plan well-balanced meals and how a consumer can use it to establish a healthful diet. What other diet planning tools can be used along with the Food Guide?
5. Create two menus for a Thanksgiving dinner, both nutritionally balanced, but one high in calories, fat and so on, and the other including the traditional foods but reduced in fat, calories, cholesterol and sodium.

WEBLINKS

National Institute of Nutrition
   www.nin.ca/
International Union of Nutritional Sciences
   www.monash.edu.au/IUNS/
Canada Food Guide
   www.hc-sc.gc.ca/hppb/nutrition/pube/foodguid/food1.htm
Jean Fremont's (Simon Fraser University Professor) Food and
   Nutrition on the Web — Finding the Right Stuff
   www.sfu.ca/~jfremont/
Food Science and Nutrition
   www.uwstout.edu/lib/subjects/foodsc.htm
Foods and Nutrition Solutions
   www.ag.uiuc.edu/~robsond/solutions/nutrition.html
Journal of Nutrition in Recipe and Menu Development
   bubl.ac.uk/journals/agr/jniramd/

CHAPTER 4
MENU PLANNING
AND
FOOD COSTING

◆◆◆

LEARNING OUTCOMES

After studying this chapter you will be able to:

◆ identify the different types and styles of menus

◆ explain the purpose of standardized recipes

◆ calculate the cost per portion for recipes

◆ convert recipe yield amounts

◆ determine menu prices and calculate food cost percentages

◆ control food costs

T

oday's professional cook must master more than the basics of béchamel, butchering and bread baking. You must be equally skilled in the business of food services. This means knowing what products cost and how much an operation should charge for its menu items.

Although computers are almost as common in kitchens as whisks, no machine can ever replace a cook's hands-on ability to apply food cost controls. Accurate measurements, portion control and proper food handling directly affect the food service operation's bottom line. In addition, cooks must, at the very least, be able to conduct yield tests, calculate recipe costs and use food cost percentages.

This chapter first introduces you to various types and styles of menus. It then explains a standardized recipe format and presents the basics of food cost controls as well as information on measurements and techniques for changing or converting recipe yields. It then describes methods for determining unit and recipe costs, including calculations for raw yield tests. It concludes with a discussion of the methods for pricing menus and controlling food costs. This chapter does not attempt to cover menu design, accounting principles or computer applications. It will, however, provide a foundation of practical techniques to be used by anyone with common sense and a calculator.

THE MENU

Whether it lists Afghan dishes, hamburgers, just desserts or classic cuisine, and whether the prices range from inexpensive to exorbitant, the menu is the soul of every food service operation. Its purposes are to identify for the consumer the foods and beverages the operation offers, to create consumer enthusiasm and to increase sales. When combined with excellent food and great service, a well-planned menu helps ensure success.

Most menus offer consumers sufficient selections to build an entire meal. A typical Canadian or American main meal consists of three courses. The first course may be a hot or cold appetizer, soup or salad. The second course is the **entree** or main dish, usually meat, poultry, fish or shellfish accompanied by a vegetable and starch. The third course is dessert, either a sweet preparation or fruit and cheese. For a more formal meal, there may be a progression of first courses, including a hot or cold appetizer and soup, as well as a fish course served before the main dish (which, in this case, would not be fish). For some meals sorbet or granité may follow the fish course as a palate cleanser. Occasionally, a light salad will be presented as a palate cleanser after the main dish and before dessert.

Entree—*the main dish of a Canadian or American meal, usually meat, poultry, fish or shellfish accompanied by a vegetable and starch; in France it is the first course, served before the fish and meat courses.*

Types of Menus

Menus are classified according to the regularity with which the foods are offered:

1. **Static menu**—All patrons are offered the same foods every day. Once a static menu is developed and established, it rarely changes. Static menus are typically found in fast-food operations, ethnic restaurants, steakhouses and the like.

   Static menus can also be used in institutional settings. For example, a static menu at an elementary school could offer students, along with a vegetable and dessert, the same luncheon choices every school day: a cheeseburger, fish sticks, chicken tacos, pizza wedges or a sandwich.

2. **Cycle menu**—A cycle menu is developed for a set time period; at the end of that period it repeats itself (i.e., on a seven-day cycle, the same menu is used every Monday). Some cycle menus are written on a seasonal basis, with a new menu for each season to take advantage of product availability. Cycle menus are used commonly in schools, hospitals and other institutions. Although cycle menus may be repetitious, the repetition is not necessarily noticeable to diners because of the length of the cycles.

3. **Market menu**—A market menu is based upon product availability during a specific time period; it is written to use foods when they are in peak season or readily available. Market menus are becoming increasingly popular with chefs (and consumers) as they challenge the chef's ingenuity in using fresh, seasonal products. Market menus are short-lived, however, because of limited product availability and perishability. In fact, they often change daily.

4. **Hybrid menu**—A hybrid menu combines a static menu with a cycle menu or a market menu of specials.

Food service operations may have separate menus for breakfast, lunch or dinner. If all three meals are available all day and are listed on the same menu, the menu is often called a California menu; California menus are typically found in 24-hour restaurants. Depending on the food service operation's objectives, separate specialty menus for drinks, hors d'oeuvres, desserts, brunch or afternoon tea, for example, are used.

Regardless of whether the menu is static, cycle, market or hybrid, it can offer consumers the opportunity to purchase their selections à la carte, semi à la carte, table d'hôte or some combination of the three.

1. **À la carte**—Every food and beverage item is priced and ordered separately.

2. **Semi à la carte**—With this popular menu style, some food items (particularly appetizers and desserts) are priced and ordered separately, while the entree is accompanied by and priced to include other items, such as a salad, starch or vegetable.

3. **Table d'hôte** or **prix fixe**—This menu offers a complete meal at a set price. (The term *table d'hôte* is French for "host's table" and is derived from the innkeeper's practice of seating all guests at a large communal table and serving them all the same meal.) A table d'hôte meal can range from very elegant to a diner's blue-plate special.

Many menus combine à la carte, semi à la carte and table d'hôte choices. For example, appetizers, salads and desserts may be available à la carte; entrees may be offered semi à la carte (they come with a salad, starch and vegetable), while the daily special is a complete (table d'hôte or prix fixe) meal.

Menu Language

The menu is the principal way in which the food service operation, including the chef, communicates with the consumer. A well-designed menu often reflects the input of design, marketing, art and other consultants as well as the chef and management. The type of folds, cover, artwork, layout, typefaces, colours and paper are all important considerations. But the most important consideration is the language.

The menu should list the foods offered. It may include descriptions such as the preparation method, essential ingredients and service method as well as the quality, cut and quantity of product. For example, the menu can list "Striploin Steak" or "Mesquite Grilled 250 g Angus Beef Striploin Steak."

Federal laws require that certain menu language be accurate. Areas of particular concern include statements about quantity, quality, grade and freshness as well as dietary and nutritional claims. Accurate references to an item's source are also important. If brand names are used, those brands must be served. If the restaurant claims to be serving "Fresh Dover Sole," it must be just that, not frozen sole from New England. (On the other hand, like French or Russian dressing, "English mint sauce" is a generic name for a style of food, so using that geographical adjective is appropriate even if the mint sauce is not made in England.) A reference to "our own fresh-baked" desserts means that the restaurant regularly bakes the desserts on premises, serves them soon after baking and does not substitute commercially prepared or frozen goods.

STANDARDIZED RECIPES

Recipe—*a set of written instructions for producing a specific food or beverage; also known as a formula.*

Standardized recipe—*a recipe producing a known quality and quantity of food for a specific operation.*

Menu writing and **recipe** development are mutually dependent activities. Once the menu is created, standardized recipes should be prepared for each item. A **standardized recipe** is one that will produce a known quality and quantity of food for a specific operation. It specifies (1) the type and amount of each ingredient, (2) the preparation and cooking procedures, and (3) the yield and portion size.

Standardized recipes may be found in books or provided by manufacturers, but usually they are recipes customized to your operation—cooking time, temperature and utensils should be based on the equipment actually available. Yield should be adjusted to an amount appropriate for your operation. A recipe must be tested repeatedly and adjusted to fit your facility and your needs before it can be considered standardized.

Standardized recipes are a tool for the chef and management. The written forms assist with training cooks, educating service staff and controlling financial matters. They also help ensure that the customer will receive a consistent quality and quantity of product. Accurate recipe costing and menu pricing depend on having and using standardized recipes.

Although formats differ, a standardized recipe form, such as that reproduced in Figure 4.1, will usually include:

+ Name of product
+ Yield
+ Portion size
+ Presentation and garnish
+ Ingredient quality and quantity
+ Preparation procedures
+ Cooking time and temperature
+ Holding procedures

INGREDIENTS	QTY/ WEIGHT	PURCH UNIT	DATE: UNIT COST	TOTAL	DATE: UNIT COST	TOTAL	DATE: UNIT COST	TOTAL	PREPARATION PROCEDURE
TOTAL COST									
COST PER PORTION									
COST % PER PORTION									

STANDARD RECIPE CARD FOR ITEM: DATE REVISED

QUANTITY PRODUCED   RECIPE FILE NO.

PORTION SIZE   RESTAURANT

NO. OF PORTIONS PRODUCED   SALES PRICE

FIGURE 4.1   *Standardized Recipe Form*

The form may also include information on costing and a photograph of the finished dish. Each form should be complete, consistent and simple to read and follow. The forms should be stored in a readily accessible place. Index cards, notebook binders or a computerized database may be used, depending on the size and complexity of the operation.

MEASUREMENTS AND CONVERSIONS

Measurement Formats

Accurate measurements are among the most important aspects of food production. Ingredients and portions must be measured correctly to ensure consistent product quality. In other words, the cook must be able to prepare a recipe the same way each time, and portion sizes must be the same from one order to the next.

In a kitchen, measurements may be made in three ways: weight, volume and count.

Weight refers to the mass or heaviness of a substance. It is expressed in terms such as kilograms, grams, ounces and pounds. Weight may be used to measure liquid or dry ingredients (for example, 800 g of eggs for a bread recipe) and portions (for example, 85 g of sliced turkey for a sandwich). As weight is generally the most accurate form of measurement, portion scales or balance scales are commonly used in kitchens.

Volume refers to the space occupied by a substance. This is mathematically expressed as *height × width × length*. It is expressed in terms such as cups, quarts, gallons, teaspoons, fluid ounces, bushels, millilitres and litres. Volume is most commonly used to measure liquids. It may also be used for dry ingredients when the amount is too small to be weighed accurately (for example, 1/4 teaspoon/1 mL of salt). Although measuring by volume is somewhat less accurate than measuring by weight, volume measurements are generally quicker to do.

Frequently, mistakes are made in food preparation by cooks who assume wrongly that weight and volume are equal. Do not be fooled—250 mL of solid food does not always equal 250 g. While it is true that 1 standard cup contains 8 *fluid* ounces, it is not true that the contents of that standard cup will *weigh* 8 ounces. For example, the weight of 1 cup of diced apples will vary depending on the size of the apple pieces. Errors are commonly made in the bakeshop by cooks who assume that 8 ounces of flour is the same as 1 cup of flour. In fact, 1 cup of flour weighs only about 4-1/2 ounces.

It is not unusual to see both weight and volume measurements used in a single recipe. When a recipe ingredient is expressed in weight, weigh it. When it is expressed as a volume, measure it. Like most rules, however, this one has exceptions. The weight and volume of water is the same. For this ingredient you may use whichever measurement is most convenient.

Count refers to the number of individual items. Count is used in recipes (for example, 4 eggs) and in portion control (for example, 2 fish fillets or 1 ear of corn). Count is also commonly used in purchasing to indicate the size of the individual items. For example, a "96 count" case of lemons means that a 40-pound (18 kg) case contains 96 individual lemons; a "115 count" case means that the same 40-pound (18 kg) case contains 115 individual lemons. So, each lemon in the 96-count case is larger than those in the 115-count case. Shrimp is another item commonly sold by count. One pound (450 g) of shrimp may contain from 8 to several hundred shrimp, depending on the size of the individual pieces. When placing an order, the chef must specify the desired count. For example, when ordering 1 pound (450 g) of 21–25-count shrimp the chef expects to receive not less than 21 nor more than 25 shrimps.

Measurement Systems

The measurement formats of weight, volume and count are used in the imperial, U.S. and metric measurement systems. Because each of these systems is used in modern food service operations, you should be able to prepare recipes written in any of the three.

The **imperial system** is used in Great Britain and a few other countries. It uses pounds and ounces for weight, and pints and fluid ounces for volume.

The **U.S. system** is the most difficult system to understand. It uses pounds for weight and cups for volume.

The **metric system**, used in Canada, is the most commonly used system in the world. Developed in France during the late 18th century, it was intended to fill the need for a mathematically rational and uniform system of measurement. The metric system is a decimal system in which the gram, litre and

◆◆◆

FANNIE MERRITT FARMER
(1857–1915)

Fannie Farmer is more than the name on a cookbook. She was an early, vigorous and influential proponent of scientific cooking, nutrition and academic training for culinary professionals.

At the age of 30, Farmer enrolled in the Boston Cooking School. The school's curriculum was not designed to graduate chefs, but rather to produce cooking teachers. After graduating from the two-year course, Farmer stayed on, first as assistant principal and then as principal.

During her years there (and, indeed, for the rest of her career) she was obsessed with accurate measurements. She waged a campaign to eliminate measurements such as a "wine glass" of liquid, a "handful" of flour, a chunk of butter the "size of an egg" or a "heaping spoonful" of salt. For, as she once wrote, "correct measurements are absolutely necessary to insure the best results." Farmer also sought to replace the European system of measuring ingredients by weight with, for her, a more scientific measurement system based on volume and level measures (e.g., a level tablespoon). To a great degree, she succeeded.

Her writings reflect her concern for accurate measurements. Her first book, *The Boston Cooking School Cookbook* (1896), includes clearly written recipes with precise measurements. Later editions add recipe yields, oven temperatures and baking times.

After leaving the Boston Cooking School, she opened "Miss Farmer's School of Cookery." The curriculum listed 60 lessons divided into 6 courses. The first course covered the basics: laying a fire and using a gas stove; making breads, eggs, soups, potatoes and coffee. The second and third courses emphasized more advanced cooking. Pastry, desserts and salads were taught during the fourth course; presentation and service were taught during the fifth course. Quite progressively for the time, her sixth course taught cooking for nurses and emphasized nutrition and the dietary needs of the sick and elderly. (This may have reflected Farmer's personal interests, for she was partially disabled and in poor health from time to time.)

Farmer wrote other cookbooks, including *Food and Cookery for the Sick and Convalescent* (1904) and *A New Book of Cookery* (first published in 1912 and republished in several revised versions). Her writings never address the joys of cooking and eating; rather, they reflect a scientific approach to cooking and rely on clearly written, accurately measured recipes for good, solid food.

---

metre are the basic units of weight, volume and length, respectively. Larger or smaller units of weight, volume and length are formed by adding a prefix to the words *gram, litre* or *metre*. Some of the more commonly used prefixes in food service operations are deca- (10), hecto- (100), kilo- (1000), deci- (1/10), centi- (1/100) and milli- (1/1000). Thus, a kilogram is 1000 grams; a decametre is 10 metres; a millilitre is 1/1000 of a litre. Because the metric system is based on multiples of 10, it is extremely easy to increase or decrease recipe amounts.

The most important thing for a cook to know about the metric system is that *you do not need to convert between the metric system and the U.S. or imperial system in recipe preparation.* If a recipe is written in metric units, use

TABLE 4.1   COMMON ABBREVIATIONS AND CONVERSIONS

teaspoon	=	tsp.
tablespoon	=	tbsp.
cup	=	c.
pint	=	pt.
quart	=	qt.
gram	=	g
millilitre	=	mL
litre	=	L
ounce	=	oz.
fluid ounce	=	fl. oz.
pound	=	lb.
kilogram	=	kg
dash	=	1/8 teaspoon
3 teaspoons	=	1 tablespoon
2 tablespoons	=	1 fl. oz.
4 tablespoons	=	1/4 cup (2 fl. oz.)
5-1/3 tablespoons	=	1/3 cup (2-2/3 fl. oz.)
16 tablespoons	=	1 cup (8 fl. oz.)
2 cups	=	1 pint (16 fl. oz.)
2 pints	=	1 quart (32 fl. oz.)
4 quarts	=	1 gallon (128 fl. oz.)*
2 gallons	=	1 peck
4 pecks	=	1 bushel
1 gram	=	0.035 ounce (1/30 oz.)
1 ounce	=	28.35 grams
454 grams	=	1 pound
2.2 pounds	=	1 kilogram (1000 grams)
1 teaspoon	=	5 millilitres
1 tablespoon	=	15 millilitres
1 cup	=	.24 litres (for practical purposes, 250 mL)

*Note that the gallon measurements in this book are based on the U.S. gallon–128 fl.oz.

metric measuring equipment; if it is written in U.S. units, use U.S. measuring equipment. Most modern measuring equipment is calibrated in both U.S. and metric increments. The need to convert amounts will arise only if the proper equipment is unavailable.

Converting Grams and Ounces

As you can see from Table 4.1, 1 ounce equals 28.35 grams. So, *to convert ounces to grams, multiply the number of ounces by 28* (rounded for convenience).

8 ounces × 28 = 224 grams (225 g for practical use)

And *to convert grams to ounces, divide the number of grams by 28.*

224 ÷ 28 = 8 ounces

To help you develop a framework for judging conversions, remember that:

+ a kilogram is about 2.2 pounds
+ a gram is about 1/30 ounce
+ a pound is about 450 grams
+ a litre is slightly more than a quart
+ a centimetre is slightly less than 1/2 inch
+ 0° Celsius is the freezing point of water (32°F)
+ 100° Celsius is the boiling point of water (212°F) at sea level

These approximations are not a substitute for accurate conversions, however. Appendix II contains additional information on equivalents and metric conversions. There is no substitute for knowing this information. In fact, it should become second nature to you. Try to avoid converting recipes, especially for baking and pastry. The results may be substandard. Remember that most recipes are based on proportions of ingredients.

RECIPE CONVERSIONS

Yield—*the total amount of a product made from a specific recipe.*

Whether 6 servings or 60, every recipe is designed to produce or **yield** a specific amount of product. A recipe's yield may be expressed in *volume, weight* or *servings* (for example, 1 litre of sauce; 4 kg of bread dough; 8 100-mL servings). If the expected yield does not meet your needs, you must convert (i.e., increase or decrease) the ingredient amounts. Recipe conversion is sometimes complicated by *portion size conversions*. For example, it may be necessary to convert a recipe that initially produces 24 250-mL servings of soup into a recipe that produces 62 180-mL servings.

It is just as easy to change yields by uneven amounts as it is to double or halve recipes. The mathematical principle is the same: *Each ingredient is multiplied by a* **conversion factor**. Do not take shortcuts by estimating recipe amounts or conversion factors. Inaccurate conversions lead to inedible foods, embarrassing shortages or wasteful excesses. Take the time to learn and apply

Conversion factor (C.F.)—*the number used to increase or decrease ingredient quantities and recipe yields.*

proper conversion techniques. Most recipes can be doubled or halved without too much quality being lost. Seasonings may need further adjustments when doing larger conversion factors.

Converting Total Yield

When portion size is unimportant or remains the same, recipe yield is converted by a simple two-step process:

Step 1: Divide the desired (new) yield by the recipe (old) yield to obtain the conversion factor (C.F.).

$$\text{new yield} \div \text{old yield} = \text{conversion factor}$$

Step 2: Multiply each ingredient quantity by the conversion factor to obtain the new quantity.

$$\text{old quantity} \times \text{conversion factor} = \text{new quantity}$$

Example 4.1

You need to convert a recipe for cauliflower soup. The present recipe yields 6 L; you need to make only 3 L.

First, determine the conversion factor:

$$3\,L \div 6\,L = .50$$

Second, the conversion factor is applied to each ingredient in the soup recipe:

CAULIFLOWER SOUP

	old quantity	×	C.F.	=	new quantity
Cauliflower, chopped	2.5 kg	×	.5	=	1.25 kg (or 1250 g)
Celery stalks	4	×	.5	=	2
Onion	1	×	.5	=	1/2
Chicken stock	2 L	×	.5	=	1 L
Heavy cream	1300 mL	×	.5	=	650 mL

Converting Portion Size

A few additional steps are necessary to convert recipes when portion sizes must also be changed.

Step 1: Determine the total yield of the existing recipe by multiplying the number of portions by the portion size.

$$\text{original portions} \times \text{original portion size} = \text{total (old) yield}$$

Step 2: Determine the total yield desired by multiplying the new number of portions by the new portion size.

$$\text{desired portions} \times \text{desired portion size} = \text{total (new) yield}$$

Step 3: Obtain the conversion factor as described above.

$$\text{total (new) yield} \div \text{total (old) yield} = \text{conversion factor}$$

Step 4: Multiply each ingredient quantity by the conversion factor.

$$\text{old quantity} \times \text{conversion factor} = \text{new quantity}$$

Example 4.2

Returning to the cauliflower soup: The original recipe produced 6 L or 48 servings of 125 mL. Now you need 72 servings of 180 mL.

STEP 1: Total original yield is 48 × 125 = 6000 mL

STEP 2: Total desired yield is 72 × 180 = 12 960 mL

STEP 3: Conversion factor is calculated by dividing total new yield by total old yield:

$$12\ 960 \div 6000 = 2.25$$

STEP 4: Old ingredient quantities are multiplied by conversion factor to determine new quantities:

CAULIFLOWER SOUP

	old quantity	×	C.F.	=	new quantity
Cauliflower, chopped	2.5 kg	×	2.25	=	5.625 kg
Celery stalks	4	×	2.25	=	9
Onion	1	×	2.25	=	2.25
Chicken stock	2 L	×	2.25	=	4.5 L
Heavy cream	1300 mL	×	2.25	=	2.925 L

Additional Conversion Problems

When making very large recipe changes—for example, from 5 to 50 portions or 600 to 36 portions—you may encounter additional problems. The mathematical conversions described above do not take into account changes in equipment, evaporation rates, unforeseen recipe errors or cooking times. Chefs learn to use their judgment, knowledge of cooking principles and skills to compensate for these factors.

Equipment

When you change the size of a recipe, you must often change the equipment used as well. Problems arise, however, when the production techniques previously used no longer work with the new quantity of ingredients. For example, if you normally make a muffin recipe in small quantities by hand and you increase the recipe size, it may be necessary to prepare the batter in a mixer. But if mixing time remains the same, the batter may become overmixed, resulting in poor-quality muffins. Trying to prepare a small amount of product in equipment that is too large for the task can also affect its quality.

Evaporation

Equipment changes can also affect product quality because of changes in evaporation rates. Increasing a soup recipe may require substituting a tilt skillet for a saucepan. But because a tilt skillet provides more surface area for evaporation than does a saucepan, reduction time must be decreased to prevent overthickening the soup. The increased evaporation caused by an increased surface area may also alter the strength of the seasonings.

Recipe Errors

A recipe may contain errors in ingredients or techniques that are not obvious when it is prepared in small quantities. When increased, however, small mistakes often become big (and obvious) ones, and the final product suffers.

The only solution is to test recipes carefully and rely on your knowledge of cooking principles to compensate for unexpected problems.

Time

Do not multiply time specifications given in a recipe by the conversion factor used with the recipe's ingredients. All things being equal, *cooking time* will not change when recipe size changes. For example, a muffin requires the same amount of baking time whether you prepare 1 dozen or 14 dozen. Cooking time will be affected, however, by changes in evaporation rate or heat conduction caused by equipment changes. *Mixing time* may change when recipe size is changed. Different equipment may perform mixing tasks more or less efficiently than previously used equipment. Again, rely on experience and good judgment or ask your supervisor.

CALCULATING UNIT COSTS AND RECIPE COSTS

Unit Costs

Food service operations purchase most foods from suppliers in bulk or wholesale packages. For example, canned goods are purchased by the case; produce by the flat, case or lug; and flour and sugar by 10- or 20-kg bags. Even fish and meats are often purchased in large cuts, not individual serving-sized portions. The purchased amount is rarely used for a single recipe, however. It must be broken down into smaller units such as kilograms, litres, grams or millilitres.

In order to allocate the proper ingredient costs to the recipe being prepared, it is necessary to convert **as-purchased costs or prices** to **unit costs or prices**. To find the unit cost (i.e., the cost of a particular unit, say a single egg) in a package containing multiple units (e.g., a 30-dozen case), divide the as-purchased cost (A.P. cost) of the package by the number of units in the package.

> **As-purchased (A.P.)**—*the condition or cost of an item as it is purchased or received from the supplier.*
>
> **Unit cost**—*the price paid to acquire one of the specified units.*

A.P. cost ÷ number of units = cost per unit

Example 4.3

A case of #10 (2.84 L) cans contains 6 individual cans. If a case of tomato paste costs $23.50, then each can costs $3.92.

$$\$23.50 \div 6 = \$3.92$$

If your recipe uses less than the total can, you must continue dividing the cost of the can until you arrive at the appropriate unit amount. Continuing with the tomato paste example, if you need only 1 cup (.225 L, or 225 mL), find out how much 1 litre costs by dividing the cost per item by the volume.

$$\$3.92 \div 2.84 \text{ L} = \$1.380 \text{ per L}$$

To calculate how much 1 cup costs, multiply this figure by the desired unit amount (.225 L):

$$1.380 \times .225 = .31 \text{ (to 2 decimal places)}$$

The whole operation can be expressed by the formula

$$\frac{\text{cost per item (\$3.92)} \times \text{unit required (.225 L, or 1 cup)}}{\text{unit size (2.84 L)}} = \$.31$$

> ◆◆◆
>
> When calculating unit costs, it is vital that the unit size and the unit required be expressed in the same measurement unit. For example, if the can is measured in fluid ounces, then the unit required must also be in fluid ounces. In the example opposite, if the cost remains the same but the can size is 100 oz., and you want to know how much a cup costs, you need to weigh one cup of tomato paste. If the item has a relatively low specific weight (or density), like rice or flour, this procedure is of even greater importance.

RECIPE COSTING FORM

Menu Item _____ Date _____

Ingredient	Quantity	COST			TOTAL COST
		As Purchased	Yield %	Edible Portion	

TOTAL COST OF RECIPE $ _____

Total Yield _____   Size of Portion _____
                                  Cost per Portion _____

Food Cost Percentage _____   Selling Price _____

FIGURE 4.2   *Recipe Costing Form*

Recipe Costs

Total recipe cost—*the total cost of ingredients for a particular recipe; it does not reflect overhead, labour, fixed expenses or profit.*

With a typical recipe, you calculate the **total recipe cost** with the following two-step procedure:

STEP 1: Determine the cost for the given quantity of each recipe ingredient with the unit costing procedures described above.

STEP 2: Add all of the ingredient costs together to obtain the total recipe cost.

The total recipe cost can then be broken down into the **cost per portion**, which is the most useful figure for food cost controls. To arrive at cost per portion, divide the total recipe cost by the total number of servings or portions produced by that recipe.

Cost per portion—*the amount of the total recipe cost divided by the number of portions produced from that recipe; the cost of one serving.*

total recipe cost ÷ number of portions = cost per portion

The Recipe Costing Form shown in Figure 4.2 is useful for organizing recipe costing information. It provides space for listing each ingredient, the quantity of each ingredient needed, the cost of each unit and the total cost for the ingredient. Total yield, portion size and cost per portion are listed at the bottom of the form. Note that there is no space for recipe procedures, as these are irrelevant in recipe costing.

YIELD TESTS

Computing the cost of recipe ingredients is a simple matter if the foods are used the way they are received and there is no waste or trim. This is rarely the case, however. The amount of a food item **as purchased (A.P.)** and the amount of the **edible portion (E.P.)** of that same item may vary considerably, particularly with meats and fresh produce. In this context, **yield** is the useable or edible quantity remaining after processing the as-purchased quantity of the food item. That is, yield refers to the amount of useable lettuce after the case of iceberg is cleaned, or the amount of meat that is served after trimming. The **yield factor or percentage** is the ratio of the useable quantity to the purchased quantity. It is always less than 100% and may be calculated in dollars or weight/volume amounts.

Because purchase specifications and fabrication techniques vary from operation to operation, there are no precise, standard yield amounts. Each kitchen must determine its own yield factors. Yield tests must be conducted on A.P. items as they are received from purveyors. To be effective, several tests must be conducted and the results averaged to arrive at a specific operation's yield factor for that item.

The method of calculating yield varies depending on whether the item's trim is all waste (for example, vegetable peelings) or whether the trim creates useable or saleable byproducts (for example, meat and poultry).

Raw Yield Tests Without Byproducts

The simplest yield test procedure is for items that have no useable or saleable byproducts. These items include most produce as well as some fish and shellfish. Unless these items are ready to serve *as received* from the purveyor, trimming is required and some trim is waste. For example, 450 g of apples may yield only 360 g of flesh after peeling and coring. If the recipe requires 450 g of peeled, cored apples, the chef must start with more than 450 g of A.P. apples. In order to determine accurate costs for such items, the trim loss must be taken into account. Even seedless grapes do not have a 100% yield factor. The weight of stems and bad grapes must be calculated and deducted from the A.P. weight to determine the correct price per 450 g of servable fruit.

There are three steps for calculating yield when all trim is waste:

STEP 1: Calculate the total weight of the trim produced from the specified A.P. quantity. This is known as **trim loss**.

STEP 2: Subtract the trim loss from the A.P. weight to arrive at the total yield weight.

STEP 3: Divide the yield weight by the A.P. weight to determine the yield factor.

Example 4.4

900 g of fresh garlic generate 126 g of trim loss. Therefore, the yield weight is 774 g and the yield factor is 86% or .86:

$$900 \text{ g} - 126 \text{ g} = 774 \text{ g}$$

$$774 \div 900 = .86 = 86\%$$

Remember, subtract trim loss from A.P. weight, then divide yield weight by A.P. weight to arrive at the yield percentage. Note that the yield factor will always be some number less than 1, and the yield percentage will always be less than 100%.

Edible portion (E.P.)—*the amount of a food item available for consumption after trimming or fabrication.*

Yield—*the total amount of a food item created or remaining after trimming or fabrication.*

Yield factor or percentage—*the ratio of the edible portion to the amount purchased.*

Trim loss—*the amount of the product removed when preparing it for consumption.*

TABLE 4.2   COMMON PRODUCE YIELD FACTORS

Produce	Yield Factor (%)	Produce	Yield Factor (%)	Produce	Yield Factor (%)
Apples	75	Grapefruit	45	Peaches	75
Apricots	94	Grapes	90	Pears	75
Artichokes	48	Kiwi	80	Peppers	82
Avocados	75	Leeks	50	Pineapple	50
Bananas	70	Lemons	45	Plums	75
Berries	95	Lettuce	75	Potatoes	80
Broccoli	70	Limes	45	Radishes	90
Cabbage	79	Melons	55	Rhubarb	85
Carrots	78	Mushrooms	90	Scallions	65
Cauliflower	55	Nectarines	86	Spinach	60
Celery	75	Okra	82	Squash, summer	90
Cherries	82	Onions	90	Squash, winter	70
Corn, cob	28	Oranges	60	Tomatoes	90
Cucumbers	95	Papayas	65	Turnips	75
Eggplant	85	Parsley	85	Watercress	90
Garlic	88	Pea pods	90	Watermelon	45

Because each operation has its own standards for cleaning and trimming raw products, yield factors should be personalized. Lists of common yield factors are available, however, as an indication of industry norms. Some of these are included in Table 4.2.

Applying Yield Factors

Now that you understand what yield factors are and how to calculate them, we look at how they are used in costing recipes. First, yield factors are used for accurate recipe costing.

Example 4.5

Carrots cost $6.50 per 10-kg bag and have a yield factor of 78%. In other words, 22% of that 10-kg bag is waste. The price should be recalculated to account for that waste; that is, the A.P. (as purchased) unit cost must be converted to an E.P. (edible portion) unit cost. This is done by dividing A.P. cost by the yield percentage.

$$\text{A.P. cost (\$)} \div \text{yield percentage} = \text{E.P. cost (\$)}$$

$$.65/\text{kg} \ (6.50 \div 10) \div .78 = .84/\text{kg}$$

Thus, the carrots have an E.P. unit cost of $0.84 per kilogram (as compared with an A.P. price of $0.65 per kilogram). Note that E.P. cost is always greater than A.P. cost. When costing a recipe, you should use the $0.84-per-kilogram price as the accurate ingredient cost.

Second, yield factors are necessary for accurate purchasing. Most recipes list ingredients in E.P. quantities. Therefore, the chef must consider waste or trim amounts when ordering these items. If only the amounts listed in the recipe are ordered and then the item requires trimming, the number of portions (or recipe yield) will be less than the desired amount.

Example 4.6

A recipe requires 12 kg of shredded cabbage. The yield factor for cabbage is 79%. Therefore, 12 kg is 79% of the A.P. quantity. Divide the amount needed by the yield factor to determine the minimum A.P. quantity.

$$\text{E.P. quantity} \div \text{yield percentage} = \text{A.P. quantity}$$

$$12 \text{ kg} \div .79 = 15.19 \text{ kg}$$

It will take 15.2 kg of cabbage to provide the 12 kg of shredded cabbage. (This figure will be increased to an even amount for purchasing because yield factors are, at best, only an estimate.) Note that the A.P. figure must always be greater than the E.P. figure in this formula.

FOOD COST

Perhaps no other cost is emphasized as much by food service managers as **food cost**. Food cost refers to the cost of all foods used in the fabrication of menu items. This figure is also known as the **cost of goods sold** or **raw food cost** ("raw" is a bit misleading as food cost includes precooked and packaged foods as well as uncooked foods).

Food cost—*the cost of the materials that go directly into the production of the menu item.*

Food costs are calculated in two ways: (1) as a total cost of all foods used during a given time period, and (2) as a cost of one particular portion or menu item. Total cost is used as a general guideline for budgeting and menu planning. The portion or item cost is used to calculate menu prices; it helps the chef stay within cost limitations.

Cost of Goods Sold

The "goods" sold by a food service operation are, of course, the foods used in producing menu items. Before you can calculate cost of goods sold you must take a physical inventory of all foodstuffs on hand. **Inventory** should be taken periodically: at the end of each week, month, quarter or other accounting period. Taking inventory requires listing and counting all foods in the kitchen, storerooms and refrigerators. The quantities are then *extended;* that is, multiplied by the unit cost. The extended prices are then added to calculate the total inventory value.

Inventory—*the listing and counting of all foods in the kitchen, storerooms and refrigerators.*

Whether prepared foods or open containers are included in the inventory depends on the operation. Often small quantities of prepared foods or open containers are not inventoried on the theory that a certain amount of such items is always on hand, the value of which is minimal but fairly consistent from one accounting period to the next.

To properly calculate the cost of goods sold you must conduct an inventory at the beginning and end of the desired period and maintain records of all purchases during the period. The time period covered by this calculation could be any duration: week, month, quarter or year. After the total value of the inventory for both the beginning and the end of the period has been established, cost of goods sold is calculated as follows:

	Value of food inventory at beginning of period
PLUS	Food purchased during period
MINUS	Inventory at end of period
	Cost of food sold

Example 4.7

The total value of food in inventory on December 1 is $7600. The restaurant purchases $2300 worth of food during December and the inventory on January 1 is worth $5600. The cost of goods sold during the month of December is $4300 (in other words, the food produced during the month of December cost $4300):

$$(7600 + 2300) - 5600 = 4300$$

Once management knows the cost of goods sold, it can compare this figure with the dollar value of sales for the same period. This comparison gives management a good idea of how the business did for that period.

Food Cost Percentages

Food cost percentage—*the ratio of the cost of food served to the food sales dollars during a given period.*

The **food cost percentage** is the ratio of costs to sales. It shows what each dollar of sales costs. For example, a 35% food cost means that $0.35 of each dollar received went to pay for the foods the operation used. Food cost percentage is determined by dividing food cost by sales.

$$\text{food cost} \div \text{sales} = \text{food cost percentage}$$

Example 4.8

Refer back to Example 4.7 and assume that sales for December totalled $10 750. The food cost percentage for the month would be 40%:

$$4300 \div 10\ 750 = .40 = 40\%$$

By itself a single food cost percentage is meaningless. To be useful, it should be compared with the food cost percentages for other months of the same year or the same month in previous years. It is also helpful to know the food cost percentages for other similarly situated food service operations.

Food cost percentages can also be calculated on individual menu items. If the food items in a sliced turkey sandwich cost $2.80 and the sandwich sells for $5.25, the food cost percentage is 53% (2.80 divided by 5.25). Many operations would find this unacceptably high. To reduce the percentage and increase gross profits, the operation must either increase the selling price or decrease the ingredient costs.

Changing menu price, raw food cost or portion size will change the food cost percentage. If the food cost percentage is too high, the gross profit will be insufficient to cover operating expenses. If the percentage is too low, customers may feel they are not getting their money's worth and take their business elsewhere. Setting an appropriate percentage requires sound judgment, knowledge of the competition and accurate cost information. Periodic evaluations are necessary to ensure that the desired objective is actually maintained.

ESTABLISHING MENU PRICES

After determining the cost of food items, you can calculate menu prices. A few of the many methods for setting menu prices are explained below. Some techniques are highly structured and closely related to food costs; others are unstructured and unrelated to actual food costs. As a practical matter, no one method is right for every operation and a combination of methods may provide the best pricing information.

Cost-Based Pricing

Food Cost Percentage Pricing

For this technique, you must first determine the food cost percentage desired for the particular facility. After calculating each item's raw food cost you determine the selling price with the following formula:

cost per portion ÷ food cost percentage = selling price

Example 4.9

If the raw food cost for 1 sandwich is $1.70 and the desired food cost percentage is 23%, the selling price must be at least $7.39:

$$1.70 ÷ .23 = 7.391$$

In this situation, 23% of the sales price for each item will go to cover the raw food cost for that item. The higher the food cost percentage, the lower the portion of the sales price available for labour, fixed expenses, overhead or profit. Determining the appropriate food cost percentage for the facility is critical to the successful use of this method.

Factor Pricing

A variation on food cost percentage pricing is factor pricing. First, you take the desired food cost percentage and divide it into 100 to arrive at a cost factor. The cost of each item is then multiplied by the cost factor to arrive at the menu price. Using the previous example, the factor is 4.35 (100 ÷ 23 = 4.35), and the menu price for a $1.70 item is $7.39 (1.70 × 4.35 = 7.39).

Both food cost percentage and factor pricings are fast and easy to use. But these methods are sometimes unreliable because they assume that other costs associated with preparing food stay the same for each menu item. These systems wrongly assume that the costs for labour, energy and overhead are the same for a rack of lamb entree and a seafood salad. These methods may be fine-tuned somewhat by adjusting the desired food cost percentage according to the type of food or menu category. Appetizers may be assigned a lower food cost percentage than, say, desserts or side dishes.

Prime Cost Pricing

The food service industry uses a figure known as **prime cost** to refer to the total of raw food cost plus direct labour. Direct labour is the labour actually required for an item's preparation. If, for example, food cost is $2.10 and direct labour is $1.50, then prime cost is $3.60. As with the food cost percentage example above, the prime cost percentage can be divided into the prime cost amount to determine menu price.

Prime cost—*the combination of food costs and direct labour.*

Example 4.10

The raw food cost for a rack of lamb is $7.50; it takes a cook a total of 9 minutes to clean and trim it for service. If that cook is paid $8.50 per hour, the direct labour cost is $1.27 (8.50 per hour = .14 per minute; .14 × 9 = $1.27).

The prime cost of the rack of lamb is $8.77 (7.50 + 1.27). A selling price is then determined by dividing prime cost by the desired prime cost percentage. If management decided that the desired prime cost percentage is 48%, then the rack of lamb should be priced at $18.27 (8.77 ÷ .48 = 18.27).

Perceived Value Pricing

This is a rather backwards way of setting prices based on what a customer will perceive as an appropriate price. First determine what the market price is for the same or a similar item. Then calculate what you can serve for that price. Assume, for example,

1. the market price for a complete fried chicken dinner is $9.95,
2. the desired profit is 7% of sales,
3. overhead expenses are 27% of sales, and
4. labour is approximately 23% of sales.

Subtract the total of these items (57%) from the $9.95 selling price and you find that your total food cost for the fried chicken dinner must not be more than $4.28. This technique requires a thorough knowledge of the market and good historical information on labour and overhead costs. With the necessary information, you can determine how much to spend on raw product for each menu item and still make the desired profit.

Noncost-Based Pricing

Noncost-based pricing techniques rely on nonmonetary factors to set menu prices. Traditional prices in the area for the same or similar items may affect an operation's ability to set prices. This is particularly true for special or loss-leader items such as 99-cent jumbo sodas or $1.99 breakfast specials.

While the competition's prices are an important consideration, you should not simply copy them. Your competition's costs are not your costs no matter how similar the final food items appear. If you must charge higher prices than your competition, seek out some way to differentiate your product or service.

Virtually all food service operations are seeking to charge the highest price possible without a loss of sales. The customer's perception of value is therefore critical. The menu can be used as a tool for educating customers. Descriptive language or an explanation of unique or special dishes can be included. Customers who understand the value of service, atmosphere, out-of-season foods and specialty products will tolerate higher prices for those items.

Psychological Impact of Pricing

Regardless of how you arrive at a menu price, you may wish to round the figure up or down for psychological impact. It is human nature to perceive some prices as higher or lower than they actually are. For example, using a 9 or 5 as the last digit in a price creates the impression of a discount; prices ending in a 9 or 5 appeal to price-conscious customers. Prices ending in a 0 are perceived as more expensive and higher quality and so are often used on fine-dining menus.

The number of digits in a price is also important: $9.95 seems much less expensive than $10.25. Likewise, the first numeral in a price affects perception. When changing menu prices, an increase from $5.95 to $6.45 is seen as greater than an increase from $6.25 to $6.75, although both are 50-cent increases.

Patrons do not like to see a large spread in menu prices. It may make them think something is wrong with one of the items or may cause confusion. For example, a lobster dinner for $14.50 may be a reasonable price, but it may be inappropriate on a menu where all other items are less than $6.00. In general, the highest price should not be more than double the lowest price within the same food category. If the least expensive appetizer is $4.00, then the most expensive appetizer should not exceed $8.00.

Establishing menu prices is one of the most difficult yet important things a chef or manager can do to affect the facility's success. No one method is best for all operations, so careful study of several approaches is recommended.

Controlling Food Costs

Many things affect food costs in any given operation; most can be controlled by the chef or manager. These controls do not require mathematical calculations or formulas, just basic management skills and a good dose of common sense. The following factors all have an impact on the operation's bottom line:

◆ menu
◆ purchasing/ordering
◆ receiving
◆ storing
◆ issuing
◆ kitchen procedures
   establishing standard portions
   waste
◆ sales and service

Chefs tend to focus their control efforts in the area of kitchen preparation. While this may seem logical, it is not adequate. A good chef will be involved in all aspects of the operation to help prevent problems from arising or to correct those that may occur.

Menu
A profitable menu is based upon many variables including customer desires, physical space and equipment, ingredient availability, cost of goods sold, employee skills and competition. All management personnel, including the chef, should be consulted when planning the menu. Menu changes, while possibly desirable, must be executed with as much care as the original design.

Purchasing/Ordering
Purchasing techniques have a direct impact on cost controls. On the one hand, **parstock** must be adequate for efficient operations; on the other hand, too much inventory wastes space and resources and may spoil. Generally, inventory should turn over on a regular basis. Approximately two and a half times per month ensures good cash flow and should minimize spoilage. Each operation must establish appropriate inventory and purchasing levels. Before any items are ordered, purchasing specifications should be established and communicated to potential purveyors. Specifications should precisely describe the item, including grade, quality, packaging and unit size. Each operation should design its own form to best meet its specific needs. A sample specification form is shown in Figure 4.3. This information can be used to obtain price quotes from several purveyors. Update these quotes periodically to ensure that you are getting the best value for your money.

Parstock (Par)—*the amount of stock necessary to cover operating needs between deliveries.*

```
Menu Item:

Product:                                      Date:

Grade/Quality:

Weight/Size:                                  Product Code:

Packaging:

Delivery Conditions:

Comments:
```

FIGURE 4.3   *Specification Form*

Receiving

Whether goods are received by a full-time clerk, as they are in a large hotel, or by the chef or kitchen manager, certain standards should be observed. The person signing for merchandise should first confirm that the items were actually ordered. Second, determine whether the items listed on the invoice are the ones being delivered and that the price and quantity listed are accurate. Third, the items, especially meats and produce, should be checked for quality, freshness, temperature and weight. Established purchase specifications should be readily available.

Storing

Proper storage of foodstuffs is crucial in order to prevent spoilage, pilferage and waste. Stock must be rotated so that the older items are used first. Such a system for rotating stock is referred to as **FIFO: First In, First Out**. Storage areas should be well ventilated and lit to prevent infestation and mold. High-cost items and liquor are often locked up separately from standard groceries.

Issuing

It may be necessary, particularly in larger operations, to limit storeroom access to specific personnel. Maintaining ongoing inventory records or par-stock sheets helps the ordering process. Controlling issuances eliminates waste caused by multiple opened containers and ensures proper stock rotation.

Kitchen Procedures: Establishing Standard Portions

Standardizing portions is essential to controlling food costs. Unless portion quantity is uniform, it will be impossible to compute portion costs accurately. Portion discrepancies can also confuse or mislead customers.

Actual portion sizes depend on the food service operation itself, the menu, the prices and the customers' desires. Some items are generally purchased preportioned for convenience (for example, steaks are sold in uniform cuts, baking potatoes are available in uniform sizes, butter comes in preportioned pats and bread comes sliced for service). Other items must be portioned by the establishment prior to service. Special equipment makes consistent portioning easy. There are machines to slice meats, cutting guides for cakes and pies and portion scales for weighing quantities. Standardized portion scoops and ladles are indispensable for serving vegetables, soups, stews, salads and similar foods. Many of these items are discussed and illustrated in Chapter 5, Tools and Equipment.

Once acceptable portion sizes are established, employees must be properly trained to present them. If each employee of a sandwich shop prepared sandwiches the way he or she would like to eat them, customers would probably never receive the same sandwich twice. Customers may become confused and decide not to risk a repeat visit. Obviously, carelessness in portioning can also drastically affect food cost.

Kitchen Procedures: Waste

The chef must also control waste from overproduction or failure to use leftovers. With an adequate sales history, the chef can accurately estimate the quantity of food to prepare for each week, day or meal. If the menu is designed properly, the chef can also use leftovers and trim from product fabrication. The less waste generated in food preparation, the lower the overall food cost will be. A periodic inspection of waste receptacles allows for monitoring of waste or carelessness. Checking refrigerators regularly helps to ensure efficient product use and handling.

Sales and Service

An improperly trained sales staff can undo even the most rigorous of food cost controls. Front-of-the-house personnel are, after all, ultimately responsible for the sales portion of the food cost equation. Proper training is once again critical. Prices charged must be accurate and complete. Poor service can lead to the need to serve for free ("comp") an excessive amount of food. Dropped or spilled foods do not generate revenues. It is important to record these items for tracking purposes.

ONCLUSION

No food service operation can become successful based on the chef's cooking ability alone. A well-designed, enticing and accurately priced menu is also necessary. By following a standardized recipe you should be able to repeatedly produce a known quality and quantity of food for your specific food service operation. Based upon the regularity with which you offer these foods, your menu can be classified as static, cycle, market or hybrid. You can offer your menu items either à la carte, semi à la carte or table d'hôte.

You must be able to understand and apply proper techniques for converting recipes, food costing, menu pricing and loss control. Although computers are useful and are becoming more common in kitchens, no machine can substitute for a chef's watchful eye and hands-on controls.

QUESTIONS FOR DISCUSSION

1. Describe the four types of menus. Can each type of menu offer foods à la carte, semi à la carte and/or table d'hôte? Explain your answer.

2. Discuss three factors in food preparation that affect successful recipe size changes.

3. Why is it important to calculate the portion cost of a recipe in professional food service operations? Why is the full recipe cost inadequate?

4. List several factors that might cause one operation's yield factor for lettuce to be higher than another operation's. Explain why standardized yield factor lists are unreliable.

5. How is food cost percentage calculated? How can this figure be used (or misused) to evaluate the success of an operation?

6. Discuss three psychological factors used in setting menu prices.

WEBLINKS

Food Service Resource List: Annotated Bibliography of Meal Planning/Preparation
www.nal.usda.gov/fnic/service/foodmp1.htm

Food Service Resource List: Annotated Bibliography of Food and Beverage Cost Control
www.nal.usda.gov/fnic/service/foodcc1.htm

Meals for You: Choose recipes and meal plans by ingredient or nutritional content
www.mymenus.com/

Foodwine.com: An Electronic Gourmet Guide, updated daily
www.foodwine.com/

Labensky: Applied Math for Food Service
www.prenticehall.ca/allbooks/ect_0138492174.html

$\mathcal{P}$ART $\mathcal{T}$WO

$\mathcal{P}$REPARATION

Mise en place *is the essence of preparation. Although it means "everything in its place," the term connotes more than merely having all ingredients and tools on hand and being ready to begin preparing a dish. Rather, it suggests that the chef can identify, appreciate and understand how the necessary tools and equipment work, how the foods are cut and what the basic flavouring ingredients and staples are.*

To assist you in preparing to cook, Part II presents information about the tools and equipment routinely found in professional kitchens, then discusses how a professional kitchen is organized. There is a chapter on knife skills as well as chapters on kitchen staples (herbs and spices, condiments, oils, vinegars, nuts, coffee and tea) and eggs and dairy products (including milk, cream, cultured milk products and cheese).

Understanding this information is critical before successful cooking can begin.

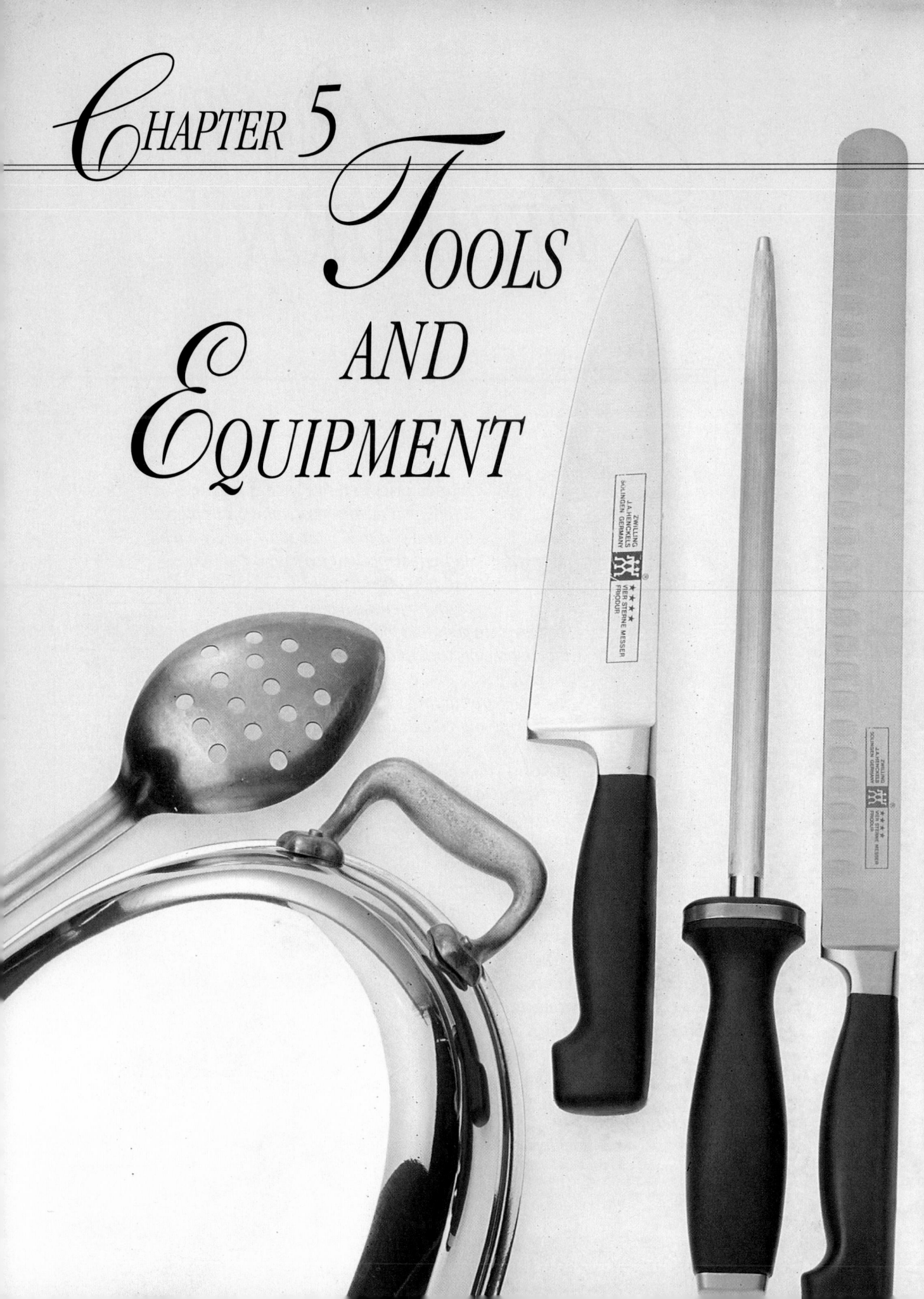

CHAPTER 5 TOOLS AND EQUIPMENT

LEARNING OUTCOMES

After studying this chapter you will be able to:

◆ recognize a variety of professional kitchen tools and equipment
◆ select and care for knives properly
◆ understand how a professional kitchen is organized

*H*aving *the proper tools and equipment for a particular task may mean the difference between a job well done and one done carelessly, incorrectly or even dangerously. This chapter introduces some of the tools and equipment typically used in a professional kitchen. Items are divided into categories according to their function: hand tools, knives, measuring and portioning devices, cookware, strainers and sieves, processing equipment, storage containers, heavy equipment, buffet equipment and safety equipment.*

A wide variety of specialized tools and equipment is available to today's chef. Breading machines, mandolines and food processors are designed to speed production by reducing handwork. Other devices—for instance, a duck press or a couscousière—are used only for unique tasks in preparing a few menu items. Much of this specialized equipment is quite expensive and found only in food manufacturing operations or specialized kitchens; a discussion of it is beyond the scope of this chapter. Brief descriptions of some of these specialized devices are, however, found in the Glossary. Baking pans and tools are discussed in Chapter 26, Principles of the Bakeshop.

This chapter is illustrated with generic drawings because manufacturers' designs differ. We end this chapter with a discussion of how a professional kitchen should be designed and organized.

Before using any equipment, study the operator's manual or have someone experienced with the particular item instruct you on proper procedures for its use and cleaning. And remember, always practise safety.

STANDARDS FOR TOOLS AND EQUIPMENT

Well-designed tools and equipment have characteristics that are beneficial to the overall efficiency and safety of the operation.

1. Equipment must be easily cleaned.
2. All food contact surfaces must be nontoxic (under intended end use conditions), nonabsorbent, corrosion resistant and nonreactive.
3. All food contact surfaces must be smooth, that is, free of pits, cracks, crevices, ledges, rivet heads and bolts.

4. Internal corners and edges must be rounded and smooth; external corners and angles must be smooth and sealed.

5. Coating materials must be nontoxic and easily cleaned; coatings must resist chipping and cracking.

6. Waste and waste liquids must be easily removed.

SELECTING TOOLS AND EQUIPMENT

In general, only commercial food service tools and equipment should be used in a professional kitchen. Household tools and appliances may not withstand the rigours of a professional kitchen. Look for tools that are well constructed. For example, joints should be welded, not bonded with solder; handles should be comfortable, with rounded borders; plastic and rubber parts should be seamless.

Before purchasing or leasing any particular piece of equipment you should evaluate several factors:

1. Is this equipment necessary for producing menu items?
2. Will this equipment perform the job required in the space available?
3. Is this equipment the most economical for the operation's specific needs?
4. Is this equipment easy to clean, maintain and repair?

HAND TOOLS

Hand tools are designed to aid in cutting, shaping, moving or combining foods. They have few, if any, moving parts. Knives, discussed separately below, are the most important hand tools. Others are metal or rubber spatulas, spoons, whisks, tongs and specialized cutters. In addition to the items shown in Figure 5.1, many hand tools designed for specific tasks, such as pressing tortillas or pitting cherries, are available. Sturdiness, durability and safety are the watchwords when selecting hand tools. Choose tools that can withstand the heavy use of a professional kitchen and those that are easily cleaned.

KNIVES

Knives are the most important items in your tool kit. With a sharp knife, the skilled cook can accomplish a number of tasks more quickly and efficiently than any machine. Good-quality knives are expensive but will last for many years with proper care. Select easily sharpened, well-constructed knives that are comfortable and balanced in your hand. Knife construction and commonly used knives are discussed here; knife safety and care as well as cutting techniques are discussed in Chapter 6, Knife Skills.

Vegetable Peeler

Melon Ball Cutter
(The smaller end is also known as a Parisian Scoop)

Zester

Perforated, Plain and Slotted Spoons

Balloon and Rigid Whisks

Straight Tongs

Table-Mounted Can Opener

Rubber Spatula

Meat Mallet

Chef's Fork

Grill Spatula

Straight Spatula (Cake Spatula)

FIGURE 5.1

Knife Construction

A good knife begins with a single piece of metal, stamped, cut or—best of all—forged and tempered into a blade of the desired shape. The metals generally used for knife blades are:

1. **Carbon steel**—An alloy of carbon and iron, it was traditionally used for blades because it is soft enough to be sharpened easily. It corrodes and discolours easily, however, especially when used with acidic foods. It is not recommended for food service applications.

2. **Stainless steel**—It will not rust, corrode or discolour and is extremely durable. But a stainless steel blade is much more difficult to sharpen than a

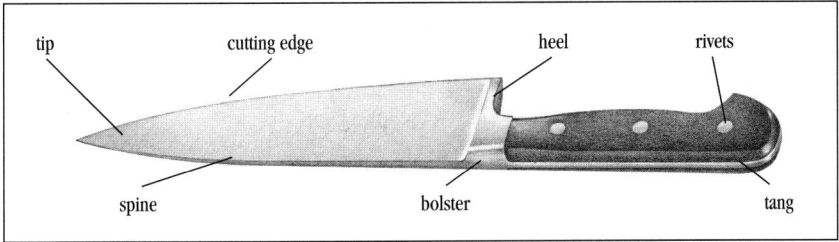

FIGURE 5.2

carbon steel one, although once an edge is established it lasts longer than the edge on a carbon steel blade.

3. **High carbon stainless steel**—An alloy combining the best features of carbon steel and stainless steel, it neither corrodes nor discolours and can be sharpened almost as easily as carbon steel. It is now the most frequently used metal for blades.

A portion of the blade, known as the tang, fits inside the handle. See Figure 5.2. The best knives are constructed with a full tang running the length of the handle; they also have a bolster where the blade meets the handle (the bolster is part of the blade, not a separate collar). Less expensive knives may have a 3/4-length tang or a thin "rattail" tang. Neither provide as much support, durability or balance as a full tang.

Knife handles are often made of hard woods infused with plastic and riveted to the tang. Molded polypropylene handles are permanently bonded to a tang without seams or rivets. Any handle should be shaped for comfort and ground smooth to eliminate crevices where bacteria can grow.

Knife Shapes and Sharpening Equipment

You will collect many knives during your career, many with specialized functions not described here. This list includes only the most basic knives and sharpening equipment. Knives and equipment described below are illustrated in Figure 5.3.

French or Chef's Knife
An all-purpose knife used for chopping, slicing and mincing. Its rigid 8- to 14-inch-long (20 to 35 cm) blade is wide at the heel and tapers to a point at the tip.

Utility Knife
An all-purpose knife used for cutting fruits and vegetables and carving poultry. Its rigid 6- to 8-inch-long (15 to 20 cm) blade is shaped like a chef's knife but narrower.

Boning Knife
A smaller knife with a thin blade used to separate meat from bone. The blade is usually 5 to 7 inches (12.5 to 17.5 cm) long and may be flexible or rigid.

Paring Knife
A short knife used for detail work or cutting fruits and vegetables. The rigid blade is from 2 to 4 inches (5 to 10 cm) long. A turning or **bird's beak knife** is similar to a paring knife but with a curved blade; it is used for shaping curved surfaces or turning vegetables.

Paring Knife

Rigid Boning Knife

Utility Knife

Cleaver

Serrated Slicer

French or Chef's Knife

Oyster Knife

Flexible Slicer

Butcher Knife

Clam Knife

Three-Sided Sharpening Stone

Steel

FIGURE 5.3

Cleaver

The large, heavy rectangular blade of this knife is used for chopping or cutting through bones.

Slicer

A knife with a long, thin blade used primarily for slicing cooked meat. The tip may be round or pointed and the blade may be flexible or rigid. A similar knife with a serrated edge is used for slicing bread or pastry items.

Butcher Knife

Sometimes known as a **scimitar** because the rigid blade curves up in a 25-degree angle at the tip, this knife is used for fabricating raw meat and is available with 6- to 14-inch (15 to 35 cm) blades.

Oyster and Clam Knives

The short, rigid blades of these knives are used to open oyster and clam shells. The tips are blunt; only the clam knife has a sharp edge.

Sharpening Stone

Also known as a **whetstone**, a sharpening stone is used to put an edge on a dull blade.

Steel

A steel is used to hone or straighten a blade immediately after and between sharpenings.

MEASURING AND PORTIONING DEVICES

Recipe ingredients must be measured precisely, especially in the bakeshop, and foods should be measured when served to control portion size and cost. The devices used to measure and portion foods are, for the most part, hand tools designed to make food preparation and service easier and more precise. The accuracy they afford prevents the cost of mistakes made when accurate measurements are ignored.

Measurements may be based upon weight (e.g., grams, ounces, pounds) or volume (e.g., millilitres, litres, quarts). Therefore it is necessary to have available several measuring devices, including liquid and dry measuring cups and a variety of scales. Thermometers and timers are also measuring devices and are discussed here (see Figure 5.4 for illustrations). When purchasing measuring devices look for quality construction and accurate markings.

Scales

Scales are necessary to determine the weight of an ingredient or a portion of food (for example, the sliced meat for a sandwich). Portion scales use a spring mechanism, round dial and single flat tray. They are available calibrated in grams, ounces or pounds. Electronic scales also use a spring mechanism but provide digital readouts. They are often required by law where foods are priced for sale by weight. Balance scales (also known as baker's scales) use a two-tray and free-weights counterbalance system. A balance scale allows more weight to be measured at one time because it is not limited by spring capacity. Any scale must be properly used and maintained to provide an accurate reading.

♦♦♦

MEASURING PRECISELY

Although many measuring devices are routinely used in kitchens, the most precise way to measure is by weight. Volume measures appear in this text for the convenience of the user

TABLE 5.1   PORTION SCOOP CAPACITIES

Scoop Number	Volume		Approximate Weight*	
	U.S.	Metric	U.S.	Metric
6	2/3 c.	160 mL	5 oz.	160 g
8	1/2 c.	120 mL	4 oz.	120 g
10	3 fl. oz.	90 mL	3 to 3-1/2 oz.	85–100 g
12	1/3 c.	80 mL	2-1/2 to 3 oz.	75–85 g
16	1/4 c.	60 mL	2 oz.	60 g
20	1-1/2 fl. oz.	45 mL	1-3/4 oz.	50 g
24	1-1/3 fl. oz.	40 mL	1-1/3 oz.	40 g
30	1 fl. oz.	30 mL	1 oz.	30 g
40	0.8 fl. oz.	24 mL	0.8 oz.	23 g
60	1/2 fl. oz.	15 mL	1/2 oz.	15 g

*Weights are approximate because they vary by food. Verify weights by scale to ensure accurate portion sizes.

Volume Measures

Ingredients may be measured by volume using measuring spoons and measuring cups. Measuring spoons sold as a set usually include 2-, 5- and 15-mL units (or the imperial equivalent). Liquid measuring cups are available in capacities from 100 mL to 1 L. They have a lip or pour spout above the top line of measurement to prevent spills. Measuring cups for dry ingredients are usually sold in sets of 1/4-, 1/3-, 1/2-, and 1-cup units. They do not have pour spouts, so the top of the cup is level with the top measurement specified. Glass measuring cups are not recommended because they can break. Avoid using bent or dented measuring cups as the damage may distort the measurement capacity.

Ladles

Long-handled ladles are useful for portioning liquids such as stocks, sauces and soups. The capacity, in ounces or millilitres, is stamped on the handle.

Portion Scoops

Portion scoops (also known as dishers) resemble ice cream scoops. They come in a range of standardized sizes and have a lever-operated blade for releasing their contents. Scoops are useful for portioning salads, vegetables, muffin batters or other soft foods. A number, stamped on either the handle or the release mechanism, indicates the number of level scoopfuls per U.S. quart. The higher the scoop number, the smaller the scoop's capacity. Metric scoops are also available. See Table 5.1 for scoop capacities.

Thermometers

Various types of thermometers are used in the kitchen.

Stem-type thermometers, including instant-read models, measure the temperature of a food. The thermometer is inserted into foods to obtain temperature readings between 0°F (–18°C) and 220°F (104°C). Temperatures are shown on either a dial noted by an arrow or a digital readout. An instant-read thermometer is a small stem-type model, designed to be carried in a pocket and used to provide quick temperature readings. An instant-read thermometer

---

♦♦♦

HOW TO CALIBRATE A STEM-TYPE THERMOMETER

All stem-type thermometers should be calibrated at least weekly as well as whenever they are dropped. To calibrate a stem-type thermometer, fill a glass with shaved ice, then add water. Place the thermometer in the ice slush and wait until the temperature reading stabilizes. Following the manufacturer's directions, adjust the thermometer's calibration nut until the temperature reads 32°F (0°C). Check the calibration by returning the thermometer to the slush.

should not be left in foods that are cooking because doing so damages the thermometer.

Candy and fat thermometers measure temperatures up to 400°F (200°C) using mercury in a column of glass. A back clip attaches to the pan, keeping the chef's hands free. Be careful not to subject glass thermometers to quick temperature changes or the glass may shatter.

Because proper temperatures must be maintained for holding and storing foods, oven and refrigerator thermometers are also useful. Select thermometers with easy-to-read dials or column divisions.

Timers

Portable kitchen timers are useful for any busy cook. Small digital timers can be carried in a pocket; some even time three functions at once. Select a timer with a loud alarm signal and long timing capability.

Measuring Spoons   Liquid Measuring Cup   Dry Measuring Cups   Portion Scoop

Portion Scale   Instant-Read Thermometer   Candy Thermometer   Ladles

Baker's Scale

FIGURE 5.4

COOKWARE

Cookware includes the sauté pans and stockpots used on the stove top as well as the roasting pans, hotel pans and specialty molds used inside the oven. Cookware should be selected for its size, shape, ability to conduct heat evenly and overall quality of construction.

Metals and Heat Conduction

Cookware that fails to distribute heat evenly may cause hot spots that burn foods. Because different metals conduct heat at different rates, and thicker layers of metal conduct heat more evenly than thinner ones, the most important considerations when choosing cookware are the type and thickness (known as the *gauge*) of the material used. No one cookware or material suits every process or need, however; always select the most appropriate material for the task at hand.

Copper

Copper is an excellent conductor: it heats rapidly and evenly and cools quickly. Indeed, unlined copper pots are unsurpassed for cooking sugar and fruit mixtures. But copper cookware is extremely expensive. It also requires a great deal of care and is often quite heavy. Moreover, because copper may react with some foods, copper cookware usually has a tin lining, which is soft and easily scratched. Because of these problems, copper is now often sandwiched between layers of stainless steel or aluminum in the bottom of pots and pans.

Aluminum

Aluminum is the metal used most commonly in commercial utensils. It is lightweight and, after copper, conducts heat best. Aluminum is a soft metal, though, so it should be treated with care to avoid dents. Do not use aluminum containers for storage or for cooking acidic foods because the metal reacts chemically with many foods. Light-coloured foods, such as soups or sauces, may be discoloured when cooked in aluminum, especially if stirred with a metal whisk or spoon.

Anodized aluminum has a hard, dark, corrosion-resistant surface that helps prevent sticking and discolouration.

Stainless Steel

Although stainless steel conducts and retains heat poorly, it is a hard, durable metal particularly useful for holding foods and for low-temperature cooking where hot spots and scorching are not problems. Stainless steel pots and pans are available with aluminum or copper bonded to the bottom or with an aluminum-layered core. Although expensive, such cookware combines the rapid, uniform heat conductivity of copper and aluminum with the strength, durability and nonreactivity of stainless steel. Stainless steel is also ideal for storage containers because it does not react with foods.

Cast Iron

Cast-iron cookware distributes heat evenly and holds high temperatures well. It is often used in griddles and large skillets. Although relatively inexpensive, cast iron is extremely heavy and brittle. It must be kept properly conditioned and dry to prevent rust and pitting.

Glass

Glass retains heat well but conducts it poorly. It does not react with foods. Tempered glass is suitable for microwave cooking provided it does not have any metal band or decoration. Commercial operations rarely use glass cookware because of the danger of breakage.

Ceramics

Ceramics, including earthenware, porcelain and stoneware, are used primarily for baking dishes, casseroles and baking stones because they conduct heat uniformly and retain temperatures well. Ceramics are nonreactive, inexpensive and generally suitable for use in a microwave oven (provided there is no metal in the glaze). Ceramics are easily chipped or cracked, however, and should not be used over a direct flame. Also, quick temperature changes may cause the cookware to crack or shatter.

Plastic

Plastic containers are frequently used in commercial kitchens for food storage or service, but they cannot be used for heating or cooking except in a microwave oven. Plastic microwave cookware is made of phenolic resin. It is easy to clean, relatively inexpensive and rigidly shaped, but its glasslike structure is brittle and it can crack or shatter.

Enamelware

Pans lined with enamel should not be used for cooking; in many areas, their use in commercial kitchens is prohibited by law. The enamel can chip or crack easily, providing good places for bacteria to grow. Also, the chemicals used to bond the enamel to the cookware can cause food poisoning if ingested.

◆◆◆

ROMAN POTS, SOUTHERN STILLS AND CRAFT FAIRS

Lead is poisonous. Ingesting it can cause severe gastrointestinal pains, anemia and central nervous system disorders including intelligence and memory deficits and behavioural changes.

The unwitting and dangerous consumption of lead is not limited to children eating peeling paint chips. Some historians suggest that the use of lead cookware and lead-lined storage vessels and water pipes may have caused pervasive lead poisoning among the elite of the Roman Empire and thus contributed to the Empire's decline. There is also ample evidence that from ancient times until just a few hundred years ago, wine was heated in lead vessels to sweeten it. This had a disastrous effect on the drinker and, for several centuries in countries throughout Europe, on the wine purveyor as well. The former could be poisoned and the latter could be punished by death for selling adulterated wine. More recently it was found that much of the moonshine whisky produced in the American South contained lead in potentially toxic ranges. The source was determined to be the lead solder used in homemade stills, some of which even included old lead-containing car radiators as condensers.

Although commercially available cookware will not contain lead, be careful of imported pottery and those lovely hand-thrown pots found at craft fairs—there could be lead in the glaze.

Nonstick Coatings

Without affecting a metal's ability to conduct heat, a polymer (plastic) known as polytetrafluoroethylene (PTFE) and marketed under the trade names Teflon® and Silverstone®, may be applied to many types of cookware. It provides a slippery, nonreactive finish that prevents food from sticking and allows the use of less fat in cooking. Cookware with nonstick coatings requires a great deal of care, however, as the coatings can scratch, chip and blister. Do not use metal spoons or spatulas in cookware with nonstick coatings.

Common Cookware

Pots

Pots are large round vessels with straight sides and two loop handles. Available in a range of sizes based on volume, they are used on the stove top for making stocks or soups, or for boiling or simmering foods, particularly where rapid evaporation is not desired. Flat or fitted lids are available. See Figure 5.5 for illustrations of pots and other common cookware.

Pans

Pans are round vessels with one long handle and straight or sloped sides. They are usually smaller and shallower than pots. Pans are available in a range of diameters and are used for general stove top cooking, especially sautéing, frying or reducing liquids rapidly.

Woks

Originally used to prepare Asian foods, woks are now found in many professional kitchens. Their round bottoms and curved sides diffuse heat and make it easy to toss or stir contents. Their large domed lids retain heat for steaming vegetables. Woks are useful for quickly sautéing strips of meat, simmering a whole fish or deep-frying appetizers. Stove top woks range in diameter from 12 to 30 inches (30 to 75 cm); larger built-in gas or electric models are also available.

Hotel Pans

Hotel pans (also known as steam table pans) are rectangular stainless steel pans designed to hold food for service in steam tables. Hotel pans may also be used for baking, roasting or poaching inside an oven. Perforated pans useful for draining, steaming or icing down foods are also available. The standard full-size pan is 12 by 20 inches (30 by 50 cm), with pans one-half, one-third, one-sixth and other fractions of this size available. Hotel pan depth is standardized at 2 inches (5 cm) (referred to as a "200 pan"), 4, 6 and 8 inches (10, 15 and 20 cm).

Molds

Pâté molds are available in several shapes and sizes, and are usually made from tinned steel. Those with hinged sides, whether smooth or patterned, are more properly referred to as *pâté en croûte* molds. The hinged sides make it easier to remove the baked pâté. Terrine molds are traditionally lidded earthenware or enamelled cast-iron containers used for baking forcemeat mixtures. They may be round, oval or rectangular. Timbale molds are small (about 4 ounces/75 to 120 mL) metal or ceramic containers used for molding aspic or baking individual portions of mousse, custard or vegetables. They may be round or oval and their slightly flared sides allow the contents to release cleanly when inverted.

Stockpot with Spigot

Sauce Pot

Sautoir (Straight Sides)

Saucepan

Cast-Iron Skillet (Griswold)

Sauteuse (Sloped Sides)

Rondeau/Brazier

Wok

Pâté en Croûte Mold

Timbales

Hotel Pans

FIGURE 5.5

STRAINERS AND SIEVES

Strainers and sieves are used primarily to aerate and remove impurities from dry ingredients and drain or purée cooked foods. Strainers, colanders, drum sieves, china caps and chinois are nonmechanical devices with a stainless steel mesh or screen through which food passes. The size of the mesh or

Chinois

Round Mesh Strainer

China Cap

Colander

Flour Sifter

Drum Sieve (Tamis)

Food Mill

Skimmer

Spider

FIGURE 5.6

screen varies from extremely fine to several millimetres wide; select the fineness best suited for the task at hand. See Figure 5.6.

Chinois and China Cap

Both the chinois and china cap are cone-shaped metal strainers. The conical shape allows liquids to filter through small openings. A chinois is made from a very fine mesh, while a china cap has a perforated metal body. Both are used for straining stocks and sauces, with the chinois being particularly useful for consommé. A china cap can also be used with a pestle to purée soft foods.

Skimmer and Spider

Both the skimmer and spider are long-handled tools used to remove foods or impurities from liquids. The flat, perforated disk of a skimmer is used for skimming stocks or removing foods from soups or stocks. The spider has a finer mesh disk, which makes it better for retrieving items from hot fat. Wooden-handled spiders are available but are less sturdy and harder to clean than all-metal designs.

Cheesecloth

Cheesecloth is a loosely woven cotton gauze used for straining stocks and sauces and wrapping poultry or fish for poaching. Cheesecloth is also indispensable for making sachets. Always rinse cheesecloth thoroughly before use; this removes lint and prevents the cheesecloth from absorbing other liquids.

Food Mill

A food mill purées and strains food at the same time. Food is placed in the hopper and a hand-crank mechanism turns a blade in the hopper against a perforated disk, forcing the food through the disk. Most models have interchangeable disks with various-sized holes. Choose a mill that can be taken apart easily for cleaning.

Flour Sifter

A sifter is used for aerating, blending and removing impurities from dry ingredients such as flour, cocoa and leavening agents. The 8-cup (2 L) hand-crank sifter shown in Figure 5.6 uses 4 curved rods to brush the contents through a curved mesh screen. The sifter should have a medium-fine screen and a comfortable handle.

PROCESSING EQUIPMENT

Processing equipment includes both electrical and nonelectrical devices used to chop, purée, slice, grind or mix foods. See Figure 5.7. Before using any such equipment, be sure to review its operating procedures and ask for assistance if necessary. Always turn the equipment off and disconnect the power before disassembling, cleaning or moving the appliance. Any problems or malfunctions should be reported to your supervisor immediately. *Never place your hand into any machinery when the power is on. Processing equipment is powerful and can cause serious injury.*

Slicer

An electric slicer is used to cut meat, bread, cheese or raw vegetables into uniform slices. It has a circular blade that rotates at high speed. Food is placed in a carrier, then passed (manually or by an electric motor) against the blade.

Slice thickness is determined by the distance between the blade and the carrier. Because of the speed with which the blade rotates, foods can be cut into extremely thin slices very quickly. An electric slicer is convenient for preparing moderate to large quantities of food, but the time required to disassemble and clean the equipment makes it impractical when slicing only a few items.

Mandoline

A mandoline is a manually operated slicer made of stainless steel with adjustable slicing blades. It is also used to make julienne and waffle-cut slices. Its narrow, rectangular body sits on the work counter at a 45-degree angle. Foods are passed against a blade to obtain uniform slices. It is useful for slicing small quantities of fruits or vegetables when using a large electric slicer would be unwarranted. To avoid injury, always use a hand guard or steel glove when using a mandoline.

Food Chopper or Buffalo Chopper

This chopper is used to process moderate to large quantities of food to a uniform size, such as chopping onions or grinding bread for crumbs. The food is placed in a large bowl rotating beneath a hood where curved blades chop it. The size of the cut depends on how long the food is left in the machine. Buffalo choppers are available in floor or tabletop models. The motor can usually be fitted with a variety of other tools such as a meat grinder or a slicer/shredder, making it even more useful.

Food Processor

A food processor has a motor housing with a removable bowl and S-shaped blade. It is used, for example, to purée cooked foods, chop nuts, prepare compound butters and emulsify sauces. Special disks can be added that slice, shred or julienne foods. Bowl capacity and motor power vary; select a model large enough for your most common tasks.

Blender

Though similar in principle to a food processor, a blender has a tall, narrow food container and a four-pronged blade. Its design is better for processing liquids or liquefying foods quickly. A blender is used to prepare smooth drinks, purée soups and sauces, blend batters and chop ice. A **vertical cutter/mixer** (VCM) operates like a very large, powerful blender. A VCM is usually floor-mounted and has a capacity of 15–80 gallons (55–300 L). Motorized blender blades at the end of a shaft are now available for blending products in large containers.

Mixer

A vertical mixer is indispensable in the bakeshop and most kitchens. The U-shaped arms hold a metal mixing bowl in place; the selected mixing attachment fits onto the rotating head. The three common mixing attachments are the whip (used for whipping eggs or cream), the paddle (used for general mixing) and the dough hook (used for kneading bread). Most mixers have several operating speeds. Bench models range in capacity from 4.5 to 20 quarts, while floor mixers can as hold as much as 140 quarts. Some mixers can be fitted with shredder/slicers, meat grinders, juicers or power strainers, making the equipment more versatile.

Juicer

Two types of juicers are available: reamers and extractors. Reamers, also known as citrus juicers, remove juice from citrus fruits. They can be manual or

Meat Slicer

Buffalo Chopper with Slicer and Meat Grinder Attachments

Mandoline

Heavy-Duty Blender

Food Processor

25-L Mixer and Attachments

Citrus Juicer

FIGURE 5.7

electric. Manual models use a lever arm to squeeze the fruit with increased pressure. They are most often used to prepare small to moderate amounts of juice for cooking or beverages. Juice extractors are electrical devices that create juice by liquefying raw fruits, vegetables and herbs. They use centrifugal force to filter out fiber and pulp.

STORAGE CONTAINERS

Proper storage containers are necessary for keeping leftovers and opened packages of food safe for consumption. Proper storage can also reduce the costs incurred by waste or spoilage.

While stainless steel pans such as hotel pans are suitable and useful for some items, the expense of stainless steel and the lack of air-tight lids makes these pans impractical for general storage purposes. Aluminum containers are not recommended because the metal can react with even mildly acidic items. Glass containers are generally not allowed in commercial kitchens because of the hazards of broken glass. The most useful storage containers are those made of high-density plastic (such as polyethylene and polypropylene).

Storage containers must have well-fitting lids and should be available in a variety of sizes, including some that are small enough to hold even minimal quantities of food without allowing too much exposure to oxygen. Round and square plastic containers are widely available. Flat, snap-on lids allow containers to be stacked for more efficient storage. Containers may be clear or opaque white, which helps protect light-sensitive foods. Larger containers may be fitted with handles and spigots, making them especially suited for storing stock. Some storage containers are marked with graduated measurements, so content quantity can be determined at a glance. See Figure 5.8.

Large quantities of dry ingredients, such as flour, sugar and rice, can be stored in rolling bins. The bins should be seamless with rounded corners for easy cleaning. They should have well-fitting but easy-to-open lids and should move easily on well-balanced casters.

FIGURE 5.8

HEAVY EQUIPMENT

Heavy equipment includes the gas-, electric- or steam-operated appliances used for cooking, reheating or holding foods. Heavy equipment also includes dishwashers and refrigeration units. Heavy equipment should be installed in a fixed location determined by the kitchen's traffic flow and space limitations.

Heavy equipment may be purchased or leased new or used. Used equipment is most often purchased in an effort to save money. While the initial cost is generally less for used equipment, the buyer should also consider the lack of a manufacturer's warranty or dealership guarantee and how the equipment was maintained by the prior owner. Functional used equipment is satisfactory for back-of-the-house areas, but it is usually better to purchase new equipment if it will be visible to the customer. Leasing equipment may be appropriate for some operations. The cost of leasing is less than purchasing and, if something goes wrong with the equipment, the operator is generally not responsible for repairs or service charges.

Stove Tops

Stove tops or ranges are often the most important cooking equipment in the kitchen. They have one or more burners powered by gas or electricity. The

FIGURE 5.9 *Gas burner and flat top range with dual ovens and an overhead broiler (salamander).*

burners may be open or covered with a cast-iron or steel plate. Open burners supply quick, direct heat that is easy to regulate. A steel plate, known as a **flat top**, supplies even but less intense heat. Although it takes longer to heat than a burner, the flat top supports heavier weights and makes a larger area available for cooking. Many stoves include both flat tops and open burner arrangements. See Figure 5.9.

Griddles are similar to flat tops except they are made of a thinner metal plate. Foods are usually cooked directly on the griddle's surface, not in pots or pans which can nick or scratch the surface. (A griddle is illustrated in Figure 5.10.) The surface should be properly cleaned and conditioned after each use. Griddles are popular for short-order and fast-food-type operations.

Ovens

An oven is an enclosed space where food is cooked by being surrounded with hot, dry air. Conventional ovens are often located beneath the stove top. They have a heating element located at the unit's bottom or floor, and pans are placed on wire racks inside the oven's cavity. (See Figure 5.9.) Conventional ovens may also be separate, free-standing units or decks stacked one on top of the other. In stack ovens, pans are placed directly on the deck or floor and not on wire racks.

Convection ovens use internal fans to circulate the hot air. This tends to cook foods more quickly and evenly. Convection ovens are almost always free-

Griddle

Steam Kettle

Deep Fryer

Stack Oven

Overhead Broiler

Tilting Skillet

Gas Grill

Convection Steamer

FIGURE 5.10

standing units, powered either by gas or electricity. Because convection ovens cook foods more quickly, temperatures may need to be reduced by 25°F to 50°F (10°C to 20°C) from those recommended for conventional ovens.

Combitherm ovens are very versatile. They can function as a low-pressure steamer, convection oven or a combination of the two. The programmable features allow for performing complex cooking procedures to achieve superior end products.

Microwave Ovens

Microwave ovens are electrically powered ovens used to cook or reheat foods. They are available in a range of sizes and power settings. Microwave ovens will not brown foods unless fitted with special browning elements. Microwave cooking is discussed in more detail in Chapter 9, Principles of Cooking.

Broilers and Grills

Broilers and grills are generally used to prepare meats, fish and poultry. For a grill, the heat source is beneath the rack on which the food is placed. For a broiler, the heat source is above the food. Most broilers are gas powered; grills may be gas or electric or may burn wood or charcoal. A **salamander** is a small overhead broiler primarily used to finish or top-brown foods. (See Figure 5.9.) A **rotisserie** is similar to a broiler except that the food is placed on a revolving spit in front of the heat source. The unit may be open or enclosed like an oven; it is most often used for cooking poultry or meats.

Tilting Skillets

Tilting skillets are large, free-standing, flat-bottomed pans about 6 inches (15 cm) deep with an internal heating element below the pan's bottom. They are usually made of stainless steel with a cover, and have a hand-crank mechanism that turns or tilts the pan to pour out the contents. Tilting skillets can be used as stockpots, braziers, fry pans, griddles or steam tables, making them one of the most versatile of modern commercial appliances.

Steam Kettles

Steam kettles (also known as steam-jacketed kettles) are similar to stockpots except they are heated from the bottom and sides by steam circulating between layers of stainless steel. The steam may be generated internally or from an outside source. Because steam heats the kettle's sides, foods cook more quickly and evenly than they would in a pot sitting on the stove top. Steam kettles are most often used for making sauces, soups, custards or stock. Steam kettles are available in a range of sizes, from a 2-gallon (9-L) tabletop model to a 100-gallon (450-L) floor model. Some models have a tilting mechanism that allows the contents to be poured out; others have a spigot near the bottom through which liquids can be drained.

Steamers

Pressure and convection steamers are used to cook foods rapidly and evenly, using direct contact with steam. Pressure steamers heat water above the boiling point in sealed compartments; the high temperature and sealed compartment increase the internal pressure in a range of 4 to 15 pounds (1.8 to 6.8 kg) per square inch. The increased pressure and temperature cook the foods rapidly. Convection steamers generate steam in an internal boiler, then release it over the foods in a cooking chamber. Both types of steamer are ideal for cooking vegetables with a minimal loss of flavour or nutrients.

Deep Fryers

Deep fryers are used only to fry foods in hot fat. The fryers may be either gas or electric and should have thermostatic controls to maintain the fat at a preset temperature. Frying procedures are discussed in Chapter 21, Deep-Fat Frying.

Refrigerators

Proper refrigeration space is an essential component of any kitchen. Many foods must be stored at low temperatures to maintain quality and safety. Most

✦✦✦
BUFFET EQUIPMENT

Food service operations that prepare buffets or cater off-premise events need specialized equipment to ensure that food is handled safely and efficiently and displayed appropriately. Proper temperatures must be maintained during transportation, display and service.

Insulated carriers hold food at a consistent temperature for a period of time. They are designed to hold hotel pans or sheet pans and are available with wheels for easy movement. Some are available with a spigot for serving hot or cold beverages. Any carrier should be easy to clean and a convenient size for the space available and the type of operation.

Temperature remains a concern when arranging food on a buffet table. Chafing dishes are commonly used for keeping hot foods hot during service. Chafing dishes are designed so that cans of solid fuel can be placed under a deep hotel pan of hot water. Like a bain marie, the hot water helps maintain the temperature of food placed in a second hotel pan suspended over the first. Chafing dishes, however, should never be used to heat food. Chafing dishes are available in several sizes and shapes, but the most convenient are those based on the size of a standard hotel pan. Round, deep chafing dishes are useful for serving soups or sauces. Exteriors can be plain or ornate, and made of silver, copper or stainless steel.

Roast beef, turkey, ham or other large cuts of meat are sometimes carved on a buffet in front of guests. Heat lamps can be used to keep these foods warm. Heat lamps are also useful for maintaining the temperature of pizza or fried foods, which might become soggy if held in a chafing dish.

Pastries, breads and cold foods can be arranged on a variety of platters, trays, baskets and serving pieces, depending on the size and style of the buffet. Some of the most elegant and traditional serving pieces are flat display mirrors. These may be plastic or glass and are available in a wide variety of shapes and sizes. The edges should be sealed in an easy-to-clean plastic to prevent chipping.

Although many of these items can be rented, operations that serve buffets on a regular basis may prefer to invest in their own transportation and serving equipment.

commercial refrigeration is of two types: walk-in units and reach-in or upright units.

A walk-in is a large, room-sized box capable of holding hundreds of kilograms of food on adjustable shelves. A separate freezer walk-in may be positioned nearby or even inside a refrigerated walk-in.

Reach-ins may be individual units or parts of a bank of units, each with shelves approximately the size of a full sheet pan. Reach-in refrigerators and freezers are usually located throughout the kitchen to provide quick access to foods. Small units may also be placed beneath the work counters. Freezers and refrigerators are available in a wide range of sizes and door designs to suit any operation.

Other forms of commercial refrigeration include chilled drawers located beneath a work area that are just large enough to accommodate a hotel pan, and display cases used to show foods to the customer.

Dishwashers
Mechanical dishwashers are available to wash, rinse and sanitize dishware, glassware, cookware and utensils. Small models clean one rack of items at a time, while larger models can handle several racks simultaneously on a conveyor belt system. Sanitizing may be accomplished with either extremely hot water (180°F/82°C) or with chemicals automatically dispensed during the final rinse cycle. Any dishwashing area should be carefully organized for efficient use of equipment and employees and to prevent recontamination of clean items.

SAFETY EQUIPMENT

There are certain items that are critical to the well-being of a food service operation although they are not used in food preparation. These are safety devices, many of which are required by provincial or local law. Failing to include safety equipment in a kitchen or failing to maintain it properly endangers workers and customers.

Fire Extinguishers
Fire extinguishers are canisters of foam, dry chemicals (such as sodium bicarbonate or potassium bicarbonate) or pressurized water used to extinguish small fires. They must be placed within sight of and easily reached from the work areas in which fires are more likely to occur. Different classes of extinguishers use different chemicals to fight different types of fire. The appropriate class must be used for the specific fire. See Table 5.2. Fire extinguishers must be recharged and checked from time to time. Be sure they have not been discharged, tampered with or otherwise damaged.

TABLE 5.2   FIRE EXTINGUISHERS

Class	Symbol	Use
Class A	▲	Fires involving wood, paper, cloth or plastic
Class B	■	Fires involving oil, grease or flammable chemicals
Class C	●	Fires involving electrical equipment or wiring

Combination extinguishers—AB, BC and ABC—are also available.

Ventilation Systems

Ventilation systems (also called ventilation hoods) are commonly installed over cooking equipment to remove vapours, heat and smoke. Most systems include fire extinguishing agents or sprinklers. A properly operating hood makes the kitchen more comfortable for the staff and reduces the danger of fire. The system must be designed, installed and inspected by professionals, then cleaned and maintained regularly. A return or makeup air system is installed to ensure air quality and good circulation.

First-Aid Kits

First-aid supplies should be stored in a clearly marked box, conspicuously located near food preparation areas. Occupational Health and Safety guidelines may specify the kit's exact contents. Generally, they should include a first-aid manual, bandages, gauze dressings, adhesive tape, antiseptics, scissors, cold packs and other supplies. The kit should be checked regularly and items replaced as needed. In addition, cards with emergency telephone numbers should be placed inside the first-aid kit and near a telephone. Emergency response procedures must be communicated to staff and a copy of them available for quick reference.

THE PROFESSIONAL KITCHEN

The kitchen is the heart of the food service operation. There, food and other items are received, stored, prepared and plated for service; dining room staff places orders, retrieves foods ready for service and returns dirty service items; dishes and other wares are cleaned and stored; and the chef conducts business. But commercial space is expensive, and most food service operators recognize that the greater the number of customers served, the greater the revenues. Often this translates into a large dining area and small kitchen and storage facilities. Therefore, when designing a kitchen, it is important to use the space wisely so that each of its functions can be accomplished efficiently.

Regardless of the kitchen's size, its design begins with a consideration of the tasks to be performed. Analyzing the menu identifies these tasks. A restaurant featuring steaks and chops, for example, will need areas to fabricate and grill meats. If it relies on commercially prepared desserts and breads, it will not need a bakeshop but will still need space to hold and plate baked goods.

Once all food preparation tasks are identified, a work area for each particular task is designated. These work areas are called **work stations**. At a steak restaurant, an important work station is the broiler. If the restaurant serves fried foods, it will also need a fry station. The size and design of each work station is determined by the volume of food the operation intends to produce.

Usually work stations using the same or similar equipment for related tasks are grouped together into **work sections**. See Table 5.3. (Note that work stations correspond to the kitchen brigade system discussed in Chapter 1, Professionalism.) For example, in a typical

TABLE 5.3	WORK SECTIONS AND THEIR STATIONS
Sections	Stations
Hot-foods section	Broiler station Fry station Griddle station Sauté/sauce station Holding
Garde-manger section	Salad greens cleaning Salad preparation Cold foods preparation Sandwich station Showpiece preparation
Bakery section	Mixing station Dough holding and proofing Dough rolling and forming Baking and cooling Dessert preparation* Frozen dessert preparation* Plating desserts*
Banquet section	Steam cooking Dry heat cooking (roasting, broiling) Holding and plating
Short-order section	Griddle station Fry station Broiler station
Beverage section	Hot beverage station Cold beverage station Alcoholic beverage station

*These stations are sometimes found in the *garde-manger* section.

◆◆◆

ALEXIS SOYER
(1809–1858)

Alexis Soyer
Photo courtesy of Barbara Wheaton.

The father of the contemporary celebrity chef was Alexis Soyer, a Frenchman whose tragically short working life was spent mostly in London. He was a flamboyant, talented and egocentric showman. He was also a renowned chef, restaurateur, social activist, author, purveyor of prepared foods and inventor.

In 1831 Soyer left his thriving catering business and restaurant in Paris for London. (A scandal was rumoured to be behind his sudden departure.) There he quickly established a reputation as a talented chef in the latest French fashion. By 1838 he was employed at a gentlemen's club called the Reform. Able to assist in planning the club's new kitchen facility, Soyer installed the most modern equipment: gas ovens with temperature controls, a steam-driven mechanical spit and a storage locker cooled by running water. From this modern kitchen he produced his signature dish: lamb chops Reform.

The Reform was founded by members of the Liberal Party, a political party interested in social reform. Their chef soon joined the party

"The Kitchen Department of the Reform Club" (1841). "To show them at one glance," wrote the *Spectator*, "the partition walls are cut away, and a bird's eye view is given of the several kitchens, larders, sculleries, and batterie de cuisine; the different functionaries are at their posts, and the accomplished chef, Monsieur Soyer, is in the act of pointing out to a favoured visitor the various contrivances suggested by his ingenuity and experience."

ranks. He developed recipes for inexpensive, nutritious soups for the working class and in 1847 went to Ireland and opened soup kitchens to feed those who were starving as a result of the Potato Famine.

His most important writings reflect his interests in good food for the masses. The intended audience for *The Modern Housewife* (1849) was the middle class; the growing urban working class was the intended audience for his second book, *A Schilling Cookery for the People* (1855).

In 1851 Soyer opened his own lavishly decorated and expensively equipped restaurant called the Gastronomic Symposium of All Nations. It closed shortly thereafter, in part because of Soyer's debts, in part because he lost his operating licence as a result of the rowdiness in the restaurant's American-style bar, at which customers were publicly served cocktails for the first time in London.

In addition to cooking and writing, Soyer created and marketed several prepared food items: Soyer's Sauce, Soyer's Nectar and Soyer's Relish. He was also fascinated with kitchen gadgets and invented several, including a sink stopper, jelly mold, egg cooker and coffeepot. The most notable, however, was a portable "Magic Stove" weighing less than 4 pounds (2 kg), similar to a modern chafing dish. Soyer's final triumph was in the Crimean War (1854–1857). He developed army rations, reorganized field and hospital kitchens and introduced one of his last inventions, the campaign stove. Portable, efficient and requiring little fuel, it was used by the British army for the next 90 years.

Stainless Steel Hood

(a)

1 Convection Oven	
2 Under-Counter Freezer Unit	
3 Griddle Top	12 Steam Table with Open Shelves Below
4 Cheese Melter	13 Stainless Steel Dual Shelf with Top Heat Rod
5 6-Burner Top/Oven Below	14 Under-Counter Freezer with Work Surface
6 Salamander	15 Conveyor Toaster
7 Under-Counter Refrigerator	16 Bain Marie with Under-Counter Refrigerator
8 Broiler Top	17 Microwave Table with Shelf
9 Stainless Steel Work Table with Open Shelves	18 Microwave
10 Deep-Fat Fryers	19 Reach-In Refrigerator Unit
11 Stainless Steel Overshelves	

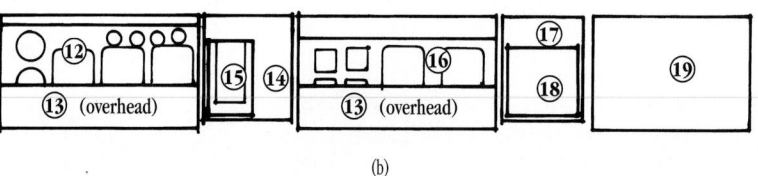

(b)

FIGURE 5.11   *Typical Hot-Foods Section Floor Plan*

full-service restaurant, there will be a single hot-foods section. It can consist of broiler, fry, griddle, sauté and sauce stations. Both advance preparation and last-minute cooking may be performed in the hot-foods section. The principal cooking equipment (a range, broiler, deep-fat fryer, oven, griddle, etc.) will be arranged in a line under a ventilation hood. A typical plan for this hot-foods section is shown in Figure 5.11. Although each work station within the hot-foods section may be staffed by a different line cook, the proximity of the stations allows one line cook to cover more than one station if the kitchen is short-handed or when business is slow.

Merely considering the plan of the work station or section is not enough, however. When designing the work area, you must also consider the elevation. That is, a kitchen designer not only examines what equipment should be placed next to the other (for example, the range next to the deep-fat fryer), but also what equipment and storage facilities can be placed beneath or on top of the other. For example, in a bakeshop, rolling storage carts for flour and sugar or an under-the-counter refrigerator for eggs and dairy products may be located beneath the work surface, while mixing bowls and dry ingredients are stored on shelves above. Figure 5.12 illustrates the elevation for the hot-foods section whose plan is shown in Figure 5.11. Ideally, each station should be designed so that the cook takes no more than three steps in any direction to perform all assigned station tasks.

In addition to the work sections where the menu items are produced, a typical restaurant kitchen includes areas dedicated to:

1. Receiving and storing foods and other items. There should be separate freezer, refrigerator and dry-goods storage facilities. Each should have

(a)

1 Convection Oven
2 Under-Counter Freezer Unit
3 Griddle Top
4 Cheese Melter
5 6-Burner Top/Oven Below
6 Salamander
7 Under-Counter Refrigerator
8 Broiler Top
9 Stainless Steel Work Table with Open Shelves
10 Deep-Fat Fryers
11 Stainless Steel Overshelves

12 Steam Table with Open Shelves Below
13 Stainless Steel Dual Shelf with Top Heat Rod
14 Under-Counter Freezer with Work Surface
15 Conveyor Toaster
16 Bain Marie with Under-Counter Refrigerator
17 Microwave Table with Shelf
18 Microwave
19 Reach-In Refrigerator Unit

(b)

FIGURE 5.12 *Typical Hot-Foods Section Elevation*

proper temperature, humidity and light controls in order to properly and safely maintain the stored items. Depending upon the operation's size and the work stations' specific needs, there can be either a central storage area or each station or section can maintain its own storage facilities. Typically, however, there is a combination of central and section storage. For example, up to 100 pounds (45 kg) of flour and sugar can be stored in rolling bins under a work table in the bakeshop, while several hundreds of pounds or kilograms more remain in a central dry goods area. Similarly, one box of salt can be stored near the hot line for immediate use, while the remainder of the case is stored in a central dry goods area. Additional storage space will be needed for cleaning and paper supplies, dishes and other service ware. *Never store cleaning supplies and other chemicals with foods.*

FIGURE 5.13   *Diagram of Kitchen*

2. *Washing dishes and other equipment.* These dish- and equipment-washing facilities should have their own sinks. Food-preparation and hand-washing sinks should be separate.

3. *Employee use.* Restrooms, locker facilities and an office are also found in most food service facilities.

The guiding principle behind a good kitchen design is to maximize the flow of goods and staff from one area to the next and within each area itself. Maximizing flow creates an efficient work environment and helps reduce preparation and service time.

Figure 5.13 shows the several sections of a professional kitchen. It includes an area for front-of-the-house staff to circulate, drop off orders, retrieve finished dishes and return dirty dishes. The design allows for the flow of foods from receiving, to storage, to food preparation areas, to holding and service areas and then to the dining room as well as the flow of dirty dishes from the dining room back into the kitchen. The work sections are arranged to take advantage of shared equipment. For instance, by placing the bakeshop next to the hot-foods section, they can share ovens. The *garde-manger* and dessert sections, both of which rely on refrigerated foods, are conveniently located near the walk-in refrigerator and freezer area. The beverage station is located near the dining room entrance so that food servers do not have to walk through food preparation areas to fill beverage orders. The office is next to receiving so that the chef can easily check and receive orders. The central storage areas are easily accessible to the receiving area as well as to the food production areas, while the cleaning-supply storage is near the dishwashing area. In general, the design eliminates the need for staff from one work station or section to cross through another station or section.

Governmental building, health, fire and safety codes will dictate, to a degree, certain aspects of a professional kitchen's design. But to make the most of these spaces, the well-designed kitchen should reflect a sound understanding of the tasks to be performed and the equipment necessary to perform them. Hiring a professional kitchen designer is a good investment when building or retrofitting a food service facility.

CONCLUSION

There are hundreds of tools and pieces of equipment that can help you prepare, cook, store and present food. Every year, manufacturers offer new or improved items. Throughout your career you will use many of them. Select those that are well constructed, durable and best suited for the task at hand. Then use them in a safe and efficient manner.

The way in which equipment is arranged and stored in a kitchen is also important. Good kitchen design emphasizes the efficient flow of goods and staff from one work section to another as well as within each work section or station.

QUESTIONS FOR DISCUSSION

1. What six characteristics should be considered in the selection of tools and equipment?
2. List the parts of a chef's knife and describe the knife's construction.
3. List six materials used to make commercial cookware and describe the advantages and disadvantages of each.
4. Describe six pieces of equipment that can be used to slice or chop foods.
5. List three classes of fire extinguishers. For each one, describe its designating symbol and identify the type or types of fire it should be used to extinguish.
6. Explain the relationship between work sections and work stations and the kitchen brigade system discussed in Chapter 1, Professionalism.

WEBLINKS

Health Canada: Cookware Safety
    www.hc-sc.gc.ca/main/hc/web/datapcb/communc/home/pubs/cooke.htm
InterTrade Systems — Foodservice Products and Services
    www.itrade.net/
Cookware Manufacturers Association
    www.cookware.org/
North American Association of Food Equipment Manufacturers
    www.nafem.org/
The Food Resource: Pictures of Culinary Equipment
    www.orst.edu/food-resource/misc/equip.html

CHAPTER 6 KNIFE SKILLS

LEARNING OUTCOMES

After studying this chapter you will be able to:

◆ care for knives properly
◆ use knives safely and properly
◆ cut foods into a variety of classic shapes

very professional must become skilled in the use of certain tools. The professional cook is no exception. One of the most important tools the apprentice cook must master is the knife. Good knife skills are critical to a cook's success because the knife is the most commonly used tool in the kitchen. Every cook spends countless hours slicing, dicing, mincing and chopping. Learning to perform these tasks safely and efficiently is an essential part of your training.

At first, professional knives may feel large and awkward and the techniques discussed below may not seem all that efficient. But as you become familiar with knives and practise your knife skills, using knives correctly will become second nature.

Knives are identified in Chapter 5, Tools and Equipment. Here we show how they are used to cut vegetables. The techniques presented, however, can be used for most any food that holds its shape when cut. Knife skills for butchering and fabricating meat, poultry, fish and shellfish are discussed in Chapters 12, Principles of Meat Cookery, through 19, Fish and Shellfish.

A note about language: Many of the classic cuts are known by their French names: julienne, *for example. Although these words are nouns and entered the English language as nouns (e.g.,* a julienne of carrot), *they are also used as verbs (to* julienne *a carrot) and adjectives (*julienned *carrots).*

USING YOUR KNIFE SAFELY

The first rule of knife safety is to *think about what you are doing.* Other basic rules of knife safety are:

1. Use the correct knife for the task at hand.

2. Always cut away from yourself.

3. Always cut on a cutting board. Do not cut on glass, marble or metal.

4. Keep knives sharp; a dull knife is more dangerous than a sharp one.

5. When carrying a knife, hold it point down, parallel to and close to your leg as you walk.

6. A falling knife has no handle. Do not attempt to catch a falling knife; step back and allow it to fall.

7. Never leave a knife in a sink of water; anyone reaching into the sink could be injured or the knife could be dented by pots or other utensils.

CARING FOR YOUR KNIFE

Knife Sharpening

A sharpening stone called a **whetstone** is used to put an edge on a dull knife blade. To use a whetstone, place the heel of the blade against the whetstone at a 20-degree angle. Keeping that angle, press down on the blade while pushing it away from you in one long arc, as if to slice off a thin piece of the stone. The entire length of the blade should come in contact with the stone during each sweep. Repeat the procedure on both sides of the blade until sufficiently sharp. With a triple-faced stone, such as that shown to the right, you progress from the coarsest to the finest surface. Any whetstone can be moistened with either water or mineral oil, but not both. Do not use vegetable oil on a whetstone as it will soon become rancid and gummy.

A **steel** does not sharpen a knife. Instead, it is used to hone or straighten the blade immediately after and between sharpenings. To use a steel, place the blade against the steel at a 20-degree angle. Then draw the blade along the entire length of the steel. Repeat the technique several times on each side of the blade.

A final note on knife care: Do not wash knives in commercial dishwashers. The heat and harsh chemicals can damage the edge and the handle. The blade can also be damaged if it knocks against cookware or utensils. In addition, the knife could injure an unsuspecting worker. Always wash and dry your knives by hand immediately after each use.

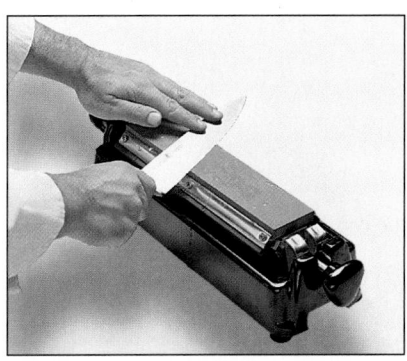

When sharpening a knife against a three-sided whetstone, go from the coarsest to the finest surface.

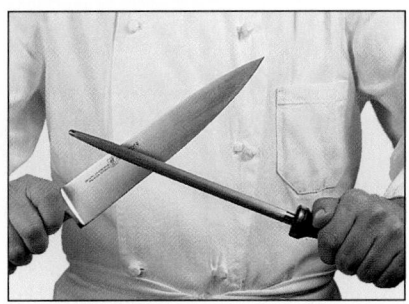

Honing a knife against a steel straightens the blade between sharpenings.

GRIPPING YOUR KNIFE

There are several ways to grip a knife. Use the grip that is most comfortable for you or the one dictated by the job at hand. Whichever grip you use should be firm but not so tight that your hand becomes tired. Gripping styles are shown below.

The most common grip: Hold the handle with three fingers while gripping the blade between the thumb and index finger.

A variation on the most common grip: Grip the handle with four fingers and place the thumb on the front of the handle.

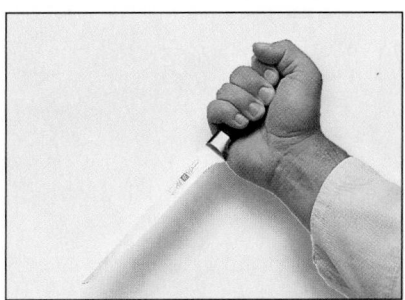

The underhand grip for a rigid boning knife: Grip the handle in a fist with four fingers and thumb. This grip allows you to use the knife tip to cut around joints and separate flesh from bone when boning meat and poultry.

CONTROLLING YOUR KNIFE

To safely produce even cuts, you must control (or guide) your knife with one hand and hold the item being cut with the other. Always allow the blade's sharp edge to do the cutting. Never force the blade through the item being cut. Smooth, even strokes should be used. Using a dull knife or excessive force with any knife produces, at best, poor results and, at worst, a significant safety risk. Cutting without using your hand as a guide may also be dangerous. Two safe cutting methods that produce good results are shown below.

Method A

1. Keep your fingertips curled back, then grip the item being cut with three fingertips and your thumb. Hold the knife in the other hand. While keeping the knife's tip on the cutting board, lift the heel of the knife.

2. Use the second joint of your index finger as a guide and cut a slice using a smooth, even, downward stroke. Adjust the position of the guiding finger after each slice to produce slices of equal size. After a few cuts, slide your fingertips and thumb down the length of the item and continue slicing. For this slicing technique, the knife's tip acts as the fulcrum.

Method B

1. Grip the item as described above. Using the second joint of your index finger as a guide, lift the knife's tip and slice by drawing the knife slightly back toward you and down through the item, cutting the item to the desired thickness.

2. The motion of the knife should come almost entirely from the wrist, not the elbow. Allow the weight of the knife to do most of the work; very little downward pressure needs to be applied to the knife. For this slicing technique, your wrist should act as the fulcrum.

CUTTING WITH YOUR KNIFE

A knife is used to shape and reduce an item's size. Uniformity of size and shape ensures even cooking and enhances the appearance of the finished product. Items are shaped by slicing, chopping, dicing, mincing or by other special cutting techniques.

Slicing

To slice is to cut an item into relatively broad, thin pieces. Slices may be either the finished cut or the first step in producing other cuts. Slicing is typically used to create three specialty cuts: the chiffonade, rondelle and diagonal. Slicing skills are also used to produce oblique or roll cuts and lozenges.

A **chiffonade** is a preparation of finely sliced or shredded leafy vegetables used as a garnish or a base under cold presentations. As shown here, slicing spinach *en chiffonade* is a relatively simple process.

1. Wash and destem the leaves as necessary. Stack several leaves on top of each other and roll them tightly like a cigar.

2. Make fine slices across the leaves while holding the leaf roll tightly.

As seen below, **rondelles** or **rounds** are easily made disk-shaped slices of cylindrical vegetables or fruits.

Peel the item (if desired) and place it on a cutting board. Make even slices perpendicular to the item being cut.

Diagonals are elongated or oval-shaped slices of cylindrical vegetables or fruits. They are produced with a cut similar to that used to cut rondelles except that the knife is held at an angle to the item being cut.

Peel the item (if desired) and place it on a cutting board. Position the knife at the desired angle to the item being cut and slice it evenly.

Oblique or **roll-cut** items are small pieces with two angle-cut sides. This relatively simple cut is most often used on carrots and parsnips.

Lozenges are diamond-shaped cuts prepared from firm vegetables such as carrots, turnips, rutabagas and potatoes.

 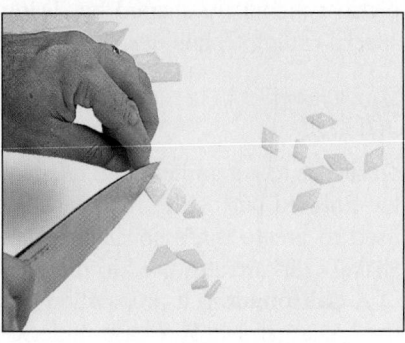

1. Slice the item into long slices of the desired thickness. Then cut the slices into strips of the desired width.

2. Cut the strips at an angle to produce diamond shapes.

Horizontal Slicing

To horizontal slice is to **butterfly** or cut a **pocket** into meats, poultry or fish. It is also a method of cutting used to thinly slice soft vegetables.

 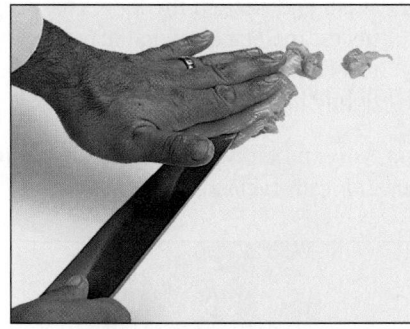

1. With your hand opened and your fingers arched upward, hold the item to be cut firmly in the centre of your palm.

2. Holding the knife parallel to the table, slice a pocket to the desired depth or cut through the item completely.

Chopping

To chop is to cut an item into small pieces where uniformity of size and shape is neither necessary (for example, coarsely chopped onions for a *mirepoix* that will be removed from the stock before service) nor feasible (for example, parsley).

Coarse Chopping

Coarse chopping does not mean carelessly hacking up food. Rather, the procedure is identical to that used for slicing but without the emphasis on uniformity. Coarsely chopped pieces should measure approximately 3/4 inch × 3/4 inch × 3/4 inch (2 cm × 2 cm × 2 cm).

Grip the knife as for slicing. Hold the item being chopped with your other hand. It may not be necessary to use your finger as a guide because uniformity is not crucial.

Chopping Parsley and Similar Foods

Parsley can be cut very coarsely or very finely. As shown below, it is easy to chop parsley and similar foods properly regardless of the desired fineness.

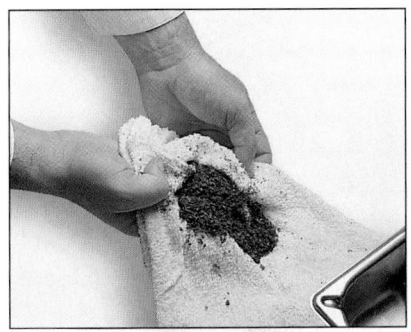

1. Wash the parsley in cold water; drain well. Remove the parsley sprigs from the stems.

2. Grip the knife in one hand. With the other hand spread flat, hold the knife's tip on the cutting board. Keeping the knife's tip on the board, chop the parsley sprigs by rocking the curved blade of the knife up and down while moving the knife back and forth over the parsley.

3. Place the chopped parsley in a clean kitchen towel or a double layer of cheesecloth. Rinse it under cold water and squeeze out as much water as possible. The chopped parsley should be dry and fluffy.

Chopping Garlic

A daily chore in many food service facilities, peeling and chopping garlic is a simple job made easy with the procedure shown here.

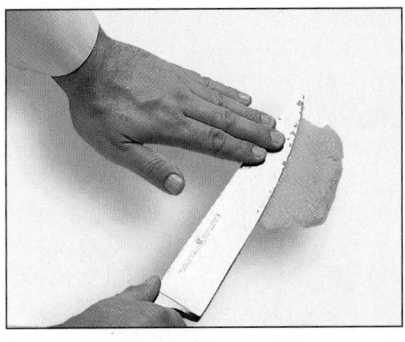

1. Break the head of garlic into individual cloves with your hands. Lightly crush the cloves using the flat edge of a chef's knife or a mallet. They will break open and the peel can be separated easily from the garlic flesh.

2. With a flat hand, hold the knife's tip on the cutting board. Using a rocking motion, chop the garlic cloves to the desired size. Garlic is usually chopped very finely.

3. Garlic paste can be made by first finely chopping the garlic and then turning the knife on an angle and repeatedly dragging the edge of the knife along the cutting board, mashing the garlic.

Cutting Sticks and Dicing

To dice is to cut an item into cubes. Before an item can be diced, it must first be cut into certain-sized sticks. These techniques are most often used when uniformity of size and shape are important (for example, julienned carrots for a salad or brunoised vegetables for a garnish).

The dicing technique is typically used to create the classic cuts known as brunoise, small dice, medium dice, large dice and paysanne. Although most cooks have some notion of what size and shape "small diced" potatoes or julienne carrots may be, there are size ranges and specific shapes for these cuts. Exact size will depend on the use or look desired.

Julienne—a stick-shaped item with dimensions of 1/16 inch × 1/16 inch × 1–2 inches (1–2 mm × 1–2 mm × 2.5–4 cm).

Allumette—a stick-shaped item with dimensions of 1/8 inch × 1/8 inch × 2 to 2-1/2 inches (3 mm × 3 mm × 5–6 cm).

Batonnet—a stick-shaped item with dimensions of 1/4 inch × 1/4 inch × 2 to 2-1/2 inches (6 mm × 6 mm × 5–6 cm).

Small dice (macedoine)—a cube-shaped item with dimensions of 1/8 inch × 1/8 inch × 1/8 inch (3 mm × 3 mm × 3 mm).

Brunoise—a cube-shaped item with dimensions of 1/16 inch × 1/16 inch × 1/16 inch (1–2 mm × 1–2 mm × 1–2 mm).

Medium dice (jardinière)—a cube-shaped item with dimensions of 1/4 inch × 1/4 inch × 1/4 inch (6 mm × 6 mm × 6 mm).

Large dice (mirepoix)—a cube-shaped item with dimensions of 1/2 inch × 1/2 inch × 1/2 inch (12 mm × 12 mm × 12 mm).

Paysanne—a flat, rectangular or triangular-shaped item with dimensions of 1/2 inch × 1/2 inch × 1/8 inch (12 mm × 12 mm × 3 mm thick).

Cutting Julienne, Allumette and Batonnet

Julienne, allumette and batonnet are matchstick-shaped cuts prepared using the same procedure as cutting sticks for dicing.

 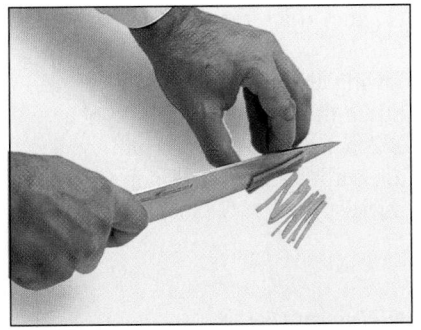

1. Peel the item (if desired) and square off the sides. Trim the item so that the slices cut from it will be the proper length. Cut even slices of the desired thickness, 1/16 inch (1–2 mm) for julienne, 1/8 inch (3 mm) for allumette or 1/4 inch (6 mm) for batonnet.

2. Stack the slices and cut them evenly into sticks (also referred to as "planks") that are the same thickness as the slices.

◆◆◆
CUT SIZES

Most cuts have a range to their size depending on the use for the item or the desired look. Generally, Canadian standards are more closely aligned with European dimensions. The cook should verify dimensions with the chef.

allumette—*literally, "matchstick." The dimensions are 1/8 × 1/8 × 2-1/2 inches (3 mm × 3 mm × 5–6 cm).*

Cutting Brunoise and Small, Medium and Large Dice

Brunoise as well as small, medium and large dice are made by first cutting the item into sticks following the procedure for cutting julienne, allumette or batonnet, then making cuts perpendicular to the length of the sticks to produce small cubes. Making a 1/6-inch (1–2 mm) cut perpendicular to the length of a julienne produces a brunoise. Making a 1/8-inch (3-mm) cut perpendicular to the length of a batonnet produces a small dice. A 1/4-inch (6-mm) cut from a 1/4-inch (6-mm) stick produces a medium dice and a 1/2-inch (12-mm) cut from a 1/2-inch (12-mm) stick produces a large dice.

Julienne, allumette and batonnet sticks and the large, medium, small and brunoise dices cut from them.

Cutting Paysanne

Paysanne is a classic vegetable cut for garnishing soups and other dishes. It resembles a 1/2-inch (12 mm) dice that has been cut in thin slices. It is produced by following the procedures for dicing, but in the final step the 1/2-inch × 1/2-inch (12 mm × 12 mm) sticks are cut into slices 1/8 inch (3 mm) thick.

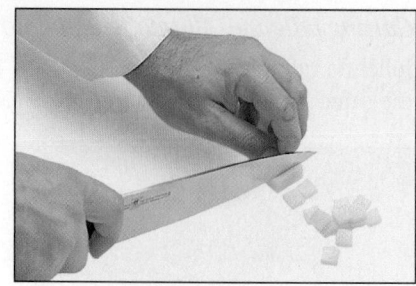

Cutting paysanne from a 1/2-inch × 1/2-inch (12 mm × 12 mm) stick.

Dicing an Onion

Onions are easily peeled and diced to any size desired using the procedure shown here.

1. Use a paring knife to remove the stem end. Trim the root end but leave it nearly intact (this helps prevent the onion from falling apart while being diced). Peel away the outer skin; be careful not to remove and waste too much onion.

2. Cut the onion in half through the stem and root. Place the cut side down on the cutting board.

3. Cut parallel slices of the desired thickness vertically through the onion from the root toward the stem end without cutting completely through the root end.

4. Make a single horizontal cut on a small onion or two horizontal cuts on a large onion through the width of the onion, again without cutting through the root end.

5. Turn the onion and cut slices perpendicular to the previous slices to produce diced onion.

Mincing

To mince is to cut an item into very small pieces. The terms "finely chopped" and "minced" are often used interchangeably and are most often used when referring to garlic, shallots, herbs and other foods that do not have to be uniform in shape.

Mincing Shallots

The procedure for mincing shallots is shown here.

1. Peel and dice the shallots, following the procedure for peeling and dicing an onion.

2. With a flat hand, hold the knife's tip on the cutting board. Using a rocking motion, mince the shallots with the heel of the knife.

Turning (Shaping)

Turning (*tourner*, "to turn" in French) is a cutting technique that results in a football-shaped finished product traditionally with seven equal sides and blunt ends. The size of the finished product may vary, the most common being 2 inches (5 cm) long. Some products are partially turned or shaped to achieve a better yield or for variety. Turned vegetables are generally associated with finer dining establishments. Due to higher labour and food cost, the practice is not prevalent. This is a more complicated procedure than other cuts and takes considerable practice to produce good results.

1. Cut the item being "turned" into pieces 2 inches × 3/4 to 1 inch (5 cm × 2–2.5 cm). Each piece should have flat ends. (Potatoes, turnips and beets may be cut into as many as 6 or 8 pieces; carrots can simply be cut into 2-inch/5-cm lengths.) Peeling is optional because in most cases the item's entire surface area is trimmed away.

2. Holding the item between the thumb and forefinger, use a turning knife or a paring knife to cut 7 curved sides on the item, creating a flat-ended, football-shaped product.

Using a Mandoline

Gaufrette—*a thin lattice or waffle-textured slice of vegetable cut on a mandoline or with a demidoff (zigzag) knife.*

The mandoline is a nonmechanical cutting tool. It does the jobs that can be done with a chef's knife, such as producing very thinly sliced apples or large quantities of julienned vegetables, quickly, easily and very accurately. It can also make cuts such as a ridged slice or **gaufrette** that cannot be done with a conventional chef's knife.

When using the mandoline always use the guard or a steel-mesh glove to protect your hand.

1. To use the mandoline, position the legs and set the blade to the desired shape and thickness.

2. Slide the guard into place.

3. To slice, slide the item against the blade with a single, smooth stroke.

4. To cut gaufrette, select the ridged blade and set it to the desired thickness. Make the first slice, turn the item 60 degrees to 90 degrees and make the second slice. Turn the item back to the original position and make another slice, and so on.

CONCLUSION

Although many slicing and dicing machines are available, none can ever completely replace a skilled chef with a sharp knife. As an apprentice, becoming efficient with your knives should be a high priority. Possessing good knife skills allows you to produce more attractive products in a safe and efficient manner. You will use the classic cuts and techniques outlined in this chapter throughout your career. You should memorize the procedures and practise them often. And remember, a dull or carelessly handled knife is dangerous.

QUESTIONS FOR DISCUSSION

1. Explain the step-by-step procedures for sharpening a knife using a three-sided whetstone.
2. What is the purpose of a steel?
3. Why is it necessary to cut vegetables into uniform shapes and sizes?
4. Describe the following cutting procedures: slicing, chopping and dicing.
5. Identify the dimensions of the following cuts: julienne, batonnet, brunoise, small dice, medium dice, large dice and paysanne.
6. Describe the procedure for making turned or shaped vegetables.
7. Describe three preparations for which a mandoline would be useful.

WEBLINKS

Sharpen Your Knife Skills
   www.extrahelp.com/extrahelp/nightknife.html
Better Homes and Gardens: Keeping Knives Sharp
   www.bhglive.com/survival/cookhelpers/knifshar.htm
General Housewares: Caring for Your Cutlery
   www.ghw.com/carving_tools/knife_care/knife_care.phtml
How to Dice an Onion
   www.eatingwell.com/recipes/abc/step/onion/

CHAPTER 7

KITCHEN STAPLES

Learning Outcomes

After studying this chapter you will be able to:

+ recognize and use a variety of herbs, spices, nuts, oils, vinegars and condiments
+ prepare a bouquet garni, sachet or oignon piqué
+ prepare and serve quality coffees and teas

*ertain foods are used in almost all stations of the kitchen with such regularity that they have become known as **staples**. Included are many of the processed, packaged items we often take for granted: salt, pepper, flour, sugar, oil and flavourings. There is, however, no single list of staples. Each food service operation will have its own list depending on the menu and the cooking methods used.*

This chapter identifies and discusses selected herbs and spices, salt, nuts, oils, vinegars and condiments as well as two popular beverages, coffee and tea. We provide identifying characteristics for some of the more common staples and set forth standards of quality and usage. Other staples, such as flour and sugar, are covered in Chapter 26, Principles of the Bakeshop.

Seasoning—*an item added to enhance the natural flavours of a food without dramatically changing its taste; salt and pepper are the most common seasonings.*

Flavouring—*an item that adds a new taste to a food and alters its natural flavours; flavourings include herbs, spices, vinegars and condiments. The terms* seasonings *and* flavourings *are often used interchangeably.*

Aromatic—*an item added to enhance the natural aromas of a food; aromatics include most flavourings, such as herbs and spices, as well as some vegetables.*

Condiment—*traditionally, any item added to a dish for flavour, including herbs, spices and vinegars; now also refers to cooked or prepared flavourings such as prepared mustards, relishes, bottled sauces and pickles.*

Herb—*any of a large group of aromatic plants whose leaves, stems or flowers are used as a flavouring; used either dried, fresh or oil-packed.*

Spice—*any of a large group of aromatic plants whose bark, roots, seeds, buds or berries are used as a flavouring; usually used in dried form, either whole or ground.*

HERBS AND SPICES

Herbs and spices are the kitchen staples used as **flavourings**. **Herbs** refer to the large group of **aromatic** plants whose leaves, stems or flowers are used to add flavours to other foods. Most herbs are available fresh or dried. Because drying alters their flavours and aromas, fresh herbs are generally preferred and should be used if possible. **Spices** are strongly flavoured or aromatic portions of plants used as flavourings, **condiments** or aromatics. Spices are the bark, roots, seeds, buds or berries of plants, most of which grow naturally only in tropical climates. Spices are almost always used in their dried form, rarely fresh, and can usually be purchased whole or ground. Some plants—dill, for example—can be used as both a herb (its leaves) and a spice (its seeds).

Herbs

Basil (Fr. *basilique*) is considered one of the great culinary herbs. It is available in a variety of "flavours"—cinnamon, garlic, lemon, even chocolate—but the most common is sweet basil. **Sweet basil** has light green, tender leaves and small white flowers. Its flavour is strong, warm and slightly peppery, with a hint of cloves. Basil is used in Mediterranean cuisines and has a special affinity for garlic and tomatoes. When purchasing fresh basil, look for bright green leaves; avoid flower buds and wilted or rust-coloured leaves. Dried sweet basil is readily available, but has a decidedly weaker flavour.

Basil

Opal basil is named for its vivid purple colour. It has a tougher, crinkled leaf and a medium-strong flavour. Opal basil may be substituted for sweet basil in cooking and its appearance makes it a distinctive garnish.

Opal basil

Bay (Fr. *laurier*), also known as sweet laurel, is a small tree from Asia that produces tough, glossy leaves with a sweet balsamic aroma and peppery flavour. Bay symbolized wisdom and glory in ancient Rome; the leaves were

Bay leaves

used to form crowns or "laurels" worn by emperors and victorious athletes. In cooking, dried bay leaves are often preferred over the more bitter fresh leaves. Essential in French cuisine, bay leaves are part of the traditional bouquet garni and court bouillon. Whole dried leaves are usually added to a dish at the start of cooking, then removed when sufficient flavour has been extracted.

Chervil

Chervil (Fr. *cerfeuil*), also known as sweet cicely, is native to Russia and the Middle East. Its lacy, fernlike leaves are similar to parsley and can be used as a garnish. Chervil's flavour is delicate, similar to parsley but with the distinctive aroma of anise. It should not be heated for long periods. Chervil is commonly used in French cuisine and is one of the traditional *fines herbes*.

Chives

Chives (Fr. *ciboulette*) are perhaps the most delicate and sophisticated members of the onion family. Their hollow, thin grass-green stems grow in clumps and produce round, pale purple flowers, which are used as a garnish. Chives may be purchased dried, quick-frozen or fresh. They have a mild onion flavour and bright green colour. Chives complement eggs, poultry, potatoes, fish and shellfish. They should not be cooked for long periods or at high temperatures. Chives make an excellent garnish when snipped with scissors or carefully chopped and sprinkled over finished soups or sauces.

Garlic chives, also known as Chinese chives, actually belong to another plant species. They have flat, solid (not hollow) stems and a mild garlic flavour. They may be used in place of regular chives if their garlic flavour is desired.

Garlic chives

Cilantro is the green leafy portion of the plant that yields seeds known as coriander. The flavours of the two portions of this plant are very different and cannot be substituted for each other.

Cilantro, also known as Chinese parsley, is sharp and tangy with a strong aroma and an almost citrus flavour. It is widely used in Asian, Mexican and South American cuisines, especially in salads and sauces. It should not be subjected to heat and cilantro's flavour is completely destroyed by drying. Do not use yellow or discoloured leaves or the tough stems.

Cilantro

Dill (Fr. *aneth*), a member of the parsley family, has tiny, aromatic, yellow flowers and feathery, delicate blue-green leaves. The leaves taste like parsley, but sharper, with a touch of anise. Dill seeds are flat, oval and brown, with a bitter flavour similar to caraway. Both the seeds and the leaves of the dill plant are used in cooking. Dill is commonly used in Scandinavian and Central European cuisines, particularly with fish and potatoes. Both leaves and seeds are used in pickling and sour dishes. Dill leaves are available fresh or dried but lose their aroma and

Dill

Epazote

Lemon grass

Lavender

flavour during cooking, so add them only after the dish is removed from the heat. Dill seeds are available whole or ground and are used in fish dishes, pickles and breads.

Epazote, also known as wormseed or stinkweed, grows wild throughout the Americas. It has a strong aroma similar to kerosene and a wild flavour. Fresh epazote is used in salads and as a flavouring in Mexican and Southwestern cuisines. It is often cooked with beans to reduce their gaseousness. Dried epazote is brewed to make a beverage.

Fine herbs (Fr. *fines herbes*) are a combination of parsley, tarragon, chervil and chives widely used in French cuisine. The mixture is available dried or you can create your own from fresh ingredients.

Lavender is an evergreen with thin leaves and tall stems bearing spikes of tiny purple flowers. Although lavender is known primarily for its aroma, which is widely used in perfumes, soaps and cosmetics, the flowers are also used as a flavouring, particularly in Middle Eastern and Provençale cuisines. These flowers have a sweet, lemony flavour and can be crystallized and used as a garnish. Lavender is also used in jams and preserves and to flavour teas and tisanes.

Lemon grass, also known as citronella grass, is a tropical grass with the strong aroma and taste of lemon. It is similar to scallions in appearance but with a woody texture. Only the lower base and white leaf stalks are used. Available fresh or quick-frozen, lemon grass is widely used in Indonesian and Southeast Asian cuisines.

Marjoram (Fr. *marjolaine*), also known as sweet marjoram, is a flowering herb native to the Mediterranean and used since ancient times. Its flavour is similar to thyme but sweeter; it also has a stronger aroma. Marjoram is now used in many European cuisines. Although it is available fresh, marjoram is one of the few herbs whose flavour increases when dried. Wild marjoram is more commonly known as oregano.

Marjoram

Mint (Fr. *menthe*), a large family of herbs, includes many species and flavours (even chocolate). **Spearmint** is the most common garden and commercial variety. It has soft, bright green leaves and a tart aroma and flavour. Mint does not blend well with other herbs, so its use is confined to specific dishes, usually fruits or fatty meats such as lamb. Mint has an affinity for chocolate. It can also be brewed into a beverage or used as a garnish.

Spearmint

Peppermint has thin, stiff, pointed leaves and a sharper menthol flavour and aroma. Fresh peppermint is used less often in cooking or as a garnish than spearmint, but peppermint oil is a common flavouring in sweets and candies.

Peppermint

Oregano (Fr. *origan*), also known as wild marjoram, is a pungent, peppery herb used in Mediterranean cuisines, particularly Greek and Italian, as well as in Mexican cuisine. It is a classic complement to tomatoes. Oregano's thin, woody stalks bear clumps of tiny, dark green leaves, which are available dried and crushed.

Oregano

Parsley (Fr. *persil)* is probably the best known and most widely used herb in the world. It grows in almost all climates and is available in many varieties, all of which are rich in vitamins and minerals. The most common type in North America and Northern Europe is **curly parsley**. It has small curly leaves and a bright green colour. Its flavour is tangy and clean. Other cuisines use a variety sometimes known as **Italian parsley**, which has flat leaves, a darker colour and coarser flavour. Curly parsley is a ubiquitous garnish; both types can be used in virtually any food except sweets. Parsley stalks have a stronger flavour than the leaves and are part of the standard bouquet garni. Chopped parsley forms the basis of many fine herb blends.

Parsley

Italian Parsley

Rosemary (Fr. *romarin*) is an evergreen bush that grows wild in warm, dry climates worldwide. It has stiff, needlelike leaves; some varieties bear pale blue flowers. It is highly aromatic, with a slight odour of camphor or pine. Rosemary is best used fresh. When dried, it loses flavour and its leaves become very hard and unpleasant to chew. Whole rosemary stems may be added to a dish such as a stew and then removed when enough flavour has been imparted. They may also be added to a bouquet garni. Rosemary has a great affinity for roasted and grilled meats, especially lamb.

Rosemary

Sage

Sage (Fr. *sauge*) was used as a medicine for centuries before it entered the kitchen as a culinary herb. Culinary sage has narrow, fuzzy, grey-green leaves and blue flowers. Its flavour is strong and balsamic, with notes of camphor. Sage is used in poultry dishes, with fatty meats or brewed as a beverage. Sage's strong flavour does not blend well with other herbs. It dries well and is available in whole or chopped leaves or rubbed (coarsely ground).

Savory (Fr. *sariette*), also known as summer savory, has been used since ancient times. Its leaves are small and narrow and it has a sharp, bitter flavour, vaguely like thyme. It dries well and is used in bean dishes, sausages and herb mixtures.

Tarragon (Fr. *estragon*), another of the great culinary herbs, is native to Siberia. It is a bushy plant with long, narrow, dark green leaves and tiny grey flowers. Tarragon goes well with fish and tomatoes and is essential in many French dishes such as béarnaise sauce and fine herb blends. Its flavour is strong and diffuses quickly through foods. It is available dried, but drying may cause haylike flavours to develop.

Savory

Tarragon

Thyme (Fr. *thym*) has been popular since 3500 B.C., when Egyptians used it as a medicine and for embalming. Thyme is a small, bushy plant with woody stems, tiny green-grey leaves and purple flowers. Its flavour is strong but refined, with notes of sage. Thyme dries well and complements virtually all types of meat, poultry, fish, shellfish and vegetables. It is often included in a bouquet garni or added to stocks.

Thyme

Spices

Allspice

Allspice, also known as Jamaican pepper, is the dried berry of a tree that flourishes in Jamaica, and one of the few spices still grown exclusively in the New World. Allspice is available whole; in berries that look like large, rough, brown peppercorns; or ground. Ground allspice is not a mixture of spices, although it does taste like a blend of cinnamon, cloves and nutmeg. Allspice is now used throughout the world, in everything from cakes to curries, and is often included in peppercorn blends.

Anise seeds

Anise (Fr. *anis*) is native to the eastern Mediterranean, where it was widely used by ancient civilizations. Today, it is grown commercially in warm climates throughout India, North Africa and southern Europe. The tiny, grey-green egg-shaped seeds have a distinctively strong, sweet flavour, similar to licorice and fennel. When anise seeds turn brown they are stale and should be discarded. Anise is used in pastries as well as fish, shellfish and vegetable dishes, and is commonly used in alcoholic beverages (e.g., Pernod and ouzo). The green leaves of the anise plant are occasionally used fresh as a herb or in salads.

Star anise, also known as Chinese anise, is the dried, star-shaped fruit of a Chinese magnolia tree. Although botanically unrelated, its flavour is similar to anise seeds but more bitter and pungent. It is an essential flavour in many Chinese dishes and one of the components of five-spice powder.

Capers

Capers (Fr. *capres*) come from a small bush that grows wild throughout the Mediterranean basin. Its unopened flower buds have been pickled and used as a condiment for thousands of years. Fresh capers are not used, as the sharp, salty-sour flavour develops only after curing in strongly salted white vinegar. The finest capers are the smallest, known as *nonpareils*, which are produced in France's Provence region. Capers are used in a variety of sauces (tartare, remoulade) and are excellent with fish and game. Capers will keep for long periods if moistened by their original liquid. Do not add or substitute vinegar, however, as this causes the capers to spoil.

◆◆◆

A Pinch of History

Spices have been used for many purposes for thousands of years. Egyptian papyri dating back to 2800 B.C. identify several spices native to the Middle and Far East that were used by the ruling and priestly classes for therapeutic, cosmetic, medicinal, ritualistic and culinary purposes.

By A.D. 300 the Romans were regularly importing spices for use as perfumes, medicines, preservatives and ingredients from China and India via long, difficult caravan journeys over sea and land. Spices were extremely expensive and unavailable to all but the wealthiest citizens.

After Rome fell in the second half of the 5th century A.D., much of the overland route through southern Europe became prey to bandits; and after Constantinople fell in 1453, the spice routes through the Middle East were controlled by the Ottoman Turks. Spice costs soared and economies based upon the spice trade, such as that of Venice, were at risk.

By then highly spiced food had become the norm, especially in wealthier households. So, in part to maintain their culinary norm, the Europeans set out to break the Ottoman Turk monopoly. These efforts led to Columbus's discovery of the Americas and Vasco de Gama's discovery of a sea route to India. Although the New World contained none of the spices for which Columbus was searching, it provided many previously unknown foods and flavourings that changed European tables forever, including chiles, vanilla, tomatoes, potatoes and chocolate.

Formation of the Dutch East India Company in 1602 marked the start of the Dutch colonial empire and made spices widely available to the growing European middle classes. The transplantation and cultivation of spice plants eventually weakened the once-powerful trading empires until, by the 19th century, no European country could monopolize trade. Prices fell dramatically.

Caraway is perhaps the world's oldest spice. Its use has been traced to the Stone Age and seeds have been found in ancient Egyptian tombs. The caraway plant grows wild in Europe and temperate regions of Asia. It produces a small, crescent-shaped brown seed with the peppery flavour of rye. Seeds may be purchased whole or ground. (The leaves have a mild, bland flavour and are rarely used in cooking.) Caraway is a very European flavour, used extensively in German and Austrian dishes, particularly breads, meats and cabbage. It is also used in cheeses and to flavour the liqueur "Kümmel."

Caraway seeds

Cardamom is one of the most expensive spices, second only to saffron in cost. Its seeds are encased in 1/4-inch-long (6 mm) light green or brown pods. Cardamom is highly aromatic. Its flavour, lemony with notes of camphor, is quite strong and is used in both sweet and savoury dishes. Cardamom is widely used in Indian and Middle Eastern cuisines, where it is also used to flavour coffee. Scandinavians use cardamom to flavour breads and pastries. Ground cardamom loses its flavour rapidly and is easily adulterated, so it is best to purchase whole seeds and grind your own as needed.

Cardamom seeds

Chiles, including paprika, chile peppers, bell peppers and cayenne, are members of the *capsicum* plant family. Although cultivated for thousands of years in the West Indies and Americas, capsicum peppers were unknown in the Old World prior to Spanish explorations during the 15th century. Capsicum peppers come in all shapes and sizes, with a wide range of flavours, from sweet to extremely hot. Some capsicums are used as a vegetable, while others are dried, ground and used as a spice. Fresh chiles and bell peppers are discussed in Chapter 22, Vegetables. Capsicums are botanically unrelated to *piper nigrum*, the black peppercorns discussed below.

For our purposes, chile *refers to the plant,* chili *refers to the stewlike dish containing chiles and* chilli *refers to the commercial spice powder.*

Cayenne, sometimes simply labelled "red pepper," is ground from a blend of several particularly hot types of dried red chile peppers. Its flavour is extremely hot and pungent; it has a bright orange-red colour and fine texture.

Paprika, also known as Hungarian pepper, is a bright red powder ground from particular varieties of red-ripened and dried chiles. The flavour ranges from sweet to pungent; the aroma is distinctive and strong. It is essential to many Spanish and eastern European dishes. Mild paprika is meant to be used in generous quantities and may be sprinkled on prepared foods as a garnish.

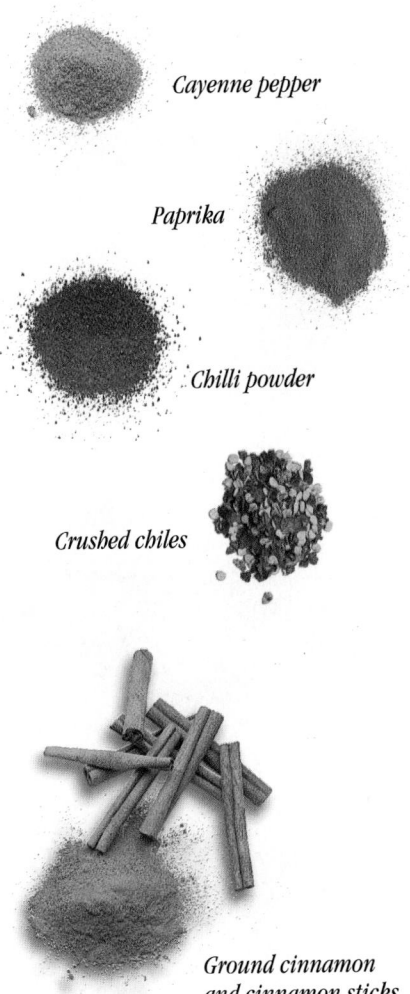

Cayenne pepper

Paprika

Chilli powder

Crushed chiles

Chile powders are made from a wide variety of dried chile peppers, ranging from sweet and mild to extremely hot and pungent. The finest pure chile powders come from dried chiles that are simply roasted, ground and sieved. Commercial chilli powder, an American invention, is actually a combination of spices—oregano, cumin, garlic and other flavourings—intended for use in Mexican dishes. Each brand is different and should be sampled before using.

Crushed chiles, also known as chile flakes, are blended from dried, coarsely crushed chiles. They are quite hot and are used in sauces and meat dishes.

Cinnamon (Fr. *cannelle*) and its cousin **cassia** are among the oldest known spices: cinnamon's use is recorded in China as early as 2500 B.C. and the Far East still produces most of these products. Both cinnamon and cassia come from the bark of small evergreen trees, peeled from branches in thin layers and dried in the sun. High-quality cinnamon should be pale brown and thin, rolled up like paper into sticks known as quills. Cassia is coarser and has a stronger, less subtle flavour than cinnamon. Consequently, it is cheaper than true cinnamon. Cinnamon is usually purchased ground because it is difficult to grind. Cinnamon sticks are used when long cooking times can be allowed in order to extract the flavour (for example, in stews or curries). Cinnamon's flavour is most often associated with pastries and sweets, but has a great affinity for lamb and spicy dishes. Labelling laws do not require that packages dis-

Ground cinnamon and cinnamon sticks

tinguish between cassia and cinnamon, so most of what is sold as cinnamon in North America is actually cassia, blended for consistent flavour and aroma.

Cloves (Fr. *clous girofle*) are the unopened buds of evergreen trees that flourish in muggy tropical regions. When dried, whole cloves have hard, sharp prongs that can be used to push them into other foods, such as onions or fruit, in order to provide flavour. Cloves are extremely pungent, with a sweet, astringent aroma. A small amount provides a great deal of flavour. Cloves are used in desserts and meat dishes, preserves and liqueurs. They may be purchased whole or ground.

Coriander seeds come from the cilantro plant. They are round and beige, with a distinctive sweet, spicy flavour and strong aroma. Unlike other plants in which the seeds and the leaves carry the same flavour and aroma, coriander and cilantro are distinct. Coriander seeds are available whole or ground and are frequently used in Indian cuisine and pickling mixtures.

Cumin is the seed of a small delicate plant of the parsley family that grows in North Africa and the Middle East. The small seeds are available whole or ground and look (but do not taste) like caraway seeds. Cumin has a powerful earthy flavour and tends to dominate any dish in which it is included. It is used in Indian, Middle Eastern and Mexican cuisines, in sausages and a few cheeses.

Fennel (Fr. *fenouil)* is a perennial plant with feathery leaves and tiny flowers long cultivated in India and China as a medicine and cure for witchcraft. Its seeds are greenish-brown with prominent ridges and short, hairlike fibres. Their taste and aroma are similar to anise, though not as sweet. Whole seeds are widely used in Italian stews and sausages; Central European cuisines use fennel with fish, pork, pickles and vegetables. Ground seeds can also be used in breads, cakes and cookies. The same plant produces a bulbous stalk used as a vegetable.

Fenugreek (Fr. *fenugrec*), grown in Mediterranean countries since ancient times, is a small, beanlike plant with a tiny flower. The seeds, available whole or ground, are pebble-shaped and transfer their pale orange colour to the foods with which they are cooked. Their flavour is bittersweet, like burnt sugar with a bitter aftertaste. Fenugreek is a staple in Indian cuisine, especially curries and chutneys.

Ginger (Fr. *gingembre*) is a well-known spice obtained from the root of a tall, flowering tropical plant. Fresh ginger root is known as a "hand" because it looks vaguely like a group of knobby fingers. It has greyish-tan skin and a pale yellow, fibrous interior. Fresh ginger should be plump and firm with smooth skin. It should keep for about a month under refrigeration. Its flavour is fiery but sweet, with notes of lemon and rosemary. Fresh ginger is widely available and is used in Indian and Asian cuisines. It has a special affinity for chicken, beef and curries. Ginger is also available peeled and pickled in vinegar, candied in sugar or preserved in alcohol or syrup. Dried, ground ginger is a fine yellow powder widely used in pastries. Its flavour is spicier and not as sweet as fresh ginger.

Juniper is an evergreen bush grown throughout the northern hemisphere. It produces round purple berries with a sweet flavour similar to pine. Juniper berries are used for flavouring gin and other alcoholic beverages, and are crushed and incorporated in game dishes, particularly venison and wild boar.

Mustard seeds (Fr. *moutarde*), available in black, brown and yellow, come from three different plants in the cabbage family. Mustard seeds are small, hard

Cloves

Coriander seeds

Cumin

Fennel

Fenugreek

Ginger root

Juniper berries

spheres with a bitter flavour. The seeds have no aroma, but their flavour is sharp and fiery hot. Yellow seeds have the mildest and black seeds the strongest flavour. All are sold whole and can be crushed for cooking. Mustard seeds are a standard component of pickling spices and are processed and blended for prepared mustards, which are discussed below. Ground or dry mustard is a bright yellow powder made from a blend of ground seeds, wheat flour and turmeric.

Mustard seeds

Ground mustard

Nutmeg (Fr. *muscade*) and **mace** come from the yellow plumlike fruit of a large tropical evergreen. These fruits are dried and opened to reveal the seed known as nutmeg. The seed is surrounded by a bright red lacy coating or aril; the aril is the spice mace. Whole nutmegs are oval and look rather like a piece of smooth wood. The flavour and aroma of nutmeg are strong and sweet, and a small quantity provides a great deal of flavour. Nutmeg should be grated directly into a dish as needed; once grated, flavour loss is rapid. Nutmeg is used in many European cuisines, mainly in pastries and sweets, but is also important in meat and savoury dishes.

Mace is an expensive spice, with a flavour similar to nutmeg but more refined. It is almost always purchased ground and retains its flavour longer than other ground spices. Mace is used primarily in pastry items.

Mace (left) and whole and ground nutmeg (right)

Peppercorns (Fr. *poivre*) are the berries of a vine plant (*piper nigrum*) native to tropical Asia. Peppercorns should not be confused with the chile (capsicum) peppers discussed above. Peppercorns vary in size, colour, pungency and flavour. Many of these differences are the result of variations in climate and growing conditions. Good-quality pepper is expensive and should be purchased whole and ground fresh in a peppermill as needed. Whole peppercorns will last indefinitely if kept dry. They should be stored well covered in a cool, dark place.

Black and **white peppercorns** are produced from the same plant, but are picked and processed differently. For black peppercorns, the berries are picked when green and simply dried whole in the sun. Black pepper has a warm, pungent flavour and aroma. Tellicherry peppercorns from the southwest coast of India are generally considered the finest black peppercorns in the world and are priced accordingly.

Black pepper (left) and white pepper (right)

For white peppercorns, the berries are allowed to ripen until they turn red. The ripened berries are allowed to ferment, then the outer layer of skin is washed off. Nowadays, white pepper may be produced by mechanically removing the outer skin from black peppercorns. This is not true white pepper, and the resulting product should be labelled "decorticated." White pepper has less aroma than black pepper but is useful in white sauces or where the appearance of black speckles is undesirable.

Green peppercorns are unripened berries that are either freeze-dried or pickled in brine or vinegar. Pickled green peppercorns are soft, with a fresh, sour flavour similar to capers. They are excellent in spiced butters and sauces or with fish.

Pink peppercorns are actually the berries of a South American tree, not a vine pepper plant. Pink peppercorns are available dried or pickled in vinegar. Although attractive, their flavour is bitter and pinelike, with less spiciness than true pepper. Pink peppercorns are no longer available in some areas because of reported toxic side effects.

Poppy seeds (Fr. *pavot*) are the ripened seeds of the opium poppy, which flourishes in the Middle East and India. (When ripe, the seeds do not contain any of the medicinal alkaloids found elsewhere in the plant.) The tiny blue-grey seeds are round and hard with a sweet, nutty flavour. Poppy seeds are used in pastries and breads.

Poppy seeds

Saffron

Sesame seeds

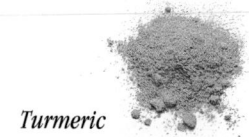

Turmeric

Saffron (Fr. *safran*) comes from the dried stigmas of the saffron crocus. Each flower bears only three threadlike stigmas, and each must be picked by hand. It takes about 250 000 flowers to produce 1 pound (450 g) of saffron, making it the most expensive spice in the world. Beware of bargains; there is no such thing as cheap saffron. Luckily, a tiny pinch is enough to colour and flavour a large quantity of food. Good saffron should be a brilliant orange colour, not yellow, with a strong aroma and a bitter, honeylike taste. Saffron produces a yellow dye that diffuses through any warm liquid. Valencia or Spanish saffron is considered the finest. It is commonly used with fish and shellfish (a necessity for bouillabaisse) and rice dishes such as paella and risotto. When using saffron threads, first crush them gently, then soak them in some hot liquid from the recipe. Powdered saffron is less expensive but more easily adulterated. It may be added directly to the other ingredients when cooking.

Sesame seeds, also known as benne seeds, are native to India. They are small, flat ovals, with a creamy white colour. Their taste is nutty and earthy, with a pronounced aroma when roasted or ground into a paste (known as tahini). Sesame seeds are the source of sesame oil, which has a mild, nutty flavour and does not go rancid easily. Sesame seeds are roasted and used in or as a garnish for breads and meat dishes. They are popular in Indian and Asian cuisines, with a black variety of seeds most popular as a Japanese condiment.

Turmeric, also known as Indian saffron, is produced from the roots of a flowering tropical plant related to ginger. Unlike ginger, fresh turmeric is not used in cooking. It is only available dried and usually ground. Turmeric is renowned for its vibrant yellow colour and is used as a food colouring and dye. Turmeric's flavour is distinctive and strong; it should not be substituted for saffron. Turmeric is a traditional ingredient in Indian curries, to which it imparts colour as well as flavour.

Spice Blends

Many countries and cuisines have created recognizable combinations of spice flavours that are found in a variety of dishes. Although many of these blends are available ready-prepared for convenience, most can be mixed by the chef as needed. A few of the more common spice blends are described here.

Chinese five-spice powder is a combination of equal parts finely ground Szechuan pepper, star anise, cloves, cinnamon and fennel seeds. This blend is widely used in Chinese and some Vietnamese foods and is excellent with pork and in pâtés.

Curry powder is a European invention that probably took its name from the Tamil word *kari*, meaning a sauce. Created by 19th-century Britons returning from colonial India, it was meant to be the complete spicing for a "curry" dish. There are as many different formulas for curry powder as there are manufacturers, some mild and sweet (Bombay or Chinese style), others hot and pungent (Madras style). Typical ingredients in curry powder are black pepper, cinnamon, cloves, coriander, cumin, ginger, mace and turmeric. Curry pastes are widely available; they are fried spices mixed with oil, onions, garlic and other flavourings.

Pickling spice

Pickling spice, as with other blends, varies by manufacturer. Most pickling spice blends are based on black peppercorns and red chiles, with some or all of the following added: allspice, cloves, ginger, mustard seeds, coriander seeds, bay leaves and dill. These blends are useful in making cucumber or vegetable pickles as well as in stews and soups.

Quatre-épices, literally "four spices" in French, is a peppery mixture of black peppercorns with lesser amounts of nutmeg, cloves and dried ginger. Sometimes cinnamon or allspice is included. Quatre-épices is used in charcuterie and long-simmered stews.

Using Herbs and Spices

Herbs and spices are a simple, inexpensive way to bring individuality and variety to foods. Their proper use leads to better-flavoured and distinctively different dishes. They add neither fat nor sodium and virtually no calories to foods; most contain only 3 to 10 calories per teaspoon (5 mL). Table 7.1 lists just a few uses for some of the more common herbs and spices.

Although the flavours and aromas of fresh herbs are generally preferred, dried herbs are widely used because they are readily available and convenient. Purchase only the amount of dried herbs that can be used within a short time. If stored in a closed container in a cool, dry place, dried herbs should last for two to three months.

Use less dried herbs than you would fresh herbs. The loss of moisture strengthens and concentrates the flavour in dried herbs. In general, you should use only one-half to one-third as much dried herb as fresh in any given recipe. For example, if a recipe calls for 1 tablespoon (15 mL) of fresh basil, you should substitute only 1 teaspoon (5 mL) of dried basil. You can usually add more later if necessary.

Spices are often available whole or ground. Once ground, they lose their flavours rapidly, however. Whole spices should keep their flavours for many months if stored in air-tight containers in a cool, dry place away from direct light. Stale spices lose their spicy aroma and develop a bitter or musty after-taste. Discard them.

Because ground spices release their flavours quickly, they should be added to cooked dishes near the end of the cooking period. In uncooked dishes that call for ground spices (for example, salad dressings), the mixture should be allowed to stand for several hours to develop good flavour.

While some combinations are timeless—rosemary with lamb, dill with salmon, nutmeg with spinach, caraway with rye bread—less common pairings can be equally delicious and far more exciting. A chef must be willing and able to experiment with new flavours. But first you must be familiar with the distinctive flavour and aroma of the herb or spice. Then you can experiment, always bearing in mind the following guidelines:

- ◆ Flavourings should not hide the taste or aroma of the primary ingredient;
- ◆ Flavourings should be combined in balance, so as not to overwhelm the palate; and
- ◆ Flavourings should not be used to disguise poor quality or poorly prepared products.

Even when following a well-tested recipe, the quantity of flavourings may need to be adjusted because of changes in brands or the condition of the ingredients. A cook should strive to develop his or her palate to recognize and correct subtle variances as necessary.

TABLE 7.1   USES FOR SOME COMMON HERBS AND SPICES

Flavouring	Form	Suggested Uses
Allspice	Whole or ground	Fruits, relishes, braised meats
Anise	Whole or ground	Asian cuisines, pastries, breads, cheeses
Basil	Fresh or dried	Tomatoes, salads, eggs, fish, chicken, lamb, cheeses
Caraway	Whole or ground	Rye bread, cabbage, beans, pork, beef, veal
Chervil	Fresh or dried	Chicken, fish, eggs, salads, soups, vegetables
Chives	Fresh or dried	Eggs, fish, chicken, soups, potatoes, cheeses
Cilantro	Fresh leaves	Salsa, salads, Mexican cuisine, fish, shellfish, chicken
Cloves	Whole or ground	Marinades, baked goods, braised meats, pickles, fruits, beverages, stocks
Cumin	Whole or ground	Chili, sausages, stews, eggs
Dill	Fresh or dried leaves; whole seeds	Leaves or seeds in soups, salads, fish, shellfish, vegetables, breads; seeds in pickles, potatoes, vegetables
Fennel	Whole seeds	Sausages, stews, sauces, pickling, lamb, eggs
Ginger	Fresh root or powder	Asian, Caribbean and Indian cuisines, pastries, curries, stews, meats
Marjoram	Fresh or dried	Sausages, pâtés, meats, poultry, stews, green vegetables, tomatoes, game
Nutmeg	Ground	Curries, relishes, rice, eggs, beverages
Rosemary	Fresh or dried	Lamb, veal, beef, poultry, game, marinades, stews
Saffron	Threads or ground	Rice, breads, potatoes, soups, stews, chicken, fish, shellfish
Sage	Fresh or dried	Poultry, charcuterie, pork, stuffings, pasta, beans, tomatoes
Tarragon	Fresh or dried	Chicken, fish, eggs, salad dressings, sauces, tomatoes
Thyme	Fresh or dried	Fish, chicken, meats, stews, charcuterie, soups, tomatoes
Turmeric	Ground	Curries, relishes, rice, eggs, breads

Bouquet Garni and Sachet

The *bouquet garni* and the *sachet* are used to introduce flavourings, seasonings and aromatics into stocks, sauces, soups and stews.

A **bouquet garni**, shown in Figure 7.1, is a selection of herbs (usually fresh) and vegetables tied into a bundle with twine. The twine makes it easy to remove the bouquet when sufficient flavour has been extracted. A standard

FIGURE 7.1 *Bouquet Garni*

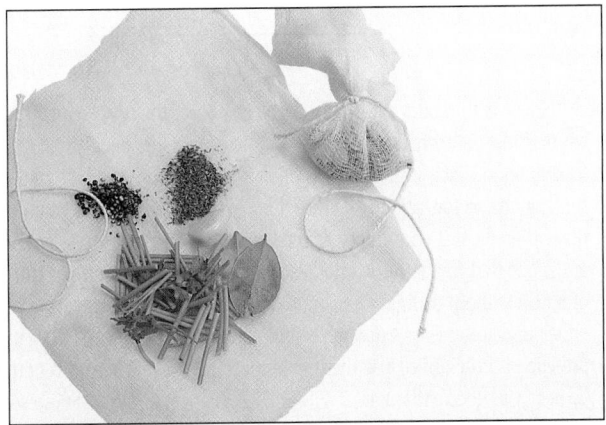

FIGURE 7.2 *Sachet*

bouquet garni consists of parsley stems, celery, thyme, leeks and carrots.

A **sachet** (also known as a *sachet d'épices*), shown in Figure 7.2, is made by tying seasonings together in cheesecloth. A standard sachet consists of peppercorns, bay leaves, parsley stems, thyme, cloves and, optionally, garlic. The exact quantity of these ingredients is determined by the amount of liquid the sachet is meant to flavour.

Bouquets garni and sachets are used to add flavours in such a way that the ingredients can be easily removed from a dish when the flavours have been extracted. A similar technique, although less commonly used, is an **oignon piqué**, or studded onion. To prepare an oignon piqué, peel the onion and trim off the root end. Attach one or two dried bay leaves to the onion using whole cloves as pins. The oignon piqué is then simmered in milk or stock to extract flavours.

SALT

Salt (Fr. *sel)* is the most basic seasoning and its use is universal. It preserves foods, heightens their flavours and provides the distinctive taste of saltiness. The presence of salt can be tasted easily but not smelled. Temperature affects saltiness. The cooler a food, the saltier it tastes, so it is best to undersalt hot foods that will be chilled prior to service (chilled soups, for example).

Culinary or **table salt** is sodium chloride (NaCl), one of the minerals essential to human life. Salt contains no calories, proteins, fats or carbohydrates. It is available from several sources, each with its own flavour and degree of saltiness.

Rock salt, mined from underground deposits, is available in both edible and nonedible forms. It is used for home freezing.

Common kitchen or table salt is produced by pumping water through underground salt deposits, then bringing the brine to the surface to evaporate, leaving behind crystals. Chemicals are usually added to prevent table salt from absorbing moisture and thus keep it free-flowing. Iodized salt is commonly used in North America. The iodine has no effect on the salt's flavour or use; it is simply added to provide an easily available source of iodine, an important nutrient, to a large number of people.

Sea salt is obtained, not surprisingly, by evaporating sea water and purifying the crystals left behind. Many chefs consider its flavour stronger or purer than mined salt.

◆◆◆

ABOUT FLAVORS

Flavor is to food what hue is to color. It is what timbre is to music. Flavor is adjective; food is noun. Each ingredient has its own particular character, which is altered by every other ingredient it encounters. A secret ingredient is one that mysteriously improves the flavor of a dish without calling attention to itself. It is either undetectable or extremely subtle, but its presence is crucial because the dish would not be nearly as good without it.

Primary flavors are those that are obvious, such as the flavors of chicken and tarragon in a chicken tarragon, shrimp and garlic in a shrimp scampi, or beef and red wine in a beef *à la Bourguignon*. Secret ingredients belong to the realm of secondary flavors. However obvious it is that you need tarragon to prepare a chicken tarragon, you would not achieve the most interesting result using *only* tarragon. Tarragon, in this case, needs secondary ingredients—a hint of celery seed and anise—to make it taste more like quintessential tarragon and at the same time more than tarragon. In

this way, primary flavors often depend on secret ingredients to make them more interesting and complex. Using only one herb or spice to achieve a certain taste usually results in a lackluster dish—each mouthful tastes the same. Whether they function in a primary or secondary way, flavors combine in only three different ways: They marry, oppose, or juxtapose.

When flavors marry, they combine to form one taste. Some secondary flavors marry with primary ones to create a new flavor greater than the sum of its parts, and often two flavors can do the job better than one. It may sound like an eccentric combination, but vanilla marries with the flavor of lobster, making it taste more like the essence of lobster than lobster does on its own. And when ginger and molasses marry, they create a flavor superior to either alone.

Opposite flavors can highlight or cancel each other; they can cut or balance each other. Sweet/sour, sweet/salty, sweet/hot, salty/sour, and salty/tart are all opposites. Salt and sugar

are so opposed, in fact, that when used in equal amounts they cancel each other entirely. Sweet relish helps to cancel the salty flavor of hot dogs. Chinese sauces usually contain some sugar to help balance the saltiness of soy sauce.

Because flavors are sensed on different parts of the tongue and palate, and because they are tasted at different times, we can juxtapose them, using flavors side by side or in layers. The layering of flavors makes the food we taste more interesting because each mouthful is different.

Knowing how to combine many flavors and aromas to achieve a simple and pure result (and knowing when not to combine flavors) will make you a better, more confident cook. Good cooks over the centuries have known these things intuitively—but they've had neither the huge variety of ingredients nor the knowledge of world cuisines that we have today.

from SECRET INGREDIENTS
by CHEF MICHAEL ROBERTS

◆◆◆

RECIPES FOR ETHNIC CUISINES

In *Ethnic Cuisine: The Flavor Principle Cookbook*, Elisabeth Rozin writes: "Every culture tends to combine a small number of flavoring ingredients so frequently and so consistently that they become definitive of that particular cuisine" (p. xiv). She calls these defining flavours "flavor principles" and notes that they are "designed to abstract what is absolutely fundamental about a cuisine and thus, to serve as a guide in cooking and developing new recipes" (p. xvii). She identifies the following "flavor principles":

Central Asia: cinnamon, fruit and nuts

China: generally—soy sauce, rice wine and ginger root
    Northern China (Mandarin/Peking)—miso and/or garlic and/or sesame

Western China (Szechuan)—sweet, sour and hot
Southern China (Canton)—black beans, garlic

Eastern Europe (Jewish): onion and chicken fat

Eastern and Northern Europe: sour cream and dill or paprika or allspice or caraway

France: generally—olive oil, garlic and basil *or* wine and herb *or* butter and/or cream and/or cheese plus wine and/or stock
    Southern France—olive oil, garlic, parsley and/or anchovy plus tomato as a variation
    Provence—olive oil, thyme, rosemary, marjoram, sage plus tomato as a variation
    Normandy—apple, cider, Calvados

Greece: tomato, cinnamon or olive oil, lemon, oregano

India: Northern—cumin, ginger, garlic
    Southern—mustard seed, coconut, tamarind, chile

Italy: generally—olive oil, garlic, basil
    Northern Italy—wine vinegar, garlic
    Southern Italy—olive oil, garlic, parsley and/or anchovy plus tomato as a variation

Japan: soy sauce, sake, sugar

Mexico: generally—tomato and chile *or* lime and chile
    Yucatan—sour orange, garlic, achiote

North Africa: cumin, coriander, cinnamon, ginger, onion and/or tomato and/or fruit

Spain: olive oil, garlic, nut or olive oil, onion, pepper, tomato

Thailand: fish sauce, curry, chile

West Africa: tomato, peanut, chile

Kosher salt has large, irregular crystals and is used in the "koshering" or curing of meats. It is purified rock salt that contains no iodine or additives. It can be substituted for common kitchen salt.

Because it is nonorganic, salt keeps indefinitely. It will, however, absorb moisture from the atmosphere, which prevents it from flowing properly. Salt is a powerful preservative; its presence stops or greatly slows down the growth of many undesirable organisms. Salt is used to preserve meats, vegetables and fish. It is also used to develop desirable flavours in bacon, ham, cheeses and fish products as well as pickled vegetables.

NUTS

A **nut** (Fr. *noix*) is the edible single-seed kernel of a fruit surrounded by a hard shell. A hazelnut is an example of a true nut. The term is used more generally, however, to refer to any seed or fruit with an edible kernel in a hard shell. Walnuts and peanuts are examples of non-nut "nuts" (peanuts are legumes that grow underground; walnuts have two kernels). Nuts are a good source of protein and B vitamins but are high in fat. Their high fat content makes them especially susceptible to rancidity and odour absorption. Nuts should be stored in nonmetal, air-tight containers in a cool, dark place. Most nuts may be kept frozen for up to one year.

Nuts are used in foods to provide texture and flavour. They are often roasted in a low (275°F/135°C) oven before use to heighten their flavour. Allowing roasted nuts to cool to room temperature before grinding prevents them from releasing too much oil.

Almonds (Fr. *amande*) are the seeds of a plumlike fruit. Native to western India, the almond was first cultivated by the ancient Greeks. It is now a major commercial crop in California. Almonds are available whole, sliced, slivered or ground. Blanched almonds have had their brown, textured skins removed; natural almonds retain their skins. Unless the brown colour of natural almond skin is undesirable, the two types can be used interchangeably in recipes. Almonds are frequently used in pastries and candies and are the main ingredient in marzipan.

Almonds

Cashews, native to the Amazon, are now cultivated in India and east Africa. The cashew nut is actually the seed of a plant related to poison ivy. Because of toxins in the shell, cashews are always sold shelled. They are expensive and have a strong flavour. Cashews are used in some Asian cuisines and make a wonderful addition to cookies and candies.

Cashews

Chestnuts (Fr. *marrons*) are true nuts that must be cooked before using. Available steamed, dried, boiled or roasted, they are often sold as a canned purée, with or without added sugar. Candied or glazed chestnuts are also available. Most chestnuts are grown in Europe, primarily Italy, but new varieties are beginning to flourish in North America. Their distinctive flavour is found in many sweet dishes and pastries. Because of their high starch content, chestnuts are also used in soups and sauces and may be served as a side dish.

Coconuts (Fr. *noix de coco*) are the seeds from one of the largest of all fruits. They grow on the tropical coconut palm tree. The nut is a dark brown oval, covered with coarse fibres. The shell is thick and hard; inside is a layer of white, moist flesh. The interior also contains a clear liquid known as coconut water. (This is not the same as coconut milk or coconut cream, both of which are prepared from the flesh.) Coconut has a mild aroma, a sweet,

Chestnuts

Coconuts

Hazelnuts

Macadamias

Peanuts

Pecans

Pine Nuts

Pistachios

nutty flavour and a crunchy, chewy texture. Fresh coconuts are readily available but require some effort to use. Coconut flesh is available shredded or flaked, with or without added sugar. Coconut is most often used in pastries and candies and is also an important ingredient in Indian and Caribbean cuisines. A good fresh coconut should feel heavy; you should be able to hear the coconut water sloshing around inside. Avoid cracked, moist or moldy coconuts.

Hazelnuts (Fr. *noisette*) are true nuts that grow wild in the northeast and upper midwest of the United States. The cultivated form, known as a **filbert**, is native to temperate regions throughout the northern hemisphere. A bit larger than the hazelnut, it has a weaker flavour than its wild cousin. Both nuts look like smooth brown marbles. Filberts are more abundant, so are generally less expensive. Hazelnuts are often ground for use in cakes or pastries. Their distinctive flavour goes well with chocolate and coffee.

To remove the hazelnut's bitter skin, roast whole nuts in a 275°F (135°C) oven for 12 to 15 minutes. They should give off a good aroma and just begin to darken. While still hot, rub the nuts in a dry towel or against a mesh sifter to remove the skin.

Macadamias, although commercially significant in Hawaii, are actually native to Australia. This small round nut is creamy white with a sweet, rich taste and high fat content. Its shell is extremely hard and must be removed by machine, so the macadamia is always sold out of the shell. Its flavour blends well with fruits, coconut and white and dark chocolate.

Peanuts (Fr. *arachide*), also known as groundnuts, are actually legumes that grow underground. The peanut is native to South America; it made its way into North America via Africa and the slave trade. Peanuts are a good source of protein and fat and became an important source of food and oil during World War II. They may be eaten raw or roasted and are available shelled or unshelled, with or without their thin red skins. Peanuts are used in Asian cuisines and are ubiquitous ground with a bit of oil into peanut butter.

Pecans (Fr. *noix de pacane*), native to the Mississippi River Valley, are perhaps the most popular nuts in America. Their flavour is rich and mapley and appears most often in breads, sweets and pastries. They are available whole in the shell or in various standard sizes and grades of pieces.

Pine nuts (Fr. *pignon*), also known as pinon nuts and pignole, are the seeds of several species of pine tree. The small, creamy white, teardrop-shaped nuts are commonly used in dishes from Spain, Italy and the American Southwest. They are rarely chopped or ground due to their small size, and will only need roasting if being used in a dish that will not receive further cooking. Pine nuts are used in breads, pastries and salads and are essential to classic pesto sauce.

Pistachios (Fr. *pistaches*) are native to central Asia, where they have been cultivated for over 3000 years. California now produces most of the pistachios marketed in this country. Pistachios are unique for the green colour of their meat. When ripe, the shell opens naturally at one end, aptly referred to as "smiling," which makes shelling the nuts quite easy. Red pistachios are dyed,

TABLE 7.2 NUTRITIONAL VALUES OF COMMON NUTS

Per 1 Ounce (28 g) Serving	Calories	Protein (g)	Carbohydrates (g)	Total Fat (g)	Saturated Fat (g)	Sodium (mg)
Almonds, whole kernels	167	5.7	5.8	14.8	1.4	3
Cashews, dry roasted	163	4.4	9.3	13.2	2.6	4
Chestnuts, roasted and peeled	70	0.9	15.0	0.6	0.1	1
Filberts, blanched	191	3.6	4.5	19.1	1.4	1
Macadamias	199	2.4	3.9	20.9	3.1	1
Peanuts, raw	159	7.2	4.5	13.8	1.9	5
Pecans	190	2.2	5.2	19.2	1.5	trace
Walnuts, English	182	4.1	5.2	17.6	1.6	3

The Corinne T. Netzer Encyclopedia of Food Values 1992

not natural. Pistachios are sold whole, shelled or unshelled, and are used in pastries and meat dishes, particularly pâtés. They should be peeled after shelling by soaking them briefly in hot water and rubbing them with a towel.

Walnuts (Fr. *noix*), relatives of the pecan, are native to Asia, Europe and North America. The black walnut, native to Appalachia, has a dark brown meat and strong flavour. The English walnut, now grown primarily in California, has a milder flavour, is easier to shell and is less expensive. Walnuts are more popular than pecans outside the United States. They are used in baked goods and are pressed for oil.

English walnuts

OILS

Oils (Fr. *huile*) are a type of fat that remains liquid at room temperature. Cooking oils are refined from various seeds, plants and vegetables. (Other fats, such as butter and margarine, are discussed in Chapter 8, Eggs and Dairy Products; animal and solid fats are discussed in Chapter 26, Principles of the Bakeshop.)

When purchasing oils you should consider their use, **smoke point**, flavour and cost. Fats, including oils and **shortenings**, are manufactured for specific purposes such as deep-fat frying, cake-baking, salad dressings and sautéing. Most food service operations purchase different ones for each of these needs.

Fats break down at different temperatures. The temperature at which a given fat begins to break down and smoke is known as its smoke point. Choose fats with higher smoke points for high temperature cooking such as deep-fat frying and sautéing. If a fat with a low smoke point is used for high temperature cooking, it may break down, burn and impart undesirable flavours.

The flavour and cost of each oil must also be considered. For example, both corn oil and walnut oil may be used in a salad dressing. Their selection may depend on balancing cost (corn oil is less expensive) against flavour (walnut oil has a stronger, more distinctive flavour).

When fats spoil they are said to go **rancid**. Rancidity is a chemical change caused by exposure to air, light or heat. It results in objectionable flavours and odours. Different fats turn rancid at different rates, but all fats benefit from refrigerated storage away from moisture, light and air. (Some oils are packaged in coloured glass containers because certain tints of green and yellow

Smoke point—*the temperature at which a fat begins to break down and smoke.*

Shortening—*a fat, usually made from vegetable oils, that is solid at room temperature.*

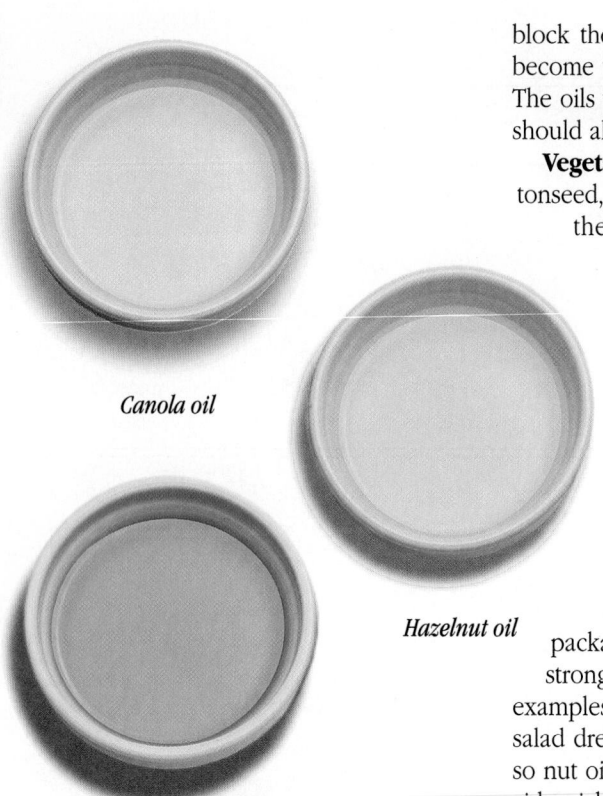

Canola oil

Hazelnut oil

Extra virgin olive oil

=== ◆◆◆ ===
THE OLIVE

Olives are the fruit of a tree native to the Mediterranean area. Green olives are those harvested unripened; black olives are fully ripened. The raw fruit is inedibly bitter and must be washed, soaked and pickled before eating. Green olives should have a smooth, tight skin. Ripe olives will be glossy but softer, with a slightly wrinkled skin. Many varieties and flavours are available, from the tiny black Niçoise to the large purplish Kalamata. Olives are packaged in a range of sizes, from medium (the smallest) to jumbo (the largest). (Colossal and super colossal olives are actually smaller than jumbos.) Pitted olives are also available. The cavity may be filled with strips of pimento, jalapeño pepper, almonds or other foods for flavour and appearance.

Olives are used as a finger food for snacks or hors d'oeuvres, or added to salads or pasta. They may even be cooked in breads, soups, sauces, stews or casseroles. A paste made of minced ripe olives, known as tapenade, is used as a dip or condiment.

block the damaging light rays that can cause an oil to go rancid.) Oils may become thick and cloudy under refrigeration. This is not a cause for concern. The oils will return to their clear, liquid states at room temperature. Stored fats should also be covered to prevent the absorption of odours.

Vegetable oils are extracted from a variety of plants, including corn, cottonseed, peanuts and soybeans, by pressure or chemical solvents. The oil is then refined and cleaned to remove unwanted colours, odours or flavours. Vegetable oils are virtually odourless and have a neutral flavour. Because they contain no animal products they are cholesterol-free. If a commercial product contains only one type of oil it is labelled "pure" (as in "pure corn oil"). Products labelled "vegetable oil" are blended from several sources. Products labelled "salad oil" are highly refined blends of vegetable oil.

Canola oil is processed from rapeseeds. Its popularity is growing rapidly because it contains no cholesterol and has a high percentage of monounsaturated fat. Canola oil is useful for frying and general cooking because it has no flavour and a high smoke point.

Nut oils are extracted from a variety of nuts and are almost always packaged as a "pure" product, never blended. A nut oil should have the strong flavour and aroma of the nut from which it was processed. Popular examples are walnut and hazelnut oils. These oils are used to give flavour to salad dressings, marinades and other dishes. But heat diminishes their flavour, so nut oils are not recommended for frying or baking. Nut oils tend to go rancid quickly and therefore are usually packaged in small containers.

Olive oil (Fr. *huile d'olive*) is the only oil that is extracted from a fruit rather than a seed, nut or grain. Olive oil is produced primarily in Spain, Italy, France, Greece and North Africa; California produces a relatively minor amount of olive oil. Like wine, olive oils vary in colour and flavour according to the variety of tree, the ripeness of the olives, the type of soil, the climate and the producer's preferences. Colours range from dark green to almost clear, depending on the ripeness of the olives at the time of pressing and the amount of subsequent refining. Colour is not a good indication of flavour, however. Flavour is ultimately a matter of personal preference. A stronger-flavoured oil may be desired for some foods, while a milder oil is better for others. Good olive oil should be thicker than refined vegetable oils, but not so thick that it has a fatty texture.

The label designations—extra virgin, virgin and pure—refer to the acidity of the oil (a low acid content is preferable) and the extent of processing used to extract the oil. The first cold-pressing of the olives results in virgin oil. (The designation "virgin" is used only when the oil is 100% unadulterated olive oil, unheated and without any chemical processing.) Virgin oil may still vary in quality depending on its acidity level. Extra virgin oil is virgin oil with an acidity level of not more than 1%; virgin oil may have an acidity level of up to 3%. Pure olive oil is processed from the pulp left after the first pressing using heat and chemicals. Pure oil is lighter in flavour and less expensive than virgin oil.

Flavoured oils, also known as **infused oils**, are an interesting and increasingly popular condiment. These oils may be used as a cooking medium or flavouring accent in marinades, dressings, sauces or other dishes. Flavours include basil and other herbs, garlic, citrus and spice. Flavoured oils are generally prepared with olive oil for additional flavour or canola oil, both considered more healthful than other fats.

Top-quality commercially flavoured oils are prepared by extracting aromatic oils from the flavouring ingredients and then emulsifying them with a high-grade oil; any impurities are then removed by placing the oil in a centrifuge.

TABLE 7.3   THE SMOKE POINT AND NUTRITIONAL VALUES OF COMMON FATS

Per 1 Ounce (28 g) Serving	Smoke Point	Calories	Total Fat (g)	Saturated Fat (g)
Olive oil	437°F/225°C	251	28.4	3.8
Peanut oil	425°F/218°C	251	28.4	4.8
Lard*	370°F/188°C	230	25.6	10.0
Canola oil	425°F/218°C	251	28.4	2.0
Walnut oil	325–400°F/ 163–204°C	240	28.0	4.0
Butter, clarified**	400°F/204°C	248	28.2	17.6
Whole butter, unsalted*	260°F/127°C	200	22.8	14.2

The Corinne T. Netzer Encyclopedia of Food Values 1992

*discussed in Chapter 26

**discussed in Chapter 8

Using the aromatic oils of the flavouring ingredients yields a more intense flavour than merely steeping the same ingredients in the oil. Flavoured oils should be stored as you would any other high-quality oil.

VINEGARS

Vinegar (Fr. *vinaigre*) is a thin, sour liquid used for thousands of years as a preservative, cooking ingredient, condiment and cleaning solution. Vinegar is obtained through the fermentation of wine or other alcoholic liquid. Bacteria attacks the alcohol in the solution, turning it into acetic acid. No alcohol will remain when the transformation is complete. The quality of vinegar depends upon the quality of the wine or other liquid on which it is based. Vinegar flavours are as varied as the liquids from which they are made.

Vinegars should be clear and clean looking, never cloudy or muddy. Commercial vinegars are pasteurized, so an unopened bottle should last indefinitely in a cool, dark place. Once opened, vinegars should last about three months if tightly capped. Any sediment that develops can be strained out; if mold develops, discard the vinegar.

Wine vinegars are as old as wine itself. They may be made from white or red wine, sherry or even champagne, and should bear the colour and flavour hallmarks of the wine used. Wine vinegars are preferred in French and Mediterranean cuisines.

Malt vinegar is produced from malted barley. Its slightly sweet, mild flavour is used as a condiment, especially with fried foods.

Distilled vinegar, made from grain alcohol, is completely clear with a stronger vinegary flavour and higher acid content than other vinegars. It is preferred for pickling and preserving.

Cider vinegar is produced from unpasteurized apple juice or cider. It is pale brown in colour with a mild acidity and fruity aroma. Cider vinegar is particularly popular in North America.

Rice vinegar is a clear, slightly sweet product brewed from rice wine. Its flavour is clean and elegant, making it useful in a variety of dishes.

Flavoured vinegars are simply traditional vinegars in which herbs, spices, fruits or other foods are steeped to infuse their flavours. They are easily produced from commercial wine or distilled vinegars, using any herb, spice or fruit

Balsamic vinegar, raspberry vinegar and cider vinegar

desired. The use of flavoured vinegars is extremely popular but definitely not new. Clove, raspberry and fennel vinegars were sold on the streets of Paris during the 13th century. Making fruit-flavoured vinegars was also one of the responsibilities of North American housewives during the 18th and 19th centuries.

Balsamic vinegar (It. *aceto Balsamico)* is newly popular in North America, though it has been produced in Italy for over 800 years. To produce balsamic vinegar, red wine vinegar is aged in a succession of wooden barrels made from a variety of woods—oak, cherry, locust, ash, mulberry and juniper—for at least 4, but sometimes up to 50, years. The resulting liquid is dark reddish-brown and sweet. Balsamic has a high acid level, but the sweetness covers the tart flavour, making it very mellow. True balsamic is extremely expensive because of the long aging process and the small quantities available. Most of the commercial products imported from Italy are now made by a quick caramelization and flavouring process. Balsamic is excellent as a condiment or seasoning and has a remarkable affinity for tomatoes and strawberries.

CONDIMENTS

Strictly speaking, a condiment is any food added to a dish for flavour, including herbs, spices and vinegars. Today, however, *condiments* more often refer to cooked or prepared flavourings, such as prepared mustards, relishes, bottled sauces and pickles. Several frequently used condiments are discussed here. These staples may be used to alter or enhance the flavour of a dish during cooking or added to a completed dish at the table by the consumer.

Prepared mustard is a mixture of crushed mustard seeds, vinegar or wine and salt or spices. It can be flavoured in many ways—with herbs, onions, peppers and even citrus zest. It can be a smooth paste or coarse and chunky, depending on how finely the seeds are ground and whether the skins are strained out. Prepared mustard gets its tangy taste from an essential oil that forms only when the seeds are crushed and mixed with water. Prepared mustard can be used as a condiment, particularly with meat and charcuterie items, or as a flavouring ingredient in sauces, stews and marinades.

Yellow mustard

Dijon mustard

Whole-grain mustard

Brown mustard

Dijon mustard takes its name from a town and the surrounding region in France that prepares about half of the world's mustard. French mustard labeled "Dijon" must, by law, be produced only in that region. Dijon and Dijon-style mustards are smooth with a rich, complex flavour. Western Canada grows the largest percentage of the world's mustard seed.

English and Chinese mustards are made from mustard flour and cool water. They are extremely hot and powerful. American or "ballpark" mustard is mild and vinegary with a bright yellow colour.

Mustard never really spoils, its flavour just fades away. Because of its high acid content, mustard does not turn rancid, but it will oxidize and develop a dark surface crust. Once opened, mustard should be kept well covered and refrigerated.

Soy sauce is a thin, dark brown liquid fermented from cooked soy beans, wheat and salt. Available in several flavours and strengths, it is ubiquitous in most Asian cuisines. Light soy sauce is thin, with a light brown colour and a very salty flavour. Dark soy sauce is thicker and dark brown, with a sweet, less salty flavour. Necessary for preparing many Asian dishes, soy sauce is also used in marinades and sauces and as an all-purpose condiment. Other soy-based condiments include tamari, teriyaki sauce and fermented bean paste (miso).

Ketchup (also known as catsup) originated in Asia and referred to any salty extract from fish, fruits or vegetables. Prepared tomato ketchup, as we know it, is really a syrupy sauce, created in America and used worldwide as a

♦♦♦

Even the most sophisticated food service operation occasionally uses prepared condiments or flavourings. The products described here are widely used and available from grocery stores or wholesale purveyors. Some are brand-name items that have become almost synonymous with the product itself; others are available from several manufacturers.

Barbecue sauce—Like ketchup, commercial barbecue sauce is a mixture of tomatoes, vinegar and spices; it tends to be hotter and sweeter than ketchup, however. Commercial barbecue sauce is used primarily for marinating or basting meat, poultry or fish. A tremendous variety of barbecue sauces is available, with various flavours, textures and aromas. Sample several before selecting the most appropriate for your specific needs.

Fish sauce—Fish sauce is a thin, dark brown liquid made from anchovy extract and salt. It is the quintessential Thai seasoning, but is used throughout Southeast Asia. It is extremely salty with a powerful aroma. There is no substitute; only a small amount is necessary for most dishes.

Hoisin—Hoisin sauce is a dark, thick, salty-sweet sauce made from fermented soy beans, vinegar, garlic and caramel. It is used in Chinese dishes or served as a dipping sauce.

Old Bay® seasoning—Old Bay® is a dry spice blend containing celery salt, dry mustard, paprika and other flavourings. It is widely used in shellfish preparations, especially boiled shrimp and crab.

Oyster sauce—Oyster sauce is a thick, dark sauce made from oyster extract. It has a salty-sweet flavour and rich aroma. Oyster sauce is often used with stir-fried meats and poultry.

Pickapeppa® sauce—Pickapeppa® sauce is a dark, thick, sweet-hot blend of tomatoes, onions, sugar, vinegar, mango, raisins, tamarinds and spices. Produced in Jamaica, West Indies, it is used as a condiment for meat, game or fish and as a seasoning in sauces, soups and dressings.

Tabasco® sauce—Tabasco® sauce is a thin, bright red liquid blended from vinegar, chiles and salt. Its fiery flavour is widely used in sauces, soups and prepared dishes; it is a popular condiment for Mexican, southern and southwestern cuisines. Tabasco® sauce has been produced in Louisiana since 1868. Other "Louisiana-style" hot sauces (those containing only peppers, vinegar and salt) may be substituted.

Worcestershire sauce—Worcestershire sauce is a thin, dark brown liquid made from malt vinegar, tamarind, molasses and spices. It is used as a condiment for beef and as a seasoning in sauces, soups, stews and prepared dishes. Its flavour should be rich and full, but not salty.

flavouring ingredient or condiment. It is bright red and thick, with a tangy, sweet-sour flavour. Ketchup, with its high sugar content, can be stored either in the refrigerator or at room temperature; it should keep well for up to four months after opening. Ketchup does not turn rancid or develop mold but it will darken and lose flavour as it ages.

COFFEES AND TEAS

Coffee and tea are the staples of most beverage menus. Despite their relatively low price a quality cup of coffee or tea can be extremely important to a customer's impression of your food service operation. A cup of coffee is often either the very first or the very last item consumed by a customer. Tea, whether iced or hot, is often consumed throughout the meal. Consequently, it is important that you learn to prepare and serve these beverages properly.

Coffee

Coffee (Fr. *café*) begins as the fruit of a small tree growing in tropical and subtropical regions throughout the world. The fruit, referred to as a cherry, is bright red with translucent flesh surrounding two flat-sided seeds. These seeds are the coffee beans. When ripe, the cherries are harvested by hand, then cleaned, fermented and hulled, leaving the green coffee beans. The beans are then roasted, blended, ground and brewed. Note that any coffee bean can be roasted to any degree of darkness, ground to any degree of fineness and brewed by any number of methods.

Only two species of coffee bean are routinely used: *arabica* and *robusta*. Arabica beans are the most important commercially and the ones from which the finest coffees are produced. Robusta beans do not produce as flavourful a drink as arabica. Nevertheless, robusta beans are becoming increasingly significant commercially, due in part to the fact that robusta trees are heartier and more fertile than arabica trees.

The conditions in which the beans are grown have almost as much effect on the final product as subsequent roasting, grinding and brewing. Because coffee takes much of its flavour and character from the soil, sunlight and air, the beans' origin is critical to the product's final quality. Each valley and mountain produces coffee distinct from all others, so geographic names are used to identify the beans regardless of whether they are from arabica or robusta trees. Thus, purveyors may offer beans known as Colombian, Chanchamayo (from Peru), Kilimanjaro (from Tanzania), Blue Mountain (from Jamaica), Java, Sumatra or Kona (from Hawaii), to name a few.

While many so-called gourmet coffees are made from a single type of bean, nearly all coffee sold in the United States and Canada is a blend of various qualities and types of bean.

Roasting Coffee

Roasting releases and enhances the flavours in coffee. It also darkens the beans and brings natural oils to the surface. Traditionally, almost everyone roasted their own coffee beans because all coffee beans were sold green. Today, however, roasting is left to experts who possess the necessary equipment.

It is important to recognize and understand some of the standard descriptions used for various types of roasting. No single international organization controls the naming of roasted coffee, however, so a coffee roaster may refer to products by any name. The following descriptions are based on the most common terminology.

Green coffee beans

City-roast beans

French-roast beans

✦ **City roast:** Also called American or brown roast, city roast is the most widely used coffee style in this country. City roast produces a beverage that may lack brilliance or be a bit flat, yet it is the roast most North Americans assume they prefer because it is the roast most often used in grocery store blends.

✦ **Brazilian roast:** Somewhat darker than a city roast, Brazilian roast should begin to show a hint of dark-roast flavour. The beans should show a trace of oil. In this context, the word Brazilian has no relationship to coffee grown in Brazil.

✦ **Viennese roast:** Also called medium-dark roast, Viennese roast generally falls somewhere between a standard city roast and French roast.

✦ **French roast:** French roast, also called New Orleans or dark roast, approaches espresso in flavour without sacrificing smoothness. The beans should be the colour of semi-sweet chocolate, with apparent oiliness on the surface.

✦ **Espresso roast:** Espresso roast, also called Italian roast, is the darkest of all. The beans are roasted until they are virtually burnt. The beans should be black with a shiny, oily surface.

Grinding Coffee

Unlike roasting, which is best left to the experts, the grinding of coffee beans is best left to the consumer or food service operation. Whole coffee beans stay fresh longer than ground coffee. Ground coffee kept in an air-tight container away from heat and light will stay fresh for three or four days. Whole beans will stay fresh for a few weeks and may be kept frozen for several months, as long as they are dry and protected from other flavours. Frozen coffee beans do not need to be thawed before grinding and brewing. Do not refrigerate coffee.

The fineness of the grind depends entirely on the type of coffee maker being used. The grind determines the length of time it takes to achieve the optimum (19%) extraction from the beans. The proper grind is simply whatever grind allows this to happen in the time it takes a specific coffee maker to complete its brewing cycle. Follow the directions for your coffee maker or ask your specialty coffee purveyor for guidance.

Brewing Coffee

Coffee is brewed by one of two methods: decoction or infusion. **Decoction** means boiling a substance until its flavour is removed. Boiling is the oldest method of making coffee, but is no longer used except in preparing extremely strong Turkish coffee. **Infusion** refers to the extraction of flavours at temperatures below boiling. Infusion techniques include steeping (mixing hot water with ground coffee), filtering (slowly pouring hot water over ground coffee held in a disposable cloth or paper filter) and dripping (pouring hot water over ground coffee and allowing the liquid to run through a strainer). Percolating is undesirable as the continuous boiling ruins the coffee's flavour.

The secrets to brewing a good cup of coffee are knowing the exact proportion of coffee to water as well as the length of time to maintain contact between the two. The best results are nearly always achieved by using 2 level tablespoons of ground coffee per 3/4 measuring cup (6 ounces, or 175 mL) of water. (A standard cup of coffee is three-quarters the size of a standard 8-ounce/250-mL measuring cup; 1 pound or about 450 g of coffee yields approximately 80 level tablespoons or enough for 40 "cups" of coffee.) An Approved Coffee Measure (ACM) was developed by the Coffee Brewing Institute to measure 2 level tablespoons accurately. ACM scoops are readily available and are often included with retail coffee packages.

Premeasured packages of ground coffee are generally used with commercial brewing equipment. These packages are available in a range of sizes for making single pots or large urns of coffee of varying strengths.

If stronger coffee is desired, use more coffee per cup of water, not a longer brewing time. For weaker coffee, prepare regular-strength coffee and dilute it with hot water. Never reuse coffee grounds.

Coffeepots and carafes should be cleaned well with hot water between each use; coffee makers should be disassembled and cleaned according to the manufacturer's directions. Unless properly cleaned, oils from coffee form an invisible film on the inside of the maker and pots, imparting a rancid or stale flavour to each subsequent batch.

Finally, coffee should be served as soon as it is brewed. Oxidation takes a toll on the aroma and flavour, which soon become flat and eventually bitter. Coffee may be held for a short time on the coffee maker's hot plate at temperatures of 185°F to 190°F (85°C to 88°C). A better holding method, however, is to immediately pour freshly brewed coffee into a thermal carafe. Never attempt to reheat cold coffee, as drastic temperature shifts destroy flavour.

Tasting Coffee

Coffee can be judged on four characteristics: aroma, acidity, body and flavour.

As a general rule, coffee will taste the way it smells. Some coffees, particularly Colombian, are more fragrant than others, however.

Acidity, also called wininess, refers to the tartness of the coffee. Acidity is a desirable characteristic that indicates snap, life or thinness. Kenyan and Guatemalan are examples of particularly acidic coffees.

Body refers to the feeling of heaviness or thickness that coffee provides on the palate. Sumatran is generally the heaviest, with Mexican and Venezuelan being the lightest.

♦♦♦
DON'T WRECK THE ENDING

Lots of time and thought are spent on selecting the wines to accompany the various savory courses of a meal, but too often at the sweet course the dessert wine finds itself up against its worst enemy: chocolate. A good sauterne, or a good quality dessert wine of almost any kind, works best with a fruit tart or with noncitrus sorbets accompanied by "dry cookie-like things," to use Richard Olney's phrase. Chocolate, whether in the form of pastry or confection, belongs with coffee, whose aromatic bitterness is a perfect foil for it.

RICHARD H. GRAFF
Chairman, CHALONE WINE GROUP

Flavour, of course, is the most ambiguous as well as the most important characteristic. Terms such as mellow, harsh, grassy or earthy are used to describe the rather subjective characteristic of flavour.

Serving Coffee

Coffee may be served unadorned, unsweetened and black (without milk or cream). The customer then adds the desired amount of sugar and milk. Other coffee beverages are made with specific additions and provide value-added menu alternatives. The most common ways of serving coffee are described here.

- ✦ **Espresso:** Espresso (Sp. *café expreso*) refers to a unique brewing method in which hot water is forced through finely ground and packed coffee under high pressure. Properly made, it will be strong, rich and smooth, not bitter or acidic. Espresso is usually made with beans that have been roasted very dark, but any type of bean may be used. A single serving of espresso uses about 1/4 ounce (7 g) of coffee to 1-1/2 ounces (45 mL) of water. Americans tend to prefer a larger portion, known as *espresso lungo*, made with 2 to 3 ounces (60–90 mL) of water.

- ✦ **Espresso machiatto:** Espresso "marked" with a tiny portion of steamed milk.

- ✦ **Cappuccino:** One-third espresso, one-third steamed milk and one-third foamed milk; the total serving is still rather small, about 4 to 6 ounces (120–180 mL).

- ✦ **Caffè latte:** One-third espresso, two-thirds steamed milk without foam; usually served in a tall glass.

- ✦ **Café au lait:** the French version of the Italian *caffe latte*, café au lait (or *café crème*) is made with strong coffee instead of espresso and hot, not steamed, milk. It is traditionally served in a handleless bowl.

- ✦ **Caffè mocha:** One-third espresso, two-thirds steamed milk, flavoured with chocolate syrup; usually topped with whipped cream and chocolate shavings or cocoa.

- ✦ **Flavoured coffees:** Dried, ground chicory root has long been added to coffee, particularly by the French who enjoy its bitter flavour. Toasted barley, dried figs and spices have also been used by various cultures for years. Coffees flavoured with vanilla, chocolate, liqueurs, spices and nuts have recently become popular in the Americas. These flavours are added to roasted coffee beans by tumbling the beans with special flavouring oils. The results are strongly aromatic flavours such as vanilla hazelnut, chocolate raspberry or maple walnut.

Steamed milk—*milk that is heated with steam generated by an espresso machine: it should be approximately 150°F to 170°F (66°C–77°C).*

Foamed milk—*milk that is heated and frothed with air and steam generated by an espresso machine: it will be slightly cooler than steamed milk.*

Decaffeinated Coffee

Caffeine is an alkaloid found in coffee beans (as well as in tea leaves and cocoa beans). It is a stimulant that can improve alertness or reduce fatigue. In excess, however, caffeine can cause some people to suffer palpitations or insomnia. Regular filtered coffee contains from 85 to 100 milligrams of caffeine per cup. Robusta beans contain more caffeine than the better-quality arabica beans. Decaffeinated coffee (with 97% or more of the caffeine removed) is designed to meet consumer desires for a caffeine-free product.

Tea

Tea (Fr. *thé*) is the name given to the leaves of *Camellia sinensis*, a tree or shrub that grows at high altitudes in damp tropical regions. Although tea comes from only one species of plant, there are three general types of tea—

✦✦✦

COFFEE'S OTHER USES

In addition to its use as a beverage, coffee is frequently an ingredient in mixed drinks such as Irish coffee (with whisky and cream) or café brulot (with orange, cloves and brandy). Coffee is also used in stews, sauces and pan gravy. It may be added to breads, such as rye and pumpernickel, cakes, custards, ice creams, dessert sauces and frostings. The flavour of coffee has a strong affinity for chocolate, nuts and rum.

A CUP OF COFFEE HISTORY

Some anthropologists suggest that coffee was initially consumed by central African warriors in the form of a paste made from mashed coffee beans and animal fat rolled into balls. Eaten before battle, the animal fat and bean protein provided nourishment; the caffeine provided a stimulant.

A hot coffee drink may first have been consumed sometime during the 9th century A.D. in Persia. Made by a decoction of ripe beans, the drink was probably very thick and acrid. Nevertheless, by the year 1000, the elite of the Arab world were regularly drinking a decoction of dried coffee beans. The beans were harvested in Abyssinia (Ethiopia) and brought to market by Egyptian merchants. Within a century or so, *kahwa* became immensely popular with members of all strata of Arab society. Coffeehouses

opened throughout the Levant, catering to customers who sipped the thick, brown brew while discussing affairs of heart and state.

Although European travellers to the Ottoman Empire had tasted coffee, and a few Arab or Turkish merchants living in Marseilles offered their guests a chance to sample the rare drink, coffee did not become popular in Europe until the 17th century. Its popularity is due in great part to Suleiman Aga, the Grand Panjandrum of the Ottoman Empire. In 1669 he arrived at the court of King Louis XIV of France as ambassador, bringing with him many exotic treasures, including *caffe*. Offered at his opulent parties, *caffe* soon became the drink of choice for the French aristocracy.

Coffee became popular in Vienna as a fortune of war. By 1683 the Turks were at the gates

of Vienna. A decisive battle was fought and the Turks fled, leaving behind stores of gold, equipment, supplies and a barely known provision—green coffee beans. One of the victorious leaders, Franz George Kolschitzky, recognized the treasure, took it as his own and soon opened the first coffeehouse in Vienna, The Blue Bottle.

Despite its growing popularity, coffee was exorbitantly expensive, in part, the result of the Sultan's monopoly on coffee beans. His agents, principally in Marseilles, controlled the sale of beans. But the monopoly was not to survive. By the end of the 17th century, the Dutch had stolen coffee plants from Arabia and began cultivating them in Java. By the early 18th century, the French had transported seedlings to the West Indies; from there coffee plantations spread throughout the New World.

A CUP OF TEA HISTORY

Some believe that the Chinese Emperor Shen Nung discovered tea drinking in 2737 B.C. Legend holds that the Emperor was boiling his drinking water beneath a tree when some leaves fell into the pot. Enchanted with the drink, he began to cultivate the plant. Whether myth or truth, it is known that a hot drink made from powdered dried tea leaves whipped into hot water was regularly consumed in China sometime after the 4th century. Later, decoctions of tea leaves (as well as rice, spices and nuts) became popular. But it was not until the Ming dynasty (A.D. 1368–1644) that infusions of tea leaves became commonplace.

By the 9th century, tea drinking had spread to Japan. In both Chinese and Japanese cultures, tea drinking developed into a ritual. For the Chinese, a cup of tea became the mirror of the soul. For the Japanese, it was the drink of immortality.

Tea was first transported from China to Europe by Dutch merchants during the early 1600s. By mid-century, it was introduced into England. In 1669 the East India Company was granted a charter by Queen Elizabeth I to import tea, a monopoly it held until 1833. To ensure a steady supply, the English surreptitiously procured plants from China and started plantations throughout the Indian subcontinent, as did the Dutch.

Tea drinking became fashionable in England, at least in court circles, through Charles II (raised in exile at The Hague in Holland, he reigned from 1660 until 1685) and his Portuguese wife, Catherine of Braganza. Queen Anne of England (reigned 1702–1714) introduced several concepts that eventually became part of the English tea custom. For example, she substituted tea for ale at breakfast

and began using large silver pots instead of tiny china pots.

The social custom of afternoon tea began in the late 1700s, thanks to Anna, Duchess of Bedford. Historians attribute to her the late afternoon ritual of snacking on sandwiches and pastries accompanied by tea. She began the practice in order to quell her hunger pangs between breakfast and dinner (which was typically served at 9:30 or 10:00 P.M.).

Eventually two distinct types of teatime evolved. Low tea was aristocratic in origin and consisted of a snack of pastries and sandwiches, with tea, served in the late afternoon as a prelude to the evening meal. High tea was bourgeois in origin, consisting of leftovers from the typically large middle-class lunch, such as cold meats, bread and cheeses. High tea became a substitute for the evening meal.

black, green and oolong. The differences among the three are the result of the manner in which the leaves are treated after picking.

Black tea is amber-brown and strongly flavoured. Its colour and flavour result from fermenting the leaves. Black tea leaves are named or graded by leaf size. Because larger leaves brew more slowly than smaller ones, teas are sorted by leaf size for efficient brewing. *Souchong* denotes large leaves, *pekoe* denotes medium-sized leaves and *orange pekoe* denotes the smallest whole leaves. (Note that *orange pekoe* does not refer to any type of orange flavour.) Broken tea, graded as either broken orange pekoe or broken pekoe, is

Fruit tea

Gunpowder *Darjeeling*

◆◆◆

TEA FLAVOURS

The following descriptions apply to some of the teas frequently available through wholesalers or gourmet suppliers. Taste several different ones to find the best for your purposes. Remember that the same tea from different blenders or distributors may taste different, and that different flavours will be more or less appropriate for different times of the day. You may wish to offer your patrons a selection of flavours.

Assam—rich black tea with a reddish colour from Northern India. It is valued by connoisseurs, especially for breakfast.

Ceylon—a full-flavoured black tea with a golden colour and delicate fragrance. Ideal for serving iced, it does not become cloudy when cold.

Darjeeling—the champagne of teas, it is a full-bodied, black tea with muscat flavour from the foothills of the Himalayas.

Earl Grey—a blend of black teas, usually including Darjeeling, flavoured with oil of bergamot. A popular choice for afternoon tea.

English Breakfast—English blend of Indian and Sri Lankan black teas; it is full-bodied and robust, with a rich colour.

Gunpowder—Green Chinese tea with a tightly curled leaf and grey-green colour. It has a pungent flavour and a light straw colour. It is often served after the evening meal.

Keemum—a mellow black Chinese tea with a strong aroma. It is less astringent than other teas and is delicious iced.

Lapsang Souchong—a large-leafed (souchong) tea from the Lapsang district of China. It has a distinctive tarry, smoky flavour and aroma, appropriate for afternoon tea or dinner.

Formosa Oolong—a unique and expensive large-leafed oolong tea with the flavour of ripe peaches. It is appropriate for breakfast or afternoon tea.

smaller, resulting in a darker, stronger brew. Broken tea is most often used in tea bags. These grades apply to both Chinese and Indian black teas.

Green tea is yellowish-green in colour with a bitter flavour. Leaves used for green tea are not fermented. Chinese green tea leaves are also graded according to leaf size and age. The finest green tea is Gunpowder, followed by Imperial and Hyson.

Oolong tea is partially fermented to combine the characteristics of black and green teas. Oolong is popular in China and Japan, often flavoured with jasmine flowers. Oolong tea leaves are also graded by size and age.

As with coffee, tea takes much of its flavour from the geographic conditions in which it is grown. Teas are named for their place of origin, for example, Darjeeling, Ceylon (now Sri Lanka) or Assam. Many popular and commercially available teas are actually blends of leaves from various sources. Blended and unblended teas may also be flavoured with oils, dried fruit, spices, flowers or herbs.

Brewing Tea

Tea may be brewed by the cup or the pot. In either case, it is important to use the following procedure.

1. Always begin with clean equipment and freshly drawn cold water. Water that has been sitting in a kettle or hot water tank contains less air and will taste flat or stale.

2. Warm the teapot by rinsing it out with hot water. This begins to relax the tea leaves and ensures that the water will stay hot when it comes in contact with the tea.

3. Place one teaspoon (5 mL) of loose tea or one tea bag per 3/4 cup (6 oz./180 mL) of water capacity in the warmed teapot.

4. As soon as the water comes to a boil, pour the appropriate amount over the tea. Do not allow the water to continue boiling as this removes the oxygen, leaving a flat taste. The water should be at a full boil when it comes in contact with the tea so that the tea leaves will uncurl and release their flavour.

5. Replace the lid of the teapot and allow the tea to infuse for three to five minutes. Time the brew. Colour is not a reliable indication of brewing time: Tea leaves release colour before flavour and different types of tea will be different colours when properly brewed.

6. Remove the tea bags or loose tea from the water when brewing is complete. This can be accomplished easily if the teapot is fitted with a removable leaf basket or if a tea bag or a perforated tea ball is used. Otherwise, decant the tea through a strainer into a second warmed teapot.

7. Serve immediately, accompanied with sugar, lemon, milk (not cream) and honey as desired. Dilute the tea with hot water if necessary.

8. Do not reuse tea leaves. One pound (450 g) of tea yields 200 cups, making it the most inexpensive beverage after tap water.

For iced tea, prepare regular brewed tea using 50% more tea. Then pour into a pitcher or glass filled with ice. The stronger brew will hold its flavour better as the ice melts. Sweeten with simple syrup as desired.

Serving Tea

Black and oolong tea may be served hot or cold, but green tea is best served hot. Black tea is served with milk or lemon and sugar; green and oolong tea are most often served plain. Adding milk to hot tea is a British preference (not normally followed in Europe or Asia) which reduces the astringency of the tea. Iced tea, an American invention, may be served plain or sweetened, and is often garnished with lemon, orange or fresh mint.

Tisanes—*herbal infusions that do not contain any "real" tea; examples include chamomile, ginseng and lemon balm. Tisanes are prepared in the same way as tea infusions.*

CONCLUSION

Kitchen staples include fresh and dried herbs, spices, salt, nuts, oils, vinegars, condiments, coffees and teas. You must be able to recognize, purchase, store and use many of these staples.

The only way to determine which brand or type of staple is best for your particular needs is to taste, smell, sample and use a variety of those available. Cost, convenience and storage factors must also be considered. By maintaining a supply of seasonings, flavourings, condiments and other staples you will be able to create new dishes or enhance standard ones at a moment's notice.

QUESTIONS FOR DISCUSSION

1. What is a staple? Does every kitchen keep the same staples on hand? Explain your answer.
2. What are the differences between a herb and a spice? Give an example of a plant that is used as both a herb and a spice.
3. If a recipe calls for a fresh herb and you have only the dried herb, what do you do? Explain your answer.
4. What is the difference between a sachet and a bouquet garni? Identify the ingredients in a standard sachet and a standard bouquet garni.
5. Discuss the importance of using proper preparation and service techniques for coffee and tea. How can these beverages be used to improve or enhance your food service operation?

WEBLINKS

Culinary Herb FAQ: Information about growing and preserving herbs and using them in cooking
sunsite.unc.edu/herbmed/culiherb.html

Flavouring the World: The FAQ about Spices
csgwww.uwaterloo.ca/~dmg/faqs/spices/node8.html

The Curry House: International Curry Recipes and Other Information
www.dwsmith.demon.co.uk/

Frequently Asked Questions about Coffee and Caffeine
daisy.uwaterloo.ca/~alopez-o/caffaq.html

The U.K. Tea Council Online
www.teacouncil.co.uk/

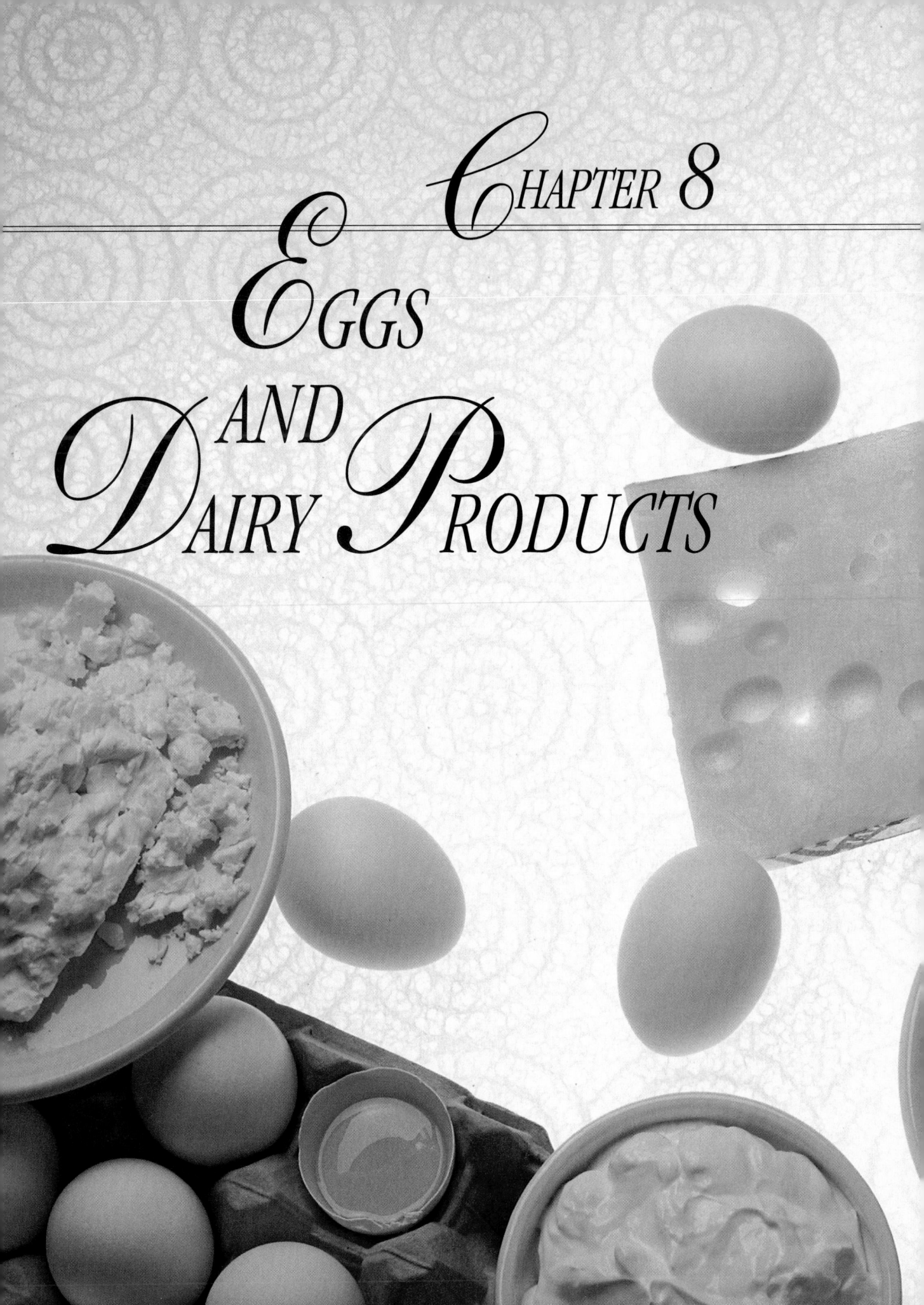

CHAPTER 8

EGGS AND DAIRY PRODUCTS

ggs and milk are unique in that they, along with seeds, are the only foods that are truly designed to support life: Eggs support chick embryos; milk supports calves. Thus they are among the most nutritious of foods. Eggs as well as milk and milk-based products (known collectively as dairy products) are also extremely versatile. They are used throughout the kitchen, either served alone or as ingredients in everything from soups and sauces to breads and pastries. High quality and freshness are critical for their proper use. Learn to select the finest products, whether they are eggs, whole milk, butter or Brie, and handle them with care.

EGGS

Nature designed eggs as the food source for developing chicks. Eggs, particularly chicken eggs, are also an excellent food for humans because of their high protein content, low cost and ready availability. Quail eggs are also used in food service operations. Duck and goose eggs are too fatty to be useful, however.

Eggs can be cooked in a variety of ways, some of which are described in Chapter 32, Breakfast and Brunch. Eggs are also incorporated into other dishes to provide texture, structure, flavour, moisture and nutrition.

Composition

The primary parts of an egg are the shell, yolk and albumen. See Figure 8.1.

The **shell**, composed of calcium carbonate, is the outermost covering of the egg. It prevents microbes from entering and moisture from escaping, and protects the egg during handling and transport. Shell colour is determined by the breed of the hen; for chickens it can range from bright white to brown. Shell colour has no effect on quality, flavour or nutrition.

The **yolk** is the yellow portion of the egg. It constitutes just over one-third of the egg and contains three-fourths of the calories, most of the minerals and

FIGURE 8.1 *An Egg*

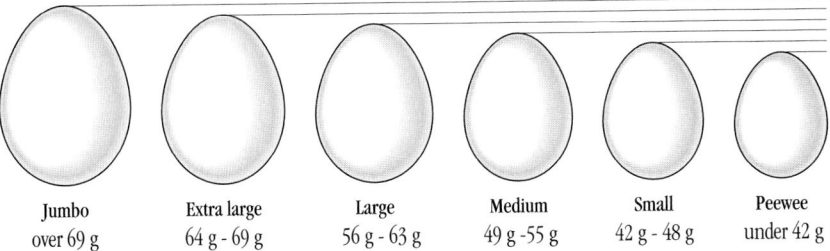

Jumbo	Extra large	Large	Medium	Small	Peewee
over 69 g	64 g - 69 g	56 g - 63 g	49 g -55 g	42 g - 48 g	under 42 g

FIGURE 8.2 *Egg Sizes*

vitamins and all of the fat. The yolk also contains lecithin, the compound responsible for emulsification in products such as hollandaise sauce and mayonnaise. Egg yolk solidifies (coagulates) at temperatures between 149°F and 158°F (65°–70°C). Although the colour of a yolk may vary depending on the hen's feed, colour does not affect quality or nutritional content.

The **albumen** is the clear portion of the egg and is often referred to as the **egg white**. It constitutes about two-thirds of the egg and contains more than half of the protein and riboflavin. Egg white coagulates, becoming firm and opaque, at temperatures between 144°F and 149°F (62–65°C).

An often misunderstood portion of the egg is the **chalazae cords**. These thick, twisted strands of egg white anchor the yolk in place. They are neither imperfections nor embryos. The more prominent the chalazae, the fresher the egg. Chalazae do not interfere with cooking or with whipping egg whites.

Eggs are sold in jumbo, extra large, large, medium, small and peewee sizes, as determined by weight per dozen. See Figure 8.2. Food service operations generally use large eggs.

Grading

Eggs are graded by the Canadian Food Inspection Agency (CFIA) (Egg and Egg Products Division). The grade A, B or C is given an egg based upon interior and exterior quality, not size. The qualities for each grade are described in Table 8.1. Grade has no effect on nutritional values.

Storage

Egg quality is quickly diminished by improper handling. Eggs should be stored at temperatures below 40°F (4°C) and at a relative humidity of 70–80%.

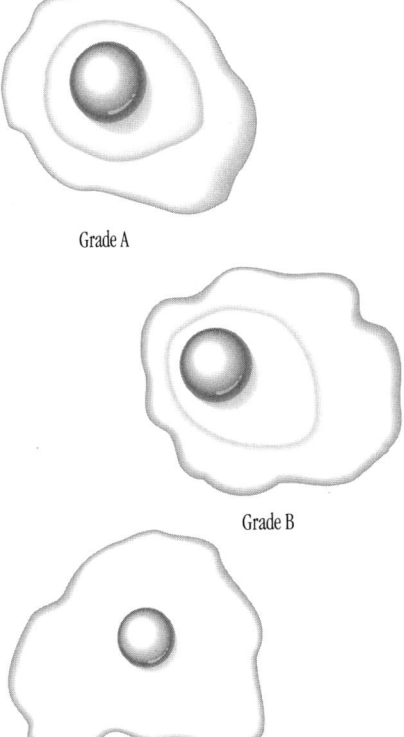

Grade A

Grade B

Grade C

TABLE 8.1	EGG GRADES		
	Grade A	Grade B	Grade C
Albumen	Firm	Watery	Thin and watery
Yolk	Round, well centred	Slightly flattened	Loose
Shell	Clean, no cracks, normal shape	No cracks, but rough texture	May be cracked
Use	Sold at retail markets for household use	Used for commercial baking or further processing	Not sold to consumers; sold to commercial processors for further processing

Eggs will age more during one day at room temperature than they will during one week under proper refrigeration. As eggs age, the white becomes thinner and the yolk becomes flatter. While this will change the appearance of poached or fried eggs, age has little effect on nutrition or behaviour during cooking procedures. Older eggs, however, should be used for hard-boiling, as the shells are easier to remove than those of fresh eggs.

Cartons of fresh, uncooked eggs will keep for at least four to five weeks beyond the pack date if properly refrigerated. Hard-boiled eggs left in their shells and refrigerated should be used within one week.

Store eggs away from strongly flavoured foods to reduce odour absorption. Rotate egg stock to maintain freshness. Do not use dirty, cracked or broken eggs as they may contain bacteria or other contaminants. Frozen eggs should be thawed in the refrigerator and used only in dishes that will be thoroughly cooked, such as baked products.

Sanitation

Eggs are a potentially hazardous food. Rich in protein, they are an excellent breeding ground for bacteria. Salmonella is of particular concern with eggs and egg products because this bacteria is commonly found in a chicken's intestinal tract. Although shells are cleaned at packing houses, some bacteria may remain. Therefore, to prevent contamination, it is best to avoid mixing a shell with the liquid egg.

Inadequately cooking or improperly storing eggs may lead to food-borne illnesses. **Pasteurization** is achieved when the whole egg stays at a temperature of 140°F (60°C) for 3.5 minutes. Hold egg dishes below 40°F (4°C) or above 145°F (63°C). Never leave an egg dish at room temperature for more than one hour, including preparation and service time. Never reuse a container after it has held raw eggs without thoroughly cleaning and sanitizing it.

Pasteurization—*the process of heating a liquid to a prescribed temperature for a specific period of time in order to destroy pathogenic bacteria.*

Whipped Egg Whites

Egg whites are often whipped into a foam that is then incorporated into cakes, custards, souffles, pancakes or other products. The air beaten into the egg foam gives products lightness and assists with leavening. Egg whites are usually whipped to a soft peak or stiff stage.

BASIC PROCEDURE FOR WHIPPING EGG WHITES

1. Use fresh egg whites that are completely free of egg yolk or other impurities. Warm the egg whites to room temperature before whipping; this causes a better foam to form.
2. Use a clean bowl and whisk. Even a tiny amount of fat can prevent the egg whites from foaming properly.
3. Whip the whites on medium speed until very foamy, then add salt or cream of tartar as directed.
4. Continue whipping until soft peaks form, then gradually add granulated sugar (or hot syrup, if preparing meringues) as directed.
5. Whip until stiff peaks form. Properly whipped egg whites should be moist and shiny; over-whipping will make the egg whites appear dry and spongy or curdled.
6. Use the whipped egg whites immediately. If liquid begins to separate from the whipped egg whites discard them; they cannot be rewhipped successfully.

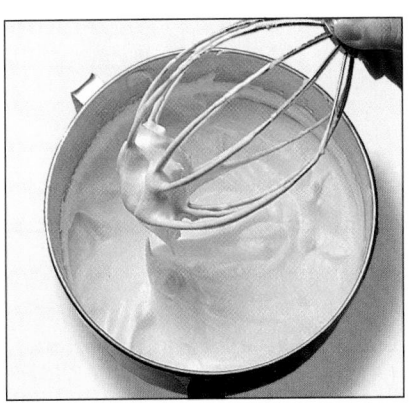

Egg whites whipped to soft peaks.   Egg whites whipped to stiff peaks.   Spongy, over-whipped egg whites.

Egg Products

Food service operations often want the convenience of buying eggs out of the shell in the exact form needed: whole eggs, yolks only or whites only. These processed items are called *egg products* and are subject to strict pasteurization standards and CFIA inspections. Egg products can be frozen, refrigerated or dried. Precooked, preportioned and blended egg products are also available.

Egg Substitutes

Concerns about the cholesterol content of eggs have increased the popularity of egg substitutes. There are two general types of substitute. The first is a complete substitute made from soy or milk proteins. It should not be used in recipes where eggs are required for thickening. The second substitute contains real albumen, but the egg yolk has been replaced with vegetable or milk products. Egg substitutes have a different flavour than real eggs, but may be useful for persons on a restricted diet.

Nutrition

Eggs contain vitamins A, D, E, K and the B-complex vitamins. They are rich in minerals but also in cholesterol. The nutritional values of an egg is listed in Table 8.2.

TABLE 8.2	NUTRITIONAL VALUES OF EGGS					
	Energy	Protein	Total Fat	Saturated Fat	Carbohydrates	Cholesterol
One large egg contains	75 calories	6 g	5 g	1.5 g	0.5 g	215 mg

Canadian Egg Marketing Agency

DAIRY PRODUCTS

Dairy products include cow's milk and foods produced from cow's milk such as butter, yogurt, sour cream and cheese. The milk of other mammals, namely goats, sheep and buffaloes, is also made into cheeses that are used in commercial food service operations. Regulations affecting dairy products are both federal and provincial, although they are being standardized under the Canadian Food Inspection Agency.

Milk

Milk is not only a popular beverage, it is also used in the preparation of many dishes. It provides texture, flavour, colour and nutritional value for cooked or baked items. Indeed, milk is considered one of the most nutritious foods available, providing proteins, vitamins and minerals (particularly calcium). But milk is also highly perishable and an excellent bacterial breeding ground. Care must be exercised in the handling and storage of milk and other dairy products.

Whole milk—that is, milk as it comes from the cow—is composed primarily of water (about 88%). It contains not less than 3.25% milkfat and 8.1% other milk solids (proteins, milk sugar [lactose] and minerals).

Fresh whole milk is not available raw, but must be processed as described below.

Processing Techniques

Pasteurization

By law, all milk must be pasteurized prior to retail sale. Pasteurization is the process of heating milk to a sufficiently high temperature for a sufficient length of time to destroy pathogenic bacteria. This typically requires holding milk at a temperature of 161°F (72°C) for 16 seconds. Pasteurization also destroys enzymes that cause spoilage thus increasing shelf life. Milk's nutritional value is not significantly affected by pasteurization.

Ultra-Pasteurization

Ultra-pasteurization is a process in which milk is heated to a very high temperature (275°F/135°C) for a very short time (2 to 4 seconds) in order to destroy virtually all bacteria. Ultra-pasteurization is most often used with whipping cream and individual creamers. Although the process may reduce cream's whipping properties, it extends its shelf life dramatically.

Ultra-High-Temperature Processing

Ultra-high-temperature processing (UHT) is a form of ultra-pasteurization in which milk is held at a temperature of 280°–300°F (138°–150°C) for 2 to 6 seconds. It is then packed in sterile containers under sterile conditions and aseptically sealed to prevent bacteria from entering the container. Unopened UHT milk can be stored without refrigeration for at least three months. Although UHT milk can be stored unrefrigerated, it should be chilled before serving and stored like fresh milk once opened. UHT processing may give milk a slightly cooked taste but it has no significant effect on milk's nutritional value. It has long been available in Europe and Canada.

Homogenization

Homogenization is a process in which the fat globules in whole milk are reduced in size and permanently dispersed throughout the liquid. This prevents the fat from clumping together and rising to the surface as a layer of cream. Although homogenization is not required, milk sold commercially is generally homogenized because it ensures a uniform consistency, a whiter colour and a richer taste.

Certification

Certification is a method of controlling the quality of milk by controlling the condition of the animals from which milk is obtained. Certification is not a true processing technique; rather it requires frequent veterinary examinations of the cows and health department inspections of the dairy farm, the equipment and the employees who handle milk. Pasteurization has replaced the need for certification, but milk from certified herds is still available in a few areas.

Milkfat Removal

Whole milk can also be processed in a centrifuge to remove all or a portion of the milkfat, resulting in **lowfat milk** or partly **skim milk**.

Partly skim milk is whole milk from which sufficient milkfat has been removed to produce a liquid with 2% to 3.25% milkfat. (All lowfat milks must still contain approximately 8.25% milk solids.) Vitamin A is added to lowfat milk to replace that removed along with the milkfat. It will be labelled with the fat content.

Skim milk, also referred to as **lowfat milk**, has had as much milkfat removed as possible. The fat content must be not more than 1%. Skim milk must also contain at least 8% milk solids and be fortified with vitamin A.

Storage

Fluid milk should be kept refrigerated at or below 40°F (4°C). Its shelf life is reduced by half for every five-degree rise in temperature above 40°F (4°C). Keep milk containers closed to prevent absorption of odours and flavours. Freezing is not recommended.

Concentrated Milks

Concentrated or condensed milk products are produced by using a vacuum to remove all or part of the water from whole milk. The resulting products have a high concentration of milkfat and milk solids and an extended shelf life.

Evaporated milk is produced by removing approximately 60% of the water from whole, homogenized milk. Evaporated milk must contain at least 7.5% milkfat and 25% milk solids. Vitamins may be added as required. The concentrated liquid is canned and heat-sterilized. This results in a cooked flavour and darker colour. Evaporated skim milk has a milkfat content of not more than .3% and less than 17% milk solids other than fat. A can of evaporated milk requires no refrigeration until opened, although the can should be stored in a cool place. Evaporated milk can be reconstituted with an equal amount of water and used like whole milk for cooking or drinking.

Sweetened condensed milk is similar to evaporated milk in that 60% of the water has been removed. But unlike evaporated milk, sweetened condensed milk contains sweeteners and a minimum of 8% milkfat. Sweetened condensed milk is also canned; the canning process darkens the colour and adds a caramel flavour. Sweetened condensed milk cannot be substituted for whole milk or evaporated milk because of its sugar content. Its distinctive flavour is most often found in desserts and confections.

Dry milk powder is made by removing virtually all of the moisture from pasteurized milk. It is a graded product. The moisture content will vary depending on the process used. Milk powder graded as Canada #1 has less than 4% moisture and 1.2% milkfat; Canada #2 has less than 1.29% milkfat and 5% moisture by weight. Dry whole milk contains a minimum of 26% milkfat.

Nonfat milk powder is made from skim milk and must contain less than 1.2% milkfat by weight. Both types of dry milk are usually fortified with vitamins A and D.

The lack of moisture prevents the growth of microorganisms and allows dry whole and nonfat milk powders to be stored for extended periods without refrigeration. However, because of its high milkfat content, dried whole milk can turn rancid if not stored in a cool place. Either type of dry milk can be reconstituted with water and used like fresh milk. Milk powder may also be added to foods directly, with additional liquid included in the recipe. This procedure is typical in bread making and does not alter the function of the milk or the flavour in the finished product.

Cream

Cream is a rich, liquid milk product containing at least 18% milkfat. It must be pasteurized or ultra-pasteurized and may be homogenized. Cream has a slight yellow or ivory colour and is more viscous than milk. It is used throughout the kitchen to give flavour and body to sauces, soups and desserts. Whipping cream, containing not less than 38% milkfat, can be whipped into a stiff foam and used in pastries and desserts. Cream is marketed in several forms with different fat contents, as described below.

Table cream is a mixture of whole milk and cream containing not less than 18% milkfat. It is often served with cereal or coffee, but does not contain enough fat to whip into a foam.

Half-and-half, light cream or **coffee cream** are all products with more than 10% but less than 18% milkfat. These products are often used in baked goods or soups as well as with coffee, fruit and cereal.

Whipping cream usually contains 35% milkfat. It is generally used for thickening and enriching sauces and making ice cream. It can be whipped into a foam and used as a dessert topping or folded into custards or mousses to add flavour and lightness.

Storage

Ultra-pasteurized cream will keep for six to eight weeks if refrigerated. Unwhipped cream should not be frozen. Whipped, sweetened cream can be frozen, tightly covered, for up to three months, then slowly thawed in the refrigerator. Keep cream away from strong odours and bright lights, as they can adversely affect its flavour.

Cultured Dairy Products

Cultured dairy products such as yogurt, buttermilk and sour cream are produced by adding specific bacterial cultures to fluid dairy products. The bacteria convert the milk sugar lactose into lactic acid, giving these products their body and tangy, unique flavours. The acid content also retards the growth of undesirable microorganisms; thus cultured products have been used for centuries to preserve milk.

Buttermilk originally referred to the liquid remaining after cream was churned into butter. Today buttermilk is produced by adding a culture (*Streptococcus lactis*) to fresh, pasteurized skim or lowfat milk. This results in a tart milk with a thick texture. Buttermilk is most often used as a beverage or in baked goods.

Sour cream is produced by adding the same culture to pasteurized, homogenized light cream. The resulting product is a white, tangy gel used as a condiment or to give baked goods a distinctive flavour. Sour cream must have the milkfat content clearly labelled.

Crème fraîche is a cultured cream popular in French cuisine. Although thinner and richer than sour cream, it has a similar tart, tangy flavour. It is used extensively in soups and sauces, especially with poultry, rabbit and lamb dishes. It is easily prepared from the following recipe.

◆◆◆

RECIPE 8.1

CRÈME FRAÎCHE

Yield: 2 cups (500 mL)

Whipping cream	16 oz.	500 mL
Buttermilk, with active cultures	1 oz.	30 mL

1. Heat the cream (preferably not ultra-pasteurized) to about 100°F (43°C).

2. Remove the cream from the heat and stir in the buttermilk.

3. Allow the mixture to stand in a warm place, loosely covered, until it thickens, approximately 12 to 36 hours.

4. Chill thoroughly before using. Crème fraîche will keep for up to 10 days in the refrigerator.

Approximate values per 1 oz. (30 g) serving:

Calories	90
Total fat	10 g
Saturated fat	6 g
Cholesterol	35 mg
Sodium	10 mg
Total carbohydrates	1 g
Protein	1 g
Vitamin A	10%
Claims—very low sodium	

Yogurt is a thick, tart, custardlike product made from milk (either whole, lowfat or nonfat) cultured with *Lactobacillus bulgaricus* and *Streptococcus thermophilus*. Though touted as a health or diet food, yogurt contains the same amount of milkfat as the milk from which it is made. Yogurt may also contain a variety of sweeteners, flavourings and fruits. Yogurt is generally eaten as is, but may be used in baked products, salad dressings and frozen desserts. It is used in many Middle Eastern cuisines.

Storage

Cultured products should be kept refrigerated at 40°F (4°C) or below. Under proper conditions sour cream will last up to four weeks, yogurt up to three weeks and buttermilk up to two weeks. Freezing is not recommended for these products, but dishes prepared with cultured products generally can be frozen.

Butter

Butter is a fatty substance produced by agitating or churning cream. Its flavour is unequalled in sauces, breads and pastries. Butter contains at least 80% milkfat, not more than 20% moisture. It may or may not contain added salt. Butter is firm when chilled and soft at room temperature. It melts into a liquid at approximately 98°F (38°C) and reaches the smoke point at 260°F (127°C).

Government grading of dairy products, including butter, is mandatory as described in the Canada Agricultural Products Act — Dairy Products Regulations. The three grades of dairy products have grade names of **Canada 1**, **Canada 2** and **Canada 3**. The Canada grade label on the butter package assures the consumer that the butter meets federal standards for the grade indicated.

◆ Canada 1: Butter of superior quality, with fresh, sweet flavour and aroma, a smooth creamy texture and good spreadability.

◆ Canada 2: Butter of very good quality, with pleasing flavour and fairly smooth texture.

◆ Canada 3: A processing grade used only for dairy products packed in bulk.

Salted butter is butter with up to 2.5% salt added. This not only changes the butter's flavour, it also extends its keeping qualities. When using salted butter in cooking or baking, the salt content must be considered in the total recipe.

Whipped butter is made by incorporating air into the butter. This increases its volume and spreadability, but also increases the speed with which the butter will become rancid. Because of the change in density, whipped butter should not be substituted in recipes calling for regular butter.

Storage

Butter should be well wrapped and stored at temperatures between 32°F and 35°F (0°–2°C). Unsalted butter is best kept frozen until needed. If well wrapped, frozen butter will keep for up to 9 months at a temperature of 0°F (–18°C).

Clarified Butter

Unsalted whole butter is approximately 80% fat. Although whole butter can be used for cooking or sauce making, sometimes a more stable and consistent product will be achieved by using butter that has had the water and milk solids removed by a process called clarification. It can be purchased commercially.

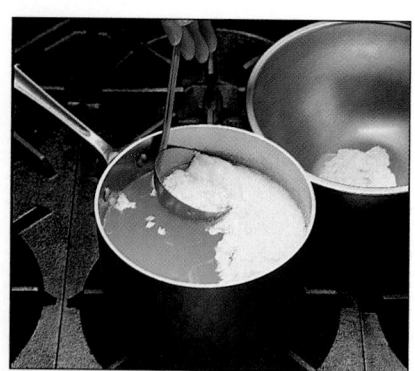

Skimming milk solids from the surface of melted butter.

BASIC PROCEDURE FOR CLARIFYING BUTTER

1. Slowly warm the butter in a saucepan over low heat without boiling or agitation. As the butter melts, the milk solids rise to the top as a foam and the water sinks to the bottom.

2. When the butter is completely melted, skim the milk solids from the top. Simmer until the oil clears.

3. When all the milk solids have been removed, ladle the butterfat into a clean saucepan, being careful to leave the water in the bottom of the pan.

4. The clarified butter is now ready to use. One pound (454 g) of whole butter will yield approximately 12 ounces (340 g) of clarified butter (a yield of 75%).

Clarified butter will keep for extended periods in either the freezer or refrigerator.

Margarine

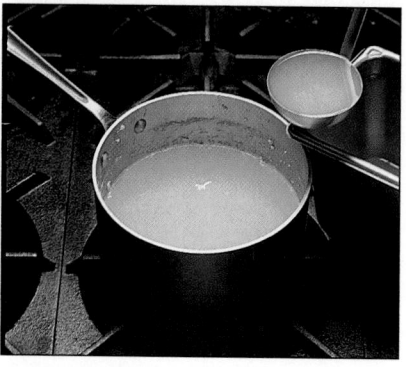

Ladling the butterfat into a clean pan.

Margarine is not a dairy product but is included in this section because it is so frequently substituted for butter in cooking, baking and table service. Margarine is manufactured from animal or vegetable fats or a combination of such fats. Flavourings, colourings, emulsifiers, preservatives and vitamins are added, and the mixture is firmed or solidified by exposure to hydrogen gas at very high temperatures, a process known as hydrogenation. Generally, the firmer the margarine the greater the degree of hydrogenation and the longer its shelf life. Like butter, margarine is approximately 80% fat and 20% moisture. But even the finest margarine cannot match the flavour of butter.

Margarine packaged in tubs is softer and more spreadable than solid products and generally contains more water and air. Indeed, diet margarine is approxi-

◆◆◆

MARGARINE:
FROM LABORATORY BENCH TO DINNER TABLE

Margarine was invented by a French chemist in 1869 after Napoleon III offered a prize for the development of a synthetic edible fat. Originally produced from animal fat and milk, margarine is now made almost exclusively from vegetable fats.

In *On Food and Cooking, The Science and Lore of the Kitchen*, Harold McGee recounts the history of margarine. He explains that margarine caught on quickly in Europe and America, with large-scale production underway by 1880. But the American dairy industry and the U.S. government put up fierce resistance. First, margarine was defined as a harmful drug and its sale restricted. Then it was heavily taxed; stores had to be licensed to sell it and, like alcohol and tobacco, it was bootlegged. The U.S. government refused to purchase it for use by the armed forces. And, in an attempt to hold it to its true colours, some states did not allow margarine to be dyed yellow (animal fats and vegetable oils are much paler than butter); the dye was sold separately and mixed in by the consumer. World War II, which brought butter rationing, probably did the most to establish margarine's respectability. But it was not until 1967 that yellow margarine could be sold in Wisconsin.

Today North Americans consume nearly three times as much margarine as butter. Both price and the concern about heart disease are responsible for this differential.

mately 50% water. Because of their decreased density, these soft products should not be substituted for regular butter or margarine in cooking or baking.

Specially formulated and blended margarine is available for commercial use in making puff pastry, croissant doughs, frostings and the like.

Nutrition

Dairy products are naturally high in vitamins, minerals and protein. Often liquid products such as milk are fortified with additional vitamins and minerals. Their fat content varies depending upon the amount of milkfat left after processing. Specific nutritional values for selected dairy products are found in Table 8.3.

TABLE 8.3 NUTRITIONAL VALUES OF DAIRY PRODUCTS

Per 250-mL Serving	Energy (Kcal)	Protein (g)	Carbohydrates (g)	Fat (g)	Cholesterol (mg)	Sodium (mg)
Whole milk (3.3% butterfat)	159	8	12	9	35	126
Skim milk	90	9	13	tr	5	133
Buttermilk	105	9	12	2	9	272
Heavy whipping cream (35% butterfat)	822	5	7	88	322	90
Half-and-half (12% butterfat)	344	8	11	31	99	105
Sour cream (14% butterfat)	385	8	11	35	99	109

Nutritional Value of Some Common Foods (Revised 1988)

Natural Cheeses

Cheese (Fr. *fromage;* It. *fromaggio*) is one of the oldest and most widely used foods known. It is served alone or as a principal ingredient in or an accompaniment to countless dishes. Cheese is commonly used in commercial kitchens, appearing in everything from breakfast to snacks to desserts.

Literally hundreds of natural cheeses are produced worldwide. Although their shapes, ages and flavours vary according to local preferences and traditions, all natural cheeses are produced in the same basic fashion as has been used for centuries. Each starts with a mammal's milk; cows, goats and sheep are the most commonly used. The milk proteins (known as *casein*) are coagulated with the addition of an enzyme, usually rennet, which is found in calves' stomachs. As the milk coagulates, it separates into solid curds and liquid whey. After draining off the whey, either the curds are made into fresh cheese, such as ricotta or cottage cheese, or the curds are further processed by cutting, kneading and cooking. The resulting substance, known as "green cheese," is packed into molds to drain. Salt or special bacteria may be added to the molded cheeses, which are then allowed to age or ripen under controlled conditions to develop the desired texture, colour and flavour.

Cheeses are a product of their environment, which is why most fine cheeses cannot be reproduced outside their native locale. The breed and feed of the milk animal, the wild spores and molds in the air and even the wind currents in a storage area can affect the manner in which a cheese develops. (Roquefort, for example, develops its distinctive flavour from aging in particular caves filled with crosscurrents of cool, moist air.) Canada has a thriving cheese industry and produces world-class products. Many are the equal in quality to the originals from other countries. Some fine cheeses are still produced from unpasteurized milk.

Some cheeses develop a natural rind or surface because of the application of bacteria (bloomy rind) or by repeated washing with brine (washed rind). Most natural rinds may be eaten if desired. Other cheeses are coated with an inedible wax rind to prevent moisture loss. Fresh cheeses have no rind whatsoever.

Moisture and fat contents are good indicators of a cheese's texture and shelf life. The higher the moisture content, the softer the product and the more perishable it will be. Low-moisture cheeses may be used for grating and will keep for several weeks if properly stored. (Reduced water activity levels prohibit bacterial growth.) Fat content ranges from low fat (less than 20% fat) to double cream (at least 60% fat) and triple cream (at least 72% fat). Cheeses with a high fat content will be creamier and have a richer taste and texture than low-fat products.

Most cheeses contain high percentages of fat and protein. Cheese is also rich in calcium, phosphorus and vitamin A. As animal products, natural cheeses contain cholesterol. Today, many low-fat, even nonfat, processed cheeses are available. Sodium has also been reduced or eliminated from some modern products. See Table 8.4.

Cheese Varieties

Cheeses can be classified by country of origin, ripening method, fat content or texture. Here we classify fine cheeses by texture; the Dairy Bureau of Canada recognizes six categories: fresh or unripened, soft, semi-soft, firm and hard. A separate section on goat's milk and other cheeses is also included.

Fresh or Unripened Cheeses

Fresh cheeses are uncooked and unripened. Referred to as *fromage blanc* or *fromage frais* in French, they are generally mild and creamy with a tart tanginess. They should not taste acidic or bitter. Fresh cheeses have a moisture content of 40% to 80% and are highly perishable.

Cream cheese is soft cow's milk cheese containing a minimum of 30% fat. It is available in various-sized solid white blocks or whipped and flavoured. It is used throughout the kitchen in baking, dips, dressings and confections and is popular as a spread for bagels or toast.

◆◆◆
MAKING MOZZARELLA

In Italy, mozzarella is made every day; it is meant to be consumed just as often. Before there was refrigeration the balls of mozzarella were stored in well water to keep them cool, which is where the tradition originated of storing fresh mozzarella in liquid.

Once the milk is coagulated and the curds are cut, the mass is slowly stirred to enhance the whey's expulsion. A few hours later, when the curds are mature, they are removed from the whey, chopped or shredded and then mixed with hot water.

To test the exact amount of maturity, a handful of curds is dipped into a bucket of hot water for 10 seconds. When the curds are removed, they should be kneaded briefly and then, holding the mass with two hands, it should be pulled and stretched out to determine its maturity. When it is exactly ready to be strung it can be stretched as thin and opaque as tissue paper. At this point, small amounts of curd are dumped into a small vat and stirred with hot water using a paddle. This is known as "stringing" the cheese because as the curds are mixed with the water they begin to melt somewhat and become stringy. The more the cheese is stirred the longer the strings are stretched. Eventually all the strings come together to make a large mass of satiny-smooth cheese. In Italian the word *filare* means "to string"; therefore, all cheeses that are strung are members of the *pasta filata* family.

When stringing is complete the cheese is ready to be shaped and hand-formed into balls. The balls are tossed immediately into vats of cool water so they will maintain the desired shapes. When cool, the balls are immersed in brine solution and then wrapped in parchment paper.

PAULA LAMBERT, *owner*
MOZZARELLA COMPANY, *Dallas, Texas*

TABLE 8.4   NUTRITIONAL VALUES OF COMMON CHEESES

Per 45-g Serving (except *)	Energy (Kcal)	Protein (g)	Carbohydrates (g)	Fat (g)	Cholesterol (mg)	Sodium (mg)
Blue	159	10	1	13	34	628
Cheddar	181	11	tr	15	47	279
Cottage* (2% butterfat, 239 g)	214	33	19	5	20	970
Cream* (15g)	52	1	tr	5	15	44
Feta	123	7	2	10	41	519
Mozzarella, part skim	118	11	1	7	27	217
Swiss	169	13	2	12	41	117
Processed cheddar	169	10	tr	14	42	644

Nutritional Value of Some Common Foods (Revised 1988)

Mascarpone is a soft cow's milk cheese originally from Italy's Lombard region. It contains 70% to 75% fat and is extremely smooth and creamy. Mascarpone is highly perishable and is available in bulk or in 8- or 16-ounce (250- or 500-g) tubs. Its pale ivory colour and rich, sweet flavour are useful in both sweet and savoury sauces as well as desserts. It is also eaten plain, with fresh fruit, or spread on bread and sprinkled with cocoa or sugar.

Ricotta is a soft cheese of Italian origin, similar to cottage cheese, made from the whey left when other cow's milk cheeses are produced. It contains from zero to 10% fat. It is white or ivory in colour and creamy in texture, with a small grain and mellow, sometimes slightly tart, flavour. Ricotta is an important ingredient in many pasta dishes and desserts.

Soft Cheeses

Soft cheeses are characterized by their bloomy rinds and creamy centres. They are among the most delicious and popular of cheeses. They ripen quickly and are at their peak for only a few days, sometimes less. Canadian soft cheeses are not cooked or pressed. Moisture content ranges from 50% to 60%.

Bel paese is a 20th-century Italian creation made from cow's milk and containing approximately 50% fat. It is mild and creamy with a fruity flavour. The inside is yellowish and the outside is brown or grey. Bel paese is excellent for snacking and melts easily.

Brie is a surface-ripened cheese of French origin made with whole cow's milk and containing a minimum of 23% milkfat. Brie is made in round, flat disks weighing 2 or 4 pounds (1 or 2 kg); it is coated with a bloomy white rind. At the peak of ripeness it is creamy and rich, with a texture that oozes. Some Bries are called double or triple cream. Selecting a properly ripened Brie is a matter of judgment and experience. Select a cheese that is bulging a bit inside its rind; there should be just the beginning of brown colouring on the rind. If underripe, Brie will be bland with a hard, chalky core. Once the cheese is cut it will not ripen any further. If overripe, Brie will have a brownish rind that may be gummy or sagging and will smell strongly of ammonia. The rind is edible. The classic after-dinner cheese, Brie is also used in soups, sauces and hors d'oeuvres. Canada produces many fine Bries, particularly in Alberta and Quebec.

Brie

Boursin is a triple-cream cow's milk cheese from France containing approximately 75% fat. Boursin is usually flavoured with peppers, herbs or garlic. It is rindless, with a smooth, creamy texture, and is packed in small, foil-wrapped cylinders. Boursin is a good breakfast cheese and a welcome addition to any cheese board. It is also a popular filling for baked chicken.

Camembert is a surface-ripened cheese originating in France and containing a minimum of 22% fat. Camembert is firmer than Brie, but milder. It is shaped in small round or oval disks and is coated with a white bloomy rind. Selecting a properly ripened Camembert is similar to selecting a Brie, but Camembert will become overripe and ammoniated even more quickly than Brie. Camembert is an excellent dessert or after-dinner cheese and goes particularly well with fruit. Like Brie, double and triple cream varieties, as well as blue-veined varieties, are available.

Semisoft Cheeses

This large category is separated into groups based on the ripening method. Moisture content ranges between 40% and 60%, while fat content is between 10% and 30%.

Mozzarella

Unripened: Pasta filata or stretched curd cheeses make up most of this group. Many of these cheeses are of Italian origin but are produced in Canada. Mozzarella is the most prevalent type and is used extensively in pizza and pasta dishes. It has a smooth, elastic character and mild flavour. Fresh mozzarella is known as bocconcini and comes packed in brine. Mild and delicate, it goes well with ripe tomatoes, virgin olive oil and a little fresh basil. Scamorza, Trecce and Fior di Latte are other types; some of these unripened cheeses are smoked or aged for flavour.

Interior Ripened: These cheeses have usually been pressed, cooked and ripened. The rind may be washed if it is firm enough as it forms. Most of these cheeses are mild and supple in texture. Havarti, with its small holes and mild flavour, may be enhanced with spices. Danish in origin, it has a creamy texture. Monterey Jack is a widely used variety that originated in the United States. It comes in blocks and is mild on its own, but it is often flavoured with chilies and other seasonings. Saint Paulin and Munster are two other interior-ripened cheeses.

Oka

Surface Ripened: These cheeses ripen from the surface to the centre. They are turned, washed and kept in cold rooms. Some have a pungent smell and flavour. Oka, Canada's most famous and true cheese, is of this type. Oka has its origins with Trappist monks in France who produced Port Salut. The conditions in Quebec produced Oka instead. Only in recent years has the original production facility become commercial. The pale yellow to red rind containing a pale yellow interior has delighted connoisseurs the world over with its mellow, buttery, nutty, flavour.

Feta

Feta is a semi-soft Greek or Italian product originally made from sheep's and/or goat's milk. Cow's milk fetas are common, too. It is a white, flaky cheese that is pickled (but not ripened) and stored in brine water, giving it a shelf life of four to six weeks. Its flavour becomes sharper and saltier with age. Feta is good for snacks and salads and melts easily for sauces and fillings.

Limburger and Stella Alpine are other examples of this cheese type.

Havarti is a cow's milk monastery-style cheese from Denmark containing 45% to 60% fat. Havarti is also known as **Danish Tilsit** or by the brand name **Dofino**. Pale yellow with many small, irregular holes, it is sold in small rounds, rectangular blocks or loaves. Havarti has a mild flavour and creamy texture. It is often flavoured with dill, caraway seeds or peppers. Havarti is very popular for snacking and on sandwiches.

Port Salut is a monastery cow's milk product from France containing approximately 50% fat. Port Salut is smooth, rich and savoury. It is shaped in thick wheels with a dense, pale yellow interior and an edible, bright orange rind. The Danish version is known as **Esrom**. Canada's most famous cheese, Oka, has its origins in Port Salut. Oka is produced in Quebec and has a worldwide reputation.

Havarti

Firm Cheeses

Firm cheeses are the largest Canadian cheese category. Some are close-textured and crumbly, like cheddar; others are dense, holey cheeses like Swiss Emmenthaler. All firm cheeses are interior ripened. Their moisture content ranges from 35% to 52%. Interior ripening is a common characteristic.

Cheddars are produced in both North America and Great Britain. Cheddar is a cow's milk cheese made primarily in the northern United States and most of Canada, containing a minimum of 31% fat. The best cheddars are non-coloured and aged two to five years. Hand-turned cheddars are now a rarity. Cheddars have a dense, crumbly texture and may be white or coloured orange with vegetable dyes, depending on local preference. "Marble" cheddar is popular in western Canada. Flavours range from mild to very sharp, depending on the age of the cheese. **Colby** and **brick** are similar to cheddars. Cheddars are sold in a variety of shapes and sizes, often coated with wax. Good-quality cheddars are welcome additions to any cheese board, while those of lesser quality are better reserved for cooking and sandwiches. **English cheddar** is a variety of cow's milk cheese produced in Great Britain containing approximately 45% fat. Perhaps the most imitated cheese in the world, true English cheddar is available in Canada. Canadian cheese manufacturers have enhanced the original English recipe and Canadian cheddar has become famous the world over. It is a moist yet sliceable cheese, aged at least six months. It is a most versatile cheese, ideal for any time of day and with nearly any meal. It is used in numerous ways for both desserts and in cooking.

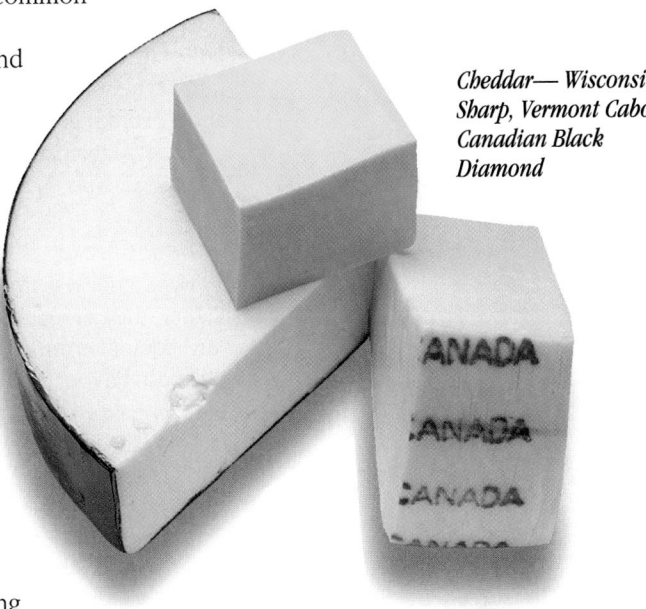

Cheddar— Wisconsin Sharp, Vermont Cabot, Canadian Black Diamond

Emmenthaler (Swiss) is a cow's milk cheese from Switzerland containing approximately 45% fat. Emmenthaler is the original Swiss cheese; it accounts for over half of Switzerland's cheese production. It is mellow, rich and nutty with a natural rind and a light yellow interior full of large holes. It is ripened in three stages with the aid of fermenting bacteria. The holes or "eyes" are caused by CO_2 gases expanding inside the cheese during fermentation. Authentic Emmenthaler is sold in 200-pound (90-kg) wheels with the word "Switzerland" stamped on the rind like the spokes of a wheel. Emmenthaler, widely used in fondues, is also popular for sandwiches,

Emmenthaler (Swiss)

snacks and after dinner with fruit and nuts.

Gouda is a Dutch cheese containing approximately 48% fat. Gouda is sold in various-sized wheels covered with red or yellow wax. The cheese is yellow with a few small holes and a mild, buttery flavour. Gouda may be sold soon after production or it may be aged for several months, resulting in a firmer, more flavourful cheese. Gouda is widely popular for snacking and in **fondue.**

Fontina is a cow's milk cheese from Italy's Piedmont region containing approximately 45% fat. The original, known as **fontina Val D'Aosta**, has a dark gold, crusty rind; the pale gold, dense interior has a few small holes. It is nutty and rich. The original must have a purple trademark stamped on the rind. Imitation fontinas (known as **fontal** or **fontinella**) are produced in Denmark, France, Sweden, the United States and other regions of Italy. They tend to be softer, with less depth of flavour, and may have a rubbery texture. Real fontina is a good after-dinner cheese; the imitations are often added to sauces, soups or sandwiches.

Jarlsberg is a Swiss-type cow's milk cheese from Norway containing approximately 45% fat. Jarlsberg closely resembles Swiss Emmenthaler in both taste and appearance. It is mild with a delicate, sweet taste and large holes. Jarlsberg has a pale yellow interior; it is coated with yellow wax and sold in huge wheels. It has a long shelf life and is popular for sandwiches, snacks and in cooking.

Other Canadian-produced cheeses in this category include Camosun, brick, Edam, Fruilano, New Bra and Saint André.

Hard Cheeses

Hard cheeses are not simply cheeses that have been allowed to dry out. Rather, they are carefully aged for extended periods of time and have a moisture content from 5% to 30%. Hard cheeses are most often used for grating; the best flavour will come from cheeses grated as needed. Even the finest hard cheeses begin to lose their flavour within hours of grating. The most famous and popular of the hard cheeses are those from Italy, where they are known as *grana*. Hard cheeses can also be served as a table cheese or with a salad.

Asiago is a cow's milk cheese from Italy containing approximately 30% fat. After only one year of aging, Asiago is sharp and nutty with a cheddarlike texture. If aged for two years or more, Asiago becomes dry, brittle and suitable for grating. Either version should be an even white to pale yellow in colour with no dark spots, cracks or strong aromas. It is sold in small wheels and keeps for long periods if well wrapped. Asiago melts easily and is often used in cooking.

Parmigiano-Reggiano (Parmesan) is a cow's milk cheese made exclusively in the region near Parma, Italy, containing from 32% to 35% fat. Parmigiano-Reggiano is one of the world's oldest and most widely copied cheeses. Used primarily for grating and cooking, it is rich, spicy and sharp with a golden interior and a hard oily rind. It should not be overly salty or bitter. Reggiano, as it is known, is produced only from mid-April to mid-November. It is shaped into huge wheels of about 80 pounds (36 kg) each, with the name stencilled repeatedly around the rind. Imitation Parmesan is produced in the United States, Argentina and elsewhere, but none can match the distinctive flavour of freshly grated Reggiano. Domestically produced Parmesan is widely available in Canada, grated, shredded or in block form.

Pecorino Romano is a sheep's milk cheese from central

Fondue—*a Swiss specialty made with melted cheese, wine and flavourings; eaten by dipping pieces of bread into the hot mixture with long forks.*

Asiago

Parmigiano-Reggiano (Parmesan)

and southern Italy containing approximately 35% fat. Romano is very brittle and sharper than other grating cheeses, with a "sheepy" tang. Its light, grainy interior is whiter than Parmesan or Asiago. It is packed in large cylinders with a yellow rind. Romano is often substituted for, or combined with, Parmesan in cooking but it is also good eaten with olives, sausages and red wine.

Provolone is a cow's milk cheese originating in southern Italy containing a minimum of 24% fat. Provolone *dolce*, aged only two months, is mild, with a smooth texture. Provolone *piccante*, aged up to six months, is stronger, with a white-yellow fibrous interior. Smoked provolone is also popular, especially for snacking. Provolone is shaped in various ways, from huge salamis to plump spheres to tiny piglets shaped by hand. It is excellent in sandwiches and for cooking, and is often used for melting and in pizza and pasta dishes.

Other Types of Cheeses

Gorgonzola is a blue-veined cow's milk cheese from Italy containing 48% fat. Gorgonzola has a white or ivory interior with bluish-green veins. It is creamier than Stilton or Roquefort, with a somewhat more pungent, spicy, earthy flavour. White Gorgonzola has no veins but a similar flavour, while aged Gorgonzola is drier and crumbly with a very strong, sharp flavour. The milder Gorgonzolas are excellent with fresh peaches or pears or crumbled in a salad. Gorgonzola is also used in sauces and in the *torta con basilico*, a cakelike cheese loaf composed of layers of cheese, fresh basil and pine nuts.

Roquefort is a blue-veined sheep's milk cheese from France containing approximately 45% fat. One of the oldest cheeses, Roquefort is intensely pungent with a rich, salty flavour and strong aroma. It is a white paste with veins of blue mold and a thin natural rind shaped into thick, foil-wrapped cylinders. Roquefort is always aged for at least three months in the limestone caves of Mount Combalou. Since 1926 no producer outside this region can legally use the name Roquefort or even "Roquefort-style." Roquefort is an excellent choice for serving before or after dinner and is, of course, essential for Roquefort dressing. Ermite is an excellent Canadian cheese produced in the Roquefort style.

Stilton is a blue-veined cow's milk cheese from Great Britain containing 45% fat. Stilton is one of the oldest and grandest cheeses in the world. It has a white or pale yellow interior with evenly spaced blue veins. Stilton's distinctive flavour is pungent, rich and tangy, combining the best of blues and cheddars. It is aged in cool ripening rooms for four to six months to develop the blue veining; it is then sold in tall cylinders with a crusty, edible rind. Stilton should be wrapped in a cloth dampened with salt water and stored at cool temperatures, but not refrigerated. It is best served alone, with plain crackers, dried fruit or vintage port.

Goat's Milk Cheeses

Because of their increasing popularity, cheeses made from goat's milk deserve a few words of their own. Although goats give less milk than cows, their milk is higher in fat and protein and richer and more concentrated in flavour. Cheeses made with goat's milk have a sharp, tangy flavour. They may range in texture from very soft and fresh to very hard, depending on age.

Chèvre (French for "goat") refers to small, soft, creamy cheeses produced in a variety of shapes: cones, disks, pyramids or logs. Chèvres are often coated with ash, herbs or seasonings. They are excellent for cooking and complement a wide variety of flavours. Unfortunately, they have a short shelf life, perhaps only two weeks. Cheese labelled *pure chèvre* must be made with 100% goat's milk, while others may be a mixture of cow's and goat's milk.

Gorgonzola

Blue Cheese—1. *A generic term for any cheese containing visible blue-green molds that contribute a characteristic tart, sharp flavour and aroma: also known as a blue-veined cheese or bleu. 2. A group of Roquefort-style cheeses made in the United States and Canada from cow's or goat's milk rather than ewe's milk and injected with molds that form blue-green veins: also known as blue mold cheese or blue-veined cheese.*

Stilton

Goat's Milk Cheeses

Some of the finest goat's milk cheeses come from France. Preferred brands include Bucheron, exported from France in 5-pound (2-kg) logs; Chevrotin, one of the mildest; and Montrachet, a tangy soft cheese from the Burgundy wine region. Spurred on by the increased popularity of chèvre, a few Canadian producers have developed excellent cheeses in a wide variety of shapes and styles.

Processed Cheeses

Pasteurized processed cheese is made from a combination of aged and green cheeses that are mixed with emulsifiers and flavourings, pasteurized and poured into molds to solidify. Manufacturers can thus produce cheeses with consistent textures and flavours. Processed cheeses are commonly used in food service operations because they are less expensive than natural cheeses. And, because they will not age or ripen, their shelf life is greatly extended. Nutritionally, processed cheeses generally contain less protein, calcium and vitamin A and more sodium than natural cheeses.

Processed cheese food contains less natural cheese (but at least 51% by weight) and more moisture than regular processed cheese. Often vegetable oils and milk solids are added, making cheese food soft and spreadable.

Cold pack is a processed cheese product made primarily of old cheddar; it is not heated in processing. Sugars are usually added to mellow the flavour.

Imitation cheese is usually manufactured with dairy byproducts and soy products mixed with emulsifiers, colourings and flavouring agents and enzymes. Although considerably less expensive than natural cheese, imitation cheese tends to be dense and rubbery, with little flavour other than that of salt.

Serving Cheeses

Cheeses may be served at any time of day. In Northern Europe they are common for breakfast; in Great Britain they are a staple at lunch. Cheeses are widely used for sandwiches, snacks and cooking in Canada, and they are often served following the entree or instead of dessert at formal dinners.

◆◆◆

CANADIAN CHEESE HISTORY

Some of the milk from cows arriving with Cartier in 1541 was likely made into cheese. The first North American dairy farm was the Champlain farm at Cap Tourmente in 1629. Nova Scotia's export of six tons of cheese in 1764 was the first documented production.

Originally produced from ewe's milk and coloured with marigolds, cheddar is a widely produced cheese in Canada, although it is made from cow's milk now. Black Diamond cheddar was the result of the wax coating protecting the cheese reacting with the mold it was transported in and turning black.

Some of Canada's finest cheeses are based on monastery production methods the monks brought with them from Europe. Oka is the most famous and is regarded as a true Canadian cheese.

Cheeseboard Set for Service

The flavour and texture of natural cheeses are best at room temperature. So, except for fresh cheeses, all cheeses should be removed from the refrigerator 30 minutes to an hour before service to allow them to come to room temperature. Fresh cheeses, such as cottage and cream, should be eaten chilled.

Any selection of fine cheeses should include a variety of flavours and textures: from mild to sharp, from soft to creamy to firm. Use a variety of shapes and colours for visual appeal. Do not precut the cheeses as this only causes them to become dry. Provide an adequate supply of serving knives so that stronger-flavoured cheeses will not combine with and overpower milder ones. Fine cheeses are best appreciated with plain bread and crackers, as salted or seasoned crackers can mask the cheese's flavour. Noncitrus fruits are also a nice accompaniment. Carefully pairing cheeses and wines can lead to a wonderful taste experience.

Storage

Most cheeses are best kept refrigerated, well wrapped to keep odours out and moisture in. Firm and hard cheeses can be kept for several weeks; fresh cheeses will spoil in 7 to 10 days because of their high moisture content. Some cheeses that have become hard or dry may still be grated for cooking or baking. Freezing is possible but not recommended because it changes the cheese's texture, making it mealy or tough.

CONCLUSION

Eggs and dairy products are versatile foods used throughout the kitchen. They may be served as is or incorporated into many dishes, including soups, sauces, entrees, breads and desserts. Fine natural cheeses are useful in

♦♦♦
CHEESE TERMINOLOGY

The following terms often appear on cheese labels and may help you identify or appreciate new or unfamiliar cheeses:

Affiné—French term for a washed-rind cheese.

Bleu—French term for blue.

Brique or *briquette*—refers to a group of French brick-shaped cheeses.

Brossé—a French term for cheeses that are brushed during ripening.

Capra—Italian for goat's milk cheese.

Carré—French term for square, flat cheeses.

Cendre—French term for cheeses ripened in ashes.

Coulant—French for "flowing," used to describe Brie, Camembert and other cheeses when their interiors ooze or flow.

Ferme or *fermier*—French term for farm-produced cheeses.

Fromage à tartiner—French term for melting cheese, often applied to processed cheeses.

Kaas—Dutch for cheese.

Kase—German for cheese.

Lait cru—French term for raw milk.

Laiterie or *laitier*—French for dairy farm or dairy farmer; appears on factory-made cheeses.

Mi chèvre—a French product so labelled must contain at least 25% goat's milk.

Ost—Scandinavian term for cheese.

Pecorino—Italian term for all sheep's milk cheeses.

Queso—Spanish term for cheese.

Râpé—French term applied to cheeses that are grated.

Tome or *tomme*—term used by the French, Italians and Swiss to refer to mountain cheeses, particularly from the Pyrenees or Savoie regions.

Tyrophile—one who loves cheese.

Vaccino—Italian term for cow's milk cheese.

❖❖❖

WINE AND CHEESE: CLASSIC COMBINATIONS

Some cheeses are delicious with beers or ales. Others are best with strong coffee or apple cider, and nothing accompanies a cheddar cheese sandwich as well as ice-cold milk. For most cheeses, however, the ultimate partner is wine. Wine and cheese bring out the best in each other. The proteins and fats in cheeses take the edge off harsh or acidic wines, while the tannins and acids in wines bring out the creamy richness of cheeses.

Because of their natural affinity, certain pairings are universal favourites: Stilton with port, Camembert with Bordeaux, Roquefort with Sauternes and English cheddar with Burgundy. Although taste preferences are an individual matter, cheese–wine marriages follow two schools of thought: Either pair likes or pair opposites.

Pairing like with like is simple: Cheeses are often best served with wines produced in the same region. For example, a white burgundy would be an excellent choice for cheeses from Burgundy such as Montrachet; and goat cheeses from the Rhone Valley go well with wines of that region. Hearty Italian wines such as Chianti, Barolo and Valpolicella are delicious with Italian cheese—Gorgonzola, provolone, taleggio. And a dry, aged Monterey Jack is perhaps the perfect mate for California zinfandel.

Opposites do attract, however. Sweet wines such as Sauternes and Gewürztraminer go well with sharp, tangy blues, especially Roquefort. And light, sparkling wines such as Champagne or Spanish Cava are a nice complement to rich, creamy cheeses like Brie and Camembert.

prepared dishes but are most important for buffets, as the cheese course during a meal or whenever cheese is the primary ingredient or dominant flavour. Eggs and dairy products spoil easily and must be handled and stored properly.

QUESTIONS FOR DISCUSSION

1. Explain the criteria used in grading eggs. Why might you prefer to use eggs with lower grades?
2. What are the differences between egg products and egg substitutes?
3. What is milkfat and how is it used in classifying milk-based products?
4. If a recipe calls for whole milk and you have only dried milk, what do you do? Explain your answer.
5. What is clarified butter and when is it used? Describe the procedure for clarifying butter.
6. The texture and shelf life of cheese depend on what two factors?
7. Cheeses are categorized as fresh, soft, semisoft, firm and hard. Give two examples of each and explain how they are generally used.

WEBLINKS

Canadian Egg Marketing Agency
   www.canadaegg.ca/
Dairy Bureau of Canada
   www.DairyBureau.org/
Canadian Food Inspection Agency/Agence canadienne
   d'inspection des aliments
   www.cfia-acia.agr.ca/
Egg Nutrition Center
   www.enc-online.org/
CheeseNet
   www.wgx.com/cheesenet/

PART THREE
COOKING

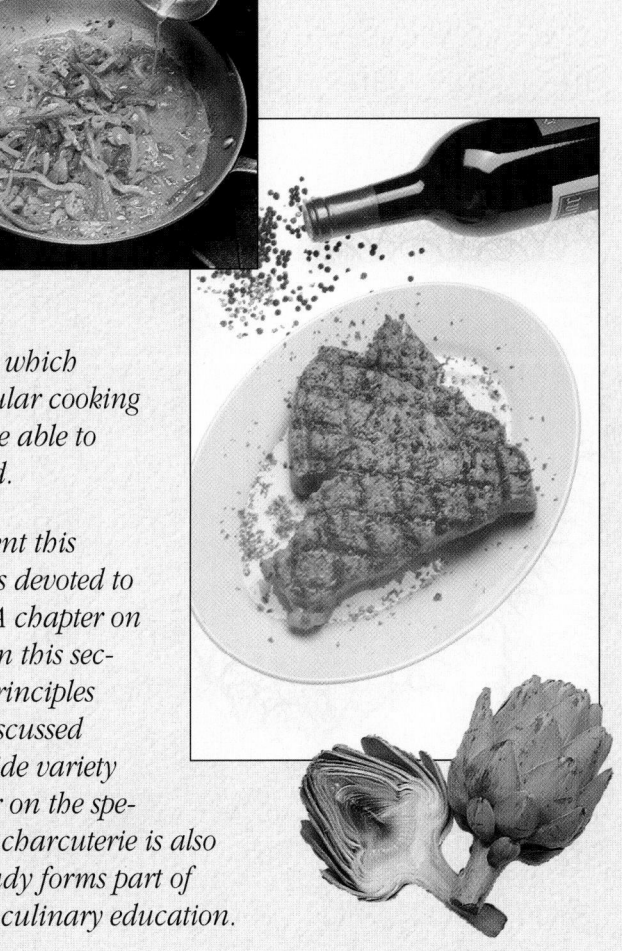

Learning to cook is not simply a matter of following recipes. You must understand and appreciate why and how chemical and physical reactions occur in foods, why foods respond to heat the way they do and which foods respond best to particular cooking techniques. You must also be able to identify the foods being used.

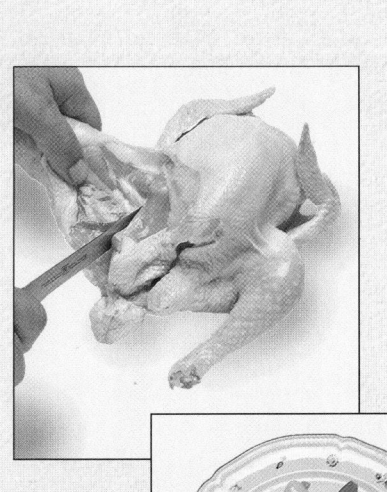

The following chapters present this information; each chapter is devoted to a specific category of food. A chapter on deep-fat frying is included in this section because the principles and techniques discussed there apply to a wide variety of foods. A chapter on the specialized subject of charcuterie is also included, as its study forms part of any well-rounded culinary education.

CHAPTER 9

PRINCIPLES OF COOKING

ooking can be defined as the transfer of energy from a heat source to a food. This energy alters the food's molecular structure, changing its texture, flavour, aroma and appearance. But why is food cooked at all? The obvious answer is that cooking makes food taste better. Cooking also destroys undesirable microorganisms and makes foods easier to ingest and digest.

To cook foods successfully, you must first understand the ways in which heat is transferred: conduction, convection and radiation. You should also understand what the application of heat does to the proteins, sugars, starches, water and fats in foods.

Perhaps most importantly, you must understand the cooking methods used to transfer heat: broiling, grilling, roasting and baking, sautéing, pan-frying, deep-fat frying, poaching, simmering, boiling, steaming, braising and stewing. Each method is used for many types of food, so you will be applying one or more of them every time you cook. The cooking method you select gives the finished product a specific texture, appearance, aroma and flavour. A thorough understanding of the basic procedures involved in each cooking method helps you produce consistent, high-quality products.

This chapter discusses each of the cooking methods in general terms without applying them to any specific food. These methods will be discussed again in more detail as they are used in the following chapters.

HEAT TRANSFER

Heat is a type of energy. When a substance gets hot its molecules have absorbed energy, which causes the molecules to vibrate rapidly, expand and bounce off one another. As the molecules move they collide with nearby molecules, causing a transfer of heat energy. The faster the molecules within a substance move, the higher its temperature. This is true whether the substance is air, water, an aluminum pot or a sirloin steak.

Heat energy may be transferred *to* foods via conduction, convention or radiation. See Figure 9.1. Heat then travels *through* foods by conduction. Only heat is transferred—cold is simply the absence of heat, so cold cannot be transferred from one substance to another.

Conduction

Conduction is the most straightforward means of heat transfer. It is simply the movement of heat from one item to another through direct contact. For example, when the flame of a gas burner touches the bottom of a sauté pan, heat is conducted to the pan. The metal of the pan then conducts heat to the surface of the food lying in that pan.

Some materials conduct heat better than others. Water is a better conductor of heat than air. This explains why a potato cooks much faster in boiling water than in an oven, and why you cannot place your hand in boiling water at a temperature of 212°F (100°C), but can place your hand, at least very briefly, into a 400°F (200°C) oven. Generally, metals are good conductors (as discussed in Chapter 5, Tools and Equipment, copper and aluminum are the best conductors), while liquids and gases are poor conductors.

Conduction is a relatively slow method of heat transfer because there must be physical contact to transfer energy from one molecule to adjacent molecules. Consider what happens when a metal spoon is placed in a pot of simmering soup. At first the spoon handle remains cool. Gradually, however, heat travels up the handle, making it warmer and warmer, until it becomes too hot to touch.

Conduction is important in all cooking methods because it is responsible for the movement of heat from the surface of a food to its interior. As the molecules near the food's exterior gather energy, they move more and more rapidly. As they move, they conduct heat to the molecules nearby, thus transferring heat *through* the food (from the exterior of the item to the interior).

In conventional heating methods (nonmicrowave) the heat source causes food molecules to react largely from the surface inward, so that layers of molecules heat in succession. This produces a range of temperatures within the food, which means that the outside can brown and form a crust long before the interior is noticeably warmer. That is why a steak can be fully cooked on the outside but still rare on the inside.

Convection

Convection refers to the transfer of heat through a fluid, which may be liquid or gas. Convection is actually a combination of conduction and a mixing in which molecules in a fluid (whether air, water or fat) move from a warmer area to a cooler one. There are two types of convection: natural and mechanical.

Natural convection occurs because of the tendency of warm liquids and gases to rise while cooler ones fall. This causes a constant natural circulation of heat. For example, when a pot of stock is placed over a gas burner, the molecules at the bottom of the pot are warmed. These molecules rise while cooler, heavier molecules sink. Upon reaching the pot's bottom, the cooler molecules are warmed and begin to rise. This ongoing cycle creates currents within the stock, and these currents distribute the heat throughout the stock.

Mechanical convection relies on fans or stirring to circulate heat more quickly and evenly. This explains why foods heat faster and more evenly when stirred. Convection ovens are equipped with fans to increase the circulation of air currents, thus speeding up the cooking process. But even conventional ovens (that is, not convection ovens) rely on the natural circulation patterns of heated air to transfer heat energy to items being baked or roasted.

Radiation

Unlike conduction and convection, **radiation** does not require physical contact between the heat source and the food being cooked. Instead, energy is transferred by waves of heat or light striking the food. Two kinds of radiant heat are used in the kitchen: infrared and microwave.

Infrared cooking uses an electric or ceramic element heated to such a high temperature that it gives off waves of radiant heat that cook the food. Radiant heat waves travel at the speed of light in any direction (unlike

FIGURE 9.1   *Arrows indicate heat patterns during conduction, convection and radiation.*

convection heat, which only rises) until they are absorbed by a food. Infrared cooking is commonly used with toasters and broilers. The glowing coals of a fire are another example of radiant heat.

Microwave cooking relies on radiation generated by a special oven to penetrate the food, where it agitates water molecules, creating friction and heat. This energy then spreads throughout the food by conduction (and by convection in liquids). Microwave cooking is much faster than other methods because energy penetrates the food up to a depth of several centimetres, setting all water molecules in motion at the same time. Heat is generated quickly and uniformly throughout the food. Microwave cooking does not brown foods, however, and often gives meats a dry, mushy texture, making microwave ovens an unacceptable replacement for traditional ovens.

Because microwave radiation affects only water molecules, a completely waterless material (such as a plate) will not get hot. Any warmth felt in a plate used when microwaving food results from heat being conducted from the food to the plate.

Microwave cooking requires the use of certain types of utensils, usually heat-resistant glass or microwaveable plastic. Even heat-resistant glass can shatter, however, and it is not recommended for professional use. The aluminum and stainless steel utensils most common in professional kitchens cannot be used because metal deflects microwaves and this can damage the oven.

THE EFFECTS OF HEAT

Foods are composed of proteins, carbohydrates (starches and sugars), water and fats, plus small amounts of minerals and vitamins. Changes in shape, texture, colour and flavour of foods may occur when heat is applied to each of these nutrients. By understanding these changes and learning to control them, you will be able to prepare foods with the characteristics desired. While volumes are written on these subjects, it is sufficient for you to know the following processes as you begin your study of cooking.

Proteins Coagulate

The proper term for the cooking of proteins is **coagulation**. Proteins are large, complex molecules found in every living cell, plant as well as animal. Coagulation refers to the irreversible transformation of proteins from a liquid or semiliquid state to a solid state. As proteins cook they lose moisture, shrink and become firm. Common examples of coagulation are the firming of meat fibres during cooking, egg whites changing from a clear liquid to a white solid when heated and the setting of the structure of wheat proteins (known as gluten) in bread during baking. Most proteins complete coagulation at 160°F to 185°F (71°C to 85°C).

Starches Gelatinize

Gelatinization is the proper term for the cooking of starches. Starches are complex carbohydrates present in plants and grains such as potatoes, wheat, rice and corn. When a mixture of starch and liquid is heated, remarkable changes occur. The starch granules absorb water, causing them to swell, soften and clarify slightly. The liquid visibly thickens because of the water being absorbed into the starch granules and the granules themselves swelling to occupy more space.

Gelatinization occurs gradually over a range of temperatures—150°F to 212°F (66°C to 100°C)—depending on the type of starch used. Starch gelatinization affects not only sauces or liquids to which starches are added for the express purpose of thickening, but also any mixture of starch and liquid that is heated. For example, the flour (a starch) in cake batter gelatinizes by absorbing the water from eggs, milk or other ingredients as the batter bakes. This causes part of the firming and drying associated with baked goods.

Sugars Caramelize

The process of cooking sugars is properly known as **caramelization**. Sugars are simple carbohydrates used by all plants and animals to store energy. As sugars cook they gradually turn brown and change flavour. Caramelized sugar is used in many sauces, candies and desserts. But caramelized sugar is also partly responsible for the flavour and colour of bread crusts and the browning of meats and vegetables. In fact, it is the process of caramelization that is responsible for most flavours we associate with cooking.

Sucrose (common table sugar) begins to brown at about 338°F (170°C). The naturally occurring sugars in other foods such as maltose, lactose and fructose also caramelize, but at varying temperatures. Because high temperatures are required for browning (i.e., caramelizing), most foods will brown only on the outside and only through the application of dry heat. Because water cannot be heated above 212°F (100°C), foods cooked with moist-heat methods do not get hot enough to caramelize. Foods cooked with dry-heat methods, including those using fats, will reach the high temperatures at which browning occurs.

Water Evaporates

All foods contain some water. Some foods, especially eggs, milk and leafy vegetables, are almost entirely water. Even as much as 75% of raw meat is water. As the internal temperature of a food increases, water molecules move faster and faster until the water turns to a gas (steam) and vaporizes. This **evaporation** of water is responsible for the drying of foods during cooking.

Fats Melt

Fat is an energy source for the plant or animal in which it is stored. Fats are smooth, greasy substances that do not dissolve in water. Their texture varies from very firm to liquid. Oils are simply fats that remain liquid at room temperature. Fats **melt** when heated; that is, they gradually soften, then liquify. Fats will not evaporate. Most fats can be heated to very high temperatures without burning, so they can be used as a cooking medium to brown foods.

COOKING METHODS

Foods can be cooked in air, fat, water or steam. These are collectively known as **cooking media**. There are two general types of cooking **methods**: dry heat and moist heat.

Dry-heat cooking methods** are those using air or fat. They are broiling, grilling, roasting and baking, sautéing, pan-frying and deep-fat frying. Foods cooked using dry-heat cooking methods have a rich flavour caused by browning.

Moist-heat cooking methods** are those using water or steam. They are poaching, simmering, boiling and steaming. Moist-heat cooking methods are used to emphasize the natural flavours of food.

Other cooking methods employ a combination of dry- and moist-heat cooking methods. The two most significant of these **combination cooking methods** are braising and stewing. See Table 9.1.

TABLE 9.1   COOKING METHODS

Method	Medium	Equipment
Dry-Heat Cooking Methods		
Broiling	Air	Overhead broiler, salamander, rotisserie
Grilling	Air	Grill
Roasting	Air	Oven
Baking	Air	Oven
Sautéing	Fat	Stove
Pan-frying	Fat	Stove, tilt skillet
Deep-fat frying	Fat	Deep-fat fryer
Moist-Heat Cooking Methods		
Poaching	Water or other liquid	Stove, oven, steam-jacketed kettle, tilt skillet
Simmering	Water or other liquid	Stove, steam-jacketed kettle, tilt skillet
Boiling	Water or other liquid	Stove, steam-jacketed kettle, tilt skillet
Steaming	Steam	Stove, convection steamer
Combination Cooking Methods		
Braising	Fat then liquid	Stove (and oven), tilt skillet
Stewing	Fat then liquid	Stove (and oven), tilt skillet

Each of these cooking methods can be applied to a wide variety of foods—meats, fish, vegetables and even pastries. Here, we discuss only the general characteristics of these cooking methods. Detailed procedures for applying these methods to specific foods are found in subsequent chapters.

Dry-Heat Cooking Methods

Cooking by dry heat is the process of applying heat either directly, by subjecting the food to the heat of a flame, or indirectly, by surrounding the food with heated air or heated fat.

Broiling

Broiling uses radiant heat from an overhead source to cook foods. The temperature at the heat source can be as high as 2000°F (1100°C). The food to be broiled is placed on a preheated metal grate. Radiant heat from overhead cooks the food, while the hot grate below marks it with attractive crosshatch marks.

Delicate foods that may be damaged by being placed directly on a metal grate or foods on which crosshatch marks are not desirable may be placed on a preheated heat-proof platter then placed under the broiler. Cooking will take place through indirect heat from the preheated platter as well as from the direct heat from the broiler's overhead heat source.

Grilling

Although similar to broiling, grilling uses a heat source located beneath the cooking surface. Grills may be electric or gas or they can burn wood or charcoal, which will add a smoky flavour to the food. Specific woods such as mesquite, hickory or vine clippings can be used to create special flavours. Grilled foods are often identified by crosshatch markings. The illustrations below show the correct procedure for positioning foods on the grill to create these markings.

1. Decide which side of the grilled food will be presented face up to the customer. Place the food on the hot grill with this side facing down. If the item is oblong, place it at a 45-degree angle to the bars on the cooking grate. Cook long enough for the food to develop dark charred lines where it touches the grate.

2. Rotate the food 90 degrees and allow it to cook long enough for the grates to char it to the same extent as in step 1.

3. Turn the food over and finish cooking it. It is usually unnecessary to create the crosshatch markings on the reverse side, as this will not be seen by the customer.

Roasting and Baking

Roasting and baking are the processes of surrounding a food with dry, heated air in a closed environment. The term *roasting* is usually applied to meats and poultry, while *baking* is used when referring to fish, fruits, vegetables, starches, breads or pastry items. Heat is transferred by convection to the food's surface, and then penetrates the food by conduction. The surface dehydrates and the food browns from caramelization, completing the cooking process.

Sautéing

Sautéing is a dry-heat cooking method that uses conduction to transfer heat from a hot sauté pan to food with the aid of a small amount of fat. Heat then penetrates the food through conduction. High temperatures are used to sauté, and the foods are usually cut into small pieces to promote even cooking.

To sauté foods properly, begin by heating a sauté pan on the stove top, then add a small amount of fat. The fat should just cover the bottom of the pan. Heat the fat or oil to the point where it just begins to smoke. The food to be cooked should be as dry as possible when it is added to the pan to promote browning and to prevent excessive spattering. Place the food in the pan in a single layer. The heat should be adjusted so the food cooks thoroughly; it should not be so hot that the outside of the food burns before the inside is cooked. The food should be turned or tossed periodically to develop the proper colour. Larger items should be turned using tongs without piercing the surface. Smaller items are often turned by using the sauteuse's sloped sides to flip them back on top of themselves. When tossing sautéed foods, keep the pan in contact with the heat source as much as possible to prevent it from cooling. Sautéing sometimes includes the preparation of a sauce directly in the pan after the main item has been removed.

Stir-frying is a variation of sautéing. A wok is used instead of a sauté pan; the curved sides and rounded bottom of the wok diffuse heat and facilitate tossing and stirring. Otherwise, stir-frying procedures are the same as those outlined for sautéing and will not be discussed separately here.

Pan-Frying

Pan-frying shares similarities with both sautéing and deep-fat frying. It is a dry-heat cooking method in which heat is transferred by conduction from the pan to the food, using a moderate amount of fat. Heat is also transferred to the food from the hot fat by convection. Foods to be pan-fried are usually coated in breading. This forms a seal that keeps the food moist and prevents the hot fat from penetrating the food, causing it to become greasy.

To pan-fry foods properly, first heat the fat in a sauté pan. Use enough fat so that the food being cooked is immersed one-third to one-half in the fat. The fat should be at a temperature somewhat lower than that used in sautéing; it should not smoke but should be hot enough so that when the food is added it crackles and spatters from the rapid vaporization of moisture. If the temperature is too low, the food will absorb excessive amounts of fat; if it is too high, the food will burn on the outside before the interior is fully cooked. When the food is properly browned on one side, turn it without piercing it, using tongs. Always turn the food away from you to prevent being burned by any fat that may splash. When the food is fully cooked, remove it from the pan, drain it on absorbent paper and serve it immediately.

Deep-Fat Frying

Deep-fat frying is a dry-heat cooking method that uses convection to transfer heat to food submerged in hot fat. Heat then penetrates the food, cooking the interior through conduction. Foods to be deep-fat fried are usually first coated in batter or breading. This preserves moisture and prevents the food from absorbing excessive quantities of fat. Deep-fat fried foods should cook thoroughly while developing an attractive deep golden-brown colour. Foods to be deep-fat fried should be of a size and shape that allows them to float freely in the fat.

Today most deep-fat frying is done in specially designed commercial fryers. These fryers have built-in thermostats, making temperature control more precise. To deep-fat fry food, first heat the fat or oil to temperatures between 325°F and 375°F (160°C–190°C). Slowly place the food in the fat, where it should float freely. Use tongs to turn it if necessary. When the food is done, remove it from the fat, drain it on absorbent paper and serve it immediately.

Moist-Heat Cooking Methods

Cooking with moist heat is the process of applying heat to food by submerging it directly into a hot liquid or by exposing it to steam. See Table 9.2.

Poaching

Poaching is a moist-heat cooking method that uses convection to transfer heat from a liquid to a food. For poaching, the food is submerged in a liquid held at temperatures between 160°F and 180°F (71°C–82°C). The surface of the liquid should show only slight movement, but no bubbles.

The flavour of the poaching liquid strongly affects the ultimate flavour of the finished product, so stock, court bouillon or broth is generally used. Poaching is most often associated with foods that do not require lengthy cooking to tenderize them, such as eggs or fish.

To poach food, first bring the poaching liquid to a boil in a suitably shaped cooking vessel. Add the food to be poached either by placing it directly into the liquid or by lowering it into the liquid using a specially designed rack. Adjust the heat as necessary to maintain the desired temperature throughout the cooking process. Do not allow the liquid to reach a boil, as the agitation will cause meats to become tough and stringy and will destroy tender foods such as fresh fruit or fish. The liquid used to poach food is sometimes used to make an accompanying sauce.

Simmering

Simmering is another moist-heat cooking method that uses convection to transfer heat from a liquid to a food. For simmering, the food is submerged in a liquid held at temperatures between 185°F and 205°F (85°C–96°C). Because simmering temperatures are slightly higher than those used for poaching, there should be more action on the liquid's surface, with a few air bubbles breaking through.

As with poaching, the liquid used for simmering has a great effect on the food's flavour. Be sure to use a well-flavoured stock or broth and to add mirepoix, herbs and seasonings as needed. Simmered foods should be moist and very tender.

Boiling

Boiling is another moist-heat cooking method that uses the process of convection to transfer heat from a liquid to a food. Boiling uses large amounts of rapidly bubbling liquid to cook foods. The turbulent waters and the relatively high temperatures cook foods more quickly than do poaching or simmering. Few foods, however, are cooked by true boiling. Most "boiled" meats are actually simmered. Even "hard-boiled" eggs are really only simmered. Starches such as pasta and potatoes are among the only types of food that are truly boiled.

TABLE 9.2   MOIST-HEAT COOKING METHODS

Method	Liquid's Temperature	Liquid's Condition	Uses
Poaching	160°F–180°F 71°C–82°C	Liquid moves slightly but no bubbles	Eggs, fish, fruits
Simmering	185°F–205°F 85°C–96°C	Small bubbles break through the liquid's surface	Meats, stews, chicken
Boiling	212°F 100°C	Large bubbles and rapid movement	Vegetables, pasta
Steaming	212°F or higher 100°C or higher	Food is in contact only with the steam generated by a boiling liquid	Vegetables, fish, shellfish

Under normal atmospheric pressure at sea level, water boils at 212°F (100°C). The addition of other ingredients or a change in atmospheric pressure can change the boiling point, however. As altitude increases, the boiling point decreases because of the drop in atmospheric pressure. For every 1000 feet (305 m) above sea level, the boiling point of water drops 2°F (1°C). In the   city of Calgary at 1100 m, for example, water boils at 206°F (97°C). Because the boiling temperature is lower it will take longer to cook foods in Calgary than in, for example, Montreal.

The addition of alcohol also lowers the boiling point of water because alcohol boils at about 175°F (80°C). In contrast, the addition of salt, sugar or other substances raises the boiling point slightly. This means that foods cooked in salted water cook faster because the boiling point is one or two degrees higher than normal.

Steaming

Steaming is a moist-heat cooking method that uses the process of convection to transfer heat from the steam to the food being cooked. The food to be steamed is placed in a basket or rack above a boiling liquid. The food should not touch the liquid; it should be positioned so that the steam can circulate around it. A lid should be placed on the steaming pot to trap the steam and also create a slight pressure within the pot, which speeds the cooking process. The liquid used to steam the food is sometimes used to make a sauce served with the item.

Another type of steaming uses a low pressure convection steamer. Convection steamers use steam to cook food very quickly in an enclosed chamber. Convection steamer cooking does not result in a flavoured liquid that can be used to make a sauce. High pressure steamers are also available.

Combination Cooking Methods

Some cooking methods employ both dry-heat and moist-heat cooking techniques. The two principal combination methods are braising and stewing. In both methods the first step is usually to brown the main item using dry heat. The second step is to complete cooking by simmering the food in a liquid. Combination methods are good for less tender but flavourful cuts of meat.

Braising

White braising and stewing—*items are seared in moderately hot fat without browning the product. Fricassees use this method.*

Braised foods benefit from the best qualities of both dry- and moist-heat cooking methods. Foods to be braised are usually large pieces that are first browned in a small amount of fat at high temperatures. As with sautéing, heat is transferred from the pan to the food mainly by the process of conduction. Vegetables and seasonings are added and enough sauce or liquid is added to come one-third to one-half up the item being cooked. The pan is covered and the heat is reduced. The food is cooked at low heat, using a combination of simmering and steaming to transfer heat from the liquid (conduction) and the air (convection) to the food. This can be done on the stove top or in the oven. A long, slow cooking period helps tenderize the main item. Braised foods are usually served with a sauce made from the cooking liquid.

Stewing

Stewing also uses a combination of dry- and moist-heat cooking methods. Stewing is most often associated with smaller pieces of food that are first cooked either by browning them in a small amount of fat or oil or by **blanching** them in a liquid. Cooking is then finished in a liquid or sauce. Stewed foods have enough liquid added to cover them completely and are simmered at a constant temperature until tender. Cooking time is generally shorter for stewing than for braising because the main items are smaller.

Blanch—*to very briefly and partially cook a food in boiling water or hot fat; used to assist preparation (for example, to loosen peels from vegetables), as part of a combination cooking method or to remove undesirable flavours.*

CONCLUSION

Cooking is the transfer of heat energy to foods by conduction, convection or radiation. Cooking changes the molecular structure of certain nutrients. When heat is applied, proteins coagulate, starches gelatinize, sugars caramelize, fats melt and water evaporates. Foods can be cooked using a variety of methods. Some use dry heat: broiling, grilling, roasting and baking, sautéing, pan-frying and deep-fat frying. Others use moist heat: poaching, simmering, boiling and steaming. Still others use a combination of the two: braising and stewing. The method used affects the texture, appearance and flavour of the cooked foods. You must understand these principles in order to ensure that foods are properly cooked.

QUESTIONS FOR DISCUSSION

1. Describe the differences between conduction and convection. Identify four cooking methods that rely on both conduction and convection to heat foods. Explain your choices.

2. Identify two cooking methods that rely on infrared heat. What is the principal difference between these methods?

3. At the same temperature, will a food cook faster in a convection oven or a conventional oven? Explain your answer.

4. Describe the process of caramelization and its significance in food preparation. Will a braised food have a caramelized surface? Explain your answer.

5. Describe the process of coagulation and its significance in food preparation. Will a pure fat coagulate if heated? Explain your answer.

6. Describe the process of gelatinization and its significance in food preparation. Will a pure fat gelatinize? Explain your answer.

WEBLINKS

National Food Safety Database: Microwave Cooking Do's and Don'ts
www.foodsafety.org/nc/nc191.htm

Induction Cooking Questions and Answers
www.ripples.co.uk/induct.html

National Food Safety Database: Commercial Broilers
www.foodsafety.org/eh/eh399.htm

Food Irradiation
www.physics.isu.edu/radinf/food.htm

CHAPTER 10
STOCKS AND SAUCES

LEARNING OUTCOMES

After studying this chapter you will be able to:

+ prepare a variety of stocks
+ caramelize bones and mirepoix
+ deglaze a pan
+ reduce a stock to a glaze
+ cook a roux and incorporate it with a liquid
+ use a liaison
+ prepare beurre blanc or beurre rouge
+ make pan gravy and coulis
+ prepare salsa and relish
+ recognize and classify sauces
+ prepare a variety of classic and modern sauces

A *stock* *is a flavoured liquid; a good stock is the key to a great soup, sauce or braised dish. The French appropriately call a stock fond ("base"), as stocks are the basis for many classic and modern dishes.*

A *sauce* *is a thickened liquid used to flavour and enhance other foods. A good sauce adds flavour, moisture, richness and visual appeal. A sauce should complement food; it should never disguise it. A sauce can be hot or cold, sweet or savoury, smooth or chunky.*

Although the thought of preparing stocks and sauces may be intimidating, the procedures are really quite simple. Carefully follow the basic procedures outlined in this chapter, use high-quality ingredients and, with practice and experience, you will soon be producing fine stocks and sauces.

This chapter addresses hot sauces as well as coulis, salsas and relishes. Cold sauces, generally based on mayonnaise, are discussed in Chapter 24, Salads and Salad Dressings; dessert sauces are discussed in Chapter 31, Custards, Creams, Frozen Desserts and Dessert Sauces.

STOCKS

There are several types of stocks. While they are all made from a combination of bones, vegetables, seasonings and liquids, each type uses specific procedures to give it distinctive characteristics.

A **white stock** is made by simmering chicken, veal or beef bones in water with vegetables and seasonings. The stock remains relatively colourless during the cooking process.

A **brown stock** is made from chicken, veal, beef or game bones and vegetables, all of which are caramelized before being simmered in water with seasonings. The stock has a rich, dark colour.

Both a **fish stock** and a **fumet** are made by slowly cooking fish bones or crustacean shells and vegetables without colouring them, then adding water and seasonings and simmering for a short period of time. For a fumet, wine and lemon juice are also added. The resulting stock or fumet is a strongly flavoured, relatively colourless liquid.

A **court bouillon** is made by simmering vegetables and seasonings in water and an acidic liquid such as vinegar or wine. It is used to poach fish or vegetables. A **vegetable stock** is made without meat products.

Ingredients

The basic ingredients of most stocks are bones, a vegetable mixture known as a **mirepoix**, seasonings and water.

Bones

Bones are the most important ingredient for producing a good stock. Bones add flavour, richness and colour. Traditionally, the kitchen or butcher shop saved the day's bones to make stock. But because many meats and poultry items are now purchased previously cut or portioned, food service operations often purchase bones specifically for stock making.

Different bones release their flavour at different rates. Even though the bones are cut into 3- to 4-inch (8 to 10 cm) pieces, a stock made entirely of beef and/or veal bones requires 6 to 8 hours of cooking time, while a stock made entirely from chicken bones requires only 3 to 5 hours.

Beef and Veal Bones

The best bones for beef and veal stock are from younger animals. They contain a higher percentage of **cartilage** and other **connective tissue** than do bones from more mature animals. Connective tissue has a high **collagen** content. Through the cooking process, the collagen is converted into **gelatin** and water. The gelatin adds richness and body to the finished stock.

The best beef and veal bones are back, neck and shank bones as they have a high collagen content. Beef and veal bones should be cut with a meat saw into small pieces, approximately 3 to 4 inches (8 to 10 cm) long, so that they can release as much flavour as possible while the stock cooks.

Chicken Bones

The best bones for chicken stock are from the neck and back. If a whole chicken carcass is used, it can be cut up for easier handling.

Fish Bones

The best bones for fish stock are from lean fish such as sole, halibut, whiting or turbot. Bones from fatty fish (e.g., salmon, tuna and swordfish) do not produce good stock because of their high fat content and distinctive flavours. The entire fish carcass can be used, but it should be cut up with a cleaver or heavy knife for easy handling and even extraction of flavours. After cutting, the pieces should be rinsed in cold water to remove blood, loose scales and other impurities.

Other Bones

Lamb, turkey, game and ham bones can also be used for white or brown stocks. While mixing bones is generally acceptable, be careful of blending strongly flavoured bones, such as those from lamb or game, with beef, veal or chicken bones. The former's strong flavours may not be appropriate or desirable in the finished product.

Mirepoix

A French classical flavouring agent made of "flavouring vegetables" is used to lay down a base flavour in stocks, soups, sauces, stews, braised dishes and pot roasts. The original mirepoix was composed of carrots, onions, celery, lardons, sprig of thyme and bay leaves. Modern chefs often omit the lardons to reduce the fat content and cost.

In many cases the mirepoix is removed before finishing or is puréed and mixed into the final product—for example, with puréed soups. For these reasons mirepoix is rough-cut. The length of cooking time dictates the size of the cut. Lengthy cooking requires large cuts while shorter times demand smaller cuts. The usual ratio is 2 parts onion to 1 part each of celery and carrot. See Figure 10.1. To introduce colour and flavour, the mirepoix is browned either by sautéing or roasting it in the oven. The dry heat caramelizes the carbohydrates in the vegetables. For a white finished product, a white mirepoix is used, made up of rough-cut onion, celery, white of leek and mushrooms.

Flavouring Vegetables

Not all vegetables are suitable for laying a foundation of flavour, for some have overpowering flavours, such as fennel. Others will impart a bitter flavour, like

Connective tissue—*tissue found throughout an animal's body that binds together and supports other tissues such as muscles.*

Cartilage—*or gristle, a tough, elastic, whitish connective tissue that helps give structure to an animal's body.*

Collagen—*a protein found in nearly all connective tissue; it dissolves when cooked with moisture.*

Gelatin—*a tasteless, odourless and brittle mixture of proteins extracted from boiling bones, connective tissue and other animal parts; when dissolved in a hot liquid and then cooled, it forms a jellylike substance used as a thickener and stabilizer.*

Mirepox—*rough-cut flavouring vegetables.*

FIGURE 10.1 *Mirepoix Ingredients*

cabbage, and some will affect colour—beets, for example. Certain root vegetables, such as potatoes, will release starch, which clouds the final product. The following vegetables are suitable to use as flavouring vegetables: carrots, celery, celeriac, mushrooms, garlic, leeks, onions, shallots and tomatoes.

Seasonings

Principal stock seasonings are peppercorns, bay leaves, thyme, parsley stems, and, optionally, garlic. These seasonings generally can be left whole. A stock is cooked long enough for all their flavours to be extracted so there is no reason to chop or grind them. Seasonings generally are added to the stock at the start of cooking. Some chefs do not add seasonings to beef or veal stock until midway through the cooking process, however, because of the extended cooking times. Seasonings can be added as a spice bag (sachet d'épices) or a bouquet garni.

Salt, an otherwise important seasoning, is not added to stock. Because a stock has a variety of uses, it is impossible for the chef to know how much salt to add when preparing it. If, for example, the stock was seasoned to taste with salt, the chef could not reduce it later; salt is not lost through reduction and the concentrated product would taste too salty. Similarly, seasoning the stock to taste with salt could prevent the chef from adding other ingredients that are high in salt when finishing a recipe. Unlike many seasonings whose flavours must be incorporated into a product through lengthy cooking periods, salt can be added at any time during the cooking process with the same effect.

Principles of Stock Making

The following principles apply to all stocks. You should follow them in order to achieve the highest-quality stock possible. See Figure 10.2.

A. Start the Stock in Cold Water

The ingredients should always be covered with cold water. When bones are covered with cold water, blood and other impurities dissolve. As the water heats, the impurities coagulate and rise to the surface, where they can be removed easily by skimming. If the bones were covered with hot water, the impurities would coagulate more quickly and remain dispersed in the stock without rising to the top, making the stock cloudy.

If the water level falls below the bones during cooking, add water to cover them. Flavour cannot be extracted from bones that are not under water, and bones exposed to the air will darken and discolour a white stock.

B. Simmer the Stock Gently

The stock should be brought to a boil and then reduced to a simmer, a temperature of approximately 185°F (85°C). While simmering, the ingredients release their flavours into the liquid. If kept at a simmer, the liquid will remain clear as it reduces and a stock develops.

Never boil a stock for any length of time. Rapid boiling of a stock, even for a few minutes, causes impurities and fats to blend with the liquid, making it cloudy.

C. Skim the Stock Frequently

A stock should be skimmed often to remove the fat and impurities that rise to the surface during cooking. If they are not removed they may make the stock cloudy.

Start the stock in cold water.

Simmer the stock gently.

Skim the stock frequently.

Strain the stock carefully.

Cool the stock quickly.

Store the stock properly.

Degrease the stock.

FIGURE 10.2   *Principles of Stock Making*

FIGURE 10.3 *Venting a Stockpot*

D. Strain the Stock Carefully

Once a stock finishes cooking, the liquid must be separated from the bones, vegetables and other solid ingredients. In order to keep the liquid clear, it is important not to disturb the solid ingredients when removing the liquid. This is easily accomplished if the stock is cooked in a steam kettle or stockpot with a spigot at the bottom.

If the stock is cooked in a standard stockpot, to strain it:

1. Skim as much fat and as many impurities from the surface as possible before removing the stockpot from the heat.
2. After removing the pot from the heat, carefully ladle the stock from the pot without stirring it.
3. Strain the stock through a china cap lined with several layers of cheescloth.

E. Cool the Stock Quickly

Most stocks are prepared in large quantities, cooled and held for later use. Great care must be taken when cooling a stock to prevent food-borne illnesses or souring. A stock can be cooled quickly and safely with the following procedure:

1. Keep the stock in a metal container. A plastic container insulates the stock and delays cooling.
2. Vent the stockpot in an empty sink by placing it on blocks or a rack. This allows water to circulate on all sides and below the pot when the sink is filled with water. See Figure 10.3 above.
3. Install an overflow pipe in the drain and fill the sink with cold water or a combination of cold water and ice. Make sure that the weight of the stock-pot is adequate to keep it from tipping over.
4. Let cold water run into the sink and drain out the overflow pipe. Stir the stock frequently to facilitate even, quick cooling.

F. Store the Stock Properly

Once the stock is cooled, transfer it to a sanitized covered container (either plastic or metal) and store it in the refrigerator. As the stock chills, fat rises to its surface and solidifies. If left intact, this layer of fat helps preserve the stock. Stocks can be stored for up to one week under refrigeration or frozen for several months. Refrigerated stocks should be reheated after 4 or 5 days and simmered for 20 minutes. This will extend their shelf life by reducing bacterial counts. Chill quickly before storing again.

G. Degrease the Stock

Degrease—*to remove fat from the surface of a liquid such as a stock or sauce by skimming, scraping or lifting congealed fat.*

Degreasing a stock is simple: When a stock is refrigerated, fat rises to its surface, hardens and is easily lifted or scraped away before the stock is reheated. See Figure 10.4.

FIGURE 10.4 *Lifting Fat from the Surface of a Cold Stock*

White Stock

A white or neutral stock may be made from beef, veal or chicken bones. The finished stock should have a good flavour, good clarity, high gelatin content and little or no colour. Veal bones are preferred usually, but any combination of beef, veal or chicken bones may be used.

Blanching Bones

Chefs disagree on whether the bones for a white stock should be blanched to remove impurities. Some chefs argue that blanching keeps the stock as clear and colourless as possible; others argue that blanching removes flavour.

BASIC PROCEDURE FOR BLANCHING BONES

If you choose to blanch the bones:

1. Wash the cut-up bones; place them in a stockpot and cover them with cold water.
2. Bring the water to a boil over high heat.
3. As soon as the water boils, skim the rising impurities. Drain the water from the bones and discard it.
4. Refill the pot with cold water and proceed with the stock recipe.

◆◆◆

RECIPE 10.1

WHITE STOCK

Yield: 2 gal. (8 L)

Bones: veal, chicken or beef	15 lb.	7 kg
Cold water	3 gal.	11 L
Mirepoix	2 lb.	1 kg
Sachet:		
Bay leaves	2	2
Dried thyme	1/2 tsp.	2 mL
Peppercorns, crushed	1/2 tsp.	2 mL
Parsley stems	8	8

1. Cut the washed bones into pieces approximately 3–4 inches (8–10 cm) long.
2. Place the bones in a stockpot and cover them with cold water. If blanching, bring the water to a boil, skimming off the scum that rises to the surface. Drain off the water and the impurities. Then add the 3 gallons (11 L) of cold water and bring to a boil. Reduce to a simmer.
3. If not blanching the bones, bring the cold water to a boil. Reduce to a simmer and skim the scum that forms.
4. Add the mirepoix and sachet to the simmering stock.

Approximate values per 1 oz. (30 mL) serving:

Calories	4
Total fat	1 g
Saturated fat	1 g
Cholesterol	0 mg
Sodium	5 mg
Total carbohydrates	0 g
Protein	.2 g
Claims—fat free; very low sodium	

5. Continue simmering and skimming the stock for 6–8 hours. (If only chicken bones are used, simmer for 3–5 hours.)
6. Strain, cool and refrigerate.

Brown Stock

A brown stock is made from chicken, veal, beef or game bones. The finished stock should have a good flavour, rich dark brown colour, good body and high gelatin content.

The primary differences between a brown stock and a white stock are that for a brown stock, the bones and mirepoix are caramelized before being simmered and a tomato product is added. These extra steps provide the finished stock with a rich dark colour and a more intense flavour.

Caramelizing

Caramelization is the process of browning the sugars found on the surface of most foods. This gives the stock its characteristic flavour and colour. Do not burn the bones or mirepoix as this will impart a bitter flavour.

BASIC PROCEDURE FOR CARAMELIZING BONES

For caramelizing, do not wash or blanch the bones as this retards browning. To caramelize:

1. Place the cut-up bones in a roasting pan one layer deep. It is better to roast several pans of bones than to overfill one pan.
2. Roast the bones for approximately one hour in a hot oven (375°F/190°C). Stirring occasionally, brown the bones thoroughly but do not allow them to burn.
3. Transfer the roasted bones from the pan to the stockpot.

Deglazing the Pan

After the bones are caramelized, the excess fat should be removed and reserved for future use. The caramelized and coagulated proteins remaining in the roasting pan are very flavourful. To utilize them, you **deglaze** the pan.

Deglaze—*to swirl or stir a liquid (usually wine or stock) in a sauté pan or other pan to dissolve cooked food particles remaining on the bottom; the resulting mixture often becomes the base for a sauce.*

BASIC PROCEDURE FOR DEGLAZING THE PAN

1. Place the pan on the stove top over medium heat and add enough water to cover the bottom of the pan approximately 1/2 inch (1 cm) deep.
2. Stir and scrape the pan bottom to dissolve and remove all of the caramelized materials while the water heats.
3. Pour the deglazing liquid (also known as the deglazing liquor) over the bones in the stockpot.

BASIC PROCEDURE FOR CARAMELIZING MIREPOIX

1. Add a little of the reserved fat from the roasted bones to the roasting pan after it has been deglazed. (Or use a sautoir large enough to contain all of the mirepoix comfortably.)
2. Sauté the mirepoix, browning all of the vegetables well and evenly without burning them. Alternatively, this may be done in an oven.
3. Add the caramelized mirepoix to the stockpot.

Remouillage—*(French for "rewetting") a stock produced by reusing the bones left from making another stock. After draining the original stock from the stockpot, add fresh mirepoix, a new sachet and enough water to cover the bones and mirepoix and a second stock can be made. A remouillage is treated like the original stock; allow it to simmer for 4–5 hours before straining. A remouillage will not be as clear or as flavourful as the original stock, however. It is often used to make glazes or in place of water when making stocks.*

Most any tomato product can be used in a brown stock: fresh tomatoes, canned whole tomatoes, crushed tomatoes, tomato purée or paste. If using a concentrated tomato product such as paste or purée, use approximately half the amount by weight of fresh or canned tomatoes. The tomato product should be added to the stockpot when the mirepoix is added.

◆◆◆

RECIPE 10.2
BROWN STOCK

Yield: 2 gal. (8 L)

Bones: veal or beef, cut in 3–4 in. (8–10 cm) pieces	15 lb.	7 kg
Cold water	3 gal.	11 L
Mirepoix	2 lb.	1 kg
Tomato paste	8 oz.	250 g
Sachet:		
Bay leaves	2	2
Dried thyme	1/2 tsp.	2 mL
Peppercorns, crushed	1/2 tsp.	2 mL
Garlic cloves, crushed	3	3
Parsley stems	12	12

1. Place the bones in a roasting pan, one layer deep, and brown in a 375°F (190°C) oven. Turn the bones occasionally to brown them evenly.
2. Remove the bones and place them in a stockpot. Pour off the fat from the roasting pan and reserve it.
3. Deglaze the roasting pan with part of the cold water.
4. Add the deglazing liquor and the rest of the cold water to the bones, covering them completely. Bring to a boil and reduce to a simmer.
5. Add a portion of the reserved fat to the roasting pan and sauté the mirepoix until evenly browned. Then add it to the simmering stock.
6. Add the tomato paste and sachet to the stock and continue to simmer for 6–8 hours, skimming as necessary.
7. Strain, cool and refrigerate.

Approximate values per 1 oz. (30 mL) serving:

Calories	3
Total fat	0 g
Saturated fat	0 g
Cholesterol	.3 mg
Sodium	105 mg
Total carbohydrates	0 g
Protein	0 g
Claims—fat free; low sodium	

1. Caramelize the bones.

2. Deglaze the pan with water.

3. Caramelize the mirepoix.

4. Add the proper amount of water.

Fish Stock and Fish Fumet

A fish stock and fish fumet are similar and can be used interchangeably in most recipes. Both are clear with a pronounced fish flavour and very light body. A fumet, however, is more strongly flavoured and aromatic.

The fish bones and crustacean shells used to make a fish stock or fumet should be washed but never blanched because blanching removes too much flavour. Because of the size and structure of fish bones and crustacean shells, stocks and fumets made from them require much less cooking time than even a chicken stock; 30 to 45 minutes is usually sufficient to extract full flavour. Mirepoix or other vegetables should be cut small so that all of their flavours can be extracted during the shorter cooking time.

The procedure for making a fish stock is very similar to that for making a white stock.

◆◆◆

RECIPE 10.3

FISH STOCK

Yield: 1 gal. (4 L)

Fish bones or crustacean shells	10 lb.	4.5 kg
Water	5 qts.	5 L
Mirepoix, small dice	1 lb.	450 g
Mushroom trimmings	8 oz.	250 g
Sachet:		
Bay leaves	2	2
Dried thyme	1/2 tsp.	2 mL
Peppercorns, crushed	1/4 tsp.	1 mL
Parsley stems	8	8

1. Combine all ingredients in a stockpot.

2. Bring to a simmer and skim impurities as necessary.

3. Simmer for 30 to 45 minutes.

4. Strain, cool and refrigerate.

Approximate values per 1 oz. (30 mL) serving:

Calories	5
Total fat	0 g
Saturated fat	0 g
Cholesterol	0 mg
Sodium	100 mg
Total carbohydrates	0 g
Protein	1 g
Claims—fat free; low sodium	

A fish stock is sometimes used to make fish fumet; if so, the resulting product is very strongly flavoured. A fish fumet is also flavoured with white wine and lemon juice. When making a fumet, **sweat** the bones and vegetables before adding the cooking liquid and seasonings.

Sweat—*to cook a food in a pan (usually covered), without browning, over low heat until the item softens and releases moisture; sweating allows the food to release its flavour more quickly when cooked with other foods.*

✦✦✦

RECIPE 10.4
FISH FUMET

Yield: 2 gal. (8 L)

Whole butter	2 oz.	60 g
Onion, small dice	1 lb.	450 g
Parsley stems	12	12
Fish bones	10 lb.	5 kg
Dry white wine	1-1/4 pint	750 mL
Lemon juice	2 oz.	60 mL
Cold water or fish stock	7 qt.	7 L
Mushroom trimmings	2 oz.	60 g
Fresh thyme	1 sprig	1 sprig
Lemon slices (1 lemon)	10	10

Approximate values per
1 oz. (30 mL) serving:

Calories	5
Total fat	7 g
Saturated fat	.2 g
Cholesterol	.5 mg
Sodium	90 g
Total carbohydrates	0 g
Protein	1 g

Claims—fat free; low sodium

1. Melt the butter in a stockpot.

2. Add the onion, parsley stems and fish bones. Cover the pot and sweat the bones on low heat.

3. Sprinkle the bones with the white wine and lemon juice.

4. Add the cold water or fish stock, mushroom trimmings, thyme and lemon slices. Bring to a boil, reduce to a simmer and cook approximately 30 minutes, skimming frequently.

5. Strain, cool and refrigerate.

1. Sweat the onions, parsley stems and fish bones.

2. Add cold water and seasonings.

Vegetable Stock

A good vegetable stock should be clear and light-coloured. Because no animal products are used, it has no gelatin content. A vegetable stock can be used instead of a meat-based stock in most recipes. This substitution is useful when preparing vegetarian dishes or as a lighter, more healthful alternative when preparing sauces and soups. Although almost any combination of vegetables can be used for stock making, more variety is not always better. Sometimes a vegetable stock made with one or two vegetables that complement the finished dish particularly well will produce better results than a stock made with many vegetables.

◆◆◆

RECIPE 10.5

VEGETABLE STOCK

Yield: 1 gal. (4 L)

Vegetable oil	2 oz.	60 mL
Mirepoix, small dice	2 lb.	900 g
Leek, whites and greens, chopped	8 oz.	250 g
Garlic cloves, chopped	4	4
Fennel, small dice	4 oz.	120 g
Tomato, diced	2 oz.	60 g
White wine	8 oz.	250 mL
Water	1 gal.	4 L
Sachet:		
Bay leaf	1	1
Dried thyme	1/2 tsp.	2 mL
Peppercorns, crushed	1/4 tsp.	1 mL
Parsley stems	8	8

Approximate values per 1 oz. (30 mL) serving:

Calories	5
Total fat	0 g
Saturated fat	0 g
Cholesterol	0 mg
Sodium	0 mg
Total carbohydrates	0 g
Protein	0 g

Claims—fat free; low calorie

1. Heat the oil. Add the vegetables and sweat for 10 minutes.
2. Add the white wine, water and sachet.
3. Bring the mixture to a boil, reduce to a simmer and cook for 45 minutes.
4. Strain, cool and refrigerate.

Court Bouillon

A court bouillon, while not actually a stock, is prepared in much the same manner as stocks so it is included here. A court bouillon (French for "short broth") is a flavoured liquid, usually water and wine or vinegar, in which vegetables and seasonings have been simmered to impart their flavours and aromas.

Court bouillon is most commonly used to poach foods such as fish and shellfish. Recipes vary depending upon the foods to be poached. Although a court bouillon can be made in advance and refrigerated for later use, its simplicity lends itself to fresh preparation whenever needed.

◆◆◆

RECIPE 10.6
COURT BOUILLON

Yield: 1 gal. (4 L)

Water	1 gal.	4 L
Vinegar	6 oz.	180 mL
Lemon juice	2 oz.	60 mL
Salt	1/2 oz.	15 g
Mirepoix	1 lb. 8 oz.	700 g
Peppercorns, crushed	1 tsp.	5 mL
Bay leaves	4	4
Dried thyme	pinch	pinch
Parsley stems	1 bunch	1 bunch

Continued

◆◆◆

COMMERCIAL BASES

Commercially produced flavour (or convenience) bases are widely used in food service operations. They are powdered or dehydrated flavourings added to water to create stocks or, when used in smaller amounts, to enhance the flavour of sauces and soups. Although inferior to well-made stocks, flavour bases do reduce the labour involved in the production of stocks, sauces and soups. Used properly, they also ensure a consistent product. Because bases do not contain gelatin, stocks and sauces made from them do not benefit from reduction.

Bases vary greatly in quality and price. Sodium (salt) is the main ingredient in most bases. Better bases are made primarily of meat, poultry or fish extracts. To judge the quality of a flavour base, prepare it according to package directions and compare the flavour to that of a well-made stock. The flavour base can be improved by adding a mirepoix, standard sachet and a few appropriate bones to the mixture, then simmering for one or two hours. It can then be strained, stored and used like a regular stock.

Although convenience bases are widely used in the industry, it is important to remember that even the best base is a poor substitute for a well-made stock.

Approximate values per
1 oz. (30 mL) serving:

Calories	3
Total fat	0 g
Saturated fat	0 g
Cholesterol	0 mg
Sodium	70 mg
Total carbohydrates	0 g
Protein	0 g

Claims—fat free; low sodium

1. Combine all ingredients and bring to a boil.
2. Reduce to a simmer and cook for 45 minutes.
3. Strain and use immediately or cool and refrigerate.

NOTE: This recipe can be used for poaching almost any fish, but it is particularly well suited to salmon, trout or shellfish. When poaching freshwater fish, replace the water and vinegar with equal parts white wine and water.

Glaze

A glaze is the reduction and concentration of a stock. One gallon (4 L) of stock produces only 8–16 ounces (250–500 mL) of glaze. *Glace de viande* is made from brown stock, reduced until it becomes dark and syrupy. *Glace de volaille* is made from chicken stock and *glace de poisson* from fish stock.

Glazes are added to soups or sauces to increase and intensify flavours. They are also used as a source of intense flavouring for several of the derivative sauces discussed below.

BASIC PROCEDURE FOR REDUCING A STOCK TO A GLAZE

1. Simmer the stock over very low heat. Be careful not to let it burn and skim it often.
2. As it reduces and the volume decreases, transfer the liquid into progressively smaller saucepans. Strain the liquid each time it is transferred into a smaller saucepan.
3. Strain it a final time, cool and refrigerate. A properly made glaze will keep for several months under refrigeration.
   See Table 10.1 for troubleshooting tips for stocks.

TABLE 10.1   TROUBLESHOOTING CHART FOR STOCKS

Problem	Reason	Solution
Cloudy	Impurities	Start stock in cold water
	Stock boiled during cooking	Strain through layers of cheesecloth
Lack of flavour	Not cooked long enough	Increase cooking time
	Inadequate seasoning	Add more flavouring ingredients
	Improper ratio of bones to water	Add more bones
		Reduce liquid
Lack of colour	Improperly caramelized bones and mirepoix	Caramelize bones and mirepoix until darker
	Not cooked long enough	Cook longer
Lack of body	Wrong bones used	Use bones with a higher content of connective tissue
	Insufficient reduction	Cook longer
	Improper ratio of bones to water	Add more bones
Too salty	Commercial base used	Change base or make own
	Salt added during cooking	stock; do not salt stock

SAUCES

With a few exceptions, a sauce is a liquid plus thickening agent plus seasonings. Any cook can produce fine sauces by learning to:

1. Make good stocks;
2. Use thickening agents properly to achieve the desired texture, flavour and appearance; and
3. Use seasonings properly to achieve the desired flavours.

Classic hot sauces are divided into two groups: **basic** (mother or leading sauces) (Fr. *sauce mère*) and **derivative** (small or compound sauces). The five classic basic sauces are béchamel, velouté, espagnole (brown), tomato and hollandaise. Except for hollandaise, basic sauces are rarely served as is; more often they are used to create the many derivative sauces.

Not all sauces fall into the traditional classifications, however. Some sauces use purées of fruits or vegetables as their base; they are known as **coulis**. Others, such as **beurre blanc** (French for "white butter") and **beurre rouge** ("red butter"), are based on an acidic reduction in which whole butter is incorporated. **Flavoured butters**, **salsas**, **relishes** and **pan gravy** are also used as sauces in modern food service operations.

Thickening Agents

Although there are exceptions, most sauces are thickened by the gelatinization of starches. As discussed in Chapter 9, Principles of Cooking, gelatinization is the process by which starch granules absorb moisture when placed in a liquid and heated. As the moisture is absorbed, the product thickens. Starches generally used to thicken sauces are flour, cornstarch and arrowroot. Gelatinization may sound easy, but it takes practice to produce a good sauce that

- ✦ is lump-free,
- ✦ has a good clean flavour that is not pasty or floury,
- ✦ has a consistency that will coat the back of a spoon (the French call this *nappé*), and
- ✦ will not separate or break when the sauce is held or reduced.

Roux

Roux is the traditional means used to thicken sauces. It is a combination of equal parts, by weight, of flour and fat, cooked together to form a paste. Cooking the flour in fat coats the starch granules with the fat and prevents them from lumping together or forming lumps when introduced into a liquid. In some production kitchens, large amounts of roux are prepared and held for use as needed. Smaller operations may make roux as required for each recipe.

There are three types of roux, as shown in Figure 10.5:

1. **White roux**—It is cooked only briefly and should be removed from the heat as soon as it develops a frothy, bubbly appearance. It is used in white sauces, such as béchamel, or in dishes where little or no colour is desired.
2. **Blond roux**—Cooked slightly longer than white roux, blond roux should begin to take on a little colour as the flour caramelizes. It is used in ivory-coloured sauces, such as velouté, or where a richer flavour is desired.

FIGURE 10.5 *White, Blond and Brown Roux*

◆◆◆

A SAUCY HISTORY

The word "sauce" is derived from the Latin word *salus*, meaning "salted." This derivation is appropriate. For millennia, salt has been the basic condiment for enhancing and/or disguising the flavour of many foods. Over the centuries, sauces have also been used for these purposes.

Cooks of ancient Rome flavoured many dishes with *garum*, a golden-coloured sauce made from fermented fish entrails combined with brine, condiments, water and wine or vinegar. They also used a sauce referred to as a "single," made from oil, wine and brine. When boiled with herbs and saffron it became a "double" sauce. To this the Byzantines later added pepper, cloves, cinnamon, cardamom and coriander or spikenard (a fragrant ointment made from grains).

During the Middle Ages chefs (and their employers) were fond of either very spicy or sweet-and-sour sauces. A typical sauce for roasted meat consisted of powdered cinnamon, mustard, red wine and a sweetener such as honey. It was thickened, if at all, with bits of stale or grilled bread. Other sauces were based on verjuice, an acidic stock prepared from the juice of unripe gapes. To it were added other fruit juices, honey, flower petals and herbs or spices. Indeed, most medieval sauces were heavily spiced. Perhaps this was done to showcase the host's wealth, perhaps to hide the taste of salt-cured or less-than-fresh meats.

Guillaume Tirel (c. 1312–1395), who called himself **Taillevent**, was the master chef for Charles V of France. Around 1375 Taillevent wrote *Le Viandier*, the oldest-known French cookbook. The cooking style he describes relies heavily on pounding, puréeing and spicing most foods so that the finished dish bears little resemblance in shape, texture or taste to the original ingredients. Included in his methods

for what can only be described as ways of masking poor-quality ingredients are 17 sauces. Among them is a recipe for a *cameline* sauce. It is made from grilled bread soaked in wine; the wine-soaked bread is then drained, squeeze-dried and ground with cinnamon, ginger, pepper, cloves and nutmeg; this mixture is then diluted with vinegar. There is also a recipe for a sauce called *taillemaslée*, made of fried onions, verjuice, vinegar and mustard. (Appropriately, on his grave marker Taillevent is dressed as a sergeant-at-arms whose shield is decorated with three cooking pots.)

Recipes for some sauces of the Renaissance, such as *poivrade* or *Robert*, are recognizable today. Most sauces enjoyed in Renaissance-era Italy and France consisted of some combination of concentrated cooking juices, wines, herbs and spices (especially pepper), sometimes thickened with bread. Sweet, fruit-based sauces were also popular. Most importantly for the development of modern cuisine, however, was the growing use of sauces based on broths

thickened with cream, butter and egg yolks and flavoured with herbs and spices.

Although he died in relative obscurity, many now consider **François Pierre de La Varenne** (1618–1678) to be one of the founding fathers of French cuisine. His treatises, especially *Le Cuisinier français* (1651), detail the early development, methods and manners of French cuisine. His analysis and recipes mark a departure from medieval cookery and a French cuisine heavily influenced by Italian traditions. His writings were uniquely modern in that he included recipes for new foods (especially fruits and vegetables native to the Americas or the Far East) and for indigenous foods (such as saltwater fish) that were gradually becoming more popular. La Varenne is credited with introducing roux as a thickening agent for sauces, especially velouté sauces. He emphasized the importance of properly prepared *fonds* and the reduction of cooking juices to concentrate flavours. He also popularized the use of bouquets garni to flavour stocks and sauces.

Sometime during the early 18th century, the chef to the French Duc de Levis-Mirepoix pioneered the use of onions, celery and carrots to enhance the flavour and aroma of stocks. The mixture, named for the chef's employer, soon became the standard way of enriching stocks. An enriched stock greatly improves the quality of the sauces derived from it.

During the early 19th century, **Antonin Carême** developed the modern system for classifying hundreds of sauces. It is unknown how many sauces Carême actually invented himself, but he wrote treatises containing the theories and recipes for many of the sauces still used today. Carême's extravagant lists of sauces were reduced and simplified by chefs later in the 19th century, most notably by **Auguste Escoffier**.

3. **Brown roux**—It is cooked until it develops a darker colour and a nutty aroma and flavour. Brown roux is used in brown sauces and dishes where a dark colour is desired. It is important to remember that cooking a starch before adding a liquid breaks down the starch granules and prevents gelatinization from occurring. Therefore, because brown roux is cooked longer than white roux, more brown roux is required to thicken a given quantity of liquid.

BASIC PROCEDURE FOR MAKING ROUX

Whether it will be white, blond or brown, the procedure for making roux is the same:

1. Using a heavy saucepan to prevent scorching, heat the clarified butter or other fat.
2. Add all of the flour and stir to form a paste. Although all-purpose flour can be used, it is better to use cake or pastry flour because they contain a higher percentage of starch. See Table 10.2. Do not use high-gluten flour because of its greatly reduced starch content. (Flours are discussed in Chapter 26, Principles of the Bakeshop.)
3. Cook the paste over medium heat until the desired colour is achieved. It should have the consistency of wet cement. Stir the roux often to avoid burning. Burnt roux will not thicken a liquid; it will simply add dark specks and an undesirable flavour.

The temperature and amount of roux being prepared determine the exact length of cooking time. Generally, however, a white roux needs to cook for only a few minutes, long enough to minimize the raw flour taste. Blond roux is cooked longer, until the paste begins to change to a slightly darker colour. Brown roux requires a much longer cooking time to develop its characteristic colour and aroma. A good roux will be stiff, not runny or pourable.

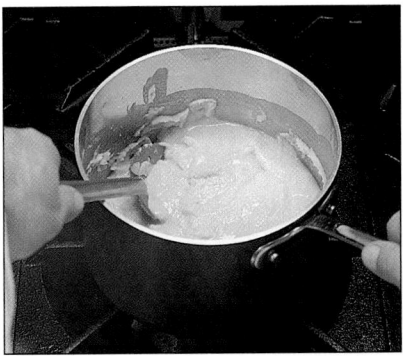

Cook the roux.

INCORPORATING ROUX INTO A LIQUID

There are two ways to incorporate roux into a liquid without causing lumps:

1. Cold stock can be added to the hot roux while stirring vigorously with a whisk.
2. Room-temperature roux can be added to a hot stock while stirring vigorously with a whisk.

When the roux and the liquid are completely incorporated and the sauce begins to boil, it is necessary to cook the sauce for a period of time to remove any raw flour taste that may remain. Most cooks feel a minimum of 20 minutes is necessary.

NOTE: Avoid using aluminium pots when using a whisk to incorporate a roux. Aluminium is a relatively soft metal and the whisk will scrape particles of aluminium into the sauce causing discolouration and off-flavour.

(a)

Cold stock

Hot roux

(b)

Cold roux

Hot stock

When thickening stock with roux, either
(a) add cold stock to hot roux, or
(b) add cold roux to hot stock.

TABLE 10.2		PROPORTIONS OF ROUX TO LIQUID				
Flour	+	Butter	=	Roux	+	Liquid	=	Sauce

Flour	+	Butter	=	Roux	+	Liquid	=	Sauce
6 oz./190 g	+	6 oz./190 g	=	12 oz./375 g	+	1 gal./4 L	=	light
8 oz./250 g	+	8 oz./250 g	=	1 lb./500 g	+	1 gal./4 L	=	medium
12 oz./375 g	+	12 oz./375 g	=	24 oz./750 g	+	1 gal./4 L	=	heavy

VARIABLES: The starch content of a flour determines its thickening power. Cake flour, being lowest in protein and highest in starch, has more thickening power than bread flour, which is high in protein and low in starch. In addition, a dark roux has less thickening power than a lighter one, so more will be needed to thicken an equal amount of liquid.

GUIDELINES FOR USING ROUX

1. Avoid using aluminum pots. The scraping action of the whisk will turn light sauces grey and will impart a metallic flavour.

2. Use sufficiently heavy pots to prevent sauces from scorching or burning during extended cooking times.

3. Avoid extreme temperatures. Roux should be no colder than room temperature so that the fat is not fully solidified. Extremely hot roux is dangerous and can spatter when combined with a liquid. Stocks should not be ice cold when combined with roux; the roux will become very cold and the solidified pieces may be very difficult to work out with a whisk.

4. Avoid overthickening. Roux does not begin to thicken a sauce until the sauce is almost at the boiling point; the thickening action continues for several minutes while the sauce simmers. If a sauce is to cook for a long time, it will also be thickened by reduction.

Cornstarch

Cornstarch, a very fine white powder, is a pure starch derived from corn. It is used widely as a thickening agent for hot and cold sauces and is especially popular in Asian cuisines for thickening sauces and soups. Liquids thickened with cornstarch have a glossy sheen that may or may not be desirable.

One unit of cornstarch thickens about twice as much liquid as an equal unit of flour. Sauces thickened with cornstarch are less stable than those thickened with roux because cornstarch can break down and lose its thickening power after prolonged heating. Products thickened with cornstarch should not be reheated.

Incorporating Cornstarch

Cornstarch must be mixed with a cool liquid before it is introduced into a hot one. The cool liquid separates the grains of starch and allows them to begin absorbing liquid without lumping. A solution of starch and cool liquid is called a **slurry**.

The starch slurry may be added to either a hot or cold liquid. If added to a hot liquid, it must be stirred continuously during incorporation. As opposed to a roux, the gelatinization of cornstarch begins almost immediately. Sauces thickened with cornstarch must be cooked gently until the raw starch flavour disappears, usually about five minutes.

Modified and Pre-gelatinized Starches

Modified starches have a cross-bonded molecular structure and can be mixed hot or cold. They are generally heat and cold stable (e.g. Ultra-Sperse). Pre-gelatinized starches are heat treated in milling and must be mixed in a cold liquid initially and then cooked (e.g. cornstarch). Follow the manufacturers directions.

Arrowroot

Arrowroot, derived from the roots of several tropical plants, is similar in texture, appearance and thickening power to cornstarch and is used in exactly the same manner. Although it is much more expensive, arrowroot does not break down as quickly as cornstarch and it produces a slightly clearer finished product.

Beurre Manié

Beurre manié is a combination of equal amounts, by volume, of flour and soft whole butter. The flour and butter are kneaded together until smooth. The mixture is then formed into pea-sized balls and whisked into a simmering sauce. Beurre manié is used for quick thickening at the end of the cooking process. The butter also adds shine and flavour to the sauce as it melts.

Liaison

Unlike the thickeners described above, a liaison does not thicken a sauce through gelatinization. A liaison is a mixture of egg yolks and heavy cream, which adds richness and smoothness with minimal thickening. Special care must be taken to prevent the yolks from coagulating when they are added to a hot liquid because this could curdle the sauce.

BASIC PROCEDURE FOR USING A LIAISON

1. Whisk together one part egg yolk and three parts whipping cream. Combining the yolk with cream raises the temperature at which the yolk's proteins coagulate, making it easier to incorporate them into a sauce without lumping or curdling.
2. **Temper** the egg yolk mixture by slowly adding a small amount of the hot liquid while stirring continuously.
3. When enough of the hot liquid has been added to the egg yolk mixture to warm it thoroughly, begin adding the warmed egg yolk mixture to the remaining hot liquid. Be sure to stir the mixture carefully to prevent the yolk from overcooking or lumping. Plain egg yolks coagulate at temperatures between 149°F and 158°F (65°C–70°C). Mixing them with cream raises the temperatures at which they coagulate to approximately 180°F–185°F (82°C–85°C). Temperatures over 185°F (85°C) will cause the yolks to curdle. Great care must be taken to hold the sauce above 140°F (60°C) for food safety and sanitation reasons, yet below 185°F (85°C) to prevent curdling.

1. Add hot liquid to the egg yolks and cream mixture.

2. Add the tempered egg yolks and cream mixture to the hot liquid.

Tempering—*gradually raising the temperature of a cold liquid by slowly stirring in a hot liquid.*

Finishing Techniques

Reduction

As sauces cook, moisture is released in the form of steam. As steam escapes, the remaining ingredients concentrate, thickening the sauce and strengthening the flavours. This process, known as **reduction**, is commonly used to thicken sauces because no starches or other flavour-altering ingredients are needed. Sauces are often finished by allowing them to reduce until the desired consistency is reached.

Straining

Smoothness is important to the success of most sauces. They can be strained through either a china cap lined with several layers of cheesecloth or a fine mesh chinois. As discussed below, often vegetables, herbs, spices and other seasonings are added to a sauce for flavour. Straining removes these ingredients as well as any lumps of roux or thickener remaining in the sauce after the desired flavour and consistency have been reached.

Monter au Beurre

Monter au beurre is the process of swirling or whisking whole butter into a sauce to give it shine, flavour and richness. Compound or flavoured butters, discussed below, can be used in place of whole butter to add specific flavours. Monter au beurre is widely used to enrich and finish derivative sauces.

TABLE 10.3   SAUCE FAMILIES

Liquid	Thickener	Basic Sauce
Milk	Roux	Béchamel
White stock	Roux	Velouté
Veal stock		Veal velouté
Chicken stock		Chicken velouté
Fish stock		Fish velouté
Brown stock	Roux	Espagnole (brown sauce)
Tomato	Roux optional	Tomato sauce
Butter	Egg yolks	Hollandaise

Sauce Families

Basic (leading or mother) **sauces** are the foundation for the entire classic repertoire of hot sauces. The five basic sauces—béchamel, velouté, espagnole (also known as brown), tomato and hollandaise—can be seasoned and garnished to create a wide variety of derivative or compound sauces. The five basic sauces are distinguished principally by the liquids and thickeners used to create them. See Table 10.3.

Derivative (small or compound) **sauces** are grouped together into families based on their basic sauce. Some derivative sauces have a variety of uses; others are traditional accompaniments for specific foods. A derivative sauce may be named for its ingredients, place of origin or creator. Although there are numerous classic derivative sauces, we have included only a few of the more popular ones following each of the basic sauce recipes.

The Béchamel Family

MILK

BÉCHAMEL

Cream   Cheddar   Mornay   Nantua   Soubise

Named for its creator, Louis de Béchamel (1630–1703), steward to Louis XIV of France, béchamel sauce is the easiest basic sauce to prepare. Traditionally it was made by adding heavy cream to a thick veal velouté. Although some chefs still believe a béchamel should contain veal stock, today the sauce is almost always made by thickening scalded milk with a white roux and adding seasonings. It is used for vegetable, egg, gratin dishes and pasta dishes.

QUALITY STANDARD

A properly made béchamel is rich, creamy and absolutely smooth with no hint of graininess. The flavours of the onion and clove used to season it should be apparent but not overwhelm the sauce's clean, milky taste. The sauce should be the colour of heavy cream and have a deep lustre. It should be thick enough to coat foods lightly but should not taste like the roux used to thicken it.

◆◆◆

RECIPE 10.7
BÉCHAMEL

Yield: 1 gal. (4 L)

Oignon piqué	1	1
Milk	1 gal.	4 L
Flour	8 oz.	250 g
Clarified butter	8 oz.	250 g
Salt and white pepper	TT	TT
Nutmeg	TT	TT

1. Add the oignon piqué to the milk in a heavy saucepan and simmer for 20 minutes.

2. In a separate stainless steel pot, make a white roux with the flour and butter.

3. Remove the oignon piqué from the milk. Gradually add the hot milk to the roux while stirring constantly with a whisk to prevent lumps. Bring to a boil.

4. Reduce the sauce to a simmer, add the seasonings and continue cooking for 30 minutes.

5. Strain the sauce through a china cap lined with cheesecloth. Melted butter can be carefully ladled over the surface of the sauce to prevent a skin from forming. Hold for service or cool in a water bath.

Approximate values per
6 oz. (180 mL) serving:

Calories	240
Total fat	15 g
Saturated fat	9 g
Cholesterol	50 mg
Sodium	180 mg
Total carbohydrates	18 g
Protein	7 g
Vitamin A	15%
Calcium	25%

Béchamel Sauce Derivatives

With a good béchamel, producing the derivative sauces in its family is quite simple. The quantities indicated below are for 1 quart (1 L) of béchamel. The final step for each recipe is to season to taste with salt and pepper.

Cheddar Add to béchamel 8 ounces (250 g) grated cheddar cheese, a dash of Worcestershire sauce and 1 tablespoon (15 mL) dry mustard.

Cream Sauce Add to béchamel 8–12 ounces (250–360 mL) scalded cream and a few drops of lemon juice.

Mornay Add to béchamel 4 ounces (120 g) grated Gruyère cheese and 1 ounce (30 g) grated Parmesan cheese. Thin as desired with scalded cream. Remove the sauce from the heat and swirl in 2 ounces (60 g) whole butter.

Nantua Add to béchamel 4 ounces (120 mL) heavy cream and 6 ounces (180 g) crayfish butter (page 219). Add paprika to achieve the desired colour. Garnish the finished sauce with diced crayfish meat.

Soubise (modern) Sweat 1 pound (500 g) diced onion in 1 ounce (30 g) butter without browning. Add béchamel and simmer until the onions are fully cooked. Strain through a fine chinois.

The Velouté Family

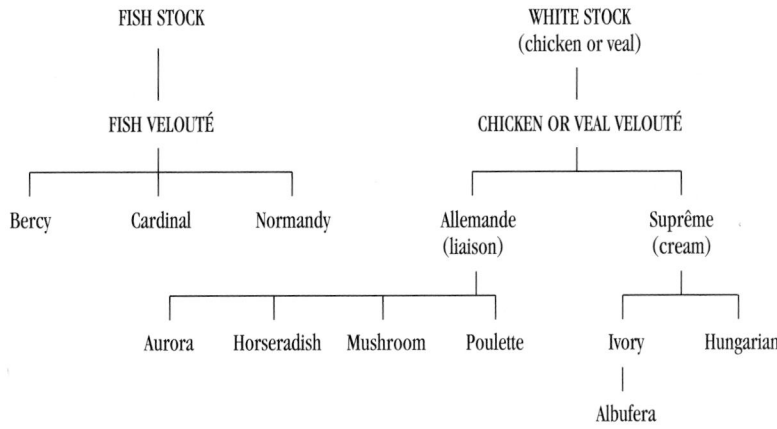

Velouté sauces are made by thickening a white stock or fish stock with roux. The white stock can be made from veal or chicken bones. A fish velouté sauce, made from fish stock, is used to create a few derivative sauces. A velouté sauce made from veal or chicken stock is usually used to make one of two intermediary sauces—allemande and suprême—from which many derivative sauces are derived. Allemande sauce is made by adding lemon juice and a liaison to either the veal or chicken velouté. (The stock used depends upon the dish with which the sauce will be served.) Suprême sauce is made by adding cream to a chicken velouté. See Table 10.4.

QUALITY STANDARD

A properly made velouté should be rich, smooth and lump-free. If made from chicken or fish stock, it should taste of chicken or fish. A velouté made from veal stock should have a more neutral flavour. The sauce should be ivory-coloured, with a deep lustre. It should be thick enough to cling to foods without tasting like the roux used to thicken it.

◆◆◆

RECIPE 10.8
VELOUTÉ

Yield: 1 gal. (4 L)

Clarified butter	8 oz.	250 g
Flour	8 oz.	250 g
Chicken, veal or fish stock	5 qt.	5 L
Salt and white pepper (optional)*	TT	TT

Approximate values per 1 oz. (30 mL) serving:

Calories	25
Total fat	1.5 g
Saturated fat	1 g
Cholesterol	5 mg
Sodium	140 mg
Total carbohydrates	2 g
Protein	1 g

1. Melt the butter in a heavy saucepan. Add the flour and cook to make a blond roux.
2. Gradually add the stock to the roux, stirring constantly with a whisk or wooden spoon to prevent lumps. Bring to a boil and reduce to a simmer.
3. Simmer and reduce to 1 gallon (4 L), approximately 30 minutes.
4. Strain through a china cap lined with cheesecloth.
5. Melted butter may be carefully ladled over the surface of the sauce to prevent a skin from forming. Hold for service or cool in a water bath.

*Seasonings are optional; their use depends upon the seasonings in the stock and the sauce's intended use.

Fish Velouté Sauce Derivatives

A few derivative sauces can be made from fish velouté. The quantities given are for 1 quart (1 L) fish velouté sauce. The final step for each recipe is to season to taste with salt and pepper.

Bercy Sauté 2 ounces (60 g) finely diced shallots in butter. Then add 8 ounces (250 mL) dry white wine and 8 ounces (250 mL) fish stock. Reduce this mixture by one-third and add the fish velouté. Finish with butter and garnish with chopped parsley.

Cardinal Add 8 ounces (250 mL) fish stock to 1 quart (1 L) fish velouté. Reduce this mixture by half and add 1 pint (500 mL) heavy cream and a dash of cayenne pepper. Bring to a boil and swirl in 1-1/2 ounces (45 g) lobster butter (page 219). Garnish with chopped lobster coral at service time.

Normandy Add 4 ounces (120 g) mushroom trimmings and 4 ounces (120 mL) shellfish liquor (oyster, clam, mussel) to 1 quart (1 L) fish velouté. Reduce by one-third and finish with an egg yolk and cream liaison. Strain through a fine chinois.

TABLE 10.4 VELOUTÉ SAUCES

Fish stock	+	Roux	=	Velouté			
Chicken stock	+	Roux	=	Velouté	+ Cream	=	Suprême
Chicken stock	+	Roux	=	Velouté	+ Liaison and lemon	=	Allemande
Veal stock	+	Roux	=	Velouté	+ Liaison and lemon	=	Allemande

❖❖❖

RECIPE 10.9

ALLEMANDE SAUCE

Yield: 1 gal. (4 L)

Veal or chicken velouté sauce	1 gal.	4 L
Egg yolks	8	8
Heavy cream	24 oz.	650 mL
Lemon juice	1 oz.	30 mL
Salt and white pepper	TT	TT

1. Bring the velouté to a simmer.

2. In a stainless steel bowl, whip the egg yolks with the cream. Ladle approximately one-third of the hot velouté sauce into this mixture, while whisking, to temper the yolk and cream mixture.

3. When one-third of the velouté has been incorporated into the now-warmed yolk and cream mixture, gradually add the liaison to the remaining velouté sauce while whisking continuously.

4. Reheat the sauce. Do not let it boil.

5. Add the lemon juice plus salt and white pepper.

6. Strain through a china cap lined with cheesecloth.

Approximate values per 1 oz. (30 mL) serving:

Calories	40
Total fat	3.5 g
Saturated fat	2 g
Cholesterol	25 mg
Sodium	95 mg
Total carbohydrates	1 g
Protein	1 g
Vitamin A	4%

Allemande Sauce Derivatives

Several derivative sauces are easily produced from an allemande sauce made with either a chicken or veal velouté. The quantities given are for 1 quart (1 L) allemande. The final step for each recipe is to season to taste with salt and pepper.

Aurora   Add to allemande 2 ounces (60 mL) tomato paste and finish with 1 ounce (30 g) butter.

Horseradish   Add to allemande 4 ounces (120 mL) heavy cream and 1 teaspoon (5 mL) dry mustard. Just before service add 2 ounces (60 g) freshly grated horseradish. The horseradish should not be cooked with the sauce.

Mushroom   Sauté 4 ounces (120 g) sliced mushrooms in 1/2 ounce (15 g) butter; add 2 teaspoons (10 mL) lemon juice. Then add the allemande to the mushrooms. Do not strain.

Poulette   Sauté 8 ounces (250 g) sliced mushrooms and 1/2 ounce (15 g) diced shallots in 1 ounce (30 g) butter. Add to the allemande; then add

2 ounces (60 mL) cream. Finish with lemon juice and 1 tablespoon (15 mL) chopped parsley.

◆◆◆

RECIPE 10.10
SUPRÊME SAUCE

Yield: 1 gal. (4 L)

Chicken velouté sauce	1 gal.	4 L
Mushroom trimmings	8 oz.	250 g
Heavy cream	1 qt.	1 L
Salt and white pepper	TT	TT

1. Simmer the velouté sauce with the mushroom trimmings until reduced by one-fourth.

2. Gradually whisk in the heavy cream and return to a simmer.

3. Adjust the seasonings.

4. Strain through a china cap lined with cheesecloth.

Approximate values per 1 oz. (30 mL) serving:

Calories	45
Total fat	4 g
Saturated fat	2.5 g
Cholesterol	15 mg
Sodium	95 mg
Total carbohydrates	1 g
Protein	1 g
Vitamin A	4%

Suprême Sauce Derivatives

The following derivative sauces are easily made from suprême sauce. The quantities given are for 1 quart (1 L) suprême sauce. The final step for each recipe is to season to taste with salt and pepper.

Albufera   Add to suprême 3 ounces (90 g) glace de volaille and 2 ounces (60 g) red pepper butter (page 219).

Hungarian   Sweat 2 ounces (60 g) diced onion in 1 tablespoon (15 mL) butter. Add 1 tablespoon (15 mL) paprika. Stir in the suprême sauce. Cook for 2–3 minutes, strain and finish with butter.

Ivory   Add to suprême 3 ounces (90 g) glace de volaille.

The Espagnole (Brown Sauce) Family

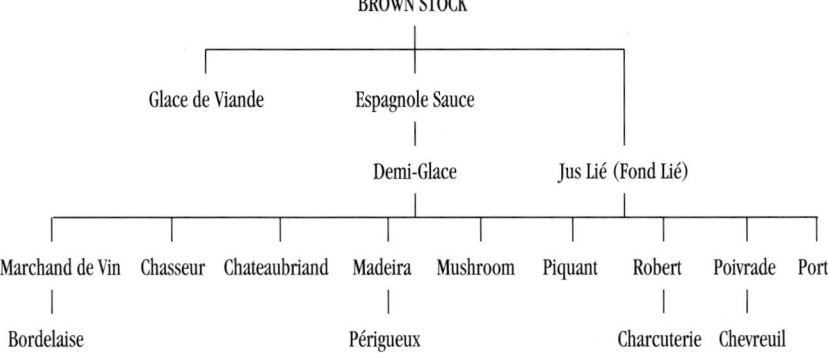

The basic sauce of the espagnole or brown sauce family is full-bodied and rich. It is made from brown stock to which brown roux, mirepoix and tomato purée are added. Most often this sauce is used to produce demi-glace. Brown stock is also used to make jus lié. Demi-glace is used to create the derivative sauces of the espagnole family.

━━━━━━━━━━━━ ◆◆◆ ━━━━━━━━━━━━

RECIPE 10.11

ESPAGNOLE
(BROWN SAUCE)

Yield: 1 gal. (4 L)

Mirepoix, medium dice	2 lb.	1 kg
Fat or clarified butter	8 oz.	250 g
Flour	8 oz.	250 g
Brown stock	5 qt.	5 L
Tomato purée	8 oz.	250 mL
Sachet:		
Bay leaf	1	1
Dried thyme	1/2 tsp.	2 mL
Peppercorns, crushed	1/4 tsp.	1 mL
Parsley stems	8	8
Salt and pepper	TT	TT

1. Sauté the mirepoix in fat until well caramelized.
2. Add the flour and cook to make a brown roux.
3. Add the brown stock and tomato purée. Stir to break up any lumps of roux. Bring to a boil; reduce to a simmer.
4. Add the sachet.
5. Simmer for approximately 1-1/2 hours, allowing the sauce to reduce. Skim the surface as needed to remove impurities.
6. Strain the sauce through a china cap lined with several layers of cheesecloth. Adjust seasonings and cool in a water bath or hold for service.

Approximate values per 1 oz. (30 mL) serving:

Calories	35
Total fat	2 g
Saturated fat	1 g
Cholesterol	5 mg
Sodium	150 mg
Total carbohydrates	4 g
Protein	1 g
Vitamin A	6%

Claims—low fat; low calorie

Demi-Glace

Brown stock is used to make the espagnole or brown sauce described above. Espagnole sauce can then be made into demi-glace, which in turn is used to make the derivative sauces of the espagnole family. Demi-glace is half brown sauce and half brown stock, reduced by half. It is usually finished with a small amount of madeira or sherry wine. Because demi-glace creates a richer, more flavourful base, it produces finer derivative sauces than those made directly from a brown sauce.

QUALITY STANDARD

A properly made demi-glace is rich, smooth and lump-free. Its prominent roasted flavour comes from the bones used for the brown stock. There should be no taste of roux. The caramelized bones and mirepoix as well as the tomato product contribute to its glossy dark brown, almost chocolate, colour. It should be thick enough to cling to food without being pasty or heavy.

Approximate values per
1 oz. (30 mL) serving:

Calories	30
Total fat	1.5 g
Saturated fat	.5 g
Cholesterol	5 mg
Sodium	200 mg
Total carbohydrates	4 g
Protein	1 g
Vitamin A	6%

Claims—low fat; low calorie

◆◆◆

RECIPE 10.12
DEMI-GLACE

Yield: 1 qt. (1 L)

Brown stock	1 qt.	1 L
Brown sauce	1 qt.	1 L

1. Combine the stock and sauce in a saucepan over medium heat.
2. Simmer until the mixture is reduced by half (i.e., a yield of 1 quart or 1 L).
3. Strain and cool in a water bath.

Jus Lié

Jus lié, or **fond lié**, are used like a demi-glace, especially to produce derivative sauces. Jus lié and fond lié are lighter and easier to make than a demi-glace, however. They are made in one of two ways:

1. A rich brown stock is thickened with cornstarch, arrowroot or modified starch and seasoned, or
2. A rich brown stock is simmered and reduced so that it thickens naturally due to concentrated amounts of gelatin and other proteins.

The starch-thickened method is a quick alternative to the long-simmering demi-glace. But because it is simply a brown stock thickened with starch or arrowroot, it will only be as good as the stock with which it was begun. Sauces made from reduced stock usually have a better flavour but can be expensive to produce because of high food costs and lengthy reduction time.

QUALITY STANDARD

A properly made jus lié is very rich and smooth. It shares many flavour characteristics with demi-glace. Its colour should be dark brown and glossy from the concentrated gelatin content. Its consistency is somewhat lighter than demi-glace, but it should still cling lightly to foods.

Espagnole (Brown) Sauce Derivatives

Demi-glace and jus lié are used to produce many derivative sauces. The quantities given are for 1 quart (1 L) demi-glace or jus lié. The final step for each recipe is to season to taste with salt and pepper.

Bordelaise Combine 1 pint (500 mL) dry red wine, 2 ounces (60 g) chopped shallots, 1 bay leaf, 1 sprig thyme and a pinch of black pepper in a saucepan. Reduce by three-fourths, then add demi-glace and simmer for 15 minutes. Strain through a fine chinois. Finish with 2 ounces (60 g) whole butter and garnish with sliced, poached beef marrow.

Chasseur (Hunter's Sauce) Sauté 4 ounces (120 g) sliced mushrooms and 1 tablespoon (15 mL) diced shallots in butter. Add 8 ounces (250 mL) white wine and reduce by three-fourths. Then add demi-glace and 6 ounces (170 g) diced tomatoes; simmer for 5 minutes. Do not strain. Garnish with chopped parsley.

Chateaubriand   Combine 1 pint (500 mL) dry white wine and 2 ounces (60 g) diced shallots. Reduce the mixture by two-thirds. Add demi-glace and reduce by half. Season to taste with lemon juice and cayenne pepper. Do not strain. Swirl in 4 ounces (120 g) butter to finish and garnish with chopped fresh tarragon.

Chevreuil   Prepare a poivrade sauce (see below) but add 6 ounces (170 g) bacon or game trimmings to the mirepoix. Finish with 4 ounces (120 mL) red wine and a dash of cayenne pepper.

Madeira or Port   Bring demi-glace to a boil, reduce slightly. Then add 4 ounces (120 mL) madeira wine or ruby red port.

Marchand de Vin   Reduce 8 ounces (250 mL) dry red wine and 2 ounces (60 g) diced shallots by two-thirds. Then add demi-glace, simmer and strain.

Mushroom   Blanch 8 ounces (250 g) mushroom caps or slices in 8 ounces (250 mL) boiling water seasoned with salt and lemon juice. Drain the mushrooms, saving the liquid. Reduce this liquid to 2 tablespoons (30 mL) and add it to the demi-glace. Just before service stir in 2 ounces (60 g) butter and the mushroom caps.

Périgueux   Add finely diced truffles to madeira sauce. *Périgourdine* sauce is the same, except that the truffles are cut into relatively thick slices.

Piquante   Combine 1 ounce (30 g) shallots, 4 ounces (120 mL) white wine and 4 ounces (120 mL) white wine vinegar. Reduce the mixture by two-thirds. Then add demi-glace and simmer for 10 minutes. Add 2 ounces (60 g) diced cornichons, 1 tablespoon (15 mL) fresh tarragon, 1 tablespoon (15 mL) fresh parsley and 1 tablespoon (15 mL) fresh chervil. Do not strain.

Poivrade   Sweat 12 ounces (340 g) mirepoix in 2 tablespoons (30 mL) oil. Add 1 bay leaf, a sprig of thyme and 4 parsley stems. Then add 1 pint (500 mL) white wine vinegar and 4 ounces (120 mL) white wine. (Red wine vinegar and red wine are also often used.) Reduce by half, add demi-glace and simmer for 40 minutes. Then add 20 crushed peppercorns and simmer for 5 more minutes. Strain through a fine chinois and finish with up to 2 ounces (60 g) butter.

Robert   Sauté 8 ounces (250 g) chopped onion in 1 ounce (30 g) butter. Add 8 ounces (250 mL) dry white wine and reduce by two-thirds. Add demi-glace and simmer for 10 minutes. Strain and then add 2 teaspoons (10 mL) prepared Dijon mustard and 1 tablespoon (15 mL) sugar. If the finished Robert sauce is garnished with sliced sour pickles, preferably cornichons, it is known as *charcutière*.

The Tomato Sauce Family

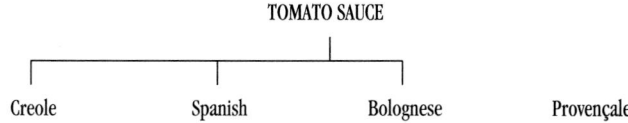

Classic tomato sauce is made from tomatoes, vegetables, seasonings and white stock and thickened with a blond or brown roux. In today's kitchens, however, most tomato sauces are not thickened with roux. Rather, they are tomatoes, herbs, spices, vegetables and other flavouring ingredients simmered together and puréed.

QUALITY STANDARD

A properly made tomato sauce is thick, rich and full-flavoured. Its texture should be grainier than most other classic sauces, but it should still be smooth. The vegetables and other seasonings should add flavour, but none should be pronounced. Tomato sauce should not be bitter, acidic or overly sweet. It should be deep red and thick enough to cling to foods.

◆◆◆

RECIPE 10.13

BASIC TOMATO SAUCE

Yield: 2 qt. (2 L)

Carrot, cut in brunoise dice	2 oz.	50 g
Celery, cut in brunoise dice	2 oz.	50 g
Onion, cut in brunoise dice	2 oz.	50 g
Garlic clove, chopped or crushed	1	1
Olive oil	3–4 oz.	90–100 mL
Tomato paste	1 lb.	450 g
White stock	2 qt.	2 L
Sugar	1 Tbsp.	5 mL
Sachet:		
Bay leaf	1/2	1/2
Sage	1/4 tsp.	1 mL
Thyme	1/2 tsp.	2 mL
Rosemary	1/2 tsp.	2 mL
Peppercorns	8	8

Approximate values per 1 oz. (30 mL) serving:

Calories	30
Total fat	.5 g
Saturated fat	.2 g
Cholesterol	.7 mg
Sodium	240 mg
Total carbohydrates	4 g
Protein	2 g
Vitamin A	6%

Claims—low fat; low calorie

1. Sweat the vegetables in the oil (to sweat an ingredient is to sauté it on medium heat, stirring regularly without letting it colour).
2. Add tomato paste and sweat for 2 minutes.
3. Add the remaining ingredients and simmer gently for about 1 hour.
4. Adjust the seasoning, and strain the sauce through a china cap, if desired.

VARIATION: Reduce the olive oil by half and sweat 4 ounces (100 g) of fine chopped bacon before adding vegetables.

Tomato Sauce Derivatives

The following derivative sauces are made by adding the listed ingredients to 1 quart (1 L) tomato sauce. The final step for each recipe is to season to taste with salt and pepper.

Bolognese Sweat 3-1/2 ounces (100 g) diced onion and 1 clove crushed garlic in 1 ounce (30 mL) olive oil. Add 10–16 ounces (300–500 g) ground veal or beef and sauté until meat browns lightly. Add tomato sauce, 2 teaspoons (10 mL) fresh basil, chopped, and 2 teaspoons (10 mL) fresh oregano leaves. Simmer. Adjust seasoning to taste. Often used with pasta dishes as garnish or to prepare lasagne.

Creole Sauté 6 ounces (170 g) finely diced onion, 4 ounces (120 g) thinly sliced celery and 1 teaspoon (5 mL) garlic in 1 ounce (30 mL) olive oil. Add tomato sauce, a bay leaf and a pinch of thyme; simmer for 15 minutes. Then add 4 ounces (120 g) finely diced green pepper, 3-1/2 ounces (100 g) diced okra, 3-1/2 ounces (100 g) sliced green olives and a dash of hot pepper sauce; simmer for 15 minutes longer. Remove bay leaf.

Spanish Sauté 5-1/2 ounces (150 g) sliced onions with 3-1/2 ounces (100 g) thinly sliced celery, 5-1/2 ounces (150 g) sliced sweet peppers, and 1 clove of garlic in 2 ounces (50 mL) olive oil. Finish with 4 ounces (120 g) sliced mushrooms, sweated, and 4 ounces (120 g) **tomato concassée**. Season with chilies, salt and pepper to taste.

Provençale This sauce is not a derivative of tomato sauce. At its simplest, it is 1 pound (500 g) peeled, seeded, diced tomatoes (**tomato concassée**) sautéed in 2 ounces (50 mL) olive oil, flavoured with 1 or 2 diced cloves of garlic. Season with salt and pepper and a pinch of sugar. Finish with 1 ounce (30 mL) chopped parsley. It goes well with light-flavoured fish, meats, or vegetables.

The Hollandaise Family

Hollandaise and the derivative sauces made from it are **emulsified** sauces. Egg yolks, which contain large amounts of lecithin, a natural emulsifier, are used to emulsify warm butter and a small amount of water, lemon juice or vinegar. By vigorously whipping the egg yolks with the liquid, while slowly adding the warm butter, the lecithin coats the individual oil droplets and holds them in suspension in the liquid.

Emulsification—*the process by which generally unmixable liquids such as oil and water are forced into a uniform distribution.*

QUALITY STANDARD

A properly made hollandaise is smooth, buttery, pale lemon-yellow-coloured and very rich. It is lump-free and should not exhibit any signs of separation. The buttery flavour should dominate but not mask the flavours of the egg, lemon and vinegar. The sauce should be frothy and light, not heavy like a mayonnaise. It should be able to be glazed under a salamander or broiler without breaking.

Glaçage—*browning or glazing a food, usually under a salamander or broiler.*

Temperatures and Sanitation Concerns

Temperatures play an important role in the proper production of a hollandaise sauce. As the egg yolks and liquid are whisked together, they are cooked over a bain marie until they thicken to the consistency of slightly whipped cream (ribbon stage). Do not overheat this mixture, because even slightly cooked eggs lose their ability to emulsify. The clarified butter used to make the sauce should be warm but not so hot as to further cook the egg yolks. Although hollandaise sauce can be made from whole butter, a more stable and consistent product will be achieved by using butter that has had the water and milk solids removed through clarification. (Clarification is described in Chapter 8, Eggs and Dairy Products.)

Tomato concassée—*peeled, seeded and diced tomato.*

Emulsified butter sauces are unique in that they must be held at the specific temperatures most conducive to bacterial growth: 40°F–140°F (4°C–60°C). If the sauce is heated above 150°F (65°C), the eggs will cook and the sauce will break and become grainy. If the sauce temperature falls below 45°F (7°C), the butter will solidify, making the sauce unuseable. In order to minimize the risk of food-borne illnesses while maintaining the integrity of the sauce:

1. Always use clean, sanitized utensils.
2. Schedule sauce production as close to the time of service as possible. Never hold hollandaise-based sauces more than 20-30 minutes.
3. Make small batches of sauce.
4. Never mix an old batch of sauce with a new one.

With practice, classic hollandaise can be produced quickly and efficiently. Nevertheless, a recipe for blender hollandaise is included for those operations with a need for this technique. In addition, many operations no longer make classic hollandaise due to health concerns or municipal regulations. These companies use a commercial base mixture.

◆◆◆

RECIPE 10.14

HOLLANDAISE

Yield: 1-1/2 qt. (1.5 L)

Black peppercorns, crushed	36	36
White wine vinegar	6 oz.	180 mL
Water	4 oz.	120 mL
Egg yolks	14	15
Lemon juice	2-1/2 oz.	75 mL
Clarified butter, warm	1 qt.	1 L
Salt and white pepper	TT	TT
Cayenne pepper	TT	TT

Approximate values per 1 oz. (30 mL) serving:

Calories	170
Total fat	18 g
Saturated fat	11 g
Cholesterol	90 mg
Sodium	180 mg
Total carbohydrates	0 g
Protein	1 g
Vitamin A	20%

1. Combine the peppercorns, vinegar and water in a small saucepan and reduce by one-half.
2. Place the egg yolks in a stainless steel bowl. Strain the vinegar and pepper reduction through a chinois into the yolks.
3. Place the bowl over a double boiler, whipping the mixture continuously with a wire whip. As the yolks cook, the mixture will thicken. When the

1. Combine the egg yolks with the vinegar and pepper reduction in a stainless steel bowl.

2. Whip the mixture over a double boiler until it is thick enough to leave a trail when the whip is removed.

3. Using a kitchen towel and saucepot to firmly hold the bowl containing the yolks, add the butter slowly while whipping continuously.

4. Hollandaise at the proper consistency.

mixture is thick enough to leave a trail across the surface when the whip is drawn away, remove the bowl from the double boiler. Do not overcook the egg yolks.

4. Whip in 1 ounce (30 mL) lemon juice to stop the yolks from cooking.
5. Begin to add the warm clarified butter to the egg yolk mixture a drop at a time, while constantly whipping the mixture to form an emulsion. Once the emulsion is started, the butter may be added more quickly. Continue until all the butter is incorporated.
6. Stir in the remaining lemon juice. Adjust the seasonings with salt, white pepper and cayenne pepper.
7. Strain the sauce through cheesecloth if necessary and hold for service in a warm (not simmering) bain marie.

◆◆◆

RECIPE 10.15

HOLLANDAISE, BLENDER METHOD

Yield: 1 qt. (1 L)

Egg yolks	9	9
Water, warm	3 oz.	90 mL
Lemon juice	1 oz.	30 mL
Cayenne pepper	TT	TT
Salt	1 tsp.	5 mL
White pepper	1/4 tsp.	1 mL
Tabasco sauce	TT	TT
Whole butter	24 oz.	750 mL

1. Place the egg yolks, water, lemon juice, cayenne pepper, salt, white pepper and Tabasco sauce in the bowl of the blender. Cover and blend on high speed for approximately 5 seconds.
2. Heat the butter to approximately 175°F (80°C). This allows the butter to cook the yolks as it is added to them.
3. Turn the blender on and immediately begin to add the butter in a steady stream. Incorporate all of the butter in 20–30 seconds. Adjust the seasonings.
4. If any lumps are present, strain the sauce through cheesecloth. Transfer the sauce to a stainless steel container and adjust the seasonings. Hold for service in a bain marie, remembering the sanitation precautions discussed previously.

Approximate values per 1 oz. (30 mL) serving:

Calories	120
Total fat	12 g
Saturated fat	7 g
Cholesterol	70 mg
Sodium	170 mg
Total carbohydrates	0 g
Protein	1 g
Vitamin A	15%

Procedure for Rescuing a Broken Hollandaise

Occasionally a hollandaise will break or separate and appear thin, grainy or even lumpy. A sauce breaks when the emulsion has not formed or the emulsified butter, eggs and liquid have separated. There are several reasons why this may happen: The temperature of the eggs or butter may have been too high or too low; the butter may have been added too quickly; the egg yolks may have been overcooked; too much butter may have been added or the sauce may not have been whipped vigorously enough to start or over-whipped.

Broken hollandaise can often be rescued and re-emulsified. To do so, you must first determine the cause of the problem.

Feel the bowl in which the sauce was prepared to determine if it is too hot or too cold. If the bowl is too hot, allow the sauce to cool. If it is too cold, reheat the sauce over a double boiler before attempting to rescue it.

For 1 quart (1 L) of broken sauce, place 1 tablespoon (15 mL) of water in a clean stainless steel bowl and slowly beat in the broken sauce. If the problem seems to be that the eggs were overcooked or too much butter was added, add a yolk to the water before incorporating the broken sauce.

Hollandaise Sauce Derivatives

The following derivative sauces are easily made by adding the listed ingredients to 1 quart (1 L) of hollandaise. The final step for each recipe is to season to taste with salt and pepper. Béarnaise is presented here as a derivative sauce as that is now general practice, although some chefs consider it a basic sauce.

Béarnaise   Combine 2 ounces (60 g) chopped shallots, 5 tablespoons (75 mL) chopped fresh tarragon, 3 tablespoons (45 mL) chopped fresh chervil and 1 teaspoon (5 mL) crushed peppercorns with 8 ounces (250 mL) white wine vinegar. Reduce to 2 ounces (60 mL). Add this reduction to the egg yolks and proceed with the hollandaise recipe. Strain the finished sauce and season to taste with salt and cayenne pepper. Garnish with additional chopped fresh tarragon.

Choron   Combine 2 ounces (60 g) tomato paste; add the mixture to a béarnaise.

Foyot   Add to béarnaise 3 ounces (90 g) melted glace de viande.

Grimrod   Infuse a hollandaise sauce with saffron.

Maltaise   Add to hollandaise 2 ounces (60 mL) blood orange juice and 2 teaspoons (10 mL) finely grated blood orange zest. Regular oranges may be used for this sauce.

Mousseline (Chantilly Sauce)   Whip 8 ounces (250 mL) heavy cream until stiff. Fold it into the hollandaise just before service. It is usually glazed under a broiler or salamander.

Beurre Blanc and Beurre Rouge

Beurre noir—*French for black butter, used to describe whole butter cooked until dark brown (not black); sometimes flavoured with vinegar or lemon juice, capers and parsley and served over fish, eggs and vegetables.*

Beurre noisette—*French for brown butter, used to describe butter cooked until it is a light brown colour, flavoured and used in much the same manner as beurre noir.*

Beurre blanc and beurre rouge are emulsified butter sauces made without egg yolks. The small amounts of lecithin and other emulsifiers naturally found in butter are used to form an oil-in-liquid emulsion. Although similar to hollandaise in concept, they are not considered either classic basic or compound sauces. Beurre blancs are thinner and lighter than hollandaise and béarnaise. They should be smooth and slightly thicker than heavy cream.

Beurre blanc and beurre rouge are made from three main ingredients: shallots, white (Fr. *blanc*) wine or red (Fr. *rouge*) wine and whole butter (not clarified). The shallots and wine provide flavour, while the butter becomes the sauce. A good beurre blanc or beurre rouge is rich and buttery, with a neutral flavour that responds well to other seasonings and flavourings, thereby lending itself to the addition of herbs, spices and vegetable purées to complement the dish with which it is served. Its pale colour changes depending upon the flavourings added. It should be light and airy yet still liquid, while thick enough to cling to food.

BASIC PROCEDURE FOR MAKING BEURRE BLANC OR BEURRE ROUGE

1. Use a nonaluminum pan to prevent discolouring the sauce. Do not use a thin-walled or nonstick pan, as heat is not evenly distributed in a thin-walled pan and a nonstick pan makes it difficult for an emulsion to set.

2. Over medium heat, reduce the wine, shallots and herbs or other seasonings, if used, until *au sec* (i.e., nearly dry). Some cooks add a small amount of heavy cream at this point and reduce the mixture. Although not necessary, the added cream helps stabilize the finished sauce.

3. Whisk in cold butter a small amount at a time. The butter should be well chilled, as this allows the butterfat, water and milk solids to be gradually incorporated into the sauce as the butter melts and the mixture is whisked.

4. When all of the butter is incorporated, strain and hold the sauce in a bain marie.

Temperature

Do not let the sauce become too hot. At 136°F (58°C) some of the emulsifying proteins begin to break down and release the butterfat they hold in emulsion. Extended periods at temperatures over 136°F (58°C) will cause the sauce to separate. If the sauce separates, it can be corrected by cooling to approximately 110°F–120°F (43°C–49°C) and whisking to reincorporate the butterfat.

If the sauce is allowed to cool below 85°F (30°C), the butterfat will solidify. If the sauce is reheated it will separate into butterfat and water; whisking will not re-emulsify it. Cold beurre blanc can be used as a soft, flavoured butter, however, simply by whisking it at room temperature until it smooths out to the consistency of mayonnaise.

◆◆◆

RECIPE 10.16
CLASSIC BEURRE BLANC

Yield: 1 qt. (1 L)

White wine	1 oz.	30 mL
White wine vinegar	4 oz.	120 mL
Salt	1-1/2 tsp.	7 mL
White pepper	1/2 tsp.	2 mL
Shallots, minced	3 Tbsp.	45 mL
Whole butter, chilled	2 lb.	1 kg

1. Combine the white wine, white wine vinegar, salt, white pepper and shallots in a small saucepan. Reduce the mixture until approximately 2 tablespoons (30 mL) of liquid remain. If more liquid than that is allowed to remain, the resulting sauce will be too thin. For a thicker sauce, reduce the mixture *au sec.*

Continued

Approximate values per	
1 oz. (30 mL) serving:	
Calories	210
Total fat	23 g
Saturated fat	14 g
Cholesterol	60 mg
Sodium	340 mg
Total carbohydrates	0 g
Protein	0 g
Vitamin A	20%

1. Reduce the shallots and wine *au sec.*

2. Whisk in the cold butter a little at a time.

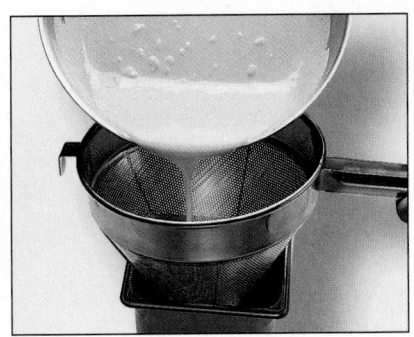

3. Strain the sauce.

2. Cut the butter into pieces approximately 1 ounce (30 g) in weight. Over low heat, whisk in the butter a few pieces at a time, using the chilled butter to keep the sauce between 100°F and 120°F (43°C–49°C).

3. Once all of the butter has been incorporated, remove the saucepan from the heat. Strain through a chinois and hold the sauce between 100°F and 130°F (38°C–54°C) for service.

VARIATIONS: *Lemon-Dill*—Heat 2 tablespoons (30 mL) lemon juice and whisk it into the beurre blanc. Stir in 4 tablespoons (60 mL) chopped fresh dill.

Pink Peppercorn—Add 2 tablespoons (30 mL) coarsely crushed pink peppercorns to the shallot-wine reduction when making beurre rouge. Garnish the finished sauce with whole pink peppercorns.

◆◆◆

RECIPE 10.17

"MY" BEURRE BLANC SAUCE

ÉCOLE HÔTELIÈRE DES LAURENTIDES, STE-ADÈLE, PQ
Chef Marcel Kretz

Marcel Kretz

Born, raised, and trained in France, Marcel has had an illustrious, award-winning career in Europe and Canada. He is credited with launching the movement to emphasize Quebec products in top Quebec restaurants, and in 1998 became the first chef ever to receive the Order of Canada.

Yield: 24 oz. (625 mL)

Dry shallots, chopped	2	2
White wine	8 oz.	250 mL
Fish stock	8 oz.	250 mL
Dried or fresh tarragon leaves	1 tsp.	5 mL
Parsley sprigs, chopped	2–3	2–3
White pepper, crushed	TT	TT
Heavy cream (35%)	18 oz.	500 mL
Unsalted butter, cubed	9 oz.	280 g
Salt	TT	TT
Lemon juice, if desired	TT	TT

1. Sauté the shallots lightly; deglaze with the white wine and fish stock.

2. Add the tarragon, parsley sprigs, crushed pepper and reduce the mixture by half. Add the cream and reduce by half again.

3. Decrease the heat and add the cubed butter piece by piece, whipping constantly, until the sauce is smooth.

4. Check and adjust the seasoning. Pass the sauce through a fine sieve.

5. Keep the sauce at a low heat in a double boiler. It will keep fairly well for a full-service period.

Serve with poached fish or seafood.

VARIATIONS: Clear chicken stock can be used instead of fish stock. It can be served with fowl or vegetable flan or mousse.

Approximate values per 1 oz. (30 mL) serving:

Calories	186
Total fat	19 g
Saturated fat	12 g
Cholesterol	62 mg
Sodium	109 mg
Total carbohydrates	1 g
Protein	1 g

Compound Butters

A compound butter is made by incorporating various seasonings into softened whole butter. These butters, also known as *beurres composés*, give flavour and colour to derivative sauces or may be served as sauces or condiments in their own right. For example, a slice of maître d'hôtel butter (parsley butter) is often placed on a grilled steak or piece of fish at the time of service. The butter quickly melts, creating a sauce for the beef or fish.

Butter and flavouring ingredients can be combined in a blender, food processor or mixer. Using parchment paper or plastic wrap, the butter is then rolled into a cylinder, chilled and sliced as needed. Or it can be piped into rosettes and refrigerated until firm. Most compound butters will keep for two to three days in the refrigerator, or they can be frozen for longer storage.

Recipes for Compound Butters

For each of the following butters, add the listed ingredients to 1 pound (450 g) of softened, unsalted butter. The compound butter should then be seasoned with salt and pepper to taste.

Basil Butter   Mince 2 ounces (50 g) basil, 2 ounces (50 g) shallots and add to butter with 2 teaspoons (10 mL) lemon juice.

Herb Butter   Add to the butter up to 1 cup (250 mL) of mixed chopped fresh herbs such as parsley, dill, chives, tarragon or chervil.

Lobster or Crayfish Butter   Grind 8 ounces (250 g) cooked lobster or crayfish meat, shells and/or coral with 1 pound (450 g) butter. Place in a saucepan and clarify. Strain the butter through a fine chinois lined with cheesecloth. Refrigerate, then remove the butterfat when firm.

Maître d'Hôtel   Mix into the butter 4 tablespoons (60 mL) finely chopped parsley, 3 tablespoons (45 mL) lemon juice and a dash of white pepper.

Montpelier   Blanch 1 ounce (30 g) parsley, 1 ounce (30 g) chervil, 1 ounce (30 g) watercress and 1 ounce (30 g) tarragon in boiling water. Refresh thoroughly. Mince two hard-boiled egg yolks, two garlic cloves and two gherkin pickles. Blend everything into the butter.

Red Pepper Butter   Purée 8 ounces (250 g) roasted, peeled red bell peppers until liquid, then add to the butter.

Shallot Butter   Blanch 8 ounces (250 g) of peeled shallots in boiling water. Dry and finely dice them and mix with the butter.

1. Place the compound butter on the plastic wrap.

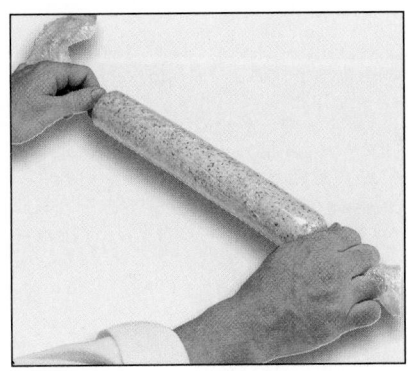

2. Roll the butter in the plastic wrap to form a cylinder.

Pan Gravy

Pan gravy is aptly named: it is made directly in the pan used to roast the poultry, beef, lamb or pork the gravy will accompany. Pan gravy is actually a sauce; it is a liquid thickened with a roux. Pan gravy gains additional flavours from the drippings left in the roasting pan and by utilizing a portion of the fat rendered during the roasting process to make the roux. This technique is used in Recipe 17.3, Roast Turkey with Chestnut Dressing and Giblet Gravy.

A properly made pan gravy should have all the characteristics of any brown sauce except that it has a meatier flavour as the result of the pan drippings.

Basic Procedure for Making Pan Gravy

1. Remove the cooked meat or poultry from the roasting pan.
2. If mirepoix was not added during the roasting process, add it to the pan containing the drippings and fat.

3. Place the roasting pan on the stove top and clarify the fat by cooking off any remaining moisture.
4. Pour off the fat, reserving it to make the roux.
5. Deglaze the pan using an appropriate stock. The deglazing liquid may be transferred to a saucepan for easier handling or the gravy may be finished directly in the roasting pan.
6. Add enough stock or water to the deglazing liquid to yield the proper amount of finished gravy.
7. Determine the amount of roux needed to thicken the liquid and prepare it in a separate pan, using a portion of the reserved fat.
8. Add the roux to the liquid and bring the mixture to a simmer. Simmer until the mirepoix is well cooked, the flavour is extracted and the flour taste is cooked out.
9. Strain the gravy and adjust the seasonings.

Coulis

The term *coulis* most often refers to a sauce made from a purée of vegetables or fruit. A vegetable coulis can be served either as a hot or cold accompaniment to other vegetables, starches, meat, poultry, fish or shellfish. It is often made from a single vegetable base (popular examples include broccoli, tomatoes and sweet red peppers) cooked with flavouring ingredients such as onions, garlic, shallots, herbs and spices and then puréed. An appropriate liquid (stock, water or cream) may be added to thin the purée if necessary. Vegetable coulis are often prepared with very little fat and served as a healthy alternative to a heavier, classic sauce.

A fruit coulis, often made from fresh or frozen berries, is generally used as a dessert sauce. It is usually as simple as puréed fruit thinned to the desired consistency with sugar syrup. (If heated and thickened with starches, it becomes a fruit sauce.)

Typically, both vegetable and fruit coulis have a texture similar to that of thin tomato sauce. But their textures can range from slightly grainy to almost lumpy, depending on their intended use. The flavour and colour of a coulis should be that of the main ingredient. The flavours of herbs, spices and other flavouring ingredients should only complement and not dominate the coulis.

BASIC PROCEDURE FOR MAKING COULIS

Here, we include a procedure for making a vegetable coulis. Procedures for making fruit coulis are included as recipes in Chapter 31, Custards, Creams, Frozen Desserts and Dessert Sauces.

1. Cook the main ingredient and any additional flavouring ingredients with an appropriate liquid.
2. Purée the main ingredient and flavouring ingredients in a food mill, blender or food processor.
3. Combine the purée with the appropriate liquid and simmer to blend the flavours.
4. Thin and season the coulis as desired.

◆◆◆

RECIPE 10.18
Red Pepper Coulis

Yield: 1 qt. (1 L)

Vegetable or olive oil	1 oz.	30 mL
Garlic, chopped	2 tsp.	10 mL
Onion, small dice	3 oz.	90 g
Red bell pepper, medium dice	3 lb.	1.25 kg
White wine	8 oz.	250 mL
Chicken stock	1 pt.	450 mL
Salt and pepper	TT	TT

1. Heat the oil and sauté the garlic and onion until translucent, without browning.
2. Add the red pepper and sauté until tender.
3. Deglaze the pan with the white wine stock.
4. Add the chicken stock, bring to a simmer and cook for 15 minutes. Season with salt and pepper.
5. Purée in a blender or food processor and strain through a china cap.
6. Adjust the consistency and seasonings and hold for service.

Approximate values per
1 oz. (30 mL) serving:

Calories	20
Total fat	1 g
Saturated fat	0 g
Cholesterol	0 mg
Sodium	45 mg
Total carbohydrates	2 g
Protein	1 g
Vitamin C	50%

Claims—low fat; low sodium; low calorie

Contemporary Sauces

Modern chefs and menu writers are relying less on traditional sauces and more on salsas, relishes, juices, broths, essences and infused oils in their work. Unlike classic sauces, these modern accompaniments do not rely on meat-based stocks and starch thickeners, but rather on fresh vegetables, vegetable juices, aromatic broths and intensely flavoured oils. The names for these sauces are not codified, as are those in the classic sauce repertoire. Chefs apply various terms freely, using whatever name best fits the dish and the overall menu. Most of these contemporary sauces can be prepared more quickly than their classic counterparts, and the use of fresh fruits and vegetables enhances the healthfulness of the dish. These so-called modern sauces may have a lighter body and less fat than classic sauces, but they are still derived from classical culinary techniques and principles. The sauces should be appropriate in flavour, texture and appearance and should complement, not overwhelm, the food they accompany.

Vegetable Juice Sauces

Juice extractors make it possible to prepare juice from fresh, uncooked vegetables such as carrots, beets and spinach. Thinner and smoother than a purée, vegetable juice can be heated, reduced, flavoured and enriched with butter to create colourful, intensely flavoured sauces. Cream or stock can be added to finish the sauce. Sauces made from vegetable juices are sometimes referred to as an **essence** or **tea** on menus.

Juice from a single type of vegetable provides the purest, most pronounced flavour, but two or more vegetables sometimes can be combined successfully. Be careful of mixing too many flavours and colours in the juice, however.

Juiced vegetable sauces are particularly appropriate with pasta, shellfish and poultry, and can be useful in vegetarian cuisine or as a healthier alternative to classic sauces.

BASIC PROCEDURE FOR MAKING A VEGETABLE JUICE SAUCE

1. Wash and peel vegetables as needed.
2. Process the vegetables through a juice extractor.
3. Place the juice in a saucepan and add stock, lemon juice, herbs or other flavourings as desired.
4. Bring the sauce to a simmer and reduce as necessary.
5. Strain the sauce through a fine chinois.
6. Adjust the seasonings and whisk in whole butter to finish.

◆◆◆

RECIPE 10.19

THYME-SCENTED CELERY ESSENCE

STOUFFER STANFORD COURT HOTEL, SAN FRANCISCO, CA
Executive Chef (formerly) Erocolino Crugnale

Yield: 1 qt. (1 L)

Celery juice	1 qt.	1 L
Tomato juice	1 pt.	500 mL
Fresh thyme, chopped	1/2 oz.	15 g
Whole butter	6 oz.	180 g
Salt	TT	TT
Tabasco sauce	TT	TT

Approximate values per 1 oz. (30 mL) serving:

Calories	50
Total fat	4.5 g
Saturated fat	2.4 g
Cholesterol	10 mg
Sodium	200 mg
Total carbohydrates	2 g
Protein	0 g

1. Combine the celery juice, tomato juice and thyme. Bring to a simmer and reduce to 1-1/2 pints (750 mL).
2. Whisk in the butter and adjust the seasonings with salt and Tabasco sauce.
3. Strain through a chinois.

Broth

Broth, which also appears on menus as **tea**, **jus**, **essence** or **nage**, is a thin, flavourful liquid served in a pool beneath the main food. The broth should not be so abundant as to turn an entree into a soup, but it should provide moisture and flavour. The essence, broth or nage is often made by simply reducing and straining the liquid in which the main food was cooked. Alternatively, a specifically flavoured stock, tomato, for example, can be prepared, then clarified like consommé to create a broth or essence to accompany an appetizer or entree.

Flavoured Oil

Small amounts of intensely flavoured oils can be used to dress or garnish a variety of dishes. Salads, soups, vegetable and starch dishes, as well as entrees, can be enhanced with a drizzle of colourful, appropriately flavoured oil. Because such small quantities are used, these oils provide flavour and moisture without adding too many calories or fat.

Unless the flavouring ingredient goes especially well with olive oil (for example, basil), select a high-quality but neutral oil such as peanut, safflower or canola. Although flavouring ingredients can be simply steeped in oil for a period of time, a better way to flavour oil is to crush, purée or cook the flavouring ingredients first.

BASIC PROCEDURE FOR MAKING A FLAVOURED OIL

1. Purée or chop fresh herbs, fruits or vegetables. Sweat dry spices or seeds in a small amount of oil to form a paste.
2. Place the selected oil and the flavouring ingredients in a jar or other tightly lidded container.
3. Allow the mixture to stand at room temperature until sufficient flavour is extracted. This may take from 1 to 24 hours. Shake the jar periodically. Do not allow the flavouring ingredients to remain in the oil indefinitely, as the flavour may become harsh or bitter.
4. Strain the oil through a chinois lined with a coffee filter.
5. Store the flavoured oil in a covered container in the refrigerator.

◆◆◆

RECIPE 10.20

SHALLOT CURRY OIL

Yield: 8 oz. (225 mL)

Canola oil	8 oz.	250 mL
Shallot, minced	1	1
Curry powder	4 Tbsp.	60 mL
Water	2 oz.	60 mL

1. In a small saucepan, heat 1 tablespoon (15 mL) of oil over medium heat. Add the shallot and sauté until softened and translucent. Do not allow the shallot to brown.
2. Add the curry powder and sauté for 1 to 2 minutes.
3. Stir in the water and bring the mixture to a boil. Reduce the heat and simmer until most of the water evaporates, leaving a paste of curry and shallots.
4. Remove from the heat and stir in the remaining oil.
5. Place the mixture in a lidded jar and set aside at room temperature for 6 to 8 hours. Shake the jar occasionally.
6. Strain the oil through a chinois lined with a coffee filter. Place the flavoured oil in a covered container and refrigerate until ready to use.

Approximate values per 1 oz. (30 mL) serving:

Calories	239
Total fat	26 g
Saturated fat	2 g
Cholesterol	0 mg
Sodium	2 mg
Total carbohydrates	2 g
Protein	0 g

Salsa and Relish

Many people think of salsa (Spanish for sauce) as a chunky mixture of raw vegetables and chiles eaten with chips or ladled over Mexican food; they think of relish as a sweet green condiment spooned on a hot dog. But salsas and relishes—generally, cold chunky mixtures of herbs, spices, fruits and/or vegetables—can be used as sauces for many meat, poultry, fish and shellfish items. They can include ingredients such as oranges, pineapple, papaya, black beans, jicama, tomatillos and an array of vegetables.

Although not members of any classic sauce family, salsas and relishes are condiments currently enjoying great popularity because of their intense fresh flavours, ease of preparation and low fat and calorie content. Salsas and

Chutney—*a sweet-and-sour condiment made of fruits and/or vegetables cooked in vinegar with sugar and spices until it has a consistency of jam. Some chutneys are reduced to a purée; others retain recognizable pieces of their ingredients.*

TABLE 10.5   USING SAUCES

Sauce	Qualities	Derivative Sauces or Flavourings	Use
Béchamel	Smooth, rich and creamy; no graininess; cream-coloured with rich sheen	Cheddar Cream sauce Mornay Nantua Soubise	Vegetables, pasta Vegetables, pasta, eggs, fish Fish, shellfish, poultry, vegetables Fish, shellfish Veal, pork, eggs

Velouté	Smooth and rich; ivory-coloured; having good flavour of the stock used; not pasty or heavy	Fish velouté
		  Bercy
		  Cardinal
		  Normandy
		Allemande (veal or chicken)
		  Aurora
		  Horseradish
		  Mushroom
		  Poulette
		Suprême (chicken)
		  Albufera
		  Hungarian
		  Ivory
			
			Poached fish
			Lobster, white fish, crab, eggs
			Delicate white fish, oysters
			
			Eggs, chicken, sweetbreads
			Roast beef, corned beef, baked ham
			Sautéed poultry, white meats
			Vegetables, sweetbreads
			
			Braised poultry, sweetbreads
			Eggs, chicken, chops, sweetbreads
			Eggs, braised poultry

Espagnole	Smooth and rich; dark brown colour; good meat flavour	Bordelaise Chasseur Chateaubriand Chevreuil Madeira/Port Mushroom Périgueux/Périgourdine Piquant Poivrade Robert	Sautéed or grilled meats Sautéed or grilled meats and poultry Broiled meats Roasted meats and game Grilled or roasted meats and game, ham Sautéed or grilled meats and poultry Sautéed poultry, grilled meats and game, sweetbreads Pork Grilled or roasted meats, game Pork
Tomato	Thick and rich; slightly grainy; full-flavoured	Tomato Bolognese Creole Provençale Spanish	Meats, poultry, vegetables, pasta and for making small sauces Pasta Fish, eggs, chicken Pasta, grilled or sautéed poultry and white meats Eggs, fish
Hollandaise/ Bérnaise	Smooth and rich; buttery flavour; light and slightly frothy; pale yellow colour; no signs of separating	Choron Foyot Grimrod Maltaise Mousseline	Grilled or sautéed meats and fish Grilled meats and fish Grilled meats and fish Eggs, poached fish Poached fish, eggs, vegetables
Beurre blanc and beurre rouge	Rich and buttery; thinner than hollandaise; light and airy; pale-coloured	Wide variety of seasonings and flavourings may be used	Steamed, grilled or poached fish; chicken or vegetables
Compound butter	Flavour ingredients should be evenly distributed	Wide variety of seasonings and flavourings may be used	Grilled meats, poultry and fish; finishing sauces, condiment, spread
Pan gravy	Smooth; deep rich colour; meaty flavour	Made from pan drippings	Roasted meats and poultry
Coulis	Rich colour; moderately thin, grainy texture; strongly flavoured	Made with a wide variety of vegetables or fruits	Vegetables, grilled or poached meats, poultry and fish
Salsa and relish	Chunky; bright colours; not watery	Made with a wide variety of vegetables, fruits and seasonings	Meats, fish, vegetables and poultry; used as a sauce or condiment

relishes are often a riot of colours, textures and flavours, simultaneously cool and hot, spicy and sweet.

BASIC PROCEDURE FOR MAKING A SALSA OR RELISH

1. Cut or chop the ingredients.
2. Precook and chill items as directed in the recipe.
3. Toss all ingredients together and refrigerate, allowing the flavours to combine for at least 30 minutes before service.

◆◆◆

RECIPE 10.21
TOMATO SALSA (PICO DE GALLO)

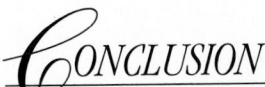

Yield: 1 qt. (1 L)

Tomatoes, seeded, small dice	5	5
Green onions, sliced	1 bunch	1 bunch
Garlic cloves, minced	3	3
Cilantro, chopped	1/2 bunch	1/2 bunch
Jalapeño peppers, chopped fine	3	3
Lemon juice	2 oz.	60 mL
Cumin, ground	1/2 tsp.	2 mL
Salt and pepper	TT	TT

Combine all ingredients and gently toss. Adjust seasonings and refrigerate.

Approximate values per 1 oz. (30 mL) serving:

Calories	5
Total fat	0 g
Saturated fat	0 g
Cholesterol	0 mg
Sodium	30 mg
Total carbohydrates	1 g
Protein	0 g

Claims—fat free; very low sodium; low calorie

USING SAUCES

Although many classic sauces were designed for or intended to be used with specific dishes, modern chefs often mix and match sauces with foods in unique or nontraditional ways. Nonclassic sauces, such as a beurre blanc, salsa or relish, may be prepared in a range of flavours using a wide variety of ingredients.

The uses shown in Table 10.5 for classic and nonclassic sauces are just suggestions. Most sauces can be used in many different dishes. It depends on your taste, creativity and judgment.

CONCLUSION

In *Le Guide culinaire*, Auguste Escoffier wrote, "Indeed, stock is everything in cooking. … Without it, nothing can be done. If one's stock is good, what remains of the work is easy; if, on the other hand, it is bad or merely mediocre, it is quite hopeless to expect anything approaching a satisfactory result." Because stocks and the sauces made from them are still the basis for much of contemporary cuisine, Escoffier's words are as true today as when he wrote them.

Both the classic basic (mother) sauces and the derivative sauces made from them as well as sauces such as beurre blanc and beurre rouge, coulis, salsas and relishes that are not based on classic recipes all share two goals: to complement the foods with which they are served and to neither mask nor disguise poorly prepared foods. With practice and care (and the right ingredients), you will be able to make great sauces.

Questions for Discussion

1. Why are the bones of younger animals preferred for making stocks?
2. Why should a stock made from beef or veal bones cook longer than a stock made from fish bones? What is the result if a stock does not cook long enough?
3. What can cause a stock to become cloudy? How can you prevent this from happening?
4. List three differences in the production of a white stock and a brown stock.
5. List the five classic basic sauces and explain how they are used to prepare derivative sauces.
6. Why is demi-glace preferred when making brown sauces? Is jus lié different from classic demi-glace? Can they be used interchangeably?
7. Why are temperatures important when making hollandaise sauce? What precautions must be taken when holding hollandaise for service?
8. Compare a beurre blanc and a hollandaise sauce. How are they similar? How are they different?
9. How are compound butters used in making sauces? What are the ingredients for a traditional maître d'hôtel butter?
10. What are the differences between a salsa, chutney and relish? Can these items be used in place of classic sauces? Explain your answer.

Additional Sauce Recipes

RECIPE 10.22

MUSHROOM TARTS WITH GARLIC CREAM

NOTE: *This dish appears in the chapter opening photograph.*

CITRUS, LOS ANGELES, CA
Chef Michel Richard

Yield: 6 Servings

GARLIC CREAM

Garlic cloves, peeled	30	30
Heavy cream	1 pt.	500 mL
Salt and pepper	TT	TT

Approximate values per serving:

Calories	670
Total fat	50 g
Saturated fat	22 g
Cholesterol	115 mg
Sodium	135 mg
Total carbohydrates	46 g
Protein	8 g
Vitamin A	35%

1. Place the garlic in a saucepan. Cover with 3 inches (8 cm) of cold water and bring to a boil. Drain and rinse with cold water. Repeat the process two more times. Then thinly slice the garlic and return it to the saucepan.
2. Add cream. Bring to a boil. Reduce the heat and simmer gently until reduced by half or to a thick, saucelike consistency, stirring occasionally.
3. Season with salt and pepper.

PUFF PASTRY

Puff pastry	8 oz.	250 g

1. Line a large baking sheet with parchment paper. Roll the pastry into a 10-inch × 9-inch (25 cm × 22.5 cm) rectangle on a lightly floured surface.
2. Cut into 6 3-inch × 5-inch (7.5 cm × 12.5 cm) squares using a fluted pastry cutter. Transfer to a baking sheet and dock the dough with a fork.
3. Cover and refrigerate at least 1 hour before baking.
4. Bake at 350°F (180°C) until puffed, browned and baked through, approximately 30 minutes.

MUSHROOMS

Fresh shiitake mushrooms	1-1/2 to 2 lb.	750 to 1000 g
Olive oil	2 Tbsp.	30 mL
Salt and pepper	TT	TT

1. Trim the ends of the mushrooms. Heat a sauté pan over medium-high heat and film with oil. Add the mushrooms and cook until lightly brown and tender, approximately 5 minutes, stirring frequently.
2. Season with salt and pepper.
3. To serve the tart, slice each piece of puff pastry in half horizontally, using a serrated knife. Arrange on 6 plates.
4. Rewarm the garlic cream and mushrooms. Spoon cream onto the bottom of each piece of pastry. Overlap the mushrooms on top of cream, alternating light and dark pieces. Set the top pieces of pastry at an angle over the mushrooms so the filling is visible.
5. Serve with marchand de vin (p. 211) and garnish with a herb sprig, if desired.

◆◆◆

RECIPE 10.23

DUXELLES SAUCE

Yield: 1-1/2 pt. (750 mL)

Mushrooms, chopped fine	8 oz.	250 g
Shallots, chopped fine	3 oz.	90 g
Clarified butter	1 oz.	30 mL
Olive oil	1 oz.	30 mL
Dry white wine	12 oz.	700 mL
Demi-glace	1 pt.	500 mL
Heavy cream	2 oz.	60 mL
Salt and pepper	TT	TT
Parsley, chopped fine	1 Tbsp.	15 mL

1. Sauté the mushrooms and the shallots in the butter and oil. The mushrooms will release their liquid and darken. Cook until completely dry.
2. Deglaze with the white wine and reduce by two-thirds.
3. Add the demi-glace. Bring to a boil, then simmer for 5 minutes.
4. Stir in the cream. Adjust seasonings. Garnish with parsley.

Approximate values per 1 oz. (30 mL) serving:

Calories	100
Total fat	10 g
Saturated fat	6 g
Cholesterol	30 mg
Sodium	40 g
Total carbohydrates	2 g
Protein	1 g
Vitamin A	15%

♦♦♦

RECIPE 10.24
BARBECUE SAUCE

Yield: 1-1/2 qt. (1.5 L)

Onion, small dice	8 oz.	250 g
Garlic, chopped	1 oz.	30 g
Vegetable oil	1 oz.	30 mL
Red wine vinegar	6 oz.	180 mL
Brown sugar	1 oz.	30 g
Honey	2 oz.	60 g
Stock (beef, chicken, pork)	8 oz.	250 mL
Ketchup	10 oz.	300 mL
Dry mustard	1 oz.	30 g
Worcestershire sauce	2 Tbsp.	30 mL
Salt and pepper	TT	TT
Cayenne pepper	TT	TT

1. Sweat the onions and garlic in the oil until tender.

2. Combine the remaining ingredients and simmer for 30 minutes.

NOTE: Spices, herbs and other flavourings may be incorporated.

Approximate values per 1 oz. (30 mL) serving:

Calories	25
Total fat	1 g
Saturated fat	0 g
Cholesterol	0 mg
Sodium	80 mg
Total carbohydrates	4 g
Protein	0 g

Claims—low fat; low sodium; low calorie

♦♦♦

RECIPE 10.25

MIGNONETTE SAUCE

Yield: 1 pt. (500 mL)

White pepper	2 tsp.	10 mL
Red wine vinegar	16 oz.	500 mL
Shallots, minced	4 oz.	120 g
Salt	TT	TT

Combine all ingredients.

Approximate values per 1 oz. (30 mL) serving:

Calories	5
Total fat	0 g
Saturated fat	0 g
Cholesterol	0 mg
Sodium	.8 mg
Total carbohydrates	1 g
Protein	0 g

Claims—fat free; very low sodium; low calorie

♦♦♦

RECIPE 10.26
FRESH TOMATO SAUCE FOR PASTA

Yield: 2-1/2 qt. (2.5 L)

Onion, small dice	8 oz.	250 g
Carrot, small dice	4 oz.	120 g
Garlic, minced	1 Tbsp.	15 mL
Olive oil	2 oz.	60 mL
Tomatoes, peeled, seeded and chopped	7 lb.	3 kg
Fresh oregano	1 Tbsp.	15 mL
Fresh thyme	2 tsp.	10 mL
Salt	1 tsp.	5 mL
Pepper	1/2 tsp.	2 mL
Fresh basil, chopped	3 Tbsp.	45 mL

1. Sweat the onion, carrot and garlic in the olive oil until tender.

Approximate values per 1 oz. (30 mL) serving:

Calories	20
Total fat	1 g
Saturated fat	0 g
Cholesterol	0 mg
Sodium	35 mg
Total carbohydrates	2 g
Protein	0 g
Vitamin C	15%

Claims—low fat; low sodium; low calorie

2. Add the tomatoes and herbs. Simmer for approximately 1 hour or until the desired consistency is reached.

3. Pass the sauce through a food mill if a smooth consistency is desired. Do not purée if a chunkier sauce is desired.

4. Adjust seasonings and add the chopped basil.

◆◆◆

RECIPE 10.27
APPLE HORSERADISH SAUCE

Yield: 1 pt. (500 mL)

Granny Smith apples	4	4
Cider vinegar	2 oz.	60 mL
Fresh horseradish, grated	2 oz.	60 g
Paprika	1 tsp.	5 mL
White wine	1 oz.	30 mL

1. Grate the apples and moisten them with vinegar.

2. Add the horseradish and paprika.

3. Add wine to thin to the desired consistency.

Approximate values per 1 oz. (30 mL) serving:	
Calories	25
Total fat	0 g
Saturated fat	0 g
Cholesterol	0 mg
Sodium	0 mg
Total carbohydrates	6 g
Protein	0 g

Claims—fat free; no sodium; low calorie

◆◆◆

RECIPE 10.28
PINE NUT AND PISTACHIO RELISH

SHAW CONFERENCE CENTRE, EDMONTON, AB
Executive Chef Simon Smotkowicz

Yield: 1 qt. (1 L)

Large eggplant, peeled and finely chopped	1	1
Virgin olive oil	8 oz.	225 mL
Spanish onion, finely chopped	1	1
Garlic cloves, peeled and minced	3	3
Tomatoes, peeled, seeded and diced	8	8
Fresh basil, minced	1 Tbsp.	15 mL
Fresh oregano, minced	1 Tbsp.	15 mL
Fresh thyme, minced	1/2 tsp.	2 mL
Celery stalks, trimmed and finely chopped	6	6
Green olives, pitted and finely chopped	6 oz.	170 g
Pine nuts, toasted	4 oz.	100 g
Green pistachio nuts, unsalted, shelled	4 oz.	100 g
Red wine vinegar	4 oz.	110 mL
Brown sugar	4-1/2 oz.	125 g
Salt and cracked black pepper	TT	TT

Simon Smotkowicz

Simon has been a member and a leader of award-winning Canadian culinary teams for many years, most recently managing Team Canada to a world championship in Glasgow in 1997. In 1995 he was elected Chef of the Year for the Western Region by his peers in the CFCC.

1. Put the chopped eggplant in a colander and sprinkle it lightly with salt. Set aside and allow to sweat for 20–30 minutes.

2. Heat the olive oil in a large skillet over medium-high heat.

3. Add the onions and garlic and sauté until translucent. Add the tomatoes, basil, oregano and thyme and sauté for 4 minutes. Add the chopped celery and olives and sauté for a further 3 minutes.

Continued

4. Thoroughly rinse the salt from the eggplant under cold running water and drain on paper towels. With the pine nuts and pistachios, sauté the eggplant in the remaining olive oil for 3 minutes.

5. Remove the pan from the heat and combine the eggplant mixture with the tomato mixture and allow to cool.

6. Mix vinegar and sugar until dissolved and add to the eggplant-tomato relish. Adjust seasoning to taste and serve warm or at room temperature.

◆◆◆

RECIPE 10.29
TOMATO VINAIGRETTE

Yield: 4 8-oz. (250 g) Servings

Vinaigrette:

Tomato, concassé	8 oz.	250 g
Fresh basil, thyme or marjoram	1 oz.	30 g
Balsamic vinegar	3 oz.	100 mL
Shallots, minced	2 Tbsp.	30 mL
Olive oil	8 oz.	250 mL
Salt and pepper	TT	TT
Pasta, cooked	1 lb.	500 g

1. Combine all vinaigrette ingredients. Season to taste with salt and pepper. Set aside for 20–30 minutes to allow the flavours to blend.

2. Toss the sauce with 1 pound (500 g) warm or cold cooked pasta such as spaghetti or fettuccine. Adjust the seasonings. Serve immediately or refrigerate and serve chilled.

◆◆◆

RECIPE 10.30
PESTO SAUCE

Yield: 1-1/2 pt. (750 mL)

Olive oil	12 oz.	350 mL
Pine nuts	3 oz.	90 g
Fresh basil leaves	6 oz.	180 g
Garlic, chopped	1 Tbsp.	15 mL
Parmesan cheese, grated	4 oz.	120 g
Romano cheese, grated	4 oz.	120 g
Salt and pepper	TT	TT

1. Place one-third of the olive oil in a blender or food processor and add all the remaining ingredients.

2. Blend or process until smooth. Add the remaining olive oil and blend a few seconds to incorporate.

VARIATION: Walnut Pesto—Substitute walnuts for pine nuts in the above recipe.

◆◆◆

RECIPE 10.31
HERB OIL

STANFORD COURT HOTEL, San Francisco, CA
Chef (formerly) Ercolino Crugnale

Yield: 4 oz. (120 mL)

Fresh parsley	2 oz.	60 g
Fresh tarragon	1 oz.	30 g
Fresh thyme	1 oz.	30 g
Olive oil	approx. 4 oz.	approx. 120 mL

Approximate values per 1 oz. (30 mL) serving:

Calories	110
Total fat	8 g
Saturated fat	1 g
Cholesterol	0 mg
Sodium	35 mg
Total carbohydrates	8 g
Protein	3 g
Vitamin A	20%
Iron	70%

Claims—no cholesterol; low sodium

1. Blanch herbs in hot water for 10 seconds. Cool and dry thoroughly.

2. Measure the volume of the herbs and put them in a blender. Add an equal volume of olive oil.

3. Purée and strain through a mesh strainer.

WEBLINKS

Searchable Online Archives of Recipes: Sauce Recipes
 SOAR.Berkeley.EDU/recipes/sauces/

Amy Gale's rec.food.recipes archive: Sauces and Marinades
 www.cs.cmu.edu/~mjw/recipes/sauces/index.html

Stephanie da Silva's rec.food.recipes archive: Sauces
 www.neosoft.com/recipes/sauces/index.html

Culinary Café: Sauces and Marinades
 www.culinarycafe.com/Sauces-Marinades.html

Culinaria Online: Collected Recipes — Sauces
 www.culinaria.com/collectedRecipes/sauces.html

CHAPTER 11

SOUPS

◆◆◆

LEARNING OUTCOMES

After studying this chapter you will be able to:

◆ prepare a variety of clear and thick soups, including broths and bouillons, consommés, cream soups, purée soups, bisques, chowders
◆ garnish and serve soups appropriately

*M*any classic soups are successfully prepared only if recipes are followed strictly. The successful preparation of other soups depends upon the mastery of specialized techniques. But where classic recipes need not be followed nor special techniques employed, perhaps no other area of the kitchen allows the cook to use his or her imagination and creativity as much as the soup station.

The variety of ingredients, seasonings and garnishes that can be used for soups is virtually endless, provided you understand the basic procedures for making different kinds of soup. Great soups can be made using the finest and most expensive ingredients or leftovers from the previous evening's dinner service and trimmings from the day's production.

This chapter extends to soups the skills and knowledge learned in Chapter 10, Stocks and Sauces. In Chapter 10 we discussed making stocks, thickening liquids, using a liaison and skimming impurities, techniques that apply to soup making as well. Here we discuss techniques such as clarifying consommés and thickening soups with vegetable purées. This chapter also covers cream soups, cold soups and guidelines for garnishing and serving a variety of soups.

Most soups can be classified by cooking technique and appearance as either clear or thick.

Clear soups include **broths** and **bouillons** made from meat, poultry, game, fish or vegetables as well as **consommés**, which are broths clarified to remove impurities.

Thickened soups include cream soups and purée soups. The most common **cream soups** are those made from vegetables cooked in a liquid that is thickened with a starch and puréed; cream is then incorporated to add richness and flavour. **Purée soups** are generally made from starchy vegetables or legumes. After the main ingredient is simmered in a liquid, the mixture—or a portion of it—is puréed. Velouté soups are basically cream soups with the addition of a liaison.

Some soups (notably **bisques** and **chowders** as well as **cold soups** such as gazpacho and fruit soup) are generally regarded as thick soups. They use special preparation methods or a combination of the methods mentioned above.

QUALITY STANDARD

A soup's quality is determined by its flavour, appearance and texture. A good soup should be full flavoured, with no off or sour tastes. Flavours from each of the soup's ingredients should blend and complement, with no one flavour overpowering another. Consommés should be crystal clear. The vegetables in vegetable soups should be brightly coloured, not grey. Garnishes should be attractive and uniform in size and shape. The soup's texture should be very precise. If it is supposed to be smooth then it should be very smooth and lump-free. If the soft and crisp textures of certain ingredients are supposed to contrast, the soup should not be overcooked, as this causes all the ingredients to become mushy and soft.

Garnishing is an important consideration when preparing soups. When applied to soups, the word *garnish* has two meanings. The first is the one more typically associated with the word. It refers to foods added to the soup as decoration—for example, a broccoli floret floated on a bowl of cream of broccoli soup. The second refers to foods that may serve not only as decorations but also as critical components of the final product—for example, noodles in a bowl of chicken noodle soup. In this context, the noodles are not ingredients because they are not used to make the chicken soup. Rather they are added to chicken soup to create a different dish. These additional items are still referred to as garnishes, however.

CLEAR SOUPS

All clear soups start as broth. Broths may be served as finished items, used as the base for other soups or refined (clarified) into consommés.

Broths and Bouillons

The techniques for making stocks, discussed in Chapter 10, are identical to those used for making broths and bouillons. Like stocks, broths are prepared by simmering flavouring ingredients in a liquid for long periods of time. Broths and stocks differ, however, in two ways. First, broths are made with meat instead of just bones. Second, broths (often with a garnish) can be served as finished dishes, while stocks are generally used to prepare other items.

Broths are made from meat, poultry, fish or vegetables cooked in a liquid. An especially full-flavoured broth results when a stock and not just water is used as the liquid. Cuts of meat from the shank, neck or shoulder result in more flavourful broths, as will the flesh of mature poultry. Proper temperature, skimming and straining help produce well-flavoured, clear broths.

BASIC PROCEDURE FOR PREPARING BROTHS

1. Truss or cut the main ingredient.
2. Brown the meat; brown or sweat the mirepoix or vegetables as necessary.
3. Place the main ingredient and mirepoix or vegetables in an appropriate stockpot and add enough cold water or stock to cover. Add a bouquet garni or sachet d'épices if desired.
4. Bring the liquid slowly to a boil; reduce to a simmer and cook, skimming occasionally, until the main ingredient is tender and the flavour is fully developed.
5. Carefully strain the broth through a china cap lined with cheesecloth; try to disturb the flavouring ingredients as little as possible in order to preserve the broth's clarity.
6. Cool and store following the procedures for cooling stocks. Or bring to a boil, garnish as desired and hold for service.

ESCOFFIER'S CLASSIFICATION OF SOUPS

In his 1903 culinary treatise *Le Guide culinaire*, Auguste Escoffier recognized many more categories of soups than we do today. They include:

Clear soups, which are always "clear consommés with a slight garnish in keeping with the nature of the consommé."

Purées, which are made from starchy vegetables and are thickened with rice, potato or soft bread crumbs.

Cullises, which use poultry, game or fish for a base and are thickened with rice, lentils, espagnole sauce or bread soaked in boiling salted water.

Bisques, which use shellfish cooked with a mirepoix as a base and are thickened with rice.

Veloutés, which use velouté sauce as a base and are finished with a liaison of egg yolks and cream.

Cream soups, which use béchamel sauce as a base and are finished with heavy cream.

Special soups, which are those that do not follow the procedures for veloutés or creams.

Vegetable soups, which are usually *paysanne* or peasant-type and "do not demand very great precision in the apportionment of the vegetables of which they are composed, but they need great care and attention, notwithstanding."

Foreign soups, "which have a foreign origin whose use, although it may not be general, is yet sufficiently common."

Because of changes in consumer health consciousness and kitchen operations, many of the distinctions between Escoffier's classic soups have now become blurred and, in some cases, eliminated. As discussed in this chapter, for example, clear consommés and vegetable soups are now made with stocks or broths; most cream soups use velouté as a base and are finished with milk or cream rather than a liaison. But not everything has changed: The procedures for making purées and bisques are essentially the same today as they were when Escoffier haunted the great kitchens of Europe.

◆◆◆

RECIPE 11.1

BEEF BROTH

Yield: 8 qt. (8 L)

Beef shank, neck or shoulder cut in 2-inch-thick (5 cm) pieces	12 lb.	5.5 kg
Vegetable oil	8 oz.	250 mL
Cold water or stock	2 gal.	8 L
Mirepoix	2 lb.	900 g
Turnip, medium dice	8 oz.	250 g
Leeks, medium dice	8 oz.	250 g
Tomato, seeded and diced	8 oz.	250 g
Sachet:		
Bay leaf	1	1
Dried thyme	1/2 tsp.	2 mL
Peppercorns, crushed	1/2 tsp.	2 mL
Parsley stems	8	8
Garlic cloves, crushed	2	2
Salt	TT	TT

Approximate values per 6 oz. (180 mL) serving:

Calories	70
Total fat	6 g
Saturated fat	1 g
Cholesterol	2 mg
Sodium	630 mg
Total carbohydrates	2 g
Protein	2 g

1. Brown the meat in 4 ounces (120 mL) of oil, then place it in a stockpot. Add the stock or water and bring to a simmer. Simmer gently for 2 hours, skimming the surface as necessary.
2. After the meat has simmered for 2 hours, caramelize the mirepoix in the remaining oil and add it to the liquid. Add the turnip, leeks, tomato and sachet.
3. Simmer until full flavour has developed, approximately 1 hour. Skim the surface as necessary.
4. Carefully strain the broth through cheesecloth and season to taste. Cool and refrigerate.

Broth-Based Soups

Broths are often used as bases for such familiar soups as vegetable, chicken noodle or beef barley.

Transforming a broth into a broth-based vegetable soup, for example, is quite simple. Although a broth may be served with a vegetable (or meat) garnish, a broth-based vegetable soup is a soup in which the vegetables (and meats) are cooked directly in the broth, adding flavour, body and texture to the finished product. Any number of vegetables can be used to make a vegetable soup; it could be a single vegetable as in onion soup or a dozen different vegetables for a hearty minestrone. Making a mixed vegetable soup allows the cook to use his or her imagination and whatever produce may be on hand.

When making broth-based vegetable soups, each ingredient must be added at the proper time so that all ingredients are cooked when the soup is finished. The ingredients must cook long enough to add their flavours and soften sufficiently but not so long that they lose their identity and become too soft or mushy.

Because broth-based vegetable soups are made by simmering ingredients directly in the broth, they are generally not as clear as plain broths. But appearance is still important. So, when cutting ingredients for the soup, pay particular attention that the pieces are uniform and visually appealing. Small dice, julienne, batonnet or paysanne cuts are recommended.

BASIC PROCEDURE FOR PREPARING BROTH-BASED VEGETABLE SOUPS

1. Sweat long-cooking vegetables in butter or fat.

2. Add the appropriate stock or broth and bring to a simmer.

3. Add seasonings such as bay leaves, dried thyme, crushed peppercorns, parsley stems and garlic, in a sachet, allowing enough time for the seasonings to fully flavour the soup.

4. Add additional ingredients according to their cooking times.

5. Simmer the soup to blend all the flavours.

6. If the soup is not going to be served immediately, cool and refrigerate it.

7. Just before service add any garnishes that were prepared separately or do not require cooking.

◆◆◆

RECIPE 11.2
HEARTY VEGETABLE BEEF SOUP

Yield: 5 qt. (5 L)

Beef, small dice	1 lb.	450 g
Butter or beef fat	6 oz.	170 g
Mirepoix, small dice	3 lb.	1.5 kg
Turnip, small dice	8 oz.	250 g
Garlic cloves, chopped	2	2
Beef broth or beef stock	4 qt.	4 L
Sachet:		
Bay leaf	1	1
Dried thyme	1/2 tsp.	2 mL
Peppercorns, crushed	1/2 tsp.	2 mL
Parsley stems	8	8
Tomato concassée	12 oz.	350 g
Corn kernels, fresh, frozen or canned	12 oz.	350 g
Salt and pepper	TT	TT

Tomato concassée—*peeled, seeded and diced tomato.*

1. Sear the beef in half the hot butter or fat and reserve meat.

2. In a soup pot, sweat the mirepoix and turnip in the remaining butter or fat until tender.

3. Add the garlic and sauté lightly.

4. Add the beef broth or stock and the seared beef; bring to a simmer. Add the sachet. Skim or degrease as necessary.

5. Simmer until the beef and vegetables are tender, approximately 1 hour.

6. Add the tomato concassée and corn; simmer for 10 minutes. Season to taste with salt and pepper.

7. Cool and refrigerate or hold for service.

VARIATIONS: A wide variety of vegetables can be added or substituted in this recipe. If leeks, rutabagas, parsnips or cabbage are used, they should be sweated to bring out their flavours before the liquid is added. Potatoes, fresh beans, summer squash and other vegetables that cook more quickly should be added according to their cooking times. Rice, barley and pasta garnishes should be cooked separately and added just before service.

Approximate values per 6 oz. (180 mL) serving:	
Calories	170
Total fat	10 g
Saturated fat	5 g
Cholesterol	30 mg
Sodium	600 mg
Total carbohydrates	12 g
Protein	7 g
Vitamin A	20%

Consommés

A consommé is a stock or broth that has been clarified to remove impurities so that it is crystal clear. Traditionally, all clear broths were referred to as consommés; a clear broth further refined using the process described below was referred to as a double consommé. The term *double consommé* is still used occasionally to describe any strongly flavoured consommé.

QUALITY STANDARD

Well-prepared consommés should be rich in the flavour of the main ingredient. Beef and game consommés should be dark in colour; consommés made from poultry should have a golden to light amber colour. They should have substantial body as a result of their high gelatin content, and all consommés should be perfectly clear with no trace of fat.

Because a consommé is a refined broth, it is absolutely essential that the broth or stock used be of the highest quality. Although the clarification process adds some flavour to the consommé, the finished consommé will be only as good as the stock or broth from which it was made.

The Clarification Process

To make a consommé, you clarify a stock or broth. The stock or broth to be clarified must be cold and grease-free. To clarify, the cold degreased stock or broth is combined with a mixture known as a **clearmeat** or **clarification**. A clearmeat is a mixture of egg whites; ground meat, poultry or fish; mirepoix, herbs and spices; and an acidic product, usually tomatoes, lemon juice or wine. (An **onion brûlé** is also often added to help flavour and colour the consommé.)

The stock or broth and clearmeat are then slowly brought to a simmer. As the albumen in the egg whites and meat begins to coagulate, it traps impurities suspended in the liquid. As coagulation continues, the albumen-containing items combine with the other clearmeat ingredients and rise to the liquid's surface, forming a **raft**. As the mixture simmers, the raft ingredients release their flavours, further enriching the consommé.

After simmering, the consommé is carefully strained through several layers of cheesecloth to remove any trace of impurities. It is then completely degreased, either by cooling and refrigerating, then removing the solidified fat or by carefully ladling the fat from the surface. The result is a rich, flavourful, crystal-clear consommé.

Onion brûlé—*literally, burnt onion, made by charring onion halves; used to flavour and colour stocks and sauces.*

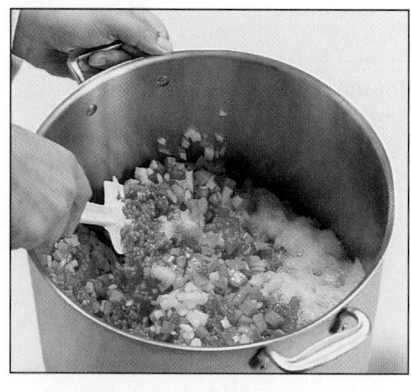

1. Combine the ingredients for the clearmeat: chill for 3-4 hours.

2. Make a hole in the raft to allow the liquid to bubble through.

BASIC PROCEDURE FOR MAKING CONSOMMÉS

1. In a suitable heavy-bottomed stockpot (one with a spigot makes it much easier to strain the consommé when it is finished), combine the ground meat, lightly beaten egg white and other clearmeat ingredients.

2. Add the cold stock or broth and stir to combine with the clearmeat ingredients.

3. Over medium heat, slowly bring the mixture to a simmer, stirring occasionally.

4. As the raft forms, make a hole in its centre so that the liquid can bubble through, cooking the raft completely and extracting as much flavour as possible from the raft ingredients.

5. Simmer the consommé until full flavour develops, approximately 1 to 1-1/2 hours.

6. Carefully strain the consommé through several layers of cheesecloth and degrease completely.

7. If the consommé will not be used immediately, it should be cooled and refrigerated, following the procedures for cooling stocks discussed in Chapter 10. When the consommé is completely cold, remove any remaining fat that solidified on its surface.

8. If, after reheating the consommé, small dots of fat appear on the surface, they can be removed by blotting with a small piece of paper towel.

◆◆◆

RECIPE 11.3
BEEF CONSOMMÉ

3. Degrease the consommé with a paper towel.

Yield: 4 qt. (4 L)

Egg whites	10	10
Ground beef, lean, preferably shank, neck or shoulder	2 lb.	1 kg
Mirepoix	1 lb.	450 g
Tomato, seeded and diced	12 oz.	350 g
Brown beef stock or broth, cold	5 qt.	5 L
Onion brûlé	2 halves	2 halves
Sachet:		
Bay leaves	2	2
Dried thyme	1/2 tsp.	2 mL
Peppercorns, crushed	1/2 tsp.	2 mL
Parsley stems	8	8
Cloves, whole	2	2
Salt	TT	TT

4. The finished consommé.

1. Whip the egg whites until slightly frothy.
2. Combine the egg whites, beef, mirepoix and tomatoes in an appropriate stockpot.
3. Add the cold beef stock or broth; mix well and add the onion brûlé and sachet.
4. Bring the mixture to a simmer over moderate heat, stirring occasionally. Stop stirring when the raft begins to form.
5. Break a hole in the centre of the raft to allow the consommé to bubble through.
6. Simmer until full flavour develops, approximately 1-1/2 hours.
7. Strain through several layers of cheesecloth, degrease and adjust the seasonings. Cool and refrigerate or hold for service.

NOTE: Guidelines for garnishing consommés as well as some classic garnishes are listed on page 249.

Approximate values per 6 oz. (180 mL) serving:	
Calories	210
Total fat	10 g
Saturated fat	3.5 g
Cholesterol	40 mg
Sodium	870 mg
Total carbohydrates	14 g
Protein	15 g
Vitamin A	20%
Vitamin C	10%

Correcting a Poorly Clarified Consommé

A clarification may fail for a variety of reasons. For example, if the consommé is allowed to boil or if it is stirred after the raft has formed, a cloudy consommé can result. If the consommé is insufficiently clear, a second clarification can be performed using the following procedure. This second clarification should be performed only once, however, and only if absolutely necessary, because the eggs not only remove impurities but also some of the consommé's flavour and richness.

1. Thoroughly chill and degrease the consommé.
2. Lightly beat one egg white per quart (litre) of consommé and combine with the cold consommé.
3. Slowly bring the consommé to a simmer, stirring occasionally. Stop stirring when the egg whites begin to coagulate.
4. When the egg whites are completely coagulated, carefully strain the consommé.

THICK SOUPS

There are two kinds of thick soups: cream velouté-based soups and purée soups. In general, cream velouté-based soups are thickened with a roux or other starch, while purée soups rely on a purée of the main ingredient for thickening. But in certain ways the two soups are very similar: Some purée soups are finished with cream or partially thickened with a roux or other starch.

Cream Soups

Most cream soups are made by simmering the main flavouring ingredient (for example, broccoli for cream of broccoli soup) in a white stock or thin velouté sauce to which seasonings have been added. The mixture is then puréed and strained. After the consistency has been adjusted, the soup is finished by adding cream. In classic cuisine, thin béchamel sauce is often used as the base for cream soups and can be substituted for velouté in many cream soup recipes, if desired.

Both hard vegetables (e.g., celery and squash) and soft or leafy vegetables (e.g., spinach, corn, broccoli and asparagus) are used for cream soups. Hard vegetables are generally sweated in butter without browning before the liquid is added. Soft and leafy vegetables are generally added to the soup after the liquid is brought to a boil. Because cream soups are puréed, it is important to cook the flavouring ingredients until they are soft and can be passed through a food mill easily.

All cream soups are finished with milk or cream. Using milk thins the soup while adding richness; using the same amount of cream adds much more richness without the same thinning effect. Cold milk and cream curdle easily if added directly to a hot or acidic soup. But there are several steps that can be taken to prevent curdling:

1. Never add cold milk or cream to hot soup. Bring the milk or cream to a simmer before adding it to the soup. Or, temper the milk or cream by gradually adding some hot soup to it and then incorporating the warmed mixture into the rest of the soup.
2. If possible, add the milk or cream to the soup just before service.
3. Do not boil the soup after the milk or cream has been added.
4. The presence of roux or other starch helps prevent curdling. Therefore, béchamel or cream sauce is often used instead of milk or cream to finish cream soups.

(Recall from Chapter 10 that a béchamel sauce is made by thickening milk with a roux, and a cream sauce is made by adding cream to a béchamel sauce.)

Basic Procedure for Making Cream Soups

1. In a soup pot, sweat hard vegetables such as squash, onions, carrots and celery in oil or butter without browning.
2. In order to thicken the soup:
   (a) add flour and cook to make a blond roux, then add the cooking liquid (i.e., the stock), or
   (b) add the stock to the vegetables, bring the stock to a simmer and add a blond roux that was prepared separately, or
   (c) add a thin velouté or béchamel sauce to the vegetables.
3. Bring to a boil and reduce to a simmer.
4. Add any soft vegetables such as broccoli or asparagus, and a sachet or bouquet garni as desired.
5. Simmer the soup, skimming occasionally, until the vegetables are very tender.
6. Purée the soup by passing it through a food mill, blender, food processor or vertical chopper mixer (VCM) and strain through a china cap. If the soup is too thick, adjust the consistency by adding boiling white stock.
7. Finish the soup by adding hot milk or cream or a thin béchamel or cream sauce. Adjust the seasonings and serve.

◆◆◆

RECIPE 11.4

Cream of Broccoli Soup

Yield: 6 qt. (6 L)

Whole butter	3 oz.	90 g
Onion, medium dice	12 oz.	350 g
Celery, medium dice	3 oz.	90 g
Broccoli stalks, chopped	3 lb.	1.4 kg
Chicken velouté sauce, hot	4 qt.	4 L
Chicken stock, hot	approx. 2 qt.	approx. 2 L
Heavy cream, hot	24 oz.	700 mL
Salt and white pepper	TT	TT
Broccoli florets	8 oz.	250 g

1. Sweat the onions, celery and broccoli in the butter, without browning, until they are nearly tender.
2. Add the velouté sauce. Bring to a simmer and cook until the vegetables are tender, approximately 15 minutes. Skim the surface periodically.
3. Purée the soup, then strain it through a fine china cap or chinois.
4. Return the soup to the stove and thin it to the correct consistency with the hot chicken stock.
5. Bring the soup to a simmer and add the hot cream. Season to taste with salt and white pepper.
6. Garnish with blanched broccoli florets just before service.

VARIATIONS: To make cream of asparagus, cauliflower, corn, pea or spinach soup, substitute an equal amount of the chosen vegetable for the broccoli. If using fresh spinach, precook the leaves slightly before proceeding with the recipe.

Approximate values per 6 oz. (180 mL) serving:

Calories	113
Total fat	9 g
Saturated fat	5 g
Cholesterol	25 mg
Sodium	453 mg
Total carbohydrates	6 g
Protein	3 g

◆◆◆

CROUTONS

A crouton is simply a piece of bread that is toasted, sautéed or dried. Two types are often used.

The more familiar ones are small seasoned cubes of bread that are baked or toasted and sprinkled over soups or salads.

A more classic variety is made by sautéing slices of bread in clarified butter or olive oil until brown and crisp. The bread may be rough slices from a baguette or cut into shapes (such as hearts, diamonds or circles) from larger slices. Sautéed croutons have two advantages over the toasted variety: They stay crisp longer after coming in contact with moist foods, and they gain flavour from the butter or olive oil in which they are cooked. Sautéed croutons can be used to decorate the border of a serving dish, as a base for canapés, a garnish for soups, an accompaniment to spreads or caviar or as a base under some meat and game dishes.

Purée Soups

Purée soups are hearty soups made by cooking starchy vegetables or legumes in a stock or broth, then puréeing all or a portion of them to thicken the soup. Purée soups are similar to cream soups in that they both consist of a main ingredient that is first cooked in a liquid, then puréed. The primary difference is that unlike cream soups, which are thickened with starch, purée soups generally do not use additional starch for thickening. Rather, purée soups depend on the starch content of the main ingredient for thickening. Also, purée soups are generally coarser than cream soups and are typically not strained after puréeing. When finishing purée soups with cream, follow the guidelines discussed above for adding cream to cream soups.

Purée soups can be made with dried or fresh beans such as peas, lentils and navy beans, or with any number of vegetables including cauliflower, celery root, turnips and potatoes. Diced potatoes or rice are often used to help thicken vegetable purée soups.

BASIC PROCEDURE FOR MAKING PURÉE SOUPS

1. Sweat the mirepoix in butter without browning.

2. Add the cooking liquid.

3. Add the main ingredients and a sachet or bouquet garni.

4. Bring to a boil, reduce to a simmer and cook until all the ingredients are soft enough to purée easily. Remove and discard the sachet or bouquet garni.

5. Reserve a portion of the liquid to adjust the soup's consistency. Purée the rest of the soup by passing it through a food mill, food processor, blender or VCM.

6. Add enough of the reserved liquid to bring the soup to the correct consistency. If the soup is still too thick, add hot stock as needed.

7. Return the soup to a simmer and adjust the seasonings.

8. Add hot cream to the soup if desired.

◆◆◆

RECIPE 11.5

PURÉE OF SPLIT PEA SOUP

Yield: 4 qt. (4 L)

Bacon, diced	3 oz.	90 g
Mirepoix, medium dice	1 lb.	450 g
Garlic cloves, chopped	2	2
Chicken stock	3 qt.	3 L
Split peas, washed and soaked	1 lb.	450 g
Ham hocks or meaty ham bones	1-1/2 lb.	675 g
Sachet:		
Bay leaves	2	2
Dried thyme	1/2 tsp.	2 mL
Peppercorns, crushed	1/2 tsp.	2 mL
Salt and pepper	TT	TT
Croutons, sautéed in butter	as needed for garnish	

Render—*to melt and clarify fat.*

1. Soak peas in water overnight.

2. In a stockpot, **render** the bacon by cooking it slowly and allowing it to release its fat; sweat the mirepoix and garlic in the fat without browning them.

3. Add the chicken stock, drained peas, ham hocks or bones and sachet. Bring to a boil, reduce to a simmer and cook until the peas are soft, approximately 1 to 1-1/2 hours.
4. Remove the sachet and ham hocks or bones. Pass the soup through a food mill and return it to the stockpot.
5. Remove the meat from the hocks or bones. Cut the meat into a medium dice and add it to the soup.
6. Bring the soup to a simmer and, if necessary, adjust the consistency by adding hot chicken stock. Adjust the seasonings with salt and pepper and serve, garnished with croutons.

VARIATIONS: White beans, yellow peas, and other dried beans or lentils can be soaked overnight in water and used instead of split peas.

Approximate values per 6 oz. (180 mL) serving:

Calories	110
Total fat	4 g
Saturated fat	1.5 g
Cholesterol	20 mg
Sodium	870 mg
Total carbohydrates	6 g
Protein	11 g

Adjusting the Consistency of Thick Soups

Cream and purée soups tend to thicken when made in advance and refrigerated. To dilute a portion being reheated, add a small amount of stock, broth, water or milk.

If the soup is too thin, additional roux, beurre manié or cornstarch mixed with cool stock can be used to thicken it. If additional starch is added to thicken the soup it should be used sparingly and the soup should be simmered a few minutes to cook out the starchy flavour. A liaison of egg yolks and heavy cream can be used to thicken cream soups when added richness is also desired. Remember, the soup must not boil after the liaison is added or it may curdle.

OTHER SOUPS

Several popular types of soup do not fit the descriptions of or follow the procedures for clear or thick soups. Soups such as bisques and chowders as well as many cold soups use special methods or a combination of the methods used for clear and thick soups.

Bisques

Traditional bisques are shellfish (crustaceans) soups thickened with cooked rice. Today bisques are prepared using a combination of the cream and purée soup procedures. They are generally made from shrimp, lobster or crayfish and are thickened with a roux instead of rice for better stability and consistency.

Much of a bisque's flavour comes from crustacean shells, which are simmered in the cooking liquid, puréed (along with the mirepoix), returned to the cooking liquid and strained after further cooking. Puréeing the shells and returning them to the soup also adds the thickness and grainy texture associated with bisques, although this is rarely done today.

Bisques are enriched with cream, following the procedures for cream soups, and can be finished with butter for additional richness. The garnish should be diced flesh from the appropriate shellfish.

BASIC PROCEDURE FOR MAKING BISQUES

1. Caramelize the mirepoix and main flavouring ingredient in fat.
2. Add a tomato product and deglaze with wine.

3. Add the cooking liquid (stock or velouté).

4. Incorporate roux if needed.

5. Simmer, skimming as needed.

6. Strain the soup, reserving the solids and liquid. Purée the solids in a food chopper or processor and return them to the liquid. Return to a simmer.

7. Strain the soup through a fine chinois or a china cap lined with cheesecloth.

8. Return the soup to a simmer and finish with hot cream.

To add even more richness to the bisque, monter au beurre with whole butter or a compound butter such as shrimp or lobster butter just before the soup is served. Also, if desired, add 3 ounces (90 mL) of sherry to each gallon (4 L) of soup just before service.

◆◆◆

RECIPE 11.6

Shrimp Bisque

Yield: 4 qt. (4 L)

Clarified butter	3 oz.	90 g
Mirepoix, small dice	1 lb.	450 g
Shrimp shells and/or lobster or crayfish shells and bodies	2 lb.	1 kg
Garlic cloves, chopped	2	2
Tomato paste	2 oz.	60 g
Brandy	4 oz.	120 mL
Dry sherry wine	12 oz.	350 mL
Fish velouté (made with shrimp stock)	4 qt.	4 L
Sachet:		
Bay leaf	1	1
Dried thyme	1/2 tsp.	2 mL
Peppercorns, crushed	1/2 tsp.	2 mL
Parsley stems	8	8
Cream, 35%, hot	1 pt.	500 mL
Salt and white pepper	TT	TT
Cayenne pepper	TT	TT
Shrimps, peeled and deveined	1 lb.	450 g

1. Caramelize the mirepoix and shrimp shells in the butter.

2. Add the garlic and tomato paste and sauté lightly.

3. Add the brandy and flambé.

4. Add the sherry wine. Deglaze and reduce the liquid by half.

5. Add the velouté and sachet and simmer for approximately 1 hour, skimming occasionally.

6. Strain, discarding the sachet and reserving the liquid and solids. Purée the solids and return them to the liquid. Return to a simmer and cook for 10 minutes.

7. Strain the bisque through a fine chinois or china cap lined with cheesecloth.

8. Return the bisque to a simmer and add the hot cream.

9. Season to taste with salt, white pepper and cayenne pepper.

10. Cook the shrimps and slice or dice them as desired. Garnish each portion of soup with cooked shrimp.

Approximate values per 4 oz. (120 mL) serving:

Calories	110
Total fat	10 g
Saturated fat	6 g
Cholesterol	60 mg
Sodium	160 mg
Total carbohydrates	2 g
Protein	4 g
Vitamin A	10%

Chowders

Although chowders are usually associated with the eastern seaboard, where fish and clams are plentiful, they are of French origin. Undoubtedly the word *chowder* is derived from the Breton phrase *faire chaudière*, which means to make a fish stew in a cauldron. The procedure was probably brought to Nova Scotia by French settlers and later introduced into New England.

Chowders are hearty soups with chunks of the main ingredients (including, virtually always, diced potatoes) and garnishes. With some exceptions (notably, Manhattan clam chowder), chowders contain milk or cream. Although there are thin chowders, most chowders are thickened with roux. The procedures for making chowders are similar to those for making cream soups except that chowders are not puréed and strained before the cream is added.

BASIC PROCEDURE FOR MAKING CHOWDERS

1. Render finely diced salt pork over medium heat.
2. Sweat mirepoix in the rendered pork.
3. Add flour to make a roux.
4. Add the liquid.
5. Add the seasoning and flavouring ingredients according to their cooking times.
6. Simmer, skimming as needed.
7. Add milk or cream.

RECIPE 11.7

NEW-ENGLAND-STYLE CLAM CHOWDER

Yield: 3 qt. (3 L)

Canned clams with juice*	2 qt.	2 L
Water or fish stock	approx. 1-1/2 qt.	approx. 1.5 L
Potato, small dice	1 lb. 4 oz.	600 g
Salt pork, small dice	8 oz.	250 g
Onion, small dice	1 lb.	450 g
Celery, small dice	8 oz.	250 g
Flour	4 oz.	120 g
Milk	1 qt.	1 L
Heavy cream	8 oz.	250 mL
Salt and pepper	TT	TT
Tabasco sauce	TT	TT
Worcestershire sauce	TT	TT
Fresh thyme	TT	TT

1. Drain the clams, reserving both the clams and their liquid. To the clam liquid add water or stock to total 2 quarts (2 L).
2. Simmer the potatoes in the clam liquid until nearly cooked through. Strain and reserve the potatoes and the liquid.
3. Render the salt pork without browning it. Add the onions and celery and sweat until tender.
4. Add the flour and cook to make a blond roux.
5. Add the clam liquid to the roux, whisking away any lumps.

Continued

6. Simmer for 30 minutes, skimming as necessary.

7. Bring the milk and cream to a boil and add to the soup.

8. Add the clams and potatoes and season to taste with salt, pepper, Tabasco, Worcestershire and thyme. (Diced green peppers are a popular addition in Western Canada.)

* If using fresh clams for the chowder, wash and steam approximately 1/2 bushel (15 L) of chowder clams in a small amount of water to yield 1-1/4 quarts (1.25 L) of clam meat. Chop the clams. Strain the liquid through several layers of cheesecloth to remove any sand that may be present. Add enough water or stock to total 2 quarts (2 L). Continue with the recipe, starting at step 2.

Cold Soups

Cold soups can be as simple as a chilled version of a cream soup or as unique as a cold fruit soup blended with yogurt. Other than the fact that they are cold, cold soups are difficult to classify because many of them use unique or combination preparation methods. Regardless, they are divided here into two categories: those that require cooking and those that do not.

Cooked Cold Soups

Many cold soups are simply chilled versions of hot soups. For example, consommé madrilène and consommé portugaise are prepared hot and served cold. Vichyssoise, probably the most popular of all cold soups, is a cold version of purée of potato-leek soup. When serving a hot soup cold, there are several considerations:

1. If the soup is to be creamed, add the cream at the last minute. Although curdling is not as much of a problem as it is with hot soups, adding the cream at the last minute helps extend the soup's shelf life.

2. Cold soups should have a thinner consistency than hot soups. To achieve the proper consistency, use less starch if starch is used as the thickener, or use a higher ratio of liquid to main ingredient if the soup is thickened by puréeing. Consistency should be checked and adjusted at service time.

3. Cold dulls the sense of taste, so cold soups require more seasoning than hot ones. Taste the soup just before service and adjust the seasonings as needed.

4. Always serve cold soups as cold as possible.

◆◆◆

RECIPE 11.8

VICHYSSOISE (COLD POTATO-LEEK SOUP)

Yield: 4 qt. (4 L)

Leek, white part only	2 lb.	1 kg
Whole butter	8 oz.	250 g
Potato, large dice	2 lb.	1 kg
Chicken stock	3-1/2 qt.	3.5 L
Salt and white pepper	TT	TT
Heavy cream	24 oz.	700 mL
Chives, snipped	as needed	as needed

1. Split the leeks lengthwise and wash well to remove all sand and grit. Slice them thinly.

2. Sweat the leeks in the butter without browning them.

3. Add the potatoes and chicken stock, season with salt and pepper and bring to a simmer.

4. Simmer until the leeks and potatoes are very tender, approximately 45 minutes.

5. Purée the soup in a food processor, blender or food mill; strain through a fine sieve.

6. Chill the soup well.

7. At service time, incorporate the heavy cream and adjust the seasonings. Serve in chilled bowls, garnished with snipped chives.

Approximate values per 6 oz. (180 mL) serving:	
Calories	300
Total fat	22 g
Saturated fat	13 g
Cholesterol	70 mg
Sodium	660 mg
Total carbohydrates	19 g
Protein	6 g
Vitamin A	20%
Vitamin C	20%

Many cooked cold soups use fruit juice (typically apple, grape or orange) as a base and are thickened with cornstarch or arrowroot as well as with puréed fruit. For additional flavour, wine is sometimes used in lieu of a portion of the fruit juice. Cinnamon, ginger and other spices that complement fruit are commonly added, as is lemon or lime juice, which adds acidity as well as flavour. Crème fraîche, yogurt or sour cream can be used as an ingredient or garnish to add richness.

RECIPE 11.9

CHILLED CHERRY SOUP

Yield: 4 qt. (4 L)

Cherries, pitted	5 lb.	2.25 kg
Apple juice	approx. 2 qt.	approx. 2 L
Sachet:		
Cinnamon sticks	2	2
Cloves, whole	4	4
Honey	6 oz.	170 g
Cornstarch	1 oz.	30 g
Lemon juice	TT	TT
Dry champagne or sparkling wine	8 oz.	250 mL
Crème fraîche	as needed for garnish	
Toasted almonds	as needed for garnish	

1. Combine the cherries, apple juice, sachet and honey. Bring to a simmer and cook for 30 minutes. Remove the sachet.

2. Dilute the cornstarch with a small amount of cold apple juice. Add it to the soup for thickening. Simmer the soup for 10 minutes to cook out the starchy taste.

3. Purée the soup in a food processor or blender and strain if desired.

4. Chill the soup thoroughly.

5. At service, adjust the seasoning with the lemon juice. Stir in the chilled champagne or sparkling wine and serve garnished with crème fraîche and toasted, slivered almonds.

Approximate values per 6 oz. (180 mL) serving:	
Calories	150
Total fat	0 g
Saturated fat	0 g
Cholesterol	0 mg
Sodium	0 mg
Total carbohydrates	34 g
Protein	1 g
Vitamin C	15%

Claims—fat free; no sodium; good source of fibre

Uncooked Cold Soups

Some cold soups are not cooked at all. Rather they rely only on puréed fruits or vegetables for thickness, body and flavour. Cold stock is sometimes used to adjust the soup's consistency. Dairy products such as cream, sour cream or crème fraîche are sometimes added to enrich and flavour the soup.

Because uncooked cold soups are never heated, enzymes and bacteria are not destroyed and the soup can spoil quickly. When preparing uncooked cold soups, always prepare small batches as close to service time as possible.

◆◆◆

RECIPE 11.10
GAZPACHO

Yield: 4 qt. (4 L)

Tomato, peeled and diced	2 lb. 8 oz.	1.2 kg
Onion, medium dice	8 oz.	250 g
Green pepper, medium dice	1	1
Red pepper, medium dice	1	1
Cucumber, peeled, seeded, medium dice	1 lb.	450 g
Garlic, minced	1 oz.	30 g
Red wine vinegar	2 oz.	60 mL
Lemon juice	2 oz.	60 mL
Olive oil	4 oz.	120 mL
Salt and pepper	TT	TT
Cayenne pepper	TT	TT
Fresh bread crumbs (optional)	3 oz.	90 g
Tomato juice	3 qt.	3 L
White stock	as needed	as needed
Garnish:		
Tomato, peeled, seeded, small dice	8 oz.	250 g
Red pepper, small dice	4 oz.	120 g
Green pepper, small dice	4 oz.	120 g
Yellow pepper, small dice	4 oz.	120 g
Cucumber, peeled, seeded, small dice	3 oz.	90 g
Green onion, sliced fine	2 oz.	60 g
Croutons	as needed	as needed

Approximate values per 6 oz. (180 mL) serving:

Calories	70
Total fat	.5 g
Saturated fat	0 g
Cholesterol	0 mg
Sodium	600 mg
Total carbohydrates	14 g
Protein	3 g
Vitamin A	15%
Vitamin C	70%
Claims—low fat; no cholesterol	

1. Combine and purée all ingredients except the tomato juice, stock and garnish in a VCM, food processor or blender.
2. Stir in the tomato juice.
3. Adjust the consistency with stock.
4. Stir in the vegetables, the garnishes and adjust the seasonings.
5. Serve in chilled cups or bowls garnished with croutons.

GARNISHING SOUPS

Garnishes can range from a simple sprinkle of chopped parsley on a bowl of cream soup to tiny profiteroles stuffed with foie gras adorning a crystal-clear bowl of consommé. Some soups are so full of attractive, flavourful and colourful foods that are integral parts of the soup (for example, vegetables and chicken in chicken vegetable soup) that no additional garnishes (as either decoration or component) are necessary. In others, the garnish determines the type of soup. For example, a beef broth garnished with cooked barley and diced beef becomes beef barley soup. See Table 11.1.

Guidelines for Garnishing Soups

Although some soups (particularly consommés) have traditional garnishes, many soups depend on the chef's imagination and the kitchen's inventory for the finishing garnish. The only rules are:

1. The garnish should be attractive.
2. The meats and vegetables used should be neatly cut into an appropriate and uniform shape and size. This is particularly important when garnishing a clear soup such as a consommé, as the consommé's clarity highlights the precise (or imprecise) cuts.
3. The garnish's texture and flavour should complement the soup.
4. Starches and vegetables used as garnishes should be cooked separately, reheated and placed in the soup bowl before the hot soup is added. If they are cooked in the soup, they may cloud or thicken the soup or alter its flavour, texture and seasoning.
5. Garnishes should be cooked just until done; meat and poultry should be tender but not falling apart, vegetables should be firm but not mushy and pasta and rice should maintain their identity. These types of garnishes are usually held on the side and added to the hot soup at the last minute to prevent overcooking.

Garnishing Suggestions

✦ Clear soups—any combination of julienne cuts of the same meat, poultry, fish or vegetable that provides the dominant flavour in the stock or broth, vegetables (cut uniformly into any shape), pasta (flat, small tortellini or tiny ravioli), gnocchi, quenelles, barley, spaetzle, white or wild rice, croutons, crepes, tortillas, or won tons.

CLASSIC CONSOMMÉS

Many consommés are known by their garnishes:

Consommé brunoise—blanched or sautéed brunoise of turnip, leek, celery, carrot and onion.

Consommé julienne—blanched or sautéed julienne of carrot, turnip, leek, celery, chervil.

Consommé madrilene—chicken consommé flavoured and garnished with tomatoes and red peppers. Serve chilled.

Consommé celestine—garnished with julienne of herb-flavoured crepe.

Consommé royale—cooked custard cut into tiny shapes.

Angels' hair consommé—cooked angel hair (vermicelli) pasta.

Consommé with profiteroles—tiny profiteroles (pâte à choux rounds) stuffed with foie gras or other mousse.

TABLE 11.1   SOUPS, THEIR THICKENING AGENTS AND FINISHES

Category	Type	Thickening Agent or Method	Finish
Clear soups	Broths	None	Assorted garnishes
	Consommés	Usually none	Assorted garnishes
Thick soups	Cream soups	Roux and/or puréeing	Assorted garnishes, cream or béchamel sauce
	Purée soups	Puréeing	Assorted garnishes; cream is optional
Other soups	Bisques	Roux or rice and puréeing	Garnish of main ingredient, cream and/or butter
	Chowders	Roux	Cream
Cold soups	Cooked cold soups	Roux, arrowroot, cornstarch, puréeing, sour cream, yogurt	Assorted garnishes, cream, crème fraîche or sour cream
	Uncooked cold soups	Puréeing	Assorted garnishes, cream, crème fraîche or sour cream

+ Cream soups, hot or cold—toasted slivered almonds, sour cream or crème fraîche, croutons, grated cheese or puff pastry fleurons; cream vegetable soups are usually garnished with slices or florets of the main ingredient.
+ Purée soups—julienne cuts of poultry or ham, sliced sausage, croutons, grated cheese, bacon bits.
+ Any soup—finely chopped fresh herbs, snipped chives, edible flower blossoms or petals, parsley or watercress.

SOUP SERVICE

Preparing Soups in Advance

Most soups can be made ahead of time and reheated as needed for service. To preserve freshness and quality, small batches of soup should be heated as needed throughout the meal service.

Clear soups are quite easy to reheat because there is little danger of scorching. If garnishes are already added to a clear soup, care should be taken not to overcook the garnishes when reheating the soup. All traces of fat should be removed from a consommé's surface before reheating.

Thick soups present more of a challenge. To increase shelf life and reduce the risk of spoilage, cool and refrigerate a thick soup when it is still a base (that is, before it is finished with milk or cream). When needed, carefully reheat the soup base just before service using a heavy-gauge pot over low heat. Stir often to prevent scorching. Then finish the soup (following the guidelines noted above) with boiling milk or cream, a light béchamel sauce or a liaison and adjust the seasonings. Always taste the soup after reheating and adjust the seasonings as needed.

Temperatures

The rule is simple: Serve hot soup hot and cold soup cold. Hot clear soups should be served near boiling. Hot cream soups should be served at slightly lower temperatures; 190°F–200°F (90°C–93°C) is acceptable. Cold soups should be served at a temperature of 40°F (4°C) or below. Preheating or chilling service bowls is required.

CONCLUSION

Soup, often served as the first course, may determine the success or failure of an entire meal. Although a wide variety of ingredients can be used to make both clear and thick soups, including trimmings and leftovers, poor-quality ingredients make poor-quality soups. By using, adapting and combining the basic techniques described in this chapter with different ingredients, you can create an infinite number of new and appetizing hot or cold soups. But exercise good judgment when combining flavours and techniques; they should blend well and complement each other. Moreover, any garnishes that are added should contribute to the appearance and character of the finished soup. And remember, always serve hot soups hot and cold soups cold.

QUESTIONS FOR DISCUSSION

1. What are the differences between a stock and a broth?
2. What are the differences between a beef consommé and a beef-based broth? How are they similar?
3. What are the differences between a cream soup and a purée soup? How are they similar?
4. Create a recipe for chicken consommé.
5. Discuss several techniques for serving soup. What can be done to ensure that soups are served at the correct temperature?
6. Explain how and why soups are garnished. Why is it sometimes said that the noodles in a chicken noodle soup are actually a garnish?

ADDITIONAL SOUP RECIPES

RECIPE 11.11 (Aboriginal)
BUTTERNUT SQUASH AND MAPLE SOUP

CULINARY PROGRAMS, H.R.T. ALLIANCE, HUMBER COLLEGE, TORONTO, ON
Program Coordinator Anthony Bevan

Yield: 10 servings

Butternut squash	3 lb.	1.35 kg
Onion	1 lb.	450 g
Grated ginger	2 Tbsp.	30 mL
Walnut oil	6 Tbsp.	90 mL
White stock (white venison stock makes an excellent base)	6 pts.	3.35 L
Maple syrup	TT	TT
Salt (optional)	TT	TT
Chiffonade of fresh mint	as needed for garnish	

1. Peel the squash. Remove the seeds and toast them in a hot oven.
2. Rough-cut the squash and onion into mirepoix.
3. Sweat the squash, onion and ginger in the walnut oil.
4. Add the stock and bring to a boil, then simmer for 40 minutes.
5. Purée the soup and strain it into a clean pot.
6. Season with the maple syrup to taste. (Although not traditional, salt may be added to taste.)
7. When serving, sprinkle the soup with the toasted seeds and mint.

Anthony Bevan
Tony is originally from Ireland, where he was Executive Chef and chef-owner at several five-star restaurants. He came to Canada in 1987, and while teaching in Sudbury became interested in Native cooking, lecturing on such subjects as Native Menus and Food Theory, and helped develop Canada's first accredited Native cooking apprenticeship program.

Approximate values per serving:

Calories	171
Total fat	10 g
Saturated fat	.1 g
Cholesterol	0 mg
Sodium	2106 mg
Total carbohydrates	18 g
Protein	3 g

◆◆◆

RECIPE 11.12
St. Louis Pumpkin Chowder

Yield: 4 servings

Corn oil	2 Tbsp.	30 mL
Bacon slices, diced	2	2
Onion, chopped	1	1
Celery stick, chopped	1	1
Pumpkin pulp, diced	1 lb.	450 g
Green chile, chopped	1	1
Water, stock and coconut milk in equal proportions to make	1 qt.	1 L
Salt	TT	TT
Honey	1 tsp.	5 mL
Fresh dairy cream or coconut cream	5 oz.	150 mL
Shrimps, cooked and peeled	16	16

1. Heat oil in a heavy bottomed pan and stir-fry the bacon and onion together for 5 minutes.

2. Add celery, pumpkin, chile and liquid combination. Boil 15 minutes, then purée the mixture.

3. Season with salt and honey. Add cream or coconut cream for a tropical finish, and garnish with shrimps.

4. Reheat gently for 4 minutes and serve. Add milk or more cream if desired.

Approximate values per serving:

Calories	462
Total fat	42 g
Saturated fat	25 g
Cholesterol	103 mg
Sodium	264 mg
Total carbohydrates	13 g
Protein	13 g

◆◆◆

RECIPE 11.13
Vichyssoise of Oysters with Caviar Chantilly

MUSTARD GRILLE, MISSISSAUGA, ON
Executive Chef Anthony Borgo

Yield: 4 Servings

Leeks	17 oz.	510 g
Onions	8 oz.	240 g
Butter	3 oz.	90 g
Potato, finely sliced	8 oz.	240 g
Fish stock	15 oz.	450 mL
Water	5 oz.	150 mL
Cream, 35%	8 oz.	240 mL
Salt and white pepper	TT	TT
Caviar Chantilly:		
Cream, 35%	4 oz.	120 mL
Iranian caviar	1 Tbsp.	15 g
Chives	4 tsp.	20 mL
Oysters, freshly shucked	8	8
Chervil sprigs	4	4

1. Clean the leeks, making sure to use only the white part of the stalks. Chop the leeks and onions very thin.

2. Sweat the leeks and onions in the butter until they are soft, but without colouring them. Then add the finely sliced raw potato, the boiling stock and water and cook over a high heat for 6 minutes.

Anthony Borgo
Since graduating in 1991, Anthony has gained a wealth of international experience working in Ireland, England, Switzerland, Japan and Canada and has risen through the ranks in the kitchen to the position of Executive Chef.

Approximate values per serving:

Calories	462
Total fat	42 g
Saturated fat	25 g
Cholesterol	103 mg
Sodium	264 mg
Total carbohydrates	13 g
Protein	13 g

3. Add the cream and cook for a further 2 minutes. Purée, then pass through a fine sieve. Season to taste.

4. Prepare the caviar chantilly by whipping the cream and folding in the caviar and finely chopped chives. To serve, place 2 of the freshly shucked oysters into each bowl. Add the hot soup. Garnish with a quenelle of the caviar/chive cream and a sprig of fresh chervil. Serve immediately.

◆◆◆

RECIPE 11.14
Moroccan Harira
(Lamb, Chicken and Lentil Soup)

Yield: 4 qt. (4 L)

Olive oil	5 oz.	140 mL
Stewing lamb, cubed	2 lb. 8 oz.	1.2 kg
Chicken pieces	3–4 lb.	1.3–1.8 kg
Garlic cloves, puréed	5	5
Onion, chopped fine	2 lb.	1 kg
Chickpeas, canned	8 oz.	250 g
Chicken stock	5 qt.	5 L
Turmeric	1-1/2 tsp.	7 mL
Ginger, ground	1-1/2 tsp.	7 mL
Coriander	1-1/2 tsp.	7 mL
Cinnamon	1-1/2 tsp.	7 mL
Tomatoes, canned, chopped	2 lb. 8 oz.	1.2 kg
Lentils, washed	8 oz.	250 g
Rice	4 oz.	120 g
Salt and pepper	TT	TT
Parsley, chopped	5 Tbsp.	75 mL
Whole eggs, beaten	5	5
Lemon juice	5 Tbsp.	75 mL

1. Heat the oil in a large, heavy sauté pan. Lightly brown the lamb, then transfer it to a large saucepot. Repeat for the chicken, garlic and onions.

2. Add the chickpeas, stock, spices, tomatoes and lentils. Cover and simmer for 40 minutes.

3. Add the rice and simmer 20 minutes longer.

4. Remove the chicken pieces from the soup. Skin them and remove the meat. Dice the meat and return it to the soup.

5. Adjust the seasonings, add the parsley and return to a simmer.

6. Immediately before service, whisk the eggs and lemon juice together. Then slowly pour them into the soup, stirring to create strands of egg throughout the soup.

7. Serve in heated bowls with lemon wedges and harissa on the side.

Approximate values per serving:

Calories	873
Total fat	38 g
Saturated fat	9 g
Cholesterol	377 mg
Sodium	883 mg
Total carbohydrates	37 g
Protein	95 g

HARISSA

Yield: 6 Tbsp. (90 mL)

Dried chile peppers, crushed	1 Tbsp.	15 mL
Cayenne pepper	1 Tbsp.	15 mL
Cumin, ground	2 tsp.	10 mL

Continued

Caraway seeds	2 tsp.	10 mL
Garlic cloves	2	2
Olive oil	3 Tbsp.	45 mL
Salt	1 tsp.	5 mL

1. Grind the spices and garlic together in a mortar and pestle, blender or spice grinder.
2. Heat the oil. Stir in the spices and salt and cook over a low flame, stirring constantly, for 3 minutes.

◆◆◆

RECIPE 11.15

FRENCH ONION SOUP

Yield: 4 qt. (4 L)

Yellow onion, thinly sliced	10 lb.	4.4 kg
Clarified butter	8 oz.	250 mL
Beef stock	4 qt.	4 L
Chicken stock	4 qt.	4 L
Fresh thyme	1/2 oz.	14 g
Salt and pepper	TT	TT
Sherry	8 oz.	250 mL
Toasted French bread slices	as needed for garnish	
Gruyère cheese, grated	as needed for garnish	

1. Sauté the onions in the butter over low heat. Carefully caramelize them thoroughly without burning.
2. Deglaze the pan with 8 ounces (250 g) of the beef stock. Cook *au sec.* Repeat this process until the onions are a very dark, even brown.
3. Add the remaining beef stock, the chicken stock and thyme.
4. Bring to a simmer and cook 20 minutes to develop flavour. Adjust the seasonings and add the sherry.
5. Serve in warm bowls. Top each portion with a slice of toasted French bread and a thick layer of cheese. Place under the broiler or salamander until the cheese is melted and lightly browned.

VARIATION: Cook 2 ounces (50 g) flour with the cooked onions and moisten with stock. The soup will have rustic quality with more body.

◆◆◆

RECIPE 11.16

MINESTRONE

Minestrone is a rich vegetable soup of Italian heritage. Northern Italian versions are made with beef stock, butter, rice and ribbon-shaped pasta. Southern Italian versions, such as the one given here, contain tomatoes, garlic, olive oil and tubular-shaped pasta. The vegetables should be fresh and varied. Substitute or change those listed as necessary to reflect the season.

Yield: 2 gal. (8 L)

Dry white beans	1 lb.	450 g
Olive oil	2 Tbsp.	30 mL
Onion, diced	10 oz.	300 g
Garlic cloves, minced	2	2
Celery, diced	1 lb.	450 g
Carrot, diced	12 oz.	340 g
Zucchini, diced	1 lb.	450 g
Green beans, cut in 1/2-inch (1.25-cm) pieces	10 oz.	300 g
Cabbage, diced	1 lb.	450 g
Vegetable stock	5 qt.	5 L
Tomato, concassée	1 lb.	450 g
Tomato paste, low-sodium	12 oz.	340 g
Fresh oregano, chopped	1 Tbsp.	15 mL
Fresh basil, chopped	2 Tbsp.	30 mL
Fresh chervil, chopped	1 Tbsp.	15 mL
Fresh parsley, chopped	2 Tbsp.	30 mL
Salt and pepper	TT	TT
Elbow macaroni, cooked	4 oz.	120 g
Parmesan cheese, grated	as needed for garnish (optional)	

1. Soak the beans in cold water overnight, then drain.
2. Cover the beans with water and simmer until tender, about 40 minutes.
3. Sauté the onions in the oil. Add garlic, celery and carrots and cook for 3 minutes.
4. Add the remaining vegetables, one type at a time, cooking each briefly.
5. Add the stock, tomatoes and tomato paste. Cover and simmer for 2-1/2 to 3 hours.
6. Stir in the chopped herbs and season to taste with salt and pepper.
7. Add the drained beans and cooked macaroni.
8. Bring the soup to a simmer and simmer 15 minutes. Serve in warm bowls, garnished with Parmesan cheese.

Approximate values per 6 oz. (180 mL) serving:

Calories	70
Total fat	1.5 g
Saturated fat	0 g
Cholesterol	1 mg
Sodium	530 mg
Total carbohydrates	10 g
Protein	3 g
Vitamin A	20%
Vitamin C	20%

Claims—low fat

◆◆◆

RECIPE 11.17 (Aboriginal)

IROQUOIS FISH SOUP

CULINARY PROGRAMS, H.R.T. ALLIANCE, HUMBER COLLEGE, TORONTO, ON
Program Coordinator Anthony Bevan

Yield: 14 portions

Onion, finely diced	6 oz.	170 g
Ginger root, grated	1 Tbsp.	15 mL
Sunflower oil	3 Tbsp.	45 mL
Garlic clove, puréed	3	3
Mushrooms, fresh, sliced (chanterelle, oyster, shiitake and/or morel)	2 lb.	900 g
Fish stock	6 pt.	3.5 L

Continued

Lima beans (fresh or frozen)	12 oz.	350 g
Sweet corn kernels, dried	6 oz.	170 g
Wild bergamot, chopped (or fresh oregano)	2 Tbsp.	30 mL
Freshwater fish fillets (trout, pickerel, perch, white fish and/or bass), cut into 1-inch (2.25-cm) squares	5 lb.	2.25 kg
Fresh dillweed, for garnish		

1. Sweat the onion and ginger in the sunflower oil.
2. Add the garlic and mushrooms.
3. Add the fish stock, lima beans and corn kernels, bring to a boil and simmer for 40 minutes.
4. Add the chopped bergamot or oregano and simmer for 5 minutes.
5. Add fish and simmer for 5 minutes.
6. Serve garnished with a feather of dillweed.

NOTE: Traditionally, the aboriginal people would use wild ginger root instead of oriental ginger; wild leek instead of onions; and wild garlic in place of garlic cloves. Water would have been the liquid used but a good fish stock lays down an excellent foundational flavour. Salt was not a part of the North American diet until the Europeans arrived; the most common seasoning used was maple sugar.

Dried Sweet Corn Kernels: Among the Iroquois, corn is held in high esteem. As one of "The Three Sisters" (corn, beans and squash), it is considered important for spiritual and physical well-being. To preserve the sweet corn, the aboriginal people dried the kernels. In the modern kitchen the same results may be achieved by removing the sweet corn kernels from the cob. Spread the kernels on a baking sheet and place in an oven at 180°F (82°C). Stir the kernels from time to time. Leave them in the oven until the corn is very hard but not burned. This may take in excess of 3 hours. Store the dried kernels in an air-tight container, where they can be stored indefinitely.

Approximate values per serving:

Calories	422
Total fat	17 g
Saturated fat	3 g
Cholesterol	119 mg
Sodium	123 mg
Total carbohydrates	20 g
Protein	46 g

David MacGillivray

From the time he was 15 years old, working in a restaurant in Picton, Ontario, David knew he wanted to be a chef. He quickly became renowned in Canada, particularly for his work in the Edith Cavell Dining Room at Jasper Park Lodge, where his creative menus and excellent service have won the restaurant several prestigious awards.

◆◆◆

RECIPE 11.18

CHOWDER OF WILD ALBERTA MUSHROOMS WITH WILD RICE, BEANS AND FIREWEED HONEY

JASPER PARK LODGE, JASPER, AB
Executive Chef David MacGillivary

Yield: 10 Servings

Butter	4 oz.	100 g
Garlic cloves, chopped	2	2
Shallots, medium, small dice	4	4
Instant flour	4 oz.	100 g
Chicken stock	70 oz.	2 L
Dried porcini mushroom powder	1 oz.	30 g
Canola oil	5 oz.	125 mL
Oyster mushrooms, sliced	4 oz.	100 g
Shiitake mushrooms, sliced	4 oz.	100 g
Chanterelle mushrooms, sliced	4 oz.	100 g

Dried morel mushrooms, soaked in water and sliced when soft	3 oz.	75 g
White wine	8 oz.	250 mL
Wild rice, cooked	3 oz. (uncooked weight)	75 g (uncooked weight)
Black beans, cooked	3 oz. (uncooked weight)	75 g (uncooked weight)
White beans, cooked	3 oz. (uncooked weight)	75 g (uncooked weight)
Potato, peeled, diced and cooked	6 oz.	150 g
Fireweed honey	2 oz.	50 mL
Fresh rosemary, chopped	4 Tbsp.	60 mL
Heavy cream	20 oz.	500 mL
Salt and cracked pepper	TT	TT

1. Melt the butter in a heavy-bottomed soup pot, over medium heat.
2. Add the garlic and shallots and cook until translucent, approximately 3 to 5 minutes.
3. Add the flour and incorporate it thoroughly to make a roux. Stir the roux constantly to avoid burning. The roux should cook for 3 to 5 minutes over medium heat.
4. In a separate pot, bring the chicken stock to a boil. Once the roux is cooked, add the stock to the roux. Whisk continuously to prevent any flour clots from developing.
5. Reduce the heat to medium-low, add the dried mushroom powder to the soup and let the soup simmer.
6. In a large frying pan over high heat, heat the canola oil and sauté the oyster mushrooms, shiitake mushrooms and chanterelles, stirring frequently.
7. Drain the excess oil from the pan and add the morels. Add white wine to deglaze the pan. Cook for 2 to 3 minutes over medium-high heat.
8. Add the mushrooms and wine mixture to the soup base. Let the soup simmer for 45 minutes, then add the rice, beans and potatoes.
9. Add the honey, rosemary and cream. Continue to cook for 15 minutes. Season with salt and pepper.
10. Serve in a large soup tureen or in individual bowls.

Approximate values per serving:

Calories	579
Total fat	42 g
Saturated fat	18 g
Cholesterol	95 mg
Sodium	124 mg
Total carbohydrates	43 g
Protein	13 g

◆◆◆

RECIPE 11.19

CHEDDAR AND LEEK SOUP

Yield: 2 qt. (2 L)

Whole butter	1 oz.	30 g
Mirepoix, chopped fine	8 oz.	250 g
Leek, chopped fine	8 oz.	250 g
Flour	2 oz.	60 g
Chicken stock	1-1/2 qt.	1.5 L
Sachet:		
Bay leaf	1	1
Dried thyme	1/4 tsp.	1 mL
Peppercorns, crushed	1/4 tsp.	1 mL
Dry white wine or flat beer	4 oz.	120 mL

Continued

Half-and-half	4 oz.	120 mL
Cheddar cheese, grated	1 lb.	500 g
Salt	TT	TT
Cayenne pepper	TT	TT
Fresh parsley, chopped	as needed for garnish	
Croutons	as needed for garnish	

Approximate values per 6 oz. (180 mL) serving:

Calories	250
Total fat	18 g
Saturated fat	11 g
Cholesterol	55 mg
Sodium	730 mg
Total carbohydrates	8 g
Protein	14 g
Vitamin A	15%
Calcium	35%

1. Sweat mirepoix and leeks in the butter until tender.
2. Stir in the flour and cook to make a blond roux.
3. Add stock and sachet and bring to a boil. Add wine (or beer), half-and-half and cheese. Simmer for 1 hour.
4. Strain; adjust seasonings with salt and cayenne pepper. Thin with additional warm half-and-half, if necessary.
5. Serve in warm bowls, garnished with parsley and croutons.

◆◆◆

RECIPE 11.20

SOUTHWESTERN BLACK BEAN SOUP

Yield: 4 qt. (4 L)

Dried black beans, soaked	1 lb.	500 g
Vegetable stock or water	5 qt.	5 L
Sachet:		
Bay leaves	2	2
Dried thyme	1/2 tsp.	2 mL
Peppercorns, cracked	10	10
Canola oil	1 Tbsp.	15 mL
Onion, diced	4 oz.	120 g
Garlic cloves, minced	2	2
Anaheim chiles, diced	1 oz.	30 g
Jalapeño or Serrano chiles, minced	1 Tbsp.	15 mL
Cumin, ground	1 tsp.	5 mL
Coriander, ground	1 tsp.	5 mL
Dried oregano	1 tsp.	5 mL
Salt and black pepper	TT	TT
Lime wedges	as needed for garnish	
Cilantro	as needed for garnish	

Approximate values per 6 oz. (180 mL) serving:

Calories	70
Total fat	2 g
Saturated fat	0 g
Cholesterol	0 mg
Sodium	1010 mg
Total carbohydrates	9 g
Protein	4 g
Claims—low fat; no saturated fat; no cholesterol	

1. Combine the beans and stock or water and bring to a simmer. Add the sachet.
2. Sauté the onions, garlic and chiles in the oil. Add to the saucepot.
3. Stir in the cumin, coriander and oregano.
4. Simmer the soup, uncovered, approximately 2–3 hours. The beans should be very soft, just beginning to fall apart. Add additional water or stock if necessary.
5. Purée about half of the soup, then stir it back into the remaining soup. Season to taste with salt and black pepper.
6. Serve in warmed bowls garnished with lime wedges and chopped cilantro.

◆◆◆

RECIPE 11.21

ROASTED CORN CHOWDER

Yield: 1 qt. (1 L)

Corn, unshucked	10 ears	10 ears
Milk, warmed	3 pt.	1500 mL
Salt pork, small dice	4 oz.	120 g
Celery, small dice	5 oz.	150 g
Onion, small dice	10 oz.	300 g
Garlic cloves, minced	4	4
Flour	2 oz.	60 g
Cream, warmed	4 oz.	120 mL
Worcestershire sauce	1 Tbsp.	15 mL
Fresh thyme	1 tsp.	5 mL
Nutmeg, ground	TT	TT
Salt and white pepper	TT	TT
Parsley, chopped fine	as needed for garnish	

1. Roast the ears of corn, in their husks, in a 400°F (200°C) oven for 45 minutes. Cool, shuck the corn and cut off the kernels. Purée half the corn kernels in a blender, adding a small amount of milk if necessary.
2. Render the salt pork. Add the celery, onions and garlic and sauté lightly.
3. Stir in the flour and cook to make a blond roux.
4. Add the remaining warm milk and bring to a simmer.
5. Add the puréed corn and the remaining corn kernels. Simmer 10 minutes.
6. Add the warm cream; adjust the seasonings with Worcestershire sauce, thyme, nutmeg, salt and white pepper.
7. Serve in warm bowls garnished with chopped parsley.

Approximate values per 6.5 oz. (200 mL) serving:	
Calories	620
Total fat	31 g
Saturated fat	16 g
Cholesterol	90 mg
Sodium	590 mg
Total carbohydrates	60 g
Protein	24 g
Vitamin A	20%
Vitamin C	35%
Calcium	45%

◆◆◆

RECIPE 11.22

CHICKEN AND SAUSAGE GUMBO

Gumbo, a thick, spicy stew, is traditional fare in the delta region of the American South. Gumbo is usually made with poultry, fish, shellfish or sausage and is thickened with dark roux. Okra or filé powder (ground sassafras leaves) may also be added for thickening. Filé powder is sometimes added at the time of service for additional flavour. Gumbo is traditionally served over white rice.

Yield: 3 qt. (3 L)

Chicken pieces	3–4 lb.	1.3–1.8 kg
Flour	as needed	as needed
Onion powder	as needed	as needed
Salt	as needed	as needed
Cayenne pepper	as needed	as needed
Vegetable oil	8 oz.	250 mL

Continued

Flour	4 oz.	120 g
Onion, medium dice	6 oz.	170 g
Celery, medium dice	3 oz.	90 g
Green bell pepper, medium dice	6 oz.	170 g
Garlic, minced	1 tsp.	5 mL
Okra, sliced and blanched	5 oz.	140 g
Chicken stock, hot	2 qt.	2 L
Jalapeño pepper, minced	1 tsp.	5 mL
Dried thyme	1/2 tsp.	2 mL
Dried oregano	1 tsp.	5 mL
Tomato paste	4 oz.	120 mL
Andouille sausage	8 oz.	250 g
Filé powder, optional	as needed	as needed
White rice, boiled	as needed	as needed

1. Dredge the chicken in flour seasoned with onion powder, salt and cayenne pepper.
2. Pan-fry in the oil until done; drain.
3. Degrease the pan, reserving 4 ounces (120 mL) of the oil.
4. Add the flour to the pan and cook to make a very dark brown roux.
5. Add the onions, celery, green pepper and garlic and sauté briefly. Add the okra.
6. Add the chicken stock. Stir in the jalapeños, thyme, oregano and tomato paste. Simmer uncovered for 30 minutes.
7. Bone the cooked chicken and cut the meat into 1/2-inch (1.2 cm) pieces.
8. Slice the sausage on a diagonal into thin pieces and sauté. Remove and drain.
9. Add the chicken and sausage pieces to the gumbo. Adjust seasoning and simmer 30 minutes.
10. If filé powder is used, stir 1–2 teaspoons (5–10 mL) into each portion at service time.
11. Serve ladled over bowls of white rice.

Approximate values per 6 oz. (180 mL) serving:

Calories	380
Total fat	25 g
Saturated fat	5 g
Cholesterol	80 mg
Sodium	640 mg
Total carbohydrates	9 g
Protein	30 g
Vitamin C	20%

♦♦♦

RECIPE 11.23

FRESH PEACH AND YOGURT SOUP

Yield: 2 qt. (2 L)

Fresh peaches	4 lb.	1.8 kg
Dry white wine	24 oz.	700 mL
Honey	4 oz.	120 mL
Lemon juice	2 oz.	60 mL
Cinnamon, ground	1/4 tsp.	1 mL
Plain yogurt	8 oz.	250 mL
Heavy cream	TT	TT
Pistachios, finely chopped	as needed for garnish	

1. Pit and coarsely chop the peaches without peeling. Place in a nonreactive saucepan. Add wine, honey and lemon juice. Cover and simmer for 30 minutes.

Approximate values per 6 oz. (180 mL) serving:

Calories	140
Total fat	0 g
Saturated fat	0 g
Cholesterol	0 mg
Sodium	20 mg
Total carbohydrates	32 g
Protein	3 g
Vitamin A	10%
Vitamin C	25%

Claims—fat free; very low sodium; good source of fibre

2. Purée the peach mixture in a blender. Strain and chill.

3. Stir in cinnamon, yogurt and heavy cream.

4. Chill thoroughly. Serve in chilled bowls, garnished with finely chopped pistachio nuts.

 # WEBLINKS

Food Institute of Canada: Soup Recipes
   foodnet.fic.ca/recipes/soups.html

Searchable Archive of Recipes: Soup Recipes
   SOAR.Berkeley.EDU/recipes/soups/

Campbell's Soup Company
   campbellsoup.com/

Soup of the Evening
   www.geocities.com/NapaValley/6188/

CHAPTER 12

PRINCIPLES OF MEAT COOKERY

LEARNING OUTCOMES

After studying this chapter you will be able to:

◆ identify the structure and composition of meats

◆ explain meat inspection and grading practices

◆ purchase meats appropriate for your needs

◆ store meats properly

◆ prepare meats for cooking

◆ apply various cooking methods to meats: broiling or grilling, roasting, sautéeing, pan-frying, simmering, braising, stewing

◆ carve a beef hip or leg of lamb

*M*eats—beef, veal, lamb and pork—often consume the largest portion of your food purchasing dollar. In this chapter we discuss how to protect your investment. You will learn how to determine the quality of meat, how to purchase meat in the form that best suits your needs and how to store it. We also discuss several of the dry-heat, moist-heat and combination cooking methods introduced in Chapter 9, Principles of Cooking, and how they can best be used so that a finished meat item is appealing to both the eye and palate. Although each of the cooking methods is illustrated with a single beef, veal, lamb or pork recipe, the analysis is intended to apply to all meats.*

In Chapters 13 through 16 you will learn about the specific cuts of beef, veal, lamb and pork typically used in food service operations, as well as some basic butchering procedures. Recipes using these cuts and applying the various cooking methods are included at the end of each of those chapters.

MUSCLE COMPOSITION

The carcasses of cattle, sheep, hogs and furred game animals consist mainly of edible lean muscular tissue, fat, connective tissue and bones. They are divided into large cuts called **primals**. Primal cuts are rarely cooked; rather, they are usually broken down to **subprimal cuts** which, in turn, can be cooked as is or used to produce **fabricated cuts**. For example, the beef primal known as a short loin can be divided into subprimals including the strip loin. The strip loin can be fabricated into other cuts including strip loin steaks. The primals, subprimals and fabricated cuts of beef, veal, lamb and pork are discussed in Chapters 13 through 16, respectively; game is discussed in Chapter 18.

Primal cuts—*the primary divisions of muscle, bone and connective tissue produced by the initial butchering of the carcass.*

Subprimal cuts—*the basic cuts produced from each primal. Secondary is used interchangeably.*

Fabricated cuts—*individual portions cut from a subprimal.*

Muscle tissue gives meat its characteristic appearance; the amount of connective tissue determines the meat's tenderness. Muscle tissue is approximately 72% water, 20% protein, 7% fat and 1% minerals. A single muscle is composed of many bundles of muscle cells or fibres held together by connective tissue. (See Figures 12.1 and 12.2.) The thickness of the cells, the size of the cell bundles and the connective tissues holding them together form the grain of the meat and determine the meat's texture. When the fibre bundles are small, the meat has a fine grain and texture. Grain also refers to the direction in which the muscle fibres travel. When an animal fattens, some of the water and proteins in the lean muscle tissue are replaced with fat, which appears as **marbling**.

Marbling—*whitish streaks of inter- and intra-muscular fat.*

Subcutaneous fat—*the fat layer between the hide and muscles, also known as **exterior fat**.*

Elastin—*a protein found in connective tissues, particularly ligaments and tendons; it often appears as the white or silver covering on meats known as **silverskin**.*

Connective tissue forms the walls of the long muscle cells and binds them into bundles. It surrounds the muscle as a membrane and also appears as the tendons and ligaments that attach the muscles to the bone. Most connective tissue is composed of either collagen or **elastin**. Collagen breaks down into gelatin and water when cooked using moist heat. Elastin, on the other hand, will not break down under normal cooking conditions. Because elastin remains stringy and tough, tendons and ligaments should be trimmed away before meat is cooked.

FIGURE 12.1 *Muscle Tissue*

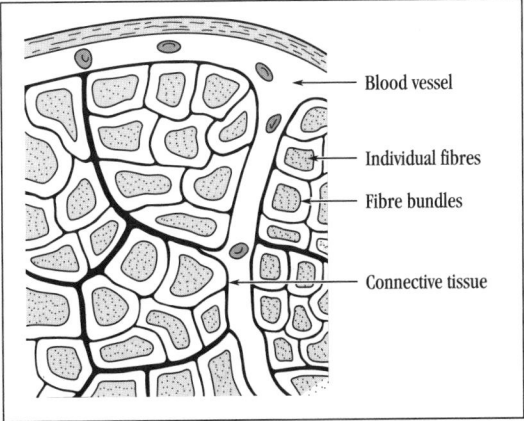

FIGURE 12.2 *Crosscut of a Bundle of Muscle Fibres*

Connective tissue develops primarily in the frequently used muscles. Therefore, cuts of meat from the shoulder (also known as the chuck), which the animal uses constantly, tend to be tougher than those from the back (also known as the loin), which are used less frequently. As an animal ages, the collagen present within the muscles becomes more resistant to breaking down through moist-heat cooking. Therefore, the meat of an older animal tends to be tougher than that of a younger one. Generally, the tougher the meat, the more flavourful it is.

Butcher—*to slaughter and dress or fabricate animals for consumption.*

Dress—*to trim or otherwise prepare an animal carcass for consumption.*

Fabricate—*to cut a larger portion of raw meat (for example, a primal or subprimal), poultry or fish into smaller portions.*

Carve—*to cut cooked meat or poultry into portions.*

NUTRITION

Although nutritional content of beef, veal, pork and lamb differs, generally, all are high in protein, saturated fats and cholesterol. See Table 12.1. Consumed in moderate quantities, however, meat can be part of a healthful diet.

TABLE 12.1   NUTRITIONAL VALUES OF MEATS

For 1 ounce (28 grams) Uncooked Lean Meat	Kcal	Protein (g)	Total Fat (g)	Saturated Fat (g)	Cholesterol (mg)	Sodium (mg)
Beef—brisket	94	4.6	8.2	3.4	22	18
Beef—T-bone steak	77	5.0	6.2	2.5	19	14
Beef—ground lean	75	5.0	5.9	2.4	21	20
Veal—chop	46	5.4	2.6	1.1	23	25
Veal—ground leg and shoulder	41	5.5	1.9	0.8	23	23
Lamb—leg	36	5.8	1.3	0.5	18	18
Lamb—chop	106	4.1	9.8	4.3	22	16
Pork—spareribs	81	4.9	6.7	2.7	22	21
Pork—shoulder (picnic)	40	5.6	1.8	0.6	18	23

The Corinne T. Netzer Encyclopedia of Food Values, 1992.

FIGURE 12.3   *Canada Health Inspection Stamp*

INSPECTION AND GRADING OF MEATS

Inspection

All meat produced for public consumption in Canada is subject to health inspection. Inspections ensure that products are processed under strict sanitary guidelines and are wholesome and fit for human consumption. Inspections do not indicate a meat's quality or tenderness, however. Whole carcasses of beef, pork, lamb and veal are labelled with a round stamp identifying the slaughterhouse. See Figure 12.3. The stamp shown in Figure 12.3 is also used for fabricated or processed meats and is found either on the product or its packaging. Imported products must also be inspected. The revised Canada Food Inspection System (CFIS) was implemented in 1998.

Grading

Canadian grading provides a voluntary, uniform system by which producers, distributors and consumers can measure differences in the quality of meats and make price/quality comparisons. There are two parts to this grading system: quality grades and yield assessments. (See Figures 12.4 and 12.5.)

Quality grades, provided and paid for by the industry as of 1996, are a guide to the eating qualities of meat: its tenderness, juiciness and flavour.

Grading takes into account three quality factors:

1. The appearance and colour of the lean and fat.
2. The texture of the lean and fat.
3. The firmness of the muscle and fat.

For beef, the intramuscular fat or marbling is taken into account also. It is assessed on the rib eye at the quarter break.

A Computer Vision System (CVS) is being tested that uses cameras to assist in grading. The rib-eye camera takes a digitized picture of the rib eye. The computer software analyzes the marbling and assigns a grade with a high degree of accuracy. The second camera takes a picture of the whole carcass and combines the information with the rib-eye scan. A yield score is calculated that provides an estimate of saleable yield. Testing has shown the computer-generated yield score to be twice as accurate as the yield ruler currently used.

In addition, a Connective Tissue (CT) probe is being developed in Canada that uses ultra-violet light to measure meat tenderness. Tests show that this probe is an extremely accurate way to determine tenderness and the device is being further refined.

Carcass pasteurization is performed in large processing plants. The process involves three steps: removing water left on the carcass surface by the final wash, exposing the carcass to a hot-water or steam blanket, and quickly chilling the carcass surface with a cold-water shower. A special chamber is used for the process.

Beef: Canada has a well-defined beef grading system with A or higher being the best. The main grades are Canada Prime, AAA, AA, A, B1, B2, B3, B4, D and E grades. Approximately 70–75% of Canadian beef production is A grade or higher, and Canada Prime represents 1–2% of production. Systems are being developed to reward producers of higher grade meat.

Veal: There are currently ten grades of veal in Canada with A1, A2, A3 and A4 being the highest. Criteria include muscle conformation, flesh colour and fat deposits. Grading is carried out for the producer but consumers

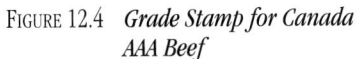

FIGURE 12.4   *Grade Stamp for Canada AAA Beef*

FIGURE 12.5   *Yield Stamp*

generally purchase based on colour. Quebec is developing a grading system for veal that includes grain-fed animals. The differences between veal and calf can be described as follows:

Characteristics	Veal	Calf
Age	10–12 weeks	3–10 months
Feed	Milk or milk replacements	Solid feed
Carcass weight	80–250 pounds (36–112 kg)	120–325 pounds (54–145 kg)
Lean colour	Pale pink	Brown
Lean texture	Fine	Coarser
Outer fat	Very little	More than veal

Pork: Pork grading is mainly done for the hog producer and for export. Domestic consumption does not show a grade stamp. The producer is paid according to the fat-to-lean ratio and most pork is trimmed at the plant. Of the 12 grades, Canada Yield Class is the most desirable. The carcass weighs 40 kg or more and the yield percentage, by probe, of lean to fat on the loin meat must be between 54.7% and 64.3% or higher.

Sheep: Most sheep are marketed as spring lamb or genuine spring lamb. Older sheep are generally processed into value added products. Spring lamb is 5–12 months old and weighs 30–65 pounds (13.5 kg–29.5 kg). The fat will be white and the flesh dark pink. The following characteristics are assessed

---

◆◆◆
YIELDS AND GRADES

Yield assessments measure the amount of useable meat (as opposed to fat and bones) on a carcass and provide a uniform method of identifying differences among carcasses. Yield assessments are critical to producers and purveyors alike. Producers of hogs are paid more for higher yield carcasses. Purveyors and retailers want high-yield carcasses in order to reduce trim costs and increase profitability. Beef and pork are the carcasses with well-defined yield assessment criteria.

Grading of meats is a voluntary program paid for by the processing industry. Ungraded meat products can be purchased; however, consumers are willing to pay a premium for the assurance of graded, top-quality products. The development of private labelling systems by industry is growing, but these private systems do not necessarily conform to Agriculture Canada's regulations and can be a source of confusion to the consumer. Ask clear, directed and concise questions of your purveyor to ensure you are getting the product you require.

◆◆◆
A HISTORY OF MEAT REGULATIONS

1929: First beef grading policy inaugurated. Jointly proposed by producer, trade and governments, it was based on the belief that beef of good eating quality should be identified by branding and grading.

1941: All beef sold to the Department of National Defence had to be grade stamped. One year later, all beef to be branded had to be graded and stamped by official graders.

1947: National beef grading regulations were passed into law.

1958: Beef and veal grading regulations were revised under the Canada Agricultural Products Standards Act. Grade discriptions reflected consumer demand for leaner beef.

1972: New beef grading system adopted. Based in part on partial ribbing and measurement of fat thickness only with some visual appraisal of rib eye muscle size and quality.

1984: Ribbing site relocated to between the twelfth and thirteenth ribs. Minimum carcass weight reintroduced. Metric measures introduced.

1988: Canada Agricultural Products Act pro-claimed. Regulated marketing of agricultural products in import, export, interprovincial trade and provincial national standards and grades.

1992: Grade names changed and marbling criteria used to be in harmony with USDA. Yield grades and stamps refined.

1995: Beef and poultry regulations amalgamated.

Late 90s: Grading privatized, Canadian Food Inspection Agency created, Canada Prime grade added to beef system.

Vacuum packaging—*a food preservation method in which fresh or cooked food is placed in an air-tight container (usually plastic). Virtually all air is removed from the container through a vacuum process, and the container is then sealed.*

and scored on a matrix grading: the appearance of the break joint; the yield; the fat level; the muscling; the colour of the pectoral muscle, and the colour of the fat. For example, muscling is rated on a scale of 1 to 5 with M5 being the highest. Grading is done primarily for the producer as most lamb is sold ungraded.

AGING MEATS

When animals are slaughtered their muscles are soft and flabby. Within 6 to 24 hours rigor mortis sets in, causing the muscles to contract and stiffen. Rigor mortis dissipates within 48 to 72 hours under refrigerated conditions. All meats should be allowed to rest, or age, long enough for rigor mortis to dissipate completely. Meats that have not been aged long enough for rigor mortis to dissipate, or that have been frozen during this period, are known as "green meats." They will be very tough and flavourless when cooked.

Typically, initial aging takes place while the meat is being transported from the slaughterhouse to the supplier or food service operation. Beef and lamb are sometimes aged for longer periods to increase their tenderness and flavour characteristics. Pork is not aged further because its high fat content turns rancid easily, and veal does not have enough fat to protect it during an extended aging period.

Wet Aging

Today, most pre-portioned or precut meats are packaged and shipped in vacuum-sealed plastic packages (sometimes known generically by the manufacturer's trade name, Cryovac®). Wet aging is the process of storing vacuum-packaged meats under refrigeration for up to six weeks. This allows natural enzymes and microorganisms time to break down connective tissue, which tenderizes and flavours the meat. As this chemical process takes place, the meat develops an unpleasant odour that is released when the package is opened and dissipates in a few minutes. Bag aging generally results in a yield loss of only 1–2%, significantly lower than dry (air) aging.

Dry Aging

Dry aging is the process of hanging fresh meats in an environment of controlled temperature, humidity and air flow for up to six weeks. This allows enzymes and microorganisms to break down connective tissues. Dry aging is actually the beginning of the natural decomposition process. Dry aged meats can lose from 5% to 20% of their weight through moisture evaporation. They can also develop mold, which adds flavour but must be trimmed off later. Moisture loss combined with additional trimming can substantially increase the cost of dry aged meats. Dry aged meats are generally available only through smaller distributors and specialty butchers.

Irradiation

This process is not currently approved for use in Canada. Other countries are irradiating meats and produce to increase shelf life and reduce the effects of some bacteria by affecting the available water.

PURCHASING AND STORING MEATS

Several factors determine the cuts of meat your food service operation should use:

1. Menu—The menu identifies the types of cooking methods used. If meats are to be broiled, grilled, roasted, sautéed or fried, more tender cuts should be used. If they are to be stewed or braised, flavourful cuts with more connective tissue can be used.

2. Menu price—Cost constraints may prevent an operation from using the best quality meats available. Generally, the more tender the meat, the more expensive it is. But the most expensive cuts are not always the best choice for a particular cooking method. For example, a beef tenderloin is one of the most expensive cuts of beef. Although excellent grilled, it will not necessarily produce a better braised dish than the fattier brisket.

3. Quality—Often, several cuts of meat can be used for a specific dish, so each food service operation should develop its own quality specifications.

Purchasing Meats

Once you have identified the cuts of meat your operation needs, you must determine the forms in which they will be bought. Meats are purchased in a variety of forms: as large as an entire carcass that must be further fabricated or as small as an individual cut (known as portion control or P.C.) ready to cook and serve. You should consider the following when deciding how to purchase meats:

1. *Employee skills*—Do your employees have the skills necessary to reduce large pieces of meat to the desired cuts?

2. *Menu*—Can you use the variety of bones, meat and trimmings that result from fabricating large cuts into individual portions?

3. *Storage*—Do you have ample refrigeration and freezer space so that you can be flexible in the way you purchase your meats?

4. *Cost*—Considering labour costs and trim usage, is it more economical to buy larger cuts of meat or P.C. units?

IMPS/NAMP/CMC

The United States Department of Agriculture (USDA) publishes Institutional Meat Purchasing Specifications (IMPS) describing products customarily purchased in the food service industry. IMPS identifications are illustrated and described in *The Meat Buyers Guide*, published by the National Association of Meat Purveyors (NAMP). The Canadian Meat Council (CMC) also publishes full-colour manuals that name and number cuts of meat. The IMPS/NAMP/CMC system is a widely accepted and useful tool in preventing miscommunications between purchasers and purveyors. Meats are indexed by a numerical system: Beef cuts are designated by the 100 series, lamb by the 200 series, veal by the 300 series, pork by the 400 series, and portion cuts by the 1000 series. Commonly used cuts of beef, veal, lamb and pork and their IMPS numbers, as well as applicable cooking methods and serving suggestions, are discussed in Chapters 13 through 16. However, there are numbering differences in some cases and it is important to communicate clearly with your supplier to ensure the correct product is ordered and received.

Storing Meats

Meat products are highly perishable, so temperature control is the most important thing to remember when storing meats. Fresh meats should be stored at temperatures of 30°F–35°F (minus 1°C to +2°C). Vacuum-packed meats should be left in their packaging until they are needed. Under proper refrigeration, vacuum-packed meats with unbroken seals have a shelf life of three to four weeks. If the seal is broken, shelf life is reduced to only a few days. Meats that are not vacuum packed should be loosely wrapped or wrapped in air-permeable paper. Do not wrap meats tightly in plastic wrap, as this creates a good breeding ground for bacteria and will significantly shorten a meat's shelf life. Store meats on trays and away from other foods to prevent cross-contamination.

Meats freeze at about 28°F (minus 2°C). When freezing meats, the faster the better. Slow freezing produces large ice crystals that tend to rupture the muscle tissues, allowing water and nutrients to drip out when the meat is thawed. Most commercially packaged meats are frozen by blast freezing, which quickly cools by blasting minus 40°F (minus 40°C) air across the meat. Most food service facilities, however, use a slower and more conventional method known as still-air freezing. Still-air freezing is the common practice of placing meat in a standard freezer at about 0°F (minus 18°C) until it is frozen.

The ideal temperature for maintaining frozen meat is minus 50°F (minus 45°C). Frozen meat should not be maintained at any temperature warmer than 0°F (minus 18°C). Moisture- and vapourproof packaging will help prevent **freezer burn**. The length of frozen storage life varies with the species and type of meat. As a general rule, properly handled meats can be frozen for up to six months. Frozen meats should be thawed at refrigerator temperatures, not at room temperature or in warm water.

Freezer burn—*the surface dehydration and discolouration of food that results from moisture loss at below-freezing temperatures.*

PREPARING MEATS

Certain procedures are often applied to meats before cooking to add flavour and/or moisture, or to enhance tenderness. These include marinating, barding and larding.

Marinating — Wet and Dry

Wet marinating is the process of soaking meat in a seasoned liquid to flavour and tenderize it. Marinades can be simple blends (herbs, seasonings and oil) or a complicated cooked recipe (red wine, fruit and other ingredients). Mild marinades should be used on more delicate meats, such as veal. Game and beef require strongly flavoured marinades. In wine-based marinades, white wine is usually used for white meats and red wine for red meats. Not only does the wine add a distinctive flavour, the acids in it break down connective tissues and help tenderize the meat.

Veal and pork generally require less time to marinate than game, beef and lamb. Smaller pieces of meat take less time than larger pieces. When marinating, be sure to cover the meat completely and keep it refrigerated. Stir or turn the meat frequently to ensure that the marinade penetrates evenly.

Dry marinating generally involves rubbing herbs and spices into the surface of the meat, fish, poultry or game. Dry rubs may have sugar and salt in them as well, although both draw moisture out of the product. Depending on the time the rub is left on the meat and on the concentrations of salts, dry marinating could be considered curing. The product may be elevated on a rack and sometimes is pressed as it undergoes the marinating process.

Barding

Barding is the process of covering the surface of meat or poultry with thin slices of pork backfat or bacon and tying them in place with butcher's twine. Barded meat or poultry is usually roasted. As the item cooks, the backfat continuously bastes it, adding flavour and moisture. A drawback to barding is that the backfat prevents the meat or poultry from developing the crusty exterior associated with roasting.

Larding

Larding is the process of inserting small strips of pork fat into meat with a larding needle. Larded meat is usually cooked by braising. During cooking, the added fat contributes moisture and flavour. Although once popular, larding is rarely used today because advances in selective breeding produce consistently tender, well-marbled meat.

Barding a Pheasant

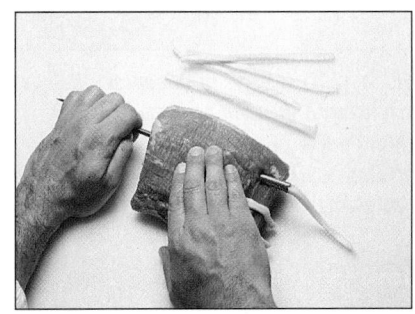

Larding Meat

APPLYING VARIOUS COOKING METHODS

In Chapter 9, Principles of Cooking, you learned the basic techniques for broiling, grilling, roasting, sautéing, pan-frying, poaching, simmering, braising and stewing. In Chapters 13 through 16 you will learn more about applying these cooking methods to beef, veal, lamb and pork. Here we apply these methods to meat cookery in general. Deep-fat frying is covered in Chapter 21, Deep-Fat Frying.

Dry-Heat Cooking Methods

Dry-heat cooking methods subject food directly to the heat of a flame (broiling and grilling), hot air (roasting) or heated fat (sautéing and pan-frying). These cooking methods firm proteins without breaking down connective tissue. They are not recommended for tougher cuts or those high in connective tissue.

Broiling and Grilling

To serve a good-quality broiled or grilled product you must start with good-quality meat. The broiling or grilling process adds flavour; additional flavours are derived from seasonings. The broiler or grill should brown and sear the meat, keeping the interior juicy. The grill should leave distinctive crosshatch marks on the meat's surface.

Selecting Meats to Broil or Grill

Only the most tender cuts should be broiled or grilled because direct heat does not tenderize. Fat adds flavour as the meat cooks, so the meat should be well marbled. Some external fat is also beneficial. Too much fat, however, will cause the broiler or grill to flare up, burning or discolouring the meat and adding objectionable flavours. Connective tissue toughens when meat is broiled or grilled. Trim away as much of it as possible.

Cooking Temperatures

Red meats should be cooked at sufficiently high temperatures to caramelize their surface, making them more attractive and flavourful. At the same time, the broiler or grill cannot be too hot or the meat's exterior will burn before the interior is cooked.

FIGURE 12.6   *Degrees of Doneness   Beef roasted rare, medium rare, medium and medium well.*

Because veal and pork are normally cooked to higher internal temperatures than beef and lamb, they should be cooked at slightly lower temperatures so their exteriors are not overcooked when their interiors are cooked properly. The exterior of white meats should be a deep golden colour when finished.

Seasoning Meats to Be Broiled or Grilled

Meats that have not been marinated should be well seasoned with salt and pepper just before being placed on the broiler or grill. If they are preseasoned and allowed to rest, the salt will dissolve and draw out moisture, making it difficult to brown the meat properly. Some chefs feel so strongly about this that they season broiled or grilled meats only after they are cooked. Pork and veal, which have a tendency to dry out when cooked, should be basted with seasoned butter or oil during cooking to help keep them moist. Meats can be glazed or basted with sauces or marinade liquids as they cook.

Degrees of Doneness

Consumers request and expect meats to be properly cooked to specific degrees of doneness. It is your responsibility to understand and comply with these requests. Meats can be cooked very rare (or bleu), rare, medium rare, medium, medium well or well done. Figure 12.6 shows the proper colour for these different degrees of doneness. This guide can be used for red meats cooked by any method.

Larger cuts of meat, such as a chateaubriand or thick chops, are often started on the broiler or grill to develop colour and flavour and then finished in the oven to ensure complete, even cooking.

Determining Doneness

Broiling or grilling meat to the proper degree of doneness is an art. Larger pieces of meat will take longer to cook than smaller ones, but how quickly a piece of meat cooks is determined by many other factors: the temperature of the broiler or grill, the temperature of the piece of meat when placed on the broiler or grill, the type of meat and the thickness of the cut. Because of these variables, timing alone is not a useful tool in determining doneness.

A thermometer is the most reliable method of determining doneness; however, its use is not very practical or accurate with cuts such as steaks. Cutting a steak to observe the colour is not acceptable to the customer. The most used method of determining doneness is by pressing the piece of meat with tongs and gauging the amount of resistance it yields. Very rare (bleu) meat will offer almost no resistance and will feel almost the same as raw meat. Meat cooked rare will feel spongy and offer slight resistance to pressure. Meat cooked medium will feel slightly firm and springy to the touch. Meat cooked well done will feel quite firm and will spring back quickly when pressed. See Table 12.2.

Accompaniments to Broiled and Grilled Meats

Because a broiler or grill cannot be deglazed to form the base for a sauce, compound butters or sauces

TABLE 12.2	DETERMINING DONENESS OF BEEF STEAK	
Degree of Doneness	Colour	Degree of Resistance
Very rare (bleu)	Very red and raw-looking centre (the centre is cool to the touch)	Almost no resistance
Rare	Large deep red centre	Spongy; very slight resistance
Medium rare	Bright red centre	Some resistance; slightly springy
Medium	Rosy pink to red centre	Slightly firm; springy
Medium well	Very little pink at the centre, almost brown throughout	Firm; springy
Well done	No red	Quite firm; springs back quickly when pressed

such as béarnaise are often served with broiled or grilled meats. Brown sauces such as bordelaise, chasseur, périgueux or brown mushroom sauce also complement many broiled or grilled items. Additional sauce suggestions are found in Table 10.5.

BASIC PROCEDURE FOR BROILING OR GRILLING MEATS

1. Heat the broiler or grill.
2. Use a wire brush to remove any charred or burnt particles that may be stuck to the broiler or grill grate. The grate can be wiped with a lightly oiled towel to remove any remaining particles and help season it.
3. Prepare the item to be broiled or grilled by trimming off excess fat and connective tissue and marinating or seasoning as desired. The meat may be brushed lightly with oil to help protect it and keep it from sticking to the grate.
4. Place the item in the broiler or on the grill. Following the example in Chapter 9, turn the meat to produce the attractive crosshatch marks associated with grilling. Use tongs to turn or flip the meat without piercing the surface in order to prevent valuable juices from escaping.
5. Cook the meat to the desired doneness while developing the proper surface colour. To do so, adjust the position of the meat on the broiler or grill or adjust the distance between the grate and heat source.

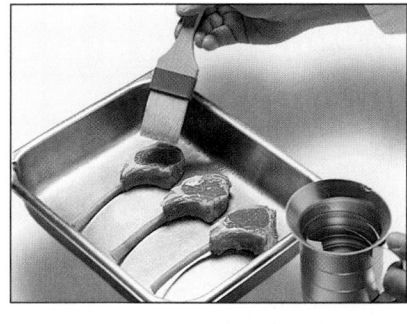

1. Brush the lamb chops with oil.

2. Place the lamb chops on the grill.

◆◆◆

RECIPE 12.1

GRILLED LAMB CHOPS WITH HERB BUTTER

Yield: 2 Servings

Lamb chops, loin or rib,		
approx. 1 in. (2.5 cm) thick	6	6
Salt and pepper	TT	TT
Oil	as needed	as needed
Herb butter	6 thin slices or	6 small rosettes

1. Preheat the grill for 15 minutes or until the grate is sufficiently heated.
2. Season the lamb chops with salt and pepper; brush with oil.
3. Place the lamb chops on the grill, turning as necessary to produce the proper crosshatching. Cook to the desired doneness.
4. Remove the lamb chops from the grill and place a slice or rosette of herb butter on each chop.
5. Serve immediately as the herb butter melts. The plate can be placed under the broiler for a few seconds to help melt the herb butter.

3. Rotate the lamb chops 90 degrees to create crosshatch marks.

4. Turn the chops over to finish them on the other side.

Roasting

Properly roasted meats should be tender, juicy and evenly cooked to the appropriate degree of doneness. They should have a pleasant appearance when whole as well as when sliced and plated.

Selecting Meats to Roast

Because roasting is a dry-heat cooking method and will not tenderize the finished product, meats that are to be roasted should be tender and well marbled. They are usually cut from the rib, loin or leg sections.

Approximate values per 6.5 oz. (195 g) serving:

Calories	623
Total fat	50 g
Saturated fat	27 g
Cholesterol	224 mg
Sodium	1186 mg
Total carbohydrates	0 g
Protein	42 g
Vitamin A	40%

TABLE 12.3

Degree of Doneness	Internal Temperature
Very rare (Bleu)	125–130°F 52–54°C
Rare	130–140°F 55–60°C
Medium	140–150°F 60–65°C
Well done	150–165°F 65–75°C

Seasoning Meats to Be Roasted

Seasonings are especially important with smaller roasts and roasts with little or no fat covering. With these roasts, some of the seasonings penetrate the meat while the remainder help create the highly seasoned crust associated with a good roast. A large roast with heavy fat covering (for example, a ponderosa hip or prime rib) does not benefit from being seasoned on the surface because the seasonings will not penetrate the fat layer, which is trimmed away before service.

When practical, a roast with excess fat should be trimmed, leaving just a thin fat layer so that the roast bastes itself while cooking. A lean roast can be barded or larded before cooking to add richness and moisture. Lamb legs are sometimes studded with garlic cloves by piercing the meat with a paring knife and then pressing slivers of raw garlic into the holes.

A roast is sometimes cooked on a bed of mirepoix, or mirepoix is added to the roasting pan as the roast cooks. The mirepoix raises the roast off the bottom of the roasting pan, preventing the bottom from overcooking. This mirepoix, however, does not add any flavour to the roast. Rather, it combines with the drippings to add flavour to the jus, sauce or gravy that is made with them.

Cooking Temperatures

Small roasts such as a rack of lamb or a beef tenderloin should be cooked at high temperatures, 375°F–450°F (190°C–230°C), so that they develop good colour during their short cooking times.

Traditionally, large roasts were started at high temperatures to sear the meat and seal in the juices; they were then finished at lower temperatures. Studies have shown, however, that roasts cooked at constant, low temperatures provide a better yield with less shrinkage than roasts that have been seared. Temperatures between 275°F and 325°F (120°C–160°C) are ideal for large roasts. These temperatures will produce a large, evenly cooked pink centre portion.

FIGURE 12.7 *The Proper Placement of an Instant-Read Thermometer*

Determining Doneness

The doneness of small roasts such as a rack of lamb is determined in much the same way as with broiled or grilled meats. With experience, the cook develops a sense of timing as well as a feel for gauging the amount of resistance by touching the meat. These techniques, however, are not infallible, especially with large roasts.

Although timing is useful as a general guide for determining doneness, there are too many variables for it to be relied upon exclusively. As a guideline, roasts will require 30 to 50 minutes per kilogram, depending on the desired doneness, type and size of roast, and beginning temperature of the cut.

The best way to determine the doneness of a large roast is to use an instant-read thermometer as shown in Figure 12.7. The thermometer is inserted into the centre or thickest part of the roast and away from any bones. The proper finished temperatures for roasted meats are listed in Table 12.3.

Carryover Cooking and Resting

Cooking does not stop the moment a roast is removed from the oven. Through conduction, the heat applied to the outside of the roast continues to penetrate, cooking the centre for several more minutes. Indeed, the internal temperature of a small roast can rise by as much as 5°F–10°F (3°C–6°C) after being removed from the oven. With a larger roast, such as a 50-pound (20-kg) beef hip, it can rise by as much as 20°F (11°C). Therefore, remove roasted meats before they reach the desired degree of doneness and allow carryover cooking to complete the cooking process. The temperatures listed in Table 12.3 are internal temperatures after allowing for carryover cooking.

As meat cooks, its juices flow towards the centre. If the roast is carved immediately after it is removed from the oven, its juices would run from the meat, causing it to lose its colour and become dry. Letting the meat rest before slicing allows the juices to redistribute themselves evenly throughout the roast, so the roast will retain more juices when carved. Small roasts, like a rack of lamb, need to rest only 5–10 minutes; larger roasts such as a hip of beef require as much as an hour.

Accompaniments to Roasted Meats

Roasts may be served with a sauce based on their natural juices (called *au jus*), as described in Recipe 12.2, Roast Prime Rib of Beef Au Jus, or with a pan gravy made with drippings from the roast. Additional sauce suggestions are found in Table 10.5.

BASIC PROCEDURE FOR ROASTING MEATS

1. Trim excess fat, tendons and silverskin from the meat. Leave only a thin fat covering, if possible, so the roast bastes itself as it cooks.

2. Season the roast as appropriate and place it in a roasting pan. The roast may be placed on a bed of mirepoix or on a rack.

3. Roast the meat, uncovered, at the desired temperature (the larger the roast, the lower the temperature), usually 275°F–425°F (135°C–220°C).

4. If a jus or pan gravy is desired and a mirepoix was not added at the start of cooking, it may be added 30–45 minutes before the roast is done, thus allowing it to caramelize while the roast finishes cooking.

5. Cook to the desired temperature.

6. Remove the roast from the oven, allowing carryover cooking to raise the internal temperature to the desired degree of doneness. Allow the roast to rest before slicing or carving it. As the roast rests, prepare the jus, sauce or pan gravy.

◆◆◆

RECIPE 12.2

ROAST PRIME RIB OF BEEF AU JUS

Yield: 18 8-oz. (250-g) boneless servings

Oven-ready rib roast		
IMPS #109, approx. 16 lbs. (7.5 kg)	1	1
Salt and pepper	TT	TT
Garlic, chopped	TT	TT
Mirepoix	1 lb.	500 g
Brown stock	2 qt.	2 L

Approximate values per 9 oz. (270 g) serving:

Calories	951
Total fat	79 g
Saturated fat	32 g
Cholesterol	214 mg
Sodium	278 mg
Total carbohydrates	1 g
Protein	56 g
Iron	40%

1. Pull back the netting, fold back the fat cap and season the roast well with the salt, pepper and chopped garlic. Replace the fat cap and netting; place the roast in an appropriate-sized roasting pan. Roast at 300°F–325°F (160°C–165°C).

2. Add the mirepoix to the pan approximately 45 minutes before the roast is finished cooking. Continue cooking until the internal temperature reaches

Continued

125°F (52°C), approximately 3–4 hours. Carryover cooking will raise the internal temperature of the roast to approximately 140°F (60°C).

3. Remove the roast from the pan and allow it to rest in a warm place for 30 minutes.

4. Drain the excess fat from the roasting pan, reserving the mirepoix and any drippings in the roasting pan.

5. Caramelize the mirepoix on the stove top; allow the liquids to evaporate, leaving only brown drippings in the pan.

6. Deglaze the pan with brown stock. Stir to loosen all the drippings.

7. Simmer the jus, reducing it slightly and allowing the mirepoix to release its flavour; season with salt and pepper if necessary.

8. Strain the jus through a china cap lined with cheesecloth. Skim any remaining fat from the surface with a ladle.

9. Remove the netting from the roast. Trim and slice the roast as described opposite and serve with approximately 1 to 2 ounces (30 to 60 mL) jus per person.

1. Drain off the excess fat.

2. Caramelize the mirepoix.

3. Deglaze the pan with brown stock.

4. Simmer the jus, reducing it slightly and allowing the mirepoix to release its flavours.

5. Strain the jus through a china cap and cheesecloth.

Carving Roasts

All the efforts that went into selecting and cooking a perfect roast will be wasted if the roast is not carved properly. Roasts are always carved against the grain; carving with the grain produces long stringy, tough slices. Cutting across the muscle fibres produces a more attractive and tender portion. Portions may be cut in a single thick slice, as with Roast Prime Rib of Beef, or in many thin slices. The photographs following illustrate several different carving procedures.

CARVING PRIME RIB

1. Remove the netting, cap fat and chine bones.

2. Trim the excess fat from the eye muscle.

3. Slice the rib in long, smooth strokes, the first cut (end cut) without a rib bone, the second cut with a rib bone, and so on.

CARVING PRIME RIB ON THE SLICER

1. When producing large quantities of prime rib, it is often more practical to slice it on a slicing machine. Following the steps illustrated above, remove the netting, cap fat and chine bone; trim excess fat from the eye muscle. Then use a long slicer, completely remove the rib eye from the rib bones, being careful to stay as close as possible to the bones to avoid wasting any meat.

2. After placing the rib on the slicing machine, set the machine to the desired thickness. The blade will have to be adjusted often because a roast's shape fluctuates.

CARVING A BEEF HIP

  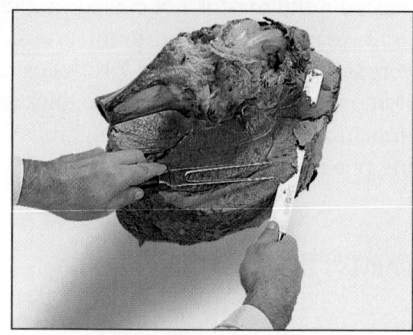

1. After setting the roast on the cutting board with the exposed femur bone (large end of the roast) down and the tibia (shank bone) or "handle" up, trim the excess exterior fat to expose the lean meat.

2. Begin slicing with a horizontal cut towards the shank bone, then make vertical cuts to release the slices of beef.

3. Keep the exposed surface as level as possible. Continue carving, turning the roast as necessary to access all sides.

CARVING A LEG OF LAMB

  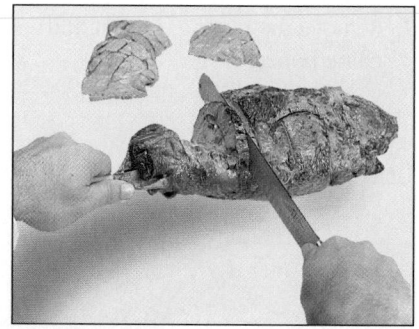

1. Hold the shank bone firmly, cut towards the bone.

2. Cut parallel to the shank bone to remove the slices.

3. Rotate the leg as needed to access the meat on all sides.

Sautéing

Sautéing is a dry-heat cooking method in which heat is conducted by a small amount of fat. Sautéed meats should be tender (a reflection of the quality of the raw product), of good colour (determined by proper cooking temperatures) and have a good overall flavour. Any accompanying sauce should be well seasoned and complement the meat without overpowering it.

Selecting Meats to Sauté

As with broiling, grilling and roasting, you should use tender meats of the highest quality in order to produce good results when sautéing. The cuts should be uniform in size and shape to promote even cooking.

Seasoning Meats to Be Sautéed

The sauces that almost always accompany sautéed meats provide much of the seasoning. The meat, however, can be marinated or simply seasoned with salt and pepper. If marinated, the meat must be patted dry before cooking to ensure proper browning. Some meats are dusted with flour before cooking to seal in juices and promote even browning.

Determining Doneness

As with broiled and grilled meats, the doneness of sautéed meats is determined by touch and timing. Red meats should be well browned; veal and pork should be somewhat lighter.

Accompaniments to Sautéed Meats

Sauces served with sautéed meats are usually made directly in the sauté pan, utilizing the **fond**. They often incorporate a previously thickened sauce. Additional sauce suggestions for sautéed meats are found in Table 10.5.

Fond—*(1) French for stock or base; (2) the concentrated juices, drippings and bits of food left in pans after foods are roasted or sautéed; it is used to flavour sauces made directly in the pans in which foods were cooked.*

BASIC PROCEDURE FOR SAUTÉING MEATS

1. Heat a sauté pan and add enough oil or clarified butter to just cover the bottom. The pan should be large enough to hold the meat in a single layer. A pan that is too large may cause the fat or meat to burn.
2. Cut the meat into **cutlets, escallopes, émincés, medallions, mignonnettes, noisettes, chops** or small even-sized pieces. Season the meat and dredge in flour if desired.
3. Add the meat to the sauté pan in a single layer. Do not crowd the pan.
4. Adjust the temperature so that the meat's exterior browns properly without burning and the interior cooks. The heat should be high enough to complete the cooking process before the meat begins to stew in its own juices.
5. Small items may be tossed using the sauté pan's sloped sides to flip them back on top of themselves. Do not toss the meat more than necessary, however. The pan should remain in contact with the heat source as much as possible to maintain proper temperatures. Larger items should be turned using tongs or a kitchen fork. Avoid splashing hot fat.
6. Larger items can be finished in an oven. Either place the sauté pan in the oven or transfer the meat to another pan. The latter procedure allows a sauce to be made in the original pan as the meat continues to cook.

Cutlet—*a relatively thick, boneless slice of meat.*

Escallope—*a thin, boneless slice of meat.*

Scallopini—*Italian for escallope*

Émincé—*a small, thin, boneless piece of meat.*

Paillarde—*a thin slice of meat pounded until thin, usually grilled.*

Medallion—*a small, round, relatively thick slice of meat.*

Mignonnette—*a medallion.*

Noisette—*a small, usually round, portion of meat cut from the rib.*

Chop—*a cut of meat including part of the rib.*

BASIC PROCEDURE FOR MAKING A SAUCE IN THE SAUTÉ PAN

1. If a sauce is to be made in the sauté pan, hold the meat in a warm spot while preparing the sauce. When the meat is removed from the pan, leave a small amount of fat as well as the fond. If there is excessive fat, degrease the pan, leaving just enough to cover its bottom. Add ingredients such as garlic, shallots and mushrooms that will be used as garnishes and sauce flavourings; sauté them.
2. Deglaze the pan with wine or stock. Scrape the pan, loosening the fond and allowing it to dissolve in the liquid. Reduce the deglazing liquid by approximately three-quarters.
3. Add fond lié (or demi-glace) or stock to the pan. Cook and reduce the sauce to the desired consistency.
4. Add any ingredients that do not require cooking such as herbs and spices. Adjust the seasonings with salt and pepper.

5. For service, the meat may be returned to the pan for a moment to reheat it and coat it with the finished sauce. The meat should remain in the sauce just long enough to reheat. Do not attempt to cook the meat in the sauce.

◆◆◆

RECIPE 12.3
SAUTÉED VEAL SCALLOPINI
WITH WHITE WINE LEMON SAUCE

Yield: 6 Servings

Veal scallopini, 3 oz. (90 g) each	12	12
Clarified butter	2 oz.	60 g
Flour	4 oz.	120 g
Salt and pepper	TT	TT
Shallots, chopped	2 Tbsp.	30 g
White wine	6 oz.	180 mL
Lemon juice	2 oz.	60 mL
Brown veal stock	4 oz.	120 mL
Unsalted butter*	2 oz.	60 g
Lemon wedges	12	12

1. Pound the scallopini to a uniform thickness, as described in Chapter 14, Veal.
2. Heat a sauté pan and add the clarified butter.
3. Dredge the scallopini in seasoned flour and add to the pan in a single layer. Sauté on each side for 1–2 minutes. As the first scallopini are done, remove them to a warm platter and sauté the remaining scallopini.
4. Add the chopped shallots to the pan and sauté.
5. Deglaze the pan with the white wine and lemon juice.
6. Add the brown veal stock and reduce by half.
7. Swirl in the unsalted butter (monter au beurre).
8. Adjust the seasonings with salt and pepper.
9. Serve 2 scallopini per person with approximately 1 ounce (30 mL) of sauce. Garnish with lemon wedges.

*The sauce may be modified to reduce the amount of butter. In Step 7, thicken the sauce with arrowroot or cornstarch and finish with 2 Tbsp. (10 g) butter.

Approximate values per 8 oz. (240 g) serving:

Calories	537
Total fat	28 g
Saturated fat	13 g
Cholesterol	208 mg
Sodium	325 mg
Total carbohydrates	17 g
Protein	47 g
Vitamin A	22%

1. Add the veal cutlets to the pan. Note the relationship of scallopini to pan size.

2. Add the chopped shallots to the pan and sauté them.

3. Deglaze the pan with white wine and lemon juice.

4. Add the brown veal stock and reduce by half.

5. Swirl in the butter and adjust the seasonings.

Pan-Frying

Pan-frying uses more fat than sautéing to conduct heat. Pan-fried meats should be tender (a reflection of the quality of the raw product), of good colour (determined by proper cooking temperatures) and with a good overall flavour. Meats to be pan-fried are usually breaded. In addition to providing flavour, breading seals the meat. The breading should be free from breaks, thus preventing the fat from coming into direct contact with the meat or collecting in a pocket formed between the meat and the breading. Pan-fried items should be golden in colour and the breading should not be soggy.

Selecting Meats to Pan-Fry

As with other dry-heat cooking methods, tender meats of high quality should be used because the meat will not be tenderized by the cooking process. Meats that are pan-fried are often cut into cutlets or escallops and may be delicated to tenderize.

Seasoning Meats to Be Pan-Fried

Pan-fried meats are usually seasoned lightly with salt and pepper either by applying them directly to the meat or adding them to the flour and crumb mixture used in the breading procedure.

Determining Doneness

The most accurate way to determine the doneness of a pan-fried item is by timing. The touch method is difficult to use because of the large amounts of hot fat. It also may not be as accurate as with broiled or grilled meats because pan-fried meats are often quite thin.

Accompaniments to Pan-Fried Meats

Any sauce served with pan-fried meats is usually made separately because there is no fond created during the pan-frying process. Sauce suggestions are listed in Table 10.5.

BASIC PROCEDURE FOR PAN-FRYING MEATS

1. Slice and pound out the meat into cutlets as described in Chapter 14, Veal.
2. Bread the meat using the standard breading procedure detailed in Chapter 21, Deep-Fat Frying.

3. Heat a moderate amount of fat or oil in a heavy pan. The temperature should be slightly lower than that used to sauté so that the breading will be nicely browned when the item is fully cooked.

4. Place the meat in the pan, being careful not to splash the hot fat. The meat should be immersed one-third to one-half. Fry until golden brown. Turn and brown the other side. Ideally, pan-fried meats should be fully cooked when they are well browned on both sides.

5. Remove the meat from the pan; drain it on absorbent paper before serving.

♦♦♦

RECIPE 12.4

BREADED PORK CUTLETS

Yield: 10 Servings

Pork cutlet, 4 oz. (120 g) each	10	10
Salt and pepper	TT	TT
Standard breading:	as needed	as needed
Flour		
Eggs		
Milk		
Bread crumbs		
Vegetable oil	as needed	as needed
Butter	6 oz.	180 g
Lemon wedges	20	20

Approximate values per 5 oz. (150 g) serving:

Calories	501
Total fat	37 g
Saturated fat	17 g
Cholesterol	193 mg
Sodium	338 mg
Total carbohydrates	5 g
Protein	36 g
Vitamin A	17%

1. Using a mallet, pound the cutlets to an even thickness, approximately 1/4 inch (0.5 cm).

2. Season the cutlets with salt and pepper.

3. Bread the cutlets using the standard breading procedure described in Chapter 21, Deep-Fat Frying.

4. Heat a heavy pan to moderate heat; add approximately 1/4 inch (0.5 cm) of oil.

5. Add the cutlets in a single layer. Do not crowd the pan. Brown on one side, then the other. Total cooking time should be approximately 4 minutes.

6. Remove the cutlets and drain on absorbent paper.

7. Melt the butter in a small pan until it foams.

8. Place one cutlet on each plate and pour approximately 1/2 ounce (15 mL) butter over each portion. Garnish with lemon wedges.

1. Add the breaded cutlets to the hot pan. Note the amount of oil in the pan.

2. Turn the cutlets to brown on the second side.

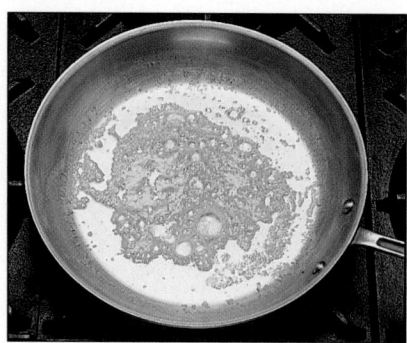

3. Melt the butter in a separate pan until it foams.

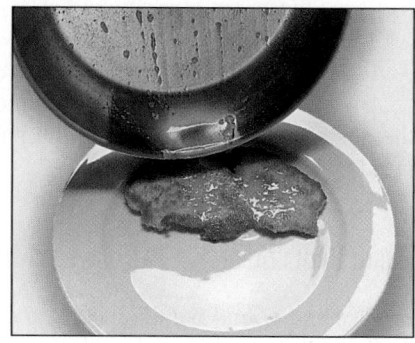

4. Pour the butter over the cutlet.

Moist-Heat Cooking Methods

Moist-heat cooking methods subject food to heat and moisture. Moist heat is often, but not always, used to tenderize tougher cuts of meat through long, slow cooking. Simmering is the only moist-heat cooking method discussed here as it is the only one frequently used with meat.

Simmering

Simmering is usually associated with specific tougher cuts of meat that need to be tenderized through long, slow, moist cooking. Quality simmered meats have good flavour and texture. The flavour is determined by the cooking liquid; the texture is a result of proper cooking temperatures and time.

Selecting Meats to Simmer

Meats such as fresh or corned beef brisket, fresh or cured hams and tongue are often simmered. Beef briskets and tongues, pork butts and hams are often simmered whole.

Seasoning Meats to Be Simmered

If the meat to be simmered was cured by either smoking (as with cured hams, ham hocks and smoked pork butt) or pickling (as with corned beef and pickled tongue), the cooking liquid will not be used to make a sauce and should not be seasoned. Indeed, simmering cured meats helps leach out some of the excess salt, making the finished dish more palatable.

Cooking Temperatures

Moist-heat cooking methods generally use lower temperatures than dry-heat cooking methods. Meats are normally simmered at temperatures between 180°F and 200°F (82°C–93°C). In larger food service operations, meats such as hams and corned beef are cooked at temperatures as low as 150°F (65°C) for up to 12 hours. Although lower cooking temperatures result in less shrinkage and a more tender finished product, cooking times can be increased to the point that very low cooking temperatures may not always be practical or healthy.

Determining Doneness

Simmered meats are almost always cooked well done, which is determined by tenderness. The size and quality of the raw product determines the cooking time. Undercooked meats will be tough and chewy. Overcooked meats will be stringy and may even fall apart.

To test large cuts of meat for doneness, a kitchen fork should be inserted into the meat and the meat should slide easily off the fork. Smaller pieces of meat should be tender to the bite or easily cut with a table fork.

Accompaniments to Simmered Meats

Simmered meats are often served with boiled or steamed vegetables, for example, corned beef and cabbage. Pickled meats are usually served with mustard or horseradish sauce on the side.

BASIC PROCEDURE FOR SIMMERING MEATS

1. Cut, trim or tie the meat according to the recipe.
2. Bring an adequate amount of liquid to a boil. There should be enough liquid to cover the meat completely. Too much liquid will leach off much of the meat's flavour; too little will leave a portion of the meat exposed, preventing it from cooking. Because the dish's final flavour is determined by the flavour of the liquid, use plenty of mirepoix, flavourings and seasonings.

3. When simmering smoked or cured items, start them in cold water. This helps draw off some of the strong pickled or smoked flavours.
4. Add the meat to the liquid.
5. Reduce the heat to the desired temperature and cook until the meat is tender. Do not allow the cooking liquid to boil. Boiling results in a tough or over-cooked and stringy product. If the simmered meat is to be served cold, a moister and juicier product can be achieved by removing the pot from the stove before the meat is fully cooked. The meat and the liquid can be cooled in a water bath like that for a stock, as described in Chapter 10, Stocks and Sauces. This allows the residual heat in the cooking liquid to finish cooking the meat.

Approximate values per serving:

Calories	1067
Total fat	58 g
Saturated fat	19 g
Cholesterol	296 mg
Sodium	3844 mg
Total carbohydrates	73 g
Protein	64 g
Vitamin A	27%
Vitamin C	200%
Iron	66%

◆◆◆

RECIPE 12.5

NEW ENGLAND BOILED DINNER

Yield: 12 6-oz. (180-g) Servings

Corned beef brisket, 8 lb. (3.6 kg)	1	1
White stock	as needed	as needed
Sachet:		
Bay leaves	2	2
Dried thyme	1/2 tsp.	2 mL
Peppercorns, cracked	1/2 tsp.	2 mL
Parsley stems	10	10
Mustard seeds	1 Tbsp.	15 mL
Cinnamon sticks	2	2
Allspice berries (whole)	4	4
Baby red beets	24	24
Baby turnips	24	24
Baby carrots	24	24
Brussels sprouts	24	24
Pearl onions	24	24
Potatoes, Red Bliss	24	24
Salt and pepper	TT	TT

1. Place the corned beef and sachet in an appropriate pot and cover with stock.

1. Place the beef in a pot and add enough stock to cover it. Add the sachet, bring to a boil and reduce to a simmer.
2. Simmer until the beef is tender, approximately 3 hours. Remove the beef and hold in a hotel pan in a small amount of the cooking liquid.
3. Peel or prepare the vegetables and potatoes as needed and cook separately in a portion of the cooking liquid.
4. Carve the beef and serve with 2 of each of the vegetables and horseradish sauce (page 207).

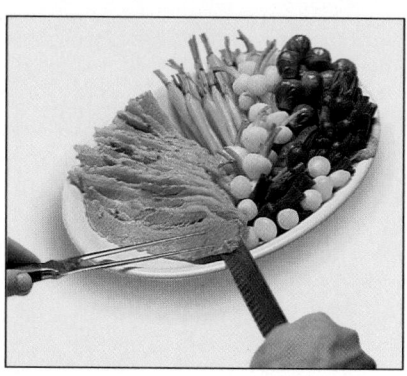

2. Carve the beef and present it with the vegetable garnish.

Combination Cooking Methods

Braising and stewing are referred to as combination cooking methods because both dry heat and moist heat are used to achieve the desired results.

Braising

Braised meats are first browned and then cooked in a liquid that serves as a sauce for the meat. A well-prepared braised dish has the rich flavour of the meat in the sauce and the moisture and flavour of the sauce in the meat. It should be almost fork tender but not falling apart. The meat should have an attractive colour from the initial browning and final glazing.

Selecting Meats to Braise

Braising can be used for tender cuts (such as those from the loin or rib) or tougher cuts (such as those from the chuck or shank). Any meat to be braised should be well marbled with ample fat content to produce a moist finished product.

If tender cuts such as veal chops or pork chops are braised, the finished dish has a uniquely different flavour and texture than if they were cooked by a dry-heat method. Tender cuts require shorter cooking times than tougher cuts because lengthy cooking is not needed to break down connective tissue.

More often, braising is used with tougher cuts that are tenderized by the long, moist cooking process. Cuts from the chuck and shank are popular choices, as they are very flavourful and contain relatively large amounts of collagen, which adds richness to the finished product.

Large pieces of meat can be braised, then carved like a roast. Portion control cuts and diced meats can also be braised.

Seasoning Meats to Be Braised

The seasoning and overall flavour of a braised dish is largely a function of the quality of the cooking liquid and the mirepoix, herbs, spices and other ingredients that season the meat as it cooks. However, braised meats can be marinated before they are cooked to tenderize them and add flavour. The marinade is then sometimes incorporated into the braising liquid. Salt and pepper may be added to the flour if the meat is dredged before it is browned, or the meat may be seasoned directly (although the salt may draw out moisture and inhibit browning).

A standard sachet and a tomato product are usually added at the start of cooking. The tomato product adds flavour and colour to the finished sauce as well as acid to tenderize the meat during the cooking process. Final seasoning should not take place until cooking is complete and the sauce will not be reduced further.

Cooking Temperatures

Braised meats are usually browned before simmering. As a general rule, smaller cuts are floured before browning; larger cuts are not. Flouring seals the meat, promotes even browning and adds body to the sauce that accompanies the meat. Whether floured or not, the meat is browned in fat. After browning, white meats should be golden to amber in colour; red meats should be dark brown. Do not brown the meat too quickly at too high a temperature, as it is important to develop a well-caramelized surface. The caramelized surface adds colour and flavour to the final product.

The meat and the braising liquid are brought to a boil over direct heat. The temperature is then reduced below boiling and the pot is covered. Cooking can be finished in the oven or on the stove top. The oven provides gentle, even heat without the risk of scorching. If the braise is finished on the stove top, proper temperatures must be maintained carefully throughout the cooking process and great care must be taken to prevent scorching or burning. Lower temperatures and longer cooking times result in more even cooking and thorough penetration of the cooking liquid, providing a more flavourful final product.

Finishing Braised Meats

Near the end of the cooking process, the lid may be removed from oven-braised meats. Finishing braised meats without a cover serves two purposes. First, the meat can be glazed by basting it often. (As the basting liquid evaporates, the meat is browned and a strongly flavoured glaze is formed.) Second, removing the lid allows the cooking liquid to reduce, thickening it and concentrating its flavours for use as a sauce.

Determining Doneness

Braised meats are done when they are tender. A fork inserted into the meat should meet little resistance. Properly braised meats should remain intact and not fall apart when handled gently.

Braised meats that fall apart or are stringy are overcooked. If the finished product is tough, it was probably undercooked or cooked at too high a temperature. If the entire dish lacks flavour, the meat may not have been properly browned or the cooking liquid may have been poorly seasoned.

Accompaniments to Braised Meats

Large braised items are often served like roasts. They are carved against the grain in thin slices and served with their sauce. Vegetables can be cooked with the braised meat, cooked separately and added when the main item has finished cooking or added at service. If the vegetables are cooked with the main item they should be added at intervals based on their individual cooking times to prevent overcooking.

BASIC PROCEDURE FOR BRAISING MEATS

The liquid used for braising is usually thickened in one of three ways:

1. With a roux added at the start of the cooking process; the roux thickens the sauce as the meat cooks.
2. Prethickened before the meat is added.
3. Thickened after the meat is cooked either by puréeing the mirepoix or by using roux, arrowroot or cornstarch.

The procedure for braising meats includes variations for whichever thickening method is selected.

1. Heat a small amount of oil in a heavy pan.
2. Dredge the meat to be braised in seasoned flour, if desired, and add it to the oil.
3. Brown the meat well on all sides and remove from the pan.
4. Add a mirepoix to the pan and caramelize it well. If using roux, it should be added at this time.
5. Add the appropriate stock or sauce so that when the meat is returned to the pan it will be immersed approximately one-third.
6. Add aromatics and seasonings.
7. Return the meat to the sauce. Tightly cover the pot and bring it to a simmer. Cook slowly either on the stove top or by placing the covered pot directly in an oven at 250°F–300°F (120°C–150°C).
8. Cook the item, basting or turning it often so that all sides of the meat benefit from the moisture and flavour of the sauce.
9. When the meat is done, remove it from the pan and hold it in a warm place while the sauce is finished.
10. The sauce may be reduced on the stove top to intensify its flavours. If the meat was braised in a stock, the stock may be thickened using a roux, arrowroot or cornstarch. Strain the sauce or, if desired, purée the mirepoix and other ingredients and return them to the sauce. Adjust the sauce's consistency as desired.

◆◆◆

RECIPE 12.6

ALBERTA BEEF CHEEKS WITH ROOT VEGETABLES, BABY ONIONS AND WILD ALBERTA MUSHROOMS, BRAISED IN A STONE CHURCH BACO NOIR SAUCE

JASPER PARK LODGE, JASPER, AB
Executive Chef David MacGillivray

This is a time-consuming dish, using the almost always neglected part of the beef carcass. However, the effort is worth it. This is a rich, soul-warming meal that can be as trashy or classy as you want it to be. Despite its fancy leanings, it really is nothing more than a beef stew, and you can use beef stewing meat as a substitute for the cheeks if they are unavailable or not to your liking.

David MacGillivray
From the time he was 15 years old, working in a restaurant in Picton, Ontario, David knew he wanted to be a chef. He quickly became renowned in Canada, particularly for his work in the Edith Cavell Dining Room at Jasper Park Lodge, where his creative menus and excellent service have won the restaurant several prestigious awards.

Yield: 6 Servings

Canola oil	2 oz.	50 mL
Beef cheeks (trimmed of excess fat)	4.5 lb.	2 kg
Salt and pepper	TT	TT
Onion, peeled and chopped	1	1
Carrot, peeled and chopped	1	1
Celery stalk, chopped	1	1
Garlic cloves, minced	6	6
Stone Church Baco Noir	18 oz.	500 mL
Bay leaf	2	2
Brown stock	100 oz.	3 L
Canola oil	2 oz.	50 mL
Carrots, medium, peeled and large dice	2	2
Purple-top turnip, peeled, large dice	1	1
Parsnip, medium, peeled, large dice	2	2
Fresh baby onions, large, cippoline if available	8–10	8–10
Chanterelles	2 oz.	50 g
Lobster mushrooms	2 oz.	50 g
Portobello mushrooms	2-1/2 oz.	75 g
Stone Church Baco Noir	9 oz.	250 mL
Roasted garlic	2 oz.	50 g
Salt and coarse ground black pepper	TT	TT
Butter	3-1/2 oz.	100 g

1. In a heavy-bottomed pot, heat canola oil, season the cheeks with salt and pepper and brown evenly and thoroughly.

2. Remove the cheeks from the pot and add the vegetables and garlic and sauté until tender.

3. Add red wine and bay leaf and deglaze the pan. Return the cheeks to the pan and add the stock.

4. Cover with a lid and place in an oven at 275°F (180°C). Cook the cheeks for 4–5 hours, checking occasionally.

5. Remove the pan from the oven. Take the cheeks out of the broth and set aside. Strain the broth through a fine chinois and set aside for finishing.

6. To finish the dish, in a heavy-bottomed saucepan, heat 2 oz. (50 mL) canola oil and sauté the root vegetables, onions and mushrooms, approximately 5 minutes.

7. Add the remaining 9 ounces (250 mL) wine from the bottle, and the poaching stock.

Continued

8. Cook the vegetables, mushrooms and the stock over medium heat for approximately 30 minutes, or until tender.
9. Add the beef cheeks to the broth to bring them back to temperature.
10. Remove the cheeks and slice them; place them on a serving platter.
11. Remove the vegetables and surround the cheeks with them. Cover and keep warm in a low oven.
12. Bring the stock to a boil, add the roasted garlic. Reduce heat to medium and cook for 15 minutes. Remove from the heat and adjust the seasoning with salt and pepper. Whisk in the butter at the last minute and ladle over the beef cheeks and vegetables.
13. Serve the cheeks on a large earthenware platter with a big bowl of creamy mashed potatoes and warm bread for sopping up the sauce.

Approximate values per serving:

Calories	1086
Total fat	63 g
Saturated fat	24 g
Cholesterol	260 mg
Sodium	378 mg
Total carbohydrates	13 g
Protein	93 g

Stewing

Stewing, like braising, is a combination cooking method. In many ways the procedures for stewing are identical to those for braising, although stewing is usually associated with smaller or bite-sized pieces of meat.

There are two main types of stews: brown stews and white stews.

When making **brown stews**, the meat is first browned in fat; then a cooking liquid is added. The initial browning adds flavour and colour to the finished product. The same characteristics apply to a good brown stew that apply to a good braised dish: It should be fork tender, have an attractive colour and rich flavour.

There are two types of **white stews**: **fricassees**, in which the meat is first cooked in a small amount of fat without colouring, then combined with a cooking liquid; and **blanquettes**, in which the meat is first blanched, then rinsed and added to a cooking liquid. White stew should have the same flavour and texture characteristics as a brown stew, but should be white or ivory in colour.

Selecting Meats to Stew
Stewing uses moist heat to tenderize meat just as braising does, therefore many of the same cuts can be used. Meats that are to be stewed should be trimmed of excess fat and connective tissue and cut into 1- to 2-inch (2.5 to 5 cm) cubes.

Seasoning Meats to Be Stewed
Stews, like braised meats, get much of their flavour from their cooking liquid. A stew's seasoning and overall flavour are a direct result of the quality of the cooking liquid and the vegetables, herbs, spices and other ingredients added during cooking.

Cooking Temperatures
Meats for brown stews are first cooked at high temperatures over direct heat until well browned. Meats for fricassees are first sautéed at low temperatures so they do not develop colour.

Once the cooking liquid has been added and the moist-heat cooking process has begun, do not allow the stew to boil. Stews benefit from low-temperature cooking. If practical, stews can be covered and finished in the oven.

Determining Doneness
Stewed meats are done when they are fork tender. Test them by removing a piece of meat to a plate and cutting it with a fork. Any vegetables that are

---

♦♦♦

STEW TERMINOLOGY

Ragout—A general term that refers to white or brown stews in which the meat is cooked by dry heat before liquid is added. In French, ragout means "to bring back the taste."

Fricassee—A white ragout usually made from white meat or small game, seared without browning and garnished with small onions and mushrooms.

Navarin—A brown ragout generally made with turnips, other root vegetables, onions, peas and lamb.

Blanquette—A white stew in which the meat is first blanched, then added to a stock or sauce to complete the cooking and tenderizing process. Blanquettes are finished with a liaison of egg yolks and heavy cream.

Chili con carne—A ragout of ground or diced meat cooked with onions, chile peppers, cumin and other spices. Despite the objections of purists, chili sometimes contains beans.

Goulash—A Hungarian stew thickened with onions, flavoured with paprika and garnished with potatoes.

cooked with the meat should be added at the proper times so that they and the meat are completely cooked at the same time.

Accompaniments to Stewed Meats

Stews are often complete meals in themselves, containing meat, vegetables and potatoes in one dish. Stews that do not contain a starch are often served with pasta or rice.

BASIC PROCEDURE FOR STEWING MEATS—*BROWN STEWS*

Red meats, lamb or game are used in brown stews. The procedure for making a brown stew is very similar to braising.

1. Trim the meat of excess fat and silverskin and cut into 1- to 2-inch (2.5 to 5 cm) pieces.
2. Dredge the meat in flour if desired. Heat an appropriate-sized pan and add enough oil to cover the bottom. Cook the meat in the oil, browning it well on all sides. Onions and garlic can be added at this time and browned.
3. Add flour to the meat and fat and cook to make a brown roux.
4. Gradually add the liquid to the roux, stirring to prevent lumps. Bring the stew to a boil and reduce to a simmer.
5. Add a tomato product and a sachet or a bouquet garni. Cover and place in the oven or continue to simmer on the stove top until the meat is tender. Add other ingredients such as vegetables or potatoes at the proper time so that they will be done when the meat is tender.
6. When the meat is tender, remove the sachet or bouquet garni. The meat may be strained out and the sauce thickened with roux, cornstarch or arrowroot or reduced to concentrate its flavours.
7. If not added during the cooking process, vegetables and other garnishes may be cooked separately and added to the finished stew.

◆◆◆

RECIPE 12.7

BROWN BEEF STEW

Yield: 8 8-oz. (250-mL) Servings

Oil	2 oz.	60 mL
Beef chuck or shank, trimmed and cut into 1-1/2 in. (3.5 cm) cubes	4 lb. 8 oz.	2 kg
Salt	2 tsp.	10 mL
Pepper	1/2 tsp.	2 mL
Onion, small dice	10 oz.	300 g
Garlic clove, chopped	1	1
Flour	1-1/2 oz.	45 g
Red wine	8 oz.	250 mL
Brown stock	1 qt.	1 L
Tomato purée	4 oz.	120 mL
Sachet:		
Bay leaves	2	2
Dried thyme	1/2 tsp.	2 mL
Peppercorns, crushed	1/2 tsp.	2 mL
Parsley stems	10	10

Continued

1. Brown the beef.

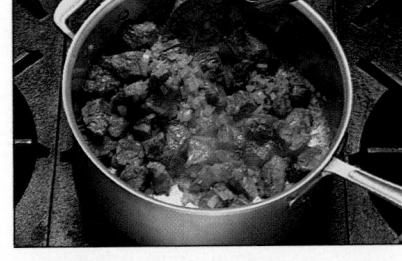

2. Sauté the garlic and onions until slightly browned.

3. Add the flour and make a roux.

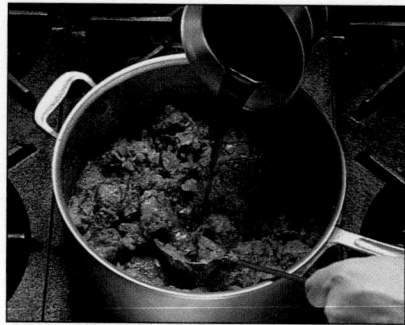

4. Add the red wine and beef stock.

5. Add the tomato purée and sachet.

6. Degrease the stew.

Approximate values per 8 oz. (240 g) serving:	
Calories	590
Total fat	32 g
Saturated fat	11 g
Cholesterol	185 mg
Sodium	710 mg
Total carbohydrates	15 g
Protein	58 g
Vitamin A	45%
Iron	40%

1. Heat a heavy pot until very hot and add the oil.

2. Season the beef and add it to the pot, browning it well on all sides. Do not overcrowd the pot. If necessary, cook the beef in several batches.

3. Add the onions and garlic and sauté until the onions are slightly browned.

4. Add the flour and stir to make a roux. Brown the roux lightly.

5. Add the red wine and brown stock slowly, stirring to prevent lumps.

6. Add the tomato purée and the sachet.

7. Bring to a simmer and cook until the beef is tender, approximately 1-1/2 to 2 hours.

8. Optional: Remove the cooked beef from the sauce and strain the sauce. Return the beef to the sauce.

9. Degrease the stew by skimming off the fat.

VARIATION: Vegetables such as turnips, carrots, celery and pearl onions can be cooked separately and added to the stew as garnish.

BASIC PROCEDURE FOR STEWING MEATS—*BRAISED WHITE STEWS (FRICASSEES)*

The procedure for making fricassees is similar to the procedure for brown stews. The primary difference is that the meat is sautéed but not allowed to brown. The braised white stew (fricassee) procedure outlined below is the basis for Recipe 14.11, Veal Fricassee.

1. Trim meat of excess fat and silverskin and cut into 1- to 2-inch (2.5 to 5 cm) pieces.

2. Heat an appropriate-sized pan and add enough oil to cover the bottom. Add the meat (and often an onion) to the pan and cook without browning.

3. Sprinkle the meat (and onion) with flour and cook to make a blond roux.

4. Gradually add the liquid, stirring to prevent lumps. Bring the stew to a boil and reduce to a simmer.

5. Add a bouquet garni and seasonings. Cover the stew and place in the oven or continue to simmer on the stove top, being careful not to burn or scorch the stew.

6. Continue to cook until the meat is tender. If the sauce is too thin, remove the meat from the sauce and hold the meat in a warm place. Reduce the sauce to the proper consistency on the stove top or thicken it by adding a small amount of blond roux, cornstarch or arrowroot.

BASIC PROCEDURE FOR STEWING MEATS—*SIMMERED WHITE STEWS (BLANQUETTES)*

Unlike fricassees, blanquettes contain meat that was blanched, not sautéed. (Because the meat is cooked only by moist heat and never by dry heat, the blanquette cooking process is not a true combination cooking method; nevertheless, because of its striking similarities to stewing, it is included here.) The most common blanquette is made with veal and is known as blanquette de veau, but any white meat or lamb can be prepared in this manner using a variety of garnishes.

1. Trim meat of excess fat and silverskin and cut into 1- to 2-inch (2.5 to 5 cm) pieces.

2. Blanch the cubed meat by placing the meat in an appropriate pot, covering with cool water, adding salt, and bringing it rapidly to a boil. Drain the water. Rinse the meat to remove any impurities.

3. Return the meat to the pot and add enough stock to cover. Add a bouquet garni, salt and pepper. Simmer until the meat is tender, approximately 1 to 1-1/2 hours.

4. Strain the meat from the stock. Discard the bouquet garni. Bring the stock to a boil, thicken it with a blond roux and simmer for 15 minutes.

5. Return the meat to the thickened stock. Add a liaison of cream and egg yolks to enrich and thicken the stew. Heat the stew to just under 185°F (85°C). Do not boil or the egg yolks will curdle.

6. If any vegetables are to be added they should be cooked separately and added to the thickened stock with the meat.

7. Adjust the seasoning with a few drops of lemon juice, nutmeg or salt and pepper as needed.

$\mathcal{C}$ONCLUSION

Because meat may account for the largest portion of your food-cost dollar, it should be purchased carefully, stored properly and fabricated appropriately. The various cuts and flavours of meat (beef, veal, lamb and pork) can be successfully broiled, grilled, roasted, sautéed, pan-fried, simmered, braised or stewed, provided you follow a few simple procedures and learn which cuts respond best to the various cooking methods.

$\mathcal{Q}$UESTIONS FOR DISCUSSION

1. Explain the difference between primals, subprimals and fabricated cuts of meat. Why is it important to be skilled in meat fabrication?

2. What is connective tissue composed of and where is it found? What happens to connective tissues at normal cooking temperatures?

3. Discuss the government's role in regulating the marketing and sale of meat.

4. Explain why meats are subject to a health inspection. What is the purpose of grading carcass meat?

5. At what temperature should fresh meat be stored? At what temperature should frozen meat be stored?

6. Would it be better to grill or braise a piece of meat that contains a great deal of connective tissue? Explain your answer.

7. List three ways to improve the cooking qualities of lean meats. What techniques can be used to compensate for the lack of fat?

8. Describe the similarities between sautéing meats and pan-frying them. Describe the differences.

9. Describe the similarities between braising meats and stewing them. Describe the differences.

$\mathcal{W}$EBLINKS

ABC's of Meat Cooking
   www.tasteofamerica.com/abc/abc_meat.html

Meat Cuts and Grading
   www.aps.uoguelph.ca/~swatland/ch3.0.htm

CHAPTER 13 BEEF

LEARNING OUTCOMES

After studying this chapter you will be able to:

◆ identify the primal, subprimal and fabricated cuts of beef

◆ perform basic butchering procedures: cutting a strip loin, trimming and cutting a tenderloin, butterflying

◆ apply appropriate cooking methods to several common cuts of beef

---

◆◆◆

NOT ALL CATTLE ARE CALLED "DAISY"

Cattle is the collective name for all domesticated oxen (genus *Bos*). Cattle are classified as:

Bulls—male cattle, usually not raised to be eaten.

Calves—young cows or bulls prized for their meat.

Cows—female cattle after their first calving, raised in this country principally for milk and calf production. In France, cows are used for beef when they are no longer needed for milk.

Heifers—young cows or cows before their first calving. Heifer meat and organs are becoming increasingly popular as a food source.

Stags—male cattle castrated after maturity, principally used for dog food.

Steers—male cattle castrated prior to maturity and principally raised for beef.

ℬeef is the meat of domesticated cattle. Most of the beef Canadians eat comes from steers, which are male cattle castrated as calves and specifically raised for beef. Although Canadians are consuming less beef today than we once did, we still consume far more beef than any other meat. The beef we are eating is leaner than that of years past, thanks to advances in animal husbandry and closer trimming of exterior fat.

PRIMAL AND SUBPRIMAL CUTS OF BEEF

After the steer or heifer is slaughtered it is cut into four pieces (called quarters) for easy handling. This is done by first splitting the carcass down the backbone into two bilateral halves. Each half is divided into the forequarter (the front portion) and hindquarter (the rear portion) by cutting along the natural curvature between the twelfth and thirteenth ribs. The quartered carcass is then further reduced into the primal cuts and the subprimal and fabricated cuts.

The primal cuts of beef are the square chuck, point brisket and shank, rib, plate, short loin, sirloin, flank and hip. Figure 13.1 shows the relationship between a steer's bone structure and the primal cuts. It is important to know the location of bones when cutting or working with meats. This makes meat fabrication and carving easier and aids in identifying cuts. Figure 13.2 shows the primal cuts of beef and their location on the carcass. An entire beef carcass can range in weight from 500 to more than 800 pounds (225–360 kg).

Forequarter

Square Chuck

The primal chuck is the animal's shoulder; it accounts for approximately 28% of carcass weight. It contains a portion of the backbone (which, in turn, consists of feather, finger and chine bones), five rib bones and portions of the blade and arm bones.

Because an animal constantly uses its shoulder muscles, chuck contains a high percentage of connective tissue and is quite tough. This tough cut of beef, however, is one of the most flavourful.

The primal chuck is used less frequently than other primal cuts in food service operations. If cooked whole, the chuck is difficult to cut or carve because of the large number of bones and relatively small muscle groups which travel in different directions.

The primal chuck produces several fabricated cuts: cross rib pot roast, chuck short ribs, cubed or tenderized steaks, stew meat and ground chuck. Because the meat is tough, the fabricated cuts usually benefit from moist-heat cooking or combination cooking methods such as stewing and braising.

Point Brisket and Shank

The brisket and shank are located beneath the primal chuck on the front half of the carcass. Together, they form a single primal that accounts for approximately 8% of the carcass weight. This primal consists of the animal's breast

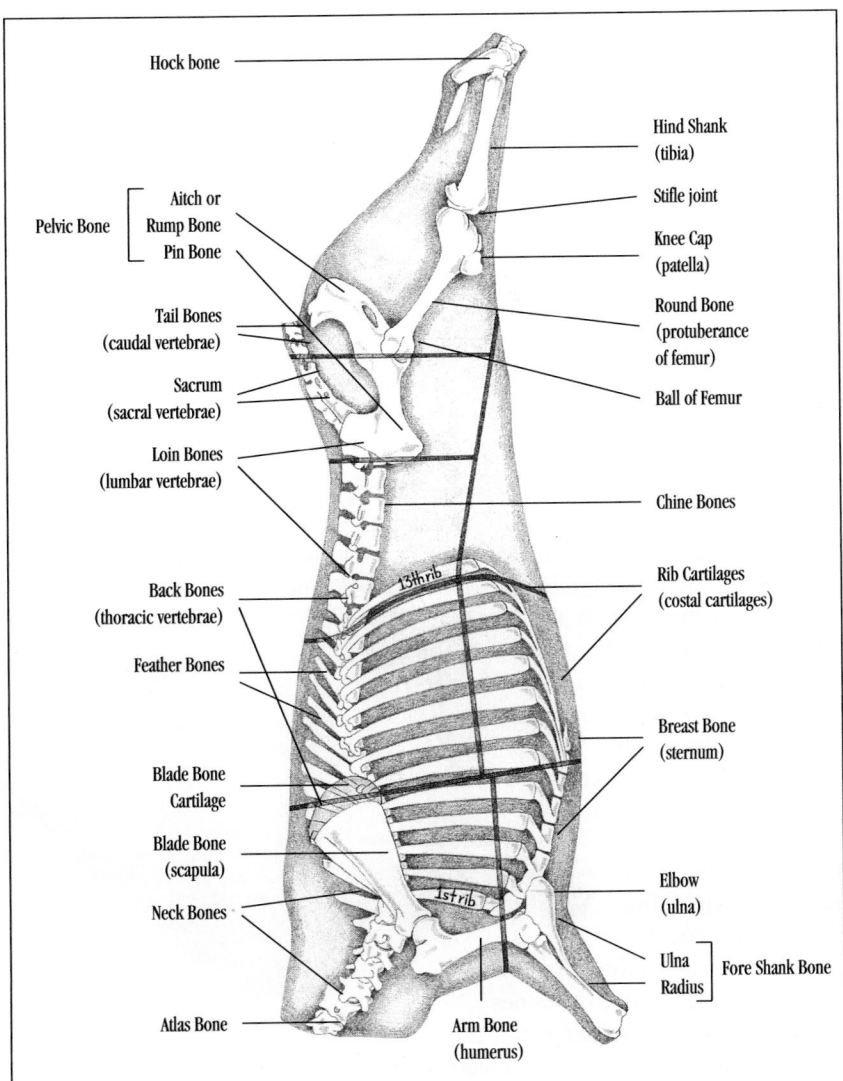

FIGURE 13.1 *The Skeletal Structure of a Steer*

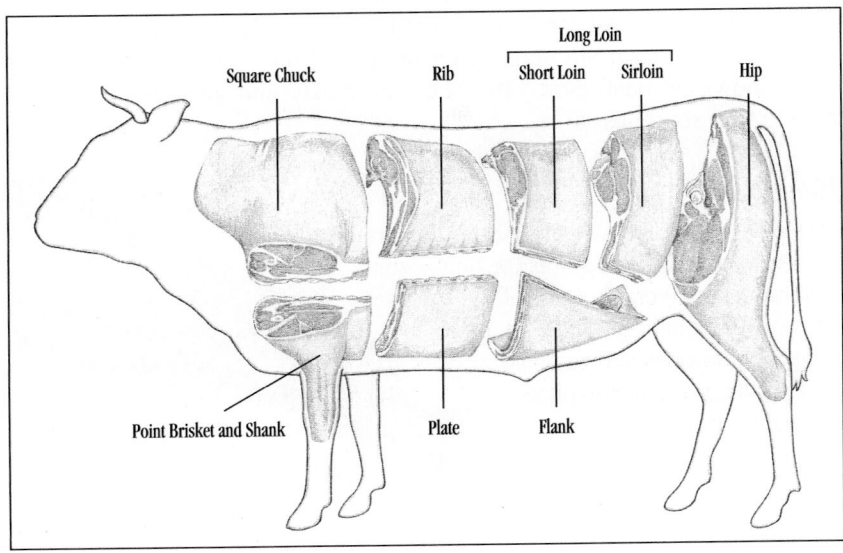

FIGURE 13.2 *The Primal Cuts of Beef*

(the brisket), which contains ribs and breast bone, and its arm (the foreshank), which contains only the shank bone.

The ribs and breast bone are always removed from the brisket before cooking. The boneless brisket is very tough and contains a substantial percentage of fat, both intermuscular and subcutaneous. It is well suited for moist-heat and combination cooking methods such as simmering or braising. It is often pickled or corned to produce corned beef brisket, or cured and peppered to make pastrami.

Beef foreshanks are very flavourful and high in collagen. Because collagen converts to gelatin when cooked using moist heat, foreshanks are excellent for making soups and stocks. Ground shank meat is often used to help clarify and flavour consommés because of its rich flavour and high collagen content.

Rib

The primal beef rib accounts for approximately 10% of carcass weight. It consists of ribs 6 through 12 as well as a portion of the backbone.

This primal is best known for yielding roast prime rib of beef. Prime rib is not named after the quality grade Canada Prime. Rather, its name reflects the fact that it constitutes the majority of the primal cut. The eye meat of the rib (the centre muscle portion) is not a well-exercised muscle and therefore is quite tender. It also contains large amounts of marbling compared to the rest of the carcass and produces rich, full-flavoured roasts and steaks. Although roasting the eye muscle on the rib bones produces a moister roast, the eye meat can be removed to produce a boneless rib eye roast or cut into rib eye steaks. The rib bones that are separated from the rib eye meat are quite meaty and flavourful and can be served as barbecued beef ribs. The ends of the rib bones that are trimmed off the primal rib to produce the rib roast are known as beef short ribs. They are meaty and are often served as braised beef short ribs.

Oven-Ready Rib Roast

Beef Rib Eye

Plate

The plate is located directly below the primal rib on a side of beef; it accounts for only a small portion of the overall weight of the carcass, approximately 9%. The plate contains rib bones and cartilage and produces the meaty plate short ribs and skirt steak.

Short ribs are meaty, yet high in connective tissue, and are best when braised.

Skirt Steak

Skirt steak is often marinated and grilled as fajitas. Other, less meaty portions of the plate are trimmed and ground.

Hindquarter

Short Loin

The short loin is the anterior (front) portion of the beef loin. It is located just behind the rib and becomes the first primal cut of the hindquarter when the side of beef is divided into a forequarter and hindquarter. It accounts for approximately 8% of carcass weight.

The short loin contains a single rib, the thirteenth, and a portion of the backbone. With careful butchering, this small primal can yield several subprimal and fabricated cuts, all of which are among the most tender, popular and expensive cuts of beef.

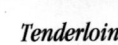

Porterhouse or T-bone Steaks

The loin eye muscle, a continuation of the rib eye muscle, runs along the top of the T-shaped bones that form the backbone. Beneath the loin eye muscle on the other side of the backbone is the tenderloin, the most tender cut of all.

When the short loin is cut in cross sections with the bone in, it produces—starting with the rib end of the short loin—club steaks (which do not contain any tenderloin), T-bone steaks (which contain only a small portion of tenderloin) and porterhouse steaks (which are cut from the sirloin end of the short loin and contain a large portion of tenderloin).

Strip Loin

The whole tenderloin also can be removed and cut into chateaubriand, filet mignon and tournedos. A portion of the tenderloin is located in the sirloin portion of the loin. When the entire beef loin is divided into the primal short loin and primal sirloin, the large end of the tenderloin (the butt tenderloin) is separated from the remainder of the tenderloin and remains in the sirloin; the smaller end of the tenderloin (the short tenderloin) remains in the short loin. If the tenderloin is to be kept whole, it must be removed before the short loin and sirloin are separated. The loin eye meat can be removed from the bones, producing a boneless strip loin, which is very tender and can be roasted or cut into boneless strip steaks.

Tenderloin

Sirloin

The sirloin is located in the hindquarter, between the short loin and the round. It accounts for approximately 7% of carcass weight and contains part of the backbone as well as a portion of the hip bone.

The sirloin produces bone-in or boneless roasts and steaks that are flavourful and tender. With the exception of the tenderloin portion, however, these subprimals and fabricated cuts are not as tender as those from the strip loin. Cuts from the sirloin are cooked using dry-heat methods such as broiling, grilling or roasting.

Top Sirloin Butt

Flank

The flank is located directly beneath the loin, posterior to (behind) the plate. It accounts for approximately 6% of carcass weight. The flank contains no bones.

Although quite flavourful, it is tough meat with a good deal of fat and connective tissue. Flank meat is usually trimmed and ground, with the exception of the flank steak or London broil. The flank also contains a small piece of meat known as the hanging tenderloin. Although not actually part of the tenderloin, it is very tender and can be cooked using any method.

Flank Steak

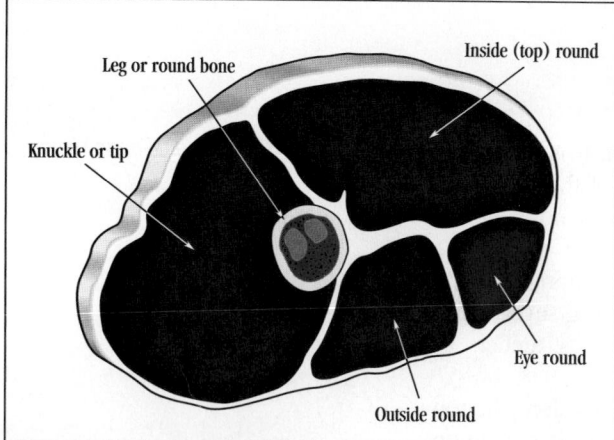

FIGURE 13.3 *Cross Cut of Muscles in a Whole Hip*

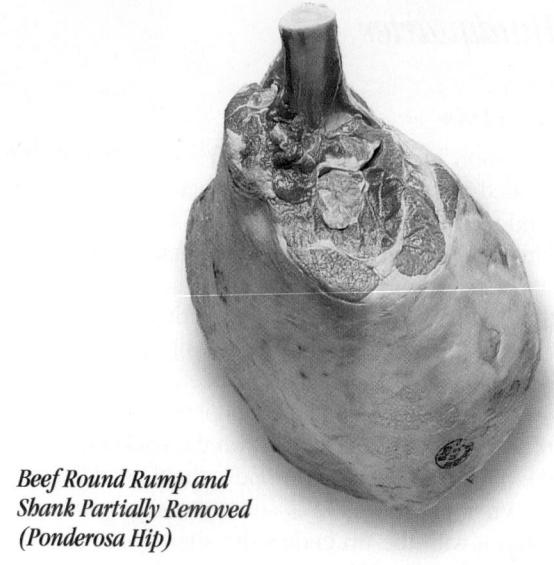

Beef Round Rump and Shank Partially Removed (Ponderosa Hip)

Inside (or Top) Round

Hip

The primal hip is very large, weighing as much as 200 pounds (90 kg) and accounting for approximately 24% of carcass weight. It is the hind leg of the animal and contains the round, aitch, shank and tail bones.

Meat from the hip is flavourful and fairly tender. The hip yields a wide variety of subprimal and fabricated cuts: the top round, outside round, eye round (the outside round and the eye round together are called the bottom round), knuckle and shank. See Figure 13.3. Steaks cut from the hip are tough, but because they have large muscles and limited intermuscular fat, the top round and knuckle make good roasts. The outside round is best when braised. The hindshank is prepared in the same fashion as the foreshank.

BEEF:
FROM COLUMBUS TO CATTLE FEEDLOTS

Although cattle have been domesticated for several thousand years, they have been in the New World only since 1493, when Columbus brought them along on his second expedition to the West Indies. During the succeeding decades, the Spanish brought cattle to Florida and Texas, where they thrived in the dry, hot climates. The French brought cattle to New France in the 1500s, establishing the first dairy and cheese facilities in North America.

The New World's desire for beef steadily grew from the 1500s to the early 1800s. By the mid-1800s, America's demand for beef outpaced the supply available from local family farms, and so cattle ranching was born. Based principally in the Southwest and West, ranchers used the open range to support large cattle herds. Texas longhorns, descended from the original Spanish cattle stock, were the animal of choice.

The first large cattle herd brought north to what is now Alberta arrived in the late 1870s. More quickly followed and, today, the foothills are still home to several large ranches. The herds today tend to be Hereford or Angus based; cross-breeding with Charolais, Limousin, Simmental and many other breeds enhances quality and production efficiencies.

Organ Meats

Several organ meats are used in food service operations. This group of products is known as **offal**. It includes the heart, kidney, tongue, tripe (stomach lining) and oxtail. Offal benefit from moist-heat cooking and are often used in soup, stew or braised dishes.

Offal— *also called variety meats, edible entrails (for example, the heart, kidneys, liver, sweetbreads and tongue) and extremities (for example, oxtail and pig's feet) of an animal.*

BUTCHERING PROCEDURES

Although many food service operations buy their beef previously cut and portioned, you still should be able to fabricate cuts of beef and perform basic butchering tasks.

BASIC PROCEDURE FOR CUTTING A STRIP LOIN STEAK FROM A BONELESS STRIP LOIN

1. Square up the strip loin by trimming off the lip so it extends 1 to 2 inches (2.5 to 5 cm) from the eye muscle.

2. Turn the strip over and trim off any fat or connective tissue.

3. Turn the strip back over and trim the fat covering to a uniform thickness of 1/4 inch (0.5 cm).

4. Cut the steaks to the thickness or weight desired.

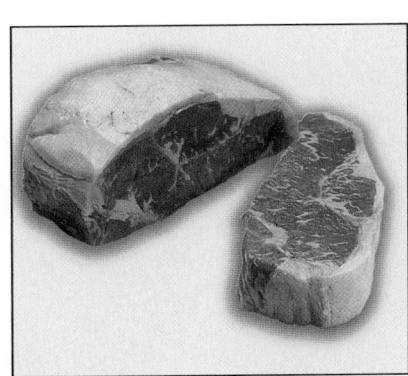

5. The eye meat of steaks located on the sirloin end of the strip is divided by a strip of connective tissue. Steaks cut from this area are called vein steaks and are inferior to steaks cut from the rib end of the strip.

BASIC PROCEDURE FOR TRIMMING A FULL BEEF TENDERLOIN AND CUTTING IT INTO CHATEAUBRIAND, FILET MIGNON AND TENDER TIPS

1. Cut and pull the excess fat from the entire tenderloin to expose the meat.

2. Remove the chain muscle from the side of the tenderloin. (Although it contains much connective tissue, the chain muscle may be trimmed and the meat used as tenderloin trimmings in various dishes.)

3. Trim away all the fat and silverskin. Do so by loosening a small piece of silverskin, then, holding the loosened silverskin tightly with one hand, cut it away in long strips, angling the knife up towards the silverskin slightly so that only the silverskin is removed and no meat is wasted.

4. Cut the tenderloin as desired into (left to right) tips, chateaubriand, filet mignon, tournedo tips, and tenderloin tips.

BASIC PROCEDURE FOR BUTTERFLYING MEATS

Many cuts of boneless meats such as tenderloin steaks and boneless pork chops can be butterflied to create a thinner cut that has a greater surface area and cooks more quickly.

1. Make the first cut nearly all the way through the meat, keeping it attached by leaving approximately 1/4 inch (0.5 cm) uncut.

2. Make a second cut, this time cutting all the way through, completely removing the steak from the tenderloin. Flatten the meat to achieve uniform thickness.

TABLE 13.1 USING COMMON CUTS OF BEEF

Primal	Subprimal or Fabricated Cut	IMPS	Cooking Methods	Serving Suggestions
Square Chuck	Chuck roll tied	116A	Combination (braise; stew)	Pot roast; beef stew
	Stew meat	135A	Combination (stew)	Beef stew
	Ground beef	136	Dry heat (broil or grill; roast)	Hamburgers; meatloaf
			Combination (braise; stew)	Chili con carne; beef stews
Point Brisket and Shank	Brisket	120	Moist heat (simmer)	Corned beef; New England boiled dinner
			Combination (braise)	Pot roast
	Shank	117	Combination (braise)	Shredded beef for tamales or hash
Rib	Oven ready rib roast	109	Dry heat (roast)	Roast prime rib
	Rib eye roll	112	Dry heat (roast)	Roast rib eye
Plate	Skirt steak	121D	Dry heat (broil or grill)	Steak; fajitas
	Short ribs	123A	Combination (braise)	Braised short ribs
Short Loin	Porterhouse or T-bone steaks	173, 174	Dry heat (broil or grill)	Steaks
	Strip loin	180	Dry heat (broil or grill; roast; sauté)	Strip loin steak; minute steak entrecôtes bordelaise
	Tenderloin	189	Dry heat (broil or grill; roast)	Tournedos Rossini; beef Wellington
Flank	Flank steak	193	Dry heat (broil or grill)	London broil
			Combination (braise)	Braised stuffed flank steak
Hip	Ponderosa hip	164A	Dry heat (roast)	Roast beef
	Top (inside) round	168	Dry heat (roast)	Roast beef
			Combination (braise)	Braised beef roulade

CONCLUSION

Antonin Carême once said that "beef is the soul of cooking." It is also the most popular meat consumed in Canada and undoubtedly will play an important role on almost any menu. Beef's assertive flavour stands up well to most any sauce and seasonings.

Prefabricated products are readily available. In fact, voluntary package labelling conventions adopted by the beef industry in 1998 (such as "grilling steak" instead of just "steak") will make it easier for consumers to know how to cook the various cuts available at the meat counter. But performing some basic fabrication procedures in your own kitchen saves money and allows you to cut the meat to your exact specifications. Each primal and subprimal cut has its own distinct characteristics. The primal rib, short loin and sirloin produce the most popular and most expensive cuts of beef. Once the beef is properly fabricated, choose the appropriate dry-heat, moist-heat or combination cooking method for that cut.

QUESTIONS FOR DISCUSSION

1. List each beef primal cut and describe its location on the carcass. For each primal cut, identify two subprimal or fabricated cuts taken from it.

2. Would it be better to use the chuck for grilling or stewing? Explain your answer.

3. Which fabricated cuts contain a portion of the tenderloin? What cooking methods are best suited for these cuts? Explain your answer.

4. Name four cuts that can be produced from a whole beef tenderloin. Describe a preparation procedure for each cut.

5. Most steaks are cut from the hindquarter. What popular steak is cut from the forequarter, and why is it tender when other cuts from the forequarter are relatively tough?

ADDITIONAL BEEF RECIPES

RECIPE 13.1

MARINATED LONDON BROIL

Yield: 6 5–8 oz. (150–250-g) Servings   **Method:** Grilling

Marinade:		
Olive oil	4 oz.	120 mL
Balsamic vinegar	4 oz.	120 mL
Fresh rosemary, chopped	2 Tbsp.	30 mL
Garlic, minced	2 oz.	60 g
Pepper	1 tsp.	5 mL
Beef flank steak, 2–3 lb. (1 to 1.5 kg)	1	1

Approximate values per 8 oz. (240 g) serving:

Calories	470
Total fat	23 g
Saturated fat	10 g
Cholesterol	152 mg
Sodium	188.24 mg
Total carbohydrates	0 g
Protein	61.46 g
Iron	40%

1. Combine the marinade ingredients in a hotel pan.
2. Add the flank steak to the marinade and coat completely. Allow the meat to marinate for at least 4 hours.
3. Grill the steak rare to medium rare. If cooked further, the meat will become extremely tough.
4. Carve into 1/4-inch-thick (0.5 cm) slices, cutting diagonally across the grain.

RECIPE 13.2

CHATEAUBRIAND

Yield: 2 Servings   **Method:** Roasting

Beef filet, cut from the "head" of the tenderloin, 16–24 ounces (500–750 g)	1	1
Salt and pepper	TT	TT
Clarified butter	as needed	as needed

1. Tie the beef with butcher's twine and season with salt and pepper.
2. Sauté the beef in clarified butter until it is well browned.
3. Transfer the beef to a 450°F (230°C) oven and roast until done, approximately 10–12 minutes for rare (internal temperature of 125°F/52°C), or 15–18 minutes for medium (140°F/60°C).

4. Remove the beef from the oven and allow it to rest for at least 5 minutes before carving.

5. At service time, slice the beef evenly on a slight diagonal bias.

Chateaubriand is traditionally served with béarnaise sauce and a bouquetiére of vegetables.

◆◆◆

RECIPE 13.3
HOME-STYLE MEATLOAF

Yield: 16 8-oz. (250-g) Servings   **Method:** Baking

Onion, small dice	1 lb.	450 g
Celery, small dice	8 oz.	250 g
Garlic, chopped	2 Tbsp.	30 mL
Oil	2 oz.	60 mL
Fresh bread crumbs	6 oz.	180 g
Tomato juice	12 oz.	350 mL
Ground beef	4 lb.	1.8 kg
Ground pork	4 lb.	1.8 kg
Eggs, beaten	6	6
Salt	1 Tbsp.	15 mL
Pepper	1 tsp.	5 mL
Parsley, chopped	2 Tbsp.	30 mL

1. Sauté the onions, celery and garlic in the oil until tender. Remove from the heat and cool.

2. Combine all ingredients; mix well.

3. Form into loaves of the desired size or place in loaf pans.

4. Bake at 350°F (180°C) until the meatloaf reaches an internal temperature of 165°F (74°C), approximately 1 to 1-1/2 hours.

5. Allow the loaves to rest 15 minutes before slicing. Cut slices of the desired thickness and serve with a tomato or mushroom sauce.

◆◆◆

RECIPE 13.4
CLAVEL OF BEEF WITH TRUFFLED POTATO RISOTTO AND SHIITAKE BREAD PUDDING

SEASONS IN THYME, SUMMERSIDE, PEI
Stefan Czapalay, Chef-Owner

Yield: 2 Servings   **Method:** Pan Roasting

Fillet of beef, 4 oz. (120 g) each	2	2
Clarified butter	2 oz.	50 mL
Salt and pepper	TT	TT
Button mushrooms, sliced	8	8
Shallot, small, sliced	1	1
Garlic clove, minced	1	1
Morel mushrooms, whole	4	4
Chanterelle mushrooms, whole	4	4
Dry red wine	2-1/2 oz.	75 mL

Continued

Approximate values per 10 oz. (300 g) serving:

Calories	705
Total fat	40 g
Saturated fat	18 g
Cholesterol	270 mg
Sodium	1350 mg
Total carbohydrates	1 g
Protein	80 g
Vitamin A	13%
Iron	66%

Approximate values per 10 oz. (300 g) serving:

Calories	755
Total fat	50 g
Saturated fat	19 g
Cholesterol	275 mg
Sodium	667 mg
Total carbohydrates	11 g
Protein	60 g
Iron	32%

Stefan Czapalay
Named provincial Chef of the Year in 1997, Stefan is the chef-owner of Seasons in Thyme restaurant in Summerside, where the menu expresses his delight in the local seafood. His other company, Canadian Cold Water, produces flavoured oils, including the flagship creation, Lobster Oil.

Star anise, crushed	1	1
Chicken stock	2-1/2 oz.	75 mL
Beef stock	2-1/2 oz.	75 mL
Veal stock	2-1/2 oz.	75 mL
Yellow-flesh potatoes, medium, peeled, brunoise	2	2
Gastrique (caramelized sugar deglazed with vinegar)	5 tsp.	25 mL
Truffle oil	3 tsp.	15 mL
Bread Pudding:		
Shiitake mushrooms, sliced	4	4
Salt-free butter	1 oz.	30 g
Egg, large	1	1
Egg yolk	1	1
Cream, 35%	2 oz.	55 mL
Truffle oil	3 tsp.	15 mL
Dry bread, cubed	1 oz.	30 g
Salt and pepper	TT	TT

1. Cut a hollow in the centre of the beef fillets to make doughnuts. Salt and pepper the beef then sear it in the clarified butter in a hot skillet. Remove the beef after it has been seared on both sides, then add the button mushrooms, shallot and garlic and cook until golden in colour. Add the morels, chanterelles and red wine. Reduce until almost dry and add the anise, stocks and the blanched brunoise potatoes. Reduce by half and add the gastrique and truffle oil. Stir until slightly thickened, then add salt and pepper to taste and reserve in a warm area.

2. To make the Bread Pudding, sauté shiitake mushrooms in butter until golden. Combine the egg and egg yolk with cream and truffle oil. Mix with the bread, season mixture with salt and pepper and let stand for 10 minutes. Place in buttered ramequin dishes and bake at 350°F (175°C) for 15 minutes in a water bath.

3. Fill the centre of the fillet doughnut with the bread pudding and place in a 275°F (185°C) oven for five minutes, or until fillet is medium rare. Allow to rest 5 minutes and serve on the potato risotto. Alternatively, cut a wedge out of the fillet at its front for presentation and place bouquet of colourful vegetables behind.

Approximate values per serving:

Calories	1030
Total fat	54 g
Saturated fat	26 g
Cholesterol	189 mg
Sodium	699 mg
Total carbohydrates	89 g
Protein	45 g

◆◆◆

RECIPE 13.5
MINUTE STEAK DIJONNAISE

Yield: 2 Servings   **Method:** Sautéing

Sirloin steak, trimmed, 6 oz. (170 g)	2	2
Dijon mustard	1 oz.	30 mL
Onion, small dice	2 oz.	60 g
Clarified butter	1 oz.	30 mL
Cream, 35%	3 oz.	90 mL
Whole butter	1 oz.	30 g
Salt and pepper	TT	TT

1. Pound the steaks to a 1/4-inch (0.5 cm) thickness.

2. Cover one side of each sirloin first with 1-1/2 teaspoons (8 mL) of the mustard and then half the onions, pressing the onions firmly into the steak.

3. Sauté the steaks in the clarified butter, presentation (onion) side down first. Remove and hold in a warm place.

4. Degrease the pan. Add the cream and reduce by half. Add the rest of the Dijon mustard.

5. Monter au beurre. Adjust the seasonings and serve the steaks with the sauce.

Approximate values per serving:

Calories	671
Total fat	45 g
Saturated fat	23 g
Cholesterol	255 mg
Sodium	2050 mg
Total carbohydrates	6 g
Protein	60 g
Vitamin A	36%
Iron	44%

◆◆◆

RECIPE 13.6

BEEF STROGANOFF

Yield: 8 8-oz. (250-g) Servings   **Method:** Sautéing

Tenderloin tips, émincé	2 lb.	1 kg
Clarified butter	1-1/2 oz.	45 mL
Onion, small dice or julienne	4 oz.	120 g
Paprika	5 Tbsp.	30 g
Mushrooms, sliced	1 lb.	450 g
Red wine	4 oz.	120 mL
Demi-glace	10 oz.	300 mL
Sour cream	8 oz.	250 mL
Dill pickle, julienne	1 cup	150 g
Fresh parsley, chopped	1 Tbsp.	15 mL
Salt and pepper	TT	TT
Egg noodles, cooked	24 oz.	700 g

1. Sauté the tenderloin tips in the butter, searing on all sides. Remove the meat and set aside.

2. Add the onion to the pan and sauté lightly then add paprika and sweat. Add the mushrooms and sauté until soft.

3. Deglaze with red wine.

4. Add the demi-glace. Bring to a boil, reduce to a simmer and cook 5 minutes.

5. Add the sour cream, dill pickle and any meat juices that accumulated while holding the meat.

6. Return the meat to the sauce to reheat. Stir in the parsley. Adjust the seasonings and serve over egg noodles.

Approximate values per serving:

Calories	635
Total fat	39 g
Saturated fat	20 g
Cholesterol	201 mg
Sodium	510 mg
Total carbohydrates	32 g
Protein	40 g
Vitamin A	41%
Iron	46%
Calcium	11%

◆◆◆

RECIPE 13.7

ENTRECÔTES BORDELAISE

Yield: 4 Servings   **Method:** Sautéing

Beef marrow	2 oz.	60 g
Strip loin steak, 7 oz. (200–225 g) each	4	4
Salt and pepper	TT	TT
Clarified butter	2 oz.	60 mL
Shallots, chopped	2 Tbsp.	30 mL
Red wine	8 oz.	250 mL
Demi-glace	12 oz.	340 mL
Whole butter	1 oz.	30 g

1. Slice the marrow into rounds and poach in salt water for 3 minutes. Drain the marrow and set it aside.

2. Season the steaks and sauté in the clarified butter to the desired doneness. Finish in the oven if desired. Remove to a platter and hold in a warm place.

Continued

3. Sauté the shallots in the same pan.

4. Deglaze the pan with the wine and reduce by half. Add the demi-glace; simmer for 5 minutes.

5. Monter au beurre.

6. Add the marrow to the sauce. Adjust the seasonings and serve the steaks with the sauce.

◆◆◆

RECIPE 13.8

PEPPER STEAK

Yield: 2 Servings   **Method:** Sautéing

Boneless strip steaks, approx. 8 oz. (250 g) each	2	2
Salt	TT	TT
Peppercorns, cracked	3 Tbsp.	45 mL
Clarified butter	1 oz.	30 mL
Cognac	1 oz.	30 mL
Cream, 35%	4 oz.	120 mL
Meat glaze	1 oz.	30 mL
Whole butter	2 oz.	60 g

1. Season the steaks with salt. Spread the peppercorns in a hotel pan and press the steaks into them, lightly coating each side.

2. Sauté the steaks in the clarified butter over high heat for 2 to 3 minutes on each side.

3. Remove the pan from the heat. Pour the cognac over the steaks, return the pan to the heat and flambé. When the flames subside, remove the steaks from the pan and keep them warm on a plate.

4. Add the cream and meat glaze to the pan. Bring to a boil and reduce for 2 minutes over high heat; monter au beurre. Pour this sauce over the steaks and serve immediately.

◆◆◆

RECIPE 13.9

SWISS STEAK

Yield: 10 Servings   **Method:** Braising

Beef bottom round steaks, 6 oz. (180 g) each	10	10
Flour	as needed	as needed
Salt and pepper	TT	TT
Oil	2 oz.	60 mL
Onion, small dice	1 lb.	450 g
Garlic cloves, crushed	3	3
Celery	8 oz.	250 g
Flour	4 oz.	120 g
Brown stock	5 pt.	2.2 L
Tomato purée	6 oz.	180 mL
Sachet:		
Bay leaves	2	2
Dried thyme	1/2 tsp.	2 mL
Peppercorns, crushed	1/2 tsp.	2 mL
Parsley stems	8	8

1. Dredge the steaks in flour seasoned with salt and pepper.
2. Heat the oil in a brazier and brown the steaks well on both sides. Remove the steaks.
3. Add the onions, garlic and celery; sauté until tender.
4. Add the flour and cook to a brown roux.
5. Gradually add the brown stock, whisking until the sauce is thickened and smooth. Add the tomato purée and sachet.
6. Return the steaks to the braising pan, cover and cook in a 300°F (150°C) oven until tender, approximately 2 hours.
7. Remove the steaks from the sauce. Discard the sachet. Strain the sauce and adjust the seasonings. Serve the steaks with the sauce.

Approximate values per serving:

Calories	601
Total fat	26 g
Saturated fat	7 g
Cholesterol	170 mg
Sodium	390 mg
Total carbohydrates	30 g
Protein	61 g
Vitamin A	49%
Vitamin C	12%
Iron	52%

◆◆◆

RECIPE 13.10
BRAISED SHORT RIBS OF BEEF

Yield: 8 8-oz. (240-g) Servings   **Method:** Braising

Flour	4 oz.	120 g
Salt	1 Tbsp.	15 mL
Pepper	1 tsp.	5 mL
Dried rosemary	1/2 tsp.	2 mL
Short ribs of beef,		
cut in 2-inch (5-cm) portions	6 lbs.	2.7 kg
Vegetable oil	1 oz.	30 mL
Onion, chopped	6 oz.	170 g
Celery, chopped	4 oz.	120 g
Brown beef stock	24 oz.	700 mL
Roux	as needed	as needed
Salt and pepper	TT	TT

1. Combine the flour, salt, pepper and rosemary. Dredge the ribs in the seasoned flour.
2. Heat the oil and brown the ribs well in a heavy brazier. Remove and hold in a warm place.
3. Add the vegetables to the brazier and sauté lightly.
4. Return the ribs to the pan, add the stock and braise in an oven until done, approximately 2-1/2 hours.
5. Remove the ribs from the liquid and skim off the excess fat.
6. Bring the liquid to a boil on the stove top; thicken it with roux to the desired consistency and simmer 15 minutes. Strain the sauce and adjust the seasonings. Return the ribs to the sauce and simmer for 5 minutes.

Approximate values per serving:

Calories	1150
Total fat	70 g
Saturated fat	27 g
Cholesterol	320 mg
Sodium	1154 mg
Total carbohydrates	18 g
Protein	110 g
Vitamin A	18%
Iron	85%

◆◆◆

RECIPE 13.11
HUNGARIAN-STYLE BEEF GOULASH

Yield: 12 8-oz. (250-mL) Servings   **Method:** Stewing

Onion, fine dice	2 lb. 12 oz.	1.3 kg
Lard or vegetable oil	8 oz.	250 mL
Beef stewing meat,		
cut in 1-inch (2.5-cm) cubes	5 lb.	2.2 kg
Hungarian paprika	1 cup	115 g
Garlic, chopped	1/2 cup	100 g

Continued

Caraway seeds, chopped	1 tsp.	5 mL
Tomato paste	4 oz.	120 mL
Marjoram, crushed	2 tsp	10 mL
Lemon zest, finely chopped	1 Tbsp.	15 mL
Bay leaf	1/2	1/2
Water	2 cup	500 mL
White vinegar	1/4 cup	50 mL
White stock	4 qt.	4 L
Salt	TT	TT
Pepper	1/2 tsp.	2 mL

Approximate values per 12 oz. (360 g) serving:

Calories	645
Total fat	32 g
Saturated fat	12 g
Cholesterol	235 mg
Sodium	910 mg
Total carbohydrates	13 g
Protein	73 g
Vitamin A	28%
Vitamin C	20%
Iron	63%

1. Sauté the onions in the lard or oil, browning lightly.
2. Add meat and sear.
3. Add the paprika, garlic, caraway seeds, tomato paste, marjoram, lemon zest and bay leaf. Stir well.
4. Add the water and vinegar and stir well.
5. Add the white stock. Bring to a boil, then reduce to a simmer.
6. Braise until the meat is very tender, approximately 1-1/2 hours. Adjust the seasonings and skim off excess fat.

◆◆◆

RECIPE 13.12

BEEF BOURGUIGNON

Yield: 10 8-oz. (250-g) Servings   **Method:** Stewing

Marinade:		
Garlic cloves, crushed	3	3
Onions, sliced	3	3
Carrots, sliced	2	2
Parsley stalks	10	10
Bouquet garni:		
Carrot stick, 4 in. (10 cm)	1	1
Leek, split, 4-in. (10-cm) piece	1	1
Fresh thyme	1 sprig	1 sprig
Bay leaf	1	1
Peppercorns, crushed	10	10
Salt	TT	TT
Dry red wine, preferably Burgundy	26 oz.	750 mL
Beef chuck, cubed for stew	4 lb.	1.8 kg
Vegetable oil	2 oz.	60 mL
Flour	2 Tbsp.	30 mL
Tomato paste	1 Tbsp.	15 mL
Tomatoes, quartered	4	4
Brown stock	1 pint	450 mL
Mushrooms, quartered	1 lb.	450 g
Unsalted butter	1-1/2 oz.	45 g
Pearl onions, boiled and peeled	30	30
Lardons of lean double smoked bacon	8 oz.	250 g
Salt and pepper	TT	TT

1. Combine the garlic, onions, carrots, parsley, bouquet garni, peppercorns, salt and wine to make a marinade.
2. Marinate the meat several hours under refrigeration.
3. Remove and drain the meat. Reserve the marinade.
4. Dry the beef and sauté it in the oil until well browned. Do this in several batches if necessary.

5. Return all the meat to the pot. Sprinkle with flour and cook to make a blond roux.

6. Stir in the tomato paste and cook for 5 minutes.

7. Add the reserved marinade, tomatoes and brown stock. Cook in a 350°F (180°C) oven until the meat is tender, approximately 2-1/2 hours.

8. Remove the meat from the sauce. Strain the sauce through a china cap, pressing to extract all of the liquid. Discard the solids. Return the liquid and beef to the pot.

9. Sauté the mushrooms in the butter and add them to the meat and sauce. Lightly sauté the lardons and add to stew. Add the onions and adjust the seasonings. Simmer for 10 minutes to blend the flavours.

Approximate values per 8 oz. (240 g) serving:	
Calories	315
Total fat	15 g
Saturated fat	6.5 g
Cholesterol	97 mg
Sodium	640 mg
Total carbohydrates	8 g
Protein	30 g
Vitamin A	27%
Vitamin C	13%
Iron	26%

=== ◆◆◆ ===

RECIPE 13.13

CHILI CON CARNE

Yield: 1 gal. (4 L)   **Method:** Braising

Onion, medium dice	1 lb.	450 g
Vegetable oil	1 Tbsp.	15 mL
Garlic, chopped	1/2 oz.	15 g
Ground beef or 1/2-inch (1-cm) diced round	2 lb. 8 oz.	1.2 kg
Tomato, crushed	2 lb.	1 kg
Tomato, diced	4 lb.	1.8 kg
Tomato paste	4 oz.	120 mL
Brown stock	1 pt.	450 mL
Chili powder	1 oz.	30 g
Cumin	2 tsp.	10 mL
Bay leaves	4	4
Salt and pepper	TT	TT
Dry kidney beans, soaked and simmered in water until tender	12 oz.	350 g

1. Sauté the onions in the oil until tender. Add the garlic and sauté 1 minute.

2. Add the beef and brown, stirring occasionally. Drain off the excess fat.

3. Add the remaining ingredients, bring to a simmer, cover and cook for 1 hour or until meat is tender.

4. Remove the bay leaves and adjust the seasonings and consistency (cornmeal will add body).

NOTE: Purists will argue that beans should not be in chili con carne.

Approximate values per 10 oz. (300 g) serving:	
Calories	310
Total fat	16 g
Saturated fat	6 g
Cholesterol	62 mg
Sodium	535 mg
Total carbohydrates	19 g
Protein	21 g
Vitamin A	20%
Vitamin C	44%
Iron	32%
Calcium	93%

𝒲EBLINKS

Beef Information Centre (Mississauga)
   www.beefinfo.org/

Beef Information Centre (Vancouver)
   www.corpinfohub.com/bic/
   bic.htm

Canada Beef Export Federation
   www.cbef.com/

Food Institute of Canada's FoodNet:
   Beef Recipes, Section 1
   foodnet.fic.ca/recipes/beef1.html

Food Institute of Canada's FoodNet:
   Beef Recipes, Section 2
   foodnet.fic.ca/recipes/beef2.html

Searchable Online Archive of Recipes:
   Beef Recipes
   SOAR.berkeley.edu/recipes/meat/
   beef/

CHAPTER 14 VEAL

After studying this chapter you will be able to:

♦ identify the primal, subprimal and fabricated cuts of veal
♦ perform basic butchering procedures: boning a leg of veal, cutting and pounding cutlets, cutting émincé, boning a veal loin, tying meats, cleaning and pressing sweetbreads, cleaning calves' liver, cleaning veal kidneys
♦ apply appropriate cooking methods to several common cuts of veal

ows must calve before they begin to give milk. These calves are the basis of today's veal industry. Veal is the meat of calves under the age of three months. Most veal comes from calves slaughtered when they are ten to twelve weeks old, however. Veal is lighter in colour than beef, has a more delicate flavour and is generally more tender. Young veal has a firm texture, light pink colour and very little fat. As soon as a calf starts eating solid food, the iron in the food begins to turn the young animal's meat red. Meat from calves slaughtered when they are older than three months is called calf. It tends to be a deeper red, with some marbling and external fat.

Veal's low fat content makes it a popular meat, especially among those looking for an alternative to beef. Its delicate flavour is complemented by both classic and modern sauces.

PRIMAL AND SUBPRIMAL CUTS OF VEAL

After slaughter, the calf carcass can be split down the backbone into two bilateral halves or, more typically, cut along the natural curvature between the eleventh and twelfth ribs into a front and a hindsaddle (rear portion). The veal carcass yields four primal cuts: one from the front (made up of the shoulder, foreshank and breast), and three from the hindsaddle (the loin, leg and flank). The veal shoulder, rib and loin may contain both bilateral portions; that is, a veal loin may contain both sides of the animal's loin.

Figure 14.1 shows the relationship between the calf's bone structure and the primal cuts. As with all meats, it is important to know the location of bones when cutting or working with veal. This makes meat fabrication and carving easier and aids in identifying cuts. Figure 14.2 shows the primal cuts of veal and their location. A veal carcass weighs in a range of 60 to 245 pounds (27–110 kg).

Front/Shoulder

Similar to the beef shoulder or chuck, the veal shoulder accounts for 21% of carcass weight. It contains four rib bones (as opposed to five in the beef chuck) and portions of the backbone, blade and arm bones.

The backbone, blade and arm bones are sometimes removed and the meat roasted or stuffed and roasted. Although shoulder chops and steaks can be fabricated, they are inferior to the chops cut from more tender areas such as the loin or rib. Often the shoulder meat is ground or cubed for stew. Because of the relatively large amount of connective tissue it contains, meat from the shoulder is best braised or stewed.

Foreshank and Breast

The foreshank and breast are located beneath the shoulder and part of the rib section on the front half of the carcass. The shank is generally purchased separately as is the breast. Combined, they account for approximately 16% of carcass weight. This section contains rib bones and rib cartilage, breast bones and shank bones. Because the calf is slaughtered young, many of the breast bones are cartilaginous rather than bony.

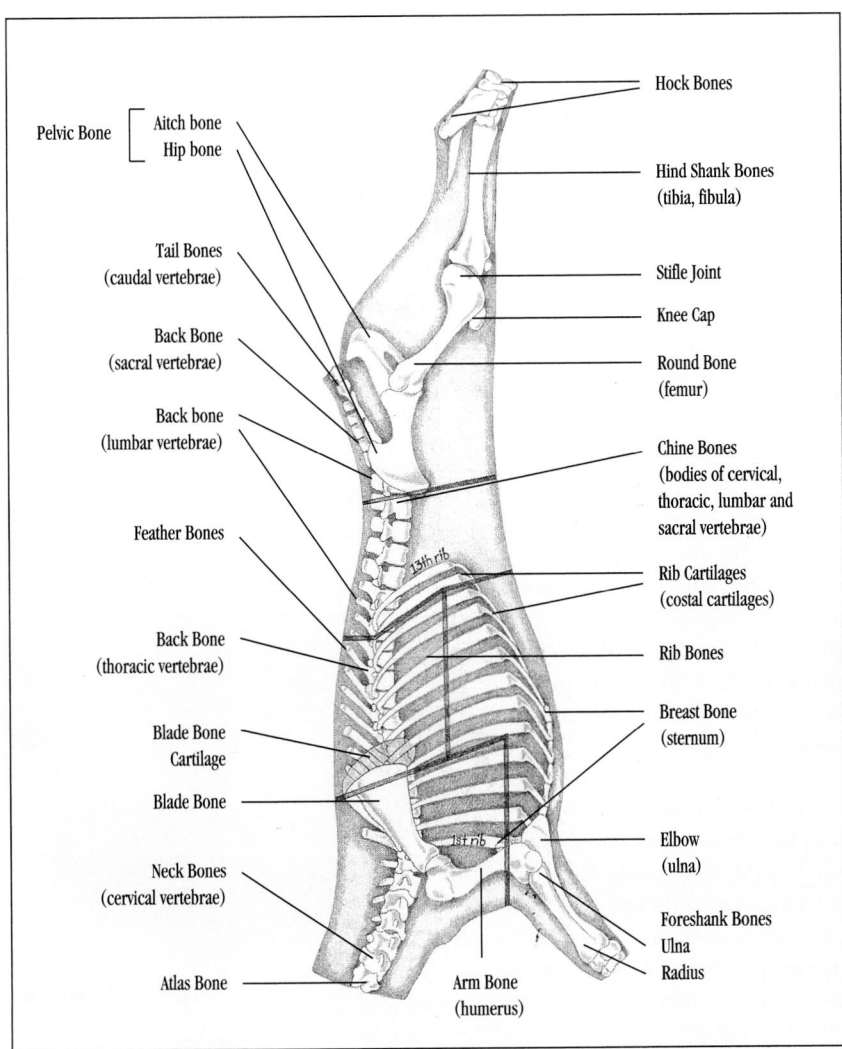

FIGURE 14.1   *The Skeletal Structure of a Calf*

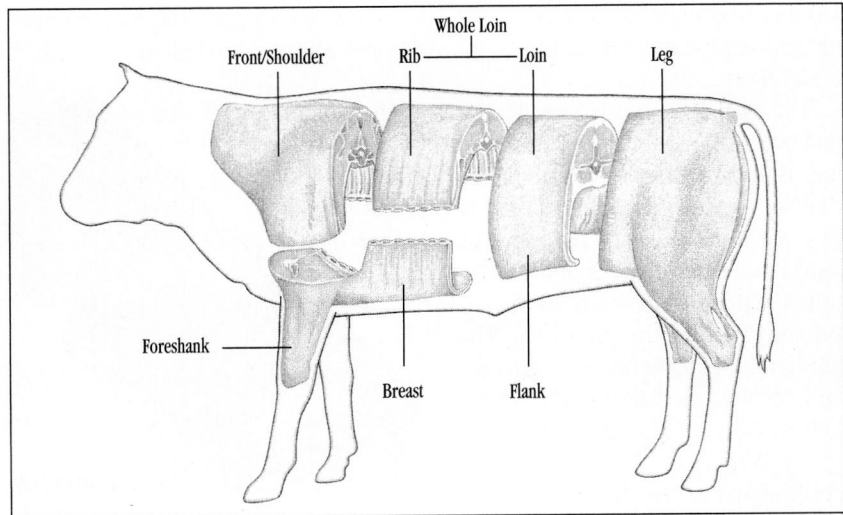

FIGURE 14.2   *The Primal Cuts of Veal*

This cartilage, as well as the ample fat and connective tissue also present in the breast, breaks down during long moist cooking, thus making the flavourful breast a good choice for braising. Veal breast can also be cubed for stews such as veal fricassee and veal blanquette, rolled and stuffed, or trimmed and ground.

The foreshank is also very flavourful but tough. It can be braised whole or sliced perpendicular to the shank bone and braised to produce osso buco.

Whole Loin

The primal whole loin contains the ribs and loin sections of the carcass. When purchased whole, it is often fabricated into chops although it may be boned for roasting or preparing loin cutlets.

Rib

The double rib, also known as a veal hotel rack, is a very tender, relatively small cut accounting for approximately 9% of carcass weight. It is very popular and very expensive. The double rack consists of two racks, each with seven rib bones and a portion of the backbone.

Veal racks can be roasted either whole or split into two sides. Veal racks can be boned out; each side produces a veal rib eye and a small piece of tenderloin known as the short tenderloin, both of which make excellent roasts. More often, veal racks are trimmed and cut into chops, which can also be bone-in or boneless, to be grilled, sautéed or braised.

Veal Hotel Rack, Split

Loin

The veal loin is posterior to the primal rib, contains two ribs (numbers 12 and 13) and accounts for approximately 10% of carcass weight. The loin consists of the loin eye muscle on top of the rib bones and the tenderloin under them.

The veal loin eye is very tender and the tenderloin is, without a doubt, the most tender cut of veal. If the veal loin is separated from the primal leg before the tenderloin is removed, the tenderloin will be cut into two pieces. The small portion (short tenderloin) remains in the loin and the large portion (butt tenderloin) remains in the sirloin portion of the primal leg. The tenderloin is sometimes removed and cut into medallions. The veal loin is often cut into chops, bone-in or boneless. It is usually cooked using dry heat such as broiling, grilling, roasting or sautéing.

Veal Loin

Loin Chops

Boneless Strip Loin

Leg

The primal veal leg consists of both the sirloin and the leg. Together they account for approximately 42% of carcass weight. The primal leg is separated from the loin by a cut perpendicular to the backbone immediately anterior to the hip bone, and it contains portions of the backbone, tail bone, hip bone, aitch bone, round bone and hind shank.

Veal Leg

Although it is tender enough to be roasted whole, the veal leg is typically fabricated into cutlets. To fabricate this cut, the leg is first broken down into its major muscles: the top round, eye round, knuckle, sirloin, bottom round (which includes the sirloin) and butt tenderloin. Each of these muscles can be reduced to cutlets by trimming all fat and visible connective tissue and slicing against the grain to the desired thickness. The cutlets then should be pounded carefully to tenderize them further and to prevent them from curling when cooked.

The hindshank is somewhat meatier than the foreshank but both are prepared and cooked in the same manner.

Because the veal carcass is small enough to be handled easily, it is sometimes purchased in forms larger than the primal cuts described above. Depending on employee skill, available equipment and storage space and an ability to utilize fully all the cuts and trimmings that fabricating meat produces, you may want to purchase veal in one of the following forms:

♦ *Foresaddle:* The anterior portion of the carcass after it is severed from the hindsaddle by a cut following the natural curvature between the eleventh and twelfth ribs. It contains the primal shoulder, foreshank and breast, and rib.

Top Round

♦ *Hindsaddle:* The posterior portion of the carcass after it is severed from the foresaddle. It contains the primal loin and leg.

♦ *Back:* The trimmed rib and loin sections in one piece. The back is particularly useful for producing large quantities of veal chops.

♦ *Veal side:* One bilateral half of the carcass, produced by cutting lengthwise through the backbone.

Hindshank Cut for Osso Buco

Organ Meats

Several calf organ meats are used in food service operations.

Sweetbreads

Sweetbreads are the thymus glands of veal and lamb. As an animal ages, its thymus gland shrinks; therefore sweetbreads are not available from older cattle or sheep. Veal sweetbreads are much more popular than lamb sweetbreads in this country. Good-quality sweetbreads should be plump and firm, with the exterior membrane intact. Delicately flavoured and tender, they can be prepared by almost any cooking method.

Sweetbreads

Calves' Liver

Calves' liver is much more popular than beef liver because of its tenderness and mild flavour. Good quality calves' liver should be firm and moist, with a shiny appearance and without any off-odour. It is most often sliced and sautéed or broiled and served with a sauce.

Calves' Liver

Kidneys

Kidneys

Kidneys are more popular in other parts of the world than in Canada. Good-quality kidneys should be plump, firm and encased in a shiny membrane. Properly prepared kidneys have a rich flavour and firm texture; they are best prepared by moist-heat cooking methods and are sometimes used in stew or kidney pie.

BUTCHERING PROCEDURES

Many food service operations purchase veal in primal or other large cuts and fabricate it in-house to their own specifications. There are several important veal fabrication and butchering techniques you should master.

BASIC PROCEDURE FOR BONING A LEG OF VEAL

1. Remove the shank by cutting through the knee joint. Remove the excess fat and flank meat.

2. Remove the butt tenderloin from the inside of the pelvic bone.

3. Remove the pelvic bone by carefully cutting around the bone, separating it from the meat. Continue until the bone is completely freed from the meat.

4. With the inside of the leg up, remove the top round by cutting along the natural seam.

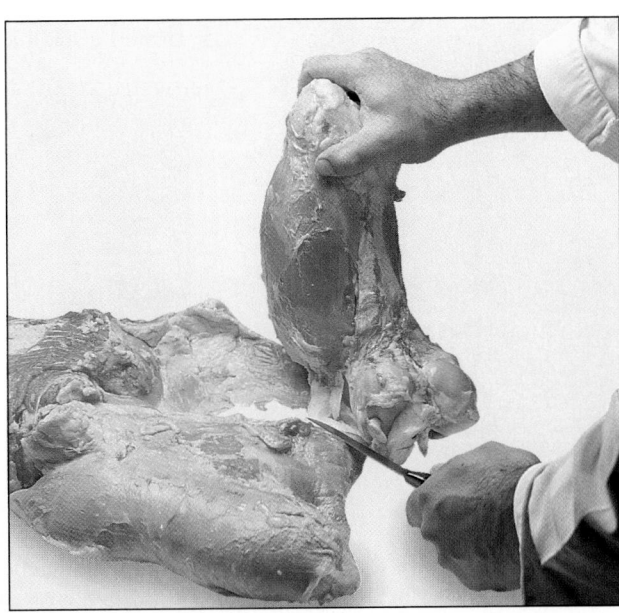

5. Remove the shank meat. (It is the round piece of meat lying between the eye round and the bone, on the shank end of the leg.)

6. Remove the round bone and the knuckle together by cutting around the bone and through the natural seams separating the knuckle from the other muscles. Separate the knuckle meat from the bone.

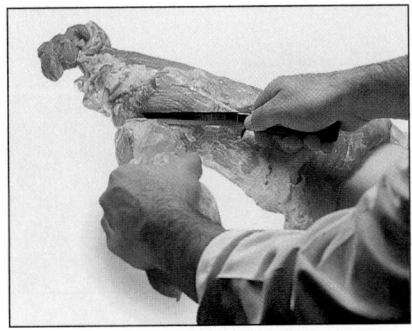

7. Remove the sirloin.

8. Remove the eye round from the bottom round.

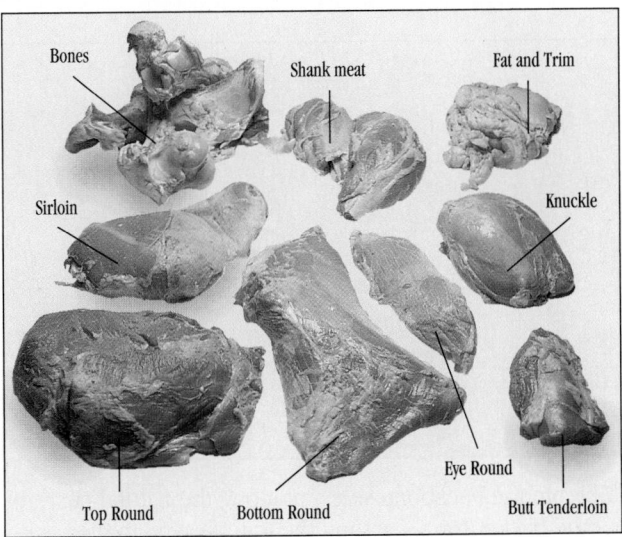

Bones   Shank meat   Fat and Trim

Sirloin   Knuckle

Top Round   Bottom Round   Eye Round   Butt Tenderloin

9. The completely boned-out veal leg, producing a top round, eye round, knuckle, shank meat, butt tenderloin, sirloin, bottom round bones and trimmings.

BASIC PROCEDURE FOR CUTTING AND POUNDING CUTLETS

1. Veal cutlets are cut from relatively large pieces of veal (here, a portion of the inside round). All fat and silverskin must be trimmed. Going against the grain, cut slices approximately 1/4 inch (0.5 cm) thick; cut on the bias to produce larger pieces.

2. Place the cutlets between two pieces of plastic wrap and pound lightly to flatten and tenderize the meat. Be careful not to tear or pound holes in the meat.

BASIC PROCEDURE FOR CUTTING ÉMINCÉ

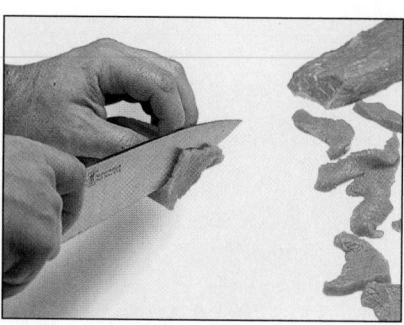

1. Émincé is cut from relatively small, lean pieces of meat. Here veal is cut across the grain into small, thin slices.

BASIC PROCEDURE FOR BONING A VEAL LOIN AND CUTTING IT INTO BONELESS VEAL CHOPS

1. Remove the tenderloin in a single piece from the inside of the loin by following the vertebrae and cutting completely around the tenderloin.

2. From the backbone side, cut along the natural curve of the backbone, separating the loin meat from the backbone.

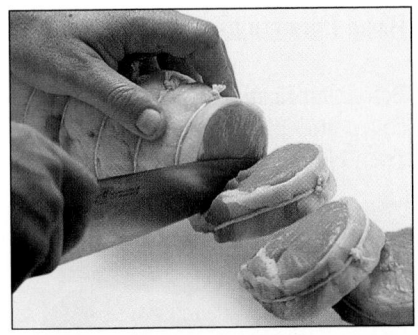

3. Trim any excess fat from the loin, and trim the flank to create a 3-inch (7.5-cm) lip. Tightly roll up the loin with the flank on the outside.

4. Tie the loin, using the procedure described below, at 1-inch (2.5-cm) intervals. Cut between the pieces of twine for individual boneless loin chops.

Basic Procedure for Tying (Trussing) Meats

Here we apply the tying procedure to a boneless veal loin; the same procedure can be used on any type of meat.

1. Cut a piece of string long enough to wrap completely around the loin. Holding one end between the thumb and forefinger, pass the other end around it and cross the strings. Loop the loose end of the string around your finger.

2. Wrap the string around itself and pass the loose end back through the hole (slip knot).

3. Pull to tighten the knot. Adjust the string so it is snug against the meat.

4. Loop one end of the string around your thumb and forefinger. Reach through with your thumb and forefinger and pull the other string back through the loop. Pull both strings to tighten the knot, thus preventing the first knot from loosening (half hitch). Trim the ends of the strings.

5. Continue in this fashion until the entire loin is tied. The strings should be tied at even intervals, just snug enough to hold the shape of the loin; they should not dig into or cut the meat.

BASIC PROCEDURE FOR CLEANING AND PRESSING SWEETBREADS

Before fabrication, you should submerge the sweetbreads in cold water and cover and place them in the refrigerator overnight to soak out any blood. Then blanch them in a court bouillon for 5 minutes.

1. Remove the sweetbreads from the poaching liquid and allow them to cool.

2. Using your hands, pull off any sinew or membranes that may be present on the surface of the sweetbreads.

3. Wrap the sweetbreads in cheese-cloth.

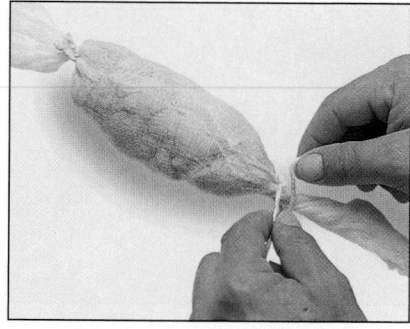

4. Tie the ends with butcher's twine.

5. Place the wrapped sweetbreads in a half hotel pan or similar container.

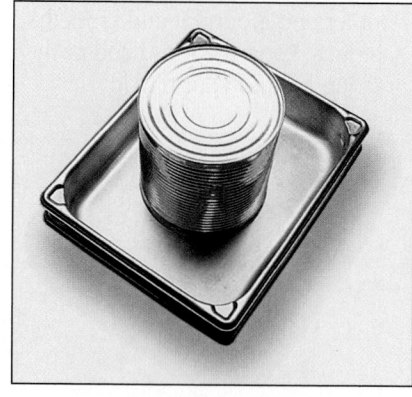

6. Place another half hotel pan on top of the sweetbreads; place a weight in the pan to press the sweetbreads. Pressing sweetbreads in this manner improves their texture.

Basic Procedure for Cleaning Calves' Liver

1. Trim the large sinew and outer membrane from the bottom of the liver.

2. Turn the liver over and peel the membrane off with your hands.

3. The liver can be cut into thick or thin slices as needed.

TABLE 14.1   USING COMMON CUTS OF VEAL

Primal	Subprimal or Fabricated Cut	Cooking Methods	Serving Suggestions
Front/ Shoulder	Cubed veal Ground veal	Combination (stew) Dry heat (broil or grill) Combination (braise)	Blanquette or fricassee Veal patties Stuffing; meatballs
Foreshank and breast	Foreshank Breast	Combination (braise) Combination (braise)	Osso buco Stuffed veal breast
Rib	Hotel rack	Dry heat (broil or grill; roast)	Grilled veal chop; roast veal with porcini mushrooms
	Rib chops	Dry heat (broil or grill) Combination (braise)	Grilled veal chop Braised veal chop with risotto
	Rib eye	Dry heat (broil or grill; roast) Combination (braise)	Broiled veal rib eye with chipotle sauce; roasted veal rib eye marchand de vin Braised rib eye
Loin	Veal loin	Dry heat (broil or grill; roast; sauté)	Roasted veal loin with wild mushrooms; Sautéed veal medallions with green peppercorn sauce
	Loin chops	Dry heat (broil or grill; sauté) Combination (braise)	Broiled or sautéed veal chops with mushroom sauce Braised veal chops Lyonnaise
	Boneless strip loin Veal tenderloin	Dry heat (broil or grill; roast; sauté) Dry heat (broil or grill; roast; sauté)	Roasted veal loin sauce poulette Grilled tenderloin; roasted tenderloin; sautéed tenderloin with garlic and herbs
Leg	Leg	Dry heat (roast; sauté) Combination (stew)	Veal scallopini Blanquette
	Inside round Outside round	Dry heat (roast; sauté) Dry heat (sauté) Combination (braise)	Veal marsala Sautéed cutlets with Calvados Stuffed veal cutlets
	Hindshank	Moist heat (simmer) Combination (braise)	Veal broth Osso buco
Offal	Sweetbreads	Dry heat (pan-fry; sauté) Combination (braise)	Sautéed sweetbreads beurre noisette Braised sweetbreads Madeira
	Calves' liver	Dry heat (broil or grill; sauté)	Broiled or sautéed calves' liver with onion and bacon
	Kidneys Tails	Combination (braise)	Kidney pie Soup and stock

BASIC PROCEDURE FOR CLEANING VEAL KIDNEYS

1. Split the kidneys lengthwise, exposing the fat and sinew.

2. With a sharp knife, trim away the fat and sinew. The kidney is now ready for cooking.

CONCLUSION

Although veal may not be as popular as beef or pork, it is versatile, easy to cook and adds variety to menus. Veal is much more delicately flavoured than beef, with a finer texture and lighter colour. Its flavour blends well with a variety of sauces and other ingredients without overpowering them. Veal can be cooked by almost any dry-heat, moist-heat or combination cooking method.

Veal quality varies greatly among purveyors. Purchase only from reputable companies to be sure you are receiving a consistently high-quality product. Because veal carcasses are relatively small, they are sometimes purchased as primal cuts for your further fabrication.

QUESTIONS FOR DISCUSSION

1. Compare and contrast the appearance and flavour of beef and veal.
2. What are the differences between formula-fed veal and free-range veal?
3. Describe two differences between a beef carcass and a veal carcass.
4. List each veal primal and describe its location on the carcass. For each primal, identify two subprimals or fabricated cuts taken from it.
5. Would it be better to use a veal loin for grilling or braising? Explain your answer.
6. What are veal sweetbreads? Describe how sweetbreads should be prepared for cooking.

*A*DDITIONAL *V*EAL *R*ECIPES

RECIPE 14.1

MIGNONS OF VEAL ON SPINACH WITH CRAYFISH

WESTIN PRINCE HOTEL, TORONTO, ON
Executive Chef Hans U. Herzig

Yield: 10 Portions (three mignons of veal and eight crayfish tails)

Method: Sautéing

Hans U. Herzig
Hans was born in Switzerland, trained in Europe, and came to Canada to work at the Windsor Arms in Toronto. Among the highlights of his career, he was captain of the Canadian team that won 10 gold medals in the 1988 World Culinary Olympics.

Crayfish tails	80	80
Fish stock	18 oz.	500 mL
Cream, 35%	18 oz.	500 mL
White wine	7 oz.	200 mL
Saffron	TT	TT
Salt and black pepper	TT	TT
Potatoes	8–10 oz.	250 g
Wild rice	2 oz.	50 g
Egg yolks	3	3
Butter	5 oz.	150 g
Nutmeg	TT	TT
Fresh spinach leaves	1 lb.	500 g
Shallots	1/2 oz.	15 g
Tomatoes	6	6
Chervil	TT	TT
Black trumpet mushrooms	2 oz.	50 g
Trimmed veal tenderloin, cut into 30 slices	2.2 lb.	1 kg

Approximate values per serving:

Calories	566
Total fat	39 g
Saturated fat	22 g
Cholesterol	290 mg
Sodium	334 mg
Total carbohydrates	11 g
Protein	39 g

1. Boil the crayfish. Remove the tails and peel them.

2. Reduce fish stock to half, add three-quarters of the cream and simmer slowly for about half an hour until sauce is reduced by half.

3. Add white wine. Add saffron, salt and pepper to taste. Add the rest of the cream and reduce until the sauce is of a consistency to coat the back of a spoon.

4. Boil the potatoes and rice them.

5. Cook the wild rice about 45 minutes. Add the rice to the potatoes along with egg yolks and a little of the butter. Mix together well and season with salt and a dash of nutmeg.

6. With two spoons, form quenelles (see Chapter 20, page 523) and poach them in either lightly salted water or chicken stock filling the pan to a depth of about 2 inches (5 cm).

7. Blanch the spinach and allow to cool. Sauté in remaining butter with the shallots.

8. Fillet the tomatoes and quickly sauté them with a little chopped chervil and the black trumpet mushrooms.

9. Season veal mignons with salt and pepper and sauté.

10. Put a ladle of sauce on a serving plate and put some spinach in the centre. Place three mignons on top and garnish with the sautéed tomatoes, chervil and mushrooms.

11. Place four wild rice quenelles on the plate and arrange the preheated crayfish tails, each garnished with a chervil leaf.

◆◆◆

RECIPE 14.2

ROSEMARY-ROASTED VEAL CHOPS WITH PORCINI MUSHROOMS

THE FOUR SEASONS, NEW YORK, NY
Chef Christian Albin

Yield: 4 Servings

Method: Roasting

Veal chops, 12–14 oz. (350–400 g) each	4	4
Salt and pepper	TT	TT
Fresh rosemary	4 sprigs	4 sprigs
Flour	as needed	as needed
Paprika	TT	TT
Clarified butter	4 oz.	120 mL
White wine	4 oz.	120 mL
Brown veal stock	1 pt.	450 mL
Unsalted butter	2 oz.	60 g

Approximate values per serving:

Calories	1138
Total fat	67 g
Saturated fat	31 g
Cholesterol	519 mg
Sodium	828 mg
Total carbohydrates	9 g
Protein	117 g
Vitamin A	50%
Iron	33%
Calcium	19%

1. Season the veal chops with salt and pepper. Press a rosemary sprig onto one side of each chop. Mix the flour and paprika and dredge the chops (both sides) in this mixture.

2. Heat the clarified butter in a sauté pan. Place the chops in the pan, rosemary side down. Roast in a preheated 375°F (190°C) oven for 7 minutes. Turn the chops carefully to keep the rosemary sprigs intact. Roast for 5–6 minutes more. Remove the chops and keep warm.

3. To make the sauce, degrease the pan and deglaze with the white wine. Add the veal stock and any juices that have accumulated under the chops. Simmer to reduce to 8 ounces (250 mL). Monter au beurre, strain and adjust the seasonings.

4. Serve the chops with grilled porcini mushrooms.

◆◆◆

RECIPE 14.3

ROAST VEAL LOIN

Yield: 6 6-oz. (180-g) Servings   **Method:** Roasting

Boneless veal loin roast, 3 lb. (1.5 kg)	1	1
Salt and pepper	TT	TT
Onions, chopped medium	2	2
Carrots, chopped medium	2	2
Garlic cloves, chopped	4	4
Fresh thyme	3 sprigs	3 sprigs
Bay leaves	2	2
Jus lié	1 pt.	500 mL

1. Tie the veal loin roast with butcher's twine.
2. Season the meat with salt and pepper and place it in a roasting pan. Scatter the onions, carrots, garlic, thyme and bay leaves around it.
3. Roast at 425°F (220°C) for approximately 45 minutes.
4. Remove the meat from the roasting pan and cut away the twine. Hold in a warm place for service.
5. Deglaze the roasting pan with the jus lié. Strain the vegetables and liquid through a chinois into a small saucepan. Discard the solids.
6. Bring the sauce to a boil and skim as much fat as possible from the surface. Season with salt and pepper. Carve the veal. Spoon a portion of the sauce over the veal; serve the remainder on the side.

Approximate values per serving:

Calories	526
Total fat	31 g
Saturated fat	12 g
Cholesterol	209 mg
Sodium	509 mg
Total carbohydrates	6 g
Protein	54 g
Vitamin A	47%
Iron	16%

◆◆◆

RECIPE 14.4

SAUTÉED VEAL CUTLETS WITH CALVADOS

Yield: 6 Servings   **Method:** Sautéing

Mushrooms, sliced	12 oz.	340 g
Clarified butter	4 oz.	120 mL
Golden Delicious apples	3	3
Veal cutlets, pounded,		
6 oz. (170 g) each	6	6
Salt and pepper	TT	TT
Shallots, minced	2	2
Calvados	2 oz.	60 mL
Crème fraîche	8 oz.	250 mL
Fresh parsley, chopped	1 Tbsp.	15 mL

1. Sauté the mushrooms in a portion of the clarified butter until dry. Remove and reserve.
2. Peel and core the apples. Cut each into 12 wedges.
3. Sauté the apple wedges in a portion of the clarified butter until slightly browned and tender. Remove and reserve.
4. Season the veal cutlets with salt and pepper. Sauté in the remaining clarified butter. (This may be done in two or three batches.) Remove and reserve.
5. Add the shallots to the pan and sauté without browning.
6. Deglaze with the Calvados. Flambé the Calvados.

Approximate values per serving:

Calories	650
Total fat	41 g
Saturated fat	21 g
Cholesterol	295 mg
Sodium	710 mg
Total carbohydrates	14 g
Protein	56 g
Vitamin A	30%

Continued

7. Add the sautéed mushrooms and crème fraîche. Bring to a boil and reduce until it thickens slightly.

8. Return the cutlets to the pan to reheat. Serve each cutlet with sauce, garnished with 6 apple slices and chopped parsley.

◆◆◆

RECIPE 14.5

SAUTÉED CALVES' LIVER WITH ONIONS

Yield: 10 Servings   **Method:** Sautéing

Onion, julienne	1 lb. 8 oz.	700 g
Clarified butter	3 oz.	90 mL
Salt and pepper	TT	TT
White wine	8 oz.	250 mL
Fresh parsley, chopped	1 Tbsp.	15 mL
Calves' liver, 6-oz. (180-g) slices	10	10
Flour	as needed	as needed

Approximate values per 6 oz. (180 g) serving:

Calories	270
Total fat	9 g
Saturated fat	3 g
Cholesterol	535 mg
Sodium	520 mg
Total carbohydrates	16 g
Protein	30 g
Vitamin A	1190%
Vitamin C	50%

1. Sauté the onions in 1 ounce (30 mL) of butter until golden brown. Season with salt and pepper.

2. Add the white wine, cover and braise until the onions are tender, approximately 10 minutes. Stir in the chopped parsley.

3. Dredge the liver in flour seasoned with salt and pepper.

4. In a separate pan sauté the liver in the remaining clarified butter until done. The liver should be slightly pink in the middle.

5. Serve the liver with a portion of the onions and their cooking liquid.

◆◆◆

RECIPE 14.6

VEAL MARENGO

Yield: 6 10-oz. (300-g) Servings   **Method:** Braising

Lean boneless veal, cut in 2-in. (5-cm) cubes	2 lb. 8 oz.	1.1 kg
Salt and pepper	TT	TT
Flour for dredging the veal	as needed	as needed
Vegetable oil	1-1/2 oz.	45 mL
Clarified butter	3 oz.	90 mL
Onion, sliced fine	12 oz.	350 g
Carrot, sliced fine	10 oz.	300 g
Garlic cloves, crushed	2	2
Tomato paste	1 oz.	30 mL
Flour	2 Tbsp.	30 mL
Dry white wine	6 oz.	170 mL
Brown veal stock	1 pt.	450 mL
Bouquet garni:		
Carrot stick, 4 in. (10 cm)	1	1
Leek, split, 4-in. (10-cm) piece	1	1
Fresh thyme	1 sprig	1 sprig
Bay leaf	1	1
Mushrooms, washed and quartered	8 oz.	250 g

| Tomato, diced | 1 lb. | 500 g |
| Pearl onions, boiled and peeled | 24 | 24 |

1. Season the veal cubes with salt and pepper and dredge in flour.

2. Sauté the veal in 1 ounce (30 mL) of oil and 1 ounce (30 mL) of butter, browning well on all sides. Remove the meat and set aside.

3. Add 1-1/2 ounces (45 mL) of butter and sauté the onions, carrots and garlic without colouring. Stir in the tomato paste and return the veal to the pan. Sprinkle with the 2 tablespoons (30 mL) flour and cook to make a blond roux.

4. Add the wine, stock and bouquet garni to the pan; bring to a boil. Cover and braise until the meat is tender, approximately 1-1/2 hours.

5. Sauté the mushrooms until dry in 1 tablespoon (15 mL) of oil and 1/2 ounce (15 mL) of butter without browning. Add the tomatoes to the pan and sauté over high heat for 3 minutes. Season with salt and pepper. Remove from the heat and reserve.

6. When the veal is tender, remove it from the pan with a slotted spoon and set aside. Strain the sauce.

7. Return the veal to the sauce along with the mushrooms, tomatoes and pearl onions. Bring to a boil and simmer for 5 minutes. Adjust the seasonings.

Approximate values per 10 oz. (300 g) serving:

Calories	340
Total fat	16 g
Saturated fat	6 g
Cholesterol	125 mg
Sodium	490 mg
Total carbohydrates	15 g
Protein	32 g
Vitamin A	70%
Vitamin C	25%

◆◆◆

RECIPE 14.7
VEAL ROULADE WITH SPINACH AND SMOKED SALMON

GALILEO RISTORANTE, Toronto, ON
Executive Chef Francisco Rivera

Yield: 8 Servings **Method:** Pan Roasting

Butter	as needed	as needed
Veal loin	2 lb. 3 oz.	1 kg
Salt and pepper	TT	TT
Ground nutmeg	TT	TT
Fresh sage, chopped	1 oz.	30 g
Spinach leaves, blanched	8 oz.	250 g
Smoked salmon, sliced thinly	8 oz.	250 g
Sauce:		
Unsalted butter	4 oz.	120 g
Pearl onions, pickled	6 oz.	180 g
Dry white wine	2 oz.	50 mL
Maple syrup	2 oz.	50 mL
Fresh rosemary	1 sprig	1 sprig
Veal stock	8 oz.	250 mL
Salt and pepper	TT	TT
Ground nutmeg	TT	TT

Francisco Rivera
Francisco trained in Toronto and has worked there for most of his career, gravitating toward Italian cuisine. He is a member of the Canadian Federation of Chefs and Cooks and the Escoffier Society of Toronto.

1. Preheat oven to 450°F (230°C). Butterfly the veal loin. Place veal between plastic wrap, cover and pound to 1/8 inch (0.3 cm).

2. Season one side of the veal with salt, pepper, nutmeg and sage. Cover the veal with the spinach, then cover the spinach with the salmon.

Continued

3. Roll the veal loin tightly and truss with butcher's twine.

4. Brown roulade on stove top. Place in roasting pan and put in oven; roast for 45 minutes. Flip veal over and roast for an additional 4 minutes.

5. Take the roulade out of the oven and let it sit for 2 minutes. Slice on the bias into 1/8-inch (3 mm) slices.

6. To make the sauce, melt half the butter in a pan over medium heat. Drain the onions and add them to the butter, cooking until they are golden brown.

7. Deglaze with white wine and reduce slightly.

8. Add maple syrup, rosemary and veal stock and bring to a boil. Adjust seasoning, then remove from heat. Monter au beurre with remaining butter.

9. Fan the veal onto a plate. Pour sauce over veal and serve hot.

Approximate values per serving:

Calories	497
Total fat	32 g
Saturated fat	17 g
Cholesterol	182 mg
Sodium	991 mg
Total carbohydrates	10 g
Protein	40 g

RECIPE 14.8

Osso Buco

ANA WESTIN HOTEL, WASHINGTON, D.C.
Chef Leland Atkinson

Yield: 4 Servings   **Method:** Braising

Veal shank, cut in 1-in. (2.5-cm) pieces	8–12 pieces	8–12 pieces
Salt and pepper	TT	TT
Flour	4 oz.	120 g
Olive oil	as needed	as needed
Garlic clove, minced	1	1
Carrot, diced	4 oz.	120 g
Lemon zest, grated	1 Tbsp.	15 mL
White wine	8 oz.	250 mL
Brown veal stock	1 qt.	1 L
Tomato purée	2 Tbsp.	30 mL
Gremolada:		
Garlic clove, chopped fine	1	1
Lemon zest	1 Tbsp.	15 mL
Fresh Italian parsley, chopped	1 Tbsp.	15 mL

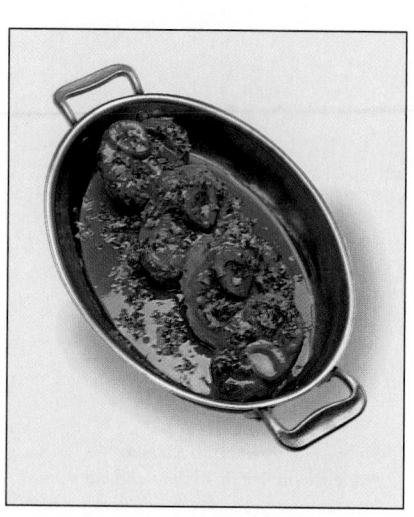

Approximate values per serving:

Calories	350
Total fat	12 g
Saturated fat	2 g
Cholesterol	55 mg
Sodium	1500 mg
Total carbohydrates	41 g
Protein	20 g
Vitamin A	80%
Vitamin C	20%
Iron	20%

1. Season the veal with salt and pepper and dredge the pieces in flour. Sauté them in olive oil until brown on both sides.

2. Add the garlic and carrot and sauté briefly.

3. Add the lemon zest, wine, stock and tomato purée. Bring to a boil and reduce to a simmer. Braise on the stove top or in a 325°F (160°C) oven until the meat is tender but not falling from the bone, approximately 40–60 minutes.

4. Remove the cover and reduce the sauce until thick. Adjust the seasonings.

5. At service time, transfer the meat to a serving platter and ladle the sauce over it. Combine the gremolada ingredients and sprinkle over the meat and sauce.

◆◆◆

RECIPE 14.9

STUFFED BREAST OF VEAL

Yield: 12 8-oz. (250-g) Servings   **Method:** Braising

Stuffing:

Onion, small dice	8 oz.	250 g
Garlic, chopped	2 tsp.	10 mL
Whole butter	1 oz.	30 g
Ground veal	1 lb.	450 g
Fresh bread crumbs	4 oz.	120 g
Nutmeg	TT	TT
Salt and pepper	TT	TT
Eggs, beaten	2	2
Mushrooms, sliced	1 lb.	450 g
Clarified butter	2 oz.	60 mL
Spinach leaves, stemmed and washed	4 oz.	120 g
Veal breast, approx. 8 lb. (3.6 kg)	1	1
Mirepoix, large dice	1 lb.	450 g
White wine	8 oz.	250 mL
Brown veal stock	3 pt.	1.5 L
Garlic, chopped	1 tsp.	5 mL
Bouquet garni:		
Carrot stick, 4 in. (10 cm)	1	1
Leek, split, 4-in. (10-cm) piece	1	1
Fresh thyme	1 sprig	1 sprig
Bay leaf	2	2

1. To make the stuffing, sauté the onions and garlic in the butter until tender. Cool. Combine with the remaining stuffing ingredients and mix well.
2. Sauté the mushrooms in 1 ounce (30 mL) of the clarified butter and cool.
3. Blanch the spinach and cool.
4. Bone the veal breast. Reserve the bones.
5. Butterfly the veal breast and open it into a large rectangular shape.
6. Spread the stuffing over the breast; leave a 1-inch (2.5-cm) border around the edges.
7. Open the spinach leaves and carefully lay them on top of the stuffing. Sprinkle the mushrooms on top of the spinach leaves.
8. Roll the breast up in a cylindrical shape so the spinach leaves form a spiral in the centre. Tie with butcher's twine.
9. Brown the breast in the remaining clarified butter.
10. Remove the breast and pour off all but 1 ounce (30 mL) of the fat. Add the mirepoix to the pan and sauté.
11. Add the reserved veal bones and place the veal breast on top of the bones.
12. Add the wine, stock, garlic and bouquet garni.
13. Cover and braise the breast until tender, approximately 2-1/2 hours.
14. Remove the breast from the pan and remove the twine. Skim any fat from the sauce.
15. Reduce the sauce and, if desired, thicken it slightly with a small amount of roux or beurre manié. Strain it through a fine chinois and adjust the seasonings.
16. Slice the veal breast and serve with the sauce.

Approximate values per serving:

Calories	750
Total fat	30 g
Saturated fat	11 g
Cholesterol	445 mg
Sodium	660 mg
Total carbohydrates	11 g
Protein	109 g
Vitamin A	165%
Iron	30%

♦♦♦

RECIPE 14.10

VEAL MARSALA

Yield: 6 Servings   **Method:** Sautéing

Veal cutlets, pounded, 3 oz. (90 g) each	12	12
Salt and pepper	TT	TT
Flour	approx. 2 oz.	approx. 60 g
Clarified butter	2 oz.	60 mL
Olive oil	2 oz.	60 mL
Dry marsala	6 oz.	170 mL
Brown veal stock	4 oz.	120 mL
Whole butter	1-1/2 oz.	45 g

Approximate values per 7 oz. (210 g) serving:

Calories	430
Total fat	28 g
Saturated fat	12 g
Cholesterol	165 mg
Sodium	650 mg
Total carbohydrates	9 g
Protein	36 g
Vitamin A	15%

1. Season the cutlets with salt and pepper. Dredge in flour and sauté the scallops in a mixture of the clarified butter and oil, a few at a time, until all are cooked.
2. Remove the cutlets and set aside. Degrease the pan and deglaze with marsala. Add the stock and reduce until it begins to thicken.
3. Return the cutlets to the sauce to reheat. Remove the cutlets to plates or a serving platter.
4. Reduce the sauce until it becomes syrupy; adjust the seasonings. Monter au beurre and spoon the sauce over the veal.

♦♦♦

RECIPE 14.11

VEAL FRICASSEE

Yield: 16 8-oz. (250-g) Servings   **Method:** Stewing

Blanquette— *similar to a fricassee but the meat is brought to a simmer in stock and cooked until tender. The liquid is thickened with a roux and finished with a liaison of cream and egg yolks.*

Veal stewing meat, cut in 2-in. (5-cm) cubes	8 lb.	3.6 kg
Salt and white pepper	TT	TT
Butter	6 oz.	180 mL
Onion, small dice	12 oz.	350 g
Garlic, chopped	1 tsp.	5 mL
Flour	6 oz.	180 g
White wine	4 oz.	120 mL
White stock	3 qt.	3 L
Bouquet garni:		
Carrot stick, 4 in. (10 cm)	1	1
Leek, split, 4-in. (10-cm) piece	1	1
Fresh thyme	1 sprig	1 sprig
Bay leaf	1	1
Cream, 35%, hot	1 pt.	450 mL

Approximate values per 8 oz. (240 g) serving:

Calories	340
Total fat	18 g
Saturated fat	8 g
Cholesterol	165 mg
Sodium	540 mg
Total carbohydrates	6 g
Protein	40 g
Vitamin A	10%

1. Season the veal with salt and pepper and sauté in the butter without browning, approximately 2 minutes.
2. Add the onions and garlic and sauté without colouring, approximately 2 minutes.
3. Add the flour and cook to make a blond roux, approximately 3 minutes.
4. Add the white wine and white stock, stir well to remove any lumps of roux and bring to a boil. Add the bouquet garni, cover and braise until the veal is tender, approximately 30 minutes.

5. Remove the veal from the sauce and reserve. Strain the sauce through a fine chinois and return it to the pan. Degrease the sauce.

6. Add the heavy cream to the sauce. Reduce slightly to thicken if necessary. Return the veal to the sauce and adjust the seasonings.

7. Serve the fricassee with rice pilaf.

WEBLINKS

Food Institute of Canada: Veal Recipes
    foodnet.fic.ca/recipes/veal.html

Searchable Archive of Recipes: Veal Recipes
    SOAR.Berkeley.edu/recipes/meat/veal/

Steak Central: Choosing the Best Veal
    www.bestbeef.com/bestbeef/choosing_best/C4_Page.html

Ontario Veal Association
    cattle.guelph.on.ca/services.htm

CHAPTER 15

LAMB

♦♦♦

LEARNING OUTCOMES

After studying this chapter you will be able to:

◆ identify the primal, subprimal and fabricated cuts of lamb
◆ perform basic butchering procedures: frenching a rack of lamb, trimming and boning a lamb leg, boning a lamb loin, cutting lamb noisettes
◆ apply appropriate cooking methods to several common cuts of lamb

*L*amb is the meat of sheep slaughtered under the age of one year. Meat from sheep slaughtered after that age is called year-ling or mutton. Spring lamb is young lamb that has not been fed grass. Because lamb is slaughtered at an early age, it is quite tender and can be prepared by almost any cooking method.

Lamb has a strong and distinctive flavour. It goes well with boldly flavoured sauces and accompaniments.

PRIMAL AND SUBPRIMAL CUTS OF LAMB

After the young sheep is slaughtered, it is usually reduced to the primal cuts: front/shoulder, breast, rack, loin and leg. Like veal, these primals are crosscut sections and contain both bilateral halves (for example, the primal leg contains both hind legs). Generally the pieces are sold separately. Lamb primals are not classified into a forequarter and hindquarter like beef, or a foresaddle and hindsaddle like veal.

Figure 15.1 shows the relationship between the lamb's bone structure and the primal cuts. As with all meats, it is important to know the location of bones when cutting or working with lamb. This makes meat fabrication and carving easier and aids in identifying cuts. Figure 15.2 shows the primal cuts of lamb and their location on the carcass. A lamb carcass generally weighs between 30 and 65 pounds (13–20 kg). Table 15.1 lists uses for common cuts of lamb.

Front/Shoulder

The primal lamb front is a relatively large cut accounting for approximately 45% of carcass weight. The front contains the shoulder, which consists of four rib bones, the arm, blade and neck bones as well as many small, tough muscles whose grains travel in different directions. The breast and shank are also part of the front.

All the bone and muscle groups make it difficult to cook and carve a whole shoulder. It may be boned and rolled with or without stuffing. Cubing for stew is a common application. Although the shanks are excellent braised, they are often made into mince along with the breast.

Flank

Located below the whole loin, the primal flank is a small part of the carcass and is not generally marketed as is. It is ground for patties or shepherd's pie.

Whole Loin

The primal whole loin accounts for approximately 21% of carcass weight. It can be purchased as a saddle, but is usually broken down into racks and loins.

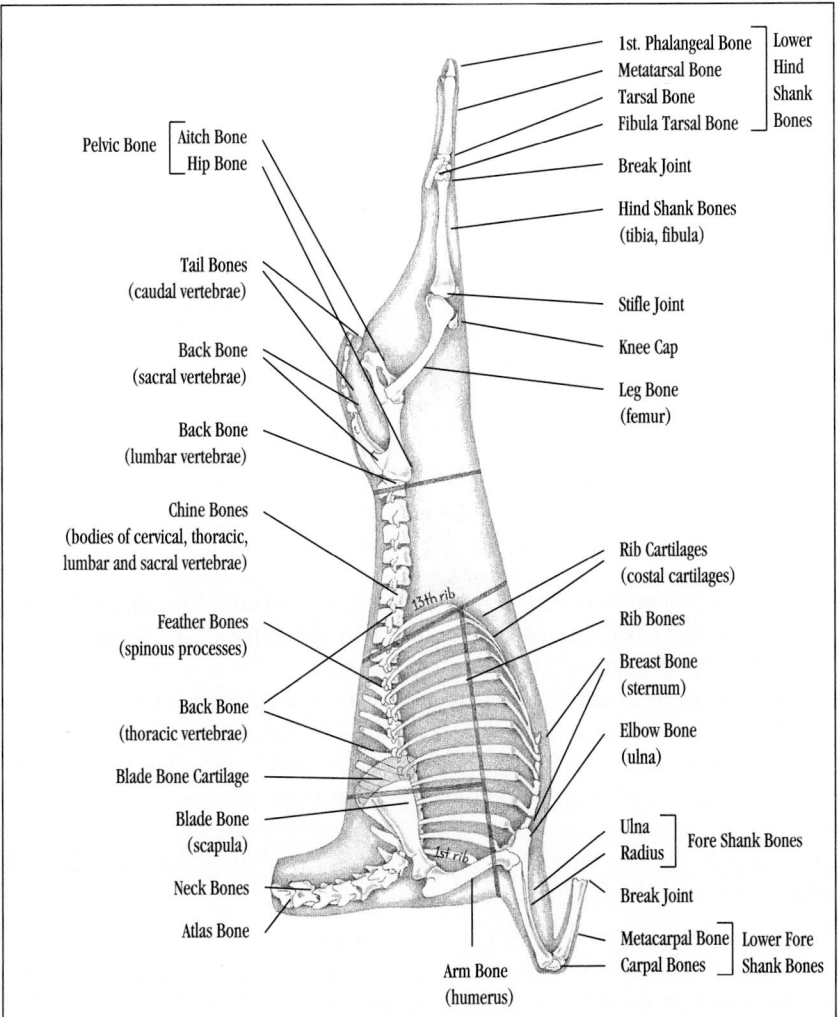

FIGURE 15.1   *The Skeletal Structure of a Lamb*

Labels (clockwise/grouped):

- Pelvic Bone [Aitch Bone / Hip Bone]
- Tail Bones (caudal vertebrae)
- Back Bone (sacral vertebrae)
- Back Bone (lumbar vertebrae)
- Chine Bones (bodies of cervical, thoracic, lumbar and sacral vertebrae)
- Feather Bones (spinous processes)
- Back Bone (thoracic vertebrae)
- Blade Bone Cartilage
- Blade Bone (scapula)
- Neck Bones
- Atlas Bone
- Arm Bone (humerus)
- 1st. Phalangeal Bone] Lower Hind Shank Bones
- Metatarsal Bone
- Tarsal Bone
- Fibula Tarsal Bone
- Break Joint
- Hind Shank Bones (tibia, fibula)
- Stifle Joint
- Knee Cap
- Leg Bone (femur)
- Rib Cartilages (costal cartilages)
- Rib Bones
- Breast Bone (sternum)
- Elbow Bone (ulna)
- Ulna / Radius] Fore Shank Bones
- Break Joint
- Metacarpal Bone] Lower Fore Shank Bones
- Carpal Bones
- 13th rib
- 1st rib

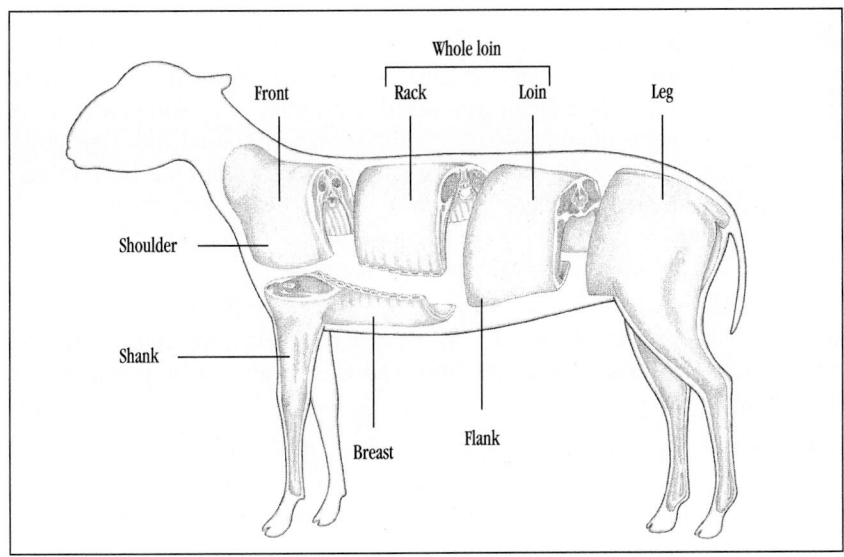

FIGURE 15.2   *The Primal Cuts of Lamb*

Labels: Front, Rack, Whole loin, Loin, Leg, Shoulder, Shank, Breast, Flank

---

IMPERIALIST, COLONIALIST AND REVOLUTIONARY SHEEP

Columbus brought sheep to the New World on his second voyage in 1493. The Spanish soon established breeding centres in the Caribbean islands, then in Mexico and Panama. In 1565 men and livestock, including sheep, settled in St. Augustine, Florida.

During the 16th and 17th centuries the Spanish established missions in Texas, New Mexico, Arizona and California in order to bridge their Florida and Mexico settlements. They brought sheep with them as an easily-cared-for source of food and wool.

Sheep raising was not as easily established in the British Colonies along the eastern seaboard. Many of the sheep brought with the early colonists were consumed for food during the harsh winters. More and more sheep had to be imported in order to satisfy the colonists' competing demands for food and clothing. By the mid-17th century, however, sheep were flourishing in the New England colonies and supplying an abundance of meat and wool.

In an attempt to maintain control of the wood trade, the British restricted the export of sheep to the American colonies and forbade the import of colonial wool and woollens. Retaliating against these restrictive trade practices, the colonists passed laws forbidding the use of sheep for food in order to preserve the flocks for wool. This protectionist scheme helped ensure a strong supply of materials for the domestic woollen industry that flourished after the Revolutionary War.

Frenched Lamb Rack

Frenched—*a method of trimming racks or individual chops of meat, especially lamb, in which the excess fat is cut away leaving the eye muscle intact; all meat and connective tissue is removed from the rib bone.*

Lamb Loin Trimmed

Lamb Leg

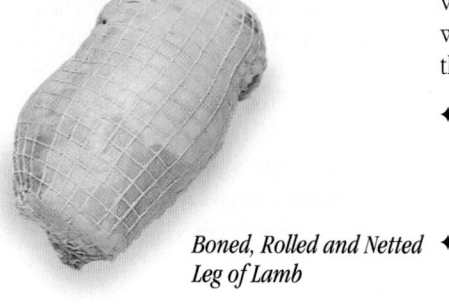

Boned, Rolled and Netted Leg of Lamb

Rack

The lamb rack is also known as the hotel rack. It is located between the front and loin. Containing eight ribs and portions of the backbone, it accounts for approximately 8% of carcass weight.

The rack is valued for its tender rib eye muscle. The hotel rack is usually split in half and trimmed so that each set of ribs can be easily cut into chops. The split racks can then be grilled, broiled or roasted as racks or cut into single or double rib chops before cooking.

Lamb Rack

Loin

The loin is located between the rib and leg. It contains rib number 13 and portions of the backbone as well as the loin eye muscle and tenderloin. It accounts for approximately 13% of carcass weight.

The loin meat is very tender and is invariably cooked using a dry-heat method such as broiling, grilling or roasting. The loin may be boned to produce boneless roasts or chops or cut into chops with the bone in. The loin eye may be removed and cut into medallions or noisettes.

Leg

The primal legs are a large section accounting for approximately 34% of carcass weight. They are the posterior portion of the carcass, separated from the loin by a straight cut anterior to the hip bone cartilage. As with veal, the cut of meat that would be the sirloin on a beef carcass is separated from the lamb loin by this cut and becomes part of the primal leg. The lamb leg contains several bones: the backbone, tail, hip, aitch, round and shank bones.

The primal leg is rarely used as is. More often it is partially or fully boned. Lamb legs are quite tender—the sirloin end more so than the shank end—and are well suited to a variety of cooking methods. A bone-in leg is often roasted for buffet service or braised with vegetables or beans for a hearty dish. Steaks can also be cut from the bone-in leg, with the sirloin end producing the most tender cuts. A boneless leg can be tied and roasted, with or without stuffing, or trimmed and cut into kebabs. The shank end can be diced for stew or ground for patties.

Because lamb carcasses are so easily handled, purveyors often sell them whole or cut in a variety of ways to better meet their customers' needs. As well as whole carcass, primal and fabricated cuts, lamb can be purchased in the following forms:

+ *Foresaddle:* The anterior portion of the carcass after it is severed from the hindsaddle by a cut following the natural curvature between the twelfth and thirteenth ribs. It contains the primal shoulder, breast and foreshank and rack.

+ *Hindsaddle:* The posterior portion of the carcass after it is severed from the foresaddle. It contains the primal loin and leg together with the kidneys.

◆ *Saddle:* The trimmed rack and loin sections in one piece. The back is particularly useful for producing large quantities of lamb chops.

BUTCHERING PROCEDURES

Lamb is unique among the common meat animals in that it is small enough to be handled easily in its carcass form. Thus, food service operations sometimes purchase lamb whole and fabricate the desired cuts themselves. This is practical if the operation has the necessary employee skills, equipment and storage space, as well as a need for all the various cuts and trimmings butchering a whole carcass produces. A few important lamb fabrication and butchering techniques follow.

BASIC PROCEDURE FOR FRENCHING A RACK OF LAMB

1. With a meat saw, trim the ribs to approximately 3 inches (7.5 cm), measuring from the rib eye on each side of the rack.

2. Turn the rack over and cut down both sides of the feather bones, completely separating the meat from the bone.

3. Turn the rack back over. Using a meat saw, cut between the ribs and the chine bone at a 45-degree angle, exposing the lean meat between the ribs and the vertebral junctures.

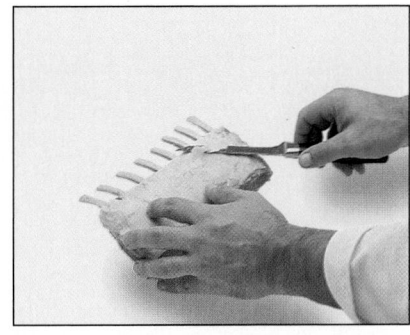

4. By pulling and cutting along the natural seam, remove the thick layers of fat and the meat between them from the rack's surface.

5. Make an even cut through the fat, perpendicular to the ribs, 1 inch (2.5 cm) from the rib eye. Trim away all meat and fat from the rib ends. The ribs should be completely clean.

6. Trim away the fat covering. Leave either a thin layer to protect the meat during cooking or trim the fat away completely to produce a very lean rack. The rack can also be cut into chops.

BASIC PROCEDURE FOR TRIMMING AND BONING A LAMB LEG FOR ROASTING OR GRILLING

1. With the tip of the knife, trim around the pelvic bone; stay close to the bone to avoid wasting any meat. Cut the sinew inside the socket and remove the bone.

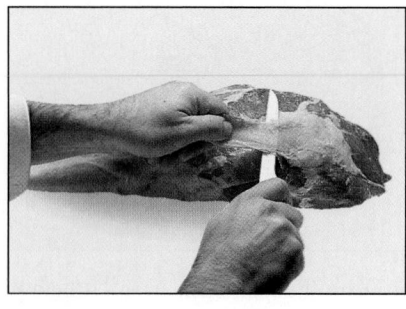

2. Trim away most of the exterior fat.

3. Cut off the shank portion completely and scrape the bone clean. This makes a handle to hold while carving the lamb.

4. Fold the flap of the sirloin over on top of the ball of the leg bone and tie with butcher's twine. This helps the leg cook evenly.

BASIC PROCEDURE FOR BONING A LAMB LOIN FOR ROASTING

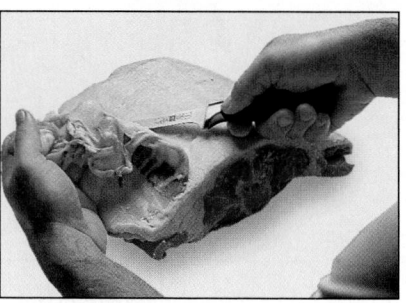

1. Start with a trimmed lamb loin (double). With the skin side up, trim the thin layer of connective tissue called the fell from the loin's surface.

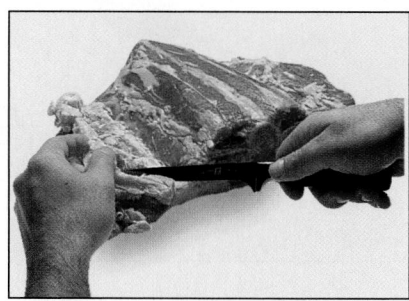

2. Turn the loin over and trim the fat from around the tenderloins.

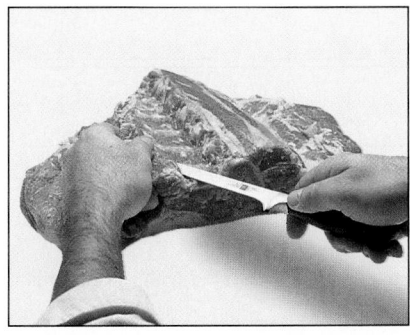

3. Starting in the middle of the backbone, cut between the tenderloin and the vertebrae, separating them but leaving the tenderloin attached to the flank. Continue until you reach the end of the vertebrae. Repeat on the other side.

4. Slide the knife under the vertebrae and rib and cut back all the way to the backbone, separating the eye muscle from the vertebrae.

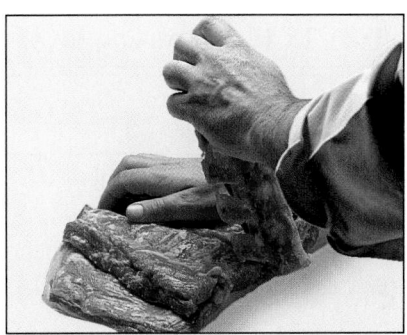

5. Pull the backbone out with your hands, keeping the loins intact.

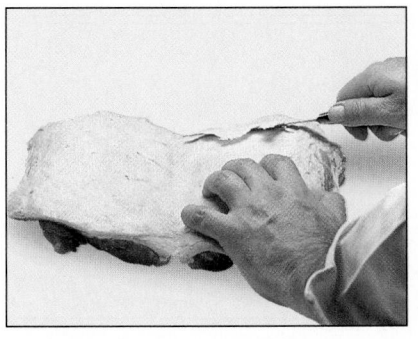

6. Turn the loins over and trim the surface fat to 1/4 inch (0.6 cm).

7. Roll the flank flaps under from each side.

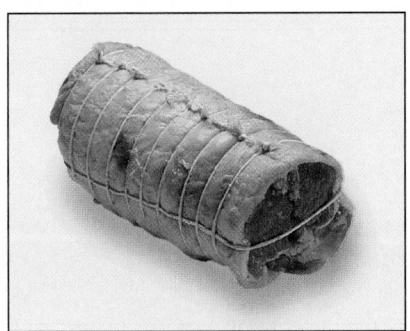

8. Tie the roast with butcher's twine at even intervals.

BASIC PROCEDURE FOR CUTTING LAMB NOISETTES FROM A LOIN

1. Remove the loin eye muscle by cutting down along the backbone and along the vertebrae. Trim the eye muscle, leaving a thin layer of fat if desired.

2. Cut the eye meat into noisettes of the desired thickness.

TABLE 15.1   USING COMMON CUTS OF LAMB

Primal	Subprimal or Fabricated Cut	IMPS	Cooking Methods	Serving Suggestions
Shoulder/ Front	Shoulder lamb chop	1207	Dry heat (broil or grill)	Broiled or grilled lamb chops
	Diced lamb	1295	Combination (stew)	Lamb stew; lamb curry
	Ground lamb	1296	Dry heat (broil or grill; sauté)	Patties
Breast	Breast	209	Combination (braise)	Lamb breast stuffed with mushrooms
Hotel Rack	Lamb rack	204	Dry heat (broil or grill; roast; sauté)	Roast rack of lamb with garlic and rosemary
	Frenched lamb rack	204C	Dry heat (broil or grill; roast; sauté)	Broiled lamb with mustard and hazelnut crust
Loin	Lamb loin trimmed	232	Dry heat (broil or grill; roast; sauté)	Noisettes of lamb with roasted garlic sauce
	Loin chops	1232	Dry heat (broil or grill; sauté)	Broiled loin chops with herb butter
Leg	Lamb leg	233A	Dry heat (broil or grill; roast)	Kebabs; roast leg of lamb
	Boned rolled tied leg of lamb	233B	Dry heat (roast)	Roast leg of lamb

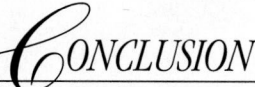

CONCLUSION

Even though lamb accounts for a small percentage of the meat consumed in this country, many people who do not prepare lamb at home will order it at a restaurant. Because lamb is slaughtered under the age of one year, its meat is tender and it can be prepared by almost any cooking method. Its distinctive flavour allows you to offer bold, robust sauces and accompaniments that might mask the flavours of other meats.

QUESTIONS FOR DISCUSSION

1. Describe the basic differences between a lamb carcass and a beef carcass.
2. List each lamb primal and describe its location on the carcass. Identify two subprimals or fabricated cuts taken from each primal.
3. Which cooking methods are most appropriate for a breast of lamb? Explain your answer.
4. Describe the procedure for preparing a frenched rack of lamb from a primal hotel rack.
5. What is the best way to purchase lamb for a food service operation that cuts its own meat and uses large quantities of lamb chops? Explain your answer.

ADDITIONAL LAMB RECIPES

RECIPE 15.1

ROAST RACK OF LAMB WITH MINT AND CELERIAC SAUCE

BISHOP'S RESTAURANT, VANCOUVER, BC
Executive Chef Dennis Green

Yield: 4 Servings   **Method:** Roasting

Lamb racks, cleaned and frenched, 2 lb. (1 kg) each	2	2
Fresh white bread cubes, crusts removed	1 pt.	500 mL
Fresh mint, chopped	2 Tbsp.	30 mL
Fresh parsley, chopped	2 Tbsp.	30 mL
Fresh chives, chopped	2 Tbsp.	30 mL
Dijon mustard	2 Tbsp.	30 mL
Salt and pepper	TT	TT
Potato and Celeriac Purée (recipe follows)	as needed	as needed
Mint and Celeriac Sauce (recipe follows)	as needed	as needed
Fresh mint sprigs	2	2

Dennis Green
Dennis was raised in Vancouver and started cooking when he was 17. He served his apprenticeship at a small bistro near his high school. He joined Bishop's in 1993, and has been the Executive Chef there since 1997.

1. Season the lamb racks with salt and pepper and sear on both sides.
2. Transfer the lamb to a roasting pan and roast in a 400°F (200°C) oven until medium rare, approximately 15–20 minutes.
3. Meanwhile, combine the bread crumbs and the herbs in a food processor and process until well blended. Set aside.
4. Remove the lamb from the roasting pan and smear with the mustard. Coat the racks with the bread crumb mixture.
5. Allow the lamb to rest for 10 minutes before carving.
6. Serve with Potato and Celeriac Purée and Mint and Celeriac Sauce. Garnish with fresh mint.

Approximate values per serving:

Calories	1240
Total fat	64 g
Saturated fat	22 g
Cholesterol	400 mg
Sodium	880 mg
Total carbohydrates	40 g
Protein	126 g
Iron	70%

POTATO AND CELERIAC PURÉE

Yield: 8 servings

Potatoes, peeled and cut into pieces	1 lb. 8 oz.	750 g
Celeriac (celery root), peeled and cut into 1-inch (2.5-cm) pieces	8 oz.	250 g
Cream, 35%	8 oz.	250 mL
Butter	2 Tbsp.	30 mL
Salt and pepper	TT	TT

1. Combine the potatoes and celeriac in a saucepan and cover with water. Bring to a boil, reduce the heat, and simmer until tender, approximately 30 minutes.
2. Strain. Mash the potatoes and celeriac using a food mill or potato ricer.
3. Heat the cream and the butter just to a boil. Add to the hot potato mixture. Using an electric mixer fitted with the whip attachment, whip the purée until fluffy. Season to taste with salt and pepper.

Approximate values per 4 oz. (120 g) serving:

Calories	225
Total fat	14 g
Saturated fat	9 g
Cholesterol	50 mg
Sodium	125 mg
Total carbohydrates	22 g
Protein	3 g
Vitamin A	15%
Vitamin C	22%

Continued

MINT AND CELERIAC SAUCE

Yield: 1 pint (500 mL)

Butter	2 Tbsp.	30 mL
Shallots, chopped fine	4 oz.	120 g
Garlic, minced	2 cloves	2 cloves
Celeriac (celery root), peeled and chopped	4 oz.	120 g
Red wine vinegar	2 oz.	30 mL
Port	4 oz.	120 mL
Fresh mint, chopped	1/2 cup	120 mL
Demi-glace	1 pt.	500 mL

Approximate values per 2 oz. (60 g) serving:

Calories	70
Total fat	6 g
Saturated fat	4 g
Cholesterol	15 mg
Sodium	90 mg
Total carbohydrates	2 g
Protein	0 g
Vitamin A	8%

Claims—low sodium; no sugar

1. Melt the butter in a saucepan. Add the shallots, garlic and celeriac and sauté until tender, but not brown.
2. Add the vinegar and reduce *au sec.*
3. Add the port and herbs and reduce by half.
4. Add the demi-glace and simmer for 30 minutes. Strain and keep warm for service. The sauce can be made up to 1 day in advance and refrigerated, then reheated as needed.

◆◆◆

RECIPE 15.2

SHISH KEBAB

Yield: 10 Servings   **Method:** Grilling or Broiling

Marinade:		
Onion, small dice	12 oz.	350 g
Garlic, chopped	1 oz.	30 g
Lemon juice	4 oz.	120 mL
Pepper	1 tsp.	5 mL
Fresh oregano, chopped	2 tsp.	10 mL
Olive oil	8 oz.	250 mL
Cumin, ground	2 tsp.	10 mL
Coriander, ground	1 Tbsp.	15 mL
Fresh mint, chopped	2 tsp.	10 mL
Lamb leg or shoulder, boneless, trimmed and cut in 2-in. (15-cm) cubes	5 lb.	2.2 kg
Salt	TT	TT

Approximate values per 7.5 oz. (255 g) serving:

Calories	410
Total fat	17 g
Saturated fat	6 g
Cholesterol	205 mg
Sodium	170 mg
Total carbohydrates	0 g
Protein	64 g
Iron	30%

1. Combine the marinade ingredients and add the lamb. Marinate for 2 hours.
2. Place 3–4 cubes of lamb on each of 10 skewers. Season with salt. Grill or broil to the desired doneness. Serve with rice pilaf.

◆◆◆

RECIPE 15.3

ROAST LEG OF LAMB

Yield: 12 Servings 5 to 6 oz. (150 to 180 g) each   **Method:** Roasting

Leg of lamb, 6–8 lb. (2.7–3.6 kg)	1	1
Dijon mustard	2 Tbsp.	30 mL
Garlic, chopped	1 Tbsp.	15 mL
Salt and pepper	TT	TT

Garlic heads	12	12
Fresh thyme	1 sprig	1 sprig
Fresh rosemary	1 sprig	1 sprig
Water	8 oz.	250 mL
Chicken glaze	2 oz.	60 g

1. Trim the leg, removing most of the fat; leave the bone intact.
2. Rub the leg with the chopped garlic.
3. Brush the lamb with Dijon mustard and season with salt and pepper.
4. Transfer the lamb to a roasting pan. Surround it with the garlic heads, thyme and rosemary. Roast at 400°F (200°C) for 45 minutes, turning the leg 3 or 4 times. When the lamb is done, remove it and the garlic from the pan and set aside.
5. To make the sauce, add the water and chicken glaze to the pan and bring to a boil. Simmer 5 minutes and strain.
6. Cut the bottoms off the garlic heads. Serve one head with each lamb portion and top each serving with 1 tablespoon (15 mL) of sauce.

Approximate values per
9 oz. (270 g) serving:

Calories	706
Total fat	42 g
Saturated fat	17 g
Cholesterol	233 mg
Sodium	267 mg
Total carbohydrates	13 g
Protein	67 g
Iron	35%

❖❖❖

RECIPE 15.4

STUFFED LEG OF LAMB

Yield: 12 Servings 5 to 6 oz. (150 to 180 g) each   **Method:** Roasting

Bacon, fine dice	3 oz.	90 g
Fennel, fine dice	1 bulb	1 bulb
Garlic cloves, chopped fine	2	2
Wild mushrooms such as shiitake, chanterelles or porcini, chopped	12 oz.	340 g
Parsley, chopped	2 Tbsp.	30 mL
Fresh thyme	1/2 tsp.	2 mL
Fresh rosemary	1/2 tsp.	2 mL
Salt and pepper	TT	TT
Dry white wine	8 oz.	250 mL
Fresh bread crumbs	3 oz.	90 g
Lamb leg 6–8 lb. (2.7–3.6 kg)	1	1
Mirepoix	1 lb.	500 g

1. To make the stuffing, sauté the bacon until crisp. Add the fennel and sauté lightly.
2. Add the garlic and sauté. Add the mushrooms, parsley, thyme, rosemary, salt and pepper and sauté an additional 2 minutes.
3. Deglaze with white wine and reduce by three-quarters. Remove from the heat.
4. Stir in the bread crumbs.
5. Completely bone out the leg, following the natural seams in the meat. Cut off the shank meat for use in another recipe. Fill the cavity left by the bone with stuffing.
6. Season the lamb with salt and pepper. Close the leg around the stuffing and seal the opening by tying with butcher's twine.
7. Place the stuffed leg in a roasting pan on a bed of mirepoix.
8. Roast at 375°F (190°C) until medium rare, approximately 1 hour. Serve au jus or with a pan gravy.

Approximate values per
10 oz. (300 g) serving:

Calories	540
Total fat	20 g
Saturated fat	7 g
Cholesterol	230 mg
Sodium	630 mg
Total carbohydrates	12 g
Protein	78 g
Iron	35%

◆◆◆

RECIPE 15.5

GRILLED RACK OF LAMB
WITH ROSEMARY AND SPICY BELL PEPPER SAUCE

VINCENT ON CAMELBACK, PHOENIX, AZ
Chef Vincent Guerithault

Yield: 8 Servings   **Method:** Grilling

Red bell peppers	2	2
Yellow bell peppers	2	2
Red Serrano chiles	8	8
Sugar	8 oz.	250 g
Lamb racks, frenched, 9 oz. (270 g) each	4	4
Salt and pepper	TT	TT
Rosemary sprigs, dried *	8	8

*Approximate values per
9 oz. (270 g) serving:*

Calories	430
Total fat	17 g
Saturated fat	6 g
Cholesterol	110 mg
Sodium	400 mg
Total carbohydrates	34 g
Protein	35 g
Vitamin A	45%
Vitamin C	280%
Iron	20%

1. To make the pepper sauce, julienne the peppers and chiles. Mix with the sugar and refrigerate overnight.
2. At service time, cook the pepper mixture (along with the liquid formed while refrigerated) over low heat for approximately 10–15 minutes. Cool and keep the pepper sauce at room temperature.
3. Cut each lamb rack in half. Season with salt and pepper.
4. Grill the lamb over mesquite to the desired temperature.
5. Cut the racks into chops and plate the lamb and pepper sauce. Garnish each plate with a dried rosemary sprig and flame. When the rosemary flames, blow it out at once and serve immediately so that the essence of rosemary is fresh.

*To dry rosemary, place fresh rosemary sprigs in a 350°F (180°C) oven for approximately 10 minutes.

◆◆◆

RECIPE 15.6

GRILLED LAMB CHOPS WITH SMOKED CORN AND WILD
MUSHROOM POLENTA AND PUMPKINSEED CREAM

THE BOULDERS RESORT, CAREFREE, AZ
Chef Jarett Forsberg

Yield: 4 Servings   **Method:** Grilling

Olive oil	1 Tbsp.	15 mL
Mushrooms, assorted fresh (such as chanterelle, morel, shiitake) cut into equal-size pieces	1 pt.	500 mL
Assorted baby braising greens (such as red chard, kale, spinach, frisée)	1-1/2 pt.	750 mL
Kosher salt	TT	TT
Freshly ground pepper	TT	TT
Lamb chops, double cut	8	8
Smoked corn polenta	1 pt.	500 mL
Pumpkinseed Cream (recipe follows)		

1. Prepare a mesquite or charcoal grill. Heat olive oil in a large sauté pan, add the mushrooms and cook until tender, approximately 15 minutes. Add the greens and wilt briefly. Season with salt and pepper.

2. Season the lamb chops with salt and pepper. Grill to desired temperature; keep warm.

3. Spoon 1/2 cup (125 mL) of the polenta onto each plate and top with one-quarter of the mushroom mixture. Arrange 2 chops on the polenta and drizzle with Pumpkinseed Cream.

SMOKED CORN POLENTA

Yield: 1-1/2 pints (750 mL)

Sweet corn	4 ears	4 ears
Chicken stock	20 oz.	600 mL
Butter	1 Tbsp.	30 mL
Olive oil	1 Tbsp.	30 mL
White onion, diced	1 small	1 small
Garlic cloves, minced	2	2
White wine	2 oz.	60 mL
Yellow cornmeal	1 pt.	500 mL
Cream, 35%	2 oz.	60 mL
Kosher salt	TT	TT
Black pepper, freshly ground	TT	TT

1. Lightly smoke the ears of corn and remove the kernels.

2. Pour 4 ounces (120 mL) of chicken stock into a blender. Add half of the corn kernels and purée. Pass the purée through a coarse strainer.

3. Heat butter and oil in a large, heavy-bottomed sauce pot. Add the onions and garlic and sauté until tender. Add the white wine and stir well; reduce *au sec.*

4. Add the remaining chicken stock, the corn purée and the remaining whole corn kernels. Bring to a boil.

5. Slowly whisk in the cornmeal. Cook for 10 minutes over medium heat, stirring constantly.

6. Add the cream and cook an additional 5 minutes. Season with salt and pepper.

PUMPKINSEED CREAM

Yield: 8 oz. (250 mL)

Olive oil	2 tsp.	10 mL
Garlic, minced	1 tsp.	5 mL
Pumpkinseeds, roasted and ground	1/4 cup	60 mL
Anaheim chile, roasted, peeled, seeded, finely chopped	1	1
Cumin, freshly toasted and ground	1/2 tsp.	3 mL
Crème fraîche	6 oz.	180 mL
Salt and pepper	TT	TT

1. Heat the olive oil in a small skillet and sauté the garlic.

2. Transfer the garlic to a mixing bowl; add the pumpkinseeds, chile and cumin. Mix well.

3. Fold in the crème fraîche and season to taste with salt and pepper.

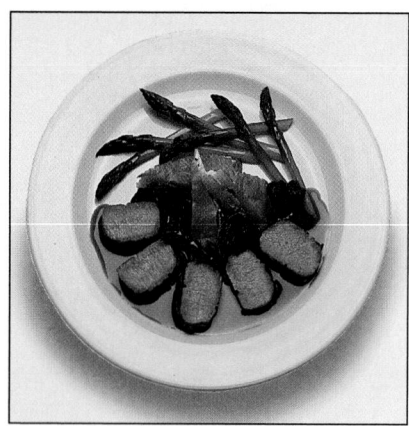

◆◆◆

RECIPE 15.7

SAUTÉED LAMB LOIN
WITH STUFFED RÖSTI POTATOES AND CHERRY CONFIT

CHEF LELAND ATKINSON, WASHINGTON, D.C.

Yield: 6 5-oz. (150-g) Servings   **Method:** Sautéing

Idaho potatoes, large	2	2
Parmesan, grated	5 oz.	150 g
Salt and pepper	TT	TT
Clarified butter	as needed	as needed
Goat cheese	6 oz.	180 g
Fresh rosemary, chopped	1 tsp.	5 mL
Fresh chives, chopped	1 tsp.	5 mL
Lamb, eye of loin, trimmed, 2 lb. 4 oz. (1 kg)	1	1
Clarified butter	2 oz.	60 mL
Port	4 oz.	120 mL
Lamb jus lié	12 oz.	350 mL
Whole butter	1 oz.	30 g
Cherry Confit (Recipe 25.13)	as needed	as needed

1. Peel and julienne the potatoes.

2. Combine the potatoes with the Parmesan, salt and pepper.

3. Heat the clarified butter in an 8-inch (20-cm) nonstick pan. Add the potato mixture and pack it tightly with the back of a spoon. Cook over moderate heat until the potatoes begin to brown.

4. Flip the rösti potatoes and place the pan in a 350°F (180°C) oven. Flipping once, cook until the potatoes are crisp and evenly browned on the outside and soft in the centre, approximately 20 minutes on each side.

5. Transfer the rösti potatoes to a wire cooling rack to rest.

6. Slice the rösti horizontally into 2 round halves. Spread the bottom half with the room-temperature goat cheese. Grind black pepper over the cheese, sprinkle the herbs evenly over the surface and carefully replace the top.

7. Season the lamb and sauté it in the 2 ounces (60 mL) of clarified butter, turning frequently, until the desired doneness is achieved, approximately 8–12 minutes.

8. Remove the lamb and allow it to rest before slicing.

9. Deglaze the pan with the port and add the lamb jus lié. Reduce by half and monter au beurre.

10. At service time, ladle the sauce onto 6 warm plates, slice the lamb and arrange over the sauce. Cut the rösti into wedges and arrange on the plate. Spoon Cherry Confit (Recipe 25.13) around the lamb and serve at once.

Approximate values per serving:

Calories	660
Total fat	39 g
Saturated fat	21 g
Cholesterol	215 mg
Sodium	1260 mg
Total carbohydrates	12 g
Protein	64 g
Vitamin A	60%
Calcium	45 %

♦♦♦

RECIPE 15.8

Roast Rack of Lamb with Crisp Potato and Vegetable Napoleon and Kalamata Olive Butter

DIVA RESTAURANT, METROPOLITAN HOTEL, Vancouver, BC
Chef Michael Noble

Michael Noble
Michael opened Diva at the Met in 1996, and within a year it was in the centre of Vancouver's culinary spotlight, winning awards from Gourmet Magazine, Vancouver Magazine, *and* GQ. *Michael also achieved Canada's highest standing ever at the Bocuse d'Or World Cuisine championship in Lyons in 1995 and 1997.*

Yield: 4 Servings

Method: Roasting

Lamb Rack:		
Lamb racks, bones frenched, 2 lb. (900 g) before cleaning	2	2
Salt and ground black pepper	TT	TT
Dijon mustard mix, grainy	1 oz.	30 g
Herbed bread crumbs	as needed	as needed
Vegetable Napoleon:		
Red pepper, seeded, cut into sections and grilled	1	1
Red onion, cut into pieces and grilled	1	1
Zucchini, sliced 1/2 inch (1 cm) thick and grilled	1/2	1/2
Japanese eggplant, sliced 1/2 inch (1 cm) thick and grilled	1/2	1/2
Salt and ground black pepper	TT	TT
Fresh basil, chopped	TT	TT
Potato Pancakes:		
Potatoes (about 2: see weight), grated coarse, water squeezed out	12 oz.	350 g
Salt and white pepper	TT	TT
Egg white	1	1
Parsley, chopped	1 Tbsp.	15 mL
Clarified butter	as needed	as needed
Kalamata Olive Butter:		
Kalamata olives, pits removed and cut into strips	2 oz.	50 g
Shallot, chopped	1	1
Lemon juice	1 lemon	1 lemon
Sherry vinegar	1 Tbsp.	15 mL
Cream, 35%	6 oz.	150 mL
Butter, cut into cubes	1-1/2 oz.	40 g
Salt and pepper	TT	TT
Parsley, chopped	as needed	as needed

1. Grill all the vegetables and let cool. Cut into dice, combine in a bowl and season. Add the chopped basil. Set aside.

2. Heat a heavy skillet over moderate heat. Place the grated potato in a bowl. Season it with salt and pepper and mix in the egg white and chopped parsley by hand. Divide the potato mixture into small pancakes (you need 12 pancakes for 4 people).

Continued

3. In a hot skillet cook the pancakes in the clarified butter until brown on one side, flip them over and cook on the other side. Remove them from the pan and drain on a paper towel. Set them aside.

4. To assemble the Napoleon, alternate layers of potato pancake and vegetable mix to create a tower assembly. Set aside and leave at room temperature.

5. To make the Kalamata Olive Butter, sauté the olives and shallot together briefly. Add the lemon juice and sherry vinegar and reduce slightly. Add the cream and reduce to a sauce consistency. Whisk in the butter, piece by piece. Season with salt and pepper, stir in the parsley and set aside in a warm (but not hot) location.

6. To assemble the dish, sear the rack of lamb in a skillet. Roast it at 350°F (180°C), until desired doneness is reached (12 to 15 minutes). Let it rest in a warm place for at least 15 minutes. Brush on the Dijon mustard mix and sprinkle with the bread crumbs, then gratinée under the broiler. Cut the rack into single bones and arrange each on the plate with the warm Vegetable Napoleon, some fine beans, the Kalamata Olive Butter and a little of the lamb jus.

Approximate values per serving:

Calories	793
Total fat	47 g
Saturated fat	22 g
Cholesterol	267 mg
Sodium	1062 mg
Total carbohydrates	25 g
Protein	64 g

David MacGillivray

From the time he was 15 years old, working in a restaurant in Picton, Ontario, David knew he wanted to be chef. He quickly became renowned in Canada, particularly for his work in the Edith Cavell Dining Room at Jasper Park Lodge, where his creative menus and excellent service have won the restaurant several prestigious awards.

◆◆◆

RECIPE 15.9

BRAISED ALBERTA LAMB SHANKS WITH LEEKS, ONIONS, BABY CARROTS AND NEW POTATOES

JASPER PARK LODGE, JASPER, AB
Executive Chef David MacGillivray

This dish was inspired by John Higgins at the King Edward Hotel in Toronto. The dish is a very rustic and hearty meal, best suited for a cold winter night.

Yield: 6 Portions

Method: Braising

Canola oil	5 oz.	150 mL
Alberta lamb shanks	6	6
Salt and pepper	TT	TT
Carrot, peeled and chopped	1	1
Onion, peeled and chopped	1	1
Celery stalk, peeled and chopped	1	1
Garlic cloves, fresh	8	8
Red wine	10 oz.	300 mL
Bay leaves	2	2
Rosemary sprigs	2	2
Lamb stock	3 qt.	3 L
Leeks (whites only)	10 oz.	250 g
Garlic cloves, finely chopped	8	8
Red onion, cut in wedges, core attached	8 oz.	200 g
Red wine	9 oz.	250 mL
Lamb poaching stock (from step 6)	50 oz.	1.5 L
New spring potatoes, smallest possible	1-1/2 lb.	650 g
Baby carrots, peeled, fresh	12 oz.	300 g
Whipped butter	3-1/2 oz.	100 g
Dijon mustard	2 oz.	60 mL
Chives, finely chopped	1/3 cup	20 g
Scallions, finely chopped	1/2 cup	25 g

| Fresh parsley, finely chopped | 1/4 cup | 10 g |
| Salt and cracked pepper | TT | TT |

1. To braise the shanks, heat the oil in a large pot. Rub the shanks with the salt and pepper and brown them evenly on all sides.
2. Remove the shanks from the pot and add the vegetables to the pot. Lightly brown the vegetables.
3. Add the red wine, bay leaves and rosemary and deglaze the pan.
4. Add the shanks to the pot and cover with the lamb stock.
5. Cover the pot and place it in an oven at 275°F (185°C). Slowly braise the shanks for 6 to 8 hours until tender. If the shanks are not whole and have been pre-sliced, cut the cooking time in half.
6. Once the shanks are tender, remove them from the broth and place them on a platter. Hold them in a low oven until needed.
7. To finish the dish, in a heavy-bottomed sauce pan, sauté the leeks, garlic and onion until tender.
8. Add the red wine and deglaze for 2 to 3 minutes.
9. Add the lamb stock and bring to a gentle boil. Add the baby potatoes and carrots and cook until tender.
10. Remove the vegetables. Place the shanks in individual, oversized soup plates or together in a large earthenware dish. Arrange the vegetables elegantly around the shanks.
11. Continue to simmer the broth for another 15 minutes.
12. Remove from heat and fold in the whipped butter, Dijon mustard, chives, scallions and fresh parsley.
13. Adjust the seasoning with salt and pepper.
14. Ladle the sauce over the shanks and vegetables and serve with biscuits.

Approximate values per serving:

Calories	1384
Total fat	84 g
Saturated fat	29 g
Cholesterol	390 mg
Sodium	1756 mg
Total carbohydrates	34 g
Protein	108 g

◆◆◆

RECIPE 15.10

IRISH LAMB STEW

Yield: 12 8-oz. (250-g) Servings **Method:** Stewing

Lamb shoulder, in 1-1/2 in. (4-cm) cubes	4 lb.	1.8 kg
White stock	3 pt.	1.5 L
Sachet:		
Bay leaf	1	1
Dried thyme	1/2 tsp.	2 mL
Peppercorns, crushed	1/2 tsp.	2 mL
Parsley stems	10	10
Garlic cloves, crushed	4	4
Onion, sliced	1 lb.	450 g
Leek, sliced	8 oz.	225 g
Potato, peeled, large dice	1 lb. 8 oz.	700 g
Salt and white pepper	TT	TT
Carrots, turned or baton	20	20
Turnips, turned or baton	20	20
Potatoes, turned or baton	20	20
Pearl onions, peeled	20	20
Parsley, chopped, fresh	1 Tbsp.	15 mL

Continued

1. Combine the lamb, stock, sachet, onions, leeks and potatoes. Season with salt and white pepper. Bring to a simmer and skim the surface. Simmer the stew on the stove or cover and cook in the oven at 350°F (180°C) until the lamb is tender, approximately 1 hour.

2. Degrease the stew; remove and discard the sachet.

3. Remove the pieces of potato and purée them in a food mill or ricer. Use the potato purée to thicken the stew to the desired consistency.

4. Simmer the stew for 10 minutes to blend the flavours.

5. Cook the turned or baton vegetables, potatoes and pearl onions separately. At service, heat the vegetable garnishes and add to each portion of stew.

6. Garnish with chopped parsley and serve.

RECIPE 15.11

Navarin of Lamb

Yield: 10 10-oz. (300-g) Servings   **Method:** Stewing

Olive oil	3 Tbsp.	45 mL
Lean lamb shoulder, large dice	3 lb.	1.5 kg
Sugar	1 Tbsp.	15 mL
Salt and pepper	TT	TT
Flour	3 Tbsp.	45 mL
White stock	1 qt.	1 L
White wine	4 oz.	120 mL
Tomato concassé	8 oz.	250 g
Bouquet garni:		
Carrot stick, 4 in. (10 cm)	1	1
Leek, split, 4-in. (10-cm) piece	1	1
Fresh thyme	1 sprig	1 sprig
Bay leaf	1	1
Potato, peeled, medium dice	1 lb. 8 oz.	650 g
Carrot, medium dice	1 lb.	450 g
White turnip, peeled, medium dice	1 lb.	450 g
Pearl onions, peeled	12	12
Green peas, fresh	6 oz.	170 g

1. In a brazier, brown the meat in the olive oil.

2. Sprinkle the meat with the sugar and season with salt and pepper.

3. Add the flour and cook to make a blond roux.

4. Add the stock and wine. Add the tomatoes and bouquet garni; bring to a boil. Cover and cook in the oven at 375°F (190°C) until the meat is almost tender, approximately 1 to 1-1/2 hours.

5. Remove the meat and hold in a warm place. Strain the sauce and skim off any excess fat.

6. Combine the sauce, meat, potatoes, carrots, turnips and onions. Cover and cook until the vegetables are almost tender, approximately 25 minutes.

7. Add the peas and cook for 10 minutes more.

8. Serve in an individual casserole (cocotte) with accompaniments on the side.

◆◆◆

RECIPE 15.12

NOISETTES OF LAMB WITH GARLIC SAUCE

Yield: 4 Servings   **Method**: Sautéing

Lamb noisettes, 2–3 oz. (60–90 g) each	8	8
Salt and pepper	TT	TT
Fresh thyme	1 tsp.	5 mL
Garlic heads	3	3
Rosemary, fresh	1 sprig	1 sprig
Olive oil	2 oz.	60 mL
Red wine	4 oz.	120 mL
Jus lié	1 pt.	450 mL

Approximate values per 5.5 oz. (165 g) serving:

Calories	370
Total fat	26 g
Saturated fat	6 g
Cholesterol	105 mg
Sodium	660 mg
Total carbohydrates	1 g
Protein	32 g

1. Season the noisettes with salt, pepper and thyme.

2. Break the garlic into cloves. Cook the cloves with the rosemary in 1 ounce (30 mL) of oil over low heat until they are very soft, approximately 10 minutes.

3. Deglaze with the wine. Add the jus lié; simmer and reduce by half.

4. Strain the sauce through a china cap, pushing to extract some of the garlic. Return the sauce to the saucepan and adjust the consistency and seasonings.

5. Sauté the noisettes to the desired degree of doneness in the remaining oil; serve with the sauce.

WEBLINKS

Lamb Informational Resources
   www.orst.edu/instruct/nfm433/p/stu/rl/info/p3_index.html

Searchable Archive of Recipes: Lamb Recipes
   SOAR.Berkeley.edu/recipes/meat/lamb/

American Sheep Industry Association: Lamb Information
   www.sheepusa.org/resource/materials.htm#Lamb

Chapter 16

Pork

LEARNING OUTCOMES

After studying this chapter you will be able to:

+ identify the primal, subprimal and fabricated cuts of pork
+ perform basic meat-cutting procedures: boning a pork loin, tying a pork roast, cutting a chop from a loin, cutting a pocket in a pork chop, trimming a pork tenderloin
+ apply appropriate cooking methods to several common cuts of pork

*P*ork is the meat of hogs usually butchered before they are one year old. With the exception of beef, Canadians consume more pork than any other meat. World pork consumption constitutes over 70% of all meats eaten. The pork we eat is leaner and healthier than it once was because of advances in animal husbandry.

Because hogs are butchered at a young age their meat is generally very tender and has a delicate flavour. It is well suited to a variety of cooking methods. A great deal of the pork marketed in North America is cured to produce products such as smoked hams and smoked bacon. Cured pork products are discussed in Chapter 20, Charcuterie.

PRIMAL AND SUBPRIMAL CUTS OF PORK

After a hog is slaughtered, it is generally split down the backbone, dividing the carcass into bilateral halves. Like the beef carcass, each side of the hog carcass is then further broken down into the primal cuts: shoulder, butt, belly, loin and fresh leg.

Hogs are bred specifically to produce long loins: The loin contains the highest-quality meat and is the most expensive cut of pork. Pork is unique in that the ribs and loin are considered a single primal cut. They are not separated into two different primals as are the ribs and loin of beef, veal and lamb.

Figure 16.1 shows the relationship between the hog's bone structure and the primal cuts. As with all meats, it is important to know the location of bones when cutting or working with pork. This makes meat fabrication and carving easier and aids in identifying cuts. Figure 16.2 shows the primal cuts of pork and their location on the carcass. A hog carcass generally weighs in a range of 120 to 210 pounds (55–110 kg).

Shoulder

Picnic Shoulder

The picnic is the lower portion of the hog's foreleg; it accounts for approximately 20% of carcass weight. The shoulder contains the arm and shank bones and has a relatively high ratio of bone to lean meat.

Because all pork comes from hogs slaughtered at a young age, the shoulder is tender enough to be cooked by any method. It is, however, one of the toughest cuts of pork. It is available smoked or fresh. The shoulder is fairly inexpensive and, when purchased fresh, it can be cut into shoulder steaks or boned and cut for stir fry or stew.

The foreshank is called the shoulder hock and is almost always smoked. Shoulder hocks are often simmered for long periods in soups, stews and braised dishes to add flavour and richness.

Shoulder Butt

The butt is a square cut located just above the picnic shoulder. It accounts for approximately 7% of carcass weight.

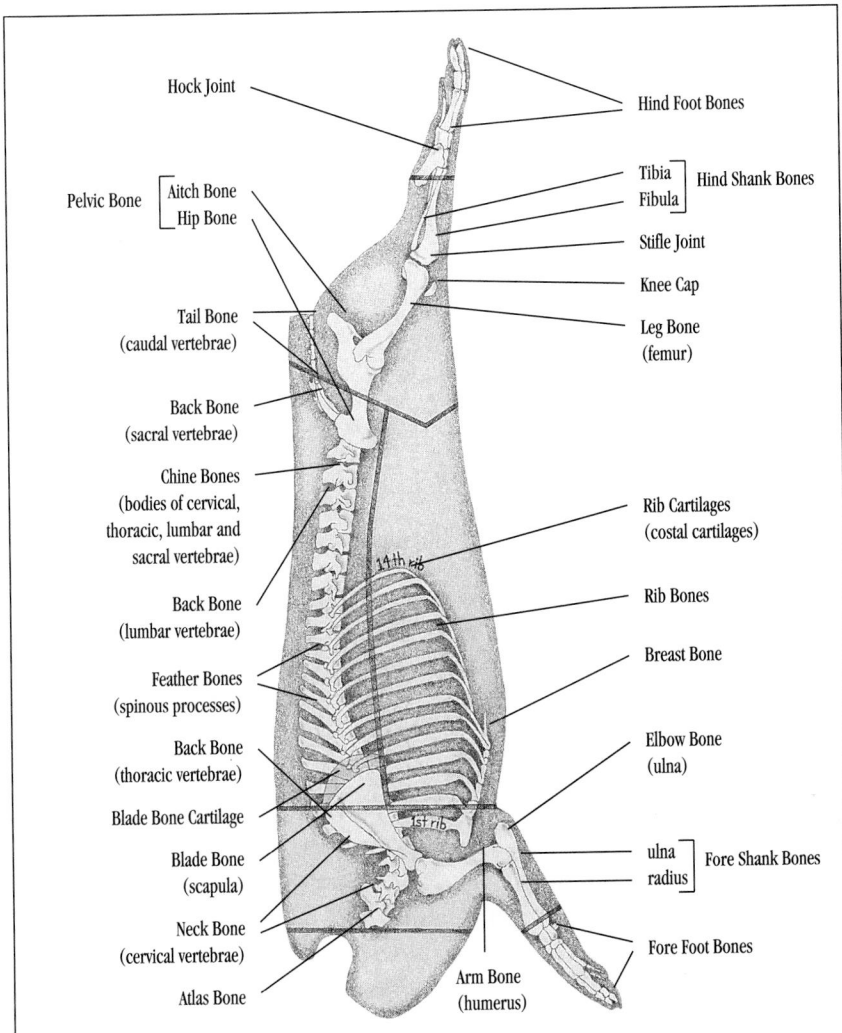

FIGURE 16.1 *The Skeletal Structure of a Hog*

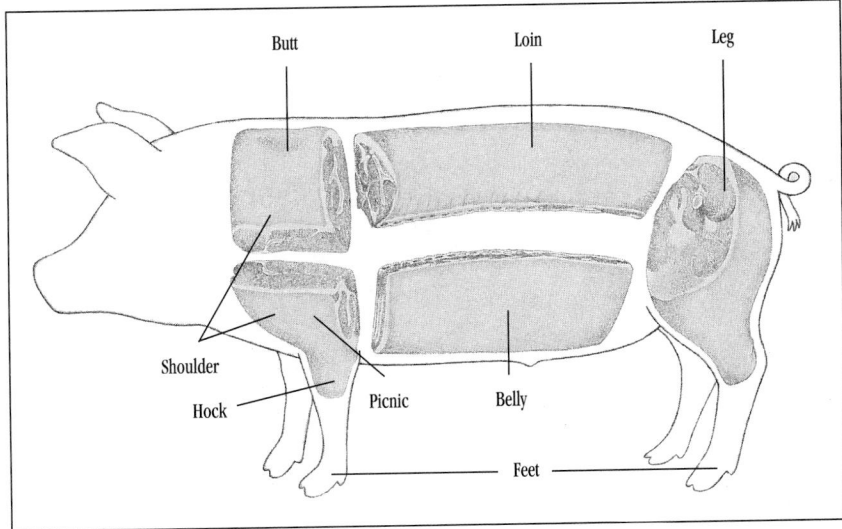

FIGURE 16.2 *The Primal Cuts of Pork*

The shoulder butt is very meaty and tender, with a good percentage of fat to lean meat. Containing only a small portion of the blade bone, the butt is a good choice when a recipe calls for a solid piece of lean pork. The fresh shoulder butt is sometimes cut into steaks or chops to be broiled or sautéed. When the butt is smoked it is usually boneless and called a cottage ham.

Shoulder Butt

Belly

The primal pork belly is located below the loin. Accounting for approximately 16% of carcass weight, it is very fatty with only streaks of lean meat. It contains the spareribs, which are always separated from the rest of the belly before cooking.

Spareribs usually are sold fresh but can also be smoked. Typically they are simmered and then grilled or baked while being basted with a spicy barbecue sauce. Radiant heat slow cooker type ovens are very effective for cooking these cuts. The remainder of the pork belly is nearly always cured and smoked to produce side bacon.

Pork Side Spareribs

Loin

The loin is cut from directly behind the shoulder butt and includes the entire rib section as well as the loin and a portion of the sirloin area. The primal loin accounts for approximately 20% of carcass weight. It contains a portion of the blade bone on the shoulder end, a portion of the hip bone on the leg end, all of the ribs and most of the backbone.

The primal pork loin is the only primal cut of pork not typically smoked or cured. Most of the loin is a single, very tender eye muscle. It is quite lean but contains enough intramuscular and subcutaneous fat to make it an excellent choice for a moist-heat cooking method such as braising. Or it can be prepared with dry-heat cooking methods such as roasting or sautéing. The loin also contains the pork tenderloin, located on the inside of the rib bones on the sirloin end of the loin. The tenderloin is the most tender cut of

Pork Loin

Pork Tenderloin

Pork Backribs

Pork Loin Chops

♦♦♦

Hogs:
A Source for Slogans

Hogs were first brought to Florida by Spanish explorers in 1539, and they thrived in this heavenly new environment. The British shipped hogs to the colonies and as early as 1639 Virginia's colonists were supplying England with ham and bacon. During colonial days, pork was packed in barrels for shipment, giving rise to the term "meat packing."

During the War of 1812, the United States government shipped pork to American soldiers. It was packed in barrels stamped with the letters "US" and the name of the meat packer, Sam Wilson. The soldiers referred to the meat as "Uncle Sam's meat," thus giving birth to the national government's nickname, Uncle Sam.

pork; it is very versatile and can be trimmed, cut into medallions and sautéed or the whole tenderloin can be roasted or braised. The most popular cut from the loin is the pork chop. Chops can be cut from the entire loin, the choicest being centre-cut chops from the primal loin after the blade bone and sirloin portions at the front and rear of the loin are removed. The pork loin can be purchased boneless or boned and tied as a roast. A boneless pork loin is smoked to produce Canadian back bacon. The rib bones, when trimmed from the loin, can be served as barbecued pork backribs.

Although not actually part of the primal loin, backfat is the thick layer of fat—sometimes more than an inch (2.5 cm) thick—between the skin and the lean eye muscle. It has a variety of uses in the kitchen, especially in the preparation of charcuterie items.

Fresh Leg

The primal fresh leg is the hog's hind leg. It is a rather large cut accounting for approximately 24% of carcass weight. The leg contains the aitch, leg and hind shank bones. Like the legs of other meat animals, it contains large muscles with relatively small amounts of connective tissue.

Fresh Leg

Like many other cuts of pork, legs are often cured and smoked. But fresh legs also produce great roasts. When boned and seamed like veal, cutlets and kebobs can be fabricated. When cured and smoked, hams are available in a variety of styles; they can be purchased bone-in, shankless or boneless, partially or fully cooked. Fully cooked hams are also available canned. There is a specific ham for nearly every use and desired degree of convenience. The shank portion of the leg is called the leg shank. It is used in the same manner as the shoulder hock.

FABRICATING PROCEDURES

Other than suckling pigs (which are very young, small whole pigs used for roasting or barbecuing), pork products generally are not purchased in forms larger than the primal cuts described previously. There are a few important pork fabrication techniques that you should master, however.

BASIC PROCEDURE FOR BONING A PORK LOIN

1. Starting on the sirloin end of a full pork loin, remove the tenderloin in one piece by making smooth cuts against the inside of the rib bones. Pull gently on the tenderloin as you cut.

2. Turn the loin over and cut between the ribs and the eye meat. Continue separating the meat from the bones, following the contours of the bones, until the loin is completely separated from the bones.

4. The fully boned loin will consist of (from left to right) the tenderloin, boneless loin and loin bones.

3. Trim around the blade bone on the shoulder end of the loin and remove it.

BASIC PROCEDURE FOR TYING A BONELESS PORK ROAST WITH THE HALF-HITCH METHOD

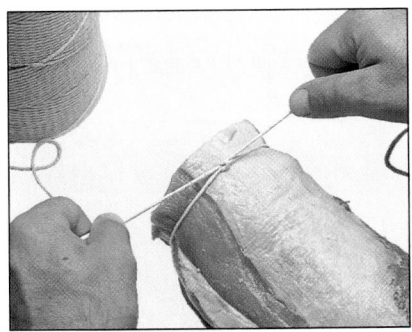

1. Wrap the loose end of the string around the pork loin and tie it with a double knot.

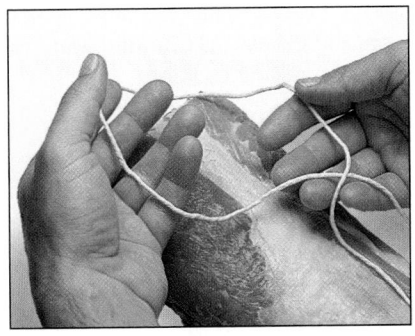

2. Make a loop and slide it down over the roast to approximately 1 inch (2.5 cm) from the first knot.

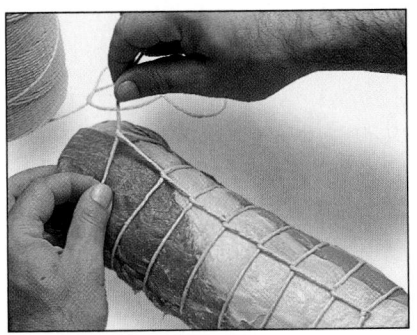

3. Make another loop and slide it down. Continue in this fashion until the whole roast has been tied.

4. Turn the roast over and cut the string, leaving enough to wrap lengthwise around the roast to the original knot.

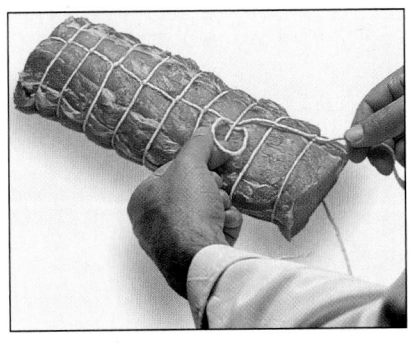

5. Wrap the string around the end of the roast, then around the string that formed the last loop. Continue in this fashion for the length of the roast, pulling the string tight after wrapping it around each loop.

6. Turn the roast back over. Wrap the string around the front end of the roast and secure it to the first loop at the point where you tied the first knot.

7. The finished roast. Note the even intervals at which the strings are tied. They should be just snug enough to hold the shape of the roast; they should not dig in or cut the meat.

BASIC PROCEDURE FOR CUTTING A CHOP FROM A PORK LOIN

Centre-cut pork chops can be cut from the centre portion of a bone-in pork loin without the aid of a saw by using a boning knife and a heavy cleaver. Trim the excess fat from the loin, leaving a 1/4-inch (0.5-cm) layer to protect the meat during cooking.

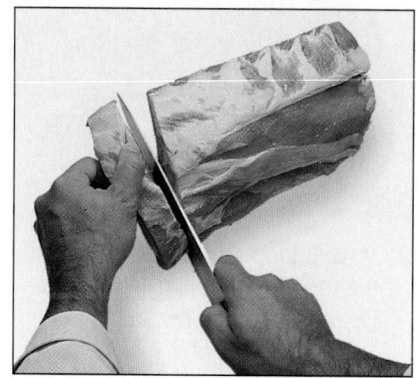

1. Cut through the meat with the knife.

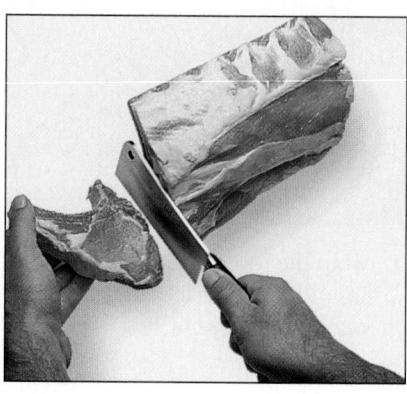

2. Use the cleaver to chop through the chine bone.

3. To produce a cleaner chop, trim the meat from the end of the rib bone. Then, with the boning knife, separate the loin meat from the chine bones and separate the chine bone from the rib with the cleaver.

BASIC PROCEDURE FOR CUTTING A POCKET IN A PORK CHOP

To make a pocket in a pork chop for stuffing, start with a thick chop or a double rib chop. Cut the pocket deep enough to hold ample stuffing, but be careful not to puncture either side of the chop.

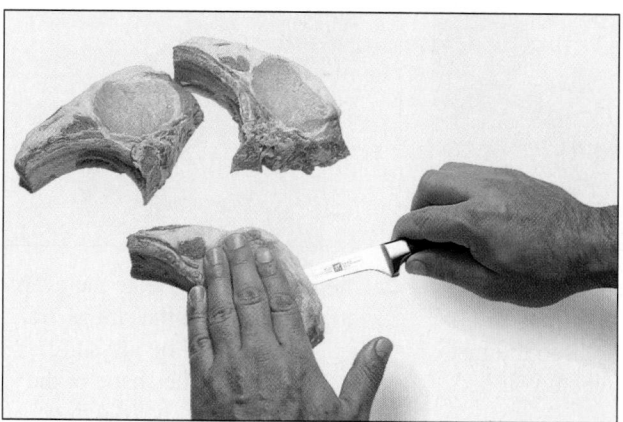

Use the tip of a boning knife to cut a pocket.

TABLE 16.1   USING COMMON CUTS OF PORK

Primal	Subprimal or Fabricated Cut	CMC/ Export	Cooking Methods	Serving Suggestions
Shoulder	Shoulder picnic	C311	Dry (baked)	Smoked shoulder picnic
	Shoulder butt	C320	Dry heat (broil or grill; sauté) Moist heat (simmer)	Broiled shoulder butt steaks Choucroute
Belly	Bacon –fresh	C400	Dry heat (sauté) Moist heat (simmer) Combination (braise)	Breakfast meat Seasoning Seasoning
	Side spareribs	C500/502	Combination (steam then grill or braise)	Barbecued spareribs
Loin	Pork loin –boneless Pork tenderloin Pork backribs Pork loin chops	C200 C201 C227 C505	Dry heat (roast) Combination (braise) Dry heat (broil or grill; sauté; roast) Combination (steam then grill) Dry heat (broil or grill) Combination (braise)	Roast pork Braised pork chops Roast pork tenderloin Barbecued backribs Broiled loin chop with mushroom sauce Braised loin chop with leeks and fennel
Fresh leg	Fresh leg	C100/101	Dry heat (roast)	Roast pork with apricots and almonds

BASIC PROCEDURE FOR TRIMMING A PORK TENDERLOIN

As with a beef tenderloin, the pork tenderloin must be trimmed of all fat and silverskin. Follow the procedures outlined in Chapter 13, Beef, for trimming a beef tenderloin.

Use a boning knife to remove the silverskin from a pork tenderloin.

CONCLUSION

Pork can be enjoyed cured, processed or fresh. The mild flavour of fresh pork blends well with many different seasonings, making it a popular menu item. It is naturally tender and can be prepared by almost any dry-heat, moist-heat or combination cooking method. Properly fabricated and prepared, it is a nutritious, healthy meat.

QUESTIONS FOR DISCUSSION

1. List each pork primal cut and describe its location on the carcass. Identify two subprimals or fabricated cuts taken from each primal.

2. What is unique about the primal pork loin as compared to the beef or veal loin?

3. Are backfat and bacon taken from the same primal? How are they different?

4. What is the only primal cut of pork that is not typically smoked or cured? How is it best cooked? Explain your answer.

ADDITIONAL PORK RECIPES

RECIPE 16.1

BARBECUED RIBS

NOTE: This dish appears in the Chapter Opening photograph.

Yield: 6 Servings, approx. 4 ribs each   **Method**: Baking

Salt and pepper	TT	TT
Crushed red pepper flakes	1 Tbsp.	30 mL
Pork backribs, 3–4 lb. (1.3–1.8 kg) slab	2	2
Cider vinegar	6 oz.	180 mL
Water	10 oz.	300 mL
Sauce:		
Onion, chopped coarse	5 oz.	150 g
Garlic cloves	3	3
Green bell pepper, chopped coarse	4 oz.	120 g
Plum tomatoes, canned	16 oz.	500 mL
Red Devil or other hot sauce	8 oz.	250 mL
Brown sugar	10 oz.	300 g
Lemon juice	2 oz.	60 mL

1. Combine the salt, pepper and red pepper flakes. Rub this mixture over both sides of the ribs, coating them well.

2. Place the ribs in a nonreactive pan and add the vinegar and water. Cover and refrigerate several hours or overnight.

3. Uncover the ribs, turn the presentation side down and bake in a 375°F (190°C) oven for 1-1/2 hours.

4. Remove the ribs from the liquid and place on a clean sheet pan, turning them so the presentation side is up. Increase the oven temperature to 400°F (200°C) and bake for an additional 30 minutes.

5. Prepare the sauce by puréeing the onion, garlic, green pepper and tomatoes in a food processor or blender. Pour this mixture into a nonreactive saucepan and add the remaining sauce ingredients.

6. Simmer the sauce over low heat until it thickens, approximately 15 to 20 minutes.

7. Brush the ribs with the sauce and serve additional sauce on the side. Serve with Creamy Coleslaw, Recipe 24.36 and Baked Beans, Recipe 22.23.

Approximate values per serving:

Calories	1410
Total fat	68 g
Saturated fat	23 g
Cholesterol	315 mg
Sodium	1280 mg
Total carbohydrates	65 g
Protein	134 g
Vitamin A	20%
Vitamin C	120%
Iron	35%

◆◆◆

RECIPE 16.2

GRILLED MEDALLIONS OF PORK ON A CORNCAKE WITH WHISKY APPLE BUTTER

CHEF LELAND ATKINSON, WASHINGTON, D.C.

Yield: 4 Servings   **Method:** Grilling

Loin medallions, 3 oz. (90 g) each	8	8
Salt and pepper	TT	TT
Lemon juice	1 oz.	30 mL
Garlic, minced	1 tsp.	5 mL
Jalapeño, minced	1 tsp.	5 mL
Corncakes (recipe follows)	4	4
Whisky Apple Butter (recipe follows)	as needed	as needed
Fresh cilantro	as needed	as needed

1. Season the pork with salt and pepper and marinate it in the lemon juice, garlic and jalapeño for 2–4 hours.
2. Grill the medallions until done, approximately 4–5 minutes per side.
3. Place the corncakes on 4 warm plates, top them with a dollop of warm Whisky Apple Butter and two pork medallions. Garnish with fresh cilantro and serve.

Approximate values per serving:

Calories	714
Total fat	29 g
Saturated fat	7 g
Cholesterol	350 mg
Sodium	506 mg
Total carbohydrates	45 g
Protein	65 g

WHISKY APPLE BUTTER

Yield: 24 oz. (700 g)

Onion, chopped fine	4 oz.	120 g
Sugar	2 oz.	60 g
Cider vinegar	1 oz.	30 mL
Granny Smith apples, peeled and chopped coarse	3	3
Rye whisky	6 oz.	180 mL
Demi-glace	8 oz.	250 mL
Cinnamon, ground	2 tsp.	10 mL
Cloves, ground	1 pinch	1 pinch
Whole butter	1 Tbsp.	15 mL
Salt and pepper	TT	TT

1. Combine the onion, sugar and vinegar; simmer for 5 minutes.
2. Add the apples, whisky, demi-glace and spices. Simmer until the apples are completely tender.
3. Purée the mixture in a blender or food processor.
4. Strain and monter au beurre. Adjust the seasonings and keep warm for service.

Approximate values per 1 oz. (30 g) serving:

Calories	28
Total fat	1 g
Saturated fat	0 g
Cholesterol	1 mg
Sodium	13 mg
Total carbohydrates	3 g
Protein	0 g

CORNCAKES

Yield: 4 4-oz. (120-g) cakes

Green onion, sliced	2 Tbsp.	30 mL
Red bell pepper, small dice	2 Tbsp.	30 mL
Jalapeño, minced	1	1
Olive oil	1 oz.	30 mL
Fresh corn kernels	8 oz.	250 g
Milk	3 oz.	90 mL

Continued

Flour	2 oz.	60 g
Cornmeal	2 oz.	60 g
Eggs	2	2
Egg yolk	1	1
Fresh cilantro, chopped	1 tsp.	5 mL
Salt and pepper	TT	TT
Clarified butter or canola oil	as needed	as needed

1. Sauté the onions, bell peppers and jalapeño in the olive oil. Drain and cool to room temperature.
2. In a food processor, blend the corn kernels with a little milk until the mixture is not quite smooth.
3. Remove the corn mixture to a bowl and stir in the remaining milk and the flour and cornmeal.
4. Beat the eggs with the yolk; add the pepper mixture to them. Add the cilantro and combine this mixture with the corn mixture. Season with salt and pepper.
5. Heat a portion of the clarified butter or oil in a sauté pan or on a griddle. Add 4 ounces (120 g) of the batter to form 5-inch (12-cm) pancakes; lightly brown them on each side.

Approximate values per 1 cake:

Calories	348
Total fat	17 g
Saturated fat	3 g
Cholesterol	180 mg
Sodium	67 mg
Total carbohydrates	41 g
Protein	10 g

♦♦♦

RECIPE 16.3

CHINESE BARBECUED SPARERIBS

Yield: 24 ribs, approximately   **Method**: Roasting

Sparerib racks, 2 lb. 8 oz. (1.1 kg) each	2	2
Garlic cloves, crushed	2	2
Tomato ketchup	2 Tbsp.	30 mL
Soy sauce	2 Tbsp.	30 mL
Hoisin sauce	2 Tbsp.	30 mL
Red wine	2 Tbsp.	30 mL
Fresh ginger, grated	1 Tbsp.	15 mL
Honey	1 Tbsp.	15 mL

1. Cut the spareribs into individual ribs and arrange them on a rack in a baking pan. Roast for 45 minutes at 300°F (150°C).
2. Combine the remaining ingredients into a sauce. Brush the spareribs lightly with the sauce. Roast for 30 minutes more.
3. Turn the spareribs and brush with more sauce. Roast until the ribs are well browned, approximately 30 minutes.

Approximate values per 8 rib (600 g) serving:

Calories	1450
Total fat	85 g
Saturated fat	29 g
Cholesterol	396 mg
Sodium	940 mg
Total carbohydrates	9 g
Protein	164 g
Iron	30%

♦♦♦

RECIPE 16.4

PORK LOIN WITH PRUNES

Yield: 6 7-oz. (210-g) Servings   **Method**: Roasting

Boneless pork loin roast, 3 lb. (1.5 kg)	1	1
Salt and pepper	TT	TT
Prunes, pitted, or other dry fruit	12 oz.	375 g
Carrot, chopped coarse	3 oz.	90 g
Onion, chopped coarse	6 oz.	170 g
Vegetable oil	1 Tbsp.	15 mL
Clarified butter	1 Tbsp.	15 mL
Fresh rosemary	1 tsp.	5 mL

Fresh thyme	1 tsp.	5 mL
Bay leaf, crushed	1	1
Garlic cloves	2	2
Apple juice	8 oz.	250 mL
White stock	8 oz.	250 mL
Sugar	2 oz.	60 g
Vinegar	2 oz.	60 mL

1. Trim and butterfly the pork loin; reserve the trimmings. (To butterfly the loin, slice it partway through the centre and open it like a book, then flatten it into a rectangular shape.) Season with salt and pepper.
2. Reserve 12 prunes and arrange the remaining prunes along the length of the loin. Roll up the loin and tie with butcher's twine.
3. Brown the pork roll and pork trimmings, carrots and onions in the oil and butter.
4. Add the herbs and garlic and roast the pork on the bed of trimmings and vegetables at 350°F (170°C), basting frequently with the fat that accumulates in the pan, until done, approximately 45–60 minutes.
5. Poach the reserved prunes in the apple juice until plump; set aside.
6. Remove the roast from the pan and keep it warm. Degrease the pan and deglaze with white stock. Simmer for 15 minutes, then strain.
7. Combine the sugar and vinegar in a saucepan. Bring to a boil and cook without stirring until the mixture turns a caramel colour. Immediately remove it from the heat and add the juices from the roasting pan. When the sputtering stops, return the pan to the heat and skim any fat from the surface; keep the sauce warm over low heat.
8. Drain the prunes. Remove the twine from the roast. Slice and serve the meat with the sauce and prunes.

VARIATION: Use dried apricots, apples or cranberries instead of prunes.

Approximate values per serving:

Calories	850
Total fat	16 g
Saturated fat	5 g
Cholesterol	185 mg
Sodium	530 mg
Total carbohydrates	110 g
Protein	66 g
Vitamin A	45%
Vitamin C	15%
Iron	30%

◆◆◆

RECIPE 16.5

MAPLE BAKED HAM

Yield: 25 6-oz (180-g) Servings   **Method:** Roasting

Ham, fully cooked, bone in, 12–14 lb. (5.4–6.3 kg)	1	1
Brown sugar	6 oz.	175 g
Cloves, ground	1/2 tsp.	2 mL
Crushed pineapple, with juice	16 oz.	500 g
Maple syrup	8 oz.	250 mL
Orange marmalade	8 oz.	250 g

1. Peel the skin from the ham and trim the exterior fat to an even thickness of 1/4 inch (0.5 cm).
2. Combine the sugar and cloves and pat this mixture evenly over the top of the ham. Roast the coated ham at 350°F (175°C) for 30 minutes.
3. Combine the pineapple, maple syrup and marmalade in a saucepan over medium heat.
4. Brush some of the sauce over the ham, reduce heat to 300°F (150°C) and cook until heated through, basting frequently, approximately 3 hours.
5. Remove the ham from the roasting pan. Keep it warm and allow it to rest 30 minutes before carving.

Approximate values per 6 oz. (180 g) serving:

Calories	727
Total fat	27 g
Saturated fat	9 g
Cholesterol	264 mg
Sodium	194 mg
Total carbohydrates	35 g
Protein	83 g

Approximate values per serving:

Calories	532
Total fat	15 g
Saturated fat	5 g
Cholesterol	188 mg
Sodium	155 mg
Total carbohydrates	36 g
Protein	61 g

◆◆◆

RECIPE 16.6

GRILLED PORK TENDERLOIN WITH CASCABEL CHILE AND HONEY GLAZE

VINCENT ON CAMELBACK, PHOENIX, AZ
Chef Vincent Guerathault

Yield: 6 6-oz. (180-g) Servings   **Method:** Grilling

Pork tenderloins, approx. 14 oz. (400 g) each	3	3
Olive oil	1 Tbsp.	15 mL
Salt	1 tsp.	5 mL
Black pepper, coarsely ground	2 tsp.	10 mL
Cascabel Chile and Honey Glaze (recipe follows)		

1. Rub the tenderloins with oil and season with salt and pepper.
2. Grill the tenderloins on all sides, a total of approximately 5 minutes. Brush with the Cascabel Chile and Honey Glaze and cook an additional 2 minutes on each side.
3. Remove the pork from the grill and allow it to rest for 5 minutes before slicing.
4. Slice each tenderloin on the bias into 12 slices. Drizzle the remaining Cascabel Chile and Honey Glaze over the sliced pork.

CASCABEL CHILE AND HONEY GLAZE

Yield: 12 oz. (350 g)

Cascabel chiles (if not available, substitute 2 jalapeños)	4	4
Honey	8 oz.	250 mL
Chicken stock	4 oz.	120 mL
Tomato purée	3 Tbsp.	45 mL
Paprika	1 tsp.	5 mL
Cumin, ground	1 tsp.	5 mL

Approximate values per 1 oz. (30 g) serving:

Calories	65
Total fat	.1 g
Saturated fat	0 g
Cholesterol	0 mg
Sodium	12 mg
Total carbohydrates	17 g
Protein	.1 g

1. Soften the cascabel chiles by soaking them in warm water for approximately 2 hours.
2. Combine all ingredients in a saucepan and simmer over medium heat for approximately 10 minutes.
3. Remove from the heat and purée in a blender.

◆◆◆

RECIPE 16.7

STUFFED PORK CHOPS

Yield: 10 Servings   **Method:** Braising

Thick-cut pork chops, approx. 8 oz. (250 g) each	10	10
Celery, small dice	3 oz.	90 g
Onion, small dice	5 oz.	150 g
Apple, small dice	2 oz.	60 g
Whole butter, melted	6 oz.	170 g
Fresh bread cubes, 1/2 in. (1.2 cm)	8 oz.	250 g
Parsley, chopped	1 Tbsp.	15 mL
Sage, fresh, chopped	2 tsp.	10 mL
Salt and pepper	TT	TT
White stock	approx. 5 oz.	approx. 150 mL

Lemon juice and zest	1/2 lemon	1/2 lemon
Canola oil	2 oz.	60 mL
Demi-glace	1 qt.	1 L

1. Cut pockets in the chops.
2. Sauté the celery, onions and apple in 2 ounces (60 g) of butter until tender.
3. Combine the celery, onions, apple and remaining butter with the bread cubes, parsley, sage, salt and pepper, lemon juice and zest. Add enough stock to moisten the dressing.
4. Stuff the mixture into each of the pork chops. Seal the pockets with toothpicks and tie with butcher's twine.
5. In a brazier, brown the stuffed chops well on each side in the canola oil.
6. Add the demi-glace. Bring to a simmer, cover and place in a 325°F (160°C) oven. Cook until tender, approximately 45 minutes.
7. Remove the chops from the pan. Degrease the sauce and reduce to the desired consistency. Strain the sauce and adjust the seasonings.

Approximate values per 10 oz. (300 g) serving:

Calories	650
Total fat	38 g
Saturated fat	16 g
Cholesterol	225 mg
Sodium	390 mg
Total carbohydrates	5 g
Protein	70 g
Vitamin A	15%
Iron	15%

◆◆◆

RECIPE 16.8

CHOUCROUTE GARNI

Yield: 12 Servings, 4 oz. (120 g) sauerkraut, 1 sausage and 5 oz. (150 g) pork   **Method:** Braising

Double smoked side bacon, medium dice	8 oz.	250 g
Onion, medium dice	12 oz.	350 g
Garlic, chopped fine	1-1/2 oz.	45 g
Granny Smith apples, medium dice	8 oz.	250 g
Sauerkraut	2 lb. 8 oz.	1 kg
Dry white wine	4 oz.	120 mL
White wine vinegar	4 oz.	120 mL
Chicken stock	1 pt.	500 mL
Sachet:		
Juniper berries	6	6
Bay leaves	3	3
Cloves	2	2
Caraway seeds	1 tsp.	5 mL
Boneless pork butt, 3 lb. (1.5 kg)	1	1
Smoked pork loin	2 lb.	1 kg
Red potatoes, peeled and quartered	3 lb.	1.5 kg
Bratwurst	12 links	12 links
Salt and pepper	TT	TT

1. Render the bacon.
2. Sauté the onions, garlic and apples in the bacon fat without browning.
3. Rinse the sauerkraut and squeeze out the liquid. Add the sauerkraut to the pan.
4. Stir in the wine, vinegar, stock and sachet.
5. Place the pork butt on the sauerkraut. Cover and braise in a 325°F (160°C) oven for 1 hour.
6. Add the smoked pork loin and potatoes and braise an additional 30 minutes.
7. Add the bratwurst and braise until all the meats are tender and the potatoes are done, approximately 30 minutes. Remove and discard the sachet. Season to taste with salt and pepper.
8. Carve the meats and serve with a portion of the sauerkraut and potatoes.

Approximate values per serving:

Calories	940
Total fat	50 g
Saturated fat	18 g
Cholesterol	255 mg
Sodium	1910 mg
Total carbohydrates	33 g
Protein	90 g
Vitamin C	35%
Iron	30%

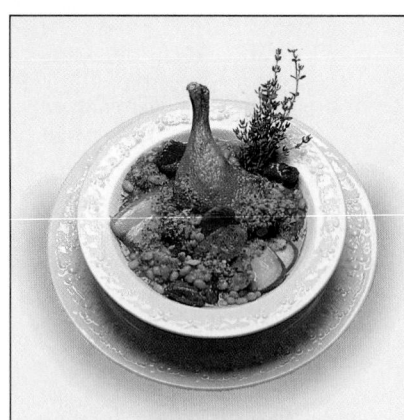

◆◆◆

RECIPE 16.9

CASSOULET

CHEF LELAND ATKINSON, WASHINGTON, D.C.

Yield: 8 Servings, 8 oz. (250 g) pork stew,   **Method:** Stewing
1-1/2 oz. (45 g) sausage and
1 piece of duck

White beans	1 lb.	500 g
White stock	2 qt.	2 L
Smoked ham, large dice	8 oz.	250 g
Bouquet garni:		
Carrot stick, 4 in. (10 cm)	1	1
Leek, split, 4-in. (10-cm) piece	1	1
Fresh thyme	1 sprig	1 sprig
Bay leaf	1	1
Lamb or other sausage	1 lb.	500 g
Onion, medium dice	6 oz.	180 g
Garlic, chopped	1/2 oz.	15 g
Pork butt, cut in 2-in. (5-cm) cubes	1 lb. 8 oz.	750 g
Salt and pepper	TT	TT
Olive oil	1 oz.	30 mL
Mirepoix	8 oz.	250 g
White wine	6 oz.	180 mL
Tomato concassé	1 lb.	250 g
Demi-glace	1 pt.	450 mL
Brown stock	8 oz.	250 mL
Sachet:		
Bay leaf	1	1
Dried thyme	1/2 tsp.	2 mL
Peppercorns, cracked	1/2 tsp.	2 mL
Parsley stems	8	8
Garlic cloves, crushed	2	2
Duck Confit (Recipe 20.14)	8 pieces	8 pieces

1. To make the bean stew, soak the white beans overnight in water. Drain and combine with the white stock, ham and bouquet garni. Bring to a simmer and cook for 30 minutes. Add the lamb sausage, onions and garlic; simmer until the beans are tender.

2. Remove and reserve the sausage.

3. Drain the beans, reserving both the beans and the cooking liquid. Reduce the cooking liquid by half and combine with the beans.

4. To make the meat stew, season the pork with salt and pepper and brown it in olive oil. Remove and reserve the meat.

5. Add the mirepoix to the pan and sauté. Deglaze with the white wine and add the tomato concassé, demi-glace, brown stock and sachet. Cover and simmer the pork until tender, approximately 45 minutes.

6. Remove the meat from the sauce and reserve. Discard the sachet. Reduce the sauce until thick; return the meat to the sauce.

7. To serve, scrape the excess fat from the duck confit. Place the duck in a roasting pan and roast at 350°F (180°C) until the meat is hot and the skin is crisp, approximately 20 minutes.

8. Place a portion of hot beans in a soup plate. Place a portion of the duck

Approximate values per serving:

Calories	630
Total fat	37 g
Saturated fat	12 g
Cholesterol	130 mg
Sodium	2360 mg
Total carbohydrates	23 g
Protein	53 g
Vitamin C	25%
Iron	30%

confit in the plate. Arrange a portion of the meat stew on top of the beans and around the duck.

9. Slice the lamb sausage and add it to the plate. Garnish with fresh herbs.

◆◆◆

RECIPE 16.10

PORK TENDERLOIN MEDALLIONS WITH SHIITAKE MUSHROOMS, GOAT CHEESE AND PORT WINE

SOUTHERN ALBERTA INSTITUTE OF TECHNOLOGY, CALGARY, AB
Chef Instructor Colin Maxwell

Yield: 4 Servings   **Method:** Sautéing

Pork tenderloin medallions, 2-1/2 oz. (75 g) each	8	8
Clarified butter	2 Tbsp.	30 mL
Shallots, chopped	2 tsp.	10 mL
Garlic, chopped	1 tsp.	5 mL
Ginger, chopped	1 tsp.	5 mL
Shiitake mushrooms, sliced	8	8
Brandy	1 oz.	30 mL
Port wine	3 oz.	90 mL
Demi-glace	6 oz.	180 mL
Cream, 35%	6 oz.	180 mL
Goat cheese slices, unripened, 1/2 oz. (15 g) each	8	8

1. Sauté the pork in clarified butter, cook to medium. Remove from pan and keep warm.
2. Sweat shallots, garlic and ginger in the same pan for about 1 minute or until soft. Add mushrooms and cook 1 more minute.
3. Flame with brandy. Add port wine and reduce liquid by half.
4. Add demi-glace and cream. Simmer until sauce thickens.
5. Place goat cheese on medallions and warm under salamander. (Do not cook cheese.)
6. Arrange the pork on the serving plate with garnishes and coat the meat with sauce.

Colin Maxwell
Currently an Instructor at SAIT, Colin had much of his training in England. He came to Canada in 1979, and quickly became the Executive Sous Chef at the Chateau Airport Hotel, where he helped run the Flight Kitchen. He was a member of Team Calgary in the 1987 World Culinary Arts Show in Vancouver, and sat on the Red Seal Exam Revision Committee in 1998.

Approximate values per serving:

Calories	621
Total fat	31 g
Saturated fat	17 g
Cholesterol	211 mg
Sodium	199 mg
Total carbohydrates	30 g
Protein	48 g

◆◆◆

RECIPE 16.11

PAPAYA MARINATED PORK

SOUTHERN ALBERTA INSTITUTE OF TECHNOLOGY, CALGARY, AB
Chef Instructor J. Otto Daniels

Yield: 6 Servings   **Method:** Sautéing

Papaya Marinade:		
Pineapple juice	5 oz.	150 mL
Soy sauce	1-1/2 oz.	50 mL
Garlic, fine chopped	3/4 oz.	25 g
Ginger, fine chopped	3/4 oz.	25 g
Papaya, fine chopped	1-1/2 oz.	50 g
Lemon juice	3/4 oz.	25 mL
Cayenne pepper	1/2 tsp.	2 mL
Honey	3 oz.	100 g

J. Otto Daniels
Otto was originally trained in Hungary. He is a Master Chef in both France and Italy, as well as a Certified Chef de Cuisine in Canada. Otto works with the culinary team at SAIT and is a coach/advisor for the Canadian national team. He recently went to Japan to help market products for Canada Export and Agriculture Canada.

Continued

Pork tenderloin	1 lb. 12 oz.	875 g
Papaya, whole, cut into 12 pieces	2	2
Vegetable oil	2 oz.	60 mL
Spring vegetable greens	10 oz.	300 g
Salt and pepper	TT	TT
Caramelized Ginger Vinaigrette (recipe follows)	TT	TT

1. Mix the marinade ingredients together.
2. Put the pork tenderloin in 10-oz. (300 mL) of the marinade and leave in refrigerator for 24 hours.
3. Slice the tenderloin into 6 medallions, about 1/2 inch (1 cm) thick.
4. Place the papaya sections in a pan in a 350°F (180°C) oven for 2 minutes.
5. In half the vegetable oil, sear the pork medallions about 1 minute on each side. The pork will be medium (slightly pink) but the carryover cooking will finish it.
6. In the remaining vegetable oil, stir-fry the spring greens just to wilt. Season to taste.
7. Serve each pork medallion on a bed of the wilted spring greens with 2 papaya sections. Drizzle equal portions of the vinaigrette over each serving.

CARAMELIZED GINGER VINAIGRETTE

Granulated sugar	4 oz.	125 mL
Rice wine vinegar	8 oz.	250 mL
Ginger, julienne	2-1/2 oz.	75 g
Salt and pepper	TT	TT

1. Place the sugar in a stainless steel pot on the stove to caramelize (be careful not to burn the sugar).
2. Add the vinegar to the caramelized sugar and liquefy completely.
3. Add ginger to liquid and simmer 2 minutes.

Approximate values per serving:

Calories	357
Total fat	17 g
Saturated fat	3 g
Cholesterol	103 mg
Sodium	165 mg
Total carbohydrates	18 g
Protein	35 g

Approximate values per serving:

Calories	461
Total fat	1 g
Saturated fat	0 g
Cholesterol	0 mg
Sodium	1174 mg
Total carbohydrates	134 g
Protein	1 g

◆◆◆

RECIPE 16.12

SMOKED WILD BOAR WITH APPLE AND CRANBERRY SAUCE

H.R.T. ALLIANCE, HUMBER COLLEGE, TORONTO, ON
Chef David Jones

Yield: 6 Servings   **Method:** Roasting/Smoking

Wild boar, saddle	6-1/2 lb.	3 kg
Brine for Smoking Wild Game (recipe follows)		
Hickory, apple and maple wood chips, for smoking		
Sauce:		
Dried cranberries	2-1/2 oz.	75 g
Apple cider	4 oz.	125 mL
Shallots, minced	3 whole	3 whole
Cider vinegar	5 tsp.	25 mL
White wine, dry	4 oz.	125 mL
Maple syrup	3 Tbsp.	45 mL
Veal stock	16 oz.	500 mL

David Jones
David was born in Wales, and trained in Canada. After working mainly in fine dining establishments, David decided to spend a year working in the James Bay area with the Cree community for a change of pace. He has been an instructor at Humber College for the last four years.

Lemon juice, fresh	2 tsp.	10 mL
Dijon-style mustard	1/2 tsp.	3 mL
Unsalted butter	1 oz.	30 g
Salt and fresh ground black pepper	TT	TT

1. Marinate the refrigerated boar in the brine for at least 2 days prior to smoking.
2. Soak the wood in water for at least 30 minutes prior to using. Drain well.
3. Hot-smoke the boar for 1-1/2 to 2 hours, replenishing the wood as required.
4. To prepare the sauce, soak the cranberries in cider for 45 minutes. Sweat shallots in a small amount of butter.
5. Add all the remaining ingredients except mustard, butter and salt and pepper.
6. Reduce sauce to the desired consistency, then add mustard.
7. Monter au beurre. Adjust seasoning with salt and pepper.
8. Allow boar to rest a few moments before slicing; serve with the sauce.

NOTE: The basic brine can be supplemented with some crushed juniper berries, cloves and orange zest.

BRINE FOR SMOKING WILD GAME

Yield: 48 oz. (1.5 L)

Cider vinegar	16 oz.	500 mL
Water	1 qt.	1 L
Salt, non-iodized	8 oz.	250 mL
Black peppercorns, cracked	1 Tbsp.	15 mL
Brown sugar	3 oz.	125 mL
Mace	1/2 tsp.	2 mL
Butter	2 Tbsp.	30 mL
Parsley, chopped	1 tsp.	5 mL
Onions, chopped	2 medium	2 medium
Carrot, sliced	1 medium	1 medium
Red wine, dry	8 oz.	250 mL

1. Bring all ingredients except wine to a boil. Simmer for 30 minutes.
2. Strain and add wine.

♦♦♦

SMOKING WILD GAME

1. Pour brine over meat and refrigerate for 3–4 days, stirring often.
2. Remove meat from marinade and air dry.
3. Smoke meat for 2—5 hours, depending on thickness of meat.
4. Finish meat on broiler or in oven.

Approximate values per serving:

Calories	783
Total fat	19 g
Saturated fat	5 g
Cholesterol	11 mg
Sodium	846 mg
Total carbohydrates	13 g
Protein	120 g

 EBLINKS

Consumer Information — Ontario Pork
   www.ontariopork.on.ca/consinfo.html

Canada Pork International
   www.cfta.ca/cpi/cpi.html

Canadian Pork Council: Pork Nutrition
   www.canpork.ca/pnf.html

U.S. National Pork Producers Council
   www.nppc.org/

CHAPTER 17 POULTRY

LEARNING OUTCOMES

After studying this chapter you will be able to:

♦ recognize the structure and composition of poultry
♦ identify various kinds and classes of poultry
♦ explain poultry inspection and grading practices
♦ purchase poultry appropriate for your needs
♦ store poultry properly
♦ prepare poultry for cooking: cutting a bird in half, cutting a bird into pieces, preparing a boneless breast, preparing a suprême or frenched breast, boning a chicken leg, trussing poultry
♦ apply various cooking methods to poultry: broiling or grilling, stuffing and roasting, sautéing and making a sauce, pan-frying, poaching or simmering, braising or stewing
♦ carve a turkey, capon or other large bird, a chicken or other small bird

*P*oultry is the collective term for domesticated birds bred for eating. They include chickens, ducks, geese, guineas, pigeons and turkeys. (Game birds such as pheasant, quail and partridge are described in Chapter 18, Game.) Poultry is generally the least expensive and most versatile of all main dish foods. It can be cooked by almost any method and its mild flavour goes well with a wide variety of sauces and accompaniments.

In this chapter we discuss the different kinds and classes of poultry and how to choose those that best suit your needs. You will learn how to store poultry properly to prevent food-borne illnesses and spoilage; how to process birds to produce the specific cuts you need and how to apply a variety of cooking methods properly.

Many of the cooking methods discussed here have been applied previously to meats. Although there are similarities with these methods, there are also many distinct differences. As you study this chapter, review the corresponding cooking methods for meats and note the similarities and differences.

MUSCLE COMPOSITION

The muscle tissue of poultry is similar to that of mammals in that it contains approximately 72% water, 20% protein, 7% fat and 1% minerals; it consists of bundles of muscle cells or fibres held together by connective tissue. Unlike red meat, poultry does not contain the intramuscular fat known as marbling. Instead, a bird stores fat in its skin, abdominal cavity and the fat pad near its tail. Poultry fat is softer and has a lower melting point than other animal fats. It is easily rendered during cooking.

As with red meats, poultry muscles that are used more often tend to be tougher than those used less frequently. Also, the muscles of an older bird

FREE-RANGE CHICKENS

Chicken has become increasingly popular in recent years, in part because it is inexpensive, versatile and considered healthier than meat. Indeed, more than 10 million chickens are processed weekly in this country. To meet an ever-increasing demand, chickens are raised indoors in huge chicken houses that may contain as many as 20,000 birds. They are fed a specially formulated mixture composed primarily of corn and soybean meal. Animal protein, vitamins, minerals and small amounts of antibiotics are added to produce quick-growing, healthy birds.

Many consumers feel that chickens raised this way do not have the flavour of chickens

that are allowed to move freely and forage for food. Some consumers are concerned about the residual effects of the vitamins, minerals and antibiotics added to the chicken feed. To meet the demand for chickens raised the "old-fashioned way," some farmers raise (and many fine establishments offer) free-range chickens.

Although the CFIA has not standardized regulations for free-range chicken, generally the term *free-range* applies to birds that are allowed unlimited access to the area outside the chicken house. Often they are raised without antibiotics, fed a vegetarian diet (no animal fat or byproducts), processed without the use of preservatives

and raised under more humane growing methods than conventionally grown birds. Most free-range chickens are marketed at 9–10 weeks old and weigh 4-1/2 to 5 pounds (2 to 2-1/2 kg)—considerably more mature and heavier than conventional broilers. They are generally sold with heads and feet intact and are more expensive than conventionally raised chickens.

Many consumers (in both the dining room and the kitchen) feel that free-range chicken is superior in flavour and quality. Others find no perceptible differences. As a consumer you will have to decide whether any difference is worth the added expense.

tend to be tougher than those of a younger one. Because the majority of poultry is marketed at a young age, however, it is generally very tender.

The breast and wing flesh of chickens and turkeys is lighter in colour than the flesh of their thighs and legs. This colour difference is due to a higher concentration of the protein myoglobin in the thigh and leg muscles. Myoglobin is the protein that stores oxygen for the muscle tissues to use. More active muscles require more myoglobin and tend to be darker than less active ones. Because chickens and turkeys generally do not fly, their breast and wing muscles contain little myoglobin and are therefore a light colour. Birds that do fly have only dark meat. Dark meat also contains more fat and connective tissue than light meat, and its cooking time is longer.

Skin colour may vary from white to golden yellow, depending on what the bird was fed. Such colour differences are not an indication of overall quality.

Cornish Game Hen

IDENTIFYING POULTRY

Agriculture Canada recognizes nine categories or **kinds** of birds: chicken, duck, goose, pheasant, quail, ostrich, guinea, pigeon and turkey. Each poultry kind is divided into **classes** based predominantly on the bird's age and tenderness. The sex of young birds is not significant for culinary purposes. It does matter, however, with older birds: Older male birds are tough and stringy and have less flavour than older female birds. Tables 17.1 through 17.6 list identifying characteristics and suggested cooking methods for each of the various kinds and classes of poultry.

Chicken Broiler/Fryer

Chicken

Chicken (Fr. *poulet*) is the most popular and widely eaten poultry in the world. It contains both light and dark meat and has relatively little fat. A young, tender chicken can be cooked by almost any method; an older bird is best stewed or braised. Chicken is extremely versatile and may be flavoured, stuffed, basted or garnished with almost anything. Chicken is inexpensive and readily available, fresh or frozen, in a variety of forms.

Capon

TABLE 17.1   CHICKEN CLASSES

Class	Description	Age	Weight	Cooking Method
Game hen	Young or immature progeny of Cornish chickens or of a Cornish chicken and a White Rock chicken; very flavourful	5–6 weeks	8 oz.–1 lb. (300–450 g)	Split and broil or grill; roast
Broiler/fryer	Young with soft, smooth-textured skin; relatively lean; flexible breastbone	6–8 weeks	up to 4 lb. (2 kg)	Any cooking method; very versatile
Roaster	Young with tender meat and smooth-textured skin; breastbone is less flexible than broiler's	8–9 weeks	4 lb. (2 kg) and over	Any cooking method
Capon	Surgically castrated male; tender meat with soft, smooth-textured skin; bred for well-flavoured meat; contains a high proportion of light to dark meat and a relatively high fat content	4–6 months	6–10 lb. (2–4 kg)	Roast
Fowl	Mature female; flavourful but less tender meat; nonflexible breastbone	Over 7 months	2 lb. (1 kg) and over	Stew or braise

TABLE 17.2   DUCK CLASSES

Class	Description	Age	Weight	Cooking Method
Young	Young bird with tender meat; rich flavour; easily dented windpipe	16 weeks or less	4–6 lb. (2–2.5 kg)	Roast
Mature	Old bird with tough flesh; hard bill and windpipe	6 months or older	4–6 lb. (2–2.5 kg)	Braise

Young Duckling

Duck

The duck (Fr. *canard*) used most often in commercial food service operations is a young duckling. It contains only dark meat and large amounts of fat. In order to make the fatty skin palatable, it is important to render as much fat as possible. Duck has a high percentage of bone and fat to meat; for example, a four-pound duck will serve only two people, while a four-pound roasting chicken will serve four people.

Goose

A goose (Fr. *oie*) contains only dark meat and has very fatty skin. It is usually roasted at high temperatures to render the fat. Roasted goose is popular at holidays and is often served with an acidic fruit-based sauce to offset the fattiness.

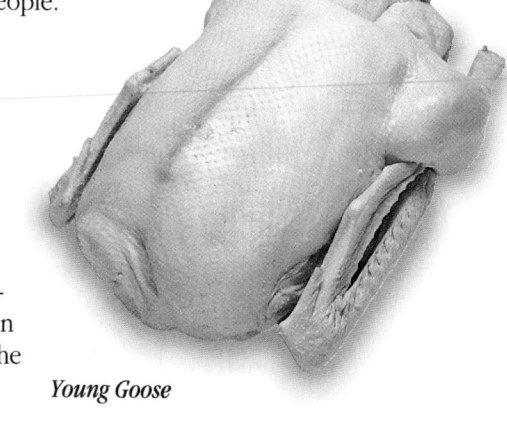

Young Goose

TABLE 17.3   GOOSE CLASSES

Class	Description	Age	Weight	Cooking Method
Young	Rich, tender dark meat with large amounts of fat; easily dented windpipe	6 months or less	6–12 lb. (2.5–5.5 kg)	Roast at high temperature, accompany with acidic sauces
Mature	Tough flesh and hard windpipe	Over 6 months	10–16 lb. (4.5–7 kg)	Braise or stew

Young Guinea

Guinea

A guinea or guinea fowl (Fr. *pintade*) is the domesticated descendant of a game bird. It has both light and dark meat and a flavour similar to pheasant. Guinea is tender enough to sauté. Because it contains little fat, a guinea is usually barded prior to roasting. Guinea, which is relatively expensive, is not as popular here as it is in Europe.

TABLE 17.4   GUINEA CLASSES

Class	Description	Age	Weight	Cooking Method
Young	Tender meat; flexible breastbone	3 months	12 oz.–1 lb. 8 oz. (.3–.7 kg)	Bard and roast; sauté
Mature	Tough flesh; hard breastbone	Over 3 months	1–2 lb. (.5–1 kg)	Braise or stew

TABLE 17.5   PIGEON CLASSES

Class	Description	Age	Weight	Cooking Method
Squab	Immature pigeon; very tender, dark flesh and a small amount of fat	4 weeks	12 oz.–1 lb. 8 oz. (.3–.7 kg)	Broil, roast or sauté
Pigeon	Mature bird; coarse skin and tough flesh	Over 4 weeks	1–2 lb. (.5–1 kg)	Braise or stew

Pigeon

The young pigeon (Fr. *pigeon*) used in commercial food service operations is referred to as squab. Its meat is dark, tender and well suited for broiling, sautéing or roasting. Squab has very little fat and benefits from barding.

Squab

Turkey

Turkey

Turkey (Fr. *dinde*) is the second most popular poultry kind in Canada. It has both light and dark meat and a relatively small amount of fat. Younger turkey is economical and can be prepared in almost any manner.

TABLE 17.6   TURKEY CLASSES

Class	Age	Weight	Cooking Method
Young	24 weeks	16–30 lb. (7–12 kg) and under	Roast or cut into cutlets and sauté or pan–fry
Mature	24+ weeks	30+ lb. (12+ kg)	Roast or stew

Livers, Gizzards, Hearts and Necks

Livers, gizzards, hearts and necks are commonly referred to as **giblets**. Although most poultry kinds are sold with giblets, chickens can be purchased with or without them, depending on your needs.

Giblets can be used in a variety of ways. Gizzards (a bird's second stomach), hearts and necks are most often used to make giblet gravy. Gizzards are sometimes trimmed and deep-fried; hearts are sometimes served sautéed and creamed. Necks are very flavourful and can be added to stocks for flavour and

♦♦♦

A TURKEY BY ANY OTHER NAME ...

In *Food In History*, Reay Tannahill explains why we call a turkey a turkey and not a peru. Turkeys were known as *uexolotl* to 16th-century native Central Americans. They were first brought to Europe by returning Spanish explorers early in the 1500s. Turkish merchants visiting Seville, Spain, on their jour- neys to and from the eastern Mediterranean brought these exotic birds to England, where the English dubbed them "turkie-cocks." This was eventually shortened to "turkeys." The Turks called these birds "hindi," suggesting that they believed the birds originated in India (as opposed to the Indies). This was a belief shared by the French, who called the bird *coq d'Inde*, which was later corrupted to *dinde* or *dindon*. The Germans followed suit, calling the bird *indianische Henn* as did the Italians, who called it *galle d'India*. Meanwhile, in India, the bird was called a *peru*—which was a little closer to the geographical mark.

richness. Livers, hearts and gizzards are not added to stocks, however, because of their strong flavours.

Chicken livers are often used in pâtés, sautéed or broiled with onions and served as an entree.

Foie Gras

Duck Foie Gras

Foie gras is the enlarged liver of a duck or goose. Considered a delicacy since Roman times, it is now produced in many parts of the world. Foie gras is produced by methodically fattening the birds by force-feeding them specially prepared corn while limiting their activity. Fresh foie gras consists of two lobes that must be separated, split and deveined. Good foie gras will be smooth, round and putty-coloured. It should not be yellow or grainy. Goose foie gras is lighter in colour and more delicate in flavour than that of duck. Duck foie gras has a deeper, winey flavour and is far more common than goose foie gras. Fresh foie gras can be grilled, roasted, sautéed or made into pâtés or terrines. No matter which cooking method is used, care must be taken not to overcook the liver. Foie gras is so high in fat that overcooking will result in the liver actually melting away. Most foie gras used in this country is pasteurized or canned. Canned foie gras may consist of solid liver or small pieces of liver compacted to form a block. Canned foie gras mousse is also available. Truffles are a natural accompaniment to foie gras and are used in many tinned preparations.

♦♦♦

FROGS

Frogs are amphibians that can be prepared like poultry or fish. Their texture and flavour are similar to those of chicken. Most of the frogs used in food service operations are farm-raised, so their meat is quite tender. Typically, only the legs are eaten. They are sold frozen, in pairs, attached by a small portion of backbone.

Ratites

Ratites are a family of flightless, bird-like animals with small wings and flat breastbones. They include the ostrich, emu and rhea. These exotic animals are farm raised and the meat is commercially available, but much of their value is in their hides, which are tanned for leather. Butchering them is specialized due to their unique bone and muscle structure.

Ratite meat, which is classified as red meat, is a dark cherry-red colour with a flavour similar to beef, but a little sweeter. Low in fat and calories, it is considered one of the healthiest red meats to eat. Most ratite meat is from animals slaughtered at 10–13 months of age. It is generally cut from the back, which contains a cut called tenderloin, the thigh (also known as the fan) and the leg. Market forms include steaks, filets, medallions, roasts, émincé, cubes or ground. A product called FIBREMIX is used by some processors to prepare consistently sized steaks.

Ratite meat is often prepared like veal or wild game. The more tender cuts can be marinated and then cooked by dry-heat cooking methods, especially broiling, grilling, pan-frying and sautéing. Because this meat has little fat, care

TABLE 17.7   NUTRITIONAL VALUES OF POULTRY

For 1 oz. (28 g) uncooked poultry with skin	Kcal	Protein (g)	Total fat (g)	Saturated fat (g)	Cholesterol (mg)	Sodium (mg)
Chicken, breast	49	5.9	2.6	0.8	18	18
Chicken, thigh	60	4.9	4.3	1.2	24	22
Duck	115	3.3	11.2	3.7	22	18
Goose	105	4.5	9.5	2.8	23	21
Squab	83	5.2	6.7	2.4	mq*	mq*
Turkey, breast	45	6.2	2.0	0.5	18	17
Turkey, leg	41	5.5	1.9	0.6	20	21

The Corinne T. Netzer Encyclopedia of Food Values, 1992
*mq = measurable quantity, but data are unavailable

must be taken to avoid over-cooking; these products are usually served rare to medium. Tougher cuts, such as those from the leg, are best ground or prepared with combination cooking methods. The meat lends itself well to charcuterie preparations and makes a fine dry cured and smoked product.

NUTRITION

Poultry is an economical source of high-quality protein. Poultry's nutritional value is similar to other meats, except that skinless chicken and turkey breast meat is lower in fat and higher in niacin than other lean meats. (Compare Table 12.1 with Table 17.7.) Generally, dark meat contains more niacin and riboflavin than white meat.

♦♦♦

The Ostrich News in 1995 reported the following nutritional values per 1 ounce (28 g):

	Ostrich	Emu
Protein	6.3 g	6.6 g
Calories	28.0 g	30.0 g
Cholesterol	18.1 mg	16.3 mg
Fat	.28 g	.48 g
Saturated fat	.07 g	.17 g
Sodium	18.0 mg	17.0 mg
Calcium	.5 mg	.3 mg
Iron	2.3 mg	1.4 mg

INSPECTION AND GRADING OF POULTRY

Inspection

All poultry produced for public consumption in Canada is subject to health inspection. Inspections ensure that products are processed under strict sanitary guidelines and are wholesome and fit for human consumption. Inspections do not indicate a product's quality or tenderness.

Grading

Grading poultry is voluntary but virtually universal. Birds are graded according to their overall quality with the grade (Canada A, B, utility or C) shown on the packaging. (See Figures 17.1 and 17.2.)

According to Agriculture Canada, Grade A poultry is free from deformities, with thick flesh and a well-developed fat layer; free of pinfeathers, cuts or tears and broken bones; the carcass is free from discolouration and, if it is frozen, free from defects that occur during handling or storage. Nearly all poultry used in wholesale and retail outlets is Grade A or utility. Grade B and C birds are used primarily for processed poultry products. In addition, poultry may be sold as "ungraded."

FIGURE 17.1 *Grade Stamp for Utility Grade*

FIGURE 17.2 *Grade Stamp for Canada Grade A Poultry*

Quality grades have no bearing on the product's tenderness or flavour. A bird's tenderness is usually indicated by its class (for example, a "young turkey" is younger and more tender than a yearling). Its grade (Canada A, B, utility or C) within each class is determined by its overall quality.

PURCHASING AND STORING POULTRY

Purchasing Poultry

Poultry can be purchased in many forms: fresh or frozen, whole or cut up, bone-in or boneless, portion controlled (P.C.), individually quick frozen (IQF), tumbled or ground. Chicken and turkey are also widely used in prepared and convenience items and are available fully cooked and vacuum-wrapped or boned and canned. Although purchasing poultry in a ready-to-use form is convenient, it is not always necessary: Poultry products are easy to fabricate and portion. Whole fresh poultry is also less expensive than precut or frozen products.

As with meats, you should consider your menu, labour costs, storage facilities and employee skills when deciding whether to purchase whole fresh poultry or some other form.

Storing Poultry

Poultry is highly perishable and particularly susceptible to contamination by salmonella bacteria. It is critical that poultry be stored at the correct temperatures.

Fresh chickens and other small birds can be stored on ice or at 32–34°F (0–2°C) for up to two days; larger birds can be stored up to four days at these temperatures. Frozen poultry should be kept at 0°F (–18°C) or below (the colder the better) and can be held for up to six months. It should be thawed gradually under refrigeration, allowing two days for chickens and up to four days for larger birds. Never attempt to cook poultry that is still partially frozen: It will be impossible to cook the product evenly and the areas that were still frozen may not reach the temperatures necessary to destroy harmful bacteria. Never partially cook poultry one day and finish cooking it later: Bacteria are more likely to grow under such conditions and result in food poisoning. Poultry should be rinsed in clear, running water before processing.

Sanitation and Cross-Contamination

Review the information in Chapter 2, Food Safety and Sanitation, before butchering any poultry. Be sure that all work surfaces, cutting boards, knives, hands and other equipment used to prepare poultry products are clean and sanitary. Be careful that juices and trimmings from poultry do not come in contact with other foods. Anything coming in contact with raw poultry should be cleaned and sanitized with a chlorine solution of 200 ppm before it comes in contact with any other food. Cooked foods should never be placed in containers that were used to hold the raw product. Kitchen towels that are used to handle poultry or clean up after butchering should be sanitized before being reused to prevent cross-contamination.

FABRICATING PROCEDURES

Poultry is easier to fabricate than meats and is often processed on-site. You should be able to perform the following commonly encountered procedures.

♦♦♦

POULTRY SAFETY MEASURES

While generally following U.S. guidelines up to 1970, Canada streamlined its inspection system for poultry in the late 1970s and early 1980s. Based on a process-controlled environment, industry assumed some of the responsibility. The Canada Poultry Inspection Program was introduced in April 1996 and will be revised in 1999.

Because the different kinds of poultry are similar in structure, these procedures apply to a variety of birds.

BASIC PROCEDURE FOR CUTTING A BIRD IN HALF

Often the first step in preparing poultry is to cut the bird in half. Broiler and fryer chickens are often split to make two portions. This procedure removes the backbone and breast bone (also known as the keel bone) for a neat finished product.

1. Square up the bird by placing it on its back and pressing on the legs and breast to create a more uniform appearance.

2. Place the bird on its breast and hold the tail tightly with the thumb and forefinger of one hand. Using a rigid boning knife and in a single swift movement, cut alongside the backbone from the bird's tail to head.

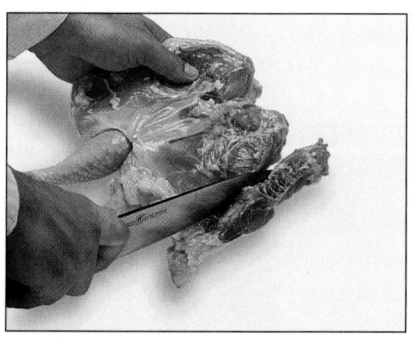

3. Lay the bird flat on the cutting board and remove the backbone by cutting through the ribs connecting it to the breast.

4. Bend the bird back, breaking the breast bone free.

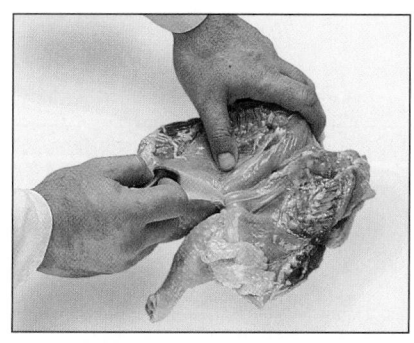

5. Run your fingers along the bone to separate the breast meat from it; pull the bone completely free. Be sure to remove the flexible cartilage completely.

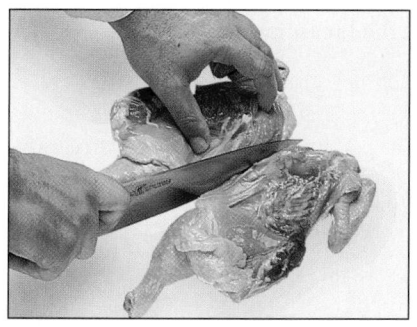

6. Cut through the skin to separate the bird into two halves. The halves are ready to be cooked; for a more attractive presentation, follow steps 7 and 8.

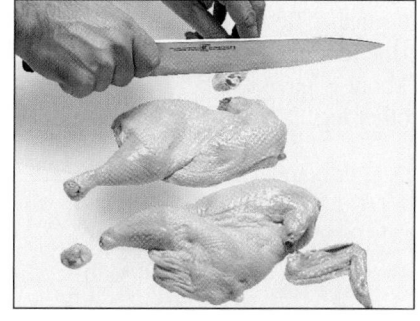

7. Trim off the wing tips and the ends of the leg bone.

8. Make a slit in the skin below the leg and tuck the leg bone into the slit.

BASIC PROCEDURE FOR CUTTING A BIRD INTO PIECES

This is one of the most common butchering procedures. It is also very simple once you understand the bird's structure and are able to find each of its joints.

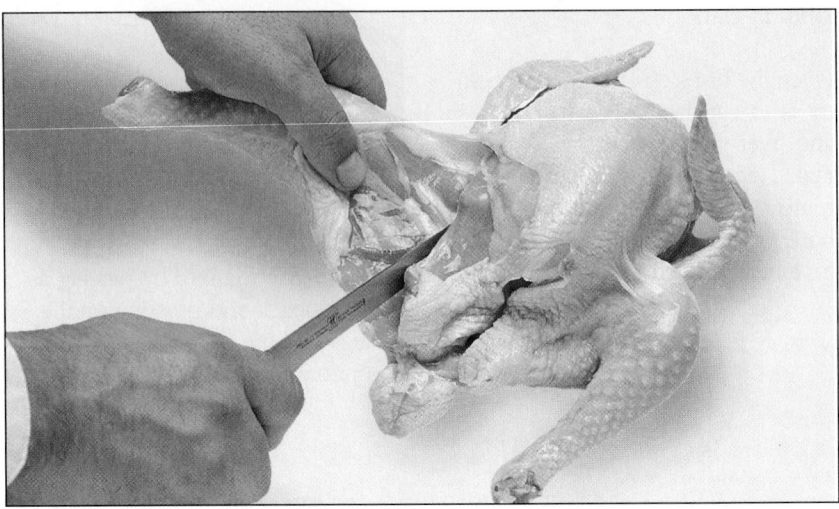

1. Remove the leg by pulling the leg and thigh away from the breast and cutting through the skin and flesh towards the thigh joint.

2. Cut down to the thigh joint, twist the leg to break the joint and cut the thigh and leg from the carcass. Be careful to trim around the oyster meat (the tender morsel of meat located next to the backbone); leave it attached to the thigh. Repeat with the other leg.

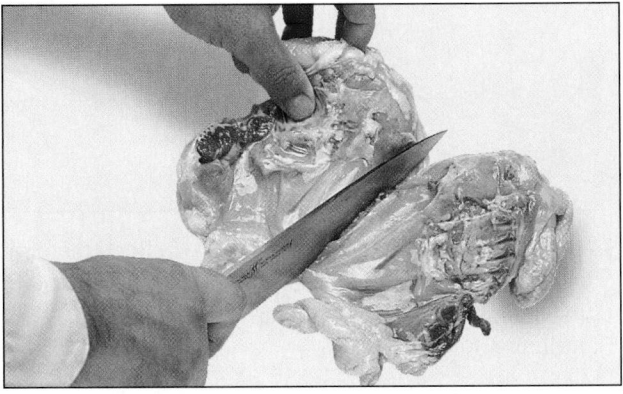

3. To split the breast, follow steps 2 through 6 for cutting a bird in half. Cut the breast into two halves.

4. The bird is now cut into four pieces.

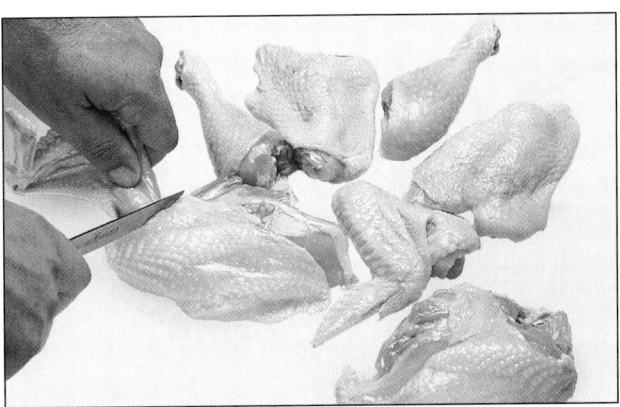

5. To cut the bird into six pieces, separate the thigh from the leg by making a cut guided by the line of fat on the inside of the thigh and leg.

6. To cut the bird into eight pieces, separate the wing from the breast by cutting through the joint, or split the breast, leaving a portion of the breast meat attached to the wing.

BASIC PROCEDURE FOR PREPARING A BONELESS BREAST

A boneless chicken breast is one of the most versatile and popular poultry cuts. It can be broiled, grilled, baked, sautéed, pan-fried or poached. Boneless turkey breast can be roasted or sliced and sautéed as a substitute for veal. The skin can be removed or left intact.

1. Remove the keel bone from the bone-in breast, following steps 4, 5 and 6 for cutting a bird in half.

2. With the chicken breast lying skin side down, separate the rib bones, wing and wishbone from the breast. Leave the two tender pieces of meat known as the tenderloins attached to the breast. Repeat the procedure on the other side, being sure to remove the small wishbone pieces from the front of the breast.

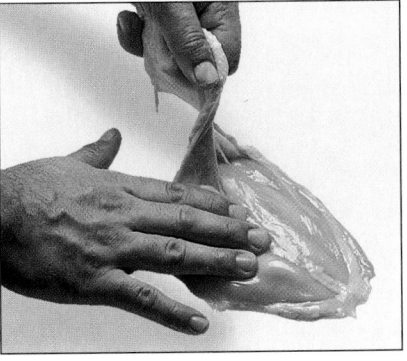

3. The skin may be left intact or removed to produce a skinless boneless breast.

BASIC PROCEDURE FOR PREPARING A SUPRÊME OR FRENCHED BREAST

A chicken suprême or frenched breast is half of a boneless chicken breast with the first wing bone attached. The tip of the wing bone is removed, yielding a neat and attractive portion that can be prepared by a variety of cooking methods. The skin can be left on or removed.

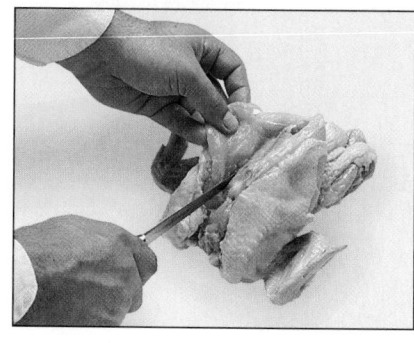

1. Remove the legs from a chicken following steps 1 and 2 for cutting a bird into pieces. Place the bird on its back. Locate the wishbone, trim around it and remove it.

2. Cut along one side of the breast bone, separating the meat from the bone.

3. Following the natural curvature of the ribs, continue cutting to remove the meat from the bones.

4. When you reach the wing joint, cut through the joint, keeping the wing attached to the breast portion. Cut the breast free from the carcass.

5. Make a cut on the back of the joint between the first and second wing bones.

6. Break the joint and pull the meat and skin back to expose a clean bone. Trim the wing bone.

7. The suprême can be prepared skin-on or skinless.

BASIC PROCEDURE FOR BONING A CHICKEN LEG

Chicken breasts are usually more popular than legs and thighs. There are, however, uses for boneless, skinless leg and thigh meat; they can be stuffed or used for ballotines, for example.

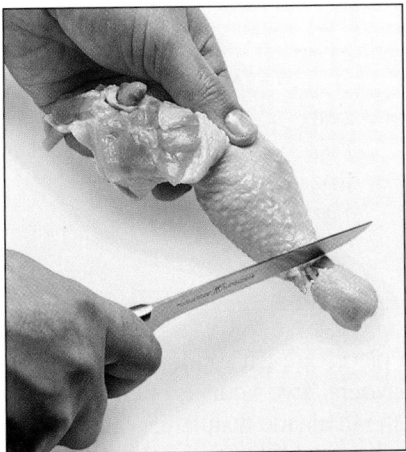

1. Carefully cut through the skin, meat and tendons at the base of the leg. Be sure to cut through completely to the bone.

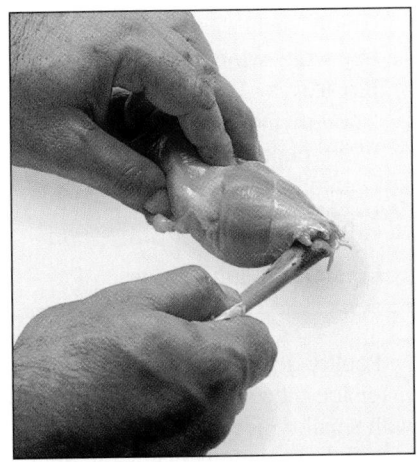

2. Pull the skin off the leg with your hands, then break the joint between the leg and thigh. Twist and pull out the leg bone.

3. Working from the inside of the thigh, cut along both sides of the thigh bone, separating it from the meat.

4. Cut around the cartilage at the joint between the leg and thigh and remove the thigh bone and cartilage.

MARINATING POULTRY

Most poultry is quite mild in flavour, so a marinade is often used to add flavour and moisture, especially to poultry that will be broiled or grilled. Barbecued chicken is one of the simplest and best-known forms of marinated poultry. Poultry is often marinated in a mixture of white wine or lemon juice, oil, pepper, herbs and spices, such as that given in Recipe 17.1.

♦♦♦

RECIPE 17.1
WHITE WINE MARINADE

Yield: 1 qt. (1 L)

Garlic, minced	2 tsp.	10 mL
Onion, small dice	5 oz.	150 g
Dry white wine	24 oz.	750 mL
Bay leaves	2	2
Dried thyme	2 tsp.	10 mL
White pepper	1 tsp.	5 mL
Lemon juice	1 oz.	30 mL
Vegetable oil	4 oz.	120 mL

Combine all ingredients.

*Approximate values per
1 oz. (30 mL) serving:*

Calories	35
Total fat	3.5 g
Saturated fat	0 g
Cholesterol	0 mg
Sodium	220 mg
Total carbohydrates	1 g
Protein	0 g

Claims—no saturated fat; no cholesterol; no sugar; low calorie

Poultry absorbs flavours quickly, so if pieces are left too long in an acidic marinade they may take on undesirable flavours. Two hours is often sufficient, with smaller pieces requiring less time in the marinade than larger ones.

If the marinade contains oil, drain it well to avoid flare-up when the item is placed on the broiler or grill. Use a clean kitchen towel or a paper towel to wipe excess moisture from the poultry's surface so that it browns more easily. The marinade can be used to baste the item during cooking, but leftover marinade should not be served uncooked or reused because of the danger of bacterial contamination from the raw poultry.

APPLYING VARIOUS COOKING METHODS

The principles of cooking discussed in Chapter 9 and applied to meats in earlier chapters also apply to poultry. Dry-heat methods are appropriate for young, tender birds. Moist-heat methods should be used with older, less-tender products.

Dry-Heat Cooking Methods

Cooking poultry with dry-heat methods—broiling and grilling, roasting, sautéing, pan-frying and deep-fat frying—presents some unique challenges. Large birds such as turkeys benefit from low-heat cooking but are better when served with the crispy skin gained through higher temperatures. Duck and goose skin contains a great deal of fat that must be rendered during the cooking process. Small birds such as squab must be cooked at sufficiently high temperatures to crisp their skins but can be easily overcooked. Boneless chicken breasts, particularly flavourful and popular when broiled or grilled, are easily overcooked and become dry because they do not contain bones to help retain moisture during cooking. Proper application of the following dry-heat cooking methods will help meet these challenges and ensure a good-quality finished product.

Broiling and Grilling

Broiled and grilled poultry should have a well-browned surface and can show crosshatched grill marks. It should be moist, tender and juicy throughout. It may be seasoned to enhance its natural flavours or marinated or basted with any number of flavoured butters or sauces.

Selecting Poultry to Broil or Grill

Smaller birds such as Cornish hens, chickens and squab are especially well suited for broiling or grilling. Whole birds should be split or cut into smaller pieces before cooking; their joints may be broken so that they lie flat. Quail and other small birds can be skewered before being broiled to help them cook evenly and retain their shape. Be especially careful when cooking breast portions or boneless pieces: The direct heat of the broiler or grill can over-cook the item very quickly.

Seasoning Poultry to Be Broiled or Grilled

Poultry is fairly neutral in flavour and responds well to marinating. Poultry may also be basted periodically during the cooking process with flavoured butter, oil or barbecue sauce. At the very least, broiled or grilled poultry should be well seasoned with salt and pepper just before cooking.

Determining Doneness

With the exception of duck breasts and squab, which are sometimes left pink, broiled or grilled poultry is always cooked well done. This makes the poultry particularly susceptible to becoming dry and tough because it contains little fat and is cooked at very high temperatures. Particular care must be taken to ensure that the item does not become overcooked.

Four methods are used to determine the doneness of broiled or grilled poultry:

1. *Touch*—When the item is done it will have a firm texture, resist pressure and spring back quickly when pressed with tongs.
2. *Temperature*—Use an instant-read thermometer to determine the item's internal temperature. This may be difficult, however, because of the item's size and the heat from the broiler or grill. Insert the thermometer in the thickest part of the item away from any bones. It should read 165–170°F (74–77°C) at the coolest point. The higher temperature (170°F/77°C) is recommended for safety; if the product is large and stuffed, the temperature should be 185°F (85°C).
3. *Looseness of the joints*—When bone-in poultry is done, the leg will begin to move freely in its socket.
4. *Colour of the juices*—Poultry is done when its juices run clear or show just a trace of pink. This degree of doneness is known in French as **à point**.

Accompaniments to Broiled and Grilled Poultry

If the item was basted with a herb butter it can be served with additional butter; if the item was basted with barbecue sauce, it should be served with the same sauce. Be careful, however, that any marinade or sauce that came in contact with the raw poultry is not served unless it is cooked thoroughly to destroy harmful bacteria. Additional sauce suggestions are found in Table 10.5.

Broiled or grilled poultry is very versatile and goes well with almost any side dish. Seasoned and grilled vegetables are a natural accompaniment, and deep-fat-fried potatoes are commonly served.

BASIC PROCEDURE FOR BROILING OR GRILLING POULTRY

As with meats, broiled or grilled poultry can be prepared by placing it directly on the grate. Poultry is also often broiled using a rotisserie.

1. Heat the broiler or grill.
2. Use a wire brush to remove any charred or burnt particles that may be stuck to the broiler or grill grate. The grate can be wiped with a lightly oiled towel to remove any remaining particles and help season it.

3. Prepare the item to be broiled or grilled by marinating or seasoning as desired; it may be brushed lightly with oil to keep it from sticking to the grate.

4. Place the item on the grate, presentation side (skin side) down. Following the example in Chapter 9, turn the item to produce the attractive crosshatch marks associated with broiling or grilling. Baste the item often. Use tongs to turn or flip the item without piercing the surface so that valuable juices do not escape.

5. Develop the proper surface colour while cooking the item until it is done *à point*. To do so, adjust the position of the item on the broiler or grill or adjust the distance between the grate and heat source. Large pieces and bone-in pieces that are difficult to cook completely on the broiler or grill can be finished in the oven.

A commonly used procedure to cook a large volume of poultry is to place the seasoned items in a broiler pan or other shallow pan and then place the pan directly under the broiler. Baste the items periodically, turning them once when they are halfway done. Items begun this way can be easily finished by transferring the entire pan to the oven.

1. Marinate the squab in white wine marinade.

2. Dry the squab.

3. Brush the squab with the melted basil butter.

◆◆◆

RECIPE 17.2

GRILLED SQUAB WITH BASIL BUTTER

Yield: 4 Servings

Squab, whole	4	4
Fresh basil leaves	16	16
White Wine Marinade (Recipe 17.1)	1 pt.	450 mL
Salt and pepper	TT	TT
Basil butter	6 oz.	170 g

1. Remove the backbone and breast bone from each squab. The birds will lie flat and remain in one piece.

2. Make a slit below each leg and tuck the leg bone into the slit.

3. Carefully slide two basil leaves under the skin over each breast to cover the meat.

4. Marinate the squab in the white wine marinade for 1–2 hours.

5. Heat and prepare the grill.

6. Remove the squab from the marinade and pat dry.

7. Melt approximately 4 ounces (120 g) of the basil butter, leaving enough for 8 thin slices to be served with the finished dish.

8. Brush the squab with basil butter and place it skin side down on the grill. Grill the squab, turning once and basting periodically with the melted basil butter. Finish in the oven if necessary.

9. Serve the squab with a slice of basil butter melting over each breast.

4. Grill the squab.

5. Serve the squab with a slice of basil butter.

Approximate values per serving:

Calories	690
Total fat	50 g
Saturated fat	26 g
Cholesterol	260 mg
Sodium	1070 mg
Total carbohydrates	0 g
Protein	60 g
Vitamin A	40%

Roasting

Properly roasted (or baked) poultry is attractively browned on the surface and tender and juicy throughout. Proper cooking temperatures ensure a crisp exterior and juicy interior. Most roasted poultry is cooked until the juices run clear. Squab and duck breasts are an exception: They are often served medium rare or pink.

Selecting Poultry to Roast

Almost every kind of poultry is suitable for roasting, but younger birds produce a more tender finished product. Because of variations in fat content, different kinds of poultry require different roasting temperatures and procedures.

BASIC PROCEDURE FOR TRUSSING POULTRY

Trussing is tying a bird into a more compact shape with thread or butcher's twine. This allows the bird to cook more evenly, helps the bird retain moisture and improves the appearance of the finished product. There are many methods for trussing poultry, some of which require a special tool called a trussing needle. Here we show a simple method using butcher's twine.

1. Square up the bird by pressing it firmly with both hands. Tuck the first joint of the wing behind the back or trim off the first and second joints as shown.

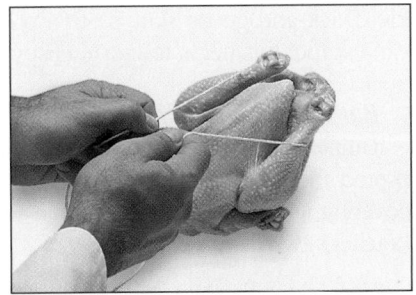

2. Cut a piece of butcher's twine approximately three times the bird's length. With the breast up and the neck towards you, pass the twine under the bird approximately one inch (2.5 cm) in front of the tail.

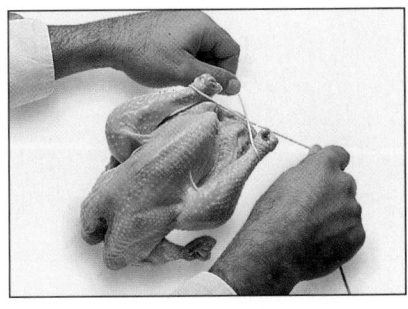

3. Bring the twine up around the legs and cross the ends, creating an X between the legs. Pass the ends of the twine below the legs.

4. Pull the ends of the twine tightly across the leg and thigh joint and across the wing if the first and second joint were trimmed off or just above the wings if they are intact.

5. Pull the string tight and tie it securely just above the neck.

6. Two examples of properly trussed birds: one with the wings intact and one with the first and second wing joints removed.

Seasoning Poultry to Be Roasted

Although the mild flavour of most poultry is enhanced by a wide variety of herbs and spices, roasted poultry is often only lightly seasoned with salt and pepper. Poultry that is roasted at high temperatures should never be seasoned with herbs on its surface because the high cooking temperatures will burn them. If herbs or additional spices are used they should be stuffed into the cavity. A mirepoix or a bouquet garni may also be added to the cavity for additional flavour. The cavities of dark-meated birds such as ducks and geese are often stuffed with fresh or dried fruits.

Cooking Temperatures

Small birds such as squab and Cornish game hens should be roasted at the relatively high temperatures of 375–400°F (190–200°C). These temperatures help produce crisp, well-coloured skins without overcooking the flesh. Chickens are best roasted at temperatures between 350 and 375°F (180–190°C). This temperature range allows the skin to crisp and the flesh to cook without causing the bird to stew in its own juices. Large birds such as capons and turkeys are started at high temperatures of 400–425°F (200–220°C) to brown the skin, then finished at lower temperatures of 275–325°F (135–160°C) to promote even cooking and produce a moister product. Ducks and geese, which are very high in fat, must be roasted at the high temperatures of 375–425°F (190–220°C) to render as much fat from the skin as possible. Duck and goose skin is often pricked before roasting so the rendered fat can escape; this helps to create crispy skin.

Barding Poultry to Be Roasted

Guineas, squabs or any skinless birds without an adequate fat covering to protect them from drying out during roasting can be barded. Bard the bird by covering its entire surface with thin slices of pork backfat, securing them with butcher's twine. See page 271.

Basting Roasted Poultry

With the exception of fatty birds such as ducks and geese, all poultry items should be basted while they roast to help retain moisture. To baste a bird, spoon or ladle the fat that collects in the bottom of the roasting pan over the bird at 15-to-20-minute intervals. Lean birds that are not barded will not produce enough fat for basting and may be brushed with butter in the same manner.

Determining Doneness

Four methods are used to determine the doneness of roasted poultry. It is best to use a combination of these methods.

1. *Temperature*—Test the internal temperature of the bird with an instant-read thermometer. The thermometer should be inserted in the bird's thigh, which is the last part to become fully cooked. It should not touch the bone and should read a minimum of 165°F (74°C). To ensure a safer product, it is recommended that poultry be cooked to 170°F (77°C) and as high as 185°F (85°C) for stuffed birds. This method works best with large birds such as capons and turkeys. Large birds are subject to some degree of carryover cooking. This is not as much of a concern with poultry as it is with meat because large birds are always cooked well done.

2. *Looseness of the joints*—The thigh and leg will begin to move freely in their sockets when the bird is done.

TABLE 17.8 GENERAL ROASTING TEMPERATURES AND TIMES

Poultry Kind or Class	Cooking Temperatures		Minutes	
Capons	350–375°F	180–190°C	18–20 min. per lb.	35–40 min. per kg
Chickens	375–400°F	190–200°C	15–18 min. per lb.	30–35 min. per kg
Ducks and geese	375–425°F	190–220°C	12–15 min. per lb.	25–30 min. per kg
Game hens	375–400°F	190–200°C	45–60 min. total	
Guineas	375–400°F	190–200°C	18–20 min. per lb.	35–40 min. per kg
Squab	400°F	200°C	30–40 min. total	
Turkeys (large)	325°F	160°C	12–15 min. per lb.	25–30 min. per kg

3. *Colour of juices*—This method is used with birds that are not stuffed. Use a kitchen fork to tilt the bird, allowing some of the juices that have collected in the cavity to run out. Clear juices may indicate that the bird is done. If the juices are cloudy or pink, the bird is undercooked.

4. *Time*—Because there are so many variables, timing alone is less reliable than other methods. It is useful, however, for planning production when large quantities are roasted and as a general guideline when used with other methods. Table 17.8 gives some general timing guidelines for roasting several kinds of poultry.

Accompaniments to Roasted Poultry

The most common accompaniments to roasted poultry are bread stuffing and gravy. Large birds, such as capons and turkeys, produce adequate drippings for making sauce or pan gravy. Small birds, such as squab and Cornish game hens, are often stuffed with wild rice or other ingredients and served with a sauce that is made separately.

Ducks and geese are complemented by stuffings containing rice, fruits, berries and nuts. They are very fatty and if stuffed, they should be roasted on a rack or mirepoix bed to ensure that the fat that collects in the pan during roasting does not penetrate the cavity, making the stuffing greasy. Ducks and geese are often served with a citrus- or fruit-based sauce. Its high acid content complements these rich, fatty birds.

BASIC PROCEDURE FOR STUFFING POULTRY

Small birds such as Cornish game hens, small chickens and squab can be stuffed successfully. Stuffing larger birds, especially for volume production, is impractical and can be dangerous for the following reasons:

1. *Safety*—Stuffing is a good bacterial breeding ground and because it is difficult to control temperatures inside a stuffed bird, there is a risk of food-borne illness.
2. *Practicality*—Stuffing poultry is labour intensive.
3. *Quality*—Stuffed poultry must be cooked longer to cook the stuffing properly; this may cause the meat to be overcooked, becoming dry and tough.

When stuffing any bird, use the following guidelines.

1. Always be aware of temperatures when mixing the raw ingredients. All ingredients should be cold when they are mixed together, and the mixture's temperature should never be allowed to rise above 40°F (4°C).

2. Stuff the bird as close to roasting time as possible.
3. The neck and main body cavities should be loosely stuffed. The stuffing will expand during cooking.
4. After the cavities are filled, their openings should be secured with skewers and butcher's twine or by trussing.
5. After cooking, remove the stuffing from the bird and store separately.

BASIC PROCEDURE FOR ROASTING POULTRY

1. Season, bard, stuff and/or truss the bird as desired.
2. Place the bird in a roasting pan. It may be placed on a rack or mirepoix bed to prevent scorching and promote even cooking.
3. Roast uncovered, basting every 15 minutes.
4. Allow the bird to rest before carving to allow even distribution of juices. As the bird rests, prepare the pan gravy or sauce.

◆◆◆

RECIPE 17.3

ROAST TURKEY WITH CHESTNUT DRESSING AND GIBLET GRAVY

Yield: 16 portions: 4 oz. (120 g) turkey,
3 oz. (90 g) dressing, 4 oz. (120 mL) gravy

Young turkey, 12–15 lb. (5.5–6.5 kg) with giblets	1	1
Salt and pepper	TT	TT
Mirepoix	20 oz.	600 g
Onion, small dice	8 oz.	250 g
Celery, small dice	6 oz.	180 g
Whole butter	4 oz.	120 g
Fresh bread cubes	2 lb.	1 kg
Eggs, beaten	2	2
Fresh parsley, chopped	1 Tbsp.	15 mL
Chicken stock	2-1/4 qt.	2 L
Chestnuts, cooked and peeled, chopped coarse	8 oz.	250 g
Pastry flour	3 oz.	90 g

1. Place the turkey in the roasting pan.

2. Add the mirepoix to the roasting pan.

1. Remove the giblets from the turkey's cavity and set aside. Season the turkey inside and out with salt and pepper. Truss the turkey.
2. Place the turkey in a roasting pan. Roast at 400°F (200°C) for 30 minutes. Reduce the temperature to 325°F (160°C) and continue cooking the turkey to an internal temperature of 170°F (77°C), approximately 2-1/2 to 3 hours. Baste the turkey often during cooking. Approximately 45 minutes before the turkey is done, add the mirepoix to the roasting pan. If the turkey begins to overbrown, cover it loosely with aluminum foil.
3. To make the dressing, sauté the diced onion and celery in the butter until tender.
4. In a large bowl, toss together the bread cubes, salt, pepper, eggs, parsley, sautéed onions and celery, 4 ounces (120 mL) of chicken stock and the chestnuts.

5. Place the dressing in a buttered hotel pan and cover with aluminum foil or buttered parchment paper. Bake at 350°F (175°C) until done, approximately 45 minutes.

6. As the turkey roasts, simmer the giblets (neck, heart and gizzard) in 1 quart (1 L) of the chicken stock until tender, approximately 1-1/2 hours.

7. When the turkey is done, remove it from the roasting pan and set aside to rest. Degrease the roasting pan, reserving 3 ounces (90 g) of the fat to make a roux.

8. Place the roasting pan on the stove top and brown the mirepoix.

9. Deglaze the pan with a small amount of chicken stock. Transfer the mirepoix and stock to a saucepot and add the remaining stock and the broth from the giblets. Bring to a simmer and degrease.

10. Make a blond roux with the reserved fat and the flour. Add the roux to the liquid, whisking well to prevent lumps. Simmer 15 minutes. Strain the gravy through a china cap lined with cheesecloth.

11. Remove the meat from the turkey neck. Trim the gizzard. Finely chop the neck meat, heart and gizzard and add to the gravy. Adjust the seasonings.

12. Carve the turkey and serve with a portion of chestnut dressing and giblet gravy.

Approximate values per serving:

Calories	720
Total fat	23 g
Saturated fat	9 g
Cholesterol	250 mg
Sodium	700 mg
Total carbohydrates	41 g
Protein	87 g
Vitamin A	6%
Iron	40%

3. Toss the dressing ingredients together.

4. Brown the mirepoix.

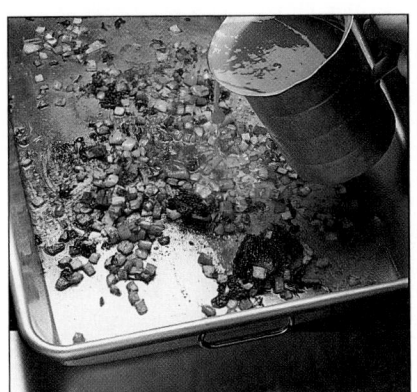

5. Deglaze the roasting pan.

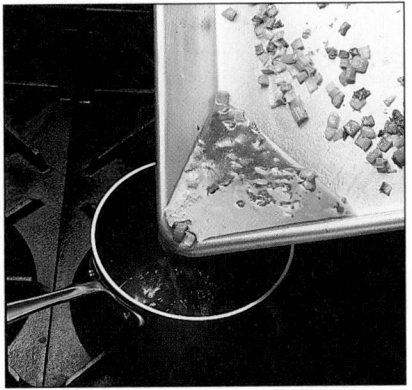

6. Transfer the mirepoix and stock to a saucepot.

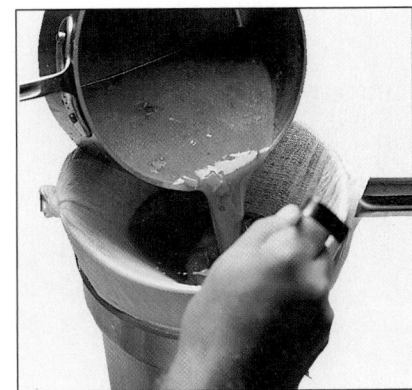

7. Strain the gravy through a china cap and cheesecloth.

Carving Roasted Poultry

Poultry can be carved in the kitchen, at tableside or on a buffet in a variety of manners. The carving methods described below produce slices of both light and dark meat.

BASIC PROCEDURE FOR CARVING A TURKEY, CAPON OR OTHER LARGE BIRD

1. After roasting, allow the turkey to stand for 20 minutes so the juices can redistribute themselves. Holding the turkey firmly with a carving fork, pry a leg outward and locate the joint. Remove the leg and thigh in one piece by cutting through the joint with the tip of a knife.

2. Repeat the procedure on the other side. Once both legs and thighs have been removed, slice the meat from the thigh by holding the leg firmly with one hand and slicing parallel to the bone.

3. Separate the thigh from the leg bone by cutting through the joint. Slice the meat from the leg by cutting parallel to the bone.

4. Cut along the breastbone, following the natural curvature of the bones to separate the breast meat from the ribs.

5. Remove an entire half breast and slice it on the cutting board as shown. Cut on an angle to produce larger slices.

6. Alternatively, the breast can be carved on the bird. Make a horizontal cut just above the wing in toward the rib bones.

7. Slice the breast meat as shown.

BASIC PROCEDURE FOR CARVING A CHICKEN OR OTHER SMALL BIRD

1. After allowing the chicken to rest for 15 minutes so the juices can redistribute themselves, cut through the skin between the leg and breast.

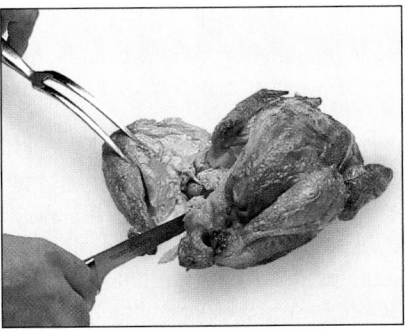

2. Use a kitchen fork to pry the leg and thigh away from the breast. Locate the thigh's ball joint and cut through it with the knife tip, separating it completely from the rest of the chicken. Be sure to cut around the delicate oyster meat, leaving it attached to the thigh.

3. With the knife tip, cut through the skin and meat on one side of the breast bone. Cut and pull the meat away from the bones with the knife.

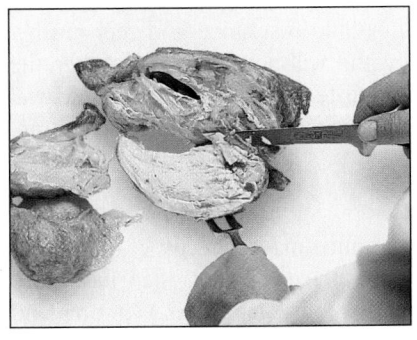

4. Cut through the wing joint, separating the breast and wing from the carcass. Repeat this procedure on the other side of the bird.

5. The chicken is now quartered.

6. To cut it into eight pieces, separate the wings from the breasts and the thighs from the legs.

Sautéing

Sautéed poultry should be tender and juicy, its flavour developed by proper browning. Additional flavours come from a sauce made by deglazing the pan, usually with wine, and adding garnishes, seasonings and liquids. Stir-frying is a popular method of sautéing poultry; boneless pieces are cut into strips and quickly cooked with assorted vegetables and seasonings.

Selecting Poultry to Sauté

Most poultry is quite tender and well suited for sautéing. Although small birds such as squab can be sautéed bone-in, large pieces and bone-in cuts from larger birds should not be sautéed. Boneless breasts, suprêmes, and cutlets are the most common and practical cuts for sautéing. Because they are high in fat, boneless duck breasts can be sautéed without additional fat.

Seasoning Poultry to Be Sautéed

Poultry has a delicate flavour that is enhanced by a wide variety of herbs, spices, condiments and marinades. Flavour combinations are limited only by your imagination. When poultry items are dusted with flour before sautéing, the seasonings may first be added to the flour.

Cooking Temperatures

The sauté pan and the cooking fat must be hot before the poultry is added. The temperature at which the poultry is then sautéed is determined by its thickness and the desired colour of the finished product. A thin, boneless slice requires relatively high temperatures so that its surface is browned before the centre is overcooked. A thicker cut such as a suprême requires lower temperatures so that neither its surface nor the fond are burned before the item is fully cooked. Adjust the temperature throughout the cooking process to achieve the desired results, never letting the pan become too cool.

If the pan is overcrowded or otherwise allowed to cool, the poultry will cook in its own juices and absorb oil from the pan, resulting in a poor-quality product.

Determining Doneness

Thin cuts of poultry cook very quickly, so timing is a useful tool; it is less useful with thicker cuts. Experienced cooks can tell the doneness of an item by judging the temperature of the sauté pan and the colour of the item being cooked.

A more practical method is to press the item with a tong and judge the resistance. Very undercooked poultry will offer little resistance and feel mushy. Slightly underdone poultry will feel spongy and will not spring back when the tong is removed. Properly cooked poultry will feel firm to the touch and will spring back when the tong is removed. Overcooked poultry will feel very firm, almost hard, and will spring back quickly.

Accompaniments to Sautéed Poultry

Sautéed poultry is usually served with a sauce made directly in the pan in which the item was cooked. The sauce uses the fond for added flavour. A wide variety of ingredients, including garlic, onions, shallots, mushrooms and tomatoes, are commonly added to the pan as well as wine and stock. Table 10.5 suggests several sauces for sautéed poultry.

Sautéed items are often served with a starch such as pasta, rice or potatoes.

BASIC PROCEDURE FOR SAUTÉING POULTRY

1. Heat a sauté pan and add enough fat or oil to just cover the bottom.
2. Add the poultry item, presentation side down, and cook until browned.
3. Turn the item, using tongs or by tossing the item back upon itself using the pan's sloped sides.
4. Larger items can be finished in an oven. Either place the sauté pan in the oven or transfer the poultry to another pan. The latter procedure allows a sauce to be made in the original pan as the poultry cooks in the oven.
   Hold smaller pieces that are thoroughly cooked in a warm place so that the pan can be used for making the sauce.

BASIC PROCEDURE FOR MAKING A SAUCE IN THE SAUTÉ PAN

1. Pour off any excess fat or oil from the sauté pan, leaving enough to sauté the sauce ingredients.
2. Add ingredients such as garlic, shallots and mushrooms that will be used as garnishes and sauce flavourings; sauté them.

3. Deglaze the pan with wine, stock or other liquids. Scrape the pan, loosening the fond and allowing it to dissolve in the liquid. Reduce the liquid.
4. Add any ingredients that do not require long cooking times such as herbs and spices. Adjust the sauce's consistency and seasonings.
5. For service, the poultry can be returned to the pan for a moment to reheat it and coat it with the sauce. The poultry should remain in the sauce just long enough to reheat. Do not attempt to cook the poultry in the sauce.
6. Serve the poultry with the accompanying sauce.

1. Sauté the breasts in butter.

◆◆◆

RECIPE 17.4

CHICKEN SAUTÉ WITH ONIONS, GARLIC AND BASIL

Yield: 6 Servings

Chicken breasts, boneless, skinless, approx. 8 oz. (250 g) each	3	3
Salt and pepper	TT	TT
Flour	as needed	as needed
Clarified butter	1 oz.	30 mL
Onion, small dice	2 oz.	60 g
Garlic cloves, chopped	6	6
Dry white wine	4 oz.	120 mL
Lemon juice	1 Tbsp.	15 mL
Tomato concassé	6 oz.	180 g
Chicken stock	4 oz.	120 mL
Fresh basil leaves, chiffonade	6	6

2. The fond left in the pan after sautéing the chicken.

1. Split the chicken breasts and remove the cartilage connecting the 2 halves.
2. Season the chicken with salt and pepper; dredge in flour.
3. Sauté the breasts in the butter, browning them and cooking *à point.* Hold in a warm place.
4. Add the onions and garlic to the fond and butter in the pan; sauté until the onions are translucent.
5. Deglaze the pan with the white wine and lemon juice.
6. Add the tomato and the chicken stock. Sauté to combine the flavours; reduce the sauce to the desired consistency.
7. Add the basil to the sauce and return the chicken breasts for reheating. Adjust the seasonings and serve 1/2 breast per portion with a portion of the sauce.

3. Sauté the onions and garlic.

4. Deglaze the pan with white wine and lemon juice.

Approximate values per 5 oz. (150 g) serving:

Calories	230
Total fat	8 g
Saturated fat	3.5 g
Cholesterol	90 mg
Sodium	580 mg
Total carbohydrates	9 g
Protein	30 g
Vitamin C	10%
Iron	10%

5. Add the tomatoes and chicken stock and simmer to combine the flavours.

6. Return the chicken to the pan to reheat.

Pan-Frying

Pan-fried poultry should be juicy. Its coating or batter should be crispy, golden brown, not excessively oily and free from any breaks that allow fat to penetrate. Both the poultry and the coating should be well seasoned.

Selecting Poultry to Pan-Fry

The most common pan-fried poultry is fried chicken. Young tender birds cut into small pieces produce the best results. Other cuts commonly pan-fried are boneless portions such as chicken breasts and turkey cutlets.

Seasoning Poultry to Be Pan-Fried

Pan-fried poultry is usually floured, breaded or battered before cooking. (Breadings and batters are discussed in Chapter 21, Deep-Fat Frying). Typically, the seasonings are added to the flour, breading or batter before the poultry item is coated. Seasonings can be a blend of any number of dried herbs and spices. But often only salt and pepper are required because the poultry will be served with a sauce or other accompaniments for additional flavours.

Cooking Temperatures

The fat should always be hot before the poultry is added. The temperature at which it is cooked is determined by the length of time required to cook it thoroughly. Pan-frying generally requires slightly lower temperatures than those used for sautéing. Within this range, thinner items require higher temperatures to produce good colour in a relatively short time. Thicker items and those containing bones require lower cooking temperatures and longer cooking times.

Determining Doneness

Even the largest pan-fried items may be too small to be accurately tested with an instant-read thermometer, so timing and experience are the best tools to determine doneness. Thin cutlets cook very quickly, so it is relatively easy to judge their doneness. On the other hand, fried chicken can take as long as 30–45 minutes to cook, requiring skill and experience to determine doneness.

Accompaniments to Pan-Fried Poultry

Because pan-frying does not produce fond or drippings that can be used to make a sauce, pan-fried poultry is usually served with lemon wedges, a vegetable garnish or a separately made sauce. Fried chicken is an exception; it is sometimes served with a country gravy made by degreasing the pan, making a roux with a portion of the fat and adding milk and seasonings.

BASIC PROCEDURE FOR PAN-FRYING POULTRY

1. Heat enough fat in a heavy sauté pan to immerse the item to be cooked one-quarter to halfway. The fat should be at approximately 325°F (160°C).
2. Add the floured, breaded or battered item to the hot fat, being careful not to splash. The fat must be hot enough to sizzle and bubble when the item is added.
3. Turn the item when the first side is the proper colour; it should be half cooked at this point. Larger items may need to be turned more than once to brown them properly on all sides.
4. Remove the browned poultry from the pan and drain it on absorbent paper.

◆◆◆

RECIPE 17.5

PAN-FRIED CHICKEN WITH PAN GRAVY

Yield: 8 2-piece Servings

Frying chickens, 2 lb. 8 oz. to 3 lb. each (1.1–1.4 kg), cut in 8 pieces	2	2
Salt and pepper	TT	TT
Garlic powder	2 tsp.	10 mL
Onion powder	2 tsp.	10 mL
Dried oregano	1 tsp.	5 mL
Dried basil	1 tsp.	5 mL
Flour	9-1/2 oz.	270 g
Buttermilk	8 oz.	250 mL
Oil	as needed	as needed
Onion, small dice	4 oz.	120 g
Half-and-half cream or chicken stock	1-1/2 pt.	750 mL

1. Dip the chicken pieces in the buttermilk.

2. Dredge the chicken in the flour mixture.

1. Season the chicken with salt and pepper.

2. Add the herbs and spices to 8 ounces (250 g) of the flour.

3. Dip the chicken pieces in the buttermilk.

4. Dredge the chicken in the seasoned flour.

5. Pan-fry the chicken in 1/4 to 1/3 inch (1 cm) of oil until done, approximately 40 minutes, turning so it cooks evenly. Reduce the heat as necessary to prevent the chicken from becoming too dark. Or remove the chicken when well browned, drain it and finish cooking it in the oven.

6. To make the pan gravy, pour off all but 1-1/2 ounces (45 mL) of oil from the pan, carefully reserving the fond.

7. Add the diced onions and sauté until translucent.

8. Add 1-1/2 ounces (45 g) of flour and cook to make a blond roux.

9. Whisk in the liquid and simmer approximately 15 minutes.

10. Strain through cheesecloth and adjust the seasonings.

11. Serve 1/4 chicken (2 pieces) per person with 4 ounces (120 mL) gravy.

Approximate values per 7 oz. (210 g) serving:	
Calories	510
Total fat	4.5 g
Saturated fat	1 g
Cholesterol	0 mg
Sodium	7780 mg
Total carbohydrates	104 g
Protein	13 g

3. Add the chicken to the oil. The bubbling fat indicates the proper cooking temperature.

4. Turn the chicken so it cooks evenly.

5. Sauté the diced onions until translucent.

6. Add the liquid to the roux.

Moist-Heat Cooking Methods

The moist-heat cooking methods most often used with poultry are poaching and simmering. Poaching is used to cook tender birds for short periods of time. Simmering is used to cook older, tougher birds for longer periods to tenderize them. Poaching and simmering are similar procedures, the principal differences being the temperature of the cooking liquid and the length of cooking time.

Poaching and Simmering

Poached or simmered poultry should be moist, tender and delicately flavoured. Although cooked in stock, overcooking will cause the poultry to be dry and tough. During cooking, some of the poultry's flavour is transferred to the cooking liquid, which can be used to make a sauce for the finished product.

Selecting Poultry to Poach or Simmer

Young birds are best suited for poaching; boneless chicken pieces are the most commonly used parts. Older, tougher birds are usually simmered. Duck and geese are rarely poached or simmered because of their high fat content.

Seasoning Poultry to Be Poached or Simmered

When poaching poultry it is especially important to use a well-seasoned and highly flavoured liquid in order to infuse as much flavour as possible into the item being cooked. Either strong stock with a sachet or a mixture of stock or water and white wine with a bouquet garni or oignon piqué produces good results. The poultry should be completely covered with liquid so that it cooks evenly. However, if too much liquid is used and it is not strongly flavoured, flavours may be leached out of the poultry, resulting in a bland finished product.

Poultry is often simmered in water instead of stock. A sachet and a generous mirepoix should be added to help flavour it. Typically, simmering birds results in a strong broth that may be used to complete the recipe or reserved for other uses.

Cooking Temperatures

For best results, poultry should be poached at low temperatures, between 165°F and 175°F (75–80°C). Cooking poultry to the proper doneness at these temperatures produces a product that is moist and tender.

Simmering is done at slightly higher temperatures, between 185°F (85°C) and just below the boiling point. When simmering, do not allow the liquid to boil, as this may result in a dry, tough and stringy finished product.

Determining Doneness

Poached poultry, whether whole or boneless, is cooked just until done. An instant-read thermometer inserted in the thigh or thicker part of the bird should read 170°F (77°C). Any juices that run from the bird should be clear.

Simmered poultry is usually cooked for longer periods to allow the moist heat to tenderize the meat. A chicken that weighs 3 pounds 8 ounces (1.5 kg), for example, may take 2-1/2 hours to cook.

Accompaniments to Poached and Simmered Poultry

Poached or simmered poultry can be served hot or cold. The meat from these birds can be served cold in salads, hot in casseroles or used in any dish that calls for cooked poultry.

Poached items are typically served with a flavoured mayonnaise or a sauce made from the reduced poaching liquid, such as sauce suprême. Poultry is also often poached as a means of producing a low-calorie dish. If so, a vegetable coulis makes a good sauce or the poultry can be served with a portion of its cooking liquid and a vegetable garnish.

Simmered poultry to be served cold will be moister and more flavourful if it is cooled in its cooking liquid. To do so, remove the pot containing the bird and the cooking liquid from the heat when the bird is still slightly undercooked. Cool the meat and broth in a water bath following the procedures in Chapter 10, Stocks and Sauces. Once cooled, remove the meat and wipe off any congealed broth before proceeding with the recipe.

Basic Procedure for Poaching or Simmering Poultry

1. Cut or truss the item to be cooked as directed in the recipe.
2. Prepare the cooking liquid and bring it to a simmer. Submerge the poultry in the cooking liquid, or arrange the items to be poached in an appropriate pan and add the poaching liquid to the pan.
3. Poach or simmer the item to the desired doneness in the oven or on the stove top. Maintain the proper cooking temperature throughout the process.
4. Remove the item and hold it for service in a portion of the cooking liquid or, using an ice bath, cool the item in its cooking liquid.
5. The cooking liquid may be used to prepare an accompanying sauce or reserved for use in other dishes.

◆◆◆

RECIPE 17.6

Poached Breast of Chicken with Tarragon Sauce

Yield: 8 Servings

Chicken breasts, boneless, skinless, approx. 8 oz. (250 g) each	4	4
Whole butter	1-1/2 oz.	45 g
Salt and white pepper	TT	TT
White wine	4 oz.	120 mL
Chicken stock	1 pt.	450 mL
Bay leaf	1	1
Dried thyme	1/4 tsp.	1 mL
Dried tarragon	1 tsp.	5 mL
Flour	1 oz.	30 g
Cream, 35%	4 oz.	120 mL
Fresh tarragon sprigs	as needed	as needed

1. Trim any rib meat and fat from the breasts. Cut the breasts into two pieces, removing the strip of cartilage that joins the halves.
2. Select a pan that will just hold the breasts when they are placed close together. Rub the pan with approximately 1/2 ounce (15 g) of butter.

Continued

*Approximate values per
4 oz. (120 g) serving:*

Calories	250
Total fat	13 g
Saturated fat	7 g
Cholesterol	105 mg
Sodium	590 mg
Total carbohydrates	4 g
Protein	29 g
Vitamin A	10%

3. Season the chicken breasts with salt and pepper and arrange them in the buttered pan, presentation side up.

4. Add the white wine, stock, bay leaf, thyme and dried tarragon.

5. Cut and butter a piece of parchment paper and cover the chicken breasts.

6. Bring the liquid to a simmer and reduce the temperature to poach the chicken.

7. Make a blond roux with 1 ounce (30 g) of butter and 1 ounce (30 g) of flour; set aside to cool.

8. When the breasts are done, remove them from the liquid. Thicken the liquid with the roux. Add the cream. Simmer and reduce to the desired consistency.

9. Strain the sauce through cheesecloth and adjust the seasonings.

10. Serve each half breast napped with approximately 2 ounces (60 mL) of sauce; garnish each portion with a sprig of fresh tarragon.

1. Arrange the breasts in an appropriate pan.

2. Add the white wine, chicken stock and seasonings to the pan.

3. Cover the breasts with a piece of buttered parchment paper.

4. Add the cream to the thickened sauce.

5. Plate the poached chicken breast.

Combination Cooking Methods

Braising and stewing use both dry and moist heat to produce a moist, flavourful product. One difference between braising and stewing when applied to meats is the size of the cut being cooked: Large cuts of meat are braised; smaller ones are stewed. Because most poultry is relatively small, this distinction does not readily apply in poultry cookery; therefore, the two cooking methods are discussed together here.

Braising and Stewing

Braised or stewed poultry should be moist and fork tender. The poultry is always served with the liquid in which it was cooked. Ducks and geese are braised or stewed in much the same way as red meats. Chicken cacciatore, coq au vin and chicken fricassee are examples of braised or stewed chicken dishes.

Selecting Poultry to Braise or Stew

Braising and stewing, being slow, moist cooking processes, are often thought of as means to tenderize tough meats. Although they can be used to tenderize older, tougher birds, these cooking methods are more often selected as a means to add moisture and flavour to poultry that is inherently tender, such as young ducks and chickens. Typically, the birds are disjointed and cooked bone-in, just until done, so that they retain their juiciness.

Seasoning Poultry to Be Braised or Stewed

Braised or stewed items obtain much of their flavour from the cooking liquid and other ingredients added during the cooking process. The main item and the cooking liquid should be well seasoned. If other seasonings such as an oignon piquet, sachet, bouquet garni or dried herbs and spices are required, they should be added at the beginning of the cooking process rather than at the end. This allows the flavours to blend and penetrate the larger pieces of poultry. If the poultry is dredged in flour prior to browning, seasonings may be added directly to the flour. As with all dishes using combination cooking methods, the finished dish should have the flavour of the poultry in the sauce and the moisture and flavour of the sauce in the poultry.

Cooking Temperatures

Some recipes, such as chicken cacciatore and coq au vin, require the main item to be thoroughly browned during the initial stages; others, such as chicken fricassee, do not. In either case, after the addition of the liquid it is important to maintain a slow simmer rather than a rapid boil. This can be done on the stove top or in the oven. Low temperatures control the cooking and produce a tender, juicy finished product.

Determining Doneness

Tenderness is the key to determining doneness. It can be determined by inserting a kitchen fork into the poultry. There should be little resistance and the poultry should freely fall off the fork. The pieces should retain their shape, however; if they fall apart they are overdone. Small boneless pieces can be tested by cutting into them with a fork.

Accompaniments to Braised or Stewed Poultry

All braises and stews are cooked in a liquid that results in a sauce or broth served as part of the finished dish. Rice, pasta or boiled potatoes are natural accompaniments to almost any braised or stewed dish, as are boiled vegetables.

BASIC PROCEDURE FOR BRAISING OR STEWING POULTRY

1. Sear the main item in butter or oil, developing colour as desired.
2. Add vegetables and other ingredients as called for in the recipe and sauté.
3. Add flour or roux if used.
4. Add the appropriate liquid.

5. Cover and simmer on the stove top or in the oven until done.
6. Add seasonings and garnishes at the appropriate times during the cooking process.
7. Finish the dish by adding cream or a liaison to the sauce or by adjusting its consistency. Adjust the seasonings.
8. Serve a portion of the main item with the sauce and appropriate garnish.

RECIPE 17.7

CHICKEN FRICASSEE

Yield: 8 2-piece Servings

Frying chickens, 2 lb. 8 oz. to 3 lb. (1.1–1.4 kg) each, cut into 8 pieces	2	2
Salt and white pepper	TT	TT
Clarified butter	3 oz.	90 mL
Onion, medium dice	10 oz.	300 g
Flour	3 oz.	90 g
Dry white wine	8 oz.	250 mL
Chicken stock	1 qt.	1 L
Sachet:		
Bay leaf	1	1
Dry thyme	1/2 tsp.	2 mL
Peppercorns, cracked	1/2 tsp.	2 mL
Parsley stems	8	8
Garlic clove, crushed	1	1
Cream, 35%	8 oz.	250 mL
Nutmeg	TT	TT

1. Season the chicken with salt and white pepper.
2. Sauté the chicken in the butter without browning. Add the onions and continue to sauté until they are translucent.
3. Sprinkle the flour over the chicken and onions and stir to make a roux. Cook the roux for 2 minutes without browning.
4. Deglaze the pan with white wine. Add the chicken stock and sachet; season with salt. Cover the pot and simmer until done, approximately 30–45 minutes.

1. Sauté the chicken and onions in butter.

2. Sprinkle the flour over the chicken.

3. Deglaze the pan with white wine.

4. Remove the chicken from the pot.

5. Strain the sauce through cheese-cloth.

6. Return the chicken to the sauce to reheat it for service.

5. Remove the chicken from the pot and hold in a warm place. Strain the sauce through cheesecloth and return it to a clean pan.

6. Add the cream and bring the sauce to a simmer. Add the nutmeg and adjust the seasonings. Return the chicken to the sauce to reheat it for service.

Approximate values per 8 oz. (250 g) serving:

Calories	700
Total fat	20 g
Saturated fat	12 g
Cholesterol	60 mg
Sodium	7950 mg
Total carbohydrates	113 g
Protein	15 g
Vitamin A	20%

CONCLUSION

The renowned French gastronome and author Jean-Anthelme Brillat-Savarin (1755–1826) once observed that "poultry is for the cook what canvas is for the painter." He meant, of course, that poultry, including chicken, duck, goose, guinea, pigeon and turkey, are wonderfully versatile foods that can be cooked by almost any method and with almost any seasonings, and can be served with many accompaniments and garnishes.

QUESTIONS FOR DISCUSSION

1. List the nine categories or kinds of poultry recognized by Agriculture Canada. How are these categories then divided into classes?
2. How should fresh poultry be stored? Discuss several procedures that should be followed carefully when working with poultry to prevent cross-contamination.
3. What is a suprême? Describe the step-by-step procedure for preparing a chicken suprême.
4. What is trussing? Why is this technique used with poultry?
5. Which poultry items are best suited for broiling or grilling? Explain your answer.
6. Describe the characteristics of properly roasted poultry. Which classes of poultry are recommended for roasting?
7. What is foie gras? Why must you be extremely careful when cooking foie gras?

ADDITIONAL POULTRY RECIPES

RECIPE 17.8
ROAST DUCK WITH RÖSTI POTATOES
NOTE: *This dish appears in the Chapter Opening photograph.*

THE FOUR SEASONS, New York, NY
Chef Christian Albin

Yield: 4 Servings   **Method:** Roasting

Ducks, 4-1/2 lb. (2 kg) each	2	2
Marinade:		
Fresh ginger, peeled and sliced thin	1 oz.	30 g
Garlic cloves, unpeeled and halved	2	2
Orange zest, julienne	1/2 orange	1/2 orange
Coriander seeds, crushed	2 tsp.	10 mL
Black peppercorns	1-1/2 tsp.	8 mL
Soy sauce	8 oz.	250 mL
Honey	2 Tbsp.	30 mL
Jasmine tea leaves, loose	4 Tbsp.	60 mL
Szechuan pepper	1 Tbsp.	15 mL
Sugared Orange Zest and Orange		
Sauce (recipe follows)	as needed	as needed
Rösti Potatoes (Recipe 23.14)		

1. Cut the wings off the ducks at the second joint and reserve. Remove the fat from the ducks' cavities.
2. Place the ducks on a rack in the refrigerator, breast sides up, a few inches (centimetres) apart. Air must circulate around the ducks so that the skin will dry. Leave the birds for 3 days.
3. Combine all of the marinade ingredients and refrigerate for 3 days, stirring daily.
4. Prick the duck skin with a knife point, except for the skin on the breast. Avoid touching or pressing on the breasts, as this will leave dark spots after roasting.
5. Place the ducks on a rack over a shallow pan. Strain the marinade and brush it liberally over the entire surface of both ducks. Spoon the remaining marinade into the ducks' cavities.
6. Let the ducks dry, breast side up, on the rack for 15 minutes. Scrape any marinade drippings from the pan into the cavities.
7. Adjust the oven racks so that one is at the lowest level and the other is directly above the first.
8. Place 3 quarts (3 L) water in a roasting pan and add the tea leaves. Place the pan on the lower rack of a 350°F (180°C) oven.
9. Position the ducks on the higher oven rack directly over the roasting pan (the ducks should not be touching). Roast undisturbed for 1-1/2 hours.
10. Remove the ducks from the oven. Drain and reserve the juices that have accumulated in the cavity.
11. Sprinkle the ducks with the Szechuan pepper; allow them to rest, then carve.
12. To serve, spoon a layer of Orange Sauce over the bottom of a warmed serving platter.

Approximate values per serving:

Calories	1200
Total fat	20 g
Saturated fat	4.5 g
Cholesterol	1390 mg
Sodium	950 mg
Total carbohydrates	7 g
Protein	249 g
Vitamin A	15%

13. Arrange a pair of drumsticks, wing bones and thighs at each end of the platter. Place the breast in the centre and garnish with orange segments. Sprinkle with the Sugared Orange Zest. Serve the duck with rösti potatoes (Recipe 23.14) and the remaining Orange sauce on the side.

SUGARED ORANGE ZEST AND ORANGE SAUCE

Yield: 12 oz. (350 mL)

Oranges	2	2
Sugar	3 oz.	90 g
Granulated sugar	as needed	as needed
Grand Marnier	2 Tbsp.	30 mL
Currant jelly	2 Tbsp.	30 mL
Basic Duck Sauce, hot (recipe follows)	12 oz.	350 mL
Lightly salted butter	2 Tbsp.	30 g
Kosher salt and black pepper	TT	TT

1. Remove the zest from the oranges and julienne. Blanch for 3 minutes in boiling water; drain.

2. Squeeze the oranges and boil the juice until reduced by one-quarter.

3. Place 3 ounces (90 g) of sugar and 8 ounces (250 mL) of water in a saucepan and bring to a boil. Add the julienned zest. Boil until the syrup begins to caramelize, turning light brown.

4. Have a bowl ready with a layer of granulated sugar. Remove the zest from the syrup and toss in the sugar until the zest is completely coated. Set the zest aside to cool.

5. Continue cooking the syrup until it becomes a dark caramel colour. Stir in the Grand Marnier, currant jelly and reduced orange juice. Whisk until smooth.

6. Pour in the Basic Duck Sauce and whisk until smooth. Cook for a few minutes to thicken slightly. Monter au beurre and season with salt and pepper.

Approximate values per serving:

Calories	100
Total fat	3 g
Saturated fat	1.5 g
Cholesterol	10 mg
Sodium	350 mg
Total carbohydrates	17 g
Protein	2 g
Vitamin A	10%

Claims—low fat; low cholesterol

BASIC DUCK SAUCE

Yield: 1-1/2 pt. (700 mL)

Vegetable oil	1 Tbsp.	15 mL
Necks and wing tips from 2 ducks		
Celery, chopped	3 oz.	90 g
Carrot, chopped	3 oz.	90 g
Onion, chopped	6 oz.	180 g
Bay leaf	1	1
Mushrooms, large, halved	3	3
Garlic cloves	4	4
Black pepper, crushed	1 Tbsp.	15 mL
Whole cloves	6	6
Tomato purée	2 Tbsp.	30 mL
Flour	2 Tbsp.	30 mL
Dry red wine	8 oz.	250 mL
Brown veal stock	2 pt.	900 mL
Cavity juices reserved from 2 roasted ducks		

1. Heat the oven to 400°F (200°C).

2. Heat the oil in a large sauté pan. Add the duck pieces and sauté until they are well caramelized. Place the pan in the oven and roast the duck pieces for 25 minutes at 350°F (180°C), stirring occasionally.

Continued

Approximate values per serving:

Calories	40
Total fat	1 g
Saturated fat	0 g
Cholesterol	5 mg
Sodium	140 mg
Total carbohydrates	5 g
Protein	2 g
Vitamin A	10%

Claims—no saturated fat; low fat; low cholesterol; low calorie

3. Add the celery, carrot, onion, bay leaf, mushrooms, garlic, pepper and cloves. Roast for 5 minutes.

4. Place the sauté pan on the stove top and add the tomato purée. Sprinkle the flour over the mixture and stir.

5. Add the red wine and brown stock. Stir; bring to a boil. Reduce the heat and simmer for 3 hours.

6. Stir in the cavity juices and cook for 10 minutes more.

7. Strain the sauce through a china cap into a saucepan. Press a ladle against the solids to remove as much liquid as possible.

8. Degrease the sauce and reduce until thick.

◆◆◆

RECIPE 17.9

ROAST CORNISH GAME HEN WITH WILD RICE STUFFING

Yield: 6 Servings   **Method:** Roasting

Whole butter, melted	6 oz.	180 g
Onion, fine dice	3 oz.	90 g
Mushrooms, chopped	6 oz.	180 g
Wild rice, cooked	1-1/2 cups	350 mL
Dried thyme, crushed	1/2 tsp.	2 mL
Dried marjoram, crushed	1/2 tsp.	2 mL
Salt and pepper	TT	TT
Cornish game hens	6	6

1. Sauté the onions and mushrooms in 2 ounces (60 g) of melted butter until tender. Cool.

2. Stir in the rice and herbs and season to taste with salt and pepper.

3. Stuff the cavity of each hen loosely with the rice mixture. Truss and place in a roasting pan.

4. Brush the hens with the remaining butter and season with salt and pepper. Roast at 400°F (200°C) for 15 minutes.

5. Reduce the oven temperature to 300°F (150°C) and roast until the juices run clear, approximately 30 minutes. Baste 2 or 3 times with melted butter.

6. Serve the hens with a pan gravy or a sauce made separately such as mushroom sauce.

NOTE: A mixture of white and wild rice also works well. Hens may be boned and shaped.

Approximate values per 14 oz. (420 g) serving:

Calories	970
Total fat	65 g
Saturated fat	26 g
Cholesterol	330 mg
Sodium	1580 mg
Total carbohydrates	12 g
Protein	86 g
Vitamin A	35%
Iron	25%

◆◆◆

RECIPE 17.10

COQ AU VIN

Yield: 8 2-piece Servings   **Method:** Braising

Chickens, 2 lb. 8 oz. to 3 lb. (1–1.4 kg)	2	2
Flour for dredging	as needed	as needed
Salt and pepper	TT	TT
Clarified butter	2 oz.	60 mL
Brandy	4 oz.	120 mL
Bouquet garni:		
Carrot stick, 4 in. (10 cm)	1	1
Leek, split, 4-in. (10-cm) piece	1	1
Fresh thyme	1 sprig	1 sprig
Bay leaf	1	1
Garlic cloves, peeled and crushed	6	6

Red wine	24 oz.	700 mL
Chicken stock	8 oz.	250 mL
Bacon **lardons**	4 oz.	120 g
Pearl onions, peeled	18	18
Mushroom caps, medium, quartered	10	10
Beurre manié	as needed	as needed
Large triangular croutons	8	8

Lardon—*bacon cut into 1/4 inch × 1/4 inch × 2 inch (6 mm × 6 mm × 5 cm) strips; used to moisten braised dishes and stews.*

1. Cut each chicken into 8 pieces and dredge in flour seasoned with salt and pepper.

2. Heat the clarified butter in a braising pan; brown the chicken.

3. Add the brandy and ignite. When the flame dies, add the bouquet garni, garlic, red wine and chicken stock. Bring to a boil, then reduce to a simmer.

4. Cover the pan and simmer until the chicken is tender, approximately 40 minutes.

5. In a separate pan, sauté the bacon until the fat begins to render. Add the onions and sauté until they begin to brown. Cook the bacon and onions covered, over low heat, until the onions are tender. Add the mushroom caps and cook them until tender.

6. Remove the chicken from the pan and adjust the sauce's consistency with the beurre manié. Strain the sauce through a china cap and adjust the seasonings.

7. Spoon the bacon, onions and mushrooms onto a serving platter, place the chicken over them and ladle the sauce over the finished dish. Serve with triangular croutons.

Approximate values per 12 oz. (360 g) serving:

Calories	860
Total fat	51 g
Saturated fat	17 g
Cholesterol	330 mg
Sodium	910 mg
Total carbohydrates	17 g
Protein	83 g
Vitamin A	60%
Iron	35%

❖❖❖

RECIPE 17.11

CHICKEN CACCIATORE

Yield: 8 2-piece Servings　　　　**Method:** Braising

Frying chickens, 2 lb. 8 oz. to 3 lb. each (1.1–1.4 kg)	2	2
Flour	2 oz.	60 g
Salt and pepper	TT	TT
Olive oil	2 oz.	60 mL
Onion, medium dice	4 oz.	120 g
Garlic cloves, chopped	3	3
Mushrooms, sliced	8 oz.	250 g
Dried thyme	1/4 tsp.	1 mL
White wine	2 oz.	60 mL
Brandy	1 oz.	30 mL
Demi-glace	16 oz.	450 mL
Tomato concassé	12 oz.	340 g

1. Cut each chicken into 8 pieces and dredge in flour seasoned with salt and pepper.

2. Heat the oil in a heavy brazier and brown the chicken well. Remove the chicken from the pan. Degrease the pan, leaving 1 tablespoon (15 mL) of fat.

3. Add the onions and garlic and sauté lightly. Add the mushrooms and thyme and continue sautéing until the mushrooms are tender.

4. Deglaze the pan with the white wine and brandy. Add the demi-glace and tomato.

5. Return the chicken to the pan and season with salt and pepper. Cover and cook until the chicken is done, approximately 30 minutes.

6. Serve 2 pieces of chicken with a portion of sauce.

Approximate values per 13 oz. (390 g) serving:

Calories	650
Total fat	29 g
Saturated fat	7 g
Cholesterol	235 mg
Sodium	500 mg
Total carbohydrates	11 g
Protein	86 g
Vitamin A	10%
Iron	25%

Dave Ryan

Canadian born and bred, Dave is one of the only chefs in Canada to win seven provincial culinary competition trophies in the last four years. He has won more than 24 medals at competitions in Canada and the U.S., and in 1996 took home a gold medal from the World Culinary Olympics in Berlin.

♦♦♦

RECIPE 17.12
CHICKEN MALIBU

LAKE OKANAGAN RESORT, KELOWNA, BC
Executive Chef Dave Ryan

Yield: 10 Servings   **Method:** Roasting

Ingredient		
Crab meat, fairly dry	10 oz.	280 g
Eggs	2 medium	2 medium
Cream, 35%	4 oz.	120 mL
Fresh white bread, crust removed and processed fine	4 slices	4 slices
Chives, chopped	3 Tbsp.	45 mL
Salt and pepper	TT	TT
Chicken breast, boneless, skinless, 5 oz. (150 g) each	10	10
Canola oil	as needed	as needed
Butter Sauce:		
Butter	2 tsp.	10 mL
Shallots, minced	2	2
Bay leaf	1	1
Okanagan Muller Thurgau	1 cup	250 mL
Cream, 35%	1-1/2 cup	375 mL
Cortina butter, chilled, cubed	1/4 lb.	110 g
Lemon juice	2 tsp.	10 mL
Salt and pepper	TT	TT
Chives, chopped	5	5
Melon balls: honey dew, cantaloupe, watermelon	3–6 pieces per serving	
Malibu rum	2–3 oz.	60–90 mL

1. For filling, in chilled bowl, mix together crab meat, eggs, cream, fresh bread, chives and salt and pepper. Reserve in refrigerator.
2. Cut pocket in chicken breasts or butterfly open.
3. Place one-tenth of the crab filling in chicken breast; repeat procedure. Shape the breasts.
4. To make the butter sauce, place 1 teaspoon (5 mL) of butter in a frying pan over low heat. Add shallots and sauté gently. Add bay leaf, then wine and reduce by half, then add cream, reduce by half again. Lower heat and whisk in the cubed butter, a little at a time. Squeeze in lemon juice and season to taste. Add chives and remove bay leaf. Keep the sauce warm.
5. Oil and season chicken breasts, then mark service side on grill. Place them in pan and finish in oven. Remove the breasts from pan. Reserve in a warm spot. Add a touch of butter to pan and sauté the melon lightly; deglaze with Malibu rum and flame off alcohol. Add butter sauce to the melon and rum mixture and pour it generously over sliced chicken breast.

Approximate values per serving:

Calories	516
Total fat	30 g
Saturated fat	17 g
Cholesterol	233 mg
Sodium	262 mg
Total carbohydrates	12 g
Protein	42 g

♦♦♦

RECIPE 17.13
CHICKEN YAKITORI

Yield: 8 Servings   **Method:** Grilling

Ingredient		
Soy sauce	8 oz.	250 mL
Sake	8 oz.	250 mL

Granulated sugar	2 oz.	60 g
Chicken breasts, boneless	2 lb.	1 kg
Cornstarch	1 Tbsp.	15 mL
Sesame seeds	1 Tbsp.	15 mL

1. Combine the soy sauce, sake and sugar. Reserve 8 ounces (250 mL) of the mixture.

2. Brush the chicken with a portion of the reserved soy sauce mixture and grill over hot charcoal until done, basting regularly.

3. To make the sauce, combine 2 ounces (60 mL) of the soy sauce mixture with the cornstarch. Bring the remainder to a boil in a small saucepan and stir in the cornstarch slurry. Stirring constantly, continue boiling until the sauce thickens. Simmer 1 minute.

4. Serve with short-grain white rice and garnish with sesame seeds.

Approximate values per
6 oz. (180 g) serving:

Calories	240
Total fat	4.5 g
Saturated fat	1 g
Cholesterol	95 mg
Sodium	1700 mg
Total carbohydrates	12 g
Protein	37 g

◆◆◆

RECIPE 17.14

CHICKEN AND SNOW PEAS IN BLACK BEAN SAUCE

Yield: 4 Servings   **Method:** Stir-frying

Chicken breasts, boneless, skinless	2 lb.	1 kg
Egg white	1	1
Chinese rice wine	6 oz.	180 mL
Cornstarch	2 Tbsp.	30 g
Soy sauce	2 oz.	60 mL
Granulated sugar	2 tsp.	10 g
Onions, small	2	2
Peanut oil	4 oz.	120 mL
Garlic, minced	1 Tbsp.	15 mL
Fresh ginger, minced	2 tsp.	10 mL
Fermented black beans, mashed	3 Tbsp.	45 mL
Snow peas, fresh	4 oz.	120 g

1. Slice the chicken into thin strips, approximately 1-1/2 inches by 1/4 inch (4 cm by 6 cm).

2. Combine the egg white, 2 oz. (60 mL) of the wine and 1 tablespoon (15 mL) of the cornstarch. Add the chicken, coat evenly and refrigerate for 2 hours.

3. For the sauce, mix the soy sauce, sugar and the remaining wine and cornstarch.

4. Quarter the onions and separate the layers.

5. In a wok, stir-fry the chicken in 3 ounces (90 mL) of oil. Remove and set aside.

6. If necessary, add all the remaining oil and stir-fry the garlic and ginger for 30 seconds. Add the onions and mashed beans and stir-fry for 30 seconds. Add the snow peas and cook for 1 minute.

7. Return the chicken to the wok, add the sauce mixture and stir-fry until hot and the sauce has thickened.

8. Serve immediately with short-grain white rice.

VARIATION: Add 2 ounces (60 g) sliced mushrooms and reduce the amount of snow peas by half or substitute broccoli.

Approximate values per serving:

Calories	750
Total fat	46 g
Saturated fat	10 g
Cholesterol	190 mg
Sodium	1050 mg
Total carbohydrates	14 g
Protein	71 g
Vitamin C	25%

◆◆◆

RECIPE 17.15

CHICKEN CURRY

Yield: 4 Servings   **Method:** Stir-frying

Onions, small dice	8 oz.	250 g
Garlic, crushed	2 tsp.	10 mL
Ghee (or clarified butter)	2 Tbsp.	30 mL
Fresh ginger, fine dice	2 oz.	60 g
Turmeric	1-1/2 tsp.	8 mL
Coriander seeds, ground	1-1/2 tsp.	8 mL
Cumin seeds, ground	1 tsp.	5 mL
Cayenne pepper	1 tsp.	5 mL
Fenugreek, ground	1/2 tsp.	3 mL
Coconut milk	20 oz.	575 mL
Roasting chicken, 3 lb. (1.3 kg), cut into 8 pieces	1	1
Salt	1 tsp.	5 mL
Jalapeño, split and seeded	1	1
Lemon juice	1 oz.	30 mL

1. Stir-fry the onions and garlic in the ghee until the onions are golden brown.
2. To make the wet masala, mix the ginger, turmeric, coriander, cumin, cayenne pepper and fenugreek; add just enough of the coconut milk to form a paste.
3. Add the wet masala to the onions and stir-fry for 8 minutes.
4. Add the chicken pieces and cook, turning them frequently, for 6–8 minutes.
5. Add the remaining coconut milk, salt and chiles. Bring to a boil, cover and reduce to a simmer. Cook until the chicken is done, approximately 45 minutes.
6. Just before service, stir in the lemon juice and adjust the seasonings. Serve with rice and a chutney.

Approximate values per serving:

Calories	1130
Total fat	64 g
Saturated fat	39 g
Cholesterol	285 mg
Sodium	1070 mg
Total carbohydrates	32 g
Protein	107 g
Vitamin C	25%
Iron	70%

◆◆◆

RECIPE 17.16

CHICKEN STUFFED
WITH SPINACH AND RICOTTA CHEESE IN SAFFRON SAUCE

CHEF LELAND ATKINSON, WASHINGTON, DC

Yield: 4 Servings   **Method:** Sautéing

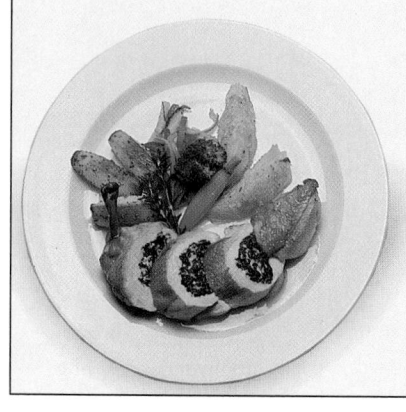

Spinach, fresh, stemmed	1 lb.	450 g
Ricotta cheese	4 oz.	120 g
Egg whites, lightly beaten	2	2
Salt and pepper	TT	TT
Frenched chicken breast, skin on, 6 oz. (180 g) each	4	4
Clarified butter	2 Tbsp.	30 mL

White wine	1 pt.	450 mL
Saffron	1 pinch	1 pinch
Chicken velouté	8 oz.	250 mL
Cream, 35%, hot	2 oz.	60 mL

1. Blanch, refresh and drain the spinach. Squeeze it tightly to remove as much moisture as possible, then chop it finely.
2. To make the stuffing, combine the cheese, egg whites and spinach in a mixing bowl; season to taste.
3. Place the chicken breasts on a cutting board, skin side down. Using a boning knife, carefully make a pocket that runs the length of each breast.
4. Put the stuffing in a pastry bag and pipe the stuffing into each pocket. Do not overfill the chicken breasts because the stuffing expands as it cooks.
5. Sauté the chicken in the clarified butter until well browned. Transfer the chicken to a sheet pan and finish in a 350°F (175°C) oven, approximately 10–12 minutes.
6. Deglaze the sauté pan with the white wine.
7. Add the saffron, bring to a boil and reduce by half.
8. Add the velouté and the cream. Adjust the seasonings and consistency; strain.
9. Ladle the sauce onto 4 warm plates. Slice and then arrange the chicken on the sauce; garnish as desired.

Approximate values per 17 oz. (540 g) serving:

Calories	880
Total fat	40 g
Saturated fat	16 g
Cholesterol	265 mg
Sodium	3190 mg
Total carbohydrates	42 g
Protein	88 g
Vitamin A	110%
Vitamin C	25%
Iron	30%

RECIPE 17.17
CHICKEN AND SAVOY CABBAGE ROULADE

L'ÉCOLE HÔTELIÈRE DES LAURENTIDES, STE-ADÈLE, PQ
Chef Marcel Kretz

Yield: 10 Servings   **Method:** Steaming

Savoy cabbage	1 medium	1 medium
Butter	2 oz.	60 g
Onion, chopped	2 oz.	60 g
Ground cumin	3 tsp.	45 mL
Salt and pepper	TT	TT
Chicken halves, deboned, without wings	5	5

1. Blanch the outer cabbage leaves in lightly salted water.
2. Thinly slice the remaining cabbage; sauté it in butter, together with onion.
3. Cover and cook for 5–6 minutes; season with cumin, salt and pepper and let it cool.
4. Slightly flatten the deboned chicken halves and season.
5. Spread cooked cabbage evenly on chicken halves. Roll them up, season them, wrap them in the blanched cabbage leaves and then in plastic food wrap. Secure both ends with string.
6. Steam for 35 minutes. Let rest 5 minutes and unwrap.
7. Slice the chicken and serve on chicken jus lié, made with chicken bones.

Marcel Kretz
Born, raised and trained in France, Marcel has had an illustrious, award-winning career in Europe and Canada. He is credited with launching the movement to emphasize Quebec products in top Quebec restaurants, and in 1998 became the first chef ever to receive the Order of Canada.

Approximate values per serving:

Calories	415
Total fat	25 g
Saturated fat	8 g
Cholesterol	143 mg
Sodium	140 mg
Total carbohydrates	4 g
Protein	42 g

◆◆◆

RECIPE 17.18

BRAISED CHICKEN
WITH APPLE CIDER AND CASHEW BUTTER

CHEF LELAND ATKINSON, WASHINGTON, DC

Yield: 8 Servings   **Method:** Braising

Clarified butter	2-1/2 oz.	75 mL
Shallots, minced	2 oz.	60 g
Calvados	4 oz.	120 mL
Fresh thyme, chopped	2 tsp.	10 mL
Cashews	3 oz.	90 g
Honey	1 Tbsp.	15 mL
Unsalted butter	3 oz.	90 g
Salt and pepper	TT	TT
Chickens, 3 lb. 8 oz. (1.6 kg) each, quartered	2	2
Flour for dredging	as needed	as needed
Mirepoix	12 oz.	350 g
Garlic head, cut in half	1	1
Apple cider	1 pt.	450 mL
Cider vinegar	1 Tbsp.	15 mL
Chicken stock	3 pt.	1.35 L
Bay leaves	2	2
Fresh thyme	1 sprig	1 sprig
Blond roux	as needed	as needed

1. To make the cashew butter, lightly sauté the shallots in 1 tablespoon (15 mL) of the clarified butter. Add 1 ounce (30 mL) of the Calvados and the chopped thyme and reduce *au sec.* Remove from the heat and cool.
2. Place the cashews in a food processor and process to a medium-fine consistency. Add the cooled shallots, honey and unsalted butter. Season with salt and pepper and process well.
3. Season the chicken with salt and pepper and dredge in flour.
4. Brown the chicken evenly in the remaining clarified butter.
5. Remove the chicken. Add the mirepoix and garlic to the pan; sauté for 1 minute.
6. Add the remaining Calvados, cider and vinegar; reduce by half.
7. Return the chicken to the pan and add the chicken stock and herbs. Cover and braise until done, approximately 15 minutes. Remove the chicken from the pan. (The breast and wing will cook more quickly and must be removed before the thigh and leg pieces.)
8. Reduce the stock by one-half. Use the roux to thicken to a light sauce consistency.
9. Strain the sauce, monter au beurre with the cashew butter and season to taste with salt and pepper. Ladle the sauce over the chicken and serve at once.

Approximate values per 17 oz. (510 g) serving:

Calories	1265
Total fat	73 g
Saturated fat	38 g
Cholesterol	80 mg
Sodium	1220 mg
Total carbohydrates	22 g
Protein	130 g
Vitamin A	60%

◆◆◆

RECIPE 17.19

WARM DUCK BREAST SALAD WITH ASIAN SPICES AND HAZELNUT VINAIGRETTE

FETZER VINEYARDS, HOPLAND, CA
Culinary Director John Ash

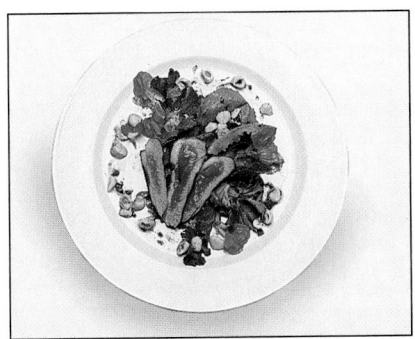

Yield: 4 Servings   **Method:** Sautéing

Whole boneless duck breasts, 12 oz. (350 g) each	2	2
Marinade:		
Garlic, minced	1 tsp.	5 mL
Green onions, minced	2 Tbsp.	30 mL
Oyster sauce	2 tsp.	10 mL
Light soy sauce	1 tsp.	5 mL
Rice wine or dry sherry	1 tsp.	5 mL
Sugar	1 tsp.	5 mL
Five spice powder	1/2 tsp.	3 mL
Hazelnut Vinaigrette:		
Garlic, minced	1 Tbsp.	15 mL
Hazelnut oil	3 oz.	90 mL
Walnut or light olive oil	3 oz.	90 mL
Chives, minced	1 Tbsp.	15 mL
Balsamic vinegar	2 Tbsp.	30 mL
Light soy sauce	1 tsp.	5 mL
Sugar	1/4 tsp.	1 mL
Mixed baby greens	4–6 oz.	120–180 g
Hazelnuts, toasted, skinned and chopped coarse	2 oz.	60 g

1. Trim the excess fat from the duck breasts and separate the breasts into halves.
2. Combine the marinade ingredients. Thoroughly coat the duck with the marinade and marinate for at least 2 hours.
3. Combine the hazelnut vinaigrette ingredients at least 2 hours before service so that the flavours will develop.
4. Wipe the marinade from the breasts and sauté them, skin side down first, in a dry sauté pan until medium rare, approximately 2-1/2 minutes per side. Do not overcook.
5. Arrange a mixture of baby greens on 4 plates. Slice the breasts on the diagonal and arrange on the plates with the greens. Drizzle the hazelnut vinaigrette over the greens, sprinkle with hazelnuts and serve.

Approximate values per 9 oz. (270 g) serving:	
Calories	820
Total fat	68 g
Saturated fat	10 g
Cholesterol	230 mg
Sodium	240 mg
Total carbohydrates	7 g
Protein	44 g
Vitamin C	20%
Iron	35%

Otto R. Daniels

Currently a teacher of professional cooking and coach/coordinator of culinary competitions, Otto is also studying for his Bachelor of Education degree. He has personally won medals and trophies in numerous competitions, and under his tutelage the St. Pius X team won four consecutive provincial championships from 1994–1997.

Approximate values per serving:

Calories	1897
Total fat	106 g
Saturated fat	51 g
Cholesterol	296 mg
Sodium	1456 mg
Total carbohydrates	199 g
Protein	41 g

◆◆◆

RECIPE 17.20

ROASTED BROME LAKE DUCKLING WITH BRAISED RED CABBAGE

ST. PIUS X CULINARY INSTITUTE, MONTREAL, PQ
Chef Otto R. Daniels, Instructor

Yield: 2 Servings   **Method:** Roasting

Brome Lake duck, quartered	1	1
Apple cider	4 oz.	110 mL
Salt and pepper	TT	TT
Demi-glace	10 oz.	300 mL
Apple cider champagne	3 oz.	110 mL
Pommettes (sweet mini apples), cored, quartered	4	4
Apple brandy	1 oz.	30 mL
Red cabbage, small head, julienne	1	1
Unsalted butter	4 oz.	125 g
Cider vinegar	10 oz.	300 mL
Brown sugar	10 oz.	300 g

1. Season the quartered duck with the apple cider and salt and pepper and let marinate for 2 hours. Place the seasoned duck on a wire rack and roast for 75 minutes at 375°F (180°C), or until the duck has achieved the proper internal temperature.

2. Simmer the demi-glace for 30 minutes then add the cider champagne. Sweat off the pommettes in a small amount of butter, then add the cooked duck and flame with the brandy. Add the flavoured demi-glace. Reduce it to a coating consistency.

3. Sauté the julienned red cabbage in butter. Add the sugar and vinegar and simmer until tender. Serve with roasted new potatoes in herb butter and steamed fiddleheads.

◆◆◆

RECIPE 17.21

LOCKPORT QUAIL MILLE-FEUILLE, ROASTED JAPANESE EGGPLANT AND RED ONION

ST. CHARLES COUNTRY CLUB, WINNIPEG, MB
Executive Chef Tony Murakami

Yield: 10 Servings   **Method:** Simmering

Poaching Stock:		
Chicken stock	2 qt.	2.5 L
Lard	1 Tbsp.	15 mL

Tony Murakami

Tony started out in Tokyo and then came to Canada, where he worked his way up to executive chef and joined the St. Charles Country Club. Tony is a Certified Master Chef, and highlights of his career include 9 gold medals and 4 grand golds in international competition. He has been recognized by the federal and Manitoba governments for his work.

Teabag (any kind)	1	1
Star anise	1	1
Cinnamon stick	1	1
Bay leaf	1	1
Salt	1 Tbsp.	15 mL
Soy sauce	2 Tbsp.	30 mL
Quail, whole, gutted and cleaned, dry (6–8 oz./170–230 g each)	10	10
Glaze:		
Glucose	2 oz.	50 mL
Vinegar	1 oz.	25 mL
Vegetable oil for deep-fat frying	2 qt.	2 L
Juniper berries	2 tsp.	10 mL
Celery, onion, carrots, diced	2 cups	400 mL
White wine	1 cup	200 mL
Veal stock	3 cups	600 mL
Red onion, medium, sliced 1/4 inch (0.5 cm) thick	2	2
Butter, clarified	1 cup	200 mL
Bread crumbs	as needed	as needed
Japanese egg plant, broiled, peeled and chopped	5	5
Salt and pepper	TT	TT

1. To make the poaching stock, mix all the ingredients together in a large pot. Bring to a boil for 10 minutes. Add the whole quail, then bring to boiling temperature. Simmer for 5 minutes. Turn off the heat and set aside, covered, for approximately 30–40 minutes.

2. Remove quail from stock. Dry the surface of the quail.

3. In the microwave, heat the glucose and vinegar for 2 minutes at medium power. Brush the glaze all over the quail, then set them aside at room temperature without covering.

4. Heat the vegetable oil for deep-fat frying to 350°F (175°C) and fry the quail in this oil until golden brown. Salt and pepper lightly.

5. Debone the quail and reserve the bones. Sprinkle the meat with juniper berries, cover it and keep it warm.

6. Sauté the mirepoix until brown. Add all the bones to the pot. Add the white wine and cook for 5 minutes, then add the veal stock and continue to simmer for 30 minutes. Strain. Skim the fat and reduce the sauce to a syrupy consistency.

7. Slice the red onion, then dip each slice in the clarified butter and bread crumbs. Roast the slices in the oven at 350°F (175°C) 5 to 10 minutes.

8. Roast the eggplant in the oven at 400°F (200°C) for 10 to 15 minutes until soft and tender (it can also be broiled). Sauté in some butter and season it with salt and pepper.

9. Place 1 slice of onion on each plate. Arrange one thinly sliced quail breast, the eggplant, the other breast and leg in layers, like a small gateau. Serve the sauce on the side.

Approximate values per quail:

Calories	469
Total fat	34 g
Saturated fat	15 g
Cholesterol	127 mg
Sodium	1114 mg
Total carbohydrates	15 g
Protein	24 g

♦♦♦

RECIPE 17.22

TURKEY SCALLOPINI WITH CAPERS AND LEMON

Yield: 4 servings   **Method:** Sautéing

Turkey breast, cut into 1/8-in. (3-mm) scallopini, 3 oz. (90 g) each	8	8
Salt and white pepper	TT	TT
Flour	as needed	as needed
Clarified butter	2 oz.	60 mL
Dry white wine	4 oz.	120 mL
Fresh lemon juice	2 oz.	60 mL
Capers	3 Tbsp.	45 mL

Approximate values per 6 oz. (180 g) serving:

Calories	390
Total fat	13 g
Saturated fat	8 g
Cholesterol	180 mg
Sodium	910 mg
Total carbohydrates	13 g
Protein	56 g
Vitamin A	10%

1. Gently pound each turkey slice with a meat mallet. Season with salt and pepper and dredge in flour.
2. Sauté the turkey in the clarified butter until golden brown. Remove and hold in a warm place.
3. Deglaze the pan with the wine, then add the lemon juice and capers. Return the turkey to the pan to coat with the sauce and reheat.
4. Serve 2 slices with a portion of the sauce.

♦♦♦

RECIPE 17.23

SPICED OSTRICH TENDERLOIN

Yield: 2 servings   **Method:** Broiling

Cumin seeds	1 Tbsp.	15 mL
Fennel seeds	1 Tbsp.	15 mL
Black peppercorns	2 tsp.	10 mL
White peppercorns	2 tsp.	10 mL
Garlic cloves, minced	2	2
Ostrich tenderloin, 4 oz. (120 g) each	2	2
Salt	TT	TT
Olive oil	1 Tbsp.	15 mL

Approximate values per 4 oz. (120 g) serving:

Calories	169
Total fat	5 g
Saturated fat	1 g
Cholesterol	91 mg
Sodium	106 mg
Total carbohydrates	5 g
Protein	27 g
Iron	46%

1. Grind the cumin, fennel, and peppercorns together in a spice grinder. Combine the ground spices with the garlic.
2. Coat the ostrich tenderloin with the spice mixture and season lightly with salt.
3. Cook the ostrich under a broiler to the desired degree of doneness.
4. Remove from the broiler and slice thinly for service.

*W*EBLINKS

Canadian Turkey Marketing Agency
www.canturkey.ca/

Chicken Farmers of Canada: Cooking Chicken
www.cdn-chicken.com/cooking.htm

U.S. National Turkey Federation: Turkey Cooking Information
www.turkeyfed.org/consumer/cookinfo.html

Carving a Turkey
www.learn2.com/04/0441/0441.html

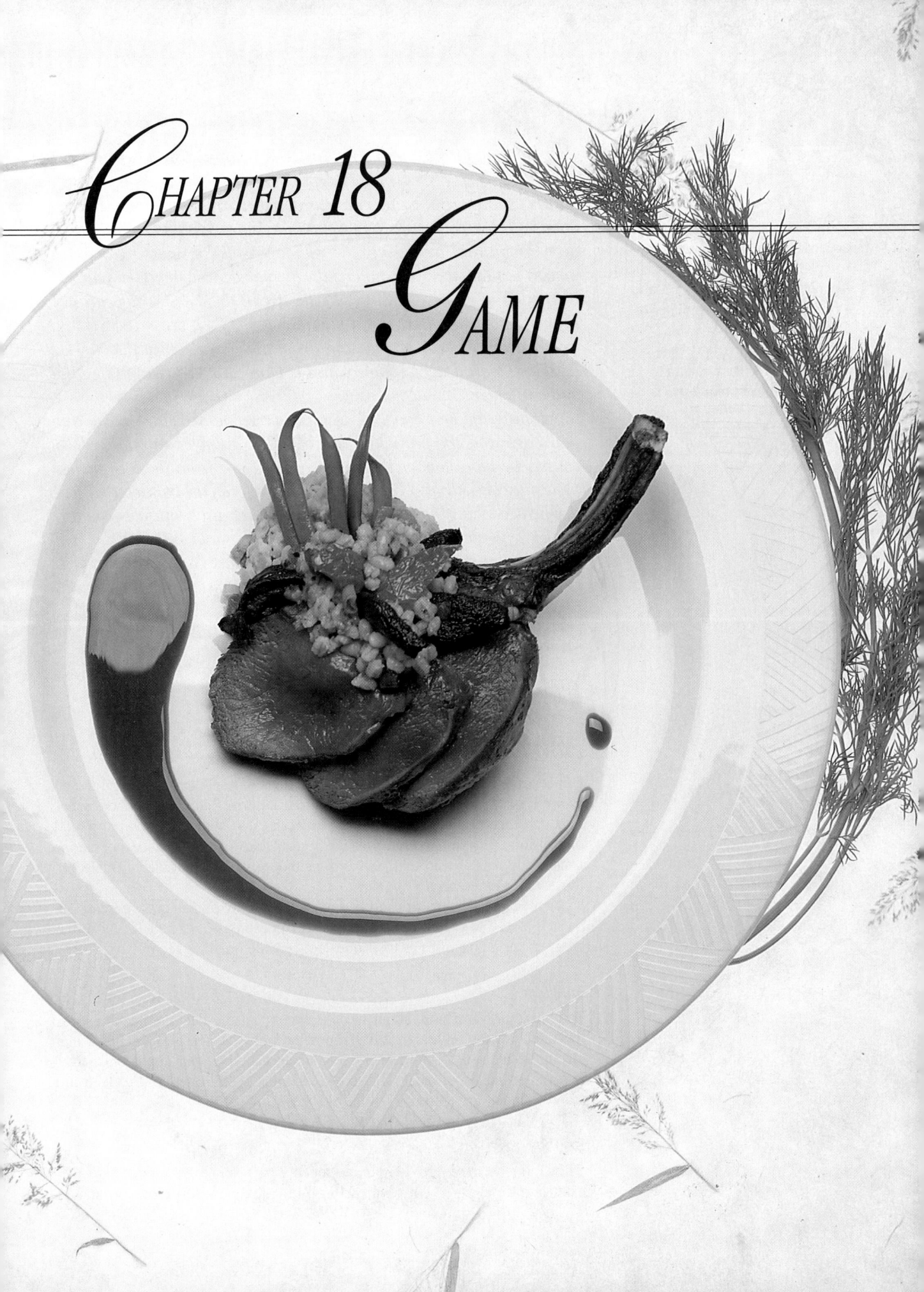

CHAPTER 18

GAME

ame (Fr. gibier) are animals hunted for sport or food. Traditionally, game supplies depended upon the season and the hunter's success. But game's increasing popularity in food service operations has led to farm-raising techniques. As a result, pheasant, quail, deer, rabbit and other animals, although still considered game, are now ranch-raised and commercially available throughout the year.

The life of game creatures is reflected in their flesh's appearance, aroma, flavour and texture. Generally, game flesh has a dark colour and a strong but not unpleasant aroma. It has a robust flavour, less fat than other meats or poultry and is more compact, becoming quite tough in older animals.

Selecting the best cooking methods for game depends on the animal's age and the particular cut of flesh. Younger animals will, of course, be more tender than older ones. Flesh from the loin or less-used muscles will also be tender and therefore can be prepared with dry-heat cooking methods. Flesh from much-used muscles, such as the leg and shoulder, will be tougher and should be prepared with combination cooking methods. Less-tender cuts can also be used in sausages, pâtés and forcemeats as discussed in Chapter 20, Charcuterie.

IDENTIFYING GAME

Furred or Ground Game

Furred game includes large animals such as deer, moose, bear, wild boar and elk as well as smaller animals such as rabbit, squirrel, raccoon and opossum. Although each of these animals (and many others) is hunted for sport and food, only bison, deer and rabbit are widely available to food service operations. Limited supplies of wild reindeer, caribou and musk ox are available. Table 18.1 lists uses for furred game.

Large game animals are rarely sold whole or in primal cuts. Instead, the meat is available precut into subprimals or portions. So, except for those that are used for rabbits, this chapter does not provide breaking techniques.

Antelope

The blackbuck antelope, about half the size of a large deer, is ranch-raised in the United States. Although it has almost no body fat, the meat retains a high amount of moisture. The meat is fine-grained, with a flavour that is only slightly stronger than deer meat (venison). It should be fabricated and cooked in a manner similar to venison.

Bison

Once found in huge herds roaming the plains, bison were hunted into near extinction during the 19th century. Bison now live on reservations or ranches,

◆◆◆

MEAT OF THE FUTURE:
BEEFALO

Beefalo is produced by cross-breeding a bison with a domestic beef animal. To be a registered full-blooded beefalo, the animal has to be three-eighths bison and five-eighths domestic beef. The five-eighths domestic beef portion is not restricted to any breed; it is often a combination of two or more breeds such as Hereford, Angus or Charolais. In 1985 the USDA approved a special label for beefalo; it is labeled as either "Beef from Beefalo" or "Beefalo Beef."

Beefalo looks and tastes much like modern beef. The animal itself is hard to distinguish from any other beef animal. Beefalo meat is tender because the animals gain weight faster and go to market at younger ages. The meat is slightly sweeter in taste than beef.

Beefalo is lower in cholesterol than beef, fish or chicken and lower in calories and fat than beef. It offers a great alternative to beef for the diet- and health-conscious guest. The per-pound cost of beefalo may be slightly higher than beef cuts, but its low amount of interior and exterior fat gives it a higher yield with a price per usable pound comparable to beef.

Because of beefalo's finer fiber and low fat content, it cooks in one-third to one-half the time of beef and should be cooked to either rare or medium-rare.

JAMES J. MUTH, *MBA, CFBE*
Chef Instructor,
GRAND RAPIDS COMMUNITY COLLEGE

where they are raised like beef cattle. Wood Buffalo National Park on the Alberta–Nunavut border is home to the largest herd of free-roaming bison. Bison meat is juicy and flavourful and may be prepared in the same manner as lean beef.

Deer

The deer family includes elk, moose, reindeer, red-tailed deer, white-tailed deer (Fr. *chevreuil*) and mule deer. Meat from any of these animals is known as venison (Fr. *venaisan*). Farm-raised venison, particularly from the Scottish red deer bred in New Zealand, Canada and the United States, is commercially available all year. Venison is typically dark red with a mild aroma. It is leaner than other meats, having almost no intramuscular fat or marbling.

Venison Saddle

The most popular commercial venison cuts are the loin, leg and rack. The loin is tender enough to roast, sauté or grill to medium rare. It can be left attached along the backbone to form a cut known as the saddle. The leg is often marinated in red wine and prepared with combination cooking methods. Other cuts can also be stewed or braised or used in sausages and pâtés. Butchering procedures for venison are similar to those for lamb discussed in Chapter 15.

Rabbit

Rabbits (Fr. *lapin*) are small burrowing animals that have long been raised for food. Rabbit has mild, lean and relatively tender flesh. Its taste and texture are similar to chicken. Ranch-raised rabbit is available all year, either whole or cut, fresh or frozen. The average weight of a whole dressed rabbit is 2 pounds 8 ounces to 3 pounds (1.2–1.4 kilograms). Young rabbit can be roasted, pan-fried, stewed or braised and is popular in rustic "country-style" dishes, especially casseroles and pâtés.

BASIC PROCEDURE FOR DISJOINTING A RABBIT

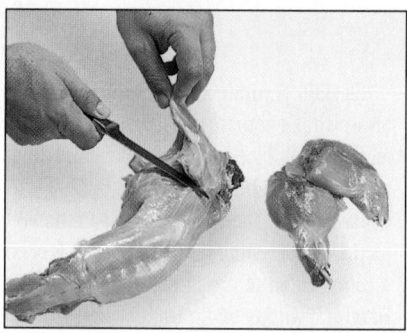

1. Place the rabbit on its back. Remove the hind legs by cutting close to the backbone and through the joint on each side. Each thigh and leg can be separated by cutting through the joint.

2. Remove the forelegs by cutting beneath the shoulder blades.

3. Cut through the breast bone and spread open the rib cage. Using a boning knife, separate the flesh from the rib bones and remove the bones.

4. Cut through the backbone to divide the loin into the desired number of pieces.

5. The cut-up rabbit: hind legs, thighs, loin in three pieces, forelegs.

TABLE 18.1   USING FURRED GAME

Animal	Commonly Purchased Cuts	Cooking Methods	Suggested Use
Antelope	Purchased and prepared in the same manner as deer		
Bison	Purchased and prepared in the same manner as lean beef		
Deer	Loin	Dry heat (roast; sauté; grill)	Sautéed medallions; whole roast loin; grilled steaks
	Leg	Combination (braise; stew)	Marinate and braise; pot roast with cranberries; chili; sausage; forcemeat
	Rack	Dry heat (roast; grill)	Grilled chops
Rabbit	Full carcass	Dry heat (sauté; pan-fry; roast; grill) Combination (braise; stew)	Pan-fried rabbit with cream gravy Braised rabbit with mushrooms
Wild Boar	Loin	Dry heat (roast)	Roast loin with mustard crust
	Chops	Combination (braise)	Marinate and braise; stew with red wine and sour cream; sausage; forcemeat

Wild Boar

A close relative of the domesticated hog, wild boar (Fr. *sanglier*) is leaner, with a stronger flavour. Though plentiful in Europe and parts of America, wild boar is available only during autumn. A limited supply of farm-raised boar is available all year, however.

Baby boar (under six months old) is considered a delicacy, but mature animals (one to two years old) have the best flavour. The meat is most often roasted, and may be used in sausages or terrines. Boar can often be substituted in recipes for venison or pork.

Boar Saddle

Feathered or Winged Game

Feathered game includes upland birds such as wild turkeys, pheasants, quails, doves and woodcocks; songbirds such as larks; and waterfowl such as wild geese and ducks. Wild birds cannot be sold in Canada but may be prepared in some private clubs. An ever-increasing number of these birds such as Muscovy duck are being farm-raised to meet increased consumer demand, however.

Game birds are available whole or precut into pieces, fresh or frozen. Butchering techniques will not be shown in this chapter as they are the same as those for domesticated poultry discussed in Chapter 17.

Because game birds tend to have less fat than other poultry, they are often barded with fat and cooked to medium rare. If cooked well done they become dry and stringy.

Partridge

The Hungarian and chukar partridges (Fr. *perdrix*) of Europe were introduced into the United States and Canada during the 19th century. Now found principally in the prairie and western mountain regions, partridges are widely raised on game preserves and farms, producing a good commercial supply.

Their flavour is less delicate than pheasant and the meat tends to be tougher. Partridge may be roasted or cut into pieces and sautéed or braised. Each bird weighs about 1 pound (450 grams) dressed.

Chukar Partridge

◆◆◆

FAISAN À LA SAINTE-ALLIANCE

Any dish prepared *à la sainte-alliance* evokes the festivities surrounding the 1815 signing of the Treaty of Paris, which ended the reign of Napoleon Bonaparte, forcing him into exile on Elba. *Faisan à la sainte-alliance* is a roast pheasant stuffed with woodcock and served on toast topped with woodcock purée. The renowned gastronome Brillat-Savarin gives the following recipe in his *Physiologie du Goût*, published in 1825:

When the pheasant has reached [its peak of ripeness], it is plucked, and not before, and it is larded carefully, with the freshest and firmest of material.... [T]he time has come to stuff it, and in the following manner:

Bone and draw a brace of woodcock, in such a way that you have one supply of the flesh, and another of the entrails.

Take the flesh and make a forcemeat of it by chopping it with some steamed beef marrow, a little scraped bacon, pepper, salt, fresh herbs, and enough fine truffles to make just the amount of stuffing needed to fill the pheasant.

Prepare a slice of bread that will be about two inches bigger on every side than the bird laid lengthwise. Then take the woodcock livers and entrails, and grind them in a mortar with two large truffles, an anchovy, a little finely minced bacon, and a sizeable lump of the best fresh butter.

Spread this paste evenly on the bread slice, and place it under the pheasant, already stuffed ... so that it will catch every drop of juice which will appear while the bird is roasting.

When the bird is done, serve it lying gracefully upon this crisp little couch; surround it with bitter oranges, and be assured of the fortunate outcome.

BRILLAT-SAVARIN,
THE PHYSIOLOGY OF TASTE,
translated and annotated by M. F. K. FISHER
(North Point Press, 1986),
pp. 374–75.

Pheasant

Pheasant

The most popular of game birds, the pheasant (Fr. *faisan*) was introduced into Europe from Asia during the Middle Ages. Its mild flavour is excellent for roasting, stewing or braising. The hen is smaller and more tender than the cock. Stock made from the carcass is often used for consommé or sauce.

Farm-raised birds are available fresh or frozen. A dressed bird weighs about 1 pound 8 ounces to 2 pounds 4 ounces (680 grams to 1 kilogram) and serves two to four people.

Quail

The quail (Fr. *caille*) is a migratory game bird related to the pheasant. The more popular European and Californian species are farm-raised and available all year.

Quail are rather small, with only about 1–2 ounces (30–60 grams) of breast meat each. Quail may be grilled (especially on skewers), roasted, broiled or sautéed and are often boned and served whole with a stuffing of forcemeat or rice. Because they are so lean, roasted quail benefit from barding.

Quail

NUTRITION

Even ranch-raised game animals live in the wild and are generally more active and less well fed than domesticated animals. This lifestyle produces animals whose meat has less fat than domesticated animals. Most game is also lower in cholesterol and has approximately one-third fewer calories than beef. Game is also generally high in protein and minerals. Compare Table 18.2 with Tables 12.1 (Meats) and 17.7 (Poultry).

TABLE 18.2   NUTRITIONAL VALUES OF GAME

For 1 oz. (28 g) Uncooked Lean Meat	Kcal	Protein (g)	Total Fat (g)	Saturated Fat (g)	Cholesterol (mg)	Sodium (mg)
Beefalo	41	6.6	1.4	0.6	13	22
Bison (American buffalo)	31	6.1	0.5	0.2	18	15
Deer (venison)	34	6.5	0.7	0.3	24	15
Rabbit	39	5.7	1.6	0.5	16	12
Wild boar	35	6.1	1.0	0.3	mq*	mq
Pheasant	51	6.4	2.6	0.8	mq	11
Quail	54	5.6	3.4	1.0	mq	15

The Corinne T. Netzer Encyclopedia of Food Values, 1992
mq* = measurable quantity but data are unavailable

◆◆◆

WILD GAME—
DELICIOUS, NUTRITIOUS AND AVAILABLE

Wild game is now widely available for use in restaurants and at home. The best of wild game provides a safe, delicious and nutritious dining experience.

In almost all states, our native game animals are protected from harvesting for commercial purposes. It is a violation of state wildlife laws to kill and sell the meat from native species such as the whitetail deer, mule deer, pronghorn antelope, etc. These laws were written when only native game was present in America. Since then, a growing number of non-native species of deer and antelope have been introduced to ranches in America and this has made it possible to harvest deer and antelope legally for meat production.

Oddly enough, however, meats such as antelope, venison, rabbit, and most other game meats are not subject to inspection under federal and most state meat inspection regulations. This is not because the authorities do not believe the meat should be inspected. When the meat inspection laws were written, these meats were not legally available and therefore were not included in the Federal Meat Act. County and city health codes, however, do require that any meat served to the public must be from "an approved source" which is interpreted as "inspected." Therefore, any game meat served in a restaurant should be certified as inspected by either state or federal meat inspection authorities.

Game meat is available from farmed (domesticated) deer and from free-ranging (ranched) deer and antelope. Most farmed deer are taken to a fixed conventional slaughterhouse where they are slaughtered and processed in the same way as cattle, sheep, and goats. Ranched deer can be properly harvested only by an elaborate procedure which involves taking a mobile slaughter facility and meat inspector to the field where the animals are killed by shooting them with a high powered rifle under the supervision of the meat inspector. The carcass is then processed inside the mobile facility to avoid any contamination of the meat. This field harvesting eliminates any stress which might occur in transport of farmed deer to the slaughterhouse.

Farmed deer tend to be relatively more uniform in size and flavor. Free-ranging deer and antelope produce meat of more complex flavor due to the variety of their diet. The difference is somewhat like the difference in cultivated mushrooms and wild mushrooms, or pen-raised chickens compared with free-range chickens. Meat from free-range animals is more expensive due to higher labor and inspection costs.

Meat from both deer and antelope can be legally labeled "venison." All venison is relatively lean when compared with conventional red meats and requires special attention when cooking to avoid drying out the meat and toughening it. Tender cuts should be cooked as little as possible (rare to medium rare) to retain the maximum amount of moisture. Quick sautéing, grilling or roasting to retain a medium rare center is most satisfactory for tender cuts such as the loin, tenderloin, and leg.

Braising is the most effective method for cooking the less tender cuts such as the shoulder, ribs and shanks. Beef broth or red wine are good liquids for braising. The toughest cut of meat will be very satisfactorily tenderized if braised for a sufficient period of time (which may be as long as two or three hours). When properly cooked, these cuts can surpass the more tender cuts in flavor.

MIKE HUGHES,
BROKEN ARROW RANCH, Ingram, Texas

INSPECTION OF GAME

The Canada Food Inspection Agency and most provinces restrict the sale of wild game. Truly wild game may be served only by those who hunt and share their kill or where a special import permit is obtained, again for private consumption. Special care must be taken to avoid cross-contamination.

Domestic Game

Bison grading—*After a carcass passes health and safety inspection, a certified grader assesses it based on maturity, conformation, fat and meat. Marbling is not a factor. Grade **A** is the top quality grade, followed by **B**, **C** and **D**. Look for the **CFIA** inspection legend.*

For resale, mandatory federal and provincial inspections for caribou, reindeer and farm- or ranch-raised game are conducted for wholesomeness. Generally, however, game is processed under the same federal inspection requirements as domesticated meats and poultry. Also, unlike meat and poultry from domesticated animals, game is not graded for quality except for bison.

Imported Game

The Canada Food Inspection Agency accepts game only from countries that have an approved inspection system. The plant processing the meat must also be an approved source. Exotic species may be subject to controls related to handling and cooking after they arrive in Canada.

PURCHASING AND STORING GAME

Purchasing Game

Furred game meats are available fresh, usually in vacuum-sealed packaging, or frozen. Game birds are available cleaned and boned, fresh or frozen. Use the same criteria to determine the freshness of game as you would for any other meat or poultry: The flesh should be firm, without slime or an off-odour.

Fresh game is sometimes **hung** before cutting to allow the meat to mature or age. During hanging, carbohydrates (glycogen) stored in muscle tissues are converted to lactic acid. This process tenderizes the flesh and strengthens its flavour. But hanging is not necessary, especially if you object to "gamy" flavours. Commercially sold game is generally fully aged and ready to use when delivered. It does not need nor will it benefit from hanging.

Storing Game

As with any fresh or frozen meat, game should be well wrapped and stored under refrigeration at temperatures below 40°F (4°C). Because the flesh is generally dry and lean, frozen game should be used within four months. Thaw frozen game slowly under refrigeration to prevent moisture loss.

◆◆◆
HOW TO HANG GAME

The following information may be useful if you find yourself with a need to hang freshly killed game. Most game should be eviscerated (drawn or gutted) as soon as possible, then suspended by either the hind legs or the head in a dry, well-ventilated place. Because the fur or feathers help prevent bacterial contamination, they should be left intact during hanging; game should be skinned or plucked just before butchering. The length of time necessary for hanging depends on the species and age of the animal. Two days may be sufficient for a rabbit, while up to three weeks may be necessary for a deer or boar. Hanging is generally complete when the first whiff of odour is detected (although traditionalists prefer pheasant to be hung until extremely ripe).

MARINATING FURRED GAME

Tradition calls for marinating game, particularly furred game, in strong mixtures of red wine, herbs and spices. Commercially raised game does not necessarily have to be marinated. Modern animal husbandry techniques used at game ranches assure the cook of receiving meat from young, tender animals.

Farm-raised game animals also have a naturally milder flavour than their truly wild cousins.

For those preferring the flavours imparted by traditional marinades, the following red wine marinade is included. After the meat is removed, the marinade may be added to the cooking liquid or reduced and used in a sauce. Do not serve uncooked marinade.

◆◆◆

RECIPE 18.1
RED-WINE GAME MARINADE

Yield: 1-1/2 qt. (1.5 L)

Carrot, chopped fine	2 oz.	60 g
Onion, chopped fine	2 oz.	60 g
Garlic, minced	1 Tbsp.	15 mL
Dried thyme	1 tsp.	5 mL
Bay leaves	2	2
Juniper berries, whole	2 tsp.	10 mL
Peppercorns, whole	1 Tbsp.	15 mL
Sage, ground	1/2 tsp.	2 mL
Red wine	1 qt.	1 L
Red wine vinegar	4 oz.	120 mL

Approximate values per 1 oz. (30 mL) serving:

Calories	5
Total fat	0 g
Saturated fat	0 g
Cholesterol	0 mg
Sodium	0 mg
Total carbohydrates	1 g
Protein	0 g
Vitamin A	6%

Claims—fat free; no saturated fat; no cholesterol; no sodium; low calorie

1. Combine all ingredients in a noncorrosive container.
2. Place the meat in the marinade and marinate for the desired time. Tender, farm-raised game may need only 30 minutes; older, wild animals may need 1–2 days.

CONCLUSION

Game is becoming increasingly popular because of consumer desires for leaner, healthier meats. Only inspected, farm-raised game can be used in food service operations. Luckily, many popular game items are now farm raised, government inspected and readily available. Generally, game flesh has a dark colour, a strong but not unpleasant aroma and a robust flavour. You should butcher, prepare and cook game according to the comparable guidelines for other meats and poultry.

QUESTIONS FOR DISCUSSION

1. Explain the differences between truly wild game and ranch-raised game.
2. What is hanging? Is it necessary for modern food service operations to hang game?
3. Which cuts of furred game are best suited to dry-heat cooking methods? Which are best for combination cooking methods?
4. Can game birds be purchased whole? How are they fabricated?
5. What degree of doneness is best suited for game birds? Explain your answer.

$\mathscr{A}$DDITIONAL GAME RECIPES

RECIPE 18.2

MARINATED LOIN OF VENISON ROASTED WITH MUSTARD, SERVED WITH CREAMY POLENTA WITH WILD MUSHROOMS

FETZER VINEYARDS, HOPLAND, CA
John Ash, Culinary Director

Yield: 8–10 6–8 oz. (180 g–250 g) Servings   **Method:** Roasting

Marinade:		
Carrots, medium	3	3
Yellow onion, large	1	1
Shallots, whole	3	3
Garlic cloves	3	3
Olive oil	2 Tbsp.	30 mL
Hearty red wine	40 oz.	1.2 L
Red wine vinegar	4 oz.	120 mL
Bay leaves	4	4
Parsley stalks	6	6
Juniper berries, whole	16	16
Sea salt	2 tsp.	10 mL
Peppercorns, black	12	12
Mustard coating:		
Garlic cloves	3	3
Green onion, chopped	2 oz.	60 g
Chardonnay	3 oz.	90 mL
Fresh sage	1 tsp.	5 mL
Fresh thyme	1 tsp.	5 mL
Dijon mustard	1 cup	250 mL
Olive oil	2 oz.	60 mL
Sea salt	1 tsp.	5 mL
Venison loin, 5 lb. (2.2 kg), well-trimmed	1	1

Approximate values per 8 oz. (250 g) serving:

Calories	340
Total fat	13 g
Saturated fat	3 g
Cholesterol	190 mg
Sodium	460 mg
Total carbohydrates	4 g
Protein	53 g
Iron	50%

1. For the marinade, coarsely chop the vegetables and sauté in the oil until lightly browned.
2. Add the wine, vinegar and remaining marinade seasonings and bring to a boil.
3. Reduce the heat and simmer 10 minutes. Cool before using.
4. For the mustard coating, place all ingredients in a food processor or blender and quickly process until smooth. The mixture should be very thick. Cover and refrigerate.
5. In a nonreactive pan, pour the cooled marinade over the loin and marinate, covered, in the refrigerator for up to 24 hours. Turn occasionally.
6. Remove the meat from the marinade and pat dry; quickly sear the meat in a hot sauté pan or on the grill.
7. Place the loin in a roasting pan and coat well with the mustard coating.

Roast at 450°F (230°C) for 5 minutes; reduce heat to 375°F (190°C) and roast for an additional 10–15 minutes, until the meat is medium rare.

8. Serve on warm plates with Creamy Polenta with Wild Mushrooms.

CREAMY POLENTA WITH WILD MUSHROOMS

Yield: 8–10 Servings

Yellow onion, chopped coarse	12 oz.	340 g
White mushrooms, chopped coarse	4 oz.	120 g
Garlic, chopped fine	2 Tbsp.	30 ml
Dried porcini or cèpes mushrooms, rinsed, soaked in water and chopped coarse	2 oz.	60 g
Olive oil	5 oz.	150 mL
Fresh basil, chopped fine	4 tsp.	20 mL
Fresh oregano, chopped fine	1 tsp.	5 mL
Chicken or vegetable stock	2 qt.	2 L
Coarse polenta cornmeal	2 cups	450 mL
Salt and pepper	TT	TT
Cream, 35%	1 pt.	450 mL
Aged Asiago or fontina cheese, grated fine	4 oz.	120 g
Fresh wild mushrooms	8–10	8–10
Fresh basil sprigs	as needed for garnish	

1. Sauté the onion, white mushrooms, garlic and porcini in 4 ounces (120 mL) olive oil until lightly coloured. Add the basil, oregano and stock; bring to a boil.

2. Slowly stir in the polenta. Simmer 10 minutes, stirring regularly. The polenta should be thick and creamy. Add more stock if necessary. Adjust the seasonings and keep warm.

3. Just before serving, add the cream and cheese and stir vigorously.

4. Sauté the fresh wild mushrooms in the remaining olive oil until tender. Spoon the polenta onto warm plates and garnish with the wild mushrooms and a sprig of fresh basil.

Approximate values per serving:	
Calories	473
Total fat	35 g
Saturated fat	15 g
Cholesterol	73 mg
Sodium	723 mg
Total carbohydrates	31 g
Protein	10 g

◆◆◆

RECIPE 18.3

ACHIOTE-BASTED RACK OF VENISON WITH SMOKED CORN PUDDING

NOTE: *This dish appears in the Chapter Opening photograph.*

THE BOULDERS RESORT, CAREFREE, AZ
Corporate Executive Chef Charles Wiley

Yield: 4 Servings   Method: Grilling

Venison chops, 6 oz. (180 g) each	4	4
Achiote Paste (recipe follows)	1/2 cup	120 mL
Kosher salt	TT	TT
Pepper	TT	TT
Olive oil	1 tsp.	5 mL
Shiitake mushroom caps	8	8

Continued

Haricots verts, blanched and shocked	24	24
Roma tomatoes, quartered	2	2
Smoked Corn Pudding (recipe follows)	2 cups	500 mL
Barley Risotto (recipe follows)	4 servings	4 servings
Venison Red Wine Jus (recipe follows)	4 oz.	120 mL

1. Prepare a mesquite or gas grill. Brush the chops with Achiote Paste and season with salt and pepper. Grill to medium rare, brushing with additional Achiote Paste. Remove the chops from the grill, cover loosely and keep warm.

2. Heat the oil in a small sauté pan and add the mushrooms. Cook for 2–3 minutes over medium heat. Add the haricot vert and tomatoes; season with salt and pepper. Cook for an additional 2–3 minutes; remove from the heat.

3. Spoon 1/2 cup (120 mL) of the Smoked Corn Pudding in the centre of a warm dinner plate. Spoon one-fourth of the haricots verts mixture on top of the pudding. Cut each chop in thirds and arrange the pieces around the pudding. Top with Barley Risotto and pour 1 ounce (30 mL) of Red Wine Jus around the venison. Serve immediately.

Approximate values per serving:

Calories	930
Total fat	37 g
Saturated fat	17 g
Cholesterol	370 mg
Sodium	1660 mg
Total carbohydrates	87 g
Protein	63 g
Vitamin A	100%
Vitamin C	60%
Iron	60%

ACHIOTE PASTE

Yield: 1/2 cup (120 mL)

Ancho chiles	3	3
Garlic clove	1	1
Allspice	1/4 tsp.	1 mL
Cumin seeds, toasted and ground	1/2 tsp.	3 mL
Annato (achiote) seeds	1 tsp.	5 mL
Olive oil	1 tsp.	5 mL
White wine vinegar	2 Tbsp.	30 mL
Orange juice	1/4 cup	60 mL
Kosher salt	1/2 tsp.	3 mL

1. Toast the ancho chiles in a skillet over medium heat for 2 minutes, or until they release some oil and have a toasted aroma. Let cool slightly, then core, seed and tear into strips.

2. Place the ancho strips in a blender with the remaining ingredients and purée until smooth.

Approximate values per 1.5 oz. (52 g) serving:

Calories	25
Total fat	1.5 g
Saturated fat	0 g
Cholesterol	0 mg
Sodium	200 mg
Total carbohydrates	3 g
Protein	0 g

SMOKED CORN PUDDING

Yield: 2 cups (500 mL)

Whole butter	3 Tbsp.	45 mL
Milk	1 pt.	500 mL
Yellow cornmeal	1/2 cup	120 mL
Kosher salt	TT	TT
Pepper	TT	TT
Corn, lightly smoked, kernels removed	2 ears	2 ears
Onion, chopped	3 Tbsp.	45 mL
Eggs, separated	3	3

1. Coat an 8-inch (20-cm) square pan with 1 tablespoon (15 mL) of butter.

2. In a medium saucepan, bring the milk to a boil. Lower the heat and gradually whisk in the cornmeal. Cook over low heat for 10 minutes, stirring with a wooden spoon.

3. Add the salt, pepper, corn, onions and remaining butter; cook for an additional 3 minutes. Remove from the heat and add the egg yolks one at a time, beating well with a wooden spoon after each addition.

4. Add a pinch of salt to the egg whites and beat with a fine whisk until stiff. Fold the whipped egg whites into the cornmeal mixture, one-half at a time. Pour into the buttered pan and bake at 350°F (175°C) until golden brown, approximately 30 minutes.

Approximate values per 1/2 cup (257 g) serving:

Calories	340
Total fat	18 g
Saturated fat	9 g
Cholesterol	200 mg
Sodium	200 mg
Total carbohydrates	31 g
Protein	12 g
Vitamin A	20%
Calcium	15%

BARLEY RISOTTO

Yield: 4 Servings

Barley	1/2 cup	120 mL
Water	1 pt.	500 mL
Whole butter	1 Tbsp.	15 mL
Garlic cloves, chopped	4	4
Chicken stock	1 cup	250 mL
Green onions or chives, sliced	3 Tbsp.	45 mL
Asiago, grated	1/4 cup	60 mL
Kosher salt	TT	TT
Pepper	TT	TT

1. Cook the barley in the water until barely done; strain.

2. Melt the butter in a large saucepan over medium heat. Add the garlic and cook until fragrant, approximately 2 minutes. Add the barley and stir with a wooden spoon to coat completely with the butter.

3. Increase the heat and add 1/2 cup (125 mL) of the chicken stock. Stir until all the stock is absorbed, then add the remaining stock. Cook until almost all of the stock is absorbed and remove from heat.

4. Stir in the green onions and cheese, and season to taste with salt and pepper.

Approximate values per serving:

Calories	180
Total fat	9 g
Saturated fat	5 g
Cholesterol	25 mg
Sodium	280 mg
Total carbohydrates	20 g
Protein	5 g
Vitamin A	10%

Claims—no sugar; good source of fibre

VENISON RED WINE JUS

Yield: 1 pt. (500 mL)

Bacon, chopped	2 Tbsp.	30 mL
Shallots, chopped	2	2
Carrots, chopped	1/2 cup	120 mL
Garlic, chopped	2 tsp.	10 mL
Celery, chopped	1 rib	1 rib
Onion, chopped	1/2 cup	120 mL
Red wine	1 pt.	500 mL
Venison or venison/veal stock	1 qt.	1 L

1. In a medium saucepan, render the bacon over low heat. Add the shallots, carrots, garlic, celery and onion, cook until tender.

2. Add the red wine and reduce to a glaze.

3. Add the stock and reduce by two-thirds. Pass through a fine strainer and check the consistency. Return to the saucepan and reduce further if necessary.

Approximate values per 1 oz. (30 mL) serving:

Calories	30
Total fat	1 g
Saturated fat	0 g
Cholesterol	1.5 mg
Sodium	228 mg
Total carbohydrates	5 g
Protein	1 g
Vitamin A	15%

Claims—low fat; low cholesterol

◆◆◆

RECIPE 18.4

VENISON MEDALLIONS GRAND VENEUR

Yield: 2 Servings   **Method:** Sautéing

Venison medallions, 3 oz. (90 g) each	4	4
Salt and pepper	TT	TT
Clarified butter	1 oz.	30 mL
White wine	1 oz.	30 mL
Poivrade sauce (p. 211)	6 oz.	180 mL
Red currant jelly	2 tsp.	10 mL
Cream, 35%	1 oz.	30 mL

*Approximate values per
6 oz. (180 g) serving:*

Calories	410
Total fat	21 g
Saturated fat	12 g
Cholesterol	195 mg
Sodium	1250 mg
Total carbohydrates	15 g
Protein	39 g
Vitamin A	15%

1. Season the medallions with salt and pepper and sauté in the clarified butter to the desired doneness. Remove and reserve.
2. Degrease the pan and deglaze with the white wine.
3. Add the poivrade sauce and bring to a simmer. Stir in the currant jelly, add the cream and adjust the seasonings.
4. Return the medallions to the sauce to reheat. Serve 2 medallions per person with a portion of the sauce.

◆◆◆

RECIPE 18.5

CARIBOU SERVED IN PUFF PASTRY
WITH BROAD BEANS AND WILD MUSHROOMS

INSTITUT DE TOURISME ET D'HÔTELLERIE DU QUÉBEC, PQ
Professeur Jean-Claude Belmont

Jean-Claude Belmont
Jean-Claude trained in France and worked in some of the most famous hotels in the world before settling in Canada. He now trains students for regional and international competitions. His Quebec Regional Junior Team won the gold medal and the prestigious Joseph Dobler Cup in Berlin in 1996. He is a dedicated promoter of regional foods.

Yield: 4 Servings   **Method:** Roasting

Sauce:		
Dry shallots, minced	6	6
Sweet butter	1 Tbsp.	15 g
Red wine	7 oz.	200 mL
Caribou Alcool, 94%	3-1/2 oz.	100 mL
Caribou brown stock	16 oz.	500 mL
Salt and pepper	TT	TT
Fresh thyme	1 sprig	1 sprig
Garnish:		
Small pearl onions	2 oz.	50 g
Sweet butter	1 Tbsp.	15 g
Morels	1 oz.	50 g
Chanterelles	1 oz.	50 g
Button mushrooms	3 oz.	150 g
Broad beans	7 oz.	200 g
Caribou loin, trimmed	1 lb.	450 g
Oil, salt and pepper	TT	TT
Puff pastry	14 oz.	400 g

1. To make the sauce, sweat the shallots in butter.
2. Add red wine and Alcool and reduce by one-half.
3. Add stock and seasonings and reduce by one-half.
4. Monter au beurre, strain and reserve.
5. To make the garnish, blanch the onions and drain well.
6. Sauté the onions with all the mushrooms in the butter.
7. Season to taste and keep hot.
8. Blanch the broad beans in salted water and keep warm.
9. Sear the trimmed, seasoned, caribou loin in oil.
10. Finish in oven, until rare (375°F/190°C). Let rest 20 minutes.
11. Roll puff pastry and cut into 4 5-inch (13-cm) rounds. Let rest 15 minutes, then bake at 375°F (190°C) for 20 minutes.
12. Split the puff pastry into 2 (top and bottom).
13. Put the bottom on a plate, then add a layer of loin slices. Cover with a layer of sauce (2 Tbsp./30 mL) and a few beans. Put the top into place.
14. To garnish, drizzle the sauce around the puff pasty. Add a few more beans and sprinkle with chopped herbs.

Approximate values per serving:

Calories	858
Total fat	40 g
Saturated fat	10 g
Cholesterol	126 mg
Sodium	626 mg
Total carbohydrates	50 g
Protein	42 g

RECIPE 18.6

BREAST OF EMU WITH SWEET GRAPEFRUIT

H.R.T. ALLIANCE HUMBER COLLEGE, CULINARY PROGRAMS
Professor Robert McCann

Robert McCann
Bob is a fellow of the Epicurean World Master Chefs Society and vice-chair of the Canadian chapter. In addition to instructing at Humber College, he judges international competitions.

Yield: 4 Servings   **Method:** Frying

Emu breasts, sliced into steaks, 5-1/2 oz. (160 g)	4	4
Cornflour	as needed	as needed
Vegetable oil	2 Tbsp.	30 mL
Red wine	5 oz.	150 mL
Sweet grapefruit juice	5 oz.	150 mL
Salt and freshly ground pepper	TT	TT
Fresh parsley, finely chopped	1 Tbsp.	15 mL
Pink grapefruit, peeled and segmented	1	1

1. Dust the emu steaks with a little cornflour on both sides.
2. Heat the oil in a frying pan and gently fry the steaks until medium rare, about 10 minutes, turning occasionally. Remove the steaks from the pan and keep warm.
3. Deglaze the pan with wine and reduce slightly.
4. Place 1 teaspoon (5 mL) of cornflour in a small bowl, add a little grapefruit juice and mix until smooth, then stir the cornflour mix, the remaining grapefruit juice, seasoning and parsley into the pan and bring to a boil, stirring constantly.
5. Put the steaks on the serving plate, garnish with the segments of grapefruit and serve with the sauce and seasonal vegetables such as boiled chickpeas with spinach, fried sweet potatoes or yam chips.

Approximate values per serving:

Calories	206
Total fat	2 g
Saturated fat	0 g
Cholesterol	74 mg
Sodium	487 mg
Total carbohydrates	10 g
Protein	31 g

♦♦♦

RECIPE 18.7

GRILLED LOIN OF RABBIT WITH SPINACH, FENNEL AND WHITE BEANS

GOTHAM BAR AND GRILL, NEW YORK, NY
Chef/Owner Alfred Portale

Yield: 6 Servings   **Method:** Grilling

Rabbit saddles	6	6
Bacon slices	6	6
Lemon, sliced thin	1	1
Shallots, minced	1 Tbsp.	15 mL
Fresh sage	1 bunch	1 bunch
Fresh rosemary	3 sprigs	3 sprigs
Fresh thyme	3 sprigs	3 sprigs
Garlic cloves, sliced thin	2	2
White peppercorns, cracked	1 Tbsp.	15 mL
Olive oil	as needed	as needed
Baby fennel, steamed until tender	12 heads	12 heads
Fresh spinach, steamed	1 lb.	450 g
White Beans (recipe follows)	as needed	as needed
Rabbit Sauce (recipe follows)	as needed	as needed

Approximate values per serving:

Calories	390
Total fat	19 g
Saturated fat	8 g
Cholesterol	140 mg
Sodium	700 mg
Total carbohydrates	20 g
Protein	36 g
Vitamin A	70%

1. Bone the saddles, removing the two loins and tenderloins.
2. Tightly wrap each loin and tenderloin together with half of a slice of bacon.
3. Place the rolled loins and tenderloins in a shallow container. Sprinkle with the lemon, shallots, herbs, garlic and cracked pepper and drizzle with olive oil; cover and refrigerate for 6–8 hours.
4. Bring the rabbit to room temperature. Remove from the marinade and grill over a medium fire until golden, approximately 6–8 minutes.
5. Cut each loin into medallions and arrange on the plates. Serve with fennel, spinach, White Beans and Rabbit Sauce.

WHITE BEANS

Yield: 2 lb. (1 kg)

Dried Great Northern beans, soaked	8 oz.	250 g
Sachet:		
Onion, small	1	1
Carrot, 3-in. (8-cm) piece	1	1
Celery, 2-in. (5-cm) piece	1	1
Fresh thyme	1 sprig	1 sprig
Fresh rosemary	1 sprig	1 sprig
Black peppercorns	1 tsp.	5 mL
Garlic clove, minced	1	1
Parsley, chopped	1 Tbsp.	15 mL
Fresh rosemary	TT	TT
Fresh thyme	TT	TT
Whole butter, softened	4 oz.	120 g
Salt and white pepper	TT	TT
Cream, 35%	2 oz.	60 mL

Approximate values per 1 oz. (30 g) serving:

Calories	45
Total fat	3.5 g
Saturated fat	2 g
Cholesterol	10 mg
Sodium	105 mg
Total carbohydrates	2 g
Protein	1 g
Vitamin A	4%

Claims—low cholesterol; low sodium; no sugar

1. Place the beans and the sachet in a large pot and cover with cold water. Bring to a simmer and cook until tender, approximately 45 minutes.

2. Cream together the garlic, parsley, rosemary, thyme and butter. Season with salt and white pepper.

3. Remove the sachet from the cooked beans and pour off all but 3–4 table-spoons (45–60 mL) of the cooking liquid. Return to the heat and swirl in the herb butter and cream. Keep warm.

RABBIT SAUCE

Yield: 1 pt. (450 mL)

Shallots, chopped	1 oz.	30 g
White peppercorns	1 Tbsp.	15 mL
Clarified butter	2 tsp.	10 mL
White wine	4 oz.	120 mL
Brown stock, made from chicken and rabbit bones	24 oz.	700 mL
Salt and white pepper	TT	TT
Whole butter	3 Tbsp.	45 mL

1. Sauté the shallots and peppercorns in the clarified butter over low heat until browned.

2. Add the white wine and reduce by one-third. Add the stock and reduce by one-third.

3. Season with salt and white pepper. Monter au beurre just before service.

Approximate values per 1 oz. (30 mL) serving:

Calories	45
Total fat	3 g
Saturated fat	2 g
Cholesterol	10 mg
Sodium	320 mg
Total carbohydrates	3 g
Protein	1 g
Vitamin A	8%

Claims—low fat, low cholesterol; no sugar

◆◆◆

RECIPE 18.8

MUSTARD-ROASTED LOIN OF BOAR WITH PAN GRAVY

Yield: 10 6-oz. (180-g) Servings   **Method:** Roasting

Crust:		
Flour	3 Tbsp.	45 mL
Brown sugar	2 Tbsp.	30 mL
Dry mustard	2 tsp.	10 mL
Dried thyme	2 tsp.	10 mL
Sage, rubbed	1 tsp.	5 mL
White wine	1 oz.	30 mL
White wine vinegar	1 oz.	30 mL
Boar loin, boneless, 4–6 lb. (2–2.7 kg)	1	1
Garlic cloves, sliced	3	3
Salt and pepper	TT	TT
Flour	2 oz.	60 g
Veal or game stock	1-1/2 qt.	1-1/2 L

1. Combine the crust ingredients to make a paste.

2. Puncture the loin with a paring knife in several places and press a slice of garlic into each hole. Season the loin with salt and pepper.

3. Coat the loin with an even layer of the crust mixture. Roast at 450°F (230°C) for 10 minutes. Reduce the temperature to 325°F (160°C) and roast until done, approximately 1 hour.

4. Remove the roast from the roasting pan. Degrease the pan, leaving about 2 ounces (60 g) of fat. Stir in 2 ounces (60 g) of flour and cook to make a blond roux. Add the stock to make a pan gravy. Strain the gravy through a chinois and adjust the seasonings.

5. Carve the boar and serve with the sauce.

Approximate values per serving:

Calories	341
Total fat	9 g
Saturated fat	2 g
Cholesterol	100 mg
Total carbohydrates	8 g
Protein	54 g

RECIPE 18.9

GRILLED BISON STEAK

Yield: 1 Serving		Method: Grilling
Bison strip loin steak, 8 oz. (250 g)	1	1
Salt and pepper	TT	TT
Oil	1 Tbsp.	15 mL

Approximate values per 8 oz. (250 g) serving, without sauce:

Calories	400
Total fat	18 g
Saturated fat	3 g
Cholesterol	140 mg
Sodium	1290 mg
Total Carbohydrates	1 g
Protein	61 g
Iron	30%

1. Season the steak well with salt and pepper.
2. Brush with oil and grill to the desired degree of doneness.
3. Serve the steak with a full-flavoured sauce such as a bordelaise (p. 210) or poivrade sauce (p. 211).

NOTE: Marinating is recommended. Cook at lower temperatures than beef.

RECIPE 18.10

ROASTED PHEASANT WITH PRAIRIE BABY LETTUCE LEAVES, WALNUT OIL AND BALSAMIC VINAIGRETTE

ST. CHARLES COUNTRY CLUB, WINNIPEG, MB
Executive Chef Tony Murakami

Tony Murakami

Tony started out in Tokyo and then came to Canada, where he worked his way up to executive chef and joined the St. Charles Country Club. Tony is a Certified Master Chef, and highlights of his career include 9 gold medals and 4 grand golds in international competition. He has been recognized by the federal and Manitoba governments for his work.

Yield: 10 Servings		Method: Roasting
Whole pheasant, each 2-1/2 to 3-1/2 lbs. (1.2–1.5 kg)	3	3
Butter, unsalted, room temperature	14 oz.	375 g
Salt and pepper	TT	TT
White wine, dry	12 oz.	350 mL
Mirepoix	3-1/2 cups	750 mL
Juniper berries	1 Tbsp.	15 mL
Mignonette (coarsely ground black pepper)	1 tsp.	5 mL
Pheasant or chicken stock	12 oz.	350 mL
Gin	1 tsp.	5 mL
Walnut Oil and Balsamic Vinaigrette:		
Dijon mustard	1 Tbsp.	15 mL
Walnut oil	12 oz.	350 mL
Balsamic vinegar	3-1/2 oz.	100 mL
Shallots, finely chopped	2 Tbsp.	30 mL
Dry red chile pepper, crushed	1 tsp.	5 mL
Salt and pepper	TT	TT
Salad:		
Assortment of baby lettuce leaves, spinach leaves or other leaves	10 portions, 8 oz. each	10 portions, 250 mL each
Potato chips (small-sized baker chipped as garnish)	30 pieces	30 pieces
Tomato petals, skinless	30 pieces	30 pieces

Approximate values per serving:

Calories	766
Total fat	56 g
Saturated fat	26 g
Cholesterol	252 mg
Sodium	342 mg
Total carbohydrates	1 g
Protein	55 g

1. Brush pheasant all over with butter and salt and pepper to season. Roast at 400°F (200°C) for 10 minutes. Reduce heat to 300°F (150°C) for 15–20 minutes. Next, pour the white wine over the bird. Take the pheasant out of the oven and let rest for 15 minutes.

2. Sauté the mirepoix until brown. Debone the pheasant and reserve the bones and skin. Set it aside and keep it warm.

3. In a heavy stainless steel pan over medium heat, add pheasant skin, bone, mirepoix, juniper berries, mignonette and anything from the roasting pan. Add pheasant or chicken stock. Simmer for 20 minutes and skim the fat.

4. Strain the stock and reduce by half or to a syrupy consistency. Add the gin.

5. Make the vinaigrette dressing. Whip the ingredients except salt and pepper with the reduction of the pheasant stock. Add salt and pepper to taste.

6. Wash the salad leaves and spin dry. Toss the salad leaves with the vinaigrette. Arrange the greens on a chilled plate, then arrange thinly sliced pheasant on the plate with small potato chips and tomato petals. To make the tomato petals, peel the tomatoes then cut them into quarters or sixths. Seed them and cut away interior flesh to produce a petal- or leaf-like shape.

Approximate values per serving (salad):

Calories	62
Total fat	3 g
Saturated fat	1 g
Cholesterol	0 mg
Sodium	59 mg
Total carbohydrates	9 g
Protein	2 g

Approximate values per serving (vinaigrette):

Calories	299
Total fat	32 g
Saturated fat	3 g
Cholesterol	0 mg
Sodium	158 mg
Total carbohydrates	3 g
Protein	.3 g

◆◆◆

RECIPE 18.11

STUFFED BREAST OF PHEASANT

Yield: 4 Servings   **Method:** Roasting

Stuffing:

Prunes, chopped fine	4 oz.	120 g
Apple, chopped fine	4 oz.	120 g
Dried apricots, chopped fine	1 oz.	30 g
Walnuts, chopped fine	2 oz.	60 g
Onion, chopped fine	2 oz.	60 g
Salt	1/4 tsp.	1 mL
Pepper	1/4 tsp.	1 mL
Fresh thyme	1/2 tsp.	3 mL
Pheasant breast, boneless	4	4
Bacon, thin slices	8	8
Ivory sauce (p. 208)	8 oz.	250 mL

1. Combine the stuffing ingredients and set aside.

2. Separate each pheasant breast into 2 pieces. Pound each to a thickness of 1/4 inch (6 mm).

3. Place a portion of the stuffing in the centre of 4 of the pieces of breast meat. Place a second piece of breast meat over the stuffing. Wrap each parcel tightly with 2 slices of bacon and tie with butcher's twine.

4. Bake at 325°F (160°C) until done, approximately 45 minutes.

5. Remove the twine, carve each bundle into slices and serve with 2 ounces (60 mL) of ivory sauce.

Approximate values per serving:

Calories	690
Total fat	20 g
Saturated fat	4.5 g
Cholesterol	210 mg
Sodium	270 mg
Total carbohydrates	33 g
Protein	93 g
Vitamin A	25%
Vitamin C	40%

◆◆◆

RECIPE 18.12
GRILLED QUAIL
WITH POTATO GALETTE, ARTICHOKE WEDGES AND BALSAMIC RASPBERRIES

STANFORD COURT HOTEL, SAN FRANCISCO, CA
Former Chef Ercolino Crugnale

Yield: 6 Servings   **Method:** Grilling

Bobwhite quail	6	6
Salt and pepper	TT	TT
Asparagus tips, 2 in. (5 cm) long, peeled and blanched	18 pieces	18 pieces
Artichoke Wedges (recipe follows)	18 pieces	18 pieces
Roma tomatoes, concassées	3	3
Cipolline onions, peeled and glazed with chicken stock and whole butter	12	12
Pure olive oil	3 oz.	90 mL
Chicken stock	6 oz.	180 mL
Dry white wine	6 oz.	180 mL
Shallots, minced	2 Tbsp.	30 mL
Fresh tarragon, chopped	2 Tbsp.	30 mL
Fresh parsley, chopped	2 Tbsp.	30 mL
Potato Galette (recipe follows)	6 pieces	6 pieces
Mixed greens such as butter lettuce, yellow frisee and radicchio, torn into 1-in. (2.5-cm) pieces	1-1/2 cups	375 mL
Basic vinaigrette dressing (Recipe 24.1)	4 Tbsp.	60 mL
Balsamic Raspberries (recipe follows)	1 qt.	1 L
Extra virgin olive oil	3 oz.	90 mL

Approximate values per serving:

Calories	534
Total fat	40 g
Saturated fat	10 g
Cholesterol	94 mg
Sodium	1534 mg
Total carbohydrates	14 g
Protein	33 g
Vitamin A	95%
Vitamin C	146%
Iron	71%

1. Season the quail with salt and pepper and grill on both sides until cooked just under medium.
2. Sauté the asparagus, artichoke wedges, tomatoes and onions in the pure olive oil.
3. Deglaze the pan with chicken stock and white wine. Add the shallots, tarragon and parsley. Season with salt and pepper.
4. To serve, place a Potato Galette on each plate. Arrange the vegetables around the potato.
5. Dress the mixed greens with the basic vinaigrette dressing and place a small amount in the centre of each plate. Place the quail on the greens.
6. Place Balsamic Raspberries around the plate; drizzle with extra virgin olive oil.

POTATO GALETTE

Yield: 6 Galettes

Approximate values per serving:

Calories	150
Total fat	4 g
Saturated fat	2.5 g
Cholesterol	10 mg
Sodium	150 mg
Total carbohydrates	25 g
Protein	2 g
Vitamin A	4%

Clarified butter	as needed	as needed
Idaho potatoes, peeled and sliced thin on a mandoline	3	3
Salt and pepper	TT	TT

1. For each galette, completely line the bottom of a buttered 8-inch (20-cm) pan with potato slices, arranging the slices in a circular, overlapping pattern.

2. Season with salt and pepper and sauté until golden brown on each side. Hold at room temperature.

ARTICHOKE WEDGES

Yield: 20 Pieces

Olive oil	4 oz.	120 mL
Artichoke bottoms, turned and cleaned, cut in quarters	5	5
Garlic, minced	2 Tbsp.	30 mL
Fresh thyme, chopped	1 Tbsp.	15 mL
Chicken stock	1 pt.	500 mL
Lemon juice	2 oz.	60 mL
White wine	4 oz.	120 mL
Salt and white pepper	TT	TT

Approximate values per serving:

Calories	60
Total fat	6 g
Saturated fat	1 g
Cholesterol	0 mg
Sodium	120 mg
Total carbohydrates	1 g
Protein	1 g
Vitamin A	0

Claims—low saturated fat; no cholesterol; low sodium; no sugar

1. Over high heat, sauté the artichokes in the olive oil for 2 minutes.

2. Add the garlic, thyme and 4 ounces (120 mL) chicken stock; reduce *au sec.*

3. Add the lemon juice, white wine and seasonings; reduce *au sec.*

4. Add another 6 ounces (180 mL) chicken stock, reduce *au sec.*

5. Add the remaining chicken stock; reduce *au sec.* The artichokes should be glazed, crisp and tender.

BALSAMIC RASPBERRIES

Yield: 1 qt. (1 L)

Raspberries, ripe but firm	1 qt.	1 L
Balsamic vinegar	6 oz.	170 mL
Pepper	1 tsp.	5 mL

Approximate values per serving:

Calories	15
Total fat	0 g
Saturated fat	0 g
Cholesterol	0 mg
Sodium	0 mg
Total carbohydrates	4 g
Protein	0 g

Claims—fat free; no saturated fat; no cholesterol; no sodium

1. Gently combine all ingredients.

2. Let the raspberries macerate for 15 minutes.

3. Strain off the vinegar and reserve.

 EBLINKS

Wild Game Recipes
   diver.ocean.washington.edu/peterl/recipes/recipemain.html

B&E Ranches and North Country Bison: Bison Cooking Tips
   www.ncbison.com/cooking_tips.html

National Food Safety Database: Preservation of Game Meats
   www.foodsafety.org/sd/sd019.htm

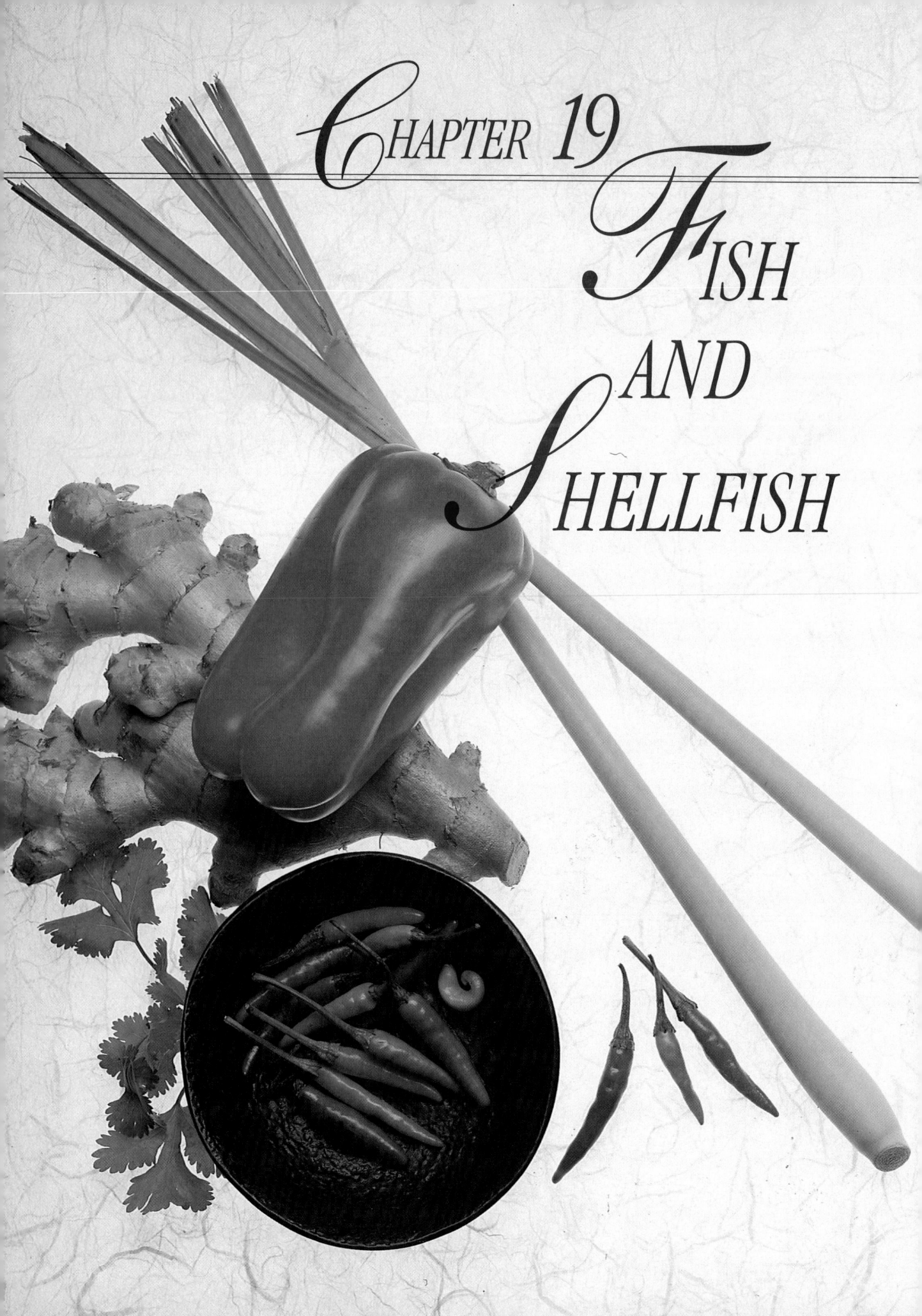

CHAPTER 19
FISH AND SHELLFISH

ish are aquatic vertebrates with fins for swimming and gills for breathing. Of the more than thirty thousand species known, most live in the seas and oceans; freshwater species are far less numerous. Shellfish are aquatic invertebrates with shells or carapaces. They are found in both fresh and salt water.

Always an important food source, fish and shellfish have become increasingly popular in recent years, due in part to demands from health-conscious consumers. Because of increased demand and improved preservation and transportation techniques, good-quality fish and shellfish, once found only along seacoasts and lakes, are now readily available to almost every food service operation.

Many fish and shellfish species are very expensive; all are highly perishable. Because their cooking times are generally shorter and their flavours more delicate than meat or poultry, special attention must be given to fish and shellfish to prevent spoilage and to produce high-quality finished products.

In this chapter you will learn how to identify a large assortment of fish and shellfish as well as how to properly purchase and store them, fabricate or prepare them for cooking and cook them by a variety of dry-heat and moist-heat cooking methods. This chapter presents many of the cooking methods applied to meats and poultry in the previous chapters. Review the corresponding procedures for meats and poultry and note the similarities and differences.

LEARNING OUTCOMES

After studying this chapter you will be able to:

+ describe the structure and composition of fish and shellfish
+ identify a variety of fish and shellfish
+ purchase fish and shellfish appropriate for your needs
+ store fish and shellfish properly
+ prepare fish and shellfish for cooking: scale fish; pan-dress flatfish; fillet round fish and flatfish; skin Dover sole and fish fillets; pull pin bones from salmon fillets; cut an escalope ; cut steaks; peel, devein and butterfly shrimp; prepare live lobster for broiling or sautéing; remove cooked lobster meat from the shell; open clams and oysters; clean and debeard mussels
+ apply various cooking methods to fish and shellfish: broiling and grilling, baking, sautéing, pan-frying, steaming, submersion and shallow poaching, simmering

---

STRUCTURE AND MUSCLE COMPOSITION

The fish and shellfish used in food service operations can be divided into three categories: fish, mollusks and crustaceans.

Fish (Fr. *poisson*) include both fresh- and saltwater varieties. They have fins and an internal skeleton of bone and cartilage. Based upon shape and skeletal structure, fish can be divided into two groups: round fish and flatfish. **Round fish** swim in a vertical position and have eyes on both sides of their heads. Their bodies may be truly round, oval or compressed. (See Figure 19.1.) **Flatfish** have asymmetrical, compressed bodies, swim in a horizontal position and have both eyes on top of their heads. Flatfish are bottom dwellers; most are found in deep ocean waters around the world. The skin on top of their bodies is dark, to camouflage them from predators, and can change colour according to their surroundings. Their scales are small and their dorsal and anal fins run the length of their bodies. (See Figure 19.2.)

Mollusks (Fr. *mollusque*) are shellfish characterized by soft, unsegmented bodies with no internal skeleton. Most mollusks have hard outer shells. Single-shelled mollusks such as abalone are known as **univalves**. Those with two shells, such as clams, oysters and mussels, are known as **bivalves**. Squid and octopus, which are known as **cephalopods**, do not have a hard outer shell. Rather, they have a single thin internal shell called a *pen* or *cuttlebone*.

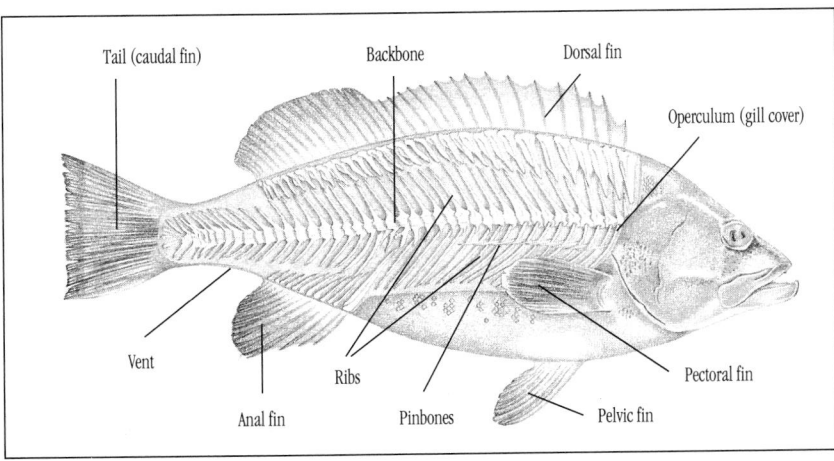

FIGURE 19.1   *Bone Structure of a Round Fish*

Crustaceans (Fr. *crustacé*) are also shellfish. They have a hard outer skeleton or shell and jointed appendages. Crustaceans include lobsters, crabs and shrimp.

The flesh of fish and shellfish consists primarily of water, protein, fat and minerals. Fish flesh is composed of short muscle fibres separated by delicate sheets of connective tissue. Fish, as well as most shellfish, are naturally tender, so the purpose of cooking is to firm proteins and enhance flavour. The absence of the oxygen-carrying protein myoglobin makes fish flesh very light or white in colour. (The orange colour of salmon and some trout comes from pigments found in their food.) Compared to meats, fish do not contain large amounts of intermuscular fat. But the amount of fat a fish does contain affects the way it responds to cooking. Fish containing a relatively large amount of fat, such as salmon and mackerel, are known as fatty or oily fish. Fish such as cod and haddock contain very little fat and are referred to as lean fish. Shellfish are also very lean.

SEAFOOD

Seafood means different things to different people. For some, the term applies just to shellfish or to shellfish and other small edible marine creatures. For others it is limited to saltwater shellfish or to saltwater shellfish and fish. For yet others, it refers to all fish and shellfish, both freshwater and saltwater. Because of the term's vagueness, it is not used here.

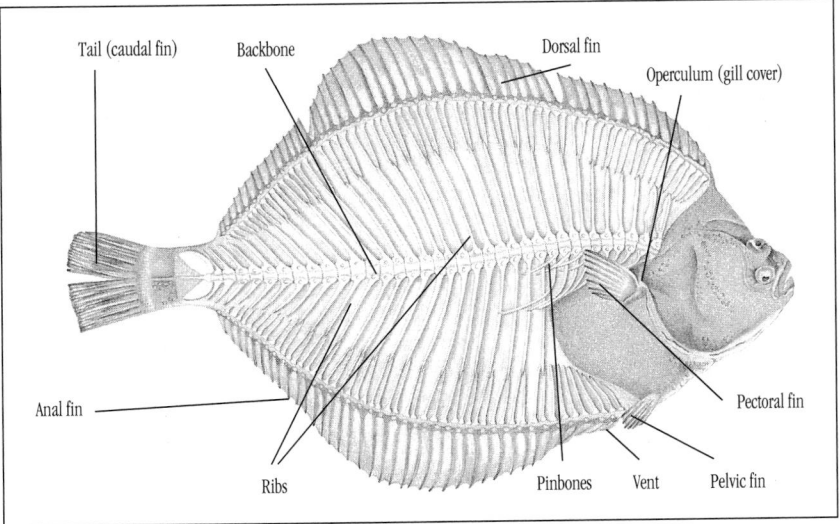

FIGURE 19.2   *Bone Structure of a Flatfish*

IDENTIFYING FISH AND SHELLFISH

Identifying fish and shellfish properly can be difficult because of the vast number of similar-appearing fish and shellfish that are separate species within each family. Adding confusion are the various colloquial names given to the same fish or the same name given to different fish in different localities. Fish with an unappealing name may also be given a catchier name or the name of a similar but more popular item for marketing purposes. Moreover, some species are referred to by a foreign name, especially on menus.

The Canadian Food Inspection Agency publishes regulations concerning acceptable nomenclature for fish and fish products.

Fish

Round Fish

Bass (Fr. *bar*) commonly refers to a number of unrelated fish. The better-known freshwater bass varieties (largemouth, smallmouth, redeye and black) are actually members of the sunfish family. They are lean and delicate but, as game, not commercially available in Canada. The saltwater bass varieties (black sea bass and striped bass) are popular commercial items.

Black sea bass are sometimes referred to as rock sea bass. They have a lean, firm white flesh with a mild flavour and flaky texture. They usually weigh from 1-1/2 to 3 pounds (675 g–1.3 kg) and are most prevalent in the Atlantic Ocean between New York and North Carolina. Black sea bass can be prepared by almost any cooking method and are often served whole in Chinese and Italian cuisines.

Striped bass, often erroneously referred to as rockfish, are ocean fish that depend on freshwater rivers to reproduce. True striped bass cannot be marketed because pollution and overfishing have damaged the supply. A hybrid of striped bass and either white bass or white perch is being **aquafarmed** for commercial use, however. It is this hybrid that food service operations receive as striped bass. Whole fish weigh from 1 to 5 pounds (450 g to 2.2 kg). Striped bass have a rich, sweet flavour and firm texture. They can be steamed, baked, poached or broiled.

Black Sea Bass

Striped Bass

Aquafarming—*also known as aquaculture, is the business, science and practice of raising large quantities of fish and shellfish in tanks, ponds or ocean pens; used especially for catfish, trout, salmon, shrimp and other popular fish and shellfish.*

Catfish are scaleless freshwater fish common in southern lakes and rivers and now aquafarmed extensively. Aquafarm raising eliminates the "muddy" taste once associated with catfish and ensures a year-round supply. The flesh is pure white with a moderate fat content, a mild, sweet flavour and firm texture. Channel catfish are the most important commercially. They usually weigh from 1-1/2 to 5 pounds (675 g to 2.2 kg). The smaller of these fish are known as **fiddlers**; they are often deep-fat fried and served whole. Catfish may be prepared by almost any cooking method, but are especially well suited to frying.

Catfish

Arctic char is a type of salmon found in the far northern rivers. It is lean and pink fleshed. It is available fresh only in August and September and March and April.

The **cod** (Fr. *cabillaud*) family includes Atlantic and Pacific cod as well as pollock, haddock, whiting and hake. Cod have a mild, delicate flavour and lean, firm white flesh that flakes apart easily. Cod can be prepared by most cooking methods, although grilling is not recommended because the flesh is too flaky.

Atlantic cod are the best-selling fish in America. They are available fresh, whole or drawn, or cut into fillets or steaks. They are also available frozen and are often used for precooked or prebreaded sticks or portions. Smoked cod and salt cod are also available. Although cod may reach 200 pounds (90 kg), most market cod weigh 10 pounds (4.5 kg) or less. **Scrod** is a marketing term for cod weighing less than 2-1/2 pounds (1.1 kg).

Atlantic Cod

Haddock, the second most commercially important fish, look like thin, small Atlantic cod and weigh about 2 to 5 pounds (900 g to 2.3 kg). They have a stronger flavour and more delicate texture than Atlantic cod.

Pacific cod, also known as grey cod, are found in the northern Pacific Ocean and are not as abundant as their Atlantic cousins. Pacific cod are most often available frozen; they should be labelled "true cod" to distinguish them from rock cod and black cod, which are unrelated.

Pollock, also known as Boston bluefish or blue cod, are plentiful in the northern Atlantic and Pacific Oceans. Their flesh is grey-pink when raw, turning white when cooked. Pollock are often frozen at sea, then reprocessed into surimi. They can also be salted or smoked.

Pollock

Eels (Fr. *anguille*) are long, snakelike freshwater fish with dorsal and anal fins running the length of their bodies. (The conger eel is from a different family and has little culinary significance.) North American and European eels are available live, whole, gutted or as fillets. Eels have a high fat content and firm flesh; they are sweet and mildly flavoured. Their tough skin should be removed before cooking. Eels may be steamed, baked, fried or used in stews. Baby eels are a springtime delicacy, especially in Spain, where they are pan-fried in olive oil and garlic with hot red peppers. Smoked eels are also available.

Eel

The **grouper** family includes almost 400 varieties found in temperate waters worldwide. The more common Atlantic Ocean varieties are the yellowfin grouper, black grouper, red grouper and gag; the Pacific Ocean varieties are the sea bass (also known as jewfish and different from the black sea bass) and spotted cabrilla. Although some species can reach 800 pounds (360 kg) or more, most commercial varieties are sold in the 5 to 20-pound (2.2 to 9-kg) range. They have lean white flesh with a mild to sweet flavour and very firm texture. Their skin, which is tough and strongly flavoured, is generally removed before cooking. Grouper fillets may be baked, deep-fat fried, broiled or grilled.

Grouper

Herring (Fr. *hareng*) are long, silvery-blue fish found in both the northern Atlantic and Pacific Oceans. Their strongly flavoured flesh has a moderate to high fat content. Whole herring weigh up to 8 ounces (225 g). Fresh herring may be butterflied or filleted and roasted, broiled or grilled. But because herring are very soft and tend to spoil quickly, they are rarely available fresh. More often, they are smoked (known as kippers) or cured in brine.

Sardines (Fr. *sardine*) are young, small herring with fatty, oily flesh that has a flaky texture. Sardines are usually sold canned, whole or as skinned and boned fillets, or fried or smoked and packed in oil or sauce. Sardines are used primarily for sandwiches and salads.

John Dory, also known as St. Peter's fish, have a distinctive round, black spot with a yellow halo on each side of the body. Their flesh is white, firm and finely flaked. They may be filleted and prepared like flounder and are a classic bouillabaisse ingredient.

John Dory

Mackerel

Mackerel (Fr. *maquereau*) of culinary importance include king and Spanish mackerel as well as tuna and wahoo, which are discussed separately later. The species known as Atlantic and Pacific mackerel are not generally used for food because of their small size and high fat content. Mackerel flesh has a high fat content, grey to pink colouring, a mild flavour and flaky texture. The flesh becomes firm and off-white when cooked. Mackerel are best broiled, grilled, smoked or baked.

Mahi-mahi is the more commonly used name for dolphin or dolphinfish; this Hawaiian name is used to distinguish them from the marine mammal of the same name. (Dolphins and porpoises are marine mammals.) Also known by their Spanish name, *dorado*, mahi-mahi are brilliantly coloured fish found in tropical seas. Mahi-mahi weigh about 15 pounds (6.6 kg) and are sold whole or as fillets. Their flesh is off-white to pink, lean and firm with a sweet flavour. Dolphinfish can be broiled, grilled or baked. The meat may become dry when cooked, however, so sauce or marinade is recommended.

Mahi-Mahi

Monkfish are also known as angler fish, goosefish, rape and lotte. These extraordinarily ugly fish are rarely seen whole, for the large head is usually discarded before reaching market. Only the tail is edible; it is available in fillets, fresh or frozen. The scaleless skin must be removed. The flesh is lean, pearly white and very firm. Its texture and flavour have earned monkfish the nickname of "poor man's lobster." Monkfish absorb flavours easily and are baked, steamed, fried, grilled or broiled. They are also used for stews and soups.

Orange roughy are caught in the South Pacific off the coasts of New Zealand and Australia. They have bright orange skin and firm, pearly-white flesh with a low fat content and extremely bland flavour. Fresh-frozen fillets are widely available year round. Orange roughy are almost always marketed as skinless, boneless frozen fillets, averaging 6 to 8 ounces (170 to 225 g) each. They can be broiled, steamed, grilled or prepared in the same manner as cod.

Red snapper is also known as the American or northern red snapper. Although there are many members of the snapper family, only one is the true red snapper. Red-skinned rockfish are often mislabelled as the more popular red snapper or Pacific snapper, a practice that is currently legal only in California. True red snapper has lean, pink flesh that becomes white when cooked; it is sweet-flavoured and flaky. They are sold whole or as fillets with the skin left on for identification.

Red Snapper

Red snapper may reach 35 pounds (15 kg), but most are marketed at only 4 to 6 pounds (1.8 to 2.7 kg) or as 1 to 3-pound (450 g to 1.3 kg) fillets. Red snapper can be prepared using almost any cooking method. The head and bones are excellent for stock.

Salmon (Fr. *saumon*) flourish in both the northern Atlantic and Pacific Oceans, returning to the freshwater rivers and streams of their birth to spawn. Salmon flesh gets its distinctive pink-red colour from fat-soluble carotenoids found in the crustaceans on which they feed. Salmon is the most popular fish in Canada.

Atlantic salmon is the most important commercially, accounting for one-quarter of all salmon produced worldwide. Extensive aquafarms in Norway, Canada and Scotland produce a steady supply of Atlantic salmon. For marketing purposes, the fish's point of origin is often added to the name (for example, Norwegian, Scottish or Shetland Atlantic salmon). Atlantic salmon have a rich pink colour and moist flesh. Their average weight is from 4 to 12 pounds (1.8 to 5.4 kg). Wild Atlantic salmon are almost never available.

Atlantic Salmon

Chinook or **king salmon** from the Pacific are also highly desirable. They average from 5 to 30 pounds (2.2 to 13.2 kg) and have red-orange flesh with a high fat content and rich flavour. Like other salmon, their flesh separates into large flakes when cooked. Chinooks are often marketed by the name of the river from which they are harvested (for example, Columbia, Yukon or Copper Chinook salmon). They are distinguished by the black interior of their mouth.

Chinook or King Salmon

Coho or **silver** salmon have pinkish flesh and are available fresh or frozen, wild or from aquafarms. Wild coho average from 3 to 12 pounds (1.3 to 5.4 kg), while aquafarmed coho are much smaller, usually less than 1 pound (450 g).

Other varieties, such as chum, sockeye, red, blueback and pink salmon, are usually canned but may be available fresh or frozen.

Salmon can be prepared by many cooking methods: broiling, grilling, poaching, steaming or baking. Frying is not recommended, however, because of their high fat content. Salmon fillets are often cured or smoked. **Gravlax** is salmon that has been cured for one to three days with salt, sugar and dill. **Lox** is salmon that is cured in a salted brine and then typically cold-smoked. **Nova** is used in the eastern U.S. to refer to a less-salty, cold-smoked salmon.

Mini Coho Salmon

Blacktip Shark

Sharks provide delicious eating, despite their less-than-appealing appearance and vicious reputation. Mako and blue sharks are the most desirable, with mako often being sold as swordfish. Sand shark, sharpnose, blacktip, angel and thresher are also available commercially. Most sharks have lean flesh with a mild flavour and firm texture. The flesh is white with tinges of pink or red when raw, turning off-white when cooked. Makos weigh from 30 to 250 pounds (13 to 110 kg); other species may reach as much as 1000 pounds (450 kg).

All sharks have cartilaginous skeletons and no bones; therefore, they are not actually fish, but rather marine invertebrates. Sharks are usually cut into loins or wheels, then into steaks or cubes. They can be broiled, grilled, baked or fried. An ammonia smell indicates that the shark was not properly treated when caught. Do not buy or eat it.

Swordfish take their name from the long, swordlike bill extending from their upper jaw. These popular fish average about 250 pounds (110 kg). Their flesh is lean and sweet with a very firm, meatlike texture; it may be grey, pink or off-white when raw, becoming white when cooked. Swordfish are most often available cut into wheels or portioned into steaks perfect for grilling or broiling.

Swordfish Wheel

Tilapia

Tilapia is the name given to several species of freshwater, aquafarm-raised fish bred worldwide. They grow quickly in warm water, reaching about 3 pounds (1.3 kg); they are available whole or filleted, fresh or frozen. The flesh is similar to catfish—lean, white and sweet, with a firm texture. Tilapia are sometimes marketed as cherry snapper or sunshine snapper, even though they are not members of the snapper family.

Trout (Fr. *truite*) are members of the salmon family. Most of the freshwater trout commercially available are aquafarm-raised rainbow trout, although brown trout and brook trout are also being aquafarmed. Some trout species spend part of their lives at sea, returning to fresh water to spawn. On the West Coast, these are called salmon trout or steelhead. Trout have a low to moderate fat content, a flaky texture and a delicate flavour that can be easily overwhelmed by strong sauces. The flesh may be white, orange or pink. Trout are usually marketed at 8 to 10 ounces (225 to 280 g) each, just right for an individual portion. Lake trout are not aquafarmed but are appearing on specialty menus, when available, as a cured and smoked product. Trout can be baked, pan-fried, smoked or steamed.

Red Mountain Trout

Rainbow Trout

Tuna (Fr. *thon*) varieties include the bluefin, yellowfin, bonito, bigeye and blackfin. Ahi is the popular market name for either yellowfin or bigeye tuna. All are members of the mackerel family and are found in tropical and subtropical waters around the world. Tuna are large fish, weighing up to several hundred pounds each. Bluefin, the finest and most desirable for sashimi, are becoming very scarce because of overfishing. Regular canned tuna is usually prepared from yellowfin or skipjack; canned white tuna is prepared from albacore, also known as longfin tuna. Pacific tuna that is frozen at sea to preserve its freshness is referred to as clipper fish. Any of these species may be found fresh or frozen, however. Tuna is usually cut into four boneless loins for market. The loins are then cut into steaks, cubes or chunks. The flesh has a low to moderate fat content (a higher fat content is preferred for sashimi) and a deep red colour. The dark, reddish-brown muscle that runs along the lateral line is very fatty and can be removed. Tuna flesh turns light grey when cooked and is very firm, with a mild flavour. Tuna work well for grilling or broiling and may be marinated or brushed with seasoned oil during cooking. Tuna are often prepared medium rare to prevent dryness.

Yellowfin Tuna

Wahoo, also known as ono, are found throughout tropical and subtropical waters, but are particularly associated with Hawaii (*ono* even means "good to eat" in Hawaiian). They are actually a type of mackerel and are cooked like any other mackerel.

Wahoo

Whitefish species inhabit the freshwater lakes and streams of North America. Lake whitefish, the most important commercially, are related to salmon. They are marketed at up to 7 pounds (3.2 kg) and are available whole or filleted. The flesh is firm and white, with a moderate amount of fat and a sweet flavour. Whitefish may be baked, broiled, grilled or smoked and are often used in processed fish products. They are the source for golden caviar.

Whitefish

Flatfish

Flounder (Fr. *flet*) have lean, firm flesh that is pearly or pinkish-white with a sweet, mild flavour. Although they are easily boned, most are deheaded and gutted at sea and sold as fresh or frozen fillets. These fillets are very thin and can dry out or spoil easily, so extra care should be taken in handling, preparing and storing them. Recipes that preserve moisture work best with flounder; poaching, steaming or frying are recommended. Many types of flounder are marketed as sole, perhaps in an attempt to cash in on the popularity of true sole. The Canadian Federal Fisheries permits this practice. (See Table 19.1.)

English sole are actually flounder caught off the West Coast of the United States and Canada. They are usually marketed simply as "fillet of sole." They are a plentiful species of fair to average quality.

Petrale sole, another West Coast flounder, are generally considered the finest of the domestic "soles." They are most often available as fillets, which tend to be thicker and firmer than other sole fillets.

English Sole

Petrale Sole

TABLE 19.1   FLOUNDER (ALSO KNOWN AS SOLE)

Atlantic Ocean	Pacific Ocean
Blackback/winter flounder/lemon sole	Arrowtooth
Fluke/summer flounder	Petrale sole
Starry flounder	Rex sole
Yellowtail	English sole
Windowpane flounder	Rock sole
Grey sole/witch flounder	Sand sole
	Yellowfin sole
	Domestic Dover sole/Pacific flounder
	Butter sole

Lemon Sole

Domestic Dover sole are also Pacific flounder. They are not as delicate or flavourful as other species of sole or flounder. Moreover, they are often afflicted with a parasite that causes the meat to have a slimy, gelatinous texture. Domestic Dover sole are not recommended if other sole or flounder are available.

Lemon sole are the most abundant and popular East Coast flounder. They are also known as blackback or winter flounder (during the winter they migrate close to shore from the deeper, colder waters). They average 2 pounds (900 g) in weight.

Alaskan Halibut

Halibut are among the largest flatfish; they often weigh up to 300 pounds (135 kg). The Canadian Federal Fisheries recognizes only two halibut species: Atlantic (eastern) and Pacific (northern, Alaskan, western) halibut. Both have lean, firm flesh that is snow-white with a sweet, mild flavour. California halibut, which are actually flounder, are similar in taste and texture but average only 12 pounds (5.4 kg) each. Halibut may be cut into boneless steaks or skewered on brochettes. The flesh, which dries out easily, can be poached, baked, grilled or broiled and is good with a variety of sauces.

True Dover Sole

Sole (Fr. *sole*) are probably the most flavourful and finely textured flatfish. Indeed, because of the connotations of quality associated with the name, "sole" is widely used for many species that are not members of the sole (*Soleidae*) family. Even though the Canadian Federal Fisheries allows many species of flatfish to be called "sole" for marketing purposes, no true sole is commercially harvested in North American waters. Any flatfish harvested in North American waters and marketed as sole is actually flounder.

True **Dover sole**, a staple of classic cuisine, are a lean fish with pearly-white flesh and a delicate flavour that can stand up to a variety of sauces and seasonings. They are a member of the *Soleidae* family and come only from the waters off the coasts of England, Africa and Europe. They are imported into this country as fresh whole fish or fresh or frozen fillets.

Turbot

Turbot are a Pacific flatfish of no great culinary distinction. In Europe, however, the species known as turbot (Fr. *turbot*) are large diamond-shaped fish highly prized for their delicate flavour and firm, white flesh. They are also marketed as brill.

Mollusks

Univalves

Univalves are mollusks with a single shell in which the soft-bodied animal resides. They are actually marine snails with a single foot, used to attach the creature to fixed objects such as rocks.

Abalone have brownish-grey, ear-shaped shells. They are harvested in California, but California law does not permit canning abalone or shipping it out of state. Some frozen abalone is available from Mexico; canned abalone is imported from Japan. Abalone are lean with a sweet, delicate flavour similar to that of clams. They are too tough to eat unless tenderized with a mallet or rolling pin. They may then be eaten raw or prepared seviche-style. Great care must be taken when grilling or sautéing abalone as the meat becomes very tough when overcooked.

Conch are found in warm waters off the Florida Keys and in the Caribbean. The beautiful peachy-pink shell of the queen conch is prized by beachcombers. Conch meat is lean, smooth and very firm with a sweet-smoky flavour and chewy texture. It can be sliced and pounded to tenderize it, eaten raw with lime juice, or slow-cooked whole.

Bivalves

Bivalves are mollusks with two bilateral shells attached by a central hinge.

Clams (Fr. *clovisses*) are harvested along both the East and West Coasts, with Atlantic clams being more significant commercially. Atlantic Coast clams include hard-shell, soft-shell and surf clams. Clams are available all year, either live in the shell or fresh-shucked (meat removed from the shell). Canned clams, whether minced, chopped or whole, are also available.

Atlantic hard-shell clams or **quahogs** have hard, blue-grey shells. Their chewy meat is not as sweet as other clam meat. Quahogs have different names, depending upon their size. **Littlenecks** are generally under 2 inches (5 cm) across the shell and usually are served on the half shell or steamed. They are the most expensive clams. **Cherrystones** are generally under 3 inches (7.5 cm) across the shell and are sometimes eaten raw but are more often cooked. **Topnecks** are usually cooked and are often served as stuffed clams. **Chowders**, the largest quahogs, are always eaten cooked, especially minced for chowder or soup.

Soft-shell clams, also known as Ipswich, steamer and long-necked clams, have thin, brittle shells that do not completely close because of the clam's protruding black-tipped siphon. Their meat is tender and sweet. They are sometimes fried but are more often served steamed.

Surf clams are deep-water clams that reach sizes of 8 inches (20 cm) across. They are most often cut into strips for frying or are minced, chopped, processed and canned.

Pacific clams are generally too tough to eat raw. The most common is the **Manila clam**, which was introduced along the Pacific Coast during the 1930s. Resembling a quahog with a ridged shell, it can be served steamed or on the half shell. **Geoducks** are the largest Pacific clam, sometimes weighing up to 10 pounds (4.5 kg) each. They look like huge soft-shell clams with a large, protruding siphon. Their tender, rich bodies and briny flavour are popular in Asian cuisines.

A freshwater **Red River clam** is commercially available in Canada.

Littlenecks

Cherrystones

Topnecks

Soft-shell Clams

Manila Clams

Cockles

Greenshell Mussels

Gulf Oysters

European Flat Oysters

Hamma-hamma Oysters

Cockles are small bivalves, about 1 inch (2.5 cm) long, with ridged shells. They are more popular in Europe than in North America and are sometimes used in dishes such as paella and fish soups or stews.

Mussels (Fr. *moule*) are found in waters worldwide. They are excellent steamed in wine or seasoned broth and can be fried or used in soups or pasta dishes.

Blue mussels are the most common edible mussel. They are found in the wild along the Atlantic Coast and are aquafarmed on both coasts. Their meat is plump and sweet with a firm, muscular texture. The orangish-yellow meat of cultivated mussels tends to be much larger than that of wild mussels and therefore worth the added cost. Blue mussels are sold live in the shell and average from 10 to 20 per pound (500 g). Although available all year, the best-quality blue mussels are harvested during the winter months.

Greenshell (or greenlip) **mussels** from New Zealand and Thailand are much larger than blue mussels, averaging 8–12 mussels per pound (500 g). Their shells are paler grey, with a distinctive bright-green edge.

Blue Mussels

Oysters (Fr. *huître*) have a rough grey shell; their soft, grey, briny flesh can be eaten raw or cooked. Most oysters available in this country are commercially grown and sold either live in the shell or shucked. Oysters are excellent live, eaten directly from the shell. They can also be steamed or baked in the shell or shucked and fried, sautéed or added to stews or chowders. There are four main domestic species.

Atlantic oysters, also called American or Eastern oysters, have darker, flatter shells than other oysters. Malpeque oysters from Prince Edward Island are considered the finest.

Bluepoint Oysters

European flat oysters are often incorrectly called Belon (true Belon oysters live only in the Belon river of France); they are very round and flat and look like giant brownish-green Olympias.

Olympias are the only oysters native to the Pacific Coast; they are tiny (about the size of a 50-cent coin).

Pacific oysters, also called Japanese oysters, *Olympias* are aquafarmed along the Pacific Coast; they have curly, thick striated shells and silvery-grey to gold to almost-white meat.

Although it may seem like there are hundreds of oyster species on the market, there are only two that are commercially significant: the Atlantic oyster and the Pacific oyster. These two species yield dozens of different varieties, however, depending on their origin. For example, Atlantic oysters may be referred to as bluepoints, Malpeque, Chesapeake Bay, Florida Gulf, Long Island and so on, while Pacific oysters include Penn Cove Select, Westcott Bay, Hamma-hamma, Kumamoto and Portuguese, among others. An oyster's flavour reflects the minerals, nutrients and salts in its water and mud bed, so a Bristol from Maine and an Apalachicola from Florida will taste very different, even though they are the same Atlantic species. New Zealand's Bluff oyster is a particularly fine product.

Scallops contain an edible white adductor muscle that holds together the fan-shaped shells. Because they die quickly, they are almost always shucked and cleaned on-board ship. The sea scallop and the bay scallop, both cold-water varieties, and the calico scallop, a warm-water variety, are the most important commercially. Sea scallops are the largest, with an average count of 20–30 per pound (per 500 g). Larger sea scallops are also available. Bay scallops average 70–90 per pound (500 g); calico scallops average 70–110 per pound (500 g). Fresh or frozen shucked, cleaned scallops are the most common market form, but live scallops in the shell and shucked scallops with roe attached (very popular in Europe) are also available. Scallops are sweet, with a tender texture. Raw scallops should be a translucent ivory colour, nonsymmetrically round and should feel springy. They can be steamed, broiled, grilled, fried, sautéed or baked. When overcooked, however, scallops quickly become chewy and dry. Only absolutely fresh scallops should be eaten raw.

Sea Scallops

Cephalopods

Cephalopods are marine mollusks with distinct heads, well-developed eyes, a number of arms that attach to the head near the mouth and a saclike fin-bearing mantle. They do not have an outer shell; instead, there is a thin internal shell called a *pen* or *cuttlebone*.

Octopus is generally quite tough and requires mechanical tenderization or long, moist-heat cooking to make it palatable. Most octopuses are imported from Portugal, though fresh ones are available on the East Coast during the winter. Octopus is sold by the pound or kilogram, fresh or frozen, usually whole. Octopus skin is grey when raw, turning purple when cooked. The interior flesh is white, lean, firm and flavourful.

Squid, known by their Italian name, *calamari*, are becoming increasingly popular in this country. Similar to octopuses but much smaller, they are harvested along both North and South American coasts and elsewhere around the world (the finest are the East Coast loligo or winter squid). They range in size from an average of 8–10 per pound (500 g) to the giant South American squid that is sold as tenderized steaks. The squid's tentacles, mantle (body tube) and fins are edible. Squid meat is white to ivory in colour, turning darker with age. It is moderately lean, slightly sweet, firm and tender, but it toughens quickly if overcooked. Squid are available either fresh, or frozen and packed in blocks. The ink is used for making black noodles.

Squid

Crustaceans

Crustaceans are found in both fresh and salt water. They have a hard outer shell and jointed appendages, and they breathe through gills.

Crayfish (Fr. *écrevisse*), generally called *crayfish* in the North and *crawfish* or *crawdad* in the South, are freshwater creatures that look like miniature lobsters. They are harvested from the wild or aquafarmed in Louisiana and the Pacific Northwest. They are from 3-1/2 to 7 inches (8 to 17.5 cm) in length when marketed and may be purchased live or precooked and frozen. The lean meat, found mostly in the tail, is sweet and tender. Crayfish can be boiled whole and served hot or cold. The tail meat can be deep-fat fried or used in soups, bisques or sauces. Crayfish are a staple of Cajun cuisine, often used in gumbo, étouffée and jambalaya. Whole crayfish become brilliant red when cooked and may be used as a garnish. Caribbean crayfish tails are often erroneously sold on menus as lobster tails. They are also found in Europe and especially Australia. Sizes range from 3-1/2 ounces (100 g) to 10 pounds (4.5 kg) for the Tasmanian crayfish.

Crabs (Fr. *crabe*) are found along the North American coasts in great numbers and are shipped throughout the world in fresh, frozen and canned forms. Crab meat varies in flavour and texture and can be used in a range of prepared dishes, from chowders to curries to casseroles. Crabs purchased live should last up to five days; dead crabs should not be used.

King crabs are very large crabs (usually around 10 pounds or 4.5 kg) caught in the very cold waters of the North Pacific. Their meat is very sweet and snow-white. King crabs are always sold frozen, usually in the shell. In-shell forms include sections or clusters, legs and claws or split legs. The meat is also available in "fancy" packs of whole leg and body meat, or shredded and minced pieces.

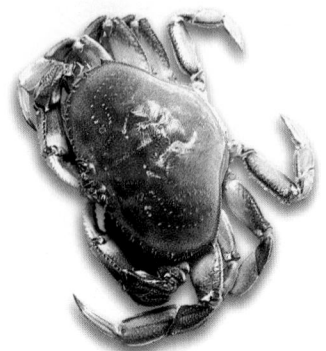

Dungeness Crab

Dungeness crabs are found along the West Coast. They weigh 1-1/2 to 4 pounds (675 g to 1.8 kg), and have delicate, sweet meat. They are sold live, precooked and frozen, or as picked meat, usually in 5-pound (2.2-kg) vacuum-packed cans.

Blue crabs are found along the entire eastern seaboard and account for approximately 50% of the total weight of all crab species harvested in the United States. Their meat is rich and sweet. Blue crabs are available as hard-shell or soft-shell. Hard-shell crabs are sold live, precooked and frozen, or as picked meat. Soft-shell crabs are those harvested within six hours after molting and are available live (generally only from May 15 to September 15) or frozen. They are often steamed and served whole. Soft-shells can be sautéed, fried, broiled or added to soups or stews. Blue crabs are sold by size, with an average diameter of 4–7 inches (10–18 cm).

Blue Crab

Soft-shell Crabs

Snow or **spider crabs** are an abundant species, most often used as a substitute for the scarcer and more expensive king crab. They are harvested from Alaskan and British Columbian waters and along the eastern coast of Canada. Snow crab is sold precooked, usually frozen. The meat can be used in soups, salads, omelettes or other prepared dishes. Legs are often served cold as an appetizer.

Stone crabs are generally available only as cooked claws, either fresh or frozen (the claws cannot be frozen raw because the meat sticks to the shell). In stone-crab fishery only the claw is harvested. After the claw is removed, the crab is returned to the water, where in about 18 months it regenerates a new claw. Claws average 2-1/2 to 5-1/2 ounces (75 to 165 g) each. The meat is firm, with a sweet taste similar to lobster. Cracked claws are served hot or cold, usually with cocktail sauce, lemon butter or other accompaniments.

Lobsters have brown to blue-black outer shells and firm, white meat with a rich, sweet flavour. Lobster shells turn red when cooked. They are usually poached, steamed, simmered, baked or grilled, and can be served hot or cold. Picked meat can be used in prepared dishes, soups or sautés. Lobsters must be kept alive until just before cooking. Dead lobsters should not be eaten. The Atlantic, also known as clawed lobster, and the spiny lobster are the most commonly marketed species.

Atlantic Lobster

Atlantic lobsters have edible meat in both their tails and claws; they are considered superior in flavour to all other lobsters. They come from the cold waters along the Northeast Coast and are most often sold live. Atlantic lobsters may be purchased by weight (i.e., 1-1/4 pound [525 g], 1-1/2 pound [650 g] or 2 pounds [900 g] each), or as chix (i.e., less than 1 pound [450 g]). Lobsters may also be purchased as culls (lobsters with only one claw) or bullets (lobsters with no claws). They are available frozen or as cooked, picked meat.

Figure 19.3 shows a cross section of an Atlantic lobster and identifies the stomach, tomalley (the olive-green liver) and coral (the roe). The stomach is not eaten; the tomalley and coral are very flavourful and are often used in the preparation of sauces and other items.

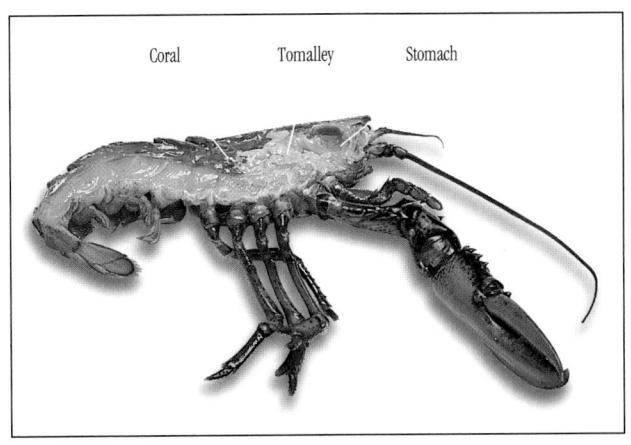

FIGURE 19.3

Spiny lobsters have very small claws and are valuable only for their meaty tails, which are notched with short spines. Nearly all spiny lobsters marketed in this country are sold as frozen tails, often identified as rock lobster. Harvested in many parts of the world, those found off Florida, Brazil and in the Caribbean are marketed as warm-water tails; those found off South Africa, Australia and New Zealand are called cold-water tails. Cold-water spiny tails are considered superior to their warm-water cousins.

Slipper lobster, lobsterette and **squat lobster** are all clawless species found in tropical, subtropical and temperate waters worldwide. Although popular in some countries, their flavour is inferior to both Atlantic and spiny lobsters. **Langoustine** are small North Atlantic lobsters.

Shrimp (Fr. *crevette*) are found worldwide and are widely popular. Gulf whites, pinks, browns and black tigers are just a few of the dozens of shrimp varieties used in food service operations. Although fresh, head-on shrimp are available, the most common form is raw, head-off (also called green headless) shrimp with the shell on. Most shrimp are deheaded and frozen at sea to preserve freshness. Shrimp are available in many forms: raw, peeled and deveined; cooked, peeled and deveined; individually quick frozen; as well as in a variety of processed, breaded or canned products. Shrimp are graded by size, which can range from 400 per pound (450 g) (titi) to 8 per pound (450 g) (extra-colossal), and are sold in counts per pound. For example, shrimp marketed as "21–26 count" means that there is an average of 21 to 26 shrimp per pound; shrimp marketed as "U-10" means that there are under 10 shrimp per pound.

Shrimp

Green Headless Shrimp

Prawn is often used interchangeably with the word *shrimp* in English-speaking countries. Although it is perhaps more accurate to refer to freshwater species as prawns and marine species as shrimp, in commercial practice prawn refers to any large shrimp. Equally confusing, *scampi* is the Italian name for the Dublin Bay prawn (which is actually a species of miniature lobster), but in this country *scampi* often refers to shrimp sautéed in garlic butter.

NUTRITION

Fish and shellfish are low in calories, fat and sodium, and are high in vitamins A, B and D and protein. (See Table 19.2.) Fish and shellfish are also high in

TABLE 19.2   NUTRITIONAL VALUES OF FISH AND SHELLFISH

Per 1 oz. (28 g) Raw	Kcal	Protein (g)	Total Fat (g)	Saturated Fat (g)	Cholesterol (mg)	Sodium (mg)
Abalone	30	4.8	0.2	<0.1	24	85
Clam, mixed species	21	3.6	0.3	<0.1	10	16
Cod, Atlantic	23	5.0	0.2	<0.1	12	15
Crab, Alaska king	24	5.2	0.2	mq*	12	237
Flatfish	26	5.3	0.3	0.1	14	23
Lobster	26	5.3	0.3	mq	27	mq
Oyster, eastern	20	2.0	0.7	0.2	16	32
Salmon	40	5.6	1.8	0.3	16	113
Sea bass	27	5.2	0.6	0.1	12	19
Shrimp, mixed species	30	5.7	0.5	0.1	43	42
Surimi	28	4.3	0.3	mq	9	41
Tuna, yellowfin	31	6.6	0.3	0.1	13	10
Whitefish	38	5.4	1.7	0.3	17	14

The Corinne T. Netzer Encyclopedia of Food Values 1992
*mq = measurable quantity, but data are unavailable

minerals, especially calcium (particularly in canned fish with edible bones), phosphorus, potassium and iron (especially mollusks). Fish are high in a group of polyunsaturated fatty acids called omega-3, which may help combat high blood cholesterol levels and aid in preventing some heart disease. Shellfish are not as high in cholesterol as was once thought. Crustaceans are higher in cholesterol than mollusks, but both have considerably lower levels than red meat or eggs.

The cooking methods used for fish and shellfish also contribute to their healthfulness. The most commonly used cooking methods—broiling, grilling, poaching and steaming—add little or no fat.

INSPECTION AND GRADING OF FISH AND SHELLFISH

Inspection

It is advisable to purchase fish and shellfish from approved sources only. The approval-granting agency is the Federal Fisheries Inspection, which is being absorbed into the Canadian Food Inspection Agency. For an operation to be an approved facility under federal regulations, it must demonstrate a Quality Management Program, which consists of a prerequisite program for the physical plant and an adherence to Hazardous Analysis Critical Control Point (HACCP) principles. In addition, there are guidelines for product quality, record keeping and a recall process.

FIGURE 19.4   *CFIA Mark and Statements*

Grading

No grading protocol for fish exists in Canada, so a buyer must rely on the integrity of the supplier. Ask the supplier if they are inspected and if they are an approved facility. The assurance of quality for yourself and the customer is well worth the extra you may pay for a superior, safe and wholesome product.

PURCHASING AND STORING FISH AND SHELLFISH

Determining Freshness

Because fish and shellfish are highly perishable, an inspection stamp does not necessarily ensure top quality. A few hours at the wrong temperature or a couple of days in the refrigerator can turn high-quality fish or shellfish into garbage. It is important that you be able to determine for yourself the freshness and quality of the fish and shellfish you purchase or use. Freshness should be checked before purchasing and again just before cooking.

Freshness can be determined by:

1. *Smell*—Smell is by far the easiest way to determine freshness. Fresh fish should have a slight sea smell or no odour at all. Any off-odours or ammonia odours are a sure sign of aged or improperly handled fish.

2. *Eyes*—The eyes should be clear and full. Sunken eyes mean that the fish is drying out and is probably not fresh.

3. *Gills*—The gills should be intact and bright red. Brown gills are a sign of age.

4. *Texture*—Generally, the flesh of fresh fish should be firm. Mushy flesh or flesh that does not spring back when pressed with a finger is a sign of poor quality or age.

5. *Fins and scales*—Fins and scales should be moist and full without excessive drying on the outer edges. Dry fins or scales are a sign of age; damaged fins or scales may be a sign of mishandling.

6. *Appearance*—Fish cuts should be moist and glistening, without bruises or dark spots. Edges should not be brown or dry.

7. *Movement*—Shellfish should be purchased alive and should show movement. Lobsters and other crustaceans should be active. Clams, mussels and oysters that are partially opened should snap shut when tapped with a finger. (Exceptions are geoduck, razor and steamer clams whose siphons protrude, preventing the shell from closing completely.) Ones that do not close are dead and should not be used. Avoid mollusks with broken shells or heavy shells that might be filled with mud or sand.

Purchasing Fish and Shellfish

Fish are available from wholesalers in a variety of market forms:

+ **Whole** or **round**—as caught, intact.
+ **Drawn**—viscera (internal organs) is removed; most whole fish are purchased this way.
+ **Dressed**—viscera, gills, fins and scales are removed.
+ **Pan-dressed**—viscera and gills are removed; fish is scaled and fins and tail are trimmed. The head is usually removed, although small fish, such as trout, may be pan-dressed with the head still attached. Pan-dressed fish are then pan-fried.
+ **Butterflied**—a pan-dressed fish, boned and opened flat like a book. The two sides remain attached by the back or belly skin.

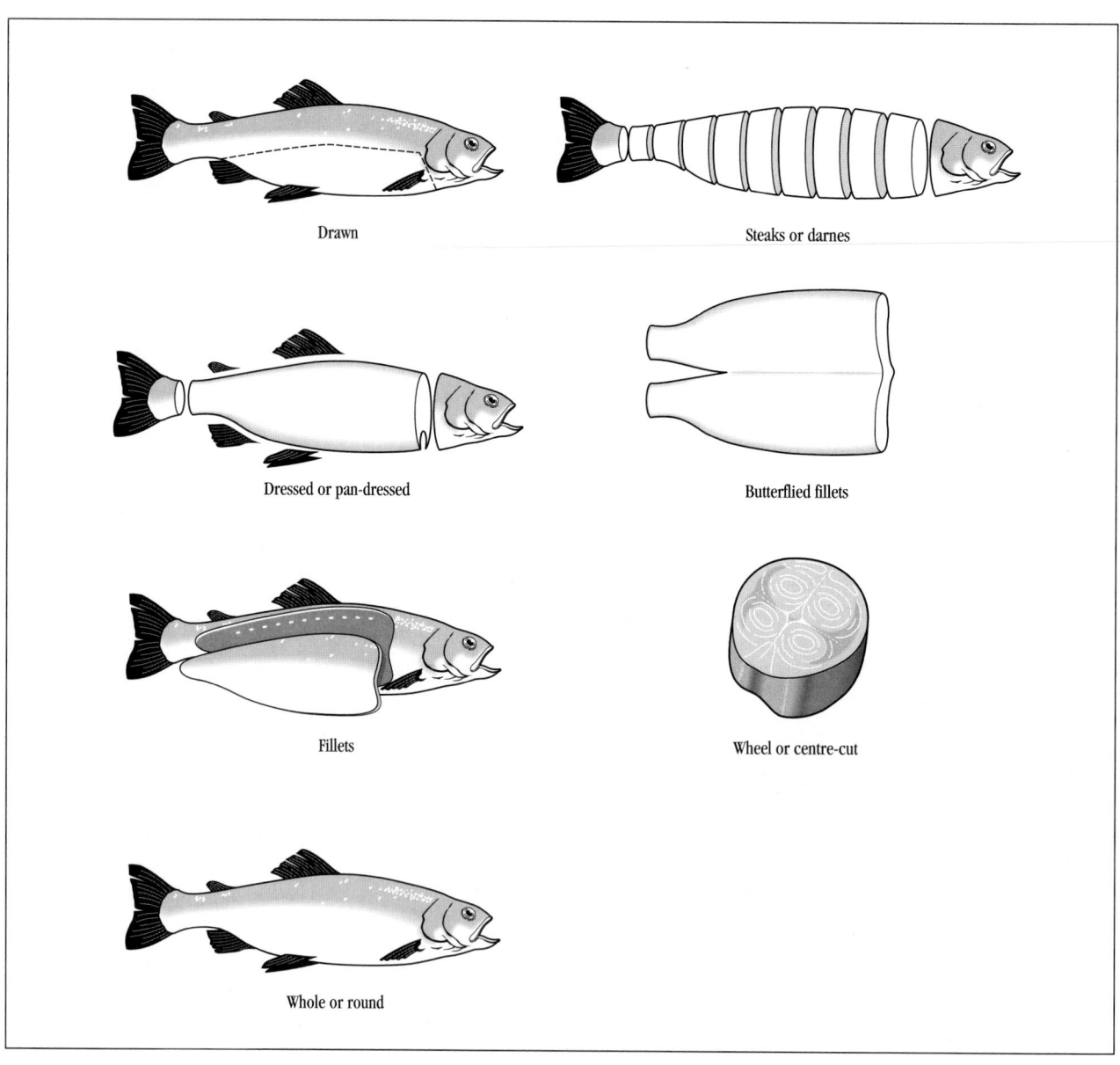

Drawn

Steaks or darnes

Dressed or pan-dressed

Butterflied fillets

Fillets

Wheel or centre-cut

Whole or round

FIGURE 19.5 *Market Forms*

- ✦ **Fillet**—the side of a fish removed intact, boneless or semi-boneless, with or without skin.
- ✦ **Steak or darne**—cross-section slice, with a small section of backbone attached; usually prepared from large round fish.
- ✦ **Wheel** or **centre-cut**—used for swordfish and sharks, which are cut into large boneless pieces from which steaks are then cut.

You should purchase fish in the market forms most practical for your operation. Although fish fabrication is a relatively simple chore requiring little specialized equipment, before you decide to cut your own fish you should consider

1. the food service operation's ability to utilize the bones and trim that cutting whole fish produces,
2. the employees' ability to fabricate fillets, steaks or portions as needed,
3. the storage facilities, and
4. the product's intended use.

Most shellfish can be purchased live in the shell, shucked (the meat removed from the shell) or processed. Both live and shucked shellfish are usually purchased by counts (i.e., the number per volume). For example, standard live Eastern oysters are packed 200–250 (the count) per bushel (the unit of volume: approximately 35 L); standard Eastern oyster meats are packed 350 per gallon. Crustaceans are sometimes packed by size based on the number of pieces per pound; for example, crab legs or shrimp are often sold in counts per pound. Or they are sold either by grades based on size (whole crabs) or by weight (lobsters).

Storing Fish and Shellfish

The most important concern when storing fish and shellfish is temperature. All fresh fish should be stored at temperatures between 30° and 34°F (-1 to 1°C). Fish stored in a refrigerator at 40°F (4°C) will have approximately half the shelf life of fish stored at 32°F (0°C).

Most fish are shipped on ice and should be stored on ice in the refrigerator immediately upon receipt. Whole fish should be layered directly in crushed or shaved ice in a perforated pan so that the melted ice water drains away. If crushed or shaved ice is not available, cubed ice may be used provided it is put in plastic bags and gently placed on top of the fish to prevent bruising and denting. Fabricated and portioned fish may be wrapped in moisture-proof packaging before icing to prevent the ice and water from damaging the exposed flesh. Fish stored on ice should be drained and re-iced daily.

Fresh scallops, fish fillets that are purchased in plastic trays, and oyster and clam meats should be set on or packed in ice. Do not let the scallops, fillets or meats come in direct contact with the ice.

Clams, mussels and oysters should be stored at 40°F (4°C), at high humidity and left in the boxes or net bags in which they were shipped. Under ideal conditions, shellfish can be kept alive for up to one week. Never store live shellfish in plastic bags and do not ice them.

If a saltwater tank is not available, live lobsters, crabs and other crustaceans should be kept in boxes with seaweed or damp newspaper to keep them moist. Most crustaceans circulate salt water over their gills; icing them or placing them in fresh water will kill them. Lobsters and crabs will live for several days under ideal conditions.

Like most frozen foods, frozen fish should be kept at temperatures of 0°F (-18°C) or colder. Colder temperatures greatly increase shelf life. Frozen fish should be thawed in the refrigerator; once thawed, they should be treated like fresh fish.

FABRICATING PROCEDURES

As discussed, fish and shellfish can be purchased in many forms. Here we demonstrate several procedures for cutting, cleaning and otherwise fabricating or preparing fish and shellfish for cooking and service.

BASIC PROCEDURE FOR SCALING FISH

This procedure is used to remove the scales from fish that will be cooked with the skin on.

Place the fish on a work surface or in a large sink. Grip the fish by the tail and, working from the tail towards the head, scrape the scales off with a fish scaler or the back of a knife. Be careful not to damage the flesh by pushing too hard. Turn the fish over and remove the scales from the other side. Rinse the fish under cold water.

BASIC PROCEDURE FOR PAN-DRESSING FLATFISH

1. Scale the flatfish. Place the fish on a cutting board and remove the head by making a V-shaped cut around it with a chef's knife. Pull the head away and remove the viscera.

2. Rinse the fish under cold water, removing all traces of blood and viscera from the cavity.

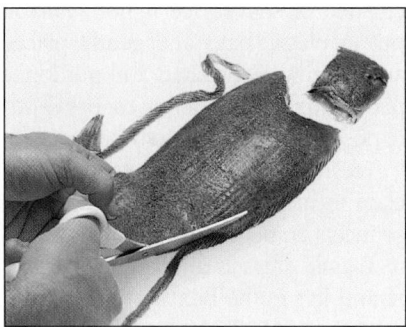

3. Using a pair of kitchen shears, trim off the tail and all of the fins.

BASIC PROCEDURE FOR FILLETING ROUND FISH

Round fish produce two fillets, one from either side.

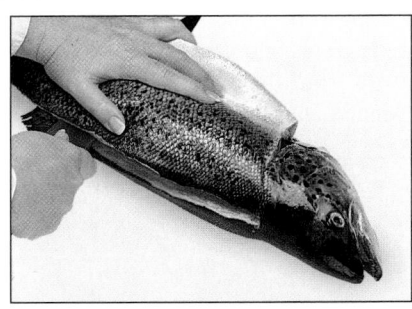

1. Using a chef's knife, cut down to the backbone just behind the gills. Do not remove the head.

2. Turn the knife towards the tail; using smooth strokes, cut from head to tail parallel to the backbone. The knife should bump against the backbone so that no flesh is wasted; you will feel the knife cutting through the small pin bones. Cut the fillet completely free from the bones. Repeat on the other side.

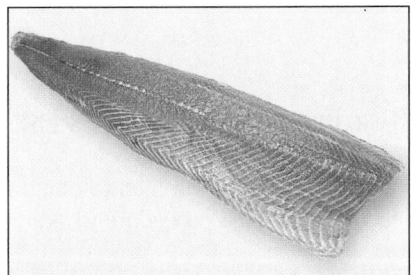

3. Trim the rib bones from the fillet with a flexible boning knife.

4. The finished fillet.

BASIC PROCEDURE FOR FILLETING FLATFISH

Flatfish produce four fillets: two large bilateral fillets from the top and two smaller bilateral fillets from the bottom. If the fish fillets are going to be cooked with the skin on, the fish should be scaled before cooking (it is easier to scale the fish before it is filleted). If the skin is going to be removed before cooking, it is not necessary to scale the fish.

1. With the dark side of the fish facing up, cut along the backbone from head to tail with the tip of a flexible boning knife.

2. Turn the knife and, using smooth strokes, cut between the flesh and the rib bones, keeping the flexible blade against the bone. Cut the fillet completely free from the fish. Remove the second fillet, following the same procedure.

3. Turn the fish over and remove the fillets from the bottom half of the fish, following the same procedure.

BASIC PROCEDURE FOR SKINNING DOVER SOLE

Dover sole is unique in that its skin can be pulled from the whole fish by following this procedure. The flesh of other small flatfish such as flounder, petrale sole and other types of domestic sole is more delicate; pulling the skin away from the whole fish could damage the flesh. These fish should be skinned after they are filleted.

Gougeons—*Thin strips or fingers cut from a fillet, often a fillet of sole. In the retail trade, they are known as fish sticks or fingers.*

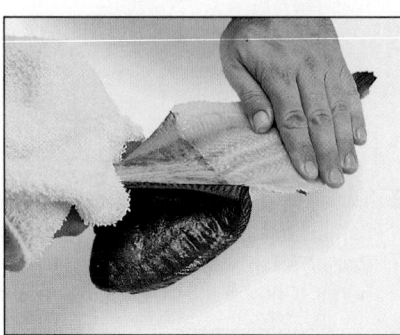

Make a shallow cut in the flesh perpendicular to the length of the fish, just in front of the tail and with the knife angled towards the head of the fish. Using a clean towel, grip the skin and pull it towards the head of the fish. The skin should come off cleanly, in one piece, leaving the flesh intact.

BASIC PROCEDURE FOR SKINNING FISH FILLETS

Here we use a salmon fillet to demonstrate the procedure for skinning fish fillets. Use the same procedure to skin all types of fish fillets.

Place the fillet on a cutting board with the skin side down. Starting at the tail, use a meat slicer or a chef's knife to cut between the flesh and skin. Angle the knife down towards the skin, grip the skin tightly with one hand and use a sawing motion to cut the skin cleanly away from the flesh.

BASIC PROCEDURE FOR PULLING PIN BONES FROM A SALMON FILLET

Round fish fillets contain a row of intramuscular bones running the length of the fillet. Known as pin bones, they are usually cut out with a knife to produce boneless fillets. In the case of salmon, they can be removed with salmon tweezers or small needle-nose pliers.

Place the fillet (either skinless or not) on the cutting board, skin side down. Starting at the front or head end of the fillet, use your fingertips to locate the bones and pull them out one by one with the pliers.

BASIC PROCEDURE FOR CUTTING AN ESCALOPE (FILLET)

A **fillet** is a boneless cut from a large flat or round fish. Usually cut on an angle, escalopes (or fillets) look large and increase plate coverage.

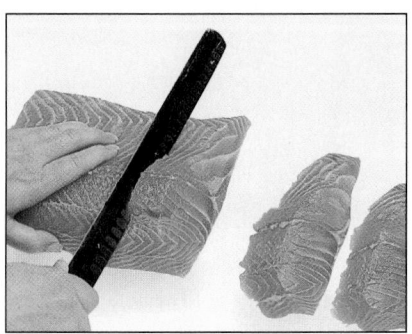

Place the fillet on the cutting board, skin side down. Using a slicer or chef's knife, cut slices of the desired weight. The escalope can be cut to the desired size by adjusting the angle of the knife. The greater the angle, the greater the surface area of the escalope.

BASIC PROCEDURE FOR CUTTING STEAKS FROM SALMON AND SIMILARLY SIZED ROUND FISH

Steaks, or darnes, are produced from salmon and similarly sized round fish by simply making crosscuts of the whole fish. First scale, gut and remove the fins from the fish. Then:

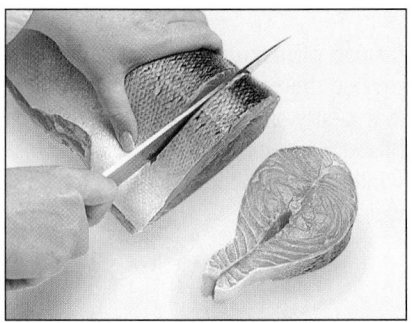

Using a chef's knife, cut through the fish, slicing steaks of the desired thickness. The steaks will contain some bones that are not necessarily removed.

BASIC PROCEDURE FOR PEELING AND DEVEINING SHRIMP

Peeling and deveining shrimp is a simple procedure done in most commercial kitchens. The tail portion of the shell is often left on the peeled shrimp to give it an attractive appearance or make it easier to eat. This procedure can be used on both cooked and uncooked shrimp.

1. Grip the shrimp's tail between your thumb and forefinger. Use your other thumb and forefinger to grip the legs and the edge of the shell.

2. Pull the legs and shell away from the flesh, leaving the tail and first joint of the shell in place if desired.

3. Place the shrimp on a cutting board and use a paring knife to make a shallow cut down the back of the shrimp, exposing the digestive tract or "vein."

4. Pull out the vein while rinsing the shrimp under cold water.

BASIC PROCEDURE FOR BUTTERFLYING SHRIMP

Butterflying raw shrimp improves their appearance and increases their surface area for even cooking. To butterfly shrimp, first peel them using the procedure outlined above, then:

Instead of making a shallow cut to expose the vein, make a deeper cut that nearly slices the shrimp into two bilateral halves. Pull out the vein while rinsing the shrimp under cold water.

BASIC PROCEDURE FOR PREPARING LIVE LOBSTER FOR BROILING

A whole lobster can be cooked by plunging it into boiling water or court bouillon. If the lobster is to be broiled, it must be split lengthwise before cooking.

1. Place the live lobster on its back on a cutting board and pierce its head with the point of a chef's knife. Then, in one smooth stroke, bring the knife down and cut through the body and tail without splitting it completely in half.

2. Use your hands to crack the lobster's back so that it lies flat. Crack the claws with the back of a chef's knife.

3. Cut through the tail and curl each half of the tail to the side. Remove and discard the stomach and brain. The tomalley (the olive-green liver) and, if present, the coral (the roe) may be removed and saved for a sauce or other preparation.

BASIC PROCEDURE FOR PREPARING LIVE LOBSTER FOR SAUTÉING

A whole lobster may also be cut into smaller pieces for sautéing or other preparations.

1. Use the point of a chef's knife to pierce the lobster's head.

2. Cut off the claws and arms.

3. Cut the tail into cross sections.

4. Split the head and thorax in half. The tomalley and coral (if present) may be removed and saved for further use. The head and legs may be added to the recipe for flavour, but there is very little meat in them and they are often discarded.

5. Crack the claws with a firm blow, using the back of a chef's knife.

BASIC PROCEDURE FOR REMOVING COOKED LOBSTER MEAT FROM THE SHELL

Many recipes call for cooked lobster meat. Cook the lobster by plunging it into a boiling court bouillon and simmering for 6–8 minutes per 500 grams. Remove the lobster and allow it to cool until it can be easily handled. Then:

1. Pull the claws and large legs away from the body. Break the claw away from the leg. Split the legs with a chef's knife and remove the meat, using your fingers or a pick.

2. Carefully crack the claw with a mallet or the back of a chef's knife without damaging the meat. Pull out the claw meat in one piece.

3. Pull the lobster's tail away from its body and use kitchen shears to trim away the soft membrane on the underside of the tail.

4. Pull the meat out of the shell in one piece.

BASIC PROCEDURE FOR OPENING CLAMS

Opening raw clams efficiently requires practice. Like all mollusks, clams should be cleaned under cold running water with a brush to remove all mud, silt and sand that may be stuck to their shells. A knife may be more easily inserted into a clam if the clam is washed and allowed to relax in the refrigerator for at least one hour before it is opened.

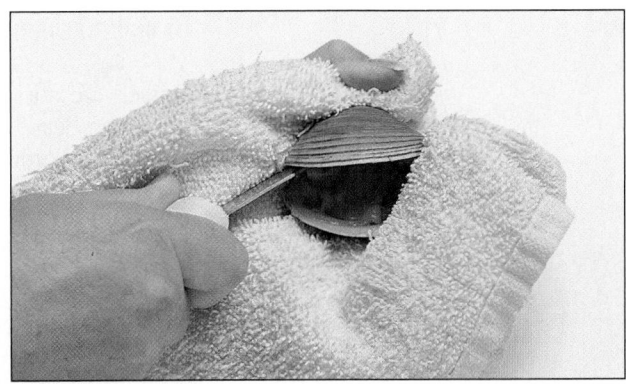

1. Hold the clam firmly in a folded towel in the palm of your hand; the notch in the edge of the shell should be towards your thumb. With the fingers of the same hand, squeeze and pull the blade of the clam knife between the clamshells. Do not push on the knife handle with your other hand; you will not be able to control the knife if it slips and you can cut yourself.

2. Pull the knife between the shells until it cuts the muscle. Twist the knife to pry the shells apart. Slide the knife tip along the top shell and cut through the muscle. Twist the top shell, breaking it free at the hinge; discard it.

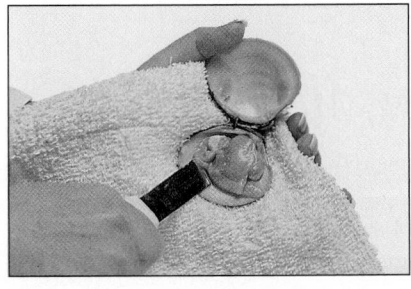

3. Use the knife tip to release the clam from the bottom shell.

BASIC PROCEDURE FOR OPENING OYSTERS

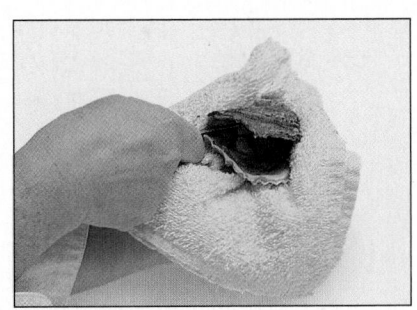

1. Clean the oyster by brushing it under running water.

2. Hold the cleaned oyster firmly in a folded towel in the palm of your hand. Insert the tip of an oyster knife in the hinge and use a twisting motion to pop the hinge apart. Do not use too much forward pressure on the knife; it can slip and you could stab yourself.

3. Slide the knife along the top of the shell to release the oyster from the shell (sever adductor muscle). Discard the top shell.

4. Use the knife tip to release the oyster from the bottom shell.

BASIC PROCEDURE FOR CLEANING AND DEBEARDING MUSSELS

Mussels are not normally eaten raw. Before cooking, a clump of dark threads called the beard must be removed. Because this could kill the mussel, cleaning and debearding must be done as close to cooking time as possible.

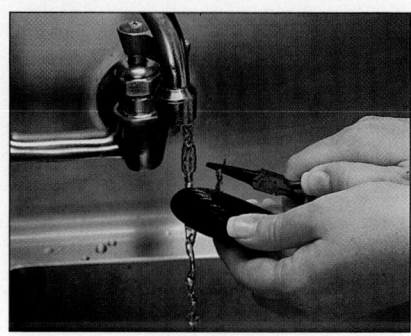

1. Clean the mussel with a brush under cold running water to remove sand and grit.

2. Pull the beard away from the mussel with your fingers or a small pair of pliers.

APPLYING VARIOUS COOKING METHODS

Fish and shellfish can be prepared by the dry-heat cooking methods of broiling and grilling, roasting (baking), sautéing, pan-frying and deep-fat frying, as well as the moist-heat cooking methods of steaming, poaching and simmering. Other than deep-fat frying, which is discussed in Chapter 21, these cooking methods are discussed below.

Determining Doneness

Unlike most meats and poultry, nearly all fish and shellfish are inherently tender and should be cooked just until done. Indeed, overcooking is the most common mistake made when preparing fish and shellfish. The Canadian Department of Fisheries recommends that all fish be cooked 10 minutes for every inch (2.5 cm) of thickness, regardless of cooking method. Although this may be a good general policy, variables such as the type and the form of fish and the exact cooking method used suggest that one or more of the following methods of determining doneness are more appropriate for professional food service operations.

1. *Translucent flesh becomes opaque*—The raw flesh of most fish and shellfish appears somewhat translucent. As the proteins coagulate during cooking, the flesh becomes opaque.
2. *Flesh becomes firm*—The flesh of most fish and shellfish firms as it cooks. Doneness can be tested by judging the resistance of the flesh when pressed with tongs. Raw or undercooked fish or shellfish will be mushy and soft. As the fish cooks, the flesh offers more resistance and springs back quickly.
3. *Flesh separates from the bones easily*—The flesh of raw fish remains firmly attached to the bones. As the fish cooks, the flesh and bones separate easily.
4. *Flesh begins to flake*—Fish flesh consists of short muscle fibres separated by

thin connective tissue. As the fish cooks, the connective tissue breaks down and the groups of muscle fibres begin to flake; that is, separate from one another. Fish is done when the flesh *begins* to flake. If the flesh flakes easily the fish will be overdone and dry.

Remember, fish and shellfish are subject to carryover cooking. Because they cook quickly and at low temperatures, it is better to undercook the item and allow carryover cooking or residual heat to finish the cooking process.

Dry-Heat Cooking Methods

Dry-heat cooking methods are those that do not require additional moisture at any time during the cooking process. The dry-heat cooking methods used with fish and shellfish are broiling and grilling, roasting (usually referred to as baking when used with fish and shellfish), sautéing, pan-frying and deep-fat frying.

Broiling and Grilling

After brushing with oil or butter, fish can be grilled directly on the grate or placed on a heated platter under the broiler. Broiled or grilled fish should have a lightly charred surface and a slightly smoky flavour as a result of the intense radiant heat of the broiler or grill. The interior should be moist and juicy. Broiled or grilled shellfish meat should be moist and tender with only slight colouration from the grill or broiler.

Selecting Fish and Shellfish to Broil or Grill

Nearly all types of fish and shellfish can be successfully broiled or grilled. Salmon, trout, swordfish and other oily fish are especially well suited to grilling, as are lean fish such as bass and snapper. Fillets of lean flatfish with delicate textures, such as flounder and sole, are better broiled. They should be placed on a preheated broiling (sizzler) platter before being placed under the broiler.

Oysters and clams are often broiled on the half shell with flavoured butters, bread crumbs or other garnishes and served sizzling hot. Squid can be stuffed, secured with a toothpick and broiled or grilled. Brushed with butter, split lobsters, king crabs and snow crabs are often broiled or grilled. Whole lobsters can be split and broiled or grilled, or their tails can be removed, split and cooked separately. Large crab legs can also be split and broiled or grilled. Shrimp and scallops are often broiled in flavoured butters or grilled on skewers for easy handling.

Seasoning Fish and Shellfish to Be Broiled or Grilled

All fish should be brushed lightly with butter or oil before being placed on the grill or under the broiler. The butter or oil prevents sticking and helps leaner fish retain moisture. For most fish, a simple seasoning of salt and pepper suffices. But most fish do respond well to marinades, especially those made with white wine and lemon juice. Because most fish are delicately flavoured, they should be marinated for only a brief period of time. (Even marinated fish should be brushed with butter or oil before cooking.) Herbs should be avoided because they will burn from the intense heat of the broiler or grill.

Clams, oysters and other shellfish that are stuffed or cooked with butters, vegetables, bacon or other accompaniments or garnishes gain flavour from these ingredients. Be careful, however, not to overpower the delicate flavours of the shellfish with the addition of too many strong flavourings.

Accompaniments to Broiled and Grilled Fish and Shellfish

Broiled fish and shellfish are served with sauces made separately. Butter sauces such as a beurre blanc are popular, as the richness of the sauce complements the lean fish. Vegetable coulis are a good choice for a healthier, lower-fat accompaniment. Additional sauce suggestions are found in Table 10.5. If the item is cooked on a broiler platter with a seasoned butter, it is often served with that butter. Lemon wedges are the traditional accompaniment to any broiled or grilled fish.

Almost any side dish goes well with broiled or grilled fish or shellfish. Fried or boiled potatoes, pasta and rice are all good choices. Grilled vegetables are a natural choice.

BASIC PROCEDURE FOR BROILING OR GRILLING FISH AND SHELLFISH

All fish is delicate and must be carefully handled to achieve an attractive finished product. When broiling whole fish or fillets with their skin still on, score the skin by making several diagonal slashes approximately 1/4 inch (5 mm) deep at even intervals. This prevents the fish from curling during cooking, promotes even cooking and creates a more attractive finished product. Be especially careful not to overcook the item. It should be served as hot as possible as soon as it is removed from the broiler or grill.

1. Heat the broiler or grill.
2. Use a wire brush to remove any charred or burnt particles that may be stuck to the broiler or grill grate. The grate can be wiped with a lightly oiled towel to remove any remaining particles and help season it.
3. Prepare the item to be broiled or grilled. For example, cut the fish into steaks or filets of even thickness; split the lobster; peel and/or skewer the shrimp. Season or marinate the item as desired. Brush the item with oil or butter.
4. Place the item (presentation side down) on a grill. If using a broiler, place the item directly on the grate or on a preheated broiler platter. Tender fish are usually broiled presentation side up on a broiler platter.
5. If practical, turn the item to produce the attractive crosshatch marks associated with grilling that are discussed in Chapter 9, Principles of Cooking. Items less than 1/2 inch (10 mm) thick cooked on a preheated broiler platter do not have to be turned over.
6. Cook the item to the desired doneness and serve immediately.

RECIPE 19.1

BROILED BLACK SEA BASS WITH HERB BUTTER AND SAUTÉED LEEKS

Yield: 1 Serving

Black sea bass fillet, skin on, approx. 7 oz. (200 g)	1	1
Salt and pepper	TT	TT
Whole butter, melted	as needed	as needed
Leek, julienne	1	1
Lemon juice	2 tsp.	10 mL
Herb butter (p. 219)	1 oz.	30 g

1. Score the skin of the bass with three diagonal cuts approximately 1/4 inch (5 mm) deep.
2. Season the bass fillet with salt and pepper and brush with melted butter.
3. Place the fillet on a preheated broiler platter, skin side up, and place under the broiler.
4. Blanch the julienned leeks in boiling water until nearly tender.
5. Drain the leeks and sauté them in 1 tablespoon (15 mL) of whole butter until tender. Add the lemon juice; season with salt and pepper.
6. Remove the fish from the broiler when done. Top with the herb butter and serve on a bed of sautéed leeks.

Approximate values per serving:

Calories	260
Total fat	15 g
Saturated fat	8 g
Cholesterol	80 mg
Sodium	790 mg
Total carbohydrates	11 g
Protein	21 g
Vitamin A	15%
Vitamin C	15%

1. Score the skin of the fish.

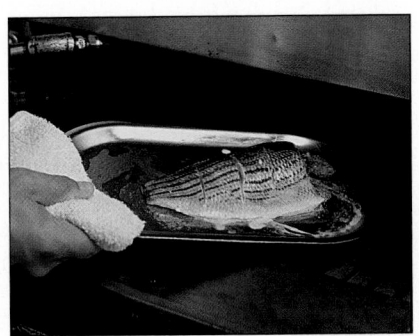

2. Place the fish on a broiler platter, under the broiler.

3. Serve the fish on a bed of sautéed leeks.

Baking

The terms *baking* and *roasting* are used interchangeably when applied to fish and shellfish. One disadvantage of baking fish is that the short baking time does not allow the surface of the fish to caramelize. To help correct this problem, fish can be browned in a sauté pan with a small amount of oil to achieve the added flavour and appearance of a browned surface, and then finished in an oven.

Selecting Fish and Shellfish to Bake

Fatty fish produce the best baked fish. Fish fillets and steaks are the best market forms to bake, as they cook quickly and evenly and are easily portioned. Although lean fish can be baked, it tends to become dry, and must be basted often.

Seasoning Fish and Shellfish to Be Baked

The most popular seasonings for baked fish are lemon, butter, salt and pepper. Fish can also be marinated before baking for added flavour. But baked fish usually depend on the accompanying sauce for much of their flavour.

Shellfish are often stuffed or mixed with other ingredients before baking. For example, raw oysters on the half shell can be topped with spinach, watercress and Pernod (oysters Rockefeller) and baked. Shrimp are often butterflied, stuffed and baked; lobsters are split, stuffed and baked. Many food service operations remove clams from their shells; mix them with bread crumbs, seasonings or other ingredients; refill the shells and bake the mixture.

Accompaniments to Baked Fish and Shellfish

Baked fish is often served with a flavourful sauce such as a Creole sauce (p. 212) or a beurre blanc (p. 217). Additional sauce suggestions are found in

Table 10.5. Almost any type of rice, pasta or potato is a good accompaniment, as is any variety of sautéed vegetable.

BASIC PROCEDURE FOR BAKING FISH AND SHELLFISH

1. Portion the fish and arrange on a well-oiled or buttered pan, presentation side up.

2. Season as desired and brush the surface of the fish or shellfish generously with melted butter; add garnishes or flavourings as desired or directed in the recipe.

3. Place the pan in a preheated oven at approximately 400°F (200°C).

4. Baste periodically during the cooking process (more often if the fish is lean). Remove from the oven when the fish is slightly underdone.

◆◆◆

RECIPE 19.2

BAKED RED SNAPPER WITH STAR FRUIT CHUTNEY

Yield: 4 Servings

Red snapper fillets, 6 oz. (170 g) each	4	4
Salt and white pepper	TT	TT
Whole butter, melted	2 oz.	60 g
Mint leaves, chopped	1 Tbsp.	15 mL
Garlic, minced	1 tsp.	5 mL
Tomato concassé	4 oz.	120 g
White wine	2 oz.	60 mL
Lemon juice	2 oz.	60 mL
Star Fruit Chutney (recipe follows)	12 oz.	350 g

Approximate values per serving:

Calories	600
Total fat	16 g
Saturated fat	8g
Cholesterol	140 mg
Sodium	850 mg
Total carbohydrates	55 g
Protein	60 g
Vitamin A	25%
Vitamin C	35%

1. Place the snapper on a buttered baking pan. Season the fillets with salt and white pepper; brush with butter.

2. Combine the mint, garlic and tomatoes and spoon on top of each portion of the fish.

3. Add the white wine and lemon juice to the pan.

4. Bake at 400°F (200°C), basting once halfway through the cooking process, until done, approximately 15 minutes.

5. Serve each portion on a bed of 3 ounces (90 grams) of Star Fruit Chutney.

1. Brush the fillets with butter.

2. Top each portion with mint and tomato concassé.

3. The finished fish.

STAR FRUIT CHUTNEY

Yield: 2 lb. (900 g)

Limes	3	3
Fresh ginger, julienne	4 oz.	120 g
Sugar	3 oz.	90 g
Apples, peeled, medium dice	2	2
Golden raisins	2 oz.	60 g
Dark raisins	2 oz.	60 g
Star fruit, medium dice	1-1/2 lb.	700 g
Cider vinegar	1 Tbsp.	15 mL
Salt and pepper	TT	TT
Cayenne pepper	TT	TT

1. Zest 2 limes.
2. Squeeze the limes to make 4 ounces (120 mL) of juice.
3. Combine the lime juice, zest, ginger and sugar. Bring to a boil and simmer until the sugar is caramelized.
4. Add the apples and raisins; simmer until the apples are soft but not mushy.
5. Add the star fruit and bring back to a boil. Remove from heat. Add the vinegar. Season to taste with salt, pepper and cayenne pepper.

Approximate values per 1 oz. (30 g) serving:

Calories	45
Total fat	0 g
Saturated fat	0 g
Cholesterol	0 mg
Sodium	0 mg
Total carbohydrates	10 g
Protein	1 g

Claims—fat free; no sodium

Sautéing

Sautéing is a very popular cooking method for fish and shellfish. It lightly caramelizes the food's surface, giving it additional flavour. Typically, other ingredients such as garlic, onions, vegetables, wine and lemon juice are added to the fond to make a sauce.

Selecting Fish and Shellfish to Sauté

Both fatty and lean fish may be sautéed. Flatfish are sometimes dressed and sautéed whole, as are small round fish such as trout. Larger fish such as salmon can be cut into steaks or filleted and cut into filets. The portions should be relatively uniform in size and thickness and fairly thin to promote even cooking. Although clams, mussels and oysters are not often sautéed, scallops and crustaceans are popular sauté items.

Seasoning Fish and Shellfish to Be Sautéed

Many types of fish—especially sole, flounder and other delicate, lean fish fillets—are often dredged in flour before sautéing. Seasoned butter is used to sauté some items, such as scampi-style shrimp. These items derive their flavour from the butter; additional seasonings should not be necessary.

Cooking Temperatures

The sauté pan and cooking fat must be hot before the fish or shellfish are added. Do not add too much fish or shellfish to the pan at one time or the pan and fat will cool, letting the foods simmer in their own juices. Thin slices and small pieces of fish and shellfish require a short cooking time, so use high temperatures in order to caramelize their surfaces without overcooking. Large, thick pieces of fish or shellfish being cooked in the shell may require slightly lower cooking temperatures to ensure that they are cooked without over-browning their surfaces.

Accompaniments to Sautéed Fish and Shellfish

Sautéed fish and shellfish are nearly always served with a sauce made directly in the sauté pan. This sauce may be as simple as browned butter (beurre noisette) or a complicated sauce flavoured with the fond. In some cases, seasoned butter is used to sauté the fish or shellfish and the butter is then served with the main item. See Table 10.5 for additional sauce suggestions.

Mildly flavoured rice and pasta are good choices to serve with sautéed fish or shellfish.

BASIC PROCEDURE FOR SAUTÉING FISH AND SHELLFISH

1. Cut or portion the fish or shellfish.
2. Season the item and dredge in seasoned flour if desired.
3. Heat a suitable sauté pan over moderate heat; add enough oil or clarified butter to cover the bottom to a depth of about 1/8 inch (3 mm).
4. Add the fish or shellfish to the pan (fish should be placed presentation side down); cook until done, turning once halfway through the cooking process. Add other foods as called for in the recipe.
5. Remove the fish or shellfish. If a sauce is to be made in the sauté pan, follow the procedures discussed in Chapter 17, Poultry.

◆◆◆

RECIPE 19.3

SAUTÉED HALIBUT
WITH THREE-COLOUR PEPPERS AND SPANISH OLIVES

Yield: 4 Servings

Halibut fillets, 6 oz. (170 g) each	4	4
Salt and pepper	TT	TT
Olive oil	2 oz.	60 mL
Onion, sliced	3 oz.	90 g
Garlic, minced	2 tsp.	10 mL
Green bell pepper, julienne	3 oz.	90 g
Red bell pepper, julienne	3 oz.	90 g
Yellow bell pepper, julienne	3 oz.	90 g
Tomato, peeled and diced	8 oz.	250 g
Spanish olives, pitted and quartered	2 oz.	60 g
Fresh thyme, chopped	2 tsp.	10 mL
Lemon juice	2 oz.	60 mL
Fish stock	2 oz.	60 mL

1. Season the fillets with salt and pepper.
2. Heat a sauté pan and add the olive oil.
3. Sauté the halibut, turning once. Remove and reserve in a warm place.
4. Add the onions and garlic to the same pan and sauté for approximately 1 minute. Add the peppers and sauté for 1–2 minutes more.
5. Add the tomato, olives and thyme; sauté briefly.
6. Add the lemon juice and deglaze the pan. Add the fish stock, simmer for 2 minutes to blend the flavours and adjust the seasonings.
7. Return the fish to the pan to reheat. Serve each fish fillet on a bed of vegetables with sauce and an appropriate garnish.

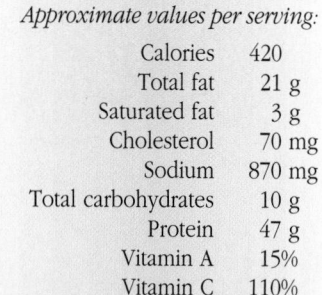

Approximate values per serving:

Calories	420
Total fat	21 g
Saturated fat	3 g
Cholesterol	70 mg
Sodium	870 mg
Total carbohydrates	10 g
Protein	47 g
Vitamin A	15%
Vitamin C	110%

Sauté the halibut fillets.

2. Sauté the onions, garlic and peppers.

3. Add the fish stock.

4. Return the fish to the pan to reheat.

Pan-Frying

Pan-frying is very similar to sautéing, but it uses more fat to cook the main item. Pan-fried fish is always coated with flour, batter or breading to help seal the surface and prevent the flesh from coming in direct contact with the cooking fat. Properly prepared pan-fried fish and shellfish should be moist and tender with a crisp surface. If battered or breaded, the coating should be intact with no breaks.

Selecting Fish and Shellfish to Pan-Fry

Both fatty and lean fish may be pan-fried. Trout and other small fish are ideal for pan-frying, as are portioned fillets of lean fish such as halibut. Pan-fried fish and shellfish should be uniform in size and relatively thin so they cook quickly and evenly.

Seasoning Fish and Shellfish to Be Pan-Fried

Although fish and shellfish can be marinated or seasoned directly, it is more common to season the flour, batter or breading that will coat them. Batters, for example, can contain cheese, and breadings can contain nuts and other ingredients to add different flavours to the fish or shellfish. Review the battering and breading procedures discussed in Chapter 21, Deep-Fat Frying. Additional seasonings come from sauces and other accompaniments served with the pan-fried fish or shellfish.

Cooking Temperatures

The fat should always be hot before the fish or shellfish are added. Breaded or battered fish fillets cook very quickly, and the fat should be hot enough to brown the coating without overcooking the interior. Whole pan-fried fish take longer to cook and therefore require a slightly lower cooking temperature so the surface does not become too dark before the interior is cooked. Oven finishing may be necessary.

Accompaniments to Pan-Fried Fish and Shellfish

Lemon wedges are the classic accompaniment to pan-fried fish and shellfish. Sauces that accompany pan-fried items are made separately. Mayonnaise-based sauces such as tartar sauce (Recipe 24.22) and rémoulade sauce are especially popular; rich wine-based sauces should be avoided. Vegetable coulis, such as tomato, also complement many pan-fried items. Additional sauce suggestions are found in Table 10.5.

BASIC PROCEDURE FOR PAN-FRYING FISH AND SHELLFISH

1. Heat enough clarified butter or oil in a heavy sauté pan to immerse one-third to one-half of the item. The fat temperature should be between 325°F and 350°F (160°C–175°C).
2. Add the floured, breaded or battered item to the pan, being careful not to splash the hot fat. Cook until done, turning once halfway through the cooking process.
3. Remove the food and drain on absorbent paper.
4. Serve it promptly with an appropriate sauce.

♦♦♦

RECIPE 19.4

BLUE CRAB CAKES WITH FRESH SALSA

Yield: 15 2-oz. (60-g) Cakes

Blue crab meat	1 lb.	450 g
Cream, 35%	6 oz.	180 mL
Red bell pepper, small dice	2 oz.	60 g
Green bell pepper, small dice	2 oz.	60 g
Clarified butter	as needed	as needed
Green onions, sliced	1 bunch	1 bunch
Fresh bread crumbs	6 oz.	180 g
Salt and pepper	TT	TT
Dijon mustard	1 Tbsp.	15 mL
Worcestershire sauce	TT	TT
Tabasco sauce	TT	TT
Egg, slightly beaten	1	1
Tomato Salsa (Recipe 10.21)	1 pt.	500 mL

1. Carefully pick through the crab meat, removing any pieces of shell. Keep the lumps of crab meat as large as possible.
2. Place the cream in a saucepan and bring to a boil. Reduce by approximately one-half. Chill the cream well.
3. Sauté the red and green bell peppers in a small amount of clarified butter until tender.
4. Combine the crab meat, reduced cream, peppers, green onions and approximately 3 ounces (90 g) of the bread crumbs along with the salt, pepper, Dijon mustard, Worcestershire sauce, Tabasco sauce and egg. Mix to combine all ingredients, trying to keep the lumps of crab meat intact.
5. Using a mould, form the crab mixture into cakes of the desired size.

1. Mix all ingredients for the crab cakes.

2. Form the crab cakes.

3. Pan-fry the crab cakes.

6. Place the remaining bread crumbs in an appropriately sized hotel pan. Place the crab cakes, a few at a time, in the hotel pan and cover with the bread crumbs. To help them adhere, press the crumbs lightly into the cakes.

7. Heat a sauté pan over moderate heat and add enough clarified butter to cover the bottom approximately 1/4 inch (0.5 cm) deep.

8. Add the crab cakes to the pan and cook until done, turning once when the first side is nicely browned. Remove and drain on absorbent paper.

9. Serve the crab cakes with fresh tomato salsa.

Approximate values per 2 oz. (60 g) cake serving:

Calories	130
Total fat	6 g
Saturated fat	3.5 g
Cholesterol	60 mg
Sodium	650 mg
Total carbohydrates	9 g
Protein	10 g
Vitamin C	15%

Moist-Heat Cooking Methods

Fish and shellfish lend themselves well to moist-heat cooking methods, especially steaming, poaching and simmering. Steaming best preserves the food's natural flavours and cooks without adding fat. Poaching is also popular, especially for fish. Poached fish can be served hot or cold, whole or as steaks, fillets or portions. Boiling, which is actually simmering, is most often associated with crustaceans.

Steaming

Steaming is a very natural way to cook fish and shellfish without adding fats. Fish are steamed by suspending them over a small amount of boiling liquid in a covered pan. The steam trapped in the pan gently cooks the food while preserving its natural flavours and most nutrients. The liquid used to steam fish and shellfish can be water or a court bouillon with herbs, spices, aromatics or wine added to infuse the item with the additional flavours. Mussels and clams can be steamed by placing them directly in a pan, adding a small amount of wine or other liquid and covering them. Their shells will hold them above the liquid as they cook. Fish and shellfish can also be steamed by wrapping them in parchment paper together with herbs, vegetables, butters or sauces as accompaniments and baking them in a hot oven. This method of steaming is called **en papillote**.

Steamed fish and shellfish should be moist and tender. They should have clean and delicate flavours. Any accompaniments or sauces should complement the main item without masking its flavour. Fish and shellfish cooked en papillote should be served piping hot so that the aromatic steam trapped by the paper escapes as the paper is cut open tableside.

Selecting Fish and Shellfish to Steam

Mollusks (e.g., clams and mussels), fatty fish (e.g., salmon and sea bass) and lean fish (e.g., sole) all produce good results when steamed. The portions should be of uniform thickness and no more than 1 inch (2.5 cm) thick to promote even cooking.

Seasoning Fish and Shellfish to Be Steamed

Steamed fish and shellfish rely heavily on their natural flavours and often require very little seasoning. Nevertheless, salt, pepper, herbs and spices can be applied directly to the raw food before steaming. Flavoured liquids used to steam fish and shellfish will contribute additional flavours. If the liquid is served with the fish or shellfish as a broth or used to make a sauce to accompany the item, it is especially important that the liquid be well seasoned. Lemons, limes and other fruits or vegetables can also be cooked with the fish or shellfish to add flavours. Clams and mussels often do not require additional salt as the liquor released when they open during cooking is sufficiently salty.

Accompaniments to Steamed Fish and Shellfish

Steamed fish and shellfish are popular partly because they are low in fat. In keeping with this perception, a low or nonfat sauce or a simple squeeze of lemon and steamed fresh vegetables are good accompaniments. If fat is not a concern, then an emulsified butter sauce such as beurre blanc (Recipe 10.16) or hollandaise (Recipe 10.14) may be a good choice. Table 10.5 lists several sauce suggestions.

Classic New England steamed clams are served with a portion of the steaming liquid; steamed mussels are served with a sauce that is created from the wine and other ingredients used to steam them.

1. Place the fish in the steamer.

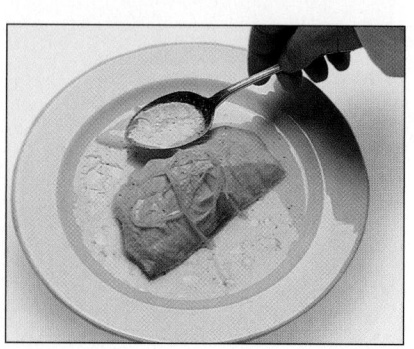

2. Spoon the dressing over the fish.

BASIC PROCEDURE FOR STEAMING FISH AND SHELLFISH

1. Portion the fish to an appropriate size. Clean the shellfish.
2. Prepare the cooking liquid. Add seasoning and flavouring ingredients as desired and bring to a boil.
3. Place the fish or shellfish in the steamer on a rack or in a perforated pan and cover tightly.
4. Steam the fish or shellfish until done.
5. Serve the fish or shellfish immediately with the steaming liquid or an appropriate sauce.

❖❖❖

RECIPE 19.5

STEAMED SALMON WITH LEMON AND OLIVE OIL

Yield: 1 Serving

Lemon zest, blanched	1 Tbsp.	15 mL
Lemon juice	2 Tbsp.	30 mL
Salt and pepper	TT	TT
Virgin olive oil	2 Tbsp.	30 mL
White wine	8 oz.	250 mL
Bay leaf	1	1
Leek, chopped	2 oz.	60 g
Fresh thyme	1 sprig	1 sprig
Peppercorns, cracked	1 tsp.	5 mL
Salmon filet or steak, approx. 6 oz. (170) g	1	1

1. To make the dressing, combine the lemon zest, lemon juice, salt and pepper. Whisk in the olive oil.
2. Combine the wine, bay leaf, leeks, thyme and peppercorns in the bottom of a steamer.
3. Season the salmon with salt and pepper and place it in the steamer basket.
4. Cover the steamer and bring the liquid to a boil. Cook the fish until done, approximately 4–6 minutes.
5. Plate the salmon and spoon the dressing over it.

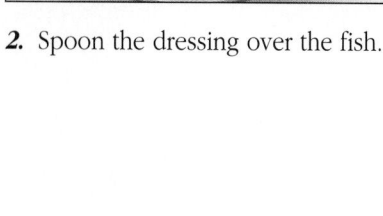

Approximate values per serving:

Calories	620
Total fat	40 g
Saturated fat	6 g
Cholesterol	95 mg
Sodium	700 mg
Total carbohydrates	16 g
Protein	48 g
Vitamin C	50%

◆◆◆

RECIPE 19.6

RED SNAPPER EN PAPILLOTE

Yield: 6 Servings

Clarified butter	as needed	as needed
Leek, julienne	3 oz.	90 g
Fennel, julienne	4 oz.	120 g
Carrot, julienne	3 oz.	90 g
Celery, julienne	3 oz.	90 g
Red bell pepper, julienne	3 oz.	90 g
Red snapper fillets, skin on, 6 oz. (170 g) each	6	6
Salt and pepper	TT	TT
Basil Butter (p. 219)	9 oz.	240 g

1. Cut 6 heart-shaped pieces of parchment paper large enough to contain the fish and vegetables when folded in half.

2. Brush each piece of parchment paper with clarified butter.

3. Toss the vegetables together. Place one-sixth of the vegetables on half of each piece of the buttered parchment paper.

4. Place 1 portion of red snapper on each portion of vegetables, skin side up; season with salt and pepper.

5. Top each portion of fish with 1-1/2 ounces (40 g) of basil butter.

Continued

Approximate values per serving:	
Calories	380
Total fat	19 g
Saturated fat	11 g
Cholesterol	125 mg
Sodium	680 mg
Total carbohydrates	6 g
Protein	46 g
Vitamin A	50%
Vitamin C	30%

1. Cut heart-shaped pieces of parchment paper.

2. Place the vegetables, red snapper and compound butter on the parchment paper.

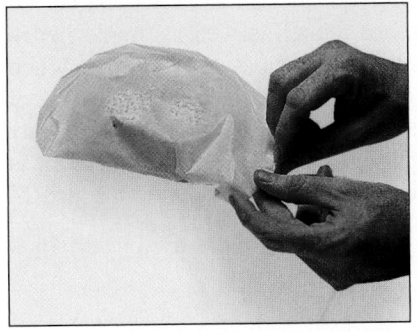

3. Crimp the edge of the parchment paper to seal it.

4. The finished papillotes.

6. Fold each piece of paper over and crimp the edges to seal it.

7. Place the envelopes (papillotes) on sheet pans and bake in a preheated oven at 450°F (230°C) for 8–10 minutes.

8. When baked, the parchment paper should puff up and brown. Remove from the oven and serve immediately. The envelope should be carefully cut open tableside to allow the aromatic steam to escape.

Poaching

Poaching is a versatile and popular method for cooking fish. Shellfish are rarely poached, however. The exception is squid, which can be quickly poached and chilled for use in salads and other preparations.

There are two distinct poaching methods.

The first is the **submersion method**, in which the fish is completely covered with a liquid, usually a court bouillon, fish stock or fish fumet. It is cooked until just done. The poached fish is then served (either hot or cold) with a sauce sometimes made from a portion of the cooking liquid but more often made separately. Whole fish (wrapped in cheesecloth to preserve its shape during cooking), filets and steaks can all be cooked by submersion poaching.

The second method, called **shallow poaching**, combines poaching and steaming to achieve the desired results. The main item, usually a fillet, filet or steak, is placed on a bed of aromatic vegetables in enough liquid to immerse half of the item. The liquid, called a **cuisson**, is brought to a simmer on the stove top. The pan is then covered with a piece of buttered parchment paper or a lid, and cooking is completed either on the stove top or in the oven. Shallow-poached fish is usually served with a sauce made with the reduced cooking liquid. (Sometimes the main item is sautéed lightly before the cooking liquid is added. If so, the cooking method is more accurately braising, as both dry- and moist-heat cooking methods are used.)

Selecting Fish to Poach

Lean white fish such as turbot, bass and sole are excellent for poaching. Some fatty fish such as salmon and trout are also excellent choices.

Seasoning Fish to Be Poached

Fish poached by either submersion or shallow poaching gain all of their seasonings from the liquid in which they are cooked and the sauce with which they are served. Therefore, it is very important to use a properly prepared court bouillon, fish fumet or a good-quality fish stock well seasoned with vegetables such as shallots, onions or fennel as well as ample herbs, spices and other seasonings. Many poached fish recipes call for wine. When using wine either in the cooking liquid or sauce, be sure to choose a wine of good quality. Most fish are very delicately flavoured, and using poor-quality wine might ruin an otherwise excellent dish. Citrus, especially lemon, is always a popular seasoning; lemon juice or zest may be added to the poaching liquid, the sauce or the finished dish.

Accompaniments to Poached Fish

Poached fish cooked by submersion go well with rich sauces like hollandaise and beurre blanc. If fat is a concern, a better choice may be a vegetable coulis (for example, broccoli or red pepper). Cold poached fish are commonly served with mayonnaise-based sauces such as sauce vert or rémoulade. Shallow-poached fish are served with sauces such as a white wine sauce or beurre blanc made from a reduction of the liquids in which the fish were poached. See Table 10.5 for additional sauce suggestions.

Poached fish are often served with rice or pasta and steamed or boiled vegetables.

BASIC PROCEDURE FOR SUBMERSION POACHING

1. Prepare the cooking liquid. Whole fish should be started in a cold liquid; gradually increasing the liquid's temperature helps preserve the appearance of the fish. Portioned fish should be started in a simmering liquid to preserve their flavour and more accurately estimate cooking time.
2. Use a rack to lower the fish into the cooking liquid. Be sure the fish is completely submerged.
3. Poach the fish at 175–185°F (80–85°C) until done.
4. Remove the fish from the poaching liquid, moisten with a portion of the liquid and hold in a warm place for service. Or remove the fish from the poaching liquid, cover it to prevent drying and allow it to cool, then refrigerate.
5. Serve the poached fish with an appropriate sauce.

RECIPE 19.7

WHOLE POACHED SALMON

Yield: 18–20 Servings

| Salmon, drawn, 4–5 lb. (1.8–2.2 kg) | 1 | 1 |
| Court bouillon | as needed | as needed |

1. Place the fish on a lightly oiled rack or screen and secure with butcher's twine.
2. Place the rack or screen in a pot and cover with cold court bouillon.
3. Bring the court bouillon to a simmer over moderate heat. Reduce the heat and poach the fish at 175–180°F (80–85°C) until done, approximately 30–45 minutes.
4. If the fish is to be served hot, remove it from the court bouillon, draining well, and serve immediately with an appropriate garnish. If it is to be served cold, remove it from the court bouillon, draining well, cool and refrigerate for several hours before decorating and garnishing as desired.

Approximate values per 4 oz. (120 g) serving:

Calories	114
Total fat	3 g
Saturated fat	1 g
Cholesterol	29 mg
Sodium	80 mg
Total carbohydrates	0 g
Protein	22 g
Calcium	6%

1. Arrange the whole fish on a rack.

2. Prepare the court bouillon.

3. Remove and drain the fish. Serve immediately or chill.

1. Arrange the sole on the bed of shallots and mushrooms.

2. Cover the fish with buttered parchment paper after the liquid is added.

3. Add the velouté to the cuisson.

Approximate values per serving:

Calories	440
Total fat	14 g
Saturated fat	5 g
Cholesterol	120 mg
Sodium	3750 mg
Total carbohydrates	27 g
Protein	42 g

BASIC PROCEDURE FOR SHALLOW POACHING

1. Butter a sauteuse and add aromatic vegetables as directed in the recipe.
2. Add the fish to the pan.
3. Add the cooking liquid to the pan.
4. Cover the pan with buttered parchment paper or a lid.
5. Bring the liquid to a simmer and cook the fish on the stove top or in the oven until done.
6. Remove the fish from the pan, moisten with a portion of the liquid and hold in a warm place for service.
7. Reduce the cuisson and finish the sauce as directed in the recipe.
8. Serve the poached fish with the sauce.

RECIPE 19.8

FILLETS OF SOLE BONNE FEMME

Yield: 2 Servings

Sole fillets, approx. 2-1/2 oz. (75 g) each	4	4
Salt and pepper	TT	TT
Whole butter	2 tsp.	10 mL
Shallots, minced	1 tsp.	5 mL
Mushrooms, sliced	4 oz.	120 g
White wine	3 oz.	90 mL
Fish stock	4 oz.	120 mL
Fish velouté	4 oz.	120 mL
Lemon juice	TT	TT
Parsley, chopped	1 tsp.	5 mL

1. Season the sole with salt and pepper.
2. Melt the butter in a sauté pan. Add the shallots and mushrooms and arrange the sole fillets over them. Add the wine and fish stock.
3. Bring the liquid to a simmer. Cover the fish with buttered parchment paper and cook on the stove top or in a 350°F (175°C) oven until done, approximately 5–8 minutes.
4. Remove the sole and reserve in a warm place.
5. Reduce the cuisson until approximately 1 ounce (30 mL) remains. Add the velouté. Add lemon juice to taste and adjust the seasonings. Serve the sauce with the fish, sprinkled with chopped parsley.

Simmering

"Boiled" lobster, crab and shrimp are not actually boiled; rather, they are cooked whole in their shells by simmering. Although they are not as delicate as some fish, these crustaceans can become tough and are easily overcooked if the cooking liquid is allowed to boil.

Selecting Shellfish to Simmer

Lobsters, crabs and shrimp are commonly cooked by simmering. Their hard shells protect their delicate flesh during the cooking process.

Seasoning Shellfish to Be Simmered

The shellfish being simmered are not seasoned. Rather, they gain flavour by being cooked in a seasoned or flavoured liquid, typically salted water or court bouillon. A sachet of pickling spice or Old Bay Seasoning is sometimes used for additional flavour.

Determining Doneness

Timing is the best method for determining the doneness of simmered shellfish. This varies depending on the size of the shellfish and how quickly the liquid returns to a simmer after the shellfish are added. Shrimp cook in as little as 3–5 minutes, crabs cook in 5–10 minutes and it can take as little as 6–8 minutes for a 1-pound (450-g) lobster to cook and 15–20 minutes for a 2-1/2 pound (1.1-kg) lobster.

Accompaniments to Simmered Shellfish

The standard accompaniments to simmered shellfish are lemon wedges and melted butter. If the shellfish is being eaten cold, there are a variety of flavourful cold sauces to select from. Nearly any type of vegetable or starch goes well with simmered shellfish, and salad preparations are popular as well as freshly baked breads.

Basic Procedure for Simmering Shellfish

1. Bring court bouillon or water to a boil.
2. Add the shellfish to the liquid. Bring the liquid back to a boil and reduce to a simmer. (Whenever an item is added to boiling water, it lowers the water's temperature. The greater the amount of water, however, the faster it will return to a boil. So, to accelerate the time within which the water returns to a boil after the shellfish are added, use as much water as possible.)
3. Cook until done.
4. Remove the shellfish from the liquid and serve immediately. Or cool by dropping them in ice water if they are to be eaten cold.

◆◆◆

RECIPE 19.9

BOILED LOBSTER

Yield: 1 Serving

Lobster, 1 lb. 8 oz. (675 g)	1	1
Boiling salted water	4 gal.	16 L
Lemon wedges	4	4
Whole butter, melted	2 oz.	60 mL

Approximate values per 1 lb. (450 g) serving:	
Calories	650
Total fat	26 g
Saturated fat	15 g
Cholesterol	390 mg
Sodium	1960 mg
Total carbohydrates	11 g
Protein	93 g
Vitamin A	35%
Vitamin C	45%

1. Drop the lobster into the boiling water. Bring the water back to a boil, reduce to a simmer and cook the lobster until done, approximately 12 minutes.
2. Remove the lobster from the pot, drain and serve immediately with lemon wedges and melted butter on the side.

Continued

3. If the lobster is to be eaten cold, drop it into a sink of ice water to stop the cooking process. When cool enough to handle, remove the meat from the shell following the procedures discussed earlier.

Combination Cooking Methods

Combination cooking methods are used with meats, game and poultry in part to tenderize them. Because fish and shellfish are inherently tender, they do not necessarily benefit from such procedures. As noted above in the section on shallow poaching, fish can, on occasion, be lightly sautéed or browned and then poached. Although this procedure is a combination cooking method, it is used to enhance flavours and not to tenderize the product.

You may encounter fish or shellfish recipes with the word "braised" or "stew" in the title. Note, however, that these recipes rarely follow the traditional combination cooking methods discussed in this book.

CONCLUSION

In part because of consumers' increased health awareness, more and more food service operations are expanding their selections of fish and shellfish. Their task is aided by the tremendous variety of high-quality fish and shellfish now available. A variety of dry-heat and moist-heat cooking methods can be used with these products and a variety of sauces and accompaniments can be served with them. Regardless of how they are served, care and attention are required in order to select, store and avoid overcooking fish and shellfish.

QUESTIONS FOR DISCUSSION

1. Discuss six techniques for determining the freshness of fish and shellfish.
2. What are the physical differences between a flatfish and a round fish? How do fabrication techniques vary for these fish?
3. List four market forms for fish and discuss several factors that may determine the form most appropriate for an operation to purchase.
4. List the three categories of mollusks and give an example of a commonly used food from each category.
5. Discuss four methods for determining the doneness of fish or shellfish. Why is it important not to overcook fish and shellfish?
6. Explain the differences between shallow poaching and submersion poaching. Why is poaching a commonly used method for preparing fish and shellfish?
7. Why are combination cooking methods rarely used with fish and shellfish? Why is boiling rarely used?

Additional Fish and Shellfish Recipes

RECIPE 19.10

Sea Bass with Thai Curry Sauce and Wok Vegetables

NOTE: *This dish appears in the Chapter Opening photograph.*

FLYING FISH, SEATTLE, WA
Chef-Owner Christine Keff

Yield: 6 Servings   **Method:** Sautéing

Chilean sea bass fillets, 5 oz. (150 g) each	6	6
Salt and pepper	TT	TT
Peanut oil	1 Tbsp.	15 mL
Wok Vegetables (recipe follows)		
Thai Curry Sauce (recipe follows)		
Fried beet frizzles (for garnish)	as needed	as needed

1. Salt and pepper both sides of the sea bass and set aside. In a large sauté pan, heat the oil over medium-high heat.
2. Gently place the sea bass fillets into the hot pan and cook to desired doneness, turning once.
3. Serve the fish over a bed of Wok Vegetables and drizzle with the Thai Curry Sauce. Top the fish with a mound of fried beet frizzles.

Approximate values per serving:

Calories	290
Total fat	13 g
Saturated fat	4 g
Cholesterol	60 mg
Sodium	617 mg
Total carbohydrates	13 g
Protein	31 g

WOK VEGETABLES

Yield: 6 Servings

Green or Napa cabbage	1/2 head	1/2 head
Zucchini	1	1
Yellow squash	1	1
Peanut oil	1 Tbsp.	15 mL
Fresh ginger root, peeled, chopped fine	1-in. knob	2.5-cm knob
Garlic, chopped fine	2 cloves	2 cloves
Cilantro, destemmed and chopped coarse	2 oz.	60 g
Peanuts, roasted, unsalted, chopped	2 Tbsp.	30 mL
Sesame oil	1 Tbsp.	15 mL
Sesame seeds	1 tsp.	5 mL
Soy sauce	2 Tbsp.	30 mL
Fresh lime juice	2 Tbsp.	30 mL
Mirin	2 Tbsp.	30 mL
Rice wine vinegar	2 Tbsp.	30 mL
Salt and pepper	TT	TT

1. Core the cabbage and cut into a rough julienne.
2. Grate the outside of the zucchini and the yellow squash, discarding the inner seeds.
3. Heat the peanut oil in a wok or large skillet over high heat. Add the ginger, garlic, cabbage, squashes, cilantro, peanuts, sesame oil and sesame seeds. Cook, tossing frequently, until the vegetables begin to wilt.

Approximate values per 6 oz. (180 g) serving:

Calories	114
Total fat	7 g
Saturated fat	1 g
Cholesterol	0 mg
Sodium	443 mg
Total carbohydrates	12 g
Protein	3 g

Claims—low saturated fat; no cholesterol; good source of fibre

Continued

4. Deglaze the pan with soy sauce, lime juice, mirin and vinegar. Season to taste with salt and pepper.

THAI CURRY SAUCE

Yield: 6 Servings

Peanut oil	as needed	as needed
Curry Paste (recipe follows)	3 Tbsp.	45 mL
Chicken stock	6 oz.	180 mL
Coconut milk	4 oz.	120 mL

1. Heat a small sauté pan and lightly coat it with peanut oil. Add the Curry Paste and sauté briefly.
2. Add the chicken stock and reduce by half.
3. Add the coconut milk and simmer until the sauce is thick enough to coat a spoon.

Approximate values per 1 oz. (30 g) serving:

Calories	35
Total fat	3 g
Saturated fat	2.5 g
Cholesterol	0 mg
Sodium	75 mg
Total carbohydrates	1 g
Protein	1 g

CURRY PASTE

Yield: 8 oz. (250 g)

Fresh galangal, peeled	1 oz.	30 g
Fresh ginger root, peeled	1 oz.	30 g
Fresh turmeric, peeled	1 oz.	30 g
Shallots, peeled	2 oz.	60 g
Garlic, peeled	6 cloves	6 cloves
Fresh cilantro	1/2 oz.	15 g
Juice of 1/2 lime		
Dried Thai chile, soaked in water to soften	1	1
Peanut oil	as needed	as needed

1. Combine all ingredients except the oil in a food processor and grind.
2. Add just enough peanut oil to make a paste. Continue to process until the paste is smooth.

Approximate values per 1 oz. (30 g) serving:

Calories	30
Total fat	1 g
Saturated fat	0 g
Cholesterol	0 mg
Sodium	15 mg
Total carbohydrates	5 g
Protein	0 g

═══════════ ◆◆◆ ═══════════

RECIPE 19.11

RED SNAPPER
WITH TOMATILLO-SERRANO CHILE VINAIGRETTE

STAGE WEST HOTEL, TORONTO, ON
Executive Chef Rudi Fischbacher

Rudi Fischbacher
Rudi trained in his native Austria and worked in Switzerland, Sweden, Spain and Germany before coming to Canada. Currently he is the Executive Chef and Food and Beverage Manager at the Stage West Hotel. He and his staff of 50 provide services for dinner theatre, banquets, the restaurant, lounge, patio and in-room dining.

Yield: 6 Servings   **Method:** Pan-frying

Peanut oil	1 oz.	30 mL
Red snapper fillets 6 oz. (180 g) each, skinned	6	6
Salt and freshly ground pepper	TT	TT
Tomatillo-Serrano Chile Vinaigrette (recipe follows)	10 oz.	300 mL

1. Heat oil in a large skillet. Add the fillets in batches and cook over moderate heat for 2 minutes. Turn and cook on the other side until the fish is

opaque throughout, about 3 minutes. Remove the fish to a large, warm platter.

2. Spoon the Tomatillo-Serrano Chile Vinaigrette onto 6 warm dinner plates and arrange the snapper fillets in the centre. Serve warm.

TOMATILLO-SERRANO CHILE VINAIGRETTE

Yield: 10 oz. (300 mL)

Fresh tomatillos, husked, rinsed and cut into small dice	4	4
Jicama, diced	2 oz.	60 g
Red bell pepper, diced	1-1/2 Tbsp.	25 g
Yellow bell pepper, diced	1-1/2 Tbsp.	25 g
Mango, peeled and cut into small dice	1/2	1/2
Serrano chile, seeded and finely diced	1	1
Peanut oil	2 oz.	60 mL
Olive oil	2 Tbsp.	30 mL
White wine vinegar	2 Tbsp.	30 mL
Balsamic vinegar	1-1/2 Tbsp.	25 mL
Fresh lime juice	1 Tbsp.	15 mL
Fresh lemon juice	1 Tbsp.	15 mL
Garlic clove, minced	1 small	1 small
Fresh coriander, minced	1–2 Tbsp.	15–30 mL
Salt	TT	TT

1. In a bowl, combine the tomatillos, jicama, red and yellow bell peppers, mango and serrano chile; toss to mix.
2. In a small bowl, combine the peanut oil, olive oil, white wine vinegar, balsamic vinegar, lime juice, lemon juice, garlic and coriander. Whisk to blend well.
3. Pour the dressing over the diced vegetables and stir lightly to mix. Season with salt to taste.

Approximate values per serving:	
Calories	297
Total fat	14 g
Saturated fat	2 g
Cholesterol	67 mg
Sodium	791 mg
Total carbohydrates	4 g
Protein	37 g

Approximate values per 1 oz. (30 mL) serving:	
Calories	51
Total fat	5 g
Saturated fat	1 g
Cholesterol	0 mg
Sodium	216 mg
Total carbohydrates	2 g
Protein	0.2 g

◆◆◆

RECIPE 19.12

CORN-CRUSTED SALMON IN BROTH WITH WILD GARLIC OIL ON SWEET CARROT AND BARLEY RISOTTO

ROYAL YORK HOTEL, TORONTO, ON
Executive Chef George McNeill

Yield: 4 Servings　　　　　　**Method:** Pan-frying

Salmon fillet, skin on, 2 oz. (60 g) each	8	8
Cornmeal	3 oz.	90 g
Salt and pepper	TT	TT
Fresh tarragon, for garnish	4 sprigs	4 sprigs

1. Prepare the Tarragon Broth, the Sweet Carrot and Barley Risotto and Wild Garlic Oil (recipes follow). Keep the broth and risotto warm.
2. Season the salmon and coat it with the cornmeal.
3. Heat the Wild Garlic Oil in the pan and pan-fry the salmon quickly (about 30 seconds per side) until the salmon is a golden colour and cooked medium rare.
4. Place a serving of hot risotto in the middle of a warm soup plate.

Continued

George McNeill
George is a Certified Master Chef (U.S.A.)—one of the few in Canada. George was captain of the 1996 Canadian National Culinary Olympic Team, which brought three gold medals home from Berlin. As Executive Chef at the Royal York Hotel, he oversees the largest hotel kitchen in the country, which produces 4000–6000 meals a day.

*Approximate values per serving,
including garnishes:*

Calories	508
Total fat	31 g
Saturated fat	5 g
Cholesterol	73 mg
Sodium	898 mg
Total carbohydrates	30 g
Protein	27 g

*Approximate values per
1 oz. (30 g) serving:*

Calories	277
Total fat	28 g
Saturated fat	2 g
Cholesterol	0 mg
Sodium	4 mg
Total carbohydrates	7 g
Protein	1 g

*Approximate values per
1 oz. (30 g) serving:*

Calories	168
Total fat	9 g
Saturated fat	5 g
Cholesterol	22 mg
Sodium	378 mg
Total carbohydrates	17 g
Protein	6 g

5. Set the warm cornmeal-salmon skin-side up on top of the risotto to build height.
6. Pour Tarragon Broth around the risotto.
7. Garnish each plate with a sprig of tarragon.

WILD GARLIC OIL

Yield: 10 oz. (300 mL)

Wild garlic bulbs, peeled and cleaned	8	8
Thyme, chopped	1 tsp.	5 mL
Shallots, chopped	2 bulbs	2 bulbs
Canola oil	10 oz.	300 mL

1. Sweat the first three ingredients in a little oil.
2. Add the remaining oil and simmer for 1 hour.
3. Remove from heat and let the oil steep for several days.
4. Strain off the oil from other ingredients. Use oil as required.

SWEET CARROT AND BARLEY RISOTTO

Yield: 1 qt. (800 mL)

Butternut squash, diced	1 oz.	30 g
Clarified butter	1–2 tsp.	5–10 mL
Salt and pepper	TT	TT
Fish or chicken stock	18 oz.	500 mL
Barley, washed and picked/cleaned	6 oz.	150 mL
Carrots, diced and blanched	1 oz.	30 g
Corn niblets	1 oz.	30 g
Lima beans, individually quick frozen, peeled	1 oz.	30 g
Sun-dried cranberries, steeped in stock	1/2 oz.	15 g
Parmesan cheese, grated	2 oz.	55 g
Whole butter, cubed	2 oz.	55 g
Herbs, chopped: Italian parsley, chives, basil	4 tsp.	20 mL

1. Place diced butternut squash in a mixing bowl, and lightly toss with clarified butter and seasoning. Put the squash in a small tray or pan and place in an oven pre-heated to 400°F (200°C) and roast until golden.
2. Bring the stock to a boil, then add the barley. Simmer until cooked, 30–35 minutes.
3. Add the remaining vegetables and cranberries. Mix well.
4. Finish with Parmesan and whole cubed butter. Season and keep warm. Sprinkle the serving dish with the chopped herbs before serving the risotto.

NOTE: Fish stock may be too strongly flavoured for risotto and the cranberries; chicken stock can be substituted.

TARRAGON BROTH

Yield: 14 oz. (400 mL)

Vegetable oil	1 oz.	30 mL
Spanish cooking onion, finely diced	3-1/2 oz.	100 g
Fresh tarragon	2 sprigs	2 sprigs
White wine	4 oz.	110 mL
White fish stock	14 oz.	400 mL

Cornstarch (optional)	as needed	as needed
Salt and pepper	TT	TT

1. Heat the vegetable oil and add the chopped onion. Sweat the onion until translucent.
2. Add one sprig of the tarragon, roughly chopped (use stems and leaves).
3. Sweat the ingredients for 2–3 minutes longer, then deglaze with the white wine. Reduce the wine by half.
4. Add the fish stock and bring to a boil.
5. Mix the cornstarch in a little of the cold fish stock and add it to the boiling stock to slightly thicken, stirring well.
6. Strain the broth through a fine sieve.
7. Finely chop the remaining sprig of tarragon, leaves only. Add tarragon to the broth and season with salt and pepper. Serve.

Approximate values per
1 oz. (30 g) serving:

Calories	30
Total fat	2 g
Saturated fat	0.1 g
Cholesterol	0 mg
Sodium	140 mg
Total carbohydrates	2 g
Protein	0.2 g

◆◆◆

RECIPE 19.13

POTATO CRUSTED SMOKED BLACK COD WITH TOMATO CHUTNEY AND SCALLION OIL

METROPOLITAN HOTEL, VANCOUVER, BC
Excutive Chef Michael Noble

Michael Noble

Michael opened Diva at the Met in 1996, and within a year it was in the centre of Vancouver's culinary spotlight, winning awards from Gourmet Magazine, Vancouver Magazine, and GQ. Michael also achieved Canada's highest standings ever at the Bocuse d'Or World Cuisine championship in Lyons, in 1995 and 1997.

Yield: 4 Servings

Method: Sautéing

Smoked black cod fillets, 2 oz. (60 g) each	4	4
Ground black pepper	TT	TT
Baker potato	1	1
Egg white	1	1
Chives, chopped	1 tsp.	5 mL
Salt	TT	TT
Flour for dredging	as needed	as needed
Olive oil	as needed	as needed
Tomato Chutney:		
Red pepper, diced fine	2 tsp.	10 mL
Shallot, minced	1	1
Raspberry vinegar	2 oz.	50 mL
Sugar	2 oz.	50 g
Tomato concassé	8 oz.	250 g
Salt and ground black pepper	TT	TT
Olive oil	as needed	as needed
Scallion Oil:		
Green onion, green part only, minced	1 bunch	1 bunch
Olive oil, extra virgin	7 oz.	200 mL
Ground white pepper	TT	TT
Rice wine vinegar	1 Tbsp.	15 mL
Pea shoots	as garnish	as garnish

1. To make the Scallion Oil, place the minced green onion, olive oil and white pepper in a bowl. Let the mixture stand for 12 to 24 hours. Purée it in a blender with the rice wine vinegar.

Approximate values per serving,
with garnishes:

Calories	230
Total fat	11 g
Saturated fat	2 g
Cholesterol	46 mg
Sodium	1177 mg
Total carbohydrates	15 g
Protein	17 g

Continued

2. Season the cod portions with the ground black pepper. Sear quickly over a hot grill or in a hot pan and let cool. Grate the potato in a coarse grater. Squeeze out the excess water without rinsing. Place the potato in a bowl. Add egg white, chives and salt. Dredge the cod lightly with flour, pat a little of the potato mixture onto the fish and sauté each piece carefully in olive oil over medium heat until golden brown and cooked through. Drain on paper towel.

3. To make the Tomato Chutney, sweat the shallots and red pepper in some olive oil. Add the vinegar and sugar and reduce by three-quarters. Add the tomato concassé and continue cooking slowly for approximately 20 minutes, or until the liquid has evaporated and the chutney is deep red in colour. Season with salt and pepper. Set aside.

4. Toss some pea shoots in olive oil. Place on a plate and then top them with the black cod. Put some Tomato Chutney on the cod, then drizzle some scallion oil on the plate and serve.

◆ ◆ ◆

RECIPE 19.14

TERIYAKI SALMON WITH PINEAPPLE PAPAYA SALSA

Yield: 4 Servings   **Method:** Grilling

Soy sauce	8 oz.	250 mL
Garlic, crushed	1 tsp.	5 mL
Ginger, minced	1 tsp.	5 mL
Brown sugar	2 oz.	60 g
Sake	4 oz.	120 mL
Salmon filets, 4 oz. (120 g) each	4	4
Vegetable oil	as needed	as needed
Pineapple Papaya Salsa (Recipe 25.9)	16 oz.	450 g

1. To make the marinade, combine the soy sauce, garlic, ginger, brown sugar and sake.

2. Marinate the salmon filets in the marinade for 15 minutes.

3. Remove the salmon from the marinade and pat dry. Brush them with vegetable oil and broil or grill until done.

4. Serve the salmon on a bed of warmed Pineapple-Papaya Salsa.

Approximate values per serving:

Calories	330
Total fat	9 g
Saturated fat	2 g
Cholesterol	65 mg
Sodium	3770 mg
Total carbohydrates	28 g
Protein	35 g
Vitamin C	60%

◆ ◆ ◆

RECIPE 19.15

CLAY POT SALMON WITH TOMATO ROSEMARY BUTTER SAUCE

Chef-Consultant Anne Milne, VANCOUVER, BC

Yield: 4 Servings   **Method:** Grilling

Salmon fillets, skinless, boneless, 5 oz. (150 g) each	4	4
Olive oil	as needed	as needed
Salt and cracked pepper	TT	TT
Tomato Rosemary Butter Sauce (recipe follows)	6 oz.	200 mL

Anne Milne

After 16 years as a successful Vancouver chef, Anne is now a self-employed chef-consultant, whose prestigious clients include the Bedford Hotel and the Butchart Gardens in Victoria. Anne is also a food writer for The Vancouver Sun, City Food Magazine, *and* City Palate *of Calgary.*

1. Rub salmon with olive oil and season with salt and fresh cracked pepper.
2. The barbecue grill should be very hot and clean. Rub the grill with oil.
3. Place fillets on the grill presentation side down. Put a clean clay pot over the fish. This "smokes" the fish and reduces cooking time. Turn fish at a 45-degree angle after 3–4 minutes. Replace the pot for another 3–4 minutes.
4. Flip fish and replace pot. Fish is done when it becomes translucent.
5. Place fish on warmed plate. Coat with Tomato Rosemary Butter Sauce.

Approximate values per serving, with sauce:	
Calories	489
Total fat	39 g
Saturated fat	19 g
Cholesterol	156 mg
Sodium	356 mg
Total carbohydrates	3 g
Protein	30 g

TOMATO ROSEMARY BUTTER SAUCE

Yield: 6 oz. (200 mL)

White wine vinegar	2 oz.	50 mL
Dry white wine	2 oz.	50 mL
Shallots, finely minced	1/4 cup	30 g
White peppercorns	4	4
Salt	pinch	pinch
Cream, 35%	few drops	few drops
Unsalted butter, cut into 16 pieces, at room temperature	8 oz.	225 g
Fresh lemon juice	TT	TT
Rosemary, fresh, finely chopped, blanched	1 Tbsp.	15 mL
Tomato, medium-sized, peeled, seeded, finely diced	1	1

1. Combine vinegar, wine, shallot, peppercorns and salt in small heavy non-corrosive saucepan. Bring to a boil over medium heat.
2. Reduce heat to very low; simmer until no more than 1/2 teaspoon (2–3 mL) of liquid remains when pan is tilted and shallot appears as a moist, mushy purée, about 10 minutes.
3. Add cream and bring to a boil. Immediately remove from heat; cool slightly.
4. Whisk butter, one piece at a time, into reduction in saucepan; add each piece just as the previous one is almost incorporated.
5. Move pan on and off very low heat as necessary to maintain smooth but not runny consistency; when all butter is added, you should have a thick, creamy emulsion with no greasy streaks. Add lemon juice to taste; strain into warm sauce boat.
6. Add blanched, finely chopped rosemary and diced, seeded and peeled tomatoes. Serve immediately.

Approximate values per 1 oz. (30 g) serving:	
Calories	292
Total fat	31 g
Saturated fat	19 g
Cholesterol	83 mg
Sodium	331 mg
Total carbohydrates	3 g
Protein	1 g

◆◆◆

RECIPE 19.16

SALMON IN RICE PAPER WITH A FRESH HERB MOSAIC AND SOY BEURRE BLANC

CHEF LELAND ATKINSON, WASHINGTON, D.C.

Yield: 4 Servings   **Method**: Sautéing

Salmon fillet portions, 6 oz. (180 g) each	4	4
Salt and pepper	TT	TT
Extra virgin olive oil	2 Tbsp.	30 mL

Continued

Rice vinegar	2 Tbsp.	30 mL
Rice paper circles, 8 in. (20 cm) in diameter	4	4
Fresh basil	4 leaves	4 leaves
Fresh dill	4 sprigs	4 sprigs
Fresh cilantro	4 leaves	4 leaves
Soy Beurre Blanc (recipe follows)	as needed	as needed

1. Season the skin side of the salmon with salt and pepper; drizzle with the olive oil and vinegar.
2. Soak the rice paper in warm water, one sheet at a time, for 30 seconds.
3. Transfer each paper to a work surface and let it stand until pliable.
4. Arrange a portion of the fresh herbs in a mosaic pattern in the centre of the rice paper.
5. Place the salmon flesh side down, centred over the mosaic.
6. Tightly fold in all four sides of the rice paper to enclose the fish.
7. Sauté the salmon, presentation (flesh) side down first, in olive oil until the rice paper is golden brown. Use caution, as the rice paper browns quickly.
8. Transfer the fish to a 350°F (180°C) oven and cook for 2–3 minutes. Do not overcook.
9. Ladle the Soy Beurre Blanc onto four warm plates and centre the fish on it.

SOY BEURRE BLANC

Yield: 12 oz. (350 g)

Shallots, chopped	1 oz.	30 g
Clarified butter	1 Tbsp.	15 mL
White wine	8 oz.	250 mL
Fresh thyme	1 sprig	1 sprig
Bay leaf	1	1
Fresh ginger, peeled, chopped	1 oz.	30 g
Cream, 35%	8 oz.	250 mL
Champagne vinegar	1 tsp.	5 mL
Butter, room temperature	4 oz.	120 g
Soy sauce	2 tsp.	10 mL
Fresh lemon juice	1 Tbsp.	15 mL

1. Sweat the shallots in clarified butter.
2. Add the wine, thyme, bay leaf and ginger. Simmer slowly, reduce *au sec.*
3. Add the cream and reduce until slightly thick.
4. Add the vinegar and whisk in the room-temperature butter.
5. Add the soy sauce and fresh lemon juice and strain.
6. Hold the sauce warm and tightly covered until service.

◆◆◆

RECIPE 19.17

RED SNAPPER VERACRUZ

Yield: 4 Servings   **Method:** Sautéing

Red snapper fillets, skinless, 6 oz. (180 g) each	4	4

Approximate values per serving:

Calories	400
Total fat	22 g
Saturated fat	5 g
Cholesterol	105 mg
Sodium	690 mg
Total carbohydrates	3 g
Protein	17 g
Vitamin A	10%

Approximate values per 1 oz. (30 g) serving:

Calories	150
Total fat	16 g
Saturated fat	10 g
Cholesterol	50 mg
Sodium	140 mg
Total carbohydrates	1 g
Protein	1 g
Vitamin A	20%

Salt and pepper	TT	TT
Flour	as needed	as needed
Olive oil	2 oz.	60 mL
Onion, medium dice	6 oz.	180 g
Garlic cloves, minced	4	4
Lemon juice	1 oz.	30 mL
Fish or chicken stock	8 oz.	250 mL
Jalapeño, seeded, small dice	1	1
Tomato concassé	1 lb. 8 oz.	650 g
Pimento-stuffed green olives, quartered	20	20
Sugar	1 tsp.	5 mL
Cinnamon stick	1	1
Dried thyme	1/2 tsp.	2 mL
Dried marjoram	1/2 tsp	2 mL
Capers	2 Tbsp.	30 mL
Fresh cilantro for garnish	as needed	as needed

1. Season the fillets with salt and pepper and dredge in flour. Sauté the fillets in olive oil until done. Remove and reserve in a warm place.

2. Add the onions and garlic to the pan and sauté until tender. Deglaze the pan with the lemon juice and add the stock, jalapeño, tomatoes, olives, sugar, cinnamon stick, thyme and marjoram.

3. Simmer 10 minutes. Remove the cinnamon stick and add the capers. Season to taste.

4. Return the fish to the pan to reheat. Serve on warm plates garnished with fresh cilantro.

VARIATIONS: Substitute bass or halibut fillets for the red snapper.

Approximate values per serving:

Calories	570
Total fat	22 g
Saturated fat	3 g
Cholesterol	80 mg
Sodium	1820 mg
Total carbohydrates	41 g
Protein	51 g
Vitamin C	70%

◆◆◆

RECIPE 19.18

PAN-FRIED TROUT WITH TOASTED GARLIC

Yield: 1 Serving   **Method:** Pan-frying

Trout, pan-dressed	1	1
Salt and pepper	TT	TT
Flour	as needed	as needed
Clarified butter	1 oz.	30 mL
Whole butter	1 Tbsp.	15 g
Garlic cloves, sliced thin	2	2
Lemon juice	1 oz.	30 mL
Fresh parsley, chopped	1 tsp.	5 mL

1. Season the trout with salt and pepper; dredge in flour.

2. Pan-fry the trout in the clarified butter until lightly browned and cooked through. Remove and reserve.

3. Degrease the pan, add the whole butter and cook until it begins to brown.

4. Add the sliced garlic and sauté a few seconds until the garlic begins to brown.

5. Add the lemon juice and parsley and swirl to combine with the butter.

6. Top the fish with the sauce and serve.

Approximate values per serving:

Calories	650
Total fat	47 g
Saturated fat	23 g
Cholesterol	165 mg
Sodium	1600 mg
Total carbohydrates	28 g
Protein	28 g
Vitamin A	45%
Vitamin C	30%

◆◆◆

RECIPE 19.19
POACHED FISH STEAKS

Yield: 8 Servings　　　　　　　　　　　　　　**Method:** Poaching

Court bouillon (Recipe 10.6)	as needed	as needed
Fish steaks (cod, salmon or turbot), 8 oz. (225 g) each	8	8

Approximate values per serving:

Calories	230
Total fat	2 g
Saturated fat	0 g
Cholesterol	125 mg
Sodium	310 mg
Total carbohydrates	0 g
Protein	52 g

Claims—low fat

1. Bring the court bouillon to a boil.
2. Arrange the steaks on a rack and lower into the court bouillon.
3. Reduce the heat, poach the fish until done, approximately 5–10 minutes.
4. Remove the fish and drain well. Remove the skin or bones, if necessary. Serve with lemon wedges and an appropriate sauce, such as hollandaise, mousseline or beurre noisette.

◆◆◆

RECIPE 19.20
NAPOLEON OF SHRIMP AND SCALLOPS

RIVERIA RESTAURANT, ATLANTA, GA
Chef Jack Shoop

Yield: 4 Servings　　　　　　　　　　　　　　**Method:** Sautéing

Puff pastry	1/2 lb.	250 g
Egg yolk	1	1
Scallops, large	12	12
Shrimp, 16–20 count, peeled and deveined	12	12
Clarified butter	1 oz.	30 mL
Sea salt	TT	TT
White pepper	TT	TT
Parsley, chopped	1 Tbsp.	15 mL
Lemon	1	1
Shallots, minced	1 Tbsp.	15 mL
Spinach leaves, washed	2 oz.	60 g
Orange segments	12	12
Sun-Dried Tomato Sauce (recipe follows)	6 oz.	180 mL
Fresh chervil	as needed	as needed

1. Roll out the puff pastry into a sheet 6 inches wide by 12 inches long by 1/8 inch thick (15 cm by 180 cm by 3 mm). Freeze the puff pastry sheet for 10 minutes.
2. Whisk the egg yolk together with 1 teaspoon (3 mL) of water and brush the puff pastry with the egg wash. Using a pastry comb, score the dough in each direction.
3. Cut the puff pastry into 4 pieces, 1-1/2 inches by 3 inches (3.75 cm by 7.5 cm). Place on a parchment-lined sheet pan and bake at 350°F (180°C) until golden brown. Let the pastry rest 30 minutes and then slice each piece in half horizontally to form the bottom and top of the Napoleon.
4. Cut the scallops in half horizontally and sauté them with the shrimp in clarified butter for approximately 3 minutes. Season to taste and add the chopped parsley and a squeeze of lemon juice.

5. In a separate pan, sauté the shallots and spinach until tender. Season to taste with salt and pepper.

6. Place the bottoms of the Napoleon shells on four plates. Place some spinach and orange segments on top of the pastry. Arrange a portion of the sliced scallops on top of the spinach and oranges and place a portion of the shrimp on top of the scallops. Spoon 1-1/2 ounces (45 mL) of the Sun-Dried Tomato Sauce over the entire arrangement. Place the top piece of puff pastry on top of the shrimp and garnish each plate with chervil.

SUN-DRIED TOMATO SAUCE

Yield: 2 qt. (2 L)

Shallots, minced	3 oz.	90 g
Sun-dried tomatoes, minced	5 Tbsp.	75 mL
Garlic cloves	7	7
Olive oil	4 oz.	120 mL
Tomato concassé	8 oz.	250 g
Champagne	6 oz.	180 mL
White stock	8 oz.	250 mL
Opal basil bouquet garni	1	1
Cream, 35%	3 qt.	3 L
Fresh orange juice	4 oz.	120 mL
Sea salt	TT	TT
Pepper	TT	TT
Whole butter	4 oz.	120 g

1. Sauté the shallots, sun-dried tomatoes and garlic in the olive oil for 2 minutes.

2. Add the tomato concassé, champagne, white stock and bouquet garni and reduce by two thirds.

3. Add the cream and simmer for 40 minutes.

4. Add the orange juice, season to taste and monter au beurre.

Approximate values per serving:

Calories	860
Total fat	32 g
Saturated fat	8 g
Cholesterol	595 mg
Sodium	980 mg
Total carbohydrates	63 g
Protein	79 g
Vitamin A	260%
Vitamin C	150%
Calcium	20%

Approximate values per 1-1/2 oz. (45 mL) serving:

Calories	155
Total fat	16 g
Saturated fat	9 g
Cholesterol	48 mg
Sodium	43 mg
Total carbohydrates	2 g
Protein	1 g
Vitamin A	15%

◆◆◆

RECIPE 19.21

SESAME SWORDFISH STEAKS

Yield: 1 Serving   **Method:** Sautéing

Leek, julienne	4 oz.	120 g
Swordfish steak, 6 oz. (170 g)	1	1
Sesame oil	1 oz.	30 mL
Sesame seeds	1 oz.	30 g
Fish stock	2 oz.	60 mL
Tamari sauce	1 Tbsp.	30 mL

1. Deep-fat fry the leeks at 280°F (140°C) until golden brown. Drain well.

2. Brush both sides of the fish with sesame oil. Coat both sides of the fish with the sesame seeds, pressing to make a solid, even coating.

3. In a very hot pan, sauté the fish in the remaining sesame oil. Turn the fish and finish cooking it in a 375°F (190°C) oven.

4. Remove the fish from the pan and hold on a warm plate. Deglaze the pan with the fish stock. Add the tamari sauce and heat thoroughly.

5. Place the fish on a bed of fried leeks, then pour the sauce over the fish and serve immediately.

VARIATIONS: Substitute a tuna or shark steak for the swordfish steak.

Approximate values per serving:

Calories	780
Total fat	52 g
Saturated fat	9 g
Cholesterol	85 mg
Sodium	1410 mg
Total carbohydrates	24 g
Protein	53 g
Vitamin C	25%
Calcium	35%

♦♦♦

RECIPE 19.22

STEAMED BLACK BASS WITH SANSHO PEPPER

THE FOUR SEASONS, NEW YORK, NY
Chef Christian Albin

Yield: 6 Servings   **Method:** Steaming

Black bass fillets, skin on, approx. 5 oz. (150 g) each	6	6
Leek, large, cleaned and cut into strips	1	1
Sansho pepper* and sea salt	TT	TT
Lime, juice and zest of	1	1
Lemon, juice and zest of	1	1
Olive oil	3 Tbsp.	45 mL
Pommeray mustard	1 tsp.	5 mL
Salt and pepper	TT	TT

1. Place the fish fillets, skin side up, and the leek in a steamer basket. Season with Sansho pepper and sea salt. Steam for approximately 5 minutes.

2. To make the vinaigrette, zest and juice the lime and lemon. Blanch the zests in water. Drain and mix the zests and juices with the olive oil and Pommeray mustard; season to taste with salt and pepper.

3. Plate the fish fillets and garnish with the leeks. Drizzle the vinaigrette over the fish and leeks.

* Sansho pepper (a slightly spicy Japanese seasoning) can be bought in specialty stores.

Approximate values per serving:

Calories	220
Total fat	7 g
Saturated fat	1.5 g
Cholesterol	125 mg
Sodium	530 mg
Total carbohydrates	5 g
Protein	35 g
Vitamin C	20%

♦♦♦

RECIPE 19.23

BAKED MONKFISH WITH BACON

Yield: 8 Servings   **Method:** Baking

Bacon, thin slices	4	4
Monkfish fillets, 6 oz. (170 g) each	8	8
Whole butter, melted	as needed	as needed
Salt and pepper	TT	TT
Lemon juice	2 Tbsp.	30 mL

1. Partially cook the bacon on a sheet pan in a 350°F (180°C) oven for 5 minutes.

2. Cut each slice of bacon in half. Wrap each portion of fish with bacon and secure with a toothpick.

3. Butter a baking pan and place the fish in it. Season with salt and pepper.

4. Brush the fish with butter and sprinkle with lemon juice.

5. Bake the fish at 450°F (230°C) until done, approximately 12–15 minutes.

6. Serve the fish with an appropriate sauce such as a tomato coulis or a tomato-based sauce such as Spanish or Creole (following Recipe 10.13).

Approximate values per serving:

Calories	190
Total fat	6 g
Saturated fat	2 g
Cholesterol	60 mg
Sodium	380 mg
Total carbohydrates	0 g
Protein	32 g

◆◆◆

RECIPE 19.24
WALNUT SOLE

Yield: 4 Servings   **Method:** Sautéing

Flour	4 oz.	120 g
Egg wash	4 oz.	120 mL
Walnuts, chopped fine	12 oz.	350 g
Sole fillets, 6 oz. (170 g) each	4	4
Whole butter	4 oz.	120 g

Approximate values per serving:

Calories	1085
Total fat	84 g
Saturated fat	22 g
Cholesterol	275 mg
Sodium	188 mg
Total carbohydrates	39 g
Protein	52 g

1. Prepare a standard breading station with the flour, egg wash and walnuts. (See Chapter 21, Deep-Fat Frying.)
2. Bread the sole fillets, pressing the walnuts onto only one side of each fillet.
3. Sauté the fish in the butter, presentation (walnut-coated) side down. Turn and finish cooking in a 375°F (190°C) oven, approximately 5–8 minutes.
4. Serve with a citrus beurre blanc.

◆◆◆

RECIPE 19.25
PAUPIETTES OF SOLE WITH MOUSSELINE OF SHRIMP

Yield: 6 Servings   **Method:** Poaching

Shrimp meat	12 oz.	360 g
Egg white	1	1
Cream, 35%	6 oz.	180 mL
Salt and white pepper	TT	TT
Lemon sole fillets,		
skinless, 4 oz. (120 g) each	12	12
Whole butter	as needed	as needed
Shallots, chopped	2 oz.	60 g
Parsley stems, chopped	6	6
White vermouth	6 oz.	180 mL
Shrimp stock	12 oz.	360 mL
Beurre manié	approx. 1-1/2 oz.	approx. 45 g

1. Purée the raw shrimp meat in a food processor.
2. Add the egg white and pulse to incorporate.
3. Slowly add 2 ounces (60 mL) of the cream to the shrimp while pulsing the processor. Season the mousseline with salt and white pepper.
4. Place the sole fillets skin side up on a cutting board and flatten lightly with a mallet.
5. Spread each fillet with a portion of the mousseline. Roll up the fillets, starting with the thickest part and finishing with the tail portion.
6. Butter a sauteuse and sprinkle with the chopped shallots and parsley stems.

Continued

7. Place the sole paupiettes in the sauteuse and add the vermouth and shrimp stock.

8. Bring the liquid to a boil, cover with a piece of buttered parchment paper and place in a 350°F (180°C) oven. Poach until nearly done.

9. Remove the sole from the sauteuse and reserve in a warm place.

10. Return the sauteuse to the heat and reduce the cuisson slightly.

11. Thicken the cuisson to the desired consistency with the beurre manié.

12. Add the remaining cream, bring the sauce to a boil and strain through a fine chinois. Adjust the seasonings.

13. Serve 2 paupiettes per portion on a pool of sauce.

1. Flatten the fillets slightly with a mallet.

2. Spread the fillets with the prepared mousseline.

3. Roll the paupiettes.

Simon Smotkowicz

Simon has been a member and a leader of award-winning Canadian culinary teams for many years, most recently managing Team Canada to a world championship in Glasgow in 1997. In 1995 he was elected Chef of the Year for the Western Region by his peers in the CFCC.

◆◆◆

RECIPE 19.26

PAN-SEARED SCALLOPS AND RAGOUT OF SUMMER VEGETABLES IN A PHYLLO FRYING PAN WITH MINTED ORANGE SAUCE

SHAW CONFERENCE CENTRE, EDMONTON, AB
Executive Chef Simon Smotkowicz

Yield: 4 Servings   **Method:** Pan-frying

Phyllo pastry	8 sheets plus 2 sheets cut in half horizontally	8 sheets plus 2 sheets cut in half horizontally
Butter, unsalted clarified	5-1/2 oz.	150 g
Fish stock	1/2 cup	110 mL
Orange juice from 3 oranges		
Lemon juice from 1/2 lemon		
Bay leaf	1	1
Mint stalks, chopped	2 Tbsp.	30 mL
Cream, 35%	1 cup	225 mL
Butter, unsalted, cold	1 oz.	25 g
Champagne vinegar	1 Tbsp.	15 mL
Salt and pepper	TT	TT

Asparagus spears	4	4
Yellow bell pepper, thinly sliced	1	1
Tomato, peeled, seeded and diced	1	1
Butter	1 tsp.	5 mL
Scallops, fresh	8 large	8 large
Olive oil	1 tsp.	5 mL
Mint leaves, julienne	1 Tbsp.	15 mL

1. To make phyllo frying pans, brush one whole phyllo sheet with butter and fold in half. Lay it in a small iron frying pan; mould it to the shape of the pan and trim off the excess. Butter a half sheet, roll it up to make a handle and lay it partly in the pan but with 3 inches (8 cm) extending up the real pan handle. To secure the handle, cover the pan area with another folded sheet. Trim this to shape and prick it all over with a fork. Brush once more with butter.

2. Bake in the iron pan for about 12 minutes, or until crisp and brown, at 375°F (190°C).

3. Repeat 3 times with remaining dough to make 4 frying pans.

4. In saucepan, mix the fish stock, fruit juices, bay leaf and mint stalks. Bring to a boil, lower heat and reduce by two-thirds. Strain, add cream and simmer for 5 minutes.

5. With a wire whip, incorporate butter in small pieces. Do not let the mixture simmer.

6. Add the champagne vinegar, then season to taste with salt and pepper and reserve.

7. Quickly blanch vegetables in boiling, salted water. Strain, add butter, season and keep warm.

8. Season scallops and sear in very hot pan in olive oil. Serve immediately in a phyllo frying pan with vegetables and orange-minted sauce. Garnish with the mint leaves.

Approximate values per serving, with vegetables and sauce:

Calories	821
Total fat	70 g
Saturated fat	41 g
Cholesterol	211 mg
Sodium	491 mg
Total carbohydrates	34 g
Protein	16 g

◆◆◆

RECIPE 19.27
PAELLA

CHEF LELAND ATKINSON, WASHINGTON, DC

Yield: 4 Servings   **Method:** Steaming

Chicken thighs	4	4
Salt and pepper	TT	TT
Olive oil	2 oz.	60 mL
Onion, medium dice	2 oz.	60 g
Garlic, chopped	1 Tbsp.	15 mL
Red bell pepper, medium dice	2 oz.	60 g
Green bell pepper, medium dice	2 oz.	60 g
Rice, long grain	12 oz.	350 g
Saffron	pinch	pinch
Chicken stock, well seasoned, hot	26 oz.	750 mL
Chorizo, cooked, sliced	4 oz.	120 g
Clams, scrubbed	12	12

Continued

Cockles, scrubbed	12	12
Shrimp, 16–20 count	12	12
Lobster, cut up	1	1
Mussels, debearded and scrubbed	12	12

1. Season the chicken with salt and pepper. Pan-fry it in the olive oil, browning it well. Cook until done, approximately 20 minutes. Remove the chicken and reserve.

2. Add the onions, garlic and peppers to the pan and sauté until tender.

3. Add the rice and sauté until it turns translucent.

4. Add the saffron to the chicken stock. Stir the chicken stock into the rice and bring to a boil.

5. Add the sliced chorizo, clams and cockles to the pan. Cover and place in a 375°F (190°C) oven for 20 minutes.

6. Add the raw shrimp and lobster, and the cooked chicken to the pan. Cover and cook for an additional 15 minutes.

7. Add the mussels to the pan and cook until the shrimp and lobster are done, the chicken is hot and all the shellfish are opened, approximately 5 minutes.

Approximate values per serving:

Calories	930
Total fat	41 g
Saturated fat	10 g
Cholesterol	650 mg
Sodium	2050 mg
Total carbohydrates	31 g
Protein	110 g
Vitamin A	25%
Vitamin C	60%
Iron	70%

◆◆◆

RECIPE 19.28

CLAMS CASINO

Yield: 36 clams   **Method:** Baking

Bacon, diced	4 slices	4 slices
Onion, minced	1 oz.	30 g
Red bell pepper, minced	1 oz.	30 g
Green bell pepper, minced	1 oz.	30 g
Whole butter	6 oz.	180 g
Lemon juice	1 Tbsp.	15 mL
Worcestershire sauce	2 tsp.	10 mL
Tabasco sauce	TT	TT
Clams, scrubbed	36	36
Fresh bread crumbs	2 oz.	60 g

1. Fry the bacon until well done. Drain the fat, reserving 2 tablespoons (30 mL).

2. Sauté the onions and peppers in the bacon fat until tender; remove from the heat and cool.

3. Combine 4 ounces (120 g) of the butter, the lemon juice, Worcestershire sauce, Tabasco sauce, bacon pieces and sautéed vegetables and chill.

4. Open the clams, leaving the meat in the bottom shell. Top each clam with 1 teaspoon (5 mL) of the vegetable-butter-bacon mixture.

5. Melt 2 ounces (60 g) of butter in a sauté pan and toss the bread crumbs in the butter. Top each clam with a portion of the bread crumbs.

6. Bake at 400°F (200°C) until light brown and bubbling, approximately 10 minutes. Serve immediately.

Approximate values per clam:

Calories	45
Total fat	4 g
Saturated fat	2.5 g
Cholesterol	10 mg
Sodium	65 mg
Total carbohydrates	1 g
Protein	0 g

♦♦♦

RECIPE 19.29

OYSTERS ROCKEFELLER

Yield: 1 Serving   **Method**: Poaching

Oysters	6	6
White wine	1 oz.	30 mL
Garlic, finely chopped	1 Tbsp.	15 g
Onion, finely chopped	1 Tbsp.	15 g
Butter	2 tsp.	10 g
Spinach, blanched	4 oz.	90 g
Nutmeg, salt, ground white pepper	TT	TT
Pernod	2 tsp.	10 mL
Rock salt	4 oz.	100 g
Cream, 35%	1 oz.	20 mL
Bread crumbs	1 Tbsp.	4 g
Parmesan cheese	1 Tbsp.	5 g
Mornay sauce (p. 205)	4 oz.	100 mL

1. Shuck the oysters; poach the shucked oysters in their own juices with the white wine.
2. Sauté the garlic and onion in butter, add the spinach, season with salt, pepper, nutmeg and flavour with the Pernod.
3. Heat the cleaned shell bottoms on rock salt for half a minute under a broiler or for 1 minute in a hot oven.
4. Stuff the shells with the spinach, and top each shell with a poached oyster. Keep them hot.
5. Add the cream to the poaching liquid and reduce by half. Add the mornay sauce to heat up.
6. Top the oyster and spinach with mornay sauce. Sprinkle with a mixture of bread crumbs and Parmesan cheese and gratinée or brown in the oven.

Approximate values per serving:

Calories	574
Total fat	39 g
Saturated fat	24 g
Cholesterol	151 mg
Sodium	406 mg
Total carbohydrates	31 g
Protein	18 g

♦♦♦

RECIPE 19.30

PAUPIETTES OF ARCTIC CHAR WITH WHITE WINE SABAYON

WESTIN PRINCE HOTEL, TORONTO, ON
Executive Chef Hans U. Herzig

Yield: 10 Servings   **Method**: Baking

Fillets of Arctic char, 2.5–2.8 oz. (70–80 g)	20	20
Salt and pepper	TT	TT
Bok choy, greens only, blanched	2 large heads	2 large heads
Butter	3-1/2 oz.	100 g
Shallots, finely diced	2	2

Continued

Hans U. Herzig

Hans was born in Switzerland and trained in Europe; he came to Canada to work at the Windsor Arms in Toronto. Among the highlights of his career, he was captain of the Canadian team that won 10 gold medals at the 1988 World Culinary Olympics.

White wine	10 oz.	300 mL
Fish stock	18 oz.	500 mL
Roma tomatoes, medium, peeled and cored	10	10
Asparagus spears, peeled and blanched, approximately 3 in. (7–8 cm) long	70	70
Yukon Gold potatoes, 1/4-in. (5-mm) thick slices, blanched	70	70
Egg yolks	5	5

1. Lay out the fish filets, season lightly and top with the bok choy greens that have been cut into size of filets.

2. Roll filets with greens on the inside and fasten with skewers.

3. Butter the baking dish, add paupiettes, sprinkle with shallots, 6 ounces (200 mL) of the wine and 16 ounces (450 mL) of the fish stock and season. Cover with buttered parchment paper and bake at 375°F (190°C) for 10–12 minutes, until firm.

4. Cut tomatoes into large square filets, season lightly and sauté. Simmer asparagus and sliced potatoes in water or stock until heated through.

5. To make the sabayon, put the egg yolks into a stainless steel bowl. Add 4 ounces (100 mL) of the wine, the remaining fish stock and a pinch of salt and pepper. Whisk vigorously over simmering water until thick.

6. Arrange 2 paupiettes on a plate and place the sliced potatoes around them. Coat the paupiettes with sabayon and garnish with tomato and the asparagus spears.

Approximate values per serving, with sabayon:

Calories	426
Total fat	23 g
Saturated fat	7 g
Cholesterol	216 mg
Sodium	492 mg
Total carbohydrates	16 g
Protein	35 g

◆◆◆

RECIPE 19.31

STEAMED SCALLOPS WITH GINGER, BASIL AND ORANGE

VINCENT ON CAMELBACK, PHOENIX, AZ
Chef Vincent Guerithault

Yield: 1 Serving   **Method:** Steaming

Oranges	2	2
Lime	1	1
Flour tortilla, 8 in. (20 cm)	1	1
Scallops, large	3	3
Ginger, grated	1 tsp.	5 mL
Carrot, julienne	2 oz.	60 g
Celery, julienne	1 oz.	30 g
Tomato, small dice	2 Tbsp.	30 mL
Fresh basil, chopped	1 Tbsp.	15 mL
Olive oil	1 Tbsp.	15 mL
Salt and pepper	TT	TT
White wine	8 oz.	250 mL
Shallot, chopped	1 tsp.	5 mL

1. Zest the oranges and then cut them in 1/2-inch (1.2-cm) slices. Peel the lime and cut into 1/4-inch (5-mm) slices.

2. Line a small bamboo steamer with the flour tortilla.

3. Place the scallops on top of the tortilla. Add the orange zest, ginger, carrot, celery, tomato, basil, olive oil, 2 slices of lime and a dash of salt and pepper. Cover.

4. Place the white wine, chopped shallots, orange slices and remaining lime slices in the bottom of the steamer pan. Steam the scallops over the seasoned wine until done, approximately 5 minutes.

Approximate values per serving:

Calories	540
Total fat	18 g
Saturated fat	2.5 g
Cholesterol	34 mg
Sodium	1660 mg
Total carbohydrates	67 g
Protein	27 g
Vitamin A	120%
Vitamin C	270%
Iron	40%

◆◆◆

RECIPE 19.32

SCALLOPS AND SHRIMP SAMBUCA

Yield: 1 9-oz. (270-g) Serving   **Method:** Sautéing

Fennel, julienne	1 oz.	30 g
Carrot, julienne	1 oz.	30 g
Celery, julienne	1 oz.	30 g
Shrimp, 8–10 count, butterflied	3	3
Whole butter	1 Tbsp.	15 mL
Bay scallops	3 oz.	90 g
Salt and white pepper	TT	TT
Sambuca	1 oz.	30 mL
Cream, 35%	3 oz.	90 mL
Puff pastry fleurons	2	2
Fresh dill	1 sprig	1 sprig

1. Blanch the fennel, carrots and celery. Refresh in cold water, drain and reserve.

2. Sauté the shrimp in the butter over high heat for 1 minute. Add the scallops and sauté for 30 more seconds. Season the shellfish with salt and pepper, remove and reserve in a warm place.

3. Deglaze the pan with sambuca. Add the cream. Boil and reduce until the sauce thickens. Add the vegetables, scallops and shrimp to the pan and simmer until the shellfish are done, approximately 2 minutes. Adjust the seasonings.

4. Serve the vegetables and shellfish mounded on a warm plate, garnished with the fleurons and dill.

Approximate values per 9 oz. (270 g) serving:

Calories	1350
Total fat	58 g
Saturated fat	31 g
Cholesterol	695 mg
Sodium	3370 mg
Total carbohydrates	117 g
Protein	90 g
Vitamin A	120%
Calcium	70%
Iron	140%

◆◆◆

RECIPE 19.33

SHRIMP POACHED IN ORANGE JUICE, GINGER AND SAUTERNE

From Allen Susser's New World Cuisine and Cookery,
by Allen Susser, North Miami Beach, FL

Yield: 4 Servings   **Method:** Poaching

Jumbo shrimp, raw	16	16
Orange juice, fresh squeezed	1 pt.	500 mL

Continued

Ginger root, julienne	2 Tbsp.	30 mL
Sauterne	4 oz.	120 mL
Shallots, julienne	1 pt.	500 mL
Carrots, julienne	1 pt.	500 mL
Kosher salt	1 tsp.	5 mL
Black pepper	1 tsp.	5 mL

Approximate values per serving:

Calories	410
Total fat	4 g
Saturated fat	1 g
Cholesterol	665 mg
Sodium	1360 mg
Total carbohydrates	21 g
Protein	73 g
Vitamin A	190%
Vitamin C	130%
Iron	60%

1. Peel, clean and butterfly the shrimp.
2. Place all of the ingredients in a low-sided pan with a lid and slowly warm over low heat to just about a simmer. Cover the pan and poach the shrimp for 3–4 minutes. The shrimp should be rosy pink and firm to the touch.
3. Remove from the heat and serve the shrimp with the vegetables and broth.

◆◆◆

RECIPE 19.34

SHELLFISH BOUILLABAISSE WITH GINGER AIOLI

SHAW CONFERENCE CENTRE, EDMONTON, AB
Executive Chef Simon Smotkowicz

Yield: Serves 4   **Method:** Sautée

Butter, unsalted	4 Tbsp.	60 g
Carrots, medium, peeled and diced	1	1
Celery, stalks, peeled and diced	2	2
Fennel bulb, cored and diced	1	1
Onion, medium, peeled and diced	1	1
Ginger root, peeled and minced	1/4 cup	50 mL
Clams	12	12
Mussels, cleaned and debearded	12	12
Fish stock	6 oz.	175 mL
Butter, unsalted	4 Tbsp.	60 g
Salt and pepper	TT	TT
Prawns, shelled	8	8
Lobsters, split lengthwise	2	2
Salt and pepper	TT	TT
Scallops	8	8
White wine	4 oz.	120 mL
Ground ginger	3 tsp.	15 mL
Vegetable Broth (recipe follows)	40 oz.	1.25 L
Saffron	pinch	pinch
Butter, unsalted, room temperature	3 Tbsp.	40 g
Salt and pepper	TT	TT
Ginger Aïoli (recipe follows)		

1. In a large saucepan, heat the butter over medium-high heat, add the vegetables and ginger and sauté until softened.
2. Remove from the pan and set aside. Add the clams, mussels and stock,

cover the pan and simmer until the shellfish are just opened. Remove the shellfish from the pan and set aside.

3. In the same pan, heat the butter. Season the prawns and lobsters and place in the pan. Sauté until pink, remove from the pan and set aside. Season the scallops, add to the pan and sauté until golden brown. Remove from the pan and set aside.

4. In the same pan, combine the wine, ginger, Vegetable Broth and saffron and reduce by half. Whisk in the butter and season. Remove from the heat and keep warm.

5. To serve, arrange the vegetables and shellfish in individual bowls, pour the reduced and seasoned broth on top, and spoon the Ginger Aïoli over the bouillabaisse as desired.

Approximate values per 19 oz. (570 g) serving:		
Calories	962	
Total fat	74 g	
Saturated fat	26 g	
Cholesterol	263 mg	
Sodium	1824 mg	
Total carbohydrates	18 g	
Protein	40 g	

VEGETABLE BROTH

Yield: 40 oz. (1.25 L)

White wine	8 oz.	225 mL
Carrots, medium, peeled and chopped	1	1
Onion, medium, peeled and chopped	1	1
Celery stalk, chopped	1	1
Tomato, medium, peeled and chopped	1	1
Ginger root, peeled and chopped	3 Tbsp.	40 mL
Water	64 oz.	1.8 L
Saffron	pinch	pinch
Bouquet garni (celery, bay leaf, thyme and cloves)	1	1

1. Put the wine in a large saucepan, add the vegetables, ginger, water, saffron and bouquet garni and bring to a boil.

2. Reduce the heat and simmer for 20 minutes or until reduced by approximately one-third. Remove from the heat, strain and reserve.

Approximate values per 19 oz. (570 g) serving:		
Calories	38	
Total fat	0 g	
Saturated fat	0 g	
Cholesterol	0 mg	
Sodium	16 mg	
Total carbohydrates	.5 g	
Protein	.1 g	

GINGER AIOLI

Yield: 6 oz. (180 mL)

Ginger root, peeled and chopped	2 tsp.	10 mL
Garlic clove	1	1
White wine	2 Tbsp.	30 mL
Saffron	pinch	pinch
Egg yolk, small	1	1
Olive oil	6 oz.	170 mL
Salt and pepper	TT	TT

1. In a small sauté pan, combine the ginger, garlic, wine and saffron. Bring the mixture to a boil, and reduce until nearly all of the liquid has evaporated.

2. Remove the reduction to the bowl of a food processor fitted with a metal blade and purée the mixture. While processing, incorporate the egg yolk and add the oil in a steady stream until the mixture is emulsified.

3. Season, remove to another bowl and set aside in the refrigerator.

Approximate values per 1 oz. (30 g) serving:		
Calories	215	
Total fat	24 g	
Saturated fat	3 g	
Cholesterol	32 mg	
Sodium	175 mg	
Total carbohydrates	.5 g	
Protein	.5 g	

◆◆◆

RECIPE 19.35

THAI CRAB CAKE

FLYING FISH, SEATTLE, WA
Chef-Owner Christine Keff

Yield: 4 Servings   **Method:** Sautéing

Crab meat	2 cups	400 g
Panko (Japanese bread crumbs)	2 cups	500 mL
Lemon Grass Mayonnaise (recipe follows)	1 cup	250 mL
Green onions, chopped fine	4	4
Basil, chopped fine	2 Tbsp.	30 mL
Cilantro, chopped fine	2 Tbsp.	30 mL
Mint, chopped fine	2 Tbsp.	30 mL
Fish sauce	TT	TT
Vegetable or canola oil	as needed for sautéing	
Mixed baby greens	as needed for garnish	
Orange supremes	as needed for garnish	
Lemon Grass Mayonnaise	as needed for garnish	

Approximate values per 6 oz. (180 g) serving:

Calories	544
Total fat	31 g
Saturated fat	6 g
Cholesterol	124 mg
Sodium	1006 mg
Total carbohydrates	45 g
Protein	21 g

1. Gently stir together the crab meat, panko, Lemon Grass Mayonnaise, green onions, herbs and fish sauce. Divide into 4 portions and form into cakes.

2. In a skillet, sauté each cake for 3 minutes on each side over medium heat, until golden brown.

3. Serve on a plate garnished with baby greens, orange supremes and additional Lemon Grass Mayonnaise.

LEMON GRASS MAYONNAISE

Yield: 1 pt. (450 mL)

Egg yolks	2	2
Rice wine vinegar	1-1/2 Tbsp.	25 mL
Mirin	1 Tbsp.	15 mL
Soy sauce	1 tsp.	5 mL
Fish sauce	1 tsp.	5 mL
Lemon Grass Oil (recipe follows)	1-1/4 cup	300 mL

Approximate values per 1 oz. (30 mL) serving:

Calories	146
Total fat	15 g
Saturated fat	3 g
Cholesterol	33 mg
Sodium	113 mg
Total carbohydrates	2 g
Protein	1 g

1. Place all of the ingredients except the Lemon Grass Oil into a food processor or blender and process for 30 seconds or until well blended.

2. With the processor running, drizzle in the oil to form an emulsion.

LEMON GRASS OIL

Yield: 10 oz. (300 mL)

Fresh ginger root, sliced thin	1/4 cup	60 mL
Lemon grass, chopped	1/4 cup	60 ml
Peanut oil	10 oz.	300 mL

Approximate values per 1 oz. (30 mL) serving:

Calories	186
Total fat	21 g
Saturated fat	4 g
Cholesterol	0 mg
Sodium	0 mg
Total carbohydrates	1 g
Protein	0 g

1. Place all of the ingredients in a small saucepan and bring to a simmer over low heat. Simmer for 5 minutes.

2. Remove from the heat and allow the flavoured oil to stand overnight at room temperature. Strain before using.

❖❖❖

RECIPE 19.36
Skillet of Lobster and Mushrooms Provençale

RIVERIA RESTAURANT, Atlanta, GA
Chef Jack Shoop

Yield: 4 Servings **Method:** Sautéeing

Olive oil	2 Tbsp.	30 mL
Shallots, minced	1 Tbsp.	15 mL
Chanterelle mushrooms, sliced	4 oz.	120 g
Shiitake mushrooms, sliced	4 oz.	120 g
Oyster mushrooms, sliced	4 oz.	120 g
Garlic, minced	1 clove	1 clove
Tomato concassé	8 oz.	250 g
Atlantic lobster tail meat, large dice	12 oz.	360 g
White wine, dry	2 Tbsp.	30 mL
Chervil, chopped	2 Tbsp.	30 mL
Tarragon, chopped	2 Tbsp.	30 mL
Sea salt	TT	TT
Pepper	TT	TT

1. Heat the olive oil in a large sauté pan; add the shallots and cook for 1 minute.
2. Add the mushrooms and sauté until tender, approximately 5 minutes.
3. Add the garlic and tomatoes and sauté for 2 minutes.
4. Add the lobster and white wine and cook for 2 to 3 minutes, or until the lobster is cooked.
5. Add the herbs and season to taste with salt and pepper.
6. Spoon the mushrooms and lobster into individual serving-size copper skillets and serve immediately.

Approximate values per 6 oz. (180 g) serving:

Calories	270
Total fat	16 g
Saturated fat	6 g
Cholesterol	130 mg
Sodium	200 mg
Total carbohydrates	13 g
Protein	18 g
Vitamin A	20%
Iron	15%

❖❖❖

RECIPE 19.37
Crayfish Etouffée

Yield: 4 Servings **Method:** Simmering

Corn oil	4 oz.	120 mL
Flour	4 oz.	120 g
Onion, chopped fine	1 large	1 large
Celery stalk, chopped fine	1	1
Green bell pepper, chopped	1/2	1/2
Garlic cloves, minced	3	3
Shrimp broth or clam juice	1-1/4 pt.	600 mL
Lemon juice	1 Tbsp.	15 mL
Crayfish fat (optional)	2 oz.	60 g

Continued

Salt	1 tsp.	5 mL
Cayenne	1/2 tsp.	3 mL
Black pepper	1/2 tsp.	3 mL
Dried thyme	1/2 tsp.	3 mL
Bay leaf	1	1
Louisiana hot sauce	1 Tbsp.	15 mL
Crayfish tails	1 lb.	450 g
Green onions, sliced	2	2
White rice, cooked	1 qt.	1 L

Approximate values per serving:

Calories	880
Total fat	32 g
Saturated fat	4 g
Cholesterol	130 mg
Sodium	1190 mg
Total carbohydrates	107 g
Protein	40 g
Vitamin A	300%
Vitamin C	480%
Calcium	45%
Iron	90%

1. Heat the oil in a large sauté pan. Whisk in the flour and cook, stirring constantly, to make a medium-dark roux.
2. Add the onion, celery, green bell pepper and garlic and sauté over medium low heat until the vegetables are tender, approximately 10 minutes.
3. Slowly add the shrimp broth or clam juice and bring to a boil. Reduce the heat to a simmer and add the lemon juice, crayfish fat and the spices. Simmer for 15 minutes to thicken.
4. Add the hot sauce and the crayfish tails and simmer for approximately 10 minutes. Add the green onions and adjust the seasonings. Serve over cooked rice.

◆◆◆

RECIPE 19.38

SHRIMP WITH OLIVE OIL AND GARLIC

Yield: 8 Servings   **Method:** Sautéing

Garlic, chopped	4 Tbsp.	60 mL
Extra virgin olive oil	4 oz.	120 mL
Shrimp, 26–30 count, in shell	2 lb. 8 oz.	1 kg
Coarse sea salt	1 Tbsp.	15 mL
Lemon juice	2 Tbsp.	30 mL

Approximate values per 5 oz. (150 g) serving:

Calories	252
Total fat	15 g
Saturated fat	2 g
Cholesterol	244 mg
Sodium	821 mg
Total carbohydrates	2 g
Protein	26 g

1. Sauté the garlic in the olive oil until translucent.
2. Add the shrimp and salt. Toss to coat the shrimp with the oil and cook just until the shrimp are pink, approximately 5 minutes. Add the lemon juice.
3. Arrange the shrimp on warm serving plates; top with the oil, garlic and lemon juice left in the pan. Serve immediately.

◆◆◆

RECIPE 19.39

SEVICHE

In a seviche, the fish and shellfish are "cooked" by the acids in the citrus juice. While a variety of fish or shellfish may be used, it is extremely important that the products be absolutely fresh. Use a nonreactive container such as stainless steel or plastic for mixing or storing the seviche. Aluminum and other metals may react with the acids in the lime juice, giving the food a metallic flavour.

Yield: 3 lb. (1.4 kg)

Raw scallops or shrimp	1 lb.	450 g
Raw firm white fish	1 lb.	450 g
Fresh lime juice	8 oz.	240 mL
Serrano pepper, minced	4	4
Red onion, fine dice	6 oz.	170 g
Fresh cilantro, minced	4 Tbsp.	60 mL
Olive oil	2 Tbsp.	30 mL
Tomato, peeled, seeded, diced	8 oz.	250 g
Garlic, chopped	2 tsp.	10 mL
Salt and pepper	TT	TT

Approximate values per 4 oz. (120 g) serving:

Calories	120
Total fat	4.5 g
Saturated fat	.5 g
Cholesterol	30 mg
Sodium	250 mg
Total carbohydrates	5 g
Protein	13 g
Vitamin A	10%
Vitamin C	20%
Claims—low saturated fat	

1. Chop the scallops or shrimp and fish coarsely but evenly. Place in a nonreactive container and add the lime juice. Cover and marinate in the refrigerator for 4 hours. The fish should turn opaque and become firm.

2. Toss in the remaining ingredients and season to taste with salt and pepper. Chill thoroughly and serve as a salad or with tortilla chips.

3. If the seviche is going to be held for more than 2 hours, drain the liquid and refrigerate separately. The reserved liquid can then be tossed with the other ingredients at service time.

WEBLINKS

Preparation of Fish
   www.cyberus.ca/~lapointefish/prepaton.html

Seafood Facts Sheet
   www.fl-seafood.com/Promo_Marketing/factshts.html

Catering UK: Seafood
   www.catering-uk.co.uk/catering-uk/features/jul-feature.html

Lobster Direct (Nova Scotia)
   www.novaweb.ca/lobster/index.html

British Columbia Salmon Marketing Council
   bcsalmon.ca

After studying this chapter you will be able to:

◆ prepare a variety of forcemeats: country-style, basic, mousseline, quenelles
◆ assemble and cook a variety of pâtés, terrines and sausages: prepare a terrine, an aspic-jelly-coated chilled mousse, assemble and bake pâtés en croûte, glaze pâté slices with aspic jelly, prepare a poultry galantine, make sausages
◆ explain the proper methods for brining, curing and smoking meats and fish
◆ identify several cured pork products

*T*raditionally, charcuterie was limited to the production of pork-based pâtés, terrines and galantines. Over the years, however, it has come to include similar products made with game, poultry, fish, shellfish and even vegetables. Many of these are discussed here.

Charcuterie is an art and science in itself. This chapter is not intended to be a complete guide to the charcutier's art. Instead, we focus on procedures for making common charcuterie items that can be prepared easily in most kitchens. We also discuss the preparation of sausages as well as curing methods, including salt curing, brining, and both cold and hot smoking. The chapter ends with information about several cured pork products.

FORCEMEATS AND THEIR USES

A **forcemeat** is a preparation made from uncooked ground meats, poultry, fish or shellfish, seasoned, then emulsified with fat. Forcemeats are the primary ingredient used to make pâtés, terrines, galantines and sausages.

The word *forcemeat* is derived from the French word *farce*, meaning stuffing. Depending on the preparation method, a forcemeat can be very smooth and velvety, well-textured and coarse, or anything in between. Regardless of its intended use, it has a glossy appearance when raw and will slice cleanly when cooked. A properly emulsified forcemeat provides a rich taste and a comforting texture on the palate.

Forcemeats are emulsified products. Emulsification is the process of binding two ingredients that ordinarily would not combine. (Emulsified sauces are discussed in Chapter 10, Stocks and Sauces; emulsified salad dressings are discussed in Chapter 24, Salads and Salad Dressings.) The proteins present in the meat, poultry, fish and shellfish combine easily with both fat and liquids. In forcemeats, these proteins act as a stabilizer that allows the fat and liquids, which ordinarily would not combine, to bind. When improperly emulsified forcemeats are cooked, they lose their fat, shrink and become dry and grainy. To ensure proper emulsification of a forcemeat:

1. the ratio of fat to other ingredients must be precise,
2. temperatures must be maintained below 40°F (4°C), and
3. the ingredients must be mixed properly.

Forcemeat Ingredients

Forcemeats are usually meat, poultry, fish or shellfish combined with binders, seasonings and sometimes garnishes. Selections from each of these basic categories are used to make an array of forcemeats. All ingredients must be of the finest quality and added in just the right proportions.

Meats

The **dominant meat** is the meat that gives the forcemeat its name and essential flavour. The dominant meat does not have to be beef, veal, lamb, pork or game. It can be poultry, fish or shellfish. When preparing meats, poultry or fish for forcemeat, it is important to trim all silverskin, gristle and small bones so that the meat will be more easily ground and will produce a smoother finished product.

Many forcemeats contain some pork. Pork adds moisture and smoothness to the forcemeat. Without it, poultry-based forcemeats tend to be rubbery, while venison and other game-based forcemeats tend to be dry. The traditional ratio is one part pork to two parts dominant meat.

Many forcemeats also contain some liver. Pork liver is commonly used, as is chicken liver. Liver contributes flavour as well as binding to the forcemeat. For a finer texture, grind the livers and then force them through a drum sieve before incorporating them into the forcemeat.

Fats

Here, **fat** refers to a separate ingredient, not the fat in the dominant meat or pork, both of which should be quite lean in order to ensure the correct ratio of fat to meat. Usually pork backfat or heavy cream is used to add moisture and richness to the forcemeat. Because fat carries flavour, it also promotes the proper infusion of flavours and smoke.

Binders

There are two principal types of binders: panadas and eggs.

A **panada** is something other than fat that is added to a forcemeat to enhance smoothness (especially in fish mousselines, which tend to be slightly grainy in texture), to aid emulsification (especially in vegetable terrines, where the protein levels are insufficient to bind on their own) or both (for example, in liver mousses). It should not make up more than 20% of the forcemeat's total weight. Usually a panada is nothing more than crustless white bread soaked in milk or, more traditionally, a heavy béchamel or rice.

Eggs or egg whites are used as a binding agent in some styles of forcemeat. If used in forcemeats that have a large ratio of liver or liquids, they also add texture. The proteins in the meat, fish or poultry are the primary binder.

Seasonings

Forcemeats are seasoned with salt, curing salt, marinades and various herbs and spices.

Salt not only adds flavour to a forcemeat but also aids in the emulsification of the meat and fat. As with other foods, a forcemeat that lacks salt will taste flat.

Curing salt is a mixture of salt and sodium nitrite. Sodium nitrite controls spoilage by inhibiting bacterial growth. Equally important, curing salt preserves the rosy pink colours of some forcemeats that might otherwise oxidize to an unappetizing grey. Although currently regarded as substantially safer than the previously used potassium nitrate (saltpetre), some studies suggest that sodium nitrite is a carcinogen. For a typical consumer, however, the amount of sodium nitrite consumed from cured meats should not pose a substantial health threat.

Traditionally, ingredients for forcemeats were marinated for long periods of time, sometimes days, before grinding. The trend today is for shorter marinating times so that the true flavours of the main ingredients shine through. Both classic and contemporary marinades include herbs, citrus zest, spices and liquors, all of which lend flavour, character and nuance to the forcemeat.

Pâté spice is a mixture of several spices and herbs that can be premixed and used as needed.

◆◆◆

RECIPE 20.1

PÂTÉ SPICE

Yield: 7-2/3 oz. (220 g)

Cloves	1 oz.	30 g
Dried ginger	1 oz.	30 g
Nutmeg	1 oz.	30 g
Paprika	1 oz.	30 g
Dried basil	2/3 oz.	20 g
Black pepper	2/3 oz.	20 g
White pepper	2/3 oz.	20 g
Bay leaf	1/3 oz.	10 g
Dried thyme	1 oz.	30 g
Dried marjoram	1/3 oz.	10 g

Grind all ingredients in a spice grinder. Pass through a sieve to remove any large pieces.

NOTE: Either use this mixture as is, or mix 1 ounce (30 g) (or any amount desired) with 1 pound (450 g) of salt. The salt and spice mixture can then be used to season forcemeats; 1/3 ounce (10 g) per pound (450 g) of forcemeat usually suffices for most pâtés.

Approximate values per 1 oz. (30 g) serving:

Calories	20
Total fat	1 g
Saturated fat	0 g
Cholesterol	0 mg
Sodium	0 mg
Total carbohydrates	3 g
Protein	1 g
Vitamin A	6%

A forcemeat's seasoning and texture can be tested by cooking a small portion before the entire forcemeat is cooked. (Unlike sauces, stews and other dishes, you cannot taste and adjust a forcemeat's flavouring during the cooking process.) A small portion of a hearty forcemeat can be sautéed; a small portion of a more delicate forcemeat should be poached for 3–5 minutes. When cooked, the forcemeat should hold its shape and be slightly firm but not rubbery. If it is too firm, add a little cream.

Garnishes

Forcemeat garnishes are meats, fat, vegetables or other foods added in limited quantities to provide contrasting flavours and textures and to improve appearance. The garnishes are usually diced, chopped or more coarsely ground than the dominant meat. Common garnishes include pistachio nuts, diced backfat, truffles or truffle peelings and diced ham or tongue.

Equipment for Preparing Forcemeats

To properly prepare forcemeats you should have a food chopper or food processor and a heavy-duty drum sieve with a metal band. You will also need a standard meat grinder or meat-grinding attachment with various-size grinding plates (see Figure 20.1).

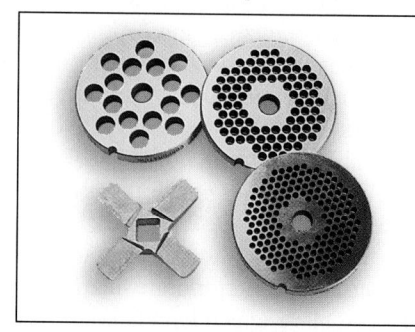

FIGURE 20.1 *A blade and assorted plates for a standard grinder.*

Preparing Forcemeats

The three common forcemeat preparations are **country-style**, **basic** and **mousseline**. Each can be produced easily in a typical food service operation. Other types of forcemeat preparations such as the emulsified mixture used to make hot dogs and bratwurst are not commonly encountered in food service operations and are not discussed here.

When preparing any forcemeat certain guidelines must be followed:

1. Forcemeat preparations include raw meats, liver, eggs and dairy products. If improperly handled, these potentially hazardous foods create a good environment for the growth of microorganisms. To avoid the risk of food-borne illness, temperatures must be carefully controlled and all cutting boards and food contact surfaces must be as sanitary as possible at all times.

2. To ensure a proper emulsification, the forcemeat must be kept cold—below 40°F (4°C)—at all times. Refrigerate all moist ingredients and keep forcemeats in progress in an ice bath. Chilling or freezing the metal grinder and food processor parts helps keep the ingredients as cold as possible.

3. Cut all foods into convenient sizes that fit easily into grinder openings. Do not overstuff grinders or overfill food processors. When grinding items twice, always begin with a larger plate, followed by a medium or small plate. For exceptional smoothness, press the forcemeat through a sieve after grinding to remove any lumps or pieces of membrane.

Country-Style Forcemeats

A traditional country-style forcemeat is heavily seasoned with onions, garlic, pepper, juniper berries and bay leaves. It is the simplest of the forcemeats to prepare and yields the heartiest and most distinctive pâtés and sausages.

The dominant meat for a country-style forcemeat is usually ground once through the grinder's large plate, then ground again through the medium plate. This produces the characteristic coarse texture. As with most forcemeats, the dominant meat for a country-style forcemeat is usually marinated and seasoned prior to grinding and then mixed with some liver.

BASIC PROCEDURE FOR PREPARING A COUNTRY-STYLE FORCEMEAT

1. Chill all ingredients and equipment thoroughly. Throughout preparation they should remain at temperatures below 40°F (4°C).

2. Cut all meats into an appropriate size for grinding.

3. Marinate, under refrigeration, the dominant meat and pork with the desired herbs, spices and liquors.

4. If using liver, grind it and force it through a sieve.

5. Cut the backfat into an appropriate size and freeze.

6. Prepare an ice bath for the forcemeat. Then grind the dominant meat, pork and fat as directed in the recipe, usually once through the grinder's largest plate and a second time through the medium plate.

7. If using liver, eggs, panada or garnishes, fold them in by hand with a spoon or spatula, remembering to keep the forcemeat over an ice bath at all times.

8. Cook a small portion of the forcemeat; adjust the seasonings and texture as appropriate.

9. Refrigerate the forcemeat until needed.

◆◆◆

RECIPE 20.2

COUNTRY-STYLE FORCEMEAT

Yield: 5 lb. (2.2 kg)

Lean pork, diced	2 lb.	900 g
Pâté spice	2 Tbsp.	30 mL
Salt	1 Tbsp.	15 mL
Pepper	TT	TT
Brandy	2 oz.	60 mL
Pork liver, cleaned and diced	1 lb.	450 g
Backfat, diced	1 lb.	450 g
Onion, small dice	3 oz.	90 g
Garlic, minced	1 Tbsp.	15 mL
Fresh parsley, chopped	3 Tbsp.	45 mL
Eggs	6	6

*Approximate values per
1 oz. (30 g) serving:*

Calories	90
Total fat	8 g
Saturated fat	3 g
Cholesterol	50 mg
Sodium	105 mg
Total carbohydrates	1 g
Protein	5 g
Vitamin A	30%

1. Combine the diced pork with the pâté spice, salt, pepper and brandy; marinate under refrigeration for several hours.
2. Grind the liver and force it through a drum sieve. Reserve.
3. Grind the marinated pork and backfat through the grinder's large plate.
4. Grind half the pork and backfat a second time through the medium plate along with the onions, garlic and parsley.
5. Working over an ice bath, combine the coarse and medium ground pork with the liver and eggs.
6. Cook and taste a small portion of the forcemeat and adjust the seasonings as necessary.

The forcemeat is now ready to use as desired in the preparation of pâtés, terrines, galantines and sausages.

1. Marinate the meat with herbs and spices.

2. Press the ground liver through a sieve.

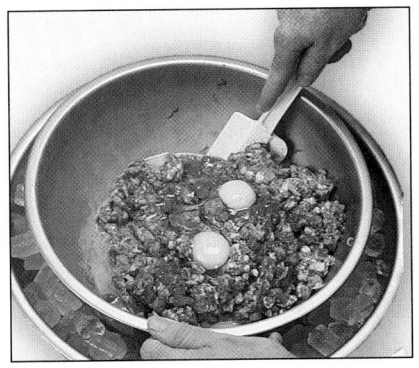

3. Grind half the meat a second time.

4. Incorporate the liver and eggs into the ground mixture over an ice bath to keep the forcemeat cold.

Basic Forcemeats

Smoother and more refined than a country-style forcemeat, a basic forcemeat is probably the most versatile of all. It should be well seasoned, but the seasonings should not mask the dominant meat's flavour. Examples of basic forcemeats are most game pâtés and terrines as well as traditional pâtés en croûte.

A basic forcemeat is made by grinding the meat and fat separately—the meat twice and the fat once. The fat is then worked into the meat, either by hand or in a food processor or chopper. A quicker method involves grinding the fat and meat together and then blending them in a food processor. Whichever method is used, some recipes call for the incorporation of crushed ice to minimize friction, reduce temperature and add moisture.

BASIC PROCEDURE FOR PREPARING A BASIC FORCEMEAT

1. Chill all ingredients and equipment thoroughly. Throughout preparation they should remain at temperatures below 40°F (4°C).

2. Cut all meats into an appropriate size for grinding.

3. Marinate, under refrigeration, the dominant meat and pork with the desired herbs, spices and liquors.

4. If using liver, grind it and force it through a sieve.

5. Cut the backfat into an appropriate size and freeze.

6. Grind the meats twice, once through the grinder's large plate and then through the medium plate; hold on an ice bath.

7. Grind the chilled or frozen fat once through the medium plate and add it to the meat mixture.

8. Work the fat into the meat over an ice bath or in a well-chilled food processor or chopping machine.

9. Over an ice bath, add any required eggs, panada and/or garnishes and work them into the mixture.

10. Cook a small portion of the forcemeat in stock or water; adjust the seasonings and texture as appropriate.

11. Refrigerate the forcemeat until needed.

An alternative method for preparing a basic forcemeat replaces steps 6 to 9 with the following procedures:

6A. Grind the meats and fats together twice.

7A. Place them in a food processor or chopper and blend until smooth.

8A. Add any required eggs or panada while the machine is running and blend them in with the meat and fat.

9A. Remove the forcemeat from the machine and, working over an ice bath, fold in any garnishes by hand.

Whichever method is used, a particularly warm kitchen or a lengthy running time in the food processor or chopping machine may necessitate the addition of small quantities of crushed ice to properly emulsify the forcemeat. Add the ice bit by bit while the machine is running.

◆◆◆

RECIPE 20.3

BASIC FORCEMEAT

Yield: 4 lb. 8 oz. (2 kg)

Veal, diced	1 lb. 8 oz.	650 g
Lean pork, diced	1 lb. 8 oz.	650 g
Brandy	2 oz.	60 mL
Pâté spice	2 tsp.	10 mL
Salt	1-1/2 tsp.	7 mL
White pepper	TT	TT
Backfat, diced	1 lb. 8 oz.	650 g
Eggs	4	4
Ham, medium dice	4 oz.	120 g
Pistachio nuts, peeled	2 oz.	60 g
Black olives, chopped coarse	2 oz.	60 g

1. Combine the veal and pork with the brandy, pâté spice, salt and white pepper; marinate under refrigeration for several hours.

2. Grind the meats through the grinder's large plate and again through the small plate.

3. Grind the backfat through the grinder's small plate.

4. Combine the meat and fat in the bowl of a food processor and blend until they are emulsified.

5. Work in the eggs until the forcemeat is smooth and well emulsified. Do not overprocess the forcemeat.

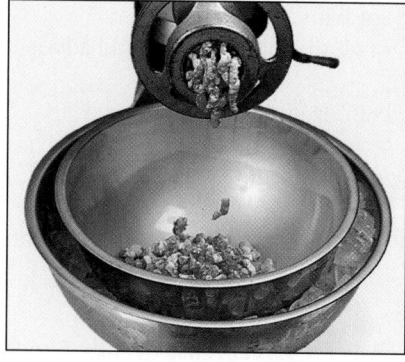

1. Grind the meat through the chilled grinder.

2. Combine the fat with the meat in the food processor.

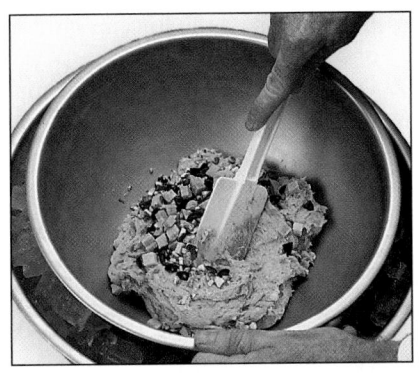

3. Add the eggs to the meat.

4. Fold the garnishes into the force-meat.

6. Fold in the ham, pistachio nuts and olives.

7. Cook a small portion of the forcemeat by poaching or sautéing it. Taste and adjust the seasonings as necessary.

The forcemeat is now ready to use as desired in the preparation of pâtés, terrines, galantines or sausages.

Approximate values per 1 oz. (30 g) serving:	
Calories	140
Total fat	12 g
Saturated fat	4.5 g
Cholesterol	45 mg
Sodium	80 mg
Total carbohydrates	1 g
Protein	7 g

Mousseline Forcemeats

A properly made mousseline forcemeat is light, airy and delicately flavoured. It is most often made with fish or shellfish but sometimes with veal, pork, feathered game or poultry. (A mousseline forcemeat is not the same as a mousse, which usually contains gelatin and is discussed on page 526.)

A mousseline forcemeat is prepared by processing ground meats and cream in a food processor; often egg whites are added to lighten and enrich the mixture. The proportion of fish to eggs to cream is very important. Too many egg whites and the mousseline will be rubbery; too few and it may not bind together. If too much cream is added, the mousseline will be too soft or will fall apart during cooking.

A mousseline forcemeat can be served hot or cold. It can be used to make fish sausages and a variety of timbales and terrines. Or it can be used to make quenelles, which are discussed on page 523. A shrimp mousseline is used with the Paupiettes of Sole, Recipe 19.25.

BASIC PROCEDURE FOR PREPARING A MOUSSELINE FORCEMEAT

1. Chill all ingredients and equipment thoroughly. Throughout preparation they should remain at temperatures below 40°F (4°C).
2. Cut all meats into an appropriate size for processing.
3. Grind the meat in a cold food processor until smooth. Do not overprocess.
4. Add eggs and pulse until just blended.
5. Add cream and seasonings in a steady stream while the machine is running. Stop the machine and scrape down the sides of the bowl once or twice during the processing. Do not run the machine any longer than necessary to achieve a smooth forcemeat.

◆◆◆ COLD, COLD, COLD

Working ground meat or fish with salt helps to extract the proteins needed for binding. The amount of heavy cream a forcemeat can hold in emulsion varies with the freshness of the meat or fish used and how cold the cream and forcemeat are. When incorporating them, do not add the cream too quickly. A temperature of 32–34°F (0–1°C) is recommended.

6. If desired, pass the forcemeat through a drum sieve to remove any sinew or bits of bone.
7. Over an ice bath, fold in any garnishes by hand.
8. Poach a small amount of the mousseline in stock or water. Taste and adjust the seasonings and texture as necessary.
9. Refrigerate until ready for use.

♦♦♦

RECIPE 20.4

MOUSSELINE FORCEMEAT

Yield: 4 lb. (1.8 kg)

Fish, scallops, skinless chicken breast or lean veal (fresh)	2 lb.	900 g
Egg whites	4	4
Salt	1 Tbsp.	15 mL
White pepper	TT	TT
Nutmeg	TT	TT
Cayenne pepper	TT	TT
Cream, 35%, very cold	up to 1 qt.	up to 1 L

1. Grind the chilled dominant meat or fish through a large plate.
2. Process the meat and salt in a food processor until smooth.
3. Add the egg whites one at a time and pulse the processor until they are incorporated.
4. Scrape down the sides of the processor's bowl and add the spices.
5. With the machine running, add the cream in a slow steady stream. Check the consistency, you may not use all the cream.
6. Scrape down the bowl again and process the mousseline until it is smooth and well mixed. Do not overprocess.
7. Remove the mousseline from the machine and hold in an ice bath. If additional smoothness is desired, force the mousseline through a drum sieve in small batches using a plastic scraper or rubber spatula.
8. Cook a small portion of the forcemeat. Taste and adjust the seasonings and texture as necessary.

The forcemeat is now ready to use as desired in the preparation of pâtés, terrines, galantines or sausages.

Approximate values per 1 oz. (30 g) serving:

Calories	80
Total fat	7 g
Saturated fat	4 g
Cholesterol	30 mg
Sodium	25 mg
Total carbohydrates	1 g
Protein	4 g
Vitamin A	8%

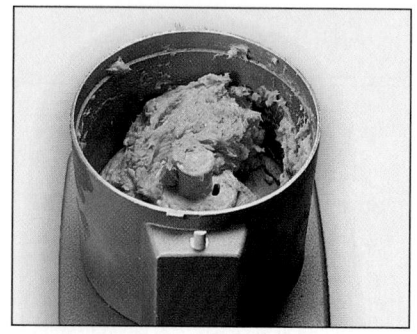

1. Process the ground meat and salt in a cold food processor just until smooth.

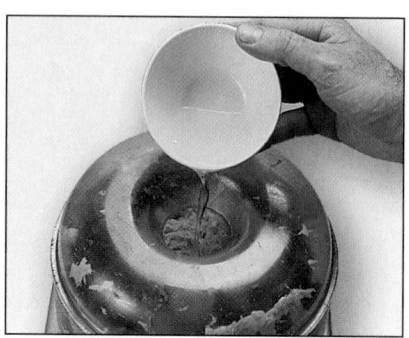

2. Add the egg whites and pulse until blended.

3. Add the cream in a steady stream while the machine runs.

4. Press the forcemeat through a drum sieve to ensure a smooth finished product.

Quenelles

Quenelles are small oblong-shaped portions of a mousseline forcemeat poached in an appropriately flavoured stock. Quenelles are a traditional garnish for many soups and a popular appetizer usually accompanied by a tomato coulis or a fish velouté-based sauce such as sauce nantua. The technique used for making and poaching quenelles is also used for testing the seasoning and consistency of a mousseline forcemeat.

BASIC PROCEDURE FOR PREPARING QUENELLES

1. Prepare a mousseline forcemeat.
2. Bring an appropriately flavoured poaching liquid to a simmer.
3. Use two spoons to form the forcemeat into oblong-shaped dumplings. For small quenelles use small spoons; for larger quenelles use larger spoons.
4. Poach the quenelles until done. Test by breaking one in half to check the centre's doneness.
5. Small soup-garnish-sized quenelles can be chilled in ice water, drained and held for service. Reheat them in a small amount of stock before garnishing the soup.

Form the quenelles using two spoons; poach gently until done.

USING FORCEMEATS

Forcemeats are used as basic components in the preparation of other foods, including terrines, pâtés, galantines and sausages. Aspic jelly is also an important component of these products.

Terrines, Pâtés and Galantines

Traditionally, a **pâté** was a fine savoury meat filling wrapped in pastry, baked and served hot or cold. A **terrine** was considered more basic, consisting of coarsely ground and highly seasoned meats baked in an earthenware mould and always served cold. (The mould is also called a terrine, derived from the French word *terre*, meaning earth.) Pâtés baked in pastry are called **pâtés en croûte**. Many types of pâté are baked in loaf-type pans, without a crust, which according to tradition would make them terrines. Today, the terms *pâté* and *terrine* are used almost interchangeably. **Galantines** are made from forcemeats of poultry, game or suckling pig wrapped in the skin of the bird or animal and poached in an appropriate stock.

◆◆◆

ASPIC JELLY

Aspic jelly is a savoury jelly produced by increasing the gelatin content of a strong stock and then clarifying the stock following the process for preparing consommé discussed in Chapter 11, Soups. Brown stock produces an amber aspic jelly; white stock produces a light aspic jelly.

Although gelatin is a natural ingredient present in all good stocks, its concentration level is not normally high enough to produce a firm aspic jelly. Additional gelatin is usually added to the stock in order to assist gelling (setting). This can be done in two ways. The first is to produce a stock with an extremely high gelatin content by using gelatinous meats and bones such as calves' feet, pigs' ears and pork skin; the second is to add plain gelatin to a finished stock. An easier method of preparing aspic jelly is to add gelatin directly to a flavourful finished consommé.

Aspic jelly has many applications throughout the kitchen. In addition to adding flavour and shine, a coating of aspic jelly prevents displayed foods from drying out and inhibits the oxidation of sliced red meats. Aspic jelly is often lightly flavoured with liquors such as madeira and cut into decorative garnishes for both plated presentations and buffet displays. It is also used to bind savoury mousses, glaze slices of pâté and coat moulded mousse. Aspic jelly is funnelled into cooked pâtés en croûte to fill the gaps created when the forcemeat shrinks during the cooking process. Aspic jelly is also the basis of aspic moulds or terrines (often simply called *aspics*), in which layers of cooked meats or vegetables are bound together and held in place by the aspic jelly. Many of these uses are discussed below.

The gelatin content of aspic jelly varies depending upon its intended use. (See Table 20.1.) Verify the bloom strength of the gelatin by testing a small batch. Aspic jelly to be used only on a display can have a very high gelatin content for easier handling. Aspic jelly to be eaten should be fairly firm when cold, gelled at room temperature but tender enough to melt quickly in the mouth when eaten. To test the gelatin content of a liquid pour a teaspoon (5 mL) onto a plate and refrigerate the plate for a few minutes. If the liquid does not gel firmly, additional gelatin can be softened in a small amount of cool liquid then added to the hot liquid.

TABLE 20.1   GELATIN CONCENTRATIONS

Type of Gel	Amount of Gelatin per U.S. Gallon (4 L) of Water	Typical Use
Soft	2 oz. (60 g)	Cubed aspic jelly for edible garnishes.
Firm	4 oz. (120 g)	Brushing slices of pâté or galantine; glazing edible centrepieces; moulding terrines, aspics and brawns that will be sliced.
Very firm	10 oz.+ (300 g+)	Nonedible purposes such as coating nonedible centrepieces or trays for presentations.

Terrines, pâtés and galantines are often made with forcemeats layered with garnishes to produce a decorative or mosaic effect when sliced. A wide variety of foods can be used as garnishes including strips of ham, backfat or tongue; mushrooms or other vegetables; truffles and pistachio nuts. Garnishes should always be cooked before they are added to the pâté, terrine or galantine or they will shrink during cooking, creating air pockets.

Pâté Pans, Moulds and Terrines

Pâté pans, moulds and terrines come in a variety of shapes and sizes. Pâtés that are not baked in a crust can be prepared in standard metal loaf pans of any shape, although rectangular ones make portioning the cooked pâté much easier. For pâté en croûte, the best pans are collapsible or hinged, thin-metal ones. They make it easier to remove the pâté after baking. Collapsible and hinged pans come in various shapes and sizes from small plain rectangles to large intricately fluted ovals. Traditional earthenware moulds and terrines as well as ones made from enamel, metal, glass or even plastic are available. Most terrines are rectangular or oval in shape. Several of these pans are illustrated in Chapter 5, Tools and Equipment.

Terrines

Terrines are forcemeats baked in a mould without a crust. The mould can be the traditional earthenware dish or some other appropriate metal, enamel or glass mould. Any type of forcemeat can be used to make a terrine. The terrine can be as simple as a baking dish filled with a forcemeat and baked until done. A more attractive terrine can be constructed by layering the forcemeat with garnishes to create a mosaic effect when sliced. A terrine can even be layered with different forcemeats; for example, a pink salmon mousseline may be layered with a white pike mousseline.

1. Line a mould with thin slices of backfat.

BASIC PROCEDURE FOR PREPARING A TERRINE

1. Prepare the desired forcemeat and garnishes and keep refrigerated until needed.
2. Line a mould with thin slices of backfat, blanched leafy vegetables or other appropriate liner. (Some chefs claim that the backfat keeps the terrine moist during cooking; most modern chefs do not agree but nevertheless use it for aesthetic purposes.) The lining should overlap slightly, completely covering the inside of the mould and extending over the edge of the mould by approximately 1 inch (2.5 cm). Alternatively, line the mould with plastic wrap.
3. Fill the terrine with the forcemeat and garnishes, being careful not to create air pockets. Tap the mould several times on a solid work surface to remove any air pockets.
4. Fold the liner or plastic wrap over the forcemeat and, if necessary, use additional pieces to completely cover its surface.
5. If desired, garnish the top of the terrine with herbs that were used in the preparation of the forcemeat.
6. Cover the terrine with its lid or aluminum foil and bake in a water bath in a 350°F (180°C) oven. Regulate the oven temperature so the water stays between 170°F and 180°F (77°C–82°C).
7. Cook the terrine to an internal temperature of 150°F (66°C) for meat-based forcemeats or 140°F (60°C) for fish- or vegetable-based forcemeats.
8. Remove the terrine from the oven and allow it to cool slightly. If desired, pour off any fat and liquid from around the terrine and cover it with cool liquid aspic jelly.

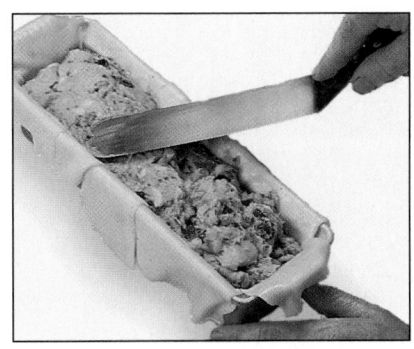

2. Fill the terrine with the forcemeat and garnish.

Several types of terrines are not made from traditional forcemeats; many others are not made from forcemeats at all. But all are nonetheless called terrines because they are moulded or cooked in the earthenware mould called a terrine. These include liver (and foie gras) terrines, vegetable terrines, brawns or aspic terrines, mousses, rillettes and confits.

Liver terrines are popular and easy to make. Puréed poultry, pork or veal livers are mixed with eggs and a panada of cream and flour, then baked in a backfat-lined terrine. Although most livers purée easily in a food processor, a smoother finished product is achieved if the livers are forced through a drum sieve after or in lieu of puréeing them in the processor.

Foie gras terrines are made with fattened geese or duck livers called foie gras. Foie gras is unique, even among other poultry livers, in that it consists almost entirely of fat. (See Chapter 17.) It requires special attention during cooking; if it is cooked improperly or too long it turns into a puddle of very expensive fat.

Vegetable terrines can be made with a relatively low fat content and are becoming increasingly popular. Beautiful vegetable terrines are made by lining

3. Decorate the top of the terrine with herbs and place the terrine in a water bath.

4. Slice the finished terrine.

a terrine with a blanched leafy vegetable such as spinach, then alternating layers of two or three separately prepared vegetable fillings to create contrasting colours and flavours. A different style of vegetable terrine is made by suspending brightly coloured vegetables in a mousseline forcemeat to create a mosaic pattern when sliced.

Brawns or **aspic terrines** are made by simmering gelatinous cuts of meat (most notably, pigs' feet and head, including the tongue) in a rich stock with wine and flavourings. The stock is enriched with gelatin and flavour from the meat, creating an unclarified aspic jelly. The meat is then pulled from the bone, diced and packed into the terrine mould. The stock is reduced to concentrate its gelatin content, strained through cheesecloth and poured over the meat in the terrine. After the terrine has set, it is removed from the mould and sliced for service. The finished product is a rustic and flavourful dish.

A more elegant-appearing brawn is made by lining a terrine mould with aspic jelly, arranging a layer of garnish (for example, sliced meats, vegetables or low-acid fruits) along the mould's bottom, adding aspic jelly to cover the garnish and repeating the procedure until the mould is full.

A **mousse** can be sweet or savoury. Sweet mousses are described in Chapter 31, Custards, Creams, Frozen Desserts and Dessert Sauces. A savoury mousse—which is not a mousseline forcemeat—is made from fully cooked meats, poultry, game, fish, shellfish or vegetables that are puréed and combined with a béchamel or other appropriate sauce, bound with gelatin and lightened with whipped cream. A mousse can be moulded in a decorated, aspic-jelly-coated mould such as that described immediately below, or it can be formed in moulds lined with plastic wrap, which is peeled off after the mousse is unmoulded. A small mousse can be served as an individual portion; a larger moulded mousse can be displayed on a buffet.

BASIC PROCEDURE FOR PREPARING AN ASPIC-JELLY-COATED CHILLED MOUSSE

A mould can be lined with aspic jelly, then decorated and filled with cold mousse. The aspic-jelly-coated mousse is then unmoulded for an attractive presentation.

1. Set a metal mould in ice water and add 8 ounces (250 mL) of cool liquid aspic jelly. Swirl the mould so the aspic jelly adheres to all sides. Pour out the excess aspic jelly. Repeat as needed to achieve the desired thickness; 1/4 inch (6 mm) or less is usually sufficient.

2. Garnish the mould by dipping pieces of vegetable or other foods in the liquid aspic jelly and placing them carefully inside the aspic-jelly-coated mould. The mould can now be filled with a cold filling such as a mousse.

3. Refrigerate the mould until it is well chilled. Unmould the aspic by dipping the mould in warm water, then inverting and tapping the mould on a plate.

Rillettes and **confits** are actually preserved meats. Rillettes are prepared by seasoning and slow-cooking pork or fatty poultry such as duck or goose in generous amounts of their own fat until the meat falls off the bone. The warm meat is mashed and combined with a portion of the cooking fat. The mixture is then packed into a crock or terrine and rendered fat is strained over the top to seal it. Rillettes are eaten cold as a spread accompanied by bread or toast.

Confit is prepared in a similar manner except before cooking the meat or poultry is often lightly salt-cured to draw out some moisture. The confit is then cooked until very tender but not falling apart. Confits are generally served hot. Like rillettes, confits can be preserved by sealing them with a layer of strained rendered fat. Properly prepared and sealed rillettes and confits will keep for several weeks under refrigeration.

Although it is sometimes incorrectly called chicken liver pâté, **chopped chicken liver** is prepared in a similar fashion to a rillette. Chopped chicken liver, however, will not have the keeping qualities of traditional rillettes or confits because it is not normally sealed in a crock or terrine with rendered fat. It should be eaten within a day or two of its preparation.

Pâté en Croûte

Considered by some to be the pinnacle of the charcutier's art, pâtés en croûte are forcemeats baked in a crust. The forcemeat can be country-style, basic or mousseline, but a basic forcemeat is most commonly used. Although pâtés en croûte can be baked without using a mould, a mould helps produce a more attractive finished product.

Pâté Dough (Pâte au Pâté)

The crust surrounding a baking forcemeat must be durable enough to hold in the juices produced as the pâté bakes and to withstand the long baking process. Unfortunately, some of the more durable crusts are tough and unpleasant to eat.

The goal is to achieve a balance so that the crust will hold the juices of the baking pâté and still be relatively pleasant to the palate. Some pâtés, especially more delicate ones such as fish mousselines, can be wrapped in brioche dough (Recipe 28.18).

♦♦♦

RECIPE 20.5

PÂTÉ DOUGH

Yield: 3 lb. 8 oz. (1.6 kg), enough for 2 or 3 pâtés

Flour, all-purpose	2 lb.	900 g
Butter, soft	10 oz.	300 g
Salt	4 tsp.	20 g
Water, lukewarm	8–10 oz.	250–300 mL
Eggs	3	3

1. Place the flour in the bowl of a mixer. Add the butter and mix on low speed until mealy.

2. Combine the salt, 8 ounces (250 mL) of water and eggs; add them to the flour and shortening mixture.

3. Knead until smooth and add more water if needed to make a pliable dough. Refrigerate. The dough will be easier to work with if allowed to rest for at least 1 hour.

Approximate values per 1 oz. (30 g) serving:

Calories	150
Total fat	9 g
Saturated fat	2 g
Cholesterol	10 mg
Sodium	100 mg
Total carbohydrates	15 g
Protein	2 g

BASIC PROCEDURE FOR ASSEMBLING AND BAKING PÂTÉ EN CROÛTE

After preparing a forcemeat and pastry dough, all that remains is to assemble and bake the pâté en croûte. The amount of pastry dough and forcemeat needed is determined by the size of the mould or pan chosen.

1. Prepare the pâté dough and the forcemeat, keeping the forcemeat refrigerated until needed.
2. Roll out the dough into a rectangular shape 1/8 inch (3 mm) thick.
3. Using the pâté mould as a pattern, determine how much dough is needed to line its inside; allow enough dough along each side of the mould's length to cover the top when folded over. Mark the dough. Cut the dough slightly larger than the marked lines. Cut a second rectangular piece of dough that is slightly larger than the top of the mould; it will be used as a lid.
4. Lightly butter the inside of the mould.
5. Lightly dust the large rectangle of dough with flour, fold it over and transfer it to the mould.
6. Use your thumbs and a dough ball made from dough trimmings to form the dough neatly into the corners of the mould. Continue until the dough is of even thickness on all sides and in the corners.
7. Trim the dough, leaving 3/4 inch (2 cm) on the ends and enough dough to cover the top along the sides.
8. Line the mould with thin slices of backfat or ham, allowing 3/4 inch (2 cm) extra around the top of the mould, or as directed in the recipe. This layer helps protect the pastry crust from coming in contact with the moist forcemeat, which would make it soggy.
9. Fill the lined mould with the forcemeat to 1/2 inch (1.2 cm) below the top of the mould, pressing it well into the corners to avoid air pockets. Layer and garnish as appropriate.
10. Fold the backfat or ham over the top of the forcemeat, using additional pieces if necessary to cover its entire surface. Fold the pastry over the forcemeat.
11. Brush the exposed surface of the pastry with egg wash; carefully cap with the top piece of dough. Press any overlapping dough down inside the sides of the mould with a small spatula.
12. Using round cutters, cut one or two holes in the top to allow steam to escape during cooking. Egg-wash the surface. Place a doughnut-shaped piece of dough around each of the holes. Egg-wash the decorations.

1. Cut the dough into a large rectangle.

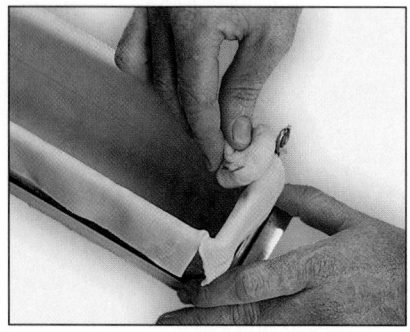

2. Press the dough into the mould with a floured dough ball and your thumbs.

3. Line the mould with thin slices of backfat.

4. Fill the lined mould with the forcemeat and garnish.

5. Use egg wash on the surface and place the top on the pâté.

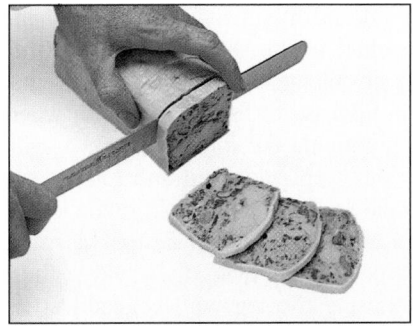

6. Insert an aluminum chimney in one of the holes of the baked pâté and pour aspic jelly into the hole.

7. Slice the pâté with a thin-bladed knife.

13. Bake the pâté in a preheated 450°F (230°C) oven for 15 minutes. Then mask the surface of the pâté with aluminum foil. Reduce the heat to 350°F (180°C) and continue baking until the internal temperature reaches 150°F (66°C) for meat pâtés or 140°F (60°C) for fish and vegetable pâtés.

14. Allow the pâté to cool for at least 1 hour or overnight. Using a funnel, pour cool liquid aspic jelly through the holes to fill the space created when the pâté shrank during cooling. Allow the pâté en croûte to chill overnight before slicing.

BASIC PROCEDURE FOR GLAZING PÂTÉ SLICES WITH ASPIC JELLY

Slices of chilled terrines, pâtés en croûte or galantines (discussed below) may be garnished and coated with aspic to preserve their colour, prevent drying and create a more attractive presentation.

1. Stir slowly to cool the clarified aspic jelly.

2. Brush or spoon the aspic jelly over slices of chilled pâté arranged on a cooling rack. Repeat the process until the coating reaches the desired thickness.

Galantines

A classic **galantine** is a boned chicken stuffed with a chicken-based forcemeat to resemble its original shape and then poached. Today, galantines are still most often prepared from whole ducks or chickens, but they can also be made from game, veal, fish or shellfish. When appropriate, the forcemeat is stuffed in the skin, which has been removed in one piece, sometimes with flesh still attached. When the skin is not available or its use is inappropriate or in the case of fish and shellfish where there is no skin, the galantine is made by forming the forcemeat into a cylindrical shape and wrapping it in cheese-cloth or plastic wrap and foil before poaching. Galantines are always served cold and are often displayed on buffets, sliced and glazed with aspic jelly.

A **ballotine** is similar to a galantine. It is made by removing the bones from a poultry leg, filling the cavity with an appropriate forcemeat and poaching or braising the leg with vegetables (it can also be made with fish or game). Ballotines are often served hot with a sauce made from the cooking liquid.

BASIC PROCEDURE FOR PREPARING A POULTRY GALANTINE

1. Bone the chicken by cutting through the skin along the length of the back-bone and then following the natural curvature of the carcass. Keep all the meat attached to the skin. Remove the legs and wings by cutting through the joints when you reach them; leave the legs and wings attached to the skin. Then cut off the wings. Bone the thighs and legs, leaving the skin and meat attached to the rest of the bird. Trim the skin to form a large rectangle.
2. Prepare a forcemeat using the meat from the skinned bird or any other appropriate meat. Reserve a portion of the meat as garnish if desired. Prepare any other garnishes. Refrigerate the forcemeat and garnishes until ready for use.
3. Spread out the skin and meat on plastic wrap or several layers of cheese-cloth with the skin side down and the flesh up.
4. Remove the chicken tenderloins and pull the tendon out of each. Butterfly the breasts and tenderloins and cover the entire skin with a thin layer of meat.
5. Arrange the forcemeat and garnishes in a cylindrical shape across the cen-tre of the skin.
6. Tightly roll the skin around the forcemeat and garnishes to form a tight cylinder. (Use the plastic or cheesecloth to assist the process.)

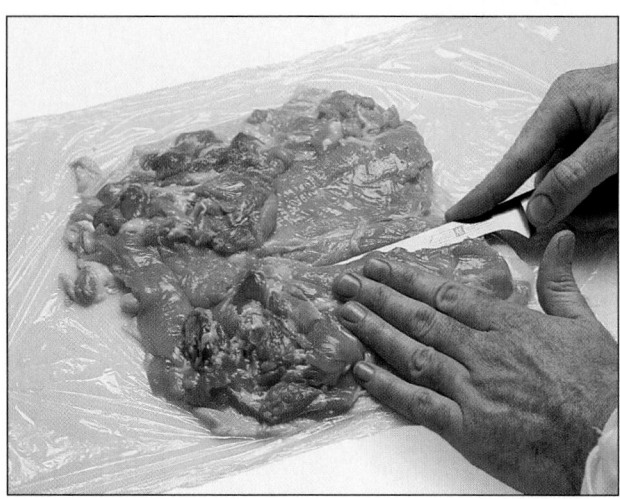

1. Butterfly the breasts and tenderloins and place a thin layer of meat over the skin.

2. Arrange the forcemeat and garnishes in a cylindrical shape across the centre of the meat.

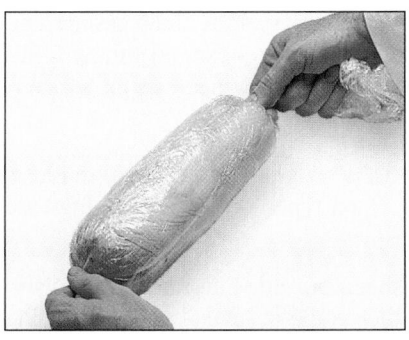

3. Use plastic wrap to roll the galantine into a tight cylinder.

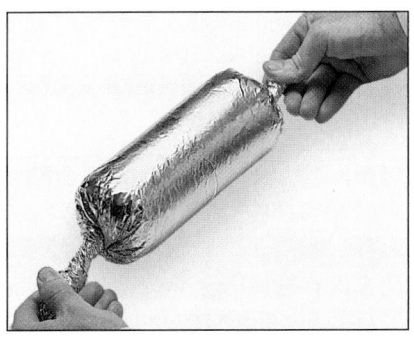

4. Secure the galantine with heavy-duty aluminum foil.

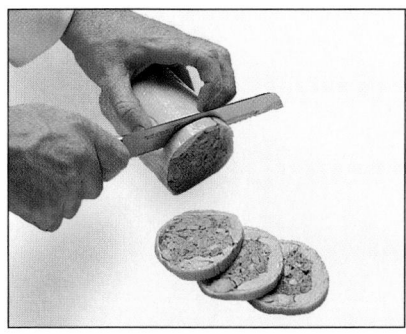

5. Slice the finished product.

7. Tie the ends of the cheesecloth with butcher's twine and secure the galantine at even intervals using strips of cheesecloth. If plastic wrap was used, wrap the galantine with heavy-duty aluminum foil.

8. Poach the galantine in a full-flavoured stock to an internal temperature of 150°F (66°C) for meat-based forcemeats or 140°F (60°C) for fish- or vegetable-based forcemeats.

9. Cool the galantine in its cooking liquid until it can be handled. Remove the cheesecloth or plastic wrap and aluminum foil and rewrap the galantine in clean cheesecloth or plastic wrap. Refrigerate overnight before decorating or slicing.

Sausages

Sausages are forcemeats stuffed into casings. For centuries, sausages consisted of ground meat, usually pork, and seasonings. Today not only are sausages made from pork, but also from game, beef, veal, poultry, fish, shellfish and even vegetables.

There are three main types of sausages:

1. Fresh sausages include breakfast sausage links and Italian sausages. They are made with fresh ingredients that have not been cured or smoked.

2. Smoked and **cooked sausages** are made with raw meat products treated with chemicals, usually the preservative sodium nitrite. Examples are kielbasa, bologna and hot dogs.

3. Dried or **hard sausages** are made with cured meats, then air-dried under controlled conditions. Dry sausages may or may not be smoked or cooked. Dried or hard sausages include salami, pepperoni, Lebanon bologna and landjäger.

Smoked and cooked sausages and dry or hard sausages are rarely prepared in typical food service operations. They are produced by specialty shops and will not be discussed here. We do discuss the ingredients and procedures for a variety of fresh sausages that can be prepared in almost any kitchen.

Sausage Components

Sausage Meats

Sausage meats are forcemeats with particular characteristics and flavourings. Coarse Italian and lamb sausages, for example, are simply a country-style forcemeat without liver and with different seasonings, stuffed into casings and formed into links. Hot dogs, bratwurst and other fine-textured sausages are variations of basic forcemeats stuffed into casings and formed into links.

Sausage Casings

Although sausage mixtures can be cooked without casings, most sausages are stuffed into casings before cooking. Two types of sausage casings are commonly used in food service operations:

1. **Natural casings** are portions of hog, sheep or cattle intestines. Their diameters are measured in millimetres and they come in several sizes depending upon the animal or portion of the intestine used. Hog casings are the most popular; sheep casings are considered the finest-quality small casings. Both hog and sheep casings are used to make hot dogs and many types of pork sausage. Beef casings are quite large and are used to make sausages such as ring bologna and Polish sausage. Most natural casings are purchased in salt packs. In order to rid them of salt and impurities, the casings must be carefully rinsed in warm water and allowed to soak in cool water for at least one hour or overnight before use.

2. **Collagen casings** are manufactured from collagen extracted from cattle hides. They are generally inferior to natural casings in taste and texture, but they do have advantages: Collagen casings do not require any washing or soaking prior to use and they are uniform in size.

Preparing Sausages

Equipment for Sausage Making

Sausage-stuffing machines are best if you engage in large-scale sausage production. Otherwise, all you need is a grinder with a sausage nozzle attachment such as the ones shown in Figure 20.2. Nozzles are available in several sizes to accommodate the various casing sizes.

FIGURE 20.2 *Sausage nozzles*

BASIC PROCEDURE FOR MAKING SAUSAGES

1. Prepare a forcemeat.
2. Thoroughly chill all parts of the sausage stuffer that will come in contact with the forcemeat.
3. Rinse and soak the casings if using natural ones. Cut the casings into 4–6-foot (1.2–1.8-m) lengths.
4. Put the forcemeat in the sausage stuffer.
5. Slide the casing over the nozzle of the sausage stuffer. Tie the end in a knot and pierce with a skewer to prevent an air pocket.

1. Slide the casing over the nozzle of the sausage stuffer.

2. Knot and pierce the casing with a skewer.

3. Support and guide the casing off the end of the nozzle as the forcemeat is extruded from the machine into the casing.

4. Twist or tie the sausage into uniform links.

6. Support and guide the casing off the end of the nozzle as the forcemeat is extruded from the nozzle into the casing.

7. After all the forcemeat has been stuffed into the casing, twist or tie the sausage into uniform links of the desired size.

SALT-CURING, BRINING AND SMOKING

Curing, brining and smoking are ancient techniques for preserving food. Today, foods such as hams, corned beef and smoked salmon are salt-cured, brined or smoked primarily for flavour. Cured meats have a characteristic pink colour caused by the reaction of sodium nitrite, which is added during processing, with the naturally occurring myoglobin protein in the meat.

Salt-Curing

Salt-curing is the process of surrounding a food with salt or a mixture of salt, sugar, nitrite-based curing salt, herbs and spices. Salt-curing dehydrates the food, inhibits bacterial growth and adds flavour. It is most often used with pork products and fish. Salt-curing is not a quick procedure—and the time involved adds money to production costs. For example, country-style hams are salt-cured. Proper curing requires approximately 1-1/2 days per pound (450 g) of ham, which means three weeks for the average ham.

Some salt-cured hams such as Smithfield and prosciutto are not actually cooked. The curing process preserves the meat and makes it safe to consume raw.

Gravlax is a well-known salmon dish prepared by salt-curing salmon fillets with a mixture of salt, sugar, pepper and dill. A recipe for gravlax (Recipe 20.20) is included at the end of this chapter.

Brining

A brine is actually a very salty marinade. Most brines have approximately 20% salinity, which is equivalent to 1 pound (450 g) of salt per gallon (4 L) of water. As with dry-salt cures, brines can also contain sugar, nitrites, herbs and spices. Brining is sometimes called pickling.

Andouille—*A very spicy smoked pork sausage, popular in Cajun cuisine.*

Chorizo—*A course, spicy smoked pork sausage flavoured with ground chiles and removed from its casing before cooking; used in Mexican and Spanish cuisines.*

Mortadella—*An Italian smoked sausage made with ground beef, pork and pork fat, flavoured with coriander and white wine; it is air-dried and has a delicate flavour; also a large American bologna-type pork sausage studded with pork fat and garlic.*

Pepperoni—*A hard, thin, air-dried Italian sausage seasoned with red and black pepper.*

Soppressata—*A hard, aged Italian sausage salami, sometimes coated with cracked peppercorns or herbs.*

Today, most cured meats are prepared in large production facilities where the brine is injected into the meat for rapid and uniform distribution. Commercially brined corned beef is cured by this process, as are most common hams. After brining, hams are further processed by smoking.

Smoking

There are two basic methods of smoking foods: cold smoking and hot smoking. The principal difference is that hot smoking actually cooks the food, cold smoking does not.

Both are done in a **smoker** specifically designed for this purpose. Smokers can be gas or electric; they vary greatly in size and operation. But they have several things in common. All consist of a chamber that holds the food being smoked, a means of burning wood to produce smoke and a heating element.

Different types of wood can be used to smoke food. Specific woods are selected to impart specific flavours. Hickory is often used for pork products; alder is excellent for smoked salmon. Maple, chestnut, juniper, mesquite and many other woods are also used. Resinous woods such as pine give food a bitter flavour and should be avoided.

Cold smoking is the process of exposing foods to smoke at temperatures of 50°F–85°F (10°C–29°C). Meat, poultry, game, fish, shellfish, cheese, nuts and even vegetables can be cold-smoked successfully. Most cold-smoked meats are generally salt-cured or brined first. Salt-curing or brining adds flavour, allows the nitrites (which give the ham, bacon and other smoked meats their distinctive pink colour) to penetrate the flesh and, most importantly, extracts moisture from the food, allowing the smoke to penetrate more easily. Cold-smoked foods are actually still raw. Some, like smoked salmon (lox), are eaten without further cooking. Others, such as bacon and hams, must be cooked before eating.

Hot smoking is the process of exposing foods to smoke at temperatures of 200°F–250°F (93°C–121°C). As with cold smoking, a great variety of foods can be prepared by hot smoking. Meats, poultry, game, fish and shellfish that are hot-smoked also benefit from salt-curing or brining. Although most hot-smoked foods are fully cooked when removed from the smoker, many are used in other recipes that call for further cooking.

Pan smoking is a process used for smaller or portion cuts. A heavy old roasting pan is heated on an open flame. Wood shavings or tea leaves and rice are placed on foil that is set in the pan. The food to be smoked is placed on a rack and set over the shavings when they begin to smoke. A lid or foil tent is placed over the food to promote even, rapid smoking. The lightly smoked food usually requires further cooking; however shellfish or thin slices may fully cook with this method. Be careful not to oversmoke or the product will be bitter.

Pork Products

Preparing hams and curing and smoking pork products are a traditional part of charcuterie. Although most bacon and ham is now produced in large commercial facilities, the chef still works with these products and must be able to identify them properly.

Most **bacon** comes from a hog's fatty belly.

Side bacon is produced by brining and cold smoking trimmed pork belly. It is available in slab or sliced form. Sliced bacon is purchased by count (number of slices) per pound;

Canadian Bacon, Sliced Bacon and Pancetta

thick-sliced bacon runs 10–14 slices per pound, while thin-sliced bacon may contain as many as 28–32 slices per pound.

Canadian bacon is produced from a boneless pork loin, trimmed so that only a thin layer of fat remains on its surface. It is then brined and smoked.

Pancetta is an Italian pork-belly bacon that is not smoked. It is salt-cured, peppered and often rolled into a cylinder shape. It can be sliced into rounds and fried; it is diced, rendered and combined with sauce to make fettuccine carbonara.

A **fresh ham** is a hog's hind leg; it is a primal cut. Many processed products produced from the primal fresh ham are also called ham.

Ham, in Canada, describes a variety of processed pork products, most of which come from the primal fresh leg. **Boneless** or **formed hams** are produced by separating a primal leg into its basic muscles, defatting the meat, curing it, stuffing the meat into various-sized and -shaped casings and cooking it. Boneless or formed hams are either smoked or liquid smoke flavouring is added during the curing process. The quality of boneless or formed hams varies greatly. The best hams are formed from only one or two large muscles, have low fat content and no added water other than that used during the curing process. Hams of lesser quality are formed from many small pieces of muscle and have a higher fat and water content. Many boneless or formed hams are listed in *The Meat Buyers Guide* and are indexed by the NAMP/IMPS system.

Country ham is a specialty of the southeastern United States. Country hams are dry-cured, smoked and hung to air-dry for a period ranging from several weeks to more than a year. During drying, a mould develops on the ham rind that must be scrubbed off before the ham is cooked. It is best cooked by first soaking, then slow simmering. The most famous country hams are Virginia hams; those from Smithfield, Virginia, are considered the finest. Only hams produced in rural areas can be called country hams; others must be labelled country-style ham.

Prosciutto is Italian for ham. What we call prosciutto in this country is called **Parma** in Italy. It is available raw (*crudo*) or cooked (*cotto*). Parma ham, produced near that Italian city, is made from hogs fed on the whey of cheese processed nearby. The ham is salt-cured and air-dried but not smoked. The curing process makes it safe and wholesome to consume raw. Several domestic varieties of prosciutto are produced (the raw variety is more popular), varying widely in quality. Imported prosciuttos are much larger than the domestic varieties because Italian hogs are larger when butchered.

Westphalian ham is dry-cured, brined and then smoked with beechwood. Authentic Westphalian hams are produced in the Westphalia region of Germany and are quite similar to prosciutto. They are sold bone-in or boneless. Their characteristic flavour is derived from the juniper berries used in the curing process and the beechwood used for smoking.

IMPS No. 501, Ham short shank, cured and smoked.

IMPS No. 510, Ham, boneless, skinless, cured and smoked, fully cooked.

CONCLUSION

The classic art of charcuterie is as popular today as ever. Consumers regularly enjoy high-quality pâtés, sausages, hams and other charcuterie products.

Although production procedures have changed as new technologies and equipment have developed, the basic principles remain the same: Terrines, pâtés and sausages can be produced only from high-quality forcemeats, and temperature control is fundamental to the proper production of forcemeats and other charcuterie products.

Armed with a basic knowledge of the procedures used for charcuterie, you can use your imagination and creativity to produce a variety of charcuterie products.

$\mathcal{Q}$UESTIONS FOR DISCUSSION

1. Explain why the art of charcuterie is relevant to the training of modern cooks.
2. Compare and contrast the three styles of forcemeat.
3. In what way is a terrine different from a pâté? How does a pâté differ from a pâté en croûte?
4. Describe the differences and the similarities between a ballotine and a galantine.
5. Describe the typical procedure for making sausages. Why is the selection of casings important?
6. Explain the difference between hot smoking and cold smoking. Describe a food typically prepared by each of these methods.

$\mathcal{A}$DDITIONAL CHARCUTERIE RECIPES

Bruno Marti

Voted National Chef of the Year in 1997 by the CFCC, Bruno was a member of the world champion Team Canada in 1984, and manager of the team that won 3 gold medals in Berlin 1996. Currently, he is the coach for the next Team Canada, as they prepare for the 2000 Culinary Olympics.

RECIPE 20.6
VEGETABLE TERRINE

LA BELLE AUBERGE, LADNER, BC
Chef-Owner Bruno Marti

Yield: 1 Terrine mould, 4 x 4 x 12 inches
(10 x 10 x 30 cm), with lid

Aubergine, cubed	8 oz.	200 g
Garlic clove, chopped	1	1
Olive oil	as needed	as needed
Shallots, chopped fine	2	2
Green beans	4 oz.	100 g
Water	2 oz.	50 mL
Salt and pepper	TT	TT
Butternut squash, peeled, de-seeded, sliced lengthwise, 1/2 inch (1 cm) thick	8 oz.	200 g
Fresh herbs, chopped: oregano, thyme, basil	TT	TT
Celeriac, peeled, sliced lengthwise, 1/2 inch (1 cm) thick	8 oz.	200 g
Shiitake mushrooms, whole, stem removed	4 oz.	100 g
Leeks, washed and cleaned, left whole (not split)	2 medium	2 medium
Carrots, peeled, cut into long thin strips, the length of the carrot	4 large	4 large
Leaf gelatin	1 pkg.	1 pkg.
Tomatoes, peeled, de-seeded, halved	8 oz.	200 g

1. Sauté aubergine in half the garlic and oil. Roast it in the oven at 375°F (190°C) for 20 minutes, then purée, adding a little water, if needed.
2. Sauté shallots in oil for 1 minute. Add the beans and the water. Season to taste, simmer until cooked, but still crisp. Allow to cool.

3. In a few drops of oil and water, simmer squash in a 400°F (200°C) oven until tender, about 10 minutes. Turn once, and season with herbs.

4. Repeat with celery root, cover and cook in moderate oven (350–375°F/ 180–190°C) for 30 minutes.

5. Sauté mushrooms in a little oil and water. Season with salt, pepper and the rest of the garlic.

6. Blanch leeks for 10 minutes and carrots for 3 minutes in boiling, salted water. Cool them in ice water.

7. Drain vegetables well.

8. Melt package of gelatin according to manufacturer's instructions.

9. Line the mould with plastic wrap. Add carrot slices, placing them across the mould with excess curving up sides and hanging over edges. Brush with gelatin.

10. Layer tomatoes, celery root, aubergine, beans (arrange them lengthwise), leeks, mushrooms and squash. Alternate ingredients to give an attractive colour combination. Brush each layer with gelatin. After brushing the final layer, fold the carrots over the gelatin to seal. Fold in plastic wrap. Place weight on top and refrigerate for at least 1 day before slicing.

Approximate values per 1/2-inch (12-mm) slice:

Calories	33
Total fat	2 g
Saturated fat	.2 g
Cholesterol	0 mg
Sodium	95 mg
Total carbohydrates	5 g
Protein	1 g

RECIPE 20.7

CARPACCIO OF SEARED BEEF WITH PARMESAN FANS AND PERFUMED MASCARPONE

SOUTHERN ALBERTA INSTITUTE OF TECHNOLOGY, CALGARY, AB
Chef Fred Malley

Yield: 10 Servings

Beef tenderloin, centre cut, trimmed and cleaned	20 oz.	600 g
Ground black pepper	TT	TT
Oil	as needed	as needed
Watercress sprigs	60	60
Artichoke hearts, halved, grilled and marinated in olive oil vinaigrette	80 pieces	80 pieces
Parmesan fans (shards, sliced from Parmesan block)	60–90	60–90
Mascarpone, flavoured with 4 roasted mashed garlic cloves	8 oz.	250 g
Espresso coffee beans, ground	pinch	pinch
Cherry tomatoes, sliced or wedged	30	30
Garlic chips (crisp deep-fat fried slices)	30	30

Fred Malley

Fred combines his passion for food with his love of teaching. Currently, among his many other professional activities, Fred is Coordinator, Curriculum and Evaluation, Hospitality Careers Dept. at SAIT. His continuing commitment to improving curriculum recently resulted in a collaboration with the federal government to produce national standards for professional cooks.

1. Sprinkle the meat with pepper and sear in the hot oil.

2. Wrap in plastic wrap to make a roll or log shape and chill for 2 hours in the freezer.

3. Slice the beef paper thin using an electric slicer, then arrange the slices in a ring on the plate.

4. Place watercress and artichokes in the centre of the meat ring with some of the vinaigrette. Top with the Parmesan fans. Pipe three rosettes of mascarpone on the plate and sprinkle espresso lightly over each. Top with the garlic chips. Place tomato pieces between the mascarpone rosettes.

Approximate values per serving:

Calories	375
Total fat	25 g
Saturated fat	12 g
Cholesterol	91 mg
Sodium	706 mg
Total carbohydrates	10 g
Protein	28 g

♦♦♦

RECIPE 20.8
VEGETABLE TERRINE IN BRIOCHE

CHEF LELAND ATKINSON, WASHINGTON, D.C.

Yield: 1 Terrine, 12 x 4 x 3 inches
(30 x 10 x 7.5 cm)

Chicken breast meat, lean	2 lb.	900 g
Egg whites	3	3
Cream, 35%	4 oz.	120 mL
Brandy	2 oz.	60 mL
Salt and pepper	TT	TT
Carrot, medium dice	3 oz.	90 g
Broccoli florets	8 oz.	250 g
Shiitake mushrooms, trimmed	12–18	12–18
Olive oil	1 oz.	30 mL
Red bell pepper, medium dice	2 oz.	60 g
Leek, white part only, medium dice	2 oz.	60 g
Fresh chives, basil and parsley, chopped	4 Tbsp.	60 mL
Nutmeg	TT	TT
Brioche dough, rolled out to approximately 1/8 inch (3 mm) thick, well chilled	1 lb.	450 g
Egg yolks, beaten	2	2
Eggs	2	2
Water	1 oz.	30 g
Madeira aspic	as needed	as needed

1. Dice or grind the chicken; place it in the bowl of a cold food processor and process.
2. Add the egg whites and then the cream and brandy in a steady stream while the motor is running.
3. Season the mousseline and poach a small amount to test for texture and seasonings.
4. Adjust the seasonings and transfer to a metal mixing bowl in an ice bath.
5. Separately blanch the carrots and broccoli; drain and blot dry on a paper towel.
6. Sauté the shiitakes in olive oil. Drain and chill. In the same pan, sauté the red peppers and leeks. Remove from the stove and add the herbs and cool. Fold the carrots, peppers, leeks and herbs into the mousseline.
7. Line a buttered pâté mould with the chilled brioche, reserving the excess for the top and garnish.
8. Fill the mould one-fourth full with the mousseline. Layer the shiitakes over the mousseline, cover them with another layer of mousseline, followed by the dry broccoli. Repeat this process until the mould is filled, finishing with a layer of mousseline.
9. Fold the ends of the brioche over the filling and brush with beaten egg yolk.
10. Make a top from the remaining brioche and place it over the mould; cut a vent and insert a foil funnel into the vent.
11. Beat the eggs with the water to make an egg wash. Brush the exposed brioche with the egg wash and bake at 425°F (220°C) until the internal temperature reaches 125°F (52°C), approximately 35–40 minutes.
12. When cold, fill the pâté with madeira aspic if there is a space between the dough and the filling.

Approximate values per slice (224 g):

Calories	450
Total fat	20 g
Saturated fat	6 g
Cholesterol	185 mg
Sodium	520 mg
Total carbohydrates	35 g
Protein	34 g
Vitamin A	45%
Vitamin C	150%

Claims—high fibre

◆◆◆

RECIPE 20.9

BASIC GAME FORCEMEAT

Yield: 4 lb. 8 oz. (2 kg)

Venison or antelope, cubed	1 lb. 8 oz.	700 g
Veal, cubed	1 lb. 8 oz.	700 g
Brandy	4 oz.	120 g
Salt and pepper	TT	TT
Dried thyme	1 tsp.	5 mL
Pork backfat, cubed	1 lb.	450 g
Eggs	3	3
Game stock, cold	1 pt.	450 mL
Fresh parsley, chopped	1 oz.	30 g
Green peppercorns	1/2 oz.	15 g

1. Combine the venison or antelope and the veal with the brandy, salt, pepper and thyme; marinate for several hours or overnight.
2. Grind the marinated meat and marinade ingredients in a chilled meat grinder once through a large plate and then once through a small plate; refrigerate.
3. Grind the backfat once through the small plate.
4. Emulsify the fat with the ground meats in the bowl of a cold food processor. This can be done in several batches. Place the forcemeat in a stainless steel bowl in an ice bath and stir to chill thoroughly.
5. Add the eggs, stock, parsley and green peppercorns to the forcemeat in several batches. Using a paddle attachment on a bench mixer, work them in.
6. Additional garnishes may be added as desired. The forcemeat can be used to make a variety of pâtés or terrines.

Approximate values per 1 oz. (30 g) serving:	
Calories	100
Total fat	7 g
Saturated fat	3 g
Cholesterol	40 mg
Sodium	110 mg
Total carbohydrates	1 g
Protein	7 g

◆◆◆

RECIPE 20.10

SALMON AND SEA BASS TERRINE
WITH SPINACH AND BASIL

Yield: 1 Terrine, 12 x 4 x 3 inches
(30 x 10 x 7.5 cm)

Salmon fillet, boneless, skinless	1 lb. 8 oz.	700 g
Egg whites	3	3
Salt	TT	TT
White pepper	TT	TT
Cayenne pepper	TT	TT
Cream, 35%	up to 24 oz.	up to 700 mL
Basil leaves	12	12
Truffle, brunoise (optional)	3/4 oz.	20 g
Spinach leaves, cleaned	6 oz.	180 g
Sea bass fillet	12 oz.	350 g

1. Grind the salmon through the large plate of a well-chilled meat grinder.
2. Place the salmon in the bowl of a food processor with salt and process until smooth and firm.
3. Add the egg whites, one at a time, pulsing the processor to incorporate.

Continued

Scrape down the bowl and season with white pepper and cayenne pepper.

4. With the machine running, add the cream in a steady stream. Scrape down the bowl again and process the mousseline until it is smooth and well mixed. You may not use all the cream.

5. Blanch the basil leaves and refresh. Chop them finely.

6. Remove the mousseline from the bowl of the processor. Fold in the basil leaves and truffles and refrigerate.

7. Blanch and refresh the spinach leaves.

8. Spread the spinach leaves on a piece of plastic wrap, completely covering a rectangle approximately the length and width of the terrine mould.

9. Cut the sea bass fillet into strips approximately 1 inch (2.5 cm) wide and place end to end on the spinach leaves. Season with salt and white pepper.

10. Use the plastic wrap to wrap the spinach leaves tightly around the fish fillets.

11. Oil terrine and line it with plastic wrap.

12. Half-fill the lined terrine with salmon mousseline.

13. Carefully unwrap the spinach and sea bass fillets and place them down the centre of the terrine. Fill the terrine with the remaining mousseline.

14. Tap the terrine mould firmly to remove any air pockets, then fold the plastic wrap over the top.

15. Cover and bake the terrine in a water bath at 300°F (150°C) to an internal temperature of 140°F (60°C), approximately 1-1/2 hours.

16. Cool the terrine well, unmould, slice or decorate and serve as desired.

Approximate values per 3-1/2 oz. (100 g) slice:

Calories	210
Total fat	16 g
Saturated fat	8 g
Cholesterol	75 mg
Sodium	180 mg
Total carbohydrates	1 g
Protein	15 g
Vitamin A	25%

Marcel Kretz

Born, raised, and trained in France, Marcel has had an illustrious, award-winning career in Europe and Canada. He is credited with launching the movement to emphasize Quebec products in top Quebec restaurants, and in 1998 became the first chef ever to receive the Order of Canada.

◆◆◆

RECIPE 20.11
CHICKEN LIVER TERRINE

L'ÉCOLE HÔTELIÈRE DES LAURENTIDES, STE-ADÈLE, PQ
Chef Marcel Kretz

Yield: 2 moulds, half-moon shaped, approximately 10 x 4 x 3 inches (25 x 10 x 7 cm)

Chicken livers, cleaned, trimmed	2 lb.	1 kg
Milk	16 oz.	500 mL
Brandy	3 oz.	90 mL
Fresh pork flank or pork cheeks, ground	8 oz.	250 g
Eggs	2	2
Cream, 35%	3 oz.	90 mL
Neutral gelatin (powder)	3 Tbsp.	45 mL
Mace	pinch	pinch
Sugar	pinch	pinch
Curing salt	pinch	pinch
Salt and pepper	TT	TT
Dry morels, soaked and chopped	1/2 oz.	15 g
Pork backfat, thinly sliced	6 oz.	180 g

1. Soak the chicken livers overnight in the milk, with a pinch of salt added. Drain and rinse carefully for 15 minutes, under running water.

2. Drain thoroughly, place in bowl, then add the brandy and a few grains salt. Marinate for 10 minutes, then drain again, reserving the brandy marinade.

3. Swiftly blanch 1-1/2 pounds (750 g) of the chicken livers in boiling salted water. Cool rapidly under running water and refrigerate.

4. Purée 8 ounces (250 g) pork and 8 ounces (250 g) raw livers in the blender with eggs, cream, gelatin, mace, sugar, marinade, curing salt and salt and pepper. When smooth, add morels, but do not purée them.

5. Line moulds with some of the thinly sliced backfat (reserve the rest for finishing). Line with half the creamy pork and liver farce, then add all the whole chicken livers and cover with remaining farce. Close with more backfat. Wrap in plastic wrap and then cover with foil.

6. Cook in a bain marie in the oven at 500°F (250°C) for 15 minutes, then reduce the heat to 350°F (175°C) and let cook for 30 minutes. The hot water should be three-quarters up the sides of the mould.

7. Remove from oven and put under a press (a foil-covered wooden board the size of the mould). Put some weight on the press and tie it down. Cool for at least 12 hours before unmoulding.

VARIATION: Replace the chicken liver with quail or duck liver.

Approximate values per 1 oz. (30 g) serving:	
Calories	59
Total fat	4 g
Saturated fat	2 g
Cholesterol	94 mg
Sodium	40 mg
Total carbohydrates	1 g
Protein	5 g

◆◆◆

RECIPE 20.12

ROASTED RED PEPPER MOUSSE

Yield: 1-1/2 pt. (700 mL)

Onion, small dice	3 oz.	90 g
Garlic, chopped	1 tsp.	5 mL
Olive oil	1 oz.	30 mL
Red bell pepper, roasted and peeled, small dice	10 oz.	300 g
Salt and pepper	TT	TT
Chicken stock	8 oz.	250 mL
Granulated gelatin	1 Tbsp.	15 mL
Dry white wine	2 oz.	60 mL
Cream, 35%, whipped	6 oz.	180 mL

1. Sauté the onions and garlic in the olive oil until tender, approximately 2 minutes.

2. Add the bell pepper, salt, pepper and chicken stock. Bring to a boil, reduce to a simmer and cook 5 minutes.

3. Soften the gelatin in the white wine, then add to the pepper mixture. Purée the pepper mixture in a blender or food processor and strain through a china cap.

4. Place the pepper purée over an ice bath. Stir until cool but do not allow the gelatin to set. Fold in the whipped cream. Pour the mousse into aspic-lined or well-oiled timbales or moulds and refrigerate several hours or overnight.

5. Unmould the mousse and serve as desired.

VARIATIONS: Substitute yellow or green bell peppers for part or all of the red bell peppers.

Broccoli Mousse: Substitute 8 ounces (250 g) of blanched, chopped broccoli for the red bell peppers.

Approximate values per 1 oz. (30 g) serving:	
Calories	60
Total fat	6 g
Saturated fat	2.5 g
Cholesterol	15 mg
Sodium	200 mg
Total carbohydrates	2 g
Protein	1 g
Vitamin C	25%

♦♦♦

RECIPE 20.13

SALMON MOUSSE

Yield: 1 lb. 8 oz. (650 g)

Salmon, boneless, skinless	12 oz.	350 g
Fish velouté, warm	8 oz.	250 mL
Cream, 35%	8 oz.	250 mL
Granulated gelatin	1-1/2 Tbsp.	20 mL
White wine	4 oz.	120 mL
Salt and white pepper	TT	TT
Cayenne pepper	TT	TT

Approximate values per 1 oz. (30 g) serving:

Calories	100
Total fat	6 g
Saturated fat	3 g
Cholesterol	25 mg
Sodium	480 mg
Total carbohydrates	6 g
Protein	5 g
Vitamin A	4%

1. Steam the salmon and transfer it to the food processor while still warm. Add the warm velouté in a steady stream while the machine is running.
2. Whip the cream to soft peaks and reserve.
3. Add the gelatin to the wine and allow it to soften for 5 minutes. Heat the gelatin mixture to liquefy the gelatin.
4. Transfer the salmon and velouté to a mixing bowl and stir in the gelatin mixture (wine aspic). Season with salt, pepper and cayenne.
5. When the mixture has cooled to near room temperature, fold in the whipped cream with a rubber spatula until just mixed.
6. The mousse is now ready to be formed into timbales, or moulded into various shapes as desired.

♦♦♦

RECIPE 20.14

DUCK CONFIT

Yield: 4 Servings

Duck, 4 lb. (1.8 kg), cut into 4 pieces	1	1
Kosher salt	2 Tbsp.	30 mL
Black pepper, cracked	1 tsp.	5 mL
Bay leaves	4	4
Fresh thyme	6 sprigs	6 sprigs
Garlic cloves, crushed	6	6
Duck or goose fat, melted	2 lb.	900 g

Approximate values per serving:

Calories	607
Total fat	51 g
Saturated fat	17 g
Cholesterol	151 mg
Sodium	1728 mg
Total carbohydrates	0 g
Protein	34 g

1. Rub the duck with the salt. Place skin side down in a roasting pan just large enough to hold the pieces in 1 layer; season with the black pepper, crumbled bay leaves, thyme and garlic. Cover and refrigerate overnight.
2. Bake the duck at 325°F (160°C) until brown, approximately 15–20 minutes. Add enough melted duck or goose fat to cover the pieces completely.
3. Cover the pan and cook in a 300°F (150°C) oven until the duck is very tender, approximately 2 hours.
4. Remove the duck from the fat and place in a narrow, deep hotel pan. Ladle enough of the cooking fat over the pieces to cover them completely. Be careful not to add any of the cooking juices.
5. Cover the pan and refrigerate for 2 days to allow the flavours to mellow.
6. To serve, remove the duck from the fat and scrape off the excess fat. Bake at 350°F (180°C) until the skin is crisp and the meat is hot, approximately 30 minutes.

◆◆◆

RECIPE 20.15
CHOPPED CHICKEN LIVER

Yield: 20 oz. (600 g)

Chicken livers, trimmed	1 lb.	450 g
Chicken fat or butter	2 oz.	60 g
Kosher salt	TT	TT
Eggs, hard-cooked	2	2
Onion, small dice	6 oz.	170 g
Salt and pepper	TT	TT

1. Sauté the livers in the chicken fat or butter until lightly browned with a slightly pink interior. Season with kosher salt.

2. Chop the livers with a chef's knife, blending in the eggs and onions. Season to taste with salt and pepper.

3. The final product should be slightly coarse and peppery. Blend in additional chicken fat or butter if necessary to make the mixture hold together.

4. Pack into a serving bowl, cover well and chill for 24 hours. Serve with crackers, toast or matzos and sliced radishes.

Approximate values per 1 oz. (30 g) serving:

Calories	60
Total fat	4 g
Saturated fat	1 g
Cholesterol	105 mg
Sodium	240 mg
Total carbohydrates	1 g
Protein	4 g
Vitamin A	70%

◆◆◆

RECIPE 20.16
RABBIT PÂTÉ EN CROÛTE

Yield: 1 Pâté, 3 x 3.5 x 16 inches
       (7.5 x 8.7 x 40 cm)

Rabbit meat, boneless, large dice	2 lb.	1 kg
Pork butt, large dice	1 lb.	450 g
Marinade:		
Pâté spice	1 Tbsp.	15 mL
Orange zest	2 Tbsp.	30 mL
Lime zest	1 Tbsp.	15 mL
Brandy	4 oz.	120 mL
Fresh thyme	1 bunch	1 bunch
Juniper berries	6	6
Salt and pepper	TT	TT
Backfat, large dice	1 lb.	450 g
Eggs	4	4
Pistachios, chopped coarse	8 oz.	250 g
Ham, diced	6 oz.	180 g
Black olives, chopped coarse	2 oz.	60 g
Rabbit loins, browned lightly in oil	4	4
Rabbit livers, browned lightly in oil	6	6
Pâté dough	1 lb. 8 oz.	700 g

1. Combine the rabbit meat and pork butt with the marinade ingredients and marinate several hours or overnight.

2. Freeze the backfat.

3. Remove the thyme and juniper berries from the marinated meat mixture and grind the meat in a well-chilled grinder first through the large plate, then through the medium plate. Hold the mixture in an ice bath.

Continued

4. Grind the frozen backfat through the medium plate and add to the meat mixture.

5. Place the meat mixture and fat in a chilled food processor bowl and process until emulsified.

6. Over an ice bath, incorporate the eggs into the forcemeat.

7. Fold the pistachios, ham and olives into the forcemeat.

8. Follow the procedure for preparing a pâté en croûte using the rabbit loins and livers as garnishes running the length of the pâté.

◆◆◆

RECIPE 20.17

TEX-MEX TURKEY SAUSAGE

Yield: 4 lb. (1.8 kg)

Canola oil	4 Tbsp.	60 mL
Onion, chopped fine	12 oz.	340 g
Garlic, minced	1 Tbsp.	15 mL
Jalapeño, chopped	1 Tbsp.	15 mL
Turkey breast meat, trimmed of fat	2 lb.	1 kg
Veal, lean	8 oz.	250 g
White wine vinegar	2 oz.	60 mL
Water	8 oz.	250 mL
Fresh cilantro, chopped	4 oz.	120 g
White pepper	1 tsp.	5 mL
Chile powder	1 tsp.	5 mL
Cumin, ground	1/2 tsp.	2 mL
Salt	1 tsp.	5 mL

1. Heat the oil and sauté the onion, garlic and jalapeño until the onions are translucent; remove and chill well.

2. Grind the turkey and veal in a cold meat grinder, first through the large plate and then through the medium plate. Working over an ice bath, combine the meats, vinegar, water and seasonings. Add the sautéed vegetables.

3. Blend well, then cook a small portion to test the flavour and texture. Adjust the seasonings.

4. Stuff into casings or portion into 2-ounce (60-g) patties and broil. Serve with papaya salsa.

◆◆◆

RECIPE 20.18

SPICY ITALIAN SAUSAGE

Yield: 5 lb. (2.2 kg)

Pork butt	5 lb.	2.2 kg
Salt	1-1/2 Tbsp.	25 mL
Black pepper	1-1/2 tsp	7 mL
Fennel seeds	1-1/2 tsp.	7 mL
Paprika	1 Tbsp.	15 mL
Red pepper, crushed	1-1/2 tsp.	7 mL

Coriander, ground	3/4 tsp.	4 mL
Ice water	5 oz.	150 mL

1. Cut the meat into 2-inch (5-cm) cubes.
2. Combine the pork with the remaining ingredients except the water.
3. Grind the meat once through the coarse plate of a well-chilled grinder.
4. Add the ice water and mix well.
5. Stuff the sausage into casings.

Approximate values per 4 oz. (120 g) serving:

Calories	220
Total fat	9 g
Saturated fat	3 g
Cholesterol	80 mg
Sodium	260 mg
Total carbohydrates	0 g
Protein	36 g

◆◆◆

RECIPE 20.19

CHORIZO

Yield: 7 lb. 8 oz. (3.4 kg)

Pork, lean	5 lb.	2.2 kg
Backfat	2 lb. 8 oz.	1.1 kg
Red pepper flakes	1 tsp.	5 mL
Garlic, chopped	1 oz.	30 g
Cumin	3 Tbsp.	45 mL
Cayenne pepper	2 Tbsp.	30 mL
Salt	4 tsp.	20 mL
Paprika	5 Tbsp.	75 mL
Red wine vinegar	3 oz.	90 mL

1. Cut the pork and backfat in 1-inch (2.5-cm) pieces. Grind the pork once using a medium plate. Grind half of the pork a second time together with the backfat through a fine plate.
2. Combine all the ingredients in the bowl of a mixer and mix, using the paddle attachment. The sausage may be used in bulk or formed into links as desired.

Approximate values per 1 oz. (30 g) serving:

Calories	120
Total fat	10 g
Saturated fat	4 g
Cholesterol	25 mg
Sodium	90 mg
Total carbohydrates	0 g
Protein	5 g

◆◆◆

RECIPE 20.20

GRAVLAX ON A WILD RICE FRITTER WITH CARROT PICKLE AND FRESH HERBS

CALGARY, AB

Chef dee Hobsbawn-Smith

This is a luxurious dish that must be started several days in advance. Use salmon, Arctic char or steelhead for the gravlax. Cut two fillets from one fish, preferably from the tail and preferably from opposite sides of the backbone so that they lie together in a perfect fit.

Yield: 12 portions

Steelhead or salmon fillet in 2 pieces of equal size and shape	2 lb.	1 kg
White sugar	1/4 cup	60 mL
Kosher salt	1/4 cup	60 mL

dee Hobsbawn-Smith

dee is a Calgary-based professional chef, caterer, culinary educator and freelance writer. Until 1994 she was chef-owner of her own restaurant, Foodsmith, considered a leader in contemporary Prairie cuisine. She contributes regularly to City Palate and Calgary City Scope and has also contributed to Canadian Living magazine.

Continued

Mustard seed, dry-roasted and ground	2 Tbsp.	30 mL
Dillweed, fresh, minced	2 Tbsp.	30 mL
Black pepper, freshly cracked	2 tsp.	10 mL
Lemon, zest only	1	1
Pickled ginger, minced (available in Japanese markets)	2 Tbsp.	30 mL
Pepper-flavoured vodka	1/4 cup	60 mL
Wild Rice Fritters (recipe follows)	1 recipe	1 recipe
Crème fraîche or sour cream	1/2 cup	120 mL
Dill, fresh, minced	1 Tbsp.	15 mL
Carrot Pickle (recipe follows)	1/4 cup	60 mL
Fresh chives and chive blossoms	as garnish	as garnish

1. Using tweezers or needle-nose pliers, pull the pinbones out of the salmon. Combine the sugar and salt, then sprinkle it evenly over the fillets. Wrap the pieces, flesh side to flesh side, snugly in plastic wrap and chill over a drip pan to catch weeping liquids for 24–48 hours.

2. Unwrap the fish and brush off any undissolved crystals of salt and sugar. Sprinkle the surface with mustard seed, dillweed, pepper, lemon zest and pickled ginger. Drizzle the vodka over the herbs and spices. Wrap and chill 12–24 hours, then slice thinly on an angle.

3. Prepare the Wild Rice Fritters and the Carrot Pickle.

4. Combine the crème fraîche or sour cream with the minced dill, then spread a little on each hot fritter. Top with a gently folded slice of gravlax, and garnish with 2–3 thin slivers of carrot pickle. Add a sprig of chives and pull apart a chive blossom, sprinkling the petals over top.

Approximate values per serving:

Calories	150
Total fat	8 g
Saturated fat	2 g
Cholesterol	56 mg
Sodium	50 mg
Total carbohydrates	2 g
Protein	17 g

WILD RICE FRITTERS

This is an adaptation of "Wild Rice and Lobster Fritters," which first appeared in Skinny Feasts (Whitecap Books, 1997).

Yield: 24 to 36 fritters, depending on size

Wild rice	1/4 cup	60 mL
Basmati rice	1 cup	250 mL
Eggs, lightly beaten	4	4
Arrowroot powder	3 Tbsp.	45 mL
Fresh dill, thyme or oregano, minced	4 Tbsp.	60 mL
Green onions, minced	1 bunch	1 bunch
Kosher salt and pepper	TT	TT
Canola oil	as needed	as needed

1. Cook the wild rice in 2 cups (500 mL) of water, covered, until the grains split open (35 to 55 minutes). Add water if needed to prevent sticking. Drain and cool. Bring 2 cups (500 mL) of water to the boil. Add the basmati rice and return to the boil. Cover and reduce heat to low and cook for 16 minutes. Cool. Combine all the ingredients except canola oil in a mixing bowl, mixing well.

2. Heat a griddle or large nonstick sauté pan, add a small amount of canola oil and drop the fritter mixture onto the hot surface in tablespoons. Flatten with the back of a spoon. When brown and crispy, turn and cook the other side. Keep warm in a slow oven or make the fritters in advance and reheat before serving.

Approximate values per serving:

Calories	38
Total fat	1 g
Saturated fat	0.2 g
Cholesterol	24 mg
Sodium	30 mg
Total carbohydrates	6 g
Protein	1 g

CARROT PICKLE

Yield: 1 qt. (1 L)

Carrots, fine julienne	2 lb.	900 g
Garlic, peeled and thinly sliced	1 head	1 head
Ginger root, peeled and thinly sliced	TT	TT
Kalonji (black onion seed)*	1-1/2 tsp.	8 mL
Fenugreek	1 tsp.	5 mL
Anise seed	1 tsp.	5 mL
Coriander seed	1/2 tsp.	3 mL
Cumin seed	1/4 tsp.	2 mL
Mustard seed	1 tsp.	5 mL
Black peppercorns, cracked	1/2 tsp.	3 mL
Lemons, juice and zest	2	2
Apple cider vinegar	1/2 cup	110 mL
Mustard oil	as needed	as needed

Approximate values per serving:

Calories	25
Total fat	1 g
Saturated fat	0.1 g
Sodium	8 mg
Total carbohydrates	3 g
Protein	0.4 g

1. Mix the carrots, garlic and ginger in a nonreactive bowl. Dry-roast the kalonji, fenugreek, anise, coriander, cumin, mustard and pepper in a small sauté pan over high heat until fragrant and beginning to colour, then add to the carrots, garlic and ginger. Add the lemon juice and zest and the vinegar. Pack into a clean 1 quart (1 L) jar and fill to the top with mustard oil.

* Kalonji is available in specialty spice stores.

RECIPE 20.21
GINGER MARINATED ATLANTIC SALMON

PALLISER HOTEL, CALGARY, AB
Executive Chef Takashi Ito

Yield: 1 Serving

Marinade:

Fresh ginger, thinly sliced	1/2 Tbsp.	10 mL
Soy sauce	4 Tbsp.	55 mL
Garlic, minced	1/2 Tbsp.	10 mL
Black pepper	TT	TT
Canola oil	1 cup	225 mL
Water	1/2 cup	110 mL
Atlantic salmon, cut in slices, marinated each piece 1-1/2 oz. (40 g)	2 pieces	2 pieces
Spinach, cleaned	1 cup	250 mL
Red pepper, julienne	1 tsp.	5 mL
Orange Kiwi Dressing (recipe follows)	1-1/2 oz.	30–40 mL

Takashi Ito
Takashi has been a Certified Chef de Cuisine since 1992, and has won several medals in competition, including the gold at the 1993 Grand Salon Culinaire in Vancouver. He is particularly notable for his skill and creativity in carving ice-sculptures, for which he has also won numerous awards.

1. Combine the marinade ingredients in a mixing bowl.
2. Place the salmon in the marinade and marinate for at least 3 hours.
3. Remove the salmon from the marinade and grill on a hot grill for about 15 seconds per side.
4. Arrange the spinach on a cold plate, cover with the salmon and red pepper.
5. Drizzle the dressing on top.

Approximate values per serving:

Calories	323
Total fat	24 g
Saturated fat	3 g
Sodium	859 mg
Total carbohydrates	5 g
Protein	23 g

ORANGE KIWI DRESSING

Yield: 1/4 cup (60 mL)

Mandarin oranges (canned)	3 pieces	3 pieces
White wine vinegar	3 tsp.	15 mL
Olive oil	4 tsp.	20 mL
Canola oil	4 tsp.	20 mL
Kiwi, ripe	1/4	1/4
Salt and black pepper	TT	TT

1. Purée the oranges in a blender.
2. Add the vinegar and oils, and blend well. Add the kiwi. Do not over-blend; keep the black seeds whole.
3. Adjust the seasoning with salt and pepper.

Approximate values per serving:

Calories	63
Total fat	6 g
Saturated fat	0.8 g
Sodium	259 mg
Total carbohydrates	2 g
Protein	0.1 g

WEBLINKS

Galloping Goose Sausage Company (B.C.)
www.islandnet.com/~sausage/
Salt Curing Meat in Brine
www.lis.ab.ca/walton/old/brine.html

DEEP-FAT FRYING

═══ ◆◆◆ ═══

LEARNING OUTCOMES

After studying this chapter you will be able to:

◆ select and maintain the proper equipment and fats for deep-fat frying
◆ use breadings and batters
◆ prepare fritters and croquettes

*D*eep-fat frying has a bad reputation. Many consumers relate it to greasy convenience foods with thick breadings or batters masking the principal ingredient's inferior quality. But, properly prepared, foods that are deep-fat fried can be deliciously tender and juicy—and their contrasting crispy crusts and moist interiors add to eating enjoyment.

Perhaps no other cooking method can be applied to such a wide variety of foods. Meats, poultry, fish and shellfish, vegetables, potatoes and other starches, fruits, pastries and even ice cream can be deep-fat fried successfully. That is why we devote a separate chapter to the process.

This versatile procedure is relatively simple provided a few basic guidelines are followed. This chapter explains those guidelines and provides recipes for breading and batters. Also included are illustrative recipes utilizing deep-fat frying techniques. Other recipes that use deep-fat frying are found in the various chapters on vegetables, fish, starches and quick breads.

Deep-fat frying is a dry-heat cooking method using fat as the cooking medium. Boiling and deep-fat frying are conceptually similar. For both cooking methods, food is placed in a liquid and heat is transferred from the hot liquid (water or fat, respectively) to the food being cooked through conduction (the transfer of heat by direct contact) and convection (the transfer of heat through the currents in a liquid or gas).

The principal difference between boiling and deep-fat frying is the temperature of the cooking medium. The boiling point, 212°F (100°C), is the hottest temperature at which food can be cooked in water. At this temperature, most foods require a long cooking period and surface sugars cannot caramelize. With deep-fat frying, temperatures up to 400°F (200°C) are used. These high temperatures cook food more quickly and allow the food's surface to brown. Even though the food is cooked in a liquid, deep-fat frying is not a moist-heat cooking method because the liquid fat contains no moisture.

SELECTING EQUIPMENT FOR DEEP-FAT FRYING

Unlike most kitchen equipment, a deep-fat fryer has only one purpose: to cook foods in a large amount of hot fat. Fryers are sized by the amount of fat they hold. Most commercial fryers range between 15 and 82 pounds (7–37 kg). Fryers can be either gas or electric and are thermostatically controlled for temperatures between 200° and 400°F (90–200°C).

When choosing a fryer, look for a fry tank with curved, easy-to-clean sloping sides. Some fryers have a cold zone (an area of reduced temperature) at the bottom of the fry tank to trap particles. This prevents them from burning, creating off-flavours and shortening the life of the fryer fat.

Deep-fat fryers usually come with steel wire baskets to hold the food during cooking. Fryer baskets are usually lowered into the fat and raised manually, although some models have automatic basket mechanisms controlled by timers.

As with any piece of equipment, read the operator's manual or have an experienced colleague show you how to operate any deep-fat fryer before using or cleaning it.

The most important factor when choosing a deep-fat fryer is **recovery time**. Recovery time is the length of time it takes the fat to return to the desired cooking temperature after food is submerged in it. When food is submerged, heat is immediately transferred to the food from the fat. This heat transfer lowers the fat's temperature. The more food added at one time, the greater the drop in the fat's temperature. If the temperature drops too much or does not return quickly to the proper cooking temperature, the food may absorb excess fat and become greasy.

Deep-fat frying foods in a sauce pot on the stove top is discouraged because it is both difficult and dangerous. Recovery time is usually very slow and temperatures are difficult to control. Also the fat can spill easily, leading to injuries or creating a fire hazard.

SELECTING FATS FOR DEEP-FAT FRYING

Many types of fats can be used for deep-fat frying. (In this chapter, the term *fat* applies to both solid fats and liquid oils.) Although animal fats, such as rendered beef fat, are sometimes used to impart their specific flavours to deep-fried foods, by far the most common fats used for deep-fat frying are vegetable oils such as soybean, safflower and canola oil.

Specially formulated deep-fat frying compounds are also available. These are usually composed of a vegetable oil or oils to which antifoaming agents, antioxidants and preservatives have been added. These additives increase useable life and raise smoke points.

A fat's **smoke point** is the temperature at which it visibly begins to smoke and chemically begins to break down. Animal fats generally have low smoke points of about 350°F (180°C), making them unsuitable for deep-fat frying. Vegetable oils generally have higher smoke points of about 475°F (250°C), thus providing the high temperatures desired for deep-fat frying. (See Chapter 7, Kitchen Staples, for a list of fat smoke points.)

Some frying fats are also hydrogenated. Hydrogenation is a chemical process that adds hydrogen to oils and turns a liquid oil into a solid (margarine is hydrogenated vegetable oil). Hydrogenated fats are more resistant to oxidation and chemical breakdown.

When fats break down, their chemical structure is altered; the triglyceride molecules that make up fat are converted into individual fatty acids. These acids add undesirable flavours to the fat and can ruin the flavour of the food being cooked. When a fat becomes very dark, foams excessively or adds off-flavours to foods, it has broken down and should be changed. (See Table 21.1.)

To choose the right fat, consider flavour, smoke point and resistance to chemical breakdown. High-quality frying fat should have a clean or natural flavour, a high smoke point and, when properly maintained, be resistant to chemical breakdown.

Maintaining Fryer Fat

Properly maintaining fryer fat greatly extends its useful life. To do so:

1. Store the fat in tightly sealed containers away from strong light; cover the fat in the fryer when not in use. Prolonged exposure to air and light turns fat rancid.

2. Skim and remove food particles from the fat's surface during frying. Food particles cause fat to break down; if they are not removed they will accumulate in the fryer and burn.

3. Do not salt food over the fat. Salt causes fat to break down chemically.

4. Prevent excessive water from coming into contact with the fat; pat-dry moist foods as much as possible before cooking and dry the fryer, baskets and utensils well after cleaning. Water, like salt, causes fat to break down.

5. Do not overheat the fat (turn the fryer down or off if not in use). High temperatures break down the fat.

6. Filter the fat each day or after each shift if the fryer is heavily used. Best results are obtained by using a filtering machine designed specifically for this purpose. Many large commercial fryers even have built-in filter systems. Less well equipped operations can simply pour the hot fat through a paper cone filter into a metal container and then transfer the filtered fat into the cleaned fryer tank.

7. Ensure proper rinsing of soap residues after washing.

TABLE 21.1

Fryer fat can be damaged by:	Change fryer fat when it:
Salt	Becomes dark
Water	Smokes
Overheating	Foams
Food particles	Develops off-flavours
Oxygen	
Soap	

PROCEDURES FOR DEEP-FAT FRYING

The temperature of the fat is critical to successful deep-fat frying. The fat must be hot enough to quickly seal the surface of the food so it does not become excessively greasy, yet it should not be so hot that the food's surface burns before the interior is cooked.

Nearly all foods that are deep-fat fried are cooked at temperatures between 325° and 375°F (160–190°C). The fat's temperature can be adjusted within this range to allow the interior of thicker foods or frozen foods to cook before their surfaces become too dark.

Try not to fry delicately flavoured foods in the same fat used for more strongly flavoured ones. For example, do not cook fruit fritters in the same fat used for catfish. If the fritters are fried in the catfish fat, they could develop an odd taste from the residual flavours left from the catfish.

Deep-Fat Frying Methods

There are two distinct deep-fat frying methods for standard electric or gas fryers: the basket method and the swimming method. Which is used depends upon the food being fried.

The **basket method** of deep-fat frying uses a basket to hold foods that are breaded, individually quick frozen or otherwise do not tend to stick together during cooking. The basket is removed from the fryer and filled as much as two-thirds full of product. (Do not fill the basket while it is hanging over the fat as this allows unnecessary crumbs, salt and food particles to fall into the fat,

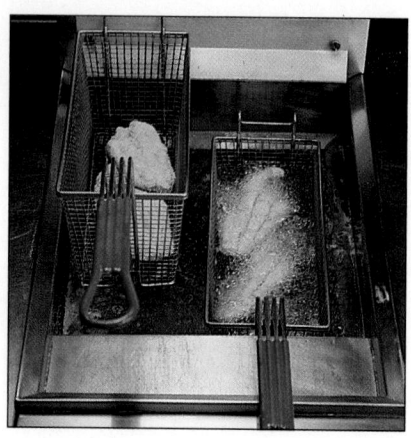

1. Basket method of deep-fat frying.

shortening its life.) The filled basket is then submerged in the hot fat. When cooking is completed, the basket is used to remove the food from the fat.

A variation on this procedure is the **double-basket method**. This variation is necessitated by the fact that many fried foods float as they cook. This may produce undesirable results because the section of the food not submerged may not cook. To prevent this and to promote even cooking, a second basket is used to keep the foods submerged in the fat.

Most battered foods initially sink to the bottom when placed in hot fat, then rise to the top as they cook. Because they would stick to a basket, the **swimming method** of deep-fat frying is used for these foods. With the swimming method, battered foods are carefully dropped directly into the hot fat. (Baskets are not used.) They will rise to the top as they cook. When the surface that is in contact with the fat is properly browned, the food is turned over with a spider or a pair of tongs so that it can cook evenly on both sides. When done, the product is removed and drained, again using a spider or tongs.

2. Double-basket method of deep-fat frying

Draining and Holding after Deep-Fat Frying

All foods that are deep-fat fried must be drained of excess oil before they are served. When removing foods from the deep-fat fryer, allow excess fat to drain into the fryer. Then transfer the foods to a hotel pan that is either lined with absorbent paper or fitted with a rack.

The foods should then be kept under a heat lamp. Steam tables do not keep these foods hot because very little of the food's crisp surface actually touches the hot surface of the steam table's pan.

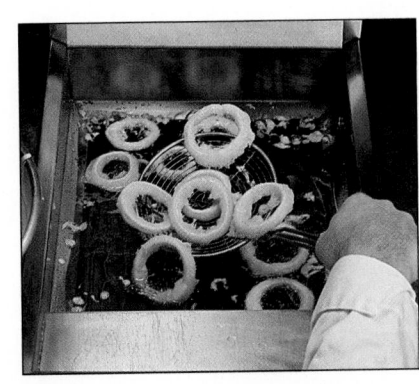

3. Swimming method of deep-fat frying

Selecting Foods for Deep-Fat Frying

Only tender foods should be deep-fat fried. Deep-fat frying cooks foods at relatively high temperatures for short periods of time and does not have a tenderizing effect. Young tender poultry is ideal, as are most types of lean fish and shellfish. Fruits and vegetables can also be deep-fat fried. Probably the most popular food for deep-fat frying is the potato, which is cooked in an endless variety of shapes and forms. (Several of the recipes found in Chapter 23, Potatoes, Grains and Pasta, call for deep-fat frying.) Foods that are deep-fat fried together should be of the same size or thickness so they cook evenly. Slow-cooking vegetables such as broccoli, cauliflower and okra can be blanched first so they cook more quickly.

Preparing Foods for Deep-Fat Frying

With some exceptions (french fries, for example), most foods for deep-fat frying are first breaded or battered. Breading and batter coat the food, keeping it moist and preventing it from becoming excessively greasy during cooking.

Seasoning Foods to Be Deep-Fat Fried

Breaded and battered foods can be seasoned before the breading or batter is applied. Seasonings may also be added to the flour, bread crumbs or batter before the main item is coated.

Food that is deep-fat fried is often salted after being removed from the fat. This should be done immediately after the food is removed from the fryer so the salt will cling more readily.

Breading Foods to Be Deep-Fat Fried

A breaded item is any food that is coated with bread crumbs, cracker meal, cornmeal or other dry meal to protect it during cooking. Breaded foods are generally cooked by deep-fat frying or pan-frying. The breading makes a solid coating that seals during cooking to prevent the fat from coming in direct contact with the food and making it greasy.

Standard Breading Procedure

Whether breading meats, poultry, fish, shellfish or vegetables, a three-step process is typically used. Called the **standard breading procedure**, it gives foods a relatively thick, crisp coating.

1. Pat the food dry and dredge it in seasoned flour. The flour adds seasoning to the food, helps seal it, and allows the egg wash to adhere.
2. Dip the floured food in an egg wash. The egg wash should contain whole eggs whisked together with approximately 1 tablespoon (15 mL) milk or water per egg. The egg wash will cause the crumbs or meal to completely coat the item and form a tight seal when the food is cooked.
3. Coat the food with bread crumbs, cracker crumbs or other dry meal. Shake off the excess crumbs and place the breaded item in a pan. As additional breaded items are added to the pan, align them in a single layer; do not stack them or the breadings will get soggy and the foods will stick together.

Figure 21.1 shows the proper setup for breading foods using the standard breading procedure.

The following procedure helps to bread foods more efficiently:

1. Assemble the mise en place as depicted in Figure 21.1.
2. With your left hand, place the food to be breaded in the flour and coat it evenly. With the same hand, remove the floured item, shake off the excess flour and place it in the egg wash.
3. With your right hand, remove the item from the egg wash and place it in the bread crumbs or meal.
4. With your left hand, cover the item with crumbs or meal and press lightly to make sure the item is completely and evenly coated. Shake off the excess crumbs or meal and place the breaded food in the empty pan for the finished product.

The key is to use one hand for the liquid ingredients and the other hand for the dry ingredients. This prevents your fingers from becoming coated with layer after layer of breading.

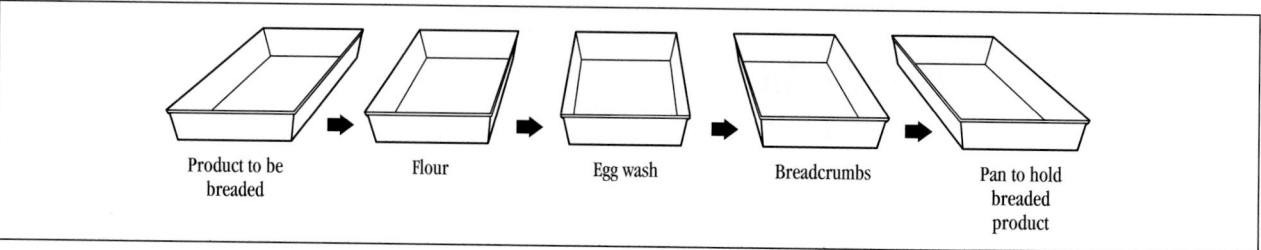

Product to be breaded → Flour → Egg wash → Breadcrumbs → Pan to hold breaded product

FIGURE 21.1   *Setup for the Standard Breading Procedure*

♦♦♦

RECIPE 21.1

DEEP-FRIED CATFISH FILLETS
WITH TARTAR SAUCE

Yield: 8 Servings

Catfish fillets, uniform-size pieces	3 lb.	1.5 kg
Salt and pepper	TT	TT
Flour	as needed	as needed
Egg wash	as needed	as needed
White cornmeal	as needed	as needed
Tartar Sauce (Recipe 24.22)	12 oz.	350 mL

Approximate values per 8 oz. (240 g) serving:

Calories	600
Total fat	46 g
Saturated fat	10 g
Cholesterol	160 mg
Sodium	910 mg
Total carbohydrates	16 g
Protein	31 g
Iron	15%

1. Season the fillets with salt and pepper.
2. Bread the fillets using the standard breading procedure (the white cornmeal is the final coating).
3. Using the basket method, deep-fat fry the fillets until done. Drain well and serve with the tartar sauce.

1. Flour the seasoned fish fillets.

2. Pass the floured fillets through the egg wash.

3. Coat the fillets with white cornmeal.

4. Deep-fat fry the fillets using the basket method.

Croquettes

Croquettes are cooked meats, poultry, vegetables, fish or potatoes, usually bound with a heavy béchamel or velouté sauce and seasoned. They are then breaded and deep-fat fried.

◆◆◆

RECIPE 21.2

SALMON CROQUETTES

Yield: 12 Croquettes

Onion, small dice	2 oz.	60 g
Whole butter	3 oz.	90 g
Flour	3 oz.	90 g
Milk	8 oz.	250 mL
Salmon, poached and flaked	1 lb.	450 g
Fresh dill, chopped	TT	TT
Salt and pepper	TT	TT
Lemon juice	1 Tbsp.	15 mL

Approximate values per croquette:

Calories	140
Total fat	9 g
Saturated fat	4.5 g
Cholesterol	40 mg
Sodium	470 mg
Total carbohydrates	7 g
Protein	9 g
Vitamin A	8%
Calcium	10%

1. Sweat the onion in the butter until translucent.
2. Add the flour and cook to make a white roux.
3. Add the milk to make a heavy béchamel sauce. Cook the sauce until very thick, approximately 5 minutes.
4. Remove the sauce from the heat and transfer it to a mixing bowl. Add the flaked salmon. Season the mixture with dill, salt, pepper and lemon juice and mix well.
5. Spread the mixture in a hotel pan, cover and refrigerate until cold.
6. Portion the mixture using a #20 portion scoop. Form each portion into a cone shape. Bread the croquettes using the standard breading procedure.
7. Using the basket method, deep-fat fry the breaded croquettes until done.

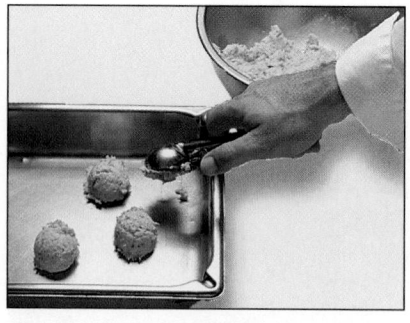

1. Portion the croquette mixture with a portion scoop.

2. Form the mixture into cones or other shapes.

3. Deep-fat fry the croquettes using the basket method.

Battering Foods to be Deep-Fat Fried

Batters, like breading, coat the food being cooked, keeping it moist and preventing it from becoming excessively greasy.

Batters consist of a liquid such as water, milk or beer, combined with a starch such as flour or cornstarch. Many batters also contain a chemical leavening agent such as baking powder. Two common batters are beer batter, which uses the beer for leavening as well as for flavour, and tempura batter.

BASIC PROCEDURE FOR BATTERING FOODS

1. Pat the food dry and dredge in flour if desired.
2. Dip the item in the batter and place it directly in hot fat.

◆◆◆

RECIPE 21.3

BEER-BATTERED ONION RINGS

Yield: 1 qt. (1 L), enough for approx. 4 lb. (1.8 kg) rings

Flour	10 oz.	300 g
Baking powder	2 tsp.	10 mL
Salt	2 tsp.	10 mL
White pepper	1/4 tsp.	1 mL
Egg	1	1
Beer	1 pt.	500 mL
Flour, for dredging	as needed	as needed
Onions, whole	4 lb.	1.8 kg

1. Sift the dry ingredients together.
2. Beat the egg in a separate bowl. Add the beer to the beaten egg.
3. Add the egg-and-beer mixture to the dry ingredients; mix until smooth.
4. Peel the onions and cut in 1/2-inch- (2-cm-) thick slices.
5. Break the slices into rings and dredge in flour.
6. Dip the rings in the batter a few at a time and fry at 375°F (190°C) until done. Drain on absorbent paper, season with additional salt and white pepper and serve hot.

Approximate values per
1 oz. (90 g) serving:

Calories	230
Total fat	10 g
Saturated fat	2.5 g
Cholesterol	5 mg
Sodium	460 mg
Total carbohydrates	31 g
Protein	4 g

1. Dredge the onion rings in flour.

2. Dip the floured rings in batter.

3. Fry the onion rings using the swimming method.

✦✦✦

RECIPE 21.4

TEMPURA SHRIMP AND VEGETABLES WITH DIPPING SAUCE

Yield: 1 qt. (1 L), enough for 4 lb. (1.8 kg) of vegetables or shrimp

Sweet potato	8 oz.	250 g
Dipping Sauce:		
Mirin	2 oz.	60 mL
Soy sauce	4 oz.	120 mL
Rice wine vinegar	2 oz.	60 mL
Lemon juice	1 Tbsp.	15 mL
Wasabi powder	1 tsp.	5 mL
Tempura Batter:		
Eggs	2	2
Sparkling water, ice cold	1 pt.	500 mL
Flour	10 oz.	300 g
Shrimp, 21–25 count, butterflied with tails on	2 lb.	1 kg
Mushrooms, small, whole	1 lb.	450 g
Zucchini, batonnet	8 oz.	250 g

1. Peel the sweet potato and cut in 1/4-inch- (6-mm-) thick slices. If the potato is large, cut each slice in half to make semicircles.
2. Combine all ingredients for the dipping sauce. Set aside.
3. To prepare the batter, beat the eggs and add the cold water.
4. Add the flour to the egg-and-water mixture and mix until the flour is incorporated. There should still be small lumps in the batter. Overmixing develops gluten, which is undesirable. Keep the batter very cold.
5. Dry the shrimp well and keep them thoroughly chilled. Holding them by the tail, dip them into the batter and drop them into the deep-fat fryer using the swimming method. Cook until done.
6. Drop the vegetables into the batter a few at a time. Remove them from the batter one at a time and drop them into the deep-fat fryer using the swimming method. Cook until done.
7. Arrange the tempura shrimp and vegetables on a serving platter. Serve the dipping sauce on the side.

Approximate values per 1 oz. (30 g) serving:

Calories	120
Total fat	5 g
Saturated fat	1 g
Cholesterol	55 mg
Sodium	370 mg
Total carbohydrates	10 g
Protein	7 g

Fritters

Fritters contain diced or chopped fish, shellfish, vegetables or fruits bound together with a thick batter and deep-fat fried. The main ingredient is usually precooked. Fritters are spooned or dropped directly into the hot fat; they form a crust as they cook. Popular examples are clam fritters, corn fritters, artichoke fritters and apple fritters.

✦✦✦

RECIPE 21.5

APPLE FRITTERS

Yield: 100 2-in. (5-cm) fritters

Eggs, separated	6	6
Milk	1 pt.	500 mL
Flour, all purpose	1 lb.	450 g

Baking powder	1 Tbsp.	15 mL
Salt	1 tsp.	5 mL
Sugar	2 oz.	60 g
Cinnamon	1/2 tsp.	2 mL
Apples, peeled, cored, medium dice	1 lb. 8 oz.	700 g
Powdered sugar	as needed	as needed

1. Combine the egg yolks and milk.
2. Sift together the flour, baking powder, salt, sugar and cinnamon. Add the dry ingredients to the milk-and-egg mixture; mix until smooth.
3. Allow the batter to rest 1 hour.
4. Stir the apples into the batter.
5. Just before the fritters are to be cooked, whip the egg whites to soft peaks and fold into the batter.
6. With a scoop drop the fritters into 350°F (180°C) deep fat, using the swimming method. Cook until done.
7. Dust with powdered sugar and serve hot.

Approximate values per 1/2 oz. (15 g) fritter:

Calories	60
Total fat	4 g
Saturated fat	1 g
Cholesterol	15 mg
Sodium	5 mg
Total carbohydrates	6 g
Protein	1 g

1. Add the dry ingredients to the liquids.

2. Fold the egg whites into the batter.

3. Drop the fritters into the deep fat.

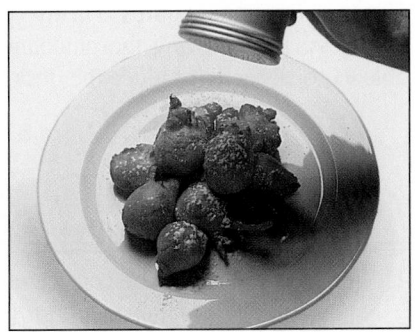

4. Dust the fritters with powdered sugar.

DETERMINING DONENESS

When deep-fat frying, it is difficult to determine the doneness of foods, especially breaded or battered ones. The keen sense of timing that develops with experience is a useful tool. Otherwise:

1. Colour is the most commonly used method for determining doneness. Most fried foods should be deep golden brown when done. But colour can be deceiving. If the temperature of the fat is too high, the food's surface will darken quickly and appear done while the centre remains raw. Also, fat becomes dark with use; dark fat prematurely darkens food, again allowing foods to appear done before they are. Similarly, foods with high sugar content darken quickly in hot fat.

2. Large items such as fried chicken can be removed from the fat and checked with an instant-read thermometer. The internal temperature should be 165–170°F (74–77°C).

3. Fish and shellfish cook quickly and are easily overcooked. If practical, remove a piece and cut it open to determine its doneness. Then rely on timing and colour for the remaining batches.

4. Vegetables should be tender when their surfaces are the proper colour.

5. Potatoes should be attractively browned and cooked to the desired crispness.

Generally, foods must be completely cooked in the deep-fat fryer. It is possible, however, to finish some foods (for example, fried chicken) in the oven after being browned in the fat. But there is a problem to doing so. As the food cooks in the oven, moisture is released that may cause the breading to become soggy on the bottom. Placing the food on a rack can help alleviate this problem.

CONCLUSION

Deep-fat frying is a useful and versatile dry-heat cooking method. To produce high-quality deep-fried foods it is important to understand which foods respond well to deep-fat frying and how to prepare them for cooking. You must also understand how to prevent deep-fried foods from becoming excessively greasy by properly coating them with batters or breadings and controlling cooking temperatures. Finally, you must understand how to determine doneness. By following the guidelines discussed in this chapter you will be able to consistently produce the desired results.

QUESTIONS FOR DISCUSSION

1. What qualities should be considered when choosing a fat for deep-fat frying?
2. Name and describe two styles of deep-fat frying.
3. List three signs that fryer fat has broken down and should be replaced. What causes fryer fat to break down? What can you do to extend the life of fryer fat?
4. Explain the differences between breading and battering foods for deep-fat frying.
5. Describe the correct mise en place for the standard breading procedure.
6. Explain several similarities and differences between fritters and croquettes.

Additional Deep-Fat Frying Recipe

RECIPE 21.6
Whole Sizzling Catfish
with Ginger and Ponzu Sauce

Note: *This dish appears in the Chapter Opening photograph.*

CHINOIS ON MAIN, Santa Monica, CA
Chef Wolfgang Puck

Yield: 4 Servings

Catfish, cleaned, 3 lb. (1.3 kg)	1	1
Salt and pepper	TT	TT
Fresh ginger, sliced and blanched	6 pieces	6 pieces
Peanut oil	as needed	as needed
Lemon juice	as needed	as needed
Ponzu Sauce:		
Soy sauce	4 oz.	120 mL
Mirin	4 oz.	120 mL
Rice vinegar	4 oz.	120 mL
Lemon juice	4 oz.	120 mL
Fresh wood ear mushrooms	as needed for garnish	
Fresh cilantro	as needed for garnish	
Green onions	as needed for garnish	

1. Season the catfish with salt and pepper. Make three 2-inch (5-cm) incisions on each side of the fish and stuff each incision with blanched ginger.
2. Deep-fat fry the catfish in peanut oil, being careful to submerge the entire fish. Cook until golden-coloured and crispy.
3. Squeeze fresh lemon juice over the top of the fish.
4. Make the Ponzu Sauce by combining the listed ingredients.
5. Serve the whole catfish on a platter garnished with wood ear mushrooms, cilantro and green onions. Serve the Ponzu Sauce on the side.

Approximate values per serving:	
Calories	970
Total fat	50 g
Saturated fat	12 g
Cholesterol	305 mg
Sodium	2710 mg
Total carbohydrates	60 g
Protein	70 g
Vitamin C	25%
Calcium	20%
Iron	40%

Weblinks

Learn2 Shop for Cooking Oils
   learn2.com/08/0864/08646.html

Canola Oil Frying Tips
   www.canolainfo.org/html/fry.html

American Council on Science and Health: The Fat Wars (article by Agnes Heinz, Ph.D., discussing public misconceptions about fat consumption)
   www.acsh.org/publications/priorities/0301/fatwars.html

Japanese Cuisine — Tempura
   www.masterstech-home.com/The_Kitchen/Articles/TempuraArticle.html

CHAPTER 22 VEGETABLES

LEARNING OUTCOMES

After studying this chapter you will be able to:

◆ identify a variety of vegetables
◆ purchase vegetables appropriate for your needs
◆ store vegetables properly
◆ explain how vegetables are preserved
◆ prepare vegetables for cooking or service: cut broccoli spears, cut cauliflower florets, cut and pit avacados, cut peppers julienne, core jalapeños, roast peppers, make tomato concassé, cut corn kernels from ear, soak dried beans, quick-soak dried beans, prepare fresh artichokes
◆ apply various cooking methods to vegetables: broiling or grilling, roasting or baking, sautéing or stir-frying, refreshing, boiling, cooking dried beans, steaming, braising and stewing, microwaving, puréeing

Vegetarian—*A person who primarily or exclusively eats plant foods.*

Ovo-lacto-vegetarian—*A vegetarian who does not eat meat, poultry or fish, but will eat eggs and dairy products.*

Vegan—*A vegetarian who does not eat any animal products.*

L̸ong overcooked and underrated, vegetables are enjoying a welcome surge in popularity. Gone are the days when a chef included vegetables as an afterthought to the "meat and potatoes" of the meal. Now, properly prepared fresh vegetables are used to add flavour, colour and variety to almost any meal. Many restaurants are featuring vegetarian entrees, an extensive selection of vegetable side dishes or an entire vegetarian menu. This trend reflects the demands of more knowledgeable and health-conscious consumers as well as the increased availability of high-quality fresh produce.

In this chapter we identify many of the vegetables typically used by food service operations. (Potatoes, although vegetables, are discussed in Chapter 23, Potatoes, Grains and Pasta, and salad greens are discussed in Chapter 24, Salads and Salad Dressings.) Here we also discuss how fresh and preserved vegetables are purchased, stored and prepared for service or cooking. Many of the cooking methods analyzed in Chapter 9, Principles of Cooking, are then applied to vegetables.

The term **vegetable** refers to any herbaceous plant that can be partially or wholly eaten. An herbaceous plant has little or no woody tissue. The portions we consume include the leaves, stems, roots, tubers, seeds and flowers. Vegetables contain more starch and less sugar than fruits. Therefore vegetables tend to be savoury, not sweet. Also unlike fruits, vegetables are most often eaten cooked, not raw.

IDENTIFYING VEGETABLES

This book presents fruits and vegetables according to the ways most people view them and use them, rather than by rigid botanical classifications. Although produce such as tomatoes, peppers and eggplants are botanically fruits, they are prepared and served like vegetables and are included here under the category we call "fruit-vegetables." Potatoes, although botanically vegetables, are discussed with other starches in Chapter 23, Potatoes, Grains and Pasta.

We divide vegetables into eleven categories based upon either botanical relationship or edible part. They are: bulb, flower/bud, fungus, leafy, pod, root, legume/pulse, shoot, stalk, tuber and fruit type. Some people recognize more and fewer categories. There is no definitive answer to what a vegetable is. A vegetable may have several names, varying from region to region or on a purveyor's whim. The names given here follow generally accepted custom and usage.

Flowers/Buds

The *Brassica* or cabbage family includes a wide range of vegetables used for their heads, flowers or leaves. They are generally quick-growing, cool-weather crops. Many are ancient plants with unknown origins. They are inexpensive, readily available and easy to prepare.

Bok Choy

Bok choy, also known as pok choy, is a white-stemmed variety of southern Chinese cabbage. The relatively tightly packed leaves are dark green, with long white ribs attached at a bulbous stem. The stalks are crisp and mild with a flavour similar to romaine lettuce. Although bok choy may be eaten raw, it is most often stir-fried or used in soups.

Choose heads with bright white stalks and dark green leaves; avoid those with brown, moist spots. Fresh bok choy is available all year. Jars of pickled and fermented bok choy (known as Korean kim chee) are also available.

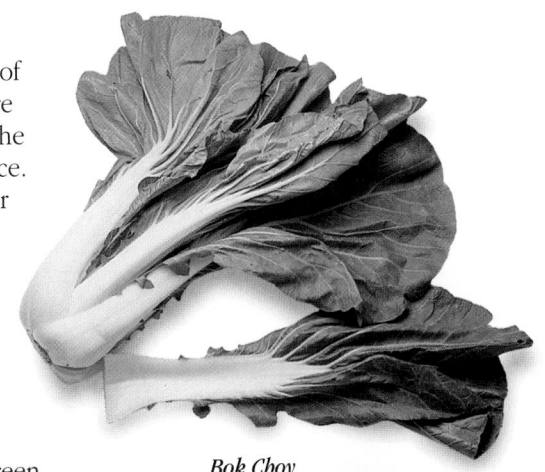

Bok Choy

Broccoli

Broccoli, a type of flower, has a thick central stalk with greyish-green leaves topped with one or more heads of green florets. Broccoli may be eaten raw or steamed, microwaved or sautéed and served warm or cold. Broccoli stalks are extremely firm and benefit from blanching. Stems are often slow-cooked for soups. Generally, broccoli leaves are not eaten.

Choose firm stalks with compact clusters of tightly closed dark green florets. Avoid stalks with yellow flowers. Broccoli is available all year.

BASIC PROCEDURE FOR CUTTING BROCCOLI SPEARS

Cut off the thick, woody portion of the stalk, then cut the florets and stems into spears.

Broccoli

Brussels Sprouts

Brussels sprouts (Fr. *choux de Bruxelles*) were first cultivated around 1700. The plant produces numerous small heads arranged in neat rows along a thick stalk. The tender young sprouts are similar to baby cabbages and are usually steamed or roasted. Brussels sprouts have a strong, nutty flavour that blends well with game, ham, duck or rich meats.

Choose small, firm sprouts that are compact and heavy. The best size is 3/4 to 1-1/2 inches (2 to 4 cm) in diameter. They should be bright green and free of blemishes. Their peak season is from September through February.

Brussels Sprouts

Cauliflower

Cauliflower (Fr. *chou-fleur*) is the king of the cabbage family. Each stalk produces one flower or head surrounded by large green leaves. The head, composed of creamy white florets, can be cooked whole or cut into separate florets for steaming, blanching or stir-frying.

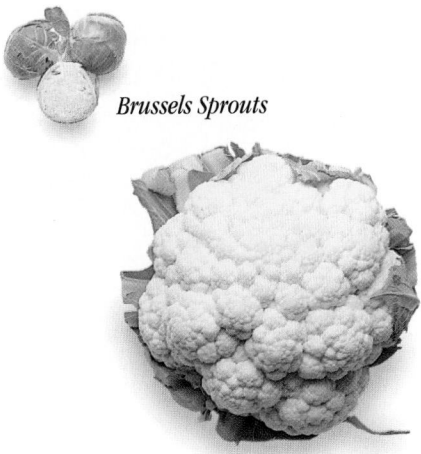

Cauliflower

Choose firm, compact heads. Any attached leaves should be bright green and crisp. A yellow colour or spreading florets indicate that the vegetable is overly mature. Cauliflower is available all year, especially from the late fall through the spring.

BASIC PROCEDURE FOR CUTTING CAULIFLOWER FLORETS

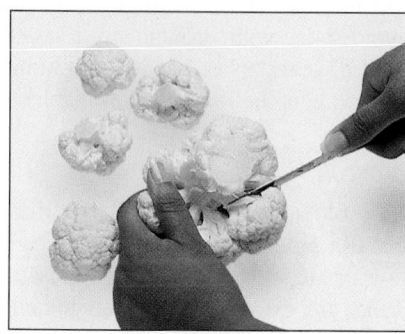

1. Cut off the stem and leaves.

2. Cut the florets off the core.

Green and Red Cabbages

Cabbage (Fr. *chou*) has been a staple of northern European cuisine for centuries. The familiar green cabbages have large, firm, round heads with tightly packed pale green leaves, which are actually flower petals. Flat and conical-shaped heads are also available. Red (or purple) cabbages are a different strain and may be tougher than green cabbages. Cabbage can be eaten raw (as in coleslaw) or used in soups or stews; it can be braised, steamed or stir-fried. The large, waxy leaves can also be steamed until soft, then wrapped around a filling of seasoned meat.

Choose firm heads without dried cores. Cabbages are available all year.

Green and Red Cabbages

Kale

Kale has large ruffled, curly or bumpy leaves. Its rather bitter flavour goes well with rich meats such as game, pork or ham. Kale is typically boiled, stuffed or used in soups.

Choose leaves that are crisp, with a greyish-green colour. Kale is available all year, with peak season during the winter months.

Ornamental or flowering kale, sometimes marketed as "savoy," is edible, but its pink, purple, yellow or white-and-green variegated leaves are best used for decoration and garnish.

Kale

Ornamental Kale

Napa Cabbage

Napa cabbage, also known as Chinese cabbage, is widely used in Asian cuisines. It has a stout, elongated head with relatively tightly packed, firm, pale green leaves. It is moister and more tender than common green and red cabbages, with a milder, more delicate flavour. Napa cabbage may be eaten raw but is particularly well suited for stir-frying or steaming.

Choose heads with crisp leaves that are free of blemishes. Napa cabbage is available fresh all year.

Napa Cabbage

Savoy

Savoy

Savoy cabbage has curly or ruffled leaves, often in variegated shades of green and purple. (The term "savoyed" is used to refer to any vegetable with bumpy, wavy or wrinkled leaves.) Savoy cabbage tends to be milder and more tender than regular cabbages and can be substituted for them, cooked or uncooked. Savoy leaves also make an attractive garnish.

Choose heads that are loose or tight, depending on the variety, with tender, unblemished leaves. Peak season is from August through the spring.

Fruit-Vegetables

Botanists classify avocados, eggplants, peppers, tomatoes, gourds and squashes as fruits because they develop from the ovary of flowering plants and contain one or more seeds. Chefs, however, prepare and serve them like vegetables; therefore they are discussed here.

Avocados

Avocados include several varieties of pear-shaped fruits with rich, high-fat flesh. This light golden-green flesh surrounds a large, inedible, oval-shaped seed (pit). Some varieties have smooth, green skin; others have pebbly, almost black skin. Avocados should be used at their peak of ripeness, a condition that lasts only briefly. Firm avocados lack the desired flavour and creamy texture. Ripe avocados should be soft to the touch but not mushy. Ripe Haas avocados have almost-black skins; the skins of the other varieties remain green when ripe. Firm avocados can be left at room temperature to ripen, then refrigerated for one or two days. Avocados are most often used raw to garnish salads, mashed or puréed for sauces, sliced for sandwiches or diced for omelets. Avocado halves are popular containers for chilled meat, fish, shellfish or poultry salads. Because avocado flesh turns brown very quickly once cut, dip avocado halves or slices in lemon juice and keep unused portions tightly covered with plastic wrap.

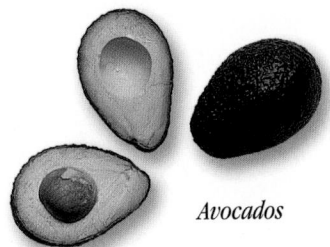

Avocados

Choose avocados that are free of blemishes or moist spots. The flesh should be free of dark spots or streaks. Available all year, the peak season for Haas avocados is April through October; for Fuertes avocados it is November through April.

BASIC PROCEDURE FOR CUTTING AND PITTING AVOCADOS

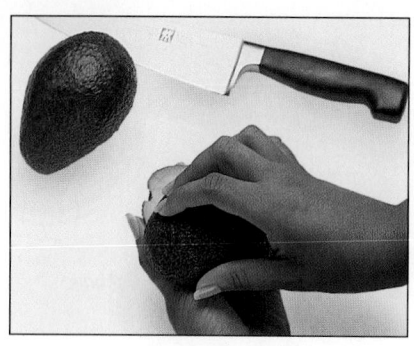

1. Cut the avocado in half length-wise. Separate the two halves with a twisting motion.

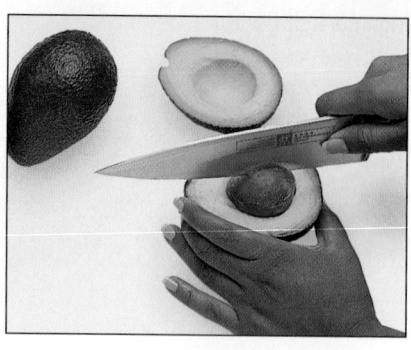

2. Insert a chef's knife into the pit and twist to remove.

3. Scoop the flesh out of the skin with a large spoon.

Western Eggplant

Eggplants

Two types of eggplants (Fr. *aubergine*) are commonly available: Asian and western. Asian varieties are either round or long and thin, with skin colours ranging from creamy white to deep purple. Western eggplants, which are more common in North America, tend to be shaped like a plump pear with shiny lavender to purple-black skin. Both types have a dense, khaki-coloured flesh with a rather bland flavour that absorbs other flavours well during cooking. Eggplants can be grilled, baked, steamed, fried or sautéed. They are commonly used in Mediterranean and East Indian cuisines (especially in vegetarian dishes), but also appear in European and North American dishes. The skin may be left intact or removed before or after cooking, as desired. Sliced eggplants may be salted and left to drain for 30 minutes to remove moisture and bitterness before cooking.

Choose plump, heavy eggplants with a smooth, shiny skin that is not blemished or wrinkled. Asian varieties tend to be softer than western. Eggplants are available all year, with peak season during the late summer.

Asian Eggplants

Peppers

Members of the *Capsicum* family are native to the New World. When "discovered" by Christopher Columbus he called them "peppers" because of their sometimes fiery flavour. These peppers, which include sweet peppers and hot peppers (chiles), are unrelated to peppercorns, the East Indian (Asian) spice for which Columbus was actually searching. Interestingly, New World peppers were readily accepted in Indian and Asian cuisines, in which they are now considered staples.

Fresh peppers are found in a wide range of colours—green, red, yellow, orange, purple or white—as well as shapes, from tiny teardrops to cones to spheres. They have dense flesh and a hollow central cavity. The flesh is lined with placental ribs (the white internal veins), to which tiny white seeds are attached. A core of seeds is also attached to the stem end of each pepper.

Chile peppers get their heat from capsaicin, which is found not in the flesh or seeds, but in the placental ribs. Thus a pepper's heat can be greatly reduced by carefully removing the ribs and attached seeds. Generally, the smaller the chile, the hotter it is. The amount of heat varies from variety to variety, however, and even from one pepper to another depending on growing conditions. Hot, dry conditions result in hotter peppers than do cool, moist conditions. A pepper's heat can be measured by Scoville Heat Units, a subjective rating in which the sweet bell pepper usually rates 0 units, the jalapeño rates from 2500 to 5000 units, the tabasco rates from 30,000 to 50,000 units and the habanero rates a whopping 100,000 to 300,000 units.

When selecting peppers, choose those that are plump and brilliantly coloured with smooth, unblemished skins. Avoid wrinkled, pitted or blistered peppers. A bright green stem indicates freshness.

Green Bell Pepper

Sweet Peppers

Common sweet peppers, known as bell peppers, are thick-walled fruits available in green, red, yellow, purple, orange and other colours. They are heart-shaped or boxy, with a short stem and crisp flesh. Their flavour is warm, sweet (red peppers tend to be the sweetest) and relatively mild. Raw bell peppers may be sliced or diced and used in salads or sandwiches. Bell peppers may also be stuffed and baked, grilled, fried, sautéed or puréed for soups, sauces or condiments. Green bell peppers are available all year; other colours are more readily available during the summer and fall.

Red and Yellow Bell Peppers

BASIC PROCEDURE FOR CUTTING PEPPERS JULIENNE

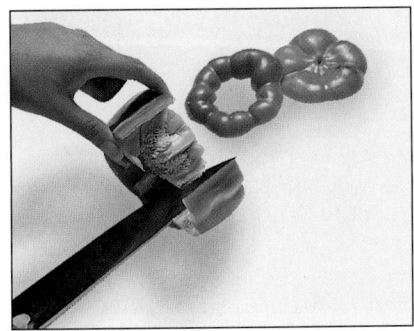

1. Trim off the ends of the pepper; cut away the seeds and core.

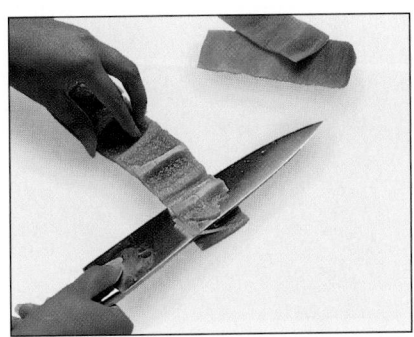

2. Cut away the pale ribs, trimming the flesh to the desired thickness.

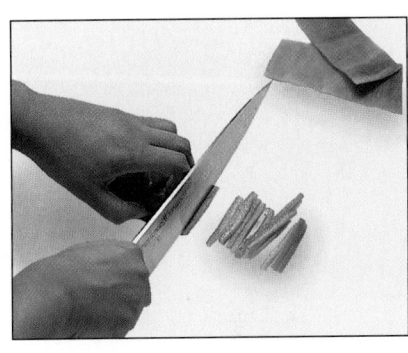

3. Slice the flesh in julienne.

Hot Peppers

Hot peppers, also known as chiles, are also members of the *Capsicum* family. Although a chile's most characteristic attribute is its pungency, each chile actually has a distinctive flavour, from mild and rich to spicy and sweet to fiery hot.

Chiles are commonly used in Asian, Indian, Mexican and Latin American cuisines. The larger (and milder) of the hot peppers, such as Anaheim and poblano, can be stuffed and baked or sautéed as a side dish. Most chiles, however, are used to add flavour and seasoning to sauces and other dishes. Fresh chiles are available all year and are also available canned in a variety of processed forms such as whole or diced roasted, pickled or marinated.

(clockwise from bottom left) Red and Green Serrano; Green and Red Jalapeño; Yellow Hot; Poblano; and Anaheim Chiles.

The popularity of Southwestern cuisine, hot condiments and salsas has brought with it a new appreciation and respect for chiles. Diners, and cooks, may find the names given to the various chiles confusing, however. Most chiles can be used either fresh or dried; drying changes not only the pepper's flavour, but also its name. Regional variations in chile names also add to the confusion. Several of the more frequently encountered chiles are listed here according to the names most commonly used for both their fresh and dried forms.

Fresh (Fresco)	Dried (Seco)
Jalapeño	Chipotle (smoked)
Mirasol	Guajillo

BASIC PROCEDURE FOR CORING JALAPEÑOS

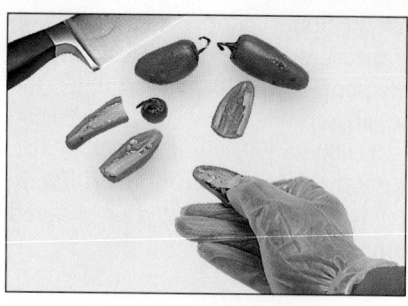

Cut the jalapeño in half lengthwise. Push the core and seeds out with your thumb. You can avoid burning your fingers by wearing rubber gloves when working with hot chiles.

Dried chiles are widely used in Mexican, Central American and southwestern cuisines. They may be ground to create a powdered spice called chilli or soaked in liquid, then puréed, for sauces or condiments. Drying radically alters the flavour of chiles, making them stronger and more pungent. Dried chiles are often called by names different from those of their fresh versions. For example, the fresh poblano becomes the dried ancho; the fresh jalapeño becomes the dried, smoked chipotle.

Choose dried chiles that are clean and unbroken, with some flexibility. Avoid any with white spots or a stale aroma.

BASIC PROCEDURE FOR ROASTING PEPPERS

1. Roast the pepper over an open flame until completely charred.

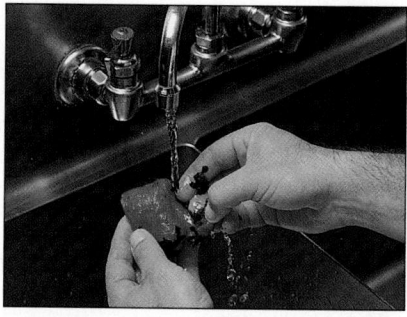

2. Remove the burnt skin and rinse under running water.

Tomatillos

Tomatillos

Tomatillos, also known as Mexican or husk tomatoes, grow on small, weedy bushes. They are bright green, about the size of a small tomato, and are covered with a thin, papery husk. They have a tart, lemony flavour and crisp, moist flesh. Although an important ingredient in southwestern and northern Mexican cuisines, tomatillos may not be readily available in other areas. Tomatillos can be used raw in salads, puréed for salsa or cooked in soups, stews or vegetable dishes.

Choose tomatillos whose husks are split but still look fresh. The skin should be plump, shiny and slightly sticky. They are available all year, with peak season during the summer and fall.

Tomatoes

Tomatoes (Fr. *tomate* or *pomme d'amour;* It. *pomodoro*) are available in a wide variety of colours and shapes. They vary from green (unripe) to golden yellow to ruby red; from tiny spheres (currant tomatoes) to huge, squat ovals (beefsteak). Some, such as the plum tomato, have lots of meaty flesh with only a few seeds; others, such as the slicing tomato, have lots of seeds and juice, but only a few meaty membranes. All tomatoes have a similar flavour, but the levels of sweetness and acidity vary depending on the species, growing conditions and ripeness at harvest.

Because tomatoes are highly perishable, they are usually harvested when mature but still green (unripe), then shipped to wholesalers who ripen them in temperature- and humidity-controlled rooms. The effect on flavour and texture is unfortunate.

Tomatoes are used widely in salads, soups, sauces and baked dishes. They are most often eaten raw, but can be grilled, pickled, pan-fried, roasted or sautéed as a side dish.

Choose fresh tomatoes that are plump with a smooth, shiny skin. The colour should be uniform and true for the variety. Tomatoes are available all year, with a summer peak season for most varieties. Many canned tomato products are also available (for example, purée, paste, sauce or stewed whole), as are dried tomatoes.

(clockwise from lower right) Pear, Cherry, Plum and Beefsteak Tomatoes

♦♦♦

THREE TREASURES OF THE NEW WORLD

In lieu of many spices, golden treasures and precious gems, early Spanish explorers returned to Spain with items of much greater significance: tomatoes, potatoes and corn. Unfortunately for those who financed the voyagers, the value of this produce was not immediately appreciated.

The Spanish and the Italians hailed the tomato (whose name comes from the Aztec name *tomatl*) as an aphrodisiac—perhaps because of its resemblance to the human heart—when it arrived from the New World during the 16th century. But even though tomatoes soon became part of Spanish and Italian cuisines, most other Europeans, New World colonists and, later, Americans considered tomatoes poisonous. (There is some truth to this notion: tomato vines and leaves contain tomatine, an alkaloid that can cause health problems.) Thus for many years and in many societies, only the adventurous ate tomatoes. Tomato historians consider September 26, 1820, a red-letter day marking the popular acceptance of the tomato. On that day, the then-well-known eccentric Colonel Robert Gibbon Johnson ate an entire bushel of toma-

toes on the Salem, New Jersey, courthouse steps before a crowd of thousands—and lived. Tomatoes soon became one of the most popular of all vegetables.

Similarly, the potato, first delivered to Europe from its native Peru by Francisco Pizarro in the 16th century, did not win wide acceptance in haute cuisine until Antoine-Augustin Parmentier (1737–1813), a French army pharmacist, induced King Louis XVI of France (reign 1775–1793) to try one. He and his courtiers liked them so much they even began wearing potato blossom boutonnières. Parmentier was ultimately honoured for his starchy contribution to French cuisine by having several potato dishes named for him. Indeed, the French still call potato soup *potage Parmentier* in his honour. Not only did Parmentier lobby for the acceptance of the potato as a food fit for a king, he also prophesied that the potato would make starvation impossible. Potatoes ultimately did become a staple of many diets. But, sadly, the converse of Parmentier's prophecy came true during the Irish Potato Famine of 1846–48, when a terrible blight destroyed the potato crop. Nearly 1.5

million people died and an equal number emigrated to North America. They brought with them a cuisine that incorporated potatoes; thus an appreciation of the common potato was reintroduced to its native land.

When returning from his second voyage to the New World, Columbus took corn with him. Called *mahiz* or *maize* by West Indian natives, corn had been a staple of Central American diets for at least 5000 years. Although Europeans did not actively shun corn as they did tomatoes and potatoes, corn never really caught on in most of Europe. (As with another famous New World import, corn's origin was mistakenly attributed by the British, Dutch, Germans and Russians to Turkey. They called corn "Turkish wheat"; the Turks simply called it "foreign grain.") Grown for human consumption mostly in Italy, Spain and southwestern France, corn was and still is usually eaten ground and boiled as polenta. But despite an unenthusiastic European reception, corn's popularity quickly spread well beyond Europe: Within 50 years of Columbus's journey, corn was being cultivated in lands as distant from the New World as China, India and sub-Saharan Africa.

BASIC PROCEDURE FOR MAKING TOMATO CONCASSÉ

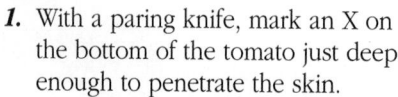

1. With a paring knife, mark an X on the bottom of the tomato just deep enough to penetrate the skin.

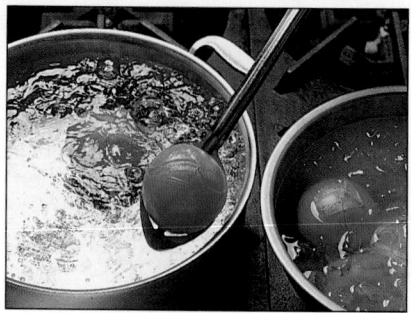

2. Blanch the tomato in boiling water for 20 seconds; refresh in ice water.

3. Using a paring knife, cut out the core and peel the tomato.

4. Cut the tomato in half horizontally and squeeze out the seeds and juice.

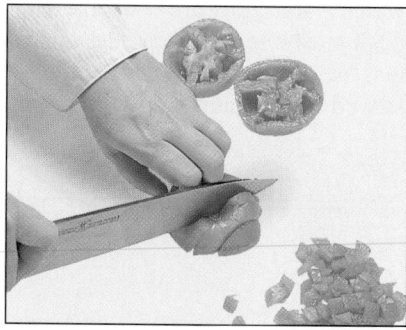

5. Chop or dice the tomato as desired for the recipe.

Cucumbers

Cucumbers can be divided into two categories: pickling and slicing. The two types are not interchangeable. Pickling cucumbers include the cornichon, dill and gherkin. They are recognizable by their sharp black or white spines and are quite bitter when raw. Slicing cucumbers include the burpless, the seedless English (or hothouse), the lemon (which is round and yellow) and the common green market cucumber. Most have relatively thin skins and may be marketed with a wax coating to prevent moisture loss and improve appearance. Waxed skins should be peeled. All cucumbers are valued for their refreshing cool taste and astringency. Slicing cucumbers are usually served raw, in salads or mixed with yogurt and dill or mint as a side dish, especially for spicy dishes. Pickling cucumbers are generally served pickled, without any further processing.

Choose cucumbers that are firm but not hard. Avoid those that are limp, yellowed or have soft spots. The common varieties are available all year, although peak season is from April through October.

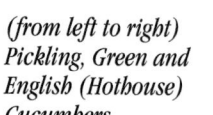

(from left to right) Pickling, Green and English (Hothouse) Cucumbers

Gourds and Squashes

The *Cucurbitaceae* or gourd family includes almost 750 species; its members are found in warm regions worldwide. Gourds are characterized by large, complex root systems with quick-growing, trailing vines and large leaves. Their flowers are often attractive and edible. Although some members of the gourd family originated in Africa, chayotes and most squashes are native to the Americas.

Chayotes

The chayote, also known as merliton or vegetable pear, is a food staple throughout Central America. The vine bears slightly lumpy, pear-shaped fruits with a smooth, light green skin and a paler green flesh. There is a single white, edible seed in the centre. Chayotes are starchy and very bland and are usually combined with more flavourful ingredients. They may be eaten raw, but their flavour and texture benefit from roasting, steaming, sautéing or grilling.

Choose chayotes that have well-coloured skin with few ridges. Avoid those with very soft spots or bruises. Their peak season is the late fall and winter.

Chayotes

Squashes

Squashes are the fleshy fruits of a large number of plants in the gourd family. Many varieties are available in a range of colours, shapes and sizes. Squashes can be classified as winter or summer based on their peak season and skin type. All squashes have a centre cavity filled with many seeds, although in winter varieties the cavity is more pronounced. Squash blossoms are also edible: They may be added to salads raw, dipped in batter and deep-fat fried or filled with cheese or meat and baked.

Choose squashes with unbroken skins and good colour for the variety. Avoid any squash with soft, moist spots.

Winter squashes include the acorn, banana, butternut, Hubbard, pumpkin and spaghetti varieties. They have hard skins (shells) and seeds. Pumpkin seeds are roasted and eaten. The flesh, which may be removed from the shell before or after cooking, tends to be sweeter and more strongly flavoured than that of summer squash. Winter squashes should not be served raw; they can be baked, steamed or sautéed. Most winter squashes can also be puréed for soups or pie fillings. Their peak season is October through March.

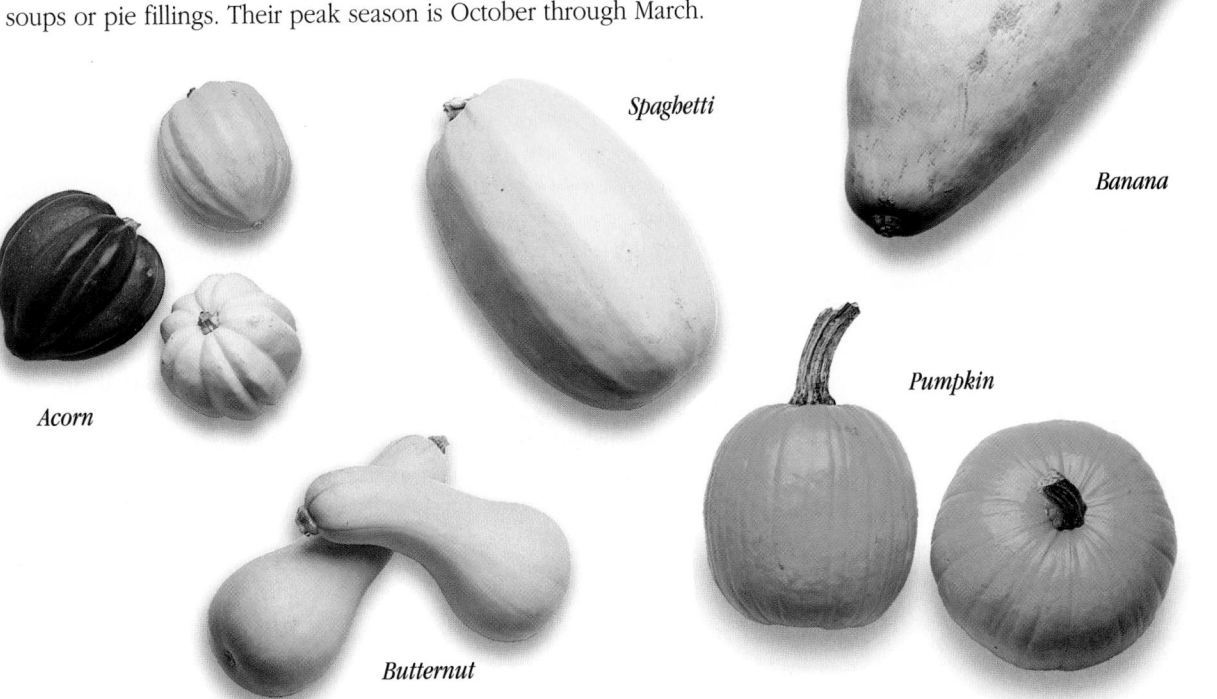

Spaghetti

Banana

Acorn

Pumpkin

Butternut

Zucchini

Summer squashes include the pattypan, yellow crookneck and zucchini varieties. They have soft edible skins and seeds that are generally not removed before cooking. Most summer squashes may be eaten raw, but are also suitable for grilling, sautéing, steaming or baking. Although summer squashes are now available all year, their peak season is April through September.

Yellow Crookneck

Leafy Greens

The term *leafy* refers to a variety of leafy green vegetables that may be served raw, but are usually cooked. Greens have long been used in the cuisines of India, Asia and the Mediterranean and are an important part of regional cuisine in the southern United States. Most have strong, spicy flavours. Mustard, sorrel, spinach, Swiss chard, dandelion and turnip greens fall into this category. The milder varieties of greens that are eaten almost always raw include the lettuces discussed in Chapter 24, Salads and Salad Dressings.

Greens have an extremely high water content, which means that cooking causes drastic shrinkage. As a general rule, allow 8 ounces (250 g) per portion before cooking.

Choose young, tender greens with good colour and no limpness. Avoid greens with dry-looking stems or yellow leaves. Most greens are available fresh all year, especially from November through June. The more popular greens are also available canned or frozen.

Mustard

Mustard, a member of the cabbage family, was brought to North America by early European immigrants. Mustard has large, dark green leaves with frilly edges. It is known for its assertive, bitter flavour. Mustard greens can be served raw in salads or used as garnish. Or they can be cooked, often with white wine, vinegar and herbs.

Choose crisp, bright green leaves without discolouration.

Mustard

Sorrel

Sorrel is an abundant and rather ordinary wild member of the buckwheat family. Its tartness and sour flavour are used in soups and sauces and to accent other vegetables. It is particularly good with fatty fish or rich meats. Sorrel leaves naturally acquire the texture of a purée after only a few minutes of moist-heat cooking.

Choose leaves that are fully formed, with no yellow blemishes.

Sorrel

Spinach

Spinach (Fr. *épinard*) is a versatile green that grows rapidly in cool climates. It has smooth, bright green leaves attached to thin stems. Spinach may be eaten raw in salads, cooked by almost any moist-heat method, microwaved or sautéed. It can be used in stuffings, baked or creamed dishes, soups or stews. Spinach grows in sandy soil and must be rinsed repeatedly in cold water to remove all traces of grit from the leaves. It bruises easily and should be handled gently during washing. Stems and large mid-ribs should be removed.

Choose bunches with crisp, tender, deep green leaves; avoid yellow leaves or those with blemishes.

Spinach

Swiss Chard

Chard—the reference to "Swiss" is inexplicable—is a type of beet that does not produce a tuberous root. It is used for its wide, flat, dark green leaves. Chard can be steamed, sautéed or used in soups. Its tart, spinachlike flavour blends well with sweet ingredients such as fruit.

Choose leaves that are crisp, with some curliness or savoying. Ribs should be an unblemished white or red.

Turnip Greens

The leaves of the turnip root have a pleasantly bitter flavour, similar to peppery mustard greens. The dark green leaves are long, slender and deeply indented. Turnip greens are best eaten steamed, sautéed, baked or microwaved.

Swiss Chard

Turnip Greens

Fungi

Mushrooms

Mushrooms (Fr. *champignon*; It. *funghi*) are members of a broad category of plants known as fungi. (Fungi have no seeds, stems or flowers; they reproduce through spores.) Mushrooms have a stalk with an umbrella-like top. Although not actually a vegetable, mushrooms are used and served in much the same manner as vegetables.

Several types of cultivated mushroom are available. They include the meadow (or white), shiitake, straw, enokidake (also called enoki) and cloud ear (also known as wood ear or Chinese black). Button mushrooms are the smallest, most immature form of the meadow mushroom. Portobello and crimini are now commonly available, along with chanterelles and lobster mushrooms.

Many wild mushrooms are gathered and sold by specialty purveyors. Because wild mushroom spores are spread around the world by air currents, the same item may be found in several areas, each with a different common name. Wild mushrooms have a stronger earthy or nutty flavour than cultivated mushrooms, and should generally be cooked before eating.

Mushrooms, whether cultivated or gathered from the wild, are available fresh, canned or dried. Because mushrooms are composed of up to 80% water, dried products are often the most economical, even though they may cost hundreds of dollars per pound. Dried mushrooms can be stored in a cool, dry place for months. When needed, they are rehydrated by soaking in warm water until soft, approximately 10–20 minutes.

Choose fresh mushrooms that are clean, without soft or moist spots or blemishes. Fresh cultivated mushrooms are generally available all year; fresh wild mushrooms are available seasonally, usually during the summer and fall. Cultivated mushrooms with exposed

Black Trumpet

Clam Shell

Pom Pom Blanc

Hen of the Woods

Morel

Porcini (cèpe or cep)

Enokidake

Oyster

Shiitake

White

gills (the ridges on the underside of the umbrellalike top) are old and should be avoided. Fresh mushrooms can be refrigerated in an open container for up to five days. Normally, it is not necessary to peel mushrooms; if they are dirty, they should be quickly rinsed (not soaked) in cool water just before use.

Truffles

Truffles are actually tubers that grow near the roots of oak or beech trees. They can be cultivated only to the extent that oak groves are planted to encourage truffle growth. The two principal varieties are the Périgord (black) and the Piedmontese (white). Fresh truffles are gathered in the fall and are rarely marketed outside their locale. Truffles, especially white ones, have a strong aroma and flavour, requiring only a small amount to add their special flavour to soups, sauces, pasta and other items. Black truffles are often used as a garnish or to flavour pâtés, terrines or egg dishes. Because fresh imported truffles can cost several hundred dollars per pound, most kitchens purchase truffles canned, dried or processed.

Black Truffles

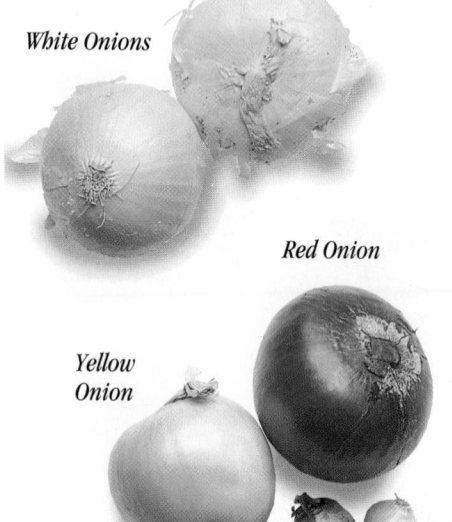

White Onions

Red Onion

Yellow Onion

Shallots   *Pearl Onions*

Fennel

Bulbs

Onions are strongly flavoured, aromatic members of the lily family and are the most widely known bulb. Most have edible grasslike or tubular leaves. Almost every culture incorporates them into its cuisine as a vegetable and for flavouring.

Bulb Onions

Common or bulb onions (Fr. *oignons*) may be white, yellow (Bermuda or Spanish) or red (purple). Medium-sized yellow and white onions are the most strongly flavoured. Larger onions tend to be sweeter and milder. Widely used as a flavouring ingredient, onions are indispensable in mirepoix. Onions are also prepared as a side dish by deep-fat frying, roasting, grilling, steaming or boiling.

Pearl onions are small, about 1/2 inch (1.25 cm) in diameter, with yellow or white skins. They have a mild flavour and can be grilled, boiled, roasted or sautéed whole as a side dish, or used in soups or stews.

Choose onions that are firm, dry and feel heavy. The outer skins should be dry and brittle. Avoid onions that have begun to sprout. They should be stored in a cool, dry, well-ventilated area. Do not refrigerate onions until they are cut. Onions are available all year.

Fennel

Fennel (Fr. *fenouil*) is a Mediterranean favourite used for thousands of years as a vegetable (the bulb), an herb (the leaves) and a spice (the seeds). The bulb (often incorrectly referred to as sweet anise) has short, tight, overlapping celerylike stalks with feathery leaves. The flavour is similar to anise or licorice, becoming milder when cooked. Fennel bulbs may be eaten raw or grilled, steamed, sautéed, baked or microwaved.

Choose fairly large, bright white bulbs on which the cut edges appear fresh, without dryness or browning. The bulb should be compact, not spreading. Fresh fennel's peak season is September through May.

Garlic

Garlic (Fr. *ail*; Sp. *ajo*) is also used in almost all of the world's cuisines. A head of garlic is composed of many small cloves. Each clove is wrapped in a thin husk or peel; the entire head is encased in several thin layers of papery husk. Of the 300 or so types of garlic known, only three are commercially significant. The most common is pure white, with a sharp flavour. A Mexican variety is pale pink and more strongly flavoured. Elephant garlic is apple-sized and particularly mild. Although whole bulbs can be baked or roasted, garlic is most often separated into cloves, peeled, sliced, minced or crushed and used to flavour a wide variety of dishes. When using garlic remember that the more finely the cloves are crushed, the stronger the flavour will be. And, cooking reduces garlic's pungency; the longer it is cooked, the milder it becomes.

Choose firm, dry bulbs with tightly closed cloves and smooth skins. Avoid bulbs with green sprouts. Store fresh garlic in a cool, well-ventilated place; do not refrigerate. Fresh garlic is available all year. Jars of processed and pickled garlic products are also available.

Garlic

Kohlrabi

Although it looks rather like a round root, kohlrabi is actually a bulbous stem vegetable created by cross-breeding cabbages and turnips. When purchased, both the leaves (which are attached directly to the bulbous stem) and roots are generally removed. Depending on the variety, the skin may be light green, purple or green with a hint of red. The interior flesh is white, with a sweet flavour similar to turnips. (Kohlrabies can be substituted for turnips in many recipes.) Younger plants are milder and more tender than large, mature ones. The outer skin must be removed from mature stems; young stems need only to be well scrubbed before cooking. Kohlrabi can be eaten raw, or it can be cooked (whole, sliced or diced) with moist-heat cooking methods such as boiling and steaming. The stems may also be hollowed out and stuffed with meat or vegetable mixtures.

Choose small, tender stems with fresh, green leaves. Peak season for kohlrabi is from June through September.

Kohlrabi

Leeks

Leeks (Fr. *poireaux*) look like large, overgrown scallions with a fat white tip and wide green leaves. Their flavour is sweeter and stronger than scallions, but milder than common bulb onions. Leeks must be carefully washed to remove the sandy soil that gets between the leaves. Leeks can be baked, braised or grilled as a side dish, or used to season stocks, soups or sauces.

Choose leeks that are firm, with stiff roots and stems. Avoid those with dry leaves, soft spots or browning. Leeks are available all year.

Leeks

Scallions

Scallions, also known as green onions or bunch onions, are the immature green stalks of bulb onions. The leaves are bright green with either a long and slender or slightly bulbous white base. Green onions are used in stir-fries and as a flavouring in other dishes. The green tops can also be sliced in small rings and used as a garnish.

Choose scallions with bright green tops and clean white bulbs. Avoid those with limp or slimy leaves. Scallions are available all year, with a peak summer season.

Scallions

Shallots

Shallots (Fr. *échalotes*) are shaped like small bulb onions with one flat side. When peeled, a shallot separates into multiple cloves, similar to garlic. They have a mild yet rich and complex flavour. Shallots are the basis of many classic sauces and meat preparations; they can also be sautéed or baked as a side dish.

Choose shallots that are plump and well shaped. Avoid those that appear dry or have sprouted. They should be stored in a cool, dry, unrefrigerated place. Shallots are available all year.

Pods and Seeds

Pod and seed vegetables include corn, legumes and okra. They are grouped together here because the parts consumed are all the seeds of their respective plants. In some cases only the seeds are eaten; in others, the pod containing the seeds is eaten as well. Seeds are generally higher in protein and carbohydrates (starch and fibre) than other vegetables.

Corn

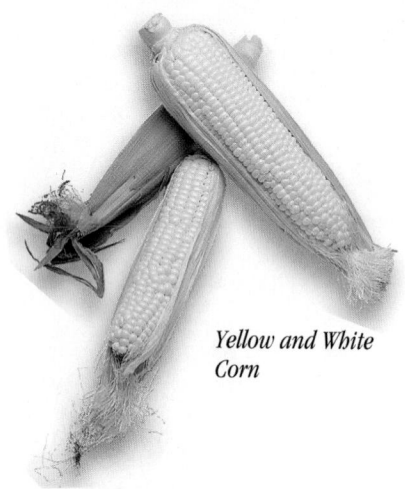

Yellow and White Corn

Sweet corn (Fr. *maïs*; Sp. *maíz*) is actually a grain, a type of grass. Corn kernels, like peas, are plant seeds. (Dried corn products are discussed in Chapter 23, Potatoes, Grains and Pasta.) The kernels, which may be white or yellow, are attached to a woody, inedible cob. The cob is encased by strands of hairlike fibres called silks and covered in layers of thin leaves called husks. The silks and husks should be shucked prior to cooking, although the husks may be left on for roasting or grilling. Shucked ears can be grilled, boiled, microwaved or steamed. The kernels can be cut off the cob before or after cooking. Corn on the cob is available fresh or frozen; corn kernels are available canned or frozen.

Choose freshly picked ears with firm, small kernels. Avoid those with mold or decay at the tip of the cob or brownish silks. Summer is the peak season for fresh corn.

BASIC PROCEDURE FOR CUTTING KERNELS OFF EARS OF CORN

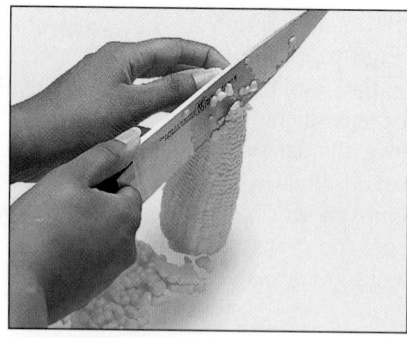

Hold the cob upright and use a chef's knife to slice off the kernels.

Legumes/Pulses

Beans (Fr. *haricots*; It. *fagiolio*) and peas (Fr. *pois*) are members of the legume family, a large group of vegetables with double-seamed pods containing a single row of seeds. Of the hundreds of known varieties of beans, some are used for their edible pods, others for shelling fresh and some only for their dried seeds. Dried beans are actually several varieties of seeds or peas left in the pod until mature, then shelled and dried.

Fresh Beans

Beans used for their edible pods, commonly referred to as green beans, string beans, runner beans or snap beans, are picked when immature. Except for the stem, the entire pod can be eaten. This category includes the green bean, the yellow wax bean and the French haricot vert, a long, slender pod with an intense flavour and tender texture. If there are any strings along the pod's seams, they should be pulled off before cooking. Beans may be left whole, cut lengthwise into thin slivers (referred to as French cut) or cut crosswise on the diagonal.

Shelling beans are those grown primarily for the edible seeds inside the pod. Common examples are flageolets, lima beans and fava (broad) beans. Their tough pods are not usually eaten.

All beans can be prepared by steaming, microwaving or sautéing. They can be added to soups or stews and they blend well with a variety of flavours, from coconut milk to garlic and olive oil. Cooked beans can be chilled and served as a salad or crudité.

Choose beans that have a bright colour without brown or soft spots. Large pods may be tough or bitter. The peak season for fresh beans is from April through December. Most bean varieties are available frozen or canned, including pickled and seasoned products.

Green Beans

Haricots Verts

Dried Beans

Anthropologists report that for thousands of years cultures worldwide have preserved some members of the legume family by drying. Common dried beans include kidney beans, pinto beans, chickpeas, lentils, black beans, black-eyed peas and split green peas. Shape is the clearest distinction among these products: Beans are oval or kidney-shaped; lentils are small, flat disks; peas are round.

Beans and peas destined for drying are left on the vine until they are fully matured and just beginning to dry. They are then harvested, shelled and quickly dried with warm air currents. Some dried legumes are sold split, which means the skin is removed, causing the seed's two halves to separate.

Most dried beans need to be soaked in water before cooking. Soaking softens and rehydrates the beans, thus reducing cooking time. Lentils and split peas generally do not require soaking, however, and will cook faster than beans. After soaking, beans are most often simmered or baked in a liquid until soft and tender. One type may be substituted for another in most recipes, although variations in colour, starch content and flavour should be considered.

Dried beans and peas are available in bulk or in poly-bags. They should be stored in a cool, dry place, but not refrigerated. Many of these beans are also available fully cooked, then canned or frozen. Some dried beans may be fermented or processed into flour, oil or bean curd.

Dried Black-Eyed Peas

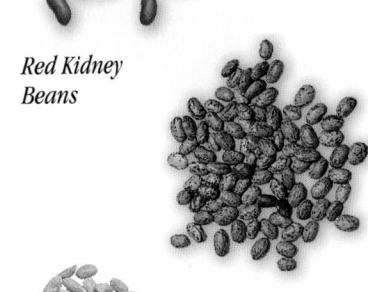

Lentils

BASIC PROCEDURE FOR SOAKING DRIED BEANS

1. Pick through the dried beans and remove any grit, pebbles or debris.
2. Place the beans in a bowl and cover with cold water; remove any skins or other items that float to the surface.
3. Drain the beans in a colander, then rinse under cold running water.
4. Return the beans to a bowl and cover with fresh cold water. Allow approximately 3 cups (750 mL) of water for each cup (250 mL) of beans.
5. Soak the beans in the cold water for the time specified in the recipe, usually several hours or overnight. Drain through a colander, discarding the water.

Red Kidney Beans

Pinto Beans

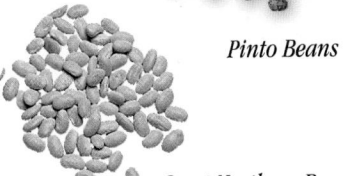

Great Northern Beans

Basic Procedure for Quick-Soaking Dried Beans

The soaking procedure can be accelerated by the following technique:

1. Rinse and pick through the beans.
2. Place the beans in a saucepan and add enough cool water to cover them by 2 inches (5 cm).
3. Bring to a boil and simmer for 2 minutes.
4. Remove from the heat, cover and soak for 1 hour.
5. Drain and discard the soaking liquid. Proceed with the recipe.

Fresh Shelling Peas

Fresh Shelling Peas

Of the shelling peas that are prepared fresh, the most common are green garden peas (English peas) and the French petit pois. Because they lose flavour rapidly after harvest, most shelling peas are sold frozen or canned. Shelling peas have a delicate, sweet flavour best presented by simply steaming until tender but still al dente. Peas may also be braised with rich meats such as ham or used in soups. Cooked peas are attractive in salads or as garnish.

Choose small fresh pea pods that are plump and moist. Peak season is April and May.

Edible Podded Peas

Snow peas, also known as Chinese pea pods, are a common variety of edible pea pod. They are very flat and have only a few very small green peas. Snow peas have a string along their seams which can be removed by holding the leafy stem and pulling from end to end. The pods can be eaten raw, lightly blanched or steamed, or stir-fried.

Snow Peas

Another variety of edible pea pod is the sugar snap pea, a cross between the garden pea and snow pea, which was developed during the late 1970s. They are plump, juicy pods filled with small, tender peas. The entire pod is eaten; do not shell the peas before cooking.

Choose pea pods that are firm, bright green and crisp. Avoid those with brown spots or a shrivelled appearance. Pea pods are available all year, with a peak season in March and April.

Okra

Okra, a common ingredient in African and Arab cuisines, was brought to the United States by slaves and French settlers. It is now integral to Creole, Cajun, southern and southwestern cuisines. Its mild flavour is similar to asparagus. Okra is not eaten raw; it is best pickled, boiled, steamed, or deep-fat fried. Okra develops a gelatinous texture when cooked for long periods, so it is used to thicken gumbos and stews. To avoid the slimy texture some find objectionable, do not wash okra until ready to cook, then trim the stem end only. Cook okra in stainless steel as other metals cause discolouration.

Okra

Choose small to medium pods (1 and 1-1/2 to 2 inches; 3.75 to 5 cm) that are deep green, without soft spots. Pale spears with stiff tips tend to be tough. Okra's peak season is from June through September. Frozen okra is widely available.

Roots and Tubers

Taproots (more commonly referred to as roots) are single roots that extend deep into the soil to supply the above-ground plant with nutrients. Tubers are fat underground stems. Most roots and tubers can be used interchangeably. All

◆◆◆

TOFU

Tofu or bean curd (Fr. *fromage de soja*) is a staple of Japanese and Chinese cuisines and is gaining acceptance in American kitchens because of its high nutritional value, low cost and flavour adaptability. Tofu is made by processing soybeans into "milk," which is then coagulated (nowadays with calcium sulfate). The curds are then placed in a perforated mould lined with cloth and pressed with a weight to remove the liquid. The result is a soft, creamy-white substance similar to cheese. Tofu is easy to digest, very high in protein, with very little fat and sodium and no cholesterol.

Tofu is an ancient foodstuff, probably created in China during the 2nd century A.D. It was introduced to Japan by Buddhist priests during the 8th century and was "discovered" by Western travellers during the 17th century. Today Japanese tofu is said to be the finest, perhaps because of the superiority of the soybeans grown in the Yamato region, near the city of Kyoto. Japanese cuisine values the natural flavour and texture of tofu and uses it in a tremendous vari-ety of ways. Chinese cuisine uses it as an additive, not as a principal ingredient.

Tofu may be eaten fresh; added to soup, broth or noodle dishes; tossed in cold salads; grilled; deep-fat fried or sautéed. Its flavour is bland, but it readily absorbs flavours from other ingredients.

Two types of tofu are widely available: cotton and silk. Cotton tofu is the most common. Its texture is firm, with an irregular surface caused by the weave of the cotton fabric in which it is wrapped for pressing. Silk tofu has a silky-smooth appearance and texture, and a somewhat more delicate flavour. Unlike cotton tofu, the water has not been pressed out of silk tofu. Consequently, silk tofu should not be cooked at high temperatures or for a long time, as it falls apart easily. The use of either type in most recipes is simply a matter of personal preference.

Fresh tofu is usually packaged in water. It should be refrigerated and kept in water until used. If the water is drained and changed daily, the tofu should last for one week.

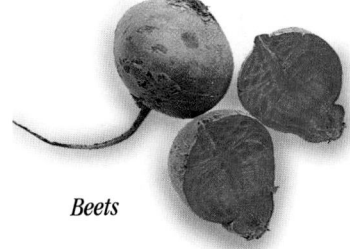

Beets

store well at cool temperatures, without refrigeration. Potatoes, the most popular tuber, are discussed in Chapter 23, Potatoes, Grains and Pasta.

Beets

Although records suggest that they were first eaten in ancient Greece, beets are most often associated with the colder northern climates, where they grow for most of the year. Beets can be boiled, then peeled and used in salads, soups or baked dishes.

Choose small to medium-sized beets that are firm, with smooth skins. Avoid those with hairy root tips, as they may be tough. Beets are available all year, with a peak season from March to October.

Carrots

Carrots (Fr. *carotte*), among the most versatile of vegetables, are large taproots. Although several kinds exist, the Imperator is the most common. It is long and pointed, with a medium to dark orange colour. It has a mild, sweet flavour. Carrots can be cut into a variety of shapes and eaten raw, used for a mirepoix or prepared by moist-heat cooking methods, grilling, microwaving or roasting. They are also grated and used in baked goods, particularly cakes and muffins.

Choose firm carrots that are smooth and well shaped, with a bright orange colour. If the tops are still attached, they should be fresh-looking and bright green. Carrots are available all year.

Carrots

Celery Root

Jicama

Parsnips

Daikon

Celery Root

Celery root, also known as celeriac, is a large, round root, long popular in northern European cuisines. It is a different plant from stalk celery, and its stalks and leaves are not eaten. Celery root has a knobby brown exterior; a creamy white, crunchy flesh and a mild, celerylike flavour. Its thick outer skin must be peeled away; the flesh is then cut as desired. Often eaten raw, celery root can be baked, steamed or boiled. It is used in soups, stews or salads and goes well with game and rich meats. Raw celery root may be placed in acidulated water to prevent browning.

Choose small to medium-sized roots that are firm and relatively clean, with a pungent smell. Their peak season is October through April.

Jicama

Jicama is actually a legume that grows underground as a tuber. It is becoming increasingly popular because of its sweet, moist flavour; crisp texture; low calorie content and long shelf life. After its thick brown skin is cut away, the crisp, moist white flesh can be cut as desired. Jicama is often eaten raw in salads, with salsa or as a crudité. It is also used in stir-fried dishes.

Choose firm, well-shaped jicamas that are free of blemishes. Size is not an indication of quality or maturity. They are available all year, with a peak season from January through May.

Parsnips

Parsnips (Fr. *panais*) are taproots that look and taste like white carrots and have the texture of sweet potatoes. Parsnips should be 5 to 10 inches (12.5 to 25 cm) in length, with smooth skins and tapering tips. Parsnips, peeled like carrots, can be eaten raw or cooked by almost any method. When steamed until very soft, they can be mashed like potatoes.

Choose small to medium-sized parsnips that are firm, smooth and well shaped; avoid large, woody ones. Parsnips are available all year, with peak supplies from December through April.

Radishes

Radishes (Fr. *radis*) are used for their peppery flavour and crisp texture. Radishes are available in many colours, including white, black and all shades of red; most have a creamy to pure white interior. Asian radishes, known as daikons, produce roots 2 to 4 inches (5 to 10 cm) in diameter and 6 to 20 inches (15 to 20 cm) long. Radishes can be steamed or stir-fried, but most often are eaten raw, in salads or used as garnish. Radish leaves can be used in salads or cooked as greens.

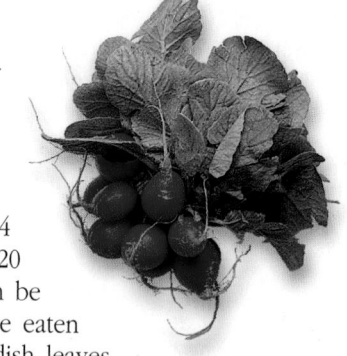

Red Radishes

Choose radishes that are firm, not limp. Their interior should be neither dry nor hollow. Radishes are available all year.

Rutabagas

Rutabagas are a root vegetable and a member of the cabbage family. Their skin is purple to yellow and they have yellow flesh with a distinctive starchy, cabbagelike flavour. Rutabagas and turnips are similar in flavour and texture when cooked and may be used interchangeably. Rutabaga leaves are not eaten. Rutabagas should be peeled with a vegetable peeler or chef's knife, then cut into quarters, slices or cubes. They are often baked, boiled and then puréed, or sliced and sautéed. They are especially flavourful when seasoned with caraway seeds, dill or lemon juice.

Choose small to medium-sized rutabagas that are smooth, firm and feel heavy. Their peak season is January through March.

Rutabagas

Turnips

Also a root vegetable from the cabbage family, turnips have white skin with a rosy-red or purple blush and white interior. Their flavour, similar to that of a radish, can be rather hot. Turnips should be peeled, then diced, sliced or julienned for cooking. They may be baked or cooked with moist-heat cooking methods, and are often puréed like potatoes.

Choose small to medium-sized turnips that have smooth skin and feel heavy. They should be firm, not rubbery or limp. Any attached leaves should be bright green and tender. Spring is their peak season.

Turnips

Stalks and Shoots

Stalk vegetables are plant stems with a high percentage of **cellulose** fibre. These vegetables should be picked while still young and tender. Tough fibres should be trimmed before cooking.

Cellulose—*A complex carbohydrate found in the cell wall of plants; it is indigestible by humans.*

Artichokes

Artichokes (Fr. *artichaut*) are the immature flowers of a thistle plant introduced to America by Italian and Spanish settlers. Young, tender globe artichokes can be cooked whole, but more mature plants need to have the fuzzy centre (known as the choke) removed first. Whole artichokes can be simmered, steamed or microwaved; they are often served with lemon juice, garlic butter or hollandaise sauce. The heart may be cooked separately, then served in salads, puréed as a filling or served as a side dish. Artichoke hearts and bottoms are both available canned.

Choose fresh artichokes with tight, compact heads that feel heavy. Their colour should be solid green to grey-green. Brown spots on the surface caused by frost are harmless. The artichoke's peak season is March through May.

Artichokes

BASIC PROCEDURE FOR PREPARING FRESH ARTICHOKES

1. Using kitchen shears or scissors, trim the barbs from the large outer leaves of the artichoke.

2. With a chef's knife, cut away the stem and the top of the artichoke. Steam or boil the artichoke as desired.

Asparagus

Asparagus

Asparagus (Fr. *asperges*), a member of the lily family, has bright green shoots with a ruffle of tiny leaves at the tip. Larger spears or shoots tend to be tough and woody, but can be used in soups or for purée. Asparagus are eaten raw or steamed briefly, stir-fried, microwaved or grilled. Fresh spring asparagus is excellent with nothing more than lemon juice or clarified butter; asparagus with hollandaise sauce is a classic preparation.

Choose firm, plump spears with tightly closed tips and a bright green colour running the full length of the spear. Asparagus should be stored, refrigerated at 40°F (4°C), upright in 1/2 inch (1.25 cm) of water or with the ends wrapped in moist paper towelling. They should not be washed until just before use. Canned and frozen asparagus are also available. Peak season is March through June.

A European variety of white asparagus is sometimes available fresh, or readily available canned. It has a milder flavour and soft, tender texture. It is produced by covering the stalks with soil as they grow; this prevents sunlight from reaching the plant and retards the development of chloro-phyll.

Celery

Celery

Once a medicinal herb, stalk celery (Fr. *céleri*) is now a common sight in kitchens worldwide. Stalk celery is pale green with stringy curved stalks. Often eaten raw in salads or as a snack, it can be braised or steamed as a side dish. Celery is also a mirepoix component.

Choose stalks that are crisp, without any sign of dryness. Celery is available all year.

Nopales

Nopales

The pads of a prickly pear cactus can be prepared as a vegetable known as nopales. Cactus pads have a flavour similar to green bell peppers. Their texture tends to be rather gelatinous or mucilaginous, making them good for stews or sauces. To prepare fresh nopales, hold the pad with tongs and cut off the thorns and "eyes" with a sharp knife or vegetable peeler. Trim off the edge all the way around. Slice the pad into julienne strips or cubes. The pieces can be boiled or steamed and served hot, or chilled and added to salads. Nopales can also be sautéed with onions, peppers and seasonings for a side dish or added to southwestern-style casseroles.

Some cultivated varieties have thin, thornless pads. Choose pads that are stiff and heavy without blemishes. They should not be dry or soggy. Fresh cactus pads are available all year, with peak season in the late spring. Canned and pickled nopales are also available.

Baby Vegetables

Many fine restaurants serve baby vegetables: tiny turnips, finger-length squash, miniature carrots and petite heads of cauliflower. First cultivated in Europe but now widely available elsewhere, baby vegetables include both hybrids bred to be true miniatures as well as regular varieties that are picked before maturity. Baby vegetables are often marketed with blossoms or greens still attached. They tend to be easily bruised and are highly perishable. Many baby vegetables can be eaten raw, but they are usually left whole, then steamed or lightly sautéed and attractively presented as an accompaniment to meat, fish or poultry entrees.

Chiogghi Beets

Baby Yellow Squash with Blossoms

Baby Zucchini with Blossoms

Baby Globe Carrots

NUTRITION

Most vegetables are more than 80% water; the remaining portions consist of carbohydrates (primarily starches) as well as small amounts of protein and fat. The relative lack of protein and fat makes most vegetables especially low in calories.

Much of a vegetable's physical structure is provided by generally indigestible substances such as cellulose and lignin, also known as fibre. This fibre produces the characteristic stringy, crisp or fibrous textures associated with vegetables.

TABLE 22.1   NUTRITIONAL VALUES OF SELECTED VEGETABLES

Per 4-oz. (112-g) serving, fresh, trimmed and prepared as noted	Kcal	Protein (g)	Carbohydrates (g)	Fibre (g)	Total Fat (g)	Vitamin A (I.U.)	Vitamin C (mg)	Calcium (mg)	Iron (mg)
Asparagus, boiled and drained	28	2.9	5	0.9 c	0.4	896	28.8	39.6	1
Broccoli, boiled and drained	32	3.4	5.7	2.9 d	0.4	1586	85	52	0.9
Cabbage, green, boiled and drained	24	1.1	5.4	0.7 c	0.3	96	27	37.5	0.4
Carrots, raw	48	1.2	11.6	3.6 d	0.4	32,404	11.2	30.4	0.6
Corn, boiled and drained	122	3.8	28.5	4.2 d	1.5	247	6.9	2.8	0.7
Mushrooms, white, raw	28	2.4	5.2	1.6 d	0.4	0	5.8	5.8	1.3
Onions, raw	44	1.2	9.6	2 d	0.3	0	6.7	21.3	0.2
Peppers, bell, green or red, raw	32	1.2	7.2	2 d	0.4	585	56.3	8.7	0.4
Pinto beans, boiled and drained	155	9.3	29.1	4.5 d	0.6	2.6	2.6	53.3	2.9
Snow peas, raw	48	3.2	8.4	2.8 d	0.4	42	17.2	12.4	0.6
Spinach, boiled and drained	26	3.4	4.3	2.5 d	0.3	7371	9	122	3.2
Tomatoes, raw	24	0.8	5.2	1.6 d	0.4	645	20.2	5	0.5
Zucchini, raw	16	1.2	3.2	0.4 d	0.3	100	2.7	4.5	0.1

The Corinne T. Netzer Encyclopedia of Food Values, 1992
c = crude fibre (a designation given to a less-accurate measurement of fibre content)
d = dietary fibre (a designation given to a newer and more accurate measurement of fibre content)

♦♦♦

ANCIENT PLANTS AND
ANCIENT WAYS VANISH

Since the days of Columbus, half of all native American crop varieties have become extinct. If this trend continues, several hundred more will become extinct in our lifetimes. Similarly, ancient farming practices have all but been abandoned. As late as the 1920s, the Tohono O'odham Indians of Arizona still used traditional methods to cultivate more than 10,000 acres without pumping groundwater. Today, only a few scattered floodwater fields remain.

When species disappear we lose an irreplaceable source of genetic diversity—a source of extraordinary genes that could someday improve modern hybrid crops. When native desert crops vanish, so does the ancient tradition of native agriculture, which has selected these crops over millennia to thrive in extreme temperatures, in alkaline soils without millions of gallons of precious water and without expensive, ecologically destructive chemicals.

Today, six highly bred species—wheat, rice, corn, sorghum, potatoes and cassava—supply most of the world's nutrition. As food crops become more and more homogeneous, they often lose their natural ability to tolerate pests, disease and drought. In the past, farmers grew thousands of food crop varieties. These traditional crop varieties contain a storehouse of genetic diversity that enables them to flourish in the most difficult environments. This broad spectrum of genetic variability is a cushion against natural predators and diseases. Wild chiles from the Sierra Madre, for example, are highly disease resistant. Their virus-tolerant genes have been bred into commercial varieties of bell pepper and jalapeños.

Native Seeds/SEARCH, one of the country's first regional seed banks, was founded to keep ancient desert plants and traditional farming methods from disappearing forever. Since 1983 we've ridden mules into remote areas and made more than 1200 collections of desert-adapted crops and wild relatives. We've gathered the seeds of chapalote (a brown popcorn), blue indigo (used for dyes), tepary (a heat- and drought-tolerant bean), teosinte (a wild relative of corn), wild chiles and other plants. These seeds are available to researchers, gardeners, farmers and seed banks. Seeds are offered free to Native Americans.

Each loss of biological and cultural diversity alters and damages the balance of life on earth, often in ways we do not understand. Each loss of leaf, stem and flower diminishes our earth's richness and beauty in ways we often don't appreciate until they're gone.

DR. GARY PAUL NABHAN
Native Seeds/SEARCH
Tucson, Arizona

Vegetables are also a good source of vitamins and minerals. (See Table 22.1.) Care must be taken during preparation to preserve their nutritional content, however. Once peeled or cut, vegetables lose nutrients to the air, or to any liquid in which they are allowed to soak. Vitamins are concentrated just under the skin, so peel vegetables thinly, if at all.

PURCHASING AND STORING FRESH VEGETABLES

Fresh vegetables should be selected according to seasonal availability. Using a vegetable at the peak of its season has several advantages: Price is at its lowest, selection is at its greatest and the vegetable's colour, flavour and texture are at their best.

Grading

The Canadian Food Inspection Agency has developed a grading system for fresh vegetables traded on wholesale markets. The system is based on appearance, condition and other factors affecting waste or eating quality. Grades for all vegetables include, in descending order of quality, Canada Fancy, Canada No. 1, Canada No. 2 and Canada Domestic Grade.

Consumer or retail grading is required for all domestic and imported vegetables. It uses alphabetical listings, with Canada No. 1 being the finest.

Purchasing

Fresh vegetables are sold by weight or count. They are packed in cartons referred to as cases, lugs, bushels, flats or crates. The weight or count packed in each of these containers varies depending on the size and type of vegetable as well as the packer. For example, celery is packed in 55-pound (25-kg) cartons containing 18 heads depending on the size of each head. Celery hearts, however, are packed in pairs in a cello pack of 12 per case.

Some of the more common fresh vegetables (e.g., onions, carrots, celery and lettuces) can be purchased from wholesalers trimmed, cleaned and cut according to your specifications. Although the unit price will be higher for diced onions than for whole onions, for example, the savings in time, labour, yield loss and storage space can be substantial. Processed vegetables may suffer a loss of nutrients, moisture and flavour, however.

Ripening

Although vegetables do not ripen in the same manner as fruits, they do continue to breathe (respire) after harvesting. The faster the respiration rate, the faster the produce ages or decays. This decay results in wilted leaves and dry, tough or woody stems and stalks. Respiration rates vary according to the vegetable variety, its maturity at harvest and its storage conditions after harvest.

Ripening proceeds more rapidly in the presence of ethylene gas. Ethylene gas is emitted naturally by fruits and vegetables and can be used to encourage further ripening in some produce, especially fruit-vegetables such as tomatoes. Items harvested and shipped when mature but green (unripe) are routinely exposed to ethylene gas to induce colour development (ripening) just before sale.

Storing

Some fresh vegetables are best stored at cool temperatures, between 40° and 60°F (4–16°C), ideally in a separate produce refrigerator. These include winter squash, potatoes, onions, shallots and garlic. If a produce refrigerator is not available, store these vegetables at room temperature in a dry area with good ventilation. Do not store them in a refrigerator set at conventional temperatures. Colder temperatures convert the starches in these vegetables to sugars, changing their texture and flavour.

Most other vegetables benefit from cold storage at temperatures between 34° and 40°F (2–4°C) with relatively high levels of humidity. Greens and other delicate vegetables should be stored away from apples, tomatoes, bananas and melons, as the latter give off a great deal of ethylene gas.

Purchasing and Storing Preserved Vegetables

Preservation techniques are designed to extend the shelf life of vegetables. These methods include irradiation, canning, freezing and drying. Except for drying, these techniques do not substantially change the vegetable's texture or flavour. Canning and freezing can also be used to preserve cooked vegetables.

FIGURE 22.1   *Irradiation Symbol*

Irradiation *processes were developed in Canada as part of the CANDU Nuclear Reactor program. The technology has been exported worldwide yet, ironically, has not yet been approved for food processing in Canada.*

Irradiated U.S. Vegetables

Although Canada does not currently allow irradiation of foods, the United States has introduced irradiated foods on their markets. The irradiation process uses ionizing radiation (usually gamma rays of cobalt 60 or cesium 137) to sterilize foods. When foods are subjected to radiation, parasites, insects and bacteria are destroyed, ripening is slowed and sprouting is prevented. Irradiation works without a noticeable increase in temperature; consequently, the flavour and texture of fresh foods are not affected. Some nutrients, however, may be destroyed. Irradiated vegetables do not need to be sprayed with post-harvest pesticides and they have an extended shelf life.

The FDA classifies irradiation as a food additive. Although it is not yet approved for all foods, grains, fruits and vegetables may be treated with low-dose radiation. Irradiated foods must be labelled "Treated with radiation" or "Treated by irradiation." The symbol shown in Figure 22.1 may also be used.

Irradiated produce is purchased, stored and used like fresh produce.

Canned Vegetables

Canned vegetables are an integral part of menu planning for many food service operations. In commercial canning, raw vegetables are cleaned and placed in a sealed container, then subjected to high temperatures for a specific period of time. Heating destroys the microorganisms that cause spoilage, and the sealed environment created by the can eliminates oxidation and retards decomposition. But the heat required by the canning process also softens the texture of most vegetables and alters their nutritional content; many vitamins and minerals may be lost through the canning process. Green vegetables may also suffer colour loss, becoming a drab olive hue.

Canned vegetables are graded by the Canadian Food Inspection Agency as Canada Fancy, Grade Choice and Grade Substandard. Canada Fancy vegetables must be top quality, tender and free of blemishes. Canada Grade Substandard vegetables may lack uniformity or flavour, but can be used in casseroles or soups if cost is a concern.

Combinations of vegetables as well as vegetables with seasonings and sauces are available canned. For example, corn kernels are available canned in water, in seasonings and sauces, combined with other vegetables or creamed. Canned vegetables are easy to serve because they are essentially fully cooked during the canning process.

Canned vegetables are purchased in cases of standard-sized cans (see Appendix II). Canned vegetables can be stored for extended periods at room temperature. Once a can is opened, any unused contents must be transferred to an appropriate storage container and refrigerated. Cans with bulges must be discarded immediately, without opening.

Frozen Vegetables

The Canadian Food Inspection Agency applies the same grading standards for frozen vegetables as for canned or preserved vegetables. Frozen vegetables are almost as convenient to use as canned. However, they often require some cooking, and expensive freezer space is necessary if an inventory is to be maintained. Regardless, freezing is a highly effective method for preserving vegetables. It severely inhibits the growth of microorganisms that cause spoilage without destroying many nutrients. Generally, green vegetables retain their colour, although the appearance and texture of most vegetables may be somewhat altered because of their high water content: Ice crystals form from the water in the cells and burst the cells' walls.

Some vegetables are available individually quick frozen (IQF). This method employs blasts of cold air, refrigerated plates, liquid nitrogen, liquid air or other techniques to chill the vegetables quickly. By speeding the freezing process, the formation of ice crystals can be greatly reduced.

Combinations of vegetables as well as vegetables with seasonings and sauces are available frozen. Some frozen vegetables are raw when frozen; others are blanched before freezing so final cooking time is reduced. Many others are fully cooked before freezing and only need to be thawed or heated for service. Frozen vegetables generally do not need to be thawed before being heated. Once thawed or cooked, they should be stored in the refrigerator and reheated in the same manner as fresh vegetables. Do not refreeze previously frozen vegetables.

Frozen vegetables are graded in the same manner as canned vegetables. They are usually packed in cases containing 2–5 pound (1–2.5 kg) boxes or bags. All frozen vegetables should be sealed in moisture-proof wrapping and kept at a constant temperature of 0°F (–18°C) or below. Temperature fluctuations can draw moisture from the vegetables, causing poor texture and flavour loss. Adequate packaging also prevents freezer burn, an irreversible change in the colour, texture and flavour of frozen foods.

Dried Vegetables

Except for beans, peas, peppers and tomatoes, few vegetables are commonly preserved by drying. Unlike other preservation methods, drying dramatically alters flavour, texture and appearance. The loss of moisture concentrates flavours and sugars and greatly extends shelf life.

APPLYING VARIOUS COOKING METHODS

Vegetables are cooked in order to break down their cellulose and gelatinize their starches. Cooking gives vegetables a pleasant flavour; creates a softer, more tender texture; and makes them more digestible. Ideally, most vegetables should be cooked as briefly as possible in order to preserve their flavour, nutrients and texture. Unfortunately, sometimes you must choose between emphasizing appearance and maintaining nutrition, because cooking methods that preserve colour and texture often remove nutrients.

Acid/Alkali Reactions

The acid or alkaline content of the cooking liquid affects the texture and colour of many vegetables. (See Table 22.2.) This is of greater concern with moist-heat cooking methods, but it is also a consideration with dry-heat cooking methods, as they often call for blanched or parboiled vegetables.

Texture

The acidity or alkalinity of the vegetable's cooking liquid influences the finished product's texture. If an acid such as lemon juice, vinegar or wine is added to the liquid for flavouring, the vegetable will resist softening and will require a longer cooking time. On the other hand, an alkaline cooking medium will quickly soften the vegetable's texture and may cause it to become mushy. Alkalinity also causes nutrient loss (especially thiamin) and may

TABLE 22.2   ACID/ALKALI REACTIONS

Vegetable	Pigment Family	Effect of Acid on:		Effect of Alkali on*:		Cook Covered?
		Colour	Texture	Colour	Texture	
Spinach, Broccoli	chlorophyll	drab olive green	firm	bright green	mushy	no
Carrots, Rutabagas	carotenoid	no change	firm	no change	mushy	no difference
Cauliflower	flavonoid	white	firm	yellow	mushy	yes
Red cabbage	flavonoid	red	firm	blue	mushy	yes

*Alkalinity always causes a loss of thiamin and other nutrients.

impart a bitter flavour. Alkalinity can be caused by tap water, detergent residue on utensils or the addition of baking soda (a base) to the cooking liquid. (You could add, for example, 1/8 teaspoon [0.5 mL] of baking soda per cup [225 mL] of navy beans to speed the softening of the dried beans.)

Colour

The acidity or alkalinity of the liquid also affects the plant's pigments, causing both desirable and undesirable colour changes. There are three principal pigment categories: chlorophyll, carotenoid and flavonoid. A plant's unique colour is the result of a combination of these pigments. Chlorophyll pigments predominate in green vegetables such as spinach, green beans and broccoli. Carotenoid pigments predominate in orange and yellow vegetables such as carrots, tomatoes, red peppers and winter squashes. Flavonoid pigments predominate in red, purple and white vegetables such as red cabbage, beets and cauliflower.

Initially, as vegetables are cooked, their original colours intensify. Exposure to heat makes pigments, especially chlorophyll, appear brighter. Exposure to acids and bases affects both chlorophyll and flavonoid pigments. Acids will gradually turn green vegetables an olive-drab colour, while a slight alkalinity promotes chlorophyll retention. The opposite occurs with vegetables containing flavonoids: They retain desirable colours in a slightly acidic environment while losing colours in an alkaline one. (Carotenoid is not affected by either acidity or alkalinity.) Colour changes alone do not affect flavour; but the altered appearance can make the product so visually unappealing as to become inedible.

Colours also change as the naturally occurring acids in vegetables are released during cooking. If the cooking pan is kept covered, the acids can concentrate, creating richer flavonoid pigments but destroying chlorophyll pigments.

Guidelines for Vegetable Cookery

The following general guidelines for vegetable cookery should be considered regardless of the cooking method used.

1. Vegetables should be carefully cut into uniform shapes and sizes to promote even cooking and provide an attractive finished product.
2. Cook vegetables for as short a time as possible to preserve texture, colour and nutrients.

3. Cook vegetables as close to service time as possible. Holding vegetables in a steam table continues to cook them.

4. When necessary, vegetables may be blanched in advance, refreshed in ice water and refrigerated. They can then be reheated as needed.

5. White and red vegetables (those with flavonoid pigments) may be cooked with a small amount of acid such as lemon juice, vinegar or white wine to help retain their colour.

6. When preparing an assortment of vegetables, cook each type separately, then combine them. Otherwise some items will be overcooked in the time required to properly cook others.

Determining Doneness

There are so many types of vegetables, with such varied responses to cooking, that no one standard for doneness is appropriate. Each item should be evaluated on a recipe-by-recipe basis. Generally, however, most cooked vegetables are done when they are just tender when pierced with a fork or the tip of a paring knife. Leafy vegetables should be wilted but still have a bright colour.

You can avoid overcooking vegetables by remembering that some carryover cooking will occur through the residual heat contained in the foods. Always rely on objective tests—sight, feel, taste and aroma—rather than the clock.

Dry-Heat Cooking Methods

Broiling and Grilling

Broiling and grilling use high heat to cook vegetables quickly. This preserves their nutritional content and natural flavours. The radiant heat of the broiler or grill caramelizes the vegetables, creating a pleasant flavour that is not generally achieved when vegetables are cooked by other methods.

Selecting and Preparing Vegetables to Broil or Grill

Broiling is often used to cook soft vegetables such as tomatoes or items that might not rest easily on a grill rack. Broiling is also used to warm and brown items just before service. If necessary, the vegetables can be basted to prevent them from drying out under the broiler's direct heat. Sometimes a cooked vegetable is napped with sauce or clarified butter and placed briefly under the broiler as a finishing touch at service time.

A large range of vegetables can be grilled. Carrots, peppers, squashes, eggplants and similar vegetables should be cut into broad, thin slices. They can then be placed on the grill in the same manner as a portion of meat or fish to create attractive crosshatchings. (See Chapter 9, Principles of Cooking.) Smaller vegetables such as mushrooms, cherry tomatoes and pearl onions can be threaded onto skewers for easy handling.

Seasoning Vegetables to Be Broiled or Grilled

Vegetables contain little fat and therefore benefit greatly from added fat when being broiled or grilled. The added fat can be a brushing of clarified butter or a marinade such as one made from olive oil and herbs. Some vegetables may be brushed with butter and coated with bread crumbs or Parmesan cheese before broiling.

◆◆◆
VEGETABLE SAUNA

"Sweating vegetables" in a little oil over low heat in a covered pot is, in effect, a vegetable sauna. All of the flavors of the vegetables emerge slowly in a juicy tangle, in a much more intense manner than if you simply added them just-cut to a stock. Like roasting garlic, it is a way to enlarge the natural flavors very dramatically.

—*from* CHINA MOON COOKBOOK
by BARBARA TROPP

BASIC PROCEDURE FOR BROILING OR GRILLING VEGETABLES

1. Heat the grill or broiler.
2. Use a wire brush to remove any charred or burnt particles that may be stuck to the broiler or grill grate. The grate may be wiped with a lightly oiled towel to remove any remaining particles and help season it.
3. Prepare the vegetables to be broiled or grilled by cutting them into appropriate shapes and sizes, then seasoning, marinating or otherwise preparing them as desired or directed in the recipe.
4. Place the vegetables on the broiler grate, broiler platter or grill grate and cook to the desired doneness while developing the proper surface colour.

◆◆◆

RECIPE 22.1

GRILLED VEGETABLE SKEWERS

Yield: 12 Skewers

Marinade:		
Rice wine vinegar	4 oz.	120 mL
Vegetable oil	8 oz.	250 mL
Garlic, chopped	1 oz.	30 g
Dried thyme	2 tsp.	10 mL
Salt	1 Tbsp.	15 mL
Pepper	1/2 tsp.	2 mL
Zucchini	6 oz.	180 g
Yellow squash	6 oz.	180 g
Broccoli florets, large	12	12
Cauliflower florets, large	12	12
Onion, large dice	24 pieces	24 pieces
Red bell pepper, large dice	12 pieces	12 pieces
Mushroom caps, medium	12	12

1. Combine all ingredients for the marinade and set aside.
2. Cut the zucchini and yellow squash into 1/2-inch-thick (1.2-cm) semicircles.
3. Blanch and refresh the zucchini, yellow squash, broccoli florets, cauliflower florets, onions and red bell pepper as discussed in the following section, Moist-Heat Cooking Methods.
4. Drain the vegetables well and combine them with the marinade. Add the mushroom caps to the marinade. Marinate the vegetables for 30–45 minutes, remove and drain well.
5. Skewer the vegetables by alternating them on 6-inch (10-cm) bamboo skewers.
6. Place the vegetable skewers on a hot grill and cook until done, turning as needed. The vegetables should brown and char lightly during cooking. Serve hot.

Skewers of grilled marinated vegetables.

Approximate values per serving:

Calories	60
Total fat	2.5 g
Saturated fat	0 g
Cholesterol	0 mg
Sodium	610 mg
Total carbohydrates	8 g
Protein	2 g
Vitamin C	90%

Claims—low fat; no cholesterol; good source of fibre

Roasting and Baking

The terms *roasting* and *baking* are used interchangeably when referring to vegetables. Roasting or baking is used to bring out the natural sweetness of many vegetables while preserving their nutritional values. The procedures are basically the same as those for roasting meats.

Selecting and Preparing Vegetables to Roast or Bake

Hearty vegetables such as winter squash and eggplant are especially well suited for roasting or baking. Vegetables such as onions, carrots and turnips are sometimes cooked alongside roasting meats or poultry. The vegetables add flavour to the finished roast and accompanying sauce, and the fats and juices released from the cooking roast add flavour to the vegetables.

Vegetables can be baked whole or cut into uniform-size pieces. Squash, for example, is usually cut into large pieces. Vegetables may be peeled or left unpeeled, depending on the desired finished product.

Seasoning Vegetables to Be Roasted or Baked

Vegetables may be seasoned with salt and pepper and rubbed with butter or oil before baking, or they may be seasoned afterward with a wide variety of herbs and spices. Some vegetables, such as winter squashes and sweet potatoes, may be flavoured with brown sugar or honey as well.

BASIC PROCEDURE FOR ROASTING OR BAKING VEGETABLES

1. Wash the vegetables. Peel, cut and prepare them as desired or directed in the recipe.
2. Season the vegetables and rub with oil or butter if desired.
3. Place the vegetables in a baking dish and bake in a preheated oven until done.

◆◆◆

RECIPE 22.2

BAKED BUTTERNUT SQUASH

Yield: 4 4-oz. (120-g) Servings

Butternut squash, medium dice	1 lb.	450 g
Salt and pepper	TT	TT
Cinnamon	1/4 tsp.	1 mL
Cardamom, ground	1/8 tsp.	0.5 mL
Brown sugar	2 Tbsp.	30 mL
Lemon juice	2 Tbsp.	30 mL
Whole butter, melted	2 oz.	60 g

1. Place the squash in a buttered pan. Season with salt, pepper, cinnamon, cardamom and brown sugar.
2. Drizzle the lemon juice and butter over the top of the squash.
3. Bake, uncovered, in a 350°F (180°C) oven until tender, approximately 50 minutes.

Approximate values per 4 oz. (120 g) serving:

Calories	190
Total fat	12 g
Saturated fat	7 g
Cholesterol	30 mg
Sodium	700 mg
Total carbohydrates	20 g
Protein	1 g
Vitamin A	90%
Vitamin C	35%

Sautéing or Stir-Frying

Sautéed or stir-fried vegetables should be brightly coloured and slightly crisp when done and show little moisture loss. When sautéing vegetables, all preparation must be complete before cooking begins because timing is important and cooking progresses rapidly. Have all vegetables, herbs, spices, seasonings and sauces ready before you begin.

Selecting and Preparing Vegetables to Sauté

A wide variety of vegetables can be sautéed. Whatever vegetables are used, they should be cut into uniform-size pieces to ensure even cooking.

Quick-cooking vegetables such as summer squashes, onions, greens, stalks, fruit-vegetables and mushrooms can be sautéed without any preparation except washing and cutting. Other vegetables such as Brussels sprouts, green beans, winter squashes, broccoli, cauliflower and most root vegetables are usually first blanched or otherwise partially cooked by baking, steaming or simmering. They are then sautéed to reheat and finish. Carrots, squash and other vegetables are sometimes finished by sautéing in butter and then adding a small amount of honey or maple syrup to glaze them. Some cooked vegetables are reheated by simply sautéing them in a small amount of stock or sauce.

Seasoning Vegetables to Be Sautéed

Sautéed vegetables can be seasoned with a great variety of herbs and spices. Seasonings should be added toward the end of the cooking process after all other ingredients have been incorporated in order to accurately evaluate the flavour of the finished dish.

Because sautéing vegetables uses slightly lower temperatures than sautéing meats and poultry, usually whole butter can be used in place of clarified butter. For additional flavours, fats such as bacon fat, olive oil, nut oils or sesame oil can be used in lieu of butter.

Basic Procedure for Sautéing Vegetables

1. Wash and cut the vegetables into uniform shapes and sizes.
2. Heat a sauté pan and add enough fat to just cover the bottom. The pan should be large enough to hold the vegetables without overcrowding.
3. When preparing an assortment of vegetables, add the ingredients according to their cooking times (first add the vegetables that take the longest to cook). Plan carefully so that all vegetables will be done at the same time. Do not overcrowd the pan; maintain high enough heat so the vegetables do not cook in their own juices.
4. Toss the vegetables using the sloped sides of the sauté pan or wok to flip them back on top of themselves. Do not toss more than necessary. The pan should remain in contact with the heat source as much as possible to maintain proper temperatures.
5. Add any sauces or vegetables with high water content, such as tomatoes, last.
6. Season the vegetables as desired with herbs or spices, or add ingredients for a glaze.

◆◆◆

RECIPE 22.3

STIR-FRIED ASPARAGUS WITH SHIITAKE MUSHROOMS

Yield: 1 lb. (450 g)

Asparagus	1 lb.	450 g
Shiitake mushrooms, fresh	6 oz.	180 g
Vegetable oil	1 Tbsp.	15 mL
Sesame oil	1 Tbsp.	15 mL
Garlic, chopped	2 tsp.	10 mL
Oyster sauce	4 oz.	120 mL
Crushed red chiles, optional	TT	TT

Approximate values per 4 oz. (120 g) serving:

Calories	140
Total fat	8 g
Saturated fat	1 g
Cholesterol	10 mg
Sodium	1130 mg
Total carbohydrates	13 g
Protein	5 g
Vitamin C	50%

1. Wash the asparagus, trim the ends and slice on the bias into 1- to 2-inch (2.5–5-cm) pieces.
2. Wash the mushrooms, trim off the stems and slice the caps into 1/2-inch-thick (1.2-cm) slices.
3. Heat the oils in a wok or sauté pan.
4. Add the garlic and stir-fry for a few seconds.
5. Add the mushrooms and asparagus and stir-fry for 1 minute.
6. Add the oyster sauce and crushed red chiles (if used) and continue to stir-fry until the asparagus is nearly tender, approximately 3 minutes.

1. Stir-fried mushrooms and asparagus.

Pan-Frying and Deep-Fat Frying

Pan-frying is not as popular as other techniques for cooking vegetables. Green tomatoes, however, are sometimes seasoned, floured and pan-fried; eggplant slices are seasoned, floured, pan-fried and used for Eggplant Parmesan. When pan-frying vegetables, follow the procedures outlined in Chapter 9, Principles of Cooking.

Deep-fat frying is a popular method of preparing vegetables such as potatoes, squashes and mushrooms. They can be served as hors d'oeuvre, appetizers or accompaniments to a main dish. Starchy vegetables may be deep-fat fried plain. Most other vegetables are first breaded or battered. Vegetables can also be grated or chopped and incorporated into fritters or croquettes. Any deep-fat fried item should have a crisp, golden exterior with a tender, non-greasy centre. See Chapter 21, Deep-Fat Frying, for additional information.

Moist-Heat Cooking Methods

Blanching and Parboiling

Blanching and parboiling are variations on boiling; the difference between them is the length of cooking time. Blanched and parboiled vegetables are often finished by other cooking methods such as sautéing.

Blanching is the partial cooking of foods in a large amount of boiling water for a very short period of time, usually only a few seconds. Besides preparing vegetables for further cooking, blanching is used to remove strong or bitter flavours, soften firm foods, set colours or loosen skins for peeling. Kale, chard, snow peas and tomatoes are examples of vegetables that are sometimes blanched for purposes other than preparation for further cooking.

Parboiling is the same as blanching, but the cooking time is longer, usually several minutes. Parboiling is used to soften vegetables and shorten final cooking times. Parboiling is commonly used for preparing root vegetables, cauliflower, broccoli and winter squashes.

Boiling

Vegetables are often boiled. Boiled vegetables can be served as is, or they can be further prepared by quickly sautéing with other ingredients, puréeing or mashing. Boiled vegetables are also chilled, then used in salads.

Starchy root vegetables are generally not boiled but rather simmered slowly so that the heat penetrates to their interiors and cooks them evenly. Green vegetables should be boiled quickly in a large amount of water in order to retain their colour and flavour.

Refreshing

Unless the boiled, blanched or parboiled vegetables will be eaten immediately, they must be quickly chilled in ice water after they are removed from the cooking liquid. This prevents further cooking and preserves (sets) their colours. This process is known as **refreshing** or **shocking** the vegetables. The vegetables are removed from the ice water as soon as they are cold. Never soak or hold the vegetables in the water longer than necessary or valuable nutrients and flavour will be leached away.

Basic Procedure for Refreshing Vegetables

1. Blanch, parboil or boil the vegetables to the desired doneness.

2. Remove the vegetables from the cooking liquid and submerge them in ice water just until they are cold.

Selecting and Preparing Vegetables to Boil

Nearly any type of vegetable can be boiled. Carrots, cabbages, green beans, turnips and red beets are just a few of the most common ones. Vegetables can be large or small, but they should be uniform in size to ensure even cooking. Some vegetables are cooked whole and only require washing before boiling. Others must be washed, peeled and trimmed or cut into smaller or more manageable sizes.

Seasoning Vegetables to Be Boiled

Often vegetables are boiled in nothing more than salted water. Lemon juice, citrus zest, wine and other acidic ingredients are sometimes added to white and red vegetables; if so, they should be added to the liquid before the vegetables. Herbs and spices in a sachet or a bouquet garni are often used to add flavour to boiled vegetables and should be added according to the recipe.

After boiling, vegetables are sometimes finished with herbs, spices, butter, cream or sauces.

Basic Procedure for Boiling Vegetables

1. Wash, peel, trim and cut the vegetables into uniform shapes and sizes.
2. Bring an adequate amount of water, stock, court bouillon or other liquid to a boil. The liquid should cover the vegetables and they should be able to move around freely without overcrowding.
3. Add seasonings if desired or as directed in the recipe.

4. Add the vegetables to the boiling liquid. If more than one vegetable is to be cooked and they have different cooking times, they should be cooked separately to ensure that all are cooked to the proper doneness. The pot may be covered if cooking white, red or yellow vegetables. Do not cover the pot when boiling green vegetables.

5. Cook the vegetables to the desired doneness.

6. Remove the vegetables from the water with a slotted spoon or a spider or drain through a colander.

7. Refresh the vegetables in ice water, drain and refrigerate until needed, or finish the hot boiled vegetables as desired and serve immediately.

◆◆◆

RECIPE 22.4

Brussels Sprouts in Pecan Butter

Yield: 6 3-oz. (90-g) Servings

Brussels sprouts	1 lb.	450 g
Whole butter	2 oz.	60 g
Pecans, chopped	4 oz.	120 g
Salt and pepper	TT	TT

Approximate values per 3 oz. (90 g) serving:

Calories	240
Total fat	21 g
Saturated fat	6 g
Cholesterol	20 mg
Sodium	480 mg
Total carbohydrates	10 g
Protein	4 g
Vitamin A	15%
Vitamin C	80%

1. Trim the Brussels sprouts and mark an X in the bottom of each with a paring knife to promote even cooking.

2. Boil the sprouts in salted water until tender, approximately 10 minutes.

3. Drain and hold the sprouts in a warm place.

4. Heat the butter in a sauté pan until it turns nut brown; this is called **beurre noisette**. Add the pecans and toss to brown them.

5. Add the Brussels sprouts and toss to reheat and blend flavours. Adjust the seasonings and serve.

Beurre noisette—*(Fr.) whole butter heated until it turns light brown and gives off a nutty aroma.*

1. Mark an X in the bottom of each Brussels sprout.

2. Boil the Brussels sprouts in the appropriate amount of water.

3. Toss the Brussels sprouts with the butter and pecans.

Basic Procedure for Cooking Dried Beans

Dried beans are best rehydrated by soaking as discussed earlier and then cooking in a boiling (actually simmering) liquid. After rehydration and cooking, the beans can be served or further cooked in baked, sautéed or puréed dishes.

1. After soaking, place the drained beans in a heavy saucepan and cover with cold water or stock. Allow approximately three times as much liquid as there are beans. Add flavouring ingredients as directed in the recipe, but do not add acids or salt until the beans have reached the desired tenderness. Acids and salt cause the exterior of beans to toughen and resist any further efforts at tenderizing.
2. Slowly bring the liquid to a boil. Boil uncovered for 10 minutes or as directed in the recipe. Use a ladle to remove any scum that rises to the surface.
3. Cover and reduce the heat. Allow the mixture to simmer until the beans are tender. Whole beans generally require 1 to 2-1/2 hours, lentils 20–35 minutes and split peas 30–60 minutes. Add additional hot liquid if necessary. Do not stir the beans during cooking.
4. Drain the cooked beans through a colander.

◆◆◆

RECIPE 22.5

CHICKPEAS WITH OLIVE OIL AND LEMON

Yield: 3 lb. (1.3 kg)

Chickpeas, dried	1 lb.	450 g
Chicken stock	3 pt.	1.5 L
Onion, medium dice	10 oz.	300 g
Bouquet garni:		
Carrot stick, 4 in. (10 cm)	1	1
Leek, split, 4-in. (10-cm) piece	1	1
Fresh thyme	1 sprig	1 sprig
Bay leaves	2	2
Salt	1 tsp.	5 mL
Lemon juice	2 oz.	60 mL
Olive oil	4 oz.	120 mL
Garlic, minced	1 oz.	30 g
Fresh oregano, chopped	1 tsp.	5 mL
Lemon zest, grated	2 Tbsp.	30 mL
Pepper	TT	TT

1. Soak the chickpeas in water for 4 hours or overnight.
2. Drain the chickpeas and combine with the chicken stock, onion and bouquet garni. Simmer, uncovered, until the chickpeas are tender, approximately 2-1/2 hours. Add the salt to the chickpeas; cook for 5 minutes.
3. Combine the lemon juice, olive oil, garlic, oregano and lemon zest to make a dressing.
4. Remove the peas from the heat; drain. Combine with the dressing and season to taste with pepper. Serve the peas hot or refrigerate and serve cold.

Approximate values per 3 oz. (90 g) serving:

Calories	140
Total fat	10 g
Saturated fat	1.5 g
Cholesterol	0 mg
Sodium	250 mg
Total carbohydrates	11 g
Protein	3 g

Steaming

Vegetables can be steamed in a convection steamer or by suspending them over boiling liquid on a rack set over a wok, saucepan or hotel pan. Vegetables can also be pan-steamed by cooking them in a covered pan with a small amount of liquid. Although the food will be touching the cooking liquid, most of the cooking is done by steam because only a small portion of the food is submerged in the liquid. Steamed vegetables can be eaten plain, partially cooked and sautéed lightly to finish, incorporated into casseroles or puréed. If they are not served immediately, they must be refreshed and refrigerated until used.

Properly steamed vegetables should be moist and tender. They generally retain their shape better than boiled vegetables. Vegetables cook very rapidly in steam and overcooking is a common mistake.

Selecting and Preparing Vegetables to Steam

Nearly any vegetable that can be boiled can also be steamed successfully. All vegetables should be washed, peeled and trimmed if appropriate and cut into uniform-size pieces. Pan-steaming is appropriate for vegetables that are small or cut into fairly small pieces such as peas and beans or broccoli and cauliflower florets.

Seasoning Vegetables to Be Steamed

Steaming produces vegetables with clean, natural flavours. Foods cooked in convection steamers can be seasoned with herbs and spices; but convection steamers use water to produce steam and the foods being cooked do not gain flavour from the cooking liquid. Vegetables steamed over liquids or pan-steamed in small amounts of liquids can be flavoured by using stocks or court bouillon as the cooking liquid. Herbs, spices and aromatic vegetables can be added to any liquid for additional flavour.

BASIC PROCEDURE FOR STEAMING VEGETABLES

1. Wash, peel, trim and cut the vegetables into uniform shapes and sizes.
2. If a convection steamer is not being used, prepare a steaming liquid and bring it to a boil in a covered pan or double boiler.
3. Place the vegetables in a perforated pan in a single layer; do not crowd the pan. Place the pan over the boiling liquid, or add the vegetables to the liquid.
4. Cover the pan and cook to the desired doneness.
5. Remove the vegetables from the steamer and serve, or refresh and refrigerate until needed.

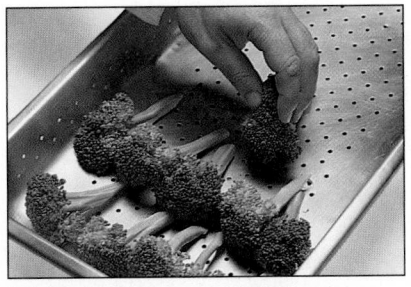

1. Place the broccoli spears in a perforated pan for steaming.

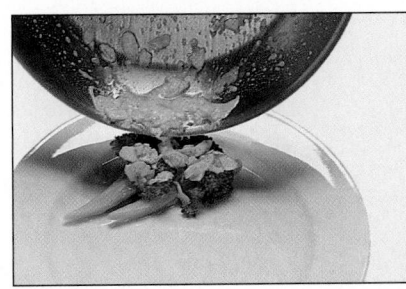

2. Drizzle the browned almonds and butter over the broccoli for service.

◆◆◆

RECIPE 22.6

BROCCOLI AMANDINE

Yield: 8 Servings

Broccoli, fresh	2 lb.	1 kg
Salt and pepper	TT	TT
Whole butter	2 oz.	60 g
Almonds, sliced	1 oz.	30 g
Garlic clove, minced	1	1
Lemon juice	2 oz.	60 mL

1. Cut the broccoli into uniform spears. Rinse and sprinkle lightly with salt and pepper.
2. Place the broccoli in a single layer in a perforated hotel pan and cook in a convection steamer until tender but slightly crisp, approximately 3 minutes.
3. Melt the butter in a sauté pan. Add the almonds and garlic and cook just until the nuts are lightly browned.
4. Arrange the broccoli on plates for service and sprinkle with the lemon juice. Drizzle the almonds and butter over the broccoli and serve immediately.

Approximate values per 6 oz. (180 g) serving:	
Calories	160
Total fat	10 g
Saturated fat	5 g
Cholesterol	20 mg
Sodium	500 g
Total carbohydrates	10 g
Protein	6 g
Vitamin A	35%
Vitamin C	110%

Combination Cooking Methods

Braising and Stewing

Braised and stewed vegetables are cooked slowly in a small amount of liquid. The liquid, including any given off by the vegetables, is reduced to a light sauce, becoming part of the finished product. Generally, a braised dish is prepared with only one vegetable; a stew is a mixture of several vegetables. The main ingredients are sometimes browned in fat before the liquid is added in order to enhance flavour and colour.

Both braises and stews can be exceptionally flavourful because they are served with all of their cooking liquid. (Boiled vegetables lose some of their flavour to the cooking liquid.) Braised and stewed vegetables generally can be held hot for service longer than vegetables prepared by other cooking methods.

Selecting and Preparing Vegetables to Braise or Stew

Various lettuces, especially romaine and Boston, are often braised. Cabbages, Belgian endive, leeks and many other vegetables are also commonly braised. Stews may contain a wide variety of vegetables such as summer squashes, eggplant, onions, peppers, tomatoes, carrots, celery and garlic. Leafy green vegetables and winter squashes are less commonly braised or stewed.

The vegetables should be washed and peeled or trimmed if appropriate. Vegetables to be braised may be left whole, cut into uniform pieces or shredded, as desired. Lettuces are usually cut into halves or quarters; cabbage is usually shredded.

Seasoning Vegetables to Be Braised or Stewed

Both braises and stews usually include flavouring ingredients such as garlic, herbs, bacon or mirepoix. The liquid may consist of water, wine, stock or tomato juice. Vegetables can even be braised in butter and sugar or honey to create a glazed dish.

Both braises and stews can be seasoned with a variety of herbs and spices. Add the seasonings before covering the pot to finish the cooking process. Strongly flavoured vegetables such as celery root and turnips are usually parboiled first in order to reduce their strong presence.

BASIC PROCEDURE FOR BRAISING AND STEWING VEGETABLES

1. Wash, peel, trim and cut the vegetables.
2. Sauté or sweat the flavouring ingredients in fat to release their flavours. Or, sauté or sweat the main ingredients in fat.
3. For a braise, add the main ingredient in a single layer. For a stew, add the ingredients according to their cooking times or as directed in the recipe.
4. Add the cooking liquid; it should partially cover the vegetables. Bring the liquid to a boil, reduce to a simmer, cover and cook in the oven or on the stove top until done.
5. If desired, remove the main ingredients from the pan and reduce the sauce or thicken it with beurre manié, cornstarch or arrowroot. Then return the main ingredients to the sauce.

◆◆◆

RECIPE 22.7
BRAISED CELERY WITH BASIL

Yield: 12 Servings

Celery	3 heads	3 heads
Onion, small dice	8 oz.	250 g
Garlic, minced	2 tsp.	10 mL
Whole butter	2 oz.	60 g
Olive oil	1 oz.	30 mL
Fresh thyme	1 tsp.	5 mL
Fresh basil, chiffonade	20 leaves	20 leaves
Dry white wine	8 oz.	250 mL
Chicken stock	1 pt.	500 mL
Salt and pepper	TT	TT

1. Trim the outer ribs from the celery heads, leaving only the tender hearts. Trim the heads to 6-inch (15-cm) lengths. Trim the root slightly, leaving each head together. Cut each head lengthwise into quarters.
2. Sauté the onions and garlic in the butter and olive oil, without colouring, until tender. Add the celery quarters to the pan and sauté, turning occasionally.
3. Add the thyme, basil, wine and chicken stock. Bring to a boil, reduce to a simmer, cover and braise in the oven at 350°F (180°C) until tender, approximately 1 hour.
4. Remove the celery and reserve. Reduce the cooking liquid on the stove top until it thickens. Adjust the liquid's seasonings and return the celery to the pan to reheat. Serve the celery with a portion of the sauce.

Approximate values per 3 oz. (90 g) serving:	
Calories	60
Total fat	4.5 g
Saturated fat	1.5 g
Cholesterol	5 mg
Sodium	170 mg
Total carbohydrates	2 g
Protein	1 g

1. Trim and cut the celery.

2. Add the liquid to the celery.

3. Reduce the sauce.

Microwaving

Fresh vegetables are among the few foods that can be consistently well prepared in a microwave oven. Often microwave cooking can be accomplished without any additional liquid, thus preserving nutrients. With microwaving, colours and flavours stay true and textures remain crisp.

Microwave cooking is actually a form of steaming. As explained in Chapter 9, Principles of Cooking, microwaves agitate water molecules, thus creating steam. The water may be the moisture found naturally in the food or may be added specifically to create the steam.

Cooking time depends on the type of microwave oven as well as on the freshness, moisture content, maturity and quantity of vegetables being prepared.

Selecting and Preparing Vegetables to Microwave

Any vegetable that can be steamed successfully can be microwaved with good results. Because typical microwave ovens are relatively small, they are impractical for producing large quantities of food. They are most useful for reheating small portions of vegetables that have been blanched or partially cooked using another cooking method.

Seasoning Vegetables to Be Microwaved

Microwaving, like steaming, brings out the natural flavours of food and produces a clean, unadulterated flavour. Herbs and spices can be added to the vegetables before they are microwaved. Or, after microwaving, the vegetables can be tossed with butter, herbs and spices or combined with a sauce.

BASIC PROCEDURE FOR MICROWAVING VEGETABLES

1. Wash, peel, trim and cut the vegetables into uniform shapes and sizes.
2. Place the vegetables in a steamer designed for microwave use or arrange the vegetables on a microwavable dish. Cover the vegetables with the lid or plastic wrap. If using plastic wrap, it should be punctured to allow some steam to escape during cooking.
3. Cook the vegetables to the desired doneness, allowing for some carryover cooking. Or reheat the previously cooked vegetables until hot. Stir or turn the vegetables as necessary to promote even cooking.
4. Serve the vegetables or refresh and refrigerate until needed.

Puréeing

Puréeing is a technique often used with vegetables. Cooked vegetable purées can be served as is, stuffed into other vegetables or be used as an ingredient in other preparations such as pumpkin pie, mashed potatoes or vegetable soufflés. Purées can also be bound with eggs, seasoned and used to make vegetable timbales and terrines.

Puréed vegetables are generally first cooked by baking, boiling, steaming or microwaving. White, red and yellow vegetables should be cooked until quite soft. They are more easily puréed when hot or warm; this also helps ensure a smooth finished purée. For most preparations, green vegetables must be refreshed after cooking and puréed while cold or they will overcook and become discoloured.

Seasoning Vegetables to Be Puréed

Vegetables for purées can be seasoned before they are puréed following the guidelines for the cooking procedure used. They can also be seasoned after they are puréed with a wide variety of ingredients such as herbs or spices, cheese, honey or brown sugar.

Finishing Puréed Vegetables

Purées can be finished with stocks, sauces, butter or cream to add richness and flavour. First purée the main ingredient, then add additional liquids to obtain the desired consistency.

BASIC PROCEDURE FOR PURÉEING VEGETABLES

1. Cook the vegetables. White, red and yellow vegetables should be cooked until very soft. Green vegetables should be cooked until tender but not overcooked to the point of being discoloured.
2. Purée the vegetables in a VCM, food processor or blender or by passing them through a food mill.
3. Season or finish the puréed vegetables as desired or directed in the recipe, or use them in another recipe.

◆◆◆

RECIPE 22.8

PARSNIP PURÉE

Yield: 2 qt. (2 L)

Parsnips	4 lb.	1.8 kg
Russet potatoes	1 lb. 8 oz.	680 g
Cream, 35%, hot	8 oz.	250 mL
Whole butter, melted	4 oz.	120 g
Salt and white pepper	TT	TT
Nutmeg	TT	TT

Approximate values per 4 oz. (120 g) serving:

Calories	240
Total fat	12 g
Saturated fat	7 g
Cholesterol	35 mg
Sodium	220 mg
Total carbohydrates	31 g
Protein	3 g
Vitamin A	10%
Vitamin C	35%

1. Peel the parsnips and potatoes and cut into large pieces of approximately the same size.
2. Boil the parsnips and potatoes separately in salted water until tender.
3. Drain the parsnips and potatoes well. Purée them together through a food mill.
4. Add the cream and butter and mix to combine. Adjust the consistency by adding cream as desired. Season the mixture with salt, white pepper and nutmeg and serve hot.

*C*ONCLUSION

Vegetables are an essential part of the human diet. They provide the body with vitamins, minerals and fibre. They appeal to the appetite with taste, colour and texture. Increased market availability of fresh, high-quality vegetables as well as new hybrids gives you an ever-increasing variety of vegetables from which to choose. Vegetables are a relatively inexpensive food that can be prepared in limitless ways. They can be served as an entire meal or as an accompaniment to or part of a wide variety of other dishes. And when cooking vegetables, remember what James Beard (1903–1985), the great American food consultant, culinary educator and writer once said: "No vegetable exists which is not better slightly undercooked."

$\mathcal{Q}$UESTIONS FOR DISCUSSION

1. Explain how season affects the price, quality and availability of vegetables.
2. List and describe three processing techniques commonly used to extend the shelf life of vegetables.
3. What special concerns exist regarding the storage of fresh vegetables? Explain why some vegetables should not be refrigerated.
4. Why is it important to cut vegetables into a uniform size before cooking?
5. Discuss several techniques used for determining the doneness of vegetables. Is carryover cooking a concern when preparing vegetables? Explain your answer.
6. Discuss the role of acid in a cooking liquid used for preparing vegetables. Which vegetables, if any, benefit from an acidic cooking environment?
7. Describe the necessary mise en place and procedure for refreshing vegetables.

$\mathcal{A}$DDITIONAL VEGETABLE RECIPES

RECIPE 22.9

SUMMER VEGETABLES WITH TARRAGON AIOLI

NOTE: *This dish appears in the Chapter Opening photograph.*

GREENS, SAN FRANCISCO, CA
Executive Chef Annie Somerville

Yield: 8–10 Servings   Method: Boiling

Baby artichokes	6	6
Carrots	8 oz.	250 g
Yellow or green zucchini	1 lb.	500 g
Sunburst squash	1 lb.	500 g
Blue lake green beans	8 oz.	250 g
Yellow wax beans	8 oz.	250 g
Broccoli florets	1 lb.	500 g
Cauliflower florets	1 lb.	500 g
Red radishes	1 bunch	1 bunch
Cherry tomatoes	1/2 pt.	250 mL
Niçoise or Gaeta olives	8 oz.	250 g
Tarragon Aïoli (recipe follows)	8 oz.	250 g

1. Trim the artichokes. Steam or boil them until tender; refresh.
2. Cut the carrots, zucchini and squash as desired. Snip the ends from the beans. Parboil the vegetables (except the radishes, tomatoes and olives), one variety at a time, in salted water until nearly tender but still crisp. Refresh each and drain well.

3. Wash the radishes. Trim the root end but leave the green tops attached.

4. Wash the cherry tomatoes and remove the stems.

5. Loosely arrange the vegetables on a platter, leaving room for the aioli unless it is to be served separately in a small bowl.

TARRAGON AIOLI

Yield: 1/2 pt. (250 mL)

Egg yolk, large	1	1
Fresh lemon juice	1 Tbsp.	15 mL
Light olive oil	8 oz.	250 mL
Garlic clove, chopped	1	1
Champagne vinegar	1 tsp.	5 mL
Fresh tarragon, chopped	2 tsp.	10 mL
Salt	TT	TT

1. Whisk the yolk and 1/2 teaspoon (3 mL) of lemon juice together until smooth.

2. Whisk in the oil, very slowly at first, until the aioli begins to emulsify. Add a few drops of lemon juice as necessary to thin the sauce. Continue until all the oil and lemon juice have been incorporated.

3. Season with the garlic, vinegar, tarragon and salt. If the aioli is too thick, thin it with a little warm water.

4. Refrigerate aïoli and use within 3 days.

Approximate values per serving:

Calories	470
Total fat	35 g
Saturated fat	5 g
Cholesterol	30 mg
Sodium	770 mg
Total carbohydrates	29 g
Protein	8 g
Vitamin A	120%
Vitamin C	150%

❖❖❖

RECIPE 22.10

SPINACH AU GRATIN

Yield: 8 8-oz. (250 g) Servings as an entree,
    16 Servings as a side vegetable

Method: Boiling

Clarified butter	2 oz.	60 mL
Flour	1 oz.	30 g
Cream, cereal	1 pt.	450 mL
Spinach, fresh chopped	2 lb. 8 oz.	1.1 kg
Garlic cloves, minced	2	2
Salt, pepper and nutmeg	TT	TT
Cheddar or Swiss cheese, shredded	1 lb. 8 oz.	700 g

1. Heat half the butter in a saucepan. Add the flour and cook to make a blond roux.

2. Add the cream, whisking to remove any lumps of roux. Bring to a simmer and cook for 15 minutes.

3. Sauté the garlic in the remaining 2 tablespoons (30 mL) of clarified butter. Add spinach and cook for 2 minutes. Remove from the heat and drain well.

4. Combine the hot spinach with the cream sauce and adjust the seasonings.

5. Fill 16 3/4-cup (150-mL) gratin dishes with the creamed spinach. Top each with 1-1/2 ounces (45 g) shredded cheese and place under the broiler until the cheese is melted and browned and the spinach is very hot. Serve immediately.

Approximate values per
8 oz. (240 g) serving:

Calories	510
Total fat	38 g
Saturated fat	24 g
Cholesterol	120 mg
Sodium	960 mg
Total carbohydrates	14 g
Protein	28 g
Vitamin A	140%
Calcium	90%

♦♦♦

RECIPE 22.11
BROILED TOMATO

Yield: 1 Serving   **Method:** Broiling

Tomato, large	1	1
Sugar	2 tsp.	10 mL
Garlic butter, melted	1 oz.	30 g
Fresh parsley, chopped	1 Tbsp.	15 mL
Fresh white bread crumbs	1 Tbsp.	15 mL

1. Core and halve the tomato.
2. Sprinkle sugar on top of each half. Place on a broiler platter and broil until tender.
3. Drizzle with butter and garnish with parsley and bread crumbs.
4. Quickly brown crumbs under broiler.

Approximate values per serving:

Calories	170
Total fat	12 g
Saturated fat	7 g
Cholesterol	30 mg
Sodium	130 mg
Total carbohydrates	14 g
Protein	1 g
Vitamin A	20%
Vitamin C	40%

♦♦♦

RECIPE 22.12
GRILLED PORTOBELLO CAPS

Yield: 3 4-oz. (120-g) Servings   **Method:** Grilling

Portobello mushroom caps	1 lb.	500 g
Olive oil	1 Tbsp.	15 mL
Garlic, chopped	1 tsp.	5 mL
Salt and pepper	TT	TT
Fresh thyme	1 tsp.	5 mL

1. Wipe the mushroom caps clean with a damp towel.
2. Combine the olive oil and garlic and brush the mixture on the mushroom caps.
3. Season the mushrooms with salt, pepper and thyme.
4. Grill or broil the mushrooms until tender, approximately 8 minutes, depending on the size of the caps. Serve with a vegetable risotto as a vegetarian entree.

Approximate values per 4 oz. (120 g) serving:

Calories	140
Total fat	10 g
Saturated fat	1.5 g
Cholesterol	0 mg
Sodium	790 mg
Total carbohydrates	8 g
Protein	6 g
Claims—no cholesterol; high fibre	

♦♦♦

RECIPE 22.13
DUXELLES

Yield: 12 oz. (360 g)   **Method:** Sautéing

Mushrooms	1 lb.	500 g
Whole butter	1 Tbsp.	15 mL
Shallots, minced	2 Tbsp.	30 mL
Garlic, chopped	1 tsp.	5 mL
Salt and pepper	TT	TT
Fresh parsley, chopped	1 Tbsp.	15 mL

1. Chop the mushrooms very finely.
2. Sauté the shallots and garlic in butter until tender. Add the mushrooms and sauté until dry.

Approximate values per 1 oz. (30 g) serving:

Calories	20
Total fat	1 g
Saturated fat	.5 g
Cholesterol	5 mg
Sodium	210 mg
Total carbohydrates	2 g
Protein	1 g
Claims—low fat; low cholesterol; low calorie	

3. Season with salt and pepper and add the parsley. Cool.

4. Use the duxelles as a stuffing for vegetables or as a flavouring ingredient in other recipes.

◆◆◆

RECIPE 22.14

STIR-FRIED SNOW PEAS WITH DRIED SHRIMP

Yield: 6 3-oz. (90-g) Servings   **Method:** Sautéing

Dried shrimp	1 oz.	30 g
Snow peas	1 lb.	500 g
Garlic, chopped	2 tsp.	10 mL
Vegetable oil	2 oz.	60 mL
Sesame oil	1 tsp.	5 mL
Water chestnuts, sliced	4 oz.	120 g
Salt	TT	TT

1. Soak the dried shrimp in hot water for 15 minutes. Drain well.

2. Snap the snow peas and remove the strings.

3. Blanch the snow peas and refresh.

4. Stir-fry the garlic and shrimp in the vegetable and sesame oils for 10 seconds. Add the water chestnuts.

5. Add the snow peas and stir-fry until tender, approximately 1 minute. Season to taste with salt.

Approximate values per 3 oz. (90 g) serving:

Calories	140
Total fat	10 g
Saturated fat	1.5 g
Cholesterol	0 mg
Sodium	590 mg
Total carbohydrates	8 g
Protein	3 g
Vitamin C	60%

◆◆◆

RECIPE 22.15

GLAZED PEARL ONIONS

Yield: 1 lb. (500 g)   **Method:** Boiling

Pearl onions, peeled	1 lb.	500 g
Whole butter	1-1/2 oz.	45 g
Sugar	1 Tbsp.	15 mL
Salt and pepper	TT	TT

1. Place the onions, butter and sugar in a sauté pan and add enough water to barely cover.

2. Boil the onions, allowing the water to evaporate. As the water evaporates, the butter-and-sugar mixture will begin to coat the onions. When the water is nearly gone, test the doneness of the onions. If they are still firm, add a small amount of water and continue to boil until the onions are tender.

3. Sauté the onions in the butter-and-sugar mixture until they are glazed.

VARIATIONS: Vegetables such as carrots, turnips, zucchini and other squashes can also be glazed with this procedure. They should be cut into appropriate shapes and be large enough so they glaze properly without overcooking. When preparing a mix of glazed vegetables, cook each type separately because each has a different cooking time.

Approximate values per 2 oz. (60 g) serving:

Calories	70
Total fat	4.5 g
Saturated fat	2.5 g
Cholesterol	10 mg
Sodium	340 mg
Total carbohydrates	8 g
Protein	1 g

◆◆◆

RECIPE 22.16

HARVARD BEETS

Yield: 8 4-oz. (120-g) Servings   **Method:** Boiling

Sugar	2 oz.	60 g
Cornstarch	2 Tbsp.	30 mL
White wine vinegar	4 oz.	120 mL
Salt and pepper	TT	TT
Beets, boiled, peeled, medium dice	2 lb.	1 kg

1. Combine the sugar, cornstarch, vinegar, salt and pepper in a heavy saucepan. Whisk until the cornstarch and sugar dissolve.
2. Bring to a boil, then cook, stirring constantly, until the mixture is thick and clear.
3. Add the beets, stirring gently to coat. Serve warm.

Approximate values per 4 oz. (120 g) serving:

Calories	97
Total fat	0 g
Saturated fat	0 g
Cholesterol	0 mg
Sodium	484 mg
Total carbohydrates	23 g
Protein	2 g

◆◆◆

RECIPE 22.17

MAPLE-GLAZED CARROTS

Yield: 16 4-oz. (120-g) Servings   **Method:** Sautéing

Carrots	4 lb.	1.8 kg
Whole butter	4 oz.	120 g
Salt and pepper	TT	TT
Maple syrup	4 oz.	120 mL
Fresh parsley, chopped	2 Tbsp.	30 mL

1. Peel the carrots and cut into a shape such as oblique, turned or rondelle.
2. Parboil the carrots in salt water and refresh. The carrots should be firm.
3. Sauté the carrots in butter until nearly tender.
4. Season with salt and pepper and add the maple syrup. Garnish with the parsley.

Approximate values per 4 oz. (120 g) serving:

Calories	120
Total fat	6 g
Saturated fat	3.5 g
Cholesterol	15 mg
Sodium	260 mg
Total carbohydrates	16 g
Protein	1 g
Vitamin A	220%
Vitamin C	15%

◆◆◆

RECIPE 22.18

CREAMED CORN WITH BASIL

Yield: 10 4-oz. (120-g) Servings   **Method:** Sautéing

Corn	12 ears	12 ears
Whole butter	2 oz.	60 g
Onion, small dice	4 oz.	120 g
Cream, 35%	8 oz.	250 mL
Basil leaves, chopped	2 Tbsp.	30 mL
Salt and white pepper	TT	TT

1. Cut the kernels from the ears.
2. Sauté the onions in the butter without browning.
3. Add the corn and sauté until hot.
4. Add the cream. Bring to a boil and reduce slightly. Add the basil and season with salt and white pepper.

Approximate values per 4 oz. (120 g) serving:

Calories	210
Total fat	14 g
Saturated fat	8 g
Cholesterol	45 mg
Sodium	290 mg
Total carbohydrates	19 g
Protein	3 g
Vitamin A	15%

◆◆◆

RECIPE 22.19

RATATOUILLE

Yield: 20 3-oz. (100-g) Servings **Method:** Sautéing

Onion, medium dice	12 oz.	350 g
Garlic, chopped	1 Tbsp.	15 mL
Olive oil	4 oz.	120 mL
Green bell pepper, medium dice	6 oz.	200 g
Red bell pepper, medium dice	6 oz.	200 g
Eggplant, medium dice	12 oz.	350 g
Zucchini, medium dice	8 oz.	250 g
Mushrooms, quartered	12 oz.	350 g
Tomato concassé	24 oz.	700 g
Fresh basil, chiffonade	1 oz.	30 g
Salt	1 oz.	30 g
Pepper	TT	TT
Tomato paste	as needed	as needed

1. Sauté the onion and garlic in the olive oil.

2. Add the peppers, eggplant, zucchini and mushrooms. Sauté until tender, approximately 10 minutes.

3. Add the tomatoes, fresh basil and seasonings. Sauté for 5 minutes. Adjust the seasonings. If the sauce is too thin, add a small amount of tomato paste to thicken.

NOTE: Fresh herbs such as oregano, thyme or others may also be used.

Approximate values per 4 oz. (120 g) serving:

Calories	90
Total fat	7 g
Saturated fat	1 g
Cholesterol	0 mg
Sodium	690 mg
Total carbohydrates	6 g
Protein	1 g
Vitamin C	35%

Claims—low saturated fat; no cholesterol

◆◆◆

RECIPE 22.20

GARLIC TIMBALES

Yield: 8 2-oz. (60-mL) Timbales **Method:** Baking

Garlic cloves, peeled	10	10
Milk	3 oz.	90 mL
Cream, 35%	8 oz.	250 mL
Eggs	2	2
Dried thyme	1 tsp.	5 mL
Salt and pepper	TT	TT

1. Butter 8 small ramekins or timbales.

2. Place the garlic in a small saucepan, add enough water to cover and bring to a boil. Drain. Repeat this blanching procedure 2 more times.

3. Place the garlic in a blender with the milk and blend. Add the cream, eggs and thyme; blend until smooth. Season with salt and pepper.

4. Divide the custard among the timbales and place in a water bath. Bake for 30–45 minutes at 325°F (160°C).

5. Run a paring knife around the rim and unmould onto the serving plate.

VARIATIONS: Broccoli or cauliflower timbales: Place 1 ounce (30 g) of blanched chopped broccoli or cauliflower in each buttered timbale before adding the garlic custard mixture.

Approximate values per 2 oz. (60 g) serving:

Calories	130
Total fat	12 g
Saturated fat	7 g
Cholesterol	95 mg
Sodium	320 mg
Total carbohydrates	3 g
Protein	3 g
Vitamin A	15%

Dennis Green

Dennis was raised in Vancouver and started cooking when he was 17. He served his apprenticeship at a small bistro near his high school. He joined Bishop's in 1993, and has been the Executive Chef there since 1997.

♦♦♦

RECIPE 22.21
WARM MUSHROOM SALAD WITH GRILLED EGGPLANT AND WHITE TRUFFLES

BISHOP'S RESTAURANT, VANCOUVER, BC
Executive Chef Dennis Green

Yield: 4 Servings   **Method:** Braising

Japanese eggplant	1 large	1 large
Olive oil	4 Tbsp.	60 mL
Salt and pepper	TT	TT
Garlic cloves, minced	2	2
Shallots, sliced	1/2 cup	120 mL
Fresh thyme, chopped	2 sprigs	2 sprigs
Oyster mushrooms	8 oz.	250 g
Dry sherry	2 Tbsp.	30 mL
Balsamic vinegar	2 Tbsp.	30 mL
Assorted baby greens, washed	4 cups	1 L
Fresh white truffle	1	1

1. Using a meat slicer or sharp knife, slice the eggplant lengthwise into 1/8-inch (3-mm) thick slices. Brush the slices with a small amount of olive oil, season with salt and pepper and grill the eggplant over a medium-hot fire. Cook on both sides, just until tender, approximately 2 minutes. Transfer to a plate to cool.

2. In a large sauté pan, heat the remaining olive oil and sauté the garlic and shallots until tender. Add the thyme and oyster mushrooms, and cook over medium heat until the mushrooms are slightly softened, approximately 3–4 minutes.

3. Add the sherry and vinegar to the pan and reduce slightly. Remove from the heat.

4. Arrange the eggplant in a ring in the centre of each serving plate. (An inverted old fashion glass may be used to help shape the eggplant.) Arrange the greens around the outside of the ring.

5. Spoon the mushroom mixture into the centre of the eggplant ring and drizzle some of the remaining liquid over the greens. Grate fresh white truffle over the salad. (If fresh truffles are not available, lightly drizzle a good quality truffle oil over the finished salad.)

Approximate values per serving:

Calories	188
Total fat	14 g
Saturated fat	2 g
Cholesterol	0 mg
Sodium	313 mg
Total carbohydrates	13 g
Protein	3 g

♦♦♦

RECIPE 22.22
MIXED BEAN SALAD

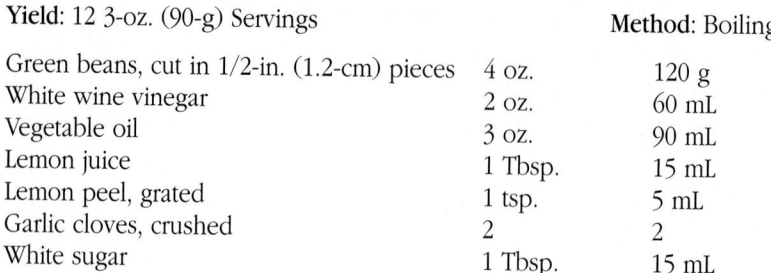

Yield: 12 3-oz. (90-g) Servings   **Method:** Boiling

Green beans, cut in 1/2-in. (1.2-cm) pieces	4 oz.	120 g
White wine vinegar	2 oz.	60 mL
Vegetable oil	3 oz.	90 mL
Lemon juice	1 Tbsp.	15 mL
Lemon peel, grated	1 tsp.	5 mL
Garlic cloves, crushed	2	2
White sugar	1 Tbsp.	15 mL

Dried red chile, chopped fine	1	1
Red kidney beans, soaked and cooked	8 oz.	250 g
Chickpeas, soaked and cooked	8 oz.	250 g
Lima or cannellini beans, soaked and cooked	8 oz.	250 g
Green onions, chopped	1 bunch	1 bunch
Red and green peppers, julienne	4 oz.	120 g
Salt and pepper	TT	TT

1. Steam the green beans until done but still crisp, approximately 3–4 minutes.

2. To make the dressing, combine the white wine vinegar, olive oil, lemon juice, lemon peel, garlic, sugar and chile.

3. Mix together all the drained beans and peas and pour the dressing over them. Add the green onions and peppers. Season with salt and pepper and toss to combine. Marinate for several hours before serving.

Approximate values per 3 oz. (90 g) serving:

Calories	150
Total fat	8 g
Saturated fat	1 g
Cholesterol	0 mg
Sodium	210 mg
Total carbohydrates	14 g
Protein	5 g
Iron	10%

Claims—low saturated fat; no cholesterol; good source of fibre

◆◆◆

RECIPE 22.23

BAKED BEANS

Yield: 60 oz. (1.8 L)   **Method:** Baking

Great Northern beans, soaked	1 lb.	450 g
Onion, small dice	4 oz.	120 g
Bacon lardons	4 oz.	120 g
Anaheim chile, small dice	1 oz.	30 g
Molasses	3 oz.	90 mL
Brown sugar	3 oz.	90 g
Catsup	8 oz.	250 mL
Dry mustard	1 tsp.	5 mL
Cider vinegar	1 Tbsp.	15 mL
Worcestershire sauce	2 Tbsp.	30 mL
Salt and pepper	TT	TT

1. Simmer the beans in water until almost tender, approximately 45 minutes. Drain well.

2. Combine the remaining ingredients, blending well.

3. Add the sauce to the beans, tossing to coat thoroughly. Adjust the seasonings.

4. Place the beans in a hotel pan or a 2-quart (2-L) baking dish. Cover and bake in a 350°F (180°C) oven until the beans are completely tender, approximately 30–40 minutes.

Approximate values per 3 oz. (90 g) serving:

Calories	120
Total fat	0 g
Saturated fat	0 g
Cholesterol	0 mg
Sodium	490 mg
Total carbohydrates	26 g
Protein	4 g
Vitamin C	15%

Claims—fat free; good source of fibre

◆◆◆

RECIPE 22.24

SORREL SAUCE

Yield: 32 oz. (1 L)   **Method:** Puréeing

Shallots, chopped coarsely	1 Tbsp.	15 mL
Whole butter	1 oz.	30 g
White wine	8 oz.	250 mL
Cream, 35%	1 pt.	500 mL
Sorrel, stemmed	8 oz.	250 g
Spinach, stemmed	8 oz.	250 g

Continued

Salt and white pepper	TT	TT
Lemon juice	1 oz.	30 mL

1. Sauté the shallots in the butter until tender.
2. Add the white wine and reduce by half.
3. Add the cream and reduce until it begins to thicken.
4. Add the sorrel and spinach leaves to the cream and cook just until the leaves are wilted.
5. Purée the sauce in a blender or food processor and season with salt, pepper and lemon juice. Serve the sauce with egg, chicken, veal or rich fish dishes.

◆◆◆

RECIPE 22.25
SWISS CHARD WITH LEMON AND PINE NUTS

Yield: 8 3-oz. (90-g) Servings   **Method:** Simmering

Swiss chard, trimmed, stems and leaves separated	2 lb.	1 kg
Water	1 pt.	500 mL
Lemon juice	2 oz.	60 mL
Extra virgin olive oil	2 oz.	60 mL
Salt and pepper	TT	TT
Pine nuts, toasted and chopped	2 oz.	60 g

1. Cut the chard into 1 to 2-inch (2.5 to 5-cm) strips on a diagonal.
2. Combine the chard, water and 1 ounce (30 g) lemon juice in a nonreactive pan. Simmer until tender, stirring frequently, approximately 10–15 minutes.
3. Drain. Toss with the remaining lemon juice and the olive oil. Season with salt and pepper and arrange on plates. Garnish with the pine nuts.

◆◆◆

RECIPE 22.26
BRAISED RED CABBAGE WITH APPLES AND WINE

Yield: 16 4-oz. (120-g) Servings   **Method:** Braising

Red cabbage	3 lb.	1.4 kg
Bacon, medium dice	12 oz.	350 g
Onions, medium dice	8 oz.	250 g
Salt and pepper	TT	TT
Medium potato, grated (optional)	1	1
Red wine	8 oz.	250 mL
White stock	8 oz.	250 mL
Cinnamon sticks	2	2
Apples, tart, cored and shredded	12 oz.	350 g
Brown sugar	1 oz.	30 g
Cider vinegar	2 oz.	60 mL
Red currant jelly	4 oz.	100 mL

1. Shred the cabbage.
2. Render the bacon. Add the onions and sweat in the bacon fat until tender.

3. Add the cabbage and sauté for 5 minutes. Season with salt and pepper. Add the stock, cinnamon sticks and the potato, if using. Cover and braise until the cabbage is almost tender, approximately 30 minutes. Moisten with additional stock if necessary.

4. Add the wine and braise 10 minutes more.

5. Add the apples, brown sugar, vinegar and red currant jelly and mix well.

6. Cover and braise until the apples are tender and dissolved, approximately 5 minutes.

NOTE: Traditionally, braised red cabbage is thickened with raw grated potato. One medium potato may be added in step 3.

Approximate values per 4 oz. (120 g) serving:	
Calories	170
Total fat	11 g
Saturated fat	4 g
Cholesterol	20 mg
Sodium	540 mg
Total carbohydrates	11 g
Protein	8 g
Vitamin C	50%

◆◆◆

RECIPE 22.27

BRAISED ROMAINE LETTUCE

Yield: 12 Servings   **Method:** Braising

Romaine lettuce	3 heads	3 heads
Onions, small dice	8 oz.	250 g
Celery, small dice	8 oz.	250 g
Carrots, small dice	8 oz.	250 g
Bacon ends and pieces, small dice	8 oz.	250 g
White stock	24 oz.	700 g
Salt and pepper	TT	TT

1. Trim the lettuce heads. Blanch them in salted boiling water and refresh and drain well.

2. Combine the onions, celery, carrots, bacon pieces and white stock in a sauce pot and simmer for 10 minutes.

3. Quarter the heads of romaine and trim off most of the core, leaving just enough to hold the leaves together.

4. Place 1 Tbsp. (15 mL) of the mirepoix in each portion of lettuce and fold to make a bundle.

5. Pour the remaining stock mixture into a hotel pan and arrange the lettuce portions in the pan. Season with salt and pepper.

6. Cover the pan and braise in a 350°F (180°C) oven for approximately 1 hour. Serve each portion with vegetables, bacon and a portion of the cooking liquid.

Approximate values per 5 oz. (150 g) serving:	
Calories	140
Total fat	10 g
Saturated fat	3.5 g
Cholesterol	15 mg
Sodium	340 mg
Total carbohydrates	6 g
Protein	7 g
Vitamin A	50%
Vitamin C	30%

◆◆◆

RECIPE 22.28

ROASTED VEGETABLE AND BOCCONCINI STACKS ON POLENTA ROUNDS

Chef-Consultant Anne Milne , VANCOUVER, BC

Yield: 8 Appetizers or   **Method:** Roasting
       4 Main Course Servings

Cornmeal	1 cup	250 mL
Butter	2 tsp.	10 mL
Salt	1 tsp.	5 mL

Continued

Anne Milne

After 16 years as a successful Vancouver chef, Anne is now a self-employed chef-consultant whose prestigious clients include the Bedford Hotel and the Butchart Gardens in Victoria. Anne is also a food writer for The Vancouver Sun, City Food Magazine, *and* City Palate *of Calgary.*

Japanese eggplant, cut into 1/2-inch (1-cm) rounds	2 large	2 large
Roma tomatoes, cut into 1/2-inch (1-cm) rounds	4 large	4 large
Zucchini, cut into 1/2-inch (1-cm) rounds	2 medium	2 medium
Red onions, cut into 1/2-inch (1-cm) rounds	2 medium	2 medium
Shiitake mushrooms	1/2 lb.	250 g
Salt and fresh cracked pepper	as needed	as needed
Olive oil	1 Tbsp.	15 mL
Balsamic vinegar	2 tsp.	10 mL
Mozzarella (bocconcini balls), fresh	8 oz.	250 g
Fresh basil leaves	4 large	4 large
Rosemary stems, fresh	4 or 8	4 or 8

1. To make the polenta, boil 4 cups (1 L) water in a heavy-bottomed pot. Whisk in cornmeal in a slow, steady stream. Stir over reduced heat until cooked, approximately 15 minutes. Stir in butter and salt.

2. Pour the polenta into a greased cookie sheet and spread to 1/2-inch (1-cm) thickness. Cool and cut out circles with a cookie cutter. (Large circles are used for main course and smaller circles for appetizers.)

3. Sprinkle cut vegetables with salt and pepper and drizzle with olive oil. Heat oven to 450°F (230°C) and brush olive oil on 2 cookie sheets. Spread the vegetables on the sheets and roast in the oven until tender and just starting to brown. (Vegetables may also be grilled.) Remove from oven and sprinkle with balsamic vinegar. Let cool.

4. Arrange the polenta circles on a clean, oiled baking sheet and stack the vegetables and cheese in the following order on top of each polenta round: polenta, bocconcini, 1 fresh basil leaf, red onion, eggplant, zucchini, tomato and shiitake mushrooms. Secure the stacks by spearing them with a bamboo skewer. Coat tops of stacks with olive oil and bake in a 375°F (190°C) oven for approximately 10 minutes, or just until cheese begins to melt.

5. Remove from the oven and replace the bamboo skewers with a stem of fresh rosemary. Serve stacks on a thin layer of marinara sauce.

Approximate values per serving:

Calories	297
Total fat	13 g
Saturated fat	7 g
Cholesterol	25 mg
Sodium	726 mg
Total carbohydrates	37 g
Protein	11 g

EBLINKS

Vegetable Categories
   www.produceoasis.com/Hierarchy_folder/
   Vegetables_folder/MainVegetable.html

History and Culinary Uses of Cucumbers
   www.lpl.arizona.edu/~bcohen/cucumbers/info.html

California Tomato Commission: Tips and Topics for Foodservice
   Professionals and Retailers
   www.tomato.org/mart-pgs/mart.htm

Mushrooms: The Mushroom Council
   www.mushroomcouncil.com/

National Onion Association
   www.onions-usa.org/

Ontario White Bean Producers — Buying, Storing, Soaking and
   Cooking Beans
   www.wwdc.com/whitepeabeans/basics.htm

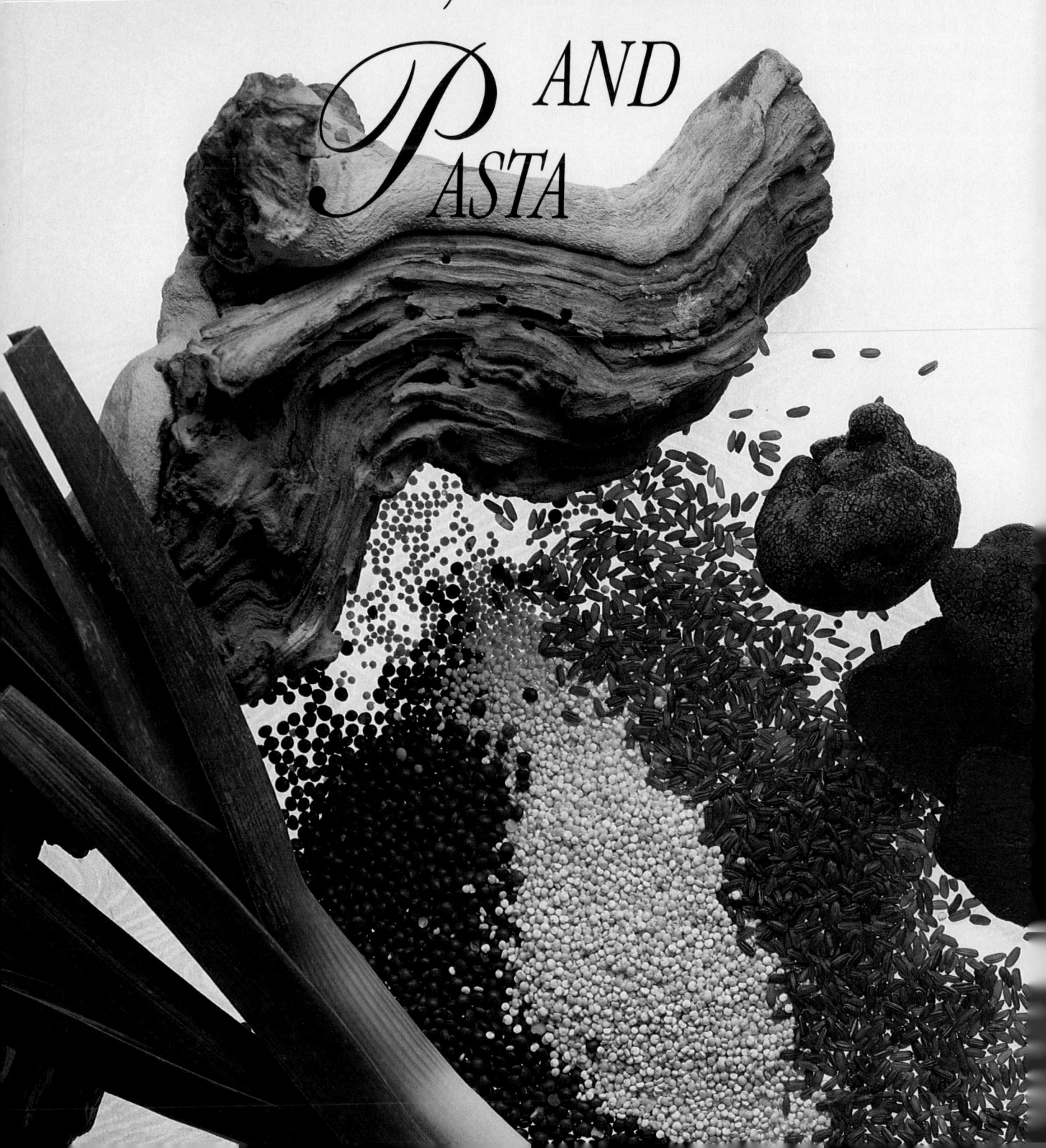

CHAPTER *23*

POTATOES, GRAINS AND PASTA

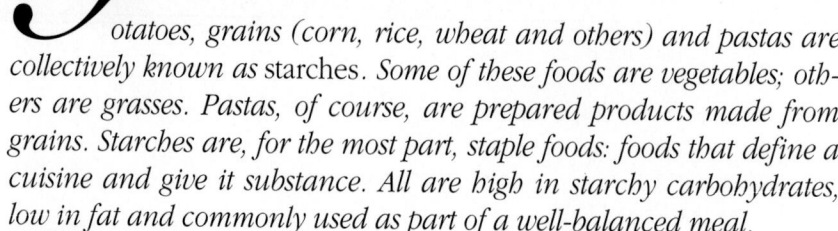

otatoes, grains (corn, rice, wheat and others) and pastas are collectively known as starches. *Some of these foods are vegetables; others are grasses. Pastas, of course, are prepared products made from grains. Starches are, for the most part, staple foods: foods that define a cuisine and give it substance. All are high in starchy carbohydrates, low in fat and commonly used as part of a well-balanced meal.*

Today's chefs are rediscovering traditional and ethnic dishes that rely on grains seldom used in typical food service operations. Pasta, made from a variety of grains in numerous shapes and flavours and accompanied by countless sauces and garnishes, now regularly appears on many menus alongside the ubiquitous potato prepared in many classic and modern styles.

◆◆◆

LEARNING OUTCOMES

After studying this chapter you will be able to:

◆ identify a variety of potatoes
◆ apply various cooking methods to potatoes: baking, baking en casserole, sautéing and pan-frying, boiling
◆ identify a variety of grains
◆ apply various cooking methods to grains: simmering, risotto method, pilaf method
◆ identify pasta products
◆ make fresh pasta: rolling and cutting the dough, making ravioli
◆ cook pasta: to order, in advance

POTATOES

Potatoes (Fr. *pommes de terre*) are one of the few vegetables native to the New World, probably originating in the South American Andes. Botanically, potatoes are succulent, nonwoody annual plants and members of the nightshade family. The portion we consume is the tuber, the swollen fleshy part of the underground stem. Potatoes are hardy and easy to grow, making them inexpensive and widely available.

Identifying Potatoes

The following are some of the more commonly used types of potatoes. Other varieties are regularly being developed or rediscovered and tested in the marketplace.

Choose potatoes that are heavy and very firm with clean skin and few eyes. Avoid those with many eyes, sprouts, green streaks, soft spots, cracks or cut edges. Most varieties are available all year.

Purple Potatoes

Purple (or blue) potatoes have a deep purple skin. The flesh is bright purple, becoming lighter when cooked. They are mealy, with a flavour and texture similar to russets. The most common varieties are All Blue and Caribe, which were quite popular in the mid-19th century.

Red Potatoes

Red potatoes have a thin red skin and crisp, white, waxy flesh, best suited to boiling or steaming. They do not have the dry, mealy texture successful baking requires. **New potatoes** are small, immature red potatoes usually marketed during the early summer as "creamers."

Russet Potatoes

Russet potatoes, also referred to as Idaho potatoes, are the standard baking potato. They are long with rough, reddish-brown skin and mealy flesh. Russets

Purple Potatoes

Red Potatoes

are excellent baked and are the best potatoes for frying. They tend to fall apart when boiled. They are marketed in several size categories and should be purchased in the size most appropriate for their intended use.

White Potatoes

White potatoes are available in round or long varieties. They have a thin, tender skin with a tender, waxy yellow or white flesh. The smaller ones are sometimes marketed as new potatoes (not to be confused with new red potatoes). Round white potatoes are also referred to as all-purpose potatoes. Yukon Gold and White Rose are common varieties. Bintje is an increasingly popular variety; it has a golden skin, creamy flesh and buttery flavour. White potatoes are usually cooked with moist heat or used for sautéing.

Russet Potatoes

White Potatoes

Sweet Potatoes

Sweet potatoes are from a different botanical family than ordinary potatoes, although they are also tubers that originated in the New World. Two types are commonly available. One has yellow flesh and a dry, mealy texture; it is known as a boniato, white or Cuban sweet potato. The other has a darker orange, moister flesh and is high in sugar; it is known as a red sweet potato. Both types have thick skins ranging in colour from light tan to brownish red. (Sometimes dark-skinned sweet potatoes are erroneously labelled *yams*.) Sweet potatoes should be chosen according to the desired degree of sweetness. They are best suited for boiling, baking and puréing, although the less sweet varieties can be deep-fat fried. The cooked flesh can also be used in breads, pies and puddings. Sweet potatoes are available canned, often in a spiced or sugary sauce.

Sweet Potatoes

Yams

Yams are a third type of tuber, botanically different from both sweet and common potatoes. Yams are less sweet than sweet potatoes, but they can be used interchangeably. The flesh of yams ranges from creamy white to deep red. Yams are Asian in origin and are now found in Africa, South America and the southern United States.

Nutrition

Potatoes contain a high percentage of easily digested complex carbohydrates and little or no fat. They are also a good source of many minerals and some vitamins. See Table 23.1, below.

TABLE 23.1 NUTRITIONAL VALUES OF SELECTED POTATOES

Per 4 oz. (112 g), baked in skin	Kcal	Protein (g)	Carbohydrates (g)	Fibre (g)	Total Fat (g)	Niacin (g)	Phosphorus (mg)	Potassium (mg)
Russet	124	2.6	28.6	0.7	0.1	1.9	64.8	475.5
Sweet potato	93	1.6	21.7	2.4	<0.1	mq	mq	mq
Yam	132	1.7	31.2	mq	0.2	0.4	33	455

The Corinne T. Netzer Encyclopedia of Food Values 1992
mq = measurable quantity, but data are unavailable

Purchasing and Storing Potatoes

Mealy Versus Waxy

One of the most important considerations in selecting potatoes is choosing between the mealy and waxy varieties. You should understand the differences and purchase the type best suited to your needs. See Table 23.2 below.

Mealy potatoes (also known as starchy potatoes) have a high starch content and thick skin. They are best for baking and are often ordered from suppliers simply as "bakers." Their low sugar content also allows them to be deep-fat fried long enough to fully cook the interior without burning the exterior. Mealy potatoes tend to fall apart when boiled, making them a good choice for whipped or puréed potatoes.

Waxy potatoes have a low starch content and thin skin. They are best for boiling. They will not develop the desired fluffy texture when baked. Because of their high moisture content they tend to become limp and soggy when deep-fat fried.

TABLE 23.2	COMPARISON OF MEALY AND WAXY POTATOES						
	Content of:			Best to:			
	Starch	Moisture	Sugar	Bake	Boil	Sauté	Deep-fat fry
Mealy: russet, white rose, purple	high	low	low	✓			✓
Waxy: red, new (red), Finnish yellow	low	high	high		✓	✓	

Grading

Potatoes sold in Canada are graded according to size and cleanliness. Canada No. 1 grade potatoes must be "reasonably free from dirt" with "not more than a slight amount of loose dirt or foreign material in the container." Round varieties of potatoes must have a minimum diameter of 2-1/4 inches (57 mm) and a maximum diameter of 3-1/2 inches (89 mm) to be graded as Canada No. 1. Long varieties must have a minimum diameter of 2 inches (51 mm) and a maximum diameter of 2-3/4 inches (70 mm). New potatoes must have a minimum diameter of 1-7/8 inches (48 mm) to be graded Canada No. 1.

Canada No. 2 grade potatoes have an "appreciable amount of dirt adhering to them" and "there is not more than a moderate amount of loose dirt or foreign material in the container" with them. Canada No. 2's must have a minimum diameter of 1-3/4 inches (44 mm) and a maximum diameter of 4-1/2 inches (114 mm).

Purchasing

Potatoes are usually packed in 50-pound (22 kg) cartons. Counts vary depending on average potato size. For example, in a 100-count carton, each potato would weigh an average of 8 ounces (250 g). Eighty-, 90- and 100-count cartons are the most common. Generally, larger-sized potatoes (i.e., smaller counts) are more expensive. Size does not affect quality, however, and selection should be based on intended use.

Storing

Temperatures between 45°–50°F (7–10°C) are best for storing potatoes. Do not store potatoes in the refrigerator. At temperatures below 40°F (4°C) potato starch turns to sugar, making the cooked product too sweet and increasing the risk that the potato will turn grey or streaky when cooked. Potatoes with a high sugar content also burn more easily when fried.

Potatoes should be stored in a dark room, as light promotes chlorophyll production, turning them green and bitter. Any green patches indicate the possible presence of solanine, a toxin harmful if eaten in large amounts, and should be peeled away. Solanine is also present in the eyes and sprouts and they, too, should be removed and discarded before cooking.

Under proper conditions, fresh potatoes should last for two months. Do not wash potatoes until ready to use, as washing promotes spoilage.

Applying Various Cooking Methods

Potatoes have a relatively neutral flavour, making them a perfect accompaniment to many savoury dishes. They can be prepared with almost any dry- or moist-heat cooking method: baking, sautéing, pan-frying, deep-fat frying, boiling or steaming. They can be combined with other ingredients in braises and stews. Potatoes are used in soups (vichyssoise), dumplings (gnocchi), breads, pancakes (latkes), puddings, salads and even vodka.

Many potato dishes, both classic and modern, employ more than one cooking method. For example, lorette potatoes require boiling and deep-fat frying; hash browns require parboiling, then sautéing. Even french fries are best when first blanched in hot oil.

Determining Doneness

Most potatoes are considered done when they are soft and tender or offer little resistance when pierced with a knife tip. Fried potatoes should have a crisp, golden-brown surface; the interior should be moist and tender.

Roasting and Baking

Potatoes may be roasted with meat or poultry, becoming coated with the fat and drippings released from the main item as it cooks. Either mealy or waxy potatoes, peeled or unpeeled, can be roasted successfully.

Mealy potatoes such as russets are ideal for baking. The skin is left intact, although it may be pierced with a fork to allow steam to escape. A true baked potato should not be wrapped in foil or cooked in a microwave; this changes the cooking method to steaming and prevents a crisp skin from forming. A properly baked potato should be white and fluffy, not yellowish or soggy. Once baked, potatoes can be eaten plain (or with butter, sour cream and other garnishes) or used in other recipes.

BASIC PROCEDURE FOR BAKING POTATOES

1. Scrub the potatoes well.
2. Using a fork, pierce the potato skins.
3. Rub the potatoes with oil and salt if desired. Do not wrap them in foil.
4. Bake the potatoes until done. A paring knife should penetrate them easily.

Approximate values per
7.5 oz. (225 g) potato:

Calories	270
Total fat	5 g
Saturated fat	.5 g
Cholesterol	0 mg
Sodium	2630 mg
Total carbohydrates	51 g
Protein	5 g
Vitamin C	45%

Claims—low saturated fat; no cholesterol; good source of fibre

♦♦♦

RECIPE 23.1

BAKED POTATOES

Yield: 8 Servings

Russet potatoes	8	8
Vegetable oil	3 Tbsp.	45 mL
Kosher salt	3 Tbsp.	45 mL

1. Scrub the potatoes well, but do not peel. Pierce the skin of each potato to allow steam to escape.
2. Rub the potatoes with the oil, then sprinkle with kosher salt.
3. Place the potato on a rack over a sheet pan. Bake in a 400°F (200°C) oven until done, approximately 1 hour. The potatoes should yield to gentle pressure and a paring knife inserted in the thickest part should meet little resistance.
4. Hold uncovered in a warm spot and serve within 1 hour.

Baking in a Casserole

Many classic potato dishes require baking either raw or parboiled potatoes with sauce, cheese, meat or other seasonings in a baking dish or casserole. Well-known examples include scalloped potatoes, which are baked in béchamel sauce, and au gratin, which are topped with cheese and baked. These dishes usually develop a crisp, brown crust, which is part of their appeal.

The casserole should hold its shape when cut; the potatoes should be tender and the sauce should be smooth, not grainy.

Potato casseroles can be fully baked, then held loosely covered in a steam table for service. Portions can be reheated or browned briefly under a broiler or salamander at service time.

BASIC PROCEDURE FOR BAKING POTATOES EN CASSEROLE

1. Prepare the potatoes by washing, peeling, slicing or partially cooking as desired or as directed in the recipe.
2. Add the potatoes to the baking pan in layers, alternating with the sauce, cream, cheese or other ingredients. Or combine the potatoes with the other ingredients and place in a buttered baking pan.
3. Bake the potatoes until done.

♦♦♦

RECIPE 23.2

GRATIN DAUPHINOIS

Yield: 4–5 lb. (1.8–2.2 kg)

Potatoes	3 lb.	1.3 kg
Whole butter	as needed	as needed
Salt and white pepper	TT	TT
Nutmeg	1/4 tsp.	2 mL

Gruyère cheese, grated	8 oz.	250 g
Cereal cream	24 oz.	650 mL
Egg yolks	3	3

1. Peel the potatoes and cut into very thin slices.
2. Place a single layer of potatoes in a well-buttered, full-size hotel pan.
3. Season with salt, pepper and a small amount of nutmeg. Sprinkle on a thin layer of cheese.
4. Add another layer of potatoes and cheese and repeat until all the potatoes and about three-quarters of the cheese are used.
5. Heat the cereal cream to a simmer. Whisk the egg yolks together in a bowl, then gradually add the hot cream.
6. Pour the cream-and-egg mixture over the potatoes. Top with the remaining cheese.
7. Bake uncovered at 350°F (180°C) until the potatoes are tender and golden brown, approximately 50–60 minutes.

Approximate values per 4 oz. (120 g) serving:

Calories	160
Total fat	8 g
Saturated fat	5 g
Cholesterol	55 mg
Sodium	160 mg
Total carbohydrates	15 g
Protein	6 g
Vitamin C	15%
Calcium	15%

Sautéing and Pan-Frying

Waxy potatoes, such as red- and white-skinned varieties, are best for sautéing or pan-frying. Often they are first parboiled or even fully cooked—a convenient way to use leftover boiled potatoes. They are then cooked in fat following the general procedures for sautéing and pan-frying discussed in Chapter 9, Principles of Cooking.

The fat can be clarified butter, oil, bacon fat or lard, depending on the desired flavour of the finished dish. The fat must be hot before the potatoes are added so that they will develop a crust without absorbing too much fat. Sautéed potatoes should have a crisp, well-browned crust and tender interior. They should be neither soggy nor greasy.

Potatoes can be sautéed or pan-fried by two methods: tossing and still-frying. The **tossing method** is used to cook relatively small pieces of potatoes in a small amount of fat. The potatoes are tossed using the pan's sloped sides so that they brown evenly on all sides. The **still-frying method** is used to create a disc-shaped potato product. The shredded or sliced potatoes are added to the pan, usually covering its bottom, and allowed to cook without stirring or flipping until they are well browned on the first side. The entire mass is then turned and cooked on the second side. When the potatoes are done, they can be cut into wedges for service.

BASIC PROCEDURE FOR SAUTÉING AND PAN-FRYING POTATOES

1. Wash, trim, peel, cut and/or cook the potatoes as desired or as directed in the recipe.
2. Heat the pan, add and heat the fat. Add the potatoes to the hot fat. Do not overcrowd the pan. Use enough fat to prevent the potatoes from sticking to the pan. Depending on the recipe, use either the tossing method or still-frying method.
3. Add garnishes, seasonings and other ingredients as desired or as directed in the recipe.
4. Cook the potatoes until done.

Approximate values per 4 oz. (120 g) serving:	
Calories	170
Total fat	12 g
Saturated fat	7 g
Cholesterol	30 mg
Sodium	650 mg
Total carbohydrates	16 g
Protein	1 g
Vitamin A	10%

◆◆◆

MORE THAN A FRENCH FRY

Thanks to the genius of Carême, Escoffier and others, few vegetables have as extensive a classic repertoire as potatoes. Some of these dishes begin with the duchesse potatoes mixture; in this regard, duchesse potatoes can be considered the mother of many classic potato preparations. For example,

Duchesse + Tomato concassé = *Marquis*
Duchesse + Chopped truffles + Almond coating + Deep-fat frying = *Berny*
Duchesse + Pâte à choux = *Dauphine*
Dauphine + Grated Parmesan + Piped shape + Deep-fat frying = *Lorette*
Duchesse + Shaping + Breading + Deep-fat frying = *Croquettes*

Other classic potato preparations not based on duchesse potatoes include:

Anna—thin slices are arranged in several circular layers in a round pan or mould coated with clarified butter; additional butter is brushed on and the potatoes are baked until crisp, then cut into wedges for service.
Boulangère—onions and potatoes are sautéed in butter, then transferred to a baking pan, stock is added and the potatoes are cooked uncovered until done.
Chateau—turned potatoes are sautéed in clarified butter until golden and soft.
Parisienne—small spheres are cut from raw, peeled potatoes with a parisienne scoop; they are seasoned and sautéed in clarified butter, then tossed with a meat glaze and garnished with chopped parsley.
Rösti—potatoes are shredded, seasoned and pan-fried in the shape of a pie, then cut into wedges for service.

◆◆◆

RECIPE 23.3

LYONNAISE POTATOES

Yield: 8 4-oz. (120-g) Servings

Potatoes, waxy variety	2 lb.	1 kg
Onion, julienne	8 oz.	250 g
Clarified butter	4 oz.	120 mL
Salt and pepper	TT	TT
Parsley, chopped	1 Tbsp.	15 mL

1. Partially cook the potatoes by baking, boiling or steaming. Allow to cool.
2. Peel and cut the potatoes into 1/4-inch- (1/2-cm-) thick slices.
3. Sauté the onions in half the butter until tender. Remove the onions from the pan with a slotted spoon and set aside.
4. Add the remaining butter to the pan. Add the potatoes and sauté, tossing as needed, until well browned on all sides.
5. Return the onions to the pan and sauté to combine the flavours. Season to taste with salt and pepper and garnish with parsley.

Deep-Fat Frying

Potato chips and french fries (Fr. *pomme frites*) are extremely popular in a variety of shapes, sizes and seasonings. While a wide range of shapes, sizes and preseasoned frozen products are available, fresh fried potatoes can be a delicious, economical menu item.

Top-quality russet potatoes are recommended for deep-fat frying. The skin may be removed or left attached. If peeled, the potatoes should be soaked in clear, cold water until ready to cut and cook. This keeps them crisp and white by leaching some of the starch that might otherwise make the potatoes gummy or cause smaller cuts to stick together when cooked.

The potatoes are usually blanched in oil ranging in temperature from 250° to 300°F (120–150°C) until tender and translucent. They are then drained and held for service, at which time they are finished in hotter oil, usually at a temperature between 350° and 375°F (180–190°C).

Deep-fat frying is also used to finish cooking several classic potato dishes such as croquettes and dauphine, in which fully cooked potatoes are puréed, seasoned, shaped and fried.

Deep-fat fried potatoes should be drained on absorbent paper briefly and served immediately.

In general, the procedures for deep-fat frying found in Chapter 21 also apply here. Specific recipes for several types of deep-fat fried potatoes are given at the end of this chapter.

Boiling

Waxy potatoes are best for all moist-heat cooking methods. Boiled potatoes (which are actually simmered) may be served as is or used in multistep preparations such as purées, salads, soups and baked casseroles. Potatoes are usually boiled in water, although stock may be used or milk added for flavour. Always begin cooking potatoes in cold liquid to ensure even cooking. Unlike other vegetables, potatoes should not be refreshed in cold water; it makes them soggy.

BASIC PROCEDURE FOR BOILING POTATOES

1. Wash, peel or trim the potatoes as desired.
2. Cut the potatoes into uniform-size pieces. The pieces should not be too small or they will absorb a large amount of water as they cook, making the final product soggy.
3. Add the potatoes to enough cool liquid to cover them by several inches. Bring to a boil, reduce to a simmer and cook until done. If a slightly firm finished product is desired, remove and drain the potatoes when they are slightly underdone and allow carryover cooking to finish cooking them.
4. Drain the potatoes in a colander and serve or use for further preparation.

◆◆◆

RECIPE 23.4

DUCHESSE POTATOES

Yield: 2 lb. (1 kg)

Potatoes, peeled and quartered	2 lb.	1 kg
Whole butter	1 oz.	30 g
Nutmeg	TT	TT
Salt and pepper	TT	TT
Eggs	1	1
Egg yolks	2	2

1. Boil the potatoes in salted water until tender. Drain and immediately turn out onto a sheet pan to allow the moisture to evaporate.
2. While still warm, press the potatoes through a ricer or food mill, or grind through a grinder's medium plate. Blend in the butter and season to taste with nutmeg, salt and pepper.
3. Mix in the eggs and egg yolks, blending well.
4. Place the duchesse mixture in a piping bag fitted with a large star tip. Pipe single portion-sized spirals onto a parchment-lined sheet pan. Brush with clarified butter and bake at 375°F (190°C) until the edges are golden brown, approximately 8–10 minutes. Serve immediately.

USAGE: Duchesse potatoes are often used to decorate platters used for buffets, tableside preparations or to present chateaubriand. To create borders and garnishes, the standard mixture for duchesse potatoes is forced through a piping bag while still very hot and relatively soft.

Approximate values per 3 oz. (90 g) serving:	
Calories	120
Total fat	3.5 g
Saturated fat	2 g
Cholesterol	65 mg
Sodium	250 mg
Total carbohydrates	18 g
Protein	3 g
Vitamin C	20%

1. Pass boiled potatoes through a food mill.

2. Pipe duchesse potatoes.

3. The finished potatoes.

GRAINS

Botanically, grains are grasses that bear edible seeds. Corn, rice and wheat are the most significant. Both the fruit (i.e., the seed or kernel) and the plant are called a grain (see Figure 23.1).

Most grain kernels are protected by a **hull** or husk. All kernels are composed of three distinct parts: the **bran**, **endosperm** and **germ**. The bran is the tough outer layer covering the endosperm. Bran is a good source of fibre and B vitamins. The endosperm is the largest part of the kernel and is a source of protein and carbohydrates (starch). It is the part used primarily in milled products such as flour. The germ is the smallest portion of the grain and is the only part that contains fat. It is also rich in thiamin. The bran, endosperm and germ are usually separated by milling.

Identifying Grains

This section presents information on corn, rice and wheat as well as several minor grains that are nutritionally significant and gaining popularity.

Some products are available in a stone-ground form. This means that the grains were ground with a stone mill rather than by the steel blades typically used for **cracking**, **grinding**, **hulling** and **pearling**. Stone grinders are gentler and more precise, so they are less likely to overgrind the grain. Stone-ground products will always be labelled as such and are usually more expensive than steel-ground ones.

Corn

Corn (Sp. *maíz*; It. *granturco*) is the only grain that is also eaten fresh as a vegetable. (Fresh corn is discussed in Chapter 22, Vegetables.) Its use as a dried grain dates back several thousand years in Central America and long preceded its use as a vegetable.

Cracking—*a milling process in which grains are broken open.*

Grinding—*a milling process in which grains are reduced to a powder; the powder can be of differing degrees of fineness or coarseness.*

Hulling—*a milling process in which the hull is removed from grains.*

Pearling—*a milling process in which all or part of the hull, bran and germ are removed from grains.*

A wheat plant.   A kernel of wheat.

FIGURE 23.1

Cornmeal

Cornmeal is made by drying and grinding a special type of corn known as *dent*, which may be yellow, white or blue. Cornmeal is most often used in breads, as a coating for fried foods or cooked as polenta or mush. Products made with cornmeal have a gritty texture and a sweet but starchy flavour.

Cornmeal

Hominy

Hominy, also known as posole or samp, is dried corn that has been soaked in hydrated lime or lye. This causes the kernels to swell, loosening the hulls. The hulls and germs are removed and the kernels dried. These white or yellow kernels resemble popcorn, but with a soft, chewy texture and smoky-sour flavour. Hominy is available dried or cooked and canned. It may be served as a side dish or used in stews or soups. **Masa harina**, a finely ground flour made from hominy, is used for making breads, tortillas, tamales and other Mexican and southwestern dishes.

Hominy

Grits

Grits are traditionally made by grinding dried hominy. These tiny white granules may be used in baked dishes but are most often served as a hot breakfast cereal, usually topped with butter or cheese. Quick-cooking and instant grits are available.

Rice

Rice (Fr. *riz*; It. *riso*; Sp. *arroz*) is the starchy seed of a semiaquatic grass. Probably originating on the Indian subcontinent or in Southeast Asia, rice is used as a staple by more than half of the world's population.

Rice can be incorporated into almost any cuisine, from Asian to Spanish to classic French. Its flavour adapts to the foods and seasonings with which the rice is cooked or served. Its texture adds an appealing chewiness to meat and poultry dishes, salads, breads and puddings. Rice is not limited to a side dish, but may be used in stews or curries, for stuffing vegetables or game birds, in puddings, salads, beverages (such as *horchata*) and breads.

Rice is divided into three types based on seed size: **long-grain, medium-grain** and **short-grain**. Long-grain rice is the most versatile and popular worldwide. The grains remain firm, fluffy and separate when cooked. (Long-grain rice can, however, become sticky if overcooked or stirred frequently during cooking.) Short-grain rice has more starch and becomes quite tender and sticky when cooked. Italian risotto, Japanese sushi and Spanish paella are all traditionally made with short-grain rice. The appearance and starch content of medium-grain rice falls somewhere in between. Medium-grain rice becomes sticky when cool, so it is best eaten freshly made and piping hot.

Long-grain, medium-grain and short-grain rice are available in different processed forms. All rice is originally brown. The grains can be left whole, with the bran attached, for **brown rice**. Or they can be pearled for the more familiar polished **white rice**. Both brown rice and white rice can be processed into converted rice and instant rice.

Converted rice is parboiled to remove the surface starch. This procedure also forces nutrients from the bran into the grain's endosperm. Therefore, converted rice retains more nutrients than regular milled white rice, although the flavour is the same. Converted rice is neither precooked nor instant; in fact, it cooks more slowly than regular milled white rice.

Instant or **quick-cooking rice** is widely available and useful if time is a concern. Instant rice is created by fully cooking then flash-freezing milled rice. Unfortunately, this processing removes some of the nutrients and flavour.

Converted Rice

Arborio Rice

Basmati Rice

Wild Pecan Rice

Wild Rice

Arborio Rice

Arborio is a round, short-grain rice used primarily in Italian dishes such as risotto. It is very sticky, with a white colour and mild flavour.

Basmati Rice

Basmati is one of the finest long-grain rices in the world. It grows in the Himalayan foothills and is preferred in Indian cuisine. It is highly aromatic, with a sweet, delicate flavour and a creamy yellow colour. Basmati rice is usually aged to improve its aromatic qualities and should be washed well before cooking.

Brown Rice

Brown rice is the whole natural grain of rice. Only the husk has been removed. Brown rice has a nutty flavour; its chewy texture is caused by the high-fibre bran. Brown rice absorbs more water and takes longer to cook than white rice.

Brown Rice

Wild Rice

Wild rice is prepared in the same manner as traditional rice, although it is actually the seed of an unrelated reedlike aquatic plant. Wild rice has long, slender grains with a dark brown to black colour. It has a nuttier flavour and chewier texture than traditional rice. Three grades are available: giant (the best quality, with very long grains); fancy (a medium-sized grain, suitable for most purposes); and select (a short grain, suitable for soups, pancakes or baked goods). Cultivated in Saskatchewan, Manitoba and Ontario, it is generally served with game, used as a stuffing for poultry or combined with regular rice for a side dish. Wild rice is expensive, but small quantities are usually sufficient.

Wild Pecan Rice

Wild pecan rice is neither wild nor made with pecans. It is a unique long-grain rice grown only in the bayou country of southern Louisiana. Wild pecan rice has a nutty flavour and exceptionally rich aroma.

Guidelines for Cooking Rice

Rice may be rinsed before cooking to remove dirt and debris, but doing so also removes some nutrients. It is not necessary to rinse most American-grown rice as it is generally clean and free of insects. Rice may also be soaked before

TABLE 23.3   GUIDELINES FOR COOKING RICE

Type of Rice	Ratio Rice: Water (by Volume)	Preparation	Cooking Time (simmering)	Yield from 1 Cup Raw Rice
Arborio	1 : 2.5–3	Do not rinse or soak	15–20 min.	2.5–3 cups
Basmati	1 : 1.75	Rinse well; soak	15 min.	3 cups
Brown, long-grain	1 : 2.5	Do not rinse; can soak	45–50 min.	3–4 cups
Converted	1 : 2.5	Do not rinse	20–25 min.	3–4 cups
White, long-grain (regular milled)	1 : 2	Do not rinse	15 min.	3 cups
Wild	1 : 3	Rinse	35–60 min., depending on grade	3–4 cups

cooking. Soaking softens the grains, removes some starch and speeds cooking.

The standard ratio for cooking rice is 2 parts liquid to 1 part rice. The actual ratio varies, however, depending on the type of rice. Guidelines for cooking rice are found in Table 23.3.

Once cooked, rice is highly perishable. Because of its neutral pH and high protein content, cooked rice is a potentially hazardous food. To avoid the risk of food-borne illnesses, be sure to store cooked rice out of the temperature danger zone.

Wheat

Wheat (Fr.: *blé*) is most often milled into the wide range of flours discussed in Chapter 26, Principles of the Bakeshop. But wheat and products derived from it are also used as starchy side dishes or ingredients in soups, salads, ground meat dishes and breads. These products include cracked wheat, bulgur and couscous. When cooked they are slightly chewy with a mild flavour. All should be fluffy; none should be soggy or sticky.

Wheat germ and *wheat bran* are widely available and highly touted for their nutritional values. Bran and germ are not generally used plain, but may be added to bread or other cooked dishes.

Cracked Wheat

Cracked wheat is the whole wheat kernel (known as a **berry**) broken into varying degrees of coarseness. It is not precooked, and the kernel's white interior should be visible. The bran and germ are still intact, so cracked wheat has a great deal of fibre but a short shelf life. Whole wheat berries must be soaked for several hours before cooking. Cracked wheat can be fully cooked by long, gentle simmering.

Bulgur

Couscous

Bulgur

Bulgur is a wheat berry that has had the bran removed; it is then steam-cooked, dried and ground into varying degrees of coarseness. Bulgur has a nutlike flavour and texture; it is a uniform golden-brown colour (uncooked cracked wheat is not) and requires less cooking time than cracked wheat. Generally, cracked wheat and bulgur cannot be substituted for one another in recipes.

Bulgur only needs to be soaked in water, then drained, for use in salads, or briefly cooked when used in stews or pilafs. Bulgur is good with grilled meats and as an alternative to rice in stuffings and other dishes. The fine grind is most often used in packaged mixes such as tabouli; the medium grind is most often available in bulk.

Couscous

Couscous is made by removing the bran and germ from **durum wheat** berries. The endosperm is then steamed, pressed to form tiny pellets and dried. Couscous is available in varying degrees of coarseness; medium-fine is the most popular. Couscous is prepared by steaming over water or stock in a pot called a couscousier. Couscous, traditionally served with North African stews, can be used or served like rice.

Durum wheat—*a species of very hard wheat with a particularly high amount of protein; it is milled into* **semolina**, *which is used for making pasta.*

Barley

Other Grains

Barley

Barley is one of the oldest culinary grains, used by humans since prehistoric times. Barley is extremely hardy, growing in climates from the tropics to the near-Arctic. Although much of the barley crop is used to make beer or feed animals, some does find its way into soups, stews and stuffings. The most common type is pearled to produce a small, round white nugget of endosperm. It has a sweet, earthy flavour similar to oats, and goes well with onions, garlic and strong herbs. Barley's texture ranges from chewy to soft, depending on the amount of water in which it is cooked. Its starchiness can be used to thicken soups or stews.

Buckwheat/Kasha

Buckwheat/Kasha

Buckwheat is not a type of wheat; it is not even a grain. Rather, it is the fruit of a plant distantly related to rhubarb. Buckwheat is included here, however, because it is prepared and served in the same manner as grains.

The whole buckwheat kernel is known as a **groat**. The product most often sold as buckwheat is actually kasha, which is a hulled, roasted buckwheat groat. Kasha is reddish brown with a strong, nutty, almost scorched flavour. It is available whole or ground to varying degrees of coarseness. Whole kasha remains in separate grains after cooking; the finer grinds become rather sticky. Kasha can be served as a side dish, usually combined with pasta or vegetables, or it can be chilled and used in salads.

Raw buckwheat groats are ground into flour typically used in pasta, blini and other pancakes. Buckwheat flour contains no gluten-forming proteins and it tends to remain grainy, with a sandy texture. Therefore, it should not be substituted for all of the white or whole wheat flour in breads or baked goods.

Oats

Oats

After rice, oats are probably the most widely accepted whole-grain product in the North American diet. Oats are consumed daily as a hot breakfast cereal (oatmeal) and are used in breads, muffins, cookies and other baked goods.

An oat groat is the whole oat kernel with only the husk removed. It contains both the bran and germ. *Steel-cut oats*, sometimes known as Irish oats, are groats that are toasted then cut into small pieces with steel blades. *Rolled oats*, marketed as "old-fashioned oats," are groats that have been steamed, then rolled into flat flakes. *Quick-cooking oats* are simply rolled oats cut into smaller pieces to reduce cooking time. *Instant oats* are partially cooked and dried before rolling so they need only to be rehydrated in boiling water. Several flavoured versions are also marketed as breakfast cereal. Rolled oats and quick-cooking oats can be used interchangeably, but instant oats should not be substituted in most recipes.

Oat bran is the outer covering of a hulled oat. It is available as a separate product, although rolled and cut oats do contain some oat bran.

The term *oatmeal* is commonly used to refer to both processed groats and the cooked porridge made from them. The processed groats known as oatmeal are a grey-white colour with a starchy texture and sweet flavour. They cook into the soft, thick porridge with a robust flavour called oatmeal.

Nutrition

Grains are an excellent source of vitamins, minerals, proteins and fibre (Table 23.4). The amount of milling or refining and the method of preparation affects their nutritional values, however. Unrefined and less-refined grains are excellent sources of dietary fibre. Rice is also quite nutritious: It is low in sodium and calories and contains all the essential amino acids. Some grains, especially white rice and oats, are usually enriched with calcium, iron and B vitamins.

TABLE 23.4   NUTRITIONAL VALUES OF SELECTED GRAINS

Per 4 oz. (120 g), cooked	Kcal	Protein (g)	Carbohydrates (g)	Fibre (g)	Total Fat (g)	Niacin (g)	Phosphorus (mg)	Potassium (mg)
Barley, pearled	139	2.6	32	0.3	0.5	1.6	42.5	72.5
Bulgur	94	3.5	21.1	0.4	0.3	0.9	36.5	62
Grits	68	1.6	14.7	0.1	0.2	0.8	15	27
Kasha	104	3.8	22.6	0.6	0.7	1.2	80	95
Oats	45	3.6	13	0.4	1	0.2	89	66
Rice, brown, long-grain	126	2.9	26	1.9	1	1.5	81	42
Rice, converted	90	1.5	21.1	mq	0.7	mq	mq	mq
Rice, white, long-grain	146	3.1	31.6	0.1	0.3	1.5	47	40
Wheat germ (toasted)	432	33.2	56.4	14.8	12	6.4	1280	1076

The Corinne T. Netzer Encyclopedia of Food Values 1992
mq = measurable quantity, but data are unavailable

Purchasing and Storing Grains

Purchasing

When buying grains, look for fresh, plump ones with a bright, even colour. Fresh grains should not be shrivelled or crumbly; there should be no sour or musty odours.

Grains are sold by weight. They come in bags or boxes ranging from 1 to 100 pounds (450 g–45 kg). Ten-, 25- and 50-pound (4.5-, 11- and 22-kg) units are usually available.

Storing

All grains should be stored in air-tight containers placed in a dark, cool, dry place. Air-tight containers prevent dust and insects from entering. Air-tight containers and darkness also reduce nutrient loss caused by oxidation or light. Coolness inhibits insect infestation; dryness prevents mould.

Vacuum-sealed packages will last for extended periods. Whole grains, which contain the oily germ, should be refrigerated to prevent rancidity.

Applying Various Cooking Methods

Three basic cooking methods are used to prepare grains: simmering, risotto and pilaf. Unlike simmered grains, those cooked by either the risotto or pilaf method are first coated with hot fat. The primary distinction between the pilaf and risotto methods is the manner in which the liquid is then added to the grains. When grains are used in puddings, breads, stuffings and baked casseroles, they are almost always first fully cooked by one of these methods.

Determining Doneness

Most grains should be cooked until tender, although some recipes do require a chewier or more al dente product. Doneness can usually be determined by cooking time and the amount of liquid remaining in the pan. Some grains, such as wild rice, are fully cooked when they puff open.

In general, grains will be fully cooked when almost all of the cooking liquid is absorbed. This is indicated by the appearance of tunnel-like holes between the grains. Grains can be cooked until almost all of the liquid is absorbed, then removed from the heat and left to stand, covered, for 5–10 minutes. This allows the cooked grains to absorb the remaining moisture without burning.

Simmering

The most commonly used method for preparing grains is simmering. To do so, simply stir the grains into a measured amount of boiling salted water in a saucepan on the stove top. When the liquid returns to a boil, lower the heat, cover, and simmer until the liquid is absorbed and the grains are tender. The grains are not stirred during cooking.

The grains can be flavoured by using stock as the cooking liquid. Herbs and spices can also be added.

BASIC PROCEDURE FOR SIMMERING GRAINS

1. Bring the cooking liquid to a boil.
2. Stir in the grains. Add herbs or spices as desired or as directed in the recipe.
3. Return the mixture to a boil, cover and reduce to a simmer.
4. Simmer the grains until tender and most of the liquid is absorbed.
5. Remove the grains from the heat.
6. Drain if appropriate or keep covered and allow the excess moisture to evaporate, approximately 5 minutes. Fluff the grains with a fork before service.

♦♦♦

RECIPE 23.5

BASIC SIMMERED RICE

Yield: 3 cups (750 mL)

Water	1 pt.	500 mL
Salt	1/2 tsp.	2 mL
White rice	1 cup	250 mL

1. Bring the water and salt to a boil in a heavy saucepan. Slowly add the rice.
2. Cover the pan and reduce the heat so that the liquid simmers gently. Cook until the rice is tender and the water is absorbed, approximately 15–20 minutes.
3. Remove from the heat and transfer to a hotel pan. Do not cover. Allow any excess moisture to evaporate for approximately 5 minutes.
4. Fluff the rice and serve, or refrigerate for use in another recipe.

Approximate values per 4 oz. (120 g) serving:

Calories	150
Total fat	0 g
Saturated fat	0 g
Cholesterol	0 mg
Sodium	0 mg
Total carbohydrates	34 g
Protein	3 g
Iron	8%

Claims—fat free; no sodium; no sugar

Risotto Method

Risotto is a classic Northern Italian rice dish in which the grains remain firm but merge with the cooking liquid to become a creamy, almost puddinglike dish. True risotto is made with a short-grain starchy rice such as Arborio, but the risotto method can also be used to cook other grains such as barley and oats.

The grains are not rinsed before cooking, as this removes the starches needed to achieve the desired consistency. The grains are coated, but not cooked, in a hot fat such as butter or oil. A hot liquid is then gradually added to the grains so that the mixture is kept at a constant simmer. The cooking liquid should be a rich, flavourful stock. Unlike simmering and the pilaf method, the risotto method requires frequent, sometimes constant, stirring.

When finished, the grains should be creamy and tender, but still al dente in the centre. Grated cheese, 35% cream, cooked meat, poultry, fish, shellfish, herbs and vegetables can be added to create a flavourful side dish or a complete meal.

BASIC PROCEDURE FOR PREPARING GRAINS BY THE RISOTTO METHOD

1. Bring the cooking liquid to a simmer.
2. Heat the fat in a heavy saucepan over moderate heat. Add any onions, garlic or other flavouring ingredients and sauté for 1–2 minutes without browning.
3. Add the grains to the saucepan. Stir well to make sure the grains are well coated with fat. Do not allow the grains to brown.
4. Add any wine and cook until it is fully absorbed.
5. Begin to add the simmering stock 4 ounces (120 mL) at a time, stirring frequently. Wait until each portion of cooking liquid is almost fully absorbed before adding the next.
6. Test for doneness after the grains have cooked for approximately 18–20 minutes.
7. Remove the saucepan from the heat and stir in any butter, grated cheese, herbs or other flavouring ingredients as directed. Serve immediately.

1. Sauté the rice and onions in butter.

◆◆◆

RECIPE 23.6

RISOTTO MILANESE

Yield: 24 4-oz. (120-g) Servings

Chicken stock	2-1/2 qt.	2.5 L
Whole butter	4 oz.	120 g
Onions, minced	5 oz.	150 g
Arborio rice	1 lb. 8 oz.	700 g
Dry white wine	8 oz.	250 mL
Saffron threads, crushed	1/2 tsp.	2 mL
Parmesan cheese, grated	4 oz.	120 g

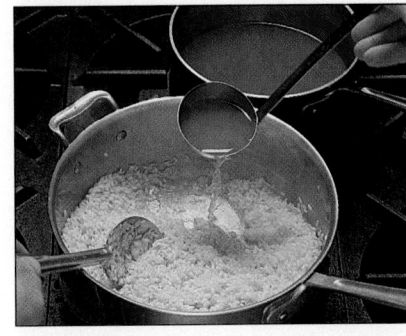

2. Add the stock gradually while stirring frequently.

1. Bring the chicken stock to a simmer.
2. Heat 3 ounces (90 g) of the butter in a large, heavy saucepan. Add the onion and sauté without browning until translucent.
3. Add the rice to the onion and butter. Stir well to coat the grains with butter but do not allow the rice to brown. Add the wine and stir until it is completely absorbed.
4. Add the saffron. Add the simmering stock, 4 ounces (120 mL) at a time, stirring frequently. Wait until the stock is absorbed before adding the next 4-ounce (120-mL) portion.
5. After approximately 18–20 minutes all of the stock should be incorporated and the rice should be tender. Remove from the heat and stir in the remaining 1 ounce (30 g) of butter and the grated cheese. Serve immediately.

Continued

3. Stir in the butter and grated cheese.

VARIATIONS: Risotto with Radicchio (*al Radicchio*)—Omit the saffron and Parmesan. Just before the risotto is fully cooked, stir in 4 ounces (120 mL) of 35% cream and 3 ounces (90 g) of finely chopped radicchio leaves.

Risotto with Four Cheeses (*al Quattro Formaggi*)—Omit the saffron. When the risotto is fully cooked, remove from the heat and stir in 2 ounces (60 g) each of grated Parmesan, Gorgonzola, fontina and mozzarella cheeses. Garnish with toasted pine nuts and chopped parsley.

Risotto with Smoked Salmon (*al Salmone Affumicato*)—Omit the butter, saffron and Parmesan. Sauté the onion in 3 ounces (90 mL) of corn or safflower oil instead of butter. When the risotto is fully cooked, remove from the heat and stir in 8 ounces (240 mL) of cereal cream, 3 ounces (90 mL) of fresh lemon juice and 8–10 ounces (240–300 g) of good-quality smoked salmon. Garnish with chopped fresh parsley and dill. Serve with lemon wedges.

Approximate values per 4 oz. (120 g) serving:	
Calories	110
Total fat	6 g
Saturated fat	3.5 g
Cholesterol	15 mg
Sodium	470 mg
Total carbohydrates	9 g
Protein	5 g

Pilaf Method

With the pilaf method, the raw grains are lightly sautéed in oil or butter, usually with onions or seasonings for additional flavour. Hot liquid, often a stock, is then added. The pan is covered and the mixture left to simmer until the liquid is absorbed.

BASIC PROCEDURE FOR PREPARING GRAINS BY THE PILAF METHOD

1. Bring the cooking liquid (either water or stock) to a boil.
2. Heat the fat in a heavy saucepan over moderate heat. Add any onions, garlic or other flavourings and sauté for 1–2 minutes without browning.
3. Add the grains to the saucepan. Stir well to make sure the grains are well coated with fat. Do not allow the grains to brown.
4. All at once, add the hot cooking liquid to the sautéed grains.
5. Return the liquid to a boil, reduce to a simmer and cover.
6. Allow the mixture to simmer, either in the oven or on the stove top, until the liquid is absorbed.

◆◆◆

RECIPE 23.7

BULGUR PILAF

Yield: 8 4-oz. (120-g) Servings

Whole butter	2 oz.	60 g
Onions, fine dice	4 oz.	120 g
Bulgur	10 oz.	300 g
Bay leaf	1	1
Chicken stock, hot	1 qt.	1 L
Salt and pepper	TT	TT

1. Melt the butter in a large, heavy saucepan over moderate heat. Add the onions and cook until translucent.
2. Add the bulgur and bay leaf. Sauté until the grains are well coated with butter.
3. Add the hot stock and season to taste with salt and pepper. Reduce the heat until the liquid barely simmers.

1. Sauté the bulgur in butter.

2. Add the hot stock to the bulgur.

3. Fluff the finished bulgur.

4. Cover and continue cooking until all of the liquid is absorbed and the grains are tender, approximately 18–20 minutes.

5. Fluff with a fork and adjust the seasonings before service.

VARIATION: Barley pilaf—Substitute 2 cups (500 mL) of pearled barley for the bulgur. Cooking time may increase by 10–15 minutes.

Approximate values per 4 oz. (120 g) serving:	
Calories	110
Total fat	7 g
Saturated fat	4 g
Cholesterol	15 mg
Sodium	470 mg
Total carbohydrates	9 g
Protein	4 g

PASTA

Pasta is made from an unleavened dough of liquid mixed with flour. The liquid is usually egg and/or water. The flour can be from almost any grain: wheat, buckwheat, rice or a combination of grains. The dough can be coloured and flavoured with puréed vegetables, herbs or other ingredients and it can be cut or **extruded** into a wide variety of shapes and sizes.

Pasta can be cooked fresh while the dough is still moist and pliable, or the dough can be allowed to dry completely before cooking. Pasta can be filled or sauced in an endless variety of ways. It can stand alone or be used in salads, desserts, soups or casseroles.

Pasta is widely used in the cuisines of Asia, North America and Europe. In Italy, pasta dishes are usually served as a separate course, referred to as the *minestre*; in other European countries, Asia and North America, pasta dishes may be served as an appetizer, entrée or side dish.

Extrusion—*the process of forcing pasta dough through perforated plates to create various shapes; pasta dough that is not extruded must be rolled and cut.*

Identifying Pastas

The better-known pastas are based on the Italian tradition of kneading wheat flour with water and eggs to form a smooth, resilient dough. This dough is rolled very thin and cut into various shapes before being boiled in water or dried for longer storage.

Macaroni—*any dried pasta made with wheat flour and water; only in North America does the term refer to elbow-shaped tubes.*

♦♦♦
THE MACARONI MYTH

The popular myth holds that noodles were first invented in China and discovered there by the Venetian explorer Marco Polo during the 13th century. He introduced the food to Italy and from there the rest of Europe. While there is little doubt that the Chinese were making noodles by the 1st century A.D., it is now equally clear that they were not alone.

Middle Eastern and Italian cooks were preparing macaroni long before Marco Polo's adventures. A clear reference to boiled noodles appears in the *Jerusalem Talmud* of the 5th century A.D. There, rabbis debate whether noodles violate Jewish dietary laws (they do, but only during Passover). Tenth-century Arabic writings refer to dried noodles purchased from

vendors. Literary references establish that dishes called lasagna, macaroni and ravioli were all well known (and costly) in Italy by the mid-13th century.

Pasta's current popularity dates from the 18th century, when mass production by machine began in Naples, Italy. English gentlemen on their Grand Tours of the Continent developed a fondness for pasta; the word *macaroni* became a synonym for a dandy or a vain young man. Macaroni arrived in America with English colonists, who preferred it with cream sauce and cheese or in a sweet custard. Domestic factories soon opened, and by the Civil War (1861–1865) macaroni was available to the working class. Pasta became a staple of the

American middle-class diet following the wave of Italian immigrants in the late 19th century.

During the 1980s pasta became ubiquitous. Restaurants began serving it in ways previously unimagined. Corner grocery stores and local supermarkets began offering at least a dozen different shapes, often fresh and sometimes flavoured. Dedicated cooks began to make pasta from scratch, though they sometimes tossed it with bottled sauce. Many also became interested in Asian noodles. Chinese, Japanese, Korean and Thai restaurants expanded their menu offerings to include traditional noodle dishes eagerly ordered by curious consumers. Pasta's popularity continues to grow as chefs discover the versatility of this inexpensive, nutritious food.

Commercially prepared dried pasta products are usually made with semolina flour. Semolina flour, ground from hard durum wheat and available from specialty purveyors, has a rich cream colour and produces a very smooth, durable dough. Semolina dough requires a great deal of kneading, however, and bread flour is an acceptable substitute when preparing fresh pasta by hand.

Asian pasta, generally known as noodles, is made from wheat, rice, bean or buckwheat flour. It is available fresh or dried from commercial purveyors and at specialty markets.

Italian-Style Pasta

Although all Italian-style pasta is made from the same type of dough, the finest commercial pastas are those made with pure semolina flour, which gives the dough a rich, yellow colour. Grey or streaked dough probably contains softer flours. Dried pasta should be very hard and break with a clean snap. The surface should be lightly pitted or dull. (A smooth or glossy surface will not hold or absorb sauces as well.)

Dried pasta, both domestic and imported, is available in a wide range of flavours and shapes. In addition to the traditional white (plain), green (spinach) and red (tomato) pastas, manufacturers are now offering such unusual flavour combinations as lemon-peppercorn, whole wheat–basil, jalapeño–black bean and carrot-ginger. Small pieces of herbs or other flavourings are often visible in these products.

There are hundreds of recognized shapes of pasta, but only two or three dozen are generally available in Canada. When experimenting with unusual flavours and shapes, be sure to consider the taste and appearance of the final dish after the sauce and any garnishes are added.

Italian-style pasta can be divided into three groups based on the shape of the final product: ribbons, tubes and shapes. There is no consistent English nomenclature for these pastas; the Italian names are recognized and applied virtually worldwide. (A specific shape or size may be given different names in different regions of Italy, however. These distinctions are beyond the scope of this text.)

Ribbons

Pasta dough can be rolled very thin and cut into strips or ribbons of various widths. All ribbon shapes work well with tomato, fish and shellfish sauces. Thicker ribbons, such as spaghetti and fettuccine, are preferred with cream or cheese sauces. Sheets of fresh pasta dough can be filled and shaped to create ravioli, cappelletti and tortellini. Filled pasta is usually served with a light cream- or tomato-based sauce that complements the filling's flavours.

Spinach Fettuccine

Fettuccine

Spaghetti

Lasagna

Capellini

Manicotti

Ziti

Penne

Rigatoni

Spira

Tubes

Cylindrical forms or tubes are made by extrusion. The hollow tubes can be curved or straight, fluted or smooth. Tubes are preferred for meat and vegetable sauces and are often used in baked casseroles.

Shapes

The extrusion process can also be used to shape pasta dough into forms. The curves and textures produced provide nooks and crevices that hold sauces well. Shaped pastas, such as conchiglie, farfalle and fusilli, are preferred with meat sauces and oil-based sauces such as pesto. Larger shaped pastas can be cooked, then stuffed with meat or cheese fillings and baked or served as a casserole.

Conchiglie

Fusilli

Rotelle

Farfalle

Orzo

Asian Noodles

Asian noodles are not cut into the same wealth of shapes and sizes as Italian-style pasta, nor are they flavoured or coloured with vegetable purées, herbs or other ingredients.

Virtually all Asian noodles are ribbons—some thin, some thick—folded into bundles and packaged. Differences arise because of the flours used for the dough.

Most dried Asian noodles benefit by soaking in hot water for several minutes before further preparation. The water softens the noddle strands; the bundles separate, and the noodles cook more evenly.

Wheat Noodles

Wheat noodles, also known as egg noodles, are the most popular and widely available of the Asian noodles. They are thin, flat noodles with a springy texture; they are available fresh or dried. Dried egg noodles can be deep-fat fried after boiling to create crisp golden noodles (chow mein) used primarily as a garnish.

Flour Stick Wheat Noodles (without egg)

Fresh Wheat and Egg Noodles

Rice Vermicelli

Cellophane Noodles

Japanese Wheat Somen

✦✦✦
DUMPLINGS

A **dumpling** is a small mound of dough cooked by steaming or simmering in a flavourful liquid. Dumplings are found in many cuisines: Italian gnocchi, Jewish matzo balls, German spaetzle, Chinese wontons and Polish pierogi. Dumplings can be sweet or savoury, plain or filled.

Plain or **drop dumplings** are made with a breadlike dough, often leavened with yeast or chemical leavening agents. They should be light and tender, but firm enough to hold their shape when cooked. Drop dumplings may be served with stews or broths, or coated with butter or sauce as an appetizer or side dish. Recipes for gnocchi and spaetzle are included at the end of this chapter.

Filled dumplings are made by wrapping noodle dough around seasoned meat, vegetables, cheese or fruit. These parcels are then steamed, fried or baked and served as a snack food, appetizer or side dish. A recipe for deep-fat fried wontons is included in Chapter 33, Appetizers and Sandwiches (Recipe 33.8).

Japanese wheat noodles, know as somen (if thick) and udon (if thin), may be round, square or flat. They are eaten in broth or with a dipping sauce.

Rice Noodles

Rice noodles are dried thin noodles made with rice flour. They should be soaked in hot water before cooking and rinsed in cool running water after boiling to remove excess starch and prevent sticking. Rice noodles are often served in soups or sautéed.

Rice vermicelli, which has very fine strands, can be fried in hot oil without presoaking. In only a few seconds the strands will turn white, puff up and become crunchy. Mounds of crunchy rice noodles can be used as a base for sautéed dishes or for presenting hors d'oeuvres.

Bean Starch Noodles

Bean starch noodles are also known as spring rain noodles, bean threads, bean noodles or cellophane noodles. They are thin, transparent noodles made from mung beans. Dried bean noodles can be fried in the same manner as rice vermicelli. Otherwise, they must be soaked in hot water before using in soups, stir-fries or braised dishes.

Buckwheat Noodles

Buckwheat flour is used in the noodles of Northern Japan and the Tokyo region, known as soba noodles. Soba noodles are available fresh or dried and do not need soaking before cooking. They are traditionally served in broth or with a dipping sauce, but may be substituted for Italian-style pasta if desired.

Nutrition

Pastas are very low in fat and are an excellent source of vitamins, minerals, proteins and carbohydrates. (See Table 23.5.) Also, the processed products are sometimes enriched with additional nutrients.

Purchasing and Storing Pasta Products

Pasta products are purchased by weight, either fresh or dried. Tubes and shapes are not generally available fresh. Dried products, by far the most common, are available in boxes or bags, usually in 1-, 10- and 20-pound (500-g, 5- and 20-kg) units. They can be stored in a cool, dry place for several months. Fresh pasta can be stored in an air-tight wrapping in the refrigerator for a few days or in the freezer for a few weeks.

TABLE 23.5   NUTRITIONAL VALUES OF SELECTED PASTA

Per 4 oz. (120 g), cooked	Kcal	Protein (g)	Carbohydrates (g)	Fibre (g)	Total Fat (g)	Niacin (g)	Phosphorus (mg)	Potassium (mg)
Noodle, Japanese soba (buckwheat)	113	5.8	24.4	mq	0.1	0.6	29	40
Pasta, wheat, dried	186	9.2	35.9	0.3	0.2	1.2	38	22
Pasta, wheat, spinach and egg, fresh	147	5.7	28.4	mq	1.10	1.2	65	42

The Corinne T. Netzer Encyclopedia of Food Values 1992

mq = measurable quantity, but data are unavailable

Preparing Fresh Pasta

Making Fresh Pasta

Fresh pasta is easy to make, requiring almost no special equipment and only a few staples. The basic form is the **sfoglia**, a thin, flat sheet of dough that is cut into ribbons, circles or squares.

Although pasta dough can be kneaded by hand, stretched and rolled with a rolling pin and cut with a chef's knife, pasta machines make these tasks easier. Pasta machines are either electric or manual. Some electric models mix and knead the dough, then extrude it through a cutting disk. An extrusion machine is most practical in a food service operation regularly serving large quantities of pasta. The pasta machine more often encountered is operated manually with a hand crank. It has two rollers that knead, press and push the dough into a thin, uniform sheet. Adjacent cutting rollers slice the thin dough into various widths for fettuccine, spaghetti, capellini or the like.

◆◆◆

RECIPE 23.8

BASIC PASTA DOUGH

Yield: 4 lb. (1.8 kg)

Eggs	15	15
Olive oil	1 oz.	30 mL
Salt	1 Tbsp.	15 mL
Bread flour or semolina	2 lb. 8 oz.	1.1 kg

1. Place the eggs, oil and salt in a large mixer bowl. Use the paddle attachment to combine.
2. Add one-third of the flour and stir until the mixture begins to form a soft dough. Remove the paddle attachment and attach the dough hook.
3. Gradually add more flour until the dough is dry and cannot absorb any more flour.
4. Remove the dough from the mixer, wrap it well with plastic wrap and set it aside at room temperature for 20–30 minutes.
5. After the dough has rested, roll it into flat sheets by hand or with a pasta machine. Work with only a small portion at a time, keeping the remainder well covered to prevent it from drying out.
6. While the sheets of dough are pliable, cut them into the desired width with a chef's knife or pasta machine. Sheets can also be used for making ravioli, as illustrated below.

VARIATIONS: Garlic-Herb—Roast 1 head of garlic. Peel and purée the cloves and add to the eggs. Add up to 2 ounces (60 g) of finely chopped assorted fresh herbs just before mixing is complete.

Spinach—Add 8 ounces (250 g) of cooked, puréed and well-drained spinach to the eggs. Increase the amount of flour slightly if necessary.

Tomato—Add 4 ounces (120 g) of tomato paste to the eggs; omit the salt. Increase the amount of flour slightly if necessary.

Note: Semolina flour can be substituted in this recipe, although it makes a stronger dough that is more difficult to work with by hand. Try half semolina (durum) and half bread flour.

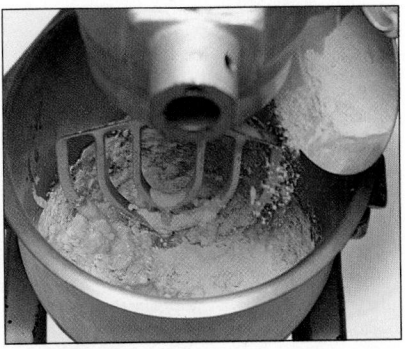

1. Add flour to the mixing bowl and use the paddle until the mixture forms a soft dough.

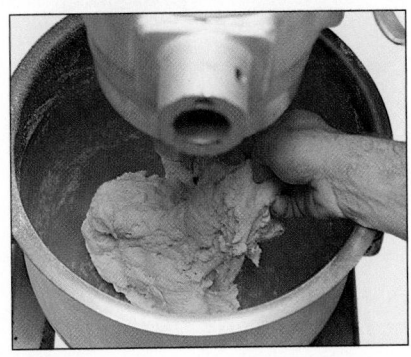

2. The finished dough.

Approximate values per 1 oz. (30 g) serving:	
Calories	80
Total fat	2 g
Saturated fat	.5 g
Cholesterol	50 mg
Sodium	125 mg
Total carbohydrates	13 g
Protein	3 g

Basic Procedure for Rolling and Cutting Pasta Dough

1. Work with a small portion of the dough. Leave the rest covered with plastic wrap to prevent it from drying out.
2. Flatten the dough with the heel of your hand.
3. Set the pasta machine rollers to their widest setting. Insert the dough and turn the handle with one hand while supporting the dough with the other hand. Pass the entire piece of dough through the rollers.
4. Dust the dough with flour, fold it in thirds and pass it through the pasta machine again.
5. Repeat the folding and rolling procedure until the dough is smooth. This may require 4–6 passes.
6. Tighten the rollers one or two marks, then pass the dough through the machine. Without folding it in thirds, pass the dough through the machine repeatedly, tightening the rollers one or two marks each time.
7. When the dough is thin enough to see your hand through, but not so thin that it begins to tear, it is ready to use or cut into ribbons. This sheet is the *sfoglia*.
8. To cut the sfoglia into ribbons, gently feed a manageable length of dough through the desired cutting blades.
9. To dry the pasta, lay it out in a single layer on a sheet pan dusted with flour. Layers of pasta ribbons can be separated with parchment paper.

1. Pass the entire piece of dough through the pasta machine.

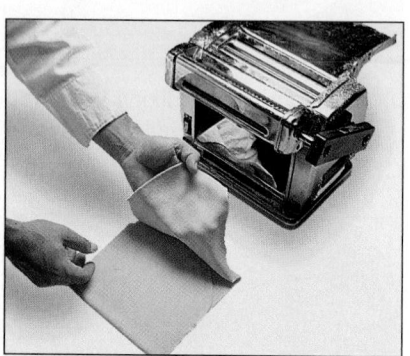

2. Fold the dough in thirds.

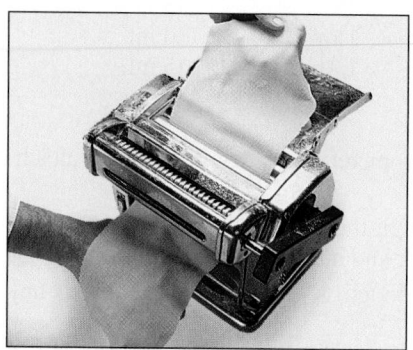

3. Pass the dough through the pasta machine to achieve the desired thickness.

4. Use the pasta machine to cut the pasta into the desired width.

Filling Pasta

Sheets of raw pasta dough can be filled or folded to create ravioli (squares), tortellini (round "hats" with a brim of dough), lunettes (circles of dough folded into half-moons), agnolotti (squares of dough folded into rectangles), cappelletti (squares of dough folded and shaped into rings) and other shapes. The filled pieces of dough are then cooked in boiling water using the procedure for cooking pasta ribbons discussed later. The filling can include almost anything—cheese, herbs, vegetables, fish, shellfish, meat or poultry. It can be uncooked or precooked. But any meat filling should be fully cooked before the pasta is assembled, as the time it takes for the dough to cook may not be sufficient to cook the filling.

Cannelloni is a different type of filled pasta: a large square of cooked dough is wrapped around a meat or cheese filling and baked. Popular lasagna dishes are similar. Lasagna pasta, which consists of wide, flat sheets, are cooked then layered with cheese, tomato sauce and meat or vegetables as desired. The finished casserole is baked and cut into portions.

Some of the larger, commercially prepared pasta shapes such as large shells (conchiglioni or rigate) or large tubes (manicotti) can be partially cooked in boiling water, then filled, sauced and baked as a casserole.

Asian noodle dough is also made into filled items such as dumplings, won tons, egg rolls (made with egg noodle dough) and spring rolls (made with rice paper). These items are usually steamed, pan-fried or deep-fat fried.

When making filled pasta, consider the flavours and textures of the filling, dough and sauce. Each should complement the others. Combinations can range from traditional unflavoured semolina pasta with herb and ricotta filling in a tomato sauce to an elegant escargot in garlic-and-herb pasta served with a beurre blanc to pork, ginger, soy and scallions in Asian egg noodle dough served with a soy-based dipping sauce.

BASIC PROCEDURE FOR PREPARING RAVIOLI

1. Prepare a basic pasta dough of the desired flavour.
2. Prepare and chill the desired filling.
3. Roll out two thin sheets of dough between the rollers of a pasta machine. Gently lay the dough flat on the work surface.
4. Using a piping bag or a small portion scoop, place small mounds of filling on one of the dough pieces. Space the fillings evenly, allowing approximately 2 inches (5 cm) between each mound.
5. Brush the exposed areas of dough with water.
6. Gently place the second sheet of dough over the mounds and press firmly around each mound to remove air pockets and seal the dough.
7. Cut between the mounds with a chef's knife, pastry wheel or circular cutter.

1. Pipe the filling onto the dough.

2. Press around the mounds of filling to seal the dough and remove any air pockets.

3. Cut around the mounds with a circular cutter.

Cooking Method

Determining Doneness

Italian-style pastas are properly cooked when they are al dente, firm but tender. Cooking times vary depending on the shape and quantity of pasta, the amount of water used, the hardness of the water and even the altitude. Fresh pasta cooks rapidly, sometimes in seconds. Noodles and dried pasta may require several minutes.

Although package or recipe directions offer some guidance, the only way to accurately test doneness is to bite into a piece. When the pasta is slightly firmer than desired, remove it from the stove and drain. It will continue to cook through residual heat.

Unlike Italian pasta, Asian noodles are not served al dente. Rather, they are either boiled until very soft or stir-fried until very crisp.

Boiling

All Italian-style pasta and most Asian noodles are cooked by just one method: boiling. The secret to boiling pasta successfully is to use ample water. Allow 1 gallon (4 L) of water for each pound (450 g) of pasta.

Use a saucepan or stockpot large enough to allow the pasta to move freely in the boiling water, otherwise the starch released by the dough will make the pasta gummy and sticky. The water should be brought to a rapid boil, then all the pasta should be added at once.

Salt should be added to the water. Pasta absorbs water and salt during cooking. Adding salt to the pasta after it is cooked will not provide the same seasoning effect.

Chefs disagree on whether to add oil to the cooking water. Purists argue against adding oil, on the theory that it makes the dough absorb water unevenly. Others think oil should be added to reduce surface foam. Another theory is that oil keeps the pasta from sticking, although this works only when oil is added to cooked, drained pasta.

Asian noodles may be prepared by boiling until fully cooked, or they may be parboiled then stir-fried with other ingredients to finish cooking.

BASIC PROCEDURE FOR COOKING PASTA TO ORDER

1. Bring the appropriate amount of water to a boil over high heat.
2. Add oil to the water if desired.
3. Add the pasta and salt to the rapidly boiling water.
4. Stir the pasta to prevent it from sticking together. Bring the water back to a boil and cook until the pasta is done.
5. When the pasta is properly cooked, immediately drain it through a colander. A small amount of oil may be gently tossed into the pasta if desired to prevent it from sticking together.
6. Serve hot pasta immediately, or refresh in cold water for use in salads or other dishes. (Do not rinse pasta that is to be served hot.)

BASIC PROCEDURE FOR COOKING DRIED PASTA IN ADVANCE

Fresh pasta is so delicate and cooks so rapidly (sometimes in as little as 15 seconds) that it should be cooked to order. Dried pasta, however, can be cooked in advance for quantity service.

1. Follow the above directions for cooking pasta, but stop the cooking process when the pasta is about two-thirds done.
2. Drain the pasta, rinse it lightly and toss it in a small amount of oil.
3. Divide the pasta into appropriate-sized portions. Individual portions can be wrapped in plastic or laid on a sheet pan and covered. Refrigerate until needed.
4. When needed, place a portion in a china cap and immerse in boiling water to reheat. Drain, add sauce and serve immediately.

Accompaniments to Pasta

Pasta is widely accepted by consumers and easily incorporated in a variety of cuisines—from Italian and Chinese to Thai and spa. It is used in broths; as a bed for stews, fish, shellfish or meat; or tossed with sauce. Today's creative chefs are constantly developing nontraditional but delicious ways of serving pasta.

TABLE 23.6 COMBINING SAUCES, PASTA AND GARNISHES

Sauce	Pasta Shape	Garnish
Ragu	Ribbons, tubes, shapes, filled	Grated cheese
Seafood	Ribbons (fettuccine and capellini)	Fish or shellfish
Vegetable	Ribbons, tubes, filled	Meatballs, sausage, grated cheese
Cream	Thick ribbons (spaghetti and fettuccine), filled	Ham, peas, sausage, mushrooms, smoked salmon, nuts, grated cheese
Garlic-oil	Ribbons, shapes, filled	Grated cheese (if uncooked or cold), herbs
Uncooked	Ribbons, shapes	Cubed or grated cheese, fresh vegetables, herbs

Pasta and Broths

Small shapes can be cooked in the broth with which they are served, or cooked separately, then added to the hot liquid at service time. Soups such as cappelletti in brodo and chicken noodle are examples of these techniques.

Pasta Sauces

There are hundreds of Italian pasta sauces as well as sauces for Italian-style pasta, but most can be divided into six categories: ragus, seafood sauces, vegetable sauces, cream sauces, garlic-oil sauces and uncooked sauces. Recipes for a selection of pasta sauces are in Chapter 10, Stocks and Sauces.

Although there are no firm rules governing the combinations of sauces and pasta, Table 23.6 offers some of the more common combinations.

◆◆◆

PASTA SAUCES

Ragus are braised dishes used as a sauce. Usually, several flavouring ingredients and meat or poultry are browned, then a liquid and often a tomato product are added. The liquid can be a combination of stock, wine, water, milk or cream.

Seafood sauces can be white or red. White seafood sauces are most often made with white wine or stock and rarely use cream. They are often flavoured with herbs. Red seafood sauces are tomato-based. Traditionally, these sauces are not garnished with cheese.

Vegetable sauces often use tomatoes as the base and a stock as the liquid. Mirepoix, garlic and red pepper flakes are commonly used for flavourings. Vegetable sauces include the traditional tomato sauce as well as primavera.

Cream sauces are based on milk or cream and are sometimes thickened with roux. Cheese is often included for flavour and richness.

Garlic-oil sauces (It. *aglio-olio*) consist mainly of garlic and oil; often herbs are added. Garlic-oil sauces can be hot or cold, cooked or uncooked. Pesto is a well-known example of an uncooked, cold garlic-oil sauce.

Uncooked sauces include a variety of dressings such as fresh tomatoes, basil and olive oil; or olive oil, lemon juice, parsley, basil and hot red pepper flakes. Other flavouring ingredients include capers, anchovies, garlic and olives as well as fresh herbs, fresh vegetables, flavoured oils and cubed cheeses.

CONCLUSION

Most meals would seem incomplete without a starch. The most popular starches are potatoes, grains (especially rice) and pasta. All are low in fat and a good source of energy. Most can be prepared with several dry- and moist-heat cooking methods. Starches can be sauced, seasoned or flavoured in limitless ways.

QUESTIONS FOR DISCUSSION

1. Explain the differences between mealy and waxy potatoes. Give two examples of each.
2. Describe the two methods of sautéing or pan-frying potatoes.
3. Explain why duchesse potatoes are regarded as the "mother" of many classic potato dishes. Name and describe two such dishes.
4. All grains are composed of three parts. Name and describe each of these parts.
5. Describe and compare the three general cooking methods used to prepare grains.
6. Name the three categories of Italian-style pasta shapes and give an example of each.
7. Why is it necessary to use ample water when cooking pasta? Should pasta be cooked in salted water? Should oil be added to the cooking water? Explain your answers.
8. Discuss the differences between cooking fresh pasta and cooking dried, factory-produced pasta.

ADDITIONAL STARCH RECIPES

RECIPE 23.9

QUINOA, RED RICE AND LENTIL SALAD WITH TRUFFLE VINAIGRETTE

Note: This dish appears in the Chapter Opening photograph.

THE RITZ CARLTON, CHICAGO, IL
Executive Chef George Bumbaris

Quinoa—*an ancient staple grain with a high protein content, bead-like shape and delicate, almost bland flavour.*

Yield: 4 Servings			Method: Simmering
Quinoa (recipe follows)	1 cup	250 mL	
Red Rice (recipe follows)	1 cup	250 mL	
Beluga Lentils (recipe follows)	1 cup	250 mL	
Carrots, brunoise, cooked	1/4 cup	60 mL	
Leeks, brunoise, cooked	1/4 cup	60 mL	
Black truffles	4 slices	4 slices	
Truffle Vinaigrette (recipe follows)	2 oz.	60 mL	
Kosher salt	TT	TT	
Pepper	TT	TT	

Herb-infused oil   as needed for garnish
Truffle Vinaigrette (recipe follows)   as needed for garnish

1. Mix the Quinoa, Red Rice, Beluga Lentils, carrots, leeks, Truffle Vinaigrette, and salt and pepper together.
2. Shape into a ring on each serving plate. Garnish with a truffle slice. Drizzle the herb oil and additional Truffle Vinaigrette around each plate.

QUINOA

Yield: 1 cup (250 mL)

Onion, diced	1/2 cup	120 mL
Olive oil	1 Tbsp.	30 mL
Quinoa	1/2 cup	120 mL
Water or vegetable stock	1 cup	250 mL
Kosher salt	TT	TT
Pepper	TT	TT

1. In a small sauce pot, sauté the onions in the olive oil over medium heat.
2. Add the quinoa and allow it to brown slightly.
3. Add the stock and season with salt and pepper. Bring the stock to a full simmer.
4. Remove from the stove and cover the pot. Allow the quinoa to steep until tender, approximately 8 minutes.

RED RICE

Yield: 1 cup (250 mL)

Onion, diced	1/4 cup	60 mL
Olive oil	1 Tbsp.	15 mL
Red rice	1/2 cup	120 mL
Water	1 cup	250 mL
Kosher salt	TT	TT
Pepper	TT	TT

1. In a small sauce pot, sauté the onions in the olive oil over medium heat.
2. Add the red rice, water, salt and pepper.
3. Cover and simmer until the rice is tender and the liquid has been absorbed, approximately 15 minutes.

BELUGA LENTILS

Yield: 1 cup (250 mL)

Olive oil	2 Tbsp.	30 mL
Onion, peeled	1 small	1 small
Clove	1	1
Carrot, peeled and cut in half lengthwise	1 large	1 large
Celery, cut in half	2 ribs	2 ribs
Garlic cloves	4	4
Shallots, minced	1/2 cup	120 mL

Approximate values per serving:

Calories	307
Total fat	23 g
Saturated fat	3 g
Cholesterol	0 mg
Sodium	581 mg
Total carbohydrates	22 g
Protein	3 g
Vitamin A	25%
Iron	50%
Claims—no cholesterol, high fibre	

Approximate values per 1/4 cup (60 mL) serving:

Calories	56
Total fat	3 g
Saturated fat	.4 g
Cholesterol	0 mg
Sodium	182 mg
Total carbohydrates	6 g
Protein	1 g
Claims—no cholesterol, high fibre	

Approximate values per 1/4 cup (60 mL) serving:

Calories	22
Total fat	2 g
Saturated fat	.3 g
Cholesterol	0 mg
Sodium	291 mg
Total carbohydrates	.9 g
Protein	.1 g
Claims—low fat, no cholesterol, no sugar	

Continued

Bay leaves	2	2
Fresh thyme	2 sprigs	2 sprigs
Kosher salt	TT	TT
Pepper	TT	TT
Beluga lentils, soaked for 1 hour	1/2 cup	120 mL
Water or vegetable stock	1 pt.	500 mL

Approximate values per 1/4 cup (60 mL) serving:

Calories	26
Total fat	2 g
Saturated fat	.2 g
Cholesterol	0 mg
Sodium	123 mg
Total carbohydrates	2 g
Protein	.7 g

Claims—low fat, no cholesterol, high fibre

1. In a large sauce pot, heat the olive oil. Stud the onion with the clove and sweat the carrots, celery and onion in the oil.
2. Add the garlic and shallots. When the shallots are translucent, add the bay leaves, fresh thyme, salt, pepper, lentils and stock.
3. Simmer until tender, approximately 40 minutes. Make sure the lentils are covered with liquid at all times.
4. After the lentils cool, remove the carrot, celery, onion, garlic cloves, bay leaves and thyme.

TRUFFLE VINAIGRETTE

Yield: 2 pt. (1 L)

Brandy	1 cup	250 mL
Madeira	1 cup	250 mL
Port	1 cup	250 mL
Truffles	7 oz.	210 g
Balsamic vinegar	1/4 cup	60 mL
Canola oil	1/4 cup	60 mL
Truffle oil	2 Tbsp.	30 mL
Kosher salt	TT	TT
Pepper	TT	TT

Approximate values per 1 oz. (30 mL) serving:

Calories	81
Total fat	2 g
Saturated fat	.1 g
Cholesterol	0 mg
Sodium	27 mg
Total carbohydrates	12 g
Protein	.1 g

Claims—no cholesterol

1. Simmer the brandy, madeira and port to remove the alcohol. Remove from the heat and add the truffles. Allow them to steep until the liquid is cool.
2. Place all of the ingredients in a blender and emulsify.

◆◆◆

RECIPE 23.10

GRILLED POTATO SALAD

GREENS RESTAURANT, SAN FRANCISCO, CA
Executive Chef Annie Somerville

Yield: 4–6 Servings　　　　　　　　　　**Method:** Baking/Grilling

New potatoes	2 lb.	1 kg
Light olive oil	as needed	as needed
Salt and pepper	TT	TT
Cherry tomatoes, sweet one hundreds or pear cherry tomatoes	4 oz.	120 g
Frisée or salad greens (optional)	4 oz.	120 g
Red and yellow bell peppers, roasted, seeded and cut into strips	1 lb.	500 g
Basil Vinaigrette (recipe follows)	4 oz.	125 mL

Champagne vinegar	as needed	as needed
Niçoise or Gaeta olives	12	12

1. Toss the potatoes with the olive oil in a baking dish; sprinkle with a few pinches of salt and pepper.
2. Cover the potatoes and place in a 400°F (200°C) oven. Cook until tender, approximately 35–40 minutes. Set aside to cool.
3. Cut the cooled potatoes in half or quarters if they are large. Thread onto skewers for grilling. (Skewers are not necessary if the grill grating is fine enough.) Grill the potatoes cut side down until they are golden and crisp with defined grill marks.
4. Cut the tomatoes in half or leave whole if small.
5. Prepare, wash and spin-dry the salad greens.
6. To assemble the salad, slide the grilled potatoes from the skewers and toss with the peppers, cherry tomatoes and Basil Vinaigrette. Adjust the seasoning, if necessary, with a splash of champagne vinegar and salt and pepper.
7. Loosely arrange the greens on plates or a platter, spoon the potatoes and other vegetables over the greens and garnish with the olives.

Approximate values per serving:

Calories	350
Total fat	22 g
Saturated fat	3 g
Cholesterol	0 mg
Sodium	1420 mg
Total carbohydrates	33 g
Protein	4 g
Vitamin C	170%
Calcium	15%
Iron	10%

BASIL VINAIGRETTE

Yield: 4 oz. (125 mL)

Champagne vinegar	1 oz.	30 mL
Extra virgin olive oil	3 oz.	90 mL
Fresh basil leaves, packed	1/2 cup	250 mL
Salt	1/2 tsp.	3 mL
Garlic clove, chopped	1	1

Combine the ingredients in a blender or food processor until smooth.

Approximate values per 1 oz. (30 mL) serving:

Calories	200
Total fat	21 g
Saturated fat	3 g
Cholesterol	0 mg
Sodium	290 mg
Total carbohydrates	1 g
Protein	0 g

◆◆◆

RECIPE 23.11

CANDIED SWEET POTATOES

Yield: 6 4-oz. (120-g) Servings   **Method:** Baking

Sweet potatoes	2 lb.	1 kg
Brown sugar	5 oz.	150 g
Water	2 oz.	60 mL
Whole butter	2 oz.	60 g
Vanilla extract	1 tsp.	5 mL

1. Wash the sweet potatoes and cut as necessary to promote even cooking.
2. Bake the sweet potatoes on a sheet pan at 350°F (180°C) until cooked but still firm, approximately 30 minutes.
3. Combine the brown sugar, water and butter and bring to a boil. Add the vanilla and remove from the heat.
4. Peel the potatoes and slice or cut as desired. Arrange the potatoes in a baking dish and pour the sugar mixture over them.
5. Sprinkle the potatoes with additional brown sugar if desired and bake for 20 minutes, basting occasionally with the sugar mixture.

Approximate values per 4 oz. (120 g) serving:

Calories	320
Total fat	8 g
Saturated fat	5 g
Cholesterol	20 mg
Sodium	105 mg
Total carbohydrates	60 g
Protein	3 g
Vitamin A	340%
Vitamin C	60%

◆◆◆

RECIPE 23.12
POTATO PANCAKES

Yield: 18 Pancakes   **Method:** Pan-frying

Eggs, whole	2	2
Egg whites	4	4
Milk	12 oz.	300 mL
Onion, grated	6 oz.	150 g
Parsley, chopped	2 Tbsp.	30 mL
Garlic clove, minced	1	1
Flour	1 cup	100 g
Sour cream	3 oz.	100 mL
Potatoes, grated	1 lb.	500 g
Bacon, fried, diced	4 oz.	120 g
Canola oil	1 Tbsp.	15 mL
Baking powder	1 Tbsp.	15 mL
Salt and pepper	TT	TT
Canola oil	as needed for cooking	

Approximate values per 4 oz. (120 g) serving:

Calories	200
Total fat	10 g
Saturated fat	1.5 g
Cholesterol	35 mg
Sodium	210 mg
Total carbohydrates	22 g
Protein	3 g
Vitamin C	15%

1. Separate the whole eggs and put all the whites in a bowl.
2. Whip the egg whites until stiff. In a separate bowl, beat the yolks, then blend into whites.
3. Fold in the milk, onions, parsley, garlic, flour, sour cream, grated potatoes, bacon, oil, baking powder, salt and pepper.
4. Heat the oil in a heavy bottomed pan. Add the potato mixture to the oil in uniform-size pancakes. Pan-fry the pancakes until tender, turning once when well browned on the first side. Remove from the pan and drain well.

◆◆◆

RECIPE 23.13
PARSNIP, POTATO AND GOAT CHEESE PIE

CANOE RESTAURANT & BAR, Toronto, ON
Co–Executive Chefs Todd Clarmo and Anthony Walsh

Yield: 6–8 Servings   **Method:** Baking

Parsnips, peeled and cut into sticks	4 large	4 large
Olive oil	2 Tbsp.	30 mL
Fresh garlic, minced	1 tsp.	5 mL
Salt and pepper, freshly ground	TT	TT
Unsalted butter, softened	1 Tbsp.	15 mL
Red onion, minced	1 medium	1 medium
Fresh thyme leaves, chopped	1 Tbsp.	15 mL
Fresh savory leaves, chopped	1 Tbsp.	15 mL
Yukon Gold potatoes, peeled and cut into rounds 1/8 in. (3 mm) thick	3	3
Soft goat cheese, crumbled	2/3–1 cup	200–250 mL
Cream, 35%	1 cup	250 mL

Todd Clarmo and Anthony Walsh
Co–Executive Chefs at Canoe, Todd and Anthony have received rave reviews since they took the helm. Canoe was named one of Toronto's top five dining restaurants by Gourmet Magazine *in 1997. Todd and Anthony have been featured in* The New York Times, Food Arts, *and* Bon Appetit.

1. Heat oven to 400°F (200°C).

2. Place the parsnips in a nonreactive bowl; toss them with the olive oil, garlic, salt and pepper. Transfer to baking dish and roast until golden brown (approximately 20 minutes); remove from oven; reserve.

3. Reduce oven heat to 350°F (175°C).

4. Grease an 8 x 8 inch (20 x 20 cm) ovenproof casserole with softened butter. Layer the bottom with the red onion; sprinkle with thyme and savory. Add half the Yukon Gold potatoes in a layer; season with salt and pepper. Cover potato layer with roasted parsnips. Sprinkle with goat cheese. Pour in 1/3 cup (80 mL) cream. Layer top of pie with remaining potatoes and season with salt and pepper.

5. Pour remaining cream on top; cover casserole with foil. Place in oven and bake for 40 minutes or until tender. Remove foil and bake another 15 minutes until golden brown.

6. Remove from oven. Cool slightly. When ready to serve, cut into squares for individual portions.

Approximate values per serving:	
Calories	361
Total fat	24 g
Saturated fat	13 g
Cholesterol	62 mg
Sodium	240 mg
Total carbohydrates	30 g
Protein	9 g

❖❖❖

RECIPE 23.14

RÖSTI POTATOES

THE FOUR SEASONS, NEW YORK, NY
Chef Christian Albin

Yield: 6 Servings

Method: Pan-frying

Boiling potatoes, large	4	4
Bacon fat	2 oz.	60 mL
Lard	2 oz.	60 mL
Kosher salt and pepper	TT	TT
Whole butter	1 oz.	30 g

1. Cook the potatoes in salted water until almost done.

2. Drain and cool the potatoes, then peel and coarsely grate them.

3. Heat the bacon fat and lard in a heavy, shallow 10-inch (25-cm) skillet with sloping sides until quite hot. Spread half the potatoes over the bottom of the pan; sprinkle with salt and pepper. Cover with the remaining potatoes and cook over medium-high heat until the bottom turns brown and crusty, approximately 10 minutes.

4. Turn the potatoes in one piece. This is easiest to do by placing a large plate over the pan and turning both together so that the potatoes fall onto the plate. Slip the turned-over potatoes off the plate back into the pan, browned side up. Cook until the bottom is browned.

5. Before serving, smooth the edges of the potatoes with a spatula. Sprinkle with salt and brush the edge of the pan with whole butter. It will melt and run into the potatoes.

VARIATION: Cheddar Cheese Rösti Potatoes—Make two thin potatoes cakes. Top one with a layer of 7 ounces (200 g) sour cream, 2 ounces (60 g) cubed sharp cheddar cheese and 2 tablespoons (30 mL) chopped chives. Top with the other cake. Dot with 1 tablespoon (15 mL) whole butter and bake in a 400°F (200°C) oven for 15 minutes.

Approximate values per serving:	
Calories	290
Total fat	23 g
Saturated fat	10 g
Cholesterol	30 mg
Sodium	430 mg
Total carbohydrates	19 g
Protein	2 g
Vitamin C	20%

Fried Potato Variations

Cottage fries.

Shoestring potatoes.

French fries.

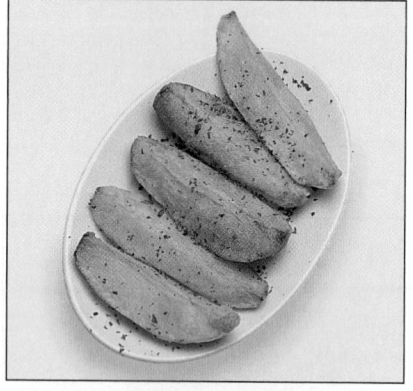

Steak fries.

Approximate values per 4 oz. (120 g) serving:	
Calories	160
Total fat	3.5 g
Saturated fat	2 g
Cholesterol	10 mg
Sodium	400 mg
Total carbohydrates	25 g
Protein	6 g
Vitamin A	10%
Calcium	15%

◆◆◆

RECIPE 23.15

POLENTA

Yield: 1 lb. 12 oz. (800 g)   **Method:** Simmering

Shallots, chopped	2 tsp.	10 mL
Whole butter	as needed	as needed
Milk, white stock or water	2 qt.	1 L
Cornmeal, yellow or white	6 oz.	180 g
Salt and pepper	TT	TT

1. Sauté the shallots in 1 tablespoon (15 mL) of butter for 30 seconds. Add the liquid and bring to a boil.
2. Slowly add the cornmeal while stirring constantly to prevent lumps, then simmer for 30 minutes.
3. Scrape the polenta into a buttered nonaluminum dish; spread to an even thickness with a spatula that has been dipped in water. Refrigerate the polenta until well chilled.
4. To serve, unmould the polenta and cut into shapes following the procedure discussed in Chapter 35, Plate Presentation. Sauté or grill the polenta for service, or sprinkle with grated Parmesan cheese and heat under a broiler or salamander.

◆◆◆

RECIPE 23.16

POLENTA WITH WILD MUSHROOMS

FETZER VINEYARDS, HOPLAND, CA
Culinary Director John Ash

Yield: 8 Servings   **Method:** Simmering

Yellow onion, chopped coarse	12 oz.	340 g
White mushrooms, chopped coarse	4 oz.	120 g

Garlic, chopped fine	2 Tbsp.	30 mL
Dried porcini or cèpes mushrooms, rinsed, soaked in water and chopped coarse	2 oz.	60 g
Olive oil	5 oz.	150 mL
Fresh basil, chopped fine	4 tsp.	20 mL
Fresh oregano, chopped fine	1 tsp.	5 mL
Chicken or vegetable stock	1-3/4 qt.	2 L
Coarse polenta cornmeal	2 cups	450 mL
Salt and pepper	TT	TT
Cream, 35%	16 oz.	450 mL
Aged Asiago or fontina, grated fine	4 oz.	120 g
Fresh wild mushrooms	8–10	8–10
Fresh basil sprigs	as needed for garnish	

1. Sauté the onion, white mushrooms, garlic and porcini or cèpes in 4 ounces (120 mL) olive oil until lightly coloured. Add the basil, oregano and stock; bring to a boil.
2. Slowly stir in the cornmeal. Simmer 10 minutes, stirring regularly. The polenta should be thick and creamy. Add more stock if necessary. Adjust the seasonings and keep warm.
3. Just before serving, add the cream and cheese and stir vigorously.
4. Sauté the fresh wild mushrooms in the remaining olive oil until tender. Spoon the polenta onto warm plates and garnish with the wild mushrooms and a sprig of fresh basil.

Approximate values per 8 oz. (240 g) serving:

Calories	550
Total fat	46 g
Saturated fat	19 g
Cholesterol	95 mg
Sodium	1090 mg
Total carbohydrates	21 g
Protein	13 g
Vitamin A	35%
Vitamin C	15%
Calcium	20%
Iron	15%

◆◆◆

RECIPE 23.17

BROWN RICE PILAF WITH PINE NUTS

Yield: 10 3-oz. (90-g) Servings   **Method:** Pilaf

Saffron threads	1/2 tsp.	2 mL
Chicken stock, hot	1 pt.	500 mL
Sesame oil	1 Tbsp.	15 mL
Vegetable oil	1 Tbsp.	15 mL
Pine nuts	2 oz.	60 g
Onion, medium dice	6 oz.	180 g
Red bell pepper, medium dice	6 oz.	180 g
Garlic, chopped	2 tsp.	10 mL
Brown rice	1 cup	250 mL
Salt	1 tsp.	10 mL
Pepper	TT	TT
Currants, dry	2 oz.	60 mL

1. Steep the saffron threads in the hot stock for 5 minutes.
2. Heat the oils and sauté the pine nuts until lightly browned.
3. Add the onion, red pepper and garlic and sauté without browning.
4. Add the rice and stir to coat the rice with the oil.
5. Add the salt and stock to the rice. Season with pepper, bring to a boil, reduce the heat and cover. Cook on the stove top or in the oven until done, approximately 30 minutes.
6. Stir in the currants, cover and allow them to soften for 5 minutes.

Approximate values per 3 oz. (90 g) serving:

Calories	150
Total fat	7 g
Saturated fat	1 g
Cholesterol	0 mg
Sodium	170 mg
Total carbohydrates	18 g
Protein	4 g
Vitamin C	25%

◆◆◆

RECIPE 23.18

WILD RICE AND CRANBERRY STUFFING

Yield: 5 pints (2.5 L)   **Method:** Simmering

Dried morels	1 oz.	30 g
Wild rice	12 oz.	340 g
Onion, minced	8 oz.	225 g
Butter or chicken fat	2 oz.	60 g
Chicken stock, hot	approx. 1 qt.	approx. 1 L
Dried cranberries	6 oz.	180 g
Salt and pepper	TT	TT
Fresh parsley, chopped fine	4 Tbsp.	60 mL

1. Soak the dried morels overnight in lightly salted water. Drain, reserving the liquid. Rinse well, drain again and chop coarsely.
2. Rinse the wild rice well in cold water.
3. Sauté the onion in the butter or chicken fat until tender. Add the mushrooms and wild rice.
4. Strain the reserved liquid from the mushrooms through several layers of cheesecloth to remove all sand and grit. Add enough chicken stock to make 3 pints (1.5 L). Add the stock mixture and cranberries to the rice. Cover and simmer until the rice is dry and fluffy, approximately 45 minutes.
5. Season to taste with salt and pepper and stir in the parsley. This rice may be served as a side dish or used for stuffing duck or game hens.

Approximate values per
4 oz. (120 g) serving:

Calories	190
Total fat	6 g
Saturated fat	3 g
Cholesterol	10 mg
Sodium	380 mg
Total carbohydrates	28 g
Protein	7 g

◆◆◆

RECIPE 23.19

RICE PILAF

Yield: 3 lb. (1.4 kg)   **Method:** Pilaf

Butter	1 oz.	30 g
Olive oil	1 oz.	30 mL
Onion, fine dice	3 oz.	90 g
Bay leaf	1	1
Long-grain rice	1 pt.	450 mL
Chicken stock, boiling	1 qt.	1 L
Salt	TT	TT

1. Heat the butter and olive oil in a heavy sautoir or sauce pot.
2. Add the onion and bay leaf and sauté until tender, but not brown.
3. Add the rice and stir to coat completely with the hot fat. Do not allow the rice to brown.
4. Pour in the boiling chicken stock and season with salt.
5. Cover the pot tightly and place it in a 350°F (175°C) oven. Bake for 18–20 minutes, until the liquid is absorbed and the rice is fluffy and tender.
6. Transfer the cooked rice to a hotel pan and fluff the rice with a fork. Remove the bay leaf and keep the rice hot for service.

Approximate values per
6 oz. (180 g) serving:

Calories	130
Total fat	7 g
Saturated fat	3 g
Cholesterol	7.5 mg
Sodium	440 mg
Total carbohydrates	12 g
Protein	4 g

RECIPE 23.20

SAFFRON RICE

Yield: 6 Servings

Basmati rice	1 pt.	450 mL
Saffron threads	1 tsp.	5 mL
Boiling water	1 qt.	1 L
Ghee (or clarified butter)	3 oz.	90 mL
Cinnamon sticks, 2 in. (5 cm) long	1	1
Cloves, whole	4	4
Onion, fine dice	5 oz.	150 g
Dark brown sugar	1 Tbsp.	15 mL
Salt	2 tsp.	10 mL
Cardamom seeds	1/4 tsp.	2 mL

1. Wash the rice and drain thoroughly.
2. Steep the saffron in 2 ounces (60 mL) of the boiling water.
3. In a saucepan, heat the ghee, add the cinnamon and cloves. Add the onions and stir-fry until they are soft and slightly brown.
4. Add the rice and stir until it is well coated with the ghee and the grains are a light golden colour.
5. Stirring constantly, add the remaining boiling water, brown sugar, salt and cardamom seeds. Bring to a boil and reduce to a simmer.
6. Gently stir in the saffron and its water, cover and simmer until the rice has absorbed all the liquid.
7. Fluff with a fork and serve at once.

Approximate values per 4 oz. (120 g) serving:

Calories	370
Total fat	16 g
Saturated fat	9 g
Cholesterol	35 mg
Sodium	780 mg
Total carbohydrates	51 g
Protein	4 g

RECIPE 23.21

BUCKWHEAT LINGUINE WITH SMOKED PHEASANT AND WILD MUSHROOMS

H.R.T. ALLIANCE, HUMBER COLLEGE, TORONTO, ON
Instructor David Jones

Yield: 4 Servings

Butter, unsalted	1 oz.	30 g
Garlic clove, minced	1	1
Wild mushrooms	4 oz.	120 g
Scallions, sliced thin	1/2 cup	45 g
Nutmeg	pinch	pinch
Dry sherry	1 oz.	30 mL
Cream, 35%, reduced by 1/3	10 oz.	30 mL
Meat glaze	1 oz.	30 mL
Smoked pheasant, sliced	6 oz.	180 g
Salt and fresh ground white pepper	TT	TT
Buckwheat Pasta (recipe follows), cut into linguini	1 lb.	500 g

David Jones

David was born in Wales and trained in Canada. After working mainly in fine dining establishments, David decided to spend a year working in the James Bay area with the Cree community for a change of pace. He has been an instructor at Humber College for the last four years.

Continued

1. Sweat the garlic in the melted butter, then add the mushrooms.
2. Add scallions (reserving some for garnish) and nutmeg. Add the sherry and deglaze, reducing *au sec.*
3. Add reduced cream, meat glaze and smoked pheasant. Reduce to sauce consistency. Season to taste.
4. Blanch buckwheat linguini in slightly salted water, drain well and toss in sauce. Garnish with reserved sliced scallions.

BUCKWHEAT PASTA

Yield: 8 Servings

Semolina flour	7 oz.	200 g
Buckwheat flour	2.25 oz	65 g
Olive oil	1 oz.	30 mL
Whole eggs	2	2
Water	2 oz.	50 mL

1. Combine the dry ingredients in a bowl.
2. Combine the eggs and oil in another bowl.
3. Make a mound of the dry ingredients on the table, and make a well in the centre. Pour the egg/oil mixture into the well and incorporate it with the dry ingredients, gradually enlarging the well as you mix in the flour.
4. Add water until the dough is firm enough to knead, then knead well for at least 15 minutes.
5. Cover and let stand at room temperature for at least 30 minutes.
6. Roll out dough as thin as possible.
7. Cut into ribbons or desired shape.

◆◆◆

RECIPE 23.22

GOAT-CHEESE RAVIOLI IN HERBED CREAM SAUCE

Yield: 72 2-in. (5-cm) Ravioli and 1-1/2 pt. (1.5 L) Sauce

Fresh goat cheese	11 oz.	300 g
Cream cheese	8 oz.	250 g
Fresh basil, chopped fine	3 Tbsp.	45 mL
Fresh thyme, chopped fine	2 tsp.	10 mL
Fresh parsley, chopped	3 Tbsp.	45 mL
Pepper	TT	TT
Pasta, fresh	2 lb.	1 kg
Cream, 35%	1 qt.	1 L
Parmesan cheese, grated	2 oz.	60 mL
Salt	TT	TT

1. To make the cheese filling, combine the goat and cream cheeses with 2 tablespoons (30 mL) basil, 1 teaspoon (5 mL) thyme and the parsley; season to taste with pepper.
2. Make ravioli using the cheese mixture and pasta.
3. To make the sauce, combine the cream with the remaining herbs and bring to a boil. Reduce by one-third and add the Parmesan cheese. Season with salt and pepper.
4. Boil the ravioli until done. Drain, toss gently with the sauce and serve.

✦✦✦

RECIPE 23.23

FETTUCCINE ALFREDO

Yield: 4 6-oz. (180-g) Servings

Fresh fettuccine	8 oz.	250 g
Whole butter	2 oz.	60 g
Cream, 35%	12 oz.	350 mL
Parmesan cheese, grated	2 oz.	60 g
Salt and white pepper	TT	TT

Approximate values per 6 oz. (180 g) serving:

Calories	630
Total fat	49 g
Saturated fat	29 g
Cholesterol	170 mg
Sodium	1000 mg
Total carbohydrates	33 g
Protein	14 g
Vitamin A	50%
Calcium	25%

1. Boil the pasta, keeping it slightly undercooked. Refresh and drain.
2. To make the sauce, combine the butter, cream and cheese in a sauté pan. Bring to a boil and reduce slightly.
3. Add the pasta to the pan and boil the sauce and pasta until the sauce is thick and the pasta is cooked. Adjust the seasonings and serve.

✦✦✦

RECIPE 23.24

PEPE PASTA WITH SHRIMP, TOMATO AND TARRAGON

THE RITZ CARLTON, CHICAGO, IL
Executive Chef George Bumbaris

Yield: 4 Servings

Olive oil	2 Tbsp.	30 mL
Onion, sliced	1/2 cup	120 mL
Garlic, minced	1 tsp.	5 mL
Tomato concassé	8 oz.	250 g
Dry white wine	4 oz.	120 mL
Fresh shrimp, peeled and deveined	16	16
Chicken or shrimp stock	3 cups	750 mL
Pepe pasta	1 cup	250 mL
Fresh lime juice	2 Tbsp.	30 mL
Whole butter	1 Tbsp.	15 g
Chives, chopped fine	1 Tbsp.	15 mL
Tarragon, chopped	1/2 tsp.	3 mL
Italian parsley, chopped	1/2 tsp.	3 mL

Approximate values per serving:

Calories	550
Total fat	15 g
Saturated fat	4 g
Cholesterol	670 mg
Sodium	1380 mg
Total carbohydrates	25 g
Protein	79 g
Vitamin A	30%
Vitamin C	35%
Iron	70%

1. In a medium-sized sauce pot over medium heat, sauté the onion in the olive oil. Add the garlic and cook for 1 additional minute.
2. Add the tomatoes, then add the white wine. Simmer until the liquid is reduced *au sec.*
3. Add the shrimp and cook for 3–4 minutes.
4. In a separate sauce pot, bring the chicken stock to a boil. Add the pepe pasta and simmer until the pasta is tender, approximately 15 minutes.
5. Drain the pasta and toss in the lime juice, butter and herbs.
6. Gently stir in the tomato and shrimp mixture and serve immediately.

Michael Noble

Michael opened Diva at the Met in 1996, and within a year it was in the centre of Vancouver's culinary spotlight, winning awards from Gourmet Magazine, Vancouver Magazine *and* GQ. *Michael also achieved Canada's highest standings ever at the Bocuse d'Or World Cuisine championship in Lyons, 1995 and 1997.*

◆◆◆

RECIPE 23.25

GRILLED PACIFIC PRAWNS WITH BAKED GARLIC AND BUTTERNUT SQUASH RISOTTO AND PISTACHIO BROWN BUTTER

METROPOLITAN HOTEL, VANCOUVER, BC
Executive Chef Michael Noble

Yield: 4 Servings   **Method:** Sautéing

Butter	3 Tbsp.	40 g
Risotto:		
Onion, medium diced	1/2	1/2
Arborio rice	7 oz.	200 g
Chicken or prawn stock (hot)	10–15 oz.	300–400 mL
Bay leaf, small	1	1
Salt and white pepper	TT	TT
Garlic bulb, roasted whole and mashed	1	1
Squash purée (butternut is best)	2 oz.	50 g
Butternut squash, diced		
and roasted in olive oil	4 Tbsp.	60 g
Parmesan cheese, grated	2 oz.	50 g
Parsley, chopped	1 oz.	15 g
Olive oil	1 Tbsp.	15 mL
Salt and ground black pepper	TT	TT
Pistachio Brown Butter (recipe follows)	as needed	as needed
Black tiger prawns or similar,		
shelled/deveined	8	8

1. Heat a pan over medium heat. Add one-third of the butter and heat until the butter is bubbly. Do not burn. Add the diced onion and sauté until translucent. Add the rice and continue stirring until the rice is warm. Add a small amount of the hot stock and the bay leaf. Lower the heat, season the rice a little and continue cooking while stirring constantly. As the rice gets dry, add more stock, a little at a time, and continue cooking until the rice is "al dente." Add the mashed, roasted garlic, the squash purée, the roasted, diced squash and a little more stock. When everything has warmed through, add the rest of the butter, the Parmesan and season to taste. Just before serving, remove the bay leaf and add the chopped parsley.

2. Just before the risotto has finished cooking, heat olive oil in a sauté pan over medium heat. Season the prawns and sauté, turning 2 or 3 times for 2 minutes or until the prawns are cooked through. Remove and set aside and make the Pistachio Butter in the same pan.

3. Serve by dividing the risotto into 4 soup plates and set the prawns decoratively on top. Drizzle the pistachio butter around the risotto.

4. Garnish with a sprinkle of tomato concassé and a herb sprig.

PISTACHIO BROWN BUTTER

Butter	4 Tbsp.	60 g
Salt and white pepper	TT	TT
Juice from 1/2 a lemon		

Approximate values per serving:

Calories	415
Total fat	19 g
Saturated fat	9 g
Cholesterol	36 mg
Sodium	555 mg
Total carbohydrates	25 g
Protein	35 g

Worcestershire sauce	dash	dash
Pistachio nuts, peeled and chopped coarse	4 tsp.	20 g

Melt the butter in a pan over medium-high heat, and season with salt and pepper. Just as the milk solids begin to colour, add the lemon juice, Worcestershire sauce and chopped nuts. Correct the seasoning.

Approximate values per serving:

Calories	558
Total fat	59 g
Saturated fat	32 g
Cholesterol	131 mg
Sodium	806 mg
Total carbohydrates	8 g
Protein	4 g

RECIPE 23.26
ANGEL HAIR WITH TOMATO VINAIGRETTE

Yield: 4 8-oz. (250-g) Servings

Vinaigrette:		
Tomato, concassé	8 oz.	250 g
Fresh basil, thyme or marjoram	1 oz.	30 g
Balsamic vinegar	3 oz.	90 mL
Shallots, minced	2 Tbsp.	30 mL
Olive oil	8 oz.	250 mL
Salt and pepper	TT	TT
Angel hair or rice noodle pasta, cooked	1 lb.	500 g

1. Combine all vinaigrette ingredients. Season to taste with salt and pepper. Set aside for 20–30 minutes to allow the flavours to blend.
2. Toss the sauce with 1 pound (500 g) warm or cold cooked pasta. Adjust the seasonings. Serve immediately or refrigerate and serve chilled.

Approximate values per serving:

Calories	216
Total fat	1 g
Saturated fat	.2 g
Cholesterol	0 mg
Sodium	304 mg
Total carbohydrates	44 g
Protein	7 g

RECIPE 23.27
PESTO SAUCE

Yield: 1-1/2 pt. (750 mL)

Olive oil	12 oz.	350 mL
Pine nuts	3 oz.	90 g
Fresh basil leaves	6 oz.	180 g
Garlic, chopped	1 Tbsp.	15 mL
Parmesan cheese, grated	4 oz.	120 g
Romano cheese, grated	4 oz.	120 g
Salt and pepper	TT	TT

1. Place one-third of the olive oil in a blender or food processor and add all the remaining ingredients.
2. Blend or process until smooth. Add the remaining olive oil and blend a few seconds to incorporate.

VARIATION: Walnut Pesto—Substitute walnuts for pine nuts in the above recipe.

Approximate values per serving:

Calories	150
Total fat	15 g
Saturated fat	3 g
Cholesterol	7 mg
Sodium	164 mg
Total carbohydrates	1 g
Protein	3 g

❖❖❖

RECIPE 23.28

CAPPELLETTI IN BRODO

Yield: 10 1-pt. (450-mL) Servings with 12 cappelletti each

Filling:

Pork, roasted	6 oz.	180 g
Mortadella	4 oz.	120 g
Ricotta cheese	6 oz.	180 g
Parmesan cheese, finely grated	6 oz.	180 g
Egg	1	1
Nutmeg	TT	TT
Basic Pasta Dough (Recipe 23.8)	1 lb. 8 oz.	750 g
Beef Broth (Recipe 11.1)	5 qt.	5 L
Parmesan cheese, shredded	8 oz.	250 g
Fresh parsley, chopped fine	3 Tbsp.	45 mL

1. To prepare the cappelletti filling, place the meats and cheeses in a food processor fitted with the metal blade. Process until finely ground. Add the egg and season lightly with nutmeg. Process until blended but not smoothly puréed.

2. Work with one-quarter of the pasta dough at a time, keeping the rest covered to prevent it from drying out. Roll out a portion of the dough until it is very thin. Cut the dough into 2-inch (5-cm) squares using a fluted pasta wheel.

3. Place 1 teaspoon (5 mL) of filling in the centre of each square. Fold the dough over the filling to form a rectangle, pinching the edges together to seal. Bring the ends of each rectangle together, overlapping them and pressing to seal.

4. Place the finished cappelletti on a paper-lined sheet pan. Leave them uncovered and turn them over once or twice so that they dry evenly. Continue working until all of the filling is used. The cappelletti may be cooked immediately or refrigerated for later use.

5. Heat the beef broth to a gentle boil. Drop the cappelletti in and cook until tender, approximately 3–5 minutes.

6. Portion the broth and cappelletti into warmed soup bowls and garnish with the shredded Parmesan and parsley.

Approximate values per serving:

Calories	270
Total fat	17 g
Saturated fat	10 g
Cholesterol	75 mg
Sodium	920 mg
Total carbohydrates	3 g
Protein	27 g
Calcium	60%

❖❖❖

RECIPE 23.29

SOBA NOODLES IN BROTH

Yield: 6 1-pt. (450-mL) Servings

Soba noodles	1 lb.	500 g
Dashi or chicken broth	1-1/2 qt.	1-1/2 L
Soy sauce	3 Tbsp.	45 mL
Mirin	1 Tbsp.	15 mL
Sugar	1 Tbsp.	15 mL
Green onions, chopped	4 Tbsp.	60 mL
White sesame seeds	1 Tbsp.	15 mL

1. Boil the noodles in salted water until tender. Drain, rinse in hot water and drain again. Set aside.

2. Heat the dashi or chicken broth with the soy sauce, mirin and sugar. Add the noodles to the hot broth, simmering just until thoroughly reheated.

3. Portion into warmed bowls and top with the green onions and sesame seeds.

Note: Dashi is a stock made with dried bonito flakes and dried kelp. It is used extensively in Japanese cuisine and is available as an instant powder or a concentrate.

Approximate values per serving:

Calories	147
Total fat	2 g
Saturated fat	1 g
Cholesterol	0 mg
Sodium	1393 mg
Total carbohydrates	22 g
Protein	10 g

◆◆◆

RECIPE 23.30
MACARONI AND CHEESE

Yield: 24 8-oz. (250-g) Servings

Cheese sauce (see p. 205)	2 qt.	2 L
Worcestershire sauce	TT	TT
Tabasco sauce	TT	TT
Elbow macaroni, boiled and refreshed	2 lb.	1 kg
Cheddar cheese, grated	2 lb.	1 kg
Whole butter	8 oz.	250 g
Bread crumbs	1 oz.	30 g

1. Season the cheese sauce with Worcestershire and Tabasco.

2. Mix the macaroni with the cheese sauce and the cheese.

3. Pour into a buttered full-size hotel pan. Sprinkle with bread crumbs.

4. Bake uncovered at 350°F (180°C) until hot, approximately 30 minutes.

VARIATIONS: Macaroni and cheese with ham and tomato—Stir 2 pounds (1 kg) each diced cooked ham and tomato concassé into the macaroni and cheese before pouring it into the hotel pan.

Approximate values per 8 oz. (240 g) serving:

Calories	457
Total fat	27 g
Saturated fat	17 g
Cholesterol	80 mg
Sodium	290 g
Total carbohydrates	36 g
Protein	17 g
Vitamin A	18%
Calcium	36%

◆◆◆

RECIPE 23.31
BAKED ZITI WITH FRESH TOMATO SAUCE

Yield: 30 Servings

Eggs	6	6
Ricotta cheese	4 lb.	1.8 kg
Fresh thyme	2 Tbsp.	30 mL
Fresh oregano	2 Tbsp.	30 mL
Fresh basil	2 Tbsp.	30 mL
Salt and pepper	TT	TT
Italian sausage links	3 lb.	1.4 kg
Ziti, cooked, refreshed and drained	4 lb.	1.8 kg
Parmesan cheese, grated	8 oz.	250 g
Fresh Tomato Sauce (Recipe 10.26)	3 qt.	3 L
Mozzarella cheese, shredded	2 lb.	1 kg

1. Combine the eggs, ricotta cheese, thyme, oregano, basil, salt and pepper. Mix well and reserve.

Continued

Approximate values per serving:

Calories	450
Total fat	23 g
Saturated fat	10 g
Cholesterol	130 mg
Sodium	1290 mg
Total carbohydrates	27 g
Protein	35 g
Vitamin A	40%
Calcium	70%
Iron	15%

2. Place the sausage links in a 2-inch-deep (5 cm) full-sized hotel pan; cook in a 350°F (180°C) oven for 20 minutes. Remove and cool. Drain the sausage. Slice the links into rounds and reserve.

3. Place the ziti in the hotel pan that was used to cook the sausage. Top with an even coating of the cheese mixture, sausage slices and Parmesan cheese.

4. Pour the tomato sauce over the top layer and stir slightly to distribute the sauce.

5. Bake at 375°F (190°C) for 1 hour. Sprinkle the mozzarella evenly over the pasta and return to the oven for 10 minutes. Serve.

6. Ziti may also be prepared in individual casseroles. Decrease baking time as necessary.

RECIPE 23.32

SPINACH AND RICOTTA LASAGNA WITH BOLOGNESE SAUCE

Yield: 28 8-oz. (250-g) Servings

Fresh spinach pasta dough, rolled into sheets	2 lb.	1 kg
Spinach, stemmed	2 lb.	1 kg
Whole butter	2 oz.	60 g
Ricotta cheese	1 lb.	500 g
Parmesan cheese, grated	6 oz.	180 g
Eggs	2	2
Salt and pepper	TT	TT
Bolognese sauce (see p. 212)	3 qt.	3 L
Béchamel sauce (Recipe 10.7)	1 qt.	1 L

1. Cut the pasta dough into 4-inch (10-cm) strips. Boil in salted water until done and drain well.

2. Sauté the spinach in the butter. Drain well and cool.

3. Combine the spinach with the ricotta cheese, 4 ounces (120 g) of the Parmesan cheese and eggs. Season to taste with salt and pepper.

4. Ladle a small amount of the Bolognese sauce into the bottom of a standard full-sized hotel pan. Cover the sauce with a layer of cooked pasta. Spread a thin layer of the spinach-and-cheese mixture on the pasta. Ladle a portion of the béchamel sauce over the spinach and spread in a thin even layer. Ladle a portion of the Bolognese sauce over the béchamel sauce and spread in an even layer.

5. Add another layer of pasta and repeat the process until all of the ingredients are used, finishing with a layer of béchamel sauce. Sprinkle the remaining Parmesan cheese on top and bake covered at 350°F (180°C) until heated through, approximately 40 minutes. Uncover the lasagna for the last 15 minutes so it browns.

Approximate values per 7 oz. (210 g) serving:

Calories	270
Total fat	8 g
Saturated fat	3.5 g
Cholesterol	200 mg
Sodium	1110 mg
Total carbohydrates	12 g
Protein	37 g
Vitamin A	30%
Vitamin C	20%
Calcium	20%
Iron	40%

Variation: Dry cottage cheese may be substituted for ricotta.

RECIPE 23.33

CHILLED CHINESE NOODLE SALAD

Yield: 8 4-oz. (120-g) Servings

Dressing:

Dark soy sauce	2 Tbsp.	30 mL
White vinegar	2 Tbsp.	30 mL
Salt	1 tsp.	5 mL
Sugar	1 Tbsp.	15 mL
Peanut oil	1 Tbsp.	15 mL
Sesame oil	1 Tbsp.	15 mL
Orange zest	1 tsp.	5 mL
Red chile flakes	1/2 tsp.	2 mL
Chinese egg noodles, fresh	8 oz.	250 g
Bean sprouts, blanched	8 oz.	250 g
Carrot, finely shredded	6 oz.	180 g
Daikon, finely shredded	3 oz.	90 g
Green onion, sliced	2 oz.	60 g
Black sesame seeds	1 Tbsp.	15 mL
Fresh cilantro leaves	as needed	as needed

1. Combine the dressing ingredients and whisk thoroughly.
2. Cook the egg noodles in rapidly boiling salted water until tender, approximately 2 minutes. Drain and refresh; drain again.
3. Toss the noodles with the bean sprouts, carrots, daikon, green onion and sesame seeds. Add the dressing and toss gently until the noodles and vegetables are thoroughly coated.
4. Chill well. Serve mounds of this noodle salad as an appetizer or an accompaniment for grilled fish or chicken. Garnish with cilantro.

Approximate values per 4 oz. (120 g) serving):

Calories	110
Total fat	4.5 g
Saturated fat	.5 g
Cholesterol	10 mg
Sodium	570 mg
Total carbohydrates	14 g
Protein	3 g
Vitamin A	40%

Claims—low cholesterol; low saturated fat

RECIPE 23.34

GNOCCHI

Yield: 3 lb. (1.4 kg)

Boiled potatoes	2 lb.	1 kg
Eggs	2	2
Salt, pepper and nutmeg	TT	TT
Flour, all-purpose	14 oz.	400 g

1. Place hot boiled potatoes on a tray and place in warm oven to dry slightly, then rice them in a food mill.
2. In mixing bowl, incorporate the potatoes, eggs and seasonings.
3. Add 12 oz. (350 g) of the flour to the ingredients in the bowl, all at once.
4. Mix lightly to form a medium-soft dough.
5. If needed, add more flour to adjust the consistency.
6. Roll the dough out to 1/2-inch (1-cm) thickness on lightly floured table, then let it cool. Cut into 3/4 × 3/4-inch (1-1/2 × 1-1/2-cm) squares. Roll the squares over the back of a table fork to make indents, forming a shell shape.
7. Cook in simmering, salted water for 3–4 minutes, or until they double in size..

Approximate values per serving:

Calories	190
Total fat	1 g
Saturated fat	0 g
Cholesterol	33 mg
Sodium	133 mg
Total carbohydrates	39 g
Protein	6 g

◆◆◆

RECIPE 23.35
SPAETZLE

Yield: 7-1/2 lb. (3.5 kg)

Eggs	30	30
Water	16 oz.	500 mL
Salt	1-1/2 Tbsp.	20 mL
Nutmeg	TT	TT
Flour, all-purpose	3 lbs. 4 oz.	1.5 kg

Approximate values per 3 oz. (90 g) serving:

Calories	250
Total fat	9 g
Saturated fat	4.5 g
Cholesterol	100 mg
Sodium	250 mg
Total carbohydrates	35 g
Protein	7 g
Vitamin A	10%
Iron	15%

1. In the bowl of the food mixer, beat the eggs, water, salt and nutmeg together. Do not overbeat or the dumplings will be tough.
2. With paddle attachment and on low speed, mix in the flour until just incorporated, then mix on high speed for 1 minute.
3. Suspend a large-holed colander over a pot of boiling water. In small batches, press the mixture through the colander so that the batter drops into the water.
4. Cook the dumplings until they float to the surface, 2–3 minutes.
5. Remove them from the water with a skimmer and refresh in ice water. *Do not leave them to soak.*
6. Drain well and reserve in refrigerator, covered with a cloth.
7. To serve, sauté the spaetzle in butter and finish with chopped parsley.

WEBLINKS

The Potato Growers of Alberta—Producers of Mother Nature's Vitamins
www.potatonet.com/
U.S. Grains Nutrition Information Center
www.wheatfoods.org/
USA Rice—Rice Facts and Background
www.usarice.com/rice.htm
Grey Owl Foods—Wild Rice Industry Reference Book
www.greyowlfoods.com/goricestuff.html
U.S. National Pasta Association: Pasta FAQs and Facts
www.ilovepasta.org/faqs.html

CHAPTER 24

SALADS

AND

SALAD DRESSINGS

LEARNING OUTCOMES

After studying this chapter you will be able to:

♦ identify and prepare a variety of salad greens: cut romaine lettuce, core iceberg lettuce, remove midribs from spinach, wash and dry greens
♦ prepare a variety of salad dressings: vinaigrette, mayonnaise, emulsified vinaigrette
♦ prepare a variety of salads: tossed salads, composed salads, vegetable salads
♦ present salads attractively

*T*his chapter discusses all types of salads: the small plate of crisp iceberg lettuce with tomato wedges, cucumber slices and ranch dressing; the dinner plate of sautéed duck breast fanned across bright red grilled radicchio and toothy green arugula, sprayed with a vinaigrette dressing; the scoop of shredded chicken, mango chutney and seasonings, bound with mayonnaise; and the bowl of artichokes and mushrooms marinated in olive oil and lemon juice.

Each of these dishes fits the definition of a salad: a single food or a mix of different foods accompanied or bound by a dressing. A salad can contain meat, grains, fruits, nuts or cheese and absolutely no lettuce. It can be an appetizer, a second course served after the appetizer, an entree (especially at lunch) or served with the main course, a course following the entree or even dessert.

The colour, texture and flavour of each salad ingredient should complement those of the others, and the dressing should complement all of the ingredients. Harmony is critical to a salad's success—no matter what type of salad is being prepared.

This chapter opens with a section identifying greens commonly used in salads. A discussion of salad dressings follows. Finally, techniques for preparing green salads (both tossed and composed), bound salads, vegetable salads and fruit salads are discussed.

SALAD GREENS

Identifying Salad Greens

Salad greens are not necessarily green: Some are red, yellow, white or brown. They are all, however, leafy vegetables. Many are members of the lettuce or chicory families.

Lettuce

Lettuce (Fr. *laitue*; It. *lattuga*) has been consumed for nearly as long as people have kept records of what they and others ate. Archaeologists found that Persian royalty were served lettuce at their banquets more than 2500 years ago. Now grown and served worldwide, lettuces are members of the genus *Lactuca*. The most common types of lettuce are butterleaf, iceberg, leaf and romaine.

Boston

Boston and bibb are two of the most popular butterleaf lettuces. Their soft, pliable, pale green leaves have a buttery texture and flavour. Boston is larger and paler than bibb. Both Boston and bibb lettuce leaves form cups when separated from the heads; these cups make convenient bases for holding other foods on cold plates or providing height and texture as part of the garnish.

Boston

Iceberg

Iceberg

Iceberg lettuce is the most common of all lettuce varieties in the United States and Canada; it outsells all other varieties combined. Its tightly packed spherical head is made up of crisp, pale green leaves with a very mild flavour. Iceberg lettuce remains crisp for a relatively long period of time after being cut or prepared. Select heads that are firm but not hard and leaves that are free of burnt or rusty tips.

Leaf

Leaf lettuce grows in bunches. It has separate, ruffle-edged leaves branching from a stalk. Because it does not grow into a firm head, it is easily damaged during harvest and transport. Both red and green leaf lettuce have bright colours, mild flavours and tender leaves. Good-quality leaf lettuce should have nicely shaped leaves free of bruises, breaks or brown spots.

*Red and Green
Leaf Lettuces*

Romaine

Romaine lettuce, also known as cos, is a loosely packed head lettuce with elongated leaves and thick midribs. Its outer leaves are dark green and although they look coarse, they are crisp, tender and tasty without being bitter. The core leaves are paler and more tender but still crisp. Romaine has enough flavour to stand up to strongly flavoured dressings such as the garlic and Parmesan cheese used in a Caesar salad. A good-quality head of romaine has dark green outer leaves that are free of blemishes or yellowing.

Baby Lettuces

Innovative chefs are always looking for new and different foods to add a twist or flair to their dishes. This has led to the popularity of baby lettuces and other specialty greens. Baby greens have similar but more subtle flavours than their mature versions. They are often less bitter and are always more tender and delicate. Because of their size and variety, they are perfect for composed salads. **Mesclun** is a mixture of several kinds of baby lettuce, herbs and flowers. Field and spring mixes are popular with food service operators.

Romaine

Brune d'Hiver

Baby Red Bibb

Red Sails

Baby Green Bibb

Lola Rosa

Baby Red Oak Leaf

Pirate

Baby Red Romaine

Belgian Endive

Curly Endive

Escarole

Radicchio

Arugula

Dandelion

Chicory

Chicories come in a variety of colours, shapes and sizes; most are slightly bitter. Chicories are quite hearty and can also be cooked, usually grilled or braised.

Belgian Endive

Belgian endive (witloof) grows in small, tight heads with pointed leaves. It is actually the shoot of a chicory root. The small sturdy leaves are white at the base with yellow fringes and tips. (A purple-tipped variety is sometimes available.) Whole leaves can be separated, trimmed and filled with soft butters, cheeses or spreads and served as an hors d'oeuvre. Or they can be used for composed salads. The leaves, cut or whole, can also be added to cold salads. Heads of Belgian endive are often braised or grilled and served with meat or poultry. Belgian endive is imported from Belgium or Holland at certain times and is grown in greenhouses locally.

Curly Endive

In this country, curly endive is often called by its family name, chicory, or its French name, frisée. The dark green outer leaves are pointed, sturdy and slightly bitter. The yellow inner leaves are more tender and less bitter. Curly endive has a strong flavour that goes well with strong cheeses, game and citrus. It is often mixed with other greens to add texture and flavour.

Escarole

Escarole, sometimes called broadleaf endive, has thick leaves and a slightly bitter flavour. It has green outer leaves and pale green or yellow centre leaves. Escarole is very sturdy and is often mixed with other greens for added texture. Its strong flavour stands up to full-flavoured dressings. It is a good accompaniment to grilled meats and poultry.

Radicchio

Radicchio resembles a small red cabbage. It retains its bright reddish colour when cooked and is popular braised or grilled and served as a vegetable side dish. Because of its attractive colour, radicchio is popular in cold salads, but it has a very bitter flavour and should be used sparingly and mixed with other greens in a tossed salad. Radicchio is quite expensive and availability is sometimes limited.

Other Salad Greens and Ingredients

Leafy vegetables besides lettuce and chicory, as well as other ingredients, are used to add texture, flavour and colour to salads. A partial listing follows.

Arugula

Arugula, also known as rocket, is a member of the cabbage family. Its individual leaves are similar to dandelion leaves in size and shape. The best are 2 to 4 inches (5 to 10 cm) long. Arugula has a very strong, spicy, peppery flavour—so strong, in fact, that it is rarely served by itself. It is best when used to add zip to salads by combining it with other greens.

Dandelion

Dandelion grows as a weed throughout most of the world. It has long, thin, toothed leaves with a prominent midrib. When purchasing dandelion for salads, look for small leaves. They are more tender and less bitter. Older, tougher leaves can be cooked and served as a vegetable.

Mâche

Mâche or lamb's lettuce is very tender and very delicately flavoured. Its small, cuplike pale to dark green leaves have a slightly nutty flavour. Because its flavour is so delicate, mâche should be combined only with other delicately flavoured greens such as Boston or bibb lettuce and dressed sparingly with a light vinaigrette dressing.

Mâche

Sorrel

Sorrel, sometimes called sourgrass, has leaves similar to spinach in colour and shape. Sorrel has a very tart, lemony flavour that goes well with fish and shellfish. It should be used sparingly and combined with other greens in a salad. Sorrel can also be made into soups, sauces and purées.

Sorrel

Spinach

Like sorrel, spinach can be cooked or used as a salad green. As a salad green, it is popular served wilted and tossed with a hot bacon dressing. Spinach is deep green with a rich flavour and tender texture. Good-quality spinach should be fairly crisp. Avoid wilted or yellowed bunches.

Sprouts

Sprouts are not salad greens but are often used as such in salads and sandwiches. Sprouts are very young alfalfa, daikon, sunflower, radish or mustard plants. Alfalfa sprouts are very mild and sweet. Daikon and mustard sprouts are quite peppery.

Sprouts

Spinach

Watercress

Watercress has tiny, dime-sized leaves and substantial stems. It has a peppery flavour and adds spice to a salad. Good-quality fresh watercress is dark green with no yellowing. To preserve its freshness, watercress must be kept very cold and moist. It is normally packed topped with ice. Individual leaves are plucked from the stems and rinsed just before service.

Watercress

Edible Flowers

Many specialty produce growers offer edible, pesticide-free blossoms. They are used for salads and as garnishes wherever a splash of colour would be appreciated. Some flowers such as nasturtiums, calendulas and pansies are grown and picked specifically for eating. Others, such as yellow cucumber flowers and squash blossoms, are byproducts of the vegetable industry.

Nasturtiums

Calendulas

Squash blossoms and other very large flowers should be cut in julienne strips before being added to salads. Pick petals from large and medium-sized flowers. Smaller whole flowers can be tossed in a salad or used as a garnish when composing a salad. Very small flowers or petals can be sprinkled on top of a salad so they are not hidden by the greens.

Pansies

◆◆◆
FLOWER SAFETY

Many flowers and blossoms are toxic, especially those grown from bulbs. Even flowers that would otherwise be edible may contain pesticides that can be harmful if ingested. Use only flowers grown specifically for use as food; purchase edible flowers only from reputable purveyors.

Fresh Herbs

Basil, thyme, tarragon, oregano, dill, cilantro, marjoram, mint, sage, savory and even rosemary are used to add interesting flavours to otherwise ordinary salads. Because many herbs have strong flavours, use them sparingly so the delicate flavours of the greens are not overpowered. Leafy herbs such as basil and sage can be cut chiffonade. Other herbs can be picked into sprigs or chopped before being tossed with the salad greens. Flowering herbs such as

TABLE 24.1   NUTRITIONAL VALUES OF SELECTED SALAD GREENS AND DRESSINGS

Salad greens per 4-oz. (112-g) serving, trimmed; Salad dressings per 1-oz. (28-g) serving	Kcal	Protein (g)	Carbohydrates (g)	Fibre (g)	Total Fat (g)	Vitamin A (I.U.)	Vitamin C (mg)	Calcium (mg)	Iron (mg)
Belgian endive	20	1.6	3.6	1.2	0.4	2052	8	52	0.8
Boston lettuce	16	1.6	2.8	1.2	0.4	816	6.7	mq	0.2
Chicory greens	28	2	5.2	0.8	0.4	14 400	88	360	3.2
Dandelion greens	52	3.2	10.4	2	0.8	mq	mq	mq	mq
Iceberg lettuce	16	1.2	2.4	1.2	0.4	383	5.8	23	0.6
Romaine lettuce	20	2	2.8	2	0.4	2912	28	40	1.2
Blue cheese dressing	143	1.4	2.1	<0.1	14.8	32	<1	12	tr
Mayonnaise	110	0.3	6.8	0	9.5	32	0	2	tr
Vinaigrette	67	<0.1	2.3	mq	6.5	0	0	0	0

The Corinne T. Netzer Encyclopedia of Food Values 1992

mq = measurable quantity, but data are unavailable   tr = trace amounts

chive blossoms are used like other edible flowers to add colour, flavour and aroma. Refer to Chapter 7, Kitchen Staples, for more information on herbs.

Nutrition

Salad greens are an especially healthful food. Greens contain virtually no fat and few calories and are high in vitamins A and C, iron and fibre. But when garnished with meat and cheese and tossed with a dressing (many of which are oil-based), fat and calories are added. In an attempt to maintain the healthful nature of greens, low-fat or fat-free dressings should be available to customers.

Purchasing and Storing Salad Greens

Purchasing

Lettuces are grown in nearly every part of the United States and Canada, both outdoors and in greenhouses; nearly all types are available year-round. Principal salad greens such as spinach are available all year; many of the specialty greens are seasonal.

Lettuce is generally packed in cases of 24 heads with varying weights. Other salad greens are packed in trays or boxes of various sizes and weights.

Because salad greens are simply washed and eaten, it is extremely important that they be as fresh and blemish-free as possible. Try to purchase salad greens daily. All greens should be fresh-looking, with no yellowing. Heads should be heavy, with little or no damage to the outer leaves.

Many types of salad greens are available precut and prewashed. These greens are often modified atmosphere-packed to increase shelf life, although delicate greens are sometimes loosely packaged in 5–10-pound (2.5–5-kg) boxes. Precut and prewashed greens are relatively expensive, but can reduce labour costs dramatically.

Storing

Although some types of salad greens are hearty enough to keep for a week or more under proper conditions, all salad greens are highly perishable.

Generally, softer-leaved varieties such as Boston and bibb tend to perish more quickly than the crisper-leaved varieties such as iceberg and romaine.

Greens should be stored in their original protective cartons in a specifically designated refrigerator. Ideally, greens should be stored at temperatures between 34° and 38°F (1–3°C) (most other vegetables should be stored at warmer temperatures of 40–50°F [4–10°C]). Greens should not be stored with tomatoes, apples or other fruits that emit ethylene gas, which causes greens to wilt and accelerates spoilage.

Do not wash greens until you need them, as excess water causes them to deteriorate quickly.

Preparing Salad Greens

Unless salad greens are purchased precut and prewashed, they will need to undergo some preparation before service, principally tearing, cutting, washing and drying. Do not leave salad greens soaking in water for storage. The nutrients will be leached out.

Tearing and Cutting

Some cooks prefer all salad greens torn by hand. Delicate greens such as butterhead and baby lettuces look nicer and it is less likely they will be bruised if hand-torn. But often it is not practical to hand-tear all greens. It is perfectly acceptable to cut hardy greens with a sharp stainless steel knife.

BASIC PROCEDURE FOR CUTTING ROMAINE LETTUCE

 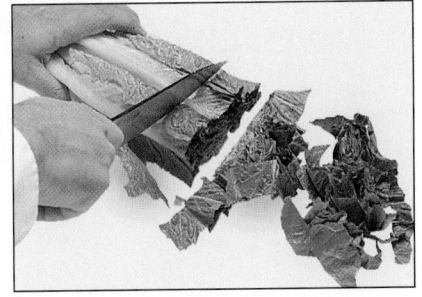

1. To cut romaine lettuce, trim the outer leaves and damaged tips with a chef's knife and split the head lengthwise.

2. Make one or two cuts along the length of the head, leaving the root intact, then cut across the width of the head.

Alternative method:

1A. Trim the outer leaves and damaged tips with a chef's knife. Pull the leaves from the core and cut the rib out of each leaf. The leaf can then be cut to the desired size. Yield and therefore food cost are affected by this method—there is more wastage.

BASIC PROCEDURE FOR CORING ICEBERG LETTUCE

1. Loosen the core by gripping the head and smacking the core on the cutting board. (Do not use too much force or you may bruise the lettuce.)

2. Remove the core and cut the lettuce as desired.

BASIC PROCEDURE FOR REMOVING THE MIDRIB FROM SPINACH

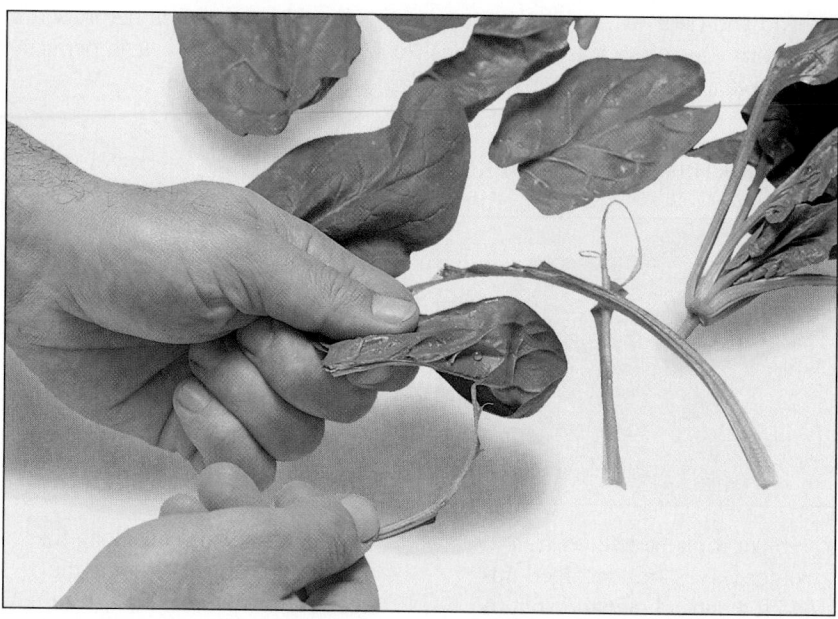

Fold the leaf in half and pull off the stem and midrib. Only the tender leaf should remain.

Washing

All lettuce and other salad greens should be washed before use. Even though they may look clean, greens may harbour hidden insects, sand, soil and pesticides. All greens should be washed after they are torn or cut. Whole heads can be washed by repeatedly dipping them in cold water and allowing them to drain. But washing whole heads is not recommended: It will not remove anything trapped near the head's centre, and water trapped in the leaves can accelerate spoilage.

BASIC PROCEDURE FOR WASHING SALAD GREENS

1. Fill a sink with cold water. Place the cut or torn greens in the water.

2. Gently stir the water and greens with your hands and remove the greens. Do not allow the greens to soak. Using fresh water each time, repeat the procedure until no grit can be detected on the bottom of the sink after the greens are removed.

Drying

Salad greens should be dried after washing. Wet greens do not stay as crisp as thoroughly dried ones. Also, wet greens tend to repel oil-based dressings and dilute their flavours. Greens may be dried by draining them well in a colander and blotting them with a clean absorbent cloth, or, preferably, they can be dried in a salad spinner, which uses centrifugal force to remove the water.

BASIC PROCEDURE FOR DRYING GREENS

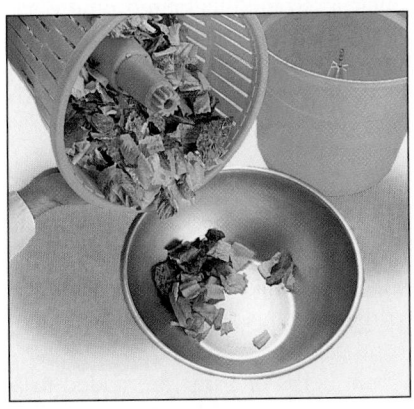

After washing the greens, place them in the basket of a salad spinner and spin for approximately 30 seconds.

SALAD DRESSINGS

A dressing is a sauce for a salad. Just as sauces for hot foods should complement rather than mask the flavour of the principal food, the sauce (dressing) for a salad should complement rather than mask the flavours of the other ingredients. Although a great many ingredients can be used to make salad dressings, most are based on either a mixture of oil and vinegar, called a vinaigrette, or a mayonnaise or other emulsified product.

Vinaigrette-style dressings can be made without oil; creamy dressings similar to mayonnaise-based dressings can be made with sour cream, yogurt or buttermilk instead of mayonnaise. Nevertheless, for all practical purposes these dressings are still prepared like vinaigrettes and mayonnaise-based dressings and they are treated that way here.

Vinaigrette Dressings

The simple vinaigrette, also known as **basic French dressing**, is a temporary emulsion of oil and vinegar seasoned with salt, pepper and mustard. The standard ratio is three parts oil to one part vinegar. The ratio can vary, however. When using strongly flavoured oils, less than three parts oil to one part vinegar generally suffices. In some recipes, all or part of the vinegar is replaced with citrus juice, in which case it may take more than one part vinegar and citrus juice to three parts oil to achieve the proper acidity level. The best way to determine the correct ratio of oil to vinegar is to taste the dressing, preferably on the food it will dress.

Oils and vinegars have unique flavours that can be mixed and matched to achieve the correct balance for a particular salad. Olive oil goes well with red wine vinegar; nut oils go well with balsamic or sherry vinegars. Neutral-flavoured oils such as canola, corn or safflower can be mixed with a flavoured vinegar.

Oil and vinegar repel each other and will separate almost immediately when mixed. They should be whisked together immediately before use.

Oils

Many types of oil can be used to make salad dressings. Light, neutral-flavoured oils such as canola, corn, cottonseed, soybean and safflower are relatively low priced and used extensively for this purpose. Other oils can be used to add flavour. Olive oil is very popular; both mild-flavoured pure olive oil and full-flavoured extra virgin olive oil are used. Nut oils such as hazelnut and walnut are expensive but they add unique and interesting flavours. Infused oils are also popular.

Vinegars

Many different vinegars can be used to make salad dressings. Red wine vinegar is the most common because it is inexpensive and its flavour blends well with many foods. But other vinegars such as cider, balsamic, white wine and rice are also used. Fruit-flavoured vinegars (particularly raspberry) are extremely popular and widely available, as are herb- and garlic-flavoured ones.

Flavoured vinegars are easy to make. Fruit, herbs or garlic are added to a wine vinegar (either red or white) and left for several days for the flavours to blend. The vinegar is then strained off and used as desired.

Acidic juices such as lemon, orange and lime are sometimes substituted for all or part of the vinegar in a salad dressing.

Other Flavouring Ingredients

Herbs, spices, shallots, garlic, mustard and sweeteners are only a few of the many flavouring ingredients used to enhance a vinaigrette dressing. Items such as herbs, shallots and garlic should be minced or chopped before being added to the dressing. If dried herbs are used, the dressing should rest for at least one hour to allow the flavours to develop. Other ingredients may be added at any time.

Basic Procedure for Preparing a Vinaigrette

1. Choose an oil and vinegar that complement each other as well as the foods they will dress.
2. Combine the vinegar, seasonings and any other flavourings in a bowl.
3. Whisk in the oil.
4. Allow the finished dressing to rest a few hours at room temperature before using so that the flavours can blend.
5. Rewhisk immediately before use.

◆◆◆

RECIPE 24.1

BASIC VINAIGRETTE DRESSING

Yield: 1 qt. (1 L)

Dry mustard	1 tsp.	5 mL
Wine vinegar	8 oz.	250 mL :1
Salt and pepper	TT	TT
Salad oil	24 oz.	750 mL :3

Ratio

1. Dissolve the mustard in a little of the vinegar.
2. Combine all ingredients and mix well.

VARIATIONS: Dijon Vinaigrette—Add 4 ounces (120 g) Dijon-style mustard to the vinegar and 3-1/2 ounces (100 g) finely chopped shallots. Proceed with the recipe.

Herbed Vinaigrette—Add 2 tablespoons (30 mL) of fresh herbs or 1 tablespoon (15 mL) dried herbs such as basil, tarragon, thyme, marjoram or chives to the vinaigrette.

Approximate values per 1 oz. (30 mL) serving:

Calories	190
Total fat	22 g
Saturated fat	3 g
Cholesterol	0 mg
Sodium	75 mg
Total carbohydrates	0 g
Protein	0 g

Claims—no cholesterol; low sodium; no sugar

Mayonnaise

Although most food service operations buy commercially made mayonnaise, every cook should know how it is made to more fully understand how to use it and why it reacts the way it does when used. Knowing how to make mayonnaise also allows you to create a mayonnaise with the exact flavourings you want.

Mayonnaise is an **emulsified sauce**. An emulsified sauce is formed when two liquids that would not ordinarily form a stable mixture are forced together and held in suspension. To make mayonnaise, oil is whisked together with a very small amount of vinegar (it is the water in the vinegar that does not normally mix with oil). As the oil and vinegar are whisked together, the oil breaks into microscopic droplets that are separated from each other by a thin barrier of vinegar. If left alone, the droplets would quickly regroup, forming a large puddle of oil and a small puddle of vinegar. To prevent the oil droplets from regrouping, an emulsifier is added. For mayonnaise, the emulsifier is lecithin, a protein found in egg yolks. (The acid in the vinegar also helps form the emulsion.) Lecithin has the unique ability to combine with both oil and water. It surrounds the oil droplets, binding them together and preventing them from coming in contact with each other and regrouping.

The balance of vinegar, oil, lecithin and agitation (whipping) is crucial to achieve a proper emulsion. The higher the proportion of oil to vinegar, the thicker the sauce will be. The higher the proportion of vinegar to oil, the thinner the sauce will be. (For example, the emulsified vinaigrette dressing discussed on pages 679 to 681 is a thin emulsion.)

There is a limit to how much oil each egg yolk can emulsify, however. One large yolk contains enough lecithin to emulsify approximately 7 ounces (200 mL) of oil. If more than that amount of oil per egg yolk is added, the sauce will break; that is, the oil and vinegar will separate and the mayonnaise will become very thin and curdled.

Ingredients

A neutral-flavoured vegetable oil is most often used for a standard mayonnaise. Other oils are used to contribute their special flavours. For example, olive oil is used to make a special garlic-flavoured mayonnaise called *aïoli*.

Rice or wine vinegar is preferable for a standard mayonnaise. Flavoured vinegars such as tarragon vinegar are often used to create unique flavours.

Seasonings vary according to the intended use but typically include dry mustard, salt, pepper and lemon juice.

Standard white or pickling vinegars are generally too acidic to make a mayonnaise with a balanced flavour.

BASIC PROCEDURE FOR PREPARING MAYONNAISE

1. Gather all ingredients and hold at room temperature. Room-temperature ingredients emulsify more easily than cold ones.
2. By hand or in an electric mixer or food processor, whip the egg yolks on high speed until frothy.
3. Add the seasonings to the yolks and whip to combine. Salt and other seasonings will dissolve or blend more easily when added at this point rather than if added to the finished mayonnaise.
4. Add a small amount of the vinegar from the recipe and whip to combine. This helps to promote the formation of an emulsion by setting the yolks slightly for better binding ability.
5. With the mixer on high or whisking vigorously by hand, begin to add the oil very slowly until an emulsion forms.
6. After the emulsion forms, the oil can be added a little more quickly but still in a slow, steady stream. The mayonnaise can now be whipped at a slightly slower speed.
7. The mayonnaise will become very thick as more oil is added. A small amount of liquid can be added if it becomes too thick. Alternate between oil and liquid two or three times until all the oil is added and the correct consistency is reached. *Important:* A large egg yolk has the ability to emulsify up to 7 ounces (200 mL) of oil; adding more oil may cause the mayonnaise to break.
8. Taste the mayonnaise and adjust the seasonings. Refrigerate immediately.

◆◆◆

RECIPE 24.2

MAYONNAISE

Yield: 1 qt. (1 L)

Egg yolks	4	4
Salt	1 tsp.	5 mL
White pepper	TT	TT
Dry mustard	1 tsp.	5 mL
Wine vinegar	3 Tbsp.	45 mL
Salad oil	28 oz.	800 mL
Lemon juice	TT	TT

1. Place the egg yolks in the bowl of a mixer and whip on high speed until frothy.
2. Add the dry ingredients and half the vinegar to the yolks; whisk to combine.
3. Begin to add the oil a drop at a time until the mixture begins to thicken and an emulsion begins to form.
4. Add the remaining oil in a slow steady stream, thinning the mayonnaise occasionally by adding a little vinegar. Continue until all oil and vinegar have been incorporated.
5. Adjust the seasonings and add lemon juice to taste.
6. Store in a covered noncorrosive container. Refrigerate until needed.

Approximate values per 1 oz. (30 g) serving:	
Calories	230
Total fat	26 g
Saturated fat	3.5 g
Cholesterol	25 mg
Sodium	75 mg
Total carbohydrates	0 g
Protein	0 g

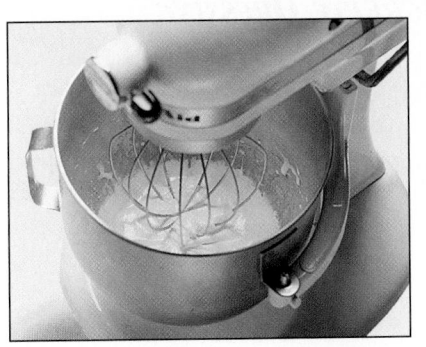

1. Whip the egg yolks until frothy.

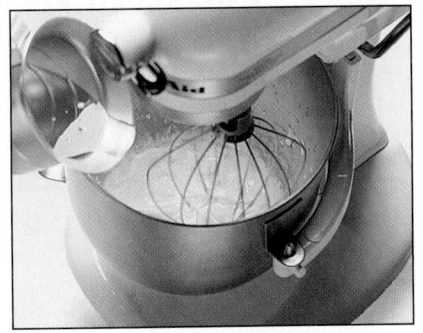

2. Add the oil very slowly, allowing the emulsion to form.

3. The finished mayonnaise.

Mayonnaise-Based Dressings

Mayonnaise-based salad dressings are sauces that use mayonnaise as a base, with other ingredients added for flavour, colour and texture. These ingredients include dairy products (especially buttermilk and sour cream), vinegar, fruit juice, vegetables (either puréed or minced), tomato paste, garlic, onions, herbs, spices, condiments, capers, anchovies and boiled eggs. Recipes for several mayonnaise-based salad dressings are at the end of this chapter.

Emulsified Vinaigrette Dressings

An emulsified vinaigrette is a standard vinaigrette dressing emulsified with whole eggs or modified starches. An emulsified vinaigrette dressing is thinner and lighter than a mayonnaise-based dressing and heavier than a basic vinaigrette. Its taste is similar to a basic vinaigrette, but it will not separate and it clings to greens quite easily. They are very popular.

BASIC PROCEDURE FOR PREPARING AN EMULSIFIED VINAIGRETTE DRESSING

1. Gather all ingredients and hold at room temperature. Room-temperature ingredients emulsify more easily than cold ones.
2. Whip the eggs until frothy.
3. Add the dry ingredients and any flavourings such as garlic, shallots and herbs.
4. Add a small amount of the liquid from the recipe and whip to incorporate the ingredients.
5. With the mixer on high or whisking vigorously by hand, begin adding the oil very slowly until the emulsion forms.
6. After the emulsion is formed, the oil can be added a little more quickly, but still in a slow, steady stream.
7. Alternate between oil and liquid two or three times until all the oil is added. The dressing should be much thinner than mayonnaise. If it is too thick it can be thinned with a little water, vinegar or lemon juice. Determine which to use by first tasting the dressing.

◆◆◆

RECIPE 24.3

EMULSIFIED VINAIGRETTE DRESSING

Yield: 1 qt. (1 L)

Eggs, whole	2	2
Salt	1 Tbsp.	15 mL
White pepper	1/2 tsp.	2 mL
Dry mustard	1 Tbsp.	15 mL
Sugar	1 Tbsp.	15 mL
Herbes de Provence	1 Tbsp.	15 mL
Cayenne pepper	TT	TT
Wine vinegar or cider vinegar	4 oz.	120 mL
Salad oil	24 oz.	700 mL
Lemon juice	3 oz.	90 mL

1. Place the eggs in the bowl of a mixer and whip at high speed until frothy.
2. Add the dry ingredients and approximately 1 ounce (30 mL) of vinegar to the eggs; whip to combine.
3. While whipping at high speed, begin adding the oil very slowly until an emulsion forms.
4. Add the remaining oil in a slow, steady stream. Occasionally thin the dressing by adding a little vinegar and lemon juice. Continue until all of the oil, vinegar and lemon juice have been incorporated.
5. Adjust the flavour and consistency.
6. Refrigerate until needed.

NOTE: Add 1 tablespoon (15 mL) paprika for an orange-coloured "American French" dressing.

Approximate values per 1 oz. (30 mL) serving:

Calories	200
Total fat	22 g
Saturated fat	3 g
Cholesterol	15 mg
Sodium	220 mg
Total carbohydrates	1 g
Protein	1 g

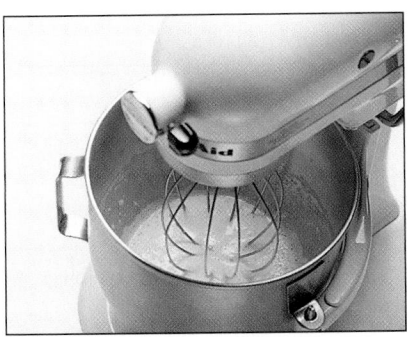

1. Whip the whole eggs.

2. Add the oil drop by drop to establish the emulsion.

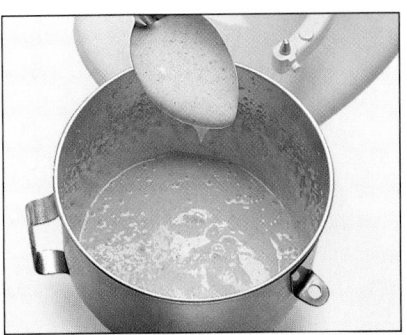

3. The finished emulsified vinaigrette dressing.

PREPARATION METHODS

There are two types of **green salads**: tossed and composed. The more informal **tossed salad** is prepared by placing the greens, garnishes and dressing in a large bowl and tossing to combine. A **composed salad** usually has a more elegant look. It is prepared by arranging each of the ingredients on plates in an artistic fashion.

Other types of salads include **bound salads**, which are cooked meats, poultry, fish, shellfish, pasta or potatoes bound with a dressing, **vegetable salads** and **fruit salads**.

Green Salads

Tossed

Tossed salads are made from leafy vegetables such as lettuce, spinach, watercress, arugula or dandelion greens. They may consist only of greens and dressing or they can be garnished with fruits, vegetables, nuts or cheese. They can be dressed with many different types of dressings, from a light oil and vinegar to a hearty hot bacon. It is important that salad dressings be added at the last possible moment before service. Acidic dressings cause most greens to wilt and become soggy.

Matching Dressings and Salad Greens

There is a simple rule to follow when choosing dressings for salads: The more delicate the texture and flavour of the greens or other ingredients, the lighter and more subtle the dressing should be. Vinaigrette-based dressings are much lighter than mayonnaise-based or similar dressings and should be used with butterleaf lettuces, mâche or other delicate greens. Crisp head lettuce like iceberg and hardy lettuce like romaine can stand up to heavier, mayonnaise-based or similar dressings. Bitter greens are balanced with tart dressings. (See Table 24.2.)

Salad Garnishes

It is impossible to make a complete list of the garnishes that can be combined with salad greens for a tossed salad. A partial list includes:

◆ Vegetables—nearly any vegetable—raw, blanched or fully cooked—cut into appropriate sizes and uniform shapes.
◆ Fruits—citrus segments, apples or pears; dried fruits such as raisins, currants or apricots.
◆ Meats, poultry, fish and shellfish—cooked meats and poultry sliced or diced neatly and uniformly; poached, grilled or cured fish, diced or flaked; small,

TABLE 24.2   MATCHING DRESSINGS AND SALAD GREENS

Dressing	Greens
Vinaigrette dressing made with vegetable oil and red wine vinegar	Any greens: iceberg, romaine, leaf lettuce, butterleaf lettuce, escarole, curly endive, Belgian endive, radicchio, baby lettuces, sorrel, arugula, dandelion
Vinaigrette dressing made with a nut oil and balsamic vinegar	Delicate greens: butterleaf lettuce, bibb lettuce, Belgian endive, radicchio, baby lettuces, arugula, mâche, watercress
Emulsified vinaigrette dressing	Any greens: romaine, leaf lettuce, butterleaf lettuce, escarole, curly endive, Belgian endive, radicchio, baby lettuces, sorrel, arugula, watercress
Mayonnaise-based dressing such as blue cheese or green goddess	Hardy greens: iceberg, romaine, leaf lettuce, escarole, curly endive, sorrel, dandelion

whole cooked shellfish such as shrimp and scallops; lobster or crab sliced, diced or chopped.

+ Cheeses—grated hard cheeses such as Parmesan, Romano or Asiago; semi-hard cheese such as cheddar and Swiss, cut julienne or shredded.
+ Nuts—nearly any are appropriate, roasted, candied or smoked.
+ Croutons—assorted breads, seasoned in various ways and toasted.

BASIC PROCEDURE FOR PREPARING TOSSED SALADS

1. Select greens with various colours, textures and flavours.
2. Carefully cut or tear, wash and dry the greens.
3. Prepare the garnishes as directed or desired.
4. Prepare the dressing.
5. Combine the greens, garnishes and dressing by tossing them together. Or toss the greens and garnishes and, using a spray bottle, spray the greens with the dressing.

◆◆◆

RECIPE 24.4

MESCLUN SALAD WITH RASPBERRY VINAIGRETTE

Yield: 6 Servings

Baby lettuces, assorted	approx. 8 heads	approx. 8 heads
Mâche	4 oz.	120 g
Fresh herbs	2 Tbsp.	30 mL
Edible flowers	approx. 12	approx. 12
Raspberry Vinaigrette (Recipe 24.9)	4 oz.	120 mL

1. Trim, wash and dry the baby lettuces and mâche.
2. Pick the fresh herbs from their stems. If using leafy herbs such as basil, they may be cut chiffonade or left as whole leaves.
3. If desired, pick the petals from the edible flowers. Small flowers may be left whole.

A simple mesclun salad.

4. Place the lettuces and mâche in a bowl and add the herbs. Ladle the dressing over them and toss gently, using two spoons.

5. Transfer the salads to cold plates. Some of the larger leaves may be used as liners if desired.

6. Garnish each salad with flowers or flower petals.

Approximate values per serving:

Calories	150
Total fat	9 g
Saturated fat	1 g
Cholesterol	0 mg
Sodium	180 mg
Total carbohydrates	14 g
Protein	4 g
Vitamin A	35%
Vitamin C	120%

Composed

Composed green salads usually use a green as a base and are built by artistically arranging other ingredients on the plate. There are usually four components: the base, body, garnish and dressing.

The **base** is usually salad greens that line or frame the plate on which the salad will be served. Depending upon the desired effect, the leaves can be cup-shaped or flat.

The **body** is the main ingredient. It can be lettuce or other greens, or another salad made from cooked or blended ingredients, such as chicken salad or fruit.

The **garnish** is added to the salad for colour, texture and flavour. It can be as substantial as a grilled, sliced duck breast or as simple as a sprinkling of chopped herbs; it can be warm or cold. The choice is unlimited but whatever is used should always complement and balance the flavour of the body.

The salad **dressing** should complement rather than mask the other flavours in the salad. If the body already contains a dressing, as in a bound salad, additional dressing may not be necessary.

Composed green salads are usually dressed by ladling the dressing over the salad after it is plated. Alternatively, the individual ingredients can be dressed before they are arranged on the plate. A third method that may be limited by the intricacy of the salad but will save precious time during a busy period is to prepare individual salads on a sheet pan. Then, just before service, mist them with dressing using a spray bottle designated for this purpose, then transfer them to chilled plates using a spatula as illustrated.

Mist salads while on a sheet pan and transfer to chilled plates for service.

BASIC PROCEDURE FOR PREPARING COMPOSED SALADS

1. Gather all ingredients for the salad and wash, trim, cut, cook, chill or otherwise prepare them as necessary or as called for in the recipe.

2. Arrange all ingredients artistically on the plates, dressing each ingredient as desired or as directed in the recipe.

3. At service time, heat or cook any items that are being served hot and add them to the salad.

♦♦♦

RECIPE 24.5

SALAD NIÇOISE

Yield: 6 Servings

Red wine vinegar	4 oz.	120 mL
Salt and pepper	TT	TT
Virgin olive oil	12 oz.	360 mL
Basil leaves, chiffonade	12	12
Belgian endive	1 head	1 head
Tomatoes, peeled	6	6
Potatoes, cooked	1 lb. 8 oz.	680 g
Green beans	12 oz.	340 g
Eggs, hard-boiled	6	6
Artichokes	6	6
Romaine lettuce leaves, washed	12	12
Tuna, fresh, grilled and chilled	1 lb. 8 oz.	680 g
Niçoise olives	4 oz.	120 g
Anchovy fillets	12	12

Approximate values per serving:

Calories	890
Total fat	70 g
Saturated fat	11 g
Cholesterol	200 mg
Sodium	760 mg
Total carbohydrates	21 g
Protein	44 g
Vitamin A	130%
Vitamin C	60%
Iron	30%

1. Make a vinaigrette dressing using the red wine vinegar, salt, pepper, olive oil and basil leaves.
2. Wash and dry the endive leaves.
3. Core and cut each tomato into 8 wedges.
4. Slice the potatoes and moisten with some of the dressing.
5. Trim and cook the green beans al dente, refresh in ice water.
6. Peel the eggs and cut into wedges.
7. Cook the artichokes. Trim the outer leaves from each artichoke leaving only the heart. Remove the choke from the heart and cut each heart into quarters.
8. Line each cold plate with romaine lettuce leaves and endive spears, then arrange the remaining ingredients artistically. Use the contrasting shapes, colours and textures to create an attractive presentation.
9. At service, whisk the dressing to combine the ingredients and pour approximately 2-1/2 ounces (75 mL) over each salad.

Bound Salads

The creative cook can prepare a wide variety of salads by combining cooked meats, poultry, fish, shellfish, potatoes, pasta, grains and/or legumes with a dressing and garnishes. Although the combinations vary greatly, these salads are grouped together here because their ingredients are all bound. That is, each salad consists of one or more ingredients held together in a cohesive mass. The binding agent can be either a vinaigrette or mayonnaise-based or similar dressing. The ingredients should be evenly distributed throughout, and the degree of cohesiveness can range from tightly packed to flaky and easily separated.

The foods that can be used to produce bound salads are so varied that it is impossible to list them all. Generalizing preparation techniques is also very difficult. There are as many ways to prepare a bound salad as there are ingredients, dressings and garnishes.

Bound salads can be used as the body of a composed salad (for instance, a serving of shrimp salad on a bed of greens). Some are used in sandwiches but not ordinarily as side dishes—for example, egg or ham salad. Some are served as side dishes but not in sandwiches, for example, potato, pasta or cucumber salad. Follow specific recipes and traditional uses for each salad until you are confident enough in your skills to let your imagination take over.

BASIC PROCEDURE FOR PREPARING BOUND SALADS

1. Preparing a salad from cooked foods is a good opportunity to use leftovers, but be sure they are fresh and of good quality. The finished salad can be only as good as each of its ingredients.
2. When making a bound salad, choose ingredients whose flavours blend well and complement each other.
3. Choose ingredients for colour; a few colourful ingredients will turn a plain salad into a spectacular one.
4. To improve appearance, generally cut all ingredients the same size and shape. If the main ingredient is diced, then dice the other ingredients. Be cautious combining diced, sliced and julienned foods in the same salad.
5. All ingredients should be cut into pieces that are small enough to be eaten easily with a fork.
6. Be sure all meats, poultry, fish and shellfish are fully cooked before using them. Undercooked foods can cause food-borne illness and spoilage.
7. Always chill cooked ingredients well before using them. Warm ingredients promote bacterial growth, especially in mayonnaise-based salads.
8. Always use dressings sparingly. They should enhance the flavours of the other salad ingredients, not mask them.

◆◆◆

RECIPE 24.6
CHUTNEY CHICKEN SALAD

Yield: 8 lb. (3.6 kg)

Chicken meat, cooked	5 lb.	2.2 kg
Celery, small dice	8 oz.	250 g
Green onion, sliced	3 oz.	90 g
Mango chutney	12 oz.	350 mL
Mayonnaise	1 lb.	500 mL
Seedless grapes	12 oz.	340 g
Salt and pepper	TT	TT

1. Remove any bones, skin and fat from the chicken and cut the meat into large dice.
2. Combine the chicken meat, celery, green onions, mango chutney and mayonnaise in a bowl; mix well.
3. Cut the grapes in half. Add them to the chicken mixture and toss gently to combine.

Approximate values per 4 oz. (120 g) serving:

Calories	230
Total fat	14 g
Saturated fat	3 g
Cholesterol	70 mg
Sodium	135 mg
Total carbohydrates	4 g
Protein	22 g

Vegetable Salads

Vegetable salads are made from cooked or raw vegetables or a combination of both. They can be served on buffets, as an appetizer or salad course. As with other salads, vegetable salads must successfully combine colour, texture and flavour. Some vegetable salads such as coleslaw and carrot-raisin salad are made with mayonnaise. Most, however, are made by either marinating the vegetables or combining them in a vinaigrette dressing.

Almost any vegetable can be successfully marinated. The amount of time depends on the vegetables and the marinade, but several hours to overnight is usually sufficient for flavours to blend. Soft vegetables such as mushrooms, zucchini and cucumbers can be added directly to a cold marinade. Hard vegetables such as carrots and cauliflower should be blanched in salted water, refreshed, drained and then added to a cold marinade. Carrots, artichokes, mushrooms, cauliflower, zucchini, pearl onions and the like are sometimes simmered quickly in a marinade flavoured with lemon juice and olive oil, and then served cold. This style is called *à la grecque*.

Many marinated salads will last several days under proper refrigeration. As the salads age in the marinade they will change in appearance and texture. This may or may not be desirable. For example, mushrooms and artichokes become more flavourful, while green vegetables are discoloured by the acids in the marinade. If marinated salads are prepared in advance, check their appearance as well as their seasonings carefully at service time.

BASIC PROCEDURE FOR PREPARING VEGETABLE SALADS

1. Gather and wash all vegetables.
2. Trim, cut, shred or otherwise prepare the vegetables as desired or as directed in the recipe.
3. Blanch or cook the vegetables if necessary.
4. Combine the vegetables with the marinade or dressing. Adjust the seasonings.

◆◆◆

RECIPE 24.7

TOMATO, ORANGE, MOZZARELLA AND BASIL SALAD

Yield: 4 Servings

Mozzarella cheese, fresh (bocconcini)	8 oz.	250 g
Tomatoes, peeled, sliced	4	4
Oranges, peeled, sliced	4	4
Basil leaves, chiffonade	8	8
Olive oil	2 oz.	60 mL
Balsamic vinegar	1 Tbsp.	15 mL
Salt and pepper	TT	TT

Approximate values per serving:

Calories	410
Total fat	32 g
Saturated fat	9 g
Cholesterol	35 mg
Sodium	370 mg
Total carbohydrates	11 g
Protein	19 g
Vitamin A	20%
Vitamin C	110%
Calcium	40%

1. Slice cheese to the same thickness as the tomato and orange slices.
2. Arrange the cheese, tomato and orange slices on plates.
3. Prepare a dressing with the olive oil and vinegar.
4. Sprinkle the slices with the basil and dressing.

Fruit Salads

There are so many different fruits with beautiful bright colours and sweet delicious flavours that preparing fruit salads is easy work. Fruit salads are a refreshing addition to buffets and can be served as the first course of a lunch or dinner. A more elaborate fruit salad can be served as a light lunch.

Always prepare fruit salads as close to service time as possible. The flesh of many types of fruit becomes soft and translucent if cut long before service. Other fruits turn brown in a matter of minutes after cutting. Refer to Chapter 25, Fruits, for more information on this browning reaction and for information on specific fruits. Fruit salad recipes are found at the end of that chapter.

If a fruit salad is dressed at all, the dressing is usually sweet and made with honey or yogurt mixed with fruit juices or purées. Alternatively, Grand Marnier, crème de menthe or other liqueurs sprinkled over the salad can serve as a dressing. Fruit salads can be tossed or composed. Either should offer the consumer a pleasing blend of colours, shapes, sizes, flavours and textures.

ONCLUSION

A salad can be a small part of a meal or the entire meal. There are many styles of salads, and a seemingly endless variety of foods can be used to prepare them. Salads are extremely popular, especially with those interested in lighter dining alternatives. You can tempt these diners by determining the appropriate style of the salads and skilfully combining the main ingredients and dressing to achieve a delicious and appealing balance of colours, textures and flavours.

QUESTIONS FOR DISCUSSION

1. Name several factors that will cause salad greens to wilt or deteriorate.
2. Describe the proper procedure for washing and drying lettuce.
3. Explain the difference between a vinaigrette and an emulsified vinaigrette dressing.
4. Describe the procedure for making mayonnaise. How can the flavour of a mayonnaise be altered?
5. Explain what happens to the ingredients when an emulsion "breaks." How can it sometimes be repaired?
6. Describe a typical bound salad. How does a bound salad differ from a dressed salad?
7. List five ways salads can be presented or offered on a menu.

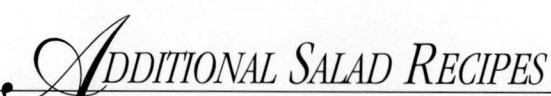

ADDITIONAL SALAD RECIPES

RECIPE 24.8

SEAFOOD SALAD

NOTE: *This dish appears in the Chapter Opening photograph.*

GOTHAM BAR AND GRILL, NEW YORK, NY
Chef/Owner Alfred Portale

Yield: 4 Servings

Lobster, 1 lb. 8 oz. (680 g)	1	1
Court bouillon	4 qt.	4 L
Sea scallops	4 oz.	120 g
Squid, cleaned	3 oz.	90 g
Mussels, debearded	12	12
Avocado	1	1
Frisée	1 head	1 head
Baby red oak	1 head	1 head
Shallot, finely minced	2 Tbsp.	30 mL
Fresh basil, chopped	1 Tbsp.	15 mL
Fresh chives, finely minced	1 Tbsp.	15 mL
Fresh Italian parsley, chopped	1 Tbsp.	15 mL
Lemon Vinaigrette (recipe follows)	as needed	as needed
Salt and white pepper	TT	TT

Approximate values per serving:

Calories	600
Total fat	34 g
Saturated fat	3.5 g
Cholesterol	230 mg
Sodium	1790 mg
Total carbohydrates	11 g
Protein	63 g
Vitamin A	30%
Vitamin C	50%
Iron	45%

1. Boil the lobster in the court bouillon, then chill it. Remove the meat from the shell; dice it.
2. Poach the sea scallops and squid in the same court bouillon. Cool and thinly slice each of them.
3. Steam the mussels in a portion of the court bouillon. Chill and remove the meat from the shells.
4. Peel, pit, quarter and thinly slice the ripe avocado.
5. Wash and dry the greens.
6. Toss the shellfish with the shallots, herbs and a portion of the vinaigrette. Dress the lettuces and avocado.
7. Season all with salt and white pepper. Arrange the lettuces, shellfish and fanned avocado on 4 plates.

LEMON VINAIGRETTE

Yield: 14 oz. (400 mL)

Dijon-style mustard	1 tsp.	5 mL
Salt and white pepper	TT	TT
Red wine vinegar	1 oz.	30 mL
Extra virgin olive oil	10 oz.	300 mL
Lemon juice	2 oz.	60 mL
Cayenne pepper	pinch	pinch

Approximate values per 1 oz. (30 mL) serving:

Calories	180
Total fat	20 g
Saturated fat	2.5 g
Cholesterol	0 mg
Sodium	170 mg
Total carbohydrates	1 g
Protein	0 g
Claims—no cholesterol; no sugar	

1. Whisk together the mustard, salt, white pepper and red wine vinegar. Slowly whisk in the olive oil.
2. Adjust the acidity with the lemon juice and add a pinch of cayenne.

◆◆◆

RECIPE 24.9

RASPBERRY VINAIGRETTE

Yield: 2 qt. (2 L)

Red wine vinegar	8 oz.	250 mL
Rice wine vinegar	8 oz.	250 mL
Lemon juice	3 Tbsp.	45 mL
Dried thyme	1 Tbsp.	15 mL
Salt	1 Tbsp.	15 mL
Pepper	1 Tbsp.	15 mL
Garlic, minced	1 Tbsp.	15 mL
Honey	4 oz.	120 g
Raspberry preserves, without seeds	8 oz.	250 g
Olive oil	12 oz.	350 mL
Salad oil	1 pt.	450 mL

Approximate values per 1 oz. (30 mL) serving:

Calories	130
Total fat	12 g
Saturated fat	1 g
Cholesterol	0 mg
Sodium	140 mg
Total carbohydrates	5 g
Protein	0 g
Claims—no cholesterol	

1. Whisk together the vinegars, lemon juice, thyme, salt, pepper and garlic.

2. Slowly whisk in the honey and raspberry preserves.

3. Whisk in the oils slowly, emulsifying the dressing.

VARIATION: Prepare Basic Vinaigrette using raspberry vinegar.

◆◆◆

RECIPE 24.10

FAT-FREE RASPBERRY VINAIGRETTE

Yield: 1 pt. (450 mL)

Raspberry vinegar	4 oz.	120 mL
Fructose	1 Tbsp.	15 mL
Garlic, minced	1 tsp.	5 mL
Worcestershire sauce	2 tsp.	10 mL
Dijon-style mustard	1 Tbsp.	15 mL
Lemon juice	2 oz.	30 mL
Water	8 oz.	250 mL
Salt and pepper	TT	TT

Approximate values per 1 oz. (30 mL) serving:

Calories	10
Total fat	0 g
Saturated fat	0 g
Cholesterol	0 mg
Sodium	50 mg
Total carbohydrates	2 g
Protein	0 g
Claims—fat free; low sodium; low calorie	

Whisk all ingredients together.

Note: Fructose is a naturally occurring simple sugar; it is readily available as a white granulated powder.

◆◆◆

RECIPE 24.11

FOUR-PEPPERCORN CRANBERRY VINAIGRETTE

Yield: 1 qt. (1 L)

White peppercorns	2 oz.	60 g
Red wine vinegar	2 oz.	60 mL
Water	6 oz.	180 mL

Continued

Sugar	7 oz.	220 g
Lemon juice	2 Tbsp.	30 mL
Cranberries	12 oz.	350 g
Orange zest	1 Tbsp.	15 mL
Green peppercorns	4 Tbsp.	60 mL
Pink peppercorns	4 Tbsp.	60 mL
Raspberry vinegar	6 oz.	180 mL
Walnut oil	4 oz.	120 mL
Salt and black pepper	TT	TT

1. Combine the white peppercorns and red wine vinegar with 2 ounces (60 mL) of water and bring to a simmer. Simmer 5 minutes, then transfer to a small container and allow to rest for at least 1 day.
2. Combine the sugar, remaining water and lemon juice. Cook until the sugar is completely dissolved and the mixture reaches a full boil.
3. Add the cranberries and orange zest and simmer 5 minutes.
4. Add the white peppercorn mixture, the green and pink peppercorns and simmer 1 minute. Remove from the heat and cool.
5. Add the raspberry vinegar and oil. Purée briefly in a blender or food processor. Season with salt and crushed black pepper.

Approximate values per serving:

Calories	53
Total fat	3 g
Saturated fat	.2 g
Cholesterol	0 mg
Sodium	46 mg
Total carbohydrates	8 g
Protein	.3 g

❖❖❖

RECIPE 24.12

RED ONION VINAIGRETTE

Yield: 1 pt. (450 mL)

Walnut oil	8 oz.	250 mL
Champagne vinegar	4 oz.	120 mL
Sugar	1 Tbsp.	15 mL
Salt and pepper	TT	TT
Red onions, fine dice	8 oz.	250 g

1. Whisk together the oil, vinegar, sugar, salt and pepper.
2. Blanch the onions for a few seconds in boiling water. Drain thoroughly.
3. Add the onions to the oil mixture and allow the dressing to rest for several hours so that the flavours blend.

Approximate values per 1 oz. (30 mL) serving:

Calories	140
Total fat	14 g
Saturated fat	1.5 g
Cholesterol	0 mg
Sodium	35 mg
Total carbohydrates	2 g
Protein	0 g

Claims—no cholesterol; low sodium

❖❖❖

RECIPE 24.13

CAESAR DRESSING

Yield: 90 oz. (2.6 L)

Dry mustard	1 tsp.	5 mL
Red wine vinegar	6 oz.	200 mL
Egg yolks	9	9
Anchovy paste	2 oz.	50 g
Worcestershire sauce	1 tsp.	5 mL
Garlic cloves, crushed	5	5
Olive oil	16 oz.	500 mL
Vegetable oil	48 oz.	1.5 L

Black pepper, ground	2 tsp.	10 mL
Salt	3 tsp.	15 mL
Lemon juice	5 oz.	150 mL
Parmesan cheese (optional)	7 oz.	200 g

1. Dissolve the mustard in half the vinegar.
2. Whisk mixture with the yolks, anchovy paste, Worcestershire sauce and garlic until frothy.
3. Slowly drizzle the olive oil into mixture while whisking.
4. Once the emulsion forms, add remaining oil in a steady stream. Adjust the consistency with vinegar while incorporating oils.
5. Add the remaining ingredients and adjust seasoning.
6. Store covered in a noncorrosive container under refrigeration.

Approximate values per serving:

Calories	193
Total fat	21 g
Saturated fat	3 g
Cholesterol	22 mg
Sodium	111 mg
Total carbohydrates	1 g
Protein	1 g

==================== ◆◆◆ ====================

RECIPE 24.14

CAESAR SALAD

Yield: 4 Servings

Crisp, chilled romaine, chopped in 1 to 1-1/2 inch (3–4 cm) pieces	1 large	1 large
Curly endive, coarse chopped	2 cups	500 mL
Garlic clove	1	1
Salad oil, preferably olive oil	1/2 cup	110 mL
Wine or tarragon vinegar	1 Tbsp.	15 mL
Salt	1/2 tsp.	2 mL
Worcestershire sauce	1 tsp.	5 mL
English dry mustard	1/2 tsp.	2 mL
Juice from half a lemon		
Anchovy fillets, chopped (or fried bacon)	2 oz.	50 g
Coddled eggs	2	2
Black pepper, fresh ground	TT	TT
Parmesan cheese, grated	1 cup	225 mL
Garlic Croutons (Recipe 24.23)	1 cup (heaping)	250 mL (heaping)

1. The romaine should be chopped, crisp, dry and chilled.
2. Line up all 12 ingredients ready for use at the tableside. Use only the very best brands of condiments.
3. In a small wooden bowl, crush the garlic with a fork and remove the pieces.
4. Add the oil, vinegar, salt, Worcestershire sauce, mustard, lemon juice and anchovies. Stir to blend. Pour over the romaine and endive and toss well.
5. Add the coddled eggs directly over the romaine. Sprinkle with pepper, scatter nearly all the Parmesan over the salad and then the croutons. Toss quickly and vigorously.
6. Serve immediately on ice cold plates, adding remaining Parmesan and more fresh pepper.

NOTE: Some customers prefer the coddled eggs to be incorporated with the dressing.

Coddled egg—*whole-shell egg immersed in hot water for 3 minutes. When cracked the white will just show traces of setting.*

Approximate values per serving:

Calories	463
Total fat	39 g
Saturated fat	10 g
Cholesterol	127 mg
Sodium	1343 mg
Total carbohydrates	10 g
Protein	19 g

♦ ♦ ♦

ALL ABOUT INFUSED OILS

These days, a cruet of olive oil is almost as common as salt and pepper shakers on dining tables. The bottle shows off olive oil's colors, and also can contain herbs and spices that infuse the oil with flavor. Customers enjoy pouring the oil into a saucer as a bread dipper or use the oil to season other dishes.

Although olive oil adds to customers' dining pleasure, care must be taken to make sure the oil is safe. If not properly refrigerated, oils containing low-acid foods such as fresh garlic, rosemary or basil could harbor botulism.

Chef Jean-Georges Vongerichten of Jo Jo, Vong and Lipstick Cafe, New York, uses flavored, infused olive oils so often that he is known as "the king of infusion." Vongerichten offers the following tips on preparing infused oils, including safety information developed in cooperation with the American Culinary Federation and the United States Department of Agriculture.

✦ Like wine, long-term storage of olive oil should be in a cool, dark place away from sunlight or heat sources. If olive oil is purchased in large containers, decant some into smaller containers for daily use. Refrigerate the small containers.

✦ If aromatics and herbs such as fresh garlic, basil or rosemary are added to olive oil, the mixture should be made in small, daily quantities and kept refrigerated until used.

✦ Infused oils in cruets or dishes used at the table or left out at room temperature should be disposed of at the end of the day.

✦ Using small cruets, bottles or dishes to served infused oils cuts down on waste.

✦ Keep cruets and bottles sparkling clean for sanitary and esthetic reasons. Do not refill cruets and bottles without washing them first.

Vongerichten also offers this recipe, which yields 2 cups of infused oil:

Place 2 Tbsp. (30 mL) fresh peeled, minced root (shallot, garlic, horseradish, ginger or leek) in a clean jar. Add 2 cups (500 mL) olive oil. Cover jar tightly; shake vigorously. Store root oil, tightly covered, in the refrigerator, at least 1 to 2 hours. Root oil will keep 2 weeks, tightly covered, in the refrigerator.

♦ ♦ ♦

RECIPE 24.15

THOUSAND ISLAND DRESSING

Yield: 1 qt. (1 L)

Red wine vinegar	1 Tbsp.	15 mL
Sugar	1 Tbsp.	15 mL
Mayonnaise	1 pt.	450 mL
Ketchup	8 oz.	250 g
Sweet pickle relish	6 oz.	180 g
Hard-cooked eggs, chopped	4	4
Fresh parsley, chopped	2 Tbsp.	30 mL
Green onions, chopped	1 bunch	1 bunch
Salt and pepper	TT	TT
Worcestershire sauce	TT	TT

Approximate values per 1 oz. (30 g) serving:

Calories	120
Total fat	11 g
Saturated fat	2 g
Cholesterol	35 mg
Sodium	270 mg
Total carbohydrates	4 g
Protein	1 g

1. Combine the vinegar and sugar; stir to dissolve the sugar.

2. Add the remaining ingredients and mix well.

3. Adjust the seasonings with the salt, pepper and Worcestershire sauce.

◆◆◆

RECIPE 24.16
GREEN GODDESS DRESSING

Yield: 1 qt. (1 L)

Fresh parsley	1 oz.	30 g
Mayonnaise	1 pt.	450 mL
Sour cream	12 oz.	340 g
Garlic, chopped	1 Tbsp.	15 mL
Anchovy fillets, minced	1 oz.	30 g
Fresh chives, chopped	1 oz.	30 g
Fresh tarragon, chopped	1 Tbsp.	15 mL
Lemon juice	1 oz.	30 mL
White wine vinegar	1 oz.	30 mL
Salt and white pepper	TT	TT
Worcestershire sauce	TT	TT

1. Rinse and chop the parsley but do not dry it or you will remove some of the chlorophyll.
2. Combine all ingredients up to and including vinegar and mix well. Season to taste with salt, white pepper and Worcestershire sauce.

Approximate values per 1 oz. (30 mL) serving:

Calories	80
Total fat	8 g
Saturated fat	2.5 g
Cholesterol	10 mg
Sodium	125 mg
Total carbohydrates	1 g
Protein	1 g

◆◆◆

RECIPE 24.17
BLUE CHEESE DRESSING

Yield: 1 qt. (1 L)

Mayonnaise	8 oz.	250 mL
Red wine vinegar	1 oz.	30 mL
Sour cream	8 oz.	250 mL
Buttermilk	4 oz.	120 mL
Garlic, chopped	1 tsp.	5 mL
Worcestershire sauce	1 tsp.	5 mL
Tabasco sauce	TT	TT
Pepper	TT	TT
Blue-veined cheese, crumbled	12 oz.	340 g

1. Combine all ingredients except the cheese; mix well.
2. Add the crumbled cheese and combine.

Approximate values per 1 oz. (30 mL) serving:

Calories	110
Total fat	10 g
Saturated fat	4 g
Cholesterol	20 mg
Sodium	240 mg
Total carbohydrates	1 g
Protein	3 g

◆◆◆

RECIPE 24.18
LOW-FAT BLUE CHEESE DRESSING

Yield: 1 qt. (1 L)

Nonfat yogurt	20 oz.	560 mL
Low-fat buttermilk	6 oz.	170 mL
Blue cheese, crumbled	4 oz.	120 g
White pepper	1/4 tsp.	1 mL
Worcestershire sauce	TT	TT
Dry mustard	1 tsp.	5 mL
Tabasco sauce	TT	TT

Combine all ingredients in the bowl of a mixer or food processor. Process until smooth.

Approximate values per 1 oz. (30 mL) serving:

Calories	25
Total fat	1 g
Saturated fat	.5 g
Cholesterol	5 mg
Sodium	65 mg
Total carbohydrates	2 g
Protein	2 g

Claims—low fat; low cholesterol; low sodium; low calorie

◆◆◆

RECIPE 24.19

CREAMY BLUE CHEESE DRESSING

Yield: 1.5 qt. (1.5 L)

Mayonnaise	24 oz.	700 mL
Sour cream	16 oz.	500 mL
Cream, 35%, whipped	7 oz.	200 mL
Blue cheese, grated	7 oz.	200 g
Green onion, finely chopped	1 Tbsp.	10 g
Worcestershire sauce	1 tsp.	5 mL
Salt	1 Tbsp.	15 g
Pepper	1/4 tsp.	1 g
Cider vinegar	2 oz.	50 mL
Lemon juice	1 oz.	20 mL

Combine all ingredients.

Approximate values per serving:

Calories	121
Total fat	13 g
Saturated fat	4 g
Cholesterol	17 mg
Sodium	215 mg
Total carbohydrates	1 g
Protein	1 g

◆◆◆

RECIPE 24.20

CUCUMBER DRESSING

Yield: 2.25 qt. (2.25 L)

Mayonnaise	32 oz.	1 L
Yogurt, plain	32 oz.	1 L
English cucumber, grated	2	2
White vinegar, white wine or rice	8 oz.	250 mL
Salt	1 Tbsp.	15 g
Pepper	1/4 tsp.	1 g
Sugar	4 tsp.	20 g

Combine all ingredients.

Approximate values per serving:

Calories	75
Total fat	8 g
Saturated fat	1 g
Cholesterol	6 mg
Sodium	117 mg
Total carbohydrates	2 g
Protein	1 g

◆◆◆

RECIPE 24.21

RANCH DRESSING

Yield: 6.5 qt. (6.5 L)

Sour cream	64 oz.	2 L
Buttermilk	64 oz.	2 L
Mayonnaise	64 oz.	2 L
Cider vinegar	10 oz.	300 mL
Worcestershire sauce	4 tsp.	20 mL
Parsley, chopped	1/2 cup	120 mL
Green onion, chopped	1 cup	250 mL
Salt	2 Tbsp.	30 g
White pepper, ground	1 tsp.	3 g

1. Combine all ingredients.
2. Adjust seasoning.

Approximate values per serving:

Calories	64
Total fat	6 g
Saturated fat	2 g
Cholesterol	7 mg
Sodium	97 mg
Total carbohydrates	1 g
Protein	1 g

◆◆◆

RECIPE 24.22

TARTAR SAUCE

Yield: 1 pt. (500 mL)

Mayonnaise	1 pt.	480 mL
Capers, chopped	2 oz.	60 g
Sweet gherkins, chopped	3 oz.	90 g
Onion, minced	2 Tbsp.	30 mL
Fresh parsley, minced	2 Tbsp.	30 mL
Lemon juice	1 Tbsp.	15 mL
Salt	TT	TT
Hard-boiled eggs, chopped	2	2

*Approximate values per
1 oz. (30 mL) serving:*

Calories	220
Total fat	23 g
Saturated fat	4 g
Cholesterol	20 mg
Sodium	420 mg
Total carbohydrates	2 g
Protein	0 g

Stir all of the ingredients together until well blended. Chill thoroughly before serving.

◆◆◆

RECIPE 24.23

GARLIC CROUTONS FOR SALADS

Yield: 1 lb. 4 oz. (550 g)

Whole butter	6 oz.	180 g
Garlic, chopped	1 Tbsp.	15 mL
French or sourdough bread cubes	1 lb. 8 oz.	700 g
Parmesan cheese, grated	1 oz.	30 g
Dried basil	2 tsp.	10 mL
Dried oregano	2 tsp.	10 mL

*Approximate values per
1 oz. (30 g) serving:*

Calories	200
Total fat	9 g
Saturated fat	5 g
Cholesterol	20 mg
Sodium	390 mg
Total carbohydrates	25 g
Protein	5 g
Iron	10%
Calcium	10%

1. Melt the butter in a small saucepan and add the garlic. Cook the garlic in the butter for 5 minutes.

2. Place the bread in a bowl, add the Parmesan cheese and herbs.

3. Pour the garlic butter over the bread cubes and immediately toss to combine.

4. Spread the bread cubes on a sheet pan in a single layer and bake at 350°F (180°C). Stir the croutons occasionally and cook until dry and lightly browned, approximately 15 minutes.

◆◆◆

RECIPE 24.24

WILTED SPINACH SALAD WITH ROASTED PEPPERS

Yield: 2 Large or 4 Small Servings

Red or yellow bell pepper, medium	1	1
Olive oil	2 oz.	50 mL
Salt and pepper	TT	TT
Red onion, sliced thin	2 oz.	60 g
Baguette, thin slices for croutons	12	12
Spinach	1 lb.	450 g

Continued

Frisée or escarole	1 head	1 head
Balsamic vinegar	3 Tbsp.	45 mL
Safflower oil	1 oz.	30 mL
Garlic clove, chopped fine	1	1
Niçoise or Gaeta olives, pitted	10	10
Parmesan cheese, grated	1 oz.	30 g

1. Roast, peel and cut the pepper into 1/4-inch (5-mm) strips. Toss the pepper strips with 1/2 tablespoon (10 mL) of olive oil and a few pinches of salt and pepper. Set aside to marinate.

2. Cover the onion slices with cold water to leach the strong onion flavour. Set aside.

3. Place the baguette slices on a baking sheet and brush them lightly with olive oil. Toast in a 375°F (190°C) oven until crisp and lightly browned, approximately 5 minutes.

4. Stem, wash and dry the spinach. Trim the stem end of the frisée or escarole and discard the tough outer leaves. Wash and dry.

5. Drain the onions. In a large bowl, combine the vinegar, 1/2 teaspoon (2 mL) salt and a few pinches of pepper. Add the greens, onions, peppers and olives.

6. Heat the safflower oil in a sauté pan with garlic until it is hot. Sauté the spinach quickly. Immediately pour it over the dressing and toss with a pair of metal tongs to coat and wilt the leaves.

7. Plate, sprinkle on the Parmesan cheese and croutons and serve immediately.

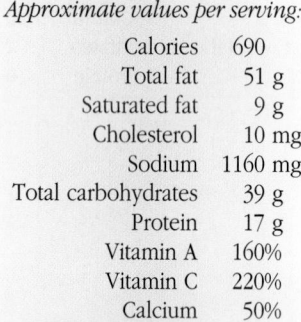

Approximate values per serving:

Calories	690
Total fat	51 g
Saturated fat	9 g
Cholesterol	10 mg
Sodium	1160 mg
Total carbohydrates	39 g
Protein	17 g
Vitamin A	160%
Vitamin C	220%
Calcium	50%
Iron	50%

❖❖❖

RECIPE 24.25

WHITE ASPARAGUS MOUSSE WITH GARDEN-FRESH LETTUCES

ARIZONA BILTMORE, PHOENIX, AZ
Executive Chef Peter Hoefler

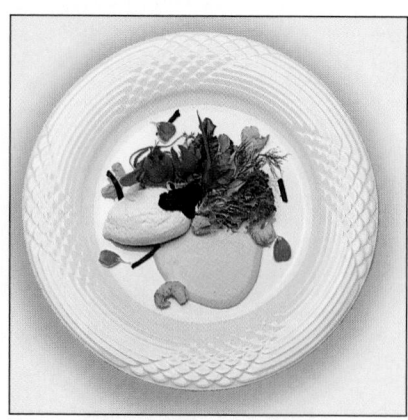

Yield: 10 Servings

White asparagus	8 oz.	250 g
Sugar	1 oz.	30 g
Béchamel sauce	3 oz.	90 mL
Gelatin powder, added to 1 oz. (30 mL) cool water	1/2 oz.	15 mL
Cream, 35%	12 oz.	350 mL
Sea salt and white pepper	TT	TT
Cayenne pepper	TT	TT
Lemon juice	1 Tbsp.	15 mL
Worcestershire sauce	TT	TT
Mâche	5 small bunches	5 small bunches
Frisée	5 small bunches	5 small bunches
Radicchio	5 small heads	5 small heads
Green oak leaf	5 small bunches	5 small bunches
Chervil sprigs	1/4 cup	60 mL
Chives, sliced	1/4 cup	60 mL

Fresh Italian parsley, leaves	1/4 cup	60 mL
Fresh dill sprigs	1/4 cup	60 mL
Basic vinaigrette	as needed	as needed
Crayfish, steamed	as needed for garnish	

1. Peel the asparagus. Depending on the stalk's toughness, trim approximately 1 inch (2.5 cm) from the end. Cook in boiling salted water with the sugar. Remove the asparagus when tender.

2. Combine the hot asparagus in a food processor with the béchamel. Add the softened gelatin and purée until smooth.

3. Pass through a sieve and cool slightly.

4. Whip the cream until stiff. Combine one-third of the cream with the asparagus mixture. Season with salt, the peppers, lemon juice and Worcestershire sauce. Fold in the remaining cream. Refrigerate for 6 hours or overnight.

5. Dress the lettuces and herbs with the basic vinaigrette dressing and arrange on plates.

6. Form quenelles of asparagus mousse and place two on each lettuce-lined plate.

7. Garnish as desired with the steamed crayfish.

Approximate values per serving:

Calories	244
Total fat	22 g
Saturated fat	10 g
Cholesterol	71 mg
Sodium	518 mg
Total carbohydrates	7 g
Protein	6 g

◆◆◆

RECIPE 24.26

FENNEL AND MUSHROOMS À LA GRECQUE

Yield: 18 3-oz. (90-g) Servings **Method:** Simmering

Mushrooms, small	1 lb.	450 g
Pearl onions, peeled	4 oz.	120 g
Olive oil	2 oz.	60 mL
White wine	4 oz.	120 mL
White stock	1 pt.	500 mL
Tomato concassé	12 oz.	350 g
Tomato paste	1 oz.	30 g
Lemon juice	1 oz.	30 mL
Coriander, ground	1 tsp.	5 mL
Bouquet garni:		
Carrot stick, 4 in. (10 cm)	1	1
Leek, split, 4-in. (10-cm) piece	1	1
Fresh thyme	1 sprig	1 sprig
Bay leaf	2	2
Salt and pepper	TT	TT
Fennel, batonnet	1 lb.	450 g

1. Wash the mushrooms and trim the stems.

2. Sauté the onions in the olive oil, browning lightly. Add the white wine, stock, tomato concassé, tomato paste, lemon juice, coriander and bouquet garni. Season to taste with salt and pepper and bring to a boil.

3. Add the fennel and mushrooms and simmer for 15 minutes.

4. Remove from the heat and allow to cool to room temperature. Remove the bouquet garni. Adjust the seasonings and refrigerate. Serve chilled.

Aproximate values per 3 oz. (90 g) serving:

Calories	60
Total fat	3.5 g
Saturated fat	0 g
Cholesterol	0 mg
Sodium	240 mg
Total Carbohydrates	5 g
Protein	2 g
Vitamin C	15%

Claims—no saturated fat; no cholesterol

◆◆◆

RECIPE 24.27

SALAD OF AHI TUNA SEARED WITH LAVENDER AND PEPPER WITH WHOLE-GRAIN MUSTARD SAUCE

FETZER VINEYARDS, HOPLAND, CA
Culinary Director John Ash

Yield: 8 Servings, 3 oz. (90 g) tuna and 1 oz. (30 g) greens each

Lavender-pepper coating:		
Coarse sea salt	1-1/2 tsp.	7 mL
Whole black peppercorns	2 tsp.	10 mL
Whole fennel seeds	2 tsp.	10 mL
White peppercorns	1 tsp.	5 mL
Dried lavender flowers	1-1/2 tsp.	7 mL
Ahi tuna, a solid 3-in.- (7.5-cm-) square piece, well trimmed	1 lb. 8 oz.	700 g
Olive oil	3 Tbsp.	45 mL
Mustard sauce:		
Whole-grain mustard	2 oz.	60 mL
Olive oil	1 oz.	30 mL
Mustard seeds, toasted	1 tsp.	5 mL
Rice wine vinegar	1 tsp.	5 mL
Sugar or honey	1 tsp.	5 mL
Baby greens	8 oz.	250 g

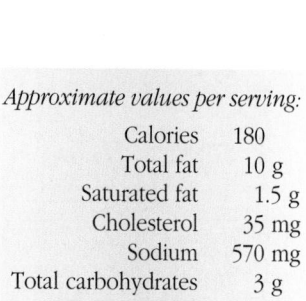

Approximate values per serving:	
Calories	180
Total fat	10 g
Saturated fat	1.5 g
Cholesterol	35 mg
Sodium	570 mg
Total carbohydrates	3 g
Protein	20 g
Vitamin C	15%

1. Using a mortar and pestle or a rolling pin, crush the ingredients for the lavender-pepper coating.

2. Lightly oil the tuna with 2 teaspoons (10 mL) of olive oil; coat lightly and evenly with the lavender-pepper mixture. Heat the remaining oil in a skillet to just smoking and quickly sear the tuna on all sides. This should not take more than 2 minutes. Immediately chill the seared tuna.

3. Mix the ingredients for the mustard sauce. Set aside.

4. To serve, thinly slice the tuna into 3 or 4 medallions per serving. Arrange on a chilled plate with baby greens and a small dollop of the mustard sauce.

◆◆◆

RECIPE 24.28

CHAR-GRILLED CALAMARI WITH WHITE BEAN AND ROASTED VEGETABLE SALAD

MUSTARD GRILLE, MISSISSAUGA, ON
Executive Chef Anthony Borgo

Anthony Borgo
Since graduating in 1991, Anthony has gained a wealth of international experience working in Ireland, England, Switzerland, Japan and Canada and has risen through the ranks in the kitchen to the position of chef.

Yield: 4 Servings

White navy beans	12 oz.	360 g
Zucchini	1 large	1 large
Olive oil	as needed	as needed
Kalamata olives, cut in quarters	12 pieces	12 pieces
Lemon zest	1 Tbsp.	15 mL
Lemon, peel	1 Tbsp.	15 mL

Capers	3 Tbsp.	45 mL
Basil, julienne	2 Tbsp.	30 mL
Chives, finely chopped	2 Tbsp.	30 mL
Red peppers roasted, deseeded, skinned, julienne	2	2
Lemon Basil Vinaigrette (recipe follows)		
Calamari tubes	12 pieces	12 pieces
Calamari tentacles	12 pieces	12 pieces
Salt and pepper	TT	TT
Olive oil	1 oz.	30 mL
Lemon juice	1 oz.	30 mL

1. Cook white beans until tender. Drain and allow to cool.

2. Slice the zucchini into paysanne cut. Roast the zucchini in a sauté pan with a little olive oil. Allow to cool.

3. In a bowl combine the beans, zucchini, olives, lemon zest and lemon peel brunoise, capers, basil, chives and red peppers. Reserve a few spoonfuls of the Lemon Basil Vinaigrette, then toss the bean mixture with the remaining vinaigrette. Set aside.

4. Place the calamari tubes and tentacles in a bowl. Season them with salt, pepper, the olive oil and lemon juice. Cook the calamari on the grill or broiler for a minute or until cooked through.

5. Position equal quantities of the bean salad in the centre of each of the 4 plates. Place 3 calamari tubes on top of each salad. Put three tentacles around the rim of each plate. Spoon the reserved Lemon Basil Vinaigrette around the plates to accent the presentation.

Approximate values per serving:

Calories	419
Total fat	21 g
Saturated fat	3 g
Cholesterol	246 mg
Sodium	815 mg
Total carbohydrates	34 g
Protein	26 g

LEMON BASIL VINAIGRETTE

Yield: 7-1/2 oz. (210 mL)

Lemon juice, squeezed fresh	1 oz.	30 mL
Lemon oil	1 oz.	30 mL
Olive oil	3 oz.	90 mL
Garlic clove	1	1
Basil leaves	8 large	8 large
Salt and pepper	TT	TT

Combine the lemon juice, lemon oil, olive oil, garlic, fresh basil, salt and pepper in a container. Using a whisk or hand-held blender, mix until the vinaigrette is emulsified.

Approximate values per 1 oz. (30 mL) serving:

Calories	182
Total fat	20 g
Saturated fat	2 g
Cholesterol	0 mg
Sodium	359 mg
Total carbohydrates	1 g
Protein	0 g

◆◆◆

RECIPE 24.29
VINE-RIPENED TOMATO SALAD

GREENS RESTAURANT, SAN FRANCISCO, CA
Executive Chef Annie Somerville

Yield: 4 Servings

Vine-ripened tomatoes	1 lb.	450 g
Cherry tomatoes	1/2 pt.	250 mL
Mixed baby greens	4 heads	4 heads
Salt and pepper	TT	TT
Cucumber, sliced on bias	1	1

Continued

Approximate values per serving:

Calories	190
Total fat	11 g
Saturated fat	1.5 g
Cholesterol	0 mg
Sodium	650 mg
Total carbohydrates	17 g
Protein	5 g
Vitamin A	35%
Vitamin C	140%

Claims—no cholesterol; good source of fibre

Extra virgin olive oil	3 Tbsp.	45 mL
Red wine vinegar	2 Tbsp.	30 mL

1. Core the vine-ripened tomatoes and cut into wedges or thick slices. Pluck the stems from the cherry tomatoes; leave whole if small or cut in half if large.
2. Wash the mixed baby greens and dry. Spread the greens on plates or a serving platter and arrange the vine-ripened tomatoes over them. Sprinkle the tomatoes with salt and pepper.
3. Garnish the tomatoes with cucumber slices.
4. Drizzle on the olive oil; follow with a light drizzle of vinegar.
5. Sprinkle the cherry tomatoes over the salad.

◆◆◆

RECIPE 24.30

COBB SALAD

Yield: 8 Entree Servings

Romaine lettuce	8 oz.	250 g
Green leaf lettuce	4 oz.	120 g
Watercress	4 oz.	120 g
Avocados	4	4
Bacon slices	16	16
Roquefort cheese, crumbled	1 lb.	450 g
Turkey breast, roasted, julienne	1 lb.	450 g
Tomato concassé	1 lb.	450 g
Eggs, hard-cooked, chopped	4	4
Dijon mustard vinaigrette	24 oz.	700 mL

Approximate values per serving:

Calories	1000
Total fat	84 g
Saturated fat	18 g
Cholesterol	215 mg
Sodium	1770 mg
Total carbohydrates	21 g
Protein	40 g
Vitamin A	45%
Vitamin C	60%
Calcium	45%
Iron	20%

1. Tear, wash and dry the lettuces. Pick over and wash the watercress.
2. Pit, peel and cut the avocados into wedges.
3. Dice the bacon and cook in a sauté pan until crisp. Remove and drain well.
4. Toss the salad greens together and arrange each of the garnishes on top in an artistic fashion.
5. Prepare a simple vinaigrette dressing using Dijon mustard; serve on the side.

◆◆◆

RECIPE 24.31

GREEK SALAD

Yield: 5 lb. 8 oz. (2.6 kg)

Extra virgin olive oil	4 oz.	120 mL
Lemon juice	1 oz.	25 mL
Red wine vinegar	1 oz.	25 mL
Fresh oregano, chopped	3 Tbsp.	45 mL
English cucumbers or field cucumbers	2	2
Feta cheese	12 oz.	350 g
Red and green peppers, diced	1 lb.	450 g
Olives, kalamata or other Greek variety	1 lb.	450 g

Tomatoes, cut into 6 wedges	3	3
Fresh parsley, chopped	1 oz.	30 g
Red onion	8 oz.	250 g
Black pepper, fresh ground	TT	TT
Romaine lettuce	1 head	1 head

1. To make the dressing, whisk together the olive oil, lemon juice, vinegar and oregano.
2. Dice the cucumber. If using field cucumber, peel and slice in half lengthwise. Remove the seeds and cut into dice
3. Dice or crumble the feta cheese into small pieces.
4. Dice the peppers into 1/2-inch (1-cm) pieces.
5. Combine the olives, cucumbers, tomatoes, chopped parsley and red onion in a bowl and add the dressing. Toss to combine and season to taste with pepper.
6. Line plates or a platter with the romaine lettuce leaves. Add the salad mixture and sprinkle on the feta cheese. Garnish as desired.

Approximate values per 6 oz. (180 g) serving:

Calories	280
Total fat	24 g
Saturated fat	7 g
Cholesterol	35 mg
Sodium	900 mg
Total carbohydrates	9 g
Protein	7 g
Vitamin A	15%
Vitamin C	35%
Calcium	25%
Iron	15%

◆◆◆

RECIPE 24.32

WARM LAMB SALAD WITH WHISKY VINAIGRETTE

Yield: 4 Servings

Lamb loin, eye only	1	1
Salt and pepper	TT	TT
Olive oil	1 Tbsp.	15 mL
New potatoes	8	8
Green onions	4	4
Radicchio	2 heads	2 heads
Garlic cloves, chopped	2	2
Fresh rosemary, chopped	1/2 tsp.	2 mL
Whole butter	2 oz.	60 g
Rye whisky	4 oz.	120 mL
Balsamic vinegar	2 oz.	60 mL
Mustard seeds	1 tsp.	5 mL
Orange supremes (fillets)	24	24

1. Cut the lamb loin into 4 portions and tie each piece so it retains its shape during cooking.
2. Season the lamb with salt and pepper. Sauté it in the olive oil. Transfer to a 350°F (180°C) oven and finish to medium rare.
3. Steam the new potatoes until tender but still firm.
4. Cut the green onions on the bias.
5. Separate the radicchio leaves from the heads.
6. To make the dressing, sauté the garlic and rosemary in the butter without browning. Whisk in the whisky, vinegar and mustard seeds, season with salt and pepper and keep hot.
7. Remove the twine and slice each portion of lamb into 6 slices. Slice the potatoes to the same thickness as the lamb.
8. Using the radicchio as the base, arrange the sliced potatoes, lamb and orange supremes on the plate. Sprinkle with the green onions. Drizzle the dressing over all the ingredients.

Approximate values per serving:

Calories	300
Total fat	17 g
Saturated fat	8 g
Cholesterol	50 mg
Sodium	680 mg
Total carbohydrates	27 g
Protein	8 g
Vitamin A	10%
Calcium	10%

◆◆◆

RECIPE 24.33

ASIAN CHICKEN SALAD

Yield: 3 lb. (1.4 kg)

Rice vinegar	6 oz.	180 mL
Soy sauce, reduced sodium	4 oz.	120 mL
Sugar	2 Tbsp.	30 mL
Fresh ginger, minced	3 Tbsp.	45 mL
White pepper	1 tsp.	5 mL
Chicken breast, boneless, skinless	1 lb. 8 oz.	700 g
Sesame oil	1 oz.	30 mL
Snow peas, julienne	4 oz.	120 g
Carrot, julienne	4 oz.	120 g
Celery, julienne	4 oz.	120 g
Jicama, julienne	4 oz.	120 g
Fresh cilantro leaves	2 Tbsp.	30 mL

Approximate values per 4 oz. (120 g) serving:

Calories	160
Total fat	4.5 g
Saturated fat	1 g
Cholesterol	50 mg
Sodium	740 mg
Total carbohydrates	10 g
Protein	19 g
Vitamin A	25%
Vitamin C	15%

1. Combine the vinegar, soy sauce, sugar, ginger and white pepper. Set aside.
2. Cut the chicken breast into strips approximately 1/2 × 1/2 × 3 inches (1 × 1 × 5 cm). Stir-fry the chicken in the sesame oil until done. Remove, cool and refrigerate.
3. Blanch the vegetables in salted water. Refresh and drain well.
4. Combine the chicken with the vegetables and the dressing; add the cilantro. Toss and serve.

◆◆◆

RECIPE 24.34

ASPARAGUS AND MINTED NEW POTATO SALAD WITH SUN-DRIED TOMATO MAYONNAISE

SHAW CONFERENCE CENTRE, EDMONTON, AB
Executive Chef Simon Smotkowicz

Simon Smotkowicz

Simon has been a member and a leader of award-winning Canadian culinary teams for many years, most recently managing Team Canada to a world championship in Glasgow in 1997. In 1995 he was elected Chef of the Year for the Western Region by his peers in the CFCC.

Yield: 4 Servings

Asparagus	1 lb	450 g
Olive oil	4 Tbsp.	60 mL
Raspberry vinegar	4 tsp.	20 mL
New potatoes, very small	16 oz.	450 g
Fresh mint, chopped	3 Tbsp.	45 mL
Salt	2 tsp.	10 mL
Sun-dried tomatoes, finely chopped	1 Tbsp.	15 mL
White wine or water	2 Tbsp.	30 mL
Mayonnaise	8 oz.	225 mL
Fresh mint, chopped	1 Tbsp.	15 mL
Spinach or pea tops	as needed	as needed

1. To prepare the asparagus, bring a large pot of salted water to a boil. Add the asparagus and cook for 3–5 minutes.
2. Cool at once in a bowl filled with iced water.
3. To prepare the vinaigrette, whisk together the olive oil and raspberry vinegar.

4. In a bowl, toss the asparagus with the vinaigrette. Season with salt and pepper and let sit for 1 hour before serving.

5. To prepare the potato salad, place the potatoes, mint and salt in a saucepan. Cover the potatoes with cold water.

6. Bring to a boil and simmer for 15–20 minutes, until done. Drain and let cool.

7. Mix together the sun-dried tomatoes, white wine and mayonnaise.

8. In a bowl, toss the potatoes with the sun-dried tomato mayonnaise.

9. To assemble, lightly cover each plate with springtime greens such as spinach (or pea tops).

10. Mound the potato salad on top of the greens and arrange the asparagus on top.

Approximate values per serving:

Calories	596
Total fat	56 g
Saturated fat	8 g
Cholesterol	31 mg
Sodium	818 mg
Total carbohydrates	20 g
Protein	6 g

◆◆◆

RECIPE 24.35
POTATO SALAD

Yield: 6 lb. 8 oz. (3 kg)

Potatoes, waxy	4 lb.	1.8 kg
Eggs, hard-cooked	6	6
Celery, medium dice	8 oz.	250 g
Green onions, sliced	1 bunch	1 bunch
Mayonnaise	10 oz.	250 mL
Sour cream	6 oz.	200 mL
Red wine or tarragon vinegar	2 oz.	50 mL
Dijon-style mustard	2 oz.	60 mL
Fresh parsley, chopped	1 oz.	30 g
Salt and pepper	TT	TT

1. Boil the potatoes in salted water until nearly cooked. Drain the potatoes, spread them on a sheet pan and refrigerate until cold.

2. Peel and cut the cold potatoes into large dice.

3. Peel and chop the eggs.

4. Combine all ingredients and adjust the seasonings with salt and pepper.

Approximate values per 4 oz. (120 g) serving:

Calories	200
Total fat	16 g
Saturated fat	3 g
Cholesterol	65 mg
Sodium	390 mg
Total carbohydrates	11 g
Protein	3 g
Vitamin C	15%

◆◆◆

RECIPE 24.36
CREAMY COLESLAW

Yield: 2 lb. (1 kg)

Mayonnaise	8 oz.	250 mL
Sour cream or crème fraîche	4 oz.	120 mL
Sugar	1 oz.	30 g
Cider vinegar	1 oz.	30 mL
Green cabbage, shredded	1 lb.	450 g
Celery, julienne	8 oz.	250 g
Carrot, shredded	4 oz.	120 g
Salt and white pepper	TT	TT

1. Combine the mayonnaise, sour cream or crème fraîche, sugar and vinegar in a bowl; whisk together.

2. Add the shredded cabbage, celery and carrots to the dressing and mix well. Season to taste with salt and pepper.

Approximate values per 4 oz. (120 g) serving:

Calories	200
Total fat	19 g
Saturated fat	4.5 g
Cholesterol	20 mg
Sodium	340 mg
Total carbohydrates	8 g
Protein	1 g
Vitamin A	20%
Vitamin C	50%

♦♦♦

RECIPE 24.37

COUSCOUS SALAD WITH ORANGE DRESSING

Yield: 3 lb. (1.4 kg)

Couscous	6 oz.	180 g
Red bell pepper, medium dice	1	1
Green bell pepper, medium dice	1	1
Green onions, sliced on the bias	1 bunch	1 bunch
Cucumbers, peeled, seeded, medium dice	6 oz.	180 g
Black olives, pitted	4 oz.	120 g
Red onion, julienne	6 oz.	180 g
Dressing:		
Orange juice concentrate	3 oz.	90 mL
Water	2 oz.	60 mL
Rice vinegar	2 oz.	60 mL
Garlic, chopped	1 tsp.	5 mL
Salt	1 tsp.	5 mL
Pepper	1 tsp.	5 mL
Fresh oregano, chopped	2 tsp.	10 mL
Salad oil	3 oz.	90 mL
Honey	1 oz.	30 mL
Fresh thyme, chopped	2 tsp.	10 mL

*Approximate values per
3 oz. (90 g) serving:*

Calories	90
Total fat	6 g
Saturated fat	.5 g
Cholesterol	0 mg
Sodium	200 mg
Total carbohydrates	7 g
Protein	1 g
Vitamin C	35%

Claims—low saturated fat; no cholesterol

1. Steam the couscous until tender; set aside to cool.
2. Combine the couscous with the vegetables.
3. Whisk together all dressing ingredients.
4. Combine the salad ingredients with the dressing. Chill thoroughly before serving.

♦♦♦

RECIPE 24.38

CUCUMBER-YOGURT SALAD

Yield: 1 qt. (1 L)

Plain yogurt	1 lb.	500 g
Cucumber, peeled and grated	12 oz.	350 g
Cumin	1 tsp.	5 mL
Salt and pepper	TT	TT
Sugar	1/2 oz.	15 g
Lime juice	1/2 oz.	15 g
Fresh cilantro, chopped	2 Tbsp.	30 mL
Jalapeño, minced	1 tsp.	5 mL
Paprika	as needed	as needed

*Approximate values per
3 oz. (90 mL) serving:*

Calories	40
Total fat	0 g
Saturated fat	0 g
Cholesterol	0 mg
Sodium	280 mg
Total carbohydrates	7 g
Protein	3 g
Calcium	10%

Claims—fat free; low calorie

1. Stir together all ingredients except the paprika. Chill for several hours before service.
2. Dust the top of the salad lightly with paprika at the time of service.

♦♦♦

RECIPE 24.39

Tabbouleh (Bulgur Wheat) Salad

Yield: 15 3-oz. (90-g) Servings

Bulgur	10 oz.	300 g
Onions, brunoise	8 oz.	250 g
Green onions, sliced	2 oz.	60 g
Fresh parsley, chopped	6 oz.	180 g
Fresh mint, chopped	2 oz.	60 g
Olive oil	8 oz.	250 mL
Lemon juice	8 oz.	250 mL
Tomato concassé	1 lb.	500 g
Salt and pepper	TT	TT
Pine nuts, toasted	4 oz.	120 g

Aproximate values per 4 oz. (120 g) serving:

Calories	280
Total fat	21 g
Saturated fat	3 g
Cholesterol	0 mg
Sodium	180 mg
Total Carbohydrates	17 g
Protein	5 g
Vitamin A	30%
Vitamin C	60%
Iron	70%

Claims—no cholesterol; good source of fibre

1. Place the bulgur in a bowl and cover with cold water. Soak the bulgur until tender, approximately 2 hours.
2. Drain the bulgur and squeeze out all of the excess water.
3. Add the onions, green onions, parsley, mint, olive oil and lemon juice. Mix well.
4. Add the tomatoes; mix to combine. Season with salt and pepper.
5. Garnish with the toasted pine nuts.

*W*EBLINKS

Salad Vegetables

    www.produceoasis.com/Hierarchy_folder/Vegetables_folder/L2SVeg_folder/MainSVeg.html

The Leafy Greens Council

    www.leafy-greens.org/

Salad Dressings

    www.cs.cmu.edu/~mjw/recipes/salad/salad-dressing/index.html

Salad Dressing Recipes

    SOAR.Berkeley.edu/recipes/dressings/

CHAPTER 25 FRUITS

After studying this chapter you will be able to:

✦ identify a variety of fruits
✦ purchase fruits appropriate for your needs
✦ store fruits properly
✦ explain how fruits are preserved
✦ prepare fruits for cooking or service: segment and zest citrus fruits, cut citrus peels, peel prickly pears, core apples, pit cherries, pit and cut mangoes, trim and slice pineapples
✦ apply various cooking methods to fruits: broil or grill, bake, sauté, poach, simmer, make preserves

Ripe—*fully grown and developed; the fruit's flavour, texture and appearance are at their peak and the fruit is ready to use as food.*

◆◆◆

HYBRIDS AND VARIETIES

Several varieties of fruits are extremely responsive to selective breeding and cross-breeding and have been toyed with by botanists and growers since at least the time of ancient Rome. Two distinct products are recognized: hybrids and varieties. **Hybrids** result from crossbreeding fruits from different species that are genetically unalike. The result is a unique product. Citrus is particularly responsive to hybridization. **Varieties** result from breeding fruits of the same species that have different qualities or characteristics. Breeding two varieties of apples, for example, produces a third variety with the best qualities of both parents.

---

*B*otanically, a fruit is an organ that develops from the ovary of a flowering plant and contains one or more seeds. Culinarily, a fruit is the perfect snack food; the basis of a dessert, colourful sauce or soup; or an accompaniment to meat, fish, shellfish or poultry. No food group offers a greater variety of colours, flavours and textures than fruit.

This chapter identifies many of the fruits typically used by food service operations. It then addresses general considerations in purchasing fresh and preserved fruits. A discussion follows about some of the cooking methods presented in Chapter 9, Principles of Cooking, as they apply to fruits. Recipes in which a fruit is the primary ingredient are presented at the end of this chapter.

IDENTIFYING FRUITS

This book presents fruits according to the ways most people view them and use them, rather than by rigid botanical classifications. Fruits are divided here into eight categories: berries, citrus, exotics, grapes, melons, pomes, stone fruits and tropicals, according to either their shape, seed structure or natural habitat. Botanically, tomatoes, beans, eggplant, capsicum peppers and other produce are fruits. But in ordinary thinking they are not; they are vegetables and are discussed in Chapter 22, Vegetables.

A fruit may have several names, varying from region to region or on a purveyor's whim. Botanists are also constantly reclassifying items to fit new findings. The names given here follow generally accepted custom and usage.

Berries

Berries are small, juicy fruits that grow on vines and bushes worldwide. Berries are characterized by thin skins and many tiny seeds that are often so small they go unnoticed. Some of the fruits classified here as berries do not fit the botanical definition (for example, raspberries and strawberries), while fruits that are berries botanically (for example, bananas and grapes) are classified elsewhere.

Berries may be eaten plain or used in everything from beer to bread, soup to sorbet. They make especially fine jams and compotes.

Berries must be fully **ripened** on the vine, as they will not ripen further after harvesting. Select berries that are plump and fully coloured. Avoid juice-stained containers and berries with whitish-grey or black spots of mould. All berries should be refrigerated and used promptly. Do not wash berries until you are ready to use them, as washing removes some of their aroma and softens them.

Blackberries   *Blackberries*

Blackberries are similar to raspberries, but are larger and shinier, with a deep purple to black colour. Thorny blackberry vines are readily found in the wild; commercial production is limited. Peak season is mid-June through August. Loganberries, ollalie berries and boysenberries are blackberry hybrids.

Blueberries

Blueberries (Fr. *myrtilles*) are small and firm, with a true blue to almost black skin and a juicy, light grey-blue interior. Cultivated berries (high-bush varieties) tend to be larger than wild (low-bush) ones. Blueberries are native to North America and are grown commercially in almost all provinces of Canada, with the Lac St. Jean region being the most famous. Peak season is short, from mid-June to mid-August.

Blueberries

Cranberries

Cranberries, another native North American food, are tart, firm fruit with a mottled red skin. They grow on low vines in cultivated bogs (swamps) throughout Ontario, British Columbia, Massachusetts, Wisconsin and New Jersey. Rarely eaten raw, they are made into sauce or relish or are used in breads, pies or pastries. Cranberries are readily available frozen, dried (candied) or made into a jelly-type sauce and canned. Although colour does not indicate ripeness, cranberries should be picked over before cooking to remove those that are soft or bruised. Peak harvesting season is from Labour Day through October, leading to the association of cranberries with Thanksgiving dinner.

Cranberries

Currants

Currants are tiny, tart fruits that grow on shrubs in grapelike clusters. The most common are a beautiful, almost translucent red, but black and golden (or white) varieties also exist. All varieties are used for jams, jellies and sauces, and black currants are made into a liqueur, crème de cassis. Although rarely grown in North America, currants are very popular and widely available in Europe, with a peak season during the late summer. (The dried fruits called currants are not produced from these berries; they are a special variety of dried grapes.)

White Currants

Red Currants

Raspberries

Raspberries (Fr. *framboises*) are perhaps the most delicate of all fruits. They have a tart flavour and velvety texture. Red raspberries are the most common, with black, purple and golden berries available in some markets. When ripe, the berry pulls away easily from its white core, leaving the characteristic hollow centre. Because they can be easily crushed and are susceptible to mould, most of the raspberries grown are marketed frozen. They grow on thorny vines in cool climates from British Columbia to the Maritimes and are imported from New Zealand and South America. The peak domestic season is from late May through November.

Raspberries

Strawberries

Strawberries (Fr. *fraises*) are brilliant red, heart-shaped fruits that grow on vines. Actually a perennial herb, the berry's flesh is covered by tiny black seeds called achenes, which are the plant's true fruits. Select berries with a good red colour and intact green leafy hull. (The hulls can be easily removed with a paring knife.) Avoid berries with soft or brown spots. Huge berries may be lovely to look at but they often have hollow centres and little flavour or juice. Although available to some extent all year, fresh strawberries are at their peak from April through June.

Strawberries

The tiny wild or Alpine berries, known by their French name *fraises des bois*, have a particularly intense flavour and aroma. They are not widely available commercially in Canada.

Citrus (genus Citrus)

Citrus fruits include lemons, limes, grapefruits, tangerines, kumquats, oranges and several hybrids. They are characterized by a thick rind, most of which is a bitter white pith (albedo) with a thin exterior layer of coloured skin known as the zest. Their flesh is segmented and juicy. Citrus fruits are acidic, with a strong aroma; their flavours vary from bitter to tart to sweet.

Citrus fruits grow on trees and shrubs in tropical and subtropical climates worldwide. All citrus fruits are fully ripened on the tree and will not ripen further after harvesting. They should be refrigerated for longest storage.

Select fruits that feel heavy and have thin, smooth skins. Avoid those with large blemishes or moist spots.

Grapefruits

Grapefruits (Fr. *pamplemousse*) are large and round with a yellow skin, thick rind and tart flesh. They are an 18th-century hybrid of the orange and pummelo (a large, coarse fruit used mostly in Middle and Far Eastern cuisines). Two varieties of grapefruit are widely available all year: white-fleshed and pink- or ruby-fleshed. White grapefruits produce the finest juice, although pink grapefruits are sweeter. Fresh grapefruits are best eaten raw or topped with brown sugar and lightly broiled. Grapefruit segments are available canned in syrup.

White Grapefruits

Ruby Grapefruits

Kumquats

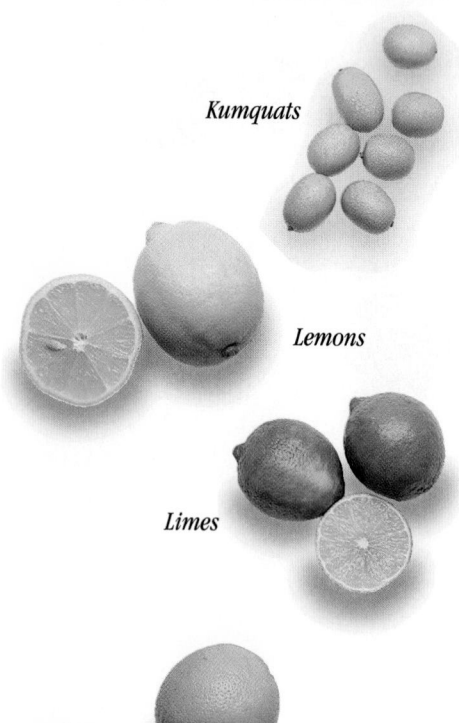
Kumquats

Kumquats are very small, oval-shaped, orange-coloured fruits with a soft, sweet skin and slightly bitter flesh. They can be eaten whole, either raw or preserved in syrup, and may be used in jams and preserves.

Lemons

Lemons

The most commonly used citrus fruits, lemons (Fr. *citrons*), are oval-shaped, bright yellow fruits available all year. Their strongly acidic flavour makes them unpleasant to eat raw but perfect for flavouring desserts and confections. Lemon juice is also widely used in sauces, especially for fish, shellfish and poultry. Lemon zest is candied or used as garnish.

Limes

Limes

Limes (Fr. *limons*) are small fruits with thin skins ranging from yellow-green to dark green. Limes are too tart to eat raw and are often substituted for lemons in prepared dishes. They are also juiced or used in cocktails, curries or desserts. Lime zest can be grated and used to give colour and flavour to a variety of dishes. Limes are available all year, with a peak season during the summer.

Oranges

Oranges are round fruits with a juicy, orange-coloured flesh and a thin, orange skin. They can be either sweet or bitter.

Valencia oranges and navel oranges (a seedless variety) are the most popular sweet oranges. They can be juiced for beverages or sauces and the flesh may be eaten raw, added to salads, cooked in desserts or used as a garnish. The zest may be grated or julienned for sauces or garnish. Sweet oranges are

Valencia Oranges

available all year, with peak season from December to April. Blood oranges are also sweet but are small, with a rough, reddish skin. Their flesh is streaked with a blood-red colour. Blood oranges are available primarily during the winter months and are eaten raw, juiced or used in salads or sauces. When selecting sweet oranges, look for fruits that feel plump and heavy, with unblemished skin. The colour of the skin depends on weather conditions; a green rind does not affect the flavour of the flesh.

Bitter oranges include the Seville and bergamot. They are used primarily for the essential oils found in their zest. Oil of bergamot gives Earl Grey tea its distinctive flavour; oil of Seville is essential to curaçao, Grand Marnier and orange flower water. Seville oranges are also used in marmalades and sauces for meats and poultry.

Navel Oranges

Blood Oranges

Tangerines

Tangerines, sometimes referred to as mandarins, are small and dark orange. Their rind is loose and easily removed to reveal sweet, juicy, aromatic segments. Tangerines are most often eaten fresh and uncooked, but are available canned as mandarin oranges.

Tangelos are a hybrid of tangerines and grapefruits. They are the size of a medium orange; they have a bulbous stem end and few to no seeds.

Tangerines

BASIC PROCEDURE FOR SEGMENTING CITRUS FRUITS

1. Citrus segments, known as fillets or *supremes*, are made by first carefully cutting off the entire peel (including the bitter white pith) in even slices.

2. Individual fillets are then removed by gently cutting alongside each membrane.

BASIC PROCEDURE FOR ZESTING CITRUS FRUITS

A five-hole zester is used to remove paper-thin strips of the coloured rind.

BASIC PROCEDURE FOR CUTTING CITRUS PEELS

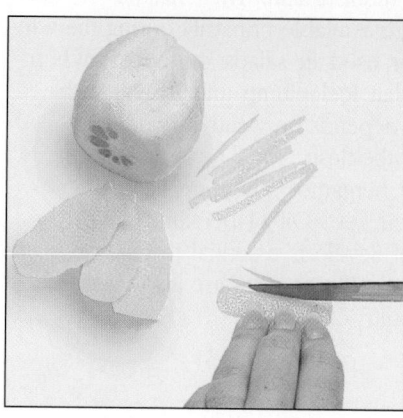

Large strips of citrus zest may be used as a garnish or to flavour soups or sauces.

Exotics

Improved transportation has led to the increasing availability (although sporadic in some areas) of exotic or unusual fresh fruits such as figs, persimmons, pomegranates, prickly pears, rhubarb and star fruits. Other exotic fruits, such as breadfruit, lychee, guava, feijoa and loquat, still are available only on a limited basis from specialty purveyors and are not discussed here.

Figs

Figs (Fr. *figues*) are the fruit of ficus trees. They are small, soft, pear-shaped fruits with an intensely sweet flavour and rich, moist texture made crunchy by a multitude of tiny seeds. Fresh figs can be sliced and served in salads or with cured meats such as prosciutto. They can also be baked, poached or used in jams, preserves or compotes.

Dark-skinned figs, known as Mission figs, are a variety planted at Pacific Coast missions during the 18th century. They have a thin skin and small seeds and are available fresh, canned or dried. The white-skinned figs grown commercially include the White Adriatic, used principally for drying and baking, and the all-purpose Kadota. The most important domestic variety, however, is the Calimyrna. These large figs have a rich yellow colour and large nutty seeds. Fresh Calimyrna figs are the finest for eating out of hand; they are also available dried.

For the best flavour, figs should be fully ripened on the tree. Unfortunately, fully ripened figs are very delicate and difficult to transport. Most figs are in season from June through October; fresh Calimyrna figs are available only during June.

Persimmons

Persimmons

Persimmons, sometimes referred to as kaki or Sharon fruits, are a bright orange, acorn-shaped fruit with a glossy skin and a large papery blossom. The flesh is bright orange and jellylike, with a mild but rich flavour similar to honey and plums. Persimmons should be peeled before use; any seeds should be discarded. Select bright orange fruits and refrigerate only after they are completely ripe. When ripe, persimmons will be very soft and the skin will have an almost translucent appearance.

Ripe persimmons are delicious eaten raw; halved and topped with cream or soft cheese; or peeled, sliced and added to fruit salads. Persimmon bread, muffins, cakes and pies are also popular. Underripe persimmons are almost inedible, however. They are strongly tannic with a chalky or cottony texture.

Persimmons are tree fruits grown in subtropical areas worldwide, although the Asian varieties—now grown in California—are the most common. Fresh persimmons are available from October through January.

Pomegranates

An ancient fruit native to Persia (now Iran), pomegranates have long been a subject of poetry and a symbol of fertility. Pomegranates are round, about the size of a large orange, with a pronounced calyx. The skin forms a hard shell with a pinkish-red colour. The interior is filled with hundreds of small, red seeds (which are, botanically, the actual fruits) surrounded by juicy red pulp. An inedible yellow membrane separates the seeds into compartments. Pomegranates are sweet-sour and the seeds are pleasantly crunchy. The bright red seeds make an attractive garnish. Pomegranate juice is a popular beverage in Mediterranean cuisines and grenadine syrup is made from concentrated pomegranate juice.

Pomegranates

Select heavy fruits that are not rock-hard, cracked or heavily bruised. Whole pomegranates can be refrigerated for several weeks. Pomegranates are available from September through December, with peak season in October.

Prickly Pears

Prickly pear fruits, also known as cactus pears and barbary figs, are actually the berries of several varieties of cactus. They are barrel- or pear-shaped, about the size of a large egg. Their thick, firm skin is green or purple with small sharp pins and nearly invisible stinging fibres. Their flesh is spongy, sweet and a brilliant pink-red, dotted with small black seeds. Prickly pears have the aroma of watermelon and the flavour of sugar-water.

Prickly Pears

Once peeled, prickly pears can be diced and eaten raw, or they can be puréed for making jams, sauces, custards or sorbets, to which they give a vivid pink colour. Prickly pears are especially common in Mexican and south-western cuisines.

Select fruits that are full-coloured, heavy and tender, but not too soft. Avoid those with mushy or bruised spots. Ripe prickly pears can be refrigerated for a week or more. Prickly pears are grown in Mexico and several states of the south-western U.S. and are available from September through December.

BASIC PROCEDURE FOR PEELING PRICKLY PEARS

1. To avoid being stung by a prickly pear, hold it steady with a fork, then use a knife to cut off both ends.

2. Cut a lengthwise slit through the skin. Slip the tip of the knife into the cut and peel away the skin by holding it down while rolling the fruit away.

Rhubarb

Rhubarb

Although botanically a vegetable, rhubarb is most often prepared as a fruit. It is a perennial plant that grows well in temperate and cold climates. Only the pinkish-red stems are edible; the leaves contain high amounts of oxalic acid, which is toxic.

Rhubarb stems are extremely acidic, requiring large amounts of sugar to create the desired sweet-sour taste. Cinnamon, ginger, orange and strawberry are particularly compatible with rhubarb. It is excellent for pies, cobblers, preserves or stewing. Young, tender stalks of rhubarb do not need to be peeled. When cooked, rhubarb becomes very soft and turns a beautiful light pink colour.

Fresh rhubarb is sold as whole stalks, with the leaves removed. Select crisp, unblemished stalks. Peak season is during the early spring, from February through May. Frozen rhubarb pieces are readily available and are excellent for pies, tarts or jams.

Star Fruits

Star fruits, also known as carambola, are oval, up to 5 inches (12.5 cm) long, with five prominent ribs or wings running their length. A cross-section cut is shaped like a star. The edible skin is a waxy orange-yellow; it covers a dry, paler yellow flesh. Its flavour is similar to plums, sweet but bland. Star fruits do not need to be peeled or seeded. They are most often sliced and added to fruit salad or used as a garnish. Unripe fruits can be cooked in stews or chutneys.

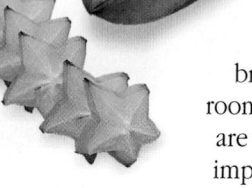

Colour and aroma are the best indicators of ripeness. The fruits should be a deep golden-yellow and the edge of the ribs should be brown. The aroma should be full and floral. Green fruits can be kept at room temperature to ripen, then refrigerated for up to two weeks. Star fruits are cultivated in Hawaii, Florida, California and Asia, though some are still imported from the Caribbean. Fresh fruits are available from August to February.

Star Fruit

Grapes (Vitis vinifera)

Grapes are the single largest fruit crop in the world, due, of course, to their use in wine making. This section, however, discusses only table grapes, those grown for eating. Grapes are berries that grow on vines in large clusters. California is the world's largest producer, with more than a dozen varieties grown for table use. Grapes are classified by colour as white (which are actually green) or black (which are actually red). White grapes are generally blander than black ones, with a thinner skin and firmer flesh.

The grape's colour and most of its flavour are found in the skin. Grapes are usually eaten raw, either alone or in fruit salads. They are also used as a garnish or accompaniment to desserts and cheeses. Dried grapes are known as raisins (usually made from Thompson Seedless or muscat grapes), currants (made from Black Corinth grapes and labelled as Zante currants) or sultanas (made from sultana grapes).

Grapes are available all year because the many varieties have different harvesting schedules. Look for firm, unblemished fruits that are firmly attached to the stem. A surface bloom or dusty appearance is caused by yeasts and indicates recent harvesting. Wrinkled grapes or those with brown spots around the stem are past their prime. All grapes should be rinsed and drained prior to use.

◆◆◆

GRAPES INTO WINE

Virtually all the fine wine made in the world comes from varieties of a single grape species, *Vitis vinifera*. Although a European species, it is also grown in the United States, Canada, South Africa, South America, the Middle East, Australia and wherever fine wine is made. The variety of grapes used in any given wine determines the wine's character, and most wine-producing countries carefully regulate the growing areas and production of grapes.

North American wines are known by their varietal names, whereas European wines are generally known by the vineyard's location. The major varietals of wine grapes and the wines in which they are used are listed below.

Grape Varietal	Wine
Pinot Noir	Red Burgundy and champagne
Chardonnay	White Burgundy, Chablis and champagne
Syrah	Côte Rotie and Hermitage
Cabernet Sauvignon	Bordeaux and red Graves
Sauvignon Blanc	Sauterne, white Graves, Fumé Blanc and Sancerre
Merlot	Saint-Emilion and for blending with Cabernet Sauvignon
Zinfandel	Red and white Zinfandel (California claims a virtual monopoly)
Chenin Blanc	Vouvray

Red Flame Grapes

Red Flame grapes are a seedless California hybrid, second only in importance to the Thompson Seedless. Red Flame grapes are large and round with a slightly tart flavour and variegated red colour.

Red Flame Grapes

Thompson Seedless Grapes

The most commercially important table grapes are a variety known as Thompson Seedless, which are pale green with a crisp texture and sweet flavour. Peak season is from June to November. Many are dried in the hot desert sun of California's San Joaquin Valley to produce dark raisins. For golden raisins, Thompson Seedless grapes are treated with sulphur dioxide to prevent browning, then dried mechanically.

Of the table grapes containing seeds, the most important varieties are the Concord, Ribier and Emperor. They range from light red to deep black in colour, and all three are in season during the autumn. Concord grapes, one of the few grape varieties native to the New World, are especially important for making juices and jellies.

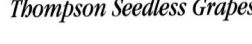

Thompson Seedless Grapes

Melons

Like pumpkins and cucumbers, melons are members of the gourd family (*Cucurbitaceae*). The dozens of melon varieties can be divided into two general types: sweet (or dessert) melons and watermelons. Sweet melons have a tan, green or yellow netted or farrowed rind and dense, fragrant flesh. Watermelon has a thick, dark green rind surrounding crisp, watery flesh.

Melons are almost 90% water, so cooking destroys their texture, quickly turning the flesh to mush. Most are served simply sliced, perhaps with a bit of lemon

Cantaloupes

Casaba Melons

Crenshaw Melons

or lime juice. Melons also blend well in fruit salads or with rich, cured meats such as prosciutto. Melons may be puréed and made into soups or sorbets.

Melons should be vine-ripened. A ripe melon should yield slightly and spring back when pressed at the blossom end (opposite the stem). It should also give off a strong aroma. Avoid melons that are very soft or feel damp at the stem end. Ripe melons may be stored in the refrigerator, although the flavour will be better at room temperature. Slightly underripe melons can be stored at room temperature to allow flavour and aroma to develop.

Cantaloupes

North American cantaloupes, which are actually muskmelons, are sweet melons with a thick, yellow-green netted rind, a sweet, moist, orange flesh and a strong aroma. (European cantaloupes, which are not generally available in this country, are more craggy and furrowed in appearance.) As with all sweet melons, the many small seeds are found in a central cavity. Cantaloupes are excellent for eating alone and are especially good with ham or rich meats.

Avoid cantaloupes with the pronounced yellow colour or mouldy aroma that indicates overripeness. Mexican imports ensure a year-round supply, although their peak season is summer.

Casaba Melons

Casaba melons are a teardrop-shaped sweet melon. They have a coarse, yellow skin and a thick, ridged rind; their flesh is creamy white to yellow. Casaba melons are used like cantaloupes. Casaba melons do not have an aroma, so selection must be based on a deep skin colour and the absence of dark or moist patches. Peak season is during September and October.

Crenshaw Melons

Crenshaw (or cranshaw) melons have a mottled, green-yellow ridged rind and orange-pink flesh. Crenshaws are large and pear-shaped, with a strong aroma. The flesh has a rich, spicy flavour and may be used like cantaloupe. Crenshaws are available from July through October, with peak season during August and September.

Honeydew Melons

Honeydew melons are large oval melons with a smooth rind that ranges from white to pale green. Although the flesh is generally pale green, with a mild, sweet flavour, pink- or gold-fleshed honeydews are also available.

Gold Honeydews

Green Honeydews

Like casaba melons, honeydew melons have no aroma. They are available almost all year, with peak season from June through October.

Santa Claus Melons

Santa Claus or Christmas melons are large, elongated melons with a green-and-yellow-striped, smooth rind. The flesh is creamy white or yellow and tastes like casaba. They are a winter variety, with peak availability during December, which explains the name.

Santa Claus Melons

Watermelons

Watermelons are large (up to 30 pounds or 13.5 kg), round or oval-shaped melons with a thick rind. The skin may be solid green, green-striped or mottled with white. The flesh is crisp and extremely juicy with small, hard, black seeds throughout. Seedless hybrids are available, although they are relatively expensive. Most watermelons have pink to red flesh, although golden-fleshed varieties are becoming more common.

   Watermelons are of a different genus from the sweet melons described above. They are native to tropical Africa and are now grown commercially in Texas and several of the southern U.S. states.

Red Seedless Watermelon

Gold Watermelon

Pomes *(family* Rosaceae*)*

Pomes are tree fruits with thin skin and firm flesh surrounding a central core containing many small seeds called pips or carpels. Pomes include apples, pears and quince.

Apples

Apples (Fr. *pommes*), perhaps the most common and commonly appreciated of all fruits, grow on trees in temperate zones worldwide. They are popular

Rome   *Red Delicious*

Granny Smith   *Golden Delicious*

McIntosh

because of their convenience, taste, variety and availability.

Apples can be eaten raw out of hand, or they can be used in a wide variety of cooked or baked dishes. They are equally useful in breads, desserts or vegetable dishes and go well with game, pork and poultry. Classic dishes prepared with apples are often referred to as *à la Normande*. Apple juice (cider) produces alcoholic and nonalcoholic beverages and cider vinegar.

Of the hundreds of known apple varieties, only 20 or so are commercially significant in Canada. Several varieties and their characteristics are noted in Table 25.1. Most have a moist, creamy white flesh with a thin skin of yellow, green or red. They range in flavour from very sweet to very tart, with an equally broad range of textures, from firm and crisp to soft and mealy.

In Europe, apples are divided into distinct cooking and eating varieties. Cooking varieties are those that disintegrate to a purée when cooked. North American varieties are less rigidly classified. Nevertheless, not all apples are appropriate for all types of cooking. Those that retain their shape better during cooking are the best choices where slices or appearance is important. Varieties with a higher malic acid content break down easily, making them more appropriate for applesauce or juicing. Either type may be eaten out of hand, depending on personal preference.

Although not native to North America, apples are now grown commercially in most provinces of Canada, with Ontario, British Columbia and Nova Scotia leading in production. Apples are harvested when still slightly underripe, then stored in a controlled atmosphere (temperature and oxygen are greatly reduced) for extended periods until ready for sale. Modern storage techniques make fresh apples available all year, although peak season is during the autumn. Also, imports ensure a constant supply.

When selecting apples, look for smooth, unbroken skins and firm fruits, without soft spots or bruises. Badly bruised or rotting apples should be discarded immediately. They emit quantities of ethylene gas that speed spoilage of nearby fruits. (Remember the saying about "one bad apple spoils the barrel.") Store apples chilled for up to six weeks. Apple peels (the skin) may be eaten or removed as desired, but in either case, apples should be washed just prior to use to remove pesticides and any wax that was applied to improve appearance. Apple slices may be frozen (often with sugar or citric acid added to slow spoilage) or dried.

TABLE 25.1   APPLE VARIETIES

Variety	Skin Colour	Flavour	Texture	Peak Season	Use
Golden Delicious	Glossy, greenish-gold	Sweet	Semifirm	Sept.–Oct.	In tarts; with cheese; in salads
Granny Smith	Bright green	Tart	Firm and crisp	Oct.–Nov.	Eating; in tarts
Jonathan	Brilliant red	Tart to acidic	Tender	Sept.–Oct.	Eating; all-purpose
McIntosh	Red with green background	Tart to acidic	Soft	Fall	Applesauce; in closed pies
Pippin (Newton)	Greenish-yellow	Tart	Semifirm	Fall	In pies; eating; baking
Red Delicious	Deep red	Sweet but bland	Soft to mealy	Sept.–Oct.	Eating
Rome	Red	Sweet-tart	Firm	Oct.–Nov.	Baking; pies; sauces
Winesap	Dark red with yellow streaks	Tangy	Crisp	Oct.–Nov.	Cider; all-purpose

BASIC PROCEDURE FOR CORING APPLES

1. Remove the core from a whole apple with an apple corer by inserting the corer from the stem end and pushing out the cylinder containing the core and seeds.

2. Alternatively, first cut an apple into quarters, then use a paring knife to cut away the core and seeds.

Pears

Pears (Fr. *poires*) are an ancient tree fruit grown in temperate areas throughout the world. Most of the pears marketed in this country are grown in California, Washington, Oregon and British Columbia.

Although literally thousands of pear varieties have been identified, only a dozen or so are commercially significant. Several varieties and their characteristics are noted in Table 25.2. Pear varieties vary widely in size, colour and flavour. They are most often eaten out of hand, but can be baked or poached. Pears are delicious with cheese, especially blue cheeses, and can be used in fruit salads, compotes or preserves.

Asian pears, also known as Chinese pears or apple-pears, are of a different species than common pears. They have the moist, sweet flavour of a pear and the round shape and crisp texture of an apple. They are becoming increasingly popular in this country, particularly those known as Twentieth Century or Nijisseiki.

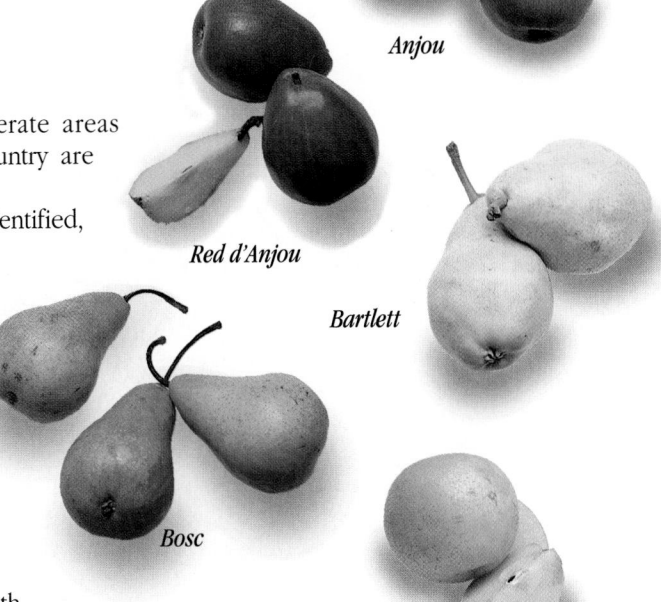

Anjou

Red d'Anjou

Bartlett

Bosc

Asian Pears

TABLE 25.2	PEAR VARIETIES				
Variety	Appearance	Flavour	Texture	Peak Season	Use
Anjou (Beurre d'Anjou)	Greenish-yellow skin; egg-shaped with short neck; red variety also available	Sweet and juicy	Firm, keeps well	Oct.–May	Eating; poaching; baking
Bartlett (Williams)	Thin yellow skin; bell-shaped; red variety also available	Very sweet, buttery, juicy	Tender	Aug.–Dec.	Eating; canning; in salads
Bosc	Golden-brown skin; long, tapered neck	Buttery	Dry, holds its shape well	Sept.–May	Poaching; baking
Comice	Yellow-green skin; large and chubby	Sweet, juicy	Smooth	Oct.–Feb.	Eating
Seckel	Tiny; brown to yellow skin	Spicy	Very firm, grainy	Aug.–Dec.	Poaching; pickling

Quince

Pectin—*a carbohydrate obtained from certain fruits; used to thicken jams and jellies.*

When selecting pears, look for fruits with smooth, unbroken skin and an intact stem. Pears will not ripen properly on the tree, so they are picked while still firm and should be allowed to soften before use. Underripe pears may be left at room temperature to ripen. A properly ripened pear should have a good fragrance and yield to gentle pressure at the stem end. Pears can be prepared or stored in the same way as apples.

Quince

Common quince (Fr. *coing*) resemble large, lumpy yellow pears. Their flesh is hard, with many pips or seeds, and they have a wonderful fragrance. Too astringent to eat raw, quince develop a sweet flavour and pink colour when cooked with sugar. Quince are used in meat stews, jellies, marmalades and pies. They have a high **pectin** content and may be added to other fruit jams or preserves to encourage gelling.

Fresh quince, usually imported from South America or southeast Europe, are available from October through January. Select firm fruits with a good yellow colour. Small blemishes may be cut away before cooking. Quince will keep for up to a month under refrigeration.

Stone Fruits (genus Prunus)

Stone fruits, also known as drupes, include apricots, cherries, nectarines, peaches and plums. They are characterized by a thin skin, soft flesh and one woody stone or pit. Although most originated in China, the shrubs and trees producing stone fruits are now grown in temperate climates worldwide.

The domestic varieties of stone fruits are in season from late spring through summer. They tend to be fragile fruits, easily bruised, difficult to transport and with a short shelf life. Do not wash them until ready to use, as moisture can cause deterioration. Avoid ingesting the pits—most contain toxic acids. Stone fruits are excellent dried and are often used to make liqueurs or brandies.

Apricots

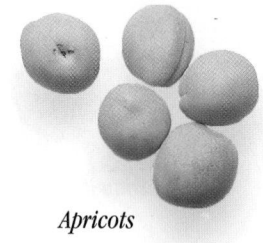

Apricots

Apricots (Fr. *abricots*) are small, round stone fruits with a velvety skin that varies in colour from deep yellow to vivid orange. Their juicy orange flesh surrounds a dark, almond-shaped pit. Apricots can be eaten out of hand, poached, stewed, baked or candied. They are often used in fruit compotes or savoury sauces for meat or poultry, and are also popular in quick breads, fruit tarts or puréed for dessert sauces, jams, custards or mousses.

Apricots enjoy a short season, peaking during June and July, and do not travel well. Select apricots that are well shaped, plump and fairly firm. Avoid those that are greenish-yellow or mushy. Fresh apricots will last for several days under refrigeration, but the flavour is best at room temperature. If fresh fruits are unavailable, canned apricots are usually an acceptable substitute. Dried apricots and apricot juice (known as nectar) are readily available.

Cherries

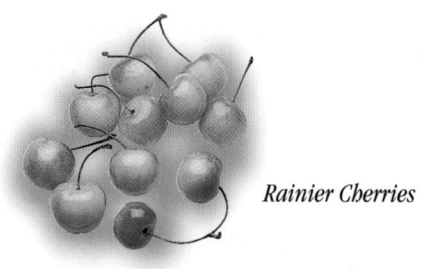

Rainier Cherries

Readily grown in most provinces of Canada are the two most important types of cherry: the sweet cherry and the sour (or tart) cherry.

Sweet cherries (Fr. *cerises*) are round to heart-shaped, about 1 inch (2.5 cm) in diameter, with skin that ranges in colour from yellow to deep red to nearly black. The flesh, which is sweet and juicy, may vary from yellow to dark red.

The most common and popular sweet cherries are the dark red Bings. Yellow-red Royal Ann and Rainier cherries are also available in some areas.

Sweet cherries are often marketed fresh, made into maraschino cherries or candied for use in baked goods. Fresh sweet cherries have a very short season, peaking during June and July. Cherries will not ripen further after harvesting. Select fruits that are firm and plump with a green stem still attached. There should not be any brown spots around the stem. A dry or brown stem indicates that the cherry is less than fresh. Once the stem is removed, the cherry will deteriorate rapidly. Store fresh cherries in the refrigerator and do not wash them until ready to use.

Sour cherries are light to dark red in colour and are so acidic they are rarely eaten uncooked. The most common sour cherries are the Montmorency and Morello. Most sour cherries are canned or frozen, or cooked with sugar and starch (usually cornstarch or tapioca) and sold as prepared pastry and pie fillings.

Both sweet and sour varieties are available dried.

Bing Cherries

BASIC PROCEDURE FOR PITTING CHERRIES

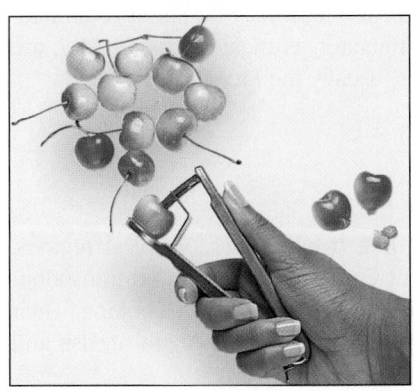

Remove the stem and place the cherry in the pitter with the indentation facing up. Squeeze the handles together to force out the pit.

Peaches and Nectarines

Peaches (Fr. *pêches*) are moderate-sized, round fruits with juicy, sweet flesh. Nectarines are a variety of peach, the main difference between the two being their skin. Peaches have a thin skin covered with fuzz, while nectarines have a thin, smooth skin. The flesh of either fruit ranges from white to pale orange. Although their flavours are somewhat different, they may be substituted for each other in most recipes.

Peaches and nectarines are excellent for eating out of hand or in dessert tarts or pastries. They are also used in jams, chutneys, preserves and savoury relishes, having a particular affinity for Asian and Indian dishes. Although the skin is edible, peaches are generally peeled before being used. (Peaches are easily peeled if blanched first.)

Peaches and nectarines are either freestones or clingstones. With freestones, the flesh separates easily from the stone; freestone fruits are commonly eaten out of hand. The flesh of clingstones adheres firmly to the stone; they hold their shape better when cooked and are the type most often canned.

Select fruits with a good aroma, an overall creamy, yellow or yellow-orange colour and an unwrinkled skin free of blemishes. Red patches are not an indication of ripeness; a green skin indicates that the fruit was picked too early and it will not ripen further. Peaches and nectarines will soften but do not become sweeter after harvesting.

Peaches

Nectarines

The United States, especially California and Georgia, is the world's largest producer of peaches and nectarines. In Canada, Ontario's Niagara Region produces abundant peach crops. Peak season is through the summer months, with July and August producing the best crop. South American peaches are sometimes available from January to May. Canned and frozen peaches are readily available.

Plums

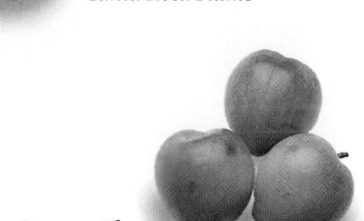

Santa Rosa Plums

Plums (Fr. *prunes*) are round to oval-shaped fruits that grow on trees or bushes. Dozens of plum varieties are known, although only a few are commercially significant. Plums vary in size from very small to 3 inches (7.5 cm) in diameter. Their thin skin can be green, red, yellow or various shades of blue-purple.

Plums are excellent for eating out of hand. Plums can also be used in pies, cobblers or tarts, or be baked or poached; they are often used in jams or preserves, and fresh slices can be used in salads or compotes.

Fresh plums are widely available from June through October, with a peak season in August and September. When selecting plums, look for plump, smooth fruits with unblemished skin. Generally, they should yield to gentle pressure, although the green and yellow varieties remain quite firm. Avoid plums with moist, brown spots near the stem. Plums may be left at room temperature to ripen, then stored in the refrigerator. Prunes, discussed later, are produced by drying special plum varieties, usually the French Agen.

Damson Plums

Tropicals

Tropical fruits are native to the world's hot, tropical or subtropical regions. Most are now readily available throughout Canada thanks to rapid transportation and distribution methods. All can be eaten fresh, without cooking. Their flavours complement each other and go well with rich or spicy meat, fish and poultry dishes.

Bananas

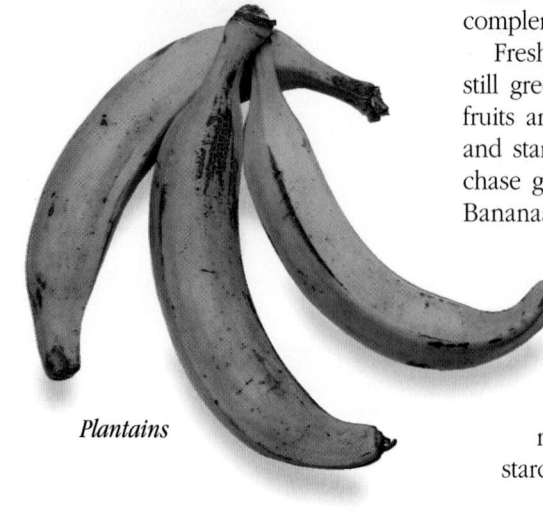

Common Yellow Bananas

Common yellow bananas (Fr. *bananes*) are actually the berries of a large tropical herb. Grown in bunches called hands, they are about 7–9 inches (17.5–22.5 cm) long, with a sticky, soft, sweet flesh. Their inedible yellow skin is easily removed. Red bananas are also available seasonally.

Properly ripened bananas are excellent eaten out of hand or used in salads. Lightly bruised or overripe fruits are best used for breads or muffins. Bananas blend well with other tropical fruits and citrus. Their unique flavour is also complemented by curry, cinnamon, ginger, honey and chocolate.

Fresh bananas are available all year. Bananas are always harvested when still green, because the texture and flavour will be adversely affected if the fruits are allowed to turn yellow on the tree. Unripe bananas are hard, dry and starchy. Because bananas ripen after harvesting, it is acceptable to purchase green bananas if there is sufficient time for final ripening before use. Bananas should be left at room temperature to ripen. A properly ripened banana has a yellow peel with brown flecks. The tip should not have any remaining green colouring. As bananas continue to age, the peel darkens and the starches turn to sugar, giving the fruits a sweeter flavour. Avoid bananas that have large brown bruises or a grey cast (a sign of cold damage).

Plantains, also referred to as cooking bananas, are larger but not as sweet as common bananas. They are frequently cooked as a starchy vegetable in tropical cuisines.

Plantains

Medjool Dates

Dates

Dates are the fruit of the date palm tree, which has been cultivated since ancient times. Dates are about 1–2 inches (2.5–5 cm) long, with a paper-thin skin and a single grooved seed in the centre. Most are golden to dark brown when ripe.

Although dates appear to be dried, they are actually fresh fruits. They have a sticky-sweet, almost candied texture and rich flavour. Dates provide flavour and moisture for breads, muffins, cookies and tarts. They can also be served with fresh or dried fruits, or stuffed with meat or cheese as an appetizer.

Pitted dates are readily available in several packaged forms: whole, chopped or extruded (for use in baking). Whole unpitted dates are available in bulk. Date juice is also available for use as a natural sweetener, especially in baked goods. Although packaged or processed dates are available all year, peak season for fresh domestic dates is from October through December. When selecting dates, look for those that are plump, glossy and moist.

Kiwis

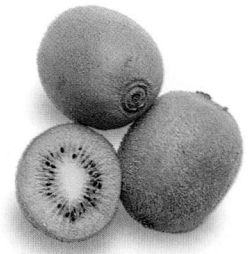

Kiwis

Kiwis, sometimes known as kiwifruits or Chinese gooseberries, are small oval fruits, about the size of a large egg, with a thin, fuzzy brown skin. The flesh is bright green with a white core surrounded by hundreds of tiny black seeds.

Kiwis are sweet, but somewhat bland. They are best used raw, peeled and eaten out of hand or sliced for fruit salads or garnish. Although kiwis are not recommended for cooking because heat causes them to fall apart, they are a perfect addition to glazed fruit tarts and can be puréed for sorbets, mousses or Bavarians. Kiwis contain an enzyme, similar to that in fresh pineapple or papaya, that has a tenderizing effect on meat and prevents gelling.

♦♦♦

FRIEDA AND THE KIWIFRUIT

How did a fuzzy brown unknown become a media darling and a hugely viable crop? The answer is thanks to Frieda Caplan. In 1962 Frieda, founder of Frieda's Inc., launched her historical worldwide promotion of kiwifruit. Acting on a suggestion that Chinese gooseberries, then grown only in New Zealand, might sell better under the name kiwifruit (the kiwi is the national bird of New Zealand), Frieda unleashed a produce giant. This story of the kiwifruit is studied throughout the world as one of the great successes in food marketing.

In 1980, after 18 years of Freida's continual, creative, aggressive and expensive marketing, the kiwifruit became a North American star when nouvelle cuisine chefs prominently featured it in their mixes of strawberry, banana, melon and pineapples. Since that time, the question asked most commonly of Frieda's Inc. is "What will be the next kiwifruit?"

The answer is that there will never be another kiwifruit. When the kiwifruit was accepted into the world's fruit vernacular, there was an unconditional paradigm shift. Today, new specialty produce does not have to go through the rigorous acceptance process inflicted on the kiwifruit. There can never be another kiwifruit because the marketing climate and consumer palate have shifted in a wonderful, irreversible way. Now when a new fruit like red bananas or yellow seedless watermelon comes onto the market, the consuming public does not react with fear and say "Bananas are supposed to be yellow" or "It really isn't watermelon if there aren't any seeds and it's not red." They respond with positive open minds (much the same as Frieda did when she purchased her first flat of kiwifruit in 1962) and a new-found knowledge that new foods will bring quality and variety, not discord, to their diets.

—KAREN CAPLAN
*Frieda's eldest daughter and
president of FRIEDA'S, INC.*

Mangoes

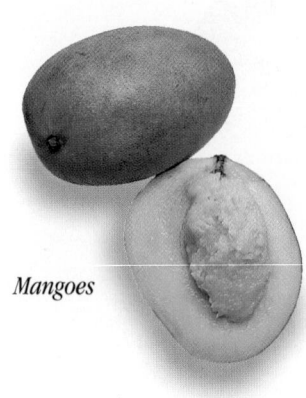

Mangoes

Mangoes are oval or kidney-shaped fruits that normally weigh between 6 ounces and 1 pound (180–500 g). Their skin is smooth and thin but tough, varying in colour from yellow to orange-red, with patches of green, red or purple. As mangoes ripen, the green disappears. The juicy, bright orange flesh clings to a large, flat pit.

A mango's unique flavour is spicy-sweet, with an acidic tang. Mangoes can be puréed for use in drinks or sauces, or the flesh can be sliced or cubed for use in salads, pickles, chutneys or desserts. Mangoes go well with spicy foods such as curry and with barbecued meats.

Although Florida produces some mangoes, most of those available in North America are from Mexico. Peak season is from May through August. Select fruits with good colour that are firm and free of blemishes. Ripe mangoes should have a good aroma, and should not be too soft or shrivelled. Allow mangoes to ripen completely at room temperature, then refrigerate for up to one week.

BASIC PROCEDURE FOR PITTING AND CUTTING MANGOES

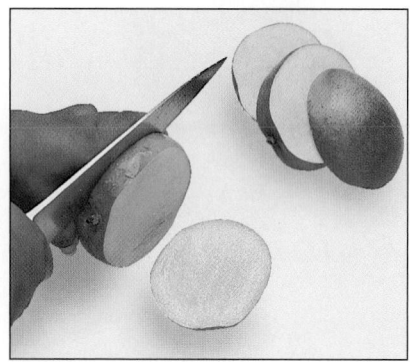

1. Cut along each side of the pit to remove two sections.

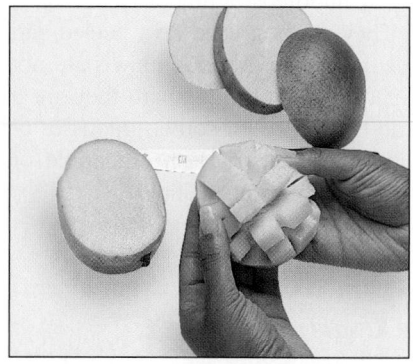

2. Each section can then be cubed using the "hedgehog" technique: Make crosswise cuts through the flesh, just to the skin; press up on the skin side of the section, exposing the cubes.

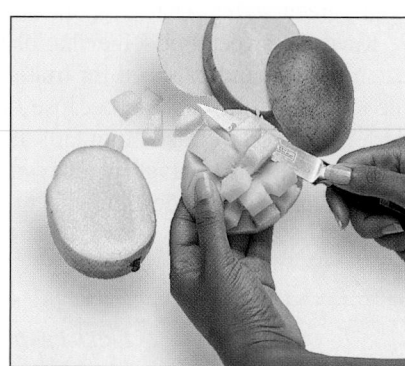

3. The mango may be served like this, or the cubes can be cut off to use in salads or other dishes.

Regular Papayas

Papain—*an enzyme found in papayas that breaks down proteins; used as the primary ingredient in many commercial meat tenderizers.*

Papayas

Papayas, also known as pawpaws, are greenish-yellow fruits shaped rather like large pears and weighing 1–2 pounds (500–1000 g). When halved, they resemble a melon. The flesh is golden to reddish-pink; its centre cavity is filled with round, silver-black seeds resembling caviar. Ripe papayas can be eaten raw, with only a squirt of lemon or lime juice. They can also be puréed for sweet or spicy sauces, chilled soups or sorbets.

Papayas contain **papain**, which breaks down proteins, and therefore papayas are an excellent meat tenderizer. Meats can be marinated with papaya juice or slices before cooking. Papain, however, makes fresh papayas unsuitable for use in gelatins because it inhibits gelling. Unripe (green) papayas are often used in pickles or chutneys, and can be baked or stewed with meat or poultry.

Papaya seeds are edible, with a peppery flavour and slight crunch. They are occasionally used to garnish fruit salads or add flavour to fruit salsas and compotes.

Papayas are grown in tropical and subtropical areas worldwide. Although available year round, peak season is from April through June. Select papayas that are plump, with a smooth, unblemished skin. Colour is a better determinant of ripeness than is softness: The greater the proportion of yellow to green skin colour, the riper the fruit. Papayas may be held at room temperature until completely ripe, then refrigerated for up to one week.

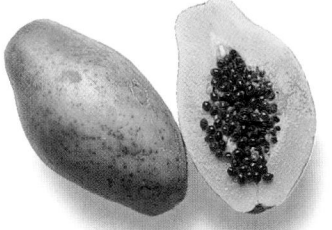

Red Papayas

Passion Fruits

Passion fruits (It. *granadillas*) have a firm, almost shell-like purple skin with orange-yellow pulp surrounding large, black, edible seeds. They are about the size and shape of large hen eggs, with a sweet, rich and unmistakable citrusy flavour. The pulp is used in custards, sauces and ice creams.

Select heavy fruits with dark, shrivelled skin and a strong aroma. Allow them to ripen at room temperature, if necessary, then refrigerate. Passion fruits are in season only during February and March. Bottles or frozen packs of purée are readily available, however, and provide a strong, true flavour.

Passion Fruits

Pineapples

Pineapples (Fr. *ananas*) are the fruit of a shrub with sharp spear-shaped leaves. Each fruit is covered with rough, brown eyes, giving it the appearance of a pine cone. The pale yellow flesh, which is sweet and very juicy, surrounds a cylindrical woody core that is edible but too tough for most uses. Most pineapples weigh approximately 2 pounds (1 kg), but dwarf varieties are also available.

Pineapples are excellent eaten raw, alone or in salads. Slices can be baked or grilled to accompany pork or ham. The cuisines of Southeast Asia incorporate pineapple into various curries, soups and stews. Pineapple juice is a popular beverage, often used in punch or cocktails. Canned or cooked pineapple can be added to gelatin mixtures, but avoid using fresh pineapple, as an enzyme (bromelin) found in fresh pineapple breaks down gelatin.

Pineapples

Pineapples do not ripen after harvesting. They must be left on the stem until completely ripe, at which time they are extremely perishable. The vast majority of pineapples come from Hawaii. Fresh pineapples are available all year, with peak supplies in March through June. Select heavy fruits with a strong, sweet aroma and rich colour. Avoid those with dried leaves or soft spots. Pineapples should be used as soon as possible after purchase. Pineapples are also available canned in slices, spears, cubes or crushed, dried or candied.

BASIC PROCEDURE FOR TRIMMING AND SLICING PINEAPPLES

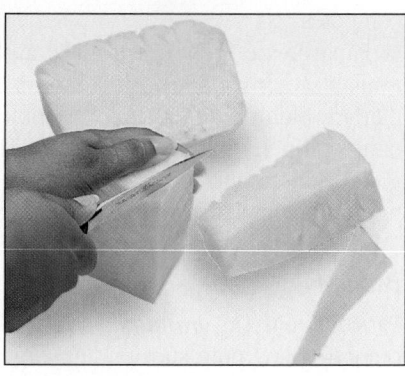

1. Slice off the leaves and stem end. Stand the fruit upright and cut the peel off in vertical strips.

2. Cut the peeled fruit in quarters, then cut away the woody core.

3. The flesh can then be cut as desired.

NUTRITION

Most fruits are quite nutritious. They have a high water content (usually 75% to 95%) and low protein and fat contents, all of which makes them low in calories. They are also an excellent source of fibre, and the sugar content of ripe fruits is a good source of energy. Some fruits, such as citrus, melons and strawberries, contain large amounts of vitamin C (which may be destroyed, however, by cooking or processing). Deep yellow and green fruits, such as apricots, mangoes and kiwis, are high in vitamin A; bananas, raisins and figs are a good source of potassium. (See Table 25.3.)

PURCHASING FRESH FRUITS

Fresh fruits have not been subjected to any processing (such as canning, freezing or drying). Fresh fruits may be ripe or unripe, depending on their condition when harvested or the conditions under which they have been stored. In order to use fresh fruits to their best advantage, it is important to make careful purchasing decisions. The size of each piece of fruit, its grade or quality, its ripeness on delivery and its nutritional content may affect your ability to use the fruit in an appropriate and cost-effective manner.

TABLE 25.3   NUTRITIONAL VALUES OF SELECTED FRUITS

Per serving, fresh, raw and/or as noted	Kcal	Protein (g)	Carbohydrates (g)	Fibre (g)	Total Fat (g)	Vitamin A (I.U.)	Vitamin C (mg)	Phosphorus (mg)	Potassium (mg)
Apple, 1 medium 2-3/4 in. (7 cm) diameter, unpeeled	81	0.3	21.1	3	0.5	74	8	10	159
Banana, peeled 4 oz. (112 g)	104	1.2	26.4	2	0.4	59.4	6.4	14.2	290
Cantaloupe, 1/2 of 5 in. (12.5 cm) diameter melon, approx. 7 oz. (210 g) of flesh	94	2.3	22.3	2.1	0.7	8608	113	45	825
Cherries, Bing, 10 medium, approx. 2.6 oz. (73 g)	49	0.8	11.3	1	0.7	146	5	13	152
Figs, 10 dried, approx. 6.6 oz. (185 g)	477	5.7	122.2	17.4	2.2	248	2	128	1332
Grapes, Thompson Seedless, 20, approx. 3.5 oz. (98 g)	72	0.6	17.8	0.8	0.6	72	10	12	186
Orange, navel, 1/2 medium, approx. 3.6 oz. (101 g)	35.6	0.8	8.9	0.3	<0.1	128	40	13.5	125
Pineapple, trimmed, 4 oz. (112 g)	56	0.4	14	1.2	0.4	25	17	8.5	125
Raisins, seedless, 4 oz. (112 g)	340	3.6	89.6	6	0.4	8	4	108	852
Strawberries, trimmed, 4 oz. (112 g)	36	0.8	8	2.5	0.4	28.7	60	19.8	175

The Corinne T. Netzer Encyclopedia of Food Values 1992

Grading

Fresh fruits traded on the wholesale market may be graded under the standards of the Canadian Food Protection Agency. The grades, based on size and uniformity of shape, colour and texture as well as the absence of defects, are Canada No. 1, Canada No. 2 and Canada Domestic. Most fruits purchased for food service operations are Canada No. 1. Fruits with lower grades are suitable for processing into sauces, jams, jellies or preserves.

Ripening

Several important changes take place in a fruit as it ripens. The fruit reaches its full size; its pulp or flesh becomes soft and tender; its colour changes. In addition, the fruit's acid content declines, making it less tart, and its starch content converts into the sugars, fructose and glucose, that provide the fruit's sweetness, flavour and aroma.

Unfortunately, these changes do not stop when the fruit reaches its peak of ripeness. Rather, they continue, deteriorating the fruit's texture and flavour and eventually causing spoilage.

Depending upon the species, fresh fruits can be purchased either fully ripened or unripened. Figs and pineapples, for example, ripen only on the plant and are harvested at or just before their peak of ripeness then rushed to market. They should not be purchased unripened as they will never attain full flavour or texture after harvesting. On the other hand, some fruits, including bananas and pears, continue to ripen after harvesting and can be purchased unripened.

With most harvested fruits, the ripening time as well as the time during which the fruits remain at their peak of ripeness can be manipulated. For instance, ripening can be delayed by chilling. Chilling slows down the fruit's respiration rate (fruits, like animals, consume oxygen and expel carbon dioxide). The slower the respiration rate, the slower the conversion of starch to sugar. For quicker ripening, fruit can be stored at room temperature.

Ripening is also effected by ethylene gas, a colourless, odourless hydrocarbon gas. Ethylene gas is naturally emitted by ripening fruits and can be used to encourage further ripening in most fruits. Apples, tomatoes, melons and bananas give off the most ethylene and should be stored away from delicate fruits and vegetables, especially greens. Fruits that are picked and shipped unripened can be exposed to ethylene gas to induce ripening just before sale. Conversely, if you want to extend the life of ripe fruits a day or two, isolate them from other fruits and keep them well chilled.

Fresh fruits will not ripen further once they are cooked or processed. The cooking or processing method applied, however, may soften the fruits or add flavour.

Purchasing

Fresh fruits are sold by weight or by count. They are packed in containers referred to as crates, bushels, cartons, cases, lugs or flats. The weight or count packed in each of these containers varies depending on the type of fruit, the purveyor and the place where the fruits were packed. For example, Texas citrus is packed in cartons equal to 7/10 of a bushel; Florida citrus is packed in cartons equal to 4/5 of a bushel. Sometimes size must be specified when ordering fruit. A 30-pound (13.5 kg) case of lemons, for example, may contain 96, 112 or 144 individual lemons, depending on their size.

Some fresh fruits, especially melons, pineapples, peaches and berries, are available trimmed, cleaned, peeled or cut, and sugar and preservatives are sometimes added. They are sold in bulk containers, sometimes packed in water. These items offer a consistent product with a significant reduction in labour costs. The purchase price may be greater than that for fresh fruits and flavour and freshness and nutritional qualities may suffer somewhat from the processing.

Purchasing and Storing Preserved Fruits

Preserving techniques are designed to extend the shelf life of fruits in essentially fresh form. These methods include irradiation, acidulation, canning, freezing and drying. Except for drying, these techniques do not substantially change the fruits' texture or flavour. Canning and freezing can also be used to preserve cooked fruits.

Preserves such as jellies and jams are cooked products and are discussed later in this chapter.

Irradiated Fruits

Some fruits can be subjected to ionizing radiation to destroy parasites, insects and bacteria. The treatment also slows ripening without a noticeable effect on the fruits' flavour and texture. Irradiated fruits must be labelled "treated with radiation," "treated by irradiation" or with a symbol when sold in the United States. Canada currently does not permit irradiation of food products.

Acidulation

Apples, pears, bananas, peaches and other fruits turn brown when cut. Although this browning is commonly attributed to exposure to oxygen, it is actually caused by the reaction of enzymes.

Enzymatic browning can be retarded by immersing cut fruits in an acidic solution such as lemon or orange juice. This simple technique is sometimes referred to as **acidulation**. Soaking fruits in water or lemon juice and water (called acidulated water) is not recommended. Unless a sufficient amount of salt or sugar is added to the water, the fruits will just become mushy. But if enough salt or sugar is added, the flavour will be affected.

Canned Fruits

Almost any type of fruit can be canned successfully; pineapple and peaches are the largest sellers. In commercial canning, raw fruits are cleaned and placed in a sealed container, then subjected to high temperatures for a specific amount of time. Heating destroys the microorganisms that cause spoilage, and the sealed environment created by the can eliminates oxidation and retards decomposition. But the heat required by the canning process also softens the texture of most fruits. Canning has little or no effect on vitamins A, B, C and D because oxygen is not present during the heating process. Canning also has no practical effect on proteins, fats or carbohydrates.

In *solid pack* cans, little or no water is added. The only liquid is from the fruits' natural moisture. *Water pack* cans have water or fruit juice added, which must be taken into account when determining costs. *Syrup pack* fruits have a sugar syrup—light, medium or heavy—added. The syrup should also be taken into account when determining food costs, and the additional sweetness should be considered when using syrup-packed fruits. Cooked fruit products such as pie fillings are also available canned.

Canned fruits are purchased in cases of standard-size cans (see Appendix II). Canned fruits can be stored for extended time periods at room temperature. Once a can is opened, any unused contents must be transferred to an appropriate storage container and refrigerated. Cans with bulges must be discarded immediately, without opening. Canned fruits are graded as follows: Canada Fancy (top quality); Canada Choice; and Canada Substandard.

Frozen Fruits

Freezing is a highly effective method for preserving fruits. It severely inhibits the growth of microorganisms that cause fruits to spoil. Freezing does not destroy nutrients, although the appearance or texture of most fruits can be affected because of their high water content. This occurs when ice crystals formed from the water in the cells burst the cells' walls.

Many fruits, especially berries and apple and pear slices, are now individually quick frozen (IQF). This method employs blasts of cold air, refrigerated plates, liquid nitrogen, liquid air or other techniques to chill the produce quickly. By speeding the freezing process, the formation of ice crystals can be greatly reduced.

Fruits can be trimmed and sliced before freezing and are also available frozen in sugar syrup, which adds flavour and prevents browning. Berries are frozen whole, while stone fruits are usually peeled, pitted and sliced. Fruit purées are also available frozen.

Frozen fruits are graded as Canada Fancy, Canada Choice or Extra Standard, or Canada Substandard. The "Canada" grade indicates that a government inspector has graded the product, but packers may use grade names without an actual inspection if the contents meet the standards of the grade indicated.

Individually quick frozen fruits can be purchased by the case. All frozen fruits should be sealed in moistureproof wrapping and kept at a constant temperature of 0°F (–18°C) or below. Temperature fluctuations can cause freezer burn.

Dried Fruits

Golden Raisins

Currants

Apricots

Persimmons

Apples

Pears

Kiwis

Drying is the oldest-known technique for preserving fruits, having been used for over 5000 years. When ripe fruits are dried they lose most of their moisture. This concentrates their flavours and sugars and dramatically extends shelf life. Although most fruits can be dried, plums (prunes), grapes (raisins, sultanas and currants), apricots and figs are the fruits most commonly dried. The drying method can be as simple as leaving ripe fruits in the sun to dry naturally or the more cost-efficient technique of passing fruits through a compartment of hot, dry air to quickly extract moisture.

Dried fruits actually retain from 16% to 25% residual moisture, which leaves them moist and soft. They are often treated with sulphur dioxide to prevent browning (oxidation) and to extend shelf life.

Dried fruits may be eaten out of hand; added to cereals or salads; baked in muffins, breads, pies or tarts; stewed for chutneys or compotes; or used as a stuffing for roasted meats or poultry. Before use, dried fruits may be softened by soaking them for a short time in a hot liquid such as water, wine, rum, brandy or other liquor. Some dried fruits should be simmered in a small amount of water before use.

Store dried fruits in air-tight containers to prevent further moisture loss; keep in a dry, cool area away from sunlight. Dried fruits may become mouldy if exposed to both air and high humidity.

JUICING

Fruit juice is used as a beverage, alone or mixed with other ingredients, and as the liquid ingredient in other preparations. Juice can be extracted from fruits (and some vegetables) in two ways: pressure and blending.

Pressure is used to extract juice from fruits such as citrus that have a high water content. Pressure is applied by hand-squeezing or with a manual or electric reamer. All reamers work on the same principle: A ribbed cone is pressed against the fruit to break down its flesh and release the juice. Always strain juices to remove seeds, pulp or fibrous pieces.

A blender or an electric juice extractor can be used to liquefy less juicy fruits and vegetables such as apples, carrots, tomatoes, beets and cabbage. The extractor pulverizes the fruit or vegetable, then separates and strains the liquid from the pulp with centrifugal action.

Interesting and delicious beverages can be made by combining the juice of one or more fruits or vegetables: Pineapple with orange, apple with cranberry, strawberry with tangerine and papaya with orange. Colour should be considered when creating mixed-juice beverages, however. Some combinations can cause rather odd colour changes. Although yellow and orange juices are not a problem, those containing red and blue flavonoid pigments (such as Concord grapes, cherries, strawberries, raspberries and blueberries) can create some unappetizing colours. Adding an acid such as lemon juice helps retain the correct red/blue hues.

Juice—*the liquid extracted from any fruit or vegetable.*

Nectar—*the diluted, sweetened juice of peaches, apricots, guavas, black currants or other fruits, the juice of which would be too thick or too tart to drink straight.*

Cider—*mildly fermented apple juice, although nonalcoholic apple juice may also be labelled cider.*

Applying Various Cooking Methods

Although most fruits are edible raw and typically served that way, some fruits can also be cooked. Commonly used cooking methods are broiling and grilling, baking, sautéing, deep-fat frying, poaching and simmering.

When cooking fruits, proper care and attention are critical. Even minimal cooking can render fruits overly soft or mushy. To combat this irreversible process, sugar can be added. When fruits are cooked with sugar, the sugar will be absorbed slowly into the cells, firming the fruits. Acids (notably lemon juice) also help fruits retain their structure. (Alkalis, such as baking soda, cause the cells to break down more quickly, reducing the fruits to mush.)

Determining Doneness

There are so many different fruits with such varied responses to cooking that no one standard for doneness is appropriate. Each item should be evaluated on a recipe-by-recipe basis. Generally, however, most cooked fruits are done when they are just tender when pierced with a fork or the tip of a paring knife. Simmered fruits, such a compotes, should be softer, cooked just to the point of disintegration.

You can avoid overcooking fruits by remembering that some carryover cooking will occur through the residual heat contained in the foods. Always rely on objective tests—sight, feel, taste and aroma—rather than the clock.

Dry-Heat Cooking Methods

Broiling and Grilling

Fruits are usually broiled or grilled just long enough to caramelize sugars. But cooking must be done quickly in order to avoid breaking down the fruits' structure. Good fruits to broil or grill are pineapples, apples, grapefruits, bananas, persimmons and peaches. The fruits may be cut into slices, chunks or halves as appropriate. A coating of sugar, honey or liqueur adds flavour, as do lemon juice, cinnamon and ginger.

When broiling fruits, use an oiled sheet pan or broiling platter. When grilling fruits, use a clean grill grate or thread the pieces onto skewers. Only thick fruit slices will need to be turned or rotated to heat fully. Broiled or grilled fruits can be served alone, as an accompaniment to meat, fish or poultry or as a topping for ice creams or custards.

BASIC PROCEDURE FOR BROILING OR GRILLING FRUITS

1. Select ripe fruits and peel, core or slice as necessary.
2. Top with sugar or honey to add flavour and aid caramelization.
3. Place the fruits on the broiler platter, sheet pan or grill grate.
4. Broil or grill at a high temperature, turning as necessary to heat the fruits thoroughly but quickly.

◆◆◆

RECIPE 25.1

BROILED GRAPEFRUIT

Yield: 8 Servings

Ruby grapefruits	4	4
Sweet sherry	2 Tbsp.	30 mL
Brown sugar	4 Tbsp.	60 mL

1. Cut each grapefruit in half (perpendicular to the segments), then section with a sharp knife, carefully removing any visible seeds.
2. Sprinkle the grapefruit halves with the sherry and sugar.
3. Arrange on a baking sheet and place under a preheated broiler. Cook briefly, only until well heated and the sugar caramelizes. Serve immediately.

Approximate values per 1/2 grapefruit (132 g) serving:

Calories	70
Total fat	0 g
Saturated fat	0 g
Cholesterol	0 mg
Sodium	0 g
Total carbohydrates	16 g
Protein	1 g
Vitamin C	80%

Claims—fat free; no sodium

Baking

After washing, peeling, coring or pitting, most pomes, stone fruits and tropicals can be baked to create hot, flavourful desserts. Fruits with sturdy skins, particularly apples and pears, are excellent for baking alone as their skin (peel) holds in moisture and flavour. They can also be used as edible containers by filling the cavity left by coring with a variety of sweet or savoury mixtures.

Combinations of fruits can also be baked successfully. Try mixing fruits for a balance of sweetness and tartness (for example, strawberries with rhubarb, apples with plums).

Several baked desserts are simply fruits (fresh, frozen or canned) topped with a crust (and called a *cobbler*), streusel (and called a *crumple* or *crisp*) or batter (and called a *buckle*). (See Recipe 29.17, Blackberry Cobbler.) Fruits, sometimes poached first, can also be baked in a wrapper of puff pastry, flaky dough or phyllo dough to produce an elegant dessert.

BASIC PROCEDURE FOR BAKING FRUITS

1. Select ripe but firm fruits and peel, core, pit or slice as necessary.
2. Add sugar or any flavourings.

3. Wrap the fruits in pastry dough if desired or directed in the recipe.

4. Place the fruits in a baking dish and bake uncovered in a moderate oven until tender or properly browned.

✦✦✦

RECIPE 25.2

BAKED APPLES

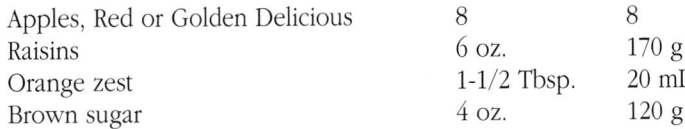

Yield: 8 Servings

Apples, Red or Golden Delicious	8	8
Raisins	6 oz.	170 g
Orange zest	1-1/2 Tbsp.	20 mL
Brown sugar	4 oz.	120 g

1. Rinse and core each apple. The peels should be scored or partially removed to allow the pulp to expand without bursting the skin during baking.

2. Plump the raisins by soaking them in boiling water for 10 minutes. Drain the raisins thoroughly.

3. Combine the raisins, orange zest and brown sugar. Fill the cavity of each apple with this mixture.

4. Stand the apples in a shallow baking dish. Add enough water to measure about 1/2 inch (1.25 cm) deep.

5. Bake the apples at 375°F (190°C) for 15 minutes. Reduce the temperature to 300°F (150°C) and continue baking until the apples are tender but still hold their shape, approximately 1 hour. Occasionally baste the apples with liquid from the baking dish.

Approximate values per apple:

Calories	220
Total fat	.5 g
Saturated fat	0 g
Cholesterol	0 mg
Sodium	10 mg
Total carbohydrates	52 g
Protein	1 g
Vitamin C	15%

Claims—low fat; no cholesterol; very low sodium; good source of fibre

Sautéing

Fruits develop a rich, syrupy flavour when sautéed briefly in butter, sugar and, if desired, spices or liqueur. Cherries, bananas, apples, pears and pineapples are good choices. They should be peeled, cored and seeded as necessary and cut into uniform-size pieces before sautéing.

For dessert, fruits are sautéed with sugar to create a caramelized glaze or syrup. The fruits and syrup can be used to fill crêpes or to top spongecakes or ice creams. Liquor may be added and the mixture flamed (flambéed) in front of diners, as with Bananas Foster (Recipe 25.14).

For savoury mixtures, onions, shallots or garlic are often added.

In both sweet and savoury fruit sautés, the fat used should be the most appropriate for the finished product. Butter and bacon fat are typical choices.

BASIC PROCEDURE FOR SAUTÉING FRUITS

1. Peel, pit and core the fruits as necessary and cut into uniform-size pieces.
2. Melt the fat in a hot sauté pan.
3. Add the fruit pieces and any flavouring ingredients. Do not crowd the pan, as this will cause the fruit to stew in its own juices.
4. Cook quickly over high heat.

♦♦♦

RECIPE 25.3

SAVOURY FRUIT FOR ROAST PORK

Yield: 1 pt. (500 mL)

Onion, fine dice	6 oz.	170 g
Butter or bacon fat	1 oz.	30 g
Apricots	3	3
Apples (tart) or peaches, peeled	3	3
Granulated sugar	4 oz.	120 g
Hot paprika	TT	TT
Salt and white pepper	TT	TT

1. Sweat the onions in the butter or bacon fat without browning.

2. Slice the apricots and apples into thin, even pieces. Add the apples to the onions and cook for 1–2 minutes. Add the apricots.

3. Sprinkle the sugar over the fruits and cook, uncovered, over medium heat until tender. Season with paprika, salt and white pepper.

4. Serve warm as an accompaniment to roast pork.

Approximate values per 1 oz. (30 mL) serving:

Calories	60
Total fat	1.5 g
Saturated fat	1 g
Cholesterol	5 mg
Sodium	50 mg
Total carbohydrates	12 g
Protein	0 g
Vitamin A	4%

Claims—low fat; low cholesterol; low sodium

Deep-Fat Frying

Few fruits are suitable for deep-fat frying. Apples, bananas, pears, pineapples and firm peaches mixed in or coated with batter, however, produce fine results. These fruits should be peeled, cored, seeded and cut into evenly sized slices or chunks. They may also need to be dried with paper towels so that the batter or coating can adhere. The procedures for deep-fat frying are found in Chapter 21, Deep-Fat Frying.

Moist-Heat Cooking Methods

Poaching

One of the more popular cooking methods for fruits is poaching. Poaching softens and tenderizes fruits and infuses them with additional flavours such as spices or wine. Poached fruits can be served hot or cold and used in tarts, pastries or as an accompaniment to meat or poultry dishes.

The poaching liquid can be water, wine, liquor or sugar syrup. (As noted above, sugar helps fruits keep their shape, although it takes longer to tenderize fruits poached in sugar syrup.) The low poaching temperature (185°F/85°C) allows fruits to soften gradually. The agitation created at higher temperatures would damage them.

Cooked fruits should be allowed to cool in the flavoured poaching liquid or syrup. Most poaching liquids can be used repeatedly. If they contain sufficient sugar, they can be reduced to a sauce or glaze to accompany the poached fruits.

BASIC PROCEDURE FOR POACHING FRUITS

1. Peel, core and slice the fruits as necessary.
2. In a sufficiently deep, nonreactive saucepan, combine the poaching liquid (usually water or wine) with sugar, spices, citrus zest and other ingredients as desired or as directed in the recipe.
3. Submerge the fruits in the liquid. Place a circle of parchment paper over the fruits to help them stay submerged.
4. Place the saucepan on the stove top over a medium-high flame; bring to a boil.
5. As soon as the liquid boils, reduce the temperature. Simmer gently.
6. Poach until the fruits are tender enough for the tip of a small knife to be easily inserted. Cooking time depends on the type of fruit used, its ripeness and the cooking liquid.
7. Remove the saucepan from the stove top and allow the liquid and fruits to cool.
8. Remove the fruits from the liquid and then refrigerate. The liquid can be returned to the stove top and reduced until thick enough to use as a sauce or glaze or refrigerated for further use.

✦✦✦

RECIPE 25.4

PEARS POACHED IN RED WINE

NOTE: *This dish appears in the Chapter Opening photograph.*

CULINARY ARTS INSTITUTE, MISSISSIPPI UNIVERSITY FOR WOMEN
Director Sarah Labensky

Yield: 8 Servings

Ripe pears, Anjou or Bartlett	8	8
Zinfandel wine	52 oz.	1.5 L
Whole peppercorns	8–10	8–10
Vanilla bean	1	1
Granulated sugar	12 oz.	340 g
Fresh basil, chopped	1 oz.	30 g
Zest of 1 orange		

1. Peel and core the pears, leaving the stems intact.
2. Combine the remaining ingredients in large nonreactive saucepan. Arrange the pears in the liquid in a single layer.
3. Place the pears on the stove top over medium-high heat. Bring to just below a boil, then immediately reduce the heat and allow the liquid to simmer gently. Cover with a round of parchment paper if necessary to keep the pears submerged.
4. Continue poaching the pears until tender, approximately 1 to 1-1/2 hours. Remove the saucepan from the stove and allow the pears to cool in the liquid.
5. Remove the pears from the poaching liquid and return the liquid to the stove top. Reduce until the liquid is thick enough to coat the back of a spoon, then strain.
6. Serve the pears chilled or at room temperature in a pool of the reduced wine syrup.

Approximate values per 7 oz. (210 g) serving:

Calories	410
Total fat	1.5 g
Saturated fat	0 g
Cholesterol	0 mg
Sodium	35 mg
Total carbohydrates	91 g
Protein	6 g
Vitamin A	40%
Calcium	90%
Iron	110%

Claims—low fat; no cholesterol; low sodium; high fibre

Simmering

Simmering techniques are used to make stewed fruits and compotes. Fresh, frozen, canned and dried fruits can be simmered or stewed. As with any moist-heat cooking method, simmering softens and tenderizes fruits. The liquid used may be water, wine or the juices naturally found in the fruits. Sugar, honey and spices may be added as desired. Stewed or simmered fruits can be served hot or cold, as a first course, a dessert or an accompaniment to meat or poultry dishes.

BASIC PROCEDURE FOR SIMMERING FRUITS

1. Peel, core, pit and slice the fruits as necessary.
2. Bring the fruits and cooking liquid, if used, to a simmer. Cook until the fruit is tender.
3. Add sugar or other sweeteners as desired or as directed in the recipe.

♦♦♦

RECIPE 25.5

DRIED FRUIT COMPOTE

Yield: 2 lb. (1 kg)

Dried apricots	5 oz.	150 g
Prunes, pitted	5 oz.	150 g
Dried pears or apples	5 oz.	150 g
Dried peaches	5 oz.	150 g
Hot water	24 oz.	720 mL
Cinnamon stick	1	1
Light corn syrup	12 oz.	340 mL
Cointreau	2 oz.	60 mL

1. Coarsely chop the fruits. Place the pieces in a nonreactive saucepan and add the water and cinnamon stick.
2. Bring the mixture to a simmer, cover and cook until tender, approximately 12–15 minutes.
3. Add the corn syrup and Cointreau. Simmer uncovered until thoroughly heated. Serve warm or refrigerate for longer storage.

Approximate values per 1 oz. (30 g) serving:

Calories	60
Total fat	0 g
Saturated fat	0 g
Cholesterol	0 mg
Sodium	15 mg
Total carbohydrates	15 g
Protein	0 g

Claims—fat free; very low sodium

Preserving

Fresh fruits can be preserved with sugar if the fruit and sugar mixture is concentrated by evaporation to the point that microbial spoilage cannot occur. The added sugar also retards the growth of, but does not destroy, microorganisms.

Pectin, a substance present in varying amounts in all fruits, can cause cooked fruits to form a semisolid mass known as a **gel**. Fruits that are visually unattractive but otherwise of high quality can be made into gels, which are more commonly known as **jams**, **jellies**, **marmalades** and **preserves**.

The essential ingredients of a fruit gel are fruit, pectin, acid (usually lemon juice) and sugar. They must be carefully combined in the correct ratio for the gel to form. For fruits with a low pectin content (such as strawberries) to form gels, pectin must be added, either by adding a fruit with a high pectin content (for example, apples or quinces) or by adding packaged pectin.

Concentrate—*also known as a fruit paste or compound, is a reduced fruit purée, without a gel structure, used as a flavouring.*

Jam—*a fruit gel made from fruit pulp and sugar.*

Jelly—*a fruit gel made from fruit juice and sugar.*

Marmalade—*a citrus jelly that also contains unpeeled slices of citrus fruit.*

Preserve—*a fruit gel that contains large pieces or whole fruits.*

BASIC PROCEDURE FOR MAKING FRUIT PRESERVES

1. Clean, peel, core, pit and cut the fruits as necessary.
2. Firm fruits should be simmered in water or juice until tender.
3. Add sugar and other flavourings to the fruits as desired or as directed in the recipe.
4. Simmer until the mixture thickens.

===== ◆◆◆ =====

RECIPE 25.6

QUINCE JAM

Yield: 1 qt. (1 L)

Water	1 qt.	1 L
Lemon juice	1 oz.	30 mL
Fresh quince	3 lb.	1.3 kg
Granulated sugar	12 oz.	340 g
Vanilla bean	1/2	1/2

1. Combine the water and 1/2 ounce (15 mL) of lemon juice in a large, nonreactive saucepan.
2. Peel, quarter and core the quince. Cut each quarter into small cubes and add to the water.
3. Bring the water to a boil, reduce the heat, cover and simmer until the quince is tender, approximately 30 minutes.
4. Remove about half the quince with a slotted spoon and set aside. Purée the remaining quince and the cooking liquid.
5. Return the purée and the quince pieces to the saucepan and bring to a simmer. Add the remaining 1/2 ounce (15 mL) of lemon juice, the sugar and vanilla bean.
6. Simmer uncovered, stirring frequently, until the jam holds its shape, approximately 15 minutes. Remove from the heat and cool over an ice bath.

Approximate values per 1 oz. (30 g) serving:

Calories	70
Total fat	0 g
Saturated fat	0 g
Cholesterol	0 mg
Sodium	0 mg
Total carbohydrates	17 g
Protein	0 g
Vitamin C	10%

Claims—no fat

CONCLUSION

Fruits, whether fresh, frozen, canned or dried, are one of the most versatile and popular of foods. Fruits can be used uncooked or incorporated into a soup, salad, bread, meat dish or dessert. When selecting fresh fruits it is important to consider seasonal availability, storage conditions and ripeness. When using them, it is important that they be at their peak of ripeness for the best flavour, texture, aroma and appearance.

QUESTIONS FOR DISCUSSION

1. Define ripeness and explain why ripe fruits are most desirable. How does the ripening process affect the availability of some fruits?
2. Describe the proper storage conditions for most fruits. Which fruits emit ethylene gas and why is this a consideration when storing fruits?

3. Explain why some apple varieties are preferred for cooking, while other varieties are preferred for eating. Which variety is generally preferred for making applesauce?

4. Which types of fruits are best for dry-heat cooking methods? Explain your answer. Why is sugar usually added when cooking any type of fruit?

5. List and describe three ways to prepare fruits for extended storage.

*A*DDITIONAL FRUIT RECIPES

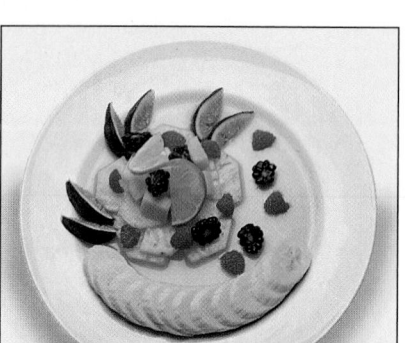

RECIPE 25.7
TROPICAL FRUIT WITH PASSION FRUIT PURÉE

CAMPTON PLACE RESTAURANT, KEMPINSKI HOTELS, SAN FRANCISCO, CA

Yield: 6 Servings

Mangoes	2	2
Papayas	2	2
Brazilian red bananas	2	2
Fresh coconut	1	1
Lime	1	1
Cherimoya (optional)	1	1
Guavas	2	2
Pineapple, medium, trimmed	1/3	1/3
Passion fruit	12	12
Sugar	4 oz.	120 g
Honey	6 oz.	180 g
Berries	as needed for garnish	

Approximate values per serving:

Calories	560
Total fat	5 g
Saturated fat	4 g
Cholesterol	0 mg
Sodium	25 mg
Total carbohydrates	123 g
Protein	4 g
Vitamin A	35%
Vitamin C	340%
Iron	10%
Claims—no cholesterol; high fibre	

1. Trim, peel and slice or cut all of the fruit, except the passion fruit, into interesting shapes. Hold in the refrigerator for service.

2. Cut the passion fruit in half and scoop out the seeds and membrane into a nonreactive saucepan. Add any fleshy trimmings from the mango, papaya, guava and pineapple. Add the sugar and honey and cook to a sauce consistency. Strain and cool.

3. Ladle 1-1/2 ounces (45 mL) of the sauce onto a cold plate or bowl. Arrange the sliced fruit attractively on the sauce. Garnish with berries.

◆ ◆ ◆

RECIPE 25.8
FIGS WITH BERRIES AND HONEY MOUSSE

GREENS RESTAURANT, SAN FRANCISCO, CA
Executive Chef Annie Somerville

Yield: 4 Servings

Raspberries or blackberries	2 cups	300 g
Fresh figs such as Black Mission, Kadota or Calimyrna	2 cups	300 g
Honey	6 oz.	170 g
Egg yolks	4	4

Salt	TT	TT
Cream, 35%	1 pt.	450 mL

1. Pick through the berries, but do not rinse them because water will dilute their flavour.
2. Rinse the figs and cut them in half, leaving the stem attached.
3. To make the mousse, whisk the honey, yolks and salt together in a bowl over a pan of barely simmering water. Whisk the mixture continuously for 8 minutes. After 5 minutes, the mousse will begin to thicken and the texture will become creamy. Whisk vigorously until the mousse leaves thick ribbons on its surface when poured over itself. Set aside to cool. The texture of the cooled mousse will be stiff and sticky.
4. Whisk 2 tablespoons (30 mL) of cream into the mousse, working it until it loosens.
5. Whip the remaining cream until it is firm, fold it into the mousse until it is just incorporated, then whisk the two together. The texture will be light and creamy.
6. Loosely arrange the figs on a platter, sprinkle with the berries and serve with the mousse.

Approximate values per serving:

Calories	680
Total fat	47 g
Saturated fat	28 g
Cholesterol	370 mg
Sodium	200 mg
Total carbohydrates	57 g
Protein	6 g
Vitamin A	60%
Vitamin C	25%

◆◆◆

RECIPE 25.9
PINEAPPLE PAPAYA SALSA

Yield: 2 qt. (2 L)

Tomatoes	3	3
Pineapple, fresh	1	1
Papaya, fresh	1	1
Green onions, sliced	1 bunch	1 bunch
Fresh cilantro, chopped	1 bunch	1 bunch
Jalapeños, seeded, minced	2	2
Lemon juice	3 Tbsp.	45 mL
Garlic, chopped	1 tsp.	5 mL
Salt	2 tsp.	10 mL

1. Core and dice the tomatoes.
2. Peel and dice the pineapple.
3. Peel, seed and dice the papaya.
4. Combine all ingredients and chill well.

Approximate values per 1 oz. (30 g) serving:

Calories	25
Total fat	0 g
Saturated fat	0 g
Cholesterol	0 mg
Sodium	330 mg
Total carbohydrates	5 g
Protein	0 g
Vitamin C	45%

Claims—fat free; low calories

◆◆◆

RECIPE 25.10
TROPICAL FRUIT SALAD WITH YOGURT DRESSING

Yield: 4 Small Salads

Mango, cut into 1/2-inch (12-mm) cubes	6 oz.	170 g
Pineapple, cut into 1/2-inch (12-mm) cubes	6 oz.	170 g

Continued

Papaya, cut into 1/2-inch (12-mm) cubes	4 oz.	120 g
Grapefruit segments	16	16
Pineapple or grapefruit juice	2 oz.	60 mL
Yogurt, plain, nonfat	4 oz.	120 mL
Honey	2 Tbsp.	30 mL
Lime juice, fresh	1 Tbsp.	15 mL
Butterleaf lettuce, large leaves, separated and cleaned	4	4
Kiwi, peeled and sliced	1	1
Poppy seeds	1 tsp.	5 mL

Approximate values per 8 oz. (240 g) serving:

Calories	170
Total fat	1 g
Saturated fat	0 g
Cholesterol	0 mg
Sodium	30 mg
Total carbohydrates	38 g
Protein	3 g
Vitamin A	20%
Vitamin C	150%

Claims—low fat; no cholesterol; very low sodium; good source of fibre

1. Mix the mango, pineapple, papaya and grapefruit together with the pineapple or grapefruit juice.
2. To make the dressing, whisk the yogurt, honey and lime juice together.
3. Line the plates with the butterleaf lettuce. Arrange the kiwi slices and the fruit salad over the lettuce.
4. Drizzle the dressing over the fruits and top with poppy seeds.

◆◆◆

RECIPE 25.11

GRATIN OF FRESH BERRIES WITH CRÈME FRAÎCHE

Yield: 1 Serving

Assorted fresh berries, such as raspberries, blueberries and blackberries	4 oz.	120 g
Crème fraîche	2 oz.	60 mL
Orange liqueur	1 tsp.	5 mL
Brown sugar	1 Tbsp.	15 mL

Approximate values per serving:

Calories	210
Total fat	7 g
Saturated fat	4 g
Cholesterol	20 mg
Sodium	30 mg
Total carbohydrates	33 g
Protein	3 g
Vitamin C	40%

Claims—very low sodium; high fibre

1. Arrange the berries in an even layer in a shallow, heatproof serving dish.
2. Stir the crème fraîche and orange liqueur together. Spoon this mixture over the berries.
3. Sprinkle the brown sugar over the crème fraîche. Place under a broiler or salamander just until the sugar melts. Serve immediately.

◆◆◆

RECIPE 25.12

GRILLED FRUIT KEBABS

Yield: 8 Skewers

Cantaloupe	6 oz.	170 g
Honeydew melon	6 oz.	170 g
Pineapple	6 oz.	170 g
Strawberries	8	8
Brown sugar	2 oz.	60 g
Lime juice	4 oz.	120 mL
Cinnamon, ground	1/4 tsp.	1 mL

1. Remove the rind and cut the melons and pineapple into 1-inch (2.5-cm) cubes. Hull the strawberries and leave whole.
2. To make the sugar glaze, combine the sugar, lime juice and cinnamon, stirring until the sugar dissolves.
3. Heat the grill and clean the grate thoroughly.
4. Thread the fruits onto kebab skewers, alternating colours for an attractive appearance.
5. Brush the fruits with the sugar glaze. Grill, rotating the skewers frequently to develop an evenly light brown surface.
6. Serve immediately as an appetizer, a garnish for ice cream or an accompaniment to rich meats such as pork or lamb.

Approximate values per skewer:

Calories	70
Total fat	0 g
Saturated fat	0 g
Cholesterol	0 mg
Sodium	10 mg
Total carbohydrates	16 g
Protein	1 g
Vitamin C	50%

Claims—fat free; very low sodium

◆◆◆

RECIPE 25.13
CHERRY CONFIT

Yield: 4 oz. (120 g)

Red onion, small dice	2 Tbsp.	30 mL
Whole butter	2 tsp.	10 mL
Dried cherries	3 oz.	90 g
Brandy	1 Tbsp.	15 mL
Port	1 Tbsp.	15 mL
Sherry vinegar	1/2 tsp.	3 mL

1. Sauté the onions in butter without colouring.
2. Add the cherries. Add the brandy and flambé.
3. Add the port and sherry vinegar; cook until almost dry. Serve warm or at room temperature with charcuterie items, or grilled or roasted meats.
4. The confit can be kept, refrigerated, for up to 1 week.

Approximate values per 1 oz. (30 g) serving:

Calories	35
Total fat	2 g
Saturated fat	1 g
Cholesterol	5 mg
Sodium	20 mg
Total carbohydrates	3 g
Protein	0 g

Claims—low fat; very low sodium; low calorie

◆◆◆

RECIPE 25.14
BANANAS FOSTER

Bananas Foster is an American classic, created in New Orleans during the 1950s and named for a local celebrity. It is usually prepared for customers tableside, using a portable burner known as a réchaud.

Yield: 1 Serving

Banana, medium	1	1
Unsalted butter	1/2 oz.	15 g
Brown sugar	1/2 oz.	15 g
Fresh orange juice	1 oz.	30 mL
Dark rum	1/2 oz.	15 mL
Brandy or crème de banana	1/2 oz.	15 mL
Cinnamon	TT	TT
Vanilla ice cream	1 portion	1 portion

1. Peel the banana and cut in half lengthwise. Cut each half into 3 chunks and set aside.
2. Melt the butter in a sauté pan. Add the brown sugar and stir until the sugar melts.

Continued

Approximate values per serving:

Calories	570
Total fat	28 g
Saturated fat	17 g
Cholesterol	100 mg
Sodium	90 mg
Total carbohydrates	72 g
Protein	8 g
Vitamin A	25%
Vitamin C	40%

Claims—low sodium; good source of fibre

3. Add the bananas and stir to coat them completely with the sauce. Cook until tender, approximately 1–2 minutes.

4. Stir in the orange juice. Add the rum and brandy, then flame the mixture. Sprinkle the cinnamon onto the bananas.

5. When the flames die, spoon the bananas and sauce over the ice cream and serve immediately.

✦✦✦

RECIPE 25.15

BANANA FRITTERS

Yield: 40 Fritters

Egg, beaten	1	1
Milk	8 oz.	250 mL
Unsalted butter, melted	2 oz.	60 g
Vanilla extract	1 tsp.	5 mL
Orange zest, finely grated	2 Tbsp.	30 mL
Orange juice	2 oz.	60 mL
Ripe banana	1 large	1 large
Pastry flour, sifted	12 oz.	340 g
Granulated sugar	4 oz.	120 g
Baking powder	1 Tbsp.	15 mL
Salt	1/2 tsp.	2 mL
Confectioner's sugar	as needed for garnish	

Approximate values per fritter:

Calories	60
Total fat	1.5 g
Saturated fat	1 g
Cholesterol	10 mg
Sodium	35 mg
Total carbohydrates	11 g
Protein	1 g

1. Whisk together the egg, milk, butter and vanilla. Add the orange zest and juice.

2. Peel and dice the banana (1/4 in./6 mm size) and add to the egg mixture.

3. Sift together the flour, sugar, baking powder and salt. Gently stir in the banana-egg mixture to form a thick batter.

4. Heat deep-fat fryer oil to 350°F (180°C). Fry 1-tablespoon (15-mL) portions of the batter until the fritters are brown and crisp, approximately 5 minutes.

5. Drain on paper towels, dust with confectioner's sugar and serve hot.

✦✦✦

RECIPE 25.16

LEMON CURD

Yield: 1-1/2 qt. (1.5 L)

Eggs, large	12	12
Egg yolks	4	4
Granulated sugar	2 lb.	900 g
Unsalted butter, cubed	1 lb.	450 g
Lemon zest	from 8 lemons	from 8 lemons
Fresh lemon juice	12 oz.	350 mL

Approximate values per 1 oz. (30 g) serving:

Calories	170
Total fat	9 g
Saturated fat	5 g
Cholesterol	90 mg
Sodium	20 mg
Total carbohydrates	20 g
Protein	2 g
Vitamin A	10%

1. Whisk all ingredients together in a large bowl.

2. Place the bowl over a pan of simmering water and cook, stirring frequently, until very thick, approximately 20–25 minutes.

3. Strain, cover and chill completely. Serve with scones or use as a filling for tartlets or layer cakes.

◆◆◆

RECIPE 25.17

BRAISED RHUBARB

Yield: 10 lb. (4.5 kg)

Tart green apples, peeled and cubed	2 lb. 8 oz.	1.1 kg
Rhubarb, Fresh or IQF pieces	7 lb.	3.2 kg
Unsalted butter	4 oz.	120 g
Sweet white wine	8 oz.	250 mL
Brown sugar	14 oz.	400 g
Vanilla extract	2 tsp.	10 mL
Cinnamon	1 Tbsp.	15 mL
Nutmeg	1/4 tsp.	1 mL
Orange juice	2 oz.	60 mL
Salt	1/2 tsp.	2 mL

1. Sauté the apples and rhubarb in the butter until they begin to soften.

2. Add the wine and reduce by half. Add the remaining ingredients. Simmer until the rhubarb is very tender.

3. Serve at room temperature in prebaked pastry cups, topped with crème chantilly, or serve warm over ice cream.

Approximate values per 1 oz. (30 g) serving:

Calories	60
Total fat	2 g
Saturated fat	.5 g
Cholesterol	0 mg
Sodium	25 mg
Total carbohydrates	11 g
Protein	0 g

Claims—low fat; no cholesterol; very low sodium

◆◆◆

RECIPE 25.18

BERRY COMPOTE

Yield: 1 pt. (450 mL)

Berries, fresh or frozen	1 pt.	500 mL
Granulated sugar	4 oz.	120 g
Oranges, juice and zest	2	2
Honey	3 oz.	90 mL
Cinnamon stick	1	1
Brandy	3 Tbsp.	45 mL

1. Select an assortment of fresh or frozen berries—strawberries, blueberries, raspberries, blackberries and cherries can be used, depending on availability.

2. Place the fruits and sugar in a nonreactive saucepan. Add the juice of 2 oranges. Bring to a simmer over low heat; cook until the fruits are soft but still intact.

3. Strain the mixture, saving both the fruits and the liquid. Return the liquid to the saucepan. Add the finely grated zest from 1 orange, the honey, cinnamon and brandy.

4. Bring to a boil and reduce until the mixture thickens enough to coat the back of a spoon. Remove from the heat and cool to room temperature.

5. Gently stir the reserved fruits into the sauce, cover and chill.

Approximate values per 1 oz. (30 g) serving:

Calories	70
Total fat	0 g
Saturated fat	0 g
Cholesterol	0 mg
Sodium	0 mg
Total carbohydrates	16 g
Protein	0 g
Vitamin C	15%

Claims—fat free; no sodium

◆◆◆

RECIPE 25.19

APPLESAUCE

Yield: 1 qt. (1 L)

McIntosh apples	4 lb.	1.8 kg
Granulated sugar	5 oz.	150 g
Lemon juice	1 Tbsp.	15 mL
Cinnamon sticks	2	2

1. Peel, core and quarter the apples. Place in a saucepan with just enough cold water to cover the bottom of the pan. Add the cinnamon sticks.

2. Bring to a simmer, cover and cook until the apples are tender, approximately 15 minutes.

3. Add the sugar and lemon juice. Simmer 10 minutes more.

4. Remove the cinnamon sticks and press the apples through a food mill.

Approximate values per 1 oz. (30 g) serving:

Calories	50
Total fat	0 g
Saturated fat	0 g
Cholesterol	0 mg
Sodium	0 mg
Total carbohydrates	13 g
Protein	0 g
Claims—fat free; no sodium	

◆◆◆

RECIPE 25.20

FRESH CRANBERRY-ORANGE SAUCE

Yield: 3 qt. (3 L)

Granulated sugar	1 lb.	450 g
Orange juice	4 oz.	120 mL
Water	8 oz.	225 mL
Fresh or frozen cranberries	1 lb. 8 oz.	700 g
Cinnamon stick	1	1
Orange liqueur	2 oz.	60 mL
Orange zest, finely grated	2 Tbsp.	30 mL
Orange segments	20	20

1. Combine the sugar, juice and water in a nonreactive saucepan; bring to a boil.

2. Add the cranberries and cinnamon stick and simmer uncovered until the berries begin to burst, approximately 15 minutes. Skim off any foam that rises to the surface.

3. Add the orange liqueur and zest and simmer for another 5 minutes.

4. Remove from the heat and remove the cinnamon stick. Add the orange segments. Cool and refrigerate.

Approximate values per 1 oz. (30 g) serving:

Calories	25
Total fat	0 g
Saturated fat	0 g
Cholesterol	0 mg
Sodium	0 mg
Total carbohydrates	6 g
Protein	0 g
Claims—fat free; no sodium; low calorie	

◆◆◆

RECIPE 25.21

MANGO CHUTNEY

Yield: 1-1/2 qt. (1.5 L)

Mango, peeled and diced	2 lb.	900 g
Onion, fine dice	4 oz.	120 g
Garlic cloves, minced	2	2
Cider vinegar	8 oz.	225 mL
Dark brown sugar	8 oz.	225 g
Golden raisins	2-1/2 oz.	75 g
Crystallized ginger	4 oz.	120 g

Salt	1/2 tsp.	2 mL
Cinnamon sticks	2	2
Red pepper flakes	1/2 tsp.	2 mL
Mustard seeds	1/2 tsp.	2 mL
Fresh ginger	1 tsp.	5 mL
Lime juice	1 oz.	30 mL

Approximate values per 1 oz. (30 g) serving:	
Calories	50
Total fat	0 g
Saturated fat	0 g
Cholesterol	0 mg
Sodium	30 mg
Total carbohydrates	12 g
Protein	0 g
Vitamin C	10%
Claims—fat free; very low sodium	

1. Combine the mango, onion, garlic, vinegar and sugar in a large, heavy saucepan. Cook until the sugar dissolves.
2. Stir in the raisins, crystallized ginger, salt and spices. Simmer until the onions and raisins are very soft, approximately 45 minutes. Skim foam from the surface as necessary.
3. Stir in the lime juice and adjust the seasonings.
4. Remove from the heat and cool uncovered. The chutney will thicken somewhat as it cools but should be thinner than fruit preserves.

RECIPE 25.22
McIntosh Apple Refreshment

WESTIN PRINCE HOTEL, Toronto, ON
Executive Chef Hans U. Herzig

Yield: 10 Servings

McIntosh apples	10	10
Sugar (or to taste)	1/2 cup	110 g
Lemons, juiced	2	2
Cream, 35%	2 cups	450 mL

1. Grate the unpeeled apples with a medium grater.
2. Mix in sugar (to taste), lemon juice and cream.
3. Keep mixture in freezer for 1–2 hours.
4. With 2 spoons, form some quenelles. You should get about 10 from the mixture.
5. Garnish to your liking. Serve instead of sherbet between courses of a meal.

Hans U. Herzig
Hans was born in Switzerland, trained in Europe, and came to Canada to work at the Windsor Arms in Toronto. Among the highlights of his career, he was Captain of the Canadian Team that won 10 gold medals at the 1988 World Culinary Olympics.

RECIPE 25.23
Parsnip and Rhubarb Soup with Dried Pear Chips

METROPOLITAN HOTEL, Vancouver, BC
Chef Michael Noble

Yield: 10 Servings

Parsnip, diced	2 lb.	800 g
Onion, diced	1	1
Rhubarb stalks, diced	4	4
Celery hearts, branch, diced	2	2
Pear, diced	2	2
Ginger, grated	3 oz.	75 g

Continued

Michael Noble
Michael opened Diva at the Met in 1996, and within a year it was in the centre of Vancouver's culinary spotlight, winning awards from Gourmet Magazine, Vancouver Magazine and GQ. Michael also achieved Canada's highest standings ever at the Bocuse d'Or World Cuisine championship in Lyons, 1995 and 1997.

Butter	4 oz.	100 g
Flour	4 oz.	100 g
Chicken stock, hot	70 oz.	2 L
Cream, 35%	20 oz.	500 mL
Salt and white pepper	TT	TT
Pear Chips (recipe follows)	as needed for garnish	

1. Sweat off the onions in the melted butter, over medium heat. Add the parsnips, rhubarb, celery, pear and grated ginger. Continue sautéing until the vegetables are slightly soft.

2. Sprinkle the flour over the vegetables to make a roux. Add the chicken stock. Bring to a simmer and add a little salt and white pepper. Continue simmering for approximately 40 minutes, adding the cream during the last 10 minutes of cooking.

3. Purée the soup, correct the seasoning and add more cream, if desired. Garnish with pear chips.

Approximate values for whole recipe:

Calories	143
Total fat	.1 g
Saturated fat	.04 g
Cholesterol	0 mg
Sodium	.1 mg
Total carbohydrates	37 g
Protein	.1 g

PEAR CHIPS

Pear, ripe, but firm	1	1
Icing sugar	to dust	to dust

1. Slice the pear into very thin slices. Lay the slices on a baking pan on silicon paper. Dust the slices with icing sugar and bake in a 325°F (165°C) oven until dry and golden brown (approximately 15 minutes).

2. Use to garnish the soup as it is being served.

WEBLINKS

Cranberry Home Page
www.scs.carleton.ca/~palepu/cranberry.html

California Strawberry Commission
www.calstrawberry.com/

Fruit Categories
www.produceoasis.com/Hierarchy_folder/MainFruits_folder/MainFruits.html

Pear Pages—Pear Varieties
www2.usapears.com/pears/pbvar.htm

U.S. National Watermelon Promotion Board: Watermelon Information
www.watermelon.org/backgrnd.html#about

U.S. Cherry Marketing Institute: Consumer Information
www.cherrymkt.org/consinfo.html

North American Blueberry Council
www.blueberry.org/

PART FOUR
BAKING

Like cooking, learning to bake fresh breads and to prepare both classic and contemporary pastries and desserts is not simply a matter of following written directions. You must understand the baking process as well as fundamental techniques and procedures.

In order to provide you with a thorough introduction to the skills needed in a bakeshop, we focus on preparing the types of breads and desserts usually found in a small retail shop or restaurant. Because this book is not designed for large wholesale or commercial bakeries, mixes, stabilizers and mechanical preparation and shaping skills are not included.

Part IV begins with a chapter on preparation and ingredients, then presents chapters on quick breads and yeast breads. We then shift to desserts with chapters on pies, pastries and cookies (including classic doughs such as puff pastry and éclair paste), cakes and frostings (including brownies), and creams, custards, frozen desserts and dessert sauces. Many of the recipes found at the end of these chapters are assembled using components from one or more other chapters.

Throughout this portion of the book, you will see the word formula used in place of recipe. This is standard terminology in the industry.

PRINCIPLES OF THE BAKESHOP

LEARNING OUTCOMES

After studying this chapter you will be able to:

✦ recognize and select ingredients used in a bakeshop
✦ control the development of gluten
✦ cook sugar correctly
✦ explain how to use sheet gelatin
✦ control the baking process
✦ recognize many of the specialized tools and equipment used in the bakeshop

F

lour, sugar, eggs, milk, butter, flavourings—with this simple list of ingredients you can produce a seemingly endless variety of goods, from breads to sauces to pastries. But to produce consistently good brioche, Bavarians, biscuits or the like, you must pay careful attention to the character and quantity of each ingredient, the way the ingredients are combined and how heat is applied to them. Unlike a cut of meat that can be grilled, roasted, sautéed or braised and still be the same cut of meat, bakeshop products depend on careful, precise preparation for their very identity.

Accurate measurements are critical in the bakeshop. It is equally important to follow bakeshop formulas carefully and completely. Unlike the rest of the kitchen, mistakes in the bakeshop often cannot be discovered until the product is finished, by which time it is too late to correct them. For example, if you omit the salt when preparing a stew, the mistake can be corrected by adding salt at service time. If you omit the salt from a loaf of bread, however, the mistake cannot be corrected after the bread has baked—and its texture and flavour may be ruined as a result. To follow a written formula, measure ingredients precisely and combine them accurately is more important in the bakeshop than anywhere else in the kitchen.

INGREDIENTS

While substituting ingredients may have little or no effect on some dishes (you can use carrots instead of turnips in a stew, for instance), this is not the case with baked goods. Different flours, fats, liquids and sweeteners function differently. Bread flour and cake flour are not the same, nor are shortening and butter. If you substitute one ingredient for another, the results will be different.

Understanding ingredients, why they function the way they do and how to adjust for their differences will make your baking experiences more successful and consistent. This chapter discusses flours, sugar and other sweeteners, fats, thickeners and flavourings such as chocolate, extracts and liquors. Eggs and dairy products, also common in baked goods, are discussed in Chapter 8, Eggs and Dairy Products.

Flours

Wheat Flour

The most frequently used—and therefore the most important—ingredient in the bakeshop is wheat flour (Fr. *farine*). Flour provides bulk and structure to baked goods.

Flour is produced by milling wheat kernels (berries). As discussed in Chapter 23, Potatoes, Grains and Pasta, a wheat kernel has an outer covering called bran. It is composed of several layers that protect the endosperm, which contains starches and proteins. The innermost part is the germ, which contains fat and serves as the wheat seed (see Figure 23.1). During milling, the kernels first pass through metal rollers to crack them, then the bran and germ are removed through repeated stages of sifting and separation. The remaining endosperm is then ground into flour. Flour derived from the portion of the endosperm closest to the germ is finer; flour derived from the portion of the endosperm nearer the bran is coarser and darker.

The character of the wheat determines the character of the flour. Wheats are classified as *soft* or *hard* depending on the kernel's hardness. The harder the wheat kernel, the higher its protein content. Soft wheat yields a soft flour with a low protein content. Soft flour, also called weak flour, is best for tender products such as cakes. Hard wheat yields a hard flour with a high protein content. Hard flour, also known as strong flour, is used for yeast breads.

Various types of flour are created by mixing or blending flours from different sources. **All-purpose flour**, a blend of hard and soft flours, is designed for use in a wide range of foods. It is also referred to in this book because it is readily available in quantities appropriate for small food service operations. Large bakeshops rarely use all-purpose flour; instead, they choose flours specifically milled and blended for industrial uses.

Aging and Bleaching

Any flour develops better baking qualities if allowed to rest for several weeks after milling. Freshly milled flour produces sticky doughs and products with less volume than those made with aged flour. While aging, flour turns white through a natural oxidation process referred to as bleaching.

Natural aging and bleaching are somewhat unpredictable, time-consuming processes, however, so chemicals are now used to do both. Benzoyl peroxide and chlorine dioxide gas rapidly ages flour. Chlorine dioxide and other chemicals bleach flour by removing yellow pigments in order to obtain a uniform white colour. Bleaching destroys small amounts of the flour's naturally occurring vitamin E, which is replaced in fortified or enriched products.

Composition of Flour

Flour is composed primarily of five nutrients: fat, minerals, moisture, starches and proteins. Fat and minerals each generally account for less than 1% of flour's content. The moisture content of flour is also relatively low—when packaged, it cannot exceed 15% under government standards. But its actual moisture content varies depending on climatic conditions and storage. In damp areas, flour absorbs moisture from the atmosphere.

Starches comprise 63% to 77% of flour, and are necessary for the absorption of moisture during baking. This process, known as **gelatinization**, occurs primarily at temperatures above 140°F (60°C). Starches also provide food for yeast during **fermentation**.

Flour proteins are important because of their gluten-forming potential. **Gluten** is the tough, rubbery substance created when wheat flour is mixed with water. Gluten strands are both plastic (i.e., they change shape under pressure) and elastic (they resume their original shape when that pressure is removed). Gluten is responsible for the volume, texture and appearance of baked goods. It provides structure and enables dough to retain the gases given off by leavening agents. Without gluten, there could be no raised breads: The gases created by yeast fermentation or chemical leaveners would simply escape if there were no network of gluten strands to trap them in the dough.

The higher a flour's protein content, the greater that flour's gluten-forming potential. The proteins responsible for gluten formation are *glutenin* and *gliadin*. Flour does not contain gluten; only a dough or batter can contain gluten. Gluten is produced when glutenin and gliadin are moistened and

TABLE 26.1   PROTEIN CONTENT OF FLOURS

Type of Flour	Percent Protein	Uses
Cake	7–9.5	Tender cakes
Pastry	7.5–10	Biscuits, pie crusts
All-purpose	10–13	General baking
Bread	12–15	Yeast breads
Whole wheat	13–14	Breads
High gluten	41–42	To increase protein content of weaker flours for bread making

manipulated, as when they are stirred or kneaded. Generally, the longer a substance is mixed, the more gluten will develop. Products requiring a dough that can be kneaded and shaped, such as French rolls, require a flour with a higher protein content than products meant to be tender, such as cakes or muffins.

Table 26.1 lists the protein content and uses for several common flours. Remember that substitutions will result in a changed and probably less desirable product.

Specialty Flours

Whole Wheat

Whole wheat flour, also referred to as graham flour, is made by milling the entire wheat kernel, except the germ. Whole wheat flour has a nutty, sweet flavour and brown, flecked colour. Products made with whole wheat flour will be denser, with less volume than those made with white flour. Whole wheat milled with the germ is not a commercial commodity in Canada because the fat content of the germ may cause rancidity. Whole wheat flour with germ is available in health food stores.

Self-Rising

Self-rising flour is an all-purpose flour to which salt and a chemical leavener, usually baking powder, have been added. It is not recommended for professional use. Chemicals lose their leavening ability over time and may cause inconsistent results. Furthermore, different formulas call for different ratios of salt and leaveners; no commercial blend is appropriate for all purposes.

Nonwheat Flours

Nonwheat flours, also referred to as composite flours, are made from grains, seeds or beans. Corn, soybeans, rice, oats, buckwheat, potatoes and other items provide flours, but none of them contain the gluten-forming proteins of wheat flour. Composite flours are generally blended with a high-protein wheat flour for baking. Substituting a composite flour for wheat flour changes the flavour and texture of the product. Specialized bakeries produce gluten-free products for sufferers of celiac sprue. Combinations of starches are used in addition to other ingredients to produce products with texture. Care must be taken not to contaminate gluten-free products with flours that form gluten.

Rye flour is commonly used in bread baking. It is milled from the rye berry much like wheat flour is milled from the wheat berry. Rye flour comes in four grades or colours: white, medium, dark and pumpernickel. White rye flour is

TABLE 26.2   NUTRITIONAL VALUES OF SELECTED FLOURS

Per 1-oz. (28-g) unit	Kcal	Protein (g)	Carbohydrates (g)	Fibre (g)	Total Fat (g)
All-purpose flour	103	2.9	21.6	0.8	0.3
Bread flour	102	3.4	20.6	mq	0.5
Rye flour, dark	92	4	19.5	mq	0.8
Whole wheat flour	96	3.9	20.6	3.6	0.5

The Corinne T. Netzer Encyclopedia of Food Values 1992
mq = measurable quantity but data are unavailable

made from only the centre of the rye berry. Medium and dark rye flours are made from the whole rye berry after the bran is removed. Pumpernickel is made by grinding the entire rye berry, including the bran. All rye flours have a warm, pungent flavour similar to caraway and a grey-brown colour. Although rye flour contains proteins, they will not form gluten, so a bread made with 100% rye flour will be dense and flat. Therefore, rye flour is usually blended with a high-protein wheat flour to produce a more acceptable product.

Nutrition

Flours are generally high in carbohydrates and low in fat. (See Table 26.2.) The grains from which they are milled are often rich in vitamins and minerals. Some of these nutrients, however, are lost during milling. In enriched flours, thiamin, riboflavin, niacin and iron are added at levels set by the government.

Purchasing and Storing

Most flours are purchased in 50- and 100-pound (20- and 40-kg) bags. They should be stored in a well-ventilated room at temperatures no higher than 80°F (27°C). Flour can be stored in a refrigerator or freezer if necessary to prevent the onset of rancidity if the germ is present. Refrigeration may cause the flour to absorb moisture, however, which will limit the flour's ability to absorb additional moisture during actual use.

An open bag of flour should be transferred to a closed container to prevent contamination. Even unopened bags of flour should not be stored near items with strong odours, as flour readily absorbs odours.

Sugar and Sweeteners

Sugar (Fr. *sucre*) and other sweeteners serve several purposes in the bakeshop: They provide flavour and colour, tenderize products by weakening gluten strands, provide food for yeasts, act as a preservative to increase shelf life (keeping qualities) by retaining moisture and act as a creaming or foaming agent to assist with leavening. Sugars also give colour to crusts.

Sugar

Sugars are carbohydrates. They are classified as either (1) single or simple sugars (monosaccharides) such as glucose and fructose, which occur naturally in honey and fruits, or (2) double or complex sugars (disaccharides) which may occur naturally, such as lactose in milk, or in refined sugars.

◆◆◆

SUGAR:
A SWEET AND SORDID PAST

Few foods have so murky an early history as sugar, now one of the most commonplace of foods. Neither botanists nor anthropologists know precisely where sugar cane first grew or when sugar was first extracted from it.

Nevertheless, there are records of a crude sugar being used as a sweetener in India over 2500 years ago. Sugar cane was being cultivated in the Middle East by the 6th century A.D. and spread from there to North Africa and Spain. Egyptians were manufacturing sugar commercially by the 10th century A.D.

Western Europeans first encountered sugar in the Middle East during the 12th-century Crusades. During the succeeding centuries, sugar remained a rare luxury in Europe. The small amounts available were traded by spice merchants and dispensed by apothecaries. At first sugar was used only as a medicine, a condiment or, occasionally, as a preservative. English cookbooks dating from the late 1300s illustrate an indiscriminate use of sugar as a condiment for meats, fish and vegetables. Like spices, sugar was used to show a person's wealth and position.

When Columbus landed in the West Indies he found an environment perfectly suited for growing sugar cane, so he brought sugar cane cuttings to the New World on his second voyage in 1493. Huge sugar cane plantations soon flourished in the New World, built and worked by enslaved Africans and their descendants.

By the 18th century European and American middle classes were able to afford sugar by the pound. Sugar was now being used principally as a sweetener, particularly in connection with three other imports: coffee, tea and chocolate. Sugar, in fact, had become one of the principal components of a vast and complex trade network involving molasses from the West Indies, distilled rum from New England, finished goods from Europe and slaves from Africa.

Early sugars bore little resemblance to the white granulated substance we use today. Until vacuum pans and centrifuges were invented in the late 19th century, pure sugars were unobtainable. All contained varying amounts of molasses and other impurities. Most of the world's sugar was sold only in large, brown cones. The price of sugar depended on its whiteness and fineness, with the whitest sugar being the most costly.

After two centuries of prosperity, the sugar cane industry began to decline in the 19th century. Several factors contributed to this: abolition of slavery, discovery of alternative sweeteners and falling sugar prices.

If cane sugar was an ancient plant exploited in the New World, then beet sugar is a modern plant fully realized in the Old World. While the ability to refine a crude sweetener from root vegetables had been known for centuries, scientists and chefs mistakenly believed that sugar could be obtained only from plants grown in tropical heat. It was not until 1747 that a German chemist, Andreas Marggraf, proved otherwise. He isolated sucrose—the same substance produced from sugar cane—from white beets. His research, however, did not have a commercial application until cane sugar supplies were threatened. During the Napoleonic Wars, the British blockade of European ports cut off supplies of cane sugar. At Napoleon's urging, research into manufacturing beet sugar progressed. The first beet sugar factory was built in France in 1812. Soon France, Germany and Belgium were virtually self-sufficient in sugar production.

Consumers accepted this new sugar with few complaints; most were totally unaware of any difference. Today about 40% of the world's sugar is manufactured from beets, primarily in Russia, Germany and the United States.

The sugar most often used in the kitchen is **sucrose**, a refined sugar obtained from both the large tropical grass called sugar cane (*saccharum officinarum*) and the root of the sugar beet (*beta vulgaris*). Sucrose is a disaccharide, composed of one molecule each of glucose and fructose. The chemical composition of beet and cane sugars is identical. The two products taste, look, smell and react the same. Sucrose is available in many forms: white granulated, light or dark brown granulated, molasses or powdered.

Sugar Manufacturing

Common **refined** or **table sugar** is produced from sugar cane or sugar beets. The first step in sugar production is to crush the cane or beet to extract the juice. This juice contains tannins, pigments, proteins and other undesirable components that must be removed through refinement. Refinement begins by dissolving the juice in water, then boiling it in large steam evaporators. The solution is then crystallized in heated vacuum pans. The uncrystallized liquid byproduct, known as **molasses**, is separated out in a centrifuge. The remaining crystallized product, known as **raw sugar**, contains many impurities and is considered unfit for direct use in food.

Raw sugar is washed with steam to remove some of the impurities. This yields a product known as **demerara sugar**. Refining continues as the demerara is heated, liquefied, centrifuged and filtered. Chemicals may be used to bleach and purify the liquid sugar. Finally, the clear liquid sugar is recrystallized in vacuum pans as **granulated white sugar**.

Pure sucrose is sold in granulated and powdered forms and is available in several grades. Because there are no government standards regulating grade labels, various manufacturers' products may differ slightly.

Demerara Sugar

Demerara sugar, sometimes called turbinado sugar, is the closest consumable product to raw sugar. It is partially refined, light brown in colour, with coarse crystals and a caramel flavour. It is sometimes used in beverages and certain baked goods. Because of its high and variable moisture content, demerara sugar is not recommended as a substitute for granulated or brown sugar.

Sanding Sugar

Sanding sugar has a large, coarse crystal structure that prevents it from dissolving easily. It is used almost exclusively for decorating cookies and pastries.

Regular Granulated Sugar

This is the all-purpose sugar used throughout the kitchen. The crystals are a fine, uniform size suitable for a variety of purposes.

Cube Sugar

Sugar cubes are formed by pressing moistened granulated sugar into moulds and allowing it to dry. Cube sugar is most often used for beverage service.

Clockwise from top left: Demerara sugar cubes, light brown sugar, icing sugar, sugar cubes, brown sugar crystals, granulated sugar

Brown Sugar

Brown sugar is simply regular refined sugar with some of the molasses returned to it. Light brown sugar contains approximately 3.5% molasses; dark brown sugar contains about 6.5%. Molasses adds moisture and a distinctive flavour. Brown sugar can be substituted for refined sugar, measure for measure, in any formula where its flavour is desired. Because of the added moisture, brown sugar tends to lump, trapping air into pockets. It should be measured by weight or if measured by volume it should be packed firmly into the measuring cup in order to remove any air pockets. Always store brown sugar in an air-tight container to prevent it from drying and hardening.

Superfine or Castor Sugar

Superfine sugar is granulated sugar with a smaller-sized crystal. Also known as castor sugar, it can be produced by processing regular granulated sugar in a food processor for a few moments. Superfine sugar dissolves quickly in liquids and produces light and tender cakes.

Icing or Confectioner's Sugar

Icing sugar (Fr. *sucre en poudre*) is made by grinding granulated sugar crystals through varying degrees of fine screens. Icing sugar cannot be made in a food processor. It is widely available in three degrees of fineness: 10X is the finest and most common; 6X and 4X are progressively coarser. Because of icing sugar's tendency to lump, 3% cornstarch is added to absorb moisture. Icing sugar is most often used in icings and glazes and for decorating baked products.

Liquid Sweeteners

Liquid sweeteners can be used to achieve the same benefits as sugar, except for leavening, in baked goods. Most of these liquids have a distinctive flavour as well as sweetness. Some liquid sweeteners are made from sugar cane; others are derived from other plants, grains or bees.

Corn Syrup

Corn syrup is produced by extracting starch from corn kernels and treating it with acid or an enzyme to develop a sweet syrup. This syrup is extremely thick or viscous and less sweet-tasting than honey or refined sugar. Its viscosity gives foods a thick, chewy texture. Corn syrup is available in light and dark forms; the dark syrup has caramel colour and flavour added. Corn syrup is a **hygroscopic** (water-attracting) sweetener, which means it will attract water from the air on humid days and lose water through evaporation more slowly than granulated sugar. Thus, it keeps products moister and fresher longer.

Honey

Honey (Fr. *miel*) is a powerful sweetener composed of fructose and glucose. It is created by honey bees from nectar collected from flowers. Its flavour and colour vary depending on the season, the type of flower the nectar came from and its age. Commercial honey is often a blend, prepared to be relatively neutral and consistent. Like corn syrup, honey is highly hygroscopic. Its distinctive flavour is found in several ethnic foods such as baklava and halvah, and beverages such as Drambuie and Benedictine.

Maple Syrup

Maple syrup is made from the sap of sugar maple trees. Sap is collected during the spring, then boiled to evaporate its water content, yielding a sweet brown syrup. One sugar maple tree produces about 12 gallons (48 L) of sap each season; 30–40 gallons (120 to 160 L) of sap will produce about 1 gallon (4 L) of syrup. Pure maple syrup must weigh not less than 11 pounds per gallon; it is graded according to colour, flavour and sugar content. The more desirable products, Canada No. 1, light and medium, have a light amber colour and delicate flavour. Pure maple syrup is expensive, but it does add a distinct flavour to baked goods, frostings and, of course, pancakes and waffles.

Maple-flavoured syrups, often served with pancakes, are usually corn syrups with artificial colourings and flavourings added. Birch tree syrup is a prized product when available.

Molasses

As mentioned earlier, molasses (Fr. *mélasse*) is the liquid byproduct of sugar refining. Edible molasses is derived only from cane sugar, as beet molasses has an unpleasant odour and bitter flavour. *Unsulphured molasses* is not a true byproduct of sugar making. It is intentionally produced from pure cane syrup and is preferred because of its lighter colour and milder flavour. *Sulphured molasses* is a byproduct and contains some of the sulphur dioxide used in secondary sugar processing. It is darker and has a strong, bitter flavour.

TABLE 26.3   NUTRITIONAL VALUES OF SELECTED SWEETENERS

Units as Noted	Kcal	Carbohydrates (g)	Sodium (mg)
Corn syrup, light, 2 Tbsp. (30 mL)	120	30	60
Honey, 2 Tbsp. (30 mL)	120	32	na
Molasses, unsulphured, 2 Tbsp. (30 mL)	140	34	56
Sugar, brown, light, 1 oz. (28 g)	106	27	1
Sugar, granulated, 1 oz. (28 g)	109	28	<1
Sugar, powdered, 1 oz. (28 g)	109	28	<1

The Corinne T. Netzer Encyclopedia of Food Values 1992

The final stage of sucrose refinement yields *blackstrap molasses*, which is somewhat popular in the American South. Blackstrap molasses is very dark and thick, with a strong, unique flavour that is unsuitable for most purposes.

Sorghum molasses is produced by cooking down the sweet sap of a brown corn plant, known as sorghum, which is grown for animal feed. The flavour and appearance of sorghum molasses are almost identical to unsulphured sugar cane molasses.

Nutrition

Sweeteners are carbohydrates. They are high in calories and contain no fibre, protein, fat, vitamin A or vitamin C. They contain only trace amounts of thiamin, riboflavin and niacin. (See Table 26.3.)

Cooking Sugar

Sugar can be incorporated into a prepared item in its dry form or first liquefied into a syrup. **Sugar syrups** (not to be confused with liquid sweeteners such as molasses) take two forms: **simple syrups**, which are mixtures of sugar and water, and **cooked syrups**, which are made of melted sugar cooked until it reaches a specific temperature. Be extremely careful when working with hot sugar syrup. Because sugar reaches very high temperatures it can cause severe burns.

Simple Sugar Syrups

Simple or stock syrups are solutions of sugar and water. They are used in the bakeshop to moisten cakes and to make sauces, fruit sorbets, buttercreams and candied fruits.

The syrup's density or concentration is dictated by its intended purpose. Cold water will dissolve up to double its weight in sugar; heating the solution forms denser, more concentrated syrups. A hydrometer, which measures specific gravity and shows degrees of concentration on the Baumé scale, is the most accurate guide to density. See the photo to the right.

Simple syrups can be prepared without the aid of a hydrometer, however. To make a simple sugar syrup, specific amounts of water and sugar are combined in a saucepan and brought to a boil. Once the solution boils, it is important not to stir, as this may cause recrystallization or lumping. For successful simple sugar syrups, the following formulas must be followed precisely.

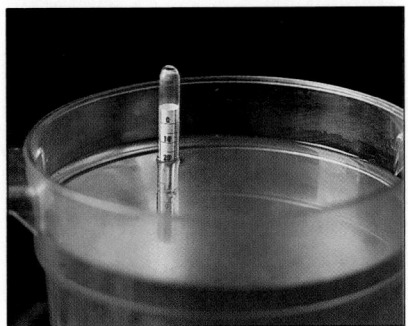

Using a Baumé hydrometer.

◆ *Light syrup*—Boil 2 parts water with 1 part sugar by weight for 1 minute. This concentration would measure 17–20° on the Baumé scale. A light syrup can be used for making sorbet or moistening spongecake.

◆ *Medium syrup*—Boil 1 part sugar with 1-1/2 parts water by weight for 1 minute. This concentration would measure 21–24° on the Baumé scale. A medium syrup can be used for candying citrus peel.

◆ *Heavy syrup*—Boil equal weights of water and sugar for 1 minute. This concentration would measure 28–30° on the Baumé scale, and the solution should be at 220°F (104°C). Heavy syrup is a basic, all-purpose syrup kept on hand in many bakeshops.

Cooked Sugars

Caramel sauce, candy and other confections often need liquid sugar that will have a cooked caramel flavour or be firm when cool. For these purposes, sugar needs to be cooked to temperatures far higher than simple syrups. A small amount of water is generally added at the beginning to help the sugar dissolve evenly. As the mixture boils, the water evaporates, the solution's temperature rises and its density increases. The syrup's concentration depends on the amount of water remaining in the final solution: The less water, the harder the syrup will become when cool.

The sugar's temperature indicates its concentration. If there is a great deal of water present, the temperature will not rise much above 212°F (100°C). As water evaporates, however, the temperature will rise until it reaches 320°F (160°C), the point at which all water is evaporated. At temperatures above 320°F (160°C), the pure sugar begins to brown or caramelize. As sugar caramelizes, its sweetening power decreases dramatically. At approximately 375°F (190°C), sugar will burn, developing a bitter flavour. If allowed to continue cooking, sugar will ignite.

1. Caramelizing sugar.

Sugar solutions are unstable because of their molecular structure. They can recrystallize because of agitation or uneven heat distribution. Several steps should be taken to prevent recrystallization:

1. Always use a heavy, clean saucepan, preferably copper.

2. Stir the solution to make sure all sugar crystals dissolve before it reaches a boil. Do not stir the solution after it begins boiling, however.

3. An interferent may be added when the solution begins to boil. Cream of tartar, vinegar, glucose (a monosaccharide) and lemon juice are known as **interferents** because they interfere with the formation of sugar crystals. Some formulas specify which interferent to use, although most are used in such small quantities that their taste cannot be detected.

2. Washing sugar crystals from the side of the pan.

4. Brush down the sides of the pan with cold water to wash off crystals that may be deposited there. These sugar crystals may seed the solution, causing more crystals (lumps) to form if not removed. Instead of using a brush to wash away crystals, you can cover the pan for a few moments as soon as the solution comes to a boil. Steam will condense on the cover and run down the sides of the pan, washing away the crystals.

The concentration of sugar syrup should be determined with a candy thermometer that measures very high temperatures. If a thermometer is not available, use the traditional but less accurate ice-water test: Spoon a few drops of the hot sugar into a bowl of very cold water. Check the hardness of the cooled sugar with your fingertips. Each stage of cooked sugar is named according to its firmness when cool—for example, soft ball or hard crack.

TABLE 26.4   STAGES OF COOKED SUGAR

Stage	Temperature	Ice-Water Test
Thread	236°F (110°C)	Spins a 2-in. (5-cm) thread when dropped
Soft ball	240°F (116°C)	Forms a soft ball
Firm ball	246°F (119°C)	Forms a firm ball
Hard ball	260°F (125°C)	Forms a hard, compact ball
Soft crack	270°F (132°C)	Separates into a hard, but not brittle, thread
Hard crack	300°F (149°C)	Separates into a hard, brittle sheet
Caramel	338°F (170°C)	Liquid turns brown

1. Soft ball stage

2. Hard ball stage

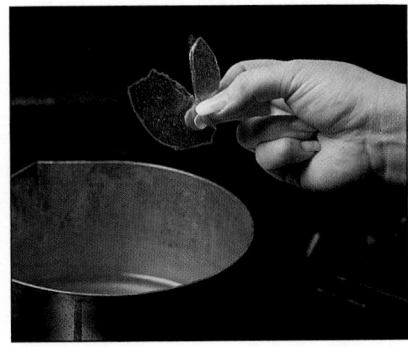

3. Hard crack stage

Table 26.4 lists the various stages of cooked sugar and the temperature for each. Each stage is also identified by the ice-water test result. Note that even a few degrees makes a difference in the syrup's concentration.

Fats

Fat is the general term for butter, lard, shortening, oil and margarine. Fats provide flavour and colour, add moisture and richness, assist with leavening, help extend a product's shelf life and shorten gluten strands.

The flavour and texture of a baked good depends on the type of fat used and the manner in which it is incorporated with other ingredients. In pastry doughs, solid fat shortens or tenderizes the gluten strands; in bread doughs, fat increases loaf volume and lightness; in cake batters, fat incorporates air bubbles and helps leaven the mixture. Fats should be selected based on their flavour, melting point and ability to form emulsions.

Most bakeshop ingredients combine completely with liquids; fats do not. Fats will not dissolve but will break down into smaller and smaller particles through mixing. With proper mixing, these fat particles are distributed, more or less evenly, throughout the other ingredients.

All-Purpose Shortening

Any fat is a shortening in baking because it shortens gluten strands and tenderizes the product. What is generally referred to as shortening, however, is a type of solid, white, generally tasteless fat, specially formulated for baking. Shortenings are made from animal fats and/or vegetable oils that are solidified through hydrogenation. These products are 100% fat with a relatively high melting point. Solid shortenings are ideal for greasing baking pans because they are tasteless and odourless.

Emulsified Shortening

Emulsifiers may be added to regular shortening to assist with moisture absorption and retention as well as leavening. Emulsified shortenings, also known as high-ratio shortenings, are used in the commercial production of cakes and frostings where the formula contains a large amount of sugar. If a formula calls for an emulsified shortening, use it. If you substitute any other fat, the product's texture suffers.

Lard

Lard (Fr. *saindoux*) is rendered pork fat. It is a solid white product of almost 100% pure fat; it contains only a small amount of water. Lard yields flaky, flavourful pastries, such as pie crusts, but is rarely used commercially because it turns rancid quickly and is not acceptable to some religious beliefs.

Butter and Margarine

Butter is prized in the bakeshop for its flavour; however, it melts at a relatively low temperature of 93°F (33°C) and burns easily. Unsalted butter is preferred for baking because it tends to be fresher, and additional salt might interfere with product formulas. Margarine melts at a slightly higher temperature than butter, making it useful for some rolled-in doughs such as puff pastry or danish. For detailed information on butter and margarine see Chapter 8, Eggs and Dairy Products.

Oil

Unlike butter and other fats, oil blends evenly throughout a mixture. It therefore coats more of the proteins, and the gluten strands produced are much shorter, a desirable result in fine-textured products such as muffins or chiffon cakes. For baking, select a neutral-flavoured oil unless the distinctive taste of olive oil is desired, as in some breads. Never substitute oil in a formula requiring a solid shortening. For detailed information on oil, see Chapter 7, Kitchen Staples.

Nutrition

Fats are high in calories and contain varying levels of saturated fats. Although they have no carbohydrates, a few fats such as butter have trace amounts of protein and minerals. (See Table 26.5.) Butter is also high in Vitamin A.

TABLE 26.5   NUTRITIONAL VALUES OF SELECTED FATS

Per 2 Tbsp. (30 mL)	Kcal	Total Fat (g)	Saturated Fat (g)	Cholesterol (mg)	Sodium (mg)
Butter, unsalted	200	22.8	14.2	62	2
Corn oil	240	27.2	3.4	0	0
Lard	230	25.6	10	24	0
Margarine	200	22	4	0	200
Margarine, diet	100	12	2	0	260
Shortening, all-purpose	226	25.6	6.4	0	0

The Corinne T. Netzer Encyclopedia of Food Values 1992

Thickeners

Starches are often used as thickening agents in bakeshop products. Cornstarch, arrowroot, instant starch, waxy maize and flour can be used as thickeners for pastry creams, sauces, custards and fruit fillings. Some of these thickeners are discussed in Chapter 10, Stocks and Sauces.

One of the most commonly used thickeners in the bakeshop is **gelatin**, a natural product derived from the animal protein collagen. It is available in two forms: granulated gelatin and sheet (also called leaf) gelatin. A two-step process is necessary to use either form: The gelatin must first be softened in a cold liquid, then dissolved in a hot liquid.

Granulated gelatin is available in bulk or in 1/4-ounce (7 g or slightly less than 1 tablespoon) envelopes. One envelope is enough to set 1 pint (500 mL) of liquid. Granulated gelatin should be softened in a cool liquid for at least 5 minutes, then heated gently to dissolve. The initial softening in a cold liquid is necessary to separate the gelatin molecules so that they will not lump together when the hot liquid is added.

Sheet or leaf gelatin is available in 1-kilogram boxes, sometimes further packaged in 5- or 6-sheet envelopes. The sheets are produced in varying thicknesses and weights. They must be separated and soaked in ice water until very soft, at least 15 minutes. They are then removed from the water and stirred into a hot liquid until completely dissolved.

BASIC PROCEDURE FOR USING SHEET GELATIN

1. Gelatin sheets are submerged in ice water for several minutes to soften.

2. Softened gelatin sheets are then removed from the ice water and incorporated into a hot liquid.

Granulated and sheet gelatin can be substituted weight for weight in any formula. Sheet gelatin, though more expensive, is preferred for its lack of flavour and colour. It also tends to dissolve more readily and evenly and has a longer shelf life than the granulated product.

Once incorporated into a product such as a Bavarian, gelatin can be frozen, or melted and reset once or twice without a loss of thickening ability. Because it scorches easily, gelatin and mixtures containing gelatin should not be allowed to boil; a double boiler or steam jacket is recommended.

Flavourings

Many spices and flavourings are used in the bakeshop. The most popular spices such as cinnamon, cloves, nutmeg and allspice are discussed in Chapter 7, Kitchen Staples. Here we discuss emulsions and extracts, vanilla, chocolate and alcoholic beverages.

Emulsions and Extracts

Emulsions and extracts are liquid flavouring agents derived from various oils.

Emulsions are flavouring oils mixed into water with the aid of emulsifiers. Lemon and orange are the most common emulsions. Emulsions are much stronger than extracts and should be used carefully and sparingly.

Extracts are mixtures of flavouring oils and ethyl alcohol. Vanilla, almond and lemon are frequently used extracts. An extract may be made with pure flavouring oils or with artificial flavours and colours. Contents are regulated and must be clearly labelled.

Emulsions and extracts are highly volatile. They should be stored in sealed containers in a cool area away from direct light.

Vanilla

Vanilla (Fr. *vanille*) is the most frequently used flavouring in the bakeshop. It comes from the pod fruit, called a bean, of a vine in the orchid family. Vanilla beans are purchased whole, individually or by weight. They should be soft and pliable, with a rich brown colour and good aroma. The finest vanilla comes from Tahiti and Madagascar.

To use a vanilla bean, cut it open lengthwise with a paring knife. Scrape out the moist seeds with the knife's tip and stir them into the mixture being flavoured. The seeds do not dissolve and will remain visible as small black or brown flecks. After all the seeds have been removed, the bean can be stored in a covered container with sugar to create vanilla sugar.

Vanilla beans should be stored in an air-tight container in a cool, dark place. During storage, the beans may develop a white coating. This is not mould, but rather crystals of vanilla flavour known as **vanillin**. It should not be removed.

Pure vanilla extract is an easy and less expensive way to give bakeshop products a true vanilla flavour. It is dark brown and aromatic, and comes in several strengths referred to as folds. Each fold requires the extract from 13.35 ounces of vanilla beans per gallon of liquid. A two-fold contains 26.7 ounces per gallon and a four-fold contains 40.5 ounces. Single or two-fold are the most commonly available; the stronger products are used only in manufacturing. By law, any product labelled vanilla extract must not contain artificial flavourings and must be at least 35% alcohol by volume.

Vanilla extract should be stored at room temperature in a closed, opaque container. It should not be frozen.

Artificial or imitation vanilla flavouring is made with synthetic vanillin. Artificial flavouring is available in a clear form, which is useful for white buttercreams where the dark brown colour of pure vanilla extract would be undesirable. Although inexpensive, artificial vanilla is, at best, weaker and less aromatic than pure extract. It can also impart a chemical or bitter taste to foods.

Scrape seeds from the interior of a vanilla bean.

Chocolate

Chocolate is one of the most—perhaps *the* most—popular flavouring for candies, cookies, cakes and pastries. Chocolate is also served as a beverage and is an ingredient in the traditional spicy Mexican molé sauce. Chocolate is available in a variety of forms and degrees of sweetness.

Chocolate Production

Chocolate (Fr. *chocolat*) begins as yellow fruit pods dangling from the trunk and main branches of the tropical cacao tree. Each pod contains about 40 almond-sized cocoa beans. After the pods ripen, the beans are placed in the sun for several days to dry and ferment. They are then cleaned, dried, cured and roasted to develop flavour and reduce bitterness. Next the beans are crushed to remove their shells, yielding the prized chocolate **nib**.

Nibs are shipped to manufacturers worldwide where they can be further roasted. They are crushed into a thick (nonalcoholic) paste known as **chocolate liquor** or **chocolate mass**. Chocolate mass contains about 53% fat, known as **cocoa butter**. The chocolate mass is further refined depending on the desired product. If **cocoa powder** is to be produced, virtually all of the cocoa butter is removed. A variety of other products are created by adding

---

♦♦♦
FROM CACAO TO CHOCOLATE CHIPS

To understand the history of chocolate a chef or chocoholic must first understand the fundamental difference between its original use as a beverage and its later transformation into a candy.

The cacao tree (called *theobroma cacao*, meaning "food of the gods") originated in the river valleys of South America and was carried into what is now Mexico by the Mayans before the 7th century A.D. It was cultivated by Mayans, Aztecs and Toltecs not only as a source of food but also as currency. Chocolate was consumed only as a treasured drink. Cacao beans were roasted, crushed to a paste and steeped in water, then thickened with corn flour to create a cold, bitter beverage. Sometimes honey, vanilla or spices, including chiles, were added. The Aztec emperor Montezuma was so enamoured with the beverage that he reportedly consumed 50 cups at each meal.

Columbus brought cacao beans to Spain from his fourth voyage to the New World in 1504. (The common term *cocoa* is actually a western European mispronunciation of the proper term *cacao*, caused by confusion with another New World delicacy, the coconut.) But almost 20 years passed before Spanish conquistadors, led by Cortez, understood the beans' value. With Montezuma's encouragement, Cortez and his soldiers slowly acquired a taste for the bitter beverage, spurred on by the intoxicating effects of caffeine.

Cortez's most important contribution to the history of chocolate was to take beans with him when he left Mexico. He planted them on the islands he passed on his return to Spain: Trinidad, Haiti and Fernando Po, from which the giant African cocoa industry grew. Through Cortez's far-sighted efforts, Spain controlled all

aspects of the cocoa trade until well into the 18th century.

The Spanish began drinking chocolate at home during the 16th century. It was usually mixed with two other expensive imports, sugar and vanilla, and frothed with a carved wooden swizzle stick known as a *molinet*. This thick, cold drink was made from tablets of crushed cocoa beans produced and sold by monks. The Spanish believed that cocoa cured all ills and supplied limitless stamina. In the early 17th century cocoa beverages, now served hot, crept into France via royal marriages.

Cocoa spread through the rest of Europe by different routes. The Dutch, who had poached on Spanish trade routes for many years, even-

Chocolate Chef, sculpted by Chef Rubin Foster, Arizona Biltmore, Phoenix, AZ.

tually realized the value of the unusual beans they found on Spanish ships. Holland soon became the most important cocoa port outside of Spain. From there, a love of cocoa spread to Germany, Scandinavia and Italy. In 1655 England acquired Jamaica and its own cocoa plantations.

Until the Industrial Revolution, cocoa was made by hand using mortar and pestle or stone-grinding disks to crush the cocoa nibs. By the 1700s cocoa factories had opened throughout Europe. James Baker opened the first cocoa factory in the United States in 1765.

Conrad van Houten, a Dutch chemist, patented "chocolate powder" in 1825. His work marked the beginning of a shift from drinking to eating chocolate. It also paved the way for everything we know as chocolate today. Van Houten developed a screw press that removed most of the cocoa butter from the bean, leaving a brown, flaky powder, essentially the same substance as modern cocoa powder.

Eventually it was discovered that the extra cocoa butter resulting from the production of cocoa powder could be added to ground beans to make the paste more malleable, smoother and more tolerant of added sugar. The English firm of Fry and Sons introduced the first eating chocolate in 1847. Their recipe was the same then as today: crushed cocoa beans, cocoa butter and sugar.

In 1876 Swiss chocolatier Daniel Peter invented solid milk chocolate using the new condensed milk created by baby food manufacturer Henri Nestlé. Pennsylvania cocoa manufacturer Milton Hershey introduced his milk chocolate bars in 1894, followed by Hershey's Kisses in 1907. Nestlé Foods introduced the chocolate chip, perfect for cookies, in 1939.

◆◆◆

MELTING CHOCOLATE

Two important rules for melting chocolate:

1. Chocolate must never exceed 120°F (49°C) or there will be a loss of flavor.
2. Water—even a drop in the form of steam—must never touch the chocolate.

When a droplet of water enters melted chocolate, the chocolate becomes lumpy (a process called *seizing*). There must be a minimum of 1 tablespoon water per ounce (15 mL/30 mL) of chocolate to keep this from happening.

If seizing does occur, the addition of fat such as vegetable shortening, clarified butter, or cocoa butter will somewhat restore the chocolate to a workable condition.

For melting chocolate, unlined copper is the traditional "chocolate pot" because it is so responsive to changes in temperature. Aluminum or heatproof glass also works well. Ideally, chocolate should be heated to 120°F (49°C), the point at which all the different fat fractions in the cocoa butter are melted.

When melting chocolate or cocoa butter, temperatures exceeding 120°F (49°C) adversely affect the flavor. There are many acceptable methods for melting dark chocolate. If the heat source does not exceed 120°F (49°C) it is fine to add the dark chocolate in large pieces and leave it to melt unmonitored. When the heat source is capable of bringing the chocolate over 120°F (49°C), however, the chocolate should be finely chopped or grated to ensure uniformity of melting. The chocolate must be carefully watched and stirred to avoid overheating. If using a double boiler, water in the lower container should not exceed 140°F (60°C) and the upper container should not touch the water. The chocolate should be stirred constantly.

Milk and white chocolate must always be stirred frequently while melting because they contain milk solids which seed (lump) if left undisturbed.

Remove chocolate from the heat source when it reaches 115°F (46°C) as the temperature may continue to rise, and stir vigorously to prevent overheating and to distribute the cocoa butter evenly.

Always melt chocolate uncovered as moisture could condense on the lid, drop back in the chocolate, and cause seizing.

—*from* THE CAKE BIBLE *by* ROSE LEVY BERANBAUM

more cocoa butter, sugar, milk solids and flavourings to the chocolate mass. Most manufacturers of fine chocolates use the Swiss technique of **conching** to increase smoothness. Conching involves stirring large vats of blended chocolate with a heavy roller or paddle to smooth out sugar crystals and improve the flavour by removing acidity from the chocolate, a process that may last from 12 hours to 3 days.

Tasting Chocolates

There are two types of chocolate beans: a very hardy, abundant African variety used as a base bean, and a very flavourful, aromatic variety from Costa Rica used for flavour. Unlike wine or coffee, you cannot taste processed chocolate and tell which beans were used. All chocolates are blends, created by their manufacturer to be unique yet consistent.

Roasting greatly affects the final flavour of chocolate. Generally, German and Spanish manufacturers use a high (or strong) roast; Swiss and American makers use a low (or mild) roast.

Refining is also a matter of national taste. Swiss and German chocolate is the smoothest, followed by English chocolates. American chocolate is noticeably more grainy.

Chocolate quality is actually the product of several factors besides taste. All these factors should be evaluated when selecting chocolates.

1. *Appearance*—colour should be even and glossy, without any discolouration.
2. *Smell*—should be chocolatey with no off-odours or staleness.
3. *Break*—should snap cleanly without crumbling.
4. *Texture*—should melt quickly and evenly on the tongue.

Unsweetened Chocolate

Unsweetened chocolate is pure hardened chocolate liquor without any added sugar or milk solids. It is frequently used in baking and is sometimes referred to as "baking chocolate." Unsweetened chocolate is approximately 53% cocoa butter and 47% cocoa solids. Its flavour is pure and chocolatey, but the absence of sugar makes it virtually inedible as is.

Bittersweet and Semisweet Chocolates

Both bittersweet and semisweet chocolates contain at least 35% chocolate liquor plus additional cocoa butter, sugar, flavourings and sometimes emulsifiers. Generally, semisweet chocolate will be sweeter than bittersweet chocolate, but there are no precise definitions so flavour and sweetness will vary from brand to brand. Both are excellent eating chocolates and can usually be substituted measure for measure in any formula.

Sweet Chocolate

Government standards require that sweet chocolate contain not less than 15% chocolate liquor and varying amounts of sugar, milk solids, flavourings and emulsifiers. As the name implies, sweet chocolate is sweeter, and thus less chocolatey, than semisweet chocolate.

Milk Chocolate

The favourite eating chocolate in North America is milk chocolate. It contains sugar, vanilla, perhaps other flavourings and, of course, milk solids. The milk solids that make the chocolate milder and sweeter than other chocolates also make it less suitable for baking purposes. Do not substitute milk chocolate for dark chocolate in any product that must be baked, as the milk solids tend to burn. If melted slowly and carefully, milk chocolate can be used in glazes, mousses or candies.

Cocoa Powder

The brown powder left after the fat (cocoa butter) is removed from cocoa beans is known as cocoa powder. It does not contain any sweeteners or flavourings and is primarily used in baked goods. Alkalized or Dutch-processed cocoa powder has been treated with an alkaline solution, such as potassium carbonate, to raise the powder's pH from 5.5 to 7 or 8. Alkalized powder is darker and milder than nonalkalized powder and has a reduced tendency to lump. Either can be used in baked goods, however.

Cocoa Butter

Chocolate liquor is approximately 53% cocoa butter. Cocoa butter has long been prized for its resistance to rancidity and its use as a cosmetic. Cocoa butter has a very precise melting point, just below body temperature.

Clockwise from lower left: Semisweet chips, disks of chocolate liquor, block of bittersweet chocolate, block of milk chocolate, disks of white chocolate, alkalized cocoa powder.

White Chocolate

This ivory-coloured substance is not the product of an albino cocoa bean. It is actually a confectionery product that does not contain any chocolate solids or liquor. (Thus it cannot be labelled "chocolate" in the United States or Canada.) The finest white chocolates contain cocoa butter, sugar, milk solids, vanilla or other flavours. Other products replace all or part of the cocoa butter with partially hydrogenated palm kernel oil. These confectionery products will be less expensive than those containing pure cocoa butter, but their flavour and texture will be noticeably inferior. White chocolate melts at a lower temperature than dark chocolate and burns easily. It is excellent for eating and candy making, but is less-often used in baked goods.

Imitation Chocolate

A less-expensive product substituted in many prepared foods, imitation chocolate is made with partially hydrogenated palm kernel oil instead of cocoa butter. The resulting product melts at a higher temperature. Products containing imitation chocolate should be labelled "chocolate flavoured." Carob is a common ingredient.

Couverture (Fr.)—*the term used by chocolate manufacturers to describe real chocolate, which consists of cocoa powder, cocoa butter and sugar that has been conched. Dark chocolate, milk and white chocolate all have varying cocoa butter content. High cocoa butter content couverture is used for glazing and is very brittle when tempered and hardened. Lower cocoa butter content results in a thicker couverture, which is usually used to prepare moulded chocolate figures.*

Coating chocolate or baker's glaze—*consists of cocoa powder, sugar and partially hydrogenated palm kernal oil. This product does not have to be tempered and is easier to use. However, it does not match the flavour of real couverture.*

TABLE 26.6   NUTRITIONAL VALUES OF SELECTED CHOCOLATES

Per 1-oz. (28-g) Unit	Kcal	Protein (g)	Carbohydrates (g)	Total Fat (g)	Sodium (mg)
Chocolate, semisweet chips (Nestlé's)	150	2	18	8	0
Chocolate, unsweetened (Baker's)	140	3	9	15	0
Cocoa powder (Hershey's)	120	7	13	4	10
Milk chocolate (Hershey's)	150	2	27	12	55
White chocolate (Nestlé's)	160	2	15	10	25

The Corinne T. Netzer Encyclopedia of Food Values 1992

✦✦✦
TO TEMPER OR NOT TO TEMPER

The number-one mystique that surrounds chocolate has to do with tempering. From the dessert maker and pastry chef's point of view, I take a radical position: I do not think it is necessary or practical to temper. But what are we talking about anyway?

Briefly, tempering is a process of slowly raising and lowering the temperature of melted chocolate, stirring constantly, until the complex fat crystals in the cocoa butter stabilize and "behave" in concert with each other. At a cool room temperature, chocolate that has been tempered will dry rapidly to a hard and shiny piece that breaks with a snap. It shrinks slightly as it dries, enabling it to release easily from a mold. A tempered chocolate piece keeps at room temperature for months without losing its luster or snap. Any bar of chocolate that you purchase to eat or to melt has been tempered. Once melted or exposed to heat, however, it loses its temper, though it can be retempered.

Chocolate that is melted but not tempered will dry slowly, at room temperature, to a soft, almost cakey texture. It will stick inside a mold. Untempered chocolate "blooms"—that is, it becomes dull and streaky, or it takes on a mottled appearance—unless it is refrigerated immediately.

Candy makers almost always temper the chocolate they use. But dessert chefs have little need to temper. There is no reason to temper the chocolate used in cake and torte batters, buttercreams, and most ganaches. The same is true for mousses, custards, and creams. Chocolate that will be stored in the refrigerator or consumed quickly need not be tempered. Chocolate glazes, properly handled, do not require tempering to remain shiny for the short life of the dessert.

—from COCOLAT: EXTRAORDINARY CHOCOLATE DESSERTS by ALICE MEDRICH

Nutrition

Chocolates are high in calories and fat. (See Table 26.6.) They contain minimal amounts of Vitamin A and trace amounts of other vitamins as well as some sodium, phosphorus, potassium and other minerals.

Storing Chocolate

All chocolates should be stored at a cool, consistent temperature, away from strong odours and moisture. Dark chocolate, white chocolate and cocoa powder can be kept for up to one year without loss of flavour. Milk chocolate will not keep as well because it contains milk solids.

Chocolate may develop greyish-white spots during storage. This is called **fatbloom**; it results from the migration of cocoa butter crystals to the surface when temperatures change. Bloom will not affect the flavour or function of chocolate and will disappear when the chocolate is melted.

Alcoholic Beverages

Liquor—*an alcoholic beverage made by distilling grains, vegetables or other foods; includes rum, whisky and vodka.*

Liqueur—*a strong, sweet, syrupy alcoholic beverage made by mixing or redistilling neutral spirits with fruits, flowers, herbs, spices or other flavourings; also known as a cordial.*

Wine—*an alcoholic beverage made from the fermented juice of grapes; may be sparkling (effervescent) or still (noneffervescent) or fortified with additional alcohol.*

Brandy—*an alcoholic beverage made from distilling the fermented mash of grapes or other fruits.*

Liquors, **liqueurs**, **wines** and **brandies** are frequently used flavourings in the bakeshop. Rum is a popular flavouring liquor because it blends well with other flavours such as chocolate and coffee. Liqueurs are selected for their specific flavours: for example, kirsch for cherry, amaretto for almond, kahlúa for coffee, crème de cassis for black current and crème de cacao for chocolate. They are used to either add or enhance flavours. Wine, both still and sparkling, is used as a flavouring (for example, in sabayon sauce) or as a cooking medium (for example, pears poached in red wine). Brandy, especially the classic orange-flavoured Grand Marnier, is another common bakeshop flavouring. Brandy complements fruits and rounds off the flavour of custards and creams.

When selecting an alcoholic beverage for baking, make quality your first concern. Only high-quality products will enhance the flavour and aroma of your baked goods.

MIXING METHODS

An important step in the production of all baked goods is the mixing of ingredients. The techniques used to mix or combine ingredients affect the baked good's final volume, appearance and texture. There are several mixing methods: **beating**, **blending**, **creaming**, **cutting**, **folding**, **kneading**, **sifting**, **stirring** and **whipping**. These terms are used throughout this part of the text, especially in procedure discussions and formulas. Use the designated mixing method as well as the appropriate equipment or tool to ensure a good-quality finished product.

THE BAKING PROCESS

Baked goods are made from doughs and batters. A **dough** has a low water content. The water-protein complex known as gluten forms the continuous medium into which other ingredients are embedded. A dough is usually prepared by beating, blending, cutting or kneading and is often stiff enough to cut into various shapes.

A **batter** generally contains more fat, sugar and liquids than a dough. Gluten development is minimized and liquid forms the continuous medium in which other ingredients are disbursed. A batter bakes into softer, moister and more crumbly products. A batter is usually prepared by blending, creaming, stirring or whipping and is generally thin enough to pour.

The changes that occur in a dough or batter as it bakes seem mysterious and complex. A pourable liquid becomes a tender, light cake; a sticky mass becomes soft, chewy cookies; a soft, elastic dough becomes firm, crusty French bread. Yet the same physical changes that occur during baking cause all of these results. Namely, gases form and are trapped within the dough or batter; starches, proteins and sugars cook; fats melt; moisture evaporates and staling begins.

By learning to control these changes, you are also learning to control the final product. Control can be exerted in the selection of ingredients and method by which those ingredients are combined as well as the baking temperature and duration.

Gases Form

A baked product's final texture is determined by the amount of leavening or rise that occurs both before and during baking. This rise is caused by the gases present in the dough or batter. These gases are carbon dioxide, air and steam. Air and carbon dioxide are present in doughs and batters before they are heated. Other gases are formed when heat is applied. For example, steam is created as the moisture in a dough is heated; yeast and baking powder rapidly release additional carbon dioxide when placed in a hot oven. These gases then expand and leaven the product. (See Table 26.7.) Additional information on baking powder and baking soda is found in Chapter 27, Quick Breads; additional information on yeast is found in Chapter 28, Yeast Breads.

Beating—*vigorously agitating foods to incorporate air or develop gluten; use a spoon or electric mixer with its paddle attachment.*

Blending—*mixing two or more ingredients until evenly distributed; use a spoon, rubber spatula, whisk or electric mixer with its paddle attachment.*

Creaming—*vigorously combining fat and sugar while incorporating air; use an electric mixer with its paddle attachment on medium speed.*

Cutting—*incorporating solid fat into dry ingredients only until lumps of the desired size remain; use pastry cutters, fingers or an electric mixer with its paddle attachment.*

Folding—*very gently incorporating ingredients, such as dry ingredients with whipped eggs; use a rubber spatula.*

Kneading—*working a dough to develop gluten; use hands or an electric mixer with its dough hook. If done by hand, the dough must be vigorously and repeatedly folded and turned in a rhythmic pattern.*

Sifting—*passing one or more dry ingredients through a wire mesh to remove lumps, combine and aerate ingredients; use a rotary or drum sifter or mesh strainer.*

Stirring—*gently mixing ingredients until blended; use a spoon, whisk or rubber spatula.*

Whipping—*beating vigorously to incorporate air; use a whisk or an electric mixer with its whip attachment.*

Gases Are Trapped

The stretchable network of proteins created in a batter or dough either by egg proteins or gluten traps gases in the product. Without an appropriate network of proteins, the gases would just escape without causing the mixture to rise.

Starches Gelatinize

When starch granules reach a temperature of approximately 140°F (60°C), they absorb additional moisture—up to 10 times their own weight—and expand. This contributes to the baked good's structure.

Proteins Coagulate

Gluten and dairy and egg proteins begin to coagulate (solidify) when the dough or batter reaches a temperature of 160°F (71°C). This process provides most of the baked good's structure.

Proper baking temperatures are important for controlling the point at which proteins coagulate. If the temperature is too high, proteins will solidify before the gases in the product have expanded fully, resulting in a product with poor texture and volume. If the temperature is too low, gases will escape before the proteins coagulate, resulting in a product that may collapse.

Fats Melt

As fats melt, steam is released and fat droplets are dispersed throughout the product. These fat droplets coat the starch (flour) granules, thus moistening and tenderizing the product by keeping the gluten strands short. Shortenings melt at different temperatures. It is important to select a fat with the proper melting point for the product being prepared.

Water Evaporates

Throughout the baking process the water contained in the liquid ingredients will turn to steam and evaporate. This steam is a useful leavener. As steam is released, the dough or batter dries out, starting from the outside, resulting in the formation of a crust.

TABLE 26.7	LEAVENING AGENTS IN BAKED GOODS
Leavening Agent	Present In
Air	All products, especially those containing whipped eggs or creamed fat
Steam	All products when liquids evaporate or fats melt
Carbon dioxide	Products containing baking soda, baking powder, baking ammonia or yeast

Sugars Caramelize

As sugars are heated above the boiling point they caramelize, adding flavour and causing the product to darken. Sugars are found in eggs, dairy products and other ingredients, not just in refined sugar and liquid sweeteners.

Carryover Baking

The physical changes in a baked good do not stop when it is removed from the oven. The residual heat contained in a product continues the baking process as the product cools. That is why a cookie or biscuit may seem a bit underbaked when removed from the oven; it will finish baking as it cools.

Staling

Staling is a change in a baked good's texture and aroma caused by both moisture loss and changes in the structure of the starch granules. Stale products have lost their fresh aroma and are firmer, drier and more crumbly than fresh goods.

Staling is not just a general loss of moisture into the atmosphere, it is also a change in the location and distribution of water molecules within the product. This process, known as **starch retrogradation**, occurs as starch molecules cool, becoming more dense and expelling moisture.

In breads, this moisture migrates from the interior to the drier crust, causing the crust to become tough and leathery. If the product is not well wrapped, moisture will escape completely into the surrounding air. In humid conditions, unwrapped bread crusts absorb moisture from the atmosphere, resulting in the same loss of crispness. The flavour and texture of breads can be revived by reheating them to approximately 140°F (60°C), the temperature at which starch gelatinization occurs. Usually, products can be reheated only once without causing additional quality loss.

The retrogradation process is temperature-dependent. It occurs most rapidly at temperatures of approximately 40°F (4°C). Therefore, baked products should not be refrigerated unless they contain perishable components such as cream fillings. It is better to store products frozen or at room temperature.

Products containing fats and sugars, which retain moisture, tend to stay fresh longer. Commercial bakeries usually add chemical emulsifiers or gums to retard staling, but these additives are not practical for small-scale production.

BAKESHOP TOOLS AND EQUIPMENT

As a beginning cook, you may find the tools of the bakeshop a bit complex. Indeed, the tools required for a professional patisserie are quite specialized. A well-equipped cook need not be concerned with possessing every gadget available, but should recognize and be familiar with most of the items shown in the photograph on page 770. Although many of these hand tools will make a task easier, most can be improvised by a creative cook. Several of the items shown, such as the springform pans, tartlet pans and petit four moulds, are used for shaping or holding batters and doughs. The various spatulas and pallet knives are used for spreading icings or fillings. The piping tools and cake comb are used for decorating and finishing baked goods.

Clockwise from centre back: Cake turntable, cake pans, flan ring, tartlet pans, cannoli forms, cake comb, offset spatulas, flat cake spatula, blade for slashing breads, flower nail, rectangular tartlet pans, piping bag and tips, metal spatula, dough cutter, rolling pin, springform pan, copper sugar pot (on cooling rack), nest of round cutters

When purchasing tools and equipment, look for quality and durability. As your baking skills grow, so will your equipment selection.

Bakeshop ovens may be conventional, convection or steam injection models. Convection ovens can reduce cooking time, but the air currents may damage delicate products such as spongecake or puff pastry. Steam injection ovens use conventional heat flow but allow the baker to automatically add steam to the cooking chamber as needed to produce crisp-crusted breads. Although expensive, steam injection ovens are a necessity for commercial bakeries and most larger restaurant and hotel bakeshops. Baking instructions in the following chapters are based on the use of a conventional oven. If a convection oven is used instead, remember that the temperature and baking time may need to be reduced.

CONCLUSION

Of the many stations of the kitchen, the bakeshop often requires the most conscientious attention to detail. The correct use of flour, thickeners, sugar, fat, chocolate and other flavourings is essential. During preparation and baking, doughs and batters go through many physical changes. One of the most important is the development of gluten, the elastic network of wheat proteins created when doughs and batters are prepared, which gives baked goods body and structure. You should understand the changes baked goods undergo and learn to control or adjust them as needed.

QUESTIONS FOR DISCUSSION

1. What is gluten? How is it produced and why is it important in the preparation of baked goods?
2. Discuss four functions of sugar and other sweeteners in baked goods.
3. Describe several steps that can be taken to prevent crystals from forming in sugar solutions.
4. Describe the effect of fat on gluten strands. Why is fat an important ingredient in baked goods?
5. Explain the difference between chocolate liquor and semisweet chocolate. Can these two types of chocolate be used interchangeably in most recipes? Explain your answer.
6. List and describe the nine steps in the baking process.
7. Name several specialized hand tools or pans often used in the bakeshop.
8. What are the differences between a steam injection oven, a convection oven and a conventional oven? Why might you select one type of oven over another?

WEBLINKS

American Institute of Baking
 www.aibonline.org/
International School of Baking: Welcome
 www.empnet.com/domocorp/
Bakery Production and Marketing
 www.cahners.com/mainmag/bpm.htm
Bakery-Net
 www.bakery-net.com/rdocs/option12.html

CHAPTER 27

QUICK BREADS

*B*uttermilk biscuits, blueberry muffins, banana-nut bread and currant scones are all quick breads. Although the origin of the name may be a mystery, why they are so named is obvious: They are quick to make and quick to bake. With only a few basic ingredients and no yeast, almost any food service operation can provide its customers with fresh muffins, biscuits, scones and loaf breads.

The variety of ingredients is virtually limitless: cornmeal, whole wheat, fruits, nuts, spices and vegetables all yield popular products. And the use of these products is not limited to breakfast service; they are equally appropriate for lunch, snacks and buffets.

CHEMICAL LEAVENING AGENTS

Quick breads are made with chemical leavening agents, principally baking soda and baking powder. This sets them apart from breads that are made with yeast and require additional time for fermentation and proofing. Understanding how chemical leavening agents operate is essential to successful quick-bread production.

Chemical leavening agents release gases through chemical reactions between acids and bases contained in the formula. These gases form bubbles or air pockets throughout the dough or batter. As the product bakes, the dough or batter sets around these air pockets, thus giving the quick bread its rise and texture.

Baking Soda

Sodium bicarbonate ($NaHCO_3$) is more commonly known as household baking soda. Baking soda is an alkaline compound (a base), which releases carbon dioxide gas (CO_2) if both an acid and moisture are present. Heat is not necessary for this reaction to occur; however, the chemical reaction will be faster at higher temperatures. Therefore, products made with baking soda must be baked at once, before the carbon dioxide has a chance to escape from the batter.

Acids commonly used with baking soda are buttermilk, sour cream, lemon juice, honey, molasses and fresh fruit. Generally, the amount of baking soda used in a formula is only the amount necessary to neutralize the acids present. If more leavening action is needed, baking powder, not more baking soda, should be used. Too much baking soda causes the product to taste soapy or bitter; it may also cause a yellow colour and brown spots to develop.

Baking Powder

Baking powder is a mixture of sodium bicarbonate and one or more acids, generally cream of tartar ($KHC_4H_4O_6$) and/or sodium aluminum sulphate ($Na_2SO_4 \cdot Al_2[SO_4]_3$). Baking powder also contains a starch to prevent lumping and to balance the chemical reactions. Because baking powder contains both the acid and the base necessary for the desired chemical reaction, the formula does not need to contain any acid. Only moisture is necessary to induce the release of gases.

There are two types of baking powder: single-acting and double-acting. An excess of either type produces undesirable flavours, textures and colours in baked products.

Single-acting baking powder requires only the presence of moisture to start releasing gas. This moisture is supplied by the eggs, milk, water or other liquids in the formula. As with baking soda, products using single-acting baking powder must be baked immediately.

Double-acting baking powder is more popular. With double-acting baking powder, there is a small release of gas upon contact with moisture and a second, stronger release of gas when heat is applied. Products made with double-acting baking powder need not be baked immediately, but can sit for a short time without loss of leavening ability. All formulas in this book rely on double-acting baking powder.

Both baking soda and baking powder are sometimes used in one formula. This is because baking soda can release CO_2 only to the extent that there is also an acid present in the formula. If the soda/acid reaction alone is insufficient to leaven the product, baking powder is needed for additional leavening.

Baking Ammonia

Baking ammonia (ammonia bicarbonate or ammonia carbonate) is also used as a leavening agent in some baked goods, primarily cookies and crackers. Baking ammonia releases ammonia and carbon dioxide very rapidly when heated. It is suitable for low-moisture products with large surface areas that are baked at high temperatures, such as crackers. Consequently, it is rarely used in quick breads.

Purchasing and Storing

Purchase chemical leaveners in the smallest unit appropriate for your operation. Although a large can of baking powder may cost less than several small ones, if not used promptly the contents of a larger container can deteriorate, causing waste or unuseable baked goods.

Chemical leavening agents should always be kept tightly covered. Not only is there a risk of contamination if left open, but they can also absorb moisture from the air and lose their effectiveness. They should be stored in a cool place, as heat deteriorates them. A properly stored and unopened container of baking powder or baking soda has a shelf life of approximately one year.

MIXING METHODS

Quick breads are generally mixed by either the **biscuit method**, the **muffin method** or the **creaming method**.

Biscuit Method

The biscuit method is used for biscuits and scones and is very similar to the technique used to make flaky pie doughs. The goal is to create a baked good that is light, flaky and tender.

BASIC PROCEDURE FOR PREPARING PRODUCTS WITH THE BISCUIT METHOD

1. Measure all ingredients.
2. Sift the dry ingredients together.
3. Cut in the fat, which should be in a solid form.
4. Combine the liquid ingredients, including any eggs.
5. Add the liquid ingredients to the dry ingredients. Mix just until the ingredients are combined. Do not overmix, as this causes toughness and inhibits the product's rise.
6. Place the dough on the bench and knead it lightly 10 or 15 times (about 20–30 seconds). The dough should be soft and slightly elastic, but not sticky. Too much kneading toughens the biscuits.
7. The dough is now ready for makeup and baking.

MAKEUP OF BISCUIT METHOD PRODUCTS

1. Roll out the dough on a floured surface to a thickness of 1/2 to 3/4 inch (1.25 to 1.8 cm). Be careful to roll it evenly. Biscuits should double in height during baking.
2. Cut into the desired shapes. Cut straight down; do not twist the cutters, as this inhibits rise. Space cuts as close together as possible to minimize scraps.
3. Position the biscuits on a lightly greased or paper-lined sheet pan. If placed with sides nearly touching, the biscuits will rise higher and have softer sides. Place farther apart for crusty sides.
4. Scraps may be rerolled one time without overtoughening the product. To do so, press the dough together gently; do not knead.
5. Tops may be brushed with egg wash before baking or with melted butter after baking. Bake immediately in a hot oven.
6. Cool the finished products on a wire rack.

◆◆◆
BISCUITS AND SCONES: A GENEALOGY

Biscuit is a French word used to describe any dry, flat cake, whether sweet or savoury. It was, perhaps, originally coined to describe twice-baked cakes (*bis* = twice + *cuit* = cooked). Crusader chronicles, for example, mention soldiers eating a "bread called 'bequis' because it is cooked twice" and still, today, the Reims biscuit is returned to the oven for further baking after it is removed from its tin.

Over the centuries the French began to use the term *biscuit* generically and appended modifiers to identify the particular type of dry, flat cake. For example, a *biscuit de guerre* [war] was the very hard, barely risen product of flour and water used from the time of the Crusades to the era of Louis XIV as an army ration; *biscuit de Savoie* is a savoury spongecake; *biscuit de pâtisserie* is a sweet biscuit.

To the British, a biscuit is what North Americans call a cracker or cookie. Yet there appears to be no British quick bread quite comparable to the North American biscuit—the closest relative would be the scone. But because a scone contains eggs and butter, it is much richer than a biscuit.

Elizabeth Alston, in *Biscuits and Scones*, proposes that the biscuit is an American variant of the scone. She theorizes that early British colonists in America brought with them traditional scone recipes. Unable to find or afford the necessary fresh butter and eggs, these practical bakers substituted lard and omitted the eggs. What they created, however, were not mock scones, but rather a new product, different from scones but still delicious. Alston further speculates that French cooks initially called the new American product "biscuit de something" and eventually dropped the "de something."

◆◆◆

RECIPE 27.1

COUNTRY BISCUITS

Yield: 36 Biscuits

Method: Biscuit

All-purpose flour	2 lb. 8 oz.	1.15 kg
Salt	3/4 oz.	20 g
Sugar	2 oz.	60 g
Baking powder	2 oz.	60 g
Unsalted butter, cold	14 oz.	400 g
Milk	1 lb. 8 oz.	680 g

Approximate values per biscuit:

Calories	210
Total fat	10 g
Saturated fat	6 g
Cholesterol	25 mg
Sodium	240 mg
Total carbohydrates	27 g
Protein	4 g
Vitamin A	10%

1. Sift the dry ingredients together, making sure they are blended thoroughly.
2. Cut in the shortening. The mixture should look mealy; do not overmix.
3. Add the milk and stir, combining only until the mixture holds together.
4. Transfer the dough to a lightly floured work surface; knead until it forms one mass, approximately 5 or 6 kneadings.
5. Roll out the dough to a thickness of 1/2 inch (1.25 cm). Cut with a floured cutter and place the biscuits on a paper-lined sheet pan.
6. Bake at 425°F (220°C) for approximately 10–15 minutes. Tops should be light brown, sides almost white and interiors still moist. Internal heat will continue to cook the biscuits after they are removed from the oven.
7. Remove the biscuits to a wire rack to cool.

NOTE: A vegetable shortening or a combination of shortening and butter is often used.

1. Sift the dry ingredients together.

2. Cut in the fat.

3. Knead the dough.

4. Cut the biscuits.

◆◆◆

RECIPE 27.2 (Aboriginal)

CORN FLOUR BANNOCK

Yield: 4 Servings

Method: Biscuit

Corn flour	8 oz.	250 g
Baking powder	1 Tbsp.	15 mL
Salt	1 tsp.	5 g
Vegetable shortening	1 oz.	30 g
Water	3 oz.	100 mL

Continued

◆◆◆

BANNOCK: THE "STAFF OF LIFE"

Bannock, a simple quick bread, is found in many Canadian native cultures. The bread is usually fried in fat or wrapped around a green hardwood stick and baked next to an open fire. The origin of the bread is not Native, however. Bannock is a "borrowed" food that arrived in Canada with the Scottish sailors of the Hudson's Bay Company just over 300 years ago.

1. Lightly grease a heavy cast-iron frying pan or baking sheet. Heat the oven to 450°F (230°C) if using the baking sheet.
2. Combine flour, baking powder and salt in a bowl. Rub in the shortening, then add the water gradually.
3. Work the mixture into a soft, sticky dough.
4. Turn the dough onto a lightly floured surface. Knead it gently 8–10 times. Roll out to 1/2 inch (1 cm) thick.
5. Turn the mixture into the frying pan or onto baking sheet. Cook in frying pan on top of stove or on baking sheet in the oven for approximately 12–15 minutes, or until golden brown. If cooking in the frying pan, turn the bannock over to brown it on both sides.

Approximate values per biscuit:

Calories	296
Total fat	10 g
Saturated fat	2 g
Cholesterol	0 mg
Sodium	859 mg
Total carbohydrates	49 g
Protein	6 g

◆◆◆

RECIPE 27.3 (Aboriginal)

MISSIIAGAAN-PAKWEJIGAN (SUNFLOWER BANNOCK)

Sunflower seeds, shelled	3-1/2 oz.	100 g
Water	7 oz.	150 mL
Salt	TT	TT
Corn flour	1 Tbsp.	12 g
Corn oil (for cooking)	2 Tbsp.	35 mL

1. Combine sunflower seeds, salt and water and simmer, covered, for 1-1/2 hours.
2. Purée seeds into a paste.
3. Add corn flour a little at a time to thicken. Work into a soft, sticky dough.
4. Knead slightly.
5. Form into flat cakes approximately 5 inches (13 cm) in diameter.
6. Heat corn oil and fry cakes until golden brown and cooked throughout.
7. Drain and serve.

Approximate values per serving:

Calories	748
Total fat	64 g
Saturated fat	7 g
Cholesterol	0 mg
Sodium	779 mg
Total carbohydrates	33 g
Protein	20 g

Muffin Method

Muffins are any small, cakelike baked good made in a muffin tin (pan). Batters for muffins and loaf quick breads are generally interchangeable. For example, banana muffin batter may be baked in a loaf pan by altering the baking time.

When preparing baked goods by the muffin method, the goal is to produce a tender product with an even shape and an even distribution of fruits, nuts or other ingredients. The most frequent problem with muffin-method products is overmixing. This causes toughness and may cause holes to form inside the baked product, a condition known as **tunnelling**.

BASIC PROCEDURE FOR PREPARING PRODUCTS WITH THE MUFFIN METHOD

1. Measure all ingredients.
2. Sift the dry ingredients together.
3. Combine the liquid ingredients, including melted fat or oil. Melted butter or shortening may resolidify when combined with the other liquids; this is not a cause for concern.

4. Add the liquid ingredients to the dry ingredients and stir just until combined. Do not overmix. The batter should be lumpy.
5. The batter is now ready for makeup and baking.

MAKEUP OF MUFFIN METHOD PRODUCTS

1. Muffin pans and loaf pans should be greased with butter, shortening or a commercial pan grease. Paper liners may be used and will prevent sticking if the batter contains fruits or vegetables. Paper liners, however, inhibit rise.
2. A portion scoop is convenient for ensuring uniform-sized muffins. Be careful not to drip or spill batter onto the edge of the muffin cups; it will burn and cause sticking.
3. Allow muffins and loaf breads to cool for several minutes before attempting to remove them from the pan.
4. Cool the finished products on a wire rack.

◆◆◆

RECIPE 27.4
BLUEBERRY MUFFINS

Yield: 12 Muffins   **Method**: Muffin

All-purpose flour	8 oz.	250 g
Sugar	5 oz.	150 g
Baking powder	2 tsp.	10 mL
Salt	1/4 tsp.	1 mL
Egg	1	1
Milk	8 oz.	250 mL
Unsalted butter, melted	2 oz.	60 mL
Vanilla	1 tsp.	5 mL
Blueberries	6 oz.	180 g
Lemon zest	1 Tbsp.	15 mL

1. Sift the dry ingredients together.
2. Stir together the liquid ingredients, including the melted butter.
3. Stir the liquid mixture into the dry ingredients. Do not overmix. The batter should be lumpy.
4. Gently fold in the blueberries and lemon zest.
5. Portion into greased or paper-lined muffin cups and bake at 350°F (180°C) until light brown and set in the centre, approximately 18 minutes.
6. Cool the muffins in the pan for several minutes before removing.

Approximate values per muffin:

Calories	180
Total fat	5 g
Saturated fat	3 g
Cholesterol	30 mg
Sodium	65 mg
Total carbohydrates	30 g
Protein	3 g
Vitamin A	6%

Claims—low sodium

1. Combine the liquid ingredients.

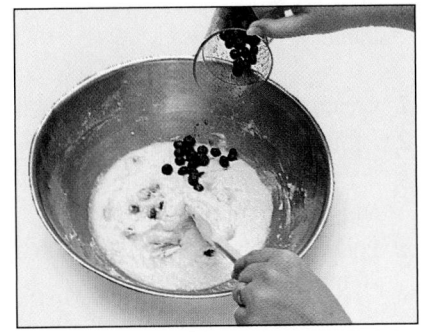

2. Fold in the blueberries.

3. Portion the batter.

Creaming Method

The creaming method is comparable to the mixing method used for many butter cakes. The final product will be cakelike, with a fine texture. There is less danger of overmixing with this method because the higher fat content shortens gluten strands and tenderizes the batter.

BASIC PROCEDURE FOR PREPARING PRODUCTS WITH THE CREAMING METHOD

1. Measure all ingredients.
2. Sift the dry ingredients together.
3. Combine softened fat and sugar in a mixer bowl. Cream until the colour lightens and the mixture fluffs.
4. Add eggs gradually, mixing well.
5. Add the dry and liquid ingredients to the creamed fat alternately. In other words, a portion of the flour is added to the fat and incorporated, then a portion of the liquid is added and incorporated. These steps are repeated until all of the liquid and dry ingredients are incorporated. By adding the liquid and dry ingredients alternately you avoid overmixing the batter and prevent the butter and sugar mixture from curdling.
6. The batter is now ready for makeup and baking.

MAKEUP OF CREAMING METHOD PRODUCTS

Panning and baking procedures are the same as those for quick breads prepared with the muffin method.

◆◆◆

RECIPE 27.5

SOUR CREAM MUFFINS

Yield: 15 Muffins   **Method:** Creaming

Unsalted butter, room temperature	8 oz.	245 g
Sugar	8 oz.	245 g
Eggs	2	2
All-purpose flour	10 oz.	300 g
Baking powder	1 tsp.	5 mL
Baking soda	1 tsp.	5 mL
Salt	1 tsp.	5 mL
Sour cream	10 oz.	300 g
Vanilla	1 tsp.	5 mL

Approximate values per muffin:

Calories	290
Total fat	17 g
Saturated fat	10 g
Cholesterol	70 mg
Sodium	260 mg
Total carbohydrates	31 g
Protein	4 g
Vitamin A	15%

1. Cream the butter and sugar until light and fluffy. Add the eggs.
2. Sift the dry ingredients together.
3. Stir the dry ingredients and sour cream, alternately, into the butter mixture. Stir in the vanilla.
4. Portion and bake at 350°F (180°C) until light brown and set, approximately 20 minutes.

5. Allow the muffins to cool briefly in the pan before removing.

VARIATIONS: Sour cream muffins can be topped with **streusel** (Recipe 27.6) or flavoured with a wide variety of fruits or nuts by adding approximately 4–6 ounces (1 cup or 120–180 g) fresh or frozen drained fruit to the batter. Blueberries, dried cherries, candied fruits, pecans and diced pears yield popular products. By adding 1/2 teaspoon (2 mL) each of cinnamon and nutmeg, basic spice muffins are produced.

Streusel—*a crumbly mixture of fat, flour, sugar and, sometimes, nuts and spices used to top baked goods.*

1. Cream the butter and sugar.

2. Add the sour cream.

3. Top the muffins with streusel.

♦♦♦

RECIPE 27.6
STREUSEL TOPPING

Yield: 3 lb. 8 oz. (1.85 kg)

All-purpose flour	8 oz.	250 g
Cinnamon	1/4 oz.	7 g
Salt	1 tsp.	5 mL
Brown sugar	8 oz.	250 g
Sugar	1 lb. 8 oz.	750 g
Whole butter, cold	1 lb. 4 oz.	600 g

1. Combine all dry ingredients. Cut in the butter until the mixture is coarse and crumbly.

2. Sprinkle on top of muffins or quick breads prior to baking. Streusel topping will keep for several weeks under refrigeration.

Aproximate values per 1 oz. (30 g) serving:

Calories	200
Total fat	8 g
Saturated fat	5 g
Cholesterol	20 mg
Sodium	130 mg
Total carbohydrates	29 g
Protein	2 g
Vitamin A	8%

Claims—low sodium

Griddlecakes

Griddlecakes or griddle breads, such as **pancakes** and **waffles**, are actually a type of quick bread. They are usually leavened with baking soda or baking powder and are quickly cooked on a very hot griddle or waffle iron with very little fat. They are described in detail in Chapter 32, "Breakfast and Brunch."

TABLE 27.1   TROUBLESHOOTING CHART FOR QUICK BREADS

Problem	Cause	Solution
Soapy or bitter taste	Chemical leaveners not properly mixed into batter	Sift chemicals with dry ingredients
	Too much baking soda	Adjust formula
Elongated holes (tunnelling)	Overmixing	Do not mix until smooth; mix only until moistened
Crust too thick	Too much sugar	Adjust formula
	Oven temperature too low	Adjust oven
Flat top with only a small peak in centre	Oven temperature too low	Adjust oven
Cracked, uneven top	Oven temperature too high	Adjust oven
No rise; dense product	Old batter	Bake promptly
	Damaged leavening agents	Store new chemicals properly
	Overmixing	Do not overmix

CONCLUSION

First you must master the three mixing methods used in producing quick breads (muffin, biscuit and creaming) and understand the interaction between chemical leaveners and other ingredients. Then, with an imaginative use of flavouring ingredients, you can successfully produce a wide array of fresh-baked breads for almost any food service operation.

QUESTIONS FOR DISCUSSION

1. Name two chemical leavening agents and explain how they cause batters and doughs to rise.
2. List three common methods used for mixing quick breads. What is the significance of the type of fat used for each of these mixing methods?
3. What is the most likely explanation for discoloured and bitter-tasting biscuits? What is the solution?
4. Describe the resulting product when muffin batter has been overmixed.

Additional Quick Bread Formulas

RECIPE 27.7
Cream Scones

Yield: 24 Scones   **Method:** Biscuit

All-purpose flour	1 lb.	500 g
Sugar	1-1/2 oz.	45 g
Baking powder	1 Tbsp.	15 mL
Baking soda	1 tsp.	5 mL
Salt	1 tsp.	5 mL
Unsalted butter, cold	4 oz.	120 g
Egg yolks	2	2
Cereal cream	11 oz.	330 mL

1. Combine all ingredients using the biscuit method.
2. Roll out the dough to a thickness of about 1/2 inch (1.25 cm). Cut as desired.
3. Bake at 400°F (200°C) for approximately 10 minutes.
4. Brush the tops with butter while hot.

VARIATIONS: One-half cup (125 mL) raisins, sultanas or currants may be added to the dry ingredients.

Approximate values per scone:

Calories	130
Total fat	6 g
Saturated fat	3.5 g
Cholesterol	35 mg
Sodium	160 mg
Total carbohydrates	17 g
Protein	3 g

◆◆◆

RECIPE 27.8
Shortcakes

Yield: 48 Large Pieces   **Method:** Biscuit

All-purpose flour	4 lb.	2 kg
Baking powder	3-3/4 oz.	110 g
Salt	2 tsp.	10 mL
Granulated sugar	13 oz.	390 g
Unsalted butter, cold	1 lb. 12 oz.	875 g
Eggs	7	7
Milk	18 oz.	550 mL
Butter, melted	as needed	as needed
Granulated sugar	as needed	as needed

1. Combine all ingredients using the biscuit method.
2. Cut into 3-inch (7.5-cm) circles and space 2 inches (5 cm) apart on a paper-lined sheet pan.
3. Bake at 400°F (200°C) until lightly browned, approximately 15–18 minutes.
4. Remove from the oven and brush the tops with melted butter, then sprinkle with granulated sugar.

Approximate values per 3 oz. (90 g) serving:

Calories	310
Total fat	15 g
Saturated fat	9 g
Cholesterol	65 mg
Sodium	250 mg
Total carbohydrates	38 g
Protein	5 g
Vitamin A	15%

♦♦♦

RECIPE 27.9

BASIC BERRY MUFFINS

STOUFFER STANFORD COURT HOTEL, SAN FRANCISCO, CA
Chef Ercolino Crugnale

Yield: 60 Muffins   **Method:** Muffin

Eggs	8	8
Cream, 35%	1 qt.	1 L
Lemon zest, finely grated	from 2 lemons	from 2 lemons
Nutmeg	1/4 tsp.	1 mL
Granulated sugar	1 lb. 4 oz.	600 g
Baking powder	6 Tbsp.	90 mL
Cake flour	3 lb.	1.4 kg
Kosher salt	1 Tbsp.	15 mL
Berries or nuts	1 to 1-1/2 qt.	1 to 1.5 L
Unsalted butter, melted	1 lb.	500 g

Approximate values per muffin:

Calories	260
Total fat	13 g
Saturated fat	8 g
Cholesterol	70 mg
Sodium	135 mg
Total carbohydrates	31 g
Protein	3 g
Vitamin A	15%

Claims—low sodium

1. Whip the eggs, cream and zest together by hand.

2. Sift the dry ingredients together. Add the berries or nuts, tossing to coat them evenly with the flour mixture.

3. Add the dry ingredients to the egg mixture and stir until about two-thirds mixed. Add the melted butter and finish mixing.

4. Portion into greased muffin tins and bake at 375°F (190°C) for approximately 15–18 minutes.

Variations: Blueberries, blackberries, raspberries, chopped pecans or walnuts may be used, as desired.

♦♦♦

RECIPE 27.10

MORNING GLORY MUFFINS

Yield: 18 Muffins   **Method:** Muffin

All-purpose flour	1 lb.	500 g
Granulated sugar	18 oz.	560 g
Baking soda	4 tsp.	20 mL
Cinnamon	4 tsp.	20 mL
Carrots, grated	14 oz.	425 g
Raisins	6 oz.	180 g
Pecan pieces	4 oz.	120 g
Coconut, shredded	4 oz.	120 g
Apple, unpeeled, grated	6 oz.	180 g
Eggs	6	6
Canola oil	12 oz.	360 mL
Vanilla extract	4 tsp.	20 mL

Approximate values per muffin:

Calories	520
Total fat	27 g
Saturated fat	5 g
Cholesterol	70 mg
Sodium	310 mg
Total carbohydrates	63 g
Protein	6 g
Vitamin A	45%

Claims—good source of fibre

1. Sift the dry ingredients together and set aside.

2. Combine the carrots, raisins, pecans, coconut and apple.

3. Combine the eggs, oil and vanilla.

4. Toss the carrot mixture in the dry ingredients. Add the liquid ingredients, stirring just until combined.

5. Bake in well-greased muffin tins at 350°F (170°C) until done, approximately 25 minutes.

◆◆◆

RECIPE 27.11

Bran Muffins

Yield: 4 Dozen   **Method:** Muffin

Brown sugar	24 oz.	720 g
Margarine	8 oz.	230 g
Baking soda	1 oz.	30 g
Eggs	6	6
Bread flour	22 oz.	650 g
Milk powder	5 oz.	150 g
Water, cold	64 oz.	2 L
Bran	12 oz.	360 g
Raisins	12 oz.	360 g

1. In a bowl, cream sugar, margarine and baking soda together.

2. Slowly add the eggs in 3 additions, creaming the batter between each addition.

3. In another bowl, blend the flour and milk powder together.

4. Add the flour to the egg mix. Blend on No. 1 speed only until moist.

5. Mix water with the bran, then blend into the rest of the mix.

6. Add the raisins when the bran is mixed in.

7. Continue to mix on No. 1 only until batter is smooth.

8. Scoop into greased or paper-lined muffin tins. Bake at 350°F (170°C) until lightly brown and firm, approximately 20 minutes.

Approximate values per muffin:

Calories	196
Total fat	6 g
Saturated fat	2 g
Cholesterol	37 mg
Sodium	221 mg
Total carbohydrates	35 g
Protein	5 g

Claims—low sodium; good source of fibre

◆◆◆

RECIPE 27.12

Zucchini Bread

Yield: 2 9-in x 5-in (24-cm x 12-cm) Loaves   **Method:** Muffin

Whole eggs	3	3
Canola oil	8 oz.	240 mL
Sugar	1 lb. 2 oz.	560 g
Vanilla	1 tsp.	5 mL
Cinnamon	2 tsp.	10 mL
Salt	1 tsp.	5 mL
Baking soda	1 tsp.	5 mL
Baking powder	1/2 tsp.	2 mL
All-purpose flour	14 oz.	420 g
Zucchini, coarsely grated	11 oz.	330 g
Pecans, chopped	4 oz.	120 g

1. Combine all ingredients using the muffin method.

2. Bake in two greased loaf pans at 350°F (170°C), approximately 1 hour.

Approximate values per 2 oz. (60 g) serving:

Calories	260
Total fat	16 g
Saturated fat	2 g
Cholesterol	30 mg
Sodium	190 mg
Total carbohydrates	27 g
Protein	2 g

━━━━━━━━━━ ✦✦✦ ━━━━━━━━━━

RECIPE 27.13
IRISH SODA BREAD

Yield: 1 8-inch-round (20-cm) Loaf   **Method:** Muffin

Currants	2 oz.	60 g
Irish whisky	1-1/2 oz.	45 mL
All-purpose flour, sifted	12 oz.	360 g
Salt	1 tsp.	5 mL
Baking powder	1-1/2 tsp.	7 mL
Baking soda	1 tsp.	5 mL
Brown sugar	1 Tbsp.	15 mL
Lowfat buttermilk	16 oz.	500 mL

1. Soak the currants in the whisky until plump, at least 1 hour.
2. Sift the dry ingredients together. Stir in the currants and whisky.
3. Stir in the buttermilk, making a stiff batter.
4. Spread the batter in a greased 8-inch-round (20-cm) cake pan. Bake at 350°F (170°C) until well browned and firm, approximately 45 minutes.

Approximate values per 3 oz. (90 g) serving:

Calories	150
Total fat	1 g
Saturated fat	0 g
Cholesterol	0 mg
Sodium	480 mg
Total carbohydrates	31 g
Protein	5 g
Calcium	10%

Claims—low fat; no cholesterol; no saturated fat

━━━━━━━━━━ ✦✦✦ ━━━━━━━━━━

RECIPE 27.14
BASIC CORN MUFFINS

Yield: 30 Muffins   **Method:** Muffin

Yellow cornmeal	12 oz.	360 g
All-purpose flour	12 oz.	360 g
Sugar	10 oz.	300 g
Baking powder	1 Tbsp.	15 mL
Baking soda	1 tsp.	5 mL
Salt	3/4 tsp.	3 mL
Buttermilk	24 oz.	720 mL
Eggs	6	6
Unsalted butter, melted	6 oz.	180 g

1. Combine all ingredients using the muffin method.
2. Portion into greased muffin tins, filling two-thirds full.
3. Bake at 375°F (190°C) for approximately 20–25 minutes.

Approximate values per muffin:

Calories	180
Total fat	6 g
Saturated fat	3.5 g
Cholesterol	55 mg
Sodium	140 mg
Total carbohydrates	28 g
Protein	4 g

━━━━━━━━━━ ✦✦✦ ━━━━━━━━━━

RECIPE 27.15
HUSH PUPPIES
(DEEP-FRIED CORNBREAD)

Yield: 60 2-inch (5-cm) Pieces   **Method:** Muffin

Yellow cornmeal	1 lb.	500 g
All-purpose flour	8 oz.	250 g
Baking powder	1 Tbsp.	15 mL
Salt	1 Tbsp.	15 mL
Black pepper	1 Tbsp.	15 mL

Continued

Sugar	2 oz.	60 g
Onion, minced	8 oz.	250 g
Eggs	4	4
Milk	16 oz.	500 mL

1. Combine all ingredients using the muffin method.
2. Drop small scoops (using a No. 60 or No. 70 portion scoop) into 375°F (190°C) deep fat. Using the swimming method, deep-fat fry until golden brown.
3. Remove from the fat and drain. Serve immediately.

Approximate values per muffin:

Calories	70
Total fat	3 g
Saturated fat	1 g
Cholesterol	5 mg
Sodium	120 mg
Total carbohydrates	10 g
Protein	1 g

◆◆◆

RECIPE 27.16

LEMON TEA BREAD

Yield: 12 Muffins or 1 Loaf   **Method:** Creaming

Unsalted butter, softened	3 oz.	90 g
Granulated sugar	10 oz.	300 g
Eggs	2	2
Milk	4 oz.	120 mL
All-purpose flour	6 oz.	180 g
Baking powder	1 tsp.	5 mL
Salt	1/2 tsp.	2 mL
Lemon zest	1 Tbsp.	15 mL
Lemon juice	4 oz.	120 mL

1. Cream the butter with 7 ounces (210 g) of the sugar. Add the eggs and milk. Mix well.
2. Sift the dry ingredients together and add to the butter mixture. Fold in the lemon zest. Portion into lightly greased pan.
3. Bake at 350°F (170°C) until tester comes out clean, approximately 35–40 minutes for a large loaf or 12–15 minutes for muffins. Remove from the pan and place on a cooling rack.
4. Combine 3 ounces (90 g) of the sugar with the lemon juice. Heat until the sugar dissolves and the mixture is hot. Slowly pour or brush the glaze over the hot bread or muffins.

Approximate values per muffin:

Calories	220
Total fat	7 g
Saturated fat	4 g
Cholesterol	50 mg
Sodium	115 mg
Total carbohydrates	36 g
Protein	3 g

WEBLINKS

Science of Foods, Oregon State University: Quickbreads
   www.orst.edu/instruct/nfm236/quickbread/index.html
Tortilla Industry Association: Consumer Information
   www.tortilla-info.com/consumer.htm
Flat Breads—A Taste of Ancient Civilizations
   www.efn.org/~sundance/FlatBreads.html
Ask the BreadLady™
   members.aol.com/BreadLady1/AskBreadLady.html

CHAPTER 28

YEAST BREADS

LEARNING OUTCOMES

After studying this chapter you will be able to:

+ select and use yeast
+ perform the 10 steps involved in yeast bread production, including kneading by hand
+ mix yeast doughs using the straight dough method and sponge method
+ prepare rolled-in doughs

Although few baked goods intimidate novice bakers as much as yeast breads, few baked goods are actually as forgiving or as comforting to prepare as yeast breads. By mastering a few basic procedures and techniques, you can offer your customers delicious, fresh yeast products.

Yeast breads can be divided into two categories: lean doughs and rich doughs. Lean doughs, such as those used for French and Italian breads, contain little or no sugar or fat. Rich doughs, such as brioche and some multigrain breads, contain significantly more sugar and fat. Rolled-in doughs, so-called because the fat is rolled into the dough in layers, are a type of rich dough used for baked goods such as croissants and sweetened danish.

The study of yeast breads could well occupy this entire text and an entire course. The focus here is narrowed to an understanding of fundamental techniques and procedures for making the most common styles of yeast breads for a small retail shop or restaurant. Some of the formulas in this chapter yield only one or two loaves or a few dozen rolls. Although most of these formulas can be increased successfully if necessary, you can best develop proper judgment skills by first preparing small quantities. We discuss hands-on mixing and makeup techniques and also include commercial (i.e., mechanical) bread production.

YEAST

Yeast is a living organism: a one-celled fungus. Various strains of yeast are present virtually everywhere. Yeast feeds on carbohydrates, converting them to carbon dioxide and alcohol in an organic process known as **fermentation**:

Yeast + Carbohydrates = Alcohol + Carbon Dioxide

Fermentation—*the process by which yeast converts sugar into alcohol and carbon dioxide; it also refers to the time that yeast dough is left to rise— that is, the time it takes for carbon dioxide gas cells to form and become trapped in the gluten network.*

When yeast produces carbon dioxide gas during bread making, the gas becomes trapped in the dough's gluten network. The trapped gas leavens the bread, providing the desired rise and texture. The small amount of alcohol produced by fermentation evaporates during baking.

As with most living things, yeast is very sensitive to temperature. It prefers temperatures between 70 and 130°F (21–54°C) depending on the type of yeast. The range used in most bakeries is 90 to 110°F (32–43°C). At temperatures below 34°F (2°C) it becomes dormant; above 138°F (59°C) it dies. (See Table 28.1.)

Salt is used in bread making because it conditions gluten, making it stronger and more elastic. Salt also affects yeast fermentation. Because salt inhibits the growth of yeast, it helps control the dough's rise. Too little salt and not only will the bread taste bland, but also it will rise too rapidly. Too much salt, however, and the yeast will be destroyed. By learning to control the

TABLE 28.1   TEMPERATURES FOR YEAST DEVELOPMENT

Temperature		Yeast Development
34°F	2°C	Inactive
60–70°F	16–21°C	Slow action
70–90°F	21–32°C	Best temperature for growth of fresh yeast
105–115°F	41–46°C	Best temperature for growth of dry yeast
125–130°F	52–54°C	Best temperature for activating instant yeast
138°F	59°C	Yeast dies

amount of food for the yeast and the temperatures of fermentation, you can learn to control the texture of your yeast-leavened products.

Though the addition of fats or shortenings to a dough will tenderize, moisturize and increase volume, it will slow down fermentation.

Types of Yeast

Baker's yeast is available in two forms: compressed and active dry. (You may also encounter a product called brewer's yeast; it is a nutritional supplement with no leavening ability.)

Compressed Yeast

Compressed yeast is a mixture of yeast and starch with a moisture content of approximately 70%. Also referred to as **fresh yeast**, compressed yeast must be kept refrigerated. It should be creamy white and crumbly with a fresh, yeasty smell. Do not use compressed yeast that has developed a sour odour, brown colour or slimy film.

Compressed yeast is available in 0.6-ounce (17-g) cubes and 1-pound (450-g) blocks. Under proper storage conditions, compressed yeast has a shelf life of two to three weeks.

Active Dry Yeast

Active dry yeast differs from compressed yeast in that virtually all of the moisture has been removed by hot air. The absence of moisture renders the organism dormant and allows the yeast to be stored without refrigeration for several months. When preparing doughs, dry yeast is generally rehydrated in a lukewarm (approximately 110°F [43°C]) liquid before being added to the other ingredients.

Dry yeast is available in 1/4-ounce (7-g) packages and 1- or 2-pound (450-g or 1-kg) vacuum-sealed bags. It should be stored in a cool, dry place and refrigerated after opening.

Instant Yeast

Instant or **quick-rise dry yeast** is also available. It must be blended with the dry ingredients in a bread formula, then activated with hot (approximately 125–130°F [52–54°C]) water. It dramatically speeds the rising process. Instant yeast can be substituted measure for measure for regular dry yeast. Instant yeast is still a living organism and will be destroyed at temperatures above 138°F (59°C).

The flavours of dry and compressed yeasts are virtually indistinguishable, but dry yeast is approximately twice as strong. Because too much yeast can ruin bread, always remember to reduce the specified weight of dry yeast when substituting for compressed yeast in a formula. Likewise, if a formula specifies dry yeast, increase the amount when substituting compressed yeast. In this text, all of the formulas requiring yeast use regular active dry yeast. Generally, 40% dry yeast is used to replace 100% fresh yeast.

Sourdough Starter

Prior to commercial yeast production, bakers relied on starters to leaven their breads. Early starters were simple but magical mixtures of flour and liquid (water, potato broth, milk) left to capture wild yeasts from the air and then ferment. Only a portion of the starter was used at a time. The rest was kept for later use, replenished periodically with additional flour and liquid so the magic could continue.

Today, starters are generally fortified with yeast to provide consistency and reliability; they are prized for the unique, sour flavours they impart. Prepared dry cultures are often used commercially to give bread a "sourdough" flavour without requiring the time and space necessary to develop and maintain an active starter.

◆◆◆

RECIPE 28.1

SOURDOUGH STARTER (FOR WHITE BREADS)

Yield: 1 qt. (1 L)

Active dry yeast	1 tsp.	5 mL
Water, warm	4 oz.	120 mL
Water, room temperature	14 oz.	400 mL
Bread flour	2 lb. 3 oz.	1 kg

1. Combine the yeast and warm water. Let stand until foamy, approximately 10 minutes.
2. Stir in the 14 ounces (400 mL) of room-temperature water, then add the flour, 2 ounces (60 mL) at a time.
3. Blend by hand or with the paddle attachment of an electric mixer on low speed for 2 minutes.
4. Place the starter in a warmed bowl and cover with plastic wrap. Let stand at room temperature overnight. The starter should triple in volume but still be wet and sticky. Refrigerate until ready to use.
5. Each time a portion of the starter is used, it must be replenished. To replenish the starter, stir in equal amounts by volume of flour and warm water. Then allow the mixture to ferment at room temperature for several hours or overnight before refrigerating.

NOTE: If liquid rises to the top of the starter it should be stirred back into the mixture. If the starter develops a pink or yellow film it has been contaminated and must be discarded.

Sourdough Starter

Approximate values per 1 oz. (30 g):

Calories	100
Total fat	0 g
Saturated fat	0 g
Cholesterol	0 mg
Sodium	0 mg
Total carbohydrates	22 g
Protein	3 g

PRODUCTION STAGES FOR YEAST BREADS

The production of yeast breads can be divided into 10 stages:

1. scaling the ingredients
2. mixing and kneading the dough
3. fermenting the dough
4. punching down the dough
5. portioning the dough
6. rounding the portions
7. shaping the portions
8. proofing the products
9. baking the products
10. cooling and storing the finished products

Stage 1: Scaling the Ingredients

As with any other bakeshop product, it is important to scale or measure ingredients accurately when making a yeast bread. Be sure that all necessary ingredients are available and at the proper temperature before starting.

The amount of flour required in a yeast bread may vary depending upon the humidity level, storage conditions of the flour and the accuracy with which other ingredients are measured. The amount of flour stated in most formulas is to be used as a guide; experience teaches when more or less flour is actually needed.

Stage 2: Mixing and Kneading the Dough

The way ingredients are combined affects the outcome of the bread. A dough must be mixed properly in order to combine the ingredients uniformly,

---

◆◆◆
THE RISE OF YEAST BREADS

How and when the first yeast-leavened bread came into being no one knows. Perhaps some wild yeasts—the world is full of them—drifted into a dough as it awaited baking. Perhaps some ancient baker substituted fermented ale or beer for water one day. In any case, the resulting bread was different, lighter and more appetizing.

Based on models, images and writings found in excavated tombs, we can be fairly certain that the ancient Egyptians saved a bit of fermented dough from one day's baking to add to the next day's. This use of sourdough starter continues today, enjoying widespread popularity.

Other cultures developed their own leavening methods. The Greeks and Romans prepared a wheat porridge with wine, which caused their doughs to ferment. The Gauls and Iberians added the foamy head from ale to their doughs. Both methods resulted in lighter breads that retained their fresh textures longer.

Since ancient times, bread baking has been one of the first household tasks readily turned over to professionals. The first cooks to work outside homes during the Greek and Roman empires were bakers. The bakery trade flourished during the Middle Ages, with a wide variety of breads being produced. Yeast-leavened breads remained the exception, not the norm, until well into the 17th century, however.

The first real collection of bread recipes is found in Nicolas Bonnefon's *Les Délices de la campagne*, published in 1654. Bonnefon's instructions, meant for those dissatisfied with commercial products of the time, included the use of beer yeast. By the end of the 17th century, published works included recipes for breads leavened with sourdough starter and the yeasts used in breweries.

Louis Pasteur finally identified yeast as a living organism in 1857. Soon after, a process for distilling or manufacturing baker's yeast was developed. By 1868, commercial baking yeast was available in stores.

distribute the yeast and develop the gluten. If the dough is not mixed properly, the bread's texture and shape suffer.

Yeast breads are usually mixed by either the **straight dough method** or the **sponge method**. A third method used for rich, flaky doughs is discussed later in the section on **rolled-in doughs**.

Once ingredients are combined, the dough must be kneaded to develop gluten, the network of proteins that gives a bread its shape and texture. Kneading can be done by hand or by an electric mixer with its dough hook attachment. Dough should be kneaded until it is smooth and moderately elastic. The presence of a few blisterlike air bubbles on the dough's surface also signals that kneading is complete. Because fat and sugar slow gluten development, rich, sweet doughs are generally kneaded longer than lean doughs. Overkneading results in dough that is, at best, difficult to shape and, in extreme cases, sticky and inelastic. Overkneading is rarely a problem, however, except when using a high-speed mixer or food processor.

BASIC PROCEDURE FOR KNEADING DOUGH BY HAND

  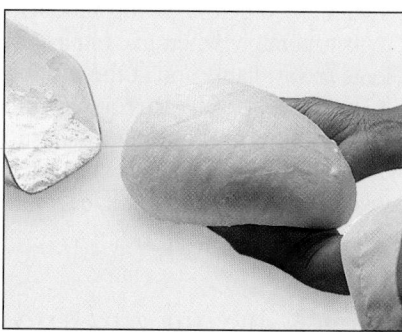

1. First, bring a portion of the dough towards you.

2. Then push the dough away from you with your fist.

3. Repeat until the dough is properly kneaded.

Straight Dough Method

The simplest and most common method for mixing yeast doughs is known as the straight dough method. With this method, all ingredients are simply combined and mixed. The yeast may or may not be combined first with a warm liquid. Be careful that the temperature of the liquid ingredients does not exceed 138°F (59°C) or the yeast will die.

Once the ingredients are combined, the dough is kneaded until it is smooth and elastic. Kneading time varies according to the kneading method used and the type of dough being produced. The straight dough method is illustrated with Recipe 28.2, Soft Yeast Dinner Rolls.

Sponge Method

The sponge method of mixing yeast doughs has two stages. During the first stage the yeast, liquid and approximately one-half of the flour are combined to make a thick batter known as a **sponge**. The sponge is allowed to rise until bubbly and doubled in size. During the second stage the fat, salt, sugar and remaining flour are added. The dough is kneaded and allowed to rise again. These two fermentations give sponge method breads a somewhat different flavour and a lighter texture than breads made with the straight dough method.

Do not confuse sponge method breads with sourdough starters. The sponge method is most often used to improve the texture of heavy doughs such as rye. Unlike a sourdough starter, the first-stage sponge is prepared only for the specific formula and is not reserved for later use. The sponge method is illustrated with Recipe 28.3, Medium Sour Rye Bread.

Stage 3: Fermenting the Dough

As mentioned earlier, fermentation is the process by which yeast converts sugar into alcohol and carbon dioxide. Fermentation also refers to the time that yeast dough is left to rise—that is, the time it takes for carbon dioxide gas to form and become trapped in the gluten network. Note that **fermentation** refers to the rise given to the entire mass of yeast dough, while **proofing** refers to the rise given to shaped yeast products just prior to baking.

For fermentation, place the kneaded dough into a lightly oiled container large enough to allow the dough to expand. The surface of the dough may be lightly oiled to prevent drying. Cover the dough and place it in a warm place—that is, at temperatures between 75° and 85°F (24–29°C). It is better to allow the dough to rise slowly in a cool place than to rush fermentation.

Fermentation is complete when the dough has approximately doubled in size and no longer springs back when pressed gently with two fingers. The time necessary varies depending on the type of dough, the temperature of the room and the temperature of the dough.

Stage 4: Punching Down the Dough

After fermentation, the dough is gently folded down to expel excessive gas pockets with a technique known as **punching down**. Punching down dough also helps even out the dough's temperature.

Stage 5: Portioning the Dough

The dough is now ready to be divided into portions. For loaves, the dough is scaled to the desired weight. For individual rolls you can first shape the dough into an even log, then cut off portions with a chef's knife or dough cutter. Weighing the cut dough pieces on a portion scale ensures even-sized portions. When portioning, work quickly and keep the dough covered to prevent it from drying out.

Stage 6: Rounding the Portions

The portions of dough must be shaped into smooth, round balls in a technique known as **rounding**. Rounding stretches the outside layer of gluten into a smooth coating. This helps hold in gases and makes it easier to shape the dough. Unrounded rolls rise unevenly and have a rough, lumpy surface.

Stage 7: Shaping the Portions

Lean doughs and some rich doughs can be shaped into a variety of forms: large loaves, small loaves, free-form or country-style rounds or individual dinner rolls. Table 28.2 identifies common pan sizes and the approximate weight of the dough used to fill them. Some shaping techniques are shown in Figures 28.1 through 28.5. Other doughs, particularly brioche, croissant and danish, are usually shaped in very specific ways. Those techniques are discussed and illustrated with their specific formulas.

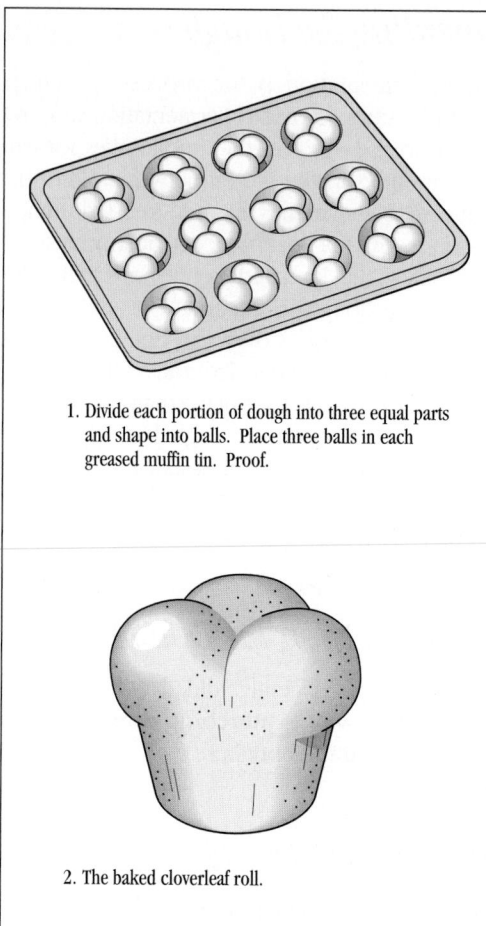

1. Divide each portion of dough into three equal parts and shape into balls. Place three balls in each greased muffin tin. Proof.

2. The baked cloverleaf roll.

FIGURE 28.1   *Cloverleaf Rolls*

TABLE 28.2   PAN SIZES FOR YEAST BREADS

Pan	Approximate Size	Weight of Dough*
Sandwich loaf	16 in. × 4 in. × 4-1/2 in.	4 lb. (1800 g)
Pullman	13 in. × 4 in. × 3 in.	3 lb. (1300 g)
Large	9 in. × 5 in. × 3 in.	2 lb. (900 g)
Medium	8 in. × 4 in. × 2 in.	1 lb. 8 oz. (680 g)
Small	7 in. × 3 in. × 2 in.	1 lb. (450 g)
Miniature	5 in. × 3 in. × 2 in.	8 oz. (225 g)

*Weights given are approximate; variations may occur based on the type of dough used as well as the temperature and time of proofing.

1. Roll dough into a thin rectangle. Brush with melted butter and cut into 1½-inch (3.75-cm) wide strips.

2. Stack 6 or 7 strips together, then cut into slices.

3. Place each slice into a greased muffin tin, cut side up. Proof.

4. The baked butterflake roll.

FIGURE 28.2 *Butterflake Rolls*

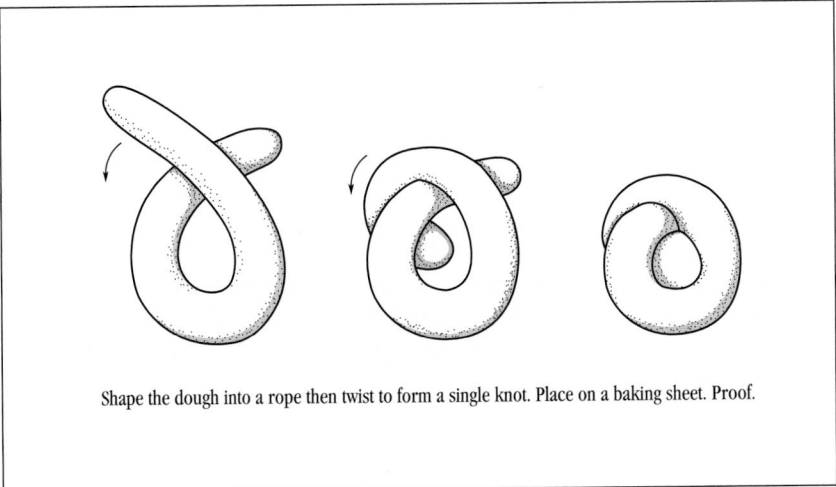

Shape the dough into a rope then twist to form a single knot. Place on a baking sheet. Proof.

FIGURE 28.3 *Bow Knot Rolls*

FIGURE 28.4　*Pan Loaves*

1. Flatten the dough into a rectangle. Fold over one short edge and press the seam together.

2. Continue to roll the dough, pressing the seam firmly with each turn. Stretch the front corners as necessary to maintain the shape.

3. Place the finished roll of dough in a greased pan, seam side down. Proof.

FIGURE 28.5　*Free-Form Loaves*

1. Roll the dough into a rectangle then roll up from the long side, jelly-roll fashion. Pinch the seam to seal.

2. Place loaf on a baking sheet, seam side down, and shape ends. Proof.

Stage 8: Proofing the Products

Proofing—*the final rise of shaped yeast products just prior to baking.*

Proofing is the final rise of shaped or panned yeast products before baking. The temperatures should be between 95° and 115°F (35–46°C), slightly higher than the temperatures for fermentation. Some humidity is also desirable to prevent the dough from drying or forming a crust. Temperature and humidity can be controlled with a special cabinet known as a **proof box**.

Proofing should continue until the product doubles in size and springs back slowly when lightly touched. Underproofing results in poor volume and texture. Overproofing results in a sour taste, poor volume and a paler colour after baking.

Stage 9: Baking the Products

As yeast breads bake, a variety of chemical and physical changes turn the dough into an edible product. These changes are discussed in Chapter 26, Principles of the Bakeshop.

Because of the expansion of gases, yeast products experience a sudden rise when first placed in a hot oven. This rise is known as **oven spring**. As the dough's temperature increases, the yeast dies, the gluten fibres become firm, the starches gelatinize, the moisture evaporates and, finally, the crust forms and turns brown.

Before baking, products can be washed and then, if desired, slashed.

Washes

The appearance of yeast breads can be altered by applying a glaze or **wash** to the dough before baking. The crust is made shiny or matte, hard or soft, darker or lighter by the proper use of washes. (Table 28.3.) Washes are also used to attach seeds, wheat germ, oats or other toppings to the dough's surface.

The most commonly used wash is an egg wash, composed of whole egg and water. Yeast products can also be topped with plain water, a mixture of egg and milk, plain milk or richer glazes containing sugar and flavourings. Even a light dusting of white flour can be used to top dough. (This is commonly seen with potato rolls.)

Avoid using too much wash, as it can burn or cause the product to stick to the pan. Puddles or streaks of egg wash on the dough will cause uneven browning.

Washes may be applied before or after proofing. If applied after proofing, be extremely careful not to deflate the product.

Occasionally a formula will specify that melted butter or oil be brushed on the product after baking. Do not, however, apply egg washes to already baked products, as the egg will remain raw and the desired effect will not be achieved.

TABLE 28.3	WASHES FOR YEAST PRODUCTS
Wash	Use
Whole egg and water	Shine and colour
Whole egg and milk	Shine and colour with a soft crust
Egg white and water	Shine with a firm crust
Water	Crisp crust
Flour	Texture and contrast
Milk or cream	Colour with a soft crust

Slashing

The shape and appearance of some breads can be improved by cutting their tops with a sharp knife or razor just before baking. This is referred to as **slashing**. Hard-crusted breads are usually slashed to allow for continued rising and the escape of gases after the crust has formed. Breads that are not properly slashed will burst or break along the sides. Slashing can also be used to make an attractive design on the product's surface.

Steam Injection

The crisp crust desired for certain breads and rolls is achieved by introducing moisture into the oven during baking. Professional bakers' ovens have built-in steam injection jets to provide moisture as needed. To create steam in any oven you can spray or mist the bread with water several times during baking, place ice cubes on the oven floor to melt or keep a pan of hot water on the oven's lowest rack. Rich doughs, which do not form crisp crusts, are baked without steam.

Determining Doneness

Baking time is determined by a variety of factors: the product's size, the oven thermostat's accuracy and the desired crust colour. Larger items require a longer baking time than smaller ones. Lean dough products bake faster and at higher temperatures than rich dough products.

Bread loaves can be tested for doneness by tapping them on the bottom and listening for a hollow sound. This indicates that air, not moisture, is present inside the loaf. If the bottom is damp or heavy, the loaf probably needs more baking time. The texture and colour of the crust are also a good indication of doneness, particularly with individual rolls. As you bake a variety of yeast products you will develop the experience necessary to determine doneness without strict adherence to elapsed time.

Stage 10: Cooling and Storing the Finished Products

The quality of even the finest yeast products suffers if they are cooled or stored improperly. Yeast products should be cooled at room temperature and away from drafts. Yeast breads and rolls should be removed from their pans for cooling. Allow loaves to cool completely before slicing.

Once cool, yeast products should be stored at room temperature or frozen for longer storage. Do not refrigerate baked goods, as refrigeration promotes staling. Do not wrap Italian or French loaves, as this causes crusts to lose the desired crispness.

◆◆◆

RECIPE 28.2

SOFT YEAST DINNER ROLLS

Yield: 75 Rolls   **Method:** Straight Dough

Water, warm	1 lb. 4 oz.	600 g
Active dry yeast	2 oz.	60 g
Bread flour	2 lb. 10 oz.	1.2 kg
Salt	1 oz.	30 g
Sugar	4 oz.	120 g
Dried milk powder	2 oz.	60 g
Shortening	2 oz.	60 g
Unsalted butter, softened	2 oz.	60 g
Eggs, whole	4 oz.	120 g
Egg wash	as needed	as needed

Approximate values per roll:

Calories	90
Total fat	1.5 g
Saturated fat	0.5 g
Cholesterol	10 mg
Sodium	160 mg
Total carbohydrates	15 g
Protein	3 g

Claims—Low fat; low saturated fat; low cholesterol

1. Combine the water and yeast in a small bowl. Combine the remaining ingredients (except the egg wash) in the bowl of an electric mixer.
2. Add the water-and-yeast mixture to the remaining ingredients; stir to combine.
3. Knead with a dough hook on second speed for 10 minutes.
4. Transfer the dough to a lightly greased bowl, cover and place in a warm spot. Let rise until doubled, approximately 1 hour.
5. Punch down the dough. Let it rest a few minutes to allow the gluten to relax.
6. Divide the dough into 1-1/4-ounce (35-g) portions and round. Shape as desired and arrange on paper-lined sheet pans. Proof until doubled in size.
7. Carefully brush the proofed rolls with egg wash. Bake at 400°F (200°C) until medium brown, approximately 12–15 minutes.

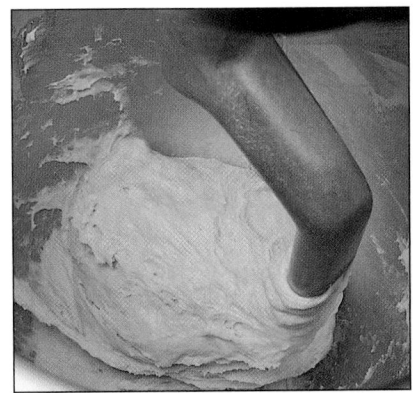

1. Mix the soft yeast dough:

    a) Combine the ingredients in a mixer bowl with the dough hook attached.

    b) Add the yeast-and-water mixture.

2. Knead the dough.

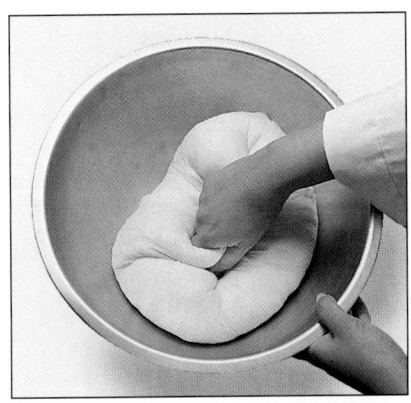

3. The dough before rising.

4. Punch down the dough:

    a) Press down on the centre of the dough with your fist.

    b) Fold the edges of the dough in towards the centre.

5. Scale the dough.

6. Round the rolls.

7. Egg-wash the rolls.

◆◆◆

RECIPE 28.3
MEDIUM SOUR RYE BREAD

Yield: 20 lb. (9.4 kg)

Dark rye flour	2 lb. 12 oz.	1.25 kg
Light rye flour	2 lb. 12 oz.	1.25 kg
Bread flour	5 lb. 6 oz.	2.5 kg
Salt	3-1/2 oz.	100 g
Dehydrated sour*	2-1/2 oz.	75 g
Yeast, fresh	5 oz.	150 g
Water, 70°F (21°C)	108 oz.	3.4 L

Approximate values per loaf:

Calories	1348
Total fat	7 g
Saturated fat	1 g
Cholesterol	0 mg
Sodium	2998 mg
Total carbohydrates	283 g
Protein	47 g

1. Blend the first 5 ingredients with a hook in mixing bowl for 1 minute on low speed.
2. Dissolve yeast in water and add to the flour.
3. Mix for 2 minutes on low speed and 5 minutes on second speed.
4. Bench for 30 minutes (benching refers to the time the dough rests in its first proofing stage at room temperature).
5. Divide dough into 1 lb. 6 oz. (620 g) rounds and rest 15 minutes.
6. Bake at 430°F (220°C) for 10–15 minutes then turn oven down to 390°F (180°C) to finish baking, approximately 30 minutes.

*Prepared dry culture (see page 792).

1. Rye bread starter.   **2.** Mix the rye dough.   **3.** Shape the rye loaves.

ROLLED-IN DOUGHS

Baked goods made with rolled-in doughs include croissants, danish pastries and the non-yeast-leavened puff pastry. (Puff pastry is discussed in Chapter 29, Pies, Pastries and Cookies.) The dough is so named because the fat is incorporated through a process of rolling and folding. Products made with a rolled-in dough have a distinctive flaky texture created by the repeated layering of fat and dough. As the dough bakes, moisture is released from the fat in the form of steam. The steam is then trapped between the layers of dough, causing them to rise and separate.

Making Rolled-In Doughs

Rolled-in doughs are made following most of the 10 production stages discussed earlier. The principal differences are: (1) the butter is incorporated through a folding process after the dough base is fermented and punched down; (2) rolled-in doughs are portioned somewhat differently than other yeast doughs; and (3) the portions are then shaped without rounding.

Butter is often used for rolled-in products because of its flavour. Unfortunately, butter is hard to work with because it cracks and breaks when cold and becomes too soft to roll at room temperature. Margarine, shortening or specially formulated high-moisture fats can be used, sometimes in combination with butter, in order to reduce costs or to make it easier to work with the dough.

The dough base should not be kneaded too much as gluten will continue to develop during the rolling and folding process. Commercial bakeries, hotels and larger restaurants generally use an electric dough sheeter to roll the dough. This saves time and ensures a more consistent product.

BASIC PROCEDURE FOR PREPARING ROLLED-IN DOUGHS

1. Mix the dough and allow it to rise.
2. Shape the butter or shortening, then chill it.
3. Roll out the dough evenly, then top with the chilled butter.
4. Fold the dough around the butter, enclosing it completely.
5. Roll out the dough into a rectangle, about 1/4 to 1/2 inch (0.6 to 1.25 cm) thick. Always be sure to roll at right angles; do not roll haphazardly or in a circle as you would pastry doughs.
6. Fold the dough in thirds. Be sure to brush off any excess flour from between the folds. This completes the first turn. Chill the dough for 20 to 30 minutes.
7. Roll out the dough and fold it in the same manner a second and third time, allowing the dough to rest between each turn. After completing the third turn, wrap the dough carefully and allow it to rest for several hours or overnight before shaping and baking.

◆◆◆

RECIPE 28.4
CROISSANTS

Yield: 60 Rolls **Method:** Rolled-In

Bread flour	2 lb. 3 oz.	1 kg
Salt	1 oz.	30 g
Sugar	6 oz.	180 g
Milk	1 lb. 6 oz.	660 g
Active dry yeast	1 oz.	30 g
Unsalted butter, soft	1 lb. 8 oz.	720 g
Egg wash	as needed	as needed

1. Stir the flour, salt and sugar together in a mixer bowl fitted with a dough hook.
2. Warm the milk to approximately 90°F (32°C). Stir in the yeast.
3. Add the milk-and-yeast mixture to the dry ingredients. Stir until combined, then knead on second speed for 10 minutes.

Continued

◆◆◆

THE CULTURED CROISSANT

A croissant brings to mind a Parisian sidewalk café and a steaming cup of café crème. It is, however, a truly international delicacy. Created by bakers in Budapest (Hungary) to celebrate the city's liberation from Turkey in 1686, its shape was derived from the crescent moon of the Turkish flag. The delicacy was soon adopted as a breakfast pastry by both the French and the Italians. The first machine for mass-producing croissants was designed by a Japanese firm and manufactured in Italy. Although croissants became popular in North America only during the last decade or so, millions of croissants are now consumed each year.

Approximate values per roll:	
Calories	200
Total fat	12 g
Saturated fat	7 g
Cholesterol	40 mg
Sodium	230 mg
Total carbohydrates	19 g
Protein	3 g
Vitamin A	10%

4. Place the dough in a large floured bowl, cover and let rise until doubled in size, approximately 1 hour.

5. Prepare the butter while the dough is rising. Place the butter in an even layer between 2 large pieces of plastic wrap and roll into a flat rectangle, approximately 8 inches × 11 inches (20 cm × 27.5 cm) and chill.

6. After the dough has risen, punch it down. Roll out the dough into a large rectangle, about 1/2 inch (1.25 cm) thick and large enough to enclose the rectangle of butter. Place the unwrapped butter in the centre of the dough and fold the dough around the butter, enclosing it completely.

7. Roll out the block of dough into a long rectangle, about 1 inch (2.5 cm) thick. Fold the dough in thirds, as if you were folding a letter. This completes the first turn. Wrap the dough in plastic and chill for approximately 20–30 minutes.

8. Repeat the rolling and folding process 2 more times, chilling the dough between each turn. When finished, wrap the dough well and chill it overnight before shaping and baking.

9. To shape the dough into croissant rolls, cut off one-quarter of the block at a time, wrapping and returning the rest to the refrigerator. Roll each quarter of dough into a large rectangle, about 1/4 inch (6 mm) thick.

10. Cut the dough into uniform triangles. Starting with the large end, roll each triangle into a crescent and place on a paper-lined sheet pan.

11. Brush lightly with egg wash. Proof until doubled, but do not allow the dough to become so warm that the butter melts.

12. Bake at 375°F (190°C) until golden brown, approximately 12–15 minutes.

1. Roll out the butter between two sheets of plastic wrap.

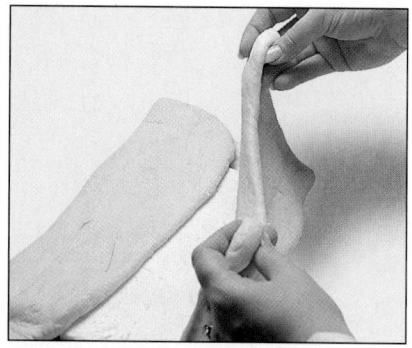

2. After positioning the butter on the rolled-out dough, fold the dough around the butter.

3. Brush the excess flour from the rolled-out dough.

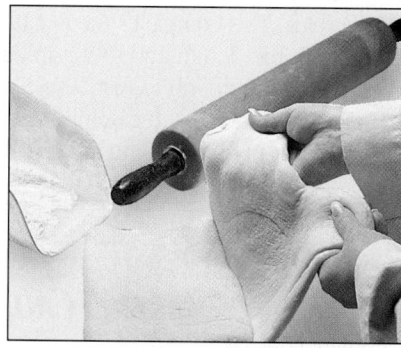

4. Fold the dough in thirds.

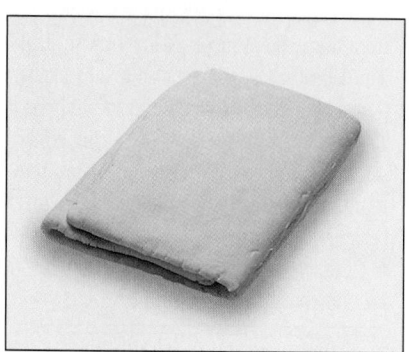

5. The finished croissant dough.

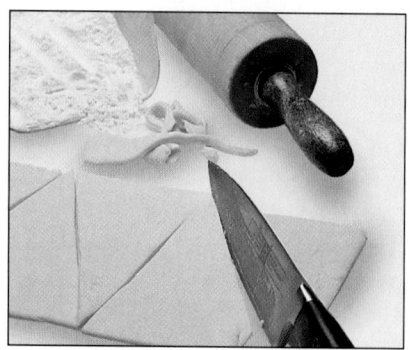

6. Cut the dough into triangles.

7. Baked croissants.

TABLE 28.4   TROUBLESHOOTING CHART FOR YEAST BREADS

Problem	Cause	Solution
Cannonball of dough	Too much flour forced into the dough	Gradually add water; adjust formula
Crust too pale	Oven temperature too low	Adjust oven
	Dough overproofed	Proof only until almost doubled, then bake immediately
Crust too dark	Oven too hot	Adjust oven
	Too much sugar in dough	Adjust formula or measure sugar carefully
Top crust separates from rest of loaf	Dough improperly shaped	Shape dough carefully
	Crust not slashed properly	Slash dough to a depth of 1/2 in. (1.25 cm)
	Dough dried out during proofing	Cover dough during proofing
Sides of loaf are cracked	Bread expanded after crust had formed	Slash top of loaf before baking
Dense texture	Not enough yeast	Adjust formula or measure yeast carefully
	Not enough fermentation time	Let dough rise until doubled or as directed
	Too much salt	Adjust formula or measure salt carefully
Ropes of undercooked dough running through the product	Insufficient kneading	Knead dough until it is smooth and elastic or as directed
	Insufficient rising time	Allow adequate time for rising
	Oven too hot	Adjust oven
Free-form loaf spreads and flattens	Dough too soft	Add flour
Large holes in bread	Too much yeast	Adjust formula or measure yeast carefully
	Overkneaded	Knead only as directed
	Inadequate punch-down	Punch down properly to knead out excess air before shaping
Blisters on crust	Too much liquid	Measure ingredients carefully
	Improper shaping	Knead out excess air before shaping
	Too much steam in oven	Reduce amount of steam or moisture in oven

CONCLUSION

Fresh yeast breads are a popular and inexpensive addition to any menu and are surprisingly easy to prepare. By understanding and appreciating the importance of each of the 10 production stages described in this chapter, you will be able to create and adapt formulas to suit your specific operation and needs.

QUESTIONS FOR DISCUSSION

1. Describe the characteristics of lean and rich doughs and give an example of each.
2. Explain the differences between active dry yeast and compressed yeast. Describe the correct procedures for working with these yeasts.
3. Explain the differences between a sponge and a sourdough starter. How are each of these items used?

4. Describe the straight dough mixing method and give two examples of products made using this procedure.

5. Briefly describe the procedure for making a rolled-in dough and give two examples of products made from rolled-in doughs.

6. List the 10 production stages for yeast breads. Which of these production stages would also apply to quick-bread production? Explain your answer.

ADDITIONAL YEAST BREAD FORMULAS

RECIPE 28.5
FRENCH BREAD

Yield: 50 lb. (22 kg)

Method: Straight Dough
Dough Temperature 82°F (28°C)

Bread flour	28 lb.	13 kg
Salt	8 oz.	230 g
Malt	5-1/4 oz.	150 g
Shortening	5-1/4 oz.	150 g
Format	4-1/2 oz.	130 g
Yeast, fresh	15-3/4 oz.	450 g
Water	264 oz.	8.2 L

1. Place flour, salt, malt and shortening into a mixing bowl.
2. Dissolve the yeast in water and add to mix.
3. Mix with a hook for 1 minute on low speed, then check the dough for consistency and continue mixing for 9 minutes at second speed.
4. Bench for 15 minutes at a dough temperature of 82°F (28°C).
5. Divide dough into 18-ounce (540-g) portions and give 10 minutes' intermediate proof.
6. Mould, proof, cut and bake at 420°F (215°C) for 35 minutes.

Approximate values per loaf:

Calories	1401
Total fat	10 g
Saturated fat	2 g
Cholesterol	0 mg
Sodium	2637 mg
Total carbohydrates	279 g
Protein	50 g

NOTE: Format is a dough conditioner that speeds up fermentation. If unavailable, proceed with the next ingredients but be aware that the proofing will take longer.

◆◆◆

RECIPE 28.6
WHITE PAN BREAD

Yield: 40 lb. (18 kg)

Method: Straight Dough
Dough Temperature 82°F (28°C)

Bread flour	22 lb.	10 kg
Sugar	15-3/4 oz.	450 g
Salt	7 oz.	200 g
Milk powder	10-1/2 oz.	300 g
Shortening	14 oz.	400 g
Yeast, fresh	13 oz.	375 g
Water	190–220 oz.	6–7 L

1. Place all ingredients except yeast and water in a mixing bowl.
2. Dissolve the yeast in water and add to the mix.

3. Mix for 2 minutes on low speed.
4. Check dough for consistency and add more flour or water as needed. Continue mixing for 9–10 minutes on second speed.
5. Divide dough into 18-ounce (540-g) units, shape into rounds and give them 10 minutes' intermediate proof.
6. Mould dough pieces and place in bread pans.
7. Proof.
8. Bake at 420°F (215°C) for about 30 minutes.
9. Cool on wire rack before slicing and bagging.

Approximate values per loaf:	
Calories	1352
Total fat	18 g
Saturated fat	4 g
Cholesterol	0 mg
Sodium	2597 mg
Total carbohydrates	256 g
Protein	44 g

❖❖❖

RECIPE 28.7
ENGLISH MUFFIN LOAVES

Yield: 2 Large Loaves   **Method:** Straight Dough

Active dry yeast	1/2 oz.	15 g
Granulated sugar	1 Tbsp.	15 mL
Baking soda	1/4 tsp.	1 mL
Salt	2 tsp.	10 mL
All-purpose flour	1 lb. 8 oz.	750 g
Milk	1 pt.	500 mL
Water	4 oz.	120 mL
Cornmeal	as needed	as needed

1. Stir together the yeast, sugar, baking soda, salt and 12 ounces (360 g) of the flour.
2. Combine the milk and water and heat to 120°F (50°C).
3. Stir the warm liquids into the dry ingredients, beating well. Add enough of the remaining flour to make a stiff batter.
4. Spoon the batter into loaf pans that have been greased and dusted with cornmeal. Proof batter until it doubles.
5. Bake at 400°F (200°C) until golden brown and done, approximately 25 minutes.
6. Remove the bread from the pans immediately and cool.

Approximate values per loaf:	
Calories	1515
Total fat	12 g
Saturated fat	6 g
Cholesterol	35 mg
Sodium	2429 mg
Total carbohydrates	296 g
Protein	48 g

❖❖❖

RECIPE 28.8
POTATO CHEDDAR CHEESE BREAD

STOUFFER STANFORD COURT, SAN FRANCISCO, CA
Executive Chef Ercolino Crugnale

Yield: 7 1 lb. 4 oz. (600 g) Loaves   **Method:** Straight Dough

Water, heated to 100°F/38°C	8 oz.	240 mL
Active dry yeast	2 oz.	60 g
Bread flour	5 lb.	2.4 kg
Potatoes, boiled, peeled and puréed	2 lb. 3 oz.	1 kg
Kosher salt	1-1/2 oz.	45 g
Cracked pepper	1 oz.	30 g
Unsalted butter, melted	3 oz.	90 g
Cheddar cheese, grated	1 lb. 2 oz.	500 g
Water, room temperature	1 lb. 2 oz.	500 mL

Continued

1. Dissolve the yeast in the warm water and set aside.
2. Combine the flour, potatoes, salt, pepper, butter and cheese. Blend on low speed for 2–3 minutes.
3. Slowly add the room temperature water and the yeast mixture. Mix on medium speed for 8–10 minutes.
4. Allow the dough to rise in a warm spot until doubled, approximately 2 hours. Punch down the dough and divide into loaves.
5. Proof until doubled in size, approximately 45 minutes. Bake at 350°F (180°C) until brown, approximately 20–30 minutes.

◆◆◆

RECIPE 28.9

SUN-DRIED TOMATO ROLLS

Yield: 20 Rolls   **Method:** Straight Dough

Bread flour	12 oz.	360 g
Semolina flour	2 oz.	60 g
Sun-dried tomatoes, diced fine	3 Tbsp.	45 mL
Granulated sugar	2 Tbsp.	30 mL
Active dry yeast	1-1/2 tsp.	8 mL
Salt	1-1/2 tsp.	8 mL
Garlic, minced	1 tsp.	5 mL
Whole butter, softened	1 oz.	30 g
Water, warm	10 oz.	300 mL

1. Combine all of the ingredients using the straight dough method. Knead until smooth and elastic, approximately 10 minutes.
2. Place the dough in a lightly greased bowl, cover and proof until it doubles.
3. Punch down the dough and proof a second time.
4. Punch down the dough again and divide into 1-1/2-ounce (45-g) portions. Round the dough and shape as desired. Proof until the rolls double in size, approximately 20 minutes.
5. Bake at 400°F (200°C) until golden brown and done, approximately 18 minutes.

◆◆◆

RECIPE 28.10

BROWN BREAD

Yield: 42 lb. (19 kg)   **Method:** Straight Dough
                                   Dough Temperature 82°F (28°C)

Bread flour	9 lb.	4.36 kg
Whole wheat flour	13 lb.	6.24 kg
Sugar	15-3/4 oz.	450 g
Shortening	14 oz.	400 g
Milk powder	10-1/2 oz.	300 g
Salt	7 oz.	200 g
Yeast, fresh	12-1/4 oz.	350 g
Water	190–260 oz.	7–8 L

1. Place flour and all ingredients except yeast and water in mixing bowl.
2. Dissolve yeast in water and add to mix.

3. Mix 2 minutes on low speed.

4. Check dough for proper consistency and add more water or flour as needed. Continue mixing for 9–10 minutes on second speed.

5. Divide dough into 18-ounce (540-g) units, round and give 10 minutes' intermediate proof.

6. Mould dough pieces and place into bread pans.

7. Proof.

8. Bake at 420°F (215°C) for about 30 minutes.

9. Cool on wire rack before slicing and bagging.

Approximate values per loaf:	
Calories	1381
Total fat	22 g
Saturated fat	6 g
Cholesterol	10 mg
Sodium	2643 mg
Total carbohydrates	261 g
Protein	48 g

❖❖❖

RECIPE 28.11

MULTIGRAIN DATE BREAD

Yield: 2 Small Loaves   **Method:** Straight Dough

Dates, chopped	8 oz.	240 g
Bread flour	1 lb. 8 oz.	720 g
Active dry yeast	1/2 oz.	15 g
Water, heated to 70°F/20°C	16 oz.	500 mL
Honey	4 oz.	120 g
Unsalted butter, melted	2 oz.	60 g
Nonfat dry milk	1-1/4 oz.	35 g
Salt	1 Tbsp.	15 mL
Whole wheat flour	6 oz.	170 g
Rye flour	2 oz.	60 g
Wheat germ	2 oz.	60 g
Bran flakes, toasted	2 oz.	60 g
Sesame seeds	2 Tbsp.	30 mL
Egg wash	as needed	as needed
Poppy or sesame seeds	2 Tbsp.	30 mL

1. In a small bowl, combine the dates with 2 ounces (60 g) of the bread flour; toss to coat and set aside.

2. In a large mixer bowl, dissolve the yeast in the warm water. Add the honey, butter, milk powder, salt and whole wheat flour. Beat at medium speed for 2 minutes.

3. Stir in the rye flour, wheat germ, bran flakes, sesame seeds and date mixture.

4. Slowly add enough of the remaining bread flour to make a soft dough. Knead until smooth and elastic, approximately 5 minutes.

5. Place the dough in a lightly greased bowl and cover. Allow to rise until doubled, approximately 1-1/2 hours.

6. Punch down the dough and knead for a few seconds.

7. Divide the dough in half. Shape each piece and place in a lightly greased loaf pan. Cover and allow to rise until almost doubled, approximately 45 minutes.

8. Slash the top of the loaves as desired and top with egg wash and poppy or sesame seeds. Bake at 375°F (190°C) until golden brown and firm, approximately 40 minutes. Loaves should be dry and sound hollow when tapped on the bottom. Remove the loaves from the pans to cool.

Approximate values per 2-1/2 oz. (75 g) serving:	
Calories	270
Total fat	4.5 g
Saturated fat	2 g
Cholesterol	30 mg
Sodium	400 mg
Total carbohydrates	49 g
Protein	8 g
Calcium	10%

1. Roll the breadstick dough.

2. Twist the breadstick dough.

Approximate values per breadstick:

Calories	60
Total fat	5 g
Saturated fat	1 g
Cholesterol	10 mg
Sodium	190 mg
Total carbohydrates	2 g
Protein	1 g

Claims—low saturated fat; low cholesterol

◆◆◆

RECIPE 28.12
BREADSTICKS

Yield: 24 Breadsticks   **Method:** Straight Dough

Active dry yeast	1/2 oz.	15 g
Water, heated to 70°F/20°C	10 oz.	300 mL
Sugar	1 oz.	30 g
Olive oil	4 oz.	120 mL
Salt	2 tsp.	10 mL
Bread flour	1 lb. 2 oz.	510 g
Egg wash	as needed	as needed
Sesame seeds	3 Tbsp.	45 mL

1. Stir the yeast, water and sugar together in a mixer bowl.

2. Blend in the oil, salt and 8 ounces (240 g) of the flour.

3. Gradually add the remaining flour. Knead the dough until it is smooth and cleans the sides of the bowl, approximately 5 minutes.

4. Remove the dough from the bowl and allow it to rest for a few minutes. Roll the dough into a rectangle, about 1/4 inch (0.5 cm) thick.

5. Cut the dough into 24 even pieces. Roll each piece into a rope and twist; bring the ends together, allowing the sides to curl together. Place on a paper-lined sheet pan.

6. Brush with egg wash and top with sesame seeds. Let the sticks rise until doubled, approximately 20 minutes.

7. Bake at 375°F (190°C) until golden brown, approximately 12–15 minutes.

VARIATIONS: *Garlic breadsticks*—Knead 1 ounce (30 g) grated Parmesan cheese and 2 tablespoons (30 mL) minced garlic into the dough.
Herbed breadsticks—Knead 3 tablespoons (45 mL) chopped fresh herbs such as basil, parsley, dill and oregano into the dough.

◆◆◆

RECIPE 28.13
ROMAN FLATBREAD

Yield: 1 Sheet Pan, 12 in. × 18 in.   **Method:** Straight Dough
              (30 cm × 45 cm)

Sugar	1 Tbsp.	15 mL
Active dry yeast	1 Tbsp.	15 mL
Water, lukewarm	12 oz.	340 mL
All-purpose flour	1 lb. 2 oz.	540 g
Kosher salt	2 tsp.	10 mL
Onion, chopped fine	3 oz.	90 g
Olive oil	2 tsp.	10 mL
Fresh rosemary, crushed	2 Tbsp.	30 mL

1. Combine the sugar, yeast and water. Stir to dissolve the yeast. Stir in the flour 4 ounces (120 g) at a time.

2. Stir in 1-1/2 teaspoons (7 mL) of salt and the onion. Mix well, then knead on a lightly floured board until smooth.

Top the flatbread dough with crushed rosemary.

3. Place the dough in an oiled bowl, cover and let rise until doubled.

4. Punch down the dough, then flatten it onto an oiled sheet pan. It should be no more than 1 inch (2.5 cm) thick. Brush the top of the dough with the olive oil. Let the dough proof until doubled, about 15 minutes.

5. Sprinkle the crushed rosemary and remaining 1/2 teaspoon (2 mL) of salt on top of the dough. Bake at 400°F (200°C) until lightly browned, approximately 20 minutes.

◆◆◆

RECIPE 28.14
PIZZA DOUGH

Yield: 1 Large or 8 Individual Pizzas   **Method:** Straight Dough

Water, heated to 70°F/20°C	2 oz.	60 mL
Active dry yeast	1 Tbsp.	15 mL
Bread flour	14 oz.	420 g
Water, cool	6 oz.	180 mL
Salt	1 tsp.	5 mL
Olive oil	1 oz.	30 mL
Honey	1 Tbsp.	15 mL

1. Stir the yeast into the warm water to dissolve. Add the flour.

2. Stir the cool water, salt, olive oil and honey into the flour mixture. Knead with a dough hook or by hand until smooth and elastic, approximately 5 minutes.

3. Place the dough in a lightly greased bowl and cover. Allow the dough to rise in a warm place for 30 minutes. Punch down the dough and divide into portions. The dough may be wrapped and refrigerated for up to 2 days.

4. On a lightly floured surface, roll the dough into very thin rounds and top as desired. Bake at 400°F (200°C) until crisp and golden brown, approximately 8–12 minutes.

◆◆◆

RECIPE 28.15
BASIC SOURDOUGH BREAD

Yield: 2 Large Loaves   **Method:** Sponge

Active dry yeast	1 Tbsp.	15 mL
Water, heated to 70°F/20°C	12 oz.	340 mL
Sourdough Starter (Recipe 28.1)	1 cup	225 mL
Honey	1 Tbsp.	15 mL
Bread flour	1 lb. 6 oz.	660 g
Kosher salt	1-1/2 tsp.	7 mL
Distilled vinegar	1 oz.	30 mL
Baking soda	1/2 tsp.	2 mL

1. Prepare a sponge by mixing the yeast, water, Sourdough Starter and honey. Stir in 4 ounces (120 g) of flour. Beat vigorously by hand or in a mixer on second speed for 3 minutes.

Continued

Approximate values per
1 oz. (30 g) serving:

Calories	100
Total fat	0.5 g
Saturated fat	0 g
Cholesterol	0 mg
Sodium	230 mg
Total carbohydrates	21 g
Protein	3 g

Claims—low fat; no saturated fat; no cholesterol

Approximate values per
2 oz. (60 g) serving:

Calories	220
Total fat	4 g
Saturated fat	0.5 g
Cholesterol	0 mg
Sodium	290 mg
Total carbohydrates	41 g
Protein	6 g

Claims—low saturated fat; no cholesterol

2. Place the sponge in a clean bowl and cover. Set aside until doubled, approximately 1–2 hours.

3. Place the risen sponge into the bowl of a mixer fitted with a dough hook. Add the salt, vinegar and baking soda. Gradually add enough bread flour to make a stiff dough. Knead for 3 minutes on second speed. The dough should clean the bowl, forming a ball around the dough hook.

4. Allow the dough to rest for 5 minutes. Then shape into 2 round or oval loaves and place on a baking sheet that has been dusted with cornmeal.

5. Cover the dough and set aside to proof until doubled, approximately 45 minutes. Slash the top of the loaf with a razor or sharp knife.

6. Bake the bread for 10 minutes in a 450°F (230°C) oven with steam added. Reduce the oven temperature to 375°F (190°C) and continue baking until golden brown and firm, approximately 30–40 minutes.

◆◆◆

RECIPE 28.16

SAN FRANCISCO SOURDOUGH BREAD

STOUFFER STANFORD COURT, SAN FRANCISCO, CA
Executive Chef Ercolino Crugnale

Yield: 1 Loaf		**Method:** Straight Dough
Water, heated to 120°F/49°C	8 oz.	240 mL
Active dry yeast	1/2 oz.	15 g
Grape Sourdough Starter (recipe follows)	1 cup	225 mL
Bread flour	1 lb.	450 g
Kosher salt	1 Tbsp.	15 mL
Egg white, beaten	1	1

1. Sprinkle the dry yeast over 2 ounces (60 mL) of the warm water and set aside until dissolved and foamy.

2. Combine the Sourdough Starter and the remaining warm water. Add 6 ounces (180 g) of bread flour.

3. Stir until a dough forms then add the yeast mixture. Knead 5 minutes on medium speed.

4. Add the remaining flour and salt. Knead until the dough is smooth and elastic, approximately 10 minutes.

5. Place the dough in a lightly greased bowl and cover with a damp cloth. Let rise in a warm place, about 80–90°F (27–32°C), until doubled.

6. Punch down the dough and shape it into a round loaf. Place the loaf on a greased and cornmeal-dusted sheet pan.

7. Let the loaf rise in a warm place, covered with a damp cloth, until increased to 2-1/2 times its original size.

8. Brush the risen loaf with the beaten egg white and score the top of the loaf with a sharp knife.

9. Bake at 450°F (230°C), with a pan of boiling water underneath the oven rack, for 10 minutes.

10. Reduce the oven temperature to 375°F (190°C), remove the water and continue baking until the loaf is well browned, approximately 35–45 minutes.

GRAPE SOURDOUGH STARTER

Grapes, off the stem	1 lb.	450 g
Water, heated to 100°F/38°C	as needed	as needed
Bread flour	12 oz.	360 g

1. Mash the grapes thoroughly and place in a covered container. Set aside at room temperature for 48 hours. (Red grapes will give some colouring to the juice; this will be eliminated gradually with continued feeding.)
2. Strain off the fermented juice and discard the pulp. Add enough warm water to the juice to make 16 ounces (450 mL).
3. Stir in the flour, cover and leave at room temperature overnight.
4. Replenish with 16 ounces (450 mL) of warm water and 12 ounces (360 g) of flour daily if starter is kept at room temperature. If kept refrigerated, replenish twice weekly.

◆◆◆

RECIPE 28.17

CHALLAH

Challah is the traditional bread for Jewish Sabbaths and celebrations. Rich with eggs and flavoured with honey, it is braided into oval loaves and topped with poppy or sesame seeds. Challah is excellent for toast or sandwiches.

Yield: 2 Large Loaves   **Method:** Straight Dough

Honey	6 oz.	180 g
Salt	1 Tbsp.	15 mL
Bread flour	1 lb. 12 oz.	840 g
Active dry yeast	1/2 oz.	15 g
Water, warm	14 oz.	420 mL
Eggs	4	4
Unsalted butter, melted	4 oz.	120 g
Egg wash	as needed	as needed
Sesame or poppy seeds	as needed	as needed

1. Stir together the honey, salt and 8 ounces (240 g) of flour in a mixer bowl. Add the yeast, water, eggs and butter. Stir until smooth.
2. Using the dough hook, knead the dough on second speed, adding the remaining flour 2 ounces (60 g) at a time until smooth and elastic, approximately 5 minutes.
3. Place the dough in a lightly greased bowl, cover and let rise until doubled, approximately 1 to 1-1/2 hours.
4. Punch down the dough and divide into 6 equal portions. Roll each portion into a long strip, about 1 inch (2.5 cm) in diameter and 12 inches (30 cm) long. Lay 3 strips side by side and braid. Pinch the ends together and tuck them under the loaf. Place the loaf on a paper-lined sheet pan. Braid the 3 remaining pieces of dough in the same manner.
5. Brush the loaves with egg wash and sprinkle with sesame or poppy seeds. Proof until doubled, approximately 45 minutes.
6. Bake at 350°F (170°C) until the loaves are golden brown and sound hollow when thumped, approximately 40 minutes.

1. Roll the challah dough into ropes.

2. Braid the challah dough.

Approximate values per 2 oz. (60 g) serving:

Calories	156
Total fat	4 g
Saturated fat	2 g
Cholesterol	44 mg
Sodium	145 mg
Total carbohydrates	25 mg
Protein	6 g

◆◆◆

RECIPE 28.18

BRIOCHE

Brioche is a rich, tender bread made with an abundance of eggs and butter. The high ratio of fat makes this dough difficult to work with, but the flavour is well worth the extra effort. Brioche is traditionally made in fluted pans and has a cap or topknot of dough; this shape is known as brioche à tête. The dough may also be baked in a loaf pan, making it perfect for toast or canapés.

Yield: 3 Large Loaves or
60 3-in. (7.5-cm) Rolls

Method: Straight Dough

Bread flour	4 lb. 7 oz.	2.13 kg
Eggs	24	24
Salt	1-3/4 oz.	50 g
Sugar	7 oz.	210 g
Active dry yeast	1-3/4 oz.	50 g
Water, heated to 70°F/20°C	7 oz.	210 mL
Unsalted butter, room temperature	3 lb.	1.35 kg

1. Place the flour, eggs, salt and sugar into the bowl of a large mixer fitted with the dough hook. Stir the ingredients together.
2. Combine the yeast and water and add to the other ingredients.
3. Knead for 20 minutes on second speed. The dough will be smooth, shiny and moist. It should not form a ball.
4. Slowly add the butter to the dough. Knead only until all the butter is incorporated. Remove the dough from the mixer and place it into a bowl dusted with flour. Cover and let rise at room temperature until doubled.
5. Punch down the dough, cover well and refrigerate overnight.
6. Shape the chilled dough as desired. Place the shaped dough in well-greased pans and proof at room temperature until doubled. Do not proof brioche in a very warm place; the butter may melt out of the dough before proofing is complete.
7. Bake at 375°F (190°C) until the brioche are a dark golden brown and sound hollow. Baking time will vary depending on the temperature of the dough and the size of the rolls or loaves being baked.

VARIATION: *Raisin brioche*—Gently warm 3 ounces (90 mL) rum with 6 ounces (180 g) raisins. Set aside until the raisins are plumped. Drain off the remaining rum into the mixture and add the raisins to the dough after the butter is incorporated.

*Approximate values per
4 oz. (120 g) serving:*

Calories	475
Total fat	30 g
Saturated fat	17 g
Cholesterol	192 mg
Sodium	138 mg
Total carbohydrates	43 g
Protein	9 g
Vitamin A	30%
Iron	16%

1. Combine the ingredients for brioche.

2. Add the yeast-and-water mixture to the dough.

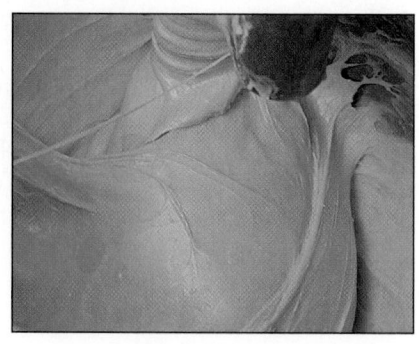

3. Brioche dough after 20 minutes of kneading.

4. Add the butter to the brioche dough.

5. The finished brioche dough ready for fermentation.

6. Shape the brioche à tête.

7. Pan the rolls.

8. A finished loaf of brioche baked in a pullman pan.

◆◆◆

RECIPE 28.19

PECAN STICKY BUNS

Yield: 12–15 Buns   **Method:** Straight Dough

Active dry yeast	1 oz.	30 g
Sugar	2 oz.	60 g
Salt	1/2 tsp.	2 mL
Milk	1 Tbsp.	15 mL
Buttermilk	5-1/2 oz.	165 mL
Vanilla	1 tsp.	5 mL
Lemon zest, grated	1 Tbsp.	15 mL
Lemon juice	1 tsp.	5 mL
Egg yolks	2	2
Bread flour	14 oz.	420 g
Unsalted butter, very soft	8 oz.	240 g
Topping:		
Honey	6 oz.	180 g
Brown sugar	6 oz.	180 g
Pecans, chopped	3 oz.	90 g
Filling:		
Cinnamon	1 tsp.	5 mL
Pecans, chopped	3 oz.	90 g
Brown sugar	4 oz.	120 g
Unsalted butter, melted	3 oz.	90 g

1. Brush melted butter over the sticky bun dough.

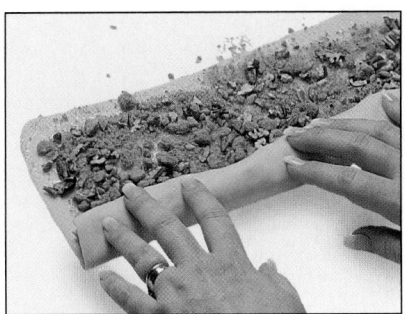

2. Roll up the filling in the sticky bun dough.

Continued

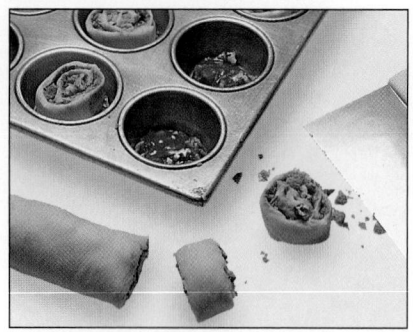

3. Cut and pan the sticky buns.

Approximate values per roll:	
Calories	480
Total fat	26 g
Saturated fat	11 g
Cholesterol	75 mg
Sodium	100 mg
Total carbohydrates	55 g
Protein	5 g
Vitamin A	15%
Iron	15%

1. Stir the yeast, sugar, and milk together in a small bowl. Set aside.

2. Stir the buttermilk, vanilla, lemon zest and lemon juice together and add to the yeast mixture.

3. Add the eggs, flour, salt and softened butter to the liquid mixture. Turn out onto a lightly floured board and knead until the butter is evenly distributed and the dough is smooth. Cover and let rise until doubled.

4. Prepare the topping and filling mixtures while the dough is rising. To make the topping, cream the honey and sugar together. Stir in the nuts. This mixture will be very stiff. To make the filling, stir the cinnamon, pecans and sugar together.

5. Lightly grease muffin cups, then distribute the topping mixture evenly, about 1 tablespoon (15 mL) per muffin cup. Set the pans aside at room temperature until the dough is ready.

6. Punch down the dough and let it rest 10 minutes. Roll out the dough into a rectangle about 1/2 inch (1.25 cm) thick. Brush with the melted butter and cover evenly with the filling mixture.

7. Starting with either long edge, roll up the dough. Cut into slices about 3/4- to 1-inch (1.8–2.5 cm) thick. Place a slice in each muffin cup over the topping.

8. Let the buns proof until doubled, approximately 20 minutes. Bake at 350°F (170°C) until very brown, approximately 25 minutes. Immediately invert the muffin pans onto paper-lined sheet pans to let the buns and their topping slide out.

◆◆◆

RECIPE 28.20

DANISH PASTRIES

Danish pastry was actually created by a French baker more than 350 years ago. He forgot to knead butter into his bread dough and attempted to cover the mistake by folding in softened butter. This rich, flaky pastry is now popular worldwide for breakfasts, desserts and snacks. The dough may be shaped in a variety of ways and is usually filled with jam, fruit, cream or marzipan.

DOUGH FOR DANISH PASTRIES

Yield: 36 Pastries   **Method:** Rolled-In

Active dry yeast	1/2 oz.	15 g
All-purpose flour	1 lb. 4 oz.	600 g
Sugar	4 oz.	120 g
Water, cold	4 oz.	120 mL
Milk, cold	4 oz.	120 mL
Eggs, room temperature	2	2
Salt	1 tsp.	5 mL
Vanilla extract	1 tsp.	5 mL
Cinnamon, ground	1/2 tsp.	2 mL
Unsalted butter, melted	1-1/2 oz.	45 g
Unsalted butter, cold	1 lb.	450 g
Filling (recipes follow)	as needed	as needed
Egg wash	as needed	as needed

1. In a large bowl, stir together the yeast and 12 ounces (360 g) of flour. Add the sugar, water, milk, eggs, salt, vanilla, cinnamon and melted butter. Stir until well combined.

2. Add the remaining flour gradually, kneading the dough by hand or with a mixer fitted with a dough hook. Knead until the dough is smooth and only slightly tacky to the touch, approximately 2–3 minutes.

3. Place the dough in a bowl that has been lightly dusted with flour. Cover and refrigerate for 1 to 1-1/2 hours.

4. Prepare the remaining butter while the dough is chilling. Start by sprinkling flour over the work surface and placing the cold butter on the flour. Then pound the butter with a rolling pin until the butter softens. Using a pastry scraper or the heel of your hand, knead the butter and flour until the mixture is spreadable. The butter should still be cold. If it begins to melt, refrigerate it until firm. Set the butter aside until the dough is ready.

5. On a lightly floured surface, roll out the dough into a large rectangle about 1/2 inch (1.25 cm) thick. Brush away any excess flour.

6. Spread the butter evenly over two-thirds of the dough. Fold the unbuttered third over the centre, then fold the buttered third over the top. Press the edges together to seal in the butter.

7. Roll the dough into a rectangle about 12 inches × 18 inches (30 cm × 45 cm). Fold the dough in thirds as before. This rolling and folding (called a turn) must be done a total of 3 times. Chill the dough between turns as necessary. After the final turn, wrap the dough well and refrigerate for at least 4 hours or overnight.

8. Shape and fill the danish dough as desired. Place the shaped pastries on a paper-lined baking sheet and allow to proof for approximately 15–20 minutes.

9. Brush the pastries with egg wash and sprinkle lightly with sugar if desired. Bake at 400°F (200°C) for 5 minutes. Decrease the oven temperature to 350°F (170°C) and bake until light brown, approximately 12–15 minutes.

Approximate values per danish:

Calories	181
Total fat	12 g
Saturated fat	7 g
Cholesterol	48 mg
Sodium	69 mg
Total carbohydrates	16 g
Protein	3 g

1. Knead the butter with the flour.

2. Spread the butter over the rolled-out dough.

3. Fold the dough in thirds to cover the butter.

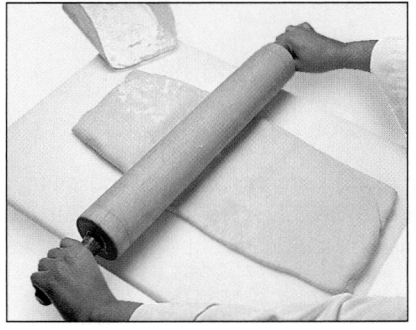

4. Roll out the dough.

5. Fold the dough in thirds to complete a turn.

6. Cut rectangles of danish dough.

Continued

7. Pipe the filling onto the danish dough.

8. Shape snails from danish dough.

FILLINGS FOR DANISH PASTRIES

CREAM CHEESE

Cream cheese	1 lb.	450 g
Sugar	8 oz.	225 g
Salt	1/4 tsp.	1 mL
Vanilla	1 tsp.	5 mL
Flour	2 Tbsp.	30 mL
Egg yolk	1	1
Lemon extract	1 tsp.	5 mL
Lemon zest	2 tsp.	10 mL

Beat the cream cheese until light and fluffy. Stir in the remaining ingredients.

ALMOND CREAM

Almond paste	10 oz.	300 g
Unsalted butter, soft	4 oz.	120 g
Salt	1/4 tsp.	1 mL
Vanilla	1 tsp.	5 mL
Egg whites	2	2

Blend the almond paste and butter until smooth. Add the salt and vanilla, then the egg whites. Blend well.

APRICOT

Dried apricots	8 oz.	225 g
Orange juice	16 oz.	500 mL
Sugar	6 oz.	180 g
Salt	1/4 tsp.	1 mL
Unsalted butter	2 oz.	60 g

1. Place the apricots and orange juice in a small saucepan. Cover and simmer until the apricots are very tender, approximately 25 minutes. Stir in the sugar and salt. When the sugar is dissolved, add the butter and remove from the heat.

2. Purée the mixture in a blender until smooth. Cool completely before using.

Approximate values per 1 oz. (30 g) serving:

Calories	103
Total fat	6 g
Saturated fat	4 g
Cholesterol	28 mg
Sodium	71 mg
Total carbohydrates	10 g
Protein	2 g

Approximate values per 1 oz. (30 g) serving:

Calories	132
Total fat	11 g
Saturated fat	4 g
Cholesterol	15 mg
Sodium	40 mg
Total carbohydrates	8 g
Protein	3 g

Approximate values per 1 oz. (30 g) serving:

Calories	55
Total fat	2 g
Saturated fat	1 g
Cholesterol	4 mg
Sodium	110 mg
Total carbohydrates	6 g
Protein	.3 g

WEBLINKS

The Bread Bakers Guild of America
    www.bbga.org/
Fleischmann's Yeast (Canada): Preparing Yeast and Dough
    www.breadworld.com/canada/tips/baking/preparing.html
Fleischmann's Yeast (Canada): Tips: Working with the Dough
    www.breadworld.com/canada/tips/baking/working.html
Breadbaking Secrets
    members.aol.com/BreadLady1/BreadTips.html
Bread Chemistry
    ericir.syr.edu/Projects/Newton/12/Lessons/bread.html

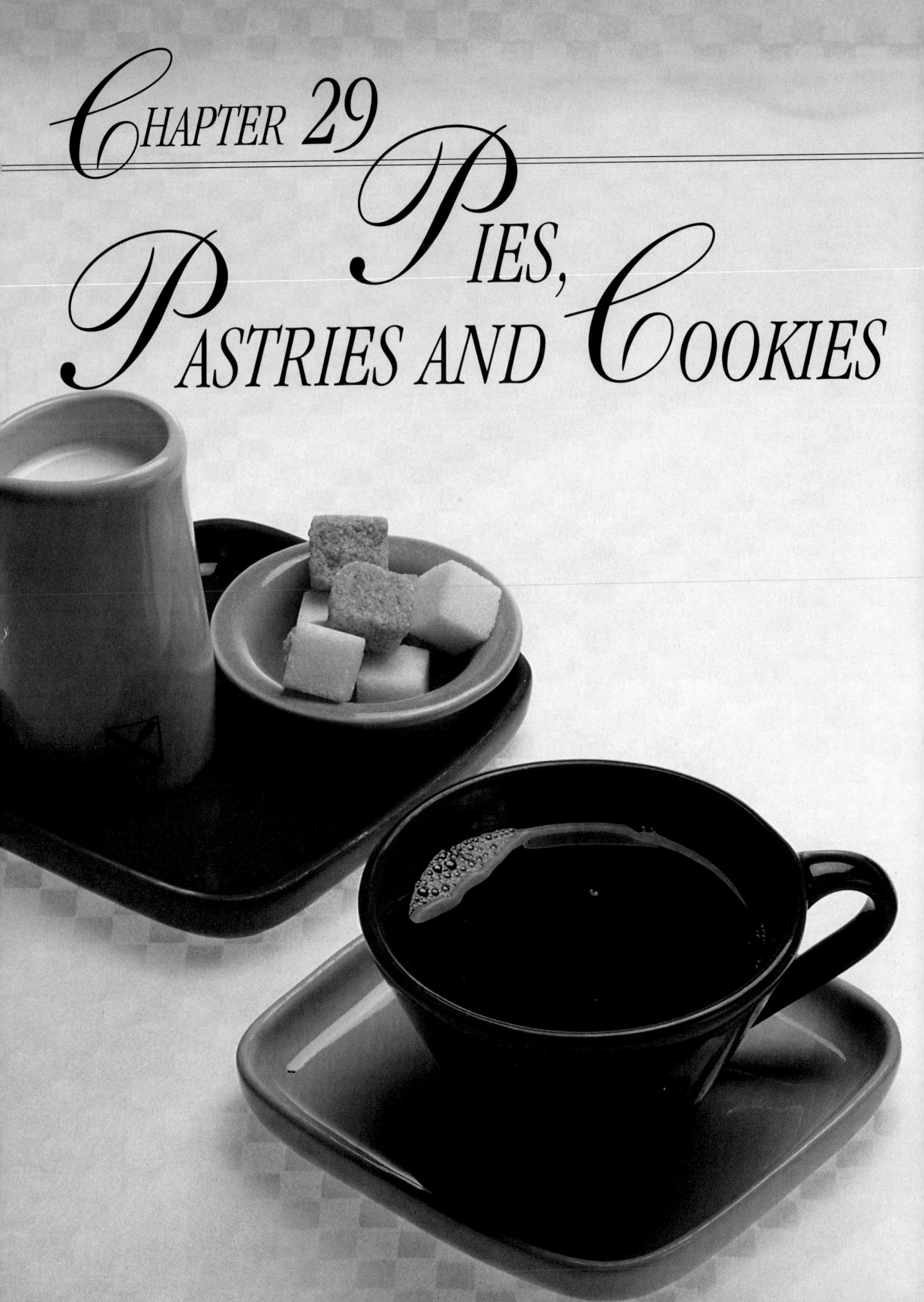

CHAPTER 29
PIES, PASTRIES AND COOKIES

LEARNING OUTCOMES

After studying this chapter you will be able to:

♦ prepare a variety of pie crusts and fillings, including flaky and mealy doughs and sweet dough
♦ prepare a variety of classic pastries, including pie crust and tart shells, tartlet shells, top crust, lattice crust, unfilled crusts, cooked fruit fillings, cooked juice fillings, baked fruit fillings, puff pastry, shape vol-au-vents and bouchées, shape feuilletées, make choux paste
♦ prepare a variety of meringues
♦ prepare a variety of cookies, including mixing cookie doughs
♦ prepare a variety of dessert and pastry items, incorporating components from other chapters

*M*ention pastry to diners and most conjure up images of buttery dough baked to crisp flaky perfection and filled or layered with rich cream, ripe fruit or smooth custard. Mention pastry to novice cooks and most conjure up images of sophisticated, complex and intimidating work. Although the diners are correct, the novice cooks are not. Pastry making is the art of creating containers for a variety of fillings. Taken one step at a time, most pastries are nothing more than selected building blocks or components assembled in a variety of ways to create traditional or unique desserts.

Perhaps the most important (and versatile) building block is the dough. Pastries can be made with flaky dough, mealy dough, sweet dough, puff pastry, éclair dough or meringue. See Table 29.1. Because pies, tarts and cookies are constructed from some of these same doughs (principally pie dough and sweet dough), they, as well as pie fillings, are discussed in the section on pies and tarts; puff pastry, choux paste and baked meringue are discussed in the section on classic pastries. The cream, custard and mousse fillings used in some of the recipes at the end of this chapter are discussed in Chapter 31, Custards, Creams, Frozen Desserts and Dessert Sauces. Cakes and frostings are covered in Chapter 30.

PIES AND TARTS

A **pie** is composed of a sweet or savoury filling in a baked crust. It can be open-faced (without a top crust) or, more typically, topped with a full or lattice crust. A pie is generally made in a round, slope-sided pan and cut into wedges for service. A **tart** is similar to a pie except it is made in a shallow, straight-sided pan, often with fluted edges. A tart can be almost any shape; round, square, rectangular and petal shapes are the most common. It is usually open-faced and derives much of its beauty from an attractive arrangement of glazed fruit.

TABLE 29.1   CLASSIFICATION OF PASTRY DOUGHS

Dough	French Name	Characteristics After Baking	Use
Flaky dough	Pâte brisée	Very flaky; not sweet	Prebaked pie shells; pie top crusts
Mealy dough	Pâte brisée	Moderately flaky; not sweet	Custard, cream or fruit pie crusts; quiche crusts
Sweet dough	Pâte sucrée	Very rich; crisp; not flaky	Tart and tartlet shells
Choux paste	Pâte à choux	Hollow with crisp exterior	Cream puffs; éclairs; savoury products
Puff pastry	Pâte feuilletée	Rich but not sweet; hundreds of light, flaky layers	Tart and pastry cases; cookies; layered pastries; savoury products
Meringue	Meringue	Sweet; light; crisp or soft depending on preparation	Topping or icing; baked as a shell or component for layered desserts; cookies

Crusts

Pie crusts and tart shells can be made from several types of doughs or crumbs. **Flaky dough, mealy dough** and **crumbs** are best for pie crusts; **sweet dough** is usually used for tart shells. A pie crust or tart shell can be shaped and completely baked before filling (known as **baked blind**) or filled and baked simultaneously with the filling.

Flaky and Mealy Doughs

Flaky and mealy pie doughs are quick, easy and versatile. Flaky dough, sometimes known as pâte brisée, takes its name from its final baked texture. It is best for pie top crusts and lattice coverings and may be used for prebaked shells that will be filled with a cooled filling shortly before service. Mealy dough takes its name from its raw texture. It is used whenever a soggy crust would be a problem (for example, as the bottom crust of a custard or fruit pie) because it resists soaking better than flaky dough. Both flaky and mealy doughs are too delicate for tarts that will be removed from the pan for service. Sweet dough, described below, is better for these types of tarts.

Flaky and mealy doughs contain little or no sugar and can be prepared from the same formula with only a slight variation in mixing method. For both types of dough a cold fat, such as butter or shortening, is cut into the flour. The amount of flakiness in the baked crust depends on the size of the fat particles in the dough. The larger the pieces of fat, the flakier the crust will be. This is because the flakes are actually the sides of fat pockets created during baking by the melting fat and steam. When preparing flaky dough, the fat is left in larger pieces, about the size of peas or peanuts. When preparing mealy dough, the fat is blended in more thoroughly, until the mixture resembles coarse cornmeal. Because the resulting fat pockets are smaller, the crust is less flaky.

The type of fat used affects both the dough's flavour and flakiness. Butter contributes a delicious flavour, but does not produce as flaky a crust as other fats. Butter is also more difficult to work with than other fats because of its lower melting point and its tendency to become brittle when chilled. All-purpose vegetable shortening produces a flaky crust but contributes nothing to its flavour. The flakiest pastry is made with lard, but because some people cannot eat pork products lard is not often used. Some chefs prefer to use a combination of butter with either shortening or lard. Oil is not an appropriate substitute as it disperses too thoroughly through the dough; when baked, the crust is stiff and crisp.

After the fat is cut into the flour, water or milk is added to form a soft dough. Less water is needed for mealy dough because more flour is already in contact with the fat, reducing its ability to absorb liquid. Cold water is normally used for both flaky and mealy doughs. The water should be well chilled to prevent softening the fat or shortening. Milk may be used to increase richness and nutritional value. It will produce a darker, less crisp crust, however. If dry milk powder is used, it should be mixed with the flour.

Hand mixing is best for small to moderate quantities of dough. You retain better control over the procedure when you can feel the fat being incorporated. It is very difficult to make flaky dough with an electric mixer or food processor, as they tend to cut the fat in too thoroughly. Overmixing makes the dough elastic and difficult to use. When an electric mixer must be used for large quantities, use the paddle attachment at the lowest speed and be sure the fat is well chilled, even frozen.

Bake blind—*to bake a pie shell before it is filled. The dough is often lined with parchment paper and filled with dried beans or pie weights to prevent the crust from rising.*

◆◆◆
OF TARTS AND TORTES

The names given to desserts can be rather confusing. One country or region calls an item a *torte* while another region calls the same item a *gâteau*. The following definitions are based on classic terms. You will, no doubt, encounter variations depending on your location and the training of those with whom you work.

Cake—In North American and British usages, *cake* refers to a broad range of pastries, including layer cakes, coffee cakes and gâteaux. *Cake* may refer to almost everything that is baked, tender, sweet and sometimes frosted. But to the French, *le cake* is a loaf-shaped fruitcake, similar to a North American pound cake with the addition of fruit, nuts and rum.

Gâteau—(pl. *gâteaux*) To the French, *gâteau* refers to various pastry items made with puff pastry, choux paste, short dough or sweet dough. In North America, *gâteau* often refers to any cake-type dessert.

Pastry—*Pastry* may refer to a group of doughs made primarily with flour, water and fat. *Pastry* can also refer to foods made with these doughs or to a large variety of fancy baked goods.

Tart—A tart is a pastry shell filled with sweet or savoury ingredients. Tarts have straight, shallow sides and are usually prepared open-face. In France and Britain the term **flan** is sometimes used to refer to the same items. A **tartlet** is a small, individual-sized tart.

Torte—In Central and Eastern European countries a *torte* (pl. *torten*) is a rich cake in which all or part of the flour is replaced with finely chopped nuts or bread crumbs. Other cultures refer to any round sweet cake as a torte.

Basic Procedure for Preparing Flaky and Mealy Doughs

1. Sift flour, salt and sugar (if used) together in a large bowl.
2. Cut the fat into the flour.
3. Gradually add a cold liquid, mixing gently until the dough holds together. Do not overmix.
4. Cover the dough with plastic wrap and chill thoroughly before using.

◆◆◆

RECIPE 29.1

Basic Pie Dough

Yield: 5 lb. (2.7 kg)

Pastry flour	3 lb.	1.5 kg
Milk powder	3 oz.	85 g
Shortening	26 oz.	800 g
Water, cold	14 oz.	425 mL
Salt	1-1/2 oz.	40 g

Approximate values per 3-1/2 oz. (105 g) pastry:

Calories	455
Total fat	30 g
Saturated fat	8 g
Cholesterol	3 mg
Sodium	560 mg
Total carbohydrates	41 g
Protein	5 g

1. Blend the flour and milk powder together.
2. Add the shortening and blend it into the flour until the fat is in pea-size or crumb-size pieces (see Note).
3. Dissolve the salt in the water.
4. Add the water all at once to the flour and fat mixture. Blend on No. 1 speed only until the mix comes together.

Note: For flaky pie crust, the fat should be pea size. For mealy pie crust, the fat should be crumb size.

1. Cut the fat into the flour coarsely for flaky dough.

2. Cut the fat into the flour finely for mealy dough.

3. The finished dough.

Sweet Dough

Sweet dough or **pâte sucrée** is a rich, nonflaky dough used for sweet tart shells. It is sturdier than flaky or mealy dough because it contains egg yolks and the fat is thoroughly blended in. It is also more cookielike than classic pie dough and has the rich flavour of butter. It creates a crisp but tender crust and is excellent for tartlets as well as for straight-sided tarts that will be removed from their pans before service. Sweet dough crusts may be prebaked then filled, or filled and baked simultaneously with the filling. The raw dough may be kept refrigerated for up to two weeks or frozen for up to three months.

BASIC PROCEDURE FOR PREPARING SWEET DOUGH

1. Cream softened butter. Add sugar and beat until the mixture is light and fluffy.
2. Slowly add eggs, blending well.
3. Slowly add flour, mixing only until incorporated. Overmixing toughens the dough.
4. Cover the dough with plastic wrap and chill thoroughly before using.

◆◆◆

RECIPE 29.2
SWEET DOUGH

Yield: 7 lb. (3.65 kg)

Unsalted butter, softened	1 lb. 8 oz.	750 g
Powdered sugar	1 lb. 5 oz.	650 g
Egg yolks	1 lb.	500 g
Whole eggs	2	2
All-purpose flour	3 lb. 8 oz.	1.75 kg

1. Cream the butter and powdered sugar in a large mixer bowl using the paddle attachment.
2. Combine the egg yolks and whole eggs. Slowly add the eggs to the creamed butter. Mix until smooth and free of lumps, scraping down the sides of the bowl as needed.
3. With the mixer on low speed, slowly add the flour to the butter-and-egg mixture. Mix only until incorporated; do not overmix. The dough should be firm, smooth and not sticky.
4. Dust a half-sheet pan with flour. Pack the dough into the pan evenly. Wrap well in plastic wrap and chill until firm.
5. Work with a small portion of the chilled dough when shaping tart shells or other products.

Approximate values per 1 oz. (30 g) serving:

Calories	120
Total fat	5 g
Saturated fat	3 g
Cholesterol	15 mg
Sodium	0 mg
Total carbohydrates	16 g
Protein	2 g
Vitamin A	4%

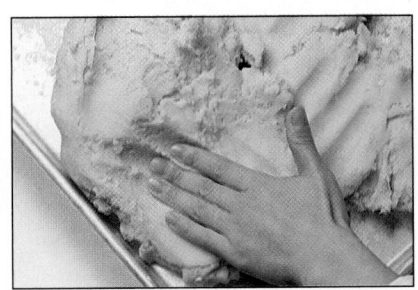

1. The sweet dough being mixed.   *2.* The finished sweet dough.

Shaping Crusts

Crusts are shaped by rolling out the dough to fit into a pie pan or tart shell (mould) or to sit on top of fillings. Mealy, flaky and sweet doughs are all easier to roll out and work with if well chilled, as chilling keeps the fat firm and prevents stickiness. When rolling and shaping the dough, work on a clean, flat surface (wood or marble is best). Lightly dust the work surface, rolling pin and dough with bread flour before starting to roll the dough. Also, work only with a manageable amount at a time: usually enough for one pie crust or a standard-sized tart or enough for 10–12 tartlet shells.

Roll out the dough from the centre, working towards the edges. Periodically, lift the dough gently and rotate it. This keeps the dough from sticking and helps produce an even thickness. If the dough sticks to the rolling pin or work surface, sprinkle on a bit more flour. Too much flour, however, makes the crust dry and crumbly and causes grey streaks.

BASIC PROCEDURE FOR ROLLING AND SHAPING DOUGH FOR A PIE CRUST OR TART SHELL

1. A typical pie crust or tart shell should be rolled to a thickness of approximately 1/8 inch (3 mm); it should also be at least 2 inches (5 cm) larger in diameter than the baking pan.

2. Carefully roll the dough up onto a rolling pin. Position the pin over the pie pan or tart shell and unroll the dough, easing it into the pan or shell. Trim the edges as necessary and flute. Bake or fill as desired.

BASIC PROCEDURE FOR ROLLING AND SHAPING DOUGH FOR TARTLET SHELLS

1. A typical crust for tartlets should be approximately 1/8 inch (3 mm) thick.
2. Roll the dough out as described above. Then roll the dough up onto the rolling pin.

3. Lay out a single layer of tartlet moulds. Unroll the dough over the moulds, pressing the dough gently into each mould.

4. Roll the rolling pin over the top of the tartlet shells. The edge of the moulds will cut the dough. Be sure the dough is pressed against the sides of each mould. Bake or fill as desired.

BASIC PROCEDURE FOR ROLLING AND SHAPING DOUGH FOR A TOP CRUST

1. Roll the dough out as before, making a circle large enough to hang over the pan's edge. The dough may be lifted into place by rolling it onto the rolling pin, as done with the bottom crust. Slits or designs can be cut in the top crust to allow steam to escape.

2. Seal the top crust to the bottom crust with egg wash or water. Crimp as desired.

BASIC PROCEDURE FOR ROLLING AND SHAPING DOUGH FOR A LATTICE CRUST

1. Roll the dough out as described before. Using a ruler as a guide, cut even strips of the desired width, typically 1/2 inch (1.25 cm). A special cutter is available to stamp out the lattice crust on the table top. The crust is then laid over the pie.

2. Using an over-under-over pattern, weave the strips together on top of the filling. Be sure the strips are evenly spaced for an attractive result. Crimp the lattice strips to the bottom crust to seal.

Streusel topping is also used for some pies, particularly fruit pies. A standard recipe is given in Chapter 27, Quick Breads.

Baking Crusts

Pie crusts can be filled and then baked, or baked and then filled. Unfilled baked crusts can be stored at room temperature for two to three days or wrapped in plastic wrap and frozen for as long as three months.

Basic Procedure for Baking Unfilled (Baked Blind) Pie Crusts

1. Roll the dough out to the desired thickness and line the pie pan or tart shell. A crimped edge or border can be added.
2. **Dock** the dough with a fork or docking wheel.
3. Cover the dough with baking parchment or greased aluminum foil. Press the paper or foil against the edge or walls of the shell. Allow a portion of the paper or foil to extend above the pan.
4. Fill the pan with baking weights, dry rice or beans. These will prevent the crust from rising.
5. Bake the weighted crust at 350°F (180°C) for 10–15 minutes.
6. Remove the weights and paper and return the crust to the oven. Bake until golden brown and fully cooked, approximately 10–15 minutes.
7. Allow to cool, then fill as desired or store.

Docking—*Pricking small holes in an unbaked dough or crust to allow steam and trapped air to escape and to prevent the dough from rising when baked.*

1. Dock the dough.

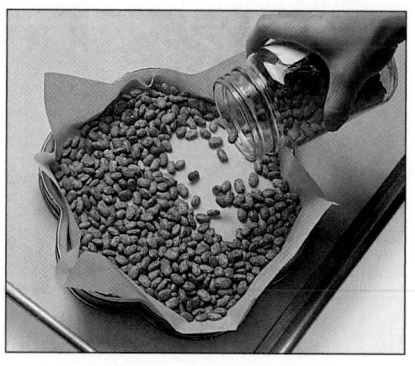

2. Use weights to prevent the crust from rising.

3. Remove weights and paper before returning the crust to the oven for browning.

Crumb Crusts

A quick and tasty bottom crust can be made from finely ground crumbs moistened with melted butter. Crumb crusts can be used for unbaked pies such as those with cream or chiffon fillings, or they can be baked with their fillings, as with cheesecakes.

Chocolate cookies, graham crackers, gingersnaps, vanilla wafers and macaroons are popular choices for crumb crusts. Some breakfast cereals such as corn flakes or bran flakes are also used. Ground nuts and spices can be added for flavour. Whatever cookies or other ingredients are used, be sure they are ground to a fine, even crumb. If packaged crumbs are unavailable, crumbs can be prepared in a food processor or blender or with a rolling pin.

The typical ratio for a crumb crust is one part melted butter, two parts sugar and four parts crumbs. For example, 8 ounces (250 g) graham crackers mixed with 4 ounces (120 g) sugar and 2 ounces (60 mL) melted butter produce enough crust to line one 9-to-10-inch (22- to 25-cm) pan. The amount of sugar may need to be adjusted depending on the type of crumbs used, however; for example, chocolate sandwich cookies need less sugar than graham crackers. If the mixture is too dry to stick together, gradually add more melted butter. Press the mixture into the bottom of the pan and chill or bake it before filling.

Press the crumb mixture into the pan.

Fillings

Fillings make pies and tarts distinctive and flavourful. Four types of fillings are discussed here: **cream**, **fruit**, **custard** and **chiffon**. There is no one correct presentation or filling-and-crust combination. The apples in an apple pie, for example, may be sliced, seasoned and topped with streusel; caramelized, puréed and blended with cream; chopped and covered with a flaky dough lattice; or poached, arranged over pastry cream and brushed with a clear glaze. Only an understanding of the fundamental techniques for making fillings—and some imagination—ensures success.

Cream Fillings

A cream filling is really nothing more than a flavoured pastry cream. Pastry cream is a type of starch-thickened egg custard discussed in Chapter 31, Custards, Creams, Frozen Desserts and Dessert Sauces. When used as a pie filling, pastry cream should be thickened with cornstarch so that it is firm enough to hold its shape when sliced. Popular flavours are chocolate, banana, coconut and lemon.

A cream filling is fully cooked on the stove top, so a prebaked or crumb crust is needed. The crust can be filled while the filling is still warm, or the filling can be chilled and later placed in the crust. A cream pie is often topped with meringue, which is then browned quickly in an oven or under a broiler.

◆◆◆

RECIPE 29.3

BASIC CREAM PIE

Yield: 2 9-inch (22-cm) Pies

Granulated sugar	1 lb.	500 g
Milk	64 oz.	2 L
Egg yolks	8	8
Eggs	4	4
Cornstarch	5 oz.	150 g
Unsalted butter	4 oz.	120 g
Vanilla extract	1 oz.	30 g

1. In a heavy saucepan, dissolve 8 ounces (250 g) of sugar in the milk. Bring just to a boil.

2. Meanwhile, whisk the egg yolks and whole eggs together in a large bowl.

3. Sift the cornstarch and remaining sugar (8 ounces/250 g) onto the eggs. Whisk until smooth.

4. **Temper** the egg mixture with approximately one-half of the hot milk. Stir the warmed egg mixture back into the remaining milk and return it to a boil, stirring constantly.

5. Stirring constantly and vigorously, allow the cream to boil until thick, approximately 30 seconds. Remove from the heat and stir in the butter and vanilla. Stir until the butter is melted and incorporated.

6. Pour the cream into prebaked pie crusts.

Temper—*to heat gently and gradually; refers to the process of slowly adding a hot liquid to eggs to raise their temperature without causing them to curdle.*

Continued

7. The pies may be topped with meringue while the filling is still warm. The meringue is then lightly browned in a 425°F (210°C) oven. Chill the pies for service or, when chilled, top with whipped cream.

VARIATIONS: *Chocolate*—Melt 12 ounces (360 g) bittersweet chocolate. Fold the melted chocolate into the hot cream after adding the butter and vanilla.

Banana—Layer 12 ounces (360 g) sliced bananas (about 3 medium bananas) into the baked shell. The juice of one lemon may be added to the bananas to help prevent browning. Fill shell with pastry cream.

Coconut I—Substitute 12 ounces (360 mL) cream of coconut for 12 ounces (360 mL) of milk and 4 ounces (120 g) of sugar. Top the pie with meringue and shredded coconut.

Coconut II—Stir 8 ounces (250 g) toasted coconut into the warm cream.

1. Fill the pie shell with chocolate pastry cream.

2. Top with meringue.

Fruit Fillings

A fruit filling is a mixture of fruit, fruit juice, spices and sugar thickened with starch. Apple, cherry, blueberry and peach are traditional favourites. The fruit can be fresh, frozen or canned. (See Chapter 25, Fruits, for comments on selecting the best fruits for fillings.) The starch can be cornstarch, tapioca or a packaged commercial instant or pregelatinized starch. The ingredients for a fruit filling are most often combined using one of three methods: **cooked fruit**, **cooked juice** or **baked**.

Cooked Fruit Fillings

The cooked fruit filling method is often used when the fruits need to be softened by cooking (for example, apples or rhubarb) or are naturally rather dry. (Poaching fruit, discussed in Chapter 25, Fruits, is a variation of this procedure.) A cooked fruit filling should be combined with a prebaked or crumb crust.

BASIC PROCEDURE FOR PREPARING COOKED FRUIT FILLINGS

1. Combine the fruit, sugar and some juice or liquid in a heavy, nonreactive saucepan and bring to a boil.

2. Dissolve the starch (usually cornstarch) in cold liquid, then add to the boiling fruit.
3. Stirring constantly, cook the fruit-and-starch mixture until the starch is clear and the mixture is thickened.
4. Add any other flavourings and any acidic ingredients such as lemon juice. Stir to blend.
5. Remove from the heat and cool before filling a prebaked pie or crumb crust.

✦✦✦

RECIPE 29.4
APPLE-CRANBERRY PIE

Yield: 1 9-inch (22-cm) Pie   **Method:** Cooked Fruit Filling

Fresh tart apples such as Granny Smiths, peeled, cored and cut in 1-inch (2.5-cm) cubes	1 lb.	500 g
Brown sugar	4 oz.	120 g
Granulated sugar	4 oz.	120 g
Orange zest	1 Tbsp.	15 mL
Ground cinnamon	1 tsp.	5 mL
Salt	1/4 tsp.	1 mL
Cornstarch	2 tsp.	10 mL
Orange juice	3 oz.	90 mL
Fresh cranberries, rinsed	1 pt.	500 mL
Partially baked mealy dough pie shell	1	1
Streusel Topping (Recipe 27.6)	4 oz.	120 g

1. Combine the apples, brown sugar, granulated sugar, orange zest, cinnamon and salt in a large, nonreactive saucepan.
2. Dissolve the cornstarch in the orange juice and add it to the apples.
3. Cover and simmer until the apples begin to soften, stirring occasionally. Add the cranberries, cover and continue simmering until the cranberries begin to soften, approximately 2 minutes. Cool the mixture to room temperature.
4. Place the apple-cranberry mixture in the pie shell and cover with the prepared streusel topping. Bake at 400°F (200°C) until the filling is bubbling hot and the topping is lightly browned, approximately 20 minutes.

VARIATION: *Apple-rhubarb pie*—Substitute cleaned rhubarb, cut into 1-inch (2.5-cm) chunks, for the cranberries. Add 1/8 teaspoon (0.5 mL) nutmeg.

Approximate values per serving:

Calories	290
Total fat	8 g
Saturated fat	2 g
Cholesterol	0 mg
Sodium	200 mg
Total carbohydrates	53 g
Protein	2 g

Claims—no cholesterol; good source of fibre

Cooked Juice Fillings

The cooked juice filling method is used for juicy fruits such as berries, especially when they are canned or frozen. This method is also recommended for delicate fruits that cannot withstand cooking such as strawberries, pineapple or blueberries. Because only the juice is cooked, the fruit retains its shape, colour and flavour better. A cooked juice filling should be combined with a prebaked or crumb crust.

Basic Procedure for Preparing Cooked Juice Fillings

1. Drain the juice from the fruit. Measure the juice and add water if necessary to create the desired volume.
2. Combine the liquid with sugar in a nonreactive saucepan and bring to a boil.
3. Dissolve the starch in cold water, then add it to the boiling liquid. Cook until the starch is clear and the juice is thickened.
4. Add any other flavouring ingredients.
5. Pour the thickened juice over the fruit and stir gently.
6. Cool the filling before placing it in a baked pie shell.

◆◆◆

RECIPE 29.5

Blueberry Pie Filling

Yield: 8 lb. (3.6 kg) Filling **Method:** Cooked Juice Filling

Canned blueberries, unsweetened	1 No. 10 can	1 No. 10 can
Sugar	1 lb. 12 oz.	840 g
Cornstarch	4-1/2 oz.	135 g
Water	8 oz.	225 mL
Cinnamon	1/2 tsp.	2 mL
Lemon juice	2 Tbsp.	30 mL
Lemon zest, grated fine	1 Tbsp.	15 mL

Approximate values per 1 oz. (30 g) serving:

Calories	40
Total fat	0 g
Saturated fat	0 g
Cholesterol	0 mg
Sodium	0 mg
Total carbohydrates	10 g
Protein	0 g

Claims—fat free; no cholesterol; no sodium; low calorie

1. Drain the juice from the canned blueberries, reserving both the fruit and the juice.
2. Measure the juice and, if necessary, add enough water to provide 1 quart (1 L) of liquid. Bring to a boil, add the sugar and stir until dissolved.
3. Dissolve the cornstarch in 8 ounces (225 mL) of water.
4. Add the cornstarch to the boiling juice and return to a boil. Cook until the mixture thickens and clears. Remove from the heat.
5. Add the cinnamon, lemon juice, lemon zest and reserved blueberries. Stir gently to coat the fruit with the glaze.
6. Allow the filling to cool, then use it to fill prebaked pie shells or other pastry items.

Baked Fruit Fillings

The baked fruit filling method is a traditional technique in which the fruit, sugar, flavourings and starch are combined in an unbaked shell. The dough and filling are then baked simultaneously. Almost any type of fruit and starch can be used. The results are not always consistent, however, because thickening is difficult to control.

Basic Procedure for Preparing Baked Fruit Fillings

1. Combine the starch, spices and sugar.
2. Peel, core, cut or drain the fruit as desired or as directed in the recipe.
3. Toss the fruit with the starch mixture, coating well.
4. Add a portion of juice to moisten the fruit. Small lumps of butter are also often added.

5. Fill an unbaked shell with the fruit mixture. Cover with a top crust, lattice or streusel and bake.

RECIPE 29.6
CHERRY PIE

Yield: 2 9-inch (22-cm) Pies   **Method:** Baked Fruit Filling

Tapioca	1-1/2 oz.	45 g
Salt	pinch	pinch
Granulated sugar	1 lb.	450 g
Almond extract	1/2 tsp.	2 mL
Canned pitted cherries, drained		
(reserve the liquid)	3 lb.	1.3 kg
Unbaked pie shells	2	2
Unsalted butter	1 oz.	30 g
Egg wash	as needed	as needed
Sanding sugar	as needed	as needed

1. Stir the tapioca, salt and sugar together. Add the almond extract and cherries.
2. Stir in up to 8 ounces (250 mL) of the liquid drained from the cherries, adding enough liquid to moisten the mixture thoroughly.
3. Allow the filling to stand for 30 minutes. Then stir gently and place the filling in an unbaked pie shell.
4. Cut the butter into small pieces. Dot the filling with the butter.
5. Place a top crust or a lattice crust over the filling; seal and flute the edges. Cut several slits in the top crust to allow steam to escape. Brush with an egg wash and sprinkle with sanding sugar.
6. Place on a preheated sheet pan and bake at 400°F (200°C) for 50–60 minutes.

Approximate values per 1/8-pie serving:

Calories	340
Total fat	9 g
Saturated fat	3 g
Cholesterol	5 mg
Sodium	170 mg
Total carbohydrates	63 g
Protein	2 g

Dot the cherry filling with butter.

Custard Fillings

A custard pie has a soft filling that bakes along with the crust. Popular examples include pumpkin, egg custard and pecan pies. As explained in Chapter 31, Custards, Creams, Frozen Desserts and Dessert Sauces, custards are liquids thickened by coagulated egg proteins. To make a custard pie, a custard sauce containing eggs is poured into a pie shell. When baked, the egg proteins coagulate, firming and setting the filling.

The procedure for making custard pies is simple: combine the ingredients and bake. But there is often a problem: baking the bottom crust completely

*Approximate values per
1/8-pie serving:*

Calories	210
Total fat	10 g
Saturated fat	2.5 g
Cholesterol	30 mg
Sodium	230 mg
Total carbohydrates	25 g
Protein	4 g
Vitamin A	6%

without overcooking the filling. For the best results, bake the pie in a 400°F (200°C) oven. After 10 minutes, reduce the heat to 325–350°F (160–180°C) to finish cooking the filling slowly.

To determine the doneness of a custard pie:

1. Shake the pie gently. It is done if it is no longer liquid. The centre should show only a slight movement.

2. Insert a thin knife about 1 inch (2.5 cm) from the centre. The filling is done if the knife comes out clean.

♦♦♦

RECIPE 29.7
PUMPKIN PIE

Yield: 4 9-inch (22-cm) Pies   **Method:** Baked Custard Filling

Eggs, beaten slightly	4	4
Pumpkin purée	2 lb.	900 g
Granulated sugar	12 oz.	340 g
Salt	1 tsp.	5 mL
Nutmeg, ground	1/2 tsp.	2 mL
Cloves, ground	1/2 tsp.	2 mL
Cinnamon, ground	2 tsp.	10 mL
Ginger, ground	1 tsp.	5 mL
Evaporated milk or cereal cream	24 oz.	700 mL
Mealy dough pie shells	4	4

1. Combine the eggs and pumpkin. Blend in the sugar.

2. Add the salt and spices, then the evaporated milk. Whisk until completely blended and smooth.

3. Allow the filling to rest for 15–20 minutes before filling the pie shells. This allows the starch in the pumpkin to begin absorbing liquid, making it less likely to separate after baking.

4. Pour the filling into unbaked pie shells. Place in the oven on a preheated sheet pan at 400°F (220°C). Bake for 15 minutes. Lower the oven temperature to 350°F (180°C) and bake until a knife inserted near the centre comes out clean, approximately 40–50 minutes.

Chiffon Fillings

A chiffon filling is created by adding gelatin to a stirred custard or a fruit purée. Whipped egg whites are then folded into the mixture. The filling is placed in a prebaked crust and chilled until firm. These preparations are the same as those for chiffons, mousses and Bavarians discussed in Chapter 31, Custards, Creams, Frozen Desserts and Dessert Sauces.

Assembling Pies and Tarts

The various types of pie fillings can be used to fill almost any crust or shell, provided the crust is prebaked as necessary. The filling can then be topped with meringue or whipped cream as desired. Garnishes such as toasted coconut, cookie crumbs and chocolate curls are often added for appearance and flavour. (See Table 29.2.)

TABLE 29.2   SUGGESTIONS FOR ASSEMBLING PIES

Filling	Crust	Topping	Garnish
Vanilla or lemon cream	Prebaked flaky dough or crumb	None, meringue or whipped cream	Crumbs from the crust
Chocolate cream	Prebaked flaky dough or crumb	None, meringue or whipped cream	Crumbs from the crust or shaved chocolate
Banana cream	Prebaked flaky dough	Meringue or whipped cream	Dried banana chips
Coconut cream	Prebaked flaky dough	Meringue or whipped cream	Shredded coconut
Fresh fruit	Unbaked mealy dough or sweet dough if shallow tart	Lattice, full crust or streusel	Sanding sugar or cut-out designs if lattice or top crust is used
Canned or frozen fruit	Unbaked mealy dough	Lattice, full crust or streusel	Sanding sugar or cut-out designs if lattice or top crust is used
Chiffon or mousse	Crumb or prebaked, sweetened flaky dough	None or whipped cream	Crumbs, fruit or shaved chocolate
Custard (e.g., pecan or pumpkin)	Unbaked mealy dough	None	Whipped cream
Vanilla pastry cream	Prebaked sweet dough	Fresh fruit	Glaze

Storing Pies and Tarts

Pies and tarts filled with cream or custard must be kept refrigerated to retard bacterial growth. Baked fruit pies should be held at refrigerator temperature.

Unbaked fruit pies or unbaked pie shells may be frozen for up to two months. Freezing baked fruit pies is not recommended unless waxy maize or modified starch, not regular cornstarch, is used in preparing the filling. Custard, cream and meringue-topped pies should not be frozen as the eggs will separate, making the product runny.

TABLE 29.3   TROUBLESHOOTING CHART FOR PIES

Problem	Cause	Solution
Crust shrinks	Overmixing	Adjust mixing technique
	Overworking dough	Adjust rolling technique
	Not enough fat	Adjust formula
Soggy crust	Wrong dough used	Use mealier dough
	Oven temperature too low	Adjust oven
	Not baked long enough	Adjust baking time
Crumbly crust	Not enough liquid	Adjust formula
	Too much fat	Adjust formula
Tough crust	Not enough fat	Adjust formula
	Overmixing	Adjust mixing technique
Runny filling	Insufficient starch	Adjust formula
	Starch insufficiently cooked	Allow starch to gelatinize completely
Lumpy cream filling	Starch not incorporated properly	Stir filling while cooking
	Filling overcooked	Adjust cooking time
Custard filling weeps or separates	Too many eggs	Reduce egg content or add starch to the filling
	Eggs overcooked	Reduce oven temperature or baking time

CLASSIC PASTRIES

Puff pastry, **choux paste** and **meringue** are classic components of French pastries; they are used to create a wide variety of dessert and pastry items. Many combinations are traditional. Once you master the skills necessary to produce these products, however, you will be free to experiment with other flavours and assembly techniques.

Puff Pastry

Puff pastry is one of the bakeshop's most elegant and sophisticated products. Also known as **pâte feuilletée**, it is a rich, buttery dough that bakes into hundreds of light, crisp layers.

Puff pastry is used for both sweet and savoury preparations. It can be baked and then filled or filled first and then baked. Puff pastry may be used to wrap beef (for beef Wellington), pâté (for pâté en croûte) or almond cream (for an apple tart). It can be shaped into shells or cases known as vol-au-vents or bouchées and filled with shellfish in a cream sauce or berries in a pastry cream. Puff pastry is essential for napoleons, pithiviers and tartes tatin.

Like croissant and danish dough (discussed in Chapter 28, Yeast Breads), puff pastry is a rolled-in dough. But unlike those doughs, puff pastry does not contain any yeast or chemical leavening agents. Fat is rolled into the dough in horizontal layers; when baked, the fat melts, separating the dough into layers. The fat's moisture turns into steam, which causes the dough to rise and the layers to further separate.

Butter is the preferred fat because of its flavour and melt-in-the-mouth quality. But butter is rather difficult to work with as it becomes brittle when cold and melts at a relatively low temperature. Therefore, specially formulated puff pastry shortenings are used to compensate for butter's shortcomings. They do not, however, provide the true flavour of butter. Some bakers use a combination of butter and specially formulated shortening.

Raw, frozen, commercially prepared puff pastry is readily available in sheets or precut in a variety of shapes. Some convenience products, especially those made with butter, provide excellent, consistent results. Their expense may be offset by the savings in time and labour. Keep these frozen doughs well wrapped to prevent drying and freezer burn, and prepare according to package directions.

Making Puff Pastry

The procedure described here for making puff pastry is just one of many. Each chef will have his or her own formula and folding method. All methods, however, depend upon the proper layering of fat and dough through a series of turns or folds to give the pastry its characteristic flakiness and rise.

Some chefs prefer to prepare a dough called **blitz** or *quick puff pastry*. It does not require the extensive rolling and folding procedure used for true puff pastry. Blitz puff pastry is less delicate and flaky but may be perfectly acceptable for some uses. A formula for it is given at the end of this chapter.

BASIC PROCEDURE FOR PREPARING PUFF PASTRY

1. Prepare the dough (**détrempe**) by combining the flour, water, salt and a small amount of fat. Do not overmix. Overmixing results in greater gluten formation; too much gluten can make the pastry undesirably tough.

English method—*fat covers two-thirds of dough and single folds are used to create layers. Either 6 × 3 or 4 × 4 folds (bookfold) can be used.*

Blitz method—*fat is incorporated as in flaky pie dough, only fat pieces are larger; dough is given two or three single folds.*

Détrempe—*a mixture made with flour and water during the first stage of preparing a pastry dough, especially rolled-in doughs.*

2. Wrap the détrempe and chill for several hours or overnight. This allows the gluten to relax and the flour to absorb the liquid.

3. Shape the butter into a rectangle of even thickness; wrap and chill until ready to use.

4. Allow the détrempe and butter to sit at room temperature until slightly softened and of the same consistency.

5. Roll out the détrempe into a rectangle of even thickness.

6. Place the butter in the centre of the dough. Fold the dough around the butter, enclosing it completely.

7. Roll out the block of dough and butter into a long, even rectangle. Roll only at right angles so that the layered structure is not destroyed.

8. Fold the dough like a business letter: Fold the bottom third up towards the centre so that it covers the centre third, then fold the top third down over the bottom and middle thirds. This completes the first turn.

9. Rotate the block of dough one-quarter turn (90 degrees) on the work surface. Roll out again into a long, even rectangle.

10. Fold the dough in thirds again, like a business letter. This completes the second turn. Wrap the dough and chill for approximately 30 minutes. The resting period allows the gluten to relax; the chilling prevents the butter from becoming too soft.

11. Repeat the rolling and folding process, chilling between every one or two turns, until the dough has been turned a total of five times.

12. Wrap well and chill overnight. Raw dough may be refrigerated for a few days or frozen for two to three months.

13. Shape and bake as needed. Baked, unfilled puff pastry can be stored at room temperature for two to three days.

BOOKFOLDS

The process of folding the dough and rolling it out and folding it again is referred to as bookfolds or turns. There are single folds (layering the dough in thirds) as described here and bookfolds, bringing both outside edges to the centre and then folding in half again. The more folds, the more layers of fat and the flakier the pastry becomes—to a point. Too many folds results in the dough becoming too thin to support the structure as it develops during baking.

RECIPE 29.8
PUFF PASTRY

Yield: 2 lb. (1 kg) **Method:** Rolled-In Dough

All-purpose flour	13 oz.	390 g
Salt	1-1/2 tsp.	7 mL
Unsalted butter, cold	3 oz.	90 g
Water, cold	7 oz.	210 mL
Unsalted butter, softened	10 oz.	300 g

1. To form the détrempe, sift the flour and salt together in a large bowl. Cut the 3 ounces (90 g) of cold butter into small pieces and then cut the pieces into the flour until the mixture resembles coarse cornmeal.

2. Make a well in the centre of the mixture and add all the water at once. Using a rubber spatula or your fingers, gradually draw the flour into the water. Mix until all of the flour is incorporated. Do not knead the dough. The détrempe should be sticky and shaggy-looking.

3. Turn the détrempe out onto a lightly floured surface. Knead the dough a few times by hand, rounding it into a ball. Wrap the dough tightly in plastic and chill overnight.

4. To roll the butter in, first prepare the 10-ounce (300-g) piece of butter by placing it between two sheets of plastic wrap. Use a rolling pin to roll the

Approximate values per 1 oz. (30 g) serving:

Calories	120
Total fat	9 g
Saturated fat	6 g
Cholesterol	25 mg
Sodium	110 mg
Total carbohydrates	9 g
Protein	1 g
Vitamin A	8%

Continued

1. Mise en place for puff pastry. The detrempe is shown on the top left.

2. Fold the dough around the butter.

3. Roll out the dough.

4. Fold the dough in thirds.

softened butter into a rectangle approximately 5 inches × 8 inches (12.5 cm × 20 cm). It is important that the détrempe and butter be of almost equal consistency. If necessary, allow the détrempe to sit at room temperature to soften or chill the butter briefly to harden.

5. On a lightly floured board, roll the détrempe into a rectangle approximately 12 inches × 15 inches (30 cm × 37.5 cm). Lift and rotate the dough as necessary to prevent sticking.

6. Use a dry pastry brush to brush away any flour from the dough's surface. Loose flour can cause grey streaks and can prevent the puff pastry from rising properly when baked.

7. Peel one piece of plastic wrap from the butter. Position the butter in the centre of the rectangle and remove the remaining plastic. Fold the four edges of the détrempe over the butter enclosing it completely. Stretch the dough if necessary; it is important that none of the butter be exposed.

8. With the folded side facing up, press the dough several times with a rolling pin. Use a rocking motion to create ridges in the dough. Place the rolling pin in each ridge and slowly roll back and forth to widen the ridge. Repeat until all of the ridges are doubled in size.

9. Using the ridges as a starting point, roll the dough out into a smooth, even rectangle approximately 8 inches × 24 inches (20 cm × 60 cm). Be careful to keep the corners of the dough at right angles.

10. Use a dry pastry brush to remove any loose flour from the dough's surface. Fold the dough in thirds, like a business letter. If one end is damaged or in worse condition, fold it in first; otherwise start at the bottom. This completes the first turn.

11. Rotate the block of dough 90 degrees, so that the folded edge is on your left and the dough faces you like a book. Roll the dough out again, repeating the ridging technique. Once again, the dough should be in a smooth, even rectangle of approximately 8 inches × 24 inches (20 cm × 60 cm).

12. Fold the dough in thirds again, completing the second turn. Cover the dough with plastic wrap and chill for at least 30 minutes.

13. Repeat the rolling and folding technique until the dough has had a total of five turns. Do not perform more than two turns without a resting and chilling period. Cover the dough completely and chill overnight before shaping and baking.

NOTES: The détrempe can be made in a food processor. To do so, combine the flour, salt and pieces of butter in a food processor bowl fitted with the metal blade. Process until a coarse meal is formed. With the processor running, slowly add the water. Turn the machine off as soon as the dough comes together to form a ball. Proceed with the remainder of the recipe.

It is not necessary to work with the entire block of dough when making bouchées, cookies or the like. Cut the block into thirds or quarters and work with one of these portions at a time, keeping the rest chilled until needed.

Shaping Puff Pastry

Once puff pastry dough is prepared, it can be shaped into containers of various sizes and shapes. Classic shapes are bouchées, vol-au-vents and feuilletées. **Bouchées** are small puff pastry shells often used for hors d'oeuvres or appetizers. **Vol-au-vents** are larger, deeper shells, often filled with savoury mixtures for a main course. Although they are most often round or square, special vol-au-vent cutters are available in the shape of fish, hearts or petals. **Feuilletées** are square, rectangular or diamond-shaped puff pastry boxes. They can be filled with a sweet or savoury mixture.

When making straight cuts in puff pastry, press the tip of your knife into the dough and cut by pressing down on the handle. Do not drag the knife through the dough or you will crush the layers and deform the pastry.

BASIC PROCEDURE FOR SHAPING VOL-AU-VENTS AND BOUCHÉES

1. Roll out the puff pastry dough to a thickness of approximately 1/4 inch (6 mm).
2. Cut the desired shape and size using a vol-au-vent cutter or rings.
3. Place the vol-au-vent or bouchée on a paper-lined sheet pan. If you used rings, place the base on the paper-lined sheet pan, brush lightly with water, then top it with the dough ring; score the edge with the back of a paring knife. Chill for 20–30 minutes to allow the dough to relax before baking.
4. Egg-wash if desired and dock the centre with a fork.

2. To shape with rings, use two rings, one approximately 1 inch (2.5 cm) smaller in diameter than the other. The larger ring is used to cut two rounds. One will be the base and is set aside. The smaller ring is then used to cut out an interior circle from the second round, leaving a border ring of dough. (The scrap of dough from the dough ring's centre has no further use in making vol-au-vents but may be used to make bouchées or fleurons.)

1. A vol-au-vent cutter looks like a double cookie cutter with one cutter about 1 inch (2.5 cm) smaller than the other. To cut the pastry, simply position the cutter and press down.

BASIC PROCEDURE FOR SHAPING FEUILLETÉES

1. Roll out the puff pastry dough into an even rectangle approximately 1/8 to 1/4 inch (3 to 6 mm) thick.
2. Using a sharp paring knife or chef's knife, cut squares that are about 2 inches (5 cm) larger than the desired interior of the finished feuilletée.

3. Fold each square in half diagonally. Cut through two sides of the dough, about 1/2 inch (1.25 cm) from the edge. Cut a "V," being careful not to cut through the corners at the centre fold.

4. Open the square and lay it flat. Lift opposite sides of the cut border at the cut corners and cross them.

5. Brush water on the edges to seal the dough. Place the feuilletées on a paper-lined sheet pan.
6. Score the edges with the back of a paring knife. Chill for 20 to 30 minutes to allow the dough to relax before baking.
7. Egg-wash if desired and dock the centre with a fork.

Puff pastry scraps cannot be rerolled and used for products needing a high rise. The additional rolling destroys the layers. Scraps (known as *rognures*), however, can be used for cookies such as palmiers (Recipe 29.26), turnovers, decorative crescents (fleurons), tart shells, napoleons (Recipe 29.24 and 29.25) or any item for which rise is less important than flavour and flakiness.

Most puff pastry products bake best in a hot oven, about 400–425°F (200–220°C).

Choux Paste

Choux paste (**pâte à choux**), sometimes called éclair paste, bakes up into golden brown, crisp pastries. The insides of these light pastries are mostly air pockets with a bit of moist dough. They can be filled with sweet cream, custard, fruit or even savoury mixtures. The dough is most often piped into rounds for **cream puffs**, fingers for **éclairs** or rings for **Paris-Brest** or **gougères.** Choux paste may also be piped or spooned into specific shapes and deep-fat fried for doughnut-type products known as **beignets**, **churros** and **crullers.**

Preparing Choux Paste

Choux paste is unique among doughs because it is cooked before baking. The cooking occurs when the flour is added to a boiling mixture of water, milk and butter. This process breaks down the starches in the flour, allowing them to absorb the liquid, speeding gelatinization. Eggs are added to the flour mixture for leavening. The paste produced is batterlike with a smooth, firm texture; it does not have the dry, elastic or crumbly texture of other doughs. Without this technique the paste would not puff up and develop the desired large interior air pockets when baked.

Cream puffs—*baked rounds of choux paste cut in half and filled with pastry cream, whipped cream, fruit or other filling.*

Profiteroles—*small baked rounds of choux paste filled with ice cream and topped with chocolate sauce.*

Croquembouche—*a pyramid of small puffs, each filled with pastry cream; a French tradition for Christmas and weddings, it is held together with caramelized sugar and decorated with spun sugar or marzipan flowers.*

Éclairs—*baked fingers of choux paste filled with pastry cream; the top is then coated with chocolate glaze or fondant.*

Paris-Brest—*rings of baked choux paste cut in half horizontally and filled with light pastry cream and/or whipped cream; the top is dusted with powdered sugar or drizzled with chocolate glaze.*

Gougères—*rings of baked, cheese-flavoured choux pastry; usually served cold.*

Beignets—*squares or strips of choux paste deep-fat fried and dusted with powdered sugar.*

Churros—*a Spanish and Mexican pastry in which sticks of choux paste flavoured with cinnamon are deep-fat fried and rolled in sugar while still hot.*

Crullers—*a Dutch pastry in which a loop or strip of twisted choux paste is deep-fat fried and glazed with a lemon-flavoured fondant.*

BASIC PROCEDURE FOR PREPARING CHOUX PASTE

1. Combine liquid ingredients and butter and bring to a boil.
2. Add all of the flour to the saucepan as soon as the water-and-butter mixture comes to a boil. If the liquid is allowed to boil, evaporation occurs; this can create an imbalance in the liquid-to-flour ratio.
3. Stir vigorously until the liquid is absorbed. Continue cooking the dough until it forms a ball that comes away from the sides of the pan, leaving only a thin film of dough in the pan.
4. Transfer the dough to a mixing bowl. Add eggs one at a time, beating well after each addition. This may be done in a mixer with the paddle attachment or by hand. The number of eggs used varies depending on the size of each egg and the moisture content of the flour mixture. Stop adding eggs when the paste just begins to fall away from the beaters.
5. The finished paste should be smooth and pliable enough to pipe through a pastry bag; it should not be runny.
6. Pipe the paste as desired and bake immediately. A high oven temperature is necessary at the start of baking; it is then reduced gradually to finish baking and dry the product. Do not open the oven door during the first half of the baking period.
7. Allow the paste to bake until completely dry. If the products are removed from the oven too soon, they will collapse.
8. Baked choux paste can be stored, unfilled, for several days at room temperature or frozen for several weeks. Once filled, the pastry should be served within two or three hours as it quickly becomes soggy.

❖❖❖

RECIPE 29.9

BASIC CHOUX PASTE

Yield: 2 lb. (1 kg) Dough

Milk, 2%	28 oz.	800 mL
Water	16 oz.	450 mL
Butter	1 lb. 2 oz.	500 g
Bread flour	1 lb.	750 g
Eggs	45 oz. approx.	1.25 kg approx.

1. Preheat the oven to 425°F (220°C). Line a sheet pan with parchment. Have a pastry bag with a large plain tip ready.
2. Place the milk, water and butter in a saucepan. Bring to a rolling boil. Make sure the butter is fully melted.
3. Remove from the heat and immediately add all the flour. Vigorously beat the dough by hand. Put the pan back on the heat and continue beating the dough until it comes away from the sides of the pan. The dough should look relatively dry.
4. Transfer the dough to a mixing bowl and allow it to cool briefly to a temperature of approximately 130°F (54°C) or lower. Using the mixer's paddle attachment, begin beating in the eggs one at a time and incorporating thoroughly.

Continued

5. Continue to add the eggs until the mixture is shiny but firm. It may not be necessary to use all the eggs. The paste should pull away from the sides of the bowl in thick threads; it will not clear the bowl.

6. Put a workable amount of dough into the pastry bag and pipe onto the sheet pan in the desired shapes at once.

7. Bake immediately, beginning at 425°F (220°C) for 10 minutes, then lowering the heat to 375°F (190°C) for another 10 minutes. Continue gradually lowering the oven temperature until the shapes are brown and dry inside. Open the oven door as little as possible to prevent rapid changes in the oven's temperature.

8. Cool completely, then fill as desired. Leftovers can be frozen or stored at room temperature.

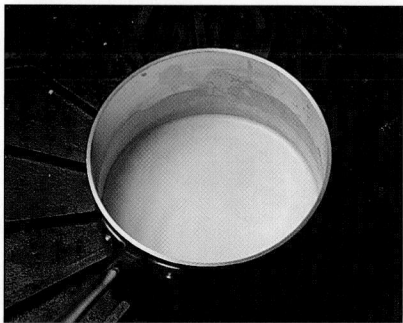

1. Heat the butter and milk.

2. Add the flour to the hot liquid.

3. Stir the dough to dry it.

4. The finished batter after the eggs have been incorporated.

5. Pipe éclairs or other shapes.

Meringues

Meringues are egg whites whipped with sugar. The texture—hard or soft—depends on the ratio of sugar to egg whites.

A low sugar content in comparison with the egg whites creates a **soft meringue**. Soft meringues can be folded into a mousse or Bavarian cream to lighten it or used in a spongecake or soufflé. Meringues with only a small amount of sugar will always be soft; they will not become crisp no matter how they are used.

Hard meringues are made with egg whites and a more than equal part of sugar. They can be incorporated into a butter cream or pastry cream or used

TABLE 29.4   MERINGUES

Type	Ratio of Sugar to Egg Whites	Preparation	Use
Common—hard	Twice as much or more	Whip or fold sugar into whipped egg whites	Baked
Common—soft	Equal parts or less	Whip or fold sugar into whipped egg whites	Pie toppings; soufflés; cake ingredient
Swiss	Varies	Warm egg whites with sugar, then whip	Buttercream; pie topping; baked
Italian	Varies	Hot sugar syrup poured into whipped egg whites	Buttercream; frosting; crème Chiboust; baked

to top a pie or baked Alaska. These toppings are usually placed briefly under a broiler to caramelize the sugar, creating an attractive brown surface.

Hard meringues with twice as much sugar as egg whites can be piped into disks or other shapes and dried in an oven. A low oven temperature evaporates the eggs' moisture, leaving a crisp, sugary, honeycomblike structure. Disks of baked meringue can be used as layers in a torte or cake. Cups or shells of baked meringue can be filled with cream, mousse, ice cream or fruit. Often baked meringues also contain ground nuts (and are then known as **japonaise**), cocoa powder or other flavourings.

Making Meringues

There are three methods for making meringues: **common**, **Swiss** and **Italian**. (See Table 29.4.) Regardless of which preparation method is used, the final product should be smooth, glossy and moist. A meringue should never be dry or spongelike. You should review the procedure for whipping egg whites given in Chapter 8, Eggs and Dairy Products.

Common Meringues

Common meringues are made by first beating egg whites to a soft foam (soft peaks). Granulated sugar is then slowly beaten or folded into the egg whites. The final product may be hard or soft depending on the ratio of sugar to egg whites.

Swiss Meringues

Swiss meringues are made by combining unwhipped egg whites with sugar and warming the mixture over a bain marie to a temperature of approximately 100°F (38°C). The syrupy solution is then whipped until cool and stiff. The final product may be hard or soft depending on the ratio of sugar to egg whites. Swiss meringues are extremely stable but rather difficult to prepare. If the mixture gets too hot it will not whip properly; the result will be syrupy and runny. Swiss meringue is often used as a topping or in buttercream.

Italian Meringues

Italian meringues are made by slowly pouring a hot sugar syrup into whipped egg whites. The heat from the syrup cooks the egg whites, adding stability. Be sure that the sugar syrup reaches the correct temperature and that it is added to the egg whites in a slow, steady stream. Italian meringues are used in buttercream (see Chapter 30, Cakes and Frostings) or folded into pastry cream to produce crème Chiboust. They may be flavoured and used as a cake filling and frosting called boiled icing.

TABLE 29.5   TROUBLESHOOTING CHART FOR MERINGUES

Problem	Cause	Solution
Weeps or beads of sugar syrup are released	Old eggs	Use fresher eggs or add starch or stabilizer
	Egg whites overwhipped	Whip only until stiff peaks form
	Not enough sugar	Increase sugar
	Not baked long enough	Increase baking time
	Browning too rapidly	Do not dust with sugar before baking; reduce oven temperature
	Moisture in the air	Do not refrigerate baked meringue
Fails to attain any volume or stiffness	Fat present	Start over with clean bowls and utensils
	Sugar added too soon	Allow egg whites to reach soft peaks before adding sugar
	Too much sugar added too quickly	Add sugar gradually.
Lumps	Not enough sugar	Add additional sugar gradually or start over
	Overwhipping	Whip only until stiff peaks form
Not shiny	Not enough sugar	Add additional sugar gradually or start over
	Overwhipping	Whip only until stiff peaks form

◆◆◆

RECIPE 29.10

JAPONAISE MERINGUE

Yield: 4 lb. (2 kg)

Egg whites	17-1/2 oz.	500 g
Granulated sugar	17-1/2 oz.	500 g
Icing sugar	17-1/2 oz.	500 g
Ground hazelnuts	17-1/2 oz.	500 g

Approximate values per 1 oz. (30 g) serving:

Calories	103
Total fat	4 g
Saturated fat	0 g
Cholesterol	0 mg
Sodium	23 mg
Total carbohydrates	15 g
Protein	2 g

1. Whip egg whites at medium speed to soft peaks.
2. With the machine still running, add the granulated sugar in small quantities. Whip to a soft peak.
3. Combine icing sugar and nuts, then fold into the meringue.
4. Using a pencil, mark circles on silicone sheets. Turn the sheets over and place on tray.
5. Pipe the japonaise mixture onto the sheets using a plain 1/2-inch (12–15 mm) tube. Using the pencilled circles as a guide, pipe in a spiral.
6. Bake at 250°F (120°C) until crisp, 1-1/2 to 2 hours. Use the meringues to make tortes.

◆◆◆

RECIPE 29.11

ITALIAN MERINGUE

Yield: Approx. 2 gal. (8 L)

Egg whites, room temperature	14 oz.	420 g
Granulated sugar	28 oz.	840 g

1. Place 18 ounces (540 g) of the sugar in a heavy saucepan and add enough water to moisten the sugar thoroughly. Attach a candy thermometer to the pan and bring the sugar to a boil over high heat.
2. Place the egg whites in the bowl of an electric mixer fitted with the whip attachment. As the temperature of the boiling sugar approaches 238°F (115°C) begin whipping the egg whites. When the whites form soft peaks, gradually add the remaining 10 ounces (300 g) of sugar. Lower the mixer speed and continue whipping.
3. When the sugar reaches 238°F (115°C) pour it into the whites, with the mixer running. Pour in a steady stream between the side of the bowl and the beater. Continue whipping the whites at medium speed until they are cool.

Approximate values per cup (225 mL):	
Calories	102
Total fat	0 g
Saturated fat	0 g
Cholesterol	0 mg
Sodium	16 mg
Total carbohydrates	25 g
Protein	1 g

Claims—no fat, no cholesterol, low sodium

COOKIES

Cookies are small, flat pastries usually eaten alone (although not singularly) and rarely used as a component in other desserts. The recent proliferation of cookie shops in malls and office buildings attests to the popularity of freshly baked cookies. They are indeed among the world's best-loved foods.

Part of the pleasure of cookies comes from their versatility. They may be eaten as a midmorning snack or as the elegant end to a formal dinner. Cookies also provide the finishing touch to a serving of ice cream, custard or fruit. Flavours are limited only by the baker's imagination; chocolate, oatmeal, cornmeal, fresh and dried fruit and nuts all find their way into several types of cookies. Several cookie formulas are given at the end of this chapter.

Mixing Methods

Most cookie doughs are mixed by the creaming method used for quick breads and cake batters. (See Chapter 27, Quick Breads, and Chapter 30, Cakes and Frostings.) Because cookie dough contains less liquid than these batters, the liquid and flour need not be added alternately, however. Cookies may be leavened with baking soda, baking powder or just air and steam. Most cookies are high in fat, which contributes taste and tenderness and extends shelf life. Overdevelopment of gluten is usually not a problem with cookies because of their high fat and low moisture contents. Careless mixing can cause the dough to become tough and dense instead of tender and flaky.

BASIC PROCEDURE FOR MIXING COOKIE DOUGHS

1. Cream the fat and sugar together to incorporate air and to blend the ingredients completely.
2. Add the eggs gradually, scraping down the bowl as needed.
3. Stir in the liquid ingredients.
4. Stir in the flour, salt, spices and leaveners.
5. Fold in any nuts, chocolate chips or chunky ingredients by hand or by mixer on low speed.

Drop Cookies

Icebox Cookies

Bar Cookies

Cut-Out or Rolled Cookies

Makeup Methods

Cookie varieties are usually classified by the way in which the individual cookies are prepared. This section describes six preparation or makeup techniques: **drop**, **icebox**, **bar**, **cut-out** or **rolled**, **pressed** and **wafer**. Some doughs can be made up by more than one method. For example, chocolate chip cookie dough can be (a) baked in sheets and cut into bars, (b) dropped in mounds or (c) rolled into logs, chilled and sliced like icebox cookies. Regardless of the makeup method used, uniformity of size and shape is important for appearance and baking time. Cookies should also be evenly spaced on sheet pans for proper air circulation and crust formation.

Drop Cookies

Drop cookies are made from a soft dough that is spooned or scooped into mounds for baking. Chunky cookies such as chocolate chip, oatmeal raisin and nut jumbles are common examples. Although a uniform appearance is not as important for drop cookies as for other types, uniform size and placement results in uniform baking time. A portion scoop is recommended for portioning the dough. Drop cookies tend to be thick with a soft or chewy texture.

Icebox Cookies

Icebox cookies are made from dough that is shaped into logs or rectangles, chilled thoroughly, then sliced into individual pieces and baked as needed. Icebox cookies can be as simple as a log of chocolate chip dough or as sophisticated as elegant pinwheel and checkerboard cookies assembled with two colours of short dough. This method usually produces uniform, waferlike cookies with a crisp texture.

Bar Cookies

Bar cookie dough is pressed or layered in shallow pans and cut into portions after baking, usually squares or rectangles to avoid waste or scraps. This category, also known as sheet cookies, contains a wide variety of layered or fruit-filled products. Brownies, often considered a bar cookie, are discussed in Chapter 30, Cakes and Frostings.

Cut-Out or Rolled Cookies

Cut-out or rolled cookies are made from a firm dough that is rolled out into a sheet and then cut into various shapes before baking. A seemingly infinite selection of cookie cutters is available, or you can use a paring knife or pastry wheel to cut the dough into the desired shapes. Always start cutting cookies from the edge of the dough, working inward. Cut the cookies as close to each other as possible to avoid scraps. Cut-out cookies are usually baked on an ungreased pan to keep the dough from spreading.

Cut-out cookies are often garnished or decorated with nuts, glaze, fruit or candies. Raw cookies should be decorated as soon as they are placed on the pan. If the dough is allowed to stand, the surface will dry out and the garnish will not adhere properly.

Pressed Cookies

Also referred to as bagged or spritz cookies, these products are made with a soft dough that is forced through a pastry tip or cookie gun. Pressed cookies are usually small, with a distinct, decorative shape. The task of piping out dozens of identical cookies may seem daunting, but the skill can be mastered with practice and an understanding of doughs. Doughs for pressed cookies often include eggs as their only liquid. Egg whites, which are a toughener, contribute body and help the cookies retain their shape. The yolks act as a tenderizer. Using too much fat or too-soft flour (i.e., one low in protein) can cause the cookies to spread and lose their shape.

Wafer Cookies

Wafer cookies are extremely thin and delicate. They are made with a thin batter that is poured or spread onto a baking sheet and baked. Then, while still hot, the wafer is moulded into a variety of shapes. The most popular shapes are the tightly rolled cigarette, the curved tuile and the cup-shaped tulip. Wafer batter is sweet and buttery and is often flavoured with citrus zest or ground nuts.

Pressed Cookies

Wafer Cookies

Cookie Textures

The textures associated with cookies—crispness, softness, chewiness or spread—are affected by various factors, including the ratio of ingredients in the dough, the oven's temperature and the pan's coating. Understanding these factors allows you to adjust formulas or techniques to achieve the desired results. See Table 29.6.

TABLE 29.6   COOKIE TEXTURES

Desired Texture	Content of					
	Fat	Sugar	Liquid	Flour	Size or Shape	Baking
Crispness	High	High; use granulated sugar	Low	Bread or pastry	Thin dough	Well done; cool on baking sheet
Softness	Low	Low; use hygroscopic sugars	High	Pastry or cake	Thick dough portion	Use parchment-lined pan; underbake
Chewiness	High	High; use hygroscopic sugars	High	Bread or pastry	Not relevant; chilled dough	Underbake; cool on rack
Spread	High	High; use coarse granulated sugar	High; especially from eggs	Pastry or cake	Not relevant; room-temperature dough	Use greased pan; low temperature

Storing Cookies

Most cookies can be stored for up to one week in an air-tight container. Do not store crisp cookies and soft cookies in the same container, however. The crisp cookies will absorb moisture from the soft cookies, ruining the texture of both. Do not store strongly flavoured cookies, such as spice, with those that are milder, such as shortbread.

Most cookies freeze well if wrapped air tight to prevent moisture loss or freezer burn. Raw dough can also be frozen, either shaped or unshaped.

CONCLUSION

Pastry making is the backbone of dessert preparation. A wide variety of pastry doughs can be prepared from flour, fat and a liquid. Proper mixing, rolling and shaping techniques are crucial to the success of the finished product. With a selection of properly prepared doughs and fillings, you can create an endless variety of tempting desserts.

QUESTIONS FOR DISCUSSION

1. How does the type of pie filling influence the selection of a pie crust? What type of crust would be best for a fresh unbaked fruit pie? Explain your answer.
2. How does rolling fat into a dough in layers (as with puff pastry) produce a flaky product? Why isn't sweet dough (which contains a high ratio of butter) flaky?
3. Explain the difference between a cream pie filling and a custard pie filling. Give two examples of each type of filling.
4. List and describe three ways of preparing fruit fillings for pies.
5. Why is it said that choux paste is the only paste that is cooked before it is baked? Why is this step necessary? List three ways for using choux paste in making classic desserts.
6. Explain the differences and similarities between common, Swiss, Italian and japonaise meringues.
7. List and describe four makeup methods for cookie doughs.

ADDITIONAL PIE, PASTRY AND COOKIE FORMULAS

Several of the formulas given below are combinations of the pastry items presented in this chapter and the creams, custards and other dessert products covered in other chapters. For example, the Strawberry Napoleon is made with the puff pastry discussed in this chapter, the pastry cream and crème Chantilly discussed in Chapter 31, Custards, Creams, Frozen Desserts and Dessert Sauces, and the fondant glaze discussed in Chapter 30, Cakes and Frostings.

◆◆◆

RECIPE 29.12

GÂTEAU ST. HONORÉ

NOTE: *This dish appears in the Chapter Opening photograph.*

CITY RESTAURANT, LOS ANGELES, CA
Chef/Owners Susan Feniger and Mary Sue Milliken

Yield: 10 Servings

Puff pastry	1 lb.	500 g
Milk	4 oz.	120 mL

Unsalted butter	1-3/4 oz.	50 g
Salt	1/8 tsp.	1/2 mL
Bread flour	2-1/2 oz.	75 g
Eggs	2	2
Pastry Cream (recipe follows)	as needed	as needed
Sugar	10 oz.	300 g
Water	4 oz.	120 mL
City Chocolate (recipe follows)	as needed	as needed
Cream, 35%, cold	1 pt.	450 mL
Semisweet chocolate, melted	3 oz.	90 g

1. Roll out the puff pastry to form a 10-inch (25-cm) square; reserve in the refrigerator.

2. Make the choux paste by combining the milk, butter and salt in a medium-heavy saucepan. Bring to a boil. Add the flour all at once. Mix quickly with a wooden spoon until a ball forms on the spoon and the flour is evenly moistened. Transfer to a bowl, cool mixture to below 130°F (54°C) and add the eggs one at a time, beating well after each addition.

3. Fit a piping bag with a large plain tip; fill it with choux paste. Line a baking sheet with parchment paper. Pipe paste onto the baking sheet to form small cream puffs about the size of quarters. With a finger dipped in cold water, flatten the point on top of each puff. Drop the pan from a height of 2 inches (5 cm) onto the counter to set the puffs.

4. Bake at 450°F (230°C) until uniformly puffed and golden, approximately 10 minutes. Reduce heat to 375°F (190°C) and bake an additional 15–20 minutes. Test for doneness by opening a puff. The inside should be totally dry. Set aside to cool on a rack.

5. Place the puff pastry on a parchment-paper-lined baking sheet and, with a 10-inch (25-cm) round cake pan inverted over the dough, trace a circle using a sharp knife. This will be the base for the cake. Prick the circle of puff pastry all over with a fork and set in the refrigerator to rest for 15 minutes.

6. Bake the puff pastry at 425°F (220°C) until puffed and golden, approximately 20 minutes. Reserve at room temperature.

7. Fit a piping bag with a No. 2 tip; fill it with pastry cream. Make a hole in the bottom of each puff using a small paring knife. Fill each puff with pastry cream and reserve.

8. To make the caramel, combine the sugar and water in a saucepan and cook until golden brown. Immediately remove from heat. Using a fork, dip half of each cream puff into the warm caramel and place on a tray lined with parchment paper. When the caramel has set, turn each puff and dip the uncoated half in the caramel. Immediately arrange the puffs, flat side up, along the edge of the cooled puff pastry to form the wall.

9. Fill the centre of the pastry with an even layer of City Chocolate.

10. Whip the cold cream until soft peaks form. Fold half of this cream into the 3 ounces (90 g) of melted chocolate and set aside.

11. Spoon the remaining whipped cream into a pastry bag fitted with a No. 8 plain tip. Pipe about 5 rows of Hershey's Kiss–shaped domes (pointy chocolate kiss shapes) over the chocolate filling, leaving even spaces between the rows. Fill the bag with the chocolate-flavoured cream and repeat, filling the spaces between rows. Chill until serving time.

Approximate values per 1/10-cake serving:

Calories	400
Total fat	25 g
Saturated fat	15 g
Cholesterol	115 mg
Sodium	65 mg
Total carbohydrates	41 g
Protein	4 g
Vitamin A	25%

Continued

PASTRY CREAM

Yield: 1-1/4 pt. (600 mL)

Sugar	4 oz.	120 g
Cornstarch	4 Tbsp.	60 mL
Egg yolks	4	4
Milk	1 pt.	450 mL
Vanilla extract	1/2 tsp.	2 mL

Approximate values per 1 oz. (30 mL) serving:

Calories	30
Total fat	1 g
Saturated fat	0 g
Cholesterol	25 mg
Sodium	10 mg
Total carbohydrates	5 g
Protein	1 g

1. Mix 2 ounces (60 g) of sugar and all of the cornstarch in a bowl. Add the egg yolks and mix until a paste is formed. Stir in 4 ounces (120 mL) of milk.
2. Combine the remaining milk and sugar in a saucepan and bring to a boil. Pour the hot milk into the egg yolk mixture, whisking constantly. Then pour the mixture back into the pan.
3. Cook over moderate heat, stirring constantly, until smooth and thick. Remove from the heat and stir for an additional minute. Stir in the vanilla and transfer to a bowl.
4. Cover with buttered parchment paper touching the top and chill a minimum of 2 hours or as long as 2 days.

CITY CHOCOLATE

Yield: 1 lb. 12 oz. (800 g)

Brandy	1-1/2 Tbsp.	20 mL
Golden raisins	1-1/2 oz.	45 g
Semisweet chocolate	9 oz.	270 g
Unsalted butter	7 oz.	210 g
Eggs, separated	5	5

Approximate values per 1 oz. (30 g) serving:

Calories	120
Total fat	9 g
Saturated fat	6 g
Cholesterol	55 mg
Sodium	15 mg
Total carbohydrates	7 g
Protein	2 g

1. Combine the brandy and raisins in a small saucepan and warm over low heat. Reserve.
2. Chop the chocolate into small pieces and melt with butter over a bain marie. Remove from the heat and stir in the raisins and brandy. Whisk in the yolks until combined.
3. Whisk the egg whites until soft peaks form. Gently fold the whites into the chocolate mixture in 2 stages.

◆◆◆

RECIPE 29.13

Cannoli Alla Siciliana

REX IL RISTORANTE, Los Angeles, CA
Executive Chef Odette Fada

Yield: 12 Pieces

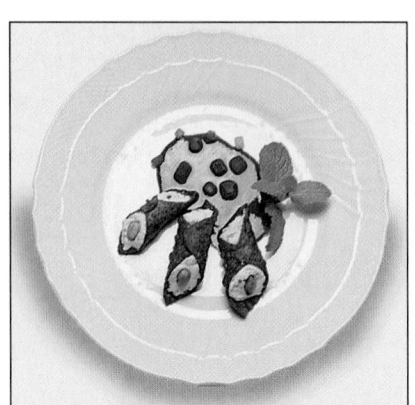

Dough:		
All-purpose flour	2 oz.	60 g
Granulated sugar	1/2 oz.	15 g
Cocoa powder	1/2 oz.	15 g
Red wine	1 Tbsp.	15 mL
Filling:		
Orange zest, candied, chopped	1 oz.	30 g
Chocolate chips	1 oz.	30 g
Pistachio nuts, chopped	1 oz.	30 g
Confectioner's sugar, sifted	1-1/2 oz.	45 g
Fresh ricotta cheese	12 oz.	360 g

1. To make the cannoli, sift the dry ingredients together, then stir in the wine. Add more wine if necessary to produce a stiff dough. Chill the dough for at least 1 hour.

2. Roll the dough very thin and cut it into 2-inch (5-cm) squares.

3. Roll each square of dough around a 3/4-inch dowel and pinch the tips of the dough together to form a tube. Deep-fat fry until crisp, approximately 1 minute. Drain on absorbent paper.

4. To make the filling, stir all filling ingredients together and chill until ready to use.

5. To assemble, fit a piping bag with a large plain tip; fill with the filling mixture and pipe it into each of the fried cannoli shells.

6. Serve with a pool of dark chocolate sauce, garnished with candied fruits.

Approximate values per piece:

Calories	100
Total fat	3.5 g
Saturated fat	1 g
Cholesterol	10 mg
Sodium	35 mg
Total carbohydrates	14 g
Protein	3 g

Claims—low saturated fat; low cholesterol; low sodium

◆◆◆

RECIPE 29.14

LINZER TART

CITY RESTAURANT, LOS ANGELES, CA
Chef/Owners Susan Feniger and Mary Sue Milliken

Yield: 8–10 Servings

Unsalted butter, softened	8 oz.	250 g
Sugar	8 oz.	250 g
Egg yolks	2	2
Orange zest	2 Tbsp.	30 mL
Lemon zest	1 Tbsp.	15 mL
All-purpose flour	11 oz.	330 g
Hazelnuts, ground fine	6 oz.	180 g
Baking powder	1 tsp.	5 mL
Cinnamon, ground	2 tsp.	10 mL
Cloves, ground	1/2 tsp.	2 mL
Salt	1/4 tsp.	1 mL
Raspberry preserves	6 oz.	180 g

1. To make the dough, cream together the butter and sugar until light and fluffy. Add the egg yolks, orange and lemon zests. Beat until well combined.

2. In another bowl, mix together the remaining ingredients except the preserves. Add the dry mixture all at once to the creamed mixture and mix briefly, until just combined. (This dough looks more like cookie dough than pastry.) Wrap in plastic and chill until firm, about 4 hours or overnight.

3. Divide the dough in half. On a generously floured board, briefly knead 1 piece of dough and flatten it with the palm of your hand. Gently roll the dough out 1/4 inch (6 mm) thick and use it to line a 9- or 10-inch (20–25 cm) tart pan with a removable bottom. This rich dough patches easily. Chill about 10 minutes.

4. Roll out the second piece of dough to form a 12-inch- × 4-inch (30 × 10 cm) rectangle. Using a sharp knife or pastry wheel, cut lengthwise strips, about 1/3 inch (0.8 cm) wide.

5. Remove the lined tart shell from the refrigerator and spread the raspberry preserves evenly over it. To create the lattice pattern with the pastry strips, first lay some strips in parallel lines, 1/2 inch (12 mm) apart. Then lay a second row of strips at a 45-degree angle to the first. Press the strips to the edge of the crust to seal.

6. Bake at 350°F (180°C) until the crust is golden brown and the filling is bubbly in the centre, approximately 45 minutes. Set aside to cool.

Approximate values per 1/10-tart serving:

Calories	300
Total fat	29 g
Saturated fat	12 g
Cholesterol	90 mg
Sodium	65 mg
Total carbohydrates	7 g
Protein	4 g
Vitamin A	20%

Claims—low sodium; good source of fibre

◆◆◆

RECIPE 29.15

SHORT CRUST PASTE

Yield: 3 8-inch (20-cm) Shells

Pastry flour	1 lb. 5 oz.	600 g
Butter, cold	8 oz.	250 g
Egg yolks	2	2
Water, cold	8–12 oz.	250–300 mL

1. Combine the flour and butter in a mixer bowl fitted with the paddle attachment. Cut in the butter until the mixture looks like coarse cornmeal.
2. Whisk the egg yolks and 8 ounces (250 mL) water to blend, then add them slowly to the dry ingredients. Blend only until the dough comes together in a ball. If the mixture does not come together, add more water.
3. Remove from the mixer, cover and chill until ready to use.

Approximate values per 8-inch (20-cm) pie shell:

Calories	1361
Total fat	72.7 g
Saturated fat	43.4 g
Cholesterol	0 mg
Sodium	0 mg
Total carbohydrates	156.3 g
Protein	19 g

◆◆◆

RECIPE 29.16

LEMON MERINGUE PIE

Yield: 2 9-inch (22-cm) Pies

Granulated sugar	1 lb. 5 oz.	600 g
Cornstarch	3 oz.	90 g
Salt	pinch	pinch
Water, cold	26 oz.	750 mL
Egg yolks	10	10
Fresh lemon juice	8 oz.	250 mL
Lemon zest, grated	2 Tbsp.	60 mL
Pie shells, prebaked	2	2
Butter	2 Tbsp.	60 g
Egg whites	8 oz.	250 mL
Granulated sugar	8 oz.	250 g

1. To make the filling, combine the 1 pound 5 ounces (600 g) of sugar, cornstarch, salt and water in a heavy saucepan. Cook over medium-high heat, stirring constantly, until the mixture becomes thick and almost clear.
2. Remove from the heat and slowly whisk in the egg yolks. Stir until completely blended. Return to the heat and cook, stirring constantly, until thick and smooth.
3. Stir in the lemon juice and zest. When the liquid is completely incorporated, remove the filling from the heat. Add the butter and stir until melted.
4. Set the filling aside to cool briefly. Fill 2 prebaked pie shells with the lemon filling.
5. To prepare the meringue, whip the egg whites until soft peaks form. Slowly add the 8 ounces (250 g) of sugar while whisking constantly. The meringue should be stiff and glossy, not dry or spongy looking.
6. Mound the meringue over the filling, creating decorative patterns with a spatula. Be sure to spread the meringue to the edge of the crust, so that all of the filling is covered.
7. Place the pie in a 400°F (200°C) oven until the meringue is golden brown, approximately 5–8 minutes. Let cool at room temperature, then refrigerate. Serve the same day.

Approximate values per 1/8-pie serving:

Calories	400
Total fat	12 g
Saturated fat	4 g
Cholesterol	135 mg
Sodium	310 mg
Total carbohydrates	67 g
Protein	5 g
Vitamin C	10%

VARIATION: *Key lime pie*—Substitute 7 ounces (200 mL) key lime juice for the lemon juice and zest. Pour the filling into two prebaked pie shells and chill. Top with whipped cream.

❖❖❖

RECIPE 29.17

BLACKBERRY COBBLER

*A **cobbler** is a home-style baked fruit dessert, usually made with a top crust of flaky pie dough, biscuit dough or streusel topping. The finished product will be slightly runny and is often served warm in a bowl or rimmed dish, accompanied by whipped cream or ice cream.*

Yield: 10 Servings

Individually quick frozen blackberries	2 qt.	2 L
Sugar	8 oz.	250 g
Tapioca	2 oz.	60 g
Water	10 oz.	300 mL
Unsalted butter	2 oz.	60 g
Lemon zest	1 Tbsp.	15 mL
Topping (see Step 3)		

1. Combine all ingredients, tossing the berries gently until well coated with the other ingredients.
2. Transfer to a lightly buttered half-size hotel pan, then set aside for at least 30 minutes before baking.
3. The cobbler can be topped with basic pie dough (about 200 g) (Recipe 29.1), biscuit dough (300–500 g) (Recipe 27.1) or streusel topping (300–500 g) (Recipe 27.6) before baking.
4. Bake at 350°F (180°C) until the berry mixture bubbles and the crust is appropriately browned, approximately 40–50 minutes.

❖❖❖

RECIPE 29.18

PECAN PIE

SOUTHERN ALBERTA INSTITUTE OF TECHNOLOGY, CALGARY, AB
Pastry Chef Albert Liu

Yield: 5 8-inch (20-cm) Pies

Brown sugar	40 oz.	1.125 kg
Corn syrup	40 oz.	1.125 kg
Butter	8 oz.	225 g
Whole eggs	28	28
Vanilla	2 tsp.	10 mL
Pecans, whole	35 oz.	1 kg
Sweet Dough (Recipe 29.2)	52-1/2 oz.	1.5 kg

1. In a saucepan, heat brown sugar, corn syrup and butter and bring to a boil. Remove from heat.
2. Mix the whole eggs and vanilla, then gradually whisk the hot sauce into the egg mixture.
3. Divide the filling evenly among the 5 prepared pie shells. Sprinkle 7 ounces (200 g) of pecans into each pie.
4. Bake at 325°F (160°C) from 45 minutes to 1 hour or until set.

Approximate values per
6 oz. (180 g) serving:

Calories	210
Total fat	5 g
Saturated fat	3 g
Cholesterol	20 mg
Sodium	10 mg
Total carbohydrates	39 g
Protein	1 g
Vitamin C	45%

Albert Liu
Albert began his career as a pâtissier at the Four Seasons Hotel in Vancouver, worked as an Executive Pastry Chef in the Bahamas, and then became the Executive Pastry Chef at the Palliser Hotel in Calgary. Currently he is a Pastry Chef Instructor at SAIT in Calgary.

Approximate values per pie:

Calories	4790
Total fat	257 g
Saturated fat	75 g
Cholesterol	1748 mg
Sodium	756 mg
Total carbohydrates	590 g
Protein	71 g

❖❖❖

RECIPE 29.19

APPLE CUSTARD FLAN

SOUTHERN ALBERTA INSTITUTE OF TECHNOLOGY, CALGARY, AB
Pastry Chef Albert Liu

Yield: 1 8-inch (20-cm) Flan

Sweet Dough (Recipe 29.2)	10-1/2 oz.	300 g
Golden apples	5	5
Whole eggs	2	2
Granulated sugar	2-1/2 oz.	75 g
Cornstarch	1/2 oz.	15 g
Milk, 2%	4 oz.	125 mL
Cream, 35%	4 oz.	125 mL
Vanilla	1/2 tsp.	2 mL
Nutmeg, grated	pinch	pinch

Approximate values per serving:

Calories	253
Total fat	12 g
Saturated fat	7 g
Cholesterol	107 mg
Sodium	29 mg
Total carbohydrates	33 g
Protein	4 g

1. Line the flan tin with the sweet paste. Set aside.
2. Peel and slice the apples.
3. Arrange the apples in the flan, overlapping them in a circle.
4. In a bowl, combine the eggs, sugar and cornstarch.
5. Add the milk, cream, vanilla and nutmeg. Whisk to blend.
6. Pour mixture over apples.
7. Bake at 350°F (170°C) until custard is set, about 45 minutes.

❖❖❖

RECIPE 29.20

FRESH BERRY TART

Yield: 1 9-inch (22-cm) Tart

Sweet Dough tart shell, fully baked (Recipe 29.2)	1	1
Pastry Cream (Recipe 31.2)	1 pt.	500 mL
Fresh berries such as strawberries, blackberries, blueberries or raspberries	3 pt.	1.5 L
Apricot glaze	as needed	as needed

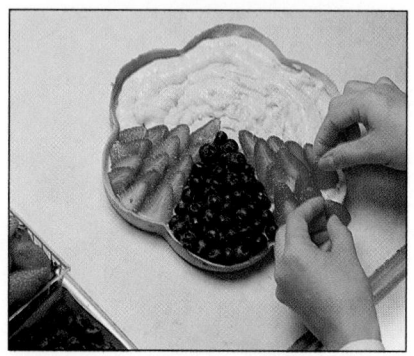

1. Arrange the fruit over the pastry cream.

2. Brush the apricot glaze over the fruit.

1. Fill a cool tart shell with pastry cream.
2. Arrange the berries over the pastry cream in an even layer. Be sure to place the berries so that the pastry cream is covered.
3. Heat the apricot glaze and brush over the fruit to form a smooth coating.

Approximate values per 1/6-tart serving:

Calories	135
Total fat	3 g
Saturated fat	1 g
Cholesterol	2 mg
Sodium	62 g
Total carbohydrates	26 g
Protein	2 g

♦♦♦

RECIPE 29.21

QUICK PUFF PASTRY

ADAPTED FROM *Nick Malgieri's Perfect Pastry*
(New York: Macmillan, 1989)

Yield: 1 lb. 4 oz. (560 g)

Unbleached bread flour	6-1/4 oz.	180 g
Cake flour	1-1/4 oz.	40 g
Unsalted butter	8 oz.	225 g
Salt	1/2 tsp.	2 mL
Water, very cold	4 oz.	120 mL

1. To mix the dough, place the bread flour in a 2-quart (2-L) mixer bowl and sift the cake flour over it. Thoroughly stir the 2 flours together.

2. Slice 1 ounce (30 g) of the butter into thin pieces and add to the bowl. Rub in the butter by hand, tossing and squeezing in the butter until no visible pieces remain.

3. Cut the remaining butter into 1/2-inch (12-mm) cubes. Add the butter cubes to the flour mixture. Toss with a rubber spatula just to separate and distribute the butter. Do not rub the butter into the flour.

4. Dissolve the salt in the water. Make a well in the flour-butter mixture and add the water. Toss gently with the spatula until the dough is evenly moistened. Add drops of water, if necessary, to complete the moistening. Press and squeeze the dough in a bowl to form a rough cylinder.

5. To turn the dough, first lightly flour the work surface and the dough. Using the palm of your hand, press down on the dough 3 or 4 times to shape the dough into a rough rectangle.

6. Press and pound the dough with a rolling pin to form an even rectangle about 1/2 inch (12 mm) thick. Roll the dough back and forth along its length once or twice until it is an even rectangle about 1/4 inch (6 mm) thick. At this stage, pieces of butter are likely to stick to the work surface. If the dough does stick, loosen it with a long spatula or scraper. Clean the surface to minimize further sticking.

7. Fold both ends of the dough in towards the centre, then fold them in towards the centre again to make 4 layers. The folded package of dough will resemble a book, with a spine on one side and the cover opening opposite it. Position the package of dough so that the spine is on the left.

8. Lightly flour the work surface and the dough and repeat the pressing as before. Roll the dough along its length as before, then roll several times along its width to form a rectangle approximately 6 inches × 18 inches (15 × 45 cm). Fold the dough, both ends in towards the centre, then over again as before. Repeat the process once more so that the dough will have 3 double turns.

9. Wrap the dough well in plastic and chill for at least 1 hour before using.

10. The dough can be refrigerated for about 3 days or frozen for up to 1 month. Defrost frozen dough in the refrigerator overnight before using it.

Approximate values per 3 oz. (90 g) serving:	
Calories	480
Total fat	37 g
Saturated fat	23 g
Cholesterol	100 mg
Sodium	240 mg
Total carbohydrates	31 g
Protein	5 g
Vitamin A	35%

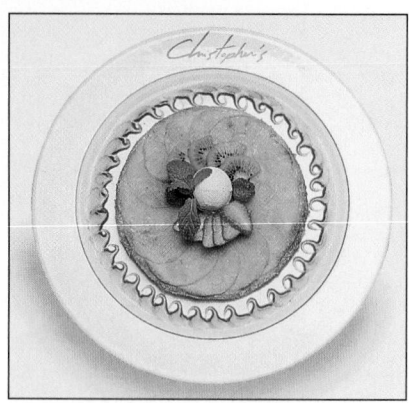

♦♦♦

RECIPE 29.22

APPLE TART
WITH VANILLA ICE CREAM

CHRISTOPHER'S AND CHRISTOPHER'S BISTRO, PHOENIX, AZ
Chef/Owner Christopher Gross

Yield: 8 Servings

Cake flour	9 oz.	270 g
Salt	1/8 tsp.	.5 mL
Unsalted butter, cut into small pieces	4-1/2 oz.	135 g
Egg	1	1
Water, very cold	2 oz.	60 mL
Green apples, peeled, cored and sliced thin	12	12
Unsalted butter, melted	4 oz.	120 g
Granulated sugar	4 oz.	120 g
Caramel sauce (See Recipe 29.25)	as needed	as needed
Vanilla Ice Cream (recipe follows)	as needed	as needed

Approximate values per serving:

Calories	510
Total fat	29 g
Saturated fat	17 g
Cholesterol	160 mg
Sodium	100 mg
Total carbohydrates	57 g
Protein	5 g
Vitamin A	30%
Claims—low sodium	

1. Combine the flour, salt, pieces of butter and egg in a food processor. Process for a few seconds, until the mixture looks like coarse meal.
2. With the processor running, add the cold water. Stop the machine as soon as the dough comes together, then knead briefly by hand if necessary. Do not overmix the dough. Cover the dough and refrigerate for 1 hour.
3. Roll the dough out very thin and cut into 8 circles 7 inches (17 cm) in diameter. Place the dough circles on a sheet pan lined with parchment paper.
4. Arrange the apple slices in a fan pattern on top of the tart dough. Brush with melted butter and top each tart with approximately 1 tablespoon (15 mL) of sugar.
5. Bake at 350°F (180°C) until brown, approximately 10 minutes. Serve warm with caramel sauce and vanilla ice cream.

VANILLA ICE CREAM

Yield: 2 qt. (2 L)

Cereal cream	1 pt.	500 mL
Milk	1 pt.	500 mL
Vanilla bean	1	1
Egg yolks	17	16
Granulated sugar	8 oz.	250 g

Approximate values per serving:

Calories	45
Total fat	2.5 g
Saturated fat	1 g
Cholesterol	60 mg
Sodium	10 mg
Total carbohydrates	4 g
Protein	1 g
Vitamin A	4%

1. Bring the cream, milk and vanilla bean to a boil.
2. Whisk the egg yolks and sugar together in a medium bowl. Temper the eggs with a portion of the hot milk mixture.
3. Return the warmed eggs to the hot milk and cook, stirring constantly, until the custard coats the back of a spoon.
4. Strain, chill and process in an ice cream machine according to the manufacturer's directions.

RECIPE 29.23

FRESH PEACH TART
WITH ALMOND CREAM

VINCENT ON CAMELBACK, Phoenix, AZ
Chef Vincent Guerithault

Yield: 8 Servings

Puff pastry	6 oz.	180 g
Almond Cream (recipe follows)	1 lb. 8 oz.	750 g
Fresh peaches, peeled, pitted and sliced	6–8	6–8
Unsalted butter, melted	3 oz.	90 g
Granulated sugar	2 Tbsp.	30 mL
Powdered sugar	as needed	as needed

1. Roll out the puff pastry into a thin strip, approximately 6 inches × 22 inches (15 cm × 55 cm) (the length of a sheet pan). Lay the dough on a sheet pan lined with parchment paper.

2. Using a large plain tip, pipe 4 rows of almond cream down the length of the puff pastry. Leave a 3/4-inch (18-mm) margin along both long edges of the dough.

3. Arrange the peach slices over the almond cream, overlapping slightly.

4. Brush the peaches with melted butter and evenly sprinkle the granulated sugar over them.

5. Bake at 400°F (200°C) until the dough is done and the peaches are lightly browned, approximately 20–30 minutes.

6. Serve warm, dusted with powdered sugar and accompanied by vanilla ice cream.

Approximate values per serving:

Calories	140
Total fat	9 g
Saturated fat	5 g
Cholesterol	25 mg
Sodium	0 mg
Total carbohydrates	15 g
Protein	1 g
Vitamin A	10%

ALMOND CREAM (FRANGIPANE)

Yield: 3 lb. (1.3 kg)

Unsalted butter, softened	8 oz.	225 g
Granulated sugar	1 lb.	450 g
Eggs	8 oz.	225 g
All-purpose flour	5 oz.	150 g
Almonds, ground	12 oz.	360 g

1. Cream the butter and sugar. Slowly add the eggs, scraping down the sides of the bowl as necessary.

2. Stir the flour and ground almonds together, then add to the butter mixture. Blend until no lumps remain.

3. Almond cream may be stored under refrigeration up to 3 weeks.

Approximate values per 1 oz. (30 g) serving:

Calories	140
Total fat	8 g
Saturated fat	3 g
Cholesterol	30 mg
Sodium	5 mg
Total carbohydrates	13 g
Protein	2 g

RECIPE 29.24
STRAWBERRY NAPOLEON

Yield: 10 Servings

Puff pastry, cut into 4-inch × 15-inch (10-cm × 37-cm) strips, docked and baked	3	3
Pastry Cream (Recipe 31.2)	1 pt.	500 mL
Fresh strawberries, sliced	1 qt.	1 L
Crème Chantilly (Recipe 31.6)	1 pt.	500 mL
Sugar Glaze (Recipe 30.13)	as needed	as needed
Dark chocolate, melted	1 oz.	30 g

1. Allow the puff pastry to cool completely before assembling.
2. Place a strip of puff pastry on a cake cardboard for support. Pipe on a layer of pastry cream, leaving a clean margin of almost 1/2 inch (12 mm) on all 4 sides.
3. Top the cream with a layer of berries.
4. Spread on a thin layer of crème Chantilly. Repeat the procedure for the second layer of puff pastry.
5. Chill while you prepare the sugar glaze. When ready to glaze, place the third strip of puff pastry on an icing rack, flat side up. Pour the sugar glaze down the length of the pastry and spread evenly with a metal cake spatula. Allow the excess to drip over the sides.
6. Immediately pipe thin lines of chocolate across the glaze. Use a toothpick to pull a spiderweb pattern in the glaze. Chill to set the glaze, then place the top in position on the napoleon.

Approximate values per 5 oz. (150 g) serving:

Calories	320
Total fat	20 g
Saturated fat	9 g
Cholesterol	115 mg
Sodium	65 mg
Total carbohydrates	29 g
Protein	4 g
Vitamin A	15%
Vitamin C	60%

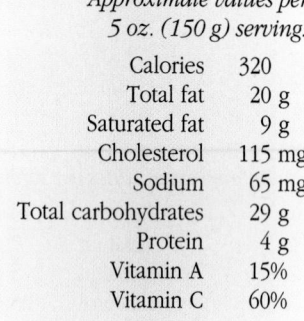

RECIPE 29.25
CRÈME BRÛLÉE NAPOLEONS WITH HAZELNUTS

CITRUS, LOS ANGELES, CA
Chef Michel Richard

Yield: 8 Servings

Crème Brûlée (recipe follows)		
Caramel Sauce (recipe follows)		
Hazelnuts	6 oz.	180 g
Granulated sugar	6 oz.	180 g
Phyllo dough, defrosted	8 sheets	8 sheets
Unsalted butter, melted	4 oz.	120 g
Powdered sugar	2 oz.	60 g

1. Prepare the crème brulée and caramel sauce up to 2 days in advance; refrigerate.
2. Place the hazelnuts on a small baking sheet and toast in a 350°F (180°C) oven until brown, approximately 15 minutes. Rub the nuts in a sieve or dry towel to remove their skins.

3. Coarsely grind the nuts with the sugar in a food processor, pulsing on/off.

4. For the pastry, line 2 large baking sheets with parchment paper. Unroll the phyllo dough and remove 1 sheet; cover the remaining phyllo with plastic wrap and a damp towel. Brush the sheet with melted butter and sprinkle generously with the hazelnut-sugar mixture. Top with a second sheet of phyllo, pressing to seal. Brush with butter and sprinkle with the nut mixture. Repeat with a third and fourth sheet.

5. Using a ruler as a guide, trim the edges of the phyllo dough with a knife or pastry wheel to form a 12-inch × 16-inch (30-cm × 40-cm) rectangle. Cut the pastry into 3 strips lengthwise and 4 strips crosswise, forming 12 4-inch (10-cm) squares.

6. Transfer the squares to prepared baking sheets in a single layer using a large spatula. Bake until brown, approximately 10 minutes.

7. Make and bake 12 more 4-inch (10 cm) squares using the remaining phyllo, butter and nut mixture.

8. Place as many phyllo squares as will fit under a broiler on a baking sheet. Sieve powdered sugar generously over the squares. Watching carefully, broil the squares several inches below the heat source until golden brown, approximately 1 minute. Transfer to racks in a single layer. Repeat with the remaining squares.

9. To serve, divide the crème brûlée among the 16 pastry squares, nut side up, spreading evenly. Make 8 napoleons by stacking 2 crème brûlée-filled squares and topping with 1 unfilled square, nut side down. Place the napoleons in the centre of 8 large plates.

10. Reheat the caramel sauce and ladle around the napoleons. Serve immediately.

Approximate values per serving:

Calories	805
Total fat	53 g
Saturated fat	24 g
Cholesterol	155 mg
Sodium	125 mg
Total carbohydrates	83 g
Protein	6 g

CRÈME BRÛLÉE

Yield: 1 pt. (500 mL)

Milk	4 oz.	120 mL
Cream, 35%	1 pt.	500 mL
Granulated sugar	4 oz.	120 g
Vanilla beans, slit lengthwise	1 or 2	1 or 2
Egg yolks, blended with a fork	2	2

1. Place the milk, cream and sugar in a heavy medium saucepan. Scrape the seeds from the vanilla beans into the milk mixture. Add the beans and bring to a boil over medium-high heat. Remove from the heat and let the beans **steep** for at least 1 hour or until the mixture cools to room temperature.

2. To prepare the water bath, place a 9 × 13 inch (22 × 32 cm) baking dish in a larger baking pan. Pour enough water into the larger pan to come three-quarters of the way up the sides of the baking dish. Remove the baking dish and place the baking pan of water in an oven to preheat.

3. Whisk the egg yolks into the cooled custard mixture. Strain through a fine sieve into the baking dish.

4. Place the baking dish of custard into the baking pan of water and bake at 300°F (150°C) until the custard is set and a knife inserted into the centre comes out dry, approximately 45 minutes to 1 hour. Remove the baking dish from the water bath. Cool, then cover and refrigerate until 15 minutes before assembling the napoleons.

Steep—*to soak food in a hot liquid in order to either extract its flavour or soften its texture.*

Approximate values per serving:

Calories	299
Total fat	25 g
Saturated fat	15 g
Cholesterol	141 mg
Sodium	33 mg
Total carbohydrates	18 g
Protein	3 g

Continued

CARAMEL SAUCE

Yield: 14 oz. (420 mL)

Granulated sugar	12 oz.	360 g
Water	as needed	as needed
Cream, 35%	10 oz.	300 mL

Approximate values per serving:

Calories	304
Total fat	14 g
Saturated fat	9 g
Cholesterol	52 mg
Sodium	15 mg
Total carbohydrates	46 g
Protein	1 g

1. Place the sugar in a heavy medium saucepan. Cover with water and cook over low heat until the sugar dissolves, occasionally swirling the pan.
2. Increase the heat and boil until the sugar caramelizes and turns a deep mahogany brown. Watch carefully so that the mixture does not burn.
3. Standing back to avoid splatters, gradually pour in the cream. Simmer the sauce, stirring occasionally, until the caramel dissolves and the sauce is smooth and thick, approximately 3 minutes. Cool and refrigerate.

◆◆◆

RECIPE 29.26

PALMIERS

Puff pastry	as needed
Granulated sugar	as needed

Approximate values per 1 oz. (30 g) serving:

Calories	130
Total fat	5 g
Saturated fat	1 g
Cholesterol	0 mg
Sodium	35 mg
Total carbohydrates	19 g
Protein	1 g

1. Roll out the puff pastry into a very thin rectangle. The length is not important but the width should be at least 7 inches (17.5 cm).
2. Sprinkle puff pastry sheet lightly with granulated sugar. Using a rolling pin, gently press the granulated sugar into the dough. Flip over and repeat.
3. Along the long edges of the dough make a 1-inch (2.5-cm) fold towards the centre. Sprinkle on additional sugar.
4. Make another 1-inch (2.5-cm) fold along the long edges towards the centre. The two folds should almost meet in the centre. Sprinkle on additional sugar.
5. Fold one side on top of the other. Press down gently with a rolling pin or your fingers so that the dough adheres. Chill for 1 hour.
6. Cut the log of dough in thin slices. Place the cookies on a paper-lined sheet pan and bake at 400°F (200°C) until the edges are brown, approximately 8–12 minutes.

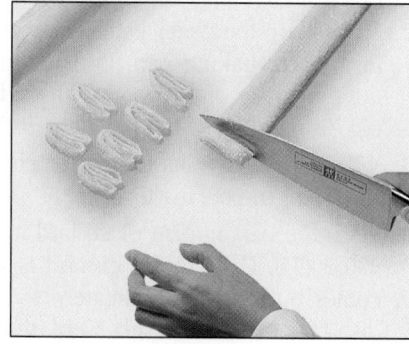

1. Fold the dough towards the centre from both edges.

2. Slice the log of dough into individual cookies.

♦♦♦

RECIPE 29.27
CHOCOLATE ÉCLAIRS

Yield: 20 Éclairs

Baked éclair shells, 4 inches (10 cm) long, made from Basic Choux Paste (Recipe 29.9)	20	20
Pastry Cream (Recipe 31.2), vanilla flavoured	1 qt.	1 L
Chocolate glaze:		
Unsweetened chocolate	4 oz.	120 g
Semisweet chocolate	4 oz.	120 g
Unsalted butter	4 oz.	120 g
White corn syrup	4 tsp.	20 mL
White chocolate, melted (optional)	as needed	as needed

1. Use a paring knife or skewer to cut a small hole into the end of each baked, cooled éclair shell.
2. Pipe the pastry cream into each shell using a piping bag fitted with a small plain tip. Be sure that the cream fills the full length of each shell. Refrigerate the filled éclairs.
3. Prepare the glaze by melting all ingredients together over a bain marie. Remove from the heat and allow to cool, occasionally stirring, until slightly thickened.
4. In a single, smooth stroke, dip the top of each filled éclair through the glaze. Only the very top of each pastry should be coated with chocolate.
5. Melted white chocolate may be piped onto the wet glaze, then pulled into patterns using a toothpick. (See sauce-pulling techniques in Chapter 35, Plate Presentation.) Keep finished éclairs refrigerated and serve within 8–12 hours.

1. Fill the éclairs with pastry cream using a piping bag.

2. Dip the éclairs in chocolate glaze.

Approximate values per 3 oz. (90 g) serving:	
Calories	410
Total fat	31 g
Saturated fat	17 g
Cholesterol	110 mg
Sodium	230 mg
Total carbohydrates	27 g
Protein	5 g
Vitamin A	20%

♦♦♦

RECIPE 29.28
CHOCOLATE DÉLICE

Yield: 1 8-inch (20-cm) Cake

Classic Dacquoise (recipe follows)
Ganache (recipe follows)
Crème Chantilly (recipe follows)
Candied Almonds (recipe follows)

1. Spread an even layer of ganache over 2 of the dacquoise disks.
2. Top 1 disk with about 6 oz. (180 mL) of crème Chantilly. Place the second disk on top, chocolate side up. Top with another 6 oz. (180 mL) of crème Chantilly. Position the third disk on top, flat side up.
3. Spread the remaining crème Chantilly over the top and sides.
4. Sprinkle candied almonds over the top and sides of the cake.
5. Freeze to firm the cream, approximately 1 hour. Remove from freezer and refrigerate for service.

Approximate values per 1/8-cake serving:	
Calories	490
Total fat	32.5 g
Saturated fat	13 g
Cholesterol	50 mg
Sodium	35 mg
Total carbohydrates	39 g
Protein	10 g
Vitamin A	16%

Continued

CLASSIC DACQUOISE

Blanched almonds	2 oz.	60 g
Granulated sugar	6 oz.	180 g
Egg whites	3 oz.	90 g

1. Preheat oven to 225°F (110°C). Line a baking sheet with parchment. Draw 3 8-inch (20-cm) circles on the parchment.
2. Grind the nuts in a food processor. They should be the consistency of cornmeal and as dry as possible. Combine with 2 ounces (60 g) of the sugar and set aside.
3. Whip the egg whites on medium speed until foamy. Increase the speed and gradually add 1 ounce (30 g) of the sugar.
4. Continue whipping until the egg whites form soft peaks. Gradually add the remaining 3 ounces (90 g) of sugar.
5. Continue whipping until smooth and glossy, about 2 minutes.
6. Sprinkle the almond-sugar mixture over the meringue and fold together by hand using a spatula.
7. Using a pastry bag with a plain tip and the circles on the parchment paper as a guide, pipe the meringue into 3 8-inch (20-cm) disks.
8. Bake until firm and crisp but not brown, approximately 60–75 minutes. Cool completely.

GANACHE

Semisweet chocolate	4 oz.	120 g
Cream, 35%	3 oz.	90 mL

1. Chop the chocolate into small pieces and place in a bowl.
2. Heat the cream just to boiling. Pour the cream over the chocolate and stir until the mixture is glossy and smooth. Allow to cool slightly before using.

CRÈME CHANTILLY

Cream, 35%	1 qt.	1 L
Sugar	3 oz.	90 g
Vanilla extract	1 tsp.	5 mL

Whip the ingredients together until soft peaks form.

CANDIED ALMONDS

Egg whites	2	2
Granulated sugar	2 oz.	60 g
Sliced almonds	8 oz.	250 g

1. Preheat oven to 325°F (160°C).
2. Whisk the egg whites and sugar together. Add the almonds. Toss with a rubber spatula to coat the nuts completely.
3. Spread the nuts in a thin layer on a lightly greased baking sheet. Bake until lightly toasted and dry, approximately 15–20 minutes. Watch closely to prevent burning.
4. Stir the nuts with a metal spatula every 5–7 minutes during baking.
5. Cool completely. Store in an air-tight container for up to 10 days.

Approximate values per serving:

Calories	100
Total fat	2.5 g
Saturated fat	0 g
Cholesterol	0 mg
Sodium	15 mg
Total carbohydrates	16 g
Protein	2 g

Claims—low fat; no saturated fat; no cholesterol; very low sodium

Approximate values per serving:

Calories	130
Total fat	10 g
Saturated fat	6 g
Cholesterol	15 mg
Sodium	0 mg
Total carbohydrates	10 g
Protein	1 g
Vitamin A	6%

Approximate values per serving:

Calories	100
Total fat	10 g
Saturated fat	6 g
Cholesterol	35 mg
Sodium	10 mg
Total carbohydrates	3 g
Protein	1 g
Vitamin A	10%

Approximate values per serving:

Calories	160
Total fat	10 g
Saturated fat	1 g
Cholesterol	0 mg
Sodium	10 mg
Total carbohydrates	10 g
Protein	6 g

Claims—low saturated fat; no cholesterol; very low sodium

◆◆◆

RECIPE 29.29

MADELEINES

Yield: 15 Large Cookies

Unsalted butter	4 oz.	120 g
Eggs	2	2
Sugar	3 oz.	90 g
Lemon zest, grated fine	1 tsp.	5 mL
Lemon juice	1/4 tsp.	1 mL
Vanilla extract	1/4 tsp.	1 mL
Baking powder	1/8 tsp.	0.5 mL
Cake flour, sifted	3 oz.	90 g

1. Melt the butter over medium heat; continue cooking until the milk solids turn a golden-brown colour. Set aside to cool.

2. Whisk the eggs and sugar over a bain marie until warm (98°F/38°C). Remove from the heat and whisk in the lemon zest, lemon juice and vanilla.

3. Sift the baking powder and flour together; stir into the egg mixture. Stir in the melted and cooled butter. Cover the bowl and allow to rest for 1 hour at room temperature.

4. Butter and flour the madeleine shells. Spoon the batter into the shells, filling each three-quarters full.

5. Bake at 450°F (230°C) until the cookies rise in the centre and are very light brown on the bottom and edges, approximately 3–4 minutes for 1-1/2-inch (3.7-cm) madeleines and 10–12 minutes for 3-inch (7.5-cm) madeleines. They should spring back when touched lightly in the centre. Remove the madeleines from the oven, invert the pan over a wire cooling rack, and tap lightly to release the cookies from the pan.

NOTE: Madeleine shells are a type of sponge cake baked in small scallop-shaped forms and eaten like a cookie.

Approximate values per cookie:

Calories	110
Total fat	7 g
Saturated fat	4 g
Cholesterol	45 mg
Sodium	10 mg
Total carbohydrates	10 g
Protein	1 g
Vitamin A	6%

◆◆◆

RECIPE 29.30

SUGAR COOKIES

Yield: 3 Dozen   **Method:** Cut-out Cookies

Pastry flour	12 oz.	360 g
Baking powder	2 tsp.	10 mL
Mace, ground	1/4 tsp.	1 mL
Unsalted butter, softened	4 oz.	120 g
Granulated sugar	8 oz.	250 g
Vanilla extract	1 tsp.	5 mL
Egg	1	1

1. Stir together the flour, baking powder and mace. Set aside.

2. Cream the butter and sugar until light and fluffy. Blend in the vanilla. Add the egg and beat again until fluffy. Gradually add the flour mixture, beating just until well combined.

Continued

Approximate values per cookie:

Calories	90
Total fat	3 g
Saturated fat	1.5 g
Cholesterol	15 mg
Sodium	0 mg
Total carbohydrates	14 g
Protein	1 g

Claims—low fat; low cholesterol; no sodium

3. Wrap the dough in plastic wrap and refrigerate until firm, about 1–2 hours.

4. Work with about half the dough at a time, keeping the remainder refrigerated. On a lightly floured board, roll out the dough to a thickness of about 1/8 inch (3 mm). Cut as desired with cookie cutters. Carefully transfer the cookies to lightly greased baking sheets.

5. Bake at 325°F (160°C) until golden brown, approximately 10–12 minutes. Let stand for about 1 minute, then transfer to wire racks to cool.

◆◆◆

RECIPE 29.31

SPRITZ COOKIES

Yield: 7 Dozen   **Method:** Pressed Cookies

Unsalted butter, softened	8 oz.	250 g
Granulated sugar	4 oz.	120 g
Salt	1/4 tsp.	1 mL
Vanilla extract	1 tsp.	5 mL
Egg	1	1
Cake flour, sifted	10 oz.	300 g

1. Cream the butter and sugar until light and fluffy. Add the salt, vanilla and egg; beat well.

2. Gradually add the flour, beating until just blended. The dough should be firm but neither sticky nor stiff.

3. Press or pipe the dough onto an ungreased sheet pan using a cookie press or a piping bag fitted with a large star tip.

4. Bake at 350°F (175°C) until lightly browned around edges, approximately 10 minutes. Transfer to wire racks to cool.

Approximate values per cookie:

Calories	40
Total fat	2.5 g
Saturated fat	1.5 g
Cholesterol	10 mg
Sodium	10 mg
Total carbohydrates	4 g
Protein	0 g

Claims—low fat; low cholesterol; very low sodium; low calories

◆◆◆

RECIPE 29.32

ALMOND TULIP MIX

Yield: Varies according to template

Almond paste	17-1/2 oz.	500 g
Sugar	7 oz.	200 g
Egg whites	10 oz.	275 g
Salt	pinch	pinch
Vanilla	dash	dash
Cinnamon	pinch	pinch
Lemon juice	1 tsp.	5 mL
Cream, 35%	4 oz.	125 mL
Bread flour	10-1/2 oz.	300 g

1. Beat the almond paste, sugar and egg whites until smooth. Add the salt, vanilla, cinnamon, lemon juice and cream and beat until smooth.

2. Add the flour and mix until smooth and free of lumps.

3. Let the batter rest for an hour or overnight.

4. Spread the mixture into a template to give it a shape. Bake at 400°F (200°C) until the edges are brown and the dough is dry, approximately 12–18 minutes.

Approximate values per 1 oz. (30 g) serving:

Calories	92
Total fat	4 g
Saturated fat	1 g
Cholesterol	3 mg
Sodium	19 mg
Total carbohydrates	13 g
Protein	3 g

❖❖❖

RECIPE 29.33
BRANDY HORNS

Yield: 100 Horns

Granulated sugar	3-2/3 cups	780 g
Yellow sugar	4-1/4 cups	780 g
Butter	10 oz.	270 g
Bread flour	4-1/3 cups	570 g
Brandy flavour	1 oz.	30 mL
Water	as needed	as needed

1. Cream the sugars and butter together, then add the flour and brandy flavour. Mix at medium speed for about 5 minutes to form a paste.

2. Add the water to make the mixture of a suitable consistency for piping, similar to choux pastry.

3. Pipe or spoon an amount of mixture no larger than 1/2 inch (1 cm) on to a silicone sheeted pan. (Mixture will spread to a circle 4–6 inches [10–15 cm] in diameter.)

4. Bake at 400°F (200°C) until mixture spreads and is bubbly. Edges should begin to appear crisp.

5. Remove from oven and shape over a cream horn tube, a dowel or rod, or over a cup or glass (to form a basket). If desired, shape hot cookies with a cutter to form perfect circles.

Approximate values per serving:

Calories	99
Total fat	2 g
Saturated fat	1 g
Cholesterol	6 mg
Sodium	3 mg
Total carbohydrates	19 g
Protein	1 g

❖❖❖

RECIPE 29.34
BANANA BUTTER TART WITH BITTER CHOCOLATE SORBET AND RUM AND RAISIN CRÈME ANGLAISE

WINSTON'S, TORONTO, ON
Pastry Chef Dean Cole

Yield: 12 servings

Cinnamon Sable Paste (recipe follows)
Butter Mix (recipe follows)
Bananas (3, sliced); sugar to glaze
Rum and Raisin Crème Anglaise (recipe follows)
Bitter Chocolate Sorbet (recipe follows)
Banana Wafers (recipe follows)

1. Prepare shells using Cinnamon Sable Paste.

2. Pour Butter Mix into shells and bake at 250°F (120°C) until set, about 15 minutes. Do not let the filling boil.

3. When filling is cold, layer thin slices of banana on top. Sprinkle with sugar and caramelize.

4. Mirror the centre of a plate with Rum and Raisin Crème Anglaise and place the butter tart in the centre.

5. Top the tart with a rounded scoop of Bitter Chocolate Sorbet.

Dean Cole
Dean trained first in Birmingham, England, where he won the "Taste of Britain" competition and Chef of the Year in 1989. He spent 3 years at the Connaught Hotel in London, specializing in patisserie. Dean moved to Toronto in 1995 and now is the Pastry Chef at the new Winston's in Toronto. He likes to teach demonstration classes in his spare time.

Approximate values per serving:

Calories	1126
Total fat	68 g
Saturated fat	40 g
Cholesterol	307 mg
Sodium	149 mg
Total carbohydrates	133 g
Protein	14 g

Continued

6. Place a Banana Wafer in the centre of the scoop, pointed side down.

7. Garnish with 2 mint leaves and serve immediately.

CINNAMON SABLE PASTE

Yield: 12 tart shells

Flour, pastry	9 oz.	270 g
Cinnamon	1/4 oz.	7 g
Sugar	3 oz.	90 g
Butter	6 oz.	180 g
Egg yolks	2	2

Approximate values per tart shell:

Calories	220
Total fat	13 g
Saturated fat	8 g
Cholesterol	67 mg
Sodium	4 mg
Total carbohydrates	24 g
Protein	2 g

1. Using the blender's paddle attachment at low speed, cut in flour, cinnamon, sugar and butter until fine crumb stage is reached.

2. Add yolks and mix just until evenly blended.

3. Place mixture on a floured surface and cream with the palm of the hand until the paste has a soft, smooth consistency.

4. Chill for several hours.

5. Line 12 3-1/2-inch (9-cm) metal rings with paste and bake at 350°F (175°C) for 7 minutes to set.

BUTTER MIX

Golden brown sugar	14 oz.	420 g
Dark corn syrup	12 oz.	360 g
Salt	1/2 tsp.	3 mL
Cinnamon	2 tsp.	10 mL
Ginger	1 tsp.	5 mL
Eggs, whole	4	4
Butter, melted	10 oz.	300 g

Approximate values per 1 oz. (30 g) serving:

Calories	109
Total fat	6 g
Saturated fat	3 g
Cholesterol	33 mg
Sodium	62 mg
Total carbohydrates	15 g
Protein	.6 g

1. Using the blender's paddle attachment at low speed, mix together brown sugar, corn syrup, salt, cinnamon and ginger until blended.

2. With machine running, add eggs 1 at a time.

3. Pour melted butter into mixture and mix thoroughly.

RUM AND RAISIN CRÈME ANGLAISE

Raisins	3 oz.	75 g
Rum	2 oz.	50 mL
Egg yolks	5	5
Sugar	2 oz.	50 g
Milk	8-1/2 oz.	250 mL
Cream, 35%	6 oz.	175 mL
Vanilla bean	1	1
Sugar	1/4 cup	50 g

Approximate values per 1 oz. (30 g) serving:

Calories	69
Total fat	4 g
Saturated fat	2 g
Total carbohydrates	7 g
Protein	1 g

1. Boil raisins in water for 1 minute.

2. Strain and add rum. Set aside.

3. Whisk together egg yolks and sugar until white and thick.

4. Scald milk, cream, vanilla bean and sugar. Infuse vanilla for 5 minutes and rescald.

5. Temper the egg mixture with the infused liquid.

6. Transfer to a clean saucepan and cook over low heat, stirring constantly until the mixture coats the back of a wooden spoon (rose stage).

7. Strain and chill quickly and thoroughly over ice.

8. Add rum-flavoured raisins.

BITTER CHOCOLATE SORBET

Cocoa powder	2 oz.	60 g
Sugar	10 oz.	280 g
Water	27 oz.	800 mL
Dark chocolate, chopped	1 lb. 2 oz.	500 g

1. Make a syrup by heating cocoa powder, sugar and water and stirring until the liquid comes to a boil.

2. Add chopped chocolate to the syrup and stir until melted. Chill over an ice bath.

3. Freeze in an ice cream freezer.

Approximate values per 1 oz. (30 g) serving:

Calories	66
Total fat	5 g
Saturated fat	3 g
Cholesterol	0 mg
Sodium	2 mg
Total carbohydrates	8 g
Protein	1 g

BANANA WAFER

Bananas, ripe	2	2
Honey	1 oz.	30 g

1. Purée banana.

2. Pass the banana purée through a fine sieve and add the honey.

3. Using a template with 5-inch (12-cm) circles, pour the mixture onto parchment paper. Each wafer should be about 1/16-inch (2-mm) thick.

4. Dry in the oven at 180°F (82°C) until golden brown.

5. Remove one by one and fold in half to form an open-fan shape.

6. If wafers harden, return them to the oven.

7. Store in a sealed container until ready to use.

Approximate values per 1 oz. (30 g) serving:

Calories	39
Total fat	.1 g
Saturated fat	.1 g
Cholesterol	0 mg
Sodium	.5 mg
Total carbohydrates	10 g
Protein	.2 g

WEBLINKS

The Pie Page
   www.teleport.com/~psyched/pie/pie.html

Baker Boulanger—Pie Crust Primer
   www.betterbaking.com/pieprimermeth.html

Tarts
   www.joyofbaking.com/tarts.html

CHAPTER 30

CAKES AND FROSTINGS

Cakes are popular in most bakeshops because a wide variety of finished products can be created from only a few basic cake, filling and frosting formulas. Many of these components can even be made in advance and assembled into finished desserts as needed. Cakes are also popular because of their versatility: They can be served as unadorned sheets in a high-volume cafeteria or as the elaborate centrepiece of a wedding buffet.

Cake making need not be difficult or intimidating, but it does require an understanding of ingredients and mixing methods. This chapter begins by explaining how typical cake ingredients interact. Each of the traditional mixing methods is then explained and illustrated with a recipe. Information on panning batters, baking temperatures, determining doneness and cooling methods follows. The second portion of this chapter presents mixing methods and formulas for a variety of frostings and icings. The third section covers cake assembly and presents some simple and commonly used cake decorating techniques. A selection of popular cake formulas concludes the chapter.

Chapter 29 covers Pies, Pastries and Cookies; Chapter 31 covers Custards, Creams, Frozen Desserts and Dessert Sauces. Some of the desserts presented in those chapters use cake or frosting formulas presented here.

CAKES

Most cakes are created from liquid batters with high fat and sugar contents. The baker's job is to combine all of the ingredients to create a structure that will support these rich ingredients, yet keep the cake as light and delicate as possible. As with other baked goods, it is impossible to taste a cake until it is fully baked and too late to alter the formula. Therefore, it is extremely important to study any formula before beginning and to follow it with particular care and attention to detail.

Ingredients

Good cakes begin with high-quality ingredients (see Chapter 26, Principles of the Bakeshop). However, even the finest ingredients must be combined in the proper balance. Too much flour and the cake may be dry; too much egg and the cake will be tough and hard. Changing one ingredient may necessitate a change in one or more of the other ingredients.

Each ingredient performs a specific function and has a specific effect on the final product. Cake ingredients can be classified by function as tougheners, tenderizers, moisteners, driers, leaveners and flavourings. Some ingredients fulfil more than one of these functions. For example, eggs contain water, so they are moisteners, and they contain protein, so they are tougheners. By understanding the function of various ingredients you should be able to understand why cakes are made in particular ways and why a preparation sometimes fails. With additional experience, you should be able to recognize and correct flawed formulas and develop your own cake formulas.

Tougheners

Flour, milk and eggs contain protein. Protein provides structure and toughens the cake. Too little protein and the cake may collapse; too much protein and the cake may be tough and coarse-textured.

Tenderizers

Sugar, fats and egg yolks shorten gluten strands, making the cake tender and soft. These ingredients also improve the cake's keeping qualities.

Moisteners

Liquids such as water, milk, juice and eggs bring moisture to the mixture. Moisture is necessary for gluten formation and starch gelatinization, as well as improving a cake's keeping qualities.

Driers

Flour, starches and milk solids absorb moisture, giving body and structure to the cake.

Leaveners

Cakes rise because gases in the batter expand when heated. Cakes are leavened by the air trapped when fat and sugar are creamed together, by carbon dioxide released from baking powder and baking soda and by air trapped in beaten eggs. All cakes rely on natural leaveners—steam and air—to create the proper texture and rise. Because baking soda and baking powder are also used in some cake formulas, you should review the material on chemical leaveners in Chapter 27, Quick Breads.

Flavourings

Flavourings such as extracts, cocoa, chocolate, spices, salt, sugar and butter provide cakes with the desired flavours. Acidic flavouring ingredients such as sour cream, chocolate and fruit also provide the acid necessary to activate baking soda.

Cake ingredients should be at room temperature, approximately 70°F (21°C), before mixing begins. If one ingredient is too cold or too warm it may affect the batter's ability to trap and hold the gases necessary for the cake to rise.

Mixing Methods

Even the finest ingredients will be wasted if the cake batter is not mixed correctly. When mixing any cake batter your goals are to combine the ingredients uniformly, incorporate air cells and develop the proper texture.

All mixing methods can be divided into two categories: *high fat*—those that create a structure that relies primarily on **creamed fat** (air) and flour, and *egg foam*—those that create a structure that relies primarily on **whipped eggs** (air) and flour. Within these broad categories are several mixing methods or types of cakes. Creamed-fat cakes include **butter cakes** (also known as **creaming method cakes**) and **high-ratio cakes**. Whipped-egg cakes include

TABLE 30.1 CAKES

Category	Mixing Method/Type of Cake	Key Formula Characteristics	Texture
Creamed fat (high fat)	Butter (creaming method)	High-fat formula; chemical leavener used	Fine grain; air cells of uniform size; moist crumb; thin and tender crust
	High-ratio (two-stage)	Emulsified shortening; two-part mixing method	Very fine grain; moist crumb; relatively high rise
Whipped egg (egg foam)	Genoise	Whole eggs are whipped with sugar; no chemical leaveners	Dry and spongy
	Sponge	Egg yolks are mixed with other ingredients, then whipped egg whites are folded in	Moister and more tender than genoise
	Angel food	No fat; large quantity of whipped egg whites; high percentage of sugar	Tall, light and fluffy
	Chiffon	Vegetable oil used; egg yolks mixed with other ingredients, then whipped egg whites folded in; baking powder may be added	Tall, light and fluffy; moister and richer than angel food

genoise, **spongecakes**, **angel food cakes** and **chiffon cakes**. See Table 30.1. Although certain general procedures are used to prepare each cake type, there are, of course, variations. Follow specific formula instructions precisely.

Creamed Fat

Creamed-fat cakes include most of the popular North American-style cakes: poundcakes, layer cakes, coffeecakes and even brownies. All are based on high-fat formulas containing chemical leaveners. A good high-fat cake has a fine grain, cells of uniform size and a crumb that is moist rather than crumbly. Crusts should be thin and tender.

Creamed-fat cakes can be divided into two classes: butter cakes and high-ratio cakes.

Butter Cakes

Butter cakes, also known as creaming method cakes, begin with softened butter or shortening creamed to incorporate air cells. Because of their high fat content, these cakes usually need the assistance of a chemical leavener to achieve the proper rise.

Modern-day butter cakes—the classic layer cakes, popular for birthdays and special occasions—are made with the creaming method. These cakes are tender yet sturdy enough to handle rich buttercreams or fillings. High-fat cakes are too soft and delicate, however, to use for roll cakes or to slice into extremely thin layers.

When making butter cakes, the fat should be creamed at low to moderate speeds to prevent raising its temperature. An increased temperature could cause a loss of air cells.

BASIC PROCEDURE FOR PREPARING BUTTER (CREAMING METHOD) CAKES

1. Preheat the oven and prepare the pans.
2. Sift the dry ingredients together and set aside.

♦♦♦
POUNDCAKES

Poundcakes are the original high-fat, creaming method cake. They are called poundcakes because early formulas specified one pound each of butter, eggs, flour and sugar. Poundcakes should have a close grain and compact texture but still be very tender. They should be neither heavy nor soggy.

As bakers experimented with poundcake formulas they reduced the amount of eggs and fat, substituting milk instead. These changes led to the development of the modern butter cake.

3. Add the sugar and cream the mixture until it is light and fluffy. Add the sugar and cream until the mixture is fluffy and smooth.
4. Add the eggs slowly, beating well after each addition.
5. Add the dry and liquid ingredients alternately. Start with flour and finish with flour.
6. Divide the batter into prepared pans and bake immediately.

RECIPE 30.1
CLASSIC POUNDCAKE

Yield: 2 12 × 4-inch (30 × 10-cm) Loaves   **Method:** Creaming

Cake flour	1 lb.	500 g
Baking powder	2 tsp.	10 mL
Salt	1/2 tsp.	2 mL
Unsalted butter, softened	1 lb.	500 g
Granulated sugar	12 oz.	340 g
Eggs	16 oz.	500 g
Vanilla extract	1 tsp.	5 mL
Lemon extract	1 tsp.	5 mL

1. Sift the cake flour, baking powder and salt together; set aside.
2. Cream the butter and sugar until light and fluffy. Add the eggs one at a time, beating well after each addition. Stir in the extracts.
3. Fold in the dry ingredients by hand. Divide the batter into greased loaf pans.
4. Bake at 325°F (160°C) until golden brown and springy to the touch, approximately 1 hour and 10 minutes.

VARIATION: *French-style fruitcake:* Add 6 ounces (180 g) finely diced nuts, raisins and candied fruit to the batter. Substitute vanilla extract for the lemon extract and add 3 tablespoons (45 mL) rum to the batter. After baking, brush the warm cake with additional rum.

Approximate values per 3 oz. (90 g) serving:

Calories	350
Total fat	21 g
Saturated fat	12 g
Cholesterol	145 mg
Sodium	90 mg
Total carbohydrates	35 g
Protein	5 g
Vitamin A	20%

1. Cream the butter.

2. Fold in the flour.

3. Pan the batter.

High-Ratio Cakes

Commercial bakers often use a special two-stage mixing method to prepare large quantities of a very liquid cake batter. These formulas require emulsified shortenings and are known as two-stage cakes because the liquids are added in two stages or portions. If emulsified shortenings are not available, do not substitute all-purpose shortening or butter as they cannot absorb the large amounts of sugar and liquid in the formula.

Because they contain a high ratio of sugar and liquid to flour, these cakes are often known as high-ratio cakes. They have a very fine, moist crumb and relatively high rise. High-ratio cakes are almost indistinguishable from modern butter cakes and may be used interchangeably.

BASIC PROCEDURE FOR PREPARING HIGH-RATIO CAKES

1. Preheat the oven and prepare the pans.
2. Place all the dry ingredients and emulsified shortening into a mixer bowl. Blend on low speed for several minutes.
3. Add approximately one-half of the liquid and blend.
4. Scrape down the mixer bowl and add the remaining liquid ingredients. Blend into a smooth batter, scraping down the bowl as necessary.
5. Pour the batter into prepared pans using liquid measurements to ensure uniform division.

RECIPE 30.2

HIGH-RATIO YELLOW CAKE

Yield: 3–4 Sheet Pans   **Method:** High-Ratio

Ingredient		
Cake flour	5 lb.	2.2 kg
Granulated sugar	5 lb. 4 oz.	2.3 kg
Emulsified shortening	2 lb. 8 oz.	1.1 kg
Salt	2 oz.	60 g
Baking powder	4 oz.	120 g
Powdered milk	8 oz.	225 g
Light corn syrup	12 oz.	340 g
Water, cold	1 qt.	1 L
Eggs	2 lb. 8 oz.	1.1 kg
Water, cold	2-1/4 qt.	2.25 L
Lemon extract	1 oz.	30 mL

1. Combine the flour, sugar, shortening, salt, baking powder, powdered milk, corn syrup and 1 quart (1 L) cold water in a large bowl of a mixer fitted with the paddle attachment. Beat for 5 minutes on low speed.
2. Combine the remaining ingredients in a separate bowl. Add these liquid ingredients to the creamed-fat mixture in three additions. Scrape down the sides of the bowl after each addition.
3. Beat for 2 minutes on low speed.
4. Divide the batter into greased and floured pans. Pans should be filled only halfway. Four quarts (4 L) of batter is sufficient for an 18-inch × 24-inch × 2-inch (45- × 60- × 5- cm) sheet pan. Bake at 340°F (170°C) until a cake tester comes out clean and the cake springs back when lightly touched, approximately 12–18 minutes.

Approximate values per 3 oz. (90 g) serving:

Calories	390
Total fat	16 g
Saturated fat	5 g
Cholesterol	60 mg
Sodium	320 mg
Total carbohydrates	57 g
Protein	5 g
Calcium	10%

Whipped Egg

Cakes based on whipped egg foams include European-style genoise as well as spongecakes, angel food cakes and chiffon cakes. Some formulas contain chemical leaveners, but the air whipped into the eggs (whether whole or separated) is the primary leavening agent. Egg-foam cakes contain little or no fat.

Genoise

Genoise is the classic European-style cake. It is based on whole eggs whipped with sugar until very light and fluffy. Chemical leaveners are not used. A small amount of oil or melted butter is sometimes added for flavour and moisture. Genoise is often baked in a thin sheet and layered with buttercream, puréed fruit, jam or chocolate filling to create multilayered specialty desserts. Because genoise is rather dry, it is usually soaked with a flavoured sugar syrup (see Chapter 26, Principles of the Bakeshop) or liquor for additional flavour and moisture.

BASIC PROCEDURE FOR PREPARING GENOISE

1. Preheat the oven and prepare the pans.
2. Sift the flour with any additional dry ingredients.
3. Combine the whole eggs and sugar in a large bowl and warm over a double boiler to a temperature of 100°F (38°C).
4. Whip the egg-and-sugar mixture until very light and tripled in volume.
5. Fold the sifted flour into the whipped eggs carefully but quickly.
6. Fold in oil or melted butter if desired.
7. Divide into pans and bake immediately.

1. Whip the eggs.

2. Fold in the flour.

◆◆◆

RECIPE 30.3

CLASSIC GENOISE

Yield: 3 Full Sheet Pans   **Method:** Whipped Egg

Cake flour	1 lb. 8 oz.	680 g
Eggs	3 lb. 4 oz.	1.6 kg
Granulated sugar	1 lb. 8 oz.	680 g
Unsalted butter, melted (optional)	4 oz.	120 g

1. Sift the flour and set aside.
2. Whisk the eggs and sugar together in a large mixer bowl. Place the bowl over a bain marie and warm the eggs to about 100°F (38°C). Stir frequently to avoid cooking the eggs.
3. When the eggs are warm, remove the bowl from the bain marie and attach to a mixer fitted with a whip attachment. Whip the egg-and-sugar mixture at medium speed until tripled in volume.
4. Quickly fold the flour into the egg mixture by hand. Be careful not to deflate the batter.
5. Pour the melted, cooled butter around the edges of the batter and fold in quickly.
6. Divide the batter immediately into parchment-lined pans. Bake at 350°F (180°C) until light brown and springy to the touch, approximately 8 minutes.

VARIATION: *Chocolate genoise*—Sift 3-1/2 ounces (100 g) of cocoa powder with the flour. Reduce flour by 3-1/2 ounces (100 g).

3. Add the melted butter.

4. Pan the batter.

Approximate values per 2 oz. (60 g) serving:

Calories	140
Total fat	4 g
Saturated fat	2 g
Cholesterol	110 mg
Sodium	30 mg
Total carbohydrates	21 g
Protein	4 g
Vitamin A	6%

Spongecakes

Spongecakes (Fr. *biscuits*) are made with whole separated eggs. A batter is prepared with the egg yolks and other ingredients, then the egg whites are whipped to firm peaks with a portion of the sugar (common meringue method) and folded into the batter. Spongecakes are primarily leavened with air, but baking powder may be included in the formula. As with genoise, oil or melted butter may be added if desired.

Spongecakes are extremely versatile. They can be soaked with sugar syrup or a liquor and assembled with buttercream as a traditional layer cake. Or they can be sliced thinly and layered, like genoise, with jam, custard, chocolate or cream filling.

BASIC PROCEDURE FOR PREPARING SPONGECAKES

1. Preheat the oven and prepare the pans.
2. Separate the eggs. Whip the egg whites with a portion of the sugar.
3. Sift the dry ingredients together and combine with liquid ingredients, including the egg yolks, as directed.
4. Carefully fold the whipped egg whites into the batter.
5. Pour the batter into the pans and bake immediately.

◆◆◆

RECIPE 30.4

CLASSIC SPONGECAKE

Yield: 2 9-inch (22-cm) Rounds　　　　　　　　**Method:** Whipped Egg

Cake flour, sifted	6 oz.	180 g
Granulated sugar	11 oz.	300 g
Eggs, separated	10 large	10 large
Vanilla extract	1-1/2 tsp.	7 mL
Cream of tartar	1-1/2 tsp.	7 mL

1. Line the bottom of two springform pans with parchment. Do not grease the sides of the pans.
2. Sift the flour and 6 ounces (180 g) of the sugar together and set aside.
3. Separate the eggs, placing the yolks and the whites in separate mixing bowls. Whip the yolks on high speed for 3–5 minutes, until thick, pale and at least doubled in volume. Whip in the vanilla extract. The yolks should be whipped "to ribbon," that is, until they fall from the beater in thick ribbons that slowly disappear into the batter's surface.
4. Place the bowl of egg whites on the mixer and, using a clean whip attachment, beat until foamy. Add the cream of tartar and 2 tablespoons (30 g) of sugar. Whip at medium speed until the whites are glossy and stiff but not dry.
5. Remove the bowl from the mixer. Pour the egg yolks onto the whipped whites. Quickly fold the two mixtures together by hand. Sprinkle the remaining sugar (3 oz./90 g) over the mixture and fold in lightly.
6. Sprinkle one-third of the sifted flour over the batter and fold in. Repeat the procedure until all of the flour is incorporated. Do not overmix; fold just until incorporated.
7. Pour the batter into the prepared pans, smoothing the surface as needed. Bake immediately at 375°F (190°C) until the cake is golden brown and

Whip the egg yolks to ribbon stage.

spongy, approximately 30 minutes. A toothpick inserted in the centre will be completely clean.

8. Invert the cake, remove from pan; run a thin metal spatula around the edge of the pan to remove the cakes if they stick. Plate on racks or parchment paper. Sprinkle with granulated sugar, then let cool.

9. When the cake is completely cool it can be frosted or wrapped in plastic wrap and frozen for 2–3 months.

Approximate values per 2 oz. (60 g) serving:

Calories	130
Total fat	2.5 g
Saturated fat	1 g
Cholesterol	105 mg
Sodium	30 mg
Total carbohydrates	23 g
Protein	4 g

Claims—low fat; low saturated fat; very low sodium

◆◆◆

RECIPE 30.5

EMULSIFIED SPONGE CAKE

Yield: 18 8-in. (20-cm) Cakes

Milk powder	6 oz.	175 g
Sugar	4 lb. 8 oz.	2.025 kg
Baking powder	2 oz.	60 g
Salt	2 oz.	60 g
Cake flour	3 lb. 8 oz.	1.69 kg
K-68 emulsifier, chilled	2 oz.	60 g
Cold water	30 oz.	900 mL
Whole eggs, chilled	58 oz.	1.69 kg
Oil	3 oz.	90 mL
Melted butter	6 oz.	180 mL

1. Place all the dry ingredients into the mixer bowl. Blend together on slow speed, using a whip attachment.

2. Add water, eggs and emulsifier to the dry ingredients. Blend on slow speed, scraping down the bowl, then whip on high speed for 3 minutes exactly.

3. Fold in the oil and melted butter by hand.

4. Scale 12 oz. (360 g) of batter per cake tin and bake at 350°F (175°C) for 20–30 minutes.

NOTE: This recipe is adjusted for an altitude of 1000 metres.

Approximate values per serving:

Calories	879
Total fat	21 g
Saturated fat	8 g
Cholesterol	351 mg
Sodium	1387 mg
Total carbohydrates	156 g
Protein	18 g

Angel Food Cakes

Angel food cakes are tall, light cakes made without fat and leavened with a large quantity of whipped egg whites. Angel food cakes are traditionally baked in ungreased tube pans, but large loaf pans can also be used. The pans are left ungreased so that the batter can cling to the sides as it rises. The cakes should be inverted as soon as they are removed from the oven and left in the pan to cool. This technique allows gravity to keep the cakes from collapsing or sinking as they cool.

Although they contain no fat, angel food cakes are not low in calories as they contain a high percentage of sugar. The classic angel food cake is pure white, but flavourings, ground nuts or cocoa powder may be added for variety. Although angel food cakes are rarely frosted, they may be topped with a fruit-flavoured or chocolate glaze. They are often served with fresh fruit, a fruit compote or whipped cream.

BASIC PROCEDURE FOR PREPARING ANGEL FOOD CAKES

1. Preheat the oven.
2. Sift the dry ingredients together.
3. Whip the egg whites with a portion of the sugar until stiff and glossy.
4. Gently fold the dry ingredients into the egg whites.
5. Spoon the batter into an ungreased pan and bake immediately.
6. Allow the cake to cool inverted in its pan.

◆◆◆

RECIPE 30.6

CHOCOLATE ANGEL FOOD CAKE

Yield: 1 10-inch (25-cm) Tube Cake   **Method:** Whipped Egg

Cocoa powder, alkalized	1 oz.	30 g
Water, warm	2 oz.	60 mL
Vanilla extract	2 tsp.	10 mL
Granulated sugar	12 oz.	340 g
Cake flour, sifted	3-1/2 oz.	100 g
Salt	1/4 tsp.	1 mL
Egg whites (large eggs)	16	16
Cream of tartar	2 tsp.	10 mL

1. Combine the cocoa powder and water in a bowl. Add the vanilla and set aside.
2. In another bowl, combine 5 ounces (150 g) of the sugar with the flour and salt.
3. Whip the egg whites until foamy, add the cream of tartar and beat to soft peaks. Gradually beat in the remaining sugar. Continue beating until the egg whites are stiff but not dry.
4. Whisk approximately 1 cup (250 mL) of the whipped egg whites into the cocoa mixture. Fold this into the remaining egg whites.
5. Sift the dry ingredients over the whites and fold in quickly but gently.
6. Pour the batter into an ungreased tube pan and smooth the top with a spatula. Bake immediately at 350°F (180°C) until the cake springs back when lightly touched and a cake tester comes out clean, approximately 40–50 minutes. The cake's surface will have deep cracks.
7. Remove the cake from the oven and immediately invert the pan onto the neck of a bottle. Allow the cake to rest upside down until completely cool.
8. To remove the cake from the pan, run a thin knife or spatula around the edge of the pan and the edge of the interior tube. If a two-piece tube pan was used, the cake and tube portion are lifted out of the pan. Use a knife or spatula to loosen the bottom of the cake, then invert it onto a cake board or serving platter.

Approximate values per serving:

Calories	210
Total fat	0.5 g
Saturated fat	0 g
Cholesterol	0 mg
Sodium	150 mg
Total carbohydrates	44 g
Protein	7 g

Claims—low fat; no saturated fat; no cholesterol

1. Fold the cocoa mixture into the whipped egg whites.

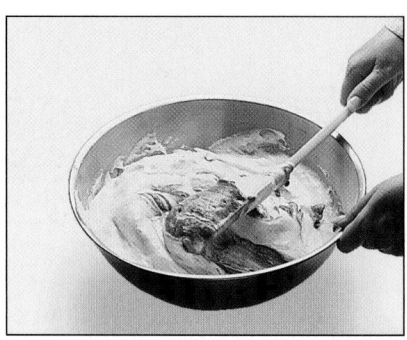

2. Fold in the flour.

3. Cool the cake upside down in its pan.

4. Remove the cake from the pan.

Chiffon Cakes

Although chiffon cakes are similar to angel food cakes in appearance and texture, the addition of egg yolks and vegetable oil makes them moister and richer. Chiffon cakes are usually leavened with whipped egg whites but may contain baking powder as well. Like angel food cakes, chiffon cakes are baked in an ungreased pan to allow the batter to cling to the pan as it rises. Chiffon cakes can be frosted with a light buttercream or whipped cream or topped with a glaze. Lemon and orange chiffon cakes are the most popular, but formulas containing chocolate, nuts or other flavourings are also common.

BASIC PROCEDURE FOR PREPARING CHIFFON CAKES

1. Preheat the oven.
2. Whip the egg whites with a portion of the sugar until almost stiff. Set aside.
3. Sift the dry ingredients together. Add the liquid ingredients, including oil.
4. Fold the whipped egg whites into the batter.
5. Spoon the batter into an ungreased pan and bake immediately.
6. Allow the cake to cool inverted in its pan.

♦♦♦

RECIPE 30.7

ORANGE CHIFFON CAKE

Yield: 1 10-inch (25-cm) Tube Cake   **Method:** Whipped Egg

Cake flour, sifted	8 oz.	250 g
Sugar	12 oz.	375 g
Baking powder	1 Tbsp.	15 mL
Salt	1 tsp.	5 mL
Vegetable oil	4 oz.	125 mL
Egg yolks (large eggs)	6	6
Water, cool	2 oz.	60 mL
Orange juice	4 oz.	125 mL
Orange zest	1 Tbsp.	15 mL
Vanilla extract	1 Tbsp.	15 mL
Egg whites	8 oz.	250 g

1. Sift together the flour, 6 ounces (170 g) of sugar, the baking powder and salt.
2. In a separate bowl mix the oil, yolks, water, juice, zest and vanilla. Add the liquid mixture to the dry ingredients.
3. In a clean bowl beat the egg whites until foamy. Slowly beat in the remaining 6 ounces (170 g) of sugar. Continue beating until the egg whites are stiff but not dry.
4. Stir one-third of the egg whites into the batter to lighten it. Fold in the remaining egg whites.
5. Pour the batter into an ungreased 10-inch (25-cm) tube pan. Bake at 325°F (160°C) until a toothpick inserted in the centre comes out clean, approximately 1 hour.
6. Immediately invert the pan over the neck of a bottle. Allow the cake to cool upside down, then remove from the pan.

Continued

♦♦♦

A BAKER CREATED CHIFFON CAKES

Chiffon cake is one of the few desserts whose history can be traced with absolute certainty. According to Gerry Schremp in her book *Kitchen Culture: Fifty Years of Food Fads*, a new type of cake was invented by Henry Baker, a California insurance salesman, in 1927. Dubbed *chiffon*, it was as light as angel food and as rich as poundcake. For years he kept the formula a secret, earning fame and fortune by selling his cakes to Hollywood restaurants. The cake's secret ingredient—vegetable oil—became public knowledge in 1947 when Baker sold the formula to General Mills, which promoted it on packages of cake flour. Chiffon cakes, in a variety of flavours, became extremely popular nationwide.

Approximate values per 1/10-cake serving:

Calories	370
Total fat	15 g
Saturated fat	2.5 g
Cholesterol	130 mg
Sodium	280 mg
Total carbohydrates	54 g
Protein	6 g
Vitamin C	10%

ORANGE GLAZE

Powdered sugar	3 oz.	90 g
Orange juice	2 Tbsp.	30 mL
Orange zest	2 tsp.	10 mL

1. Sift the sugar, then stir in the juice and zest.

2. Drizzle the glaze over the top of the cooled cake.

VARIATION: *Lemon chiffon cake*—Substitute 2 ounces (60 mL) fresh lemon juice and 2 ounces (60 mL) water for the orange juice. Substitute lemon zest for the orange zest. Top with Basic Sugar Glaze, Recipe 30.13.

Panning, Baking and Cooling

Preparing Pans

To prevent cakes from sticking, most baking pans are coated with fat or a nonstick baking parchment. (See Table 30.3.) Pans should be prepared before the batter is mixed, so that they may be filled and the cakes baked as soon as the batter is finished. If the batter stands while the pans are prepared, air cells within the batter will deflate and volume may be lost.

Solid shortening is better than butter for coating pans because it does not contain any water; butter and margarine do contain water and this may cause the cake to stick in places. Solid shortening is also less expensive, tasteless and odourless. Finally, solid shortening does not burn as easily as butter and it holds a dusting of flour better.

Pan-release sprays are useful but must be applied carefully and completely. Although relatively expensive, sprays save time and are particularly effective when used with parchment pan liners.

In kitchens where a great deal of baking is done, it may be more convenient to prepare quantities of pan coating to be kept available for use as needed. Pan coating is a mixture of equal parts oil, shortening and flour, creamed together, that can be applied to cake pans with a pastry brush. It is used whenever pans need to be greased and floured. Pan coating will not leave a white residue on the cake's crust as a dusting of flour often does.

TABLE 30.2   NUTRITIONAL VALUES OF SELECTED CAKES

Per 1/12 Portion of a 9-inch (22.5-cm) Cake, Unfrosted	Kcal	Protein (g)	Carbohydrates (g)	Total Fat (g)	Saturated Fat (g)	Sodium (mg)
Angel food	130	3	30	0	0	170
Butter cake	260	3	37	11	6	350
Chiffon, lemon	200	4	36	5	mq	200
Devil's food	260	4	35	12	3	450
Sponge (2-in./5-cm square)	80	1	11	3	1	125

All cakes are prepared from a typical mix according to package directions.
The Corinne T. Netzer Encyclopedia of Food Values 1992
mq = measurable quantity but data are unavailable

TABLE 30.3   PAN PREPARATIONS

Pan Preparation	Used For
Ungreased	Angel food and chiffon cakes
Ungreased sides; paper on bottom	Genoise layers
Greased and papered	High-fat cakes, sponge sheets
Greased and coated with flour	High-fat cakes, chocolate cakes, anything in a bundt or shaped pan
Greased, floured and lined with paper	Cakes containing melted chocolate, fruit chunks or fruit or vegetable purées

◆◆◆

RECIPE 30.8
PAN COATING

Yield: 3 lb. (1.5 kg)

Vegetable oil	1 lb.	500 g
All-purpose shortening	1 lb.	500 g
Bread flour	1 lb.	500 g

1. Combine all ingredients in a mixer fitted with the paddle attachment. Blend on low speed for 5 minutes or until smooth.
2. Store in an air-tight container at room temperature for up to 2 months.
3. Apply to baking pans in a thin, even layer using a pastry brush.

Pan coating is not appropriate for all cakes, however. Those containing chocolate, raisins or fruit should still be baked in pans lined with parchment paper to prevent sticking.

Angel food and chiffon cakes are baked in ungreased, unlined pans because these fragile cakes need to cling to the sides of the pan as they rise.

◆◆◆
BROWNIES

Where do you draw the line between cakes and brownies? The decision must be a matter of texture and personal preference, for the preparation methods are nearly identical. Brownies are generally chewy and fudgy, sweeter and denser than even the richest of butter cakes.

Brownies are a relatively inexpensive and easy way for a food service operation to offer its customers a fresh-baked dessert. Although not as sophisticated as an elaborate gâteau, a well-made brownie can always be served with pride (and a scoop of ice cream).

Brownies are prepared using the same procedures as those for high-fat cakes. Good brownies are achieved with a proper balance of ingredients: A high percentage of butter to flour produces a dense, fudgy brownie; less butter produces a more cakelike brownie. Likewise, the higher the ratio of sugar, the gooier the finished brownie. In some formulas, the fat is creamed to incorporate air, as with butter cakes. In others, the fat is first melted and combined with other liquid ingredients. Brownies are rarely made with whipped egg whites, however, as this makes their texture too light and cakelike.

Each customer and cook has his or her own idea of the quintessential brownie. Some are cloyingly sweet, with a creamy texture and an abundance of chocolate; others are bitter and crisp. Baked brownies can be frozen for 2–3 months if well wrapped.

TABLE 30.4   CAKE PAN SIZES

Pan Shape and Size		Quantity of Batter*
Round, 2 inch (5 cm) deep	6 inch (15 cm)	1 pt. (500 mL)
	8 inch (20 cm)	3 cups (750 mL)
	10 inch (25 cm)	1-1/2 qt. (1–1.5 L)
	12 inch (30 cm)	1 qt. + 3-1/2 cups (1.75 L)
	14 inch (35 cm)	2-1/2 qt. (2.5 L)
Square, 2 inch (5 cm) deep	8 inch (20 cm)	1 qt. (1 L)
	10 inch (25 cm)	1-1/2 qt. (1.5 L)
	12 inch (30 cm)	2-1/2 qt. (2.5 L)
	14 inch (35 cm)	3 qt. + 1-1/2 cups (3.5 L)
Rectangular	6 × 8 inch (15 × 20 cm)	2-1/2 cups (500 mL)
	9 × 13 inch (22.5 × 32.5 cm)	2 qt. (2 L)
	16 × 12 inch (40 × 30 cm)	2 qt. + 3 cups (2.75 L)

* Quantities given are approximate and are based on filling the pans two-thirds full of batter.

Spongecakes and genoise are often baked in pans with a paper liner on the bottom and ungreased sides. While the ungreased sides give the batter a surface to cling to, the paper liner makes removing the cake from the pan easier.

Filling Pans

Pans should be filled no more than one-half to two-thirds full. This allows the batter to rise during baking without spilling over the edges. (See Table 30.4.)

Pans should be filled to uniform depths. High-fat and egg-foam cake batters can be ladled into each pan according to weight. High-ratio cake batter is so liquid that it can be measured by volume and poured into each pan. Filling the pans uniformly prevents both uneven layers and over- or underfilled pans. If you are baking three 8-inch (20-cm) layers to be stacked for one presentation and the amount of batter is different in each pan, the baking times will vary and the final product will suffer.

The cake batter should always be spread evenly in the pan. Use an offset spatula. Do not work the batter too much, however, as this destroys air cells and prevents the cake from rising properly.

Baking

Temperatures

Always preheat the oven before preparing your batter. If the finished batter must wait while the oven reaches the correct temperature, valuable leavening will be lost and the cake will not rise properly.

Most cakes are baked at temperatures between 325° and 375°F (160–190°C). The temperature must be high enough to create steam within the batter and cause that steam and other gases in the batter to expand and rise quickly. If the temperature is too high, however, the cake may rise unevenly and the crust may burn before the interior is completely baked. The temperature must also be low enough that the batter can set completely and evenly without drying out. If the temperature is too low, however, the cake will not rise sufficiently and may dry out before baking completely.

If no temperature is given in a formula or you are altering the dimensions of the baking pan from those specified, use common sense in setting the oven temperature. Usually, the larger the surface area, the higher the temperature can be. Tall cakes, such as bundt or tube cakes, should be baked at a lower temperature than thin layer or sheet cakes. Tube or loaf cakes take longer to bake than thin sheet cakes; butter cakes, because they contain more liquid, take longer to bake than genoise or spongecakes.

Altitude Adjustments

As you learned in Chapter 9, Principles of Cooking, altitude affects the temperatures at which foods cook. The decreased atmospheric pressure at altitudes above 3000 feet (900 m) affects the creation of steam and the expansion of hot air in cake batters. These factors must be considered when making cakes. Because gases expand more easily at higher altitudes, your cake may rise so much that its structure cannot support it and the cake can collapse.

Therefore, the amount of leavening should be decreased at higher altitudes. (See Figure 30.1.) Chemical leaveners should usually be reduced by 20% at 3500 feet (1050 m) and by 40% at altitudes over 5000 feet (1500 m). Eggs should be underwhipped to avoid incorporating too much air, and the volume should be increased by approximately 10%. An additional 10% of liquid may be required. In general, oven temperatures should also be increased by 25°F (4°C) at altitudes over 3500 feet (1050 m) to help the cake's structure to set rapidly.

Because the boiling point decreases at higher altitudes, more moisture will evaporate from your cake during baking. This may cause dryness and an excessive proportion of sugar, which shows up as white spots on the cake's surface. Correct this by reducing every 8 ounces (225 g) of sugar by 1/2 ounce (15 g) at 3000 feet (900 m) and by 1-1/2 ounces (45 g) at 7000 feet (2100 m).

Attempting to adjust typical (i.e., sea level) formulas for high altitudes is somewhat risky, especially in a commercial operation. Try to find and use formulas developed especially for your area.

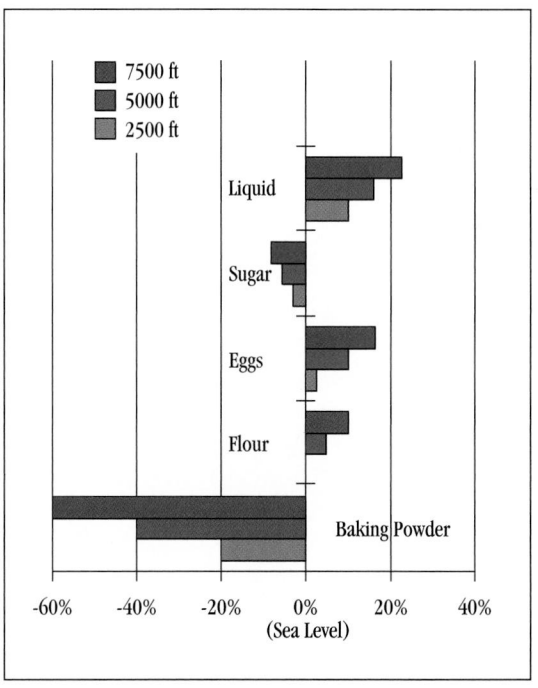

FIGURE 30.1 *Altitude Adjustments*
Source: Andreas Schwarzer, SAIT.

Determining Doneness

In addition to following the baking time suggested in a formula, several simple tests can be used to determine doneness. Whichever test or tests are used, avoid opening the oven door to check the cake's progress. Cold air or a drop in oven temperature can cause the cake to fall. Use a timer to note the minimum suggested baking time. Then, and only then, should you use the following tests to evaluate the cake's doneness:

◆ *Appearance*—The cake's surface should be a light to golden brown. Unless noted otherwise in the formula, the edges should just begin to pull away from the pan. The cake should not jiggle or move beneath its surface.
◆ *Touch*—Touch the cake *lightly* with your finger. It should spring back quickly without feeling soggy or leaving an indentation.
◆ *Cake tester*—If appearance and touch indicate that the cake is done, test the interior by inserting a toothpick, bamboo skewer or metal cake tester into the cake's centre. With most cakes, the tester should come out clean. If wet crumbs cling to the tester the cake probably needs to bake a bit longer.

If a formula provides particular doneness guidelines, they should be followed. For example, some flourless cakes are fully baked even though a cake tester will not come out clean.

TABLE 30.5   TROUBLESHOOTING CHART FOR CAKES

Problem	Cause	Solution
Batter curdles during mixing	Ingredients too warm or too cold	Eggs must be room temperature and added slowly
	Incorrect fat used	Use correct ingredients
	Fat inadequately creamed before liquid was added	Add a portion of the flour, then continue adding the liquid
	Too much liquid was added	Add a portion of the flour, then continue adding the liquid
Cake lacks volume	Flour too strong	Use a weaker flour
	Old chemical leavener	Replace with fresh leavener
	Egg foam underwhipped	Use correct mixing method, do not deflate eggs during folding
	Oven too hot	Adjust oven temperature
Crust burst or cracked	Too much flour or too little liquid	Adjust formula
	Oven too hot	Adjust oven temperature
Cake shrinks after baking	Weak internal structure	Adjust formula
	Too much sugar or fat for the batter to support	Adjust formula
	Cake not fully baked	Test cake for doneness before removing from oven
	Cake cooled too rapidly	Cool away from drafts
Texture is dense or heavy	Too little leavening	Adjust formula
	Too much fat or liquid	Cream fat or whip eggs properly
	Oven too cool	Adjust oven temperature
Texture is coarse with an open grain	Overmixing	Alter mixing method
	Oven too cool	Adjust oven temperature
Poor flavour	Poor ingredients	Check flavour and aroma of all ingredients
	Unclean pans	Do not grease pans with rancid fats
Uneven shape	Butter not incorporated evenly	Incorporate fats completely
	Batter spread unevenly	Spread batter evenly
	Oven rack not level	Adjust oven racks
	Uneven oven temperature	Adjust oven temperature

Cooling

Generally, a cake is allowed to cool for 10–15 minutes in its pan after being removed from the oven. This helps prevent the cake from cracking or breaking after it is removed from its pan.

To remove the partially cooled cake from its pan, run a thin knife or spatula blade between the pan and the cake to loosen it. Place a wire rack, cake board or sheet pan over the cake and invert. Then remove the pan. The cake can be left upside down to cool completely or inverted again to cool top side up. Wire racks are preferred for cooling cakes because they allow air to circulate, speeding the cooling process and preventing steam from making the cake soggy.

Angel food and chiffon cakes should be turned upside down immediately after they are removed from the oven. They are left to cool completely in their

TABLE 30.6	FROSTINGS	
Frosting	Preparation	Texture/Taste
Buttercream	Mixture of sugar and fat (usually butter); can contain egg yolks or egg whites	Rich but light; smooth, fluffy
Foam	Meringue made with hot sugar syrup	Light, fluffy; very sweet
Fudge	Cooked mixture of sugar, butter and water or milk; applied warm	Heavy, rich and candylike
Fondant	Cooked mixture of sugar and water; applied warm	Thick; opaque; sweet
Glaze	Confectioner's sugar with liquid	Thin
Royal icing	Uncooked mixture of confectioner's sugar and egg whites	Hard and brittle when dry
Ganache	Blend of melted chocolate and cream	Rich, smooth, intense flavour

pans to prevent the cake from collapsing or shrinking. The top of the pan should not touch the countertop so that air can circulate under the inverted pan.

All cakes should be left to cool away from drafts or air currents that might cause them to collapse. Cakes should not be refrigerated to speed the cooling process, as rapid cooling can cause cracking. Prolonged refrigeration also causes cakes to dry out.

FROSTINGS

Frosting, also known as **icing**, is a sweet decorative coating used as a filling between the layers or as a coating over the top and sides of a cake. It is used to add flavour and to improve the cake's appearance. Frosting can also extend a cake's shelf life by forming a protective coating.

There are seven general types of frosting: **buttercream, foam, fudge, fondant, glaze, royal icing** and **ganache**. (See Table 30.6.) Each type can be produced with a number of formulas and in a range of flavourings.

Because frosting is integral to the flavour and appearance of many cakes, it should be made carefully using high-quality ingredients and natural flavours and colours. A good frosting is smooth; it is never grainy or lumpy. It should complement the flavour and texture of the cake without overpowering it.

Buttercream

A buttercream is a light, smooth, fluffy mixture of sugar and fat (butter, margarine or shortening). It may also contain egg yolks for richness or whipped egg whites for lightness. A good buttercream will be sweet, but not heavy; buttery, but not greasy.

Buttercreams are popular and useful for most types of cakes and may be flavoured or coloured as desired. They may be stored, covered, in the refrigerator for several days but must be softened before use and creamed again.

Although there are many types of buttercream and many formula variations, we discuss the three most popular styles: **simple**, **Italian** and **French**.

Simple Buttercream

Simple buttercream is made by creaming butter and powdered sugar together until the mixture is light and smooth. Cream, eggs, preferably pasteurized (whole, yolks or whites) and flavourings may be added as desired. Simple buttercream is quick and easy to prepare.

If cost is a consideration, high-ratio or emulsified shortening can be substituted for a portion of the butter, but the flavour and mouth-feel will be different. Buttercream made with shortening tends to taste greasier and heavier because shortening does not melt on the tongue like butter. It will be more stable than buttercream made only with butter, however, and is useful for products that will be on display.

BASIC PROCEDURE FOR PREPARING SIMPLE BUTTERCREAM

1. Cream softened butter or shortening until the mixture is light and fluffy.
2. Beat in egg, if desired.
3. Beat in sifted powdered sugar, scraping down the sides of the bowl as needed.
4. Beat in the flavouring ingredients.

RECIPE 30.9

SIMPLE BUTTERCREAM

Yield: 3 lb. (1.5 kg)

Lightly salted butter, softened	1 lb.	450 g
Egg (optional)	1	1
Powdered sugar, sifted	2 lb.	900 g
Vanilla extract	2 tsp.	10 mL

1. Using a mixer fitted with the paddle attachment, cream the butter until light and fluffy.
2. Beat in the egg if using. Gradually add the sugar, frequently scraping down the sides of the bowl.
3. Add the vanilla and continue beating until the frosting is smooth and light.

VARIATIONS: *Light chocolate*—Dissolve 1 ounce (30 g) sifted cocoa powder in 2 ounces (60 mL) cool water. Add to the buttercream along with the vanilla.

Lemon—Decrease the vanilla extract to 1 teaspoon (5 mL). Add 1 teaspoon (5 mL) lemon extract and the finely grated zest of one lemon.

Approximate values per 1 oz. (30 g) serving:

Calories	170
Total fat	6 g
Saturated fat	4 g
Cholesterol	25 mg
Sodium	70 mg
Total carbohydrates	28 g
Protein	0 g
Vitamin A	10%

Italian Buttercream

Italian buttercream, also known as **meringue buttercream**, is based on an Italian meringue, that is, whipped egg whites enriched with hot sugar syrup. (See Chapter 29, Pies, Pastries and Cookies.) Softened butter is then whipped into the cooled meringue and the mixture is flavoured as desired. This type of buttercream is extremely soft and light. It can be used on most types of cakes and is particularly popular for multilayered genoise and spongecakes.

BASIC PROCEDURE FOR PREPARING ITALIAN BUTTERCREAM

1. Whip the egg whites until soft peaks form.
2. Beat granulated sugar into the egg whites and whip until firm and glossy.
3. Meanwhile, combine additional sugar with water and cook to soft ball stage (238°F/115°C).

4. With the mixer on medium speed, pour the sugar syrup into the whipped egg whites. Pour slowly and carefully to avoid splatters.
5. Continue whipping the egg-white-and-sugar mixture until completely cool.
6. Whip softened, but not melted, butter into the cooled egg-white-and-sugar mixture.
7. Add flavouring ingredients as desired.

—— ◆◆◆ ——

RECIPE 30.10

ITALIAN BUTTERCREAM

Yield: 5 lb. (2.2 kg)

Egg whites	14 oz.	400 g
Sugar	1 lb. 11 oz.	750 g
Lightly salted butter, softened but not melted	2 lb. 12 oz.	1.25 kg

1. All ingredients should be at room temperature before beginning.
2. Place the egg whites in a mixer bowl. Have 9 ounces (250 g) of sugar nearby.
3. Place 1 pound 2 ounces (500 g) of sugar in a heavy saucepan with enough water to moisten. Bring to a boil over high heat.
4. As the sugar syrup's temperature approaches a soft ball stage (238°F/115°C), begin whipping the egg whites. Watch the sugar closely so that the temperature does not exceed 238°F (115°C).
5. When soft peaks form in the egg whites, gradually add the 9 ounces (250 g) of sugar to them. Reduce mixer speed to medium and continue whipping the egg whites to stiff peaks.
6. When the sugar syrup reaches soft ball stage, immediately pour it into the whites while the mixer is running. Pour the syrup in a steady stream between the side of the bowl and the beater. If the syrup hits the beater it will splatter and cause lumps. Continue beating at medium speed until the egg whites are completely cool. At this point the product is known as Italian meringue.
7. Gradually add the softened butter to the Italian meringue. When all of the butter is incorporated, add flavouring ingredients as desired.

VARIATION: *Chocolate:* Add 1 tablespoon (15 mL) vanilla extract and 10 ounces (300 g) melted and cooled bittersweet chocolate.

Approximate values per 1 oz. (30 g) serving:

Calories	175
Total fat	13 g
Saturated fat	8 g
Cholesterol	34 mg
Sodium	140 mg
Total carbohydrates	16 g
Protein	1 g
Vitamin A	10%

1. Add the sugar syrup to the whipped egg whites.

2. Add the softened butter to the cooled Italian meringue.

3. Finished Italian buttercream.

French Buttercream

French buttercream, also known as **mousseline buttercream**, is similar to Italian buttercream except that the hot sugar syrup is whipped into beaten egg yolks (not egg whites). Softened butter and flavourings are added when the sweetened egg yolks are fluffy and cool. An Italian meringue such as the one created in the above formula is sometimes folded in for additional body and lightness. French buttercream is perhaps the most difficult type of buttercream to master, but it has the richest flavour and smoothest texture. Like a meringue buttercream, mousseline buttercream may be used on almost any type of cake.

BASIC PROCEDURE FOR PREPARING FRENCH BUTTERCREAM

1. Prepare a sugar syrup and cook to soft ball stage (238°F/115°C).
2. Beat egg yolks to a thin ribbon.
3. Slowly beat the hot sugar syrup into the egg yolks.
4. Continue beating until the yolks are pale, stiff and completely cool.
5. Gradually add softened butter to the cooled yolks.
6. Fold in Italian meringue.
7. Stir in flavouring ingredients.

RECIPE 30.11

FRENCH BUTTERCREAM

Yield: 2 qt. (2 L)

Granulated sugar	1 lb. 10 oz.	800 g
Water	8 oz.	250 mL
Egg yolks	16 large	16 large
Lightly salted butter, softened but not melted	3 lb.	1.5 kg
Italian Meringue (Recipe 29.11)	1 qt.	1 L

Approximate values per 1 oz. (30 mL) serving:

Calories	230
Total fat	20 g
Saturated fat	12 g
Cholesterol	105 mg
Sodium	190 mg
Total carbohydrates	12 g
Protein	1 g
Vitamin A	20%

1. Combine the sugar and water in a small saucepan and bring to a boil. Continue boiling until the syrup reaches 238°F (115°C).
2. Meanwhile, beat the egg yolks in a mixer fitted with a wire whisk on low speed. When the sugar syrup reaches 238°F (115°C), pour it slowly into the egg yolks, gradually increasing the speed at which they are whipped. Continue beating at medium-high speed until the mixture is very pale, stiff and cool.
3. Gradually add the softened butter to the egg mixture, frequently scraping down the sides of the bowl.
4. Fold in the Italian meringue with a spatula. Stir in flavouring extracts as desired.

Foam Frosting

Foam frosting, sometimes known as **boiled icing**, is simply a meringue made with hot sugar syrup. Foam frosting is light and fluffy but very sweet. It may be flavoured with extract, liqueur or melted chocolate.

Foam frosting is rather unstable. It should be used immediately and served the day it is prepared. Refrigeration often makes the foam weep beads of sugar. Freezing causes it to separate or melt.

An easy foam frosting can be made by following the formula for Italian Buttercream (Recipe 30.10). As soon as the meringue has cooled to room temperature it can be flavoured with extracts as desired.

Fudge Frosting

A fudge frosting is a warmed mixture of sugar, butter and water or milk. It is heavy, rich and candylike. It is also stable and holds up well. A fudge frosting should be applied warm and allowed to dry on the cake or pastry. When dry, it will have a thin crust and a moist interior. A fudge frosting can be vanilla- or chocolate-based and is used on cupcakes, layer cakes and sheet cakes.

BASIC PROCEDURE FOR PREPARING FUDGE FROSTINGS

1. Blend sifted powdered sugar with corn syrup, beating until the sugar is dissolved and the mixture is smooth.
2. Blend in warm melted shortening and/or butter.
3. Blend in hot liquids. Add extracts or flavourings.
4. Use fudge frosting while still warm.

Cocoa fudge frosting.

♦♦♦

RECIPE 30.12
BASIC FUDGE FROSTING

Yield: 4 lb. (2 kg)

Icing sugar, sifted	3 lb.	1.5 kg
Salt	1/4 tsp.	1 mL
Light corn syrup	2 oz.	60 mL
Shortening, melted	4 oz.	120 g
Water, hot (140°F/60°C)	10 oz.	300 mL
Vanilla extract	2 Tbsp.	30 mL

1. Blend the sugar, salt and corn syrup. Beat until smooth.
2. Add the melted shortening and blend well.
3. Add the hot water and vanilla and blend well. If the fudge is too stiff it may be thinned with a simple sugar syrup. Use before the icing cools.

VARIATION: *Cocoa fudge frosting:* Sift 4 ounces (120 g) cocoa powder with the powdered sugar. Add 2 ounces (60 mL) melted unsalted butter with the shortening.

Approximate values per 1 oz. (30 g) serving:

Calories	140
Total fat	2.5 g
Saturated fat	0.5 g
Cholesterol	0 mg
Sodium	15 mg
Total carbohydrates	30 g
Protein	0 g

Claims—low fat; low saturated fat; no cholesterol; very low sodium

Fondant

Fondant is a thick, opaque sugar paste commonly used for glazing napoleons, petit fours and other pastries as well as some cakes. It is a cooked mixture of sugar and water, with **glucose** or corn syrup added to encourage the correct type of sugar crystallization. Poured over the surface being coated, fondant

Glucose—*a thick, sweet syrup made from cornstarch, composed primarily of dextrose. Light corn syrup can usually be substituted for it in baked goods or candy making.*

quickly dries to a shiny, nonsticky coating. It is naturally pure white and can be tinted with food colouring. Fondant can also be flavoured with melted chocolate.

Fondant is rather difficult to make, so it is almost always purchased prepared. To use, warm fondant to 100°F (38°C) over medium heat, stirring constantly to prevent overheating. If necessary, thin fondant with water or simple syrup after warming up the fondant. Commercially prepared fondant will keep for several months at room temperature in an air-tight container. The surface of the fondant should be coated with simple syrup, however, to prevent a crust from forming.

Glaze

A glaze is a thin coating meant to be poured or dripped onto a cake or pastry. A glaze is usually too thin to apply with a knife or spatula. It is used to add moisture and flavour to cakes on which a heavy frosting would be undesirable—for example, a chiffon or angel food cake.

Flat icing or **water icing** is a specific type of glaze used on danish pastries and coffeecakes. It is pure white and dries to a firm gloss.

BASIC PROCEDURE FOR PREPARING GLAZES

1. Blend sifted powdered sugar with a small amount of liquid and flavourings.
2. Use immediately.

◆◆◆

RECIPE 30.13

BASIC SUGAR GLAZE

Yield: 13 oz. (370 g)

Icing sugar, sifted	9-1/2 oz.	270 g
Light cream or milk	2 oz.	60 mL
Unsalted butter, melted	1 oz.	30 g
Vanilla extract	2 tsp.	10 mL

1. Stir the ingredients together in a small bowl until smooth.
2. Adjust the consistency by adding more cream or milk to thin the glaze if necessary.
3. Adjust the flavour as necessary.
4. Use immediately, before the glaze begins to dry.

VARIATION: Another extract, such as lemon or almond, may be used if desired.

Approximate values per 1 oz. (30 g) serving:

Calories	110
Total fat	2 g
Saturated fat	1.5 g
Cholesterol	5 mg
Sodium	0 mg
Total carbohydrates	23 g
Protein	0 g

Claims—low fat; low cholesterol; no sodium

Royal Icing

Royal icing, also known as **decorator's icing**, is similar to flat icing except it is much stiffer and becomes hard and brittle when dry. It is an uncooked mixture of icing sugar and egg whites. It may be dyed with food colouring pastes.

Royal icing is used for making decorations, particularly intricate flowers or lace patterns. Prepare royal icing in small quantities and always keep any unused portion covered with a damp towel to prevent hardening.

◆◆◆

CONVENIENCE PRODUCTS

A wide selection of prepared icings, glazes and toppings are available. Often, chocolate and vanilla fudge icing bases are purchased, then flavoured or coloured as needed. Foam frostings can be purchased in powder form, to which you add water and then whip. Even prepared "buttercreams" are available, although they contain little or no real butter.

Prepared icings are often exceedingly sweet and overpowered by artificial flavours and chemical preservatives. These products save time but often cost more than their counterparts made from scratch. They should be used only after balancing the disadvantages against the benefits for your particular operation.

BASIC PROCEDURE FOR PREPARING ROYAL ICING

1. Combine egg white and lemon juice, if used.
2. Beat in sifted icing sugar until the correct consistency is reached.
3. Beat until very smooth and firm enough to hold a stiff peak.
4. Colour as desired with paste food colourings.
5. Store covered with a damp cloth and plastic wrap.

◆◆◆

RECIPE 30.14

ROYAL ICING

Yield: 7 oz. (200 g)

Icing sugar	6 oz.	180 g
Egg white, room temperature	1	1
Lemon juice	1/4 tsp.	1 mL

1. Sift the sugar and set aside.
2. Place the egg white and lemon juice in a stainless steel bowl.
3. Add 4 ounces (120 g) of sugar and beat with an electric mixer or metal spoon until blended. The mixture should fall from a spoon in heavy globs. If it pours, it is too thin and will need the remaining 2 ounces (60 g) of sugar.
4. Once the consistency is correct, continue beating for 3–4 minutes. The icing should be white, smooth and thick enough to hold a stiff peak. Food colouring paste can be added at this time if desired.
5. Cover the icing with a damp towel and plastic wrap to prevent it from hardening.

Approximate values per 1 oz. (30 g) serving:

Calories	120
Total fat	0 g
Saturated fat	0 g
Cholesterol	0 mg
Sodium	10 mg
Total carbohydrates	28 g
Protein	1 g

Claims—fat free; no saturated fat; no cholesterol; very low sodium

Ganache

Ganache is a blend of chocolate and cream. It may also include butter, liquor or other flavourings. Any bittersweet, semisweet or dark chocolate may be used; the choice depends on personal preference and cost considerations.

Depending on its consistency, ganache may be used as a filling, frosting or glaze-type coating on cakes or pastries. The ratio of chocolate to cream determines how thick the cooled ganache will be. Equal parts chocolate and cream generally are best for frostings and fillings. Increasing the percentage of chocolate produces a thicker ganache. Warm ganache can be poured over a cake or pastry and allowed to harden as a thin glaze, or the ganache may be cooled and whipped to create a rich, smooth frosting. If it becomes too firm, ganache can be remelted over a bain marie.

BASIC PROCEDURE FOR PREPARING GANACHE

1. Melt finely chopped chocolate with cream in a double boiler. Or,
2. Bring cream just to a boil. Then pour it over finely chopped chocolate and allow the cream's heat to gently melt the chocolate.
3. Whichever method is used, cool the cream and chocolate mixture over an ice bath.

Do not attempt to melt chocolate and then add cool cream. This will cause the chocolate to resolidify and lump.

RECIPE 30.15

CHOCOLATE GANACHE

Yield: 2.2 lb. (1 kg)

Bittersweet chocolate	1 lb. 1 oz.	500 g
Cream, 35%	1 lb. 1 oz.	500 mL
Almond or coffee liqueur	1 oz.	30 mL

Approximate values per 1 oz. (30 g) serving:

Calories	130
Total fat	10 g
Saturated fat	6 g
Cholesterol	20 mg
Sodium	5 mg
Total carbohydrates	8 g
Protein	1 g
Vitamin A	6%

1. Chop the chocolate into small pieces and place in a large metal bowl.
2. Bring the cream just to a boil, then immediately pour it over the chocolate, whisking to blend. Stir gently until all the chocolate has melted.
3. Stir in the liqueur.
4. Allow to cool, stirring frequently until the desired consistency is achieved. An ice bath may be used to speed the cooling process.

1. Pour the hot cream over the chopped chocolate.

2. Cool, firm ganache.

TABLE 30.7   TROUBLESHOOTING CHART FOR FROSTINGS

Problem	Cause	Solution
Frosting breaks or curdles	Fat added too slowly or eggs too hot when fat was added	Add shortening or sifted confectioner's sugar
Frosting is lumpy	Confectioner's sugar not sifted	Sift dry ingredients
	Ingredients not blended	Use softened fat
	Sugar syrup lumps in frosting	Add sugar syrups carefully
Frosting is gritty	Granulated sugar not dissolved	Cook sugar syrups properly; cook fudge frostings as directed
Frosting is too stiff	Not enough liquid	Adjust formula; add small amount of water or milk to thin frosting
	Too cold	Bring frosting to room temperature
Frosting will not adhere to cake	Cake too hot	Cool cake completely
	Frosting too thin	Adjust frosting formula

ASSEMBLING AND DECORATING CAKES

Much of a cake's initial appeal lies in its appearance. This is true whether the finished cake is a simple sheet cake topped with swirls of buttercream or an elaborate wedding cake with intricate garlands and bouquets of royal icing roses. Any cake assembled and decorated with care and attention to detail is preferable to a carelessly assembled or garishly overdecorated one.

Thousands of decorating styles or designs are possible, of course. This section describes a few simple options that can be prepared by beginning pastry cooks using a minimum of specialized tools. In planning your cake's design consider the flavour, texture and colour of the components used as well as the number of guests or portions that must be served. Consider who will be cutting and eating the cake and how long the dessert must stand before service.

Assembling Cakes

Before a cake can be decorated, it must be assembled and coated with frosting. Most cakes can be assembled in a variety of shapes and sizes: sheet cakes, round layer cakes and rectangular layer cakes are the most common. When assembling any cake, the goal is to fill and stack the cake layers evenly and to apply an even coating of frosting that is smooth and free of crumbs.

◆◆◆

ADVANCED PÂTISSERIE

Sugar can be used to create a number of doughs, pastes and syrups used for artistic and decorative work. Mastering even some of these products takes years of experience and practice. Although formulas and preparation methods are beyond the scope of this book, it is important that all pastry cooks be able to recognize and identify certain decorative sugar products.

Blown sugar—a boiled mixture of sucrose, glucose and tartaric acid that is coloured and shaped (in a manner very similar to glass blowing) using an air pump. It is used for making pieces of fruit and containers such as bowls and vases.

Gum paste—a smooth dough made of sugar and gelatin; it dries relatively slowly, becoming very firm and hard. The paste can be coloured and rolled out, cut and shaped, or moulded. It is used for making flowers, leaves and small figures.

Marzipan—a mixture of almond paste and sugar that may be coloured and used like modelling clay for sculpting small fruits, flowers or other objects. Marzipan may also be rolled out and cut into various shapes or used to cover cakes or pastries.

Nougat—a candy made of caramelized sugar and almonds that can be moulded into shapes or containers. Unlike other sugar decorations, nougat remains deliciously edible.

Pastillage—a paste made with sugar, cornstarch and gelatin. It can be rolled into sheets, then cut into shapes. It dries in a very firm and sturdy form, like plaster. Naturally pure white, it can be painted with cocoa or food colourings. Pastillage is used for showpieces and large decorative items.

Pulled sugar—a doughlike mixture of sucrose, glucose and tartaric acid that is coloured, then shaped by hand. Pulled sugar is used for making birds, flowers, leaves, bows and other items.

Spun sugar—made by flicking dark caramelized sugar rapidly over a dowel to create long, fine, hairlike threads. Mounds or wreaths of these threads are used to decorate ice cream desserts, croquembouche and gâteaux.

Most of the photographs used in this section show the assembly and decoration of a wedding cake. The finished cake is shown in the photograph that introduces this chapter. The complete formula is found in Recipe 30.16.

BASIC PROCEDURE FOR ASSEMBLING CAKES

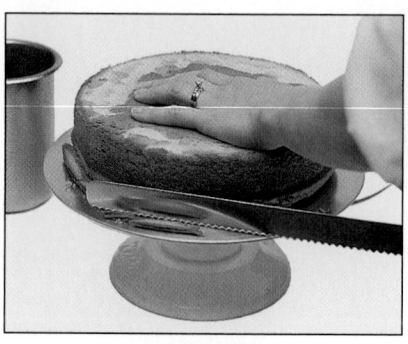

1. Begin by levelling the cake and trimming the edges as needed with a serrated knife.

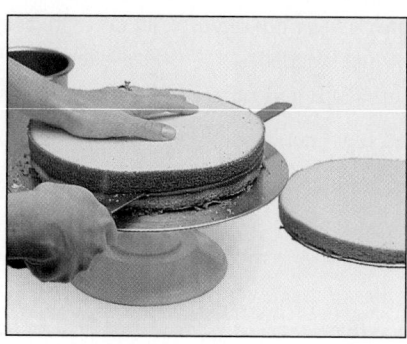

2. Split the cake horizontally into thin layers if desired. Use cake boards to support each layer as it is removed. Brush away any loose crumbs with a dry pastry brush.

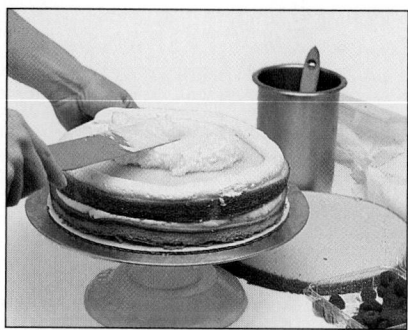

3. Position the bottom layer on a cake board. Place the layer on a revolving cake stand, brush cake with a flavoured simple syrup. Top the layer with a mound of frosting or filling, then use a cake spatula to spread it evenly to the edges.

4. Position the next cake layer over the filling and continue layering and filling the cake as desired.

5. Place a mound of frosting in the centre of the cake top. Push it to the edge of the cake with a cake spatula. Do not drag the frosting back and forth or lift the spatula off the frosting, as these actions tend to pick up crumbs.

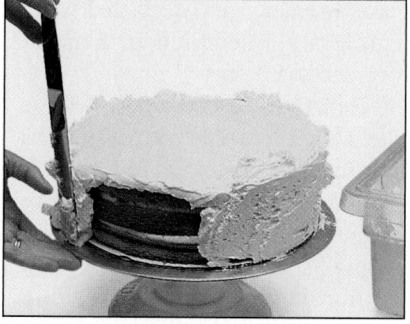

6. Cover the sides with excess frosting from the top, adding more as necessary. Hold the spatula upright against the side of the cake and, pressing gently, turn the cake stand slowly. This smooths and evens the sides. When the sides and top are smooth, the cake is ready to be decorated as desired.

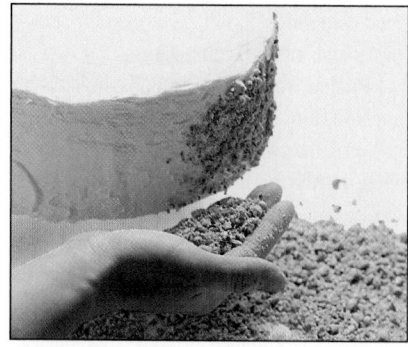

Side masking—coating the sides of a carrot cake with chopped pecans.

Simple Decorating Techniques

An extremely simple yet effective way to decorate a frosted cake is with a garnish of chopped nuts, fruit, toasted coconut, shaved chocolate or other foods arranged in patterns or sprinkled over the cake. Be sure to use a garnish that complements the cake and frosting flavours or reflects one of the cake's ingredients. For example, finely chopped pecans would be an appropriate garnish for a carrot cake that contains pecans; shaved chocolate would not.

Side masking is the technique of coating only the sides of a cake with garnish. The top may be left plain or decorated with icing designs or a message. Be sure to apply the garnish while the frosting is still damp enough for it to adhere.

Stencils can be used to apply patterns of finely chopped garnishes, confectioner's sugar or cocoa powder to the top of a cake. A design can be cut from cardboard, or thin plastic forms can be purchased. Even simple strips of parchment paper can be used to create an attractive pattern. If using a stencil on a frosted cake allow the frosting to set somewhat before laying the stencil on top of it. After the garnishes have been sprinkled over the stencil, carefully lift the stencil to avoid spilling the excess garnish and messing the pattern.

A **cake** or **baker's comb** or a serrated knife can be used to create patterns on a cake iced with buttercream, fudge or ganache. Hold the comb against the frosted cake and rotate the cake slowly and evenly to create horizontal lines in the icing.

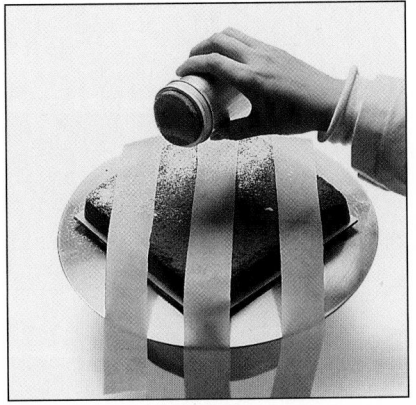

Stencils—creating a design with confectioner's sugar and strips of parchment paper.

Cake comb—creating a pattern on a frosted cake.

Piping Techniques

More elaborate and difficult decorations can be produced with the aid of a piping bag and an assortment of pastry tips. With these tools, frosting or royal icing can be used to create borders, flowers and messages. Before applying any decoration, however, plan a design or pattern that is appropriate for the size and shape of the item being decorated.

When used properly, coloured frostings can bring cake decorations to life. Buttercream, royal icing and fondant are easily tinted using paste food colouring. Liquid food colourings are not recommended as they may thin the frosting too much. Always add colouring gradually with a toothpick. Frosting colours tend to darken as they sit. It is easy to add more later to darken the colour if necessary, but it is difficult to lighten the colour if too much is added.

Piping bags made from plastic, nylon or plastic-coated canvas are available in a range of sizes. A disposable piping cone can also be made from parchment paper.

Most decorations and designs are made by using a piping bag fitted with a pastry tip. Pastry tips are available with dozens of different openings and are referred to by standardized numbers. Some commonly used tips are shown on page 896. You can produce a variety of borders and designs by changing the pressure, the angle of the bag and the distance between the tip and the cake surface.

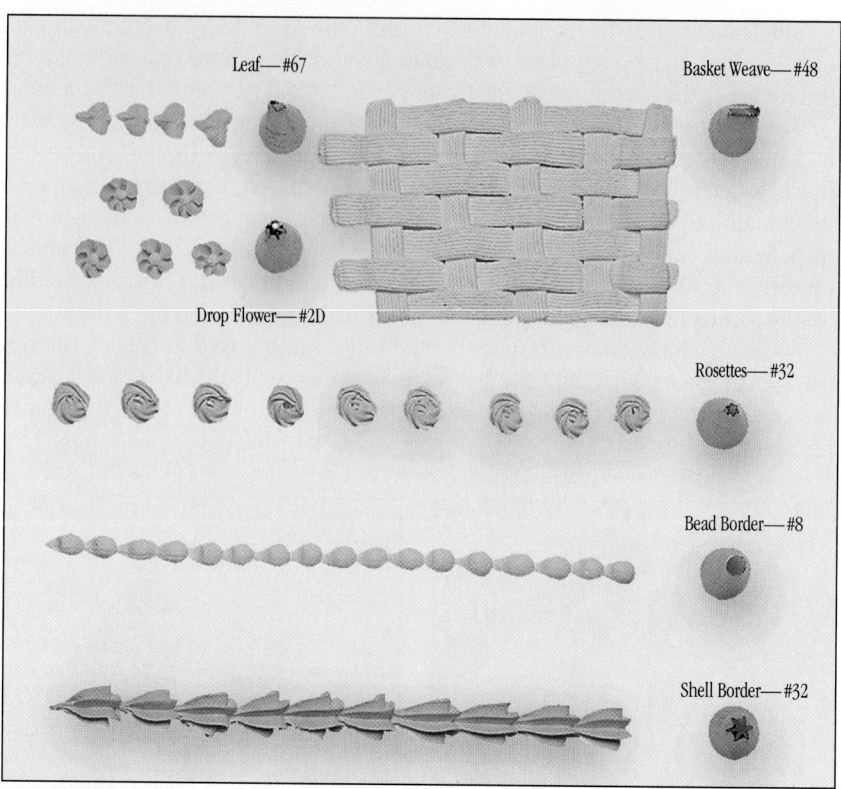

Leaf—#67

Basket Weave—#48

Drop Flower—#2D

Rosettes—#32

Bead Border—#8

Shell Border—#32

Tip Patterns

BASIC PROCEDURE FOR FILLING A PIPING BAG

1. Select the proper size piping bag for your task. Insert the desired tip.

2. Fold down the top of the bag, then fill approximately half full with frosting. Do not overfill the bag.

3. Be sure to close the open end tightly before you start piping. Hold the bag firmly in your palm and squeeze from the top. Do not squeeze from the bottom or you may force the contents out the wrong end. Use the fingers of your other hand to guide the bag as you work.

◆◆◆

MAKING A PARCHMENT-PAPER CONE

A disposable piping bag or cone is easily made from parchment paper. Begin with an equilateral triangle of uncreased paper. Shape it into a cone as shown, folding the top edges together to hold the shape. The point of the cone can be cut as desired. Paper cones are especially useful for writing messages or piping melted chocolate.

1. Wrap opposite ends of the parchment triangle.

2. Fold the ends together to seal.

3. Cut the tip of the filled parchment cone.

Piped-On Decorating Techniques

Instead of leaving the sides of a frosted cake smooth or coating them with chopped nuts or crumbs, you can pipe on frosting designs and patterns. A simple but elegant design is the basket weave, shown below.

Normally a border pattern will be piped around the base of the cake and along the top edge. Borders should be piped on after nuts or any other garnishes are applied.

Each slice or serving of cake can be marked with its own decoration. For example, a rosette of frosting or a whole nut or piece of fruit could be used as shown below. This makes it easier to portion the cake evenly.

Delicate flowers such as roses can be piped, allowed to harden, then placed on the cake in attractive arrangements. Royal icing is particularly useful for making decorations in advance because it dries very hard and lasts indefinitely.

Applying a basket weave pattern to the sides of the wedding cake.

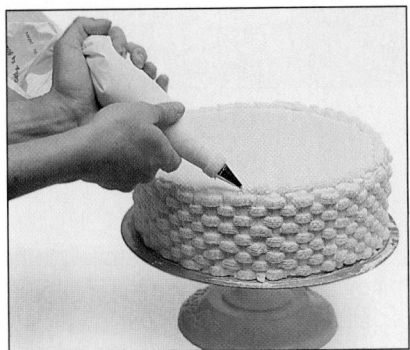

Applying a shell border to the wedding cake.

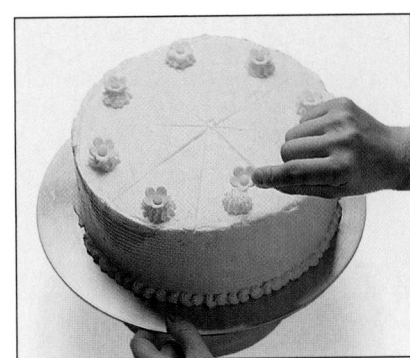

Placing royal icing flowers onto cake portions.

BASIC PROCEDURE FOR PIPING A BUTTERCREAM ROSE

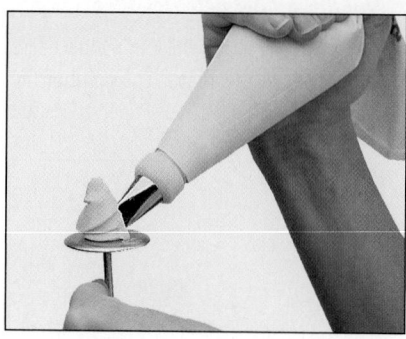

1. Using a #104 tip, pipe a mound of icing onto a rose nail.

2. Pipe a curve of icing around the mound to create the centre of the rose.

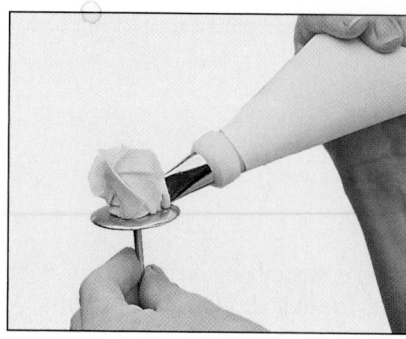

3. Pipe 3 overlapping petals around the centre.

4. Pipe 5 more overlapping petals around the first 3 petals.

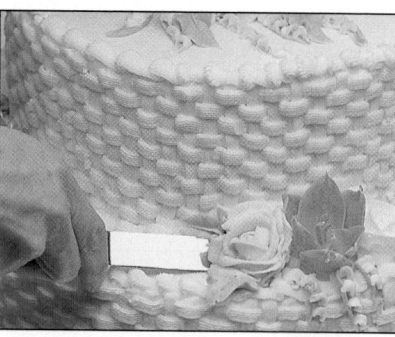

5. The finished rose is placed on the cake.

The key to success with a piping bag is practice, practice, practice. Use plain all-purpose shortening piped onto parchment paper to practise and experiment with piping techniques. Once you are comfortable using a piping bag, you can apply these newfound skills directly to cakes and pastry decorating. Piping skills are also used in other areas of food preparation.

Storing Cakes

Unfrosted cake layers or sheets can be stored at room temperature for two or three days if well covered. Frosted or filled cakes are usually refrigerated to prevent spoilage. Simple buttercreams or sugar glazes, however, can be left at room temperature for one or two days. Any cake containing custard filling or whipped cream, as well as cakes finished with buttercream containing eggs, must be refrigerated. Cakes made with foam-type frosting should be eaten the day they are prepared.

Cakes can usually be frozen with great success; this makes them ideal for baking in advance. Unfrosted layers or sheets should be well covered with plastic wrap and frozen at 0°F (–18°C) or lower. High-fat cakes will keep for up to six months; egg foam cakes begin to deteriorate after two or three months.

Frostings and fillings do not freeze particularly well, often losing flavour or changing texture when frozen. Buttercreams made with egg whites or sugar syrups tend to develop crystals and graininess. Foam frostings weep, expelling beads of sugar and becoming sticky. Fondant will absorb moisture and separate from the cake. If you must freeze a filled or frosted cake, it is best to freeze it unwrapped first, until the frosting is firm. The cake can then be covered with plastic wrap without damaging the frosting design. Leave the cake wrapped until completely thawed. It is best to thaw cakes in the refrigerator if time permits. Do not refreeze thawed cakes.

Conclusion

The ability to produce good cakes and frostings depends on using the right balance of high-quality ingredients and combining them with the proper techniques. When preparing cakes and frostings, always combine flavours and textures with care; apply frostings, garnishes and decorations with care also. Avoid overly rich, cloyingly sweet or garishly decorated products. With study and practice, you can learn the mixing techniques and assembly skills necessary for producing good cakes. Additional practice will develop the decorating and garnishing skills of a fine pastry chef.

Questions for Discussion

1. Raw cake ingredients can be classified by function into six categories. List them and give an example of each.
2. What is the primary leavening agent in cakes made with the foaming method? How is this similar to or different from cakes made with the creaming method?
3. What is the difference between a spongecake and a classic genoise?
4. Describe the procedures for making three types of frosting or icing as discussed in this chapter.
5. List the steps employed in assembling and frosting a three-layer cake.

ADDITIONAL CAKE AND FROSTING FORMULAS

RECIPE 30.16

VANILLA RASPBERRY LAYER CAKE WITH WHITE CHOCOLATE BUTTERCREAM

NOTE: *This dish appears in the Chapter Opening photograph.*

HYATT REGENCY SCOTTSDALE AT GAINEY RANCH, SCOTTSDALE, AZ
Executive Pastry Chef Judy Doherty

VANILLA CAKES

Yield: 1 8-inch (20-cm), 1 10-inch (25-cm) and   **Method:** Two-Stage
1 14-inch (35-cm) tier for Wedding Cake

Cake flour	1 lb. 14 oz.	850 g
Granulated sugar	2 lb. 8 oz.	1.13 kg
Baking powder	2-1/2 oz.	70 g
Eggs	48 oz.	1.4 kg
Salt	1 oz.	28 g
Fluid Flex	1 lb. 4 oz.	570 g
Milk	1 pt.	450 mL

Approximate values per 6 oz. (180 g) serving:

Calories	600
Total fat	28 g
Saturated fat	7 g
Cholesterol	240 mg
Sodium	520 mg
Total carbohydrates	75 g
Protein	10 g
Vitamin A	10%
Calcium	20%

1. Prepare the pans by spraying with pan release and lining with parchment paper.
2. Combine the flour, sugar, baking powder, eggs and salt in a large mixer bowl. Whip on high speed for 8 minutes.
3. Add Fluid Flex (an emulsifier for spongecakes) and milk. Mix for 8 more minutes at medium speed.
4. Divide the batter between 1 8-inch (20-cm), 1 10-inch (25-cm) and 1 14-inch (35-cm) cake pan. Fill each pan halfway.
5. Bake at 350°F (180°C) for 35–60 minutes, depending upon tier size. The cake is done when it springs back when lightly touched in the centre. Allow to cool, then remove from the pans and freeze.

RASPBERRY SYRUP

Water	16 oz.	450 mL
Granulated sugar	1 lb.	450 g
Raspberry liqueur	2 oz.	60 mL

Bring the sugar and water to a boil, then cool to room temperature. Add the raspberry liqueur.

DIPLOMAT CREAM FILLING

Pastry cream, chilled	1 gal.	4 L
Raspberry liqueur	4 oz.	120 mL
Gelatin	1-1/2 oz.	42 g
Water	6 oz.	170 mL
Whipped cream	1 qt.	1 L

1. Place the pastry cream in a large mixer bowl and whip on high speed until smooth. Add the raspberry liqueur.

2. Soften the gelatin in the water, then place over a low flame and heat to dissolve.

3. Add 1 pint (450 mL) of the raspberry-flavoured pastry cream to the gelatin. Place over a low flame and whip by hand until smooth and the gelatin is incorporated. Add this mixture to the remainder of the pastry cream.

4. Fold in the whipped cream.

WHITE CHOCOLATE BUTTERCREAM

Sugar	5 lb. 8 oz.	2.5 kg
Water	1 lb. 6 oz.	625 mL
Egg whites	1 lb. 12 oz.	800 g
Unsalted butter, softened	7 lb.	3.15 kg
White crème de cacao	9 oz.	260 mL
White chocolate, melted	1 lb. 8 oz.	680 g

Approximate values per 1 oz. (30 g) serving:	
Calories	40
Total fat	2 g
Saturated fat	1 g
Cholesterol	30 mg
Sodium	10 mg
Total carbohydrates	5 g
Protein	1 g

1. Cook the sugar and water to 242°F (117°C), then pour into a measuring container with a handle for easier pouring.

2. Start whipping the egg whites when the sugar reaches 235°F (113°C).

3. When the whites are whipped to firm peaks, add the hot sugar syrup slowly while continuing to whip at low speed. Whip until completely cool.

4. Add the butter and whip until smooth.

5. Add the crème de cacao to the white chocolate. Whip until smooth, then add to the buttercream.

ASSEMBLY: Each cake tier is sliced horizontally into 3 layers. The layers are brushed with the raspberry syrup, then filled with diplomat cream and fresh raspberries. The top and sides of each tier are coated with the white chocolate buttercream; the sides are coated with a basketweave design; and the tiers are decorated with pulled sugar and royal icing roses. The assembly is illustrated in the photographs appearing throughout this chapter.

Approximate values per 1 oz. (30 g) serving:	
Calories	140
Total fat	11 g
Saturated fat	7 g
Cholesterol	25 mg
Sodium	10 mg
Total carbohydrates	10 g
Protein	1 g
Vitamin A	8%

━━━━━ ◆◆◆ ━━━━━

RECIPE 30.17

CARROT CAKE WITH CREAM CHEESE FROSTING

Yield: 5 Sheet Cakes or 16 10-inch (25-cm) Rounds   **Method:** Creaming

Vegetable oil	3 lb. 8 oz.	1.75 kg
Granulated sugar	3 lb. 11 oz.	1.85 kg
Eggs	1 lb. 12 oz.	875 g
Carrots, shredded	5 lb.	2.5 kg
Crushed pineapple, with juice	3 lb. 4 oz.	1.625 kg
Baking soda	1-1/2 oz.	45 g
Cinnamon	2 oz.	60 g
Pumpkin pie spice	1-1/2 oz.	45 g
Salt	1-1/2 oz.	45 g
Baking powder	1-1/4 oz.	40 g
Cake flour	4 lb. 10 oz.	2.3 kg
Coconut, shredded	1 lb.	500 g
Walnut pieces	1 lb.	500 g

Continued

Approximate values per serving:

Calories	390
Total fat	22 g
Saturated fat	4 g
Cholesterol	40 mg
Sodium	490 mg
Total carbohydrates	44 g
Protein	5 g
Vitamin A	100%

Approximate values per serving:

Calories	130
Total fat	6 g
Saturated fat	3 g
Cholesterol	15 mg
Sodium	45 mg
Total carbohydrates	17 g
Protein	1 g
Vitamin A	6%

1. Blend the oil and sugar in a large mixer bowl fitted with the paddle attachment. Add the eggs, beating to incorporate.

2. Blend in the carrots and pineapple.

3. Sift the dry ingredients together, then add them to the batter. Stir in the coconut and walnuts.

4. Divide the batter into greased and floured pans, scaling at 5 pounds (2.2 kg) per sheet pan or 1 pound 8 ounces (680 g) per 10-inch (25-cm) round.

5. Bake at 340°F (170°C) until springy to the touch and a cake tester comes out almost clean.

CREAM CHEESE FROSTING

Unsalted butter, softened	12 oz.	350 g
Cream cheese, softened	3 lb.	1.5 kg
Margarine	12 oz.	350 g
Vanilla extract	1 oz.	30 mL
Icing sugar, sifted	6 lb.	3 kg

1. Cream the butter and cream cheese until smooth. Add the margarine and beat well.

2. Beat in the vanilla extract. Slowly add the sugar, scraping down the bowl frequently. Beat until smooth.

RECIPE 30.18

Sacher Torte

SOUTHERN ALBERTA INSTITUTE OF TECHNOLOGY, Calgary, AB
Pastry Chef Andreas Schwarzer

Yield: 6 9-inch (22-cm) Cakes

Butter	1 lb.	500 g
Sugar	1 lb.	500 g
Sweet chocolate, melted	1 lb. 6 oz.	625 g
Egg yolks	1 lb.	500 g
Vanilla	1/2 oz.	15 mL
Egg whites	1 lb. 10 oz.	750 g
Salt	1/8 oz.	4 g
Sugar	13 oz.	375 g
Cake flour, sifted	1 lb.	500 g
Apricot jam	as needed	as needed
Chocolate icing	as needed	as needed
Chocolate glaze	as needed	as needed

1. Grease the sides of 6 9-inch (22-cm) springform pans with some butter and line the bottoms with parchment circles.

2. Cream the butter until light and add sugar, beating until fluffy.

3. Beat in melted chocolate until smooth.

4. Add egg yolks in 5 stages, beating well after each addition.

5. Beat in vanilla.

Andreas Schwarzer

Andreas worked in pastry shops and bakeries in Germany before coming to Canada. He has won several medals for his pastries and showpieces, and has worked on banquets for such celebrities as Clint Eastwood, Arnold Schwarzenegger, Margaret Thatcher, and Prince Philip.

6. Whip egg whites and salt to soft peaks.

7. Gradually whisk in sugar to form soft meringue.

8. Add flour in stages. Fold in meringue last for maximum aeration.

9. Pan batter. Bake at 375°F (180°C) for 45–60 minutes.

10. Cool cakes for 5 minutes and depan. Cool completely, then cut each cake horizontally into 2 layers. Spread apricot jam between layers and stack to make 6 cakes.

11. Ice cakes with chocolate icing and refrigerate.

12. Pour chocolate glaze over each cake to form a complete, smooth, glossy coating.

Note: This recipe has been adjusted for preparation at an altitude of 1200 metres.

Approximate values per serving:

Calories	280
Total fat	15 g
Saturated fat	8 g
Cholesterol	129 mg
Sodium	88 mg
Total carbohydrates	35 g
Protein	5 g

RECIPE 30.19

Zuppa Romana

SOUTHERN ALBERTA INSTITUTE OF TECHNOLOGY, Calgary, AB
Master Pâtissier Hermann Greineder

Yield: 12 to 16 Servings

White sponge cake, 9 inches (22 cm)	1	1
Simple syrup	10 oz.	300 mL
Brandy	2 oz.	50 mL
Rum	2 oz.	50 mL
Pastry Cream Filling:		
Pastry cream	7 oz.	200 g
Cream, 35%, whipped	1 qt.	1 L
Fruit Filling:		
Cherry pie filling	5 oz.	150 g
Mandarin sections	2-1/2 oz.	75 g
Fresh strawberries	2-1/2 oz.	75 g
Lemon, juice and grated rind	1	1
Cream, 35%	4 cups	1 L

Hermann Greineder
Currently a pastry instructor at SAIT, Hermann got his German Master Certification as "Chef Pâtissier" in 1971. He has 41 years of experience in a wide range of establishments, and has won several medals for his lovely chocolate showpieces.

1. Slice sponge cake into 3 1/4-inch- (6-mm-) thick layers. Place first sponge layer in appropriate dish (a silver platter, for example). Soak the cake well with about a third of the simple syrup, flavoured with brandy and rum.

2. Make the pastry cream filling by mixing the pastry cream and whipped cream together. Prepare the fruit filling by mixing the cherry pie filling, mandarin sections, strawberries and lemon juice and rind.

3. Spread pastry cream 1/8-inch (3-mm) thick on the bottom layer. Place all the fruit filling on top of the pastry cream. Add the next sponge layer, another third of the syrup and a layer of pastry cream. Place final sponge layer on top of filling and soak it very well with the remaining syrup. Ice with whipped cream and decorate.

Approximate values per serving:

Calories	562
Total fat	29 g
Saturated fat	17 g
Cholesterol	225 mg
Sodium	172 mg
Total carbohydrates	64 g
Protein	7 g

✦✦✦

RECIPE 30.20

DEVIL'S FOOD CAKE

Yield: 5 Sheet Pans or
30 8-inch (20-cm) Rounds

Method: High-Ratio (2-stage method)

Cake flour	5 lb.	2.5 kg
Granulated sugar	6 lb.	3 kg
Emulsified shortening	3 lb.	1.5 kg
Cocoa powder	1 lb.	500 g
Salt	2-1/2 oz.	75 g
Baking powder	3 oz.	90 g
Baking soda	1-1/2 oz.	45 g
Nonfat dry milk powder	9-1/2 oz.	270 g
Vanilla extract	1-1/2 oz.	45 mL
Corn syrup	1 lb.	500 g
Water, cold	2 qt. 8 oz.	2.25 L
Eggs	4 lb.	2 kg

*Approximate values per
3.5 oz. (105 g) serving:*

Calories	400
Total fat	17 g
Saturated fat	5 g
Cholesterol	80 mg
Sodium	460 mg
Total carbohydrates	55 g
Protein	6 g
Calcium	10%
Iron	15%

1. Mix the cake flour, sugar and emulsified shortening in a large mixer bowl on low speed for 5 minutes.
2. Add the cocoa powder, salt, baking powder, baking soda, milk powder, vanilla, corn syrup and 1 quart (1 L) cold water. Blend well, then scrape down the bowl.
3. Combine the eggs with the remaining 1 quart 8 ounces (1250 mL) cold water and add to the batter in 3 equal parts, blending well and scraping down the bowl after each addition.
4. After all ingredients are incorporated, blend on low speed for 2 minutes.
5. Divide into greased and floured pans, scaling 1 gallon (4 L) of batter for each sheet pan or 1 pound (450 g) for each 8-inch (20-cm) round layer.
6. Bake at 340°F (170°C) until springy and a toothpick inserted in the centre comes out clean.

✦✦✦

RECIPE 30.21

BÛCHE DE NOËL

Yield: 10–12 Servings

Genoise (Recipe 30.3), freshly baked	one-half sheet	one-half sheet
Simple syrup	as needed	as needed
Buttercream—coffee, chocolate or vanilla	1 qt.	1 L

1. Roll up the genoise in a spiral, starting with the long side. Wrap in parchment paper and cool.
2. Carefully unroll the cake. Brush the interior with simple syrup and coat with buttercream, leaving a 1-inch (2.5-cm) unfrosted rim around each edge.
3. Reroll the cake tightly and position it with the seam down on a cake cardboard.
4. Cut 1 end from the cake on a diagonal. Place the cut piece on top of the log, securing with toothpicks.

5. Pipe additional buttercream onto the cake log using a large star tip. Pipe the buttercream onto the ends in a spiral pattern. Decorate as desired with buttercream flowers, baked meringue mushrooms or marzipan figures.

Approximate values per serving:

Calories	650
Total fat	21 g
Saturated fat	6 g
Cholesterol	0 mg
Sodium	330 mg
Total carbohydrates	115 g
Protein	2 g
Vitamin C	70%

Claims—no cholesterol

1. Roll the cake filled with buttercream.

2. Attach the cut end to the log.

3. Pipe on the buttercream.

◆◆◆

RECIPE 30.22

LADYFINGERS

Yield: 80 4-inch (10-cm) Cookies

Cornstarch	3 oz.	90 g
Bread flour	4 oz.	120 g
Eggs, separated	6	6
Granulated sugar	6 oz.	180 g
Lemon juice	1/2 tsp.	2 mL

1. Sift the cornstarch and bread flour together.

2. Whip the egg yolks with 2 ounces (60 g) of sugar until thick and creamy.

3. Whip the egg whites until foamy. Gradually add 2 ounces (60 g) of the sugar and the lemon juice. Continue whipping to soft peaks, then add the remaining sugar gradually and whip to stiff peaks.

4. Fold approximately one-quarter of the egg whites into the whipped yolks to lighten them, then gently fold in the remaining whites. Fold in the flour mixture.

5. Place the batter into a pastry bag fitted with a large plain tip. Pipe 4-inch-long (10-cm-) cookies onto paper-lined sheet pans.

6. Bake immediately at 425°F (220°C) until lightly browned, approximately 8 minutes.

Approximate values per cookie:

Calories	20
Total fat	0 g
Saturated fat	0 g
Cholesterol	15 mg
Sodium	0 mg
Total carbohydrates	4 g
Protein	1 g

Claims—fat free; no saturated fat; low cholesterol; no sodium; low calorie

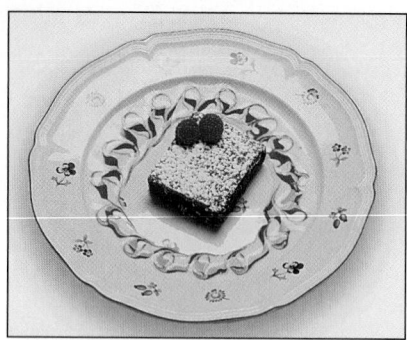

Approximate values per
4 oz. (120 g) serving:

Calories	470
Total fat	35 g
Saturated fat	20 g
Cholesterol	250 mg
Sodium	65 mg
Total carbohydrates	32 g
Protein	8 g
Vitamin A	25%

◆◆◆

RECIPE 30.23

CHOCOLATE FLOURLESS CAKE

VINCENT ON CAMELBACK, PHOENIX, AZ
Chef Vincent Guerithault

Yield: 21 Servings

Unsalted butter	1 lb.	450 g
Chocolate	1 lb. 11 oz.	800 g
Eggs, separated	20	20
Granulated sugar	7 oz.	200 g
Powdered sugar	as needed	as needed

1. Melt the butter and chocolate over a bain marie.
2. Whisk the yolks into the melted chocolate.
3. Whip the egg whites until shiny. Add the granulated sugar and whip until very stiff. Fold into the chocolate. Pour the batter into a full-sized hotel pan that is lined with buttered parchment.
4. Bake at 400°F (200°C) for 10 minutes. Reduce the oven temperature to 350°F (180°C) and continue baking until done, approximately 40 minutes. A cake tester will not come out clean, even though the cake will be done.
5. Invert the cake onto the back of a sheet pan. Cool completely; then dust with powdered sugar.

◆◆◆

RECIPE 30.24

CHOCOLATE TRUFFLE CAKE

FLYING FISH, SEATTLE, WA
Pastry Chef Robin Reiels

Yield: 12 Servings

Semisweet chocolate	8 oz.	250 g
Unsalted butter, softened	8 oz.	250 g
Granulated sugar	5 oz.	150 g
Eggs, separated	6 large	6 large
Cream of tartar	1/2 tsp.	3 mL
Ganache Filling (recipe follows)		
Ganache Coating (recipe follows)		
Whipped cream	as needed for garnish	
Fresh berries	as needed for garnish	

1. Melt the chocolate over a bain marie and set aside.
2. Cream the butter and 2 tablespoons (30 mL) of the sugar until light and fluffy. Slowly add the egg yolks, one at a time.
3. Scrape down the sides of the mixing bowl and add the melted chocolate.
4. In a clean, dry mixing bowl, whip the egg whites and cream of tartar to soft peaks. Gradually sprinkle in the remaining sugar and continue beating until stiff but not dry.

5. Fold one-quarter of the egg whites into the chocolate mixture to lighten. Gently fold the remaining egg whites into the chocolate, then pour the batter into an ungreased 9-inch (23-cm) springform pan. Bake at 325°F (160°C) until a toothpick inserted in the centre comes out clean, approximately 45 minutes.

6. Allow the cake to cool, then remove from the pan. When the cake is completely cool and firm to the touch, top it with the Ganache Filling, using a spatula to form the ganache into a dome shape.

7. Refrigerate until the filling is firm. Place the cake on an icing rack over a baking pan and pour the Ganache Coating over the entire cake. Refrigerate briefly to set the coating before serving.

GANACHE FILLING

Yield: 34 oz. (1020 g)

Cream, 35%	2-1/2 cups	600 mL
Semisweet chocolate, chopped	14 oz.	420 g

1. Bring the cream to a boil, remove from the heat and whisk in the chocolate. Stir until the chocolate is completely melted. Refrigerate until firm.

2. Just before use, gently whip the ganache to lighten.

GANACHE COATING

Yield: 17 oz. (510 g)

Cream, 35%	8 oz.	240 mL
Semisweet chocolate, chopped	8 oz.	240 g
Unsalted butter	1 oz.	30 g

Bring the cream to a boil, remove from the heat and add the chocolate and butter. Stir gently to melt the chocolate and butter, but do not whisk the ganache.

Approximate values per serving:

Calories	681
Total fat	61 g
Saturated fat	36 g
Cholesterol	247 mg
Sodium	60 mg
Total carbohydrates	39 g
Protein	8 g

Approximate values per 1 oz. (30 g) serving:

Calories	107
Total fat	11 g
Saturated fat	6 g
Cholesterol	34 mg
Sodium	10 mg
Total carbohydrates	3.5 g
Protein	1 g

Approximate values per 1 oz. (30 g) serving:

Calories	122
Total fat	11 g
Saturated fat	6 g
Cholesterol	23 mg
Sodium	5 mg
Total carbohydrates	8 g
Protein	1 g

◆◆◆

RECIPE 30.25

APPLESAUCE BROWNIES

Yield: 1 Sheet Pan

Unsweetened chocolate	4 oz.	120 g
Cake flour, sifted	1 lb.	500 g
Cocoa powder	9 oz.	270 g
Salt	2 tsp.	10 mL
Egg whites	12	12
Whole eggs	8	8
Granulated sugar	2 lb. 2 oz.	1 kg
Light corn syrup	2 lb.	1 kg
Unsweetened applesauce	1-1/2 pt.	750 mL
Canola oil	7 oz.	210 mL
Vanilla extract	2 Tbsp.	30 mL

Continued

Approximate values per 2-inch (5-cm) square:

Calories	150
Total fat	5 g
Saturated fat	.8 g
Cholesterol	19 mg
Sodium	82 mg
Total carbohydrates	26 g
Protein	2 g

1. Coat a sheet pan with pan-release spray.
2. Melt the chocolate over a bain marie and set aside.
3. Sift the flour, cocoa powder and salt together and set aside.
4. Whisk the egg whites and eggs together. Add the sugar, corn syrup, apple-sauce, oil and vanilla. Whisk in the chocolate.
5. Fold the flour mixture into the egg mixture. Pour into the prepared pan and bake at 350°F (180°C) until a cake tester comes out clean, approximately 25 minutes.

Peter Phillips

Peter hails from Nipawin, Saskatchewan. He trained at Humber College in Toronto, where he was inspired to specialize in pastries. He was a member of Team Saskatchewan until joining Team Canada, and recently won a silver medal in Singapore.

✦✦✦

RECIPE 30.26

TIRAMISU TORTE

BOFFINS, SASKATOON, SK
Peter Phillips, Executive Chef and Manager

Yield: 1 9-inch (22-cm) torte

Gelatin leaves	4	4
Water	1 oz.	30 mL
Egg yolks	6	6
Mascarpone	18 oz.	500 g
Egg whites	6	6
Sugar	3 oz.	90 g
Espresso	4 oz.	125 mL
Ladyfingers and Cake (recipe follows)		
Cocoa powder, dutched	TT	TT

1. Soak gelatin in cold water until soft, approximately 10 minutes.
2. At medium speed, whisk the egg yolks until light and fluffy.
3. Add the egg yolks to the gelatin in small quantities and continue mixing, until well blended.
4. Add the mascarpone and mix well.
5. In a separate bowl, whip the egg whites until foamy. Continue to whip while gradually adding sugar, until soft peaks form.
6. Fold egg-white mixture into cheese mixture in three stages, mixing well.
7. Place the 9-inch (22.5-cm) cake layer in a 9-inch (22.5-cm) cake ring on a 12-inch (30-cm) cake board and brush lightly with espresso.
8. Cut each ladyfinger in half and place upright around the inside of the cake ring.
9. Pour in half the cheese mixture.
10. Place the remaining cake layer on top of the mixture and brush well with espresso.
11. Pour in the remaining cheese mixture.
12. Refrigerate for 2 to 3 hours.
13. Dust with cocoa powder.

Approximate values per serving:

Calories	472
Total fat	24 g
Saturated fat	13 g
Cholesterol	308 mg
Sodium	274 mg
Total carbohydrates	51 g
Protein	16 g

LADYFINGERS AND CAKE

Yield: 20 ladyfingers, 1 9-inch (22.5-cm) layer and
1 7-inch (17.5-cm) layer

Egg yolks	6	6
Vanilla	1 tsp.	5 mL
Sugar	6-1/2 oz.	190 g
Egg whites	6	6
Bread flour, sifted	5 oz.	145 g
Cornstarch	1 oz.	30 g

1. At medium speed, whisk the egg yolks, vanilla and 1 oz. (30 g) of sugar until light and fluffy.

2. In a separate bowl, whip the egg whites until foamy. Continue to whip while gradually adding the remaining sugar, until soft peaks form.

3. Fold approximately one third of the egg whites into the whipped yolks to lighten them; fold in another third and then the remaining third.

4. Sift together flour and cornstarch, and fold into the egg mixture.

5. Place batter in a piping bag fitted with a plain No. 8 tip.

6. To make the ladyfingers, pipe 20 4-inch-long (10-cm-long) cookies onto paper-lined sheet pans. Allow for some spreading during baking.

7. To make the base and centre layers of cake, draw one 9-inch (22.5-cm) circle and one 7-inch (17.5-cm) circle on parchment paper to make a template and turn over onto a sheet pan (allow for some spreading during baking). Pipe batter onto the circles.

8. Sprinkle both trays with sugar and bake at 425°F (218°C) until golden brown, 8–10 minutes.

Approximate values per 1 oz. (30 g) serving:	
Calories	77
Total fat	1 g
Saturated fat	.4 g
Cholesterol	53 mg
Sodium	35 mg
Total carbohydrates	14 g
Protein	2 g

WEBLINKS

American Cake Decorating Magazine
  www.cakemag.com/
Wedding Cake Decorating
  www.pastrywiz.com/season/wedding.htm
Cakes
  www.joyofbaking.com/cakes.html

CHAPTER 31

CUSTARDS, CREAMS, FROZEN DESSERTS AND DESSERT SAUCES

*T*he bakeshop is responsible for more than just quick breads, yeast breads, pies, pastries, cookies and cakes. It also produces many delightfully sweet concoctions that are not baked and often not even cooked. These include sweet custards, creams, frozen desserts and dessert sauces. Sweet custards are cooked mixtures of eggs, sugar and milk; starch may be added. Sweet custards can be flavoured in a variety of ways and eaten hot or cold. Some are served alone as a dessert or used as a filling, topping or accompaniment for pies, pastries or cakes. Creams include whipped cream and mixtures lightened with whipped cream such as Bavarians, chiffons and mousses. Frozen desserts include ice cream and sorbet as well as the still-frozen mousses called semifreddi.

Sauces for these desserts, including fruit purées, caramel sauces and chocolate syrup, are also made in the bakeshop and are discussed in this chapter. Indeed, many of the items presented in this chapter are components, meant to be combined with pastries (Chapter 29) or cakes (Chapter 30) to form complete desserts. Guidelines for assembling desserts are given at this chapter's end.

CUSTARDS

A **custard** is any liquid thickened by the coagulation of egg proteins. A custard's consistency depends on the ratio of eggs to liquid and the type of liquid used. The more eggs used, the thicker and richer the final product will be. The richer the liquid (cream versus milk, for example), the thicker the final product. Most custards, with the notable exception of pastry creams, are not thickened by starch.

A custard can be stirred or baked. A **stirred custard** tends to be soft, rich and creamy. A **baked custard**, typically cooked in a bain marie, is usually firm enough to unmould and slice.

Stirred Custards

A stirred custard is cooked on the stove top either directly in a saucepan or over a double boiler. It must be stirred throughout the cooking process to prevent curdling (overcooking).

A stirred custard can be used as a dessert sauce, incorporated into a complex dessert or eaten alone. The stirred custards most commonly used in food service operations are **vanilla custard sauce** and **pastry cream**. Other popular stirred custards are lemon curd (Recipe 25.16) and **sabayon** (Recipe 31.3).

Vanilla Custard Sauce

A custard sauce is made with egg yolks, sugar and milk or cereal cream. Usually flavoured with vanilla bean or pure vanilla extract, a custard sauce can also be flavoured with liquor, chocolate, ground nuts or other extracts.

It is prepared on the stove top over direct heat. When making custard sauce, be extremely careful to stir the mixture continually and not allow it to boil, or it will curdle. A properly made custard sauce should be smooth and thick enough to coat the back of a spoon. It should not contain any noticeable bits of cooked egg.

Vanilla custard sauce (Fr. *crème anglaise*) is served with cakes, pastries, fruits and soufflés and is often used for decorating dessert plates. It may be served hot or cold. It is also used as the base for many ice creams.

A very thick version of custard sauce can be made using 35% cream and additional egg yolks. Its consistency is more like a pudding than a sauce. This custard is often served over fruit in a small ramekin or other container and then topped with caramelized sugar for a dessert known as **crème brûlée** (burnt cream). See Recipe 31.15.

Pastry Cream

Pastry cream (Fr. *crème pâtissière*) is a stirred custard made with egg yolks, sugar and milk and thickened with cornstarch. Because starch protects the egg yolks from curdling, pastry cream can be boiled. In fact, it must be boiled to fully gelatinize the starch and eliminate the taste of raw starch.

Pastry cream can be flavoured with chocolate, liquors, extracts or fruits. (Pudding is nothing more than flavoured pastry cream.) It is used for filling éclairs, cream puffs, napoleons, fruit tarts and other pastries. Pastry cream is also the filling for cream pies (see Chapter 29, Pies, Pastries and Cookies). Pastry cream is thick enough to hold its shape without making pastry doughs soggy.

Pastry cream can be rather heavy. It can be lightened by folding in whipped cream to produce a **mousseline**, or Italian meringue can be folded in to produce a **crème Chiboust**.

BASIC PROCEDURE FOR PREPARING VANILLA CUSTARD SAUCE AND PASTRY CREAM

1. Place milk and/or cream in a heavy, nonreactive saucepan; add vanilla bean if desired.
2. In a mixing bowl, whisk together the egg yolks, sugar and starch (if used). Do not use an electric mixer as it incorporates too much air.
3. Bring the liquid just to a boil. **Temper** the egg mixture with approximately one-third of the hot liquid.
4. Pour the tempered eggs into the remaining hot liquid and return the mixture to the heat. The stove's temperature can be as hot as you dare: The lower the temperature, the longer the custard will take to thicken; the higher the temperature, the greater the risk of curdling. The thickening agent for custard sauce is eggs. The thickener for pastry cream is cornstarch.
5. Cook, stirring constantly, until thickened. Custard sauce should reach a temperature of 185°F (85°C). Pastry cream should be allowed to boil for a few moments.
6. Immediately remove the cooked custard from the hot saucepan to avoid overcooking. Butter or other flavourings can be added at this time.
7. Cool over an ice bath. Store in a clean, shallow container, cover and refrigerate.

BASIC PROCEDURE FOR SALVAGING CURDLED VANILLA CUSTARD SAUCE

1. Strain the sauce into a bowl. Place the bowl over an ice bath and whisk vigorously.
2. If this does not smooth out the overcooked sauce, place the sauce in a blender and process for a few moments.

Temper—*to heat gently and gradually; refers to the process of slowly adding a hot liquid to eggs to raise their temperature without causing them to curdle.*

♦♦♦

RECIPE 31.1

VANILLA SAUCE

Yield: 40 oz. (1.2 L)

Cereal cream	1 qt.	1 L
Vanilla bean, split	1	1
Egg yolks	12	12
Granulated sugar	10 oz.	300 g

Approximate values per 1 fl. oz. (30 mL) serving:

Calories	80
Total fat	4.5 g
Saturated fat	2.5 g
Cholesterol	75 mg
Sodium	15 mg
Total carbohydrates	8 g
Protein	2 g
Vitamin A	6%

1. Using a heavy, nonreactive saucepan, bring the cream and vanilla bean just to a boil.
2. Whisk the egg yolks and sugar together in a mixing bowl. Temper the egg mixture with approximately one-third of the hot cream, then return the entire mixture to the saucepan with the remaining cream.
3. Cook the sauce over medium heat, stirring constantly, until it is thick enough to coat the back of a spoon. Do not allow the sauce to boil.
4. As soon as the sauce thickens, remove it from the heat and pour it through a fine mesh strainer into a clean bowl. Chill the sauce over an ice bath, then cover and keep refrigerated. The sauce should last 3–4 days.

1. Mise en place for vanilla sauce.

2. Temper the eggs.

3. The properly cooked sauce.

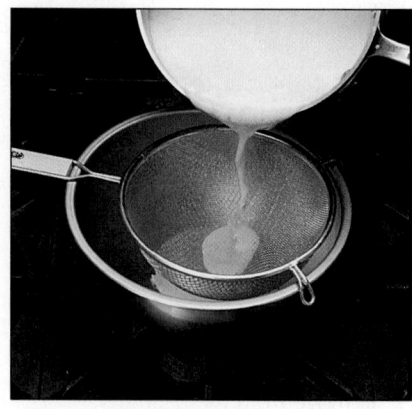

4. Strain the sauce into a bowl.

◆◆◆

RECIPE 31.2

PASTRY CREAM

Yield: 1-1/2 qt. (1.5 L)

Cornstarch	3 oz.	90 g
Sugar	6 oz.	180 g
Milk	32 oz.	1 L
Egg yolks	6	6
Butter (optional)	1-3/4 oz.	50 g

1. Dilute the cornstarch and half the sugar with 8 oz. (250 mL) of cold milk and egg yolks. Whisk until very smooth.
2. Bring the remaining milk and sugar to a boil.
3. Blend the two mixtures together gradually, stirring constantly.
4. Place back on the heat and cook for a few minutes, stirring constantly, until thickened.
5. Remove the pan from the heat and stir in butter if desired. Transfer mixture to a clean bowl.
6. Cover with plastic film and cool over ice bath.

Approximate values per
1 oz. (30 g) serving:

Calories	47
Total fat	2 g
Saturated fat	1 g
Cholesterol	30 mg
Sodium	11 mg
Total carbohydrates	6 g
Protein	1 g

1. Stir the pastry cream as it comes to a boil.

2. Fold butter into the cooked pastry cream.

Sabayon

Sabayon (It. *zabaglione*) is a foamy, stirred custard sauce made by whisking eggs, sugar and wine over low heat. The egg proteins coagulate, thickening the mixture, while the whisking incorporates air to make it light and fluffy. Usually a sweet wine is used; marsala and champagne are the most popular choices.

The mixture can be served warm, or it can be chilled. Sabayon may be served alone or as a sauce or topping with fruit or pastries such as sponge-cake or ladyfingers.

BASIC PROCEDURE FOR PREPARING SABAYON

1. Combine egg yolks, sugar and wine in the top of a double boiler.
2. Place the double boiler over low heat and whisk constantly until the sauce is foamy and thick enough to form a ribbon when the whisk is lifted.
3. Remove from the heat and serve immediately, or whisk over an ice bath until cool. If allowed to sit, the hot mixture may separate.

The thickened sabayon.

Approximate values per 1 fl. oz. (30 mL) serving:	
Calories	50
Total fat	4 g
Saturated fat	2 g
Cholesterol	60 mg
Sodium	25 mg
Total carbohydrates	4 g
Protein	1 g
Vitamin A	6%

♦♦♦

RECIPE 31.3
CHAMPAGNE SABAYON

Yield: 1 qt. (1 L)

Egg yolks	8	8
Granulated sugar	4 oz.	120 g
Salt	1/4 tsp.	1 mL
Marsala wine	2 oz.	60 mL
Dry champagne	6 oz.	180 mL
Cream, 35% (optional; see Variation)	8 oz.	250 mL

1. Combine the egg yolks, sugar and salt in a stainless steel bowl.

2. Add the marsala and champagne to the egg mixture.

3. Place the bowl over a pan of barely simmering water. Whisk vigorously until the sauce is thick and pale yellow, approximately 10 minutes. Serve immediately.

VARIATION: To prepare a sabayon mousseline, place the bowl of sabayon over an ice bath and continue whisking until completely cold. Whip the cream to soft peaks and fold it into the cold sabayon.

Baked Custards

A baked custard is based on the same principle as a stirred custard: A liquid thickens by the coagulation of egg proteins. However, with a baked custard, the thickening occurs in an oven. The container of custard is usually placed in a water bath (bain marie) to protect the eggs from curdling. Even though the water bath's temperature will not exceed 212°F (100°C), care must be taken not to bake the custards for too long or at too high a temperature. An over-baked custard will be watery or curdled; a properly baked custard should be smooth-textured and firm enough to slice.

Baked custards include simple mixtures of egg yolks, sugar and milk such as **crème caramel** as well as custard mixtures in which other ingredients are suspended, for example, **cheesecake**, rice pudding, **bread pudding** and quiche.

Crème Caramel

Crème caramel, crème renversée and flan all refer to an egg custard baked over a layer of caramelized sugar and inverted for service. The caramelized sugar produces a golden-brown surface on the inverted custard and a thin caramel sauce.

♦♦♦

RECIPE 31.4
TOFFEE CARAMEL FLAN

Yield: 10 6-ounce (180-mL) Ramekins

Granulated sugar	1 lb. 4 oz.	600 g
Water	8 oz.	250 mL
Milk	24 oz.	720 mL
Cream, 35%	24 oz.	720 mL
Cinnamon sticks	2	2

Vanilla bean, split	1	1
Whole eggs	8	8
Egg yolks	4	4
Brown sugar	6 oz.	180 g
Molasses	1 Tbsp.	15 mL
Amaretto liqueur	2 Tbsp.	30 mL

Fill the ramekins for flans.

1. Combine the granulated sugar with the water in a small, heavy saucepan; bring to a boil. Cook until the sugar reaches a deep golden brown. Immediately pour about 2 tablespoons (30 mL) of the sugar into each of the lightly greased ramekins. Tilt each ramekin to spread the caramel evenly along the bottom. Arrange the ramekins in a 2-inch- (5-cm-) deep hotel pan and set aside.

2. Combine the milk, cream, cinnamon sticks and vanilla bean in a large saucepan. Bring just to a boil, cover and remove from the heat. Allow this mixture to **steep** for about 30 minutes.

3. Whisk the eggs, egg yolks, brown sugar, molasses and amaretto together in a large bowl.

4. Uncover the milk mixture and return it to the stove top. Bring just to the boil. Temper the egg-and-sugar mixture with approximately one-third of the hot milk. Whisk in the remaining hot milk.

5. Strain the custard through a fine mesh strainer. Pour into the caramel-lined ramekins, filling to just below the rim.

6. Pour enough warm water into the hotel pan to reach halfway up the sides of the ramekins. Bake at 325°F (160°C) for approximately 30–40 minutes. The custards should be almost set, but still slightly soft in the centre.

7. Completely chill the baked custards before serving. To unmould, run a small knife around the edge of the custard, invert onto the serving plate and give the ramekin a firm sideways shake. Garnish with fresh fruit or caramelized almonds.

Steep—*to soak food in a hot liquid in order to either extract its flavour or soften its texture.*

Approximate values per serving:

Calories	670
Total fat	33 g
Saturated fat	19 g
Cholesterol	355 mg
Sodium	120 mg
Total carbohydrates	82 g
Protein	10 g
Vitamin A	40%
Calcium	20%

Cheesecake

Cheesecakes, which are almost as old as western civilization, have undergone many changes and variations since the ancient Greeks devised the first known recipe. Americans revolutionized the dessert with the development of cream cheese in 1872.

Cheesecake is a baked custard that contains a smooth cheese, usually a soft, fresh cheese such as cream, ricotta, cottage or farmer cheese. A cheesecake may be prepared without a crust or it may have a base or sides of short dough, cookie crumbs, ground nuts or spongecake. The filling can be dense and rich (New York style) or light and fluffy (Italian style). Fruit, nuts and flavourings may also be included in the filling. Cheesecakes are often topped with fruit or sour cream glaze. Recipes for both dense and light cheesecakes are at the end of this chapter.

Some cheesecakes are unbaked and rely on gelatin for thickening; others are frozen. These are not really custards, however, but are more similar to the chiffons or mousses discussed later.

Bread Pudding

Bread pudding is a home-style dessert in which chunks of bread, flavourings and raisins or other fruit are mixed with an egg custard and baked. The result is somewhat of a cross between a cake and a pudding. It is often served with custard sauce, ice cream, whipped cream or a whisky-flavoured butter sauce. Bread pudding is a delicious way to use stale or leftover bread or overripe fruit. A recipe for bread pudding with bourbon sauce (Recipe 31.20) appears at the end of this chapter.

Soufflés

A soufflé is made with a custard base that is lightened with whipped egg whites and then baked. The air in the egg whites expands to create a light, fluffy texture and tall rise. A soufflé is not as stable as a cake or other pastry item, however, and will collapse very quickly when removed from the oven.

Soufflés can be prepared in a wide variety of sweet and savoury flavours. The flavourings may be incorporated into the custard, as in the following recipe. Alternatively, an unflavoured pastry cream can be used as the base; the liqueur, fruit or chocolate are then added to each portion separately.

When making a soufflé, the custard base and egg whites should be at room temperature. First, the egg whites will whip to a better volume, and second, if the base is approximately the same temperature as the egg whites, the two mixtures can be more easily incorporated. The egg whites are whipped to stiff peaks with a portion of the sugar for stability. The whipped egg whites are then gently folded into the base immediately before baking.

A soufflé is baked in a straight-sided mould or individual ramekin. The finished soufflé should be puffy with a lightly browned top. It should rise well above the rim of the baking dish. A soufflé must be served immediately, before it collapses. A warm custard sauce (crème anglaise) is often served as an accompaniment to a sweet soufflé.

A frozen soufflé is not a true soufflé. Rather, it is a creamy custard mixture thickened with gelatin, lightened with whipped egg whites or whipped cream and placed in a soufflé dish wrapped with a tall paper collar. When the paper is removed, the mixture looks as if it has risen above the mould like a hot soufflé.

BASIC PROCEDURE FOR PREPARING BAKED SOUFFLÉS

1. Butter the mould or ramekins and dust with granulated sugar. Preheat the oven to approximately 425°F (220°C).
2. Prepare the custard base. Add flavourings as desired.
3. Whip the egg whites and sugar to stiff peaks. Fold the whipped egg whites into the base.
4. Pour the mixture into the prepared mould or ramekins and bake immediately.

◆◆◆

RECIPE 31.5
CHOCOLATE SOUFFLÉS

Yield: 8 Servings

Orange juice	1 pt.	500 mL
Eggs, separated	8	8
Sugar	4 oz.	120 g
All-purpose flour	3 oz.	90 g
Bittersweet chocolate, chopped fine	8 oz.	225 g
Orange liqueur	2 oz.	60 mL

Approximate values per serving:

Calories	350
Total fat	15 g
Saturated fat	8 g
Cholesterol	210 mg
Sodium	65 mg
Total carbohydrates	48 g
Protein	10 g
Vitamin A	10%
Vitamin C	50%

| Butter, melted | as needed | as needed |
| Granulated sugar | as needed | as needed |

1. To prepare the base, heat the orange juice to lukewarm in a heavy saucepan.

2. Whisk the egg yolks with 3 ounces (90 g) of the sugar in a large mixing bowl. Whisk in the flour and warm orange juice, then return the mixture to the saucepan.

3. Cook over medium-low heat, stirring constantly, until the custard is thick. Do not allow it to boil. Remove from the heat.

4. Stir in the chocolate until completely melted. Stir in the liqueur. Cover the base mixture with plastic to prevent a skin from forming. Hold for use at room temperature. (Unused base can be keep overnight in the refrigerator; it should be brought to room temperature before mixing with the egg whites.)

5. To prepare the soufflés, brush individual-serving-sized ramekins with melted butter and dust with granulated sugar.

6. Preheat the oven to 425°F (220°C). Place a sheet pan in the oven, onto which you will place the soufflés for baking. (This makes it easier to remove the hot soufflé cups from the oven.)

7. Whip the egg whites to stiff peaks with the remaining 1 ounce (30 g) of sugar. Fold the whites into the chocolate base and spoon the mixture into the prepared ramekins. The ramekins should be filled to within 1/4 inch (6 mm) of the rim. Smooth the top of each soufflé with a spatula and bake immediately.

8. The soufflés are done when well risen, golden brown on top and the edges appear dry. Do not touch a soufflé to test doneness.

9. Sprinkle the soufflés with powdered sugar if desired and serve immediately.

1. Fold the whipped egg whites into the chocolate base.

2. Fill the ramekins.

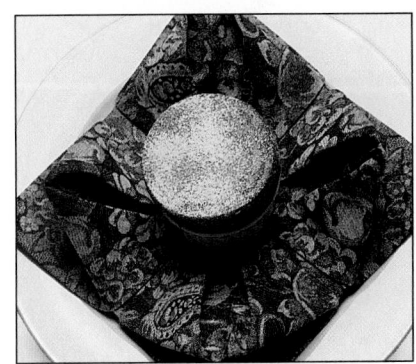

3. The finished soufflé, ready for service.

CREAMS

Creams (Fr. crèmes) include light, fluffy or creamy-textured dessert items made with whipped egg whites or cream. Some, such as **Bavarian creams** and **chiffons**, are thickened with gelatin. Others, such as **mousses** and **crèmes Chantilly**, are softer and lighter. The success of all, however, depends on the proper whipping and incorporation of egg whites or heavy cream.

You should review the material on whipping cream found in Chapter 8, Eggs and Dairy Products. Note that whipping cream has a butterfat content of 30–40 percent. When preparing any whipped cream be sure that the cream, the mixing bowl and all utensils are well chilled and clean. A warm bowl can melt the butterfat, destroying the texture of the cream. Properly whipped cream should increase two to three times in volume.

Crème Chantilly

Crème Chantilly is simply heavy cream whipped to soft peaks and flavoured with sugar and vanilla. It can be used for garnishing pastry or dessert items, or it can be folded into cooled custard or pastry cream and used as a component in a pastry.

Properly whipped crème Chantilly

Approximate values per 1 fl. oz. (30 mL) serving:	
Calories	60
Total fat	6 g
Saturated fat	3.5 g
Cholesterol	20 mg
Sodium	5 mg
Total carbohydrates	2 g
Protein	0 g

When making crème Chantilly, the vanilla extract and sugar should be added after the cream begins to thicken. Either granulated or icing sugar may be used; there are advantages and disadvantages to both. Granulated sugar assists in forming a better foam than icing sugar, but it may cause the cream to feel gritty. Icing sugar dissolves more quickly and completely than granulated sugar, but does nothing to assist with foaming. Whichever sugar is used, it should be added just before the whipping is complete to avoid interfering with the cream's volume and stability.

◆◆◆

RECIPE 31.6
CRÈME CHANTILLY

Yield: 2 to 2-1/2 qt. (2 to 2.5 L)

Cream, 35%, chilled	1 qt.	1 L
Icing sugar	3 oz.	90 g
Vanilla extract	2 tsp.	10 mL

1. Place the cream in a chilled mixing bowl. Using a balloon whisk, whisk the cream until slightly thickened.
2. Add the sugar and vanilla and continue whisking to the desired consistency. The cream should be smooth and light, not grainy. Do not overwhip.
3. Crème Chantilly may be stored in the refrigerator for several hours. If the cream begins to soften, gently rewhip as necessary.

Bavarian Cream

A Bavarian cream (Fr. *bavarois*) is prepared by first thickening custard sauce with gelatin, then folding in whipped cream. The final product is poured into a mould and chilled until firm enough to unmould and slice. Although a Bavarian cream can be moulded into individual servings, it is most often poured into a round mould lined with jellyroll slices or ladyfingers to create the classic desserts known as **charlotte royale** and **charlotte russe**.

Bavarians may be flavoured by adding chocolate, puréed fruit, chopped nuts, extracts or liquors to the custard sauce base. Layers of fruit or liquor-soaked spongecake may also be added for flavour and texture.

When thickening a dessert cream with gelatin, it is important to use the correct amount of gelatin. If not enough gelatin is used or it is not incorporated completely the cream will not become firm enough to unmould. If too much gelatin is used, the cream will be tough and rubbery. The recipes given here use sheet gelatin, although an equal amount by weight of granulated gelatin can be substituted. Refer to Chapter 26, Principles of the Bakeshop, for information on using gelatin.

BASIC PROCEDURE FOR PREPARING BAVARIAN CREAMS

1. Prepare a custard sauce of the desired flavour.
2. While the custard sauce is still quite warm, stir in softened gelatin. Make sure the gelatin is completely incorporated.

3. Chill the custard until almost thickened, then fold in the whipped cream.

4. Pour the Bavarian into a mould or charlotte form. Chill until set.

◆◆◆

RECIPE 31.7
FRESH FRUIT BAVARIAN

Yield: 1 1-qt. (1-L) Mould

Fresh fruit such as 2 kiwis, 1 banana
        or 1/2 pint (225 mL) raspberries, blueberries or wild strawberries

Honey	1 Tbsp.	15 mL
Kirsch	2 Tbsp.	30 mL
Egg yolks	4	4
Sugar	4 oz.	120 g
Milk	8 oz.	250 mL
Vanilla bean	1/2	1/2
Gelatin, softened	1/2 oz.	15 g
Cream, 35%	12 oz.	375 mL

1. Lightly spray the bottom of a 1-quart (1-L) mould with pan release spray. If a smooth mould is being used, line it with a sheet of plastic wrap, allowing the wrap to extend beyond the mould's edges.

2. Peel and thinly slice the fruit if necessary. Mix the honey and kirsch and pour over the fruit. Chill while preparing the Bavarian cream.

3. Prepare a vanilla custard sauce using the yolks, sugar, milk and vanilla. Remove from the saucepan.

4. Add softened gelatin to the hot custard. Chill until thick, but do not allow the custard to set.

5. Whip the cream until stiff and fold it into the chilled and thickened custard. Pour about one-third of this mixture (the Bavarian cream) into the mould. Arrange one-half of the fruit on top. Pour half of the remaining Bavarian cream on top of the fruit and top with the remaining fruit. Fill with the rest of the Bavarian cream. Chill until completely set, approximately 2 hours.

6. Unmould onto a serving dish. Garnish the top with additional fruit and whipped cream as desired.

NOTE: Gelatin may separate in the freezer, so quick chilling is not recommended. Products made with gelatin keep well for 1–2 days but stiffen with age.

VARIATION: *Charlotte*—Line a 1- to 1-1/2-quart (1- to 1.5-L) charlotte mould with ladyfingers (Recipe 30.22) before filling with layers of fruit and Bavarian. Invert onto a serving platter when firm and garnish with whipped cream.

◆◆◆
CHARLOTTE, SWEET CHARLOTTE

The original charlotte was created during the 18th century and named for the wife of King George III of England. It consisted of an apple compote baked in a round mould lined with toast slices. A few decades later, the great French chef Carême adopted the name but altered the concept in response to a kitchen disaster. When preparing a grand banquet for King Louis XVIII, he found that his gelatin supply was insufficient for the Bavarian creams he was making, so Carême steadied the sides of his sagging desserts with ladyfingers. The result became known as charlotte russe, probably due to the reigning fad for anything Russian. A fancier version, known as charlotte royale, is made with pinwheels or layers of spongecake and jam instead of ladyfingers. The filling for either should be a classic Bavarian cream.

Approximate values per
3-1/2 oz. (105 g) serving:

Calories	230
Total fat	15 g
Saturated fat	9 g
Cholesterol	135 mg
Sodium	30 mg
Total carbohydrates	19 g
Protein	3 g
Vitamin A	20%
Vitamin C	25%

1. Add gelatin to the custard base.

2. Fold in the whipped egg whites.

TABLE 31.1   CREAM (CRÈME) COMPONENTS

For a:	Begin with a Base of:	Thicken with:	Then Fold in:
Bavarian	Custard	Gelatin	Whipped cream
Chiffon	Custard or starch-thickened fruit	Gelatin	Whipped egg whites
Mousse	Melted chocolate, puréed fruit or custard	Nothing or gelatin	Whipped cream, whipped egg whites or both

Chiffon

A chiffon is similar to a Bavarian except that whipped egg whites instead of whipped cream are folded into the thickened base. The base may be a custard or a fruit mixture thickened with cornstarch. Although a chiffon may be moulded like a Bavarian, it is most often used as a pie or tart filling.

BASIC PROCEDURE FOR PREPARING CHIFFONS

1. Prepare the base, which is usually a custard or a fruit mixture thickened with cornstarch.
2. Add gelatin to the warm base.
3. Fold in whipped egg whites.
4. Pour into a mould or pie shell and chill.

RECIPE 31.8

LIME CHIFFON

Yield: 1 10-inch (25-cm) Pie or 8 Servings

Granulated gelatin	1/4 oz.	7 g
Water	5 oz.	150 mL
Granulated sugar	7 oz.	210 g
Fresh lime juice	3 oz.	90 mL
Lime zest	1 Tbsp.	15 mL
Eggs, separated	4	4

1. Soften the gelatin in 1 ounce (30 mL) of the water.
2. Combine 4 ounces (120 g) of the sugar, the remaining water, lime juice, zest and egg yolks in a bowl over a pan of simmering water.
3. Whisk the egg-and-lime mixture together vigorously until it begins to thicken. Add the softened gelatin and continue whipping until very thick and foamy.
4. Remove from the heat, cover and refrigerate until cool and as thick as whipping cream.
5. Meanwhile, whip the egg whites to soft peaks. Whip in the remaining sugar (3 ounces/90 g) and continue whipping until stiff but not dry.
6. Fold the whipped egg whites into the egg-and-lime mixture. Pour into a prepared pie crust or serving dishes and chill for several hours, until firm.

VARIATIONS: *Lime Chiffon*—Substitute lemon juice and lemon zest for the lime juice and zest.

Orange Chiffon—Substitute orange juice for the lime juice and for 4 ounces (120 mL) of the water. Substitute orange zest for the lime zest. Reduce the amount of sugar in the egg yolk mixture to 1 ounce (30 g).

Approximate values per serving:

Calories	140
Total fat	2.5 g
Saturated fat	1 g
Cholesterol	105 mg
Sodium	35 mg
Total carbohydrates	26 g
Protein	4 g

Claims—low fat; low saturated fat; low sodium

Mousse

The term *mousse* applies to an assortment of dessert creams not easily classified elsewhere. A mousse is similar to a Bavarian or chiffon in that it is lightened with whipped cream, whipped egg whites or both. A mousse is generally softer than these other products, however, and only occasionally contains a small amount of gelatin. A mousse is generally too soft to mould.

A mousse may be served alone as a dessert or used as a filling in cakes or pastry items. Sweet mousses may be based on a custard sauce, melted chocolate or puréed fruit.

BASIC PROCEDURE FOR PREPARING MOUSSES

1. Prepare the base, which is usually a custard sauce, melted chocolate or puréed fruit.
2. If gelatin is used, it is softened first, then dissolved in the warm base.
3. Fold in whipped egg whites, if used. If the base is slightly warm when the egg whites are added their proteins will coagulate, making the mousse firmer and more stable.
4. Allow the mixture to cool completely, then fold in whipped cream, if used.

NOTE: The egg whites are folded in before any whipped cream. Although the egg whites may deflate somewhat during folding, if the cream is added first it may become overwhipped when the egg whites are added, creating a grainy or coarse product.

♦♦♦

RECIPE 31.9

CLASSIC CHOCOLATE MOUSSE

SOUTHERN ALBERTA INSTITUTE OF TECHNOLOGY, Calgary, AB
Pastry Chef Andreas Schwarzer

Yield: 10-1/2 lb. (5.3 kg)

Couverture	57 oz.	1.7 kg
Cream, 35%	80 oz.	2.4 L
Egg yolks	19 oz.	560 g
Granulated sugar	17 oz.	500 g
Water	5 oz.	150 mL

1. Melt the couverture in a double boiler to not more than 104°F (40°C).
2. Whip the cream to soft peaks, being careful not to overwhip.
3. In a bowl, start mixing the yolks on slow speed.
4. At the same time, make the syrup by mixing the sugar and water and bringing to a boil—256°F (125°C).
5. Add the syrup in a steady stream to the egg yolks while mixing at a medium speed.
6. Add the melted couverture to the cool, whipped egg yolk mixture.
7. Fold in the whipped cream, carefully.

NOTE: The temperature of the sugar syrup will determine the thickness of the mousse. If you like a softer chocolate mousse, cook the syrup to only

Continued

Andreas Schwarzer
Andreas worked in pastry shops and bakeries in Germany before coming to Canada. He has won several medals for his pastries and showpieces, and has worked on banquets for such celebrities as Clint Eastwood, Arnold Schwarzenegger, Margaret Thatcher, and Prince Philip.

Approximate values per 1 oz. (30 g) serving:	
Calories	108
Total fat	9 g
Saturated fat	5 g
Cholesterol	56 mg
Sodium	6 mg
Total carbohydrates	7 g
Protein	1 g

240°F (115°C). A good couverture (a fine grade of chocolate with a high cocoa butter content) gives the mousse a pure chocolate taste, which chocolate lovers will appreciate. Chocolate coating will not give a rich and tasteful chocolate mousse. The mousse will be soft and weak in flavour.

FROZEN DESSERTS

Frozen desserts include **ice cream** and **gelato** and desserts assembled with ice cream such as baked Alaska, bombes and parfaits. Frozen fruit purées, known as **sorbets** and **sherbets**, are also included in this category. Still-frozen desserts, known as **semifreddi**, are made from custards or mousses that are frozen without churning.

When making any frozen mixture, remember that cold dulls flavours. Although perfect at room temperature, flavours seem weaker when the mixture is cold. Thus, it may be necessary to oversweeten or overflavour creams or custards that will be frozen for service. Although liquors and liqueurs are common flavouring ingredients, alcohol drastically lowers a liquid mixture's freezing point. Too much alcohol as well as too much sugar will prevent the mixture from freezing; thus any liqueurs or liquors and sugar must be used in moderation.

Ice Cream and Gelato

Ice cream and gelato are custards that are churned during freezing. They can be flavoured with a seemingly endless variety of fruits, nuts, extracts, liqueurs and the like. Gelato is an Italian-style ice cream. It is denser than American-style products because less air is incorporated during churning.

◆◆◆

ICE CREAM:
FROM ANCIENT CHINA TO DOUBLE FUDGE BROWNIE CHOCOLATE CHIP
WITH COOKIE DOUGH AND TOASTED ALMOND SLIVERS

Despite claims to the contrary, it is impossible to identify any one country as having invented ice cream. More likely, it was invented in several places around the world at various times.

Early ancestors of today's ice creams were flavoured water ices, which have been popular in China since prehistoric times. They have also been popular in the Mediterranean and Middle East since the Golden Age of Greece. In fact, Alexander the Great had a penchant for wine-flavoured ices, made with ice brought down from the mountains by runners. The Roman Emperor Nero served his guests mixtures of fruit crushed with snow and honey. The Saracens brought their knowledge of making flavoured ices with them when they migrated to Sicily in the 9th century. And 12th-century Crusaders returned to western Europe with memories of Middle Eastern sherbets.

The Italians are said to have developed gelato from a recipe brought back from China by Marco Polo in the 13th century. Somehow the dish spread to England by the 15th century, where it was recorded that King Henry V served it at his coronation banquet. Catherine de Medici brought the recipe with her when she married the future king of France in 1533. A different flavour was served during each of the 34 days of their marriage festivities.

Ice cream was first served to the public in Paris during the late 17th century. It was available at fashionable cafés serving another new treat: coffee. French chefs quickly developed many elaborate desserts using ice creams including bombes, coupes and parfaits.

Many of the founders of the United States —Thomas Jefferson, Alexander Hamilton, James and Dolly Madison—were confirmed ice cream addicts. George Washington spent over $200, a very princely sum, for ice cream during the summer of 1790.

The mechanized ice cream freezer was invented in 1846, setting the stage for mass production and wide availability. By the late 19th century ice cream parlours were popular gathering places. (Many of today's ice cream parlours take their décor from "Gay Nineties" motifs.)

Despite the disappearance of most ice cream wagons, soda fountains and lunch counters, all of which were popular ice cream purveyors for much of the 20th century, ice cream sales have never waned. Today, over 80% of all ice cream is sold in supermarkets or convenience stores. The public's demand for high-fat, homemade-style "super-premium" ice creams with rich and often-elaborate flavour combinations shows no sign of declining.

The CFIA requires that products labelled "ice cream" contain not less than 10% milk fat and 20% milk solids, and have no more than 50% **overrun**. "Ice milk" refers to products that do not meet the standards for ice cream. Low-fat products made without cream or egg yolks are also available for the health conscious. Frozen yogurt uses yogurt as its base. Although touted as a nutritious substitute for ice cream, frozen yogurt may have whole milk or cream added for richness and smoothness.

One hallmark of good ice cream and gelato is smoothness. The ice crystals that would normally form during freezing can be avoided by constant stirring or churning. Churning, usually accomplished mechanically, also incorporates air into the product. The air causes the mixture to expand. Gelato has little incorporated air. Good-quality ice creams and sorbets have enough air to make them light; inferior products often contain overrun. The difference becomes obvious when equal volumes are weighed.

Many food service operations use ice cream makers that have internal freezing units to chill the mixture while churning it. Most commercial machines are suitable for churning either ice cream or sorbet. Follow the manufacturer's directions for using and cleaning any ice cream maker.

Overrun—*the amount of air churned into an ice cream.*

BASIC PROCEDURE FOR PREPARING ICE CREAMS

1. Place the milk and/or cream in a heavy saucepan. If vanilla bean is being used it may be added at this time.
2. Whisk the egg yolks and sugar together in a mixing bowl.
3. Bring the liquid just to a boil. Temper the egg mixture with approximately one-third of the hot liquid.
4. Pour the tempered eggs into the remaining hot liquid and return the mixture to the heat.
5. Cook, stirring constantly, until warm (183°F [84°C]).
6. Remove the cooked custard sauce from the hot saucepan immediately. If left in the hot saucepan, it will overcook. Flavourings may be added at this time.
7. Cool the cooked custard sauce over an ice bath. Store covered and refrigerated until ready to process.
8. Process according to the machine manufacturer's directions.

◆◆◆

RECIPE 31.10

ICE CREAM BASE

Yield: 2-1/2 qt. (2.5 L)

Whole milk	1-1/2 qt.	1.5 L
Cream, 35%	1 pt.	500 mL
Vanilla bean, optional	1	1
Egg yolks	16	16
Granulated sugar	20 oz.	600 g

1. Combine the milk and cream in a heavy saucepan and bring to a boil. Add the vanilla bean if desired.
2. Whisk the egg yolks and sugar together in a mixing bowl.

Continued

3. Temper the eggs with one-third of the hot milk. Return the egg mixture to the saucepan.

4. Cook over medium heat until slightly thickened. Pour through a fine mesh strainer into a clean bowl.

5. Chill the cooked custard sauce completely before processing.

VARIATIONS: *Chocolate*—Add approximately 9 ounces (270 g) of finely chopped bittersweet chocolate per quart (litre) of ice cream base. Add the chocolate to the hot mixture after it is strained. Stir until completely melted.

Cappuccino—Steep the hot milk and cream with the vanilla bean and 2–3 cinnamon sticks. After the ice cream base is made, stir in 2 tablespoons (30 mL) coffee extract.

Brandied Cherry—Drain the liquid from 1 16-ounce (500-g) can of tart, pitted cherries. Soak the cherries in 3 tablespoons (45 mL) brandy. Prepare the ice cream base as directed, omitting the vanilla bean. Add the brandy-soaked cherries to the cooled custard before processing.

Approximate values per 6 fl. oz. (180 mL) serving:

Calories	370
Total fat	20 g
Saturated fat	11 g
Cholesterol	270 mg
Sodium	65 mg
Total carbohydrates	41 g
Protein	7 g
Vitamin A	25%

Sherbets and Sorbets

Sherbet and sorbet are frozen mixtures of fruit juice or fruit purée. Sherbet contains milk and/or egg yolks for creaminess; sorbet contains neither.

Sorbet can be prepared in a wide variety of fruit (and even some vegetable) flavours; it is often flavoured with an alcoholic beverage. It is served as a first course, a palate refresher between courses or a dessert. Because of its milk content, sherbet tends to be richer than a sorbet, so it is generally reserved for dessert.

Sorbet and sherbet may be made with fresh, frozen or canned fruit. Granulated sugar or sugar syrup is added for flavour and body. The ratio of sugar to fruit purée or juice depends to some extent on the natural sweetness of the specific fruit as well as personal preference. If too much sugar is used, however, the mixture will be soft and syrupy. If too little sugar is used, the sorbet will be very hard and grainy. Egg whites may also be added to sorbets during churning for body.

✦✦✦

RECIPE 31.11

LEMON SORBET

Yield: 4–5 qt. (4–5 L)

Water	64 oz.	2 L
Sugar	2 lb. 3 oz.	1 kg
Juice of lemons	10	10
Zest of lemons	4	4

1. Place all ingredients in a pan, bring to a boil and reduce until the syrup registers 22°B on the Baumé hydrometer and is the consistency of a light syrup.

2. Pass the syrup through a fine strainer and cool over ice.

3. Pour the syrup into an ice-cream machine, filling it half full, and churn-freeze for approximately 10–12 minutes or until set.

Approximate values per 1 oz. (30 mL) serving:

Calories	34
Total fat	0 g
Saturated fat	0 g
Cholesterol	0 mg
Sodium	1 mg
Total carbohydrates	9 g
Protein	0 g

Serving Suggestions for Ice Creams and Sorbets

Ice creams and sorbets are usually served by the scoop, often in cookie cones. Or they can be served as **sundaes**. More formal presentations include **baked Alaska**, **bombes**, **coupes** and **parfaits**.

Still-Frozen Desserts

Still-frozen desserts (It. *semifreddi*) are made with frozen mousse, custard or cream. Layers of spongecake and/or fruit may be added for flavour and texture. Because these mixtures are frozen without churning, air must be incorporated by folding in relatively large amounts of whipped cream or meringue. The air helps keep the mixture smooth and prevents it from becoming too hard. Still-frozen desserts develop ice crystals quicker than churned products, so they tend to have a shorter shelf life than ice creams or sorbets.

Still-frozen products include frozen soufflés, **marquise**, mousses and **neapolitans**. No gelatin is used for a still-frozen dessert. The Chocolate Hazelnut Marquis recipe later in this chapter (Recipe 31.28) is an example of a still-frozen dessert.

Sundae—*a great and gooey concoction of ice cream, sauces (hot fudge, marshmallow and caramel, for example), toppings (nuts, candies, and fresh fruit to name a few) and whipped cream.*

Baked Alaska—*ice cream set on a layer of spongecake and encased in meringue, then baked until the meringue is warm and golden.*

Bombe—*two or more flavours of ice cream, or ice cream and sherbet shaped in a spherical mould; each flavour is a separate layer that forms the shell for the next flavour.*

Coupe—*ice cream served with a fruit topping.*

Parfait—*ice cream served in a long, slender glass with alternating layers of topping or sauce.*

Marquise—*a frozen mousse-like dessert, usually chocolate.*

Neapolitan—*a three-layered loaf or cake of ice cream; each layer is a different flavour and a different colour, a typical combination being chocolate, vanilla and strawberry.*

Dessert Sauces

Pastries and desserts are often accompanied by sweet sauces. Dessert sauces provide flavour and texture and enhance plate presentation. Vanilla sauce (Recipe 31.1) is the principal dessert sauce. It can be flavoured and coloured with chocolate, coffee extract, liquor or fruit compound as desired. Other dessert sauces include fruit purées, caramel sauces and chocolate syrups. Techniques for decorating plates with sauces are discussed in Chapter 35, Plate Presentation.

Fruit Purées

Many types of fruit can be puréed for dessert sauces: Strawberries, raspberries, blackberries, apricots, mangoes and papayas are popular choices. They produce thick sauces with strong flavours and colours. Fresh or individually quick frozen (IQF) fruits are recommended.

Puréed fruit sauces, known as **coulis**, are uncooked. Fruit sauce generally denotes a cooked product. Cooking thickens sauces by reduction and allows the starch thickener to gelatinize. Fruit sauces cooked and thickened with waxy maize or modified starches tend to have a better shine than cornstarch achieves. Glucose contributes to a better consistency, particularly for coulis. They can also be sweetened with granulated sugar or a sugar syrup. The amount of sweetener will vary depending upon the fruit's natural sweetness.

Raspberry Coulis

◆◆◆

RECIPE 31.12

RASPBERRY COULIS

Yield: 1 qt. (1 L)

Raspberries, fresh or IQF	2 lb.	1 kg
Granulated sugar	1 lb.	500 g
Lemon juice	1 oz.	30 mL

1. Purée the berries and strain through a fine chinois.
2. Stir in the sugar and lemon juice. Adjust the flavour with additional sugar if necessary.

Approximate values per 1 oz. (30 mL) serving:	
Calories	70
Total fat	0 g
Saturated fat	0 g
Cholesterol	0 mg
Sodium	0 mg
Total carbohydrates	17 g
Protein	0 g
Claims—fat free; no saturated fat; no cholesterol; no sodium	

Caramel Sauce

Caramel sauce is a mixture of caramelized sugar and heavy cream. A liqueur or citrus juice may be used for added flavour. Review the material on caramelizing sugar in Chapter 26, Principles of the Bakeshop, before making caramel sauce.

Caramel Sauce

Approximate values per 1 fl. oz. (30 mL) serving:	
Calories	130
Total fat	7 g
Saturated fat	4 g
Cholesterol	25 mg
Sodium	5 mg
Total carbohydrates	16 g
Protein	0 g
Vitamin A	8%

◆◆◆

RECIPE 31.13
CARAMEL SAUCE

Yield: 4 qt. (4 L)

Granulated sugar	4 lb. 8 oz.	2 kg
Water	1 pt.	500 mL
Lemon juice	2 oz.	60 mL
Cream, 35%, room temperature	2 qt.	2 L
Unsalted butter, cut into pieces	5 oz.	150 g

1. Combine the sugar, lemon juice and water in a large, heavy saucepan. Stir to moisten the sugar completely. Place the saucepan on the stove top over high heat and bring to a boil. Brush down the sides of the pan with water to remove any sugar granules.
2. Do not stir the sugar. Continue boiling until the sugar caramelizes, turning a dark golden brown and producing a rich aroma.
3. Remove the saucepan from the heat. Gradually add the cream. Be extremely careful, as the hot caramel may splatter. Whisk in the cream to blend.
4. Add the pieces of butter. Stir until the butter melts completely. If necessary, return the sauce to the stove to reheat enough to melt the butter.
5. Strain the sauce and cool completely at room temperature. The sauce may be stored for several weeks under refrigeration. Stir before using.

Chocolate Syrup

Chocolate syrup or sauce can be prepared by adding finely chopped chocolate to warm vanilla custard sauce. A darker syrup can also be made with unsweetened chocolate or cocoa powder. Fudge-type sauces, like the one at the end of this chapter, are really just variations on ganache, discussed in Chapter 30, Cakes and Frostings.

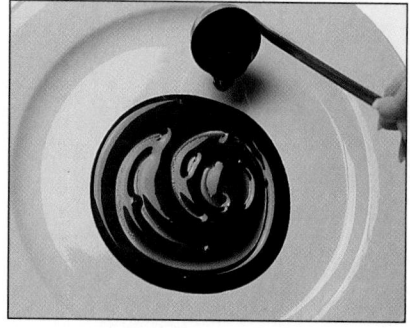

Dark Chocolate Syrup

◆◆◆

RECIPE 31.14
DARK CHOCOLATE SYRUP

Yield: 1 pt. (500 mL)

Cocoa powder	2 oz.	60 g
Water	12 oz.	360 mL
Granulated sugar	8 oz.	250 g
Unsalted butter	3 oz.	90 g
Cream, 35%	1 oz.	30 mL

1. Mix the cocoa powder with just enough water to make a smooth paste.

2. Bring the sugar and remaining water to a boil in a small, heavy saucepan. Immediately add the cocoa paste, whisking until smooth.

3. Simmer for 15 minutes, stirring constantly, then remove from the heat.

4. Stir the butter and cream into the warm cocoa mixture. Serve warm or at room temperature.

Approximate values per 1 fl. oz. (30 mL) serving:	
Calories	120
Total fat	6 g
Saturated fat	3 g
Cholesterol	15 mg
Sodium	0 mg
Total carbohydrates	16 g
Protein	1 g
Vitamin A	6%

ASSEMBLING DESSERTS

As noted previously, many pastries and other desserts are assembled from the baked doughs discussed in Chapter 29, Pies, Pastries and Cookies; the cakes, icings and glazes discussed in Chapter 30, Cakes and Frostings; and the creams, custards and other products discussed in this chapter. Many of these desserts are classic presentations requiring the precise arrangement of specific components. Formulas for some of these desserts are found at the end of the chapters in this part. But once you begin to master the basic skills presented in these chapters, you can use your creativity, taste and judgment to combine these components into a wide selection of new, unique and tempting desserts.

Assembled pastries and other desserts generally consist of three principal components: the base, the filling and the garnish. The **base** is the dough, crust or cake product that provides structure and forms the foundation for the final product. The **filling** refers to whatever is used to add flavour, texture and body to the final product. The **garnish** is any glaze, fruit, sauce or accompaniment used to complete the dish.

BASIC GUIDELINES FOR ASSEMBLING DESSERTS

1. There should be a proper blend of complementary and contrasting flavours. For example, pears, red wine and blue cheese go well together, as do chocolate and raspberries. Do not combine flavours simply for the sake of originality, however.

2. There should be a proper blend of complementary and contrasting textures. For example, crisp puff pastry, soft pastry cream and tender strawberries are combined for a strawberry napoleon.

3. There should be a proper blend of complementary and contrasting colours. For example, a garnish of red raspberries and green mint looks great.

4. Garnishes should not be overly fussy or garish.

5. The base should be strong enough to hold the filling and garnish without collapsing, yet thin or tender enough to cut easily with a fork.

6. The filling or garnish may cause the base to become soft or even soggy. This may or may not be desirable. If you want a crisp base, assemble the product very close to service. If you want this softening to occur, assemble the product in advance of service.

7. Consider the various storage and keeping qualities of the individual components. It may be best to assemble or finish some products at service time.

8. The final construction should not be so elaborate or fragile that it cannot be portioned or served easily or attractively.

9. Consider whether the product would be better prepared as individual portions or as one large item. This may depend on the desired plate presentation and the ease and speed with which a large product can be cut and portioned for service.

♦♦♦

PLATING DESSERTS

There are four different ways to plate and present desserts.

1. The dessert by itself.

2. The dessert with fruit, sugar or chocolate garnish.

3. The dessert and sauce painting.

4. The complex presentation: two or more desserts on one plate. One or more sauces, garnishes or both may also be included.

CONCLUSION

If pastry doughs are the backbone of dessert preparations, then custards, creams, mousses and the like are the heart. The skills and techniques presented in this chapter are essential to successful pastry production. Many of these skills, such as whipping cream or preparing custards, will be useful in other areas of the kitchen as well. Once you have mastered these skills as well as those discussed in Chapter 29, Pies, Pastries and Cookies, and Chapter 30, Cakes and Frostings, you will be able to prepare a wide variety of tempting desserts.

QUESTIONS FOR DISCUSSION

1. Eggs and dairy products are susceptible to bacterial contamination. What precautions should be taken to avoid food-borne illnesses when preparing custards?

2. Explain why pastry cream should be boiled and why custard sauce should not be boiled.

3. Identify three desserts that are based on a baked custard.

4. Compare a classically prepared Bavarian, chiffon, mousse and soufflé. How are they similar? How are they different?

5. Describe the procedure for making a typical still-frozen dessert. What is the purpose of including whipped cream or whipped egg whites?

6. Explain three ways in which sweet sauces can be used in preparing or presenting a dessert.

ADDITIONAL CUSTARD, CREAM, FROZEN DESSERT AND DESSERT SAUCE FORMULAS

RECIPE 31.15
CRÈME BRÛLÉE

VINCENT ON CAMELBACK, PHOENIX, AZ
Chef Vincent Guerithault

Yield: 3-1/2 qt. (3.5 L)

Cream, 35%	2 qt.	2 L
Vanilla beans, split	2	2
Egg yolks	50	50
Granulated sugar	20 oz.	600 g
Fresh berries	as needed	as needed
Almond Tulip Mix (Recipe 29.32)		
Granulated sugar		as needed for caramelized topping

1. Place the cream and the vanilla beans in a large, heavy saucepan. Heat just to a boil.
2. Whisk the egg yolks and sugar together until smooth and well blended.
3. Temper the eggs with one-third of the hot cream. Return the egg mixture to the saucepan and cook, stirring constantly, until very thick. Do not allow the custard to boil.
4. Remove from the heat and strain into a clean bowl. Cool over an ice bath, stirring occasionally.
5. To serve, place fresh berries in the bottom of each cookie cup. Top with several spoonfuls of custard.
6. Sprinkle granulated sugar over the top of the custard and caramelize with a propane torch. Serve immediately.

Approximate values per 5 oz. (150 mL) serving:	
Calories	460
Total fat	36 g
Saturated fat	20 g
Cholesterol	480 mg
Sodium	135 mg
Total carbohydrates	26 g
Protein	7 g
Vitamin A	50%

‡‡‡

RECIPE 31.16
CRÈME CHIBOUST

CONA SUCRE D'ART, NANAIMO, BC
Pâtissier Confiseur George Wagner

Yield: 2 qt. (2 L)

Egg yolks	7 oz.	210 g
Sugar	5 oz.	150 g
Lemon juice	5 oz.	150 mL
Cream, 35%	10 oz.	300 mL
Cornstarch	1 Tbsp.	15 mL
Gelatin leaves (soaked in cold water)	6	6
Egg whites	12-1/4 oz.	350 g
Sugar	8 oz.	250 g

1. Whisk yolks, 5 ounces of sugar (150 g) and lemon juice in a double boiler until warm and foamy.
2. Blend cream and cornstarch in a heavy-bottomed saucepan.
3. Add yolk mixture to cream mixture and bring to a boil for 4 minutes.
4. Squeeze excess moisture from gelatin leaves and add to hot mixture. Stir until dissolved.
5. Whip egg whites and remaining sugar to form soft meringue.
6. Gently fold meringue into hot sauce.

George Wagner
Born and raised in France, George was apprenticed at the age of 14 and later specialized in pâtisserie. He came to Canada in 1966 and was Pastry Instructor at Malaspina University College from 1978 to 1994. George now owns his own school, where he instructs students in the art of sugar and chocolate confections.

Approximate values per 1 oz. (30 g) serving:	
Calories	70
Total fat	4 g
Saturated fat	2 g
Cholesterol	62 mg
Sodium	17 mg
Total carbohydrates	8 g
Protein	2 g

‡‡‡

RECIPE 31.17
CHOCOLATE POT DE CRÈME

Yield: 8 4-oz. (120-mL) Servings

Milk	1 pt.	500 mL
Bittersweet chocolate	8 oz.	250 g
Granulated sugar	7 oz.	210 g
Vanilla extract	1 tsp.	5 mL

Continued

Coffee liqueur	2 Tbsp.	30 mL
Egg yolks	7	7

1. Heat the milk just to a simmer. Add the chocolate and sugar. Stir constantly until the chocolate melts; do not allow the mixture to boil. Remove from the heat and add the vanilla and liqueur.
2. Whisk the egg yolks together, then slowly whisk them into the chocolate mixture.
3. Pour the custard into ramekins. Place the ramekins in a hotel pan and add enough hot water to reach halfway up the sides of the ramekins.
4. Bake at 325°F (160°C) until custards are almost set in the centre, approximately 30 minutes. Remove from the water bath and refrigerate until thoroughly chilled. Serve garnished with whipped cream and chocolate shavings.

◆◆◆

RECIPE 31.18

PEAR TART CHIBOUST

CONA SUCRE D'ART, Nanaimo, BC
Pâtissier Confiseur George Wagner

Yield: 1 Torte/Cake (6 servings)

Puff Pastry (Recipe 29.8)	4 oz.	120 g
Crème Chiboust (Recipe 31.16)	2 oz.	60 mL
Pears, freshly poached or canned,		
thinly sliced	3–4	3–4
Sugar	1/3 cup	75 mL
Pear Liqueur Caramel Sauce (recipe follows)		

1. Cut a circle of puff pastry 8 inches (20 cm) in diameter.
2. Spread a thin layer of chiboust on it.
3. Arrange pear slices so they overlap on top of crème Chiboust.
4. Bake at 400°F (200°C) for approximately 15–20 minutes.
5. Place an 8-inch (20-cm) cake ring over the tart and fill with crème Chiboust to a height of 1-1/2 inches (3.75 cm). Let cool.
6. When firm, sprinkle sugar on top. Using a torch, caramelize the top and let set for a few minutes.
7. Remove the ring and serve with Caramel Sauce.

PEAR LIQUEUR CARAMEL SAUCE

Yield: 2 cups (500 mL)

Sugar	16 oz.	500 g
Cream, 35%	10 oz.	300 mL
Pear William liqueur	2-1/2 oz.	75 mL

1. Stir dry sugar in a heavy-bottomed, shallow pan on medium heat, stirring constantly with a wooden spoon, until the sugar begins to turn golden but is not melting.
2. Deglaze with cream.
3. When cool, stir in pear William liqueur.

RECIPE 31.19

NEW YORK–STYLE CHEESECAKE

Yield: 2 10-inch (25-cm) Cakes
        12–16 servings per cake

Cream cheese, softened	3 lb. 6 oz.	1.6 kg
Cake flour	2 oz.	60 g
Granulated sugar	18 oz.	540 g
Eggs	8	8
Cream, 35%	5 oz.	150 mL
Vanilla extract	1 Tbsp.	15 mL
Orange zest, minced	1 Tbsp.	15 mL
Lemon zest, minced	1 tsp.	5 mL

1. Cream the cheese at low speed until smooth. Incorporate the flour and sugar.

2. Blend in the eggs slowly, then add the cream, vanilla and lemon and orange zests.

3. Pour the batter into well-buttered springform pans. Bake at 300°F (150°C) until set, approximately 1 to 1-1/2 hours.

4. Cool completely before removing the sides of each pan.

NOTE: Pans may be lined with a crumb or short paste crust.

Approximate values per 1/10-cake serving:

Calories	450
Total fat	32 g
Saturated fat	20 g
Cholesterol	180 mg
Sodium	260 mg
Total carbohydrates	31 g
Protein	9 g
Vitamin A	40%

RECIPE 31.20

BREAD PUDDING WITH BOURBON SAUCE

Yield: 20 Servings

Raisins	8 oz.	250 g
Brandy	4 oz.	120 mL
Unsalted butter, melted	2 oz.	60 g
White bread, day-old	24 oz.	720 g
Cream, 35%	2 qt.	2 L
Eggs	6	6
Granulated sugar	1 lb. 10 oz.	800 g
Vanilla extract	2 oz.	60 mL
Bourbon Sauce (recipe follows)	as needed	as needed

1. Combine the raisins and brandy in a small saucepan. Heat just to a simmer, cover and set aside.

2. Use a portion of the butter to thoroughly coat a 2-inch-deep (5 cm) hotel pan. Reserve the remaining butter.

3. Tear the bread into chunks and place in a large bowl. Pour the cream over the bread and set aside until soft.

4. Beat the eggs and sugar until smooth and thick. Add the remaining ingredients, including the melted butter, raisins and brandy.

5. Gently toss the egg mixture with the bread to blend. Pour into the hotel pan and bake at 350°F (180°C) until browned and almost set, approximately 45 minutes.

6. Serve warm with 2–3 tablespoons (30–45 mL) of the Bourbon Sauce.

Approximate values per serving:

Calories	700
Total fat	44 g
Saturated fat	26 g
Cholesterol	270 mg
Sodium	260 mg
Total carbohydrates	67 g
Protein	9 g
Vitamin A	50%
Calcium	10%
Iron	10%

Continued

Approximate values per
1 oz. (30 g) serving:

Calories	150
Total fat	8 g
Saturated fat	5 g
Cholesterol	40 mg
Sodium	50 mg
Total carbohydrates	19 g
Protein	1 g
Vitamin A	8%

Clafouti—*a country-style French dessert, similar to a quiche, in which dark cherries are baked in an egg custard.*

Approximate values per
1/10-cake serving:

Calories	170
Total fat	3.5 g
Saturated fat	1.5 g
Cholesterol	90 mg
Sodium	4.5 mg
Total carbohydrates	30 g
Protein	5 g
Vitamin A	6%

BOURBON SAUCE

Unsalted butter	8 oz.	250 g
Granulated sugar	1 lb.	500 g
Eggs	2	2
Bourbon	8 oz.	250 mL

1. Melt the butter; stir in the sugar and eggs and simmer to thicken.
2. Add the bourbon and hold in a warm place for service.

◆◆◆

RECIPE 31.21

CHERRY CLAFOUTI

Yield: 1 10-inch (25-cm) Cake

Dark cherries, fresh or canned, pitted	1 lb.	500 g
Eggs	4	4
Milk	12 oz.	360 mL
Granulated sugar	2 oz.	60 g
Vanilla extract	1 tsp.	5 mL
All-purpose flour	2 oz.	60 g
Powdered sugar	as needed	as needed

1. Drain the cherries and pat them completely dry with paper towels. Arrange them evenly on the bottom of a buttered 10-inch (25-cm) pan. Do not use a springform pan or removable-bottom tartlet pan.
2. Make the custard by whisking the eggs and milk together. Add the sugar, vanilla and flour and continue whisking until all the lumps are removed.
3. Pour the custard over the cherries and bake at 325°F (160°C) for 1 to 1-1/2 hours. The custard should be lightly browned and firm to the touch when done.
4. Dust with powdered sugar and serve the clafouti while still warm.

◆◆◆

RECIPE 31.22

WARM CHOCOLATE SOUFFLÉ

MANGO, CHICAGO, IL
Chef Steve Chiappetti

Yield: 6 Servings

Bittersweet chocolate	12 oz.	360 g
Unsalted butter	20 oz.	600 g
Egg yolks	12	12
Granulated sugar	8 oz.	250 g
All-purpose flour	1 cup	250 mL
Egg whites	12	12

1. Melt the chocolate and butter in a bowl over a bain marie.
2. Combine the egg yolks and 4 ounces (120 g) of the sugar and beat at high speed until the yolks are pale and form a thick ribbon.
3. When the yolks are fully whipped, add the flour and beat at low speed. Slowly pour the melted chocolate into the yolk mixture.

4. In a separate bowl, beat the egg whites at medium speed until soft peaks form. Slowly add the remaining 4 ounces (130 g) of sugar and beat at high speed until stiff peaks form.

5. Gently fold the egg whites into the yolk mixture.

6. Pour into 6 buttered and sugared ramekins or soufflé moulds and bake at 400–425°F (200–220°C) until done, approximately 12–15 minutes.

Approximate values per serving:

Calories	1563
Total fat	118 g
Saturated fat	61 g
Cholesterol	1055 mg
Sodium	157 mg
Total carbohydrates	99 g
Protein	28 g
Vitamin A	110%
Iron	33%

=== ◆◆◆ ===

RECIPE 31.23

MAPLE SYRUP MOUSSE "TEEPEE IROQUOIS" WITH STRAWBERRY COULIS

SOUTHERN ALBERTA INSTITUTE OF TECHNOLOGY, CALGARY, AB
Master Pâtissier Hermann Greineder

Yield: 4–6 portions

Egg yolks	4	4
Maple syrup	3-1/2 oz.	100 mL
Cream, 35%, cold	10 oz.	300 mL
Pure white gelatin powder	1/4 oz.	7 g
Strawberry Coulis (recipe follows)		
Almond Tulip Mix (Recipe 29.32)	as needed	as needed

1. Whip the egg yolks and maple syrup in a bowl over boiling water until the mixture thickens to ribbon stage. It should not get too hot, otherwise the egg yolks will curdle. The mixture should have a nice creamy texture.

2. Whip the cold cream.

3. Dissolve gelatin in a few drops of water, let it bloom, then melt over heat.

4. Pour it into syrup mixture. Add whipped cream and mix well, but slowly.

5. Divide the mousse between 4–6 ramekins. Refrigerate.

6. To serve, dip ramekins into hot water to loosen mousse. Turn upside down on a dessert plate. Pour the Strawberry Coulis around the mousse and garnish with Almond Tulip shards to represent a teepee.

STRAWBERRY COULIS

Strawberries	as needed	as needed
Sugar	TT	TT

Blend fresh or frozen strawberries with sugar, to taste, in a blender.

Hermann Greineder

Currently a Pastry Instructor at SAIT, Hermann received his German Master Certification as "Chef Pâtissier" in 1971. He has 41 years of experience in a wide range of establishments, and has won several medals in competition for his beautiful chocolate showpieces.

Approximate values per serving:

Calories	521
Total fat	37 g
Saturated fat	20 g
Cholesterol	320 mg
Sodium	63 mg
Total carbohydrates	41 g
Protein	9 g

=== ◆◆◆ ===

RECIPE 31.24

CHOCOLATE CHIFFON PIE

Yield: 2 9-inch (22-cm) Pies

Gelatin	1/2 oz.	15 g
Milk	20 oz.	600 mL
Unsweetened chocolate	4 oz.	120 g
Granulated sugar	6 oz.	180 g
Salt	1/4 tsp.	1 mL

Continued

Eggs, separated	6	6
Vanilla extract	2 tsp.	10 mL
Crumb-crust pie shells	2	2
Unsweetened whipped cream	as needed	as needed
Chocolate shavings	as needed	as needed

1. Soften the gelatin and set aside.
2. Combine the milk and chocolate in a heavy saucepan and warm over low heat until the chocolate melts.
3. Beat the egg yolks into 4 ounces (120 g) of the sugar and the salt. Add to the chocolate sauce. Continue cooking, stirring constantly, until the mixture thickens.
4. Remove from the heat and add the gelatin, stirring until completely dissolved. Pour the mixture into a bowl and chill until very thick.
5. Whip the egg whites to soft peaks. Add the vanilla and the remaining sugar and whip to stiff peaks. Fold the whites into the chocolate.
6. Mound the chiffon into the pie shells and chill for several hours before serving. Garnish with unsweetened whipped cream and chocolate shavings.

Approximate values per 1/10-pie serving:

Calories	210
Total fat	12 g
Saturated fat	4.5 g
Cholesterol	70 mg
Sodium	160 mg
Total carbohydrates	21 g
Protein	5 g

RECIPE 31.25

RASPBERRY MOUSSE

Yield: 1 qt. (1 L)

Gelatin	6 sheets	6 sheets
Raspberries, puréed	12 oz.	360 g
Granulated sugar	3 oz.	90 g
Raspberry brandy	2 Tbsp.	30 mL
Cream, 35%	8 oz.	250 mL

1. Soften the gelatin in ice water and set aside.
2. Place the raspberry purée, sugar and brandy in a nonreactive saucepan and warm just to dissolve the sugar. Remove from the heat and strain through a fine chinois.
3. Add the gelatin, stirring until it is dissolved. Chill the mixture until thick but not set.
4. Whip the cream to soft peaks and fold it into the raspberry mixture.

Approximate values per 3 oz. (90 mL) serving:

Calories	180
Total fat	11 g
Saturated fat	7 g
Cholesterol	40 mg
Sodium	15 mg
Total carbohydrates	16 g
Protein	5 g
Vitamin A	10%

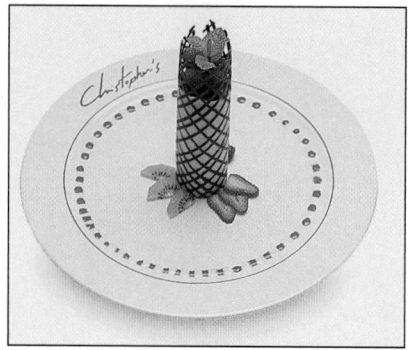

RECIPE 31.26

PARNASSIENNE DE MOUSSE AU CHOCOLAT (CHOCOLATE TOWER)

CHRISTOPHER'S AND CHRISTOPHER'S BISTRO, PHOENIX, AZ
Chef/Owner Christopher Gross

Yield: 8 Servings

Parchment paper moulds	8	8
Dark chocolate, chopped	5-1/2 oz.	165 g

Unsalted butter	3 Tbsp.	45 mL
Cream, 35%	2 oz.	60 mL
Egg whites	10	10
Superfine sugar	4 Tbsp.	60 mL
Dark chocolate, bakers' glaze, melted	2 oz.	60 g
White chocolate, bakers' glaze, melted	5 oz.	150 g
Espresso Sauce (recipe follows)	as needed	as needed
Fresh berries	as needed	as needed

1. To make the moulds, cut parchment paper into 16 strips, each 3-1/2 inches (8.75 cm) high and 5 inches (12.5 cm) long. Roll 8 of these strips into tubes and tape closed. Stand these 8 tubes upright on a parchment-lined sheet pan. Reserve the remaining strips for the tower coating.
2. To make the mousse, melt the 5-1/2 ounces (165 g) of chocolate and the butter in a medium bowl over a bain marie.
3. Whip the cream to stiff peaks and refrigerate.
4. Whip the egg whites and the superfine sugar to stiff peaks.
5. Fold the egg whites into the melted chocolate, then fold in the whipped cream.
6. Using a large piping bag fitted with a plain tip, pipe the mousse into the 8 parchment paper tubes. Freeze until completely solid, several hours or overnight.
7. To make the tower coating, pipe a pattern of melted dark chocolate onto the 8 remaining strips of parchment paper. When the dark chocolate hardens, coat the same side of the parchment with the melted white chocolate. Immediately remove a tube of mousse from the freezer. Remove the paper wrapping and wrap the chocolate-coated parchment strip around the frozen mousse, placing the chocolate side next to the mousse. Refreeze for 5 minutes, then carefully peel the paper off the tower. The dark and white chocolate coating will remain wrapped around the mousse.
8. Repeat the procedure for wrapping the frozen mousse with chocolate-coated paper for the remaining pieces.
9. For service, ladle espresso sauce onto 8 plates, place a mousse tower in the centre of each plate and garnish with fresh berries.

Approximate values per serving:

Calories	458
Total fat	35 g
Saturated fat	21 g
Cholesterol	176 mg
Sodium	173 mg
Total carbohydrates	34 g
Protein	13 g

ESPRESSO SAUCE

Yield: 1-1/2 pt. (700 mL)

Egg yolks	8	8
Granulated sugar	3-1/2 oz.	100 g
Cereal cream	1 pt.	450 mL
Espresso beans	3 oz.	90 g
Vanilla bean	1/2	1/2

1. Whisk the egg yolks and sugar together in a medium bowl.
2. Bring the cream, espresso beans and vanilla bean to a simmer in a heavy saucepan.
3. Temper the egg yolks with a portion of the hot cream, then return the mixture to the saucepan. Cook over low heat, stirring constantly, until the sauce is thick enough to coat the back of a spoon. Strain and cool over an ice bath.

Approximate values per serving:

Calories	60
Total fat	4 g
Saturated fat	2 g
Cholesterol	75 mg
Sodium	10 mg
Total carbohydrates	5 g
Protein	2 g
Vitamin A	6%
Claims—very low sodium	

◆◆◆

RECIPE 31.27

BANANA GALETTE WITH NUTMEG ICE CREAM

CONA SUCRE D'ART, NANAIMO, BC

Pâtissier Confiseur George Wagner

Yield: 12 Portions

Phyllo pastry	6 sheets	6 sheets
Melted butter	as needed	as needed
Sugar	1/8 cup	30 mL
Cake crumbs	1/8 cup	30 mL
Pastry Cream (Recipe 31.2)	48 oz.	1.3 L
Banana slices, thin	as needed	as needed
Sugar	1-1/2 oz.	45 mL
Nutmeg Ice Cream (recipe follows)		
Crème Anglaise (recipe follows)		

1. Brush 1 layer of phyllo pastry with the melted butter. Mix the sugar and cake crumbs together and sprinkle a fifth of it evenly over the phyllo.
2. Place a second sheet of phyllo pastry on the first one and repeat the first step 4 more times.
3. Cut the phyllo in 3 × 3-inch (7.5 × 7.5-cm) squares and bake at 375°F (185°C) for about 20 minutes.
4. When the squares are baked and cooled pipe 2 ounces (60 mL) of pastry cream on each one. Arrange the banana slices on top and sprinkle with 1-1/2 ounces (45 mL) of sugar. Use a torch to caramelize. Transfer the towers to individual plates.
5. Add 1 scoop of Nutmeg Ice Cream to each and drizzle Crème Anglaise on plate. Serve immediately.

NUTMEG ICE CREAM

Milk	32 oz.	1 L
Cream, 35%	32 oz.	1 L
Sugar	12 oz.	400 g
Egg yolks, beaten	12	12
Nutmeg, grated and sifted	1/2 nutmeg	1/2 nutmeg

1. Boil the milk with the cream and half the sugar. Add nutmeg. Remove from heat.
2. Blend yolks and remaining sugar.
3. Pour boiling liquid over the yolk mixture, stirring constantly.
4. Return mixture to heat and, using a thermometer, cook to 183°F (84°C).
5. Pass through a china cap immediately. Let cool.
6. Churn-freeze the mixture in an ice cream freezing machine.

CRÈME ANGLAISE

Milk	32 oz.	1 L
Cream, 35%	32 oz.	1 L
Sugar	12 oz.	400 g
Yolks	12	12
Vanilla bean	1	1

1. Boil the milk with the cream, half the sugar and the vanilla bean. Remove from heat.
2. Blend yolks and remaining sugar.
3. Pour boiling liquid over the yolk mixture, stirring constantly.
4. Return mixture to heat and, using a thermometer, cook to 183°F (84°C).
5. Pass through a china cap immediately. Let cool.

Approximate values per
9 oz. (270 g) serving:

Calories	519
Total fat	31 g
Saturated fat	18 g
Cholesterol	291 mg
Sodium	129 mg
Total carbohydrates	53 g
Protein	8 g

Approximate values per
1 oz. (30 g) serving:

Calories	67
Total fat	5 g
Saturated fat	3 g
Cholesterol	45 mg
Sodium	11 mg
Total carbohydrates	5 g
Protein	1 g

Approximate values per
1 oz. (30 g) serving:

Calories	67
Total fat	5 g
Saturated fat	3 g
Cholesterol	45 mg
Sodium	11 mg
Total carbohydrates	5 g
Protein	1 g

◆◆◆

RECIPE 31.28

Chocolate Hazelnut Marquise with Frangelico Sauce

Yield: 12 Servings

Dark chocolate	1 lb.	500 g
Unsalted butter	4 oz.	120 g
Hazelnuts, roasted, skinned and chopped coarse	4 oz.	120 g
Eggs, separated	6	6
Frangelico (hazelnut liqueur)	2 oz.	60 mL
Salt	pinch	pinch
Frangelico Sauce (recipe follows)	as needed	as needed
Hazelnuts, roasted and chopped coarse	as needed	as needed
Raspberries	as needed	as needed
Mint	as needed	as needed

1. Line a terrine mould with melted butter and parchment paper.

2. Melt the chocolate and butter over a bain marie. Remove from the heat and stir in the nuts, egg yolks and hazelnut liqueur. Set aside to cool to room temperature but do not use an ice bath as the chocolate will solidify.

3. Whip the egg whites with the salt until stiff but not dry. Fold the whipped egg whites into the chocolate mixture.

4. Pour the mixture into the mould and freeze overnight.

5. Remove the marquise from the mould and peel off the paper. (Work quickly because this melts quickly.) While the loaf is still frozen, use a hot knife to slice it into 1/3-inch (8-mm) slices. Freeze the slices until just before service.

6. Serve 2 slices on a pool of Frangelico Sauce. Garnish with coarsely chopped hazelnuts, fresh raspberries and mint.

Approximate values per serving:	
Calories	380
Total fat	28 g
Saturated fat	14 g
Cholesterol	125 mg
Sodium	35 mg
Total carbohydrates	25 g
Protein	6 g
Vitamin A	10%

FRANGELICO SAUCE

Prepare a vanilla sauce (Recipe 31.1), omitting the vanilla bean. Stir in 1/2 teaspoon (2 mL) vanilla and 2–3 tablespoons (30–45 mL) of Frangelico (hazelnut liqueur), to taste.

◆◆◆

RECIPE 31.29

Walnut and Chocolate Tart

ROYAL YORK HOTEL, Toronto, ON
Executive Chef George McNeill

Yield: 1 11-inch (28-cm) Tart

Corn syrup	4 oz.	250 mL
Dark chocolate pieces	2 oz.	55 g
Granulated sugar	4 oz.	110 g
Whole eggs	5	5
Melted butter	1/3 oz.	10 mL
Walnut crumbs	14 oz.	400 g
Sugar Pastry Flan (recipe follows)		

George McNeill

George is a Certified Master Chef (U.S.A.)—one of the few in Canada. George was Captain of the 1996 Canadian National Culinary Olympic Team, which brought three gold medals home from Berlin. As Executive Chef at the Royal York Hotel, he oversees the largest hotel kitchen in the country, which produces 4000–6000 meals a day.

Continued

Approximate values per 1/12-pie serving:	
Calories	514
Total fat	32 g
Saturated fat	8 g
Cholesterol	122 mg
Sodium	71 mg
Total carbohydrates	55 g
Protein	10 g

1. Warm the corn syrup over low heat and add the chocolate pieces. Melt together, then allow the mixture to cool slightly.
2. Add the sugar and eggs. Combine well.
3. Stir in the melted butter.
4. Pour the mixture into an 11-inch (28-cm) sugar pastry flan.
5. Sprinkle the top evenly with walnut crumbs. Bake at 350°F (175°C) for approximately 35 minutes. Serve with raspberry or other fruit sorbet and garnish with caramelized peaches, or a compote of fruit or berries.

SUGAR PASTRY FLAN

Butter	4 oz.	100 g
Granulated sugar	2 oz.	50 g
Whole egg	1	1
Flour, sieved	8 oz.	200 g

1. Cream the butter and sugar until fluffy.
2. Add the egg slowly and combine well.
3. Fold in the flour and knead into a dough.
4. Allow the dough to rest in the refrigerator for approximately half an hour.
5. Pin or roll the pastry 1/4 inch (0.5 cm) thick and 11 inches (28 cm) in diameter.

Approximate values per 1 oz. (30 g) serving:	
Calories	122
Total fat	6 g
Saturated fat	4 g
Cholesterol	31 mg
Sodium	6 mg
Total carbohydrates	15 g
Protein	2 g

Michael Noble

Michael opened Diva at the Met in 1996, and within a year it was in Vancouver's culinary spotlight, winning awards from Gourmet Magazine, Vancouver Magazine, *and* GQ. *Michael also achieved Canada's highest standings ever at the Bocuse d'Or World Cuisine championship in Lyons, in 1995 and 1997.*

◆◆◆

RECIPE 31.30

MARINATED FIELD BERRIES WITH LEMON COOKIES AND MISSION HILL ICE SABAYON

METROPOLITAN HOTEL, VANCOUVER, BC
Chef Michael Noble

Yield: 4 servings

Eggs, separated	5	5
Lemon zest	1 tsp.	5 mL
Sugar	5-1/2 oz.	150 g
Flour, cake	3-1/2 oz.	100 g
Icing sugar	to dust	to dust
Marinated Field Berries (recipe follows)		
Mission Hill Ice Sabayon (recipe follows)		

1. To make the cookies, in a stainless steel mixing bowl, place the egg yolks, lemon zest and sugar. Using a small fine whisk, whip the mixture until it becomes light, fluffy and rather stiff.
2. In a separate bowl, whip the egg whites until they form stiff peaks. Fold the egg whites into the yolk mixture and then fold the flour in to form a batter-like consistency.
3. Using a pastry bag with a straight tube, immediately pipe the batter into round shapes, approximately 2-3/4 inches (7 cm) in diameter, by piping in a spiral motion.

4. When the shapes are piped, dust them lightly with icing sugar and place immediately into a 340°F (170°C) oven; bake for approximately 7 minutes, or until golden brown. Remove from the oven and let cool.

5. On a dessert plate, place one of the cookies. Spoon some of the berry mixture over it with some of the juice from the marinade. Set another cookie on top and repeat the procedure. Generously spoon some sabayon over it until it completely covers the cookies and berries, flowing over them. Using a small torch, burn the surface until it is a light golden brown all over. Garnish with a mint sprig and serve.

MARINATED FIELD BERRIES

Strawberries, cut into wedge-like quarters	8 oz.	250 g
Blueberries	8 oz.	250 g
Granulated sugar	2-1/2 Tbsp.	40 g
Lemon juice	1 lemon	1 lemon
Ice wine	2 oz.	60 mL

. Place the berries in a nonreactive bowl with the sugar, lemon juice and ice wine. Let marinate in the refrigerator, covered, for 3 hours.

MISSION HILL ICE SABAYON

Whole eggs	2	2
Egg yolks	2	2
Sugar	2 oz.	60 g
Ice wine, reduced by half	5 oz.	150 mL
Ice wine, not reduced	2 oz.	60 mL

Place the eggs, egg yolks, sugar and ice wine in a stainless-steel mixing bowl. Using a balloon whisk, whip the mixture over a simmering pot of water, taking care to remove the bowl from the water occasionally to keep the eggs from curdling or scrambling. Continue whisking until the sabayon is warm and holds its shape slightly after falling from the whisk.

◆◆◆

RECIPE 31.31

BUTTERSCOTCH SAUCE

Yield: 2 qt. (2 L)

Granulated sugar	1 lb. 8 oz.	720 g
Light corn syrup	2 lb. 3 oz.	1 kg
Unsalted butter	4 oz.	120 g
Cream, 35%	10 oz.	300 mL
Scotch whisky	4 oz.	120 mL

1. Caramelize the sugar to a dark brown. Add the corn syrup.

2. Remove the sugar from the heat and slowly add the butter and the cream, stirring until the butter is completely melted.

3. Stir in the scotch and cool.

Approximate values per serving:

Calories	634
Total fat	12 g
Saturated fat	4 g
Cholesterol	482 mg
Sodium	123 mg
Total carbohydrates	109 g
Protein	15 g

Approximate values per 1 oz. (30 g) serving:

Calories	18
Total fat	.1 g
Saturated fat	0 g
Cholesterol	0 mg
Sodium	1 mg
Total carbohydrates	4 g
Protein	.2 g

Approximate values per serving:

Calories	52
Total fat	1 g
Saturated fat	.4 g
Cholesterol	57 mg
Sodium	10 mg
Total carbohydrates	7 g
Protein	1 g

Approximate values per 1 fl. oz. (30 mL) serving:

Calories	120
Total fat	3 g
Saturated fat	2 g
Cholesterol	23 mg
Sodium	20 mg
Total carbohydrates	23 g
Protein	0 g
Vitamin A	4%

Claims—low fat; low cholesterol; very low sodium

◆◆◆

RECIPE 31.32
CHOCOLATE FUDGE SAUCE

Yield: 1 gal. (4 L)

Cream, 35%	2 qt.	2 L
Light corn syrup	6 oz.	180 g
Granulated sugar	8 oz.	225 g
Bittersweet chocolate	4 lb.	2 kg

1. Combine the cream, corn syrup and sugar in a saucepan and bring just to a boil, stirring frequently.
2. Chop the chocolate and place in a large bowl.
3. Pour the hot cream over the chocolate and stir until completely melted.
4. Store well covered and refrigerated. Gently rewarm over a bain marie if desired.

Approximate values per
1 oz. (30 mL) serving:

Calories	130
Total fat	9 g
Saturated fat	6 g
Cholesterol	20 mg
Sodium	10 mg
Total carbohydrates	10 g
Protein	1 g
Vitamin A	6%

Michéal McFadden

Michéal has been helping turn out new chefs at Humber College for the past 13 years. Prior to that, he was the executive Pastry Chef at the former Harbour Castle Hilton. His love of cooking emerged early in life, as he helped his mother around the house in his native Ireland.

◆◆◆

RECIPE 31.33
BLACKCURRANT MOUSSE

HRT ALLIANCE, HUMBER COLLEGE, ON
Chef Michéal McFadden

Yield: 1-1/2 qt. (1.5 L)

Granulated sugar	10-1/2 oz.	300 g
Water	3-1/2 oz.	100 mL
Egg whites	5	5
Icing sugar	2 oz.	50 g
Blackcurrants, puréed	17-1/2 oz.	500 g
Gelatin leaves	6	6
Cream, 35%	35 oz.	1 L
Whipped cream	TT	TT
Blackcurrants, fresh	TT	TT

1. Bring granulated sugar and water to (244°F) 118°C to make a syrup.
2. Whip egg whites and icing sugar together to make a soft meringue.
3. Pour hot syrup into the meringue and whip until cold.
4. Soak gelatin in ice water until soft and then dissolve over a warm-water bath.
5. Add gelatin to the blackcurrant purée and mix well.
6. Whip cream until it forms soft peaks.
7. Add blackcurrant mixture to the cool meringue.
8. Fold in cream and transfer to a stainless steel bowl.
9. Cover with plastic wrap and refrigerate for approximately 2 hours.
10. Using a piping bag with a #10 star tip, pipe mixture into glasses and decorate with whipped cream and fresh blackcurrants.

Approximate values per
1 oz. (30 g) serving:

Calories	72
Total fat	6 g
Saturated fat	3 g
Cholesterol	21 mg
Sodium	10 mg
Total carbohydrates	5 g
Protein	1 g

EBLINKS

Ice Cream
 www.foodsci.uoguelph.ca/dairyedu/icecream.html
The Ice Cream Parlor: Frozen Desserts
 www.dsuper.net/~zaz/icecream/frame.html
Tiramisu
 www.geocities.com/NapaValley/2490/
Sweet Soufflés
 www.cs.cmu.edu/~mjw/recipes/souffle/sweet/index.html
Cheesecakes
 SOAR.Berkeley.edu/recipes/baked-goods/desserts/cheesecakes/

MEAL SERVICE AND PRESENTATION

Part V begins with a chapter on Breakfast and Brunch and another on Appetizers and Sandwiches. In each, we discuss the preparation and presentation of foods typically associated with these categories. This information is designed to synthesize many of the skills presented earlier in the book.

We then present material on several international cuisines. We emphasize each cuisine's distinguishing flavours and cooking procedures; we do not attempt to provide an array of representative recipes.

Part V concludes with a chapter on plate presentation in which we demonstrate simple yet effective techniques for making foods visually appealing.

CHAPTER 32
BREAKFAST AND BRUNCH

After studying this chapter you will be able to:

◆ prepare eggs using a variety of cooking methods: shirred, quiches, scrambled, omelettes, frittatas, pan-fried, soft-cooked and hard-cooked, poached
◆ prepare pancakes and other griddlecakes, such as crepes and French toast
◆ prepare a variety of cereals
◆ identify a variety of breakfast meats
◆ offer your customers a variety of breakfast foods

Mom always said breakfast was the most important meal of the day, and she was probably right. Breakfast (from the expression "to break fast") gives you the energy to get going after a night's sleep. It should provide at least one-fourth of the calories and nutrients consumed during the day.

Breakfast is often an on-the-go, rushed experience, hence the popularity of breakfast sandwiches, jumbo muffins and take-out coffee. Brunch, on the other hand, is a leisurely experience, combining breakfast and lunch into a social occasion. Brunch menus include traditional breakfast foods along with almost anything else. Unlike breakfast, brunch is often accompanied by champagne or other alcoholic beverages and concludes with a pastry or dessert.

Food service operations must offer a variety of breakfast options to appeal to a wide range of consumers. Hotels and resorts may offer a complimentary continental-style breakfast of coffee, juice and simple rolls; a full-service à la carte dining room; a room service menu and a casual snack bar. The grand hotel Sunday and holiday brunch buffet is an institution for celebrations and special occasions.

Office, retail and commercial complexes are peppered with small shops selling coffee, muffins, bagels and sweet rolls. Coffee houses offering a variety of coffee blends and drinks, pastries, breads and quiche are also popular. Even fast-food facilities have expanded their menus and hours of operation to meet the needs of early-morning diners.

The foods served at breakfast include most of the foods served at other times during the day. A diner's perception of the proper breakfast depends on his cultural, ethnic, economic and geographic background as well as sleep patterns and work schedule.

Breakfast menus typically include:

◆ Coffee, tea or other hot beverages
◆ Fruits or fruit juices
◆ Eggs
◆ Breads, including sweet breads
◆ Cereals and grains
◆ Potatoes
◆ Pancakes, waffles and French toast
◆ Meats or fish
◆ Dairy products, including milk, cheese and yogurt

Although few people could sit down to a breakfast including all of these components even occasionally, most food service operations find it necessary to offer some items from each category in order to meet their customers' expectations.

This chapter discusses cooking methods used for eggs, breakfast meats, pancakes and other griddlecakes and cereals. Other foods typically served at breakfast are noted on the following pages and discussed in more detail elsewhere in this text.

BEVERAGES

Few breakfast menus would be complete without offering coffee, tea or other hot beverages. Whether it's black tea in St. Petersburg or café au lait in Paris, cinnamon-spiced chocolate in Mexico City or a cup of fresh-brewed Colombian in Vancouver, people everywhere enjoy starting their day with hot, aromatic, caffeine-laced beverages. Coffees and teas are identified and discussed in Chapter 7, Kitchen Staples. Recipes for a rich hot chocolate and spiced apple cider are at the end of this chapter.

FRUITS

Fruits are popular breakfast foods because they are light and flavourful, require little or no preparation and provide vitamins and natural sugars for energy. Citrus fruits, melons, berries and bananas are breakfast staples. Fruits, whether raw or cooked, fresh, canned, frozen or dried, can be served alone, with a topping of cream or yogurt or as a garnish for cereals, pancakes or French toast. Fresh seasonal fruits can be served at the beginning of the meal, as garnish with the main course, as a light brunch dessert or as juice. Fruits are identified and discussed in Chapter 25, Fruits.

BREADS

Breads, usually rich, sweet and loaded with fruits and nuts, are a staple of many breakfast menus. Sticky pecan buns, glazed cinnamon rolls, fruit-filled muffins, danish pastries and buttery croissants, which seem too rich later in the day, somehow seem perfect in the morning. Even a humble slice of toast rounds out a breakfast menu, especially if topped with butter and jam. Breakfast breads can be served as an accompaniment to eggs, fruits or other dishes or they can be the complete meal. Chapter 27, Quick Breads; Chapter 28, Yeast Breads; and Chapter 29, Pies, Pastries and Cookies, include several recipes for breakfast breads and pastries.

POTATOES

Potatoes are often served at breakfast and brunch, usually sautéed or pan-fried as hash browns, cottage fries or lyonnaise. Potatoes may be served as a side dish or incorporated into hash or egg casseroles. Unlike breads or fruits, which may be the entire breakfast, potatoes are usually just part of a hearty breakfast, especially one that includes meat and eggs. Potatoes are identified and discussed in Chapter 23, Potatoes, Grains and Pasta.

DAIRY PRODUCTS

Some dairy products are indispensable at breakfast: milk and cream, for example. Other dairy products such as yogurt, crème fraîche and cheese are less commonly served but just as appropriate. Like milk, yogurt and crème fraîche can be used to top cold cereals or fruit. Cheeses are commonly used in omelettes and frittatas, blintzes and danish pastries; an assortment of mild cheeses offered with crusty bread and fresh fruit is a delicious breakfast or brunch alternative. Dairy products are identified and discussed in Chapter 8, Eggs and Dairy Products.

EGGS

No other breakfast food is as popular or as versatile as the egg. Eggs can be cooked by almost any method and served with a wide array of seasonings, accompaniments and garnishes. Whatever cooking method is selected, be sure to prepare the eggs carefully: Overcooked eggs and those cooked at too high a temperature will be tough and rubbery. Eggs are described in Chapter 8, Eggs and Dairy Products.

The following cooking methods are those most often used for egg-based breakfast dishes. They include dry-heat cooking methods (baking, sautéing and pan-frying) and moist-heat cooking methods (in-shell cooking and poaching).

Dry-Heat Cooking Methods

Baking

Shirred Eggs

Baked eggs, also referred to as shirred eggs, are normally prepared in individual ramekins or baking dishes. The ramekins can be lined or partially filled with ingredients such as bread, ham, creamed spinach or artichokes. The eggs are often topped with grated cheese, fresh herbs or a sauce. When properly cooked, the egg whites should be set and the yolks should be soft and creamy. They are not often seen on modern menus although skillet meals are sometimes available.

1. Add the eggs to the ramekin on top of the ham.

2. The finished shirred eggs with ham.

Approximate values per serving:

Calories	280
Total fat	22 g
Saturated fat	10 g
Cholesterol	470 mg
Sodium	300 mg
Total carbohydrates	2 g
Protein	17 g
Vitamin A	30%

BASIC PROCEDURE FOR PREPARING SHIRRED EGGS

1. Coat each ramekin with melted butter. Add flavouring ingredients as desired.
2. Break one or two eggs into each ramekin. Do not break the yolks. Season with salt and pepper.
3. Bake the eggs until the white is firm, approximately 12–15 minutes. Approximately 3–5 minutes before the eggs are done, add cream or top the eggs with grated cheese, diced ham, fresh herbs or other ingredients as desired.

◆◆◆

RECIPE 32.1

SHIRRED EGGS WITH HAM

Yield: 1 Serving

Whole butter, melted	as needed	as needed
Baked ham, sliced thin	1/2 oz.	15 g
Eggs	2	2
Salt and pepper	TT	TT
Cream, 35%, hot	1 Tbsp.	15 mL
Swiss cheese, grated	1 Tbsp.	15 mL

1. Brush the interior of a 6-ounce (180-mL) ramekin with melted butter. Line the ramekin with the ham.
2. Break the eggs into a cup and pour them carefully into the ramekin on top of the ham. Season with salt and pepper.
3. Bake at 325°F (160°C) until the eggs begin to set, approximately 8–10 minutes. Remove from the oven, add the cream and grated cheese. Return to the oven until the eggs are cooked and the cheese is melted. Serve immediately.

Quiche

Quiche is a classic breakfast and brunch entrée. It consists of an egg custard (eggs, cream or milk and seasonings) and fillings baked in a crust.

The filling usually includes at least one type of cheese, and can also include any number of other ingredients such as cooked, diced meats (for example, sausage, crumbled bacon, ham, fish or shellfish) or blanched vegetables (for example, mushrooms, sautéed onions, asparagus or broccoli). The flavour and texture of these ingredients should complement each other without overpowering the delicate egg custard. Quiche is a good way of using leftovers, but the ingredients should still be fresh and of good quality.

The crust may be made with whole wheat flour, cornmeal or other grains for added flavour and texture.

BASIC PROCEDURE FOR PREPARING QUICHE

1. Prepare and parbake a pie shell.
2. Prepare the garnishes and flavouring ingredients and add them to the pie shell.
3. Prepare a custard and add it to the pie shell. Ratios of eggs to milk or heavy cream vary depending on the specific recipe, but 6–8 eggs to 1 quart (1 L) of liquid is usually sufficient to bind the custard.
4. Bake the quiche until set; allow it to cool slightly before cutting.

◆◆◆

RECIPE 32.2

QUICHE LORRAINE

Yield: 1 8-inch (20-cm) Tart

Short crust pastry (savoury)	10-1/2 oz.	300 g
Bacon, diced	3-1/2 oz.	100 g
Onion, small dice	3-1/2 oz.	100 g
Gruyère cheese, grated	10-1/2 oz.	300 g
Flour	2 oz.	50 g
Milk	2/3 cup	170 mL
Cream, 35%	2 oz.	60 mL
Egg yolks	2	2
Egg whites, beaten to soft peak	2	2

1. Line the tart tin with the pastry.
2. Sauté the bacon and onion until the onion is translucent, 2–3 minutes, then cool.
3. Spread the cooled bacon and onion evenly in the shell.
4. Distribute the cheese over the bacon mix.
5. Mix the flour, milk, cream and egg yolks together until smooth.
6. Fold in the beaten egg whites and pour over the cheese. Distribute evenly over the entire pie to cover it completely. The egg white foam makes the top crust.
7. Bake at 350°F (175°C) for about 25 minutes or until a knife inserted about 1 inch (3 cm) from the edge comes out clean.

Approximate values per 4 oz. (120 g) serving:

Calories	357
Total fat	25 g
Saturated fat	13 g
Cholesterol	165 mg
Sodium	287 mg
Total carbohydrates	17 g
Protein	17 g

Sautéing

Scrambled Eggs

Scrambled eggs are eggs whisked with seasonings and then sautéed. They are stirred nearly constantly during cooking. The finished eggs should be light and fluffy with a tender, creamy texture. A small amount of milk or cream may be added to the eggs near the end of cooking to provide a more delicate finished product. Overcooking or cooking at too high a temperature causes the eggs to become tough and rubbery.

Scrambled eggs are often flavoured by sautéing other foods (for example, onions, mushrooms or diced ham) in the pan before adding the eggs or by adding other foods (for example, grated cheeses or herbs) to the eggs just before cooking is complete. Suggested additions include finely diced bell peppers, onions, mushrooms, zucchini or tomatoes; cottage cheese or any variety of shredded firm cheese; crumbled bacon; diced ham, turkey or beef; bits of smoked salmon, cooked shrimp or cooked sausage; and fresh herbs.

BASIC PROCEDURE FOR PREPARING SCRAMBLED EGGS

1. Break the eggs into a mixing bowl. Season lightly with salt and pepper.
2. Heat a sauté pan, add clarified butter or oil and heat until the fat begins to sizzle.
3. Sauté any additional ingredients in the hot fat.
4. Pour the eggs into the pan all at once. As the eggs begin to set, stir and shake them with a wooden spoon. When they are half-cooked you may add 1 scant tablespoon (12 mL) of milk or cream per egg and whisk everything together.
5. Sprinkle on additional ingredients such as cheese or herbs.
6. Cook just until the eggs are set, but still shiny and moist. Remove from the pan and serve immediately.

◆◆◆

RECIPE 32.3

GREEK-STYLE SCRAMBLED EGGS

Yield: 6 6-oz. (180-g) Servings

Eggs	12	12
Cream, 35%	2 oz.	60 mL
Salt and pepper	TT	TT
Onion, fine dice	2 oz.	60 g
Clarified butter	3 oz.	90 mL
Spinach, chiffonade	2 oz.	60 g
Feta cheese, crumbled	4 oz.	120 g
Greek olives, pitted and chopped	3 Tbsp.	45 mL

1. Combine the eggs, cream, salt and pepper in a mixing bowl. Whisk until well blended.
2. Sauté the onion in the butter until translucent but not brown.
3. Pour the egg mixture into the pan and cook, stirring frequently, for approximately 1 minute.
4. Add the spinach to the eggs and continue cooking. Just before the eggs are fully cooked, sprinkle on the cheese.
5. Spoon the cooked egg mixture onto serving plates and garnish with the olives. Serve immediately.

Approximate values per 5 oz. (150 g) serving:

Calories	340
Total fat	29 g
Saturated fat	15 g
Cholesterol	485 mg
Sodium	490 mg
Total carbohydrates	4 g
Protein	16 g
Vitamin A	45%
Calcium	15%

Omelettes

Omelettes are needlessly intimidating egg creations that begin as scrambled eggs. They are usually prepared as individual servings using two or three eggs. The cooked eggs are then folded around a warm filling. Fillings may be cooked into the omelette or a plain omelette may be cut and the filling placed inside.

The filling may contain vegetables, cheeses or meats. Any filling ingredient that needs cooking should be cooked before being added to the omelette. Because the eggs cook relatively quickly, raw fillings would not be properly cooked until the eggs were overcooked. Traditionally, omelettes are formed into a cigar shape.

1. Lift the edge of the eggs to allow them to cook evenly.

BASIC PROCEDURE FOR PREPARING FOLDED OMELETTES

1. Fully cook any meats and blanch or otherwise cook any vegetables that will be incorporated into the omelette.
2. Heat an omelette pan over moderately high heat and add clarified butter.
3. Whisk the eggs together in a small bowl. Season with salt and pepper if desired.
4. Pour the eggs into the pan and stir until they begin to set, approximately 10 seconds.
5. Pull cooked egg from the sides of the pan towards the centre, allowing raw egg to run underneath. Continue doing so for 20–30 seconds.
6. Spoon any fillings on top of the eggs or add any other garnishes.
7. When cooked as desired, flip one side of the omelette towards the centre with a spatula or a shake of the pan. Slide the omelette onto the serving plate so that it lands folded in thirds with the seam underneath.
8. Spoon any sauce or additional filling on top, garnish as desired and serve immediately.

2. Add the filling to the eggs.

3. Fold the eggs.

◆◆◆

RECIPE 32.4

SHRIMP AND AVOCADO OMELETTE

Yield: 1 Serving

Shrimp, peeled, deveined and cut into pieces	3 oz.	90 g
Green onion, sliced	1 Tbsp.	15 mL
Clarified butter	1 oz.	30 mL
Eggs	3	3
Salt and pepper	TT	TT
Avocado, peeled and diced	1/4	1/4
Cilantro, chopped	2 tsp.	10 mL

1. Sauté the shrimp and onion in half of the butter for 1 minute. Remove from the heat and set aside.
2. Heat an omelette pan and add the remaining butter.
3. Whisk the eggs together in a small bowl, season with salt and pepper and pour into the omelette pan.
4. Stir the eggs as they cook. Stop when they begin to set. Lift the edges as the omelette cooks to allow the raw eggs to run underneath.
5. When the eggs are nearly set, add the shrimp filling, avocado and cilantro. Fold one-third of the eggs over and roll the omelette onto a plate.

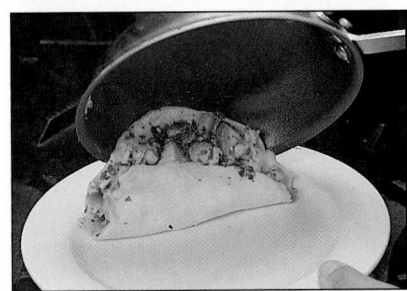

4. Roll the omelette onto the plate. Ensure the seam is on the bottom.

Approximate values per serving:

Calories	590
Total fat	47 g
Saturated fat	19 g
Cholesterol	865 mg
Sodium	620 mg
Total carbohydrates	4 g
Protein	39 g
Vitamin A	60%
Vitamin C	20%
Iron	30%

Frittatas

Frittatas are essentially open-faced omelettes of Spanish-Italian heritage. They may be cooked in small pans as individual portions or in large pans, then cut into wedges for service. A relatively large amount of hearty ingredients are mixed directly into the eggs. The eggs are first cooked on the stove top, then the pan is transferred to an oven or placed under a salamander or broiler to finish cooking.

BASIC PROCEDURE FOR PREPARING FRITTATAS

1. Fully cook any meats and blanch or otherwise prepare any vegetables that will be incorporated into the frittata.
2. Heat a sauté pan and add clarified butter.
3. Whisk the eggs, flavourings and any other ingredients together; pour into the pan.
4. Stir gently until the eggs start to set. Gently lift the cooked eggs at the edge of the frittata so that the raw eggs can run underneath. Continue cooking until the eggs are almost set.
5. Place the pan in a hot oven or underneath a salamander or broiler to finish cooking and lightly brown the top.
6. Slide the finished frittata out of the pan onto a serving platter.

◆◆◆

RECIPE 32.5

GARDEN FRITTATA

Yield: 1 Serving

Chicken breast, 4 oz. (120 g), boneless, skinless	1	1
Garlic, chopped	1 tsp.	5 mL
Cumin	TT	TT
Salt and pepper	TT	TT
Mushrooms, sliced	2 oz.	60 g
Unsalted butter	3 Tbsp.	45 g
Jalapeño, seeded, minced	1 tsp.	5 mL
Red bell pepper, roasted, seeded, peeled, julienne	2 oz.	60 g
Green onions, sliced	1 oz.	30 g
Cilantro	2 tsp.	10 mL
Eggs, beaten	2	2
Monterey Jack or cheddar cheese	2 oz.	60 g

1. Rub the chicken breast with the garlic, cumin, salt and pepper. Grill or broil the chicken until done. Allow it to rest briefly, then cut into strips.
2. In a well-seasoned 9-inch (23-cm) sauté pan, sauté the mushrooms in the butter until tender. Add the jalapeño and sauté for 30 seconds. Add the chicken, roasted pepper, green onions and cilantro and sauté until hot.
3. Add the eggs and season with salt and pepper. Cook the mixture, stirring and lifting the eggs to help them cook evenly, until they begin to set.
4. Sprinkle the cheese over the eggs and place under a salamander or broiler to melt the cheese and finish cooking the eggs. Slide the frittata onto a plate or cut into wedges for smaller portions.

Approximate values per serving:

Calories	1210
Total fat	72 g
Saturated fat	39 g
Cholesterol	720 mg
Sodium	1630 mg
Total carbohydrates	52 g
Protein	89 g
Vitamin A	440%
Vitamin C	790%
Calcium	70%
Iron	60%

Pan-Frying

Pan-fried eggs are commonly referred to as sunny-side-up or over-easy, over-medium or over-hard. These are visibly different products produced with proper timing and technique. Very fresh eggs are best for pan-frying as the yolk holds its shape better and the white spreads less.

Sunny-side-up eggs are not turned during cooking; their yellow yolks remain visible. They should be cooked over medium-low heat long enough to firm the whites and partially firm the yolks: approximately 4 minutes if cooked on a 250°F (120°C) cooking surface.

For "over" eggs, the egg is partially cooked on one side, then gently flipped and cooked on the other side until done. The egg white should be firm and its edges should not be brown. The yolk should never be broken regardless of the degree of doneness. Not only is a broken yolk unattractive, the spilled yolk will coagulate on contact with the hot pan, making it difficult to serve.

For over-easy eggs, the yolk should remain very runny; on a 250°F (120°C) cooking surface, the egg should cook for about 3 minutes on the first side and 2 minutes on the other. Eggs fried over-medium should be cooked slightly longer, until the yolk is partially set. For over-hard eggs, the yolk should be completely cooked.

Most establishments prepare this style of egg on a griddle.

BASIC PROCEDURE FOR PREPARING PAN-FRIED EGGS

1. Select a sauté pan just large enough to accommodate the number of eggs being cooked. (An 8-inch-diameter [20-cm] pan is appropriate for up to 3 eggs.)
2. Add a small amount of clarified butter and heat until the fat just begins to sizzle.
3. Carefully break the eggs into the pan.
4. Continue cooking over medium-low heat until the eggs reach the appropriate degree of firmness. Sunny-side-up eggs are not flipped during cooking; "over" eggs are flipped once during cooking.
5. When done, gently flip the "over" eggs once again so that the first side is up, then gently slide the cooked eggs out of the pan onto the serving plate. Use a lifter to move the eggs. Blot the lifter on a clean towel before placing the eggs on a plate. Serve immediately.

Basted eggs are a variation of sunny-side-up eggs. Basted eggs are cooked over low heat with the hot butter from the pan spooned over them as they cook. Another version of basted eggs is made by adding 1–2 teaspoons (5–10 mL) of water to the sauté pan and then covering the pan. The steam cooks the top of the eggs.

Moist-Heat Cooking Methods

In-Shell Cooking (Simmering)

The difference between **soft-cooked eggs** (also called soft-boiled) and **hard-cooked eggs** (also called hard-boiled) is time. Both styles refer to eggs cooked in their shell in hot water. Despite the word "boiled" in their names, eggs cooked in the shell should never be boiled. Boiling toughens eggs and causes discolouration. Instead, eggs should be simmered. Soft-cooked eggs are usually simmered for 3–5 minutes; hard-cooked eggs may be simmered for

♦♦♦

TIPS AND TECHNIQUES

♦ Cool boiled eggs quickly once the cooking time is up. This rapid cooling helps prevent a green ring from forming around the yolk.
♦ Handle eggs with care to minimize cracking egg shells before cooking.

as long as 12–15 minutes depending on customer preference and the altitude where you are.

Sometimes it is difficult to remove the shell from very fresh eggs. Eggs that are a few days old are better for cooking in the shell.

BASIC PROCEDURE FOR PREPARING SOFT-COOKED EGGS

1. Fill a saucepan or stockpot with sufficient water to cover the eggs. Bring the water to a simmer.
2. Carefully lower each egg into the simmering water. Simmer uncovered for 3–5 minutes, depending on the firmness desired and the altitude.
3. Lift each egg out of the water with a slotted spoon or spider. Crack the large end of the shell carefully and serve immediately.

BASIC PROCEDURE FOR PREPARING HARD-COOKED EGGS

1. Follow steps 1 and 2 for soft-cooked eggs, simmering the eggs for 12–15 minutes depending on the altitude and the size of the eggs.
2. Lift each egg out of the water with a slotted spoon or spider and place in an ice bath.
3. When the eggs are cool enough to handle, peel them and use as desired or cover and refrigerate for up to 5 days.

Poaching

Eggs that are to be poached should always be very fresh. They should also be kept very cold until used. Cold egg whites stay together better when dropped into hot water. Poached eggs should be soft and moist; the whites should be firm enough to encase the yolk completely, but the yolk should still be runny.

Some chefs add salt to the poaching water for flavour; others feel the salt causes the egg whites to separate. To help the egg whites cling together, add 2 tablespoons (30 mL) of white vinegar per 1 quart (1 L) of water.

BASIC PROCEDURE FOR PREPARING POACHED EGGS

1. Fill a saucepan or stockpot with at least 3 inches (7.5 cm) of water. Add salt and vinegar if desired. Bring the water to a simmer and hold at a temperature of approximately 200°F (90°C).
2. One at a time, crack the eggs into a small ramekin or cup. If a piece of shell falls into the egg, it can be removed; if the yolk breaks, the egg can be set aside for some other use.
3. Gently slide each egg into the simmering water and cook for 3–5 minutes.
4. Lift the poached egg out of the water with a slotted spoon. Trim any ragged edges with a paring knife. Serve immediately.

For quantity service, eggs can be poached in advance and held for up to one day. To do so, cook the eggs as described above. As each egg is removed from the hot water, set it in a hotel pan filled with ice water. This stops the cooking process. The eggs can be stored in the ice water until needed. For banquet-style service, all of the eggs can be reheated at once by placing the entire pan on the stove top. Or, the eggs can be reheated one or two at a time by placing them in a pan of barely simmering water until they are hot.

◆◆◆

RECIPE 32.6

POACHED EGGS

Yield: 1 Serving

Water	1 qt.	1 L
Salt	1 tsp.	5 mL
Vinegar	2 Tbsp.	30 mL
Eggs	2	2

1. Bring the water to a simmer; add the salt and vinegar.

2. Crack 1 egg into a cup and carefully add it to the water. Repeat with the other egg.

3. Cook the eggs to the desired doneness, approximately 3–5 minutes. Remove them from the water with a slotted spoon and serve as desired or carefully lower them into ice water and refrigerate for later use.

Approximate values per 3-1/2 oz. (105 g) serving:	
Calories	140
Total fat	10 g
Saturated fat	3 g
Cholesterol	425 mg
Sodium	280 mg
Total carbohydrates	1 g
Protein	12 g
Vitamin A	20%

1. Add eggs to a pot of simmering water.

2. Lower the eggs into ice water to cool them for future use.

BREAKFAST MEATS

At other meals, meat is typically the principal food, but at breakfast it is usually an accompaniment. Breakfast meats tend to be spicy or highly flavoured. A hearty breakfast menu may include a small beef steak (usually sirloin and often pan-fried) or pork chop. Corned beef, roast beef or roast turkey can be diced or shredded, then sautéed with potatoes and other ingredients for a breakfast hash. Fish, particularly smoked products, are also served at breakfast.

But the most popular breakfast meats are bacon, ham and sausages. They are all discussed in Chapter 20, Charcuterie. Bacon can be cooked on a flat griddle, in a heavy skillet or baked on a sheet pan. Regardless of the method used, the cooked bacon should be drained on absorbent paper towels to remove excess fat. Canadian back bacon is very lean and requires little cooking, although slices are usually sautéed briefly before serving. The round slices may be served like ham and are essential for eggs Benedict. A ham steak is simply a thick slice ideal for breakfast. Fully cooked ham needs only to be heated briefly on a griddle or in a sauté pan before service. The most popular breakfast sausages are made from uncured, uncooked meats. They can be mild to spicy, slightly sweet or strongly seasoned with sage. Recipes for country-style and other sausages are included in Chapter 20. Breakfast sausage is available in bulk, links or preformed patties. Link sausage is often steamed, then browned by sautéing at service time. It should be drained on absorbent paper towels to remove excess fat before service.

GRIDDLECAKES AND FRENCH TOAST

Griddlecakes

Pancakes and **waffles** are types of griddlecakes or griddle breads. They are usually leavened with baking soda or baking powder and are quickly cooked on a very hot griddle or waffle iron with very little fat. Griddlecakes should be more than just an excuse for eating butter and maple syrup, however. They should have a rich flavour and a light, tender, moist interior.

Pancake and waffle batters may be flavoured with tangy buckwheat flour, fruits, whole grains or nuts. Both pancakes and waffles are usually served with plain or flavoured butter and fruit compote or syrup.

Waffles must be cooked in a special waffle iron. This gives the cakes a distinctive gridlike pattern and crisp texture. Electric waffle irons are available with square, round and even heart-shaped moulds. The grids should be seasoned well, then never washed. (Follow the manufacturer's directions for seasoning.) Crispy Belgian waffles are made in a waffle iron with extra deep grids. They are served for breakfast or as a dessert, topped with fresh fruit, whipped cream or ice cream.

BASIC PROCEDURE FOR PREPARING PANCAKES

1. Prepare the batter.
2. Heat a flat griddle or thick big-bottomed flat pan over moderately high heat. Lightly coat with vegetable oil.
3. Portion the pancake batter onto the hot griddle using a portion scoop, ladle or adjustable batter dispenser. Pour the portioned batter in one spot; it should spread into an even circle. Pour the batter so that no two pancakes will touch after the batter spreads.
4. Cook until bubbles appear on the surface and the bottom of the cake is set and golden brown. Flip the pancake using an offset spatula.
5. Cook the pancake until the second side is golden brown. Avoid flipping the pancake more than once as this causes it to deflate.

◆◆◆

RECIPE 32.7

BUTTERMILK PANCAKES

Yield: 24 Pancakes

All-purpose flour	1 lb.	450 g
Granulated sugar	4 Tbsp.	60 mL
Baking powder	4 tsp.	20 mL
Baking soda	2 tsp.	10 mL
Salt	1-1/2 tsp.	7 mL
Buttermilk	32 oz.	1 L
Unsalted butter, melted	4 oz.	120 g
Eggs, beaten	4	4

1. Sift the flour, sugar, baking powder, baking soda and salt together.
2. Combine the liquid ingredients and add them to the dry ingredients. Mix just until the ingredients are combined.
3. If the griddle is not well seasoned, coat it lightly with vegetable oil. Once its temperature reaches 375°F (190°C), drop the batter onto it in 2-ounce (60-g) portions using a ladle, portion scoop or batter portioner. If the batter is too thick and does not spread enough, thin with a little water.
4. When bubbles appear on the pancake's surface and the bottom is browned, flip the pancake to finish cooking.

Approximate values per pancake:

Calories	136
Total fat	5 g
Saturated fat	3 g
Cholesterol	47 mg
Sodium	359 mg
Total carbohydrates	18 g
Protein	4 g

Crepes and Blintzes

Crepes are thin, delicate, unleavened pancakes. They are made with a very liquid batter cooked in a small, very hot sauté pan. Crepe batter can be flavoured with buckwheat flour, cornmeal or other grains. Crepes are not eaten as is, but are usually filled and garnished with sautéed fruits, scrambled eggs, cheese or vegetables. Crepes can be prepared in advance, then filled and reheated in the oven.

Blintzes are crepes that are cooked on only one side, then filled with cheese, browned in butter and served with sour cream, fruit compote or preserves. A recipe for cheese blintzes is provided at the end of this chapter.

BASIC PROCEDURE FOR PREPARING CREPES

1. Prepare the batter.
2. Heat a well-seasoned crepe pan over moderately high heat. Add a small amount of clarified butter.
3. Ladle a small amount of batter into the pan. Tilt the pan so that the batter spreads to coat the bottom evenly.
4. Cook until the crepe is set and the bottom begins to brown, approximately 1 minute. Flip the crepe over with a quick flick of the wrist or by lifting it carefully with a spatula.
5. Cook for an additional 30 seconds. Slide the finished crepe from the pan. Crepes can be stacked between layers of parchment paper for storage.

◆◆◆

RECIPE 32.8

SWEET CREPES

Yield: 30 6-inch (15-cm) Crepes

Whole eggs	6	6
Egg yolks	6	6
Water	12 oz.	350 mL
Milk	18 oz.	540 mL
Granulated sugar	6 oz.	180 g
Salt	1 tsp.	5 mL
Flour	14 oz.	420 g
Unsalted butter, melted	5 oz.	150 g
Clarified butter	as needed	as needed

Continued

Approximate values per
2 oz. (60 g) serving:

Calories	140
Total fat	7 g
Saturated fat	3.5 g
Cholesterol	95 mg
Sodium	100 mg
Total carbohydrates	17 g
Protein	4 g

1. Whisk together all liquid ingredients except the melted butter. Add the sugar, salt and flour; whisk together. Stir in the melted butter. Cover and set aside to rest for at least 1 hour before cooking.
2. Heat a small sauté or crepe pan; brush lightly with clarified butter. Pour in 1 to 1-1/2 ounces (30–45 mL) of batter; swirl to coat the bottom of the pan evenly.
3. Cook the crepe until set and light brown, approximately 30 seconds. Flip it over and cook a few seconds longer. Remove from the pan.
4. Cooked crepes may be used immediately or covered and held briefly in a warm oven. Crepes can also be wrapped well in plastic wrap and refrigerated for 2–3 days or frozen for several weeks.

1. Coat the bottom of the pan evenly with the batter.

2. Flip the crepe. Notice the proper light brown colour.

French Toast

Like a pancake, French toast is sautéed on a griddle and served with butter and syrup. Unlike a pancake, French toast begins with slices of day-old bread. (It is known in France as *pain perdu*, meaning "lost bread," probably because it provided a way to use bread that would otherwise have been discarded.) French bread, sourdough, raisin bread, challah, whole wheat, even stale croissants can be used. The bread is dipped into a batter of eggs, sugar, milk or cream and flavourings, then sautéed in butter. French toast should be served very hot. It may be topped with powdered sugar, fresh fruit, fruit compote or maple syrup as desired.

BASIC PROCEDURE FOR PREPARING FRENCH TOAST

1. Prepare the batter. Store the batter in a hotel pan that is large enough to accommodate the bread slices. Keep the batter refrigerated until ready to use.
2. Slice the bread as desired. Dip each slice of bread into the batter. Allow the bread to absorb the batter through to the centre. Turn the bread so that both sides are coated.
3. Heat a griddle or sauté pan and add clarified butter.
4. Place the batter-dipped bread onto the hot griddle. Cook until the bottom is set and golden brown. The cooking time will be determined by the thickness of the bread.
5. Flip the bread with an offset spatula and cook the toast on the other side. The toast is done when it is not runny in the middle; however, it should not be dry. Remove and serve immediately.

◆◆◆

RECIPE 32.9
CINNAMON FRENCH TOAST

Yield: 6 Servings

Eggs, beaten	10	10
Cream, 35%	4 oz.	120 mL
Salt	TT	TT
Cinnamon, ground	TT	TT
Thick-sliced bread such as sourdough, cinnamon, banana or brioche	12 slices	12 slices
Unsalted butter	as needed	as needed
Powdered sugar	as needed	as needed

1. Whisk together the eggs, cream, salt and cinnamon.
2. Place the egg mixture in a shallow pan. Place the slices of bread in the egg mixture and let soak for 2–3 minutes, turning them over after the first minute or so.
3. Cook the slices of French toast in a lightly buttered, preheated sauté pan or griddle set at 350°F (180°C) until well browned. Turn the slices and cook on the second side until done.
4. Cut each slice of bread into 2 triangles.
5. Arrange 4 triangles on each plate and dust with powdered sugar.

Approximate values per 5 oz. (150 g) serving:

Calories	320
Total fat	17 g
Saturated fat	7 g
Cholesterol	380 mg
Sodium	420 mg
Total carbohydrates	28 g
Protein	15 g
Vitamin A	25%
Iron	15%

CEREALS AND GRAINS

Oats, rice, corn and wheat are perhaps the most widely eaten breakfast foods. Processed breakfast cereals are ready-to-eat products made from these grains. Most consumers now think of breakfast cereal as a cold food, but not so long ago only hot grains were breakfast staples. Oatmeal served as a hot porridge

◆◆◆

FROM HEALTH FOOD TO SUGAR SNACK

The century old, multibillion-dollar-a-year North American breakfast cereal industry, unlike any other in the world, is rooted in health foods. During the 1890s, Dr. John Harvey Kellogg directed a sanitarium in Battle Creek, Michigan. Among the healthful foods prescribed for his patients was his special mixture of whole grains called "granula." John, along with his brother Will, next created and began marketing wheat flakes as a nutritious breakfast food. They were not an immediate success, however; people found a cold breakfast unappealing. Undeterred, Will continued toy-ing with cold cereals, eventually creating flakes made from toasted corn and malt. Thanks to a massive advertising campaign, the American public finally embraced corn flakes and a financial empire was born.

Charles W. Post was a patient of Dr. Kellogg's Battle Creek Sanitarium in 1891. He adopted the principles of healthful eating espoused by the Kellogg brothers and soon opened his own spa, complete with a factory producing his "Post Toasties" and grape nuts. He promoted them as a cure for appendicitis, consumption and malaria.

Soon Battle Creek became a boomtown, home to more than 40 breakfast cereal companies. Unfortunately for the consumer, not all manufacturers—then and now—were as concerned about health as John, Will and C.W. The addition of sugar, sometimes totalling more than half the cereal's weight, makes some of today's breakfast products more sugary than candy bars. Even some of the granola cereals touted as a healthier alternative to other breakfast cereals and snacks contain 20% or more sugar. But at least they no longer claim to cure malaria.

is still popular, especially with toppings such as cream, brown sugar, fresh or dried fruit or fruit preserves. Grits, made from ground corn, are another grain product served hot at breakfast. Grits may be topped with butter and presented as a starch side dish or served in a bowl as a porridge with cream and brown sugar. Oats and oatmeal, grits and other grains are discussed in Chapter 23, Potatoes, Grains and Pasta.

Ready-to-eat (cold) cereal is usually topped with milk or light cream and sugar. Fresh or dried fruits may be added. Many products are enriched or fortified with vitamins and minerals to compensate for the nutrients lost during processing. Creative cooks can avoid overly sweet, artificially flavoured commercial products by making their own ready-to-eat breakfast cereals such as granola, a toasted blend of whole grains, nuts and dried fruits. The results are less expensive, more nutritious and far more interesting.

❖❖❖

RECIPE 32.10
CRUNCHY GRANOLA

Yield: 12 cups (3 L)

Brown sugar	8 oz.	250 g
Water, hot	4 oz.	120 mL
Canola oil	6 oz.	180 mL
Old-fashioned oats	18 oz.	500 g
Wheat germ	4 oz.	120 g
Coconut, shredded	2-1/2 oz.	75 g
Salt (optional)	1 Tbsp.	15 mL
Whole wheat flour	2 oz.	60 g
Amaranth flour	2 oz.	60 g
Unbleached all-purpose flour	2 oz.	60 g
Yellow cornmeal	2 oz.	60 g
Pecans, chopped	4 oz.	120 g

1. Dissolve the brown sugar in the hot water. Add the oil.
2. Combine the dry ingredients in a large bowl. Mix thoroughly by hand.
3. Add the brown-sugar-and-oil mixture to the dry ingredients; toss to combine.
4. Spread out the granola in a thin layer on a sheet pan. Bake at 200°F (90°C) until crisp, approximately 1-1/2 to 2 hours. Toss lightly with a metal spatula every 30 minutes.
5. Let the baked granola cool completely at room temperature, then store in an air-tight container. Chopped dried fruits, additional nuts or fresh fruits can be added at service time.

Approximate values per 1 oz. (30 g) serving:

Calories	118
Total fat	6 g
Saturated fat	15 g
Cholesterol	15 mg
Sodium	120 mg
Total carbohydrates	15 g
Protein	3 g

NUTRITION

Most nutritionists agree that you and your customers should start the day with a nutritious breakfast. Depending upon what is eaten, a breakfast can supply a good percentage of the day's proteins, carbohydrates, fats, vitamins and minerals. (See Table 32.1.)

TABLE 32.1   NUTRITIONAL VALUES OF SELECTED BREAKFAST FOODS

Per Portion as Noted	Kcal	Protein (g)	Carbohydrates (g)	Total Fat (g)	Saturated Fat (g)	Cholesterol (mg)	Sodium (mg)
Coffee, brewed, 6 oz. (180 mL)	4	0.1	0.8	0	0	0	4
Cream, light, 1 oz. (30 mL)	55	0.8	1	5.5	3.4	19	11
Sugar, granulated, 1 Tbsp. (15 mL)	46	0	11.9	0	0	0	trace
Orange juice, fresh, 6 oz. (180 mL)	83	1.3	19.3	0.4	<0.1	0	2
Egg, hard-cooked, 1 large	77	6.3	0.6	5.3	1.6	213	62
Egg, pan-fried in margarine, 1 large	91	6.2	0.6	6.9	1.9	211	162
Bacon, cooked, 3 slices (20 slices per lb.)	109	5.8	0.1	9.4	3.3	16	303
English muffin, 1	130	4.3	25.4	1.3	na	0	206
Corn flakes, 1 oz. (28 g)	100	2	24	0	0	0	250
Milk, 8 oz. (240 mL)	88	7.2	11.2	1.6	0.8	8	240

The Corrine T. Netzer Encyclopedia of Food Values 1992
na = not available

CONCLUSION

Breakfast is an important meal for consumers and food service operations alike. Breakfast menus may offer a variety of items, including fruits, cereals, eggs, pancakes and cured meats, or they can be devoted to one or two specialty items such as coffee and cinnamon rolls. Whatever is served should be prepared and served with care.

QUESTIONS FOR DISCUSSION

1. Explain the differences between a typical breakfast and a typical brunch. Create a sample menu for each of these meals.
2. Explain the difference between an omelette and a frittata.
3. Describe four different types of fried eggs and explain how each is prepared.
4. What is the difference between a soft-cooked egg and a hard-cooked egg? Why are these eggs simmered instead of boiled?
5. List three types of griddlecakes and explain how they are prepared.
6. What problems might be encountered when preparing French toast with very thick slices of bread? How can you avoid these problems?
7. Should meats be fully cooked before being incorporated into egg dishes such as omelettes and quiches? Explain your answer.

ADDITIONAL BREAKFAST RECIPES

RECIPE 32.11

CAMPTON PLACE BAGELS
WITH SMOKED TROUT CREAM CHEESE

NOTE: *This dish appears in the Chapter Opening photograph.*

CAMPTON PLACE RESTAURANT, KEMPINSKI HOTELS, SAN FRANCISCO, CA
Chef Jan Birnbaum

Yield: 24 Bagels; 24-oz. (720-g) Spread

Dry yeast	1 Tbsp.	15 mL
Water (95°F/35°C)	8 oz.	250 mL
Granulated sugar	3 Tbsp.	45 mL
Malt	3 Tbsp.	45 mL
Flour	1 lb.	450 g
Salt	1 Tbsp.	15 mL
Vegetable oil	2 Tbsp.	30 mL
Egg wash	as needed	as needed
Cream cheese	1 lb.	450 g
Crème fraîche or sour cream	4 oz.	120 mL
Pepper, cracked	1/2 tsp.	3 g
Chives, cut	4 Tbsp.	60 mL
Smoked trout	1 lb.	450 g
Eggs, poached or basted	24	24

Approximate values per serving:

Calories	352
Total fat	9 g
Saturated fat	5 g
Cholesterol	33 mg
Sodium	522 mg
Total carbohydrates	55 g
Protein	11 g

1. To make the bagels, dissolve the yeast in the water.
2. Thoroughly combine the sugar, malt, flour and salt.
3. Add the oil to the yeast solution, then add the liquid ingredients to the dry ingredients. Mix thoroughly and knead the dough until hands and board come clean. Cover with a moist towel and allow to proof in a warm place (70–85°F/21–29°C) until doubled.
4. Punch down and cut into 1-ounce (30-g) pieces. Roll into doughnut shapes. Proof the bagels for 15 minutes.
5. Blanch the bagels in simmering water for 4 minutes, turning once. Remove and place on a sheet pan lined with parchment paper.
6. Brush with egg wash and bake at 350°F (180°C) until golden, approximately 20 minutes.
7. To make the cream cheese with smoked trout, beat the cream cheese in an electric mixer with the paddle attachment for approximately 5 minutes to incorporate air.
8. Add the crème fraîche and whisk for 2–3 minutes.
9. Add the pepper and chives and mix until incorporated, approximately 30 seconds.
10. Fold in 4 ounces (120 g) of small diced trout by hand.
11. To assemble, spread 2 ounces (60 g) of smoked trout spread on one half of each bagel. Top with 2 or 3 thin slices of smoked trout.
12. Place a poached or basted egg on the other half of the bagel.
13. Garnish the plate with fresh tomatoes and baby greens. Serve immediately.

◆◆◆

RECIPE 32.12

RICH HOT CHOCOLATE

Yield: 2 Servings

Milk	8 oz.	250 mL
Cream, 35%	8 oz.	250 mL
Chocolate Fudge Sauce, Recipe 31.32	3 oz.	90 mL

1. Heat the milk with 4 ounces (120 mL) of the cream and the fudge sauce over moderate heat, stirring constantly, until almost boiling.
2. Whip the remaining cream to soft peaks.
3. Portion the hot chocolate into warmed cups. Serve the whipped cream on the top.

Approximate values per serving:

Calories	674
Total fat	64 g
Saturated fat	40 g
Cholesterol	210 mg
Sodium	117 mg
Total carbohydrates	23 g
Protein	9 g

◆◆◆

RECIPE 32.13

SPICED CIDER

Yield: 64 oz. (2 L)

Apple cider	32 oz.	1 L
Orange or cranberry juice	32 oz.	1 L
Brown sugar	2 oz.	60 g
Cinnamon sticks	2	2
Cloves, whole	5	5
Allspice, whole	5	5

1. Combine all ingredients in a nonreactive saucepan over medium-low heat.
2. Bring the mixture to a simmer, cover and remove from the heat. Let steep for 10–15 minutes. Strain and serve garnished with sliced lemon or a cinnamon stick.

Approximate values per 6 oz. (180 mL) serving:

Calories	99
Total fat	0 g
Saturated fat	0 g
Cholesterol	0 mg
Sodium	5 mg
Total carbohydrates	24 g
Protein	1 g

◆◆◆

RECIPE 32.14

ARTICHOKE FRITTATA

THE INN OF THE WHITE SALMON, WHITE SALMON, WA

Yield: 1 9-inch-round (22-cm) Frittata

Artichoke hearts, cooked, fresh or canned	8 oz.	250 g
Unsalted butter	1 oz.	30 g
Parmesan cheese, grated	2 oz.	60 g
Eggs	10	10
Cereal cream	6 oz.	180 mL
Monterey Jack cheese, grated	4 oz.	120 g

1. Quarter the artichoke hearts.
2. Melt the butter in a sauté pan. Add the artichokes and sauté until heated through but not browned.
3. Distribute the artichokes in an even layer on the bottom of a 9-inch-round

Continued

Approximate values per 1/8-pie (137 g) serving:

Calories	250
Total fat	18 g
Saturated fat	9 g
Cholesterol	300 mg
Sodium	320 mg
Total carbohydrates	5 g
Protein	16 g
Vitamin A	20%
Calcium	25%

(22-cm) nonstick pan. Sprinkle with 1 ounce (30 g) of the Parmesan cheese.

4. In a small mixing bowl, whisk the eggs together with the cream. Pour over the artichokes.

5. Sprinkle the Monterey Jack cheese over the entire pan.

6. Bake for 30 minutes at 350°F (180°C). Remove from the oven and sprinkle the remaining 1 ounce (30 g) of Parmesan cheese over the frittata. Return to the oven until the cheese is melted and light brown, approximately 5 minutes.

❖❖❖

RECIPE 32.15

CRABCAKES BENEDICT

PHOENIX BREWING CO., ATLANTA, GA
Executive Chef Kevin Fonzo

Yield: 6 Servings

English muffins, split and toasted	6	6
Crab Cakes (recipe follows)	12	12
Eggs, poached	12	12
Tomato Chile Hollandaise (recipe follows)	12 oz.	360 mL

1. Place an open English muffin on each plate. Top each muffin half with a Crab Cake, a poached egg and 2 ounces (60 mL) of Tomato Chile Hollandaise sauce.

2. Garnish with gaufrette potatoes and fresh fruit.

CRAB CAKES

Approximate values per serving:

Calories	715
Total fat	43 g
Saturated fat	20 g
Cholesterol	539 mg
Sodium	2620 mg
Total carbohydrates	53 g
Protein	32 g
Vitamin A	48%
Vitamin C	15%
Calcium	35%
Iron	27%

Yield: 12 cakes

Whole butter	3 Tbsp.	45 mL
Onion, chopped	1 cup	250 mL
Green bell pepper, chopped	1/2 cup	120 mL
Green onion, chopped	1/2 cup	120 mL
Salt	1/2 tsp.	3 mL
Cayenne pepper	1/4 tsp.	1 mL
Worcestershire sauce	1 tsp.	5 mL
Old Bay® Seasoning (or other seasoning salt)	1 tsp.	5 mL
Cilantro, chopped	1 tsp.	5 mL
Egg	1	1
Lump crab meat	1 lb.	500 g
Bread crumbs	1–1-1/2 cup	250–360 mL
Olive oil	3 Tbsp.	45 mL

1. Heat the butter in a sauté pan over medium-high heat. Add the onion, bell pepper and green onion. Cook until tender then remove from the pan and cool completely.

2. In a large bowl combine the salt, cayenne, Worcestershire sauce, Old Bay, cilantro and egg. Mix well. Add the cooled vegetables and crab.

3. Add enough bread crumbs to bind the mixture. Divide into 12 portions and shape into patties.

4. Heat the olive oil in a large sauté pan. Sauté the crab cakes until golden brown on both sides.

Approximate values per cake:

Calories	139
Total fat	8 g
Saturated fat	3 g
Cholesterol	55 mg
Sodium	381 mg
Total carbohydrates	8 g
Protein	9 g

TOMATO CHILE HOLLANDAISE

Yield: 1 qt. (1 L)

Hollandaise sauce (Recipe 10.14)	1 qt.	1 L
Chilli powder	1 Tbsp.	15 mL
Tomato paste	1 Tbsp.	15 mL

Stir the chilli powder and tomato paste into the hollandaise sauce.

Approximate values per 4 oz. (120 mL) serving:

Calories	129
Total fat	11 g
Saturated fat	6 g
Cholesterol	26 mg
Sodium	830 mg
Total carbohydrates	8 g
Protein	3 g
Vitamin A	15%

❖❖❖

RECIPE 32.16

EGGS BENEDICT

Yield: 1 Serving

English muffin, split	1	1
Canadian back bacon slices, 1/4 in. (5 mm) thick	2	2
Eggs, poached	2	2
Salt	TT	TT
Vinegar	2 Tbsp.	30 mL
Hollandaise sauce (Recipe 10.14)	4 oz.	120 mL
Truffle slices or black olive halves	2	2

1. Toast the English muffin.
2. Sauté or griddle the bacon slices until hot.
3. Bring 1 quart (1 L) of water to a boil and add the salt and vinegar.
4. Add the eggs and poach until done. Drain well and dress.
5. Place the muffins on a plate and top with the bacon slices. Place an egg on each slice of bacon and cover with the Hollandaise sauce. Gratinée until golden.
6. Garnish each egg with a truffle slice or black olive half and serve.

VARIATIONS: *Poached eggs Sardou*—poached eggs and creamed spinach on an artichoke bottom with hollandaise sauce.

Poached eggs princess style—poached eggs on an English muffin with asparagus tips and hollandaise sauce.

Approximate values per serving:

Calories	970
Total fat	69 g
Saturated fat	33 g
Cholesterol	610 mg
Sodium	2480 mg
Total carbohydrates	53 g
Protein	33 g
Vitamin A	80%
Iron	25%

❖❖❖

RECIPE 32.17

APPLE PANCAKES

Yield: 24 Pancakes

Lemon juice	1 oz.	30 mL
Apples, peeled, cored and chopped fine	3	3
All-purpose flour	5 oz.	150 g
Salt	1/2 tsp.	2 mL
Granulated sugar	1 Tbsp.	15 mL
Eggs	4	4
Milk	12 oz.	350 mL
Butter, melted	2 oz.	60 mL
Powdered sugar	as needed	as needed
Cinnamon, ground	as needed	as needed

Continued

Approximate values per pancake:

Calories	65
Total fat	3 g
Saturated fat	1 g
Cholesterol	41 mg
Sodium	43 mg
Total carbohydrates	8 g
Protein	2 g

1. Sprinkle the lemon juice over the apples to prevent browning, then set aside.

2. Sift the flour, salt and sugar into a bowl. Beat the eggs with the milk.

3. Stir the egg mixture into the flour mixture, blending well. Fold in the apples.

4. Heat the butter in a sauté pan over medium-high heat. Spoon the batter into the pan, in 2-ounce (60-g) portions. Cook the pancakes, turning once, until golden brown on both sides. Dust with powdered sugar and cinnamon and serve immediately.

◆◆◆

RECIPE 32.18

BUCKWHEAT CREPES
WITH SAUSAGE AND APPLE STUFFING

THE CONYERS HOUSE, SPERRYVILLE, VA

Yield: 8 Servings

All-purpose flour	3 oz.	90 g
Buckwheat flour	1 oz.	30 g
Eggs	2	2
Salt	1/4 tsp.	1 mL
Milk	4 oz.	120 mL
Water	6 oz.	180 mL
Unsalted butter, melted	1 oz.	30 g
Oil	as needed	as needed
Pork sausage, bulk	1 lb.	450 g
Unsalted butter	2 oz.	60 g
Apples, peeled, cored and diced	6 medium	6 medium
Cinnamon, ground	1 tsp.	5 mL
Apple cider	4 oz.	120 mL
Sour cream	8 oz.	250 mL
Fresh sage	2 Tbsp.	30 mL

1. To make the crepes, mix the flours together in a medium bowl. Add the eggs and salt. Stir to make a thick batter.

2. Whisk in the milk, then add the water a little at a time. Whisk in the melted butter. Set the batter aside to rest for 20 minutes.

3. Heat a crepe pan and coat it lightly with oil. Pour 1-1/2 ounces (45 mL) of batter into the pan, lifting and tilting to coat the pan evenly.

4. Brown the crepe lightly on one side, cooking until the surface is set. Remove from the pan and hold in a warm oven until ready to fill and serve.

5. To make the filling, crumble the sausage into a sauté pan; cook over medium-high heat until fully cooked. Remove the sausage from the pan with a slotted spoon and place in a mesh strainer to drain excess fat.

6. Pour off all but 1 tablespoon (15 mL) of fat. Add the butter to the pan and melt over medium heat. Add the diced apples and sauté until soft.

7. Sprinkle the cinnamon over the apples and pour in the apple cider. Cook until the cider is reduced by half.

8. Return the drained sausage to the pan. Add the sour cream and sage. Mix well and heat thoroughly.

9. To assemble, spoon a portion of the filling onto each crepe. Roll the crepe around the filling and serve immediately.

Approximate values per 6 oz. (180 g) serving:

Calories	240
Total fat	11 g
Saturated fat	6 g
Cholesterol	75 mg
Sodium	140 mg
Total carbohydrates	29 g
Protein	5 g
Vitamin A	10%

Claims—good source of fibre

◆◆◆

RECIPE 32.19

CHEESE BLINTZES

Yield: 16 Blintzes

Eggs	3	3
Milk	8 oz.	250 mL
Vegetable oil	1 oz.	30 mL
Salt	1/2 tsp.	2 mL
Flour	4 oz.	120 g
Clarified butter	as needed	as needed
Ricotta cheese	12 oz.	350 g
Egg yolk	1	1
Salt	1/4 tsp.	1 mL
Lemon juice	1 tsp.	5 mL
Vanilla extract	1 tsp.	5 mL
Butter	2 oz.	60 g

1. To make the batter, whisk together the eggs, milk and oil. Add the salt. Stir in the flour and mix until smooth. Allow the batter to rest for 30 minutes.

2. Heat a crepe pan and add a small amount of clarified butter.

3. Add 1 ounce (30 g) of the batter to the pan. Tip the pan so the batter coats the entire surface in a thin layer.

4. Cook the pancake until lightly browned on the bottom. Remove it from the pan and reserve. Do not stack the pancakes.

5. To make the filling, drain the cheese in a china cap. Combine the remaining ingredients (except the butter) with the cheese and mix well.

6. To assemble, place a pancake on the work surface with the uncooked side down. Place 1 ounce (30 g) of the filling in the centre of the pancake. Fold the opposite ends in and then roll up to form a small package.

7. Sauté each blintz in butter until hot. Serve with sour cream or fruit compote as desired.

Approximate values per 2 oz. (60 g) serving:	
Calories	110
Total fat	7 g
Saturated fat	3.5 g
Cholesterol	65 mg
Sodium	170 mg
Total carbohydrates	7 g
Protein	5 g

◆◆◆

RECIPE 32.20

BANANA BRIOCHE FRENCH TOAST

CAMPTON PLACE RESTAURANT, KEMPINSKI HOTELS, SAN FRANCISCO, CA
Executive Chef Jan Birnbaum

Yield: 4 Servings

Bananas, sliced	3	3
Lemon juice	2 Tbsp.	30 mL
Zest of two lemons		
Brioche, sliced 1-1/2 inches (3.7 cm) thick	12 slices	12 slices
Eggs	10	10
Cream, 35%	11 oz.	300 mL
Salt	pinch	pinch
Cinnamon, ground	1/2 tsp.	2 mL
Nutmeg	1/4 tsp.	1 mL
Granulated sugar	3 oz.	90 g

Continued

Vanilla extract	1 tsp.	5 mL
Unsalted butter	as needed	as needed
Powdered sugar	as needed	as needed
Mango preserves	as needed	as needed
Macadamia nuts, chopped	as needed	as needed

1. Toss the bananas with the lemon juice and zest.
2. Cut into one side of each slice of bread to create a deep pocket. Stuff the pocket with the banana slices.
3. Whisk together the eggs, cream, salt, cinnamon, nutmeg, sugar and vanilla. Soak the stuffed bread in this mixture until very soggy. Remove carefully from the egg mixture and drain briefly.
4. Sauté the soaked bread in butter until golden brown on each side. Place in a 375°F (190°C) oven and bake until the bread puffs, approximately 3–4 minutes.
5. Dust with powdered sugar and top with mango preserves and macadamia nuts.

Approximate values per serving (3 slices):

Calories	1220
Total fat	87 g
Saturated fat	40 g
Cholesterol	735 mg
Sodium	750 mg
Total carbohydrates	90 g
Protein	27 g

RECIPE 32.21

CORNED BEEF HASH

Yield: 5 Servings   **Method:** Sautéing

Onion, diced fine	4 oz.	110 g
Vegetable oil	2 Tbsp.	30 mL
Corned beef, cooked and diced finely	1 lb.	450 g
Potatoes, cooked, diced	8 oz.	225 g
Tomato paste	1 oz.	25 g
Tomato concassée	1 lb.	225 g
Parsley, chopped fine	1/2 oz.	15 g
Salt and pepper	TT	TT

1. Sauté onions in oil until they are clear.
2. Add the corned beef and sauté until meat is heated through.
3. Add potatoes and sauté mixture until it is lightly browned. Stir periodically.
4. Add tomato paste and concassée. Simmer until liquid is reduced by two-thirds.
5. Add chopped parsley and adjust seasoning with salt and pepper.
6. Cool the mixture and refrigerate until needed.
7. To serve, preheat the skillet and lubricate it with a small amount of oil. Place a portion of the hash in the skillet and sauté until lightly browned, stirring constantly.
8. Shape and transfer to plate.
9. Serve with fried or poached eggs.

Alternative Method: Reheat and brown mixture in a sauté pan and shape like a cigar.

Approximate values per serving:

Calories	336
Total fat	19 g
Saturated fat	6 g
Cholesterol	77 mg
Sodium	1178 mg
Total carbohydrates	14 g
Protein	26 g

EBLINKS

American Egg Board: Breakfast and Brunch Recipes
   www.aeb.org/recipes/breakfast/index.html
Breakfast
   www.efn.org/~sundance/Breakfast.html
Creole/Cajun: Breakfast and Breads
   www.gumbopages.com/breakfast-home.html

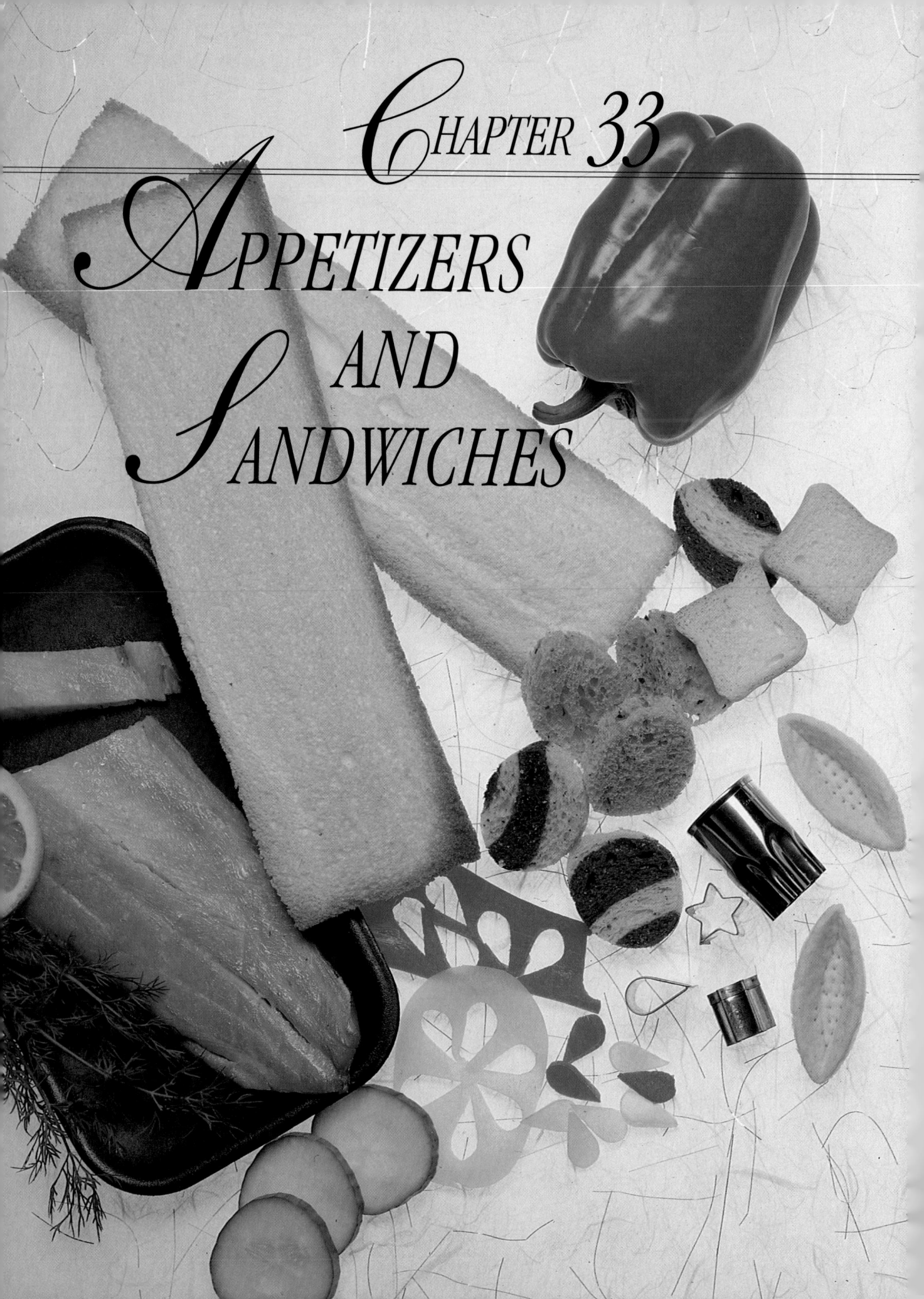

CHAPTER 33

APPETIZERS AND SANDWICHES

*H*ors d'oeuvres and canapés, whether hot or cold, are very small portions of foods served before or at the beginning of the meal to stimulate the appetite or at a reception as the accompaniment to liquid refreshments. Hors d'oeuvres can be passed elegantly by waiters or displayed on buffets. Appetizers, whether hot or cold, are generally the first course or introduction to a meal; they are more typically served with dinner than with lunch. Sometimes there is very little difference between an hors d'oeuvre and an appetizer.

Sandwiches, which are usually quick and easy to assemble, also lend themselves to a cook's creativity. Fancy sandwiches can become sensational menu additions in even the most formal restaurants, and amazing sandwiches can keep lunch customers visiting regularly.

The preparation of hors d'oeuvres and sandwiches uses skills from almost every work station. Because they can consist of meat, poultry, fish, shellfish, vegetables, potatoes, grains, pasta, fruits, baked goods and sauces, they require a detailed knowledge of these foods and how they are prepared.

Although hors d'oeuvres and sandwiches can be divided into hot and cold varieties, it is difficult (and unnecessary) to categorize them further because of the vast variety possible and the absence of any one dominant food type or style.

HORS D'OEUVRES

The French term *hors d'oeuvre* translates as "outside the work" although we generally use it to mean appetizer. Its usage was correct under the classic kitchen brigade system, for it was the service staff's responsibility to prepare small tidbits for guests to enjoy while the kitchen prepared the meal. Today, however, the kitchen staff prepares the hors d'oeuvres as well as the meals. Cold hors d'oeuvres are usually prepared by the *garde-manger*; hot ones are prepared in the main kitchen.

There are really only two limitations on the type of food and manner of preparation that can be used for hors d'oeuvres: the cook's imagination and the foods at his or her disposal. There are, however, a few guidelines.

BASIC GUIDELINES FOR PREPARING HORS D'OEUVRES

1. They should be small, one to two bites.
2. They should be flavourful and well seasoned without being overpowering.
3. They should be visually attractive.
4. They should complement the foods to follow without duplicating their flavours.

Cold Hors d'Oeuvres

Cold hors d'oeuvres are divided here into five broad categories based upon preparation method, principal ingredient or presentation style. They are: canapés, caviars, crudités, dips and sushi. These categories may vary somewhat from classical teachings, but they are completely appropriate for modern menus and food service operations.

Canapés

Canapés are, essentially, tiny, open-faced sandwiches. They are constructed from a base, a spread and one or more garnishes.

The most common **canapé base** is a thin slice of bread cut into an interesting shape and toasted. Although most any variety of bread can be used, spiced, herbed or otherwise flavoured breads may be inappropriate for some spreads or garnishes. Melba toasts, crackers, or slices of firm vegetables such as cucumbers or zucchini or meat slices are also popular canapé bases. The base must be strong enough to support the weight of the spread and garnish without falling apart when handled.

The **canapé spread** provides much of the canapé's flavour. Spreads are usually flavoured butters, cream cheese or a combination of the two. Examples of spreads are listed in Table 33.1. Each of the spreads is made by adding the desired amount of the main ingredient (chopped or puréed as appropriate) and seasonings to softened butter or cream cheese and mixing until combined. Quantities and proportions vary according to individual tastes. Other canapé spreads include bound salads (for example, tuna or egg), finely chopped shrimp or liver mousse. Any of a number of ingredients can be combined for spreads, provided the following guidelines are followed.

BASIC GUIDELINES FOR PREPARING CANAPÉ SPREADS

1. The spread's texture should be smooth enough to produce attractive designs if piped through a pastry bag fitted with a decorative tip.
2. The spread's consistency should be firm enough to hold its shape when piped onto the base, yet soft enough to stick to the base and hold the garnishes in place.
3. The spread's flavour should complement the garnishes and be flavourful enough to stimulate the appetite without being overpowering.

A spread may be a substantial portion of the canapé as well as its distinguishing characteristic. Or it can be applied sparingly and used more as a means of gluing the garnish to the base than as a principal ingredient.

Canapés with bread bases tend to become soggy quickly from both the moisture in the spread and the moisture in the refrigerator where they are stored. Using a spread made with butter will help keep the bread bases crispier, as will buttering the base with a thin coat of softened plain butter before piping on the spread. The best way to ensure a crisp base is to make the canapés as close to service time as possible.

The variety of **canapé garnishes** is vast. The garnish can dominate or complement the spread, or it can be a simple herb sprig intended to provide visual appeal but little flavour. Although several ingredients can be used to garnish the same canapé, remember the limitations imposed by the canapé's size and purpose.

TABLE 33.1   A SELECTION OF CANAPÉ SPREADS AND SUGGESTED GARNISHES

Spread	Suggested Garnishes
Anchovy butter	Hard-cooked eggs, capers, green or black olive slices
Blue cheese	Grape half, walnuts, roast beef roulade, pear slice, currants, watercress
Caviar butter	Caviar, lemon, egg slice, chives
Deviled ham	Cornichons, mustard butter, sliced radish
Horseradish butter	Smoked salmon, roast beef, smoked trout, marinated herring, capers, parsley
Lemon butter	Shrimp, crab, caviar, salmon, chives, parsley, black olive slices
Liver pâté	Truffle slice, cornichon
Mustard butter	Smoked meats, pâté, dry salami coronet, cornichon
Pimiento cream cheese	Smoked oyster, sardine, pimiento, parsley
Shrimp butter	Poached bay scallops, shrimp, caviar, parsley
Tuna salad	Capers, cornichons, sliced radish

BASIC PROCEDURE FOR PREPARING CANAPÉS

This procedure can be adapted and used with a variety of ingredients to produce a variety of canapés. If the canapé base is a bread crouton, begin with step 1. If some other product is used as the base, prepare that base and begin with step 4.

1. Trim the crust from an unsliced loaf of bread. Slice the bread lengthwise approximately 1/3 inch (8 mm) thick.
2. Cut the bread slices into the desired shapes using a serrated bread knife or canapé cutter.
3. Brush the bread shapes with melted butter and bake in a 350°F (180°C) oven until they are toasted and dry. Remove and cool.
4. If desired, spread each base with a thin layer of softened plain butter.
5. Apply the spread to the base. If a thin layer is desired, use a palette knife. If a thicker or more decorative layer is desired, pipe the spread onto the base using a pastry bag and decorative tip.
6. Garnish the canapé as desired.
7. If desired, glaze each canapé with a thin coating of aspic jelly. The aspic jelly can be applied with a small spoon or a spray bottle designated for that purpose.

Barquettes, Tartlets and Profiteroles

Barquettes, tartlets and profiteroles are all adaptations of the basic canapé. A **barquette** is a tiny boat-shaped shell made from a savoury dough such as pâte brisée. A **tartlet** is simply a round version of a barquette. A **profiterole** is a small puff made from pâte à choux. These three items can be prepared like canapés by filling them with flavoured spreads and garnishing as desired.

Other Types of Canapés

Vegetables such as cherry tomatoes, blanched snow peas, mushroom caps and Belgian endive leaves are sometimes used as canapé bases. They are filled and garnished in the same manner as barquettes, tartlets and profiteroles.

Caviar

Caviar, considered by many to be the ultimate hors d'oeuvre, is the salted roe (eggs) of the sturgeon fish. In Canada, only sturgeon roe can be labelled as simply "caviar." Roe from other fish must be qualified as such on the label (e.g., salmon caviar or lumpfish caviar).

Most of the world's caviar comes from sturgeon harvested in the Caspian Sea and imported from Russia and Iran. Imported sturgeon caviar, classified according to the sturgeon species and the roe's size and colour, includes **beluga**, **osetra** and **sevruga** as well as **pressed caviar**. Belugia is the most expensive caviar; it comes from the largest species (the sturgeon can weigh up to 1750 pounds/800 kg); the dark grey and well-separated eggs are the largest and most fragile kind. Osetra is considered by some connoisseurs to be the best caviar; the eggs are medium-sized, golden yellow to brown in colour and quite oily. Sevruga is harvested from small sturgeon; the eggs are quite small and light to dark grey in colour. Pressed caviar is a processed caviar from osetra and sevruga roes. The eggs are cleaned, packed in linen bags and hung to drain; as salt and moisture drain away, the natural shape of the eggs is destroyed and the eggs are pressed together. Approximately 3 pounds (1.3 kg) of roe produce only 1 pound (450 g) of pressed caviar; pressed caviar has a spreadable, jamlike consistency. Most of the caviar consumed in North America, however, comes from either domestic sturgeon or other fish and is labelled **American sturgeon caviar**, **golden whitefish caviar**, **lumpfish caviar** or **salmon caviar**. American sturgeon caviar is not considered of the same quality as Russian or Iranian caviars; nevertheless, roe from sturgeon harvested in the coastal waters of the American northwest and the Tennessee River is becoming increasingly popular, due in part to its relatively low price. Golden whitefish caviar is a small and very crisp roe; the roe is a natural golden colour and comes from whitefish native to the northern Great Lakes. Lumpfish caviar is readily available and reasonably priced; it is produced from lumpfish harvested in the North Atlantic. The small and very crisp eggs are dyed black, red or gold; the food colouring is not stable, however, and when used to garnish foods, coloured lumpfish caviar has a tendency to bleed. Salmon caviar is the eggs of the chum and silver salmon and is a very popular garnish. The eggs are large with a good flavour and natural orange colour.

Purchasing and Storing Caviars

Although all caviar is processed with salt, the best caviar is labelled **malassol**, which means "little salt." Caviar should smell fresh, with no off-odours. The eggs should be whole, not broken, and they should be crisp and pop when pressed with the tongue. Excessive oiliness may be caused by a large number of broken eggs. The best way to test a caviar's quality is to taste it. Remember, price alone does not necessarily indicate quality.

Most caviar can be purchased fresh or pasteurized in tins or jars ranging from 1 ounce (28 g) to over 4 pounds (2 kg). Some caviars are also available frozen. (Frozen caviar should be used only as a garnish and should not be served by itself.) In order to ensure the freshest possible product, always purchase caviar in small quantities as often as necessary based on your needs.

Fresh caviar should be stored at 32°F (0°C). Because most refrigerators are considerably warmer than that, store the caviar on ice in the coldest part of the refrigerator and change the ice often. If properly handled, fresh caviar will last one to two weeks before opening and several days after opening. Pasteurized caviar does not require refrigeration until it is opened and will last several days in the refrigerator after opening.

Serving Caviars

Fine caviar should be served in its original container or a nonmetal bowl on a bed of crushed ice, accompanied only by lightly buttered toasts or blinis and sour cream. Connoisseurs prefer china, bone or other nonmetal utensils for serving caviar because metal reacts with the caviar, producing off-flavours.

Lesser-quality caviars are often served on ice, accompanied by minced onion, chopped hard-cooked egg whites and yolks (separately), lemon, sour cream and buttered toasts.

Lumpfish and other nonsturgeon caviars are usually not served by themselves. Rather, they are used as ingredients in or garnishes for other dishes.

An Artful Array of Crudités and Dip.

Chafing dish—*a metal dish with a heating unit (flame or electric) used to keep foods warm at tableside or during buffet service.*

Crudités

Crudité, a French word meaning "raw thing," generally refers to raw or slightly blanched vegetables served as an hors d'oeuvre. Although almost any vegetable will do, the most commonly used are broccoli, cauliflower, carrots, celery, asparagus and green beans, all of which are often blanched, and cucumbers, zucchini, yellow squash, radishes, green onions, cherry tomatoes, Belgian endive leaves, mushrooms, peppers and jicama, which are served raw.

When preparing crudités, use only the freshest and best-looking produce available. Because crudités are displayed and eaten raw, blemishes and imperfections cannot be disguised. Vegetables, both blanched and raw, should be cut into attractive shapes. Crudités are usually served with one or more dips.

Dips

Dips can be served hot or cold and as an accompaniment to crudités, crackers, chips, toasts, breads or other foods.

Cold dips often use mayonnaise, sour cream or cream cheese as a base. The methods for preparing mayonnaise- and sour-cream-based dips are identical to those for making mayonnaise-based salad dressings discussed in Chapter 24, Salads and Salad Dressings. The principal difference is that dips are normally thicker than dressings.

To use cream cheese as a base, first soften it by mixing it in an electric mixer with a paddle attachment. Then add the flavouring ingredients such as chopped cooked vegetables, chopped cooked fish or shellfish, herbs, spices, garlic or onions. Adjust the consistency of the dip by adding milk, buttermilk, cream, sour cream or other appropriate liquid.

Some cold dips such as guacamole and hummus use purées of fruits, vegetables or beans as the base.

Hot dips often use a béchamel, cream sauce or cheese sauce as a base and usually contain a dominant flavouring ingredient such as chopped spinach or shellfish. The traditional Italian bagna cauda is an example of a hot, oil-based dip. It is made with olive oil, garlic and anchovies and is kept hot over a small burner while guests dip raw vegetables in it.

Dips can be served in small bowls or hollowed-out cabbages, squash, pumpkins or other vegetables. Hot dips are often served in **chafing dishes**.

The combinations of ingredients and seasonings that can be used to make dips as well as the foods that are dipped in them are limited only by the chef's imagination.

◆◆◆

RECIPE 33.1

CLAM DIP

Yield: 3 pt. (1.5 L)

Cream cheese	1 lb.	450 g
Worcestershire sauce	1 oz.	30 mL
Dijon mustard	1 Tbsp.	15 mL
Sour cream	1 lb.	450 mL
Canned clams, drained	1 lb.	450 g
Lemon juice	1 oz.	30 mL
Salt and pepper	TT	TT
Tabasco sauce	TT	TT
Green onions, sliced	2 oz.	60 g

1. Soften the cream cheese in the bowl of an electric mixer, using the paddle attachment.
2. Add the Worcestershire sauce, Dijon mustard and sour cream; mix until smooth.
3. Add the clams and lemon juice and season with salt, pepper and Tabasco.
4. Add the green onions and mix well.

Approximate values per 1 oz. (30 g) serving:

Calories	70
Total fat	5 g
Saturated fat	3.5 g
Cholesterol	20 mg
Sodium	55 mg
Total carbohydrates	1 g
Protein	4 g
Iron	15%

Claims—low sodium; low sugar

Sushi

Generally, **sushi** refers to cooked or raw fish and shellfish rolled in or served on seasoned rice. **Sashimi** is raw fish eaten without rice. In Japan, the word sushi (or **zushi**) refers only to the flavoured rice. Each combination of rice and another ingredient or ingredients has a specific name. These include: *nigiri zushi* (rice with raw fish), *norimaki zushi* (rice rolled in seaweed), *fukusa zushi* (rice wrapped in omelette), *inari zushi* (rice in fried bean curd) and *chirashi zushi* (rice with fish, shellfish and vegetables). Although a Japanese sushi master spends years perfecting style and technique, many types of sushi can be produced in any professional kitchen with very little specialized equipment.

Ingredients

Fish—The key to good sushi and sashimi is the freshness of the fish. All fish must be of the highest quality and absolutely fresh, preferably no more than one day out of the water. Ahi and yellowfin tuna, salmon, flounder and sea bass are typically used for sushi. Cooked shrimp and eel are also popular.

Rice—Sushi rice is prepared by adding seasonings such as vinegar, sugar, salt and rice wine (sake or mirin) to steamed short-grain rice. The consistency of the rice is very important. It must be sticky enough to stay together when formed into finger-shaped oblongs, but not too soft.

Seasonings—These include:

+ Shoyu—Japanese soy sauce, which is lighter and more delicate than the Chinese variety.
+ Wasabi—A strong aromatic root, purchased as a green powder. It is sometimes called green horseradish although it is not actually related to the common horseradish.
+ Pickled ginger—fresh ginger pickled in vinegar, which gives it a pink colour.
+ Nori—a dried seaweed purchased in sheets; it adds flavour and is sometimes used to contain the rolled rice and other ingredients.

◆◆◆

RECIPE 33.2

ZUSHI
(SUSHI RICE)

Yield: 2 lb. (1 kg)

Short-grain rice	1 lb.	480 g
Water	20 oz.	600 mL
Rice vinegar	2 oz.	60 mL
Sugar	3 Tbsp.	45 mL
Salt	2-1/2 tsp.	12 mL
Mirin	1 oz.	30 mL

Continued

Approximate values per 1 oz. (30 g) serving:

Calories	60
Total fat	0 g
Saturated fat	0 g
Cholesterol	0 mg
Sodium	140 mg
Total carbohydrates	13 g
Protein	1 g

Claims—fat free

1. Form a finger-shaped rice mound.

2. Press the fish onto the rice.

Approximate values per piece:	
Calories	80
Total fat	2 g
Saturated fat	0 g
Cholesterol	10 mg
Sodium	310 mg
Total carbohydrates	11 g
Protein	5 g
Claims—low fat; low cholesterol; no sugar	

1. Wash the rice and allow it to drain for 30 minutes.
2. Combine the rice and water in a saucepan. Bring to a boil, reduce to a simmer, cover and steam for 20 minutes.
3. Disolve the sugar and salt in warmed mirin. Add the rice vinegar and cool.
4. Spread the rice in a shallow bowl or tray.
5. Sprinkle the vinegar mixture over the rice and gently stir it in. Fan the rice to cool while stirring with chopsticks.
6. Keep cooled mixture covered with a damp cloth. Use immediately.

◆◆◆

RECIPE 33.3

NIGIRI ZUSHI

Yield: 24 Pieces

Sushi-quality fish fillets such as ahi, salmon, flounder or sea bass	1 lb.	450 g
Wasabi powder	1 oz.	30 g
Water	1 oz.	30 mL
Zushi (Recipe 33.2)	2 lb.	900 g
Pickled ginger, sliced	2 oz.	60 g
Shoyu	3 oz.	90 mL

1. Trim the fish fillets of any skin, bone, imperfections or blemishes. Cut the fillets into 24 thin slices approximately 2 inches long by 1 inch wide (5 cm by 2.5 cm).
2. Mix the wasabi powder and water to form a paste.
3. With your hands, form a 1-1/2-ounce (50-g) portion of rice into a finger-shaped mound.
4. Rub a small amount of wasabi on one side of a slice of fish.
5. Holding the rice mound in one hand, press the fish, wasabi side down, onto the rice with the fingers of the other hand.
6. Serve with additional wasabi, pickled ginger and shoyu.

◆◆◆

RECIPE 33.4

NORIMAKI ZUSHI

Yield: 36 Pieces

Dried shiitake mushrooms	4	4
Shoyu	4 oz.	120 mL
Brown sugar	1 Tbsp.	15 mL
Cucumber	1/2	1/2
Sushi-quality fish fillets such as ahi, salmon, flounder or sea bass	5 oz.	150 g
Nori	3 sheets	3 sheets
Zushi (Recipe 33.2)	18 oz.	500 g
Pickled ginger	2 oz.	60 g
Wasabi paste	2 oz.	60 mL

1. Soak the mushrooms in hot water for 20 minutes. Remove the mushrooms and reserve 4 ounces (120 mL) of the liquid. Trim off the mushroom stems.

2. Julienne the mushroom caps. Combine the reserved soaking liquid with 2 tablespoons (30 mL) of the shoyu and the brown sugar. Simmer the caps in this liquid and reduce *au sec*. Remove from the heat and refrigerate.

3. Peel and seed the cucumber; cut it into strips the size of pencils, approximately 6 inches (15 cm) long.

4. Trim the fish fillets of any skin, bone, imperfections or blemishes. Cut the fillets into strips the same size as the cucumbers.

5. Cut the sheets of nori in half and place one half sheet on a napkin or bamboo rolling mat. Divide the rice into 6 equal portions; spread 1 portion over each half sheet of nori, leaving a 1/2 inch (12 mm) border of nori exposed.

6. Spread 1 teaspoon (5 mL) of wasabi evenly on the rice.

7. Lay 1/6 of the mushrooms, cucumber and fish strips in a row down the middle of the rice.

8. Use the napkin or bamboo mat to roll the nori tightly around the rice and garnishes.

9. Slice each roll into 6 pieces and serve with the remaining shoyu, pickled ginger and wasabi.

Approximate values per piece:

Calories	40
Total fat	0 g
Saturated fat	0 g
Cholesterol	5 mg
Sodium	220 mg
Total carbohydrates	6 g
Protein	2 g
Vitamin C	15%

Claims—fat free; low cholesterol; low calorie

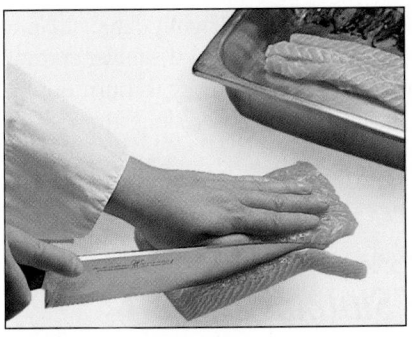

1. Prepare the garnishes for the sushi roll.

2. Spread the rice over the nori.

3. Add the garnishes in a row down the middle of the rice.

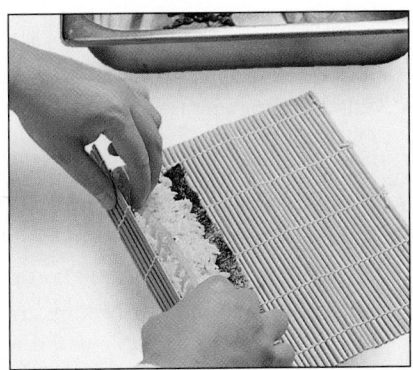

4. With the mat roll the nori around the rice and garnishes.

5. Slice the roll into 6 pieces.

Hot Hors d'Oeuvres

To provide a comprehensive list of hot hors d'oeuvres would be virtually impossible; therefore we discuss just a few of the more commonly encountered ones that can be easily made in most any kitchen.

Filled Pastry Shells

Because savoury (unsweetened) barquettes and tartlets, choux puffs and bouchées can hold a small amount of liquid, they are often baked then filled with warm meat, poultry or fish purées or ragouts, garnished and served hot. They become soggy quickly, however, and must be prepared at the last possible minute before service.

Brochettes

Hors d'oeuvre brochettes are small skewers holding a combination of meat, poultry, game, fish, shellfish or vegetables. They are normally baked, grilled or broiled and are often served with a dipping sauce. Brochettes can be small pieces of boneless chicken breast marinated in white wine and grilled; beef cubes glazed with teriyaki sauce; lamb or chicken satay (saté) with peanut sauce or rabbit and shiitake mushrooms skewered on a sprig of fresh rosemary.

In order to increase visual appeal, the main ingredients should be carefully cut and consistently sized and shaped. The ingredients are normally diced, but strips of meat and poultry can also be threaded onto the skewers. Often, ingredients are first marinated.

As hors d'oeuvres, the skewers should be very small, slightly larger than a toothpick. When assembling brochettes, leave enough exposed skewer so diners can pick them up easily. Wooden skewers have a tendency to burn during cooking. Soaking them in water before using them helps reduce the risk of burning.

RECIPE 33.5

RABBIT AND SHIITAKE SKEWERS

Yield: 12 Skewers

Rabbit	1	1
Shiitake mushrooms	2 lb.	1 kg
Rosemary sprigs	12	12
Salt and pepper	TT	TT
Olive oil	2 oz.	60 mL

1. Bone the rabbit and cut the pieces into 1/2-inch (1.2-cm) cubes. One rabbit should produce 36 cubes.
2. Wash the mushrooms. Trim and discard the stems.
3. Cut enough of the mushrooms into 1/2-inch (1.2-cm) dice to produce 24 pieces.
4. Skewer 3 pieces of rabbit and 2 pieces of mushroom alternately onto each rosemary sprig.
5. Season the skewers and the remaining mushrooms with salt and pepper and brush with olive oil. Grill the skewers and the mushroom caps over medium heat, being careful not to burn the rosemary sprigs.
6. Slice the mushroom caps. Arrange a portion of sliced mushrooms and 2 rabbit skewers on each plate.

Approximate values per skewer:	
Calories	160
Total fat	8 g
Saturated fat	1.5 g
Cholesterol	30 mg
Sodium	20 mg
Total carbohydrates	11 g
Protein	12 g

Meatballs

Meatballs made from ground beef, veal, pork or poultry and served in a sauce buffet-style are a popular hot hors d'oeuvre. One of the best known is the Swedish meatball. It is made from ground beef, veal and pork bound with eggs and bread crumbs and served in a velouté or cream sauce seasoned with dill. Other sauces that can be used in the same manner are mushroom sauce, red wine sauce or any style of tomato sauce.

◆◆◆

RECIPE 33.6

SWEDISH MEATBALLS

Yield: 4 lb. 8 oz. (2 kg)

Onions, small dice	8 oz.	250 g
Whole butter	2 oz.	60 g
Ground beef	2 lb.	1 kg
Ground pork	2 lb.	1 kg
Bread crumbs, fresh	4 oz.	120 g
Eggs	3	3
Salt	1 Tbsp.	15 mL
Pepper	TT	TT
Nutmeg	TT	TT
Allspice	TT	TT
Lemon zest, grated	1 tsp.	5 mL
Demi-glace, hot	1 qt.	1 L
Cream, 35%, hot	8 oz.	250 mL
Fresh dill, chopped	2 Tbsp.	30 mL

1. Sauté the onions in butter without colouring. Remove and cool.
2. Combine the onions with all the ingredients except the demi-glace, cream and dill. Mix well.
3. Portion the meat with a #20 scoop; form into balls with your hands and place on a sheet pan.
4. Bake the meatballs at 400°F (200°C) until firm, approximately 15 minutes. Remove the meatballs from the pan with a slotted spoon, draining well, and place in a hotel pan.
5. Combine the demi-glace, cream and dill; pour over the meatballs.
6. Cover the meatballs and bake at 350°F (180°C) until done, approximately 20 minutes. Skim off the grease from the surface and serve.

Approximate values per 5 oz. (150 g) serving:

Calories	250
Total fat	16 g
Saturated fat	7 g
Cholesterol	105 mg
Sodium	420 mg
Total carbohydrates	7 g
Protein	20 g
Calcium	30%

Rumaki

Traditionally, rumaki were made by wrapping chicken livers in bacon and broiling or baking them. Today, however, many other foods prepared in the same fashion are called rumaki. For example, blanched bacon can be wrapped around olives, pickled watermelon rind, water chestnuts, pineapple, dates or scallops. These morsels are then broiled, baked or fried and served piping hot.

◆◆◆

RECIPE 33.7

DATE AND CHORIZO RUMAKI

Yield: 32 Pieces

Bacon, thin-cut slices	16	16
Chorizo (Recipe 20.19)	8 oz.	250 g
Cream cheese	4 oz.	120 g
Whole dates, pitted	32	32

1. Partially cook the bacon on a sheet pan in a 350°F (180°C) oven, approximately 5 minutes.
2. Cook the chorizo to render the excess fat. If the chorizo is in links, remove the meat from the casings before cooking.
3. Remove the cooked chorizo from the pan and drain in a mesh strainer or china cap to remove excess fat. Then blend the cream cheese into the meat.
4. Cut the dates open, butterfly style. Stuff each date with a portion of the chorizo mixture.
5. Wrap each date with a half slice of bacon, securing with a toothpick.
6. Arrange the rumaki on a rack placed over a sheet pan. Bake at 350°F (180°C) until the bacon is crisp and the dates are hot, approximately 15–20 minutes.

Approximate values per piece:

Calories	90
Total fat	5 g
Saturated fat	2.5 g
Cholesterol	15 mg
Sodium	150 mg
Total carbohydrates	7 g
Protein	3 g

Stuffed Wonton Skins

Wonton skins are an Asian noodle dough used to produce a wide variety of hors d'oeuvres such as a miniature version of the traditional egg roll or a puff filled with a mixture of seasoned cream cheese and crab. Or they can be stuffed with a wide variety of pork, chicken, shellfish and vegetables before cooking. As hors d'oeuvres, stuffed wonton skins can be steamed, but they are more often pan-fried or deep-fat fried.

◆◆◆

RECIPE 33.8

STUFFED WONTONS WITH APRICOT SAUCE

Yield: 24 Pieces

Cream cheese	8 oz.	250 g
Crab meat	8 oz.	250 g
Garlic, chopped	1 tsp.	5 mL
Green onion, sliced	1 oz.	30 g
Salt and pepper	TT	TT
Worcestershire sauce	TT	TT
Sesame oil	TT	TT
Wonton skins	24	24
Apricot Sauce (recipe follows)	as needed	as needed

1. Place the cream cheese in the bowl of a mixer and mix until soft.

2. Add the crab, garlic and green onion. Season with salt and pepper, Worcestershire sauce and a drop or two of sesame oil.

3. Place several wonton skins on a work surface. Brush the edges with water. Place 1 tablespoon (15 mL) of the cream cheese mixture in the centre of each skin. Fold the wonton skin in half to form a triangle; seal the edges.

4. Deep-fat fry the wontons using the swimming method, at 350°F (180°C) for 10 seconds. Remove the wontons, drain well and refrigerate.

5. At service, deep-fat fry the wontons at 350°F (180°C) until crisp, approximately 1 minute. Serve with Apricot Sauce.

Approximate values per piece:	
Calories	70
Total fat	3.5 g
Saturated fat	2 g
Cholesterol	20 mg
Sodium	120 mg
Total carbohydrates	5 g
Protein	3 g

APRICOT SAUCE

Yield: 8 oz. (250 g)

Apricot preserves	8 oz.	250 g
Fresh ginger, grated	1 Tbsp.	15 mL
Dry mustard	1 tsp.	5 mL
Red wine vinegar	1 Tbsp.	15 mL

Combine all ingredients and heat until the preserves melt and the flavours blend.

Other Hot Hors d'Oeuvres

Other types of hot hors d'oeuvres include layers of phyllo dough wrapped around various fillings; vegetables such as mushrooms that are stuffed and baked; tiny red potatoes filled with sour cream and caviar or Roquefort cheese and walnuts; tiny artichoke or clam fritters or any of the hundreds of varieties of chicken wings that are seasoned or marinated, baked, fried, broiled or grilled and served with a cool and soothing or outrageously spicy sauce.

The secret is to let your imagination be your guide, to keep the ingredients harmonious and, if the hors d'oeuvres are to precede dinner, not to allow them to duplicate the foods to be served or overpower them with excessively spicy flavours.

Serving Hors d'Oeuvres

Hors d'oeuvres are not only served as a precursor to dinner. At many events the only food served may be butlered hors d'oeuvres, an hors d'oeuvre buffet or a combination of the two. Whether the hors d'oeuvres are being served before dinner or as dinner, butler style or buffet style, they must always be attractively prepared and displayed.

All events have themes and varying degrees of formality. Long buffets with overflowing baskets of crudités and sweet potato chips with dips presented in hollowed squashes and cabbages may be appropriate for one event, while elegant silver trays of carefully prepared canapés passed among guests by white-gloved, tuxedoed service staff may be appropriate for another. When preparing and serving hors d'oeuvres, always keep the event's theme in mind and plan accordingly.

When choosing hors d'oeuvres, select an assortment that contrasts flavours, textures and styles. There are no limits to the variety of hors d'oeuvres that can be served, but three to four cold and three to four hot selections are sufficient for most occasions. The following is a small selection of hot and cold hors d'oeuvres that contrast flavours, textures and styles as well as types of food.

Cold:

✦ Canapés of smoked salmon on brioche
✦ Barquettes filled with Roquefort cheese and garnished with grapes
✦ Tiny tortilla cups filled with grilled chicken and spicy tomato salsa

Hot:

✦ Spanakopita (Recipe 33.14)
✦ Date and chorizo rumaki (Recipe 33.7)
✦ Rabbit and shiitake mushroom brochettes on rosemary sprigs (Recipe 33.5)

Generally, calculating three hors d'oeuvres per person per hour is sufficient when determining how many to prepare. If no other food will be available, four or five pieces may be appropriate. One must also consider whether they are a meal replacement, in which case larger quantities may be needed.

Butler Service

Butler service hors d'oeuvres or "passed" hors d'oeuvres are presented to guests on trays by the service staff. The hors d'oeuvres can be hot or cold and should be very small to make it easier for the guests to eat them without the aid of a knife or fork. Hot and cold hors d'oeuvres should be passed separately so that they can be kept at the correct temperatures. For a one-hour cocktail reception before a dinner, three to five hors d'oeuvres per person is usually sufficient.

Buffet Service

An hors d'oeuvre buffet should be beautiful and appetizing. It may consist of a single table to serve a small group of people or several huge multilevel displays designed to feed thousands. Colours, flavours and textures must all be taken into account when planning the menu.

Both hot and cold hors d'oeuvres may be served on buffets. Hot hors d'oeuvres are often kept hot by holding them in chafing dishes. Alternatively, hot hors d'oeuvres can be displayed on trays or platters; the trays and platters, however, must be replaced frequently to ensure that the food stays hot. Cold hors d'oeuvres can be displayed on trays, mirrors, platters, baskets, leaves, papers or other serving pieces to create the desired look.

Arranging Buffet Platters

When displaying hors d'oeuvres and other foods on mirrors, trays or platters, the foods should be displayed in a pattern that is pleasing to the eye and flows towards the guest or from one side to the other. An easy and attractive method for accomplishing this is to arrange the items on a mirror or tray with an attractive centrepiece. The food can be placed in parallel diagonal lines, alternating the various styles and shapes. Be careful not to make the tray or mirror too fussy or cluttered, however; often the best approach is to keep it simple. The diagrams in Figure 33.1 may be used as guides for arranging canapés and other foods on trays.

APPETIZERS OR FIRST COURSES

Because eating habits have changed over the years, the types of foods chefs prepare have also changed. Today, only the most elaborate banquets include hors d'oeuvres, soup, salad, entrée and dessert and perhaps separate fish and

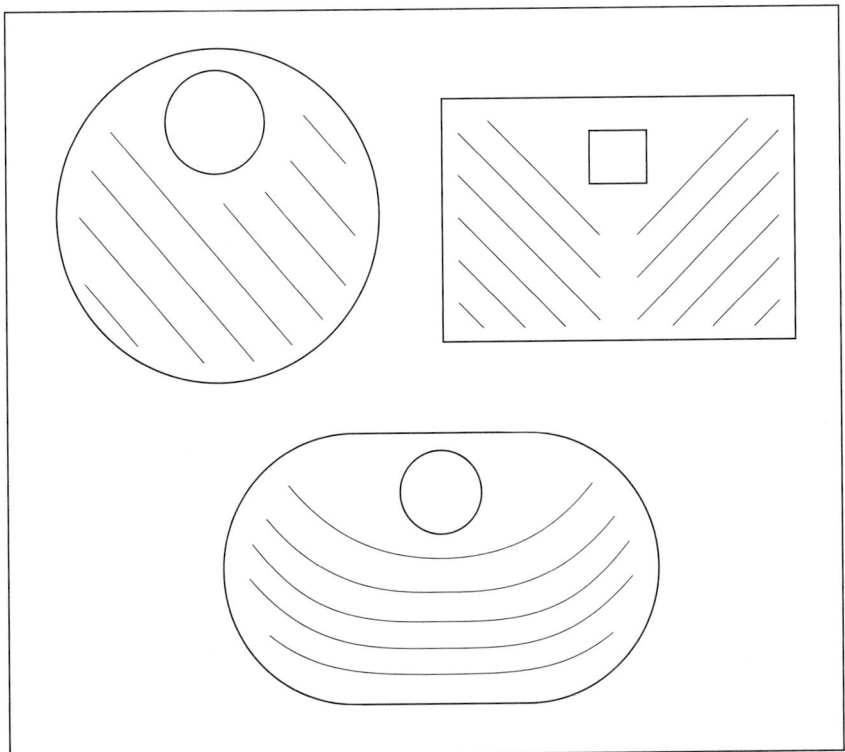

FIGURE 33.1 *Simple patterns that can be used to effectively display canapés and other foods on trays or mirrors.*

cheese courses. A more likely progression may be soup (which serves as the appetizer), salad, entrée and dessert, or a salad with a small portion of grilled meat or fish that doubles as both appetizer and salad, followed by an entrée and dessert. Because of these changes the term **first course** may be more fitting than appetizer.

Generally, appetizers and first courses are small portions of foods intended to whet the appetite in anticipation of more substantial courses to follow. Unlike foods prepared as entrees, appetizers rarely contain the traditional combination of meat or other main item, vegetable and starch. More often, appetizers consist only of the main item accompanied by a sauce and/or garnish. Appetizers do not need to contain any meat, poultry, fish or shellfish, however. Soups, salads, charcuterie items, vegetables, pizzas, pastas and other starch dishes may be served as appetizers. Because they are very rich, some foods such as foie gras and escargots are traditionally served as appetizers. These foods are generally consumed in small amounts and are rarely served as entrées.

Although there are few limitations on what can be served as an appetizer or first course, a few guidelines should be followed to ensure that whatever is served will be well received.

BASIC GUIDELINES FOR PREPARING APPETIZERS

1. The first course should be small. Remember, there are other, more substantial courses to follow. As the name implies, an appetizer should stimulate the appetite rather than satisfy it. Remember that rich cream-based sauces tend to satisfy appetites quickly, even when the portions are small. Two to 3 ounces (60–90 g) of pasta and 2 ounces (60 g) of sauce is an ample appetizer portion. Many recipes, such as Ahi Tuna Seared with Lavender and Pepper with Whole Grain Mustard Sauce (Recipe 24.27) and Chinese Barbecued Spareribs (Recipe 16.3), can be prepared as an appetizer by simply serving smaller portions.

2. Avoid very spicy foods that may deaden the palate and detract from any more delicate flavours that follow.

3. The first course should harmonize with the rest of the meal with respect to the types of foods as well as the style. For example, an appetizer of a roasted Anaheim chile stuffed with grilled corn and goat cheese followed by an entrée of paupiettes of sole vin blanc would be a poor combination: The strong spices and flavours of the chile would overpower the delicate flavours of the sole; the chile has strong southwestern ties, the sole is a classic French dish.

4. Avoid duplication of foods within the meal. If fish or shellfish is served as the first course, do not serve fish or shellfish as the main course.

5. For more variety, use several methods of preparation within the meal. If the entrée will be grilled or roasted, serve a first course that is poached or sautéed.

6. A first course should always be attractively presented. Remember that often it is the first food the customer sees. It should set the standard for the rest of the meal.

SANDWICHES

A sandwich is often the first meal a person learns to prepare. Even those who claim to be unable to cook often make delicious hot and cold sandwiches without considering it cooking. Mastering a grilled cheese sandwich or assembling the quintessential BLT may not require a degree in culinary arts, but it does require the ability to select and use ingredients wisely.

Sandwiches offer food service operations economical opportunities for using leftovers and offer customers, especially those with smaller budgets or appetites, meals to eat out of hand. Thus, the ability to correctly prepare hot and cold sandwiches to order is a fundamental skill in many food service operations.

Ingredients for Sandwiches

Sandwiches are constructed from bread, a spread and one or more fillings. These components should be selected and combined carefully so that the finished sandwich is flavourful and visually appealing.

Bread

Bread provides more than a convenient means for handling a sandwich. It holds or contains the spread and fillings and gives the sandwich its shape. Bread also adds flavour, texture, nutrition and colour, and often determines the overall look of the finished product.

Health consciousness and consumer willingness to try new and unusual foods give today's cooks the freedom to create sandwiches without relying on two slices of white bread. Virtually any bread can be used in sandwich-making: rolls, biscuits, bagels, croissants, fruit and nut breads, whole grain breads and savoury breads, as well as flatbreads such as naan, lavosh and tortillas, pocket breads such as pitas and flavourful breads such as focaccia and Swedish limpa.

Whatever bread is used and whether its flavour is mild or intense, the bread should complement the fillings and not overpower them. The bread should be fresh (although day-old bread is easier to slice and is excellent toasted) and its texture should be able to withstand moisture from the spread and fillings without becoming soggy or pasty. An overly hard or crusty bread, however, may make the sandwich difficult to eat.

Spread

A spread is used to add flavour, moisture and richness to the sandwich and, sometimes, it helps hold or bind it together. Some spreads, especially plain or flavoured butters, also act as a barrier to prevent the moisture in the filling from soaking into the bread.

There are three principal spreads:

Butter—One of the most common spreads, plain butter adds flavour and richness; it is also an excellent moisture barrier. Flavoured or compound butters, discussed in Chapter 10, Stocks and Sauces, make excellent sandwich spreads, adding flavour dimensions to the finished product. For example, try caper butter on a Cajun-style blackened beef sandwich or a red chile honey butter on a smoked turkey sandwich. Any butter spread should be softened or whipped so that it will spread easily without tearing the bread.

Mayonnaise—Perhaps the most popular sandwich spread, mayonnaise adds moisture, richness and flavour and complements most meat, poultry, fish, shellfish, vegetable, egg and cheese fillings. Like butter, mayonnaise can be made more exciting by adding flavouring ingredients. Condiments (for example, coarse-grained mustard or grated horseradish), herbs, spices and spice blends (for example, curry or chile powder) and other ingredients such as sun-dried tomatoes and pesto sauce can be stirred into fresh or commercially prepared mayonnaise. Fresh mayonnaise can also be prepared with flavoured oils, such as olive oil, walnut oil or chile oil. See Chapter 24, Salads and Salad Dressings, for recipes and additional information on mayonnaise.

Vegetable purées—Puréed vegetables are often used as sandwich spreads; after all, lunch boxes everywhere would be incomplete without a purée of roasted peanuts (more commonly known as peanut butter) and fruit jelly. More sophisticated examples include finely chopped black olives flavoured with fresh thyme, oregano and a few drops of olive oil for a sandwich of Italian meats and cheeses, or a well-seasoned chickpea purée with lemon and tahini paste for a vegetarian sandwich. Unlike butter, vegetable purées usually will not provide a moisture barrier between the bread and the fillings.

Filling

The filling is the body of the sandwich, providing most of its flavour. A sandwich often contains more than one filling. For example, the filling in a Reuben sandwich is corned beef, Swiss cheese and sauerkraut and in a BLT it is bacon, lettuce and tomato. Most fillings for cold sandwiches must be precooked and properly chilled, although some hot sandwich fillings may be cooked to order.

When choosing fillings, be sure that the flavours complement each other. Their textures may be similar or contrasting. If an ingredient, such as lettuce, is supposed to be crisp, it should be very crisp, not limp. If an ingredient is supposed to be tender and moist, make sure it is so. Improperly prepared, poor quality or mishandled filling ingredients can ruin an otherwise wonderful sandwich.

Popular fillings include:

Beef—Although the classic hot beef sandwich is the hamburger, other hot or cold beef products are commonly used. For example, hot or cold small steaks, slices of larger cuts such as the tenderloin, thin slices of roast beef, and so on, make excellent fillings. Also popular are hot or cold slices of cured beef products, including corned beef, pastrami and tongue as well as beef sausages such as salami, bologna and hot dogs.

Pork—Various ham and bacon products, served either hot or cold, are extremely popular. In addition, pork loin and tenderloin are light, white meats that adapt well to various flavour combinations and cooking methods. Barbecued pork, pork sausages and pork hot dogs are also popular.

Poultry—Sliced turkey breast, either roasted or smoked, and processed turkey are often used in hot or cold sandwiches. Moreover, food substitutes such as turkey bologna, turkey pastrami, turkey hot dogs and turkey ham are becoming increasingly popular because they generally have a lower fat content than the beef or pork original. Boneless chicken breast, either sliced or whole, is also quite popular as it can be prepared by a variety of methods; it complements a broad range of flavours and it has a relatively low fat content.

Fish and shellfish—Although fried fish fillets are an old standard, grilled fish sandwiches are gaining in popularity. Canned fish products, particularly tuna and salmon, are also widely used. Often fish and shellfish, especially tuna, shrimp and crab, are used for mayonnaise-based bound salads. Sardines and anchovies are less popular than other fish, but are sometimes mixed into bound salads or arranged on open-faced sandwiches.

Vegetables—Vegetables add texture, moisture, flavour and nutrition to most any sandwich. Fresh vegetables such as lettuce, onions and tomatoes are commonly used in combination with meat, cheese and other fillings. Vegetables, however, can stand on their own as sandwich fillings. Marinated, grilled vegetables can be used in hot or cold sandwiches and a combination of sliced, fresh vegetables and a flavourful dressing wrapped in soft lavosh or a tortilla becomes a portable salad.

Eggs—Hard-cooked eggs are most often used as an ingredient in a mayonnaise-based salad, where they are chopped and combined with pickle relish and seasonings. Hard-cooked eggs can also be sliced thin and used as an attractive garnish on open-faced sandwiches. Fried or scrambled eggs can be layered between pieces of bread or rolled in a tortilla for a breakfast sandwich.

Cheese—Cheese is available in such a variety of textures, flavours, colours and styles that it is a welcome addition to nearly any sandwich. Sliced cheese can be used as a filling in hot or cold sandwiches and melted cheese or a cheese sauce makes an excellent topping for hot open-faced sandwiches. Flavoured cream cheese is also used as a spread or filling, particularly with bagels and fruit or nut breads.

Bound Salads—Protein salads bound with mayonnaise or salad dressing are popular sandwich fillings. Examples include chicken, tuna, egg and ham salads. Bound salads are discussed in Chapter 24, Salads and Salad Dressings.

Types of Sandwiches

Sandwiches can be hot or cold, closed or open-faced, depending on the way in which the ingredients are assembled and presented.

Hot Sandwiches

Hot closed sandwiches include those in which the filling ingredients are served hot, such as a hamburger or hot dog, and those where the entire sandwich is heated for service, such as a grilled cheese or Monte Cristo. Hot closed sandwiches can be categorized as basic, grilled or deep-fat fried.

Basic hot closed sandwiches are generally those in which the principal filling is served hot between two pieces of bread. These sandwiches may also include fillings that are not hot, such as tomato slices and lettuce leaves. Variations of the basic hot closed sandwich include tacos, quesadillas, burros (or burritos) and wraps, in which the hot and/or cold fillings are folded or wrapped in a tortilla or other supple flatbread.

BASIC PROCEDURE FOR PREPARING WRAP SANDWICHES

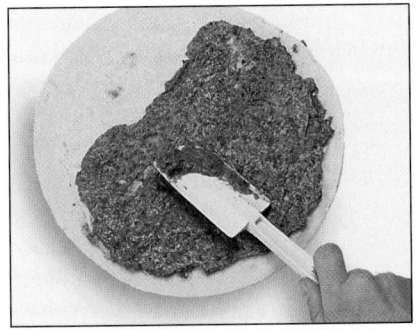

1. Top the tortilla with a spread or dressing.

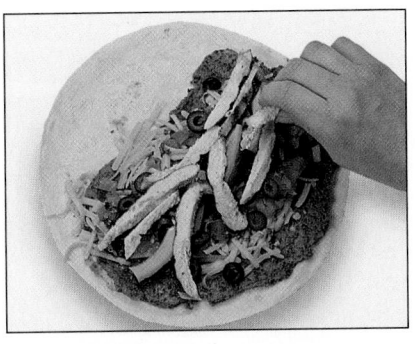

2. Place vegetables and meat, fish or poultry items in a mound across the tortilla.

3. Roll the tortilla tightly around the filling.

Grilled sandwiches are those in which the filling is placed between two pieces of bread, which are buttered on the outside and then browned on a griddle or in a sauté pan. The filling will be warmed during this procedure but will not cook. Therefore, filings such as bacon or sliced meat should be fully cooked before the sandwich is assembled and grilled.

Deep-fat fried sandwiches are made by dipping a closed sandwich in egg batter or bread crumbs and then deep-fat frying it. The most common example is the Monte Cristo: white bread filled with sliced ham, Swiss cheese and Dijon mustard.

The hot open-faced turkey or steak sandwich proved long ago that sandwiches do not need to be eaten out of hand. In the typical **hot open-faced sandwich**, bread (grilled, toasted or fresh) is placed on a serving plate, covered with hot meat or other filling and topped with an appropriate gravy, sauce or cheese. The completed dish is often browned under a broiler before service. Condiments and garnishes are usually served on the side.

Perhaps the ultimate hot open-faced sandwich is the pizza. Bread dough is topped with sauce, cheese, meat and vegetables, then baked. Small personal-sized pizzas are a popular menu item even in upscale restaurants.

Grilled Cheese Sandwiches

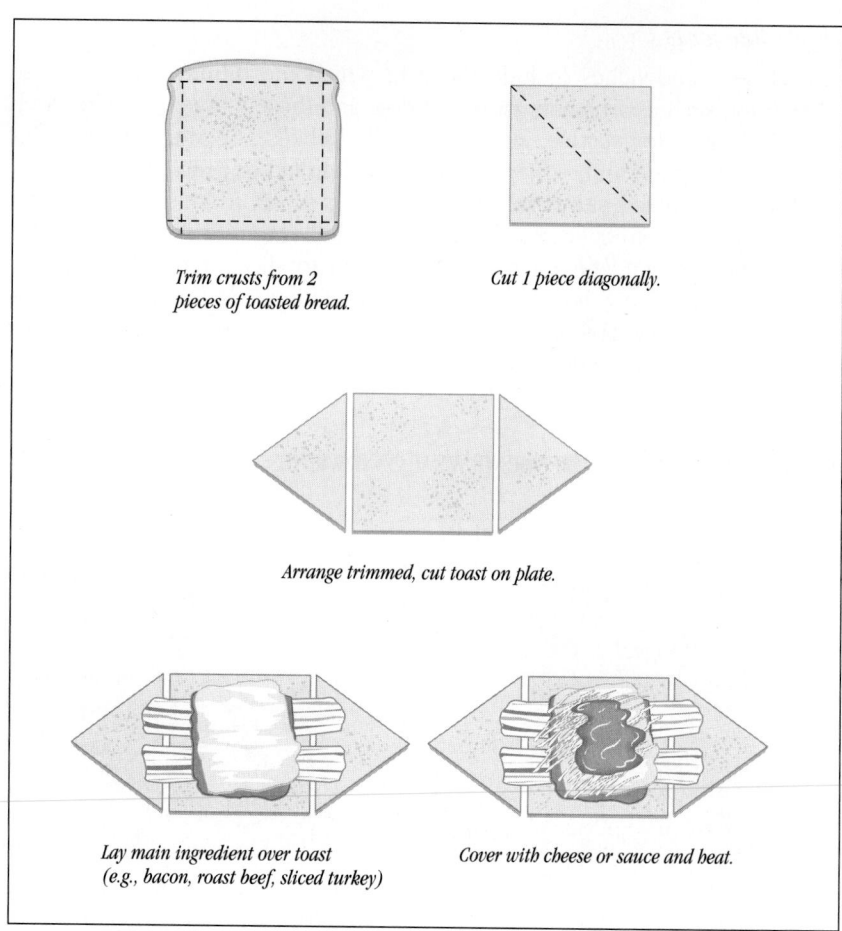

Trim crusts from 2
pieces of toasted bread.

Cut 1 piece diagonally.

Arrange trimmed, cut toast on plate.

Lay main ingredient over toast
(e.g., bacon, roast beef, sliced turkey)

Cover with cheese or sauce and heat.

FIGURE 33.2   *The arrangement of a hot open-faced sandwich.*

Cold Sandwiches

Cold sandwiches are simply sandwiches that are eaten cold. They are made with raw ingredients that are not intended to be cooked, such as vegetables and cheese, or with meat, poultry, fish or shellfish that is precooked then chilled before use as a filling. As with hot sandwiches, cold sandwiches may be closed or open-faced.

Cold closed sandwiches are those that contain two or more pieces of bread with one or more fillings and one or more spreads. Cold closed sandwiches are usually eaten with the hands and come in three styles: basic, multi-decker and tea.

Basic cold sandwiches are made with two pieces of bread or one split roll, one spread and one or more fillings. A tuna salad sandwich or an Italian-style submarine are both examples of basic cold closed sandwiches. A variation of the basic cold sandwich is a wrap with cold fillings, for example, a herb-flavoured tortilla spread with peanut sauce and wrapped around spinach leaves, diced grilled chicken and cold cooked rice.

Multi-decker cold sandwiches are made with three or more pieces of bread, one or more spreads and two or more fillings. The club sandwich, in which sliced turkey, bacon, lettuce and tomato are layered with three slices of toasted bread, is a classic example of a multi-decker sandwich, although it is actually served warm.

BASIC PROCEDURE FOR PREPARING COLD MULTI-DECKER SANDWICHES

1. Spread butter or mayonnaise on the first slice of toasted bread and top with meat and vegetables.

2. Add the second slice of bread and spread with mayonnaise.

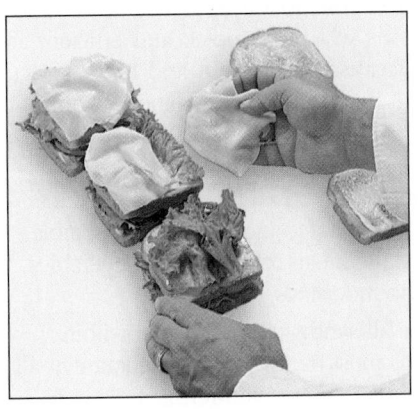

3. Add a second layer of vegetables and meat.

4. Cut the finished sandwich into quarters for service.

Tea sandwiches are small, fancy constructions made with light, soft, trimmed breads and delicate fillings and spreads. They are usually cut or rolled into shapes such as diamonds, circles or pinwheels and served as a finger food at parties and receptions.

Cold open-faced sandwiches are simply larger versions of canapés, discussed earlier in this chapter. The most popular style is the open-faced Norwegian sandwich known as smørbrød. As with canapés, much emphasis is placed on visual appeal. A single slice of bread is coated with a spread, a small lettuce leaf may be used, then covered with thin slices of meat, poultry or fish, or a portion of a bound salad. Carefully cut and arranged garnishes such as hard-cooked eggs, fresh herbs, pickles, onions and radishes are used to complete the presentation. A simpler version of an open-faced cold sandwich is a delicatessen classic—a bagel with lox and cream cheese.

FIGURE 33.3   *Cold open-faced sandwiches.*

Preparing Sandwiches

Sandwiches are generally prepared to order and their preparation usually requires a great deal of handwork. Therefore, the goal is to assemble all ingredients and equipment so that your motions will be as quick and efficient as possible at the time of final assembly. Because each menu and food service operation has its own requirements, there is no one correct station setup, but there are a few basic guidelines.

1. *Prepare ingredients.* All sandwich ingredients should be cooked, mixed, sliced and prepared ahead of service to facilitate quick, efficient assembly at service time. So, before service, slice the meats, cheeses and vegetables, blend the flavoured spreads, mix the bound salads, and so on.

2. *Arrange and store ingredients.* Arrange all sandwich ingredients within easy reach of the work area. Cold items must be properly refrigerated at all times. A sandwich bar, similar to a steam table but with refrigerated compartments, is frequently used for this purpose. Under-counter refrigeration can be used for backup supplies and less frequently used ingredients. Sliced meats, cheeses and vegetables must be well covered to prevent dehydration or contamination. Many ingredients can be preportioned, either by weight or count, then wrapped in individual portions for storage.

♦♦♦
SANDWICH SANITATION

Sandwiches, whether hot or cold, present a particularly dangerous environment for the spread of food-borne illnesses. The use of pre-cooked, high protein foods, the combination of hot and cold ingredients and the presence of uncooked eggs in spreads such as mayonnaise offer bacteria attractive homes. Cross-contamination can be an especially common problem because of the repeated use of spatulas, spreaders, scales, knives, cutting boards and, deadliest of all, human hands. Take extra care to wash hands frequently and to clean work surfaces and tools with a sanitizer often during service. Latex gloves provide false security. They often cause more problems than they solve. The cardinal rule for proper food handling applies as well: *Keep hot foods hot, keep cold foods cold.* Please review Chapter 2, Food Safety and Sanitation for further information.

FIGURE 33.4   *A typical sandwich bar.*

3. *Select and arrange equipment.* The heavy equipment needed for making sandwiches can include preparation equipment such as meat slicers, griddles, grills, fryers and broilers as well as storage equipment such as refrigerated sandwich bars for cold ingredients and steam tables for hot ingredients. Even the simplest sandwich menu requires the use of basic hand tools such as spatulas, spreaders, portion scoops, knives and cutting boards. Be sure that the supply of such items is adequate to permit quick handwork and to avoid delays at service time.

Presenting and Garnishing Sandwiches

Sandwiches, especially cold closed sandwiches, are usually cut into halves, thirds or quarters for service. See Figure 33.5 for examples. Cutting makes a sandwich easier for the customer to handle and allows for a more attractive presentation: the sandwich wedges can be arranged to add height to the plate and to expose the fillings' colours and textures. Hot closed sandwiches such as hamburgers are often presented open-faced. Condiments, such as mustard and mayonnaise, and garnishes, such as sliced tomatoes, onions, relish and lettuce leaves, are served on the side or on one of the open bun halves. This tends to be a more attractive presentation and it allows the customer to assemble and add ingredients to the sandwich as desired.

Although a sandwich can be a meal unto itself, it may be served with a salad or starch accompaniment. Potato chips or french-fried potatoes are, of

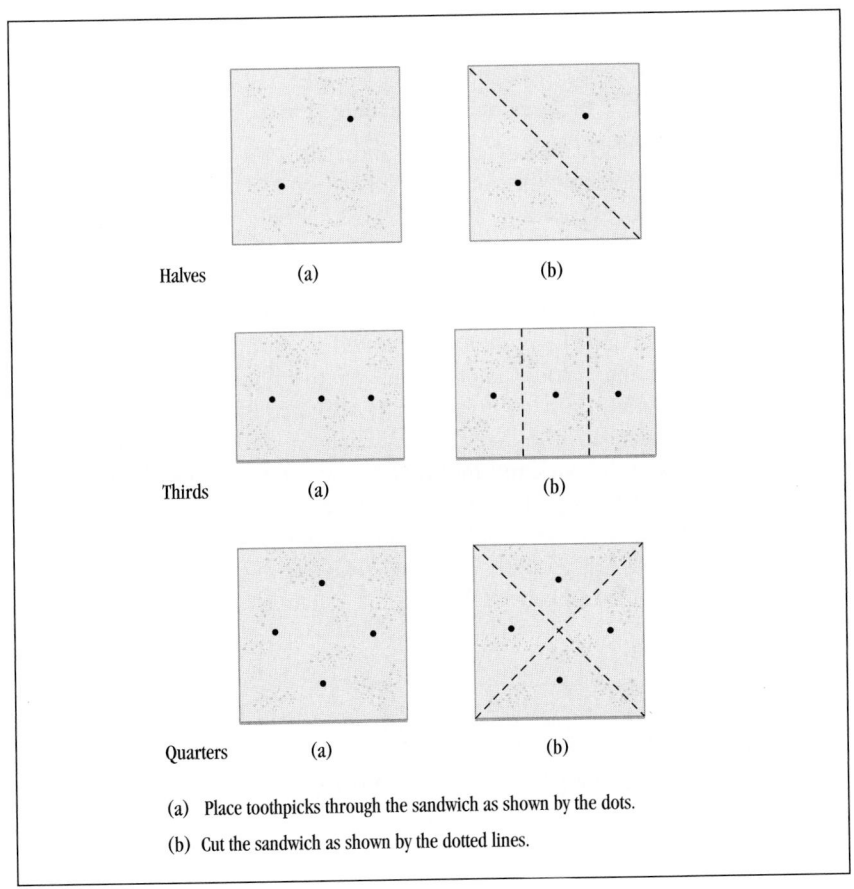

Halves   (a)   (b)

Thirds   (a)   (b)

Quarters   (a)   (b)

(a) Place toothpicks through the sandwich as shown by the dots.

(b) Cut the sandwich as shown by the dotted lines.

FIGURE 33.5   *Cutting sandwiches.*

TABLE 33.2 NUTRITIONAL VALUES FOR SELECTED FAST-FOOD SANDWICHES

	Kcal	Protein (g)	Carbohydrates (g)	Total Fat (g)	Cholesterol (mg)	Sodium (mg)
McDonald's Big Mac	560	25.2	42.5	32.4	103	950
McDonald's Egg McMuffin	290	18.2	28.1	11.2	226	740
McDonald's Filet-O-Fish	440	13.8	37.9	26.1	50	1030
Burger King Whopper	614	27.0	45.0	36.0	90	865
Wendy's Grilled Chicken	340	24.0	37.0	13.0	60	815

The Corrine T. Netzer Encyclopedia of Food Values, 1992

course, standard fare, perhaps because they also are finger foods and they provide a crunchy texture. Bound salads, such as potato and macaroni, are also common starch accompaniments. Plated sandwiches have long been served with cole slaw, fruit salad or a small mixed green salad as side dishes. Even the standard soup-and-sandwich combo—half of a sandwich with a cup of soup—remains a popular lunch selection.

CONCLUSION

The preparation of hors d'oeuvres and sandwiches provides an opportunity for the cook to demonstrate his or her creativity, knowledge of food and skills in presentation and garnishing. Because hors d'oeuvres and canapés often serve as the guests' introduction to the foods you serve, it is especially important that these foods be properly prepared and of the highest quality.

Quality is equally important for sandwiches, which should be made from fresh, carefully prepared ingredients, presented in an appetizing and appealing manner. Flavours, colours and textures of the bread, spread and filling should be appropriate and complementary. Breads should be fresh, never stale, and appropriate for the finished sandwich. Spreads should be carefully chosen to add extra flavours and moisture to the sandwich but should not be used to cover or mask dry or poor-quality fillings or breads. Fillings provide the dominant flavour and are usually the source of the sandwich's name; they should be flavourful and properly prepared. The appearance of even the most basic sandwich can be improved by careful assembly and precise trimming and cutting.

QUESTIONS FOR DISCUSSION

1. Discuss four guidelines that should be followed when preparing hors d'oeuvres.
2. Identify and describe the three parts of a canapé.

3. Describe the differences between beluga, osetra and sevruga caviars and explain how these foods differ from domestic caviars.

4. Create an hors d'oeuvre menu for a small cocktail party. Include three hot and three cold items and explain the reasons for your selections.

5. List and explain five guidelines that should be followed when preparing appetizers or first courses.

6. List examples for each of the three primary sandwich components.

7. Explain the differences between a hot open-faced and a hot closed sandwich.

8. List several hand tools used in sandwich production and explain the need for an ample supply of these tools.

9. Why is cross-contamination a concern when preparing sandwiches? What simple steps can be taken to avoid the spread of pathogenic microorganisms?

ADDITIONAL APPETIZER AND SANDWICH RECIPES

RECIPE 33.9

STUFFED SQUASH BLOSSOMS AND BUCKWHEAT BLINI WITH SMOKED SALMON AND CAVIAR

Yield: 24 Servings

Chevre cheese	8 oz.	250 g
Cream cheese	4 oz.	120 g
Assorted fresh herbs, chopped	2 tsp.	10 mL
Garlic cloves, minced	2	2
Black pepper	TT	TT
Baby squash with blossoms	24	24
Tempura Batter (Recipe 21.4)	24 oz.	700 g
Olive oil	1 Tbsp.	15 mL
Bell peppers, red, yellow and green, julienne	12 oz.	360 g
Salt	TT	TT
Buckwheat Blinis (recipe follows)	24	24
Blackberry preserves	3 oz.	90 g
Smoked salmon, sliced	1 lb.	500 g
Caviar	2 oz.	60 g
Fresh basil sprigs	24	24

1. Blend the chevre cheese and cream cheese in the bowl of an electric mixer until smooth. Fold in the herbs and garlic and season with black pepper.

2. Using a pastry bag fitted with a round tip, fill each of the squash blossoms with the cheese mixture and pinch the flowers shut.

3. Dip each of the squash in tempura batter and deep-fat fry until lightly browned, approximately 1 minute. Remove and drain well.

4. Sauté the peppers in olive oil until tender. Season with salt and pepper.

5. Carefully split each squash and blossom in half. Arrange 2 squash halves on each plate and garnish with the julienne peppers.

Continued

Approximate values per serving:

Calories	190
Total fat	7 g
Saturated fat	4 g
Cholesterol	49 mg
Sodium	416 mg
Total carbohydrates	22 g
Protein	10 g

6. Spread each of the blini with blackberry preserves. Form rosettes out of the salmon slices and place one on each blini.

7. Place the blini on the plate with the squash and peppers and garnish with 2 dollops of caviar and a sprig of basil.

BUCKWHEAT BLINI

Yield: 24 Blini

Granulated sugar	2 tsp.	10 mL
Dry yeast	1/4 oz.	7 g
Milk, lukewarm	14 oz.	420 mL
Buckwheat flour	4 oz.	120 g
All-purpose flour	3 oz.	90 g
Salt	1/2 tsp.	2 mL
Unsalted butter, melted	3 Tbsp.	45 mL
Vegetable oil	2 Tbsp.	30 mL
Egg yolks	3	3
Egg whites	2	2

Approximate values per pancake:

Calories	43
Total fat	1 g
Saturated fat	.4 g
Cholesterol	2 mg
Sodium	90 mg
Total carbohydrates	8 g
Protein	2 g

1. Stir the sugar and yeast into the warmed milk and let stand until foamy, approximately 5 minutes.

2. Whisk in the flours, salt, butter, oil and egg yolks. Beat until smooth.

3. Cover the batter and allow it to rise in a warm place until doubled, approximately 1 hour.

4. Beat the egg whites to stiff peaks, then fold them into the risen batter.

5. Lightly oil and pre-heat a large sauté pan. Drop 2 tablespoons (30 mL) of batter into the sauté pan, spacing the blini at least 1 inch (2.5 cm) apart. Cook until the bottom of each blini is golden, approximately 1 minute. Turn the blini and cook an additional 30 seconds. Remove from the pan and keep warm for service.

◆◆◆

RECIPE 33.10

HUMMUS

Yield: 1 qt. (1 L)

Chickpeas, cooked	1 lb.	500 g
Tahini paste	8 oz.	250 g
Garlic, chopped	2 tsp.	10 mL
Cumin	1/2 tsp.	2 mL
Lemon juice	4 oz.	120 mL
Salt	1 tsp.	5 mL
Cayenne pepper	TT	TT
Olive oil	2 oz.	60 mL
Fresh parsley, chopped	2 tsp.	10 mL

Approximate values per 2 oz. (60 g) serving:

Calories	210
Total fat	16 g
Saturated fat	1 g
Cholesterol	0 mg
Sodium	250 mg
Total carbohydrates	10 g
Protein	7 g
Iron	8%

1. Combine the chickpeas, tahini, garlic, cumin and lemon juice in a food processor; process until smooth. Season with salt and cayenne.

2. Spoon the hummus onto a serving platter and smooth the surface. Drizzle the olive oil over the hummus and garnish with the chopped parsley. Serve with warm pita bread that has been cut into quarters.

◆◆◆

RECIPE 33.11

GUACAMOLE

Yield: 1 qt. (1 L)

Avocados	6	6
Lemon juice	2-1/2 oz.	75 mL
Green onion, sliced	4 Tbsp.	60 mL
Cilantro, chopped	3 Tbsp.	45 mL
Tomatoes, seeded, diced	3 Tbsp.	45 mL
Garlic, chopped	1 tsp.	5 mL
Dried oregano	1/2 tsp.	2 mL
Jalapeños, seeded, chopped	1	1
Salt	TT	TT

1. Cut each avocado in half. Remove the seed and scoop out the pulp.

2. Add the lemon juice to the avocado pulp and mix well, mashing the avocado pulp.

3. Add the remaining ingredients. Season with salt and mix well.

Approximate values per
2 oz. (60 mL) serving:

Calories	120
Total fat	12 g
Saturated fat	0 g
Cholesterol	0 mg
Sodium	25 mg
Total carbohydrates	1 g
Protein	2 g
Vitamin C	15%

Claims—no saturated fat; no cholesterol; no sugar; high fibre

◆◆◆

RECIPE 33.12

SUN-DRIED TOMATO
AND BASIL AIOLI

Yield: 1 qt. (1 L)

Garlic cloves, mashed to a paste	4	4
Egg yolks	4	4
Lemon juice	2 Tbsp.	30 mL
Olive oil	1-1/2 pt.	650 mL
Sun-dried tomatoes, packed in olive oil	4 oz.	120 g
Fresh basil, chopped	4 Tbsp.	60 mL
Salt	1 tsp.	5 mL
Pepper	1/2 tsp.	2 mL

1. Combine the garlic, egg yolks and a few drops of the lemon juice in a bowl and whip until frothy.

2. While whipping the egg yolk mixture, slowly add the olive oil until an emulsion begins to form. Continue adding the oil while whipping until all of the oil is incorporated. A few drops of lemon juice may be added from time to time to thin the sauce.

3. Finely chop the sun-dried tomatoes. Add them, a portion of the olive oil in which they were packed, and the basil to the aïoli.

4. Season with salt, pepper and lemon juice.

Approximate values per
1 oz. (30 mL) serving:

Calories	194
Total fat	21 g
Saturated fat	3 g
Cholesterol	28 mg
Sodium	157 mg
Total carbohydrates	3 g
Protein	1 g

RECIPE 33.13

LAMB SATAY WITH PEANUT SAUCE

Yield: 16 Skewers

Lamb leg meat, boned, trimmed	2 lb.	1 kg
Vegetable oil	2 oz.	60 mL
Lemon grass, chopped	2 Tbsp.	30 mL
Garlic, chopped	1 Tbsp.	15 mL
Red pepper flakes, crushed	1 tsp.	5 mL
Curry powder	1 Tbsp.	15 mL
Honey	1 Tbsp.	15 mL
Fish sauce	1 Tbsp.	15 mL
Peanut Sauce (recipe follows)	as needed	as needed

Approximate values per skewer and 1/2 oz. (15 mL) sauce:

Calories	144
Total fat	7 g
Saturated fat	2 g
Cholesterol	56 mg
Sodium	58 mg
Total carbohydrates	1 g
Protein	18 g

1. Cut the lamb into 2-ounce (60-g) strips approximately 4 inches (10 cm) long. Lightly pound the strips with a mallet. Thread the strips onto 6-inch (15-cm) bamboo skewers that have been soaked in water.
2. To make the marinade, combine the remaining ingredients in the bowl of a food processor and purée until smooth.
3. Brush the meat with the marinade and allow to marinate for 1 hour.
4. Grill the skewers until done, approximately 2 minutes. Serve with Peanut Sauce.

PEANUT SAUCE

Yield: 28 oz. (800 mL)

Garlic, chopped	1 tsp.	5 mL
Onion, small dice	6 oz.	180 g
Red pepper flakes, crushed	1 tsp.	5 mL
Kaffir lime leaves (optional)	4	4
Curry powder	2 tsp.	10 mL
Lemon grass, minced	1 oz.	30 mL
Vegetable oil	1 oz.	30 mL
Coconut milk	8 oz.	250 mL
Cinnamon sticks	2	2
Bay leaves	4	4
Lime juice	1 oz.	30 mL
Rice wine vinegar	4 oz.	120 mL
Chicken stock	10 oz.	300 mL
Peanut butter	10 oz.	300 g

Approximate values per 1 oz. (30 g) serving:

Calories	100
Total fat	8 g
Saturated fat	3 g
Cholesterol	0 mg
Sodium	115 mg
Total carbohydrates	5 g
Protein	3 g

1. Sauté the garlic, onion, red pepper flakes, lime leaves, curry powder and lemon grass in the vegetable oil for 5 minutes.
2. Add the remaining ingredients and simmer for 30 minutes. Stir often, as the sauce can easily burn.
3. Remove bay and lime leaves and cinnamon sticks. Serve warm.

VARIATIONS: Beef or chicken satay can be made by substituting well-trimmed beef or boneless, skinless chicken meat for the lamb.

❖❖❖

RECIPE 33.14

SPANAKOPITA

Yield: 90 Triangles

Onion, small dice	4 oz.	120 g
Unsalted butter, melted	6 oz.	180 g
Fresh spinach, cooked and cooled, or frozen spinach, thawed	24 oz.	700 g
Fresh mint, chopped	1 Tbsp.	15 mL
Feta cheese, crumbled	1 lb.	450 g
Eggs, beaten	3	3
Salt and pepper	TT	TT
Phyllo dough	1 lb.	450 g

1. Sauté the onions in 1 tablespoon (15 mL) of butter until tender. Remove and cool.

2. Squeeze the water from the spinach. Combine the cooled onions, spinach, mint, feta cheese and beaten eggs. Season with salt and pepper and mix well.

3. Spread 1 sheet of phyllo dough on the work surface; brush with melted butter. Place another sheet of phyllo on top of the first; brush it with butter. Place a third sheet of phyllo on top of the second and brush it with butter as well.

4. Cut the dough into 2-inch-wide (5 cm) strips.

5. Place 1 tablespoon (15 mL) of the spinach on the end of each strip of phyllo.

6. Starting at the end with the spinach, fold one corner of the dough over the spinach to the opposite side of the strip to form a triangle. Continue folding the dough, keeping it in a triangular shape, like point-folding a flag (see photograph below).

7. Place the phyllo triangles on a sheet pan and brush with melted butter. Bake at 375°F (190°C) until brown and crispy, approximately 20 minutes.

Approximate values per piece:	
Calories	45
Total fat	3 g
Saturated fat	2 g
Cholesterol	15 mg
Sodium	105 mg
Total carbohydrates	3 g
Protein	2 g
Vitamin A	8%
Claims—low fat; low cholesterol; no sugar	

1. Brush and stack the layers of phyllo pastry with butter.

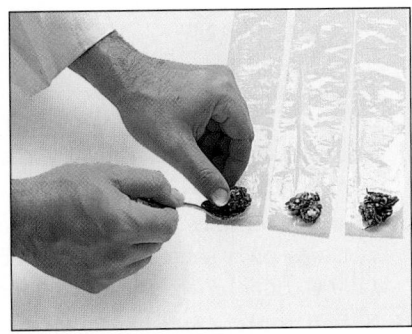

2. Place the filling on the pastry.

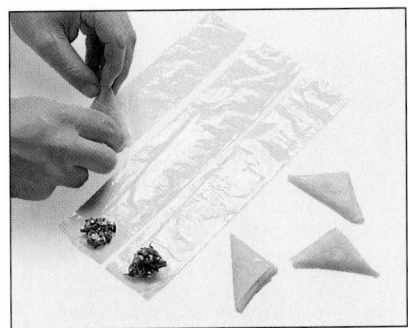

3. Fold the pastry and filling into triangles.

◆◆◆

RECIPE 33.15

KALAMATA OLIVE AND ASIAGO CHEESE CROSTINI

Yield: 12 Pieces

French baguette	1/2 loaf	1/2 loaf
Butter, melted	2 oz.	60 mL
Basil leaves, chopped	50	50
Tomato concassé	4 oz.	120 g
Garlic, chopped	2 tsp.	10 mL
Kalamata olives, pitted, chopped	15	15
Asiago cheese, grated	2 oz.	60 g

Approximate values per serving:

Calories	93
Total fat	8 g
Saturated fat	4 g
Cholesterol	15 mg
Sodium	181 mg
Total carbohydrates	4 g
Protein	2 g

1. Slice the bread 1/4-inch (6-mm) thick.
2. Brush bread slices with butter and bake until golden and crisp.
3. Combine the remaining ingredients and mix well.
4. Spread 1 tablespoon (20 g) of the mixture on each slice of bread. Place under the broiler or salamander until hot and the cheese is melted, approximately 2 minutes.

◆◆◆

RECIPE 33.16

RED POTATOES WITH WALNUTS AND GORGONZOLA CHEESE

Yield: 80 Pieces

New red potatoes	40	40
Salt and pepper	TT	TT
Fresh thyme	2 tsp.	10 mL
Olive oil	2 oz.	60 mL
Cream cheese	8 oz.	250 g
Gorgonzola cheese	3 oz.	90 g
Bacon, medium dice, cooked	1 oz.	30 g
Sour cream	4 oz.	120 mL
Walnuts, chopped coarse	1-1/2 oz.	45 g
Worcestershire sauce	TT	TT
Tabasco sauce	TT	TT
Chives, minced	3 Tbsp.	45 g

Approximate values per serving:

Calories	38
Total fat	3 g
Saturated fat	1 g
Cholesterol	5 mg
Sodium	61 mg
Total carbohydrates	2 g
Protein	1 g

1. Cut the new potatoes in half and scoop out a portion of the inside with a parisienne scoop.
2. Toss the potatoes with the salt, pepper, thyme and olive oil. Arrange the potatoes on a sheet pan with their flat surfaces down and bake at 400°F (200°C) until brown and cooked through, approximately 15 minutes.
3. Soften the cream cheese in the bowl of an electric mixer. Add the Gorgonzola cheese, bacon bits, sour cream and walnuts. Mix until smooth. Season with the Worcestershire and Tabasco sauces.
4. Using a pastry bag and plain tip, fill each hot potato half with the cold cheese mixture and sprinkle with chopped chives.

VARIATION: Fill the cooked potatoes with crème fraîche, top with caviar and sprinkle with chopped chives instead of using the bacon-and-cheese mixture.

RECIPE 33.17

Stuffed Mushroom Caps

Yield: 48 Pieces

White mushrooms, medium	60	60
Clarified butter	2 oz.	60 mL
Onion, minced	4 oz.	120 g
Flour	1 Tbsp.	15 mL
Cream, 35%	4 oz.	120 mL
Shrimp or crabmeat, chopped	4 oz.	120 g
Fresh parsley, chopped	2 Tbsp.	30 mL
Salt and pepper	TT	TT
Swiss cheese, shredded	2 oz.	60 g

1. Wash the mushrooms. Remove and chop the stems and 12 of the caps.

2. Sauté the whole mushroom caps in 1 ounce (30 mL) of clarified butter until partially cooked but still firm. Remove from the pan and reserve.

3. Add the remaining butter to the pan. Sauté the onion and chopped mushrooms until dry.

4. Add the flour and cook 1 minute. Add the cream; bring to a simmer and cook for 2 minutes.

5. Add the shellfish and parsley, season to taste with salt and pepper; stir to combine. Remove from the pan and cool slightly.

6. Stuff the mushroom caps with the shellfish mixture and sprinkle with shredded Swiss cheese.

7. Bake the mushrooms at 350°F (180°C) until hot, approximately 10–15 minutes.

Approximate values per piece:	
Calories	280
Total fat	11 g
Saturated fat	3 g
Cholesterol	185 mg
Sodium	200 mg
Total carbohydrates	22 g
Protein	21 g
Vitamin A	21%
Iron	35%

RECIPE 33.18

Poached Pear Appetizer

GALILEO RISTORANTE, Toronto, ON
Executive Chef Francisco Rivera

Yield: 4 Portions

Bosc pears, peeled and halved	4 whole	4 whole
Amaretto	1 oz.	15 mL
Brandy	1 oz.	15 mL
Cinnamon stick	1	1
Rosemary, fresh	1 pinch	1 pinch
Cashews, chopped	1-1/2 oz.	50 g
Sun-dried tomatoes, julienne	2 slices	2 slices
Pancetta (or smoked goose)	1-1/2 oz.	50 g
Olive oil	1 Tbsp.	15 mL
Butter	1 oz.	30 mL
Shiitake mushrooms, julienne	4 oz.	125 g
Plum, halved, sliced thin	1 whole	1 whole
Salt and pepper	TT	TT
Nutmeg, grated	TT	TT
Cereal cream	2 Tbsp.	30 mL
Veal stock	1/3 pt.	150 mL

Francisco Rivera

Francisco trained in Toronto and has worked there for most of his career, gravitating toward Italian cuisine. He is a member of the Canadian Federation of Chefs and Cooks and the Escoffier Society of Toronto.

Continued

1. Remove core and seeds from pear halves. Keep stems attached.
2. Simmer pear halves in enough water to cover along with amaretto, brandy, cinnamon, rosemary, 1 ounce (15 mL) cashews and 1 sun-dried tomato slice.
3. Remove pear halves when tender. Sauté pancetta in oil until browned. Remove excess oil and add butter. Add mushrooms, remaining sun-dried tomato slice, cashews and plum.
4. Season to taste with salt and pepper and nutmeg.
5. Add cream and veal stock. Simmer until slightly thickened.
6. Add drained pears.
7. To serve, fill pear halves with mushroom mixture.
8. Coat pears with remaining sauce. Serve warm.

Approximate values per serving:

Calories	181
Total fat	12 g
Saturated fat	4 g
Cholesterol	17 mg
Sodium	428 mg
Total carbohydrates	16 g
Protein	4 g

❖❖❖

RECIPE 33.19

GRILLED SHRIMP WITH PROSCIUTTO AND BASIL

Yield: 12 Pieces

Shrimp, 16–20 count, peeled and deveined, tails removed	12	12
Dry white wine	2 oz.	60 mL
Rice wine vinegar	1 oz.	30 mL
Thyme	2 tsp.	10 mL
Onion, minced	2 oz.	60 g
Cumin, ground	1 Tbsp.	15 mL
Salt and pepper	TT	TT
Vegetable oil	3 oz.	100 mL
Dried basil	2 tsp.	10 mL
Garlic cloves, chopped	2	2
Prosciutto slices	3	3
Fresh basil leaves	6	6

1. Combine all of the ingredients except the prosciutto and fresh basil in a stainless-steel bowl. Marinate for 30 minutes.
2. Remove the shrimps from the marinade and drain them well.
3. Cut each slice of prosciutto into quarters.
4. Wrap each shrimp first with 1/2 leaf of basil, then a piece of prosciutto; secure with a toothpick.
5. Grill for 1 to 1-1/2 minutes per side. Be careful not to overcook. Remove the toothpick and serve hot or cold.

Approximate values per piece:

Calories	220
Total fat	15 g
Saturated fat	2 g
Cholesterol	170 mg
Sodium	250 mg
Total carbohydrates	2 g
Protein	18 g
Iron	15%

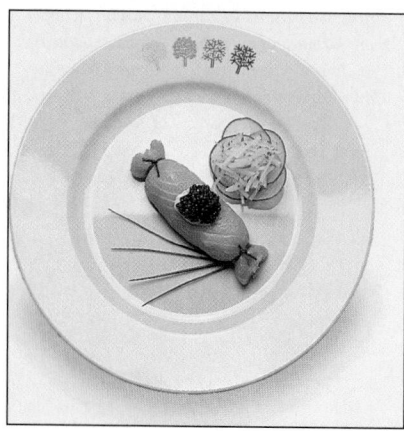

❖❖❖

RECIPE 33.20

SMOKED SALMON ROULADE

THE FOUR SEASONS, NEW YORK, NY
Chef Christian Albin

Yield: 4 Servings

Smoked salmon, sliced	10 oz.	300 g
Wasabi powder	1 tsp.	5 mL
Celery root (or celery), small dice	8 oz.	250 g
Sour cream	3 oz.	90 mL
Chives, blanched and refreshed	1 bunch	1 bunch
Black caviar	4 oz.	120 g

Radish, cut into strips
        (placed in ice water to crisp)   4   4
Cucumber, cut in rounds
        (placed in ice water to crisp)   1/2   1/2

1. Form the slices of smoked salmon into 4 rectangles. Reserve any salmon trimmings for the stuffing.
2. To make the stuffing, dilute the wasabi powder with 2 teaspoons (10 mL) of water. Mix the celery root with the sour cream, diluted wasabi and smoked salmon trimmings.
3. To make the roulades, place an equal portion of stuffing on each smoked salmon rectangle. Roll up each piece of salmon, neatly locking the stuffing in place.
4. Tie each roulade with a chive "string" at each end. Trim the strings.
5. Place each roulade on a plate. Garnish with caviar, radish strips and cucumber rounds.

Approximate values per serving:

Calories	233
Total fat	13 g
Saturated fat	5 g
Cholesterol	203 mg
Sodium	1088 mg
Total carbohydrates	7 g
Protein	23 g

◆◆◆

RECIPE 33.21

ESCARGOT IN GARLIC BUTTER

Yield: 6 8-Piece Servings

Snails, canned	48	48
Butter, softened	1 lb.	500 g
Shallots, minced	2 Tbsp.	30 mL
Garlic, chopped	2 tsp.	10 mL
Fine bread crumbs	2 Tbsp.	30 mL
Brandy	1 Tbsp.	15 mL
Parsley, chopped	3 Tbsp.	45 mL
Salt and pepper	TT	TT
Nutmeg	pinch	pinch
Mushroom caps, medium	48	48

1. Drain and rinse the snails.
2. Combine the butter, shallots, garlic, bread crumbs, brandy, parsley, salt, pepper and nutmeg in a mixer or food processor and mix or process until well blended.
3. Sauté the mushroom caps in a small amount of the butter mixture until cooked but still firm. Remove from the heat and place 6 caps in each of 8 shallow ramekins.
4. Place a snail in each cap and top with a generous amount of the garlic butter.
5. Bake the mushrooms and snails at 450°F (230°C) for 5 to 7 minutes and serve hot.

VARIATIONS:

1. If snail shells are available, place a small amount of the butter in each shell. Push a snail into the buttered shell and add more butter to completely cover the snail. Place the shells in a specially designed escargot dish or a shallow ramekin with 1/2 inch (10 mm) of rock salt to hold them in place and cook as above.
2. Prepare 48 small bouchées from puff pastry or brioche. Sauté the snails in a generous amount of the garlic butter and place 1 snail in each bouchée. Drizzle the snail with the garlic butter and serve as a hot hors d'oeuvre.

Approximate values per serving:

Calories	491
Total fat	47 g
Saturated fat	29 g
Cholesterol	153 mg
Sodium	58 mg
Total carbohydrates	7 g
Protein	12 g

◆◆◆

RECIPE 33.22

TERIYAKI SALMON WITH PINEAPPLE-PAPAYA SALSA

Yield: 4 Servings

Soy sauce	8 oz.	250 mL
Garlic, crushed	1 tsp.	5 mL
Ginger, minced	1 tsp.	5 mL
Brown sugar	2 oz.	60 g
Sake	4 oz.	120 mL
Salmon, slices, 3 oz. (100 g) each	4	4
Vegetable oil	as needed	as needed
Pineapple Papaya Salsa (Recipe 25.9)	16 oz.	450 g

1. To make the marinade, combine the soy sauce, garlic, ginger, brown sugar and sake.

2. Marinate the salmon slices in the sauce for 15 minutes.

3. Remove the salmon slices from the marinade and pat dry. Brush them with vegetable oil and broil or grill until done.

4. Serve the salmon on a bed of warmed Pineapple-Papaya Salsa.

Approximate values per 8 oz. (240 g) serving:

Calories	223
Total fat	10 g
Saturated fat	1 g
Cholesterol	55 mg
Sodium	1510 mg
Total carbohydrates	10 g
Protein	22 g

◆◆◆

RECIPE 33.23

MUSSELS CHEF STEFAN STYLE

SEASONS IN THYME, SUMMERSIDE, PEI
Chef Stefan Czapalay

Stefan Czapalay
Named provincial Chef of the Year in 1997, Stefan is the chef-owner of Seasons in Thyme restaurant in Summerside, where the menu expresses his delight in the local seafood. His other company, Canadian Cold Water, produces flavoured oils, including the flagship creation, Lobster Oil.

Yield: 2 Servings **Method:** Steaming

Unsalted butter	2 Tbsp.	30 mL
Shallot, finely minced	1	1
Garlic cloves, finely minced	2	2
Celery stalk, finely chopped	1	1
Ginger, finely minced	1 Tbsp.	15 mL
Baby blue mussels	30	30
White wine	3 oz.	90 mL
Tomato, small	1	1
Fennel seeds	5	5
Basil, chopped	1/2 tsp.	3 mL
Curry powder	pinch	pinch
Pink peppercorns	5	5
Cream, 35%	2 oz.	60 mL

1. In a saucepan, melt 1 tablespoon (15 mL) of butter over moderate heat. Add shallot, garlic, celery and ginger and sweat gently.

2. Add mussels, wine, tomato, fennel, basil, curry powder and peppercorns and cook until the mussel shells open (5–7 minutes).

3. Remove the mussels and place in a bowl.

4. Meanwhile, bring the broth to a boil on high heat. Reduce volume by half by boiling rapidly.

5. Add the cream and return to boil.

6. Remove the sauce from the heat, swirl in the remaining butter and adjust seasoning.

7. Pour the sauce over the mussels and serve with crusty bread.

Approximate values per serving:

Calories	440
Total fat	28 g
Saturated fat	15 g
Cholesterol	129 mg
Sodium	408 mg
Total carbohydrates	15 g
Protein	26 g

RECIPE 33.24
SNOW CRAB AND BROCCOLI FLAN

ÉCOLE HÔTELIÈRE DES LAURENTIDES, STE. ADÈLE, PQ
Chef Marcel Kretz, CM

Marcel Kretz

Born, raised, and trained in France, Marcel has had an illustrious, award-winning career in Europe and Canada. He is credited with launching the movement to emphasize Quebec products in top Quebec restaurants, and in 1998 became the first chef ever to receive the Order of Canada.

Yield: 10 Servings   **Method:** Poaching

Butter	2 oz.	50 g
Snow crab meat, cooked	8 oz.	200 g
Broccoli florets, cooked	8 oz.	200 g
Eggs	6	6
Milk	8 oz.	200 mL
Cream, 35%	8 oz.	200 mL
Salt, white pepper, nutmeg	TT	TT

1. Butter 10 ramekins well.
2. Layer the crab and broccoli alternately in the ramekins.
3. In a bowl, mix the eggs, milk and cream thoroughly and add seasonings.
4. Pour the mixture into ramekins. Put the ramekins in a bain marie.
5. Poach slowly in the oven at 350°F (175°C) for 30 minutes, or until firm.
6. Unmould and serve with beurre blanc sauce (try "My" Beurre Blanc—Recipe 10.17) or a white wine sauce.

NOTE: Lobster or shrimps can be substituted for crab meat.

Approximate values per serving:

Calories	196
Total fat	17 g
Saturated fat	9 g
Cholesterol	188 mg
Sodium	402 mg
Total carbohydrates	3 g
Protein	9 g

RECIPE 33.25
EGGPLANT AND SUN-DRIED TOMATO PIZZA

GREENS RESTAURANT, SAN FRANCISCO, CA
Executive Chef Annie Somerville

Yield: 1 15-in. (37-cm) or 2 9-in. (22-cm) Pizzas

Japanese eggplants	2	2
Extra virgin olive oil	2 oz.	60 mL
Garlic, chopped	2 tsp.	10 mL
Salt and pepper	TT	TT
Pizza Dough (Recipe 28.14)	1 lb.	480 g
Sun-dried tomatoes, packed in oil	5	5
Provolone cheese, grated	4 oz.	120 g
Mozzarella cheese, grated	2 oz.	60 g
Parmesan cheese, grated	1/2 oz.	15 g
Fresh basil, chiffonade	12 leaves	12 leaves

1. Slice the eggplant diagonally into 1/2-inch (10-mm) slices.
2. Toss the eggplant with 1 ounce (30 mL) of olive oil and the garlic; season with salt and pepper.
3. Place the eggplant slices on a baking sheet and roast at 375°F (190°C) until soft in the centre, approximately 15–20 minutes. Cool and slice into strips.
4. Preheat the oven to 500°F (260°C). Roll out the dough and place it on a

Continued

lightly oiled pizza pan or well-floured wooden peel; brush it lightly with the remaining olive oil. Lay the eggplant and sun-dried tomatoes on top. Toss the provolone and mozzarella cheeses together and sprinkle onto the pizza.

5. Bake the pizza until the crust is golden and crisp, approximately 8–12 minutes. Remove from the oven and sprinkle with the Parmesan cheese and basil.

◆◆◆

RECIPE 33.26
SPRING ROLLS

Yield: 36 Rolls

Peanut oil	2 oz.	60 mL
Sesame oil	3 Tbsp.	45 mL
Onions, julienne	12 oz.	350 g
Red bell peppers, julienne	12 oz.	350 g
Snow peas, julienne	12 oz.	350 g
Fresh ginger, grated	1 Tbsp.	15 mL
Garlic, chopped	1 Tbsp.	15 mL
Napa cabbage, julienne	8 oz.	250 g
Bean sprouts	1 lb.	450 g
Cashews, unsalted, crushed	1 lb.	450 g
Cayenne pepper	1 tsp.	5 mL
Salt and pepper	TT	TT
Rice paper wrappers	36	36

1. Heat the oils and sauté the onions and peppers for 30 seconds.
2. Add the snow peas, ginger and garlic; sauté for 15 seconds.
3. Add the cabbage, bean sprouts, cashews, cayenne, salt and pepper. Cook for 15 seconds more.
4. Remove from the heat, cool and refrigerate.
5. Soak the rice paper wrappers in water for a few seconds to soften them. Place 2 ounces (60 g) of filling in each wrapper, fold the sides over towards the middle and roll up into a cigar shape. Brush the edge with water and press to seal.
6. Deep-fat fry the spring rolls at 350°F (180°C) until hot and crispy, approximately 45 seconds.

VARIATION: Wrap the filling in large wonton wrappers, seal and deep-fat fry.

◆◆◆

RECIPE 33.27
CHICKEN, PESTO AND FETA CHEESE SANDWICH

WILDFLOWER BREAD CO., SCOTTSDALE, AZ

Yield: 8 Sandwiches

Mushrooms, sliced thin	8 oz.	240 g
Balsamic vinaigrette	1 oz.	30 mL
Red bell peppers, roasted	8 oz.	240 g
Tomatoes, medium	4	4
Chicken breasts, boneless, skinless 4 oz. (120 g) each	8	8

Italian roll	8	8
Pesto (Recipe 10.30)	8 oz.	240 g
Feta	8 oz.	240 g

1. Marinate the mushrooms in the balsamic vinaigrette for at least 24 hours under refrigeration, stirring occasionally.
2. Slice the peppers into 1/4-inch (6-mm) wide strips.
3. Slice the tomatoes into 1/4-inch (6-mm) thick slices.
4. Trim any fat or rib meat from the chicken breasts and then grill until done.
5. To assemble each sandwich, slice one roll in half lengthwise. Spread 1 ounce (30 g) of the pesto on the bottom half of the roll, then crumble 1 ounce (30 g) of the feta on top of the pesto, covering the entire surface. Place a chicken breast on top of the feta, then 1/2 ounce (15 g) of the mushrooms on the chicken, 1 ounce (30 g) of the roasted red pepper strips on top of the mushrooms and finish with 3 tomato slices and the top half of the roll. Insert 2 toothpicks, slice and serve.

Approximate values per sandwich:

Calories	540
Total fat	20 g
Saturated fat	7 g
Cholesterol	135 g
Sodium	830 mg
Total carbohydrates	39 g
Protein	51 g
Vitamin A	20%
Vitamin C	60%
Calcium	30%
Iron	25%

RECIPE 33.28
GROUPER SANDWICH WITH LEMON RÉMOULADE

PHOENIX BREWING CO., ATLANTA, GA
Executive Chef Kevin Fonzo

Yield: 6 Sandwiches

Olive oil	2 Tbsp.	30 mL
Grouper fillets, 5 oz. (150 g) each	6	6
Salt and pepper	TT	TT
Lemon Rémoulade (recipe follows)	6 Tbsp.	90 mL
Kaiser rolls, sliced, toasted	6	6
Mixed greens	3 cups	720 mL
Tomato slices	6	6

1. Heat the olive oil in a large sauté pan. Season the grouper fillets with salt and pepper and then sauté the fish until golden brown and cooked through.
2. To assemble each sandwich, spread 1 tablespoon (15 mL) of the lemon rémoulade on the bottom half of the roll, then top with 1/2 cup (120 mL) of mixed greens, a tomato slice and the cooked fish. Cover with remaining half of the roll and serve.

LEMON RÉMOULADE

Yield: 20 oz. (600 mL)

Mayonnaise	1 pt.	500 mL
Sweet pickle relish	3 oz.	90 g
Onion, chopped fine	2 Tbsp.	30 mL
Parsley, chopped	2 Tbsp.	30 mL
Fresh lemon juice	2 Tbsp.	30 mL
Salt and black pepper	TT	TT
Worcestershire sauce	TT	TT
Tabasco	TT	TT

Mix all of the ingredients together until thoroughly blended.

Approximate values per serving:

Calories	330
Total fat	8 g
Saturated fat	1 g
Cholesterol	40 mg
Sodium	380 mg
Total carbohydrates	36 g
Protein	28 g
Vitamin A	15%
Vitamin C	60%

Approximate values per 1 oz. (30 mL) serving:

Calories	170
Total fat	18 g
Saturated fat	2.5 g
Cholesterol	15 mg
Sodium	160 mg
Total carbohydrates	2 g
Protein	0 g

◆◆◆

RECIPE 33.29

HAMBURGER

Yield: 1 Sandwich

Ground hip or chuck	4–6 oz.	120–180 g
Salt and pepper	TT	TT
Hamburger bun or an appropriate bread	1	1
Garnishes	as desired	as desired

1. Form the ground hip or chuck into a patty, handling the beef as little as possible.

2. Season the patty with salt and pepper and broil or grill to the desired doneness, turning once. While the patty is cooking, toast the bun or bread if desired.

3. Remove the patty from the broiler or grill, place on one-half of the bun or on 1 slice of bread and garnish the other half with a lettuce leaf, a slice of onion, a slice of tomato and/or pickles. Serve with condiments such as ketchup and mustard.

Approximate values per sandwich:

Calories	580
Total fat	32 g
Saturated fat	9 g
Cholesterol	99 mg
Sodium	355 mg
Total carbohydrates	40 g
Protein	29 g

VARIATIONS: *Cheeseburger*—Place 1 or 2 slices of American, cheddar, Swiss or other cheese on the cooking patty approximately 1 minute before it is done.

Approximate values per sandwich:

Calories	680
Total fat	42 g
Saturated fat	15 g
Cholesterol	130 mg
Sodium	520 mg
Total carbohydrates	42 g
Protein	36 g
Calcium	20%

Bacon cheeseburger—Prepare a cheeseburger and place 2 slices of crisp bacon on top of the cheese when the patty is done.

Approximate values per sandwich:

Calories	650
Total fat	39 g
Saturated fat	12 g
Cholesterol	110 mg
Sodium	560 mg
Total carbohydrates	41 g
Protein	33 g

Mushroom burger—Sauté 2 ounces (60 g) of sliced mushrooms in 1 to 2 teaspoons (5 to 10 mL) of butter or olive oil. Top the cooked hamburger or cheeseburger with the cooked mushrooms.

Approximate values per sandwich without cheese:

Calories	660
Total fat	37 g
Saturated fat	12 g
Cholesterol	110 mg
Sodium	400 mg
Total carbohydrates	48 g
Protein	33 g

Approximate values per sandwich without cheese:

Calories	690
Total fat	40 g
Saturated fat	9 g
Cholesterol	100 mg
Sodium	770 mg
Total carbohydrates	50 g
Protein	33 g
Vitamin C	20%

California burger—Prepare a hamburger or cheeseburger and serve on a whole wheat bun accompanied by 2 ounces (60 g) of guacamole, 1 ounce (30 g) of alfalfa sprouts, 2 slices of ripe tomato and 1 thin slice of red onion.

◆◆◆

RECIPE 33.30

GRILLED RED SNAPPER BURGER WITH MANGO KETCHUP

from *Allen Susser's New World Cuisine and Cookery*
by ALLEN SUSSER, NORTH MIAMI BEACH, FL

Yield: 4 Sandwiches

Red snapper fillets, fresh	1 lb.	450 g
Egg whites	3	3
Kosher salt	1-1/2 tsp.	7 mL
Cayenne pepper	1/4 tsp.	1 mL
Thai fish sauce	1 Tbsp.	15 mL
Scallions, chopped	2 Tbsp.	30 mL
Fresh dill, chopped	1 tsp.	5 mL
Fresh bread crumbs	1/4 cup	60 mL
Olive oil	2 Tbsp.	30 mL
French bread, quartered	1 loaf	1 loaf
Spinach, cleaned and dried	1 cup	225 mL
Mango Ketchup (recipe follows)	1 Tbsp.	15 mL

1. Chop the red snapper by hand or with a steel blade in a food processor. Place the chopped snapper into a large stainless-steel bowl.

2. Add the egg whites, salt, cayenne, fish sauce, scallions and dill. Mix well.

3. Add enough bread crumbs to bind all of the ingredients together.

4. Form into 4 burgers 1/2-inch (1.25-cm) thick and chill for approximately 30 minutes in the refrigerator.

5. Heat a grill or broiler until very hot. Drizzle a little olive oil over the burgers just before cooking. Grill or broil over high heat for about 1-1/2 minutes on each side, being careful not to overcook the fish.

6. Serve the burgers immediately on the French bread with one-quarter of the spinach leaves and 1 tablespoon (15 mL) of Mango Ketchup on each.

Approximate values per sandwich:

Calories	445
Total fat	11 g
Saturated fat	2 g
Cholesterol	55 mg
Sodium	1620 mg
Total carbohydrates	47 g
Protein	40 g
Vitamin A	50%
Calcium	20%

MANGO KETCHUP

Yield: 2 qt. (2 L)

Mangoes, medium	5	5
Vinegar	3 Tbsp.	45 mL
Fresh ginger, chopped	1 Tbsp.	15 mL
Cinnamon, ground	dash	dash
Kosher salt	1 tsp.	5 mL
Granulated sugar	4 oz.	120 g
White wine	4 oz.	120 mL
Allspice, ground	1/2 tsp.	2 mL
Cayenne pepper	1/2 tsp.	2 mL
Clove, whole	1	1

1. Peel and pit the mangoes. Purée the pulp in a food processor fitted with a stainless-steel blade.

2. Add all of the remaining ingredients and pulse together.

3. In a heavy-sided saucepan cook the mixture over low heat for 1 hour, until well reduced and thickened.

4. Remove from the heat and cool.

5. Strain through a fine sieve. Let set, refrigerated, for 24 hours.

Approximate values per 1 oz. (30 mL) serving:

Calories	26
Total fat	0 g
Saturated fat	0 g
Cholesterol	0 mg
Sodium	47 mg
Total carbohydrates	6 g
Protein	0 g

◆◆◆

RECIPE 33.31

BLACKENED STEAK SANDWICH

Yield: 2 Sandwiches

Strip loin steak, 10 oz. (280 g)	1	1
Blackened Steak Seasoning (recipe follows)	as needed	as needed
Clarified butter	1 oz.	30 mL
Capers	1 Tbsp.	15 mL
Whole butter, softened	1 oz.	30 g
French bread, cut on the bias	2 slices	2 slices
Baby lettuce, cleaned	4 oz.	120 g
Roma tomatoes, sliced	2	2
Red onions, sliced	1 oz.	30 g

1. Heat a cast-iron skillet over high heat for 10 minutes. Pat the steak dry with a clean towel. Coat the steak in the blackened steak seasoning.

2. Carefully place the steak into the hot skillet and ladle 1/2 ounce (15 mL) of clarified butter over the steak. Be very careful, the butter may flare up. There will be intense smoke and the steak will form a black crust. Cook the steak for approximately 2 minutes.

3. Turn the steak, ladle the remaining clarified butter over it and allow it to cook to the desired degree of doneness. Remove the steak from the pan and hold in a warm place.

4. Chop the capers and combine them with the softened butter. Spread each slice of bread with half of the caper butter.

5. Slice the steak on the bias.

6. To assemble each sandwich, place one-half of the warm steak on a slice of buttered bread and arrange half of the greens, tomatoes and onions attractively on the plate and serve.

VARIATION: To serve this sandwich cold, allow the steak to cool after cooking then refrigerate it until completely cold. Proceed with the recipe.

Approximate values per sandwich:

Calories	610
Total fat	38 g
Saturated fat	20 g
Cholesterol	180 mg
Sodium	650 mg
Total carbohydrates	21 g
Protein	44 g
Vitamin A	30%
Vitamin C	40%

BLACKENED STEAK SEASONING

Yield: 1-1/2 oz. (45 g)

Paprika	1 Tbsp.	15 mL
Salt	2 tsp.	10 mL
Onion powder	1 tsp.	5 mL
Garlic powder	1 tsp.	5 mL
Cayenne pepper	1 tsp.	5 mL
White pepper	1/2 tsp.	3 mL
Black pepper	1/2 tsp.	3 mL
Dried thyme	1/2 tsp.	3 mL

Combine all ingredients and mix well.

RECIPE 33.32
GRILLED BBQ PORTOBELLO MUSHROOM SANDWICH ON FOCACCIA

PHOENIX BREWING CO., ATLANTA, GA
Executive Chef Kevin Fonzo

Yield: 6 Sandwiches

Focaccia, cut into 6- in. (15-cm) squares	6	6
Portobello mushrooms	6	6
Barbecue Sauce (Recipe 10.24)	2 oz.	60 mL
Red bell peppers, roasted, peeled and julienne	2	2
Basil leaves	30	30
Goat cheese, crumbled	6 Tbsp.	90 mL

Approximate values per sandwich:

Calories	330
Total fat	12 g
Saturated fat	3.5 g
Cholesterol	15 mg
Sodium	660 mg
Total carbohydrates	45 g
Protein	11 g
Vitamin C	80%
Iron	15%

Claims–good source of fibre

1. Slice the focaccia squares horizontally and toast.

2. Brush the portobello mushrooms with the barbecue sauce and grill until hot and tender.

3. To assemble each sandwich, place 1 mushroom on the bottom half of a focaccia square and top with one-sixth of the roasted pepper strips, 5 basil leaves and 1 tablespoon (15 mL) of goat cheese. Top with the second half of the focaccia square, cut in half and serve.

RECIPE 33.33
REUBEN SANDWICH

Yield: 1 Sandwich

Dark rye bread	2 slices	2 slices
Thousand Island Dressing (Recipe 24.15)	1 oz.	30 mL
Cooked corned beef, hot, sliced very thin	4 oz.	120 g
Sauerkraut, hot, drained well	2 oz.	60 g
Swiss cheese	2 slices	2 slices
Whole butter, softened	as needed	as needed

Approximate values per sandwich:

Calories	560
Total fat	27 g
Saturated fat	10 g
Cholesterol	85 mg
Sodium	2150 mg
Total carbohydrates	39 g
Protein	40 g
Vitamin A	10%
Vitamin C	30%

1. Spread each slice of bread with approximately 1 tablespoon (15 mL) of Thousand Island dressing.

2. Place the hot corned beef, hot sauerkraut and Swiss cheese on 1 slice of bread. Top with the second slice of bread, keeping the dressing side down.

3. Butter the top slice of bread and place the sandwich on a hot griddle, top down. Carefully butter the second slice of bread.

4. Fry the sandwich, turning once when the first side is well browned. The sandwich is done when both sides are well browned, the fillings are very hot and the cheese is melted.

5. Cut the sandwich in half diagonally and arrange as desired for service.

✦✦✦

RECIPE 33.34

SOUTHWESTERN GRILLED CHEESE SANDWICH WITH CHIPOTLE PURÉE AND AVOCADO

Yield: 1 Sandwich

Whole grain bread	2 slices	2 slices
Monterey Jack cheese with peppers	2 slices	2 slices
Chipotle Purée (recipe follows)	1 tsp.	5 mL
Crème fraîche	1 Tbsp.	15 mL
Avocado, sliced thin	2 oz.	60 g
Red onion, sliced thin	1/2 oz.	15 g
Cilantro leaves	1 Tbsp.	15 mL
Whole butter, soft	1 oz.	30 g

Approximate values per sandwich:

Calories	730
Total fat	55 g
Saturated fat	28 g
Cholesterol	140 mg
Sodium	800 mg
Total carbohydrates	35 g
Protein	24 g
Vitamin A	45%
Calcium	60%

1. Top each slice of bread with a slice of cheese. Spread each slice with half of the chipotle purée and half of the crème fraîche.
2. Arrange the avocado slices, sliced red onion and cilantro leaves on 1 slice of the bread. Close the sandwich and press together lightly.
3. Butter the top slice of bread and place the sandwich, butter side down, on a hot griddle. Carefully butter the top of the second slice of bread.
4. Fry the sandwich, turning once when the first side is well browned. The sandwich is done when both sides are well browned and the cheese is melted.
5. Cut the sandwich in half diagonally and arrange as desired for service.

CHIPOTLE PURÉE

Yield: 8-1/2 oz (250 g)

Chipotle peppers in adobo sauce	7 oz.	200 g
Vegetable oil	1 oz.	30 g
Lime	1	1

1. Place the chipotle peppers and the oil in the bowl of a food processor; squeeze the lime and add the juice.
2. Process the mixture until smooth.

✦✦✦

RECIPE 33.35

MONTE CRISTO SANDWICH

Yield: 1 Sandwich

White bread	2 slices	2 slices
Whole butter, softened	as needed	as needed
Cooked turkey breast, sliced thin	1 oz.	30 g
Ham, sliced thin	1 oz.	30 g
Swiss cheese	2 slices	2 slices
Egg	1	1
Milk	1 oz.	30 mL

1. Spread 1 side of each slice of bread with butter.

2. Arrange the turkey breast, ham and cheese on top of the butter on the slice of bread.

3. Place the other slice of bread on top of the cheese, butter side against the cheese.

4. Beat the egg and milk together. Dip the sandwich in the egg batter and allow the batter to soak into the bread.

5. Deep-fat fry the sandwich in 375°F (190°C) oil until it is evenly browned. Remove from the oil and drain well. Cut the sandwich into 4 pieces and arrange as desired.

VARIATION: Wedge the sandwich before dipping and soaking.

Approximate values per sandwich:

Calories	630
Total fat	42 g
Saturated fat	24 g
Cholesterol	345 mg
Sodium	1050 mg
Total carbohydrates	27 g
Protein	35 g
Vitamin A	40%

◆◆◆

RECIPE 33.36

FALAFEL

Yield: 12 Sandwiches

Chickpeas, dry	1 lb.	500 g
Garlic cloves, minced	6	6
Parsley, chopped	1/2 oz.	15 g
Chives, minced	1/2 oz.	15 g
Cumin, ground	1 Tbsp.	15 mL
Coriander, ground	2 tsp.	10 mL
Cayenne pepper	TT	TT
Eggs	3	3
Salt	TT	TT
Flour	5 oz.	150 g
Plain yogurt	6 oz.	180 mL
Lemon juice	2 oz.	60 mL
Pita bread	12	12
Iceberg lettuce, shredded	6 oz.	180 g
Tomatoes, diced	6 oz.	180 g

1. To make the falafel, soak the chickpeas following the procedures for dried beans outlined in Chapter 22, Vegetables. Drain the chickpeas, place them in a pot and cover with cool water. Simmer until tender, approximately 2 to 3 hours, remove from the heat and drain well.

2. Process the chickpeas in a food processor or a food chopper until coarsely chopped. Add the garlic, parsley, chives, cumin, coriander and cayenne pepper and process for a few seconds.

3. Add the eggs, salt and flour and process briefly. Remove the falafel from the machine and chill in the refrigerator for 1 hour.

4. Combine the yogurt and lemon juice and mix well. Set aside.

5. Portion the falafel using a No. 50 scoop (there should be approximately 60 balls) and deep-fat fry the balls at 375°F (190°C) until crisp and hot. Drain well and hold in a warm place.

6. To assemble each sandwich, cut a pita in half or open it to form a pocket, stuff with several balls of falafel and 1 ounce (30 g) of the shredded lettuce and diced tomatoes, and dress with the yogurt sauce. Arrange the sandwiches as desired and serve hot.

Approximate values per sandwich:

Calories	290
Total fat	3 g
Saturated fat	0.5 g
Cholesterol	55 mg
Sodium	470 mg
Total carbohydrates	55 g
Protein	12 g

Claims–low fat; low saturated fat; good source of fibre

❖❖❖

RECIPE 33.37

HOT TURKEY SANDWICH

Yield: 6 Sandwiches

Cream, 35%, hot	6 oz.	180 mL
Romano, grated	6 oz.	180 g
Velouté sauce, hot	1 qt.	1 L
Dry sherry	1 oz.	30 mL
White toast, crust removed	12 slices	12 slices
Turkey breast, sliced	1 lb. 8 oz.	720 g
Parmesan, grated	2 oz.	60 g
Tomato wedges	12	12
Bacon, lean, cooked crisp	12 slices	12 slices

Approximate values per sandwich:

Calories	270
Total fat	34 g
Saturated fat	17 g
Cholesterol	185 mg
Sodium	2180 mg
Total carbohydrates	45 g
Protein	59 g
Vitamin A	20%
Calcium	50%

1. To make the sauce, add the cream and the Romano to the velouté sauce and bring to a simmer. Simmer for 1 minute, then strain the sauce through a china cap. Stir in the sherry. Hold in a warm place for service.
2. Cut the toast diagonally into triangles.
3. To assemble each sandwich, arrange 4 toast triangles in a gratin dish and top with 4 ounces (120 g) of turkey and 4 ounces (120 mL) of sauce. Bake at 350°F (225°C) until brown, approximately 15 minutes.
4. Top each sandwich with parmesan, 2 tomato wedges and 2 strips of bacon and serve very hot.

❖❖❖

RECIPE 33.38

ROAST BEEF AND BLUE CHEESE SANDWICH

WILDFLOWER BREAD CO., SCOTTSDALE, AZ

Yield: 4 Sandwiches

Red bell peppers, roasted	8 oz.	240 g
Herb Mayonnaise (recipe follows)	8 Tbsp.	120 mL
White sourdough bread slices	8	8
Blue cheese, crumbled	6 oz.	180 g
Roast beef, rare, cold, sliced thin	1 lb.	440 g
Red onion, sliced thin	2 oz.	60 g
Tomato slices	12	12
Romaine lettuce	4 leaves	4 leaves

Approximate values per sandwich:

Calories	679
Total fat	42 g
Saturated fat	17 g
Cholesterol	105 mg
Sodium	1061 mg
Total carbohydrates	41 g
Protein	34 g
Vitamin A	73%
Vitamin C	170%
Calcium	30%
Iron	28%

1. Slice the peppers into strips 1/4-inch (6-mm) wide.
2. To assemble 1 sandwich, spread 2 tablespoons (30 mL) of herb mayonnaise on a slice of bread and top with 1-1/2 ounces (45 g) of blue cheese. Then place 3-1/2 ounces (110 g) of the roast beef on top of the cheese and cover with the 1/2 ounce (15 g) of red onions, 2 ounces (60 g) of red bell pepper strips, 3 tomato slices, 1 leaf of romaine lettuce and a slice of bread.

HERB MAYONNAISE

Yield: 1 cup (250 mL)

Mayonnaise	1 cup	250 mL
Fresh basil, chopped	1 Tbsp.	15 mL

| Fresh cilantro, chopped | 1 tsp. | 5 mL |
| Fresh parsley, chopped | 1 tsp. | 5 mL |

Stir all of the ingredients together until the herbs are evenly distributed throughout the mayonnaise. Chill until ready to use.

◆◆◆

RECIPE 33.39

NEW ORLEANS–STYLE MUFFALETTA SANDWICH

Yield: 1 Sandwich, 4-6 Servings

Red bell pepper, roasted chopped	1	1
Niçoise or Gaeta olives, pitted, chopped	4 oz.	120 g
Olives, green, pitted, chopped	4 oz.	120 g
Virgin olive oil	4 oz.	120 mL
Italian parsley, chopped	2 Tbsp.	30 mL
Anchovy fillets, mashed	2	2
Dried oregano	1 tsp.	5 mL
Lemon juice	1 Tbsp.	15 mL
Round Italian bread, 8 in. (18 cm) diameter	1	1
Arugula or curly endive, chiffonade	1-1/2 oz.	45 g
Tomato concassé	6 oz.	180 g
Mortadella, sliced thin	6 oz.	180 g
Soppressata, sliced thin (see page 533)	4 oz.	120 g
Provolone or fontina, sliced thin	4 oz.	120 g
Pepper	TT	TT

1. To make the olive salad, combine the red pepper, olives, olive oil, parsley, anchovies, oregano and lemon juice and marinate for several hours.
2. Cut the loaf of bread in half horizontally. Remove some of the soft interior of the bread to create a slight hollow area.
3. Drain the olive salad, reserving the oil. Brush the interior of the bread with the reserved oil, using it all.
4. Arrange the olive salad, greens, tomato, mortadella, soppressata and cheese in layers on the bottom portion of the loaf of bread, finishing with a thick layer of olive salad. Season the layers with pepper as desired.
5. Place the top on the sandwich and wrap tightly with plastic wrap. Refrigerate the sandwich for several hours so that the layers will remain in place when the sandwich is cut.
6. Cut the sandwich into 4 to 6 wedges and arrange as desired for service.

Approximate values per sandwich:

Calories	670
Total fat	57 g
Saturated fat	14 g
Cholesterol	60 mg
Sodium	2200 mg
Total carbohydrates	16 g
Protein	24 g
Vitamin C	80%
Calcium	30%

◆◆◆

RECIPE 33.40

SOUTHWESTERN GRILLED CHICKEN WRAP

Yield: 12 Sandwiches

Chicken breast, boneless, skinless	3 lb.	1.36 kg
Salt and pepper	TT	TT
Avocados	3	3
Red bell peppers	2	2

Continued

Red onion	1	1
Tomatoes	2	2
Tortillas, 10 in. (24 cm)	12	12
Black Bean Spread (recipe follows)	3 lb.	1.3 kg
Black olives, sliced	1 cup	250 mL
Cilantro, chopped	2 bunches	2 bunches
Cheddar cheese, grated	1 lb. 8 oz.	750 g
Jalapeños, minced	2	2

Approximate values per sandwich:

Calories	642
Total fat	37 g
Saturated fat	16 g
Cholesterol	118 mg
Sodium	695 mg
Total carbohydrates	37 g
Protein	41 g
Vitamin A	37%
Vitamin C	76%
Calcium	50%
Iron	22%

1. Season the chicken breast with salt and pepper and grill or broil until done. Chill and cut into strips.
2. Peel the avocados and cut each into 12 slices. Clean the bell peppers and cut into strips. Slice the onions thinly. Dice the tomatoes.
3. To make each sandwich, place 1 tortilla on a cutting board and spread with approximately 4 ounces (120 g) of black bean spread.
4. Sprinkle one-twelfth of the pepper, onions, tomatoes, olives, cilantro, cheese and jalapeños over the bean spread.
5. Top with one-twelfth of the chicken.
6. Roll the tortilla around the ingredients tightly enough so that the sandwich will hold its shape. Cut the sandwich as desired for service.

BLACK BEAN SPREAD

Yield: 3 lb. (1.3 kg)

Black beans, soaked and drained	1 lb. 8 oz.	750 g
Water	4 qt.	4 L
Onion, diced	4 oz.	120 g
Tomatoes, diced	6 oz.	180 g
Cilantro, chopped	2 Tbsp.	30 mL
Salt and pepper	TT	TT
Cumin	1 tsp.	5 mL
Chilli powder	1 tsp.	5 mL

Approximate values per 2 oz. (60 g) serving:

Calories	100
Total fat	0.5 g
Saturated fat	0 g
Cholesterol	0 mg
Sodium	51 mg
Total carbohydrates	37 g
Protein	12 g

Claims–low fat; no cholesterol, low sodium

1. Combine the beans and the water, bring to a boil, reduce to a simmer and cook until tender, approximately 1 to 1-1/2 hours.
2. Add the remaining ingredients and simmer for 10 minutes.
3. Drain the beans, reserving the cooking liquid. Chill the beans and the liquid.
4. Purée the beans in a food processor, adding enough of the cooking liquid to make a soft, spreadable purée.

◆◆◆

RECIPE 33.41

VEGGIE WRAP

Yield: 1 Sandwich

Spinach-flavoured tortilla	1	1
Garlic Yogurt Dressing (recipe follows)	2 Tbsp.	30 mL
Jasmine rice, cooked	3 oz.	90 g
Roma tomato, diced	2 Tbsp.	30 mL

Cucumber, julienne	1 oz.	30 g
Alfalfa sprouts	as needed	as needed
Broccoli florets	1 oz.	30 g
Red onion, sliced thin	1 oz.	30 g
Capers	1 Tbsp.	15 mL

Approximate values per sandwich:

Calories	464
Total fat	3 g
Saturated fat	.5 g
Cholesterol	0 mg
Sodium	296 mg
Total carbohydrates	95 g
Protein	12 g
Vitamin A	12%
Vitamin C	45%
Calcium	14%
Iron	15%

1. Spread the tortilla with 1 tablespoon (15 mL) of the garlic yogurt dressing.
2. Arrange the rice in a mound across the centre of the tortilla. Top the rice with the vegetables and capers.
3. Drizzle the remaining garlic yogurt dressing over the vegetables.
4. Using a piece of parchment paper as a wrapper, roll the tortilla tightly around the filling, then chill and serve.

GARLIC YOGURT DRESSING

Yield: 1 pt. (500 mL)

Nonfat yogurt, plain	1 pt.	500 mL
Parsley, minced	1 Tbsp.	15 mL
Garlic, minced	2 Tbsp.	30 mL
Dijon mustard	2 Tbsp.	30 mL
Black pepper	1/4 tsp.	1 mL
Tabasco sauce	TT	TT

Combine all of the ingredients and chill until ready to use.

Approximate values per 1 oz. (30 mL) serving:

Calories	19
Total fat	0 g
Saturated fat	0 g
Cholesterol	1 mg
Sodium	46 mg
Total carbohydrates	3 g
Protein	2 g

◆◆◆

RECIPE 33.42

CLUB SANDWICH

Yield: 1 Sandwich

Sliced bread, toasted	3 slices	3 slices
Mayonnaise	as needed	as needed
Lettuce leaves	2	2
Tomato	3 slices	3 slices
Bacon, cooked crisp	3 slices	3 slices
Salt and pepper	TT	TT
Cooked turkey breast, sliced thin	3 oz.	90 g

1. Spread 1 side of each slice of toasted bread with mayonnaise.
2. Arrange the lettuce, tomato and bacon on 1 slice of toast. Season with salt and pepper.
3. Place another slice of toast on top of the bacon.
4. Arrange the turkey breast on top of the second slice of toast.
5. Place the third slice of toast on top of the turkey breast, mayonnaise side down.
6. Place 4 frilled toothpicks in the sandwich, 1 on each side, approximately 1 inch (2.5 cm) in from the edge. Cut the sandwich diagonally into quarters and arrange as desired for service.

Approximate values per sandwich:

Calories	530
Total fat	24 g
Saturated fat	6 g
Cholesterol	95 mg
Sodium	830 mg
Total carbohydrates	38 g
Protein	39 g
Vitamin A	4%
Vitamin C	10%

♦♦♦

RECIPE 33.43
GRILLED SALMON CLUB WITH CILANTRO AIOLI

PHOENIX BREWING CO., ATLANTA, GA
Executive Chef Kevin Fonzo

Yield: 4 Sandwiches

Salmon fillets, 5 oz. (150 g), each	4	4
Salt and pepper	TT	TT
Olive oil	1 Tbsp.	15 mL
Wheat bread, toasted	12 slices	12 slices
Watercress	2 cups	500 mL
Red onions, cut in rings, 1/8-in (3-mm) thick	8 rings	8 rings
Tomato, thick slices	8	8
Cilantro Aïoli (recipe follows)	4 Tbsp.	60 mL

Approximate values per sandwich:

Calories	471
Total fat	24 g
Saturated fat	3 g
Cholesterol	87 mg
Sodium	410 mg
Total carbohydrates	30 g
Protein	34 g
Vitamin A	27%
Vitamin C	36%
Iron	16%

1. Season the salmon with salt and pepper and rub with the olive oil, then grill the salmon until just cooked. Do not overcook.

2. To assemble each sandwich, top 1 slice of toasted bread with 1/2 cup (120 mL) of watercress, then 2 red onion rings and 2 slices of tomato. Top with a second slice of bread.

3. Place 1 salmon fillet on the second slice of bread.

4. Spread the third slice of bread with 1 tablespoon (15 mL) of the cilantro aïoli and place on top of the salmon. Cut the sandwich and serve.

CILANTRO AIOLI

Yield: 1 qt. (1 L)

Egg yolks	4	4
Salt	1 tsp.	5 mL
White pepper	TT	TT
Dijon mustard	1 tsp.	5 mL
White vinegar	3 Tbsp.	45 mL
Cilantro, chopped	3 Tbsp.	45 mL
Lime juice	TT	TT
Salad oil	28 oz.	840 mL

Approximate values per 2 oz. (60 mL) serving:

Calories	455
Total fat	51 g
Saturated fat	6 g
Cholesterol	53 mg
Sodium	140 mg
Total carbohydrates	.5 g
Protein	.8 g

1. Combine all of the ingredients except the oil in a blender. Process until thoroughly combined.

2. With the blender running, slowly pour the oil into the egg yolk mixture to form an emulsion.

EBLINKS

Enormous Appetizer Collection
    www.cs.cmu.edu/~mjw/recipes/appetizers/enorm-appetizer-coll.html

A Sushi Glossary
    www.cis.unisa.edu.au/~cisjpm/Sushi/Full/glossary.html

Dim Sum
    www.cris.com/~lkarper/dim_sum.html

CHAPTER 34

INTERNATIONAL FLAVOUR PRINCIPLES

After studying this chapter you will be able to:

+ describe the flavour principles of several cuisines
+ prepare chicken and starch dishes incorporating the flavour principles and representative cooking methods of each of these cuisines

*P*eople worldwide share a love of food. But the ingredients, flavourings, seasonings and cooking methods they use are not the same. Whether defined by geography, history, ethnicity, politics or religion, various societies eat different foods seasoned and prepared in distinctive manners. These differences shape and define their particular cuisine.

Because this book is a guide to understanding the hows and whys of cooking and is not simply a collection of recipes, we will not explore here all of the world's cuisines nor provide a comprehensive selection of recipes illustrating the cuisines discussed. Instead, we delve into the flavour principles that distinguish several important cuisines from European and North American traditions.

Once you understand these principles, you should be able to prepare a variety of dishes that reflect a particular cuisine's flavour principles and cooking methods. To illustrate this point, and because most societies eat chicken, we include a chicken and starch recipe from each of the cuisines discussed.

Cookery—*the art, practice or work of cooking.*

Cuisine—*the ingredients, seasonings, cooking procedures and styles and eating habits attributable to a particular group of people; the group can be defined by geography, history, ethnicity, politics, culture or religion.*

National cuisine—*the characteristic cuisine of a nation.*

Regional cuisine—*a set of recipes based upon local ingredients, traditions and practices; within a larger geographical, political, cultural or social unit, regional cuisines are often variations of each other that blend together to create a national cuisine.*

Ethnic cuisine—*the cuisine of a group of people having a common cultural heritage as opposed to the cuisine of a group of people bound together by geography or political factors.*

Professional cooking—*a system of cooking based upon a knowledge of ingredients and procedures.*

RECIPES FOR ETHNIC CUISINES

In *Ethnic Cuisine: The Flavor Principle Cookbook*, Elisabeth Rozin writes: "Every culture tends to combine a small number of flavoring ingredients so frequently and so consistently that they become definitive of that particular cuisine" (p. xiv). She calls these defining flavours "flavor principles" and notes that they are "designed to abstract what is absolutely fundamental about a cuisine and, thus, to serve as a guide in cooking and developing new recipes" (p. xvii). She identifies the following flavour principles for European cuisines:

Greek:
Tomato, cinnamon *or* olive oil, lemon, oregano

Italian:
Generally—olive oil, garlic, basil
Northern Italy—wine vinegar, garlic
Southern Italy—olive oil, garlic, parsley and/or anchovy plus tomato as a variation

French:
Generally—olive oil, garlic, basil *or* wine, herb *or* butter and/or cream and/or cheese plus wine and/or stock
Southern France—olive oil, garlic, parsley and/or anchovy plus tomato as a variation
Provence—olive oil, thyme, rosemary, marjoram, sage plus tomato as a variation
Normandy—apple, cider, Calvados

Spanish:
Olive oil, garlic, nut *or* olive oil, onion, pepper, tomato

Hungarian:
Onion, lard, paprika

Eastern European Jewish:
Onion, chicken fat

Eastern and Northern European:
Sour cream, dill *or* paprika *or* allspice *or* caraway

CHINESE CUISINES

China, a large, geographically diverse country, nurtures several distinctive regional cuisines, the most prominent of which are called here Northern, Southern, Western and Eastern. All Chinese cuisines emphasize a sophisticated contrast and harmony of flavours (sweet, sour, bitter, spicy and salty) and textures (crisp, crunchy, chunky, chewy, smooth and liquid) and rely on the quick cooking of attractively cut, bite-sized pieces of food. Reducing all foods to bite-sized pieces promotes the quick infusion of flavourings. Most cooking is done in a wok that can be used for stir-frying, deep-fat frying and steaming. Anthropologists suggest that the reliance on quick cooking methods was the result of chronic fuel shortages. Although these quick cooking methods can produce fully cooked foods in minutes, the careful cutting and preparation techniques often require far more time.

Staples include several varieties of rice, noodles (made from rice, beans and wheat) and soy beans (eaten as seeds, beans, sprouts and curd, and used for oil and sauce). Pork, poultry (particularly chicken and duck), fish (particularly pike, carp and bass) and shellfish are regularly consumed, as are a large assortment of vegetables (including varieties of mushrooms, several cabbages, bamboo shoots, water chestnuts and snow peas) and fruits (including litchi, pears, plums and various citrus fruits).

Common spices are star anise, cinnamon, cloves, fennel and Szechuan peppercorns (these are sometimes blended for five spice powder), lemon balm, tangerine peel, coriander, sesame seeds and oil, lotus nut paste, lotus root and hot chiles (a New World import). Commonly used sauces include plum, oyster, hoisin and both light and dark soy.

Chinese—(clockwise from top left) chicken in black bean sauce, white rice, rolls of moo shu chicken, plum sauce, moo shu chicken

◆◆◆
ON TASTE

Taste is composed of about 10,000 compounds. When we think of taste we normally think in terms of the language we are familiar with and the foods we grew up with. The structure of our taste is formed very early, basically when we start eating baby food. As Westerners we divide taste into four major groups: sweet, salty, bitter and sour. The Chinese include a fifth: hot (spicy), and Southeast Asians add aromatic and pungent. So, there are actually seven or more types. Americans, however, basically rely on sweet and salty. They don't use sour and bitter very much. They certainly don't use hot very much. Nor do they use aromatic or strong pungent things like fish paste very often. We really only use about 30% of our palate. To compare this to sight, it's as if we are colorblind, unable to perceive and enjoy fully five out of every seven colors we see. This is why we sometimes have trouble "acquiring" a taste for ethnic foods.

Westerners have a lineal palate, which is set up on sweet, salty, with very few counterpoints and harmonies. When I say lineal, for instance, if you eat in the European manner, you usually begin with an appetizer, which may be salty or hot. Then you have soup, then a fish course, then a meat course, then a sweet. You are using different parts of your palate, but linearly. In Asian cuisines, however, you use sweet, hot, bitter and sour at the same time. You're eating circularly. The meal is not a lineal progress to some point, like dessert. You may have already had fruit or a sweet in the meal, which is a much more satisfying and actually much more healthy way to eat. European food, like European art, is more concerned with finished form. Most ethnic things are concerned with process and expression.

You must train your mind to go after flavor characteristics and become involved in the process of eating. You must look for flavors in different parts of your mouth. Think about how quickly flavors appear in the mouth and how long the flavors are. Think about the finish. You must develop a very good sensitivity to the finish of the product, otherwise you overseason and lose the compositional balance.

—*from* MARK MILLER, *chef/owner RED SAGE, WASHINGTON D.C., and COYOTE CAFE, SANTA FE, NM*

Northern China

Northern China includes Beijing, the capital. Some consider this region's cuisine to be the most aristocratic of the regional cuisines; indeed, it is sometimes referred to as Mandarin cuisine, named for the centuries-old Chinese aristocratic and bureaucratic classes.

Northern Chinese dishes are generally lightly spiced and contain little residual oil. Because northern China is relatively dry, rice is not a regional staple, as rice needs an abundance of water to grow. Instead, wheat and millet, eaten as noodles, dumplings and pancakes, are popular. *Chao mian* is a dish of thin wheat noodles stir-fried with other ingredients. Freshwater fish are regularly consumed, as is lamb, a meat rarely eaten elsewhere in China. Meats and poultry are most often roasted or barbecued; Peking duck is a well-known example. Mongol influence still exists in the form of the Mongolian hot pot: a simmering broth into which each diner submerges bits of meat, poultry, vegetables or bean curd.

A classic Northern Chinese dish is Moo Shu Chicken: The wood ears (mushrooms) and bamboo shoots provide contrasting textures, the duck sauce (also known as plum sauce) is a delicate condiment and the pancakes are classically Mandarin. The dish is best enjoyed by spreading 1/2 teaspoon (3 mL) of the duck sauce on each pancake, then topping with green onions and 2–3 tablespoons (30–45 mL) of the moo shu. The pancake is then rolled up with the ends folded in.

◆◆◆
RECIPE 34.1
MOO SHU CHICKEN

Yield: 4 Servings

Chicken breast, boneless, skinless	8 oz.	240 g
Marinade:		
Chinese rice wine	1 tsp.	5 mL
Salt	TT	TT
Egg white, beaten	1	1
Soy sauce	1/2 tsp.	3 mL
Wood ear mushrooms, dried	5	5
Eggs	3	3
Vegetable oil	4 oz.	120 mL
Garlic, chopped	1 tsp.	5 mL
Hoisin sauce	2 oz.	60 mL
Bamboo shoots, shredded	3 oz.	90 g
Bok choy, shredded	3 oz.	90 g
Carrot, shredded	3 oz.	90 g
Salt	1 tsp.	5 g
Chicken stock	2 oz.	60 mL
Green onions, shredded	1 oz.	30 g

1. Slice the chicken into thin strips, approximately 1-1/2 inches by 1/4 inch (4 cm by 0.6 cm), and marinate in the rice wine, salt, egg white and soy sauce for 15 minutes.

2. Soak the wood ears in hot water until soft. Break off the hard stems and shred the mushrooms.

3. Beat the eggs. Heat 1 tablespoon (15 mL) of the oil in a wok and cook the eggs. Do not let them brown. Remove the eggs, shred and set aside.

4. Stir-fry the garlic in 2 ounces (60 mL) of oil until golden. Add the chicken and stir-fry until the chicken is very lightly browned. Remove the chicken, drain and set aside.

5. Add the hoisin sauce and 2 tablespoons (30 mL) of oil to the wok; quickly stir-fry the sauce. Add the bamboo shoots, bok choy, carrots and shredded mushrooms and cook for 5 minutes.

6. Add the chicken, salt, chicken stock and shredded eggs. Stir-fry over high heat for 1 minute.

7. Serve hot, garnished with green onions.

Approximate values per serving:

Calories	435
Total fat	33 g
Saturated fat	3 g
Cholesterol	194 mg
Sodium	891 mg
Total carbohydrates	15 g
Protein	21 g

◆◆◆

RECIPE 34.2
DUCK SAUCE

Yield: 4 oz. (110 g)

Sweet bean sauce	3 Tbsp.	45 mL
Hoisin sauce	3 Tbsp.	45 mL
Sugar	1 tsp.	5 mL
Sesame oil	1 Tbsp.	15 mL

Combine and stir all the ingredients until smooth. Serve at room temperature.

Approximate values per 1 oz. (30 g) serving:

Calories	68
Total fat	4 g
Saturated fat	1 g
Cholesterol	0 mg
Sodium	293 mg
Total carbohydrates	7 g
Protein	1 g

◆◆◆

RECIPE 34.3
MANDARIN PANCAKES

Yield: 16 5-inch (12.5-cm) Pancakes

All-purpose flour	8 oz.	240 g
Sesame oil	1 Tbsp.	15 mL
Salt	pinch	pinch
Boiling water	6 oz.	180 mL

1. Place the flour, 1/2 teaspoon (2 mL) of sesame oil and a pinch of salt in a bowl. Add the boiling water and gradually mix with a spoon to make a soft dough.

2. On a lightly floured surface, gently knead the dough until smooth. Cover with a damp cloth and let rest for 15 minutes.

3. Shape the dough into a cylinder about 1 inch (2.5 cm) in diameter, adding more flour if necessary. Slice the log into 16 equal pieces; roll each piece into a ball and then flatten each to make a disk.

4. Brush the tops of 8 disks with the remaining sesame oil. Then place an unoiled disk on top of each oiled disk. Using a rolling pin, flatten each pair of disks into a 5-inch (12.5-cm) circle. Cover the pancakes with a dry towel.

5. Heat an ungreased 8-inch (20-cm) skillet over high heat for 30 seconds to 1 minute. Reduce the heat to medium.

6. Place 1 pancake pair into the skillet. When it puffs and bubbles appear on its surface, turn it over and cook the other side until it is speckled brown, approximately 1 minute. Then turn the pancake and cook the first side until it too is speckled brown, approximately 30 seconds. Remove the pancake and wrap it in a clean, dry towel.

Continued

Approximate values per pancake:

Calories	63
Total fat	1 g
Saturated fat	.2 g
Cholesterol	0 mg
Sodium	1 mg
Total carbohydrates	12 g
Protein	2 g

7. Repeat until each pancake pair is cooked.

8. Just before service, separate each pancake pair by gently pulling apart at the edges. Serve warm.

Southern China

Southern Chinese cuisine is centred in Canton, a fertile area rich with rice paddies, vegetable farms and fruit orchards. All these ingredients are found in the cuisine, along with an abundance of saltwater and freshwater fish and shellfish as well as more exotic ingredients such as abalone, sea urchin, snake, shark fins, turtle, snails and eel. Both rice and wheat noodle dishes are very popular.

Southern Chinese cuisine emphasizes the freshness of its local ingredients; therefore stir-frying is a popular cooking method. When stir-frying, most of the spices and nonliquid flavouring ingredients are added at the start. Their flavours are released by quickly sautéing them in hot oil. The liquid flavouring ingredients are usually mixed with a thickening agent (often cornstarch) and added towards the end of cooking. This mixture then boils and thickens, coating the foods with the flavouring sauce.

◆◆◆

RECIPE 34.4

CHICKEN AND SNOW PEAS IN BLACK BEAN SAUCE

Yield: 4 Servings

Chicken breasts, boneless, skinless	2 lb.	1 kg
Egg white	1	1
Chinese rice wine	6 oz.	180 mL
Cornstarch	2 Tbsp.	30 g
Soy sauce	2 oz.	60 mL
Granulated sugar	2 tsp.	10 g
Onions, small	2	2
Peanut oil	4 oz.	120 mL
Garlic, minced	1 Tbsp.	15 mL
Fresh ginger, minced	2 tsp.	10 mL
Fermented black beans, mashed	3 Tbsp.	45 g
Snow peas, fresh	4 oz.	120 g

1. Slice the chicken into thin strips, approximately 1-1/2 inches by 1/4 inch (4 cm by 0.6 cm).

2. Combine the egg white, one-third of the wine and 1 tablespoon (15 g) of the cornstarch. Add the chicken and refrigerate for 2 hours.

3. For the sauce, mix the soy sauce, sugar and the remaining wine and cornstarch.

4. Quarter the onions and separate the layers.

5. Stir-fry the chicken in 3 ounces (90 mL) of oil. Remove and set aside.

6. If necessary, add all the remaining oil and stir-fry the garlic and ginger for 30 seconds. Add the onions and mashed beans and stir-fry for 30 seconds. Add the snow peas and cook for 1 minute.

7. Return the chicken to the wok, add the sauce mixture and stir-fry until hot and the sauce has thickened.

8. Serve immediately with short-grain white rice.

VARIATION: Add 2 ounces (60 g) sliced mushrooms and reduce the amount of snow peas by half.

Approximate values per serving:

Calories	727
Total fat	28 g
Saturated fat	7 g
Cholesterol	188 mg
Sodium	1588 mg
Total carbohydrates	26 g
Protein	78 g

Western China

Encompassing the cookery of both Szechuan and Hunan provinces, Western Chinese cuisine is distinguished by its spiciness. Favourite seasonings include ginger, vinegar, garlic, sesame oil, green onions and hot chiles. Szechuan recipes usually incorporate chiles in paste form, while Hunan dishes use fresh chiles. Hunan cuisine is typically more sweet and sour than Szechuan cuisine. Both, however, include countless dishes that offer diners several competing spices. After the first fiery sensation passes, these multiple flavours should be recognizable and savoured.

Both rice and wheat are grown in western China. Fresh and dried freshwater fish, pork, beef and poultry are common ingredients, as are several types of mushrooms. Often the meats are subjected to several preparations for one dish.

◆◆◆

RECIPE 34.5

JAR GAI
(SZECHUAN-STYLE FRIED CHICKEN)

Yield: 4 Servings

Chicken breasts, boneless, skinless	1 lb.	500 g
Cornstarch	5 Tbsp.	75 g
Salt	1 tsp.	5 g
Five spice powder	3/4 tsp.	4 mL
Chicken stock	8 oz.	240 mL
Granulated sugar	2 tsp.	10 g
Light soy sauce	1 Tbsp.	15 mL
Sesame oil	1/2 tsp.	3 mL
Rice wine vinegar	1 tsp.	5 mL
Chinese rice wine	2 tsp.	10 mL
Black pepper, ground	1/4 tsp.	2 mL
Cold water	1 Tbsp.	15 mL
Canola or corn oil	4 oz.	120 mL
Red chiles, dried and seeded	15	15
Garlic, chopped fine	2 tsp.	10 mL
Fresh ginger, peeled and chopped fine	2 tsp.	10 mL
Green onions, trimmed and cut into 2-in. (5-cm) lengths	4	4

1. Slice the chicken into thin strips, approximately 1-1/2 inches by 1/4 inch (4 cm by 0.6 cm).

2. Combine 4 tablespoons (60 g) of the cornstarch, the salt and 1/2 teaspoon

Approximate values per serving:

Calories	617
Total fat	39 g
Saturated fat	5 g
Cholesterol	94 mg
Sodium	920 mg
Total carbohydrates	28 g
Protein	38 g

Continued

(3 mL) of the five spice powder. Toss the chicken pieces in the mixture; dust off any excess cornstarch.

3. Mix 4 ounces (120 mL) of the stock with the sugar, soy sauce, sesame oil, vinegar, wine, pepper and the remaining five spice powder.

4. In a separate bowl, mix the water and remaining cornstarch.

5. Heat the oil and stir-fry the chicken in small batches.

6. Degrease the pan, reserving 2 tablespoons (30 mL) of the oil. Add the chiles, garlic and ginger; stir-fry until the garlic and ginger are golden and the chiles turn dark.

7. Add the green onions and toss for a few seconds. Add the stock mixture and bring to a boil.

8. Thicken the sauce with the remaining cornstarch-and-water mixture.

9. Return the chicken to the pan and toss to heat thoroughly.

10. Serve immediately with short-grain white rice.

Eastern China

Shanghai, a large city on China's east coast, has been the principal point of contact between foreigners and Chinese since the 19th century. Its cuisine reflects this contact. For example, dairy products, which rarely appear in Chinese cuisine, are sometimes used in Eastern Chinese recipes. Similarly, meats are often subjected to slow cooking methods more typical of Europe, such as red-cooking, a form of simmering named for the rich, red-brown sauce that results from cooking the meat in soy sauce. Wine, soy sauces, vinegars (especially an aged vinegar known as Chinkiang) and sugar are the predominant flavourings.

Eastern Chinese cuisine also reflects the fertile area's year-round growing season, many rivers and long shoreline. While most other regional Chinese cuisines incorporate only one or two vegetables in a dish, Shanghai chefs will blend six or more, often cutting them into different shapes.

◆◆◆

RECIPE 34.6

SEE YO GAI
(RED-COOKED CHICKEN)

Yield: 4 Servings

Roasting chicken, 3–4 lb. (1.3–1.8 kg)	1	1
Cold water	12 oz.	350 mL
Dark soy sauce	12 oz.	350 mL
Chinese rice wine	2 oz.	60 g
Fresh ginger, peeled and sliced thin	2 oz.	60 g
Garlic, chopped	1 tsp.	5 mL
Star anise	10	10
Granulated sugar	1-1/2 Tbsp.	20 g
Sesame oil	2 tsp.	10 mL

1. Place the washed chicken, breast side down, in a covered saucepan small enough so that the liquid ingredients will cover the chicken completely.

2. Add all other ingredients except the sesame oil and slowly bring to a boil. Reduce the heat and simmer for 15 minutes. Turn the chicken and simmer for 20 minutes, basting the bird every 5 minutes.

3. Remove the pot from the heat and leave covered until cool.*

4. Remove the chicken and brush it with the sesame oil. The chicken can be carved in joints or, in the traditional Chinese manner, split lengthwise and chopped into strips 1-1/2 inches (4 cm) wide.

5. Serve the chicken at room temperature* with the leftover sauce for dipping and a noodle dish as an accompaniment.

Note: Allowing cooked chicken to cool in this manner and then serving it at room temperature is not consistent with sound food-handling procedures; it is, however, an authentic practice.

Approximate values per serving:

Calories	952
Total fat	50 g
Saturated fat	14 g
Cholesterol	293 mg
Sodium	6341 mg
Total carbohydrates	18 g
Protein	99 g

JAPANESE CUISINE

As with their arts, the Japanese strive for a cuisine that reflects *sappari*: clarity, lightness, simplicity and order. Small portions of subtly combined ingredients, flavours and textures beautifully presented on dishes that complement the food are its hallmarks.

Rice, both sweet and savoury, is the staple of the Japanese diet; indeed, *gohan*, a Japanese word for rice, also refers to a meal. Rice is served steamed, pressed into cakes or made into noodles. Other staples are soybean products

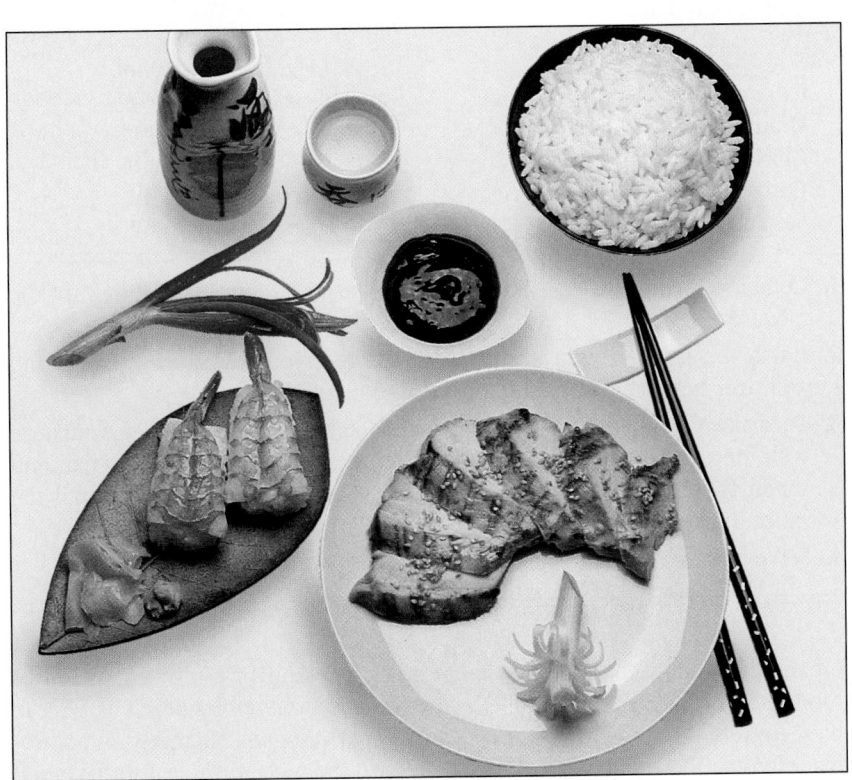

Japanese—(clockwise from top left) sake, white rice, chicken yakitori with dipping sauce, ebi sushi

✦✦✦
A JAPANESE MEAL

The aesthetics of a Japanese meal are of great importance. The aesthetic considerations relate to both the beauty of the food as well as to its presentation. Great care is often taken to cut, carve and form foods into delightful shapes: a carrot slice can be cut like a blossom for spring and a maple leaf in the autumn; a nigiri zushi can be tied with a bow of green onion; a choice morsel of raw fish can be formed into the shape of a rose. Lacquered and porcelain trays, dishes and covered bowls are commonly used for service, and care is taken to make sure the shape, material, size, colour and pattern complement the food.

Traditional dinners cooked by highly trained chefs known as *kappo* consist of at least four different courses. They combine liquid, crisp and simmered foods, some spicey and others bland. Alternating consistencies and tastes is a golden rule of Japanese cuisine. Generally tofu and invariably rice are served. Bites of rice are often eaten along with the other foods. Tea and sake are common dinner drinks.

Approximate values per serving:

Calories	677
Total fat	21 g
Saturated fat	5 g
Cholesterol	188 mg
Sodium	5495 mg
Total carbohydrates	27 g
Protein	75 g

including bean curd (tofu), bean paste (miso), sprouts, seeds and sauce. Japanese cuisine also relies on a variety of noodles, including ones made from wheat (the thin ramen, the thicker somen and the very thick udon), buckwheat (soba) and mung beans.

Fish and shellfish play important roles in Japanese cuisine for two reasons. First, Japan is a nation of mountainous islands that depends on the sea as the source for much of its protein. And, second, until the 19th century much of the Japanese population followed Buddhist teachings that prescribed a vegetarian diet supplemented with fish and shellfish. During this century, however, there has been a marked increase in the consumption of meat (especially beef) and poultry (especially chicken).

Typical seasonings—used, for the most part, quite judiciously—include rice wine vinegar, wasabi (a pungent green root erroneously called green horseradish), daikon (a white radish), pepper, sesame oil and seeds, ginger, soy sauce (known as *shoyu*, generally lighter and more delicate than Chinese soy sauce), rice wine (mirin, which is light and sweet and used only for cooking, and sake, a finer product used for cooking and drinking), tamari sauce, seaweed and pressed algae products (from the delicate to the very fishy), dried fish and shellfish and a variety of pickled foods (collectively known as *zuke*) as well as fresh herbs. Many dishes are marinated before cooking.

Yakitori, a classic Japanese flavouring combination of soy sauce, rice wine and sugar, is often used for broiled or grilled dishes.

✦✦✦
RECIPE 34.7
CHICKEN YAKITORI

Yield: 8 Servings

Soy sauce	8 fl. oz.	240 mL
Sake	8 fl. oz.	240 mL
Granulated sugar	2 oz.	60 g
Chicken breasts, boneless	2 lb.	1 kg
Cornstarch	1 Tbsp.	15 mL
Sesame seeds	1 Tbsp.	15 mL

1. Combine the soy sauce, sake and sugar. Reserve 8 ounces (240 mL) of the mixture.

2. Brush the chicken with a portion of the reserved soy sauce mixture and grill over hot charcoal until done, basting regularly.

3. To make the sauce, combine 2 ounces (60 mL) of the soy sauce mixture with the cornstarch. Bring the remainder to a boil in a small saucepan and stir in the cornstarch slurry. Stirring constantly, continue boiling until the sauce thickens. Simmer 1 minute.

4. Serve with short-grain white rice and garnish with sesame seeds.

Japanese cooking generally relies on quick cooking of bite-sized pieces of food. Foods can be grilled (called *yakimono*; if done tableside, as is typical, they are referred to as *nabemon*), steamed (*mushimono*), simmered in an aromatic broth (these liquid-based dishes often start with *dashi*, a fish-flavoured stock made from kelp and bonito; the cooking process is referred to as *nimono*) or deep-fat fried (*agemono*). The deep-fat frying technique and batter

---

♦♦♦

ASIAN FLAVORS
IN AN AMERICAN KITCHEN

Asian flavors now play an increasingly important role in Western food preparations. Whether called "East-West," "Pan-Asian," or "Pacific Style" food, this type of cooking ranges from ideas as simple as swirling butter into a classic Chinese black-bean sauce for a more velvet texture to drizzling an Asian sauce across the top of barbecued salmon to brushing butter infused with ginger, garlic, and cilantro on sourdough baguettes.

Several trends have led to this merging of cuisines. During the late 1960s the environmental movement and the rising popularity of health foods caused many Americans to reevaluate their diet and move away from meals based heavily on fats, sugar, and starches. Within a few years, starting in the 1970s, the growing interest in a healthier diet resulted in a new type of French cooking, *nouvelle cuisine*, which included experimentation with Asian seasonings. At about the same time, Richard Nixon's 1972 trip to China caused an enormous surge in the popularity of Chinese food in America. Chinese and other Asian seasonings became commonplace in supermarkets.

While many of us were traveling through Asia, fascinated with these new flavors, a huge Asian emigration to America began. Thai, Vietnamese, Korean, Japanese, and Filipino restaurants now proliferate. The new dishes offered in these restaurants, the "exotic" condiments and fresh herbs available in local Asian markets, and a flood of Asian cookbooks reinforce this ongoing trend. Examples of Asian and Pacific Style food appear on the menus of many of America's top young chefs. The fresh tastes of the Pacific are becoming a common part of contemporary cuisine.

—*from* CHOPSTIX *by* HUGH CARPENTER

---

known as tempura are actually derived from cooking techniques and recipes Portuguese Jesuits introduced to the Japanese during the late 16th century.

Japanese cuisine also offers a variety of raw foods, collectively known as *namamono*. Sashimi, small slices of fresh fish served with a soy sauce spiked with mustard and wasabi, is popular; as are *nigiri zushi* (small balls of sushi—vinegar-flavoured rice—topped with a slice of raw fish or shellfish) and *maki zushi* (raw fish or shellfish rolled in sushi and crisp seaweed). Recipes and techniques for these are given in Chapter 33, Appetizers and Sandwiches.

INDIAN CUISINES

Indian cuisine offers more than curry. The Indian subcontinent is home to many peoples, including Hindus, Buddhists and Muslims; each has a distinctive cuisine, and each cuisine has influenced the others, giving rise to several regional cuisines. Kasmir in the far north is famous for its meat and chickpeas, while the northern areas of Delhi and Bengal are famous for their tandoori and intensely sweet desserts, respectively. The western seaport of Bombay is known for its pork and vinegar, while vegetarian dishes made with tamarind, semolina and coconut are popular in the southern seaport of Madras.

The heart of Indian cookery is the masala, the combination of spices that gives each dish its distinctive taste. A masala's preparation, subtlety and sophistication are the tests by which chefs are often judged. The timing of its incorporation into the dish is critical. Common spices for masalas are turmeric, cumin seeds, coriander seeds, fenugreek, saffron, fennel seeds, mace, nutmeg, cardamom, clove, cinnamon, mustard seeds, sesame seeds, and black, red and white peppercorns. Garlic, onions and chiles are also popular flavourings, as are several herbs including coriander leaves, mint leaves and sweet basil. Souring agents include vinegar, lemon juice and imli (water with extract of tamarind). Curry powder is really nothing more than a commercial masala typically containing fenugreek, coriander, cumin, turmeric, ginger, celery seeds,

♦♦♦

When discussing foreign—that is, not French—foods, Escoffier opined that "if only for the sake of novelty or variety, it is occasionally permissible to poach upon the preserves of foreign nations."

Indian—(clockwise from top) naan, chicken tandoor, mango chutney, saffron rice

mace and pepper. The word *curry* is probably derived from the Tamil word *kari*, meaning sauce or combination of seasonings; the product is considered an inferior British invention never used in true Indian cooking.

◆◆◆

RECIPE 34.8

MASALA

Yield: 10 Tbsp. (90 g)

Coriander seeds	4 Tbsp.	60 g
Cumin seeds	2 Tbsp.	30 g
Black peppercorns, whole	1 Tbsp.	15 g
Cardamom seeds (measure after removing pods)	2 tsp.	10 g
Cinnamon, 3 inch (7.5-cm) sticks	4	4
Cloves, whole	1 tsp.	5 g
Nutmeg, whole	1	1

Approximate values per 1 oz. (30 g) serving:

Calories	92
Total fat	4 g
Saturated fat	.2 g
Cholesterol	0 mg
Sodium	19 mg
Total carbohydrates	16 g
Protein	3 g

1. In a small saucepan, separately dry-roast the coriander seeds, cumin seeds, peppercorns, cardamom seeds, cinnamon and cloves. As each begins to smell fragrant, remove from the pan to cool. After dry-roasting the cardamom, peel it, remove the seeds and discard the pods.

2. With a mortar and pestle or spice grinder, blend all the roasted spices to a fine powder.

3. Finely grate the nutmeg and mix it in with the other spices.

4. Store tightly covered and away from light.

The staples of Indian cuisine are rice, dals and bread. The rice is usually long-grain and served steamed and mixed with flavourings and garnishes. For special occasions, aromatic rices such as basmati are eaten. Dals are pulses such as lentils, beans and peas; nearly 60 varieties of protein-rich pulses are used in Indian cookery. These include the small, sweet yellow *chana dal, moong dal* (mung beans) and the salmon-coloured split pea called *masoor dal*. Breads, called *roti*, include *capitis* (flat, unleavened rounds made of whole wheat flour), *naan* (one of the few leavened breads), *paratha* (a flaky bread fried on a pan called a *tava*) and *poori* (a deep-fat-fried puffy bread). Many pan-fried breads are stuffed with savoury mixtures or dusted with flavourings. Rice and lentil flours are also used for breads.

Devout Muslims do not eat pork; devout Hindus do not eat beef and devout Buddhists do not eat any meat, poultry, fish, shellfish or dairy product.

For those who do eat meat and poultry, the most commonly eaten are mutton and chicken, prepared in a variety of ways: stewed with spices; marinated and grilled; braised in yogurt or cream (called *kormas*); sautéed and baked (called *bhoona*) or formed into meatballs (called *koftas*). A wide variety of freshwater and saltwater fish and shellfish are also consumed. Dairy products include a mild white fresh cheese known as *paneer*.

The long tradition of vegetarianism and the variety of vegetables and spices available have made for a vegetarian cuisine rich in flavours and textures. Vegetables are usually fried with spices and served without any sauce. These pungent dishes are known as *foogath* in the South and *bhujia* in the North. Vegetables can be puréed and delicately spiced (called *bharta*); or mashed, shaped into balls and fried.

Chutneys are relishes made from fruits, vegetables and herbs. Sometimes their flavours are tempered by marinating or cooking, although most fresh chutneys are nothing more than a mixture of raw foods, ground or finely cut and blended with seasonings. Chutneys are used to add contrast to the highly spiced dishes that dominate Indian cuisines.

Clarified butter made from water buffalo milk, known as *ghee*, is an important cooking medium, although ghee's expense has made a hydrogenated vegetable fat called *vanaspati* more popular. Usually, only meat is cooked in ghee; vegetable oils are used for vegetables.

The *degchi* is a commonly used cooking vessel. Traditionally made of brass but now also made of aluminum, it is a tall, straight-sided, flat-rimmed pot used for boiling, stewing, braising or steaming. When lidded, it can be used as an oven by placing coals below the pot as well as on the lid.

Northern India

The cuisine of Northern India reflects the strong Muslim presence found in northern and central India since the 16th-century Mogul invasions. This presence has given rise to a regional cuisine using meat. The area's geography favours wheat, not rice, so capitis is a dietary staple. Generally, Northern Indian cuisine produces dryer foods with thick sauces. A typical Northern masala calls for cumin, fenugreek, ginger and garlic. After the spices are ground and mixed, they are added to the dish without further preparation.

One of the best-known Northern Indian dishes is tandoori chicken. The tandoor is a jar-shaped clay oven usually buried in the earth and heated by placing hot coals inside. The meat or poultry is threaded on skewers and placed inside the oven to cook. The finished product has a wonderfully dry, crusty surface. Although it is difficult to reproduce the surface in a conventional oven, it is possible to reproduce the flavours.

◆◆◆

RECIPE 34.9

TANDOORI MURGH
(CHICKEN TANDOOR)

Yield: 4 Servings

Roasting chicken, 3 lb. (1.3 kg)	1	1
Saffron strands	1/2 tsp.	3 mL
Boiling water	1 Tbsp.	15 mL
Garlic, chopped	2 Tbsp.	30 mL
Fresh ginger, peeled and minced	1 Tbsp.	15 mL
Lemon juice	2 Tbsp.	30 mL
Chilli powder	1 tsp.	5 mL
Paprika	1-1/2 tsp.	8 mL
Masala (Recipe 34.8)	2 tsp.	10 mL
Salt	1 tsp.	5 g
Ghee (or clarified butter or canola oil)	3 Tbsp.	45 mL
Lemons, wedged	2	2

1. Quarter and skin the chicken, making slits in the drumsticks, thighs and breasts to allow the spices to penetrate.

2. Steep the saffron in boiling water for 10 minutes. Then combine it with the garlic, ginger, lemon juice, chilli powder, paprika, masala and salt; blend until smooth.

3. Season the chicken with the spice mixture, covering the entire surface, especially the slits. Cover and marinate, under refrigeration, for at least 2 hours or overnight.

4. Roast the chicken on a rack at 350°F (180°C), basting periodically with ghee, until done, approximately 45 minutes.

5. Serve hot, garnished with lemon wedges and accompanied by naan.

Approximate values per serving:

Calories	898
Total fat	55 g
Saturated fat	19 g
Cholesterol	311 mg
Sodium	757 mg
Total carbohydrates	7 g
Protein	90 g

Southern India

The cuisine of Southern India is heavily influenced by Hindus. It offers a wide range of meatless dishes with rich, spicy sauces. Rice is the principal crop and it is eaten with almost every meal, as plain or flavoured rice or as rice-flour breads such as *idli* and *dosa*. Southern Indian cuisine uses more fresh herbs than Northern Indian cuisine and its masalas are wet; that is, the ground spices are mixed into a paste with vinegar, water or coconut milk. (Wet masalas must be used immediately.) Typical spices used in Southern Indian masalas include mustard seed, tamarind and asafetida (a fennel-like resin). Chiles are more popular in the south than in the north, as is garlic.

◆◆◆

RECIPE 34.10

MURGHI KARI
(CHICKEN CURRY)

Yield: 4 Servings

Onions, small dice	8 oz.	250 g
Garlic, crushed	2 tsp.	10 mL

Ghee (or clarified butter)	2 Tbsp.	30 mL
Fresh ginger, fine dice	2 oz.	60 g
Turmeric	1-1/2 tsp.	8 mL
Coriander seeds, ground	1-1/2 tsp.	8 mL
Cumin seeds, ground	1 tsp.	5 mL
Cayenne pepper	1 tsp.	5 mL
Fenugreek, ground	1/2 tsp.	3 mL
Coconut milk	20 oz.	600 mL
Roasting chicken, 3 lb. (1.3 kg), cut into 8 pieces	1	1
Salt	1 tsp.	5 g
Green chiles, slit lengthwise	3	3
Lemon juice	1 oz.	30 mL

1. Stir-fry the onions and garlic in the ghee until the onions are golden brown.
2. To make the wet masala, mix the ginger, turmeric, coriander, cumin, cayenne pepper and fenugreek; add just enough of the coconut milk to form a paste.
3. Add the wet masala to the onions and stir-fry for 8 minutes.
4. Add the chicken pieces and cook, turning them frequently, for 6–8 minutes.
5. Add the remaining coconut milk, salt and chiles. Bring to a boil, cover and reduce to a simmer. Cook until the chicken is done, approximately 45 minutes.
6. Just before service, stir in the lemon juice and adjust the seasonings. Serve with saffron rice and a chutney.

Approximate values per serving:

Calories	1198
Total fat	83 g
Saturated fat	44 g
Cholesterol	303 mg
Sodium	781 mg
Total carbohydrates	22 g
Protein	95 g

◆◆◆

RECIPE 34.11

KESAR CHAVAL (SAFFRON RICE)

Yield: 6 Servings

Basmati rice	1 pt.	450 mL
Saffron threads	1 tsp.	5 mL
Boiling water	1 qt.	900 mL
Ghee (or clarified butter)	3 oz.	90 mL
Cinnamon, 2-inch (5-cm) sticks	1	1
Cloves, whole	4	4
Onion, fine dice	5 oz.	150 g
Dark brown sugar	1 Tbsp.	15 mL
Salt	2 tsp.	10 g
Cardamom seeds	1/4 tsp.	2 mL

1. Wash the rice and drain thoroughly.
2. Steep the saffron in 2 ounces (60 mL) of the boiling water.
3. In a saucepan, heat the ghee, add the cinnamon and cloves. Add the onions and stir-fry until they are soft and slightly brown.
4. Add the rice and stir until it is well coated with the ghee and the grains are a light golden colour.

Approximate values per serving:

Calories	374
Total fat	16 g
Saturated fat	9 g
Cholesterol	38 mg
Sodium	659 mg
Total carbohydrates	54 g
Protein	5 g

Continued

5. Stirring constantly, add the remaining boiling water, brown sugar, salt and cardamom seeds. Bring to a boil and reduce to a simmer.
6. Gently stir in the saffron and its water, cover and simmer until the rice has absorbed all the liquid.
7. Fluff with a fork and serve at once.

━━━━━━━━━━━━━━━━━━━━━

Throughout India, many foods are eaten in the form of savoury snacks (collectively known as *chat*), which are served as appetizers or at teatime. Examples include *chanachur* (made from split peas, peanuts, lemon, peppers and lentil flour, all the ingredients being fried separately), *samosas* (deep-fat fried tidbits like turnovers, stuffed with meat, potatoes or vegetables), *pakoras* (vegetables or other foods dipped in chickpea flour and deep-fat fried), spiced fish balls and eggplant fritters served with chutney.

Sweet snacks (collectively known as *meethai*) are also an integral part of Indian cuisines. Many are made from milk that is condensed into a thick mass called *mawa*. *Mawa* is then cooked with sugar and flavourings such as coconut, almond, pistachio or kewra (a perfumed flower essence). *Jelebis* are pretzel-like sweets made from a batter of wheat and chickpea flour, oil and curds that is deep-fat fried and then dipped into a sugar syrup.

NORTH AFRICAN AND MIDDLE EASTERN CUISINES

Stretching from Morocco at the northwest tip of Africa, along the southern and eastern portions of the Mediterranean Sea and north to Lebanon, is a land primarily populated by Arabs. It is rich in religious and culinary traditions and offers a range of national cuisines. These various cuisines can be divided into two main groups: North African and Middle Eastern.

All of the cuisines, however, share certain staples, seasonings and a fondness for sweets. Wheat in various forms is eaten throughout the area. Legumes, including lentils, beans and peas, provide starch. Pork is virtually nonexistent for religious reasons; lamb is the principal meat, chicken the principal poultry. Fish from the Mediterranean is also popular. Garlic, onions, peppers, tomatoes and citrus are commonly used flavouring ingredients. Spices include cumin, ginger and peppercorns; herbs include mint, coriander and parsley. Eggplants, cucumbers, squash, okra, tomatoes, quinces, dates, figs, melons, pomegranates, mangoes and bananas are popular. A consistent theme among the various cuisines is a combination of fruits and nuts cooked with savoury meat dishes.

North African

The cuisines of North Africa include those of Morocco, Algeria and Tunisia as well as those of the more nomadic Bedouin tribes. This area, often referred to as the Maghreb, was once the granary for Imperial Rome. More recently, France was the dominant foreign influence. North African cuisine is based on cereals, vegetables, dried fruits and grilled meats. The national cuisines differ to a degree: Foods are more highly seasoned in Algeria and Tunisia and more subtly spiced in Morocco.

A principal spice mixture (known as *ras al hanout* in Morocco) consists of cinnamon, cumin, coriander, ginger and turmeric. Other North African season-

Middle Eastern—(clockwise from top left) baklava, medjool dates, pita bread, harissa, Tangier couscous

ings and flavouring ingredients include garlic, onions, tomatoes, olives, fresh coriander leaves, fresh mint leaves, parsley and dried limes or lemons.

Many North African meat dishes include fruit or other sweet foods. For example, *tajine*, a type of slow-cooked ragout, may be made with mutton or rabbit with prunes and accompanied by fennel with lemon; chicken is cooked with cinnamon, kumquats and onions, and mutton is cooked with quinces and honey. Meats, often reduced to bite-sized chunks or ground balls, are often grilled or spit-roasted as kebabs. Fish can be grilled or fried. Vegetables are cooked in a sauce and frequently served with scrambled eggs, marinated and served in a salad or stuffed with sweet and savoury foods. Soups are always highly aromatic and often associated with religious festivities. The soups often combine dried vegetables or cereals (lentils, beans, chickpeas, unripe wheat) with meat (diced mutton or chicken) or fish.

Wheat is the principal grain and it is used to make one of the better-known North African dishes: couscous. Couscous refers to both the starch and the completed dish. The starch is made of semolina flour produced from hard durum wheat. It is steamed over a watery stew of lamb, chicken, beef (usually in the form of meatballs), fish or tripe and vegetables in a couscousier. A couscousier consists of two bulbous pots. The bottom one sits on the heat and holds the watery stew. The second sits on top of the first; it has a perforated bottom and holds the couscous. As the stew simmers, steam rising from it gently cooks the couscous and infuses flavours. The dish can be flavoured with saffron (Morocco), tomato purée (Algeria) or ginger and pepper (Tunisia). Traditionally mixed with smeun fat, a sort of rancid butter, the couscous and stew are more typically served with harissa, a hot and pungent sauce (see Recipe 11.14). Couscous is eaten by taking a small amount of the couscous along with a morsel of meat or vegetable, rolling it into a ball and popping it into the mouth. This entire action should be accomplished with only the first three fingers of the right hand.

=== ◆◆◆ ===

RECIPE 34.12
SEKSU TANJAOUI (TANGIER COUSCOUS)

Yield: 4 Servings

Ingredient		
Roaster chicken, quartered with giblets, 3–4 lb. (1.3–1.8 kg)	1	1
Salt	2 tsp.	10 mL
Pepper	1 Tbsp.	15 mL
Ginger, ground	2-1/2 tsp.	12 mL
Saffron, pulverized and mixed with turmeric	1/2 tsp.	3 mL
Cayenne pepper	pinch	pinch
Onions, medium, quartered	3	3
Bouquet garni:		
Fresh coriander	4 sprigs	4 sprigs
Fresh parsley	4 sprigs	4 sprigs
Whole butter	8 oz.	240 g
Water	5 pt.	2.5 L
Couscous	1 lb. 8 oz.	700 g
Onion, large, julienne	1	1
Raisins	3 oz.	90 g
Chicken stock	as needed	as needed

1. Place the chicken, salt, pepper, ginger, saffron, cayenne, onion quarters, bouquet garni and half the butter in the bottom of the couscousier. Melt the butter and stir the ingredients to coat them with the melted butter. Add 5 pints (2.5 L) of water; bring to a boil, reduce to a simmer and cook 1 hour.
2. Combine the couscous with 3 quarts (3 L) of cold water; mix and drain. Gently break apart any lumps.
3. After the stew has simmered for 1 hour, place the couscous in the top pot or a metal colander suspended over the pot, lower the heat and steam for 20 minutes. Do not cover the couscous while it steams.
4. Remove the colander and add the sliced onions and raisins to the stew; adjust its consistency with water or chicken stock if necessary. Replace the colander and steam for 15 minutes. Dot the couscous with the remaining butter and steam for 5 minutes. Fluff the couscous with a fork to distribute the melted butter.
5. Serve the couscous with the stew and Harissa: see Recipe 11.14.

Approximate values per serving:

Calories	392
Total fat	25 g
Saturated fat	11 g
Cholesterol	115 mg
Sodium	399 mg
Total carbohydrates	14 g
Protein	28 g

Middle Eastern

The cuisines of the Middle East include those of Egypt, Jordan, Syria and Lebanon. This is the southern portion of the Levant, an area that stretches from Egypt through Israel, north to Turkey and east through Greece. Now predominantly Arab, the area has been ruled by the Egyptians, Romans, Turks, British and French, to name a few. Each nationality has left its mark.

Generally, rice and wheat (wheat for bread flour and bulgur) are the principal staples, as are legumes, especially chickpeas. Chickpeas are used in many dishes, most notably *hummus*, in which they are mashed with sesame seed paste, and *ful medames*, an ancient Egyptian dish in which the beans are flavoured with garlic and dressed with lemon juice and oil. Important spices include cinnamon, cumin, ginger, coriander, allspice and hot peppers, as well as some more unusual spices such as *mahlab* (ground black-cherry pits, which gives food a slightly fruity flavour), *zatar* (a variety of thyme that tastes like a cross between thyme and oregano) and *sumac* (which gives meats a woody taste). Dried whole limes and verjuice are also used for flavourings.

Yogurt is used as a beverage, pudding and flavouring ingredient. Olive oil is a typical cooking medium as well as a dressing and a basic ingredient in many of the vegetable dishes called *yakhni*. Sesame seed oil is also used, especially in Lebanese dishes. Tahini is a popular paste made from crushed sesame seeds. Produce of importance includes garlic, okra, cucumbers, eggplants and lemons as well as tomatoes and peppers (New World imports).

Several varieties of freshwater and saltwater fish are enjoyed grilled, baked or poached. Little beef is consumed, although camel is eaten (hump meat is the choicest). Lamb, however, dominates Middle Eastern cuisine. It can be grilled, roasted, braised, stewed with vegetables or made into a variety of meatballs (called *kofta*) and kebabs. It is also the basic ingredient in the Lebanese and Syrian dish known as *kibbeh*. For kibbeh, ground lamb is mixed with onion-flavoured bulgur, parsley and pine nuts. It is then shaped into cakes and grilled, deep-fat fried or baked, or stuffed with savoury ingredients and deep-fat fried. Chicken is also popular, whether spit-roasted, marinated in oil and citrus or stuffed with rice and pine nuts and baked in an earthenware casserole.

❖❖❖

RECIPE 34.13

DAJAJ MAHSHY
(CHICKEN STUFFED WITH RICE, CURRANTS AND PINE NUTS)

Yield: 4 Servings

Long-grain white rice	1 cup	250 mL
Whole butter	4 oz.	120 g
Onions, fine dice	3 oz.	90 g
Pine nuts	3 Tbsp.	45 mL
Water	1 pt.	500 mL
Dried currants	2 Tbsp.	30 mL
Salt	2 Tbsp.	30 g
Pepper	TT	TT
Fryer chicken, 3 to 3-1/2 lb. (1.3 to 1.5 kg), including coarsely chopped giblets	1	1
Yogurt	2 oz.	60 mL

1. Wash the rice and set aside.
2. Sauté the onions in the butter until transparent.
3. Add the coarsely chopped giblets and pine nuts and sauté until the pine nuts are browned.

Approximate values per serving:	
Calories	1327
Total fat	79 g
Saturated fat	30 g
Cholesterol	376 mg
Sodium	3208 mg
Total carbohydrates	49 g
Protein	103 g

Continued

4. Stir in the rice and cook until the grains are coated with butter.

5. Add the water, currants, 1 tablespoon (15 g) of the salt and pepper to taste; cover and cook until the rice is done.

6. Remove from the heat and mix in the remaining butter.

7. Stuff the chicken's cavity with the rice mixture and truss.

8. Season the yogurt with the remaining salt and pepper. Brush half of the mixture over the chicken. Roast the chicken at 350°F (180°C), basting periodically with the yogurt mixture until done, approximately 1 hour.

9. Carve the chicken and serve it with the rice.

Middle Eastern sweets are very sweet; they include *ataif* (pancakes drenched with syrup and topped with chopped nuts and thick clotted cream), *muhallabia* (a milk pudding flavoured with orange flower water) and *ma'amoul* (pastries stuffed with dates or nuts and coated with powdered sugar or served in cream) as well as the more familiar halva, candied dates, baklava and Turkish delight.

MEXICAN CUISINE

Mexican cuisine is rooted in its pre-Columbian past and nurtured by centuries of Spanish influence. For thousands of years before Columbus's arrival, the people of Mexico lived on a diet of squash, corn (maize) and beans supplemented with fresh vegetables (avocados, peppers, tomatoes), fruit (manioc and bananas) and occasionally fish, shellfish, game and wild poultry. The population relied on steaming and slow cooking methods such as wrapping meats, poultry and fish in leaves and slow-roasting them over hot embers or stewing foods with little liquid in tightly lidded earthenware pots.

In the wake of Cortez's conquest of Mexico in 1521 came pigs, cattle and dairy products, chicken, wheat, rice, sesame seeds, citrus and almonds. The Spanish also brought with them a new manner of cooking: rendering fat from meat and using the rendered fat and vegetable oils to fry foods. All of these foods, to one degree or another, were soon integrated into the local cuisines; sautéing and pan-frying became standard cooking methods. (Although the people of Mexico quickly adopted European foods and cooking methods, Europeans waited centuries before adopting Mexican foods and appreciating Mexican cuisine.)

Mexico has given rise to several regional cuisines of note. Unfortunately, many consumers in this country erroneously believe that Mexican cuisine starts and ends with tacos and refried beans.

The most characteristic feature of Mexican cookery is the widespread use of chiles. There are about 100 varieties, many of which have a hot, pungent taste. (Unlike English, Mexican Spanish differentiates between the word *hot* as applied to a food's temperature—*caliente*—and *hot* as applied to its degree of spiciness—*chiloso*.) Fresh chiles can be served raw; stuffed and baked; stewed; chopped with tomatoes, herbs and oil for a salsa; or minced and used as a seasoning. Or they can be dried and used whole or ground as a seasoning. Other seasonings include garlic, cinnamon, cumin, oregano, onion, achiote seeds, basil, peppercorns, cilantro and other fresh herbs.

Fresh vegetable salsas accompany many dishes. Guacamole, for example, is an ancient dish made from avocados and flavourings such as onions and tomatoes. The numerous fresh salsas are usually categorized as either red or green. Red salsa, called *salsa roja*, is made from chiles (usually dried), onions

Mexican—(clockwise from top left) poblano rice, poblano chili, coconut candies, chicken mole on corn tortillas, hibiscus water

and tomato. Green salsa, called *salsa verde*, is made from chiles (usually fresh), onions and tomatillos.

Corn flour is used to make a dough called *masa*. Popular throughout Mexico, smooth masa is pressed (traditionally by hand) into flat rounds and quickly cooked on a griddle to make tortillas. Tortillas are eaten like bread, filled with savoury mixtures for burritos, fried crisp and topped for tostadas, folded around savoury mixtures and fried for tacos, or used for turnovers (quesadillas, empañadas and enchiladas). Tamales are made from a coarser masa dough that is stuffed with a savoury mixture of beans, meats or poultry, encased in corn husks and steamed. Many of these masa-based dishes are considered snack foods known as *antojitos*, the traditional portable snacks of the Mexican marketplace.

Wheat flour is also used for tortillas (especially in north Mexico) as well as for a variety of leavened breads. Rice, although not indigenous, is also a staple of Mexican diets.

As they were during pre-Columbian times, beans are still a staple. They are usually dried, then reconstituted in water and served in a soupy fashion, or mashed and fried in lard or oil to make a smooth paste called *frijoles refritos* (refried beans).

Chicken is popular throughout the country. Meat is used somewhat sparingly in most Mexican regional cuisines. Beef and dairy products are more widely consumed in the north, while goat and goat cheese are more typical of the country's central regions. Fish and shellfish are eaten along both coasts.

The ancient manner of slow cooking is still used for meats, poultry and fish; there is a great variety of stews and soups. The ancient cooking method known as *pibil*, in which meats were wrapped in maguey or banana leaves and cooked in a pit lined with hot coals, is often replaced today by steaming banana-leaf-wrapped meats. Some meats and vegetables are also grilled (called *al carbon*) or seared and roasted. A popular meat marinade known as *adobado* combines chiles, garlic and herbs.

Sauce making is very different from European traditions and includes a step known as "frying the sauce." Most sauces start with dried peppers that are soaked, seeded and ground to a paste and then mixed with herbs, spices and vegetables. The mixture, sometimes thickened with ground toasted pumpkin seeds or nuts, is then puréed and fried in oil or lard. This sauce is added to partially cooked and drained meat or poultry and the dish is then simmered to blend the flavours.

Moles are dishes made with a classic cooking method that incorporates this sauce-making technique. The meat or poultry is cooked and then steeped or simmered in a sauce made from chiles and other ingredients.

◆◆◆

RECIPE 34.14
MOLE ROJO CON POLLO
(RICH RED MOLE WITH CHICKEN)

Yield: 4 Servings

Chiles, dried, stemmed, seeded and deveined:		
Chiles anchos	2 oz.	60 g
Chiles mulatos	1 oz.	30 g
Chiles pasilla	1/3 oz.	10 g
Vegetable oil	3 oz.	90 mL
Tomato, medium, roasted, cored, peeled and diced	1	1
Medium tomatillos, husked, washed and simmered until tender	3	3
Mexican chocolate, chopped	1 oz.	30 g
Oregano, dried	1/2 tsp.	3 mL
Thyme, dried	1/4 tsp.	2 mL
Bay leaf	1	1
Peppercorns	8	8
Cloves	3	3
Cinnamon stick	1 in.	2.5 cm
Sesame seeds	2 Tbsp.	30 mL
Raisins	2 Tbsp.	30 mL
Garlic, chopped	1 tsp.	5 mL
Onion, thickly sliced	2 oz.	60 g
Peanuts	1 oz.	30 g
Plantain, small, peeled and diced (optional)	4 oz.	120 g
Corn tortilla, stale	1/2	1/2
White bread slice, stale	1	1
Chicken stock	1 qt.	900 mL
Chicken, 3-1/2 lb. (1.6 kg), quartered	1	1
Salt	1 tsp.	5 mL
Granulated sugar	1 Tbsp.	15 mL

1. Sauté the chiles in 3 tablespoons (45 mL) of oil until nutty brown.

Remove, reserving the oil. Cover the chiles with boiling water and soak for 1 hour. Drain and set aside.

2. Combine the tomatoes, tomatillos, chocolate, oregano and thyme in a large bowl. Pulverize the bay leaf, peppercorns, cloves and cinnamon and combine with the tomato mixture.

3. Toast the sesame seeds and add them to the tomato mixture.

4. Sauté the raisins in the reserved chile oil until they puff; add them to the tomato mixture.

5. In the same oil, sauté the garlic, onion and peanuts until they are well browned; add to the tomato mixture.

6. Sauté the plantain until golden brown; add to the tomato mixture.

7. Sauté the tortilla until brown; shred it and add to the tomato mixture.

8. Lay the bread in the pan and quickly flip it to coat both sides with the fat; then brown it on both sides. Tear it into pieces and add to the tomato mixture.

9. Stir the tomato mixture well. Purée it with 6 ounces (180 mL) of chicken stock and strain through a china cap.

10. Purée the reconstituted chiles with 2 ounces (60 mL) of chicken stock; strain through a china cap in a separate bowl and set aside.

11. Sauté the chicken in oil. Remove and degrease the pan. In the same pan, sauté the chile purée until it is thick and dark. Add the tomato purée and cook until thick.

12. Add 1-1/2 pints (700 mL) of chicken stock. Simmer the sauce 45 minutes. Season with salt and sugar. If the sauce is thicker than whipping cream, dilute it with additional chicken stock.

13. Add the chicken to the pan and braise until done.

14. Degrease the sauce. Garnish the chicken with sesame seeds and serve with the sauce and Arroz a la Poblana (see Recipe 34.15).

Approximate values per serving:

Calories	844
Total fat	54 g
Saturated fat	12 g
Cholesterol	132 mg
Sodium	1468 mg
Total carbohydrates	42 g
Protein	52 g

◆◆◆

RECIPE 34.15

Arroz a la Poblana
(Rice with Poblano Chiles)

Yield: 4 Servings

Vegetable oil	1-1/2 Tbsp.	20 mL
Onion, small dice	5 oz.	150 g
Long- or medium-grain rice	1 cup	250 mL
Chicken stock, hot	14 oz.	400 mL
Salt	TT	TT
Chiles poblanos, fresh, roasted and peeled, seeded, julienne	3	3
Fresh corn kernels	6 oz.	180 g
Mexican queso fresco (or feta or farmer's cheese), crumbled	5 oz.	150 g
Parsley or cilantro sprigs	as needed	as needed

Approximate values per serving:

Calories	333
Total fat	11 g
Saturated fat	6 g
Cholesterol	33 mg
Sodium	629 mg
Total carbohydrates	48 g
Protein	11 g

1. Sauté the onion in oil until translucent. Add the rice and sauté without colouring.

Continued

2. Add the hot stock, salt, chiles and corn to the rice mixture; bring to a boil, reduce to a simmer, cover and cook until all liquid has evaporated.

3. Add the crumbled cheese to the rice and toss to combine.

4. Serve as a side dish garnished with parsley or cilantro sprigs.

Sweets, especially candies, candied fruits and hard cookies or cakes, are popular throughout Mexico. The more commonly encountered desserts such as flans and caramels are derived from the Spanish tradition.

Mexico is a country rich in regional cuisines. A few observations about them follow.

Central (Mexico City)

Blended with tomatoes, the fiery hot *guajillos* or smoky *chipotles* are the principal chiles used for sauces. Also popular are the common black chile and the *pasilla*. A great variety of beans are used, but the purplish *flor de mayo* and the tan *bayo* are the most popular. Cooking methods include mole. A typical meat dish would be lamb wrapped in maguey or banana leaves cooked in brick pits and served with a sauce of fermented maguey juice and pasilla.

West Central (Guadalajara)

The defining sauce is made with a purée of the very hot *de arbol* chiles, sometimes thickened with tomatillos. De arbol also come bottled, pickled with vinegar. A great variety of beans are used, but as with Central Mexican cuisine, flor de mayo and bayo are the most popular. A typical meat dish would be kid (young goat) marinated in chiles and slow-cooked in a sealed container. From the west coast also comes seviche, a dish of finely chopped fish and shellfish marinated in lime juice, cilantro, tomato chunks and herbs.

Central East Coast (Veracruz)

Although still used in abundance, chiles play a less prominent role. Herbs (especially cilantro, basil, bay leaves, parsley and oregano) and spices (peppercorns and cinnamon) are a vital part of the cuisine. The area is known for its fish and shellfish cooked in a chunky broth of olives, herbs and chiles (usually jalapeños). The basic bean is black and usually cooked with a sprig of epazote.

Northern (Sonora, Chihuahua)

As in West Central Mexico, the defining sauce is made with a purée of the very hot de arbol chiles, sometimes thickened with tomatillos. This region is known for its wheat and beef, which is sometimes dried and called *carne seca*. A typical pork dish is the simmered *carne con chile colorado*. Popular beans are pintos and the yellowish-tan *piruano*.

Southeastern (Yucatan)

This regional cuisine is unique, using achiote seeds as the principal seasoning. Fresh chiles are usually ground with salt and lime or purchased in a bottled form. A vinegary orange-red and a green sauce made with the local *habañero* chiles are especially popular. Seasonings are added to most dishes in the form of a paste that can be brick red (made from achiote seeds ground with oregano, black pepper, cloves and cumin mixed with garlic and vinegar), olive-amber (a mild blend of garlic, allspice, cinnamon and other spices) or coal black (made from burnt chiles, achiote, spices and garlic). A typical pork dish is flavoured with achiote and wrapped in banana leaves, then slowly steamed or roasted. The most commonly used bean is black and usually cooked with a sprig of epazote.

Southern (Oaxaca)

A wide range of dried peppers are used in many different stews and sauces, some of which combine sweeter spices such as cloves and cinnamon with savoury foods. A typical meat or poultry dish would be kid or chicken marinated in chiles, then wrapped in avocado leaves and steamed. Some consider this region to produce the finest *chorizo*, a pork sausage made with herbs, spices, a touch of vinegar and deep red chiles. The basic black bean is also regularly used throughout the south.

CONCLUSION

Although the foods and flavourings may differ from the cuisine of one culture to the cuisine of another, the fundamentals of cookery do not: Quality ingredients need to be prepared, seasoned and cooked, then presented in an attractive and appropriate manner. With a good purveyor, a little practice and an understanding of the principles discussed throughout this book, a world of great cooking and eating is available to you and your customers.

QUESTIONS FOR DISCUSSION

1. Which of the cuisines discussed rely on slow-cooking methods for meats? Which rely on quick-cooking methods?
2. Identify the flavour principle for each of the cuisines discussed.
3. Which New World product plays an important role in some Asian cuisines?
4. Compare and contrast the cuisines of Japan and North Africa.
5. Compare and contrast one of the cuisines of India and one of the cuisines of China.
6. Explain why there may be several cuisines within a single country.

WEBLINKS

Moroccan Recipes
  www.Maghreb.Net/countries/morocco/recipes.html
Web Resources for Japanese Food
  www.bento.com/morefood.html
Cuisine of India
  www.incore.com/india/cuisine.html
Jewish Food Recipe Archives
  www.eskimo.com/~jefffree/recipes/
Hungarian Cuisine
  www.fsz.bme.hu/hungary/cuisine/cuisine.html
Chinascape: Chinese Food and Tea
  www.chinascape.org/china/culture/food/index.html

CHAPTER 35
PLATE PRESENTATION

hile food preparation is very much a science, food presentation is an art. Good plate presentation results from careful attention to the colours, shapes, textures and arrangements of the foods. Great plate presentation requires experience and style.

In this chapter we describe several methods of presenting foods. We realize that for every guideline we suggest, there are exceptions. Nor are our examples meant to take the place of more traditional techniques. They are intended only to spark your imagination. As you gain experience, you will undoubtedly develop your own style.

The final step in food preparation is to justify the hours of hard work spent cooking the food by serving and presenting it properly.

Service is the process of delivering the selected foods to diners in the proper fashion. Hot foods should be served very hot and on heated plates; cold foods should be served very cold and on chilled plates. Foods should be cooked to the proper degree of doneness: A roast rack of lamb ordered medium rare should be medium rare—not medium, not rare. Pasta should be served al dente—slightly chewy, not mushy. Bread should be fresh, not stale. Portion sizes should be appropriate. First courses and appetizers should be small enough so that the diner can still appreciate the courses that follow. Rich foods should be served in smaller portions than other foods.

Presentation is the process of offering the selected foods to diners in a fashion that is visually pleasing. When presenting foods, always bear in mind that diners eat first with their eyes and then with their mouths. The foods must be pleasantly and appropriately coloured, cut or moulded. And the colours, textures, shapes and arrangements of all foods must work together to form a pleasing composition on the plate. Any decorative touches such as the manipulation of sauces or the addition of garnishes should be done thoughtfully and well. Most importantly, plates should be neat and clean. Inspect all plates before they leave the kitchen; wipe drops of sauce or specks of food from plate rims with a clean towel.

Presentation techniques are divided here into two broad categories: Those applied to specific foods and those applied to the plate as a whole. The techniques described here use some foods or recipes that appear elsewhere in the text.

THE FOOD

The most attractive foods will always be the ones that are properly prepared, but they can be made even more attractive by cutting or moulding them into various shapes. Both of these techniques preserve the integrity of the food; that is, neither changes the food itself, they only change the way the food is presented.

◆◆◆

GARNISHES
(AN ADMITTEDLY CRANKY ADMONITION)

I am a strong believer in the simple, edible garnish that has a close flavor kinship to the dish. In my world, dyed daikon flamingos, writhing carrot dragons, and blinking Christmas lights in the empty eye sockets of a stir-fried lobster—all garnishes of the Hong Kong sort—are out. So, too, are radish flowers, tomato rosettes, and vegetable pellets sculpted to look like suppositories. I find all of this loathsome.

In my own rather minimalist style, the fanciest I get is an occasional scallion brush. Otherwise, a leggy piece of coriander or a flourish of scallion rings are all that our already colorful dishes require. Or, if the dish is green, a confetti of finely diced red bell pepper will do the job.

The issue is a visible one, but it needs to make sense on your tongue. A garnish is primarily designed to tickle the eye, but it also should meld seamlessly with the other flavors on the plate or contrast with them in a meaningful way.

Garnishing the rims of plates—a current feature of trendy restaurants in the 90s—is something I find very peculiar. I spill and splatter my own food quite nicely, thank you, and don't want the kitchen to do it for me.

Ditto the rage for a whole chive aloft each appetizer or a cage of spun sugar looming above a dessert. It is admittedly wonderful to give a little height to a dish: One can arrange cold shrimp, for example, in a lively tumble with just a touch or two. But the unrelated vertical garnish is often absurd, a bit of Dr. Seuss on the plate.

I sound cranky, and perhaps I am! Restaurant cooks frequently spend too much time decorating their food, and too little time paying attention to its taste. This, I think, is sad.

—from CHINA MOON COOKBOOK
by BARBARA TROPP

Preparing Foods Properly

Foods look best when prepared properly. A sirloin steak grilled medium rare should be pink inside; its surface should glisten and be branded with well-defined and neatly executed crosshatch marks. When serving asparagus with hollandaise the stalks should be bright green and crisp looking; the hollandaise sauce should be smooth and shiny, not grainy and dingy. A lemon meringue pie should be attractively browned on top; the filling should be a true lemony yellow and the crust golden brown and without cracks.

Whether a recipe calls for browning foods under a salamander before service, poaching a galantine of chicken wrapped in cheesecloth to maintain its shape or adding vinegar when braising red cabbage, proper cooking procedures can enhance the texture, shape and colour of many cooked foods. Throughout this text we have discussed the proper cooking procedures for many, many foods. Use them.

Cutting Foods

The careful cutting of foods often increases their visual appeal and reflects the chef's attention to detail. Here we distinguish between cutting foods to decorate the plate and cutting the foods to be consumed. Decorative garnishes such as tomato and radish roses, frizzed scallions, watermelon boats and the like fall within the former category. Cutting foods into beautiful garnishes is an art unto itself, requiring skill and practice. While beyond the scope of this text, books on creating food garnishes are listed in the Bibliography.

The latter category includes the meats, poultry, fish, vegetables and starches that are the meal. Each should be carefully cut. Vegetables can be cut into uniform shapes and sizes such as julienne, batonnet or turned. If serving sliced meats or poultry, the slices should be of even thickness; fish can be cut into fillets. Individual stew ingredients and soup or salad garnishes should be of uniform sizes. All of these techniques are simple, fundamental and effective.

Some foods take the shape of the pan in which they are cooked. Polenta and gratin or scalloped potatoes, for example, can be presented attractively when baked in and removed from individual casseroles, or they can be baked in a hotel pan and then cut into various shapes.

BASIC PROCEDURE FOR CUTTING POLENTA

1. Cook the polenta according to the recipe. When it is done, pour it onto a well-oiled or buttered half sheet pan. Then chill it in the refrigerator until firm.
2. Once the polenta is firm, flip the pan over onto a work table. Lift off the pan; the polenta will come out easily. Using a chef's knife or circular cutters, cut the polenta into the desired shape. The polenta can be sautéed or grilled for service.

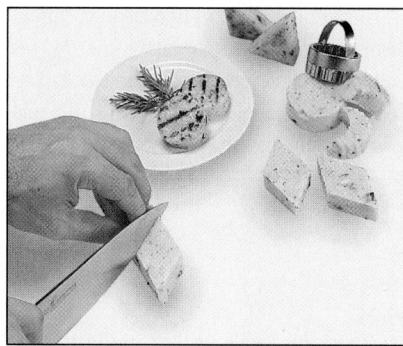

Cutting polenta into various shapes.

BASIC PROCEDURE FOR CUTTING GRATIN OR SCALLOPED POTATOES

1. Select a recipe that produces a firm finished product so that the finished dish will hold its shape after cutting.
2. Bake the potatoes in a well-greased hotel pan and refrigerate until cold and firm. Then cut the potatoes into various shapes with a chef's knife or circular cutters and remove them to a clean pan with a spatula.
3. For service, reheat the potatoes in a 325°F (160°C) oven until hot.

Cutting potatoes with a circular cutter.

Moulding Foods

Some foods, particularly grains or vegetables bound by sauces, can be moulded into attractive, hard-edged shapes by using metal rings, circular cutters or other forms. These moulded forms create height and keep the plate neat and clean.

BASIC PROCEDURE FOR MOULDING GRAINS

1. Fill a timbale, soup cup or other mould of the appropriate size and shape with the hot grains, firmly pressing them together.

2. For à la carte service, immediately unmould the grains onto the serving plate by placing the mould upside down on the plate and tapping its rim.

3. For banquet service, place the filled moulds in a hotel pan and refrigerate until needed. Shortly before service, fill the hotel pan with hot water to a point about two-thirds up the side of the moulds. Be careful not to splash any water onto the grains. Cover the pan with foil and place in the oven. Heat until the grains are hot, then plate as desired.

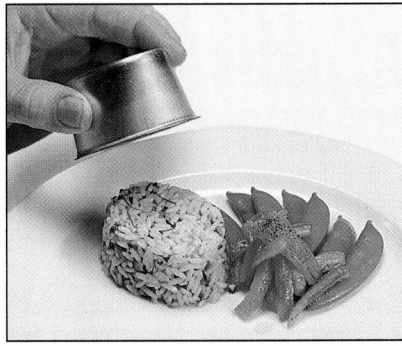

Unmoulding a timbale of rice.

BASIC PROCEDURE FOR MOULDING VEGETABLES

1. Position a ring mould on the plate and fill it with the vegetables. Press the foods into the ring to help them hold the shape. Level the top.

2. Carefully lift off the ring.

THE PLATE

Properly cooked, carefully cut and appropriately moulded foods should not be haphazardly slapped onto a plate. Rather, you should choose and position the foods carefully to achieve a plate presentation with a balanced, harmonious composition.

The composition can be further enhanced by decorating the plate with garnishes, crumbs or sauces. Some of these techniques (for example, decorating the plate with powdered sugar) do not substantially affect the flavours of the foods, they only make the completed presentation more attractive. Other techniques (for example, garnishing a dessert with finely chopped nuts or painting a plate with two sauces) add flavour and texture to the finished dish.

Composition—*a completed plate's structure of colours, textures, shapes and arrangements.*

Choosing Plates

Restaurant china is available in many different shapes, sizes, colours and patterns. (See Figure 35.1.) It is often the chef's responsibility to choose the appropriate piece of china for a particular dish.

Sizes and Shapes

Most plates are round, but oval plates, often referred to as platters, are becoming more common. Plates are available in a variety of sizes from a small 4-inch (10-cm) bread plate to a huge 14-inch (35-cm) charger or base plate. Plates are typically concave; their depths vary within a limited range of about 1 inch (2.5 cm). Most plates have rims; rim diameters also vary. Soup bowls can be rimmed or rimless. Soup plates are usually larger and shallower than soup bowls and have wide rims. Soup cups are also available. There are also dozens of plate designs intended for a specific purpose, such as plates with small indentations for holding escargots, or long, rectangular plates with grooves for holding asparagus.

Choose plates large enough to hold the food comfortably without overcrowding or spilling. Oversized, rimmed soup plates are becoming quite popular for serving any food with a sauce. Be careful when using oversized plates, however, as the food may look sparse, creating poor value perception.

Regardless of whether you choose a round, oval or less conventionally shaped plate, be sure to choose one with a size and shape that best highlights the food and supports the composition.

FIGURE 35.1   *Common Restaurant China*

Colours and Patterns

White and cream are by far the most common colours for restaurant china. Almost any food looks good on these neutral colours.

Coloured and patterned plates can be used quite effectively to accent food, however. The obvious choice is to contrast dark plates with bright- or light-coloured foods and light plates with dark-coloured foods.

The food should always be the focal point of any plate. Be careful in selecting restaurant china with intricate designs and brightly coloured patterns that can conflict or compete with the colours, shapes and arrangements of the foods. The colours and shapes in the pattern should blend well and harmonize with the foods served. The swirling patterns of blues, greys, pinks and yellows along the plate rim shown to the right, for example, harmonize well with the colours of the smoked salmon, squash blossoms and accompaniments.

Stuffed Squash Blossoms, Blini and Smoked Salmon (Recipe 33.9)

Arranging Foods on Plates

You should strive for a well-balanced plate composition. This can be achieved by carefully considering colours, textures, shapes and arrangements.

Colours

Foods come in a rainbow of colours and, to the extent appropriate, foods of different colours should be presented together. Generally, the colours should provide balance and contrast. But no matter how well prepared or planned, some dishes simply have dull, boring or similar colours. If so, try adding another ingredient or garnish for a splash of colour. The vivid red lobster claws and the shiny black mussel shells shown here add striking colour notes to a paella dish that would otherwise be dominated by yellow rice, tan chicken, brown sausages and grey clam shells.

Paella (Recipe 19.27)

Textures

Visual texture refers to how smooth or rough, coarse or fine a food looks. Mashed potatoes and carrot purée both look smooth and soft. Salmon mousseline and spinach soufflé both have slightly grainy surfaces. Rösti potatoes and meatloaf both appear coarse. The flavours of each food in these pairs differ; their visual textures do not.

Typically, foods with similar textures look boring together; foods with different textures look more exciting. Serve carrots cut julienne with the mashed potatoes to achieve a balance of hard and soft textures; steamed leaf spinach with the salmon mousseline for a combination of smooth and grainy textures; and a baked potato with the meatloaf for pairing fluffy and coarse textures. These pairs generally maintain the same range of flavours as the first set of pairs while providing different visual textures.

The cassoulet shown to the right harmoniously combines several textures in one dish: the pebbly beans, the slices of smooth slab bacon and coarse sausage and the bumpy skin of the duck leg. Indeed, the variation in textures is so dramatic and appealing that many diners may not even notice that all the principal ingredients are essentially the same colour.

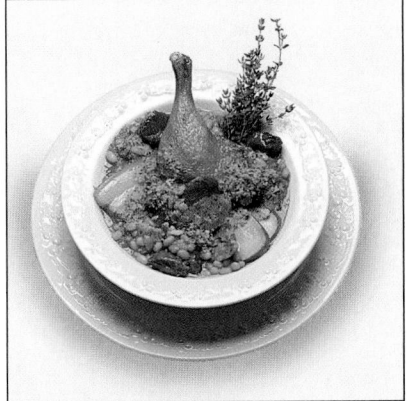

Cassoulet (Recipe 16.9)

Shapes

For a more dramatic presentation, combine foods with different shapes on one plate. The plate shown on page 1056 is an excellent example of simple shapes artfully combined: ovals of evenly sliced lamb loin with cleanly cut tri-

Lamb Loin with Rösti Potatoes (Recipe 15.7)

angles of crisp potatoes and long, thin spears of asparagus. The three very different shapes lend contrast and character to the dish.

Arrangements

Having decided on the colours, textures and shapes of the foods that will go on the plate, you must next decide where to place each individual item to achieve a balanced and unified composition. Mostly this takes judgment and style, but there are a few general guidelines.

BASIC GUIDELINES FOR ARRANGING FOODS ON A PLATE

1. Strike a balance between overcrowding the plate and leaving large gaps of space. Foods should not touch the plate rim nor necessarily be confined to the very centre.
2. Choose a focal point for the plate—that is, the point to which the eye is drawn. This is usually the highest point on the plate. Design the plate with the highest point to the rear or centre. Avoid placing foods of equal heights around the edge of the plate leaving a hole in the centre—the eye will naturally be drawn to that gap.
3. The plate's composition should flow naturally. For example, make the highest point the back of the plate and have the rest of the food become gradually shorter towards the front of the plate. Slicing and fanning foods can attract the eye and help establish a flow.

The grilled duck with roasted vegetables shown below elegantly illustrates these principles. Height is established by a structure composed of the duck leg and thigh, sliced turnips and baby carrots. The structure sits towards the back of the plate. Its height, placement and striking appearance make it the focal point. The neatly sliced duck breast is then fanned across the plate in front of this focal point, drawing the viewer's attention into the plate.

Grilled Duck with Roasted Vegetables

Decorating Plates

The colours, textures, shapes and arrangements of foods on a plate can be improved or highlighted by decorating a plate with herbs, spices and other garnishes, baked hippen masse dough and sauces. If any of these are to be applied after the principal food is placed on the plate, be prepared to do so quickly so that the food is served at its proper temperature.

Plate Dusting

An attractive method for decorating dessert plates is to cover the entire plate with a dusting of powdered sugar, cocoa powder or both before placing the dessert on the plate. Use sugar on dark-coloured plates and cocoa on light-coloured plates. These items can be dusted onto the plate with a shaker can or sifter in a free-form fashion or into any desired pattern by using a template. The template can be a doily or a stencil placed over the plate before it is dusted.

BASIC PROCEDURE FOR DUSTING DESSERT PLATES

1. Place a template over the plate. Dust the sugar or cocoa over the template.

2. Carefully remove the template.

Provided they complement the food, very finely chopped nuts can also be used to decorate plates for sweet or savoury foods. See, for example, the plate of French toast garnished with chopped macadamia nuts shown here. Plates for savoury foods can be decorated in a similar fashion by sprinkling them with finely chopped herbs such as thyme or minced vegetables such as a combination of brightly coloured peppers.

Garnishing Plates with Herbs

Using fresh herbs is one of the easiest ways to add colour, texture and flow to a plate. Whether the herb is an ingredient in the dish or merely a decoration, it should always complement the foods and be consistent with their seasonings. A sprig of fresh rosemary garnishing a beautifully roasted rack of lamb, or tiny leaves of chervil garnishing delicately poached fillets of sole are natural combinations. Sprigs of fresh green mint (often with a fresh berry or two or a strawberry cut in a fan) are often the perfect decoration for a dessert plate.

Banana Brioche French Toast (Recipe 32.20)

Using herbs to garnish a plate.

Garnishing Plates with Hippen Masse

An increasingly popular presentation technique is to pipe batters into intricate designs and then bake them to form crisp, rigid, cookielike garnishes. These garnishes are then used to create height and add texture.

RECIPE 35.1
Savoury Hippen Masse

ARIZONA BILTMORE, Phoenix, AZ

Yield: 1 lb. (450 g)

Egg whites, room temperature	8 oz.	250 g
Wondra flour	4 oz.	120 g
Cream, 35%	3 oz.	90 mL
Granulated sugar	1 oz.	30 g
Salt and white pepper	TT	TT
Dried thyme, crushed	1 tsp.	5 mL

1. Stir the egg whites together to blend. Stir in all of the flour at once.

2. Blend in the cream, then add the remaining ingredients.

3. Strain the batter through a china cap and allow to rest for 30 minutes.

4. Lightly oil the back of a very flat sheet pan. Pipe the hippen masse onto the pan using a plastic squeeze bottle. Pipe the batter into decorative patterns appropriate for the desired plate presentation.

5. Bake at 375°F (190°C) until set and lightly browned. Remove from the oven, then remove the decorations from the sheet pan while still slightly warm.

1. Pipe the batter onto an oiled sheet pan.

2. The baked batter as a component of the finished design.

Decorating Plates with Sauces

The sauce is an integral part of most any dish: It adds flavour and moisture; it also adds colour, texture and flow to the plate. A rich, glossy bordelaise or

Madeira sauce pooled beneath sautéed tournedos of beef is a classic example. A chunky salsa of tomatoes, papaya and pineapple beneath a juicy piece of grilled salmon is a more contemporary approach.

Sauces are also used in other, less traditional ways to add visual appeal. For example, if using a vinaigrette dressing for grilled foods, let the oil and vinegar separate and pool on the plate, creating the interesting effect illustrated here.

One or more coloured sauces can also be used to paint plates. One technique is simply to drizzle or splatter the sauce onto the plate.

Alternatively, one or more coloured sauces can be applied to a plate using squirt bottles to create abstract patterns or representational designs. Painting plates with different-coloured sauces also facilitates flow and adds colour. Although this technique can be used with hot sauces, it is more often used with cold sauces (such as vanilla, caramel, chocolate and fruit-flavoured ones) for dessert presentations. The sauces must be thick enough to hold the pattern once it is created and they should all be of the same viscosity.

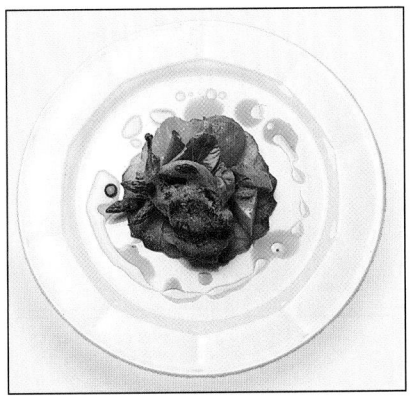

Grilled Quail with Balsamic Raspberries (Recipe 18.12)

BASIC PROCEDURE FOR PAINTING A DESIGN WITH SAUCES

1. Apply the sauces to the plate in parallel lines of alternating colours.

2. Carefully pull a toothpick through the sauces, perpendicular to the parallel lines in the sauces.

BASIC PROCEDURE FOR PAINTING A SPIDER WEB DESIGN

1. Pool one sauce evenly across the entire base of the plate, then apply a contrasting sauce onto the base sauce in a spiral.

2. Draw a thin-bladed knife or a toothpick through the sauces from the centre point towards the edge. Then, leaving a half inch (1.2 cm) space along the edge, draw a knife blade or toothpick from the edge to the centre.

Other patterns can be produced by squirting the sauces onto the plate in different patterns or by pulling the knife or toothpick through the sauces in different directions. As shown to the left, a circle of chocolate-sauce dots in a pool of vanilla sauce is pulled to create a leaf wreath.

CONCLUSION

Although the techniques described in this chapter—as well as many other ones—can be used to create a variety of effects, often the most elegant plates are those with the simplest designs. Thoughtful presentation improves the appeal and appearance of any food as well as the completed plate, but it cannot mask poor-quality, poorly prepared or bland-tasting foods.

QUESTIONS FOR DISCUSSION

1. Explain why proper service and presentation are important in food service operations.
2. Distinguish between cutting and moulding foods for visual appeal and creating garnishes out of foods.
3. How can the selection of service ware such as bowls and platters affect the visual appeal of the foods served?
4. List and describe four techniques for garnishing plates.
5. Describe how colour, texture, shape and arrangement can be used to create a well-balanced plate composition.

WEBLINKS

Learn2 Set a Table—Intro
  learn2.com/06/0608/0608.html
Garnishing Tools & Gadgets
  www.chef-harvey.com/tools/toolink.htm
Napkin Folding Tips
  www.ywh.com/Tips/Napkin/napkins.html

TWENTY SUGGESTED MENUS

The following menus are designed for beginning students. They use basic skills and techniques that students should master before progressing to more difficult items.

BEGINNING MENU 1:

RECIPE 24.4   **MESCLUN SALAD WITH RASPBERRY VINAIGRETTE**

RECIPE 13.8   **PEPPER STEAK**

RECIPE 22.6   **BROCCOLI ALMONDINE**

RECIPE 27.1   **COUNTRY BISCUITS**

RECIPE 31.17   **CHOCOLATE POT DE CRÈME**

BEGINNING MENU 2:

RECIPE 24.34   **ASPARAGUS AND MINTED NEW POTATO SALAD WITH SUN-DRIED TOMATO MAYONNAISE**

RECIPE 19.1   **BROILED BLACK SEA BASS WITH HERB BUTTER AND SAUTÉED LEEKS**

RECIPE 23.5   **BASIC SIMMERED RICE**

RECIPE 25.4   **PEARS POACHED IN RED WINE**

BEGINNING MENU 3:

RECIPE 11.2   **HEARTY VEGETABLE BEEF SOUP**

Tossed salad with

    RECIPE 24.17   **ROQUEFORT DRESSING** and

    RECIPE 24.23   **GARLIC CROUTONS**

RECIPE 17.22   **TURKEY SCALLOPINE**

RECIPE 23.17   **BROWN RICE PILAF WITH PINENUTS**

RECIPE 31.9   **CLASSIC CHOCOLATE MOUSSE**

BEGINNING MENU 4:

RECIPE 11.19   **CHEDDAR AND LEEK SOUP**

RECIPE 19.6   **RED SNAPPER EN PAPILLOTE WITH JULIENNE VEGETABLES AND BASIL BUTTER**

RECIPE 23.4   **DUCHESSE POTATOES**

RECIPE 31.21   **CHERRY CLAFOUTI**

BEGINNING MENU 5:

RECIPE 11.15   **FRENCH ONION SOUP**

RECIPE 12.1   **GRILLED LAMB CHOPS WITH HERB BUTTER**

RECIPE 23.15   **POLENTA**

RECIPE 22.14   **STIR-FRIED SNOW PEAS**

RECIPE 25.11   **GRATIN OF FRESH BERRIES WITH CRÈME FRAÎCHE**

BEGINNING MENU 6:

RECIPE 11.4   **CREAM OF BROCCOLI SOUP**

RECIPE 13.1   **LONDON BROIL**

RECIPE 22.11   **BROILED TOMATO**

RECIPE 28.2   **SOFT YEAST DINNER ROLLS**

RECIPE 31.19   **NEW YORK–STYLE CHEESECAKE**

BEGINNING MENU 7:

RECIPE 11.23   **FRESH PEACH AND YOGURT SOUP**

RECIPE 17.19   **DUCK BREAST SALAD WITH HAZELNUTS**

RECIPE 28.12   **BREADSTICKS**

RECIPE 29.28   **CHOCOLATE DÉLICE**

BEGINNING MENU 8:

Tossed salad with

    RECIPE 24.3   **EMULSIFIED VINAIGRETTE DRESSING**

RECIPE 12.2   **ROAST PRIME RIB OF BEEF AU JUS**

RECIPE 23.1   **BAKED POTATOES**

RECIPE 22.17   **MAPLE GLAZED CARROTS**

RECIPE 28.5   **BASIC FRENCH BREAD**

RECIPE 29.6   **CHERRY PIE**

BEGINNING MENU 9:

RECIPE 12.5　*NEW ENGLAND BOILED DINNER*

RECIPE 28.10　*WHOLE WHEAT BREAD*

RECIPE 25.2　*BAKED APPLES*

BEGINNING MENU 10:

RECIPE 11.5　*PURÉE OF SPLIT PEA SOUP*

RECIPE 13.3　*HOME-STYLE MEATLOAF* with mushroom sauce

RECIPE 22.2　*BAKED BUTTERNUT SQUASH*

RECIPE 23.3　*LYONNAISE POTATOES*

RECIPE 31.10　*CHOCOLATE ICE CREAM*

RECIPE 29.30　*SUGAR COOKIES*

The following menus are designed for intermediate-level students. They include dishes that integrate multiple techniques in order to build upon skills previously learned.

INTERMEDIATE MENU 1:

RECIPE 19.29　*OYSTERS ROCKEFELLER*

RECIPE 24.32　*WARM LAMB SALAD WITH BOURBON VINAIGRETTE*

RECIPE 28.4　*CROISSANTS*

RECIPE 31.28　*CHOCOLATE HAZELNUT MARQUISE*

INTERMEDIATE MENU 2:

RECIPE 20.16　*RABBIT PÂTÉ EN CROÛTE*

RECIPE 11.8　*VICHYSSOISE*

RECIPE 17.21　*LOCKPORT QUAIL MILLE-FEUILLE*

RECIPE 23.33　*SPAETZLE*

RECIPE 29.4　*APPLE CRANBERRY PIE* with
　　RECIPE 31.10　*VANILLA ICE CREAM*

INTERMEDIATE MENU 3:

RECIPE 20.8　*VEGETABLE TERRINE IN BRIOCHE*

RECIPE 19.25　*PAUPIETTES OF SOLE WITH MOUSSELINE OF SHRIMP*

RECIPE 23.14　*RÖSTI POTATOES*

Salad of baby greens with shaved Parmesan cheese and
　　RECIPE 24.11　*FOUR-PEPPERCORN CRANBERRY VINAIGRETTE*

RECIPE 29.27　*CHOCOLATE ÉCLAIRS*

INTERMEDIATE MENU 4:

RECIPE 11.3　*BEEF CONSOMMÉ*

RECIPE 23.22　*GOAT'S CHEESE RAVIOLI IN HERBED CREAM SAUCE*

RECIPE 19.5　*STEAMED SALMON WITH LEMON AND OLIVE OIL*

RECIPE 22.3　*STIR-FRIED ASPARAGUS WITH SHIITAKE MUSHROOMS*

RECIPE 23.7　*BULGUR PILAF*

RECIPE 29.24　*STRAWBERRY NAPOLEON*

INTERMEDIATE MENU 5:

Tossed green salad with
　　RECIPE 24.1　*BASIC VINAIGRETTE DRESSING* and
　　RECIPE 20.12　*RED PEPPER MOUSSE*

RECIPE 16.9　*CASSOULET*

RECIPE 28.16　*SAN FRANCISCO SOURDOUGH BREAD*

RECIPE 31.9　*CLASSIC CHOCOLATE MOUSSE* in tuile cup

INTERMEDIATE MENU 6:

RECIPE 20.7　*CARPACCIO OF SEARED BEEF WITH PARMESAN FANS AND PERFUMED MASCARPONE*

RECIPE 11.16　*MINESTRONE*

RECIPE 12.3　*SAUTÉED VEAL SCALLOPINI WITH WHITE WINE LEMON SAUCE*

RECIPE 29.13　*CANNOLI ALLA SICILIANA*

INTERMEDIATE MENU 7:

RECIPE 19.4　*BLUE CRAB CAKES WITH FRESH SALSA*

Romaine lettuce with
　　RECIPE 24.12　*RED ONION VINAIGRETTE*

RECIPE 17.16　*CHICKEN STUFFED WITH SPINACH IN SAFFRON SAUCE*

RECIPE 23.2　*GRATIN DAUPHINOIS*

RECIPE 31.7　*FRESH FRUIT BAVARIAN CHARLOTTE* made with
　　RECIPE 30.22　*LADYFINGERS*

INTERMEDIATE MENU 8: BRUNCH BUFFET

RECIPE 24.29　*VINE-RIPENED TOMATO SALAD*

RECIPE 32.3　*GREEK-STYLE SCRAMBLED EGGS*

RECIPE 32.5　*GARDEN FRITTATA*

RECIPE 32.2　*QUICHE LORRAINE*

RECIPE 27.4　*BLUEBERRY MUFFINS*

RECIPE 28.20　*DANISH PASTRIES*

RECIPE 29.14　*LINZER TART*

RECIPE 25.8　*FIGS WITH BERRIES AND HONEY MOUSSE*

RECIPE 32.12　*HOT CHOCOLATE MOUSSE*

INTERMEDIATE MENU 9:

RECIPE 24.24　*WILTED SPINACH SALAD WITH ROASTED PEPPERS*

RECIPE 17.9　*ROAST CORNISH GAME HEN*

RECIPE 22.4　*BRUSSELS SPROUTS IN PECAN BUTTER*

RECIPE 28.17　*CHALLAH*

RECIPE 31.30　*MARINATED FIELD BERRIES WITH LEMON COOKIES AND MISSION HILL ICE SABAYON*

INTERMEDIATE MENU 10:

RECIPE 24.25　*WHITE ASPARAGUS MOUSSE WITH GARDEN FRESH LETTUCES*

RECIPE 19.34　*SHELLFISH BOUILLABAISSE WITH GINGER AÏOLI*

RECIPE 28.13　*ROMAN FLATBREAD*

RECIPE 29.23　*FRESH PEACH TART WITH ALMOND CREAM*

MEASUREMENT AND CONVERSION CHARTS

MEASUREMENT CONVERSION CHART

Formulas for Exact Measures	When you know:	Multiply by:	To find:	Rounded Measures for Quick Reference		
Mass	ounces	28.35	grams	1 oz.		= 30 g
(Weight)	pounds	0.45	kilograms	4 oz.		= 120 g
	grams	0.035	ounces	8 oz.		= 225 g
	kilograms	2.2	pounds	16 oz.	= 1 lb.	= 450 g
				32 oz.	= 2 lb.	= 900 g
				36 oz.	= 2 1/4 lb.	= 1000 g (1 kg)
Volume	teaspoons	5.0	millilitres	1/4 tsp.	= 1/24 oz.	= 1 ml
(Capacity)	tablespoons	15.0	millilitres	1/2 tsp.	= 1/12 oz.	= 2 ml
	fluid ounces	29.57	millilitres	1 tsp.	= 1/6 oz.	= 5 ml
	cups	0.24	litres	1 Tbsp.	= 1/2 oz.	= 15 ml
	pints	0.47	litres	1 c.	= 8 oz.	= 250 ml
	quarts	0.95	litres	2 c. (1 pt.)	= 16 oz.	= 500 ml
	gallons	3.785	litres	4 c. (1 qt.)	= 32 oz.	= 1 lt
	millilitres	0.034	fluid ounces	4 qt. (1 gal.)	= 128 oz.	= 3 3/4 lt
Temperature	Fahrenheit	5/9 (after subtracting 32)	Celsius	32°F	= 0°C	
	Celsius	9/5 (then add 32)	Fahrenheit	122°F	= 50°C	
				212°F	= 100°C	

CONVERSION GUIDELINES

1 gallon	=	4 quarts
		8 pints
		16 cups (8 ounces)
		128 ounces
1 fifth bottle	=	approximately 1 1/2 pints or exactly 26.5 ounces
1 measuring cup	=	8 ounces (a coffee cup is generally 6 ounces)
1 large egg white	=	1 ounce (average)
1 lemon	=	1 to 1 1/4 ounces of juice
1 orange	=	3 to 3 1/2 ounces of juice

SCOOP SIZES

Scoop Measure	Level Measure
6	2/3 cup
8	1/2 cup
10	2/5 cup
12	1/3 cup
16	1/4 cup
20	3 1/5 tablespoons
24	2 2/3 tablespoons
30	2 1/5 tablespoons
40	1 3/5 tablespoons

The number scoop determines the number of servings in each quart of a mixture, for example, with a No. 16 scoop, one quart of mixture will yield 16 servings.

LADLE SIZES

Size	Portion of a Cup	Number per Quart	Number per Litre
1 oz.	1/8	32	34
2 oz.	1/4	16	17
2 2/3 oz.	1/3	12	13
4 oz.	1/2	8	8.6
6 oz.	3/4	5 1/3	5.7

CANNED GOOD SIZES

Size	No. of Cans per Case	Average Weight	Average No. Cups per Can
No. 1/2	8	8 oz.	1
No. 1 tall (also known as 303)	2 & 4 doz.	16 oz.	2
No. 2	2 doz.	20 oz.	2 1/2
No. 2 1/2	2 doz.	28 oz.	3 1/2
No. 3	2 doz.	33 oz.	4
No. 3 cylinder	1 doz.	51 oz.	5 2/3
No. 5	1 doz.	3 lb. 8 oz.	5 1/2
No. 10	6	6 lb. 10 oz.	13

BIBLIOGRAPHY AND RECOMMENDED READING

GENERAL INTEREST

Bickel, Walter, ed. and trans. *Hering's Dictionary of Classical and Modern Cookery.* 12th Eng. ed. London: Virtue & Company Limited, 1991.

Culinary Institute of America. *The New Professional Chef.* 5th ed. New York: Van Nostrand Reinhold, 1991.

Dawson, Hannelore. *Great Food for Great Numbers.* New York: Van Nostrand Reinhold, 1991.

Escoffier, Auguste. *Le Guide culinaire.* (Translation entitled *The Escoffier Cookbook and Guide to the Fine Art of Cookery for Connoisseurs, Chefs, Epicures*). New York: Crown Publishers, 1969.

Gisslen, Wayne. *Professional Baking.* New York: John Wiley & Sons, Inc., 1985.

————. *Professional Cooking.* 2nd ed. New York: John Wiley & Sons, Inc., 1989.

The Grand Masters of the French Cuisine. Selected and adapted by Celine Vence and Robert Courtine. New York: G.P. Putnam & Sons, 1978.

Haines, Robert G. *Food Preparation.* Homewood, Ill.: American Technical Publishers, Inc., 1988.

Lang, Jennifer Harvey, ed. *Larousse Gastronomique.* American ed. New York: Crown Publishers, Inc., 1988.

Leith, Prue. *The Cook's Handbook.* New York: A & W Publishers, Inc., 1981.

Pauli, Eugen, *Classical Cooking the Modern Way.* 2nd ed. New York: Van Nostrand Reinhold, 1989.

Pepin, Jacques. *The Art of Cooking.* New York: Alfred A. Knopf, 1987.

————. *La Technique.* New York: Wallaby/Pocket Books, 1976.

Rombauer, Irma von Starkloff and Marion Rombauer Becker. *Joy of Cooking.* New York: The Bobbs-Merrill Co., Inc., Macmillan, 1975.

Shugart, Grace and Mary Molt. *Food for Fifty.* 9th ed. New York: Macmillan, 1993.

Willan, Anne. *La Varenne Pratique.* New York: Crown Publishers, 1989.

FOOD HISTORY

Clair, Colin. *Kitchen & Table: A Bedside History of Eating in the Western World.* New York: Abelard-Schuman Limited, 1965.

Fussell, Betty. *The Story of Corn.* New York: Borzoi Books, Alfred A. Knopf, Inc., 1992.

Hale, William Harlan, and The Editors of Horizon Magazine. *The Horizon Cookbook and Illustrated History of Eating and Drinking Through the Ages.* New York: American Heritage Publishing Co., Inc., 1968.

Mintz, Sidney W. *Sweetness and Power: The Place of Sugar in Modern History.* New York: Penguin Books, 1985.

Montagné, P., and Dr. Gottschalk. *Larousse Gastronomique.* Eds. Nina Froud and Charlotte Turgeon. London: The Hamlyn Publishing Group Ltd., 1974.

Norman, Barbara. *Tales of the Table: A History of Western Cuisine.* Englewood Cliffs, N.J.: Prentice-Hall, 1972.

Revel, Jean-François. *Culture and Cuisine.* (Trans. of *Un Festin en paroles.*) New York: Da Capo Press, Inc., 1982.

Rupp, Rececca. *Blue Corn and Square Tomatoes.* Pownal, Vt.: Garden Way Publishing, 1987.

Schremp, Gerry. *Kitchen Culture: Fifty Years of Food Fads.* New York: Pharos Books, A Scripps Howard Co., 1991.

Shapiro, Laura. *Perfection Salad: Women and Cooking at the Turn of the Century.* New York: Farrar, Straus and Giroux, 1986.

Tannahill, Reay. *Food in History.* New York: Crown Publishers, Inc., 1988.

Toussaint-Samat, Maguelonne. *A History of Food.* Translated by Anthea Bell. Cambridge, Mass.: Blackwell Publishers, 1992.

Wheaton, Barbara Ketcham. *Savoring the Past.* Philadelphia: The University of Pennsylvania Press, 1983.

Willan, Anne. *Great Cooks and Their Recipes: From Taillevent to Escoffier.* Boston: Little, Brown and Co., A Bulfinch Press Book, 1992.

SANITATION AND SAFETY

Canadian Restaurant and Food Services Association publications.

————. *ServSafe: Serving Safe Food.* Workbooks and videos. Distributed in Canada by Kostuch Publications Ltd., Toronto. The Educational Foundation of the National Restaurant Association. *Applied Foodservice Sanitation: A Foundation Textbook.* 4th ed. John Wiley & Sons, Inc., 1992.

Guthrie, Rufus K. *Food Sanitation.* 3d ed. New York: Van Nostrand Reinhold, 1988.

National Assessment Institute. *Handbook for Safe Food Service Management.* Englewood Cliffs, N.J.: Regents/Prentice Hall, 1994.

Southern Alberta Institute of Technology and Calgary Regional Health Authority. *Food Safety and Sanitation Modules.* SAIT, 1998.

NUTRITION

Brody, Jane E. *Jane Brody's Nutrition Book.* New York: Bantam Books, Inc., 1982.

Freyberg, Nicholas, and Willis A. Gortner. *The Food Additives Book.* New York: Bantam Books, Inc., 1982.

Hamilton, Eva Mae Nunnelley, Eleanor Noss Whitney, and Frances Sienkiewicz Sizer. *Nutrition: Concepts and Controversies.* 4th ed. St. Paul, Minn.: West Publishing Co., 1988.

Netzer, Corinne T. *The Corinne T. Netzer Encyclopedia of Food Values.* New York: Dell Publishing, 1992.

Spiller, Gene. *The Super Pyramid Eating Program: Introducing the Revolutionary Five New Food Groups.* New York: Times Books, Random House, Inc., 1993.

FOOD COSTING AND MENU PRICING

Coltman, Michael M. *Financial Control for Your Foodservice Operation.* New York: Van Nostrand Reinhold, 1991.

Keister, Douglas C. *Food and Beverage Control.* 2nd ed. Englewood Cliffs, N.J.: Prentice Hall, 1990.

McVety, Paul J., and Bradley J. Ware. *Fundamentals of Menu Planning.* New York: Van Nostrand Reinhold, 1989.

Miller, Jack E. *Menu Pricing and Strategy.* 2nd ed. New York: Van Nostrand Reinhold, 1987.

Schmidt, Arno. *Chef's Book of Formulas, Yields, and Sizes.* New York: Van Nostrand Reinhold, 1990.

TOOLS

Bridge, Fred, and Jean F. Tibbetts. *The Well-Tooled Kitchen.* New York: William Morrow and Co., 1991.

GENERAL INGREDIENTS

DeMers, John. *The Community Kitchens Complete Guide to Gourmet Coffee.* New York: Simon & Schuster, 1986.

Dowell, Philip, and Adrian Bailey. *Cook's Ingredients.* New York: William Morrow and Co., 1980.

Jordan, Michele Anna. *The Good Cook's Book of Oil & Vinegar.* Reading, Mass.: Addison-Wesley, 1992.

Norman, Jill. *The Complete Book of Spices.* American ed. New York: Viking Studio Books, 1991.

Ortiz, Elisabeth Lambert. *The Encyclopedia of Herbs, Spices and Flavorings.* 1st American ed. New York: Dorling Kindersley, Inc., 1992.

Schapira, Joel, and Karl Schapira. *The Book of Coffee and Tea.* New York: St. Martin's Press, 1975.

Schuler, Stanley, ed. *Simon & Schuster's Guide to Herbs and Spices.* New York: Fireside and Simon & Schuster, 1990.

Stobart, Tom. *Herbs, Spices and Flavorings.* Woodstock, N.Y.: The Overland Press, 1982.

EGGS, DAIRY AND CHEESE

Dairy Farmers of Canada. *Fundamentals of Canadian Cheeses and Their Use in Fine Cuisine.* Montreal: Les Éditions de la Chenelière Inc., 1992.

Eggcyclopedia. 2nd ed. Park Ridge, Ill.: American Egg Board, revised 1989.

Jones, Evan. *The World of Cheese.* New York: Alfred A. Knopf, 1984.

Marquis, Vivienne, and Patricia Haskell. *The Cheese Book.* New York: Simon & Schuster, 1985.

FOOD SCIENCE

Freeland-Graves, H., and Gladys C. Peckham. *Foundations of Food Preparation.* 5th ed. New York: Macmillan, 1987.

McGee, Harold. *On Food and Cooking.* New York: Charles Scribner's Sons, 1984.

McWilliams, Margaret. *Food Fundamentals.* 4th ed. New York: Macmillan, 1985.

Potter, Norman N. *Food Science.* 4th ed. Westport, Conn.: The AVI Publishing Co. Inc., 1986.

STOCKS, SAUCES AND SOUPS

Clayton, Bernard. *The Complete Book of Soups and Stews.* New York: Simon & Schuster, 1984.

Davis, Deidre. *A Fresh Look at Saucing Foods.* Reading, Mass.: Addison-Wesley, 1993.

Larousse, David Paul. *The Sauce Bible: Guide to the Saucier's Craft.* New York: John Wiley & Sons, Inc., 1993.

Peterson, James. *Sauces: Classical and Contemporary Sauce Making.* New York: Van Nostrand Reinhold, 1991.

Sokolov, Raymond A. *The Saucier's Apprentice.* New York: Alfred A. Knopf, 1976.

MEAT

Libby, James A. *Meat Hygiene.* Philadelphia: Lea & Febiger, 1975.

The Meat Buyers Guide. Reston, Va.: National Association of Meat Purveyors, 1990.

Thomas, John R., and P. Thomas Ziegler. *The Meat We Eat.* Danville, Ill.: Interstate Printers & Publishers, Inc., 1985.

The Editors of Time-Life Books. *The Good Cook: Lamb.* London: Time Life International (Nederland) B.V., 1981.

The Editors of Time-Life Books. *The Good Cook: Beef and Veal.* London: Time Life International (Nederland) B.V., 1978.

POULTRY

The Editors of Time-Life Books. *The Good Cook: Poultry.* London: Time Life International (Nederland) B.V., 1978.

GAME

Cameron, Angus, and Judith Jones. *The L.L. Bean Game and Fish Cookbook.* New York: Random House, 1983.

Little, Carolyn. *The Game Cookbook.* Wiltshire, England: The Crowood Press, 1988.

Marrone, Teresa. *Dressing and Cooking Wild Game.* New York: Prentice Hall Press, 1987.

FISH AND SHELLFISH

Cronin, Isaac, Jay Harlow, and Paul Johnson. *The California Seafood Cookbook.* Berkeley, Calif.: Harris Publishing Co., Inc. (Aris Books), 1983.

The Fish List: FDA Guide to Acceptable Market Names for Food Fish Sold in Interstate Commerce. Washington, D.C.: U.S. Government Printing Office, 1988.

Howarth, A. Jan. *The Complete Fish Cookbook.* New York: St. Martin's Press, 1983.

King, Shirley. *Fish, The Basics.* New York: Simon & Schuster, 1990.

———. *Saucing the Fish.* New York: Simon & Schuster, 1976.

Loomis, Susan Herrmann. *The Great American Seafood Cookbook*. New York: Workman Publishing, 1988.

McClane, A. J. *The Encyclopedia of Fish Cookery*. New York: Holt, Rinehart and Winston, 1977.

The Seafood Handbook: Seafood Standards. Rockland, Maine: Seafood Business Magazine, 1991.

CHARCUTERIE

Ehlert, Friedrich W., et al. *Pâtés and Terrines*. Reprint. London: Hearst Books, 1990.

Grigson, Jane. *The Art of Charcuterie*. Reprint. New York: The Echo Press, 1991.

Sonnenschmidt and Nicolas. *The Art of Garde Manger*. 4th ed. New York: Van Nostrand Reinhold, 1988.

The Editors of Time-Life Books. *The Good Cook: Terrines, Pâtés and Galantines*. London: Time Life International (Nederland) B.V., 1981.

VEGETABLES AND FRUITS

Andrews, Jean. *Peppers: The Domesticated Capsicums*. Austin, Tex.: University of Texas Press, 1984.

Bauer, Cathy, and Juel Andersen. *The Tofu Cookbook*. Emmaus, Pa.: Rodale Press, 1979.

Beck, Bruce. *Produce: A Fruit and Vegetable Lovers' Guide*. New York: Friendly Press, 1984.

Brennan, Georgeanne, Isaac Cronin, and Charlotte Glenn. *The New American Vegetable Cookbook*. Berkeley, Calif.: Harris Publishing Co., 1985.

Brown, Marlene. *International Produce Cookbook and Guide*. Los Angeles: HP Books, 1989.

Davidson, Alan. *Fruit: A Connoisseur's Guide and Cookbook*. New York: Simon & Schuster, 1991.

DeWitt, Dave, and Nancy Gerlach. *The Whole Chile Pepper Book*. Boston: Little, Brown and Co., 1990.

Holthaus, Fusako. *Tofu Cookery*. Tokyo: Kodansha International, 1992.

Miller, Mark, with John Harrisson. *The Great Chile Book*. Berkeley, Calif.: Ten Speed Press, 1991.

Murdich, Jack. *Buying Produce*. New York: William Morrow and Co., 1986.

Payne, Rolce Redard, and Dorrit Speyer Senior. *Cooking With Fruit*. New York: Crown Publishers, Inc., 1992.

Schmidt, Jimmy. *Cooking For All Seasons*. New York: Macmillan, 1991.

Schneider, Elizabeth. *Uncommon Fruits and Vegetables: A Commonsense Guide*. New York: Harper & Row, 1986.

GRAINS AND PASTA

Bugialli, Giuliano. *On Pasta*. New York: Simon & Schuster, 1988.

Della Croce, Julia. *Pasta Classica*. San Francisco: Chronicle Books, 1987.

Gelles, Carol. *The Complete Whole Grain Cookbook*. New York: Donald I. Fine, Inc., 1989.

Greene, Bert. *The Grains Cookbook*. New York: Workman Publishing, 1988.

Kummer, Corby. "Pasta." *The Atlantic*, 258, no. 1 (July 1986): 35–47.

Leblang, Bonnie Tandy, and Joanne Lamb Hayes. *Rice*. New York: Harmony Books, 1991.

Scott, Marisa Luisa, and Jack Denton Scott. *Rice*. New York: Times Books, 1985.

Spier, Carol. *Food Essentials: Grains and Pasta*. New York: Crescent Books, 1993.

SALADS AND SALAD DRESSINGS

Blair, Eulalia. C. *Salads for Foodservice Menu Planning*. New York: Van Nostrand Reinhold, 1988.

Idone, Christopher. *Christopher Idone's Salad Days*. New York: Random House, 1989.

Muller, Veronika. *Salads*. New York: Van Nostrand Reinhold, 1989.

Nathan, Amy. *Salad*. San Francisco: Chronicle Books, 1985.

BREADS

Albright, Barbara, and Leslie Weiner. *Mostly Muffins*. New York: St. Martin's Press, 1984.

Alston, Elizabeth. *Biscuits and Scones*. New York: Clarkson N. Potter, Inc., 1988.

Amendola, Joseph. *The Bakers' Manual*. 4th ed. New York: Van Nostrand Reinhold, 1993.

Clayton, Bernard. *Bernard Clayton's New Complete Book of Breads*. Rev. ed. New York: Simon & Schuster, 1987.

Cunningham, Marion. *The Fannie Farmer Baking Book*. New York: Alfred A. Knopf, 1984.

David, Elizabeth. *English Bread and Yeast Cookery*. Notes by Karen Hess. American ed. New York: The Viking Press, 1980.

Jones, Judith, and Evan Jones. *The Book of Bread*. New York: Harper & Row, 1982.

Ortiz, Joe. *The Village Baker: Classic Regional Breads from Europe and America*. Berkeley, Calif.: Ten Speed Press, 1993.

Weiner, Leslie, and Barbara Albright. *Simply Scones*. New York: St. Martin's Press, 1988.

PASTRIES AND DESSERTS

Bernachon, Maurice, and Jean-Jacques Bernachon. *A Passion for Chocolate*. Translated and adapted for the American kitchen by Rose Levy Beranbaum. New York: William Morrow and Co., Inc., 1989.

Braker, Flo. *The Simple Art of Perfect Baking*. Shelburne, Vt.: Chapters Publishing, Ltd., 1992.

Fletcher, Helen S. *The New Pastry Cook*. New York: William Morrow and Co., Inc., 1986.

Friberg, Bo. *The Professional Pastry Chef*. 2nd ed. New York: Van Nostrand Reinhold, 1990.

Healy, Bruce, and Paul Bugat. *Mastering the Art of French Pastry*. Woodbury, N.Y.: Barron's, 1984.

Hyman, Philip, and Mary Hyman, trans. *The Best of Gaston Lenotre's Desserts*. Woodbury, N.Y.: Barron's, 1983.

London, Sheryl, and Mel London. *Fresh Fruit Desserts: Classic and Contemporary*. New York: Prentice Hall Press, 1990.

Purdy, Susan G. *A Piece of Cake*. New York: Macmillan, 1989.

Roux, Michel, and Albert Roux. *The Roux Brothers on Pâtisserie*. New York: Prentice Hall Press, 1986.

Silverton, Nancy. *Desserts by Nancy Silverton*. New York: Harper & Row, 1986.

Sultan, William J. *The Pastry Chef*. New York: Van Nostrand Reinhold, 1983.

Sultan, William J. *Practical Baking*. 5th ed. New York: Van Nostrand Reinhold, 1990.

MEAL SERVICE

Alston, Elizabeth. *Breakfast with Friends: Seasonal Menus to Celebrate the Morning*. New York: McGraw-Hill, 1989.

Bristow, Linda Kay. *Bread and Breakfast*. San Ramon, Calif.: 101 Productions, 1985.

Janericco, Terence. *The Book of Great Hors d'Oeuvre*. New York: Van Nostrand Reinhold, 1990.

Kolpas, Norman. *Breakfast and Brunch Book*. Los Angeles: HP Books, 1988.

Kotschevar, Lendal H. *Short Order Cooking*. New York: Van Nostrand Reinhold, 1990.

International Cuisines

Bayless, Rick, with Deann Groen Bayless. *Authentic Mexican: Regional Cooking from the Heart of Mexico*. New York: William Morrow and Co., Inc., 1987.

Bugialli, Giuliano. *The Fine Art of Italian Cooking*. New York: Random House, 1990.

Casas, Penelope. *The Foods and Wines of Spain*. New York: Alfred A. Knopf, 1991.

Curnonsky [Maurice Edmond Sailland]. *Traditional French Cooking*. Translation of *Cuisine et vins de France*, English ed. Jeni Wright. New York: Doubleday, 1989.

Devi, Yamuna. *The Art of Indian Vegetarian Cooking*. New York: E.P. Dutton, 1987.

Downer, Lesley. *At the Japanese Table*. San Francisco: Chronicle Books, 1993.

Efrain, Martinez. *Classic Spanish Cooking with Chef Ef*. Los Angeles: Lowell House, 1993.

Field, Carol. *Celebrating Italy*. New York: William Morrow & Co., Inc., 1990.

Gin, Maggie. *Regional Cooking of China*. San Francisco: 101 Productions, 1984.

Grigson, Jane. *Jane Grigson's Book of European Cookery*. New York: Atheneum, 1983.

Hazan, Marcella. *Essentials of Classic Italian Cooking*. New York: Alfred A. Knopf, 1993.

Jaffrey, Madhur. *An Invitation to Indian Cooking*. New York: Vintage Books, 1973.

———. *A Taste of India*. New York: Atheneum, 1986.

Kasper, Lynn Rossetto. *The Splendid Table: Recipes from Emilia-Romagna the Heartland of Northern Italian Food*. New York: William Morrow & Co., Inc., 1992.

Kennedy, Diana. *The Cuisines of Mexico*. Rev. ed. New York: Harper & Row, 1986.

Lo, Kenneth. *The Encyclopedia of Chinese Cooking*. New York: Bristol Books, 1979.

McDermott, Nancie. *Real Thai: The Best of Thailand's Regional Cooking*. San Francisco: Chronicle Books, 1992.

Olaore, Ola. *Traditional African Cooking*. London: Foulsham & Company Ltd., 1990.

Randelman, Mary Urrutia, and Joan Schwartz. *Memories of a Cuban Kitchen*. New York: Macmillan, 1992.

Richie, Donald. *A Taste of Japan*. New York: Kodansha, 1985.

Roden, Claudia. *A Book of Middle Eastern Food*. New York: Vintage Books, 1972.

Rojas-Lombardi, Felipe. *The Art of South American Cooking*. New York: HarperCollins, 1991.

Rose, Evelyn. *The New Complete International Jewish Cookbook*. New York: Carroll & Graf Publishers, Inc., 1992.

Routhier, Nicole. *The Foods of Vietnam*. New York: Stewart, Tabori & Chang, 1989.

Rozin, Elisabeth. *Ethnic Cuisine: The Flavor-Principle Cookbook*. Lexington, Mass.: S. Green Press, 1983. Reprint. New York: Penguin Books USA Inc., Viking Penguin, 1992.

Sandler, Bea. *The African Cookbook*. New York: World Publishing, 1970.

Scharfenberg, Horst. *The Cuisines of Germany: Regional Specialties and Traditional Home Cooking*. New York: Poseidon Press, 1980.

Solomon, Charmaine. *The Complete Asian Cookbook*. New York: McGraw-Hill, 1976.

———. *Charmaine Solomon's Thai Cookbook*. Rutland, Vt.: Charles E. Tuttle Co., 1991.

Toomre, Joyce. *Classic Russian Cooking: Elena Molokhovets' A Gift to Young Housewives*. Translated, introduced, and annotated by Joyce Toomre. Bloomington, Ind.: Indiana University Press, 1992.

Volokh, Anne, with Mavis Manus. *The Art of Russian Cuisine*. New York: Collier Books, 1983.

Von Bremzen, Anya, and John Welchman. *Please To The Table: The Russian Cookbook*. New York: Workman Publishing Co., 1990.

Wolfert, Paula. *Couscous and Other Good Food from Morocco*. New York: Harper & Row, 1973.

Presentation and Garnishing

Budgen, June. *The Book of Garnishes*. Los Angeles: HP Books, 1986.

Grotz, Peter. *Successful Cold Buffets*. New York: Van Nostrand Reinhold, 1990.

Haydock, Robert, and Yukiko Haydock. *Japanese Garnishes*. New York: Holt, Rinehart and Winston, 1980.

Larousse, David Paul. *Edible Art: Forty-Eight Garnishes for the Professional*. New York: Van Nostrand Reinhold, 1987.

Lynch, Francis Talyn. *Garnishing: A Feast for Your Eyes*. Los Angeles: HP Books, 1987.

Books by Contributing Chefs

Ash, John, and Sid Goldstein. *American Game Cooking*. Reading, Mass.: Addison-Wesley (Aris Books), 1991.

Beranbaum, Rose Levy. *The Cake Bible*. New York: William Morrow and Co., Inc., 1988.

Carpenter, Hugh, and Teri Sandison. *Chopstix: Quick Cooking with Pacific Flavors*. New York: Stewart, Tabori & Chang, 1990.

Golden, Harris. *Golden's Kitchen: The Artistry of Cooking and Dining on the Light Side*. Rev. 2nd ed. Phoenix, Ariz.: Quail Run Books, 1989.

Kerr, Graham. *Graham Kerr's Minimax Cookbook*. New York: Doubleday, 1992.

Malgieri, Nick. *Nick Malgieri's Perfect Pastry*. New York: Macmillan, 1989.

Medrich, Alice. *Cocolat*. New York: Warner Books, 1990.

Milliken, Mary Sue, and Susan Feniger. *City Cuisine*. New York: William Morris and Co., Inc., 1989.

Miller, Mark. *Coyote Cafe*. Berkeley, Calif.: Ten Speed Press, 1989.

Puck, Wolfgang. *Adventures in the Kitchen: 175 New Recipes from Spago, Chinois on Main, Postrio and Eureka*. New York: Random House, 1991.

———. *The Wolfgang Puck Cookbook*. New York: Random House, 1986.

Richard, Michel. *Michel Richard's Home Cooking with a French Accent*. New York: William Morrow and Co., Inc., 1993.

Roberts, Michael. *Secret Ingredients*. New York: Bantam Books, 1988.

Somerville, Annie. *Fields of Greens: New Vegetarian Recipes from the Celebrated Greens Restaurant*. New York: Bantam Books, 1993.

Tropp, Barbara. *China Moon Cookbook*. New York: Workman Publishing Co., 1992.

GLOSSARY

Acid—foods such as citrus juice, vinegar and wine that have a sour or sharp flavour (most foods are slightly acidic); acids have a pH of less than 7.

Acidulation—the browning of cut fruit caused by the reaction of an enzyme (polyphenoloxidase) with the phenolic compounds present in these fruits; this browning is often mistakenly attributed to exposure to oxygen.

Additives—substances added to foods to prevent spoilage or to improve appearance, texture, taste or nutritional value.

Aerobes—bacteria that thrive on oxygen.

Aging—(1) the period of time during which freshly killed meat is allowed to rest so that the effects of rigor mortis dissipate; (2) the period during which freshly milled flour is allowed to rest so that it will whiten and produce less sticky doughs; the aging of flour can be chemically accelerated.

Airline breast—a boneless chicken breast with the first wing bone attached.

À la carte—(1) a menu on which each food and beverage is listed and priced separately; (2) foods cooked to order as opposed to foods cooked in advance and held for later service.

Albumen—the principal protein found in egg whites.

Al dente—(ahl den-tay) cooked foods (usually vegetables and pasta) that are prepared firm to the bite, not soft or mushy.

Alkali—also known as a base, any substance with a pH higher than 7; baking soda is one of the few alkaline foods.

Alkaloid—a number of bitter organic substances with alkaline properties; found most often in plants and sometimes used in drugs.

Allemande—(ah-luh-mahnd) a sauce made by adding lemon juice and a liaison to a velouté made from veal or chicken stock; used to make several derivative sauces of the velouté family.

Allumette—(al-u-met) (1) a matchstick cut 1/8 inch × 1/8 inch × 2–2-1/2 inches (3 mm × 3 mm × 5–6 cm) long; usually used for potatoes; (2) a strip of puff pastry with a sweet or savoury filling.

American service—restaurant service where the waiter takes the orders and brings the food to the table; the food is placed on dishes (plated) in the kitchen, making it a relatively fast method for seated service.

Amino acid—the basic molecular component of proteins; each of the approximately two dozen amino acids contain oxygen, hydrogen, carbon and nitrogen atoms.

Anaerobes—bacteria that are able to live and grow without the presence of oxygen.

Animal husbandry—the business, science and practice of raising domesticated animals.

Anterior—at or toward the front of an object or place; opposite of *posterior*.

Appetizers—also known as first courses, usually small portions of hot or cold foods intended to whet the appetite in anticipation of the more substantial courses to follow.

Aquafarming—also known as aquaculture, the business, science and practice of raising large quantities of fish and shellfish in tanks, ponds or ocean pens.

Aromatic—a food added to a preparation to enhance flavour and aroma; includes herbs and spices as well as some vegetables.

Aspic or aspic jelly—a clear jelly usually made from a clarified stock thickened with gelatin; used to coat foods, especially charcuterie items, and for garnish.

As-purchased (A.P.)—the condition or cost of an item as it is purchased or received from the supplier.

Au gratin—(ah graw-ton) foods with a browned or crusted top; often made by browning a food with a bread crumb, cheese and/or sauce topping under a broiler or salamander.

Au jus—(ah zhew) roasted meats, poultry or game served with their natural, unthickened juices.

Au sec—(ah sec) cooked until nearly dry.

Backfat—fresh pork fat from the back of the pig, used primarily for barding.

Bacteria—single-celled microorganisms, some of which can cause diseases, including food-borne diseases.

Bain marie—(bane mah-ree) (1) a hot water bath used to gently cook food or keep cooked food hot; (2) a container for holding food in a hot water bath.

Baking—a dry-heat cooking method in which foods are surrounded by hot, dry air in a closed environment; similar to roasting, the term baking is usually applied to breads, pastries, vegetables and fish.

Baking powder—a mixture of sodium bicarbonate and one or more acids, generally cream of tartar and/or sodium aluminum sulphate, used to leaven baked goods; it releases carbon dioxide gas if moisture is present in a formula. *Single-acting baking powder* releases carbon dioxide gas in the presence of moisture only; *double-acting baking powder* releases some carbon dioxide gas upon contact with moisture, more gas is released when heat is applied.

Baking soda—sodium bicarbonate, an alkaline compound that releases carbon dioxide gas when combined with an acid and moisture; used to leaven baked goods.

Ballotine—(bahl-lo-teen) similar to a galantine, it is usually made by stuffing a deboned poultry leg with forcemeat; it is then poached or braised and normally served hot.

Barbecue—(1) to cook foods over dry heat created by the burning of hardwood or hardwood charcoals; (2) a tangy tomato- or vinegar-based sauce used for grilled foods; (3) foods cooked by this method and/or with this sauce.

Barding—tying thin slices of fat, such as bacon or pork backfat, over meats or poultry that have little to no natural fat covering in order to protect and moisten them during roasting.

Basic sauces—also known as mother or leading sauces; the foundation for the entire classic repertoire of hot sauces; the five leading sauces (béchamel, velouté, espagnole [also known as brown], tomato and hollandaise) are distinguished by the liquids and thickeners used to make them. They can be seasoned and garnished to create a wide variety of derivative sauces.

Basting—moistening foods during cooking (usually roasting, broiling or grilling) with melted fat, pan drippings, sauce or other liquids to prevent drying and to add flavour.

Batonnet—(bah-toh-nah) foods cut into matchstick shapes of 1/4 inch × 1/4 inch × 2–2-1/2 inches (6 mm × 6 mm × 5–6 cm).

Batter—(1) a semiliquid mixture containing flour or other starch used to make cakes and breads. The gluten development is minimized and the liquid forms the continuous medium in which other ingredients are disbursed; generally contains more fat, sugar and liquids than a dough; (2) a semiliquid mixture of liquid and starch used to coat foods for deep-fat frying.

Baumé scale—(boh-may) see **Hydrometer**.

Bavarian cream—a sweet dessert mixture made by thickening custard sauce with gelatin and then folding in whipped cream; the final product is poured into a mould and chilled until firm.

Beard—a clump of dark threads found on a mussel.

Béarnaise—(bare-naze) a sauce made of butter and egg yolks and flavoured with a reduction of vinegar, shallots, tarragon and peppercorns.

Beating—a mixing method in which foods are vigorously agitated to incorporate air or develop gluten; a spoon or electric mixer with its paddle attachment is used.

Béchamel—(bay-shah-mell) a leading sauce made by thickening milk with a white roux and adding seasonings.

Beef—the meat of domesticated cattle.

Beefalo—the product of crossbreeding a bison (North American buffalo) and a domestic beef animal.

Berry—(1) the kernel of certain grains such as wheat; (2) small, juicy fruits that grow on vines and bushes.

Beurre blanc—(burr blanhk) (Fr. for white butter) an emulsified butter sauce made from shallots, white wine and butter.

Beurre composé—(burr kom-poz-a) see **Compound butter**.

Beurre manié—(burr man-yay) a combination of equal amounts by weight of flour and soft, whole butter; it is whisked into a simmering sauce at the end of the cooking process for quick thickening and added sheen and flavour.

Beurre noir—(burr nwar) (Fr. for black butter) whole butter heated until dark brown; sometimes flavoured with vinegar.

Beurre noisette—(burr nwah-zett) whole butter heated until it turns light brown, giving off a nutty aroma.

Beurre rouge—(burr rooge) (Fr. for red butter) an emulsified butter sauce made from shallots, red wine and butter.

Bilateral—symmetrical halves arranged along a central axis.

Biological hazard—a danger to the safety of food from disease-causing microorganisms such as bacteria, moulds, yeasts, viruses or fungi.

Biscuit method—a mixing method used to make biscuits, scones and flaky doughs; it involves cutting cold fat into the flour and other dry ingredients before any liquid is added.

Bisque—(bisk) a soup made from shellfish; classic versions are thickened with rice.

Bivalves—mollusks such as clams, oysters and mussels that have two bilateral shells attached at a central hinge.

Blanching—very briefly and partially cooking a food in boiling water or hot fat; usually used to assist preparation (for example, to loosen peels from vegetables), as part of a combination cooking method, to remove undesirable flavours or to prepare a food for freezing.

Blanquette—(blang-kett) a white stew made of a white sauce and meat or poultry that is simmered without first browning.

Blending—a mixing method in which two or more ingredients are combined just until they are evenly distributed; a spoon, rubber spatula, whisk or electric mixer with its paddle attachment is used.

Blown sugar—a boiled mixture of sucrose, glucose and tartaric acid coloured and shaped using an air pump; used to make fruits and containers.

Boiling—a moist-heat cooking method that uses convection to transfer heat from a hot (approximately 212°F [100°C]) liquid to the food submerged in it; the turbulent waters and higher temperatures cook foods more quickly than do poaching or simmering.

Bordelaise—(bor-da-lays) a brown sauce flavoured with a reduction of red wine, shallots, pepper and herbs and garnished with marrow.

Bouchées—(boo-shays) small puff pastry shells often filled with a savoury mixture and used for hors d'oeuvres.

Bound salad—a salad composed of cooked meats, poultry, fish, shellfish, pasta or potatoes combined with a dressing.

Bouquet garni—(boo-kay gar-nee) a selection of herbs (usually fresh) and vegetables tied into a bundle with twine and used to flavour stocks, sauces, soups and stews.

Bouquetière—(buk-a-tyer) a garnish (bouquet) of carefully cut and arranged fresh vegetables.

Braising—a combination cooking method in which foods are first browned in hot fat, then covered and slowly cooked in a small amount of liquid over low heat; braising uses a combination of simmering and steaming to transfer heat from the liquid (conduction) and the air (convection) to the foods.

Bran—the tough outer layer of a cereal grain and the part highest in fibre.

Brandy—an alcoholic beverage made by distilling the fermented mash of grapes or other fruits.

Brawn—also called an *aspic terrine*, made from simmered meats packed into a terrine and covered with aspic.

Brazier or **brasier**—a pan designed for braising; usually round with two handles and a tight-fitting lid.

Breading—(1) a coating of bread or cracker crumbs, cornmeal or other dry meal applied to foods that will typically be deep-fat fried or pan-fried; (2) the process of applying this coating.

Brigade—also known as the kitchen brigade, a system of staffing a kitchen so that each worker is assigned a set of specific tasks; these tasks are often related by cooking method, equipment or the type of foods being produced.

Brine—a mixture of salt, water and seasonings used to preserve foods.

Brioche—(bree-yohsh) a rich yeast bread containing large amounts of eggs and butter.

Brochettes—(bro-shetts) skewers, either small hors d'oeuvre or large entrée size, threaded with meat, poultry, fish, shellfish and/or vegetables and grilled, broiled or baked; sometimes served with a dipping sauce.

Broiling—a dry-heat cooking method in which foods are cooked by heat radiating from an overhead source.

Broth—a flavourful liquid obtained from the long simmering of meats and/or vegetables.

Browning—see **Caramelization**.

Brown sauce—see **Espagnole**.

Brown stew—a stew in which the meat is first browned in hot fat.

Brown stock—a richly coloured stock made of chicken, veal, beef or game bones and vegetables, all of which are caramelized before they are simmered in water with seasonings.

Brunch—a late morning to early afternoon meal that takes the place of both breakfast and lunch; a brunch menu often offers breakfast foods as well as almost anything else.

Brunoise—(broo-nwah) (1) foods cut into cubes of 1/16 inch × 1/16 inch × 1/16 inch (1–2 mm × 1–2 mm × 1–2 mm); (2) foods garnished with vegetables cut in this manner.

Buffet service—diners generally serve themselves foods arranged on a counter or table or are served by workers assigned to specific areas of the buffet. Usually buffet-service-style restaurants charge by the meal; restaurants offering buffet service that charge by the dish are known as cafeterias.

Butcher—(1) to slaughter and dress or fabricate animals for consumption; (2)

the person who slaughters and fabricates animals.

Butler service—the use of servers to pass foods (typically hors d'oeuvres) or drinks arranged on trays.

Buttercream—a light, smooth, fluffy frosting of sugar, fat and flavourings; egg yolks or whipped egg whites are sometimes added. There are three principal kinds: simple, Italian and French.

Butterflying—slicing boneless meat, fish or shrimp nearly in half lengthwise so that they spread open like a book; used to increase surface area and speed cooking.

Cafeteria—see **Buffet service**.

Caffeine—an alkaloid found in coffee beans, tea leaves and cocoa beans that acts as a stimulant.

Cake—in North American usage, refers to a broad range of pastries including layer cakes, coffeecakes and gâteaux; can refer to almost anything that is baked, tender, sweet and sometimes frosted.

Calf—(1) a young cow or bull; (2) the meat of calves slaughtered when they are older than three months.

Calorie—the unit of energy measured by the amount of heat required to raise 1000 grams of water one degree Celsius; it is also written as kilocalorie or kcal and is used as a measure of food energy.

Canada's Food Guide to Healthy Eating—a dietary guide published by Health Canada that prioritizes and proportions food choices among food groups and promotes nutritious eating.

Canapé—(kahn-ah-pay) tiny open-faced sandwich served as an hors d'oeuvre; usually composed of a small piece of bread or toast topped with a savoury spread and garnish.

Canning—a preservation method in which the food is sealed in a glass or metal container and subjected to high temperatures for a specific period of time in order to destroy microorganisms that cause spoilage; the sealed environment eliminates oxidation and retards decomposition.

Capon—(kay-pahn) the class of surgically castrated male chickens; they have well-flavoured meat and soft, smooth skin.

Capsaicin—(kap-say-ih-sin) an alkaloid found in a chile pepper's placental ribs that provides the pepper's heat.

Caramelization—the process of cooking sugars; the browning of sugar enhances the flavour and appearance of foods.

Carbohydrates—a group of compounds composed of oxygen, hydrogen and carbon that supply the body with energy (4 calories per gram); carbohydrates are classified as *simple* (including certain sugars) and *complex* (including starches and fibre).

Carotenoid—a naturally occurring pigment that predominates in red and yellow vegetables such as carrots and red peppers.

Carryover cooking—the cooking that occurs after a food is removed from a heat source; it is accomplished by the residual heat remaining in the food.

Cartilage—also known as *gristle*, a tough, whitish elastic connective tissue that helps give structure to an animal's body.

Carve—to cut cooked meat or poultry into portions.

Casings—membranes used to hold force-meat for sausages; they can be natural animal intestines or manufactured from collagen extracted from cattle hides.

Casserole—(1) a heavy dish, usually ceramic, for baking foods; (2) foods baked in a casserole dish.

Caul fat—a fatty membrane from pig or sheep intestines; it resembles fine netting and is used to bard roasts and pâtés and to encase forcemeat for sausages.

Cellulose—a complex carbohydrate found in the cell wall of plants; it is edible but indigestible by humans.

Cephalopods—mollusks with a single, thin internal shell called a pen or cuttlebone, well-developed eyes, a number of arms that attach to the head and a saclike fin-bearing mantle; include squid and octopus.

Chafing dish—a metal dish with a heating unit (flame or electric) used to keep foods warm at tableside or during buffet service.

Chalazae cords—thick, twisted strands of egg white that anchor the yolk in place.

Charcuterie—the production of pâtés, terrines, galantines, sausages and similar foods.

Cheesecloth—a light, fine mesh gauze used to strain liquids and make sachets.

Chef de cuisine—also known simply as *chef*, the person responsible for all kitchen operations, developing menu items and setting the kitchen's tone and tempo.

Chef de partie—also known as *station chef*, produces the menu items under the direct supervision of the chef or sous-chef.

Chef's knife—an all-purpose knife used for chopping, slicing and mincing; its tapering blade is 20 to 35 cm long.

Chemical hazard—a danger to the safety of food caused by chemical substances, especially cleaning agents, pesticides and toxic metals.

Chemical leavening agents—see **Baking powder** and **Baking soda**; through chemical reactions between acids and bases, these products release gases used to leaven baked goods.

Chèvre—(shev-ruh) (Fr. for goat) generally refers to a cheese made from goat's milk.

Chiffonade—(cheh-fon-nahd) (1) to finely slice or shred leafy vegetables or herbs; (2) the finely cut leafy vegetables or herbs often used as a garnish or bedding.

Chile—pepper; a member of the *capsicum* plant family.

Chili—the stewlike dish containing chiles.

Chilled—a food that has been refrigerated.

Chilli—a commercial spice powder containing a blend of seasonings.

China cap—a cone-shaped strainer made of perforated metal.

Chinois—(shen-wasz) a conical strainer made of fine mesh, used for straining and puréeing foods.

Chlorophyll—a naturally occurring pigment that predominates in green vegetables such as cabbage.

Cholesterol—a fatty substance found in foods derived from animal products and in the human body; it has been linked to heart disease.

Chop—(1) a cut of meat including part of the rib; (2) to cut an item into small pieces where uniformity of size and shape is neither feasible nor necessary.

Choux paste—also known as *éclair paste*, a soft dough that produces hollow baked products with crisp exteriors; used for making éclairs, cream puffs and savoury products.

Chowder—a hearty soup made from fish, shellfish and/or vegetables, usually containing milk and potatoes and often thickened with roux.

Chutney—a sweet-and-sour condiment made of fruits and/or vegetables cooked in vinegar with sugar and spices; some chutneys are reduced to a purée, while others retain recognizable pieces of their ingredients.

Cider—mildly fermented apple juice; nonalcoholic apple juice may also be labelled cider.

Citrus—fruits characterized by a thick rind, most of which is a bitter white pith (albedo) with a thin exterior layer of coloured skin (zest); their flesh is segmented, juicy and varies from bitter to tart to sweet.

Clarification—(1) the process of transforming a broth into a clear consommé by trapping impurities with a clearmeat consisting of the egg white protein albumen, ground meat, an acidic product, mirepoix and other ingredients; (2) the clearmeat used to clarify a broth.

Clarified butter—purified butterfat; the butter is melted and the water and milk solids are removed.

Classes—the subdivisions of poultry kinds based on the bird's age and tenderness.

Classic cuisine—a late 19th- and early 20th-century refinement and simplification of French *grande cuisine*. Classic (or classical) cuisine relies upon the thorough exploration of culinary principles and techniques and emphasizes the refined preparation and presentation of superb ingredients.

Clean—to remove visible dirt and soil.

Clearmeat—see **Clarification**.

Clear soups—unthickened soups including broths, consommés and broth-based soups.

Coagulation—the irreversible transformation of proteins from a liquid or semi-liquid state to a drier, solid state; usually accomplished through the application of heat.

Cocoa butter—the fat found in cocoa beans and used in fine chocolates.

Colander—a perforated bowl, with or without a base or legs, used to strain foods.

Collagen—a protein found in nearly all connective tissues; it dissolves when cooked with moisture.

Combination cooking methods—cooking methods, principally braising and stewing, that employ both dry-heat and moist-heat procedures.

Composed salad—a salad prepared by arranging each of the ingredients (the base, body, garnish and dressing) on individual plates in an artistic fashion.

Compound butter—also known as a beurre composé, a mixture of softened whole butter and flavourings used as a sauce or to flavour and colour other sauces.

Compound sauces—see **Derivative sauces**.

Concasser—(kon-kaas-say) to pound or chop coarsely; usually used for tomatoes or parsley.

Condiment—traditionally, any item added to a dish for flavour, including herbs, spices and vinegars; now also refers to cooked or prepared flavourings such as prepared mustards, relishes, bottled sauces or pickles.

Conduction—the transfer of heat from one item to another through direct contact.

Confit—meat or poultry (often lightly salt-cured) slowly cooked and preserved in its own fat and served hot.

Connective tissues—tissues found throughout an animal's body that hold together and support other tissues such as muscles.

Consommé—a rich stock or broth that has been clarified with clearmeat to remove impurities.

Contaminants—biological, chemical or physical substances that can be harmful when consumed in sufficient quantities.

Contamination—the presence, generally unintentional, of harmful organisms or substances.

Convection—the transfer of heat caused by the natural movement of molecules in a fluid (whether air, water or fat) from a warmer area to a cooler one.
Mechanical convection is the movement of molecules caused by stirring.

Cookery—the art, practice or work of cooking.

Cookies—small, sweet, flat pastries; usually classified by preparation or makeup techniques as drop, icebox, bar, cutout, pressed and wafer.

Cooking—the transfer of energy from a heat source to a food; this energy alters the food's molecular structure, changing its texture, flavour, aroma and appearance.

Cooking medium—the air, fat, water or steam in which a food is cooked.

Coring—the process of removing the seeds or pit from a fruit or fruit-vegetable.

Cost of goods sold—the total cost of food items sold during a given period; calculated as beginning inventory plus purchases minus ending inventory.

Cost per portion—the cost of one serving; calculated as the total recipe cost divided by the number of portions produced from that recipe.

Coulis—(koo-lees) a sauce made from a purée of vegetables or fruit; may be hot or cold.

Count—the number of individual items in a given measure of weight or volume.

Court bouillon—(cort boo-yon) water simmered with vegetables, seasonings and an acidic product such as vinegar or wine; used for simmering or poaching fish, shellfish or vegetables.

Couscoussier—two bulbous pots, the top one has a perforated bottom and sits snugly on the bottom pot; used to cook couscous.

Cows—female cattle after their first calving, principally raised for milk and calf production.

Cream filling—a pie filling made of flavoured pastry cream thickened with cornstarch.

Creaming—a mixing method in which softened fat and sugar are vigorously combined to incorporate air; used for making some quick breads, cookies and high-fat cakes.

Creams—also known as crèmes, include light, fluffy or creamy-textured dessert foods made with whipped cream or whipped egg whites, such as Bavarian creams, chiffons, mousses and crème Chantilly.

Cream soup—a soup made from vegetables cooked in a liquid that is thickened with a starch and puréed; cream is then incorporated to add richness and flavour.

Crème anglaise—(crem ahn-glas) or *crème a l'anglaise*; see **Vanilla custard sauce**.

Crème caramel—(crem cah-rah-mel) like crème renversée and flan, a custard baked over a layer of caramelized sugar and inverted for service.

Crème Chantilly—(crem shan-tee) heavy cream whipped to soft peaks and flavoured with sugar and vanilla; used to garnish pastries or desserts or folded into cooled custard or pastry cream for fillings.

Crème Chiboust—(crem chee-boos) a pastry cream lightened by folding in Italian meringue.

Crème pâtissière—(crem pah-tees-syehr) see **Pastry cream**.

Crepe—(krayp) a thin, delicate unleavened griddlecake made with a very thin egg batter cooked in a very hot sauté pan; used in sweet and savoury preparations.

Critical control point—under the HACCP system, it is any step during the processing of a food when a mistake can result in the transmission, growth or survival of pathogenic bacteria.

Croissant—(krwah-san) a crescent-shaped roll made from a rich, rolled-in yeast dough.

Croquette—(crow-kett) a food that has been puréed or bound with a thick sauce (usually béchamel or velouté), made into small shapes, then breaded and deep-fat fried.

Cross-contamination—the transfer of bacteria or other contaminants from one food, work surface or equipment to another.

Croûte, en—(awn croot) a food encased in a bread or pastry crust.

Crouton—a bread or pastry garnish, usually toasted or sautéed until crisp.

Crudités—(croo-dee-tays) generally refers to raw or blanched vegetables served as an hors d'oeuvre and often accompanied by a dip.

Crustaceans—shellfish characterized by a hard outer skeleton or shell and jointed appendages; include lobsters, crabs and shrimp.

Cuisine—the ingredients, seasonings, cooking procedures and styles attributable to a particular group of people; the group can be defined by geography, history, ethnicity, politics, culture or religion.

Cuisson—(kwee-zon) the liquid used for shallow poaching.

Curdle—the separation of milk or egg mixtures into solid and liquid components; caused by overcooking, high heat or the presence of acids.

Curing salt—a mixture of salt and sodium nitrite that inhibits bacterial growth; used as a preservative, often for charcuterie items.

Custard—any liquid thickened by the coagulation of egg proteins; its consistency depends on the ratio of eggs to liquid and the type of liquid used. Custards can be baked in the oven or cooked in a bain marie or on the stove top.

Cutlet—a relatively thick boneless slice of meat.

Cutting—(1) reducing a food to smaller pieces; (2) a mixing method in which solid fat is incorporated into dry ingredients until only lumps of the desired size remain.

Cutting loss—the unavoidable and unrecoverable loss of food during fabrication; the loss is usually the result of food particles sticking to the cutting board or the evaporation of liquids.

Cuttlebone—also known as the pen, the single, thin internal shell of cephalopods.

Cycle menu—a menu that changes every day for a certain period and then repeats the same daily items in the same order (i.e., on a seven-day cycle, the same menu is used every Monday).

Dairy products—include cow's milk and foods produced from cow's milk such as butter, yogurt, sour cream and cheese.

Decline phase—a period during which bacteria die at an accelerated rate, also known as the *negative growth phase*.

Decoction—(1) boiling a food until its flavour is removed; (2) a procedure used for brewing coffee.

Decorator's icing—see **Royal icing**.

Deep-fat frying—a dry-heat cooking method using convection to transfer heat to a food submerged in hot fat; foods to be deep-fat fried are usually first coated in batter or breading.

Deglaze—to swirl or stir a liquid (usually wine or stock) in a sauté pan or other pan to dissolve cooked food particles remaining on the bottom; the resulting mixture often becomes the base for a sauce.

Degrease—to skim the fat from the top of a liquid such as a sauce or stock.

Demi-glace—(deh-me glass) (Fr. for half-glaze) a mixture of half brown stock and half brown sauce reduced by half.

Derivative sauces—also known as compound or small sauces, they are made by adding one or more ingredients to a leading sauce and are grouped together into families based on their leading sauce.

Some derivative sauces have a variety of uses; others are traditional accompaniments for specific foods.

Détrempe—(day-tromp) a paste made with flour and water during the first stage of preparing a pastry dough, especially rolled-in doughs.

Deveining—the process of removing a shrimp's digestive tract.

Devilled—meat, poultry or other food seasoned with mustard, vinegar and other spicy seasonings.

Diagonals—elongated or oval-shaped slices of cylindrical vegetables or fruits.

Dice—(1) to cut foods into cubes: 1/8 inch (3 mm) for small, 1/4 inch (6 mm) for medium and 1/2 inch (12 mm) for large; (2) the cubes of cut food.

Dietary fibre—see **Fibre**.

Dip—a thick, creamy sauce, served hot or cold, to accompany crudités, crackers, chips or other foods, especially as an hors d'oeuvre; dips are often based on sour cream, mayonnaise or cream cheese.

Direct contamination—the contamination of raw foods in their natural setting or habitat.

Docking—pricking small holes in an unbaked dough or crust to allow steam to escape and prevent the dough from rising when baked.

Dough—a mixture of flour and other ingredients used in baking; has a low moisture content and gluten forms the continuous medium into which other ingredients are embedded; it is often stiff enough to cut into shapes.

Drawn—a market form for fish in which the viscera is removed.

Dredging—coating a food with flour or finely ground crumbs; usually done prior to sautéing or frying or as the first step of the standardized breading procedure.

Dressed—(1) an animal carcass trimmed or otherwise prepared for consumption; (2) a market form for fish in which the viscera, gills, fins and scales are removed.

Drupes—see **Stone fruits**.

Dry-heat cooking methods—cooking methods, principally broiling, grilling, roasting and baking, sautéing, pan-frying and deep-fat frying, that use air or fat to transfer heat through conduction and convection; dry-heat cooking methods allow surface sugars to caramelize.

Drying—a preservation method in which the food's moisture content is dramatically reduced; drying changes the food's texture, flavour and appearance.

Duchesse potatoes—(duh-shees) a purée of cooked potatoes, butter and egg yolks, seasoned with salt, pepper and nutmeg; can be eaten as is or used to prepare several classic potato dishes.

Dumpling—any of a variety of small starchy products made from doughs or batters that are simmered or steamed; can be plain or filled.

Durum—a type of hard wheat milled into semolina flour, which is used for making pasta.

Duxelles—(duke-sell) a coarse paste made of finely chopped mushrooms sautéed with shallots in butter.

Edible portion (E.P.)—the amount of a food item available for consumption after trimming or fabrication.

Egg wash—a mixture of beaten eggs (whole eggs, yolks or whites) and a liquid, usually milk or water, used to coat doughs before baking to add sheen.

Elastin—a protein found in connective tissues, particularly ligaments and tendons, it often appears as the white or silver covering on meats known as *silverskin*; elastin does not dissolve when cooked.

Émincé—(eh-manss) a small, thin boneless piece of meat.

Emulsification—the process by which generally unmixable liquids, such as oil and water, are forced into a uniform distribution.

Emulsion—(1) a uniform mixture of two unmixable liquids; (2) flavouring oils such as orange and lemon, mixed into water with the aid of emulsifiers.

Endosperm—the largest part of a cereal grain and a source of protein and carbohydrates (starch); it is the part used primarily in milled products.

Entrée—(ahn-tray) the main dish of a Canadian or American meal, usually meat, poultry, fish or shellfish accompanied by a vegetable and starch; in France it is the first course, served before the fish and meat courses.

Enzymatic browning—see **Acidulation**.

Enzyme—proteins that aid specific chemical reactions in plants and animals.

Escallop—(Fr. **escallope**) a thin, boneless slice of meat or fish.

Espagnole—(ess-spah-nyol) also known as *brown sauce*, a basic sauce made of brown stock, mirepoix and tomatoes thickened with brown roux; often used to produce demi-glace.

Essential nutrients—nutrients that must be provided by food because the body cannot or does not produce them in sufficient quantities.

Ethnic cuisine—generally, the cuisine of a group of people having a common cultural heritage, as opposed to the cuisine of a group of people bound together by geography or political factors.

Ethylene gas—a colourless, odourless hydrocarbon gas naturally emitted from fruits and fruit-vegetables that encourages ripening.

Evaporation—the process by which heated water molecules move faster and faster until the water turns to a gas (steam) and vaporizes; evaporation is responsible for the drying of foods during cooking.

Extracts—concentrated mixtures of ethyl alcohol and flavouring oils such as vanilla, almond and lemon.

Extrusion—the process of forcing pasta dough through perforated plates to create various shapes; pasta dough that is not extruded must be rolled and cut.

Fabricate—to cut a large item into smaller portions; often refers to the butchering of fish or shellfish.

Fabricated cuts—individual portions of meat cut from a subprimal.

Facultative bacteria—those that can adapt and will survive with or without oxygen.

Fancy—(1) fish that has been previously frozen; (2) a quality grade for fruits, especially canned or frozen.

Fatbloom—(1) a white, powdery layer that sometimes appears on chocolate if the cocoa butter separates.

Fats—(1) a group of compounds composed of oxygen, hydrogen and carbon atoms that supply the body with energy (9 calories per gram); fats are classified as saturated, monounsaturated or polyunsaturated; (2) the general term for butter, lard, shortening, oil and margarine used as cooking media or ingredients.

Fermentation—(1) the process by which yeast converts sugar into alcohol and carbon dioxide; (2) the period of time that yeast bread dough is left to rise.

Feuillettes—(fuh-yuh-lyeth) square, rectangular or diamond-shaped puff pastry boxes that can be filled with a sweet or savoury mixture.

Fibre—also known as *dietary fibre*, indigestible carbohydrates found in grains, fruits, and vegetables; fibre aids digestion.

FIFO (First In, First Out)—an inventory storage and utilization process in which the oldest product is always used first.

Filé—(fee-lay) a seasoning and thickening agent made from dried, ground sassafras leaves.

Filet, fillet—(fee-lay) (1) filet: the boneless tenderloin of meat; (2) fillet: the side of a fish removed intact, boneless or semiboneless, with or without skin; (3) to cut such a piece.

Fish scaler—an inflexible, rasplike tool used to remove scales from fish.

Fish velouté—a velouté sauce made from fish stock.

Flambé—(flahm-bay) food served flaming; produced by igniting brandy, rum or other liquor.

Flash-frozen—food that has been frozen very rapidly using metal plates, extremely low temperatures or chemical solutions.

Flatfish—fish with asymmetrical, compressed bodies that swim in a horizontal position and have both eyes on the top of the head; include sole, flounder and halibut.

Flat icing—a white, glossy glaze used on danish pastries. Also called *water icing*.

Flavonoid—a naturally occurring pigment that predominates in red, purple and white vegetables such as cauliflower, red cabbage and beets.

Flavouring—an item that adds a new taste to a food and alters its natural flavours; flavourings include herbs, spices, vinegars and condiments.

Fleuron—(floor-ahn) a crescent-shaped piece of puff pastry used as a garnish.

Flour—a powdery substance of varying degrees of fineness made by milling grains such as wheat, corn or rye.

Foie gras—(fwah grah) liver of specially fattened geese.

Fold—a measurement of the strength of vanilla extract.

Folding—a mixing method used to gently incorporate light, airy products into heavier ingredients (for example, mixing dry ingredients with whipped eggs).

Fond—(fahn) (1) Fr. for stock or base; (2) the concentrated juices, drippings and bits of food left in pans after foods are roasted or sautéed; used to flavour sauces made directly in the pans in which the foods were cooked.

Fondant—(fahn-dant) a sweet, thick opaque sugar paste commonly used for glazing pastries such as napoleons or making candies.

Fond lié—(fahn lee-ay) See **Jus lié**.

Food cost—the cost of the materials that go directly into the production of menu items.

Food cost percentage—the ratio of the cost of foods served to the food sales dollars during a given period.

Food danger zone—the temperature range of approximately 40–140°F (5–60°C), which is most favourable for bacterial growth.

Forcemeat—a preparation made from uncooked ground meats, poultry, fish or shellfish, seasoned, and emulsified with fat; commonly prepared as country-style, basic and mousseline and used for pâtés, sausages and other charcuterie items.

Formula—a recipe; the term is most often used in the bakeshop.

Formula-fed veal—also known as milk-fed veal, it is the meat of calves fed only a nutrient-rich liquid and kept tethered in pens; this meat is whiter and more mildly flavoured than that of free-range calves.

Frangipane—(fran-juh-pahn) a sweet almond and egg filling cooked inside pastry.

Free-range chickens—chickens allowed to move freely and forage for food, as opposed to chickens raised in coops.

Free-range veal—the meat of calves that are allowed to roam freely and eat grasses and other natural foods; this meat is pinker and more strongly flavoured than that of formula-fed calves.

Freezer burn—the surface dehydration and discolouration of food that results from moisture loss at below-freezing temperatures.

French service—restaurant service where one waiter (a captain) takes the order, does the tableside cooking and

brings the drinks and food, the secondary or back waiter serves bread and water, clears each course, crumbs the table and serves the coffee.

Fresh—a food that is not and has never been frozen.

Fresh-frozen—a food that has been frozen while still fresh.

Fricassee—(frick-a-see) a white stew in which the meat is cooked in fat without browning before the liquid is added.

Frittata—(free-tah-ta) an open-faced omelette of Spanish-Italian heritage.

Frosting—also known as *icing*, a sweet decorative coating used as a filling between the layers or as a coating over the top and sides of a cake.

Fruit—refers to the edible organ that develops from the ovary of a flowering plant and contains one or more seeds (pips or pits).

Fruit-vegetables—foods such as avocados, eggplants, chile peppers and tomatoes that are botanically fruits but are most often prepared and served like vegetables.

Frying—a dry-heat cooking method in which foods are cooked in hot fat; includes sautéing and stir-frying, pan-frying and deep-fat frying.

Fumet—(foo-may) a stock made from fish bones or crustacean shells and vegetables simmered in a liquid with flavourings.

Fungi—a large group of plants ranging from single-celled organisms to giant mushrooms; the most common are moulds and yeasts.

Galantine—similar to a ballotine, it is a charcuterie item made from a forcemeat of poultry, game or suckling pig; usually wrapped in the skin of the bird or animal and poached in an appropriate stock; often served cold, usually in aspic.

Game—birds and animals hunted for sport or food; many game birds and animals are now ranch-raised and commercially available.

Game hen—the class of young or immature progeny of Cornish chickens or of a Cornish chicken and White Rock chicken; they are small and very flavourful.

Ganache—(ga-nosh) a rich blend of chocolate and heavy cream and, optionally, flavourings, used as a pastry or candy filling or frosting.

Garde-manger—(gar mawn-zhay) (1) also known as the *pantry chef*, the cook in charge of cold food production, including salads and salad dressings, charcuterie items, cold appetizers and buffet items; (2) the work area where these foods are prepared.

Garnish—(1) food used as an attractive decoration; (2) a subsidiary food used to add flavour or character to the main ingredient in a dish (for example, noodles in chicken noodle soup).

Gastronomy—the art and science of eating well.

Gâteau—(ga-toe) (1) in North American usage, refers to any cake-type dessert; (2) in French usage, refers to various pastry items made with puff pastry, choux paste, short dough or sweet dough.

Gaufrette—a thin lattice or waffle-textured slice of vegetable cut on a mandoline or with a zigzag knife.

Gelatin—a flavourless and odourless mixture of proteins (especially collagen) extracted from bones, connective tissues and other animal parts; when dissolved in a hot liquid and then cooled, it forms a jellylike substance used as a thickener and stabilizer.

Gelatinization—the process by which starch granules are cooked. They absorb moisture when placed in a liquid and heated; as the moisture is absorbed, the product swells, softens and clarifies slightly.

Gelato—(jah-laht-to) an Italian-style ice cream that is denser than North American-style ice cream.

Genoise—(zhen-waahz) (1) a form of whipped-egg cake that uses whole eggs whipped with sugar; (2) a French sponge cake.

Germ—the smallest portion of a cereal grain and the only part that contains fat.

Giblets—the collective term for edible poultry viscera including gizzards, hearts, livers and necks.

Gizzard—a bird's second stomach.

Glaçage—browning or glazing a food, usually under a salamander or broiler.

Glace de poisson—(glahss duh pwah-sawng) a syrupy glaze made by reducing a fish stock.

Glace de viande—(glahss duh vee-awnd) a dark, syrupy meat glaze made by reducing a brown stock.

Glace de volaille—(glahss duh vo-lahy) a light brown, syrupy glaze made by reducing a chicken stock.

Glaze—(1) any shiny coating applied to food or created by browning; (2) the dramatic reduction and concentration of a stock; (3) a thin, flavoured coating poured or dripped onto a cake or pastry.

Gliaden—see **Gluten**.

Glucose—an important energy source for the body; also known as blood sugar.

Gluten—a tough elastic substance created when flour is moistened and mixed; it gives structure and strength to baked goods and is responsible for their volume, texture and appearance. The proteins necessary for gluten formation are glutenin and gliaden.

Glutenin—see **Gluten**.

Grading—a designation given by the Canadian Food Inspection Agency (CFIA) to indicate a food's overall quality; grade has no effect on nutritional value.

Grains—(1) grasses that bear edible seeds, including corn, rice and wheat; (2) the fruit (i.e., seed or kernel) of such grasses.

Gram—the basic unit of weight in the metric system; equal to approximately one-thirtieth of an ounce.

Grande cuisine—the rich, intricate and elaborate cuisine of the 18th- and 19th-century French aristocracy and upper classes. It is based upon the rational identification, development and adoption of strict culinary principles.

Grate—to cut a food into small, thin shreds by rubbing it against a serrated metal plate known as a grater.

Green meats—freshly slaughtered meats that have not had sufficient time to age and develop tenderness and flavour.

Gremolada—(greh-moa-lah-dah) an aromatic garnish of chopped parsley, garlic and lemon zest used for osso buco.

Grilling—a dry-heat cooking method in which foods are cooked by heat radiating from a source located below the cooking surface; the heat can be generated by electricity or by burning gas, hardwood or hardwood charcoals.

Grind—to pulverize or reduce food to small particles using a mechanical grinder or food processor.

Grinding—a milling process in which grains are reduced to a powder; the powder can be of differing degrees of fineness or coarseness.

Gristle—see **Cartilage**.

Gum paste—a smooth dough of sugar and gelatin that can be coloured and used to make decorations, especially for pastries.

HACCP—see **Hazard Analysis Critical Control Points**.

Hanging—the practice of allowing eviscerated (drawn or gutted) game to age in a dry, well-ventilated place; hanging helps tenderize the flesh and strengthen its flavour.

Hazard Analysis Critical Control Points (HACCP)—a rigorous system of self-inspection used to manage and maintain sanitary conditions in all types of food service operations; it focuses on the flow of food through the food service facility to identify any point or step in preparation (known as a critical control point) where some action must be taken to prevent or minimize a risk or hazard.

Heifers—young cows; cows before their first calving.

Heimlich manoeuvre—the first aid procedure for victims of choking in which sudden upward pressure is applied to the upper abdomen in order to force any foreign object from the windpipe.

Herbs—any of a large group of aromatic plants whose leaves, stems or flowers are used to add flavours to other foods.

High-ratio cake—a form of creamed-fat cake that uses emulsified shortening and has a two-stage mixing method.

Hollandaise—(holl-uhn-daze) an emulsified sauce made of butter, egg yolks and flavourings (especially lemon juice).

Homogenization—the process by which milk fat is prevented from separating out of milk products.

Hors d'oeuvres—(ohr durvs) very small portions of hot or cold foods served before the meal to stimulate the appetite.

Hotel pan—a rectangular, stainless steel pan with a lip allowing it to rest in a storage shelf or steam table; available in several standard sizes.

Hull—also known as the husk, the outer covering of a fruit, seed or grain.

Hybrid—the result of crossbreeding different species that are genetically not alike; it is often a unique product.

Hybrid menu—a menu combining features of a static menu with a cycle menu or a market menu of specials.

Hydrogenation—the process used to harden oils: Hydrogen atoms are added to unsaturated fat molecules, making them partially or completely saturated and thus solid at room temperature.

Hydrometer—a device used to measure specific gravity; it shows degrees of concentration on the Baumé scale.

Hygroscopic—the characteristic of a food to readily absorb moisture from the air.

Icing—see **Frosting**.

IMPS/NAMP/CMC—see **NAMP**.

Induction cooking—a cooking method that uses a special coil placed below the stove top's surface in combination with specially designed cookware to generate heat rapidly with an alternating magnetic field.

Infection—in the food safety context, a disease caused by the ingestion of live pathogenic bacteria that continue their life processes in the consumer's intestinal tract.

Infrared cooking—a heating method that uses an electric or ceramic element heated to such a high temperature that it gives off waves of radiant heat that cook the food.

Infusion—(1) the extraction of flavours from a food at a temperature below boiling; (2) a group of coffee brewing techniques including steeping, filtring and dripping; (3) the liquid resulting from this process.

Instant-read thermometer—a thermometer used to measure the internal temperature of foods; the stem is inserted in the food, producing an instant temperature readout.

Intoxication—in the food safety context, a disease caused by the toxins that bacteria produce during their life processes.

Inventory—the listing and counting of all foods in the kitchen, storerooms and refrigerators.

IQF (Individually Quick Frozen)—the technique of rapidly freezing each individual item of food such as slices of fruit, berries or pieces of fish before packaging; IQF foods are not packaged with syrup or sauce.

Irradiation—a preservation method used in the United States for certain fruits, vegetables and grains in which ionizing radiation sterilizes the food, slows ripening and prevents sprouting; irradiation has little effect on the food's texture, flavour or appearance; Canada does not currently allow irradiation foods.

Jam—a fruit gel made from fruit pulp and sugar.

Jelly—a fruit gel made from fruit juice and sugar.

Juice—the liquid extracted from any fruit or vegetable.

Julienne—(ju-lee-en) (1) to cut foods into stick-shaped pieces, approximately 1/16 inch × 1/16 inch × 1–2 inches (1–2 mm × 1–2 mm × 2.5–4 cm); (2) the stick-shaped pieces of cut food.

Jus lié—(zhew lee-ay) also known as *fond lié*, a sauce made by thickening brown stock with cornstarch or similar starch; often used like a demi-glace, especially to produce derivative sauces.

Kinds—the nine categories of poultry recognized by Agriculture Canada: chicken, duck, goose, pheasant, quail, ostrich, guinea, pigeon and turkey. See also **Classes**.

Kitchen brigade—see **Brigade**.

Kneading—working a dough to develop gluten.

Kosher—prepared in accordance with Jewish dietary laws.

Lag phase—a period, usually following transfer from one place to another, during which bacteria do not experience much growth.

Lamb—the meat of sheep slaughtered under the age of one year.

Lard—the rendered fat of hogs.

Larding—inserting thin slices of fat, such as pork backfat, into low-fat meats in order to add moisture.

Lardon—bacon cut into 6 mm × 6 mm × 5 cm strips; used to moisten braised dishes and stews.

Leading sauces—see **Basic sauces**.

Lean doughs—yeast doughs that contain little or no sugar or fat; used for French or Italian breads.

Leavener—an ingredient or process that produces or incorporates gases in a baked product in order to increase volume, provide structure and give texture.

Lecithin—a natural emulsifier found in egg yolks.

Legumes—(lay-gyooms) (1) Fr. for vegetables; (2) a large group of vegetables with double-seamed seed pods; depending upon the variety, the seeds, pod and seeds together, or the dried seeds are eaten.

Liaison—(lee-yeh-zon) a mixture of egg yolks and heavy cream used to thicken and enrich sauces.

Liqueur—a strong, sweet, syrupy alcoholic beverage made by mixing or redistilling neutral spirits with fruits, flowers, herbs, spices or other flavourings; also known as a *cordial*.

Liquor—an alcoholic beverage made by distilling grains, vegetables or other foods; includes rum, whisky and vodka.

Litre—the basic unit of volume in the metric system, equal to slightly more than a quart.

Log phase—a period of accelerated growth for bacteria.

Macaroni—(1) any dried pasta made with wheat flour and water; (2) in North American usage, an elbow-shaped pasta tube.

Macerate—to soak foods in a liquid, usually alcoholic, to soften them.

Macronutrients—the nutrients needed in large quantities: carbohydrates, proteins, fats and water.

Madeira—a Portuguese fortified wine heated during aging to give it a distinctive flavour and brown colour.

Maître d'hotel (maître d')—(may-tr doh-tel) (1) the leader of the dining room brigade, also known as the dining room manager, he oversees the dining room or "front of the house" staff; (2) a compound butter flavoured with chopped parsley and lemon juice.

Mandoline—a stainless steel, hand-operated slicing device with adjustable blades.

Marbling—whitish streaks of inter- and intramuscular fat.

Marinade—the liquid used to marinate foods; it generally contains herbs, spices and other flavouring ingredients as well as an acidic product such as wine, vinegar or lemon juice.

Marinate—to soak a food in a seasoned liquid in order to tenderize the food and add flavour to it.

Market menu—a menu based upon product availability during a specific time period; it is written to use foods when they are in peak season or readily available.

Marmalade—a citrus jelly that also contains unpeeled slices of citrus fruit.

Marsala—a flavourful fortified sweet-to-semidry Sicilian wine.

Marzipan—a paste of ground almonds, sugar and egg whites used to fill and decorate pastries.

Matzo—thin, crisp unleavened bread made only with flour and water; can be ground into meal that is used for matzo balls and pancakes.

Mayonnaise—a thick, creamy sauce consisting of oil and vinegar emulsified with egg yolks, usually used as a salad dressing.

Mealy potatoes—also known as *starchy potatoes*, those with a high starch content and thick skin; they are best for baking.

Medallion—a small, round, relatively thick slice of meat.

Melt—the process by which certain foods, especially those high in fat, gradually soften then liquefy when heated.

Menu—a list of foods and beverages available for purchase.

Meringue—(muh-reng) a foam made of beaten egg whites and sugar.

Metabolism—all of the chemical reactions and physical processes that continually occur in living cells and organisms.

Metre—the basic unit of length in the metric system, equal to slightly more than one yard.

Mezzaluna—a two-handled knife with one or more thick, crescent-shaped blades used to chop and mince herbs and vegetables.

Micronutrients—the nutrients needed only in small amounts: vitamins and minerals.

Microorganisms—single-celled organisms as well as tiny plants and animals that can be seen only through a microscope.

Microwave cooking—a heating method that uses radiation generated by a special oven to penetrate the food. It agitates water molecules, creating friction and heat; this energy then spreads throughout the food by conduction (and by convection in liquids).

Mignonette—a medallion of meat.

Milling—the process by which grain is ground into flour or meal.

Mince—to cut a food item into very small pieces.

Mineral—inorganic micronutrients necessary for regulating body functions and proper bone and teeth structures.

Mirepoix—(meer-pwa) a mixture of coarsely chopped onions, carrots and celery used to flavour stocks, stews and other foods; generally, a mixture of 50% onions, 25% carrots and 25% celery, by weight, is used.

Mise en place—(meez on plahs) (Fr. for putting in place) refers to the preparation and assembly of all necessary ingredients and equipment.

Mix—to combine ingredients in such a way that they are evenly dispersed.

Moist-heat cooking methods—cooking methods, principally simmering, poaching, boiling and steaming, that use water or steam to transfer heat through convection; moist-heat cooking methods are used to emphasize the natural flavours of foods.

Moulding—the process of shaping foods, particularly grains and vegetables bound by sauces, into attractive, hard-edged shapes by using metal rings, circular cutters or other forms.

Moulds—(1) algaelike fungi that form long filaments or strands; for the most part, moulds affect only food appearance and flavour; (2) containers used for shaping foods.

Mollusks—shellfish characterized by a soft, unsegmented body, no internal skeleton and a hard outer shell.

Monounsaturated fats—see **Unsaturated fats**.

Monter au beurre—(mohn-tay ah burr) to finish a sauce by swirling or whisking in butter (raw or compound) until it is melted; used to give sauces shine, flavour and richness.

Mortar and pestle—a hard bowl (the mortar) in which foods such as spices are ground or pounded into a powder with a club-shaped tool (the pestle).

Mother sauces—(Fr. *sauce mère*), see **Basic sauces**.

Mousse—(moose) a soft, creamy food, either sweet or savoury, lightened by adding whipped cream, beaten egg whites or both.

Mousseline—(moose-uh-leen) (1) a delicately flavoured forcemeat based on white meat, fish or shellfish lightened

with cream and egg whites; (2) a sauce or cream lightened by folding in whipped cream.

Muffin method—a mixing method used to make quick bread batters; it involves combining liquid fat with other liquid ingredients before adding them to the dry ingredients.

Muscles—animal tissues consisting of bundles of cells or fibres that can contract and expand; they are the portions of a carcass usually consumed.

Mushrooms—members of a broad category of plants known as fungi; they are often used and served like vegetables.

Mutton—the meat of sheep slaughtered after they reach the age of one year.

NAMP/IMPS/CMC—the United States Department of Agriculture publishes Institutional Meat Purchasing Specifications (IMPS); the IMPS are illustrated and described in *The Meat Buyers Guide* published by the National Association of Meat Purveyors (NAMP); the Canadian Meat Council (CMC) also publishes full-colour manuals that name and number cuts of meat.

Nappé—(nap) (1) the consistency of a liquid, usually a sauce, that will coat the back of a spoon; (2) to coat a food with sauce.

National cuisine—the characteristic cuisine of a nation.

Nectar—the diluted, sweetened juice of peaches, apricots, guavas, black currants or other fruits, the juice of which would be too thick or too tart to drink straight.

Noisette—(nwah-zet) (1) a small, usually round, portion of meat cut from the rib or loin; (2) Fr. for hazelnut.

Noodles—flat strips of pasta-type dough that contains eggs; may be fresh or dried.

Nouvelle cuisine—(Fr. for new cooking) a mid-20th-century movement away from many classic cuisine principles and toward a lighter cuisine based on natural flavours, shortened cooking times and innovative combinations.

Nut—(1) the edible single-seed kernel of a fruit surrounded by a hard shell; (2) generally refers to any seed or fruit with an edible kernel in a hard shell.

Nutrients—the chemical substances found in food that nourish the body by promoting growth, facilitating body functions and providing energy; there are six categories of nutrients: proteins, carbohydrates, fats, water, minerals and vitamins.

Nutrition—the science that studies nutrients.

Oblique cuts—also known as *roll cuts*; small pieces of food, usually vegetables, with two angle-cut sides.

Offal—also called *variety meats*; the edible entrails (for example, the heart, kidneys, liver, sweetbreads and tongue) and extremities (for example, oxtail and pig's feet) of an animal.

Oignon piquet—(ohn-nawng pee-kay) (Fr. for pricked onion) a bay leaf tacked with a clove to a peeled onion; used to flavour sauces and soups.

Oil—a type of fat that remains liquid at room temperature.

Onion brûlée—(ohn-nawng brew-lay) (Fr. for burnt onion) charred onion halves; used to flavour and colour stocks and sauces.

Organic farming—a method of farming that does not rely on synthetic pesticides, fungicides, herbicides or fertilizers.

Oven spring—the rapid rise of yeast goods in a hot oven, resulting from the production and expansion of trapped gases.

Paillard—(pahy-lahrd) a thin slice of meat pounded until thin; it is usually grilled.

Panada or **panade**—(1) something other than fat added to a forcemeat to enhance smoothness, aid emulsification or both; it is often béchamel, rice or crustless white bread soaked in milk; (2) a mixture for binding stuffings and dumplings, notably quenelles, often choux pastry, bread crumbs, frangipane, puréed potatoes or rice.

Pan-dressed—a market form for fish in which the viscera, gills and scales are removed and the fins and tail are trimmed.

Pan-frying—a dry-heat cooking method in which food is placed in a moderate amount of hot fat.

Pan gravy—a sauce made by deglazing pan drippings from roast meat or poultry and combining them with a roux or other starch and stock.

Papillote, en—(awn poppy-yote) a cooking method in which food is wrapped in paper or foil and then heated so that the food steams in its own moisture.

Parboiling—partially cooking a food in a boiling or simmering liquid; similar to blanching but the cooking time is longer.

Parchment (paper)—heat-resistant paper used throughout the kitchen for tasks such as lining baking pans, wrapping foods to be cooked en papillote and covering foods during shallow poaching.

Parcooking—partially cooking a food by any cooking method.

Paring knife—a short knife used for detail work, especially cutting fruits and vegetables; it has a rigid blade approximately 5 to 10 cm long.

Parstock or par—the amount of stock necessary to cover operating needs between deliveries.

Pasta—(1) an unleavened paste or dough made from wheat flour (often semolina), water and eggs; the dough can be coloured and flavoured with a wide variety of herbs, spices or other ingredients and cut or extruded into a wide variety of shapes and sizes; it can be fresh or dried and is boiled for service; (2) general term for any macaroni product or egg noodle.

Pasteurization—the process of heating a liquid to a prescribed temperature for a specific period of time in order to destroy pathogenic bacteria.

Pastillage—a paste made of sugar, cornstarch and gelatin; it may be cut or moulded into decorative shapes.

Pastry cream—also known as *crème pâtissière*, a stirred custard made with egg yolks, sugar and milk and thickened with starch; used for pastry and pie fillings.

Pâte—(paht) Fr. for dough.

Pâté—(pah-tay) traditionally, a fine savoury meat filling wrapped in pastry, baked and served hot or cold as opposed to a terrine, which was a coarsely ground and highly seasoned meat mixture baked in an earthenware mould and served cold; today the words pâté and terrine are generally used interchangeably.

Pâte au pâté—(paht ah pah-tay) a specially formulated pastry dough used for wrapping pâté when making pâté en croûte.

Pâte brisée—(paht bree-zay) a dough that produces a very flaky baked product containing little or no sugar; flaky dough is used for prebaked pie shells or pie top crusts; mealy dough is a less flaky product used for custard, cream or fruit pie crusts.

Pâté en croûte—(pah-tay awn croot) a pâté baked in pastry dough such as pâte au pâté.

Pâte feuilletée—see **Puff pastry**.

Pâte sucrée—(paht sew-kra) a dough containing sugar that produces a very rich, crisp (not flaky) baked product; also known as sweet dough, it is used for tart shells.

Pathogen—any organism that causes disease; usually refers to bacteria.

Pâtissier—(pah-tees-sir-yair) a pastry chef, the person responsible for all baked items, including breads, pastries and desserts.

Paupiette—(po-pee-et) thin slices of meat, poultry or fish spread with a savoury stuffing and rolled, then braised or poached.

Paysanne—(pahy-sahn) foods cut into flat squares of 1/2 inch × 1/2 inch × 1/8 inch (12 mm × 12 mm × 3 mm thick).

Pearling—a milling process in which all or part of the hull, bran and germ are removed from the grain.

Pectin—a gelatinlike carbohydrate obtained from certain fruits, used to thicken jams and jellies.

Persillade—(payr-se-yad) (1) a food served with or containing parsley; (2) a mixture of bread crumbs, parsley and garlic used to coat meats, usually lamb.

pH—a symbol for the level of acidity or alkalinity of a solution; expressed on a scale of 0 to 14.0, 7.0 is considered neutral or balanced; the lower the pH value, the more acidic the substance, the higher the pH value, the more alkaline the substance.

Phyllo—(fee-low) pastry dough made with very thin sheets of a flour and water mixture; several sheets are often layered with melted butter and used in sweet or savoury preparations.

Physical hazard—a danger to the safety of food caused by particles such as chips, metal shavings, bits of wood or other foreign matter.

Picked—refers to the crab or lobster meat removed from the shell with a fine, needle-like tool called a pick.

Pigment—any substance that gives colour to an item.

Pilaf—a cooking method for grains in which the grains are lightly sautéed in hot fat and then a hot liquid is added; the mixture is simmered without stirring until the liquid is absorbed.

Poaching—a moist-heat cooking method that uses convection to transfer heat from a hot (approximately 160–180°F [71–82°C]) liquid to the food submerged in it.

Polyunsaturated fats—see **Unsaturated fats**.

Pomes—members of the Rosaceae family, they are tree fruits with a thin skin and firm flesh surrounding a central core containing many small seeds (called pips or carpels); include apples, pears and quince.

Pork—the meat of hogs usually slaughtered under the age of one year.

Posterior—at or toward the rear of an object or place; opposite of *anterior*.

Potentially hazardous foods—foods on which bacteria thrive.

Poultry—the collective term for domesticated birds bred for eating; they include chickens, ducks, geese, guineas, pigeons and turkeys.

Preserve—(1) a fruit gel that contains large pieces or whole fruits; (2) to extend the shelf life of a food by subjecting it to a process such as irradiation, canning, vacuum-packing, drying or freezing and/or by adding preservatives.

Primal cuts—the primary divisions of muscle, bone and connective tissue produced by the initial butchering of the carcass; primals are further broken down into smaller, more manageable cuts.

Prime cost—the combination of food costs and direct labour.

Prix fixe—(pree feks) (Fr. for fixed price) refers to a menu offering a complete meal for a set price, also known as *table d'hôte*.

Professional cooking—a system of cooking based upon the application of procedures to maintain the integrity of ingredients while providing wholesome and safe food.

Profiterole—(pro-feet-uh-roll) small round pastry made from choux paste filled with a savoury filling and served as an hors d'oeuvre or filled with ice cream and served as a dessert.

Proofing—the rise given shaped yeast products just prior to baking.

Proteins—a group of compounds composed of oxygen, hydrogen, carbon and nitrogen atoms necessary for manufacturing, maintaining and repairing body tissues and as an alternative source of energy (4 calories per gram); protein chains are constructed of various combinations of amino acids.

Puff pastry—also known as *pâte feuilletée*, it is a rolled-in dough used for pastries, cookies and savoury products; it produces a rich and buttery but not sweet baked product with hundreds of light, flaky layers.

Pulled sugar—a doughlike mixture of sucrose, glucose and tartaric acid that can be coloured and shaped by hand.

Pulses—dried seeds from a variety of legumes.

Pumpernickel—(1) coarsely ground rye flour; (2) bread made with this flour.

Purée—(pur-ray) (1) to process food to achieve a smooth pulp; (2) food that is processed by mashing, straining or fine chopping to achieve a smooth pulp.

Purée soup—a soup usually made from starchy vegetables or legumes; after the main ingredient is simmered in a liquid, the mixture, or a portion of it, is puréed.

Putrefactives—bacteria that spoil food without rendering it unfit for human consumption.

Quenelle—(cuh-nell) a small, dumpling-shaped portion of a mousseline forcemeat poached in an appropriately flavoured stock; it is shaped by using two spoons.

Quiche—a savoury tart or pie consisting of a custard baked in a pastry shell with a variety of flavourings and garnishes.

Quick bread—a bread, including loaves and muffins, leavened by chemical leaveners or steam rather than yeast.

Radiation cooking—a heating process that does not require physical contact between the heat source and the food being cooked; instead, energy is transferred by waves of heat or light striking the food. Two kinds of radiant heat used in the kitchen are *infrared* and *microwave*.

Raft—formed during the clarification process from the clearmeat and impurities from the stock; it rises to the top of the simmering stock and releases additional flavours.

Ragout—(rah-goo) (1) traditionally, a well-seasoned, rich stew containing meat, vegetables and wine; (2) any stewed mixture.

Ramekin—a small, ovenproof dish, usually ceramic.

Rancidity—a chemical change in fats caused by exposure to air, light or heat that results in objectionable flavours and odours.

Recipe—a set of written instructions for producing a specific food or beverage; also known as a *formula*.

Recommended Daily Intake (RDI)—a standard for the daily intake of various nutrients established by Health Canada.

Recovery time—the length of time it takes hot fat to return to the desired cooking temperature after food is submerged in it.

Reduce—to cook a liquid mixture, often a sauce, until its quantity decreases because of evaporation; typically done to concentrate flavours and thicken liquids.

Refreshing—submerging a food in cold water to quickly cool it and prevent further cooking, also known as *shocking*; usually used for vegetables.

Regional cuisine—a set of recipes based on local ingredients, traditions and practices; within a larger geographical, political, cultural or social unit, regional cuisines are often variations of each other that blend together to create a national cuisine.

Relishes—cooked or pickled sauces usually made with vegetables or fruits and often used as a condiment.

Remouillage—(Fr. for rewetting) a stock produced by reusing the bones from another stock.

Render—(1) to melt and clarify fat; (2) to cook meats in order to remove the fat.

Ricer—a sieve-like utensil with small holes through which soft food is forced; it produces particles about the size of a grain of rice.

Rich doughs—yeast doughs such as those used for brioche and some multi-grain breads that contain a significant amount of sugar and fat.

Rillette—(ree-yet) meat or poultry slowly cooked, mashed and preserved in its own fat and served cold and usually spread on toast.

Ripe—(1) fully grown and developed fruit; the fruit's flavour, texture and appearance are at their peak and the fruit is ready to eat; (2) an unpleasant odour indicating that a food, especially meat, poultry, fish or shellfish, may be past its prime.

Risotto—(re-zot-toe) (1) a cooking method for grains in which the grains are lightly sautéed in butter and then a liquid is gradually added; the mixture is simmered with near-constant stirring until the still-firm grains merge with the cooking liquid; (2) a Northern Italian rice dish prepared this way.

Roasting—a dry-heat cooking method that heats food by surrounding it with hot, dry air in a closed environment or on a spit over an open fire; similar to baking, the term roasting is usually applied to meats, poultry, game and vegetables.

Roe—(roh) fish eggs.

Roll cuts—see **Oblique cuts**.

Rolled-in dough—a dough in which a fat is incorporated in many layers by using a rolling and folding procedure; it is used for flaky baked goods such as croissants, puff pastry and danish.

Rondeau—(ron-doe) a shallow, wide, straight-sided pot with two loop handles.

Rondelles—(ron-dells) or rounds, disk-shaped slices of cylindrical vegetables or fruits.

Rotisserie—cooking equipment that slowly rotates meat or other foods in front of a heating element.

Roulade—(roo-lahd) (1) a slice of meat, poultry or fish rolled around a stuffing; (2) a filled and rolled spongecake.

Round fish—fish with round, oval or compressed bodies that swim in a vertical position and have eyes on both sides of their heads; include salmon, swordfish and cod.

Rounding—the process of shaping dough into smooth, round balls; used to stretch the outside layer of gluten into a smooth coating.

Roux—(roo) a cooked mixture of equal parts flour and fat, by weight, used as a thickener for sauces and other dishes; cooking the flour in fat coats the starch granules with the fat and prevents them from lumping together or forming lumps when introduced into a liquid.

Royal icing—also known as *decorator's icing*, an uncooked mixture of confectioner's sugar and egg whites that becomes hard and brittle when dry; used for making intricate cake decorations.

Russian service—restaurant service in which the entrée, vegetables and starches are served from a platter onto the diner's plate by a waiter.

Sabayon—(sa-by-on) also known as *zabaglione*, a foamy, stirred custard sauce made by whisking eggs, sugar and wine over low heat.

Sachet d'épices or **sachet**—(sah-shay day-pea-say) (Fr. for bag of spices) aromatic ingredients tied in a cheesecloth bag and used to flavour stocks and other foods; a standard sachet contains parsley stems, cracked peppercorns, dried thyme, bay leaf, cloves and, optionally, garlic.

Salad—a single food or a mix of different foods accompanied or bound by a dressing.

Salad dressing—a sauce for a salad; most are based on a vinaigrette, mayonnaise or other emulsified product.

Salad greens—a variety of leafy vegetables that are usually eaten raw.

Salamander—a small broiler used primarily for browning or glazing the tops of foods.

Salsa—(sahl-sah) (Sp. for sauce) (1) generally, a cold chunky mixture of fresh herbs, spices, fruits and/or vegetables used as a sauce for meat, poultry, fish or shellfish; (2) in Italian usage, a general term for pasta sauces.

Salt curing—the process of surrounding a food with salt or a mixture of salt, sugar, nitrite-based curing salt, herbs and spices; salt curing dehydrates the food, inhibits bacterial growth and adds flavour.

Sanitation—the creation and maintenance of conditions that will prevent food contamination or food-borne illness.

Sanitize—to reduce pathogenic organisms to safe levels, usually with heat or chemical disinfectants.

Sashimi—(sah-shee-mee) raw fish eaten without rice; usually served as the first course of a Japanese meal.

Saturated fats—fats found mainly in animal products and tropical oils; they are usually solid at room temperature, the body has more difficulty breaking down saturated fats than either monounsaturated or polyunsaturated fats.

Sauce—generally, a thickened liquid used to flavour and enhance other foods.

Sausage—a seasoned forcemeat usually stuffed into a casing; a sausage can be fresh, smoked and cooked, dried or hard.

Sautéing—(saw-tay-ing) a dry-heat cooking method that uses conduction to transfer heat from a hot pan to food with the aid of a small amount of hot fat; cooking is usually done quickly over high temperatures.

Sauteuse—(saw-toose) the basic sauté pan with sloping sides and a single long handle.

Sautoir—(saw-twahr) a sauté pan with straight sides and a single long handle.

Savoury—(1) spiced or seasoned, as opposed to sweet, foods; (2) a highly seasoned last course of a traditional English dinner.

Scald—to heat a liquid, usually milk, to just below the boiling point.

Score—to cut shallow gashes across the surface of a food before cooking.

Scoville Heat Units—a subjective rating for measuring a chile's heat; the sweet bell pepper usually rates 0, the tabasco rates from 30 000 to 50 000 and the habañera rates from 100 000 to 300 000 units.

Seafood—an inconsistently used term encompassing some or all of the following: saltwater fish, freshwater fish, saltwater shellfish, freshwater shellfish, other edible marine life.

Sear—to brown food quickly over high heat; usually done as a preparatory step for combination cooking methods.

Season—(1) traditionally, to enhance flavour by adding salt; (2) more commonly, to enhance flavour by adding salt and/or pepper as well as herbs and spices; (3) to mature and bring a food (usually beef or game) to a proper condition by aging or special preparation; (4) to prepare a pot, pan or other cooking surface to prevent sticking.

Seasoning—traditionally, an item added to enhance the natural flavours of a food without dramatically changing its taste; salt is the most common seasoning although all herbs and spices are often referred to as seasonings.

Semi à la carte—a menu on which some foods (usually appetizers and desserts) and beverages are priced and ordered separately, while the entrée is accompanied by and priced to include other dishes such as a salad, starch or vegetable.

Semifreddi—(seh-mee-frayd-dee) also known as *still-frozen desserts*, made with frozen mousse, custard or cream into which large amounts of whipped cream or meringue are folded in order to incorporate air; layers of spongecake and/or fruits may be added for flavour and texture; includes frozen soufflés, marquis, mousses and neapolitans.

Semolina—see **Durum**.

Sfoglia—(sfo-glee-ah) a thin, flat sheet of pasta dough that can be cut into ribbons, circles, squares or other shapes.

Shallow poaching—a moist-heat cooking method that combines poaching and steaming; the food (usually fish) is placed on a vegetable bed and partially covered with a liquid (cuisson) and simmered.

Shellfish—aquatic invertebrates with shells or carapaces.

Sherbet—a frozen mixture of fruit juice or fruit purée that contains milk and/or egg yolks for creaminess.

Shocking—see **Refreshing**.

Shortening—(1) a white, flavourless, solid fat formulated for baking or deep-fat frying; (2) any fat used in baking to tenderize the product by shortening gluten strands.

Shred—to cut into thin but irregular strips.

Shuck—(1) a shell, pod or husk; (2) to remove the edible portion of a food (e.g., clam meat, pea and ear of corn) from its shell, pod or husk.

Side masking—the technique of coating only the sides of a cake with garnish.

Sift—(1) to shake a dry, powdered substance through a sieve or sifter to remove lumps and incorporate air; (2) to mix together powdery substances by sifting.

Silverskin—the tough connective tissue that surrounds certain muscles; see **Elastin**.

Simmering—(1) a moist-heat cooking method that uses convection to transfer heat from a hot (approximately 185–205°F [85–96°C]) liquid to the food submerged in it; (2) maintaining the temperature of a liquid just below the boiling point.

Skim—to remove fat and impurities from the surface of a liquid during cooking.

Slashing—cutting the top of a bread with a sharp knife to improve appearance and allow for continued rising and the escape of gases after the crust has formed.

Slice—to cut an item into relatively broad, thin pieces.

Slurry—a mixture of raw starch and cold liquid used for thickening.

Small sauces—see **Derivative sauces**.

Smoke point—the temperature at which a fat begins to break down and emit smoke.

Smoking—any of several methods for preserving and flavouring foods by exposing them to smoke, includes cold smoking (in which the foods are not fully cooked) and hot smoking (in which the foods are cooked). Pan smoking is used for smaller cuts.

Solid pack—canned fruits or vegetables with little or no water added.

Sorbet—(sore-bay) a frozen mixture of fruit juice or fruit purée; similar to sherbet but without milk products.

Soufflé—(soo-flay) either a sweet or savoury fluffy dish made with a custard base lightened with whipped egg whites and then baked; the whipped egg whites cause the dish to puff when baked.

Sous-chef—(soo-shef) a cook who supervises food production and who reports to the executive chef; he or she is second in command of a kitchen.

Specifications or specs—standard requirements to be followed in procuring items from suppliers.

Spices—any of a group of strongly flavoured or aromatic portions of plants (other than leaves) used as flavourings, condiments or aromatics.

Springform pan—a circular baking pan with a separate bottom and a side wall held together with a clamp that is released to free the baked product.

Spring lamb—the meat of sheep slaughtered before they have fed on grass or grains.

Spun sugar—a decoration made by flicking dark caramelized sugar rapidly over a dowel to create long, fine, hairlike threads.

Squab—the class of young pigeon used in food service operations.

Staling—also known as *starch retrogradation*, a change in the distribution and location of water molecules within baked products; stale products are firmer, drier and more crumbly than fresh baked goods.

Standard breading procedure—the procedure for coating foods with crumbs or meal by passing the food through flour, then an egg wash and then the crumbs; it gives foods a relatively thick, crisp coating when deep-fat fried or pan-fried.

Standardized recipe—a recipe producing a known quality and quantity of food for a specific operation.

Staples—(1) certain foods regularly used throughout the kitchen; (2) certain foods, usually starches, that help form the basis for a regional or national cuisine and are principal components in the diet.

Starch—(1) complex carbohydrates from plants that are edible and either digestible or indigestible (fibre); (2) a rice, grain, pasta or potato accompaniment to a meal.

Starch retrogradation—see **Staling**.

Starchy potatoes—see **Mealy potatoes**.

Static menu—a menu offering patrons the same foods every day.

Station chef—the cook in charge of a particular department in a kitchen.

Steak—(1) a cross-section slice of a round fish with a small section of the bone attached; (2) a cut of meat, either with or without the bone.

Steamer—(1) a set of stacked pots with perforations in the bottom of each pot, they fit over a larger pot filled with boiling or simmering water and are used to steam foods; (2) a perforated insert made of metal or bamboo placed in a pot and used to steam foods; (3) a type of soft-shell clam from the East Coast; (4) a piece of gas or electric equipment in which foods are steamed in a sealed chamber.

Steaming—a moist-heat cooking method in which heat is transferred from steam to the food being cooked by direct contact; the food to be steamed is placed in a basket or rack above a boiling liquid in a covered pan.

Steel—a tool, usually made of steel, used to hone or straighten knife blades.

Steep—to soak a food in a hot liquid in order to extract its flavour or impurities or to soften its texture.

Steers—male cattle castrated prior to maturity and principally raised for beef.

Sterilize—to destroy all living microorganisms.

Stewing—a combination cooking method similar to braising but generally involving smaller pieces of meat that are first blanched or browned, then cooked in a small amount of liquid that is served as a sauce.

Stir-frying—a dry-heat cooking method similar to sautéing in which foods are cooked over very high heat using little fat while stirring constantly and briskly; often done in a wok.

Stirring—a mixing method in which ingredients are gently mixed by hand until blended, usually with a spoon, whisk or rubber spatula.

Stock—(Fr. *fond*) a clear, unthickened liquid flavoured by soluble substances extracted from meat, poultry or fish and their bones as well as from a mirepoix, other vegetables and seasonings.

Stone fruits—members of the genus *Prunus* and also known as drupes, they are tree or shrub fruits with a thin skin, soft flesh and one woody stone or pit; include apricots, cherries, nectarines, peaches and plums.

Straight dough method—a mixing method for yeast breads in which all ingredients are simply combined and mixed.

Strain—to pour foods through a sieve, mesh strainer or cheesecloth to separate or remove the liquid component.

Streusel—(stroo-zel) a crumbly mixture of fat, flour, sugar and sometimes nuts and spices; used to top baked goods.

Subcutaneous fat—also known as *exterior fat*, the fat layer between the hide and muscles.

Submersion poaching—a poaching method in which the food is completely covered with the poaching liquid.

Subprimal cuts—the basic cuts produced from each primal.

Sucrose—the chemical name for refined or table sugar, it is refined from the raw sugars found in the large tropical grass called sugar cane and the root of the sugar beet; it is available as white or brown granules, molasses or powdered sugar.

Sugar—a carbohydrate that provides the body with energy and gives a sweet taste to foods.

Sugar syrups—either simple syrups (thin mixtures of sugar and water) or cooked syrups (melted sugar cooked until it reaches a specific temperature).

Suprême—(su-prem) (1) a sauce made by adding cream to a velouté made from chicken stock; it is used to make several derivative sauces of the velouté family; (2) a boneless, skinless chicken breast with the first wing segment attached.

Sushi—(szu-she) cooked or raw fish or shellfish rolled in or served on seasoned rice.

Sweating—cooking a food (typically vegetables) in a small amount of fat, usually covered, over low heat without browning until the food softens and releases moisture; sweating allows the food to release its flavour more quickly when cooked with other foods.

Sweetbreads—the thymus glands of a calf or lamb.

Sweet dough—see Pâte sucrée.

Syrup—sugar that is dissolved in liquid, usually water, and often flavoured with spices or citrus zest.

Syrup pack—cans of fruits with a light, medium or heavy syrup added.

Table d'hôte—(tab-bluh dote) see **Prix fixe**.

Tang—the portion of a knife's blade that extends inside the handle.

Taproots—more commonly referred to as *roots*, includes edible single roots that extend deep into the ground to provide the above-ground plant with nutrients.

Tart—a sweet or savoury filling in a baked crust made in a shallow, straight-sided pan without a top crust.

Tartlet—a small, single-serving tart.

Temperature danger zone—the broad range of temperatures between 40 and 140°F (4 and 60°C) at which bacteria multiply rapidly.

Tempering—(1) heating gently and gradually; (2) refers to the process of slowly adding a hot liquid to eggs or other foods to raise their temperature without causing them to curdle; (3) refers to a process for melting chocolate.

Terrine—(1) traditionally, a loaf of coarse forcemeat cooked in a covered earthenware mould and without a crust; today, the word is used interchangeably with pâté; (2) the mould used to cook such items, usually a rectangle or oval shape and made of ceramic.

Thickening agents—ingredients used to thicken sauces, include starches (flour, cornstarch and arrowroot), gelatin and liaisons.

Timbale—(tim-bull) (1) a small pail-shaped mould used to shape foods; (2) a preparation made in such a mould.

Tisanes—(teh-zahns) beverages made from herbal infusions that do not contain any tea.

Tomato concassé—(kon-kaas say) peeled, seeded and diced tomato.

Tomato sauce—a basic sauce made from tomatoes, vegetables, seasonings and white stock; it may or may not be thickened with roux.

Toque—(toke) the tall white hat worn by chefs.

Torte—in Central and Eastern European usage, refers to a rich cake in which all or part of the flour is replaced with finely chopped nuts or bread crumbs.

Tossed salad—a salad prepared by placing the greens, garnishes and salad dressing in a large bowl and tossing to combine.

Tourner—(toor-nay) (Fr. for to turn), to cut foods, usually vegetables, into football-shaped pieces with seven equal sides and blunt ends.

Toxins—byproducts of living bacteria that can cause illness if consumed in sufficient quantities.

Tranche—(tranch) an angled slice cut from fish fillets.

Trim loss—the amount of a food item removed when preparing it for consumption.

Tripe—the edible lining of a cow's stomach.

Truffles—(1) flavourful tubers that grow near the roots of oak or beech trees; (2) rich chocolate candies made with ganache.

Truss—to tie poultry with butcher's twine into a compact shape for cooking.

Tube pan—a deep round baking pan with a hollow tube in the centre.

Tuber—the fleshy root, stem or rhizome of a plant from which a new plant will grow; some, such as potatoes, are eaten as vegetables.

Tunnelling—the holes that may form in baked goods as the result of overmixing.

Unit cost or **price**—the price paid to acquire one specified unit.

Univalves—single-shelled mollusks with a single muscular foot, such as abalone.

Unsaturated fats—fats that are normally liquid (oils) at room temperature; they may be *monounsaturated* (from plants such as olives and avocados) or *polyunsaturated* (from grains and seeds such as corn, soybeans and safflower as well as from fish).

Vanilla custard sauce—also known as *crème anglaise*, a stirred custard made with egg yolks, sugar and milk or half-and-half and flavoured with vanilla; served with or used in dessert preparations.

Vanillin—(1) whitish crystals of vanilla flavour that often develop on vanilla beans during storage; (2) synthetic vanilla flavouring.

Variety—the result of breeding plants of the same species that have different qualities or characteristics; the new plant often combines features from both parents.

Variety meats—see **Offal**.

Veal—the meat of calves under the age of 10–12 weeks.

Vegetable—refers to any herbaceous plant (one with little or no woody tissue) that can be partially or wholly eaten; vegetables can be classified as cabbages, fruit-vegetables, gourds and squashes, greens, mushrooms and truffles, onions, pods and seeds, roots and tubers, and stalks.

Velouté—(veh-loo-tay) a basic sauce made by thickening a white stock (either fish, veal or chicken) with roux.

Venison—meat from any member of the deer family including elk, moose, reindeer, red-tailed deer, white-tailed deer and mule deer; it is typically a lean, dark red meat with a mild aroma.

Vent—(1) to allow circulation or escape of a liquid or gas; (2) to cool a pot of hot liquid by setting the pot on blocks in a cold water bath and allowing cold water to circulate around it.

Vinaigrette—(vin-nay-greht) a temporary emulsion of oil and vinegar (usually three parts oil to one part vinegar) seasoned with herbs, salt and pepper; used as a salad dressing or sauce. Also known as *basic French dressing*.

Vinegar—a thin, sour liquid used as a preservative, cooking ingredient and cleaning solution.

Viruses—the smallest known form of life; they invade the living cells of a host and take over those cells' genetic material, causing the cells to produce more viruses; some viruses can enter a host through the ingestion of food contaminated with those viruses.

Viscera—internal organs.

Vitamins—compounds present in foods in very small quantities; they do not provide energy but are essential for regulating body functions.

Vol-au-vent—(vul-oh-van) a large, deep puff pastry shell often filled with a savoury mixture for a main course.

Volume—the space occupied by a substance; volume measurements are commonly expressed as litres, teaspoons, tablespoons, cups, pints and gallons.

Wash—a glaze applied to dough before baking; a commonly used wash is made with whole egg and water.

Water bath—see **Bain marie**.

Water pack—canned fruits with water or fruit juice added.

Waxy potatoes—those with a low starch content and thin skin; they are best for boiling.

Weight—the mass or heaviness of a substance; weight measurements are commonly expressed as kilograms, grams, ounces and pounds.

Wheel—(1) a large boneless piece of fish (such as swordfish or tuna) from which steaks are cut, also known as a centre cut; (2) a cylindrical-shaped cheese.

Whetstone—a dense, grained stone used to sharpen or hone a knife blade.

Whipping—a mixing method in which foods are vigorously beaten in order to incorporate air; a whisk or an electric mixer with its whip attachment is used.

White stew—see **Fricassee** and **Blanquette**.

White stock—a light-coloured stock made from chicken, veal, beef or fish bones simmered in water with vegetables and seasonings.

Whitewash—a thin mixture or slurry of flour and cold water used like cornstarch for thickening.

Wine—an alcoholic beverage made from the fermented juice of grapes; may be sparkling (effervescent) or still (noneffervescent) or fortified with additional alcohol.

Work section—see **Work station**.

Work station—a work area in the kitchen dedicated to a particular task, such as broiling or salad making; work stations using the same or similar equipment for related tasks are grouped together into *work sections*.

Yeasts—microscopic fungi whose metabolic processes are responsible for fermentation; they are used for leavening bread and in cheese, beer, and wine making.

Yield—(1) the total amount of a food item created or remaining after trimming or fabrication; (2) the total amount of a product made from a specific recipe.

Yield factor or percentage—the ratio of the edible portion to the amount purchased.

Zest—the thin, coloured part of a citrus peel.

Zushi—(zhoo-she) the seasoned rice used for sushi.

$\mathcal{I}$NDEX